Marketing

Best Practices

Marketing

Best Practices

K. Douglas Hoffman
Colorado State University

Michael R. Czinkota
Georgetown University

Peter R. Dickson
Florida International University

Patrick Dunne
Texas Tech University

Abbie Griffin
University of Illinois–
Urbana-Champaign

Michael D. Hutt
Arizona State University

Balaji C. Krishnan
University of Memphis

John H. Lindgren, Jr.
University of Virginia

Robert F. Lusch
Texas Christian University

Ilkka A. Ronkainen
Georgetown University

Bert Rosenbloom
Drexel University

Jagdish N. Sheth
Emory University

Terence A. Shimp
University of South Carolina

Judy A. Siguaw
Cornell University

Penny M. Simpson
Southeastern Oklahoma
State University

Thomas W. Speh
Miami University–Ohio

Joel E. Urbany
University of Notre Dame

THOMSON

SOUTH-WESTERN

Australia · Canada · Mexico · Singapore · Spain · United Kingdom · United States

THOMSON

SOUTH-WESTERN

Marketing: Best Practices, 2e

K. Douglas Hoffman, Michael R. Czinkota, Peter R. Dickson, Patrick Dunne, Abbie Griffin, Michael D. Hutt, John H. Lindgren, Jr., Balaji C. Krishnan, Robert F. Lusch, Ilkka A. Ronkainen, Bert Rosenbloom, Jagdish N. Sheth, Terence A. Shimp, Judy A. Siguaw, Penny M. Simpson, Thomas W. Speh, and Joel E. Urbany

Editor-in-Chief:
Jack W. Calhoun

Team Leader:
Melissa S. Acuña

Acquisitions Editor:
Steven W. Hazelwood

Senior Developmental Editor:
Trish Taylor

Marketing Manager:
Nicole Moore

Production Editor:
Amy A. Brooks

Manufacturing Coordinator:
Diane Lohman

Compositor:
Stratford Publishing Services, Inc.

Printer:
Quebecor World Versailles
Versailles, KY

Design Project Manager:
Casey Gilbertson

Internal Designer:
Casey Gilbertson

Cover Designer:
Ann Small
a small design studio,
Cincinnati, OH

Cover Image:
Photonica

Photography Manager:
Deanna Ettinger

Photo Editor:
Fred M. Middendorf
Script Pict Ink Ltd.

Library of Congress Cataloging-in-
Publication Data

Marketing : best practices /
K. Douglas Hoffman . . . [et al.]—
2nd ed.
      p.   cm.
Includes bibliographical references
and indexes.
ISBN: 0-03-034999-0
1. Marketing. I. Hoffman,
K. Douglas.
HF5415 .M297453 2003
658.8—dc21

                2002021786

To the students of Marketing—
past, present, and future:

It is our collective wish that this text play some role toward
improving marketing practice throughout the 21st century.

—The *Best Practices* author team

Preface

NOTES FROM THE *BEST PRACTICES* AUTHOR TEAM

In a market full of traditional and established principles of marketing textbooks, there are at least 17 good reasons to take notice of the groundbreaking approach taken by *Marketing: Best Practices*. This project combines the expertise of 17 leading marketers into one high-powered principles text. Each chapter is penned by an authority in a particular field of marketing. The end result is a principles text that successfully communicates a strong sense of passion and insight and one that sets a new standard for principles of marketing textbooks.

The *Best Practices* author team consists of current South-Western textbook authors and selected individuals who are specialists in their respective fields. *Marketing: Best Practices* allowed us as authors to showcase our areas of expertise for the principles market. As a result, *Marketing: Best Practices* covers the latest issues and topics from the field while equipping students with a solid foundation in marketing basics. The *Best Practices* author team and their respective areas of specialization are as follows:

Introduction to Strategic Marketing	Peter R. Dickson, *Florida International University*
Marketing and Social Responsibility	Peter R. Dickson, *Florida International University*
International Marketing	Michael R. Czinkota, *Georgetown University* Ilkka A. Ronkainen, *Georgetown University*
Marketing Research and Information Systems	Peter R. Dickson, *Florida International University*
Consumer Behavior	Jagdish N. Sheth, *Emory University* Balaji C. Krishnan, *University of Memphis*
Business-to-Business Marketing	Michael D. Hutt, *Arizona State University* Thomas W. Speh, *Miami University, Ohio*
Market Segmentation and Target Markets	Penny M. Simpson, *Southeastern Oklahoma State University*
Marketing's Role in New Product Development and Product Decisions	Abbie Griffin, *University of Illinois, Urbana-Champaign*
Services Marketing	K. Douglas Hoffman, *Colorado State University*
Marketing Channels and Distribution	Bert Rosenbloom, *Drexel University*
Retailing and Wholesaling	Patrick Dunne, *Texas Tech University* Robert F. Lusch, *Texas Christian University*
Integrated Marketing Communications: Advertising, Promotions, and Other MarCom Tools	Terence A. Shimp, *University of South Carolina*
Personal Selling and Sales Management	Judy A. Siguaw, *Cornell University*
Pricing Strategies and Determination	Joel E. Urbany, *University of Notre Dame*
E-Marketing	John H. Lindgren, Jr., *University of Virginia*

If we may say so ourselves, the *Best Practices* author team is an intriguing group of individuals. Writing is this group's forte—throughout our collective careers, the *Best Practices* author team has published 125 books and more than 1085 articles. As a group, we are genuinely excited to be collaborating with one another and to have the opportunity to influence, educate, and challenge students of marketing. As the dedication to the book indicates, we sincerely wish to make an impact on improving the practice of marketing.

NOTES FROM THE PUBLISHER

Seventeen Experts, One Voice

While *Marketing: Best Practices* includes insight from 17 marketing experts, it offers a single, uniform voice. In addition to his chapter on services marketing, Dr. Doug Hoffman once again served as consulting editor on the project, bringing to this innovative text the valued expertise of many but the succinct voice of one.

Since the onset of the project, the publisher, the authors, and the editorial and marketing teams have been committed to the highest level of quality possible. And achieving that uncompromising quality required a very thorough writing, editing, and review process.

As a result of these efforts, each chapter is consistent in format and pedagogy, the writing level is uniform, topics are linked throughout the text, and the copy maintains a lively, energetic tone. However, consistency was not achieved at the expense of content or the authors' individual personalities. Each chapter is intentionally a true reflection of its author's personal style and individual marketing expertise.

Real-World Emphasis

Students receive "an insider's view" of marketing issues throughout the text, as the authors relate myriad firsthand accounts from their personal experiences in consulting and research. Readers gain additional insight into real-world marketing practice through experiential exercises, leadership applications, career development, cases, and much more. The text and package alike have a strong emphasis on careers, giving students insight into the marketing opportunities available after graduation. For example, each chapter features a **Careers in Marketing** box spotlighting successful individuals—former students and personal acquaintances of the authors—in their various career paths.

Careers in Marketing

Global Experience Leads to the Top

E. V. Goings, president of Tupperware, took part in a total-immersion program in Spanish—his third language—but he hardly stands out on his company's executive committee. The eight other members of the group speak two to four languages each, and all can boast of international work experience.

International exposure has long been trumpeted as essential for global managers in multinationals, but these days, even chief executives are going global. To keep up with the growing importance of foreign markets, more companies are requiring candidates for top management positions to have strong international resumes. Victor J. Menezes, a native of Puna, India, has worked for Citigroup since 1972—in Hong Kong, China, Brussels, Latin America, and Africa—and is now head of the corporate emerging markets planning group. During a trip to a recent acquisition in Poland, Menezes met with executives: several Poles, three Indians, an Englishman, an Argentinian, a Belgian, an Irishman, and a Chinese-Singaporean—and no Americans.

Executives who climbed the corporate ladder in the past typically ran successively bigger operations of a single product line or specialized in one discipline like finance. Leaving the United States for an overseas post was often perceived as dangerous, taking executives far from the center of power. Today, however, international experience is often a top priority for executive headhunters. Executive-search firms report that major corporations required candidates with international experience in 28 percent of senior-level searches [in 1995], up from 4 percent in 1990.

"It sends the most powerful signal you can send [to the employees] if the CEO has international experience or has been selected for that reason," says Jean-Pierre Rosso, the president and CEO of Case Corp. Rosso spent 12 years at Honeywell Inc. in France and Belgium. Dana Mead, the CEO of Tenneco Inc. and the person responsible for picking Rosso for the job, says that he "showed he could operate in both [American and French] cultures."

Combining high-profile roles abroad and at home seems to be the formula of success for many top management candidates. The Egyptian-born CEO of Goodyear Tire and Rubber, Samir Gibara, caught the eye of his predecessor Stanley Gault by turning around Goodyear's losses in its European operation in the early 1990s. Then Gibara took on several key U.S. jobs at the tire maker's Akron, Ohio, headquarters before becoming CEO.

Other types of foreign exposure can also offer executives the opportunity for great upward mobility. Expertise in the bigger and more challenging emerging markets such as Brazil, China, and India can often pave the way to success. A key reason why Andrea Jung was elected president of Avon Products Inc. was that she served the firm as president and COO of global marketing, with operating responsibility for all of Avon's global units.

Sources: Joann S. Lublin, "An Overseas Stint Can Be a Ticket to the Top," *Wall Street Journal*, 29 January 1996, B1; Paul Beckett, "To Fuel Its Growth, Citigroup Depends on Menezes' Work in Emerging Markets," *Wall Street Journal*, 21 February 2001, C1; http://www.avon.com.

Technologically Focused

A technology focus is integrated throughout the text and package, as well. Chapter 15 is devoted to e-marketing. In addition, **Marketing Technologies** boxes pertaining to technology's impact on marketing are frequently featured throughout the text, integrating chapter concepts with Internet applications and exercises. Web addresses of companies highlighted as text examples are included throughout, and Internet exercises are included in the end-of-chapter material. In addition, the text includes its own comprehensive, interactive Web site:
http://bestpractices.swcollege.com

Marketing Technologies

Meet Mya—The Virtual Service Provider

In an attempt to expand sales, many traditional PC manufacturers are looking for new product development ideas that involve mobile methods of using the Internet. For example, Motorola has recognized that many consumers are away from their computer when they would most like to use it. Motorola's response to this consumer need is Mya, a mobile platform that integrates voice and data. According to Motorola, Mya is essentially a voice-enabled browser that eliminates the middleman—the computer.

Mya has been designed specifically to act as a sort of digital secretary. Subscribers to Mya's services are given an 800 number and PIN that provides 24-hour access to the Net, 7 days a week. Theoretically, a subscriber can call Mya and ask for a list of Italian restaurants within a specified location. If a restaurant's Web site has been designed to take reservations, Mya can book the reservation. The limitation is that Mya can only access what is on the Internet. So, if a restaurant does not have a Web site, Mya has no way of knowing that it exists. Other services that Mya can provide include checking subscribers' e-mail and reminding them of upcoming appointments, birthdays, and anniversaries.

Although Mya is virtual, she has been given a human voice and physical appearance in order to assist in Motorola's marketing efforts. Mya's voice is that of Gabrielle Carteris, an actress who played Andrea on Fox television's *Beverly Hills 90210*. Mya's physical appearance is digitally animated—she is a tall, thin blonde with spiked hair, wearing a silver pantsuit. She was created by the same firm that generated the special effects for *Terminator 2* and *Titanic*. Mya's services are currently available to BellSouth subscribers. Other networks have yet to be finalized.

Source: Tobey Grumet, "Mya Desires Your Attention," *Revolution* 1, no. 5, (2000): 23.

SUPPORT MATERIALS: A POWERHOUSE PACKAGE

Marketing: Best Practices combines a collection of the strongest names in the market with one of the most innovative and comprehensive packages available. The accompanying ancillary package features a wealth of valuable teaching tools for instructors and a variety of interactive learning tools for students.

Incredible PowerPoint Instructor CD-ROMs

Created by Jack Lindgren of the University of Virginia, the PowerPoint Instructor multimedia presentation brings lectures and classroom discussions to life. Organized by chapter, this extremely user-friendly program enables instructors to custom design their own multimedia classroom presentations, using overhead transparencies, figures, tables, graphs, ads, and more from the text, as well as video segments and additional material from outside sources.

Instructors will receive two CD-ROMs with over 2 hours of TV commercials demonstrating the concepts in each of the chapters. In addition, approximately 75 to 125 Power-Point slides per chapter are provided, which can be easily modified to fit the needs of individual instructors. The software is available in PowerPoint 2000. Users of PowerPoint 97and 95 can obtain a converter/player from Microsoft: **http://www.microsoft.com/office/powerpoint/downloads/default.asp.**

Cutting-Edge Video Package

Completely integrated with the text, 19 videos provide students with valuable insight into how real companies apply chapter concepts to their own marketing operations. Videos feature such companies as Neiman Marcus, the Timberland Company, Tower Records, ESPN, Fisher-Price, Fresh Samantha juice products, and many others. Videos include interviews with top business executives and successful entrepreneurs. Integrated video cases, found at the back of the textbook, create an even stronger link between the video package and the text.

The videos illustrate such themes as quality, customer satisfaction, brand equity, relationship marketing, teamwork, product revitalization, regulation, and ethics. Additionally, many segments conclude with career profiles of key marketing managers and executives, who discuss their career paths, marketing successes, key managerial skills, and the role of marketing, as well as offer personal advice to students entering the field.

Best Practices Web Site

The *Marketing: Best Practices* Web site, **http://bestpractices.swcollege.com**, is an incredible resource for instructors and students alike. The *Best Practices* Web site gives students hands-on experience using the Internet as a marketing tool. For example, through the online exercises, students can review chapter material and explore the vast resources available online, while a reading room section links users to business journals, daily newspapers, magazines, and marketing publications from across the country and around the world. Interactive quizzes, Internet applications, crossword puzzles, and learning objectives also help students absorb chapter content.

Customized Instructor's Manual

Designed to support novice instructors and marketing veterans alike, this comprehensive *Instructor's Manual* includes key term definitions, learning objectives, lecture outlines, answers to critical-thinking questions, answers to the end-of-chapter review questions, teaching notes for the Internet exercises, and answers to the chapter case questions. The *Instructor's Manual* was compiled by Anne M. Gogela of Colorado State University.

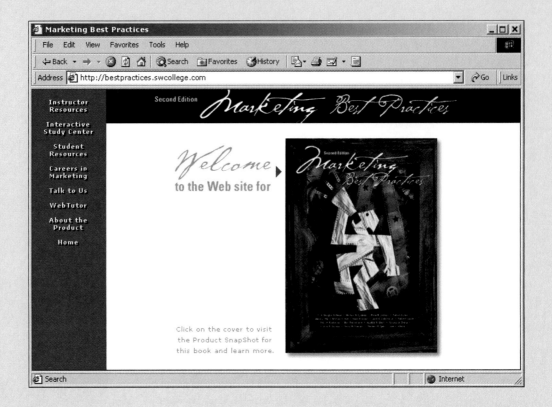

Test Bank

Thoroughly reviewed for accuracy, the *Test Bank* includes approximately 3,000 true/false, multiple-choice, short-answer, and essay questions. The *Test Bank* has been reviewed, revised, and checked for accuracy by John E. Weiss, Colorado State University, who is also the author of the *Study Guide*. The test questions are tied directly to chapter learning objectives, have corresponding page references, and each question is rated according to its level of difficulty.

ExamView

With ExamView from South-Western, you can easily create and customize tests! ExamView's Quick Test Wizard guides you step-by-step through the process of creating and printing a test in minutes. And ExamView is the only test generator that offers a WYSIWYG (what-you-see-is-what-you-get) feature that allows you to see the test you are creating on the screen exactly as it will print! You can also enter an unlimited number of new questions or edit existing questions using ExamView's complete word-processing capability. Undo, cut, copy, paste, find

and replace, and spellchecking functions are available at the touch of a key. ExamView allows you to easily create Internet tests and study guides. You can then deliver the test via the Internet, and student results will be automatically e-mailed back to you.

Comprehensive Study Guide

Designed to enhance student understanding and provide additional practice application of chapter content, this comprehensive learning tool includes chapter outlines, experiential exercises, self-quizzes, matching exercises for key terms and concepts, multiple-choice review questions, Internet application problems, marketing plan exercises, and solutions to study questions. The *Study Guide* was written by John E. Weiss, Colorado State University.

Marketing: Best Practices greatly benefited from the quality of reviews provided by numerous colleagues representing a variety of academic institutions. In particular, the *Best Practices* author team is very grateful to the following colleagues for giving their time and insightful direction:

Tim Aurand	*Northern Illinois University*	Charles Harrington	*Pasadena City College*
Arni Authorsson	*College of St. Francis*	Braxton Hinchey	*University of Massachusetts–Lowell*
Mike Barone	*Iowa State University*	Earl Honeycutt	*Old Dominion University*
Francine Beaty	*Miami University*	Susan Meyer	*Colorado State University*
Mark Bennion	*Bowling Green University*	Ina Midkiff	*Austin Community College*
Edward Bond	*Bradley University*	Russ Moorehead	*Des Moines Area Community College*
Anne Brumbaugh	*Wake Forest University*	Terry Paul	*Ohio State University*
Bill Carner	*University of Texas–Austin*	Tom Pritchett	*Kennesaw State University*
Jerome Christia	*Coastal Carolina University*	Glen Reicken	*East Tennessee State University*
Janice Cox	*Miami University, Oxford Ohio*	Alan Sawyer	*University of Florida*
Erwin Daneels	*Worcester Polytechnic Institute*	Regina P. Schlee	*Seattle Pacific University*
George Dollar	*Clearwater Christian College*	Don Schreiber	*Baylor University*
Carl Dresden	*Coastal Carolina University*	Jane Sojka	*Ohio University*
Sean Dwyer	*Louisiana Tech University*	Ruth Taylor	*Southwest Texas State University*
Dave Fallin	*Kansas State University*	John Weiss	*Colorado State University*
Dwayne Gremler	*University of Idaho*	Rama Yelkur	*University of Wisconsin–Eau Claire*
Steve Grove	*Clemson University*	Joyce Young	*Indiana State University*
Diane Hambley	*University of South Dakota*		

We would also like to thank the many good folks at South-Western, many of whom we have had the pleasure of knowing for many years through our other text projects. Special thanks to Melissa Acuña, Vice President/Team Director; Lise Johnson, Vice President/Director of Marketing; and Steve Hazelwood, Acquisitions Editor, for generating and maintaining the level of enthusiasm associated with this project throughout the entire process.

We would especially like to thank Trish Taylor, who acted as Senior Developmental Editor. Trish, words are inadequate to express our gratitude for your monumental efforts in coordinating an author team of 17 academics. Thank you, Trish!

Additional thanks are extended to Amy Brooks, Production Editor; Lara Stelmaszyk, Project Manager; Casey Gilbertson, Designer; Fred Middendorf, Photo Editor; and Christie Loehrke, Editorial Assistant, for putting the project together. A number of other good people focused on putting together the *Instructor's Manual, Test Bank, Study Guide,* and video cases. We would like to extend our special thanks to John E. Weiss and Dawna Susa for their support and dedication to the project.

We would also like to thank the South-Western sales force for supporting this unique project and stirring up the worldwide principles of marketing market. We truly appreciate your efforts in bringing this package to the marketplace and offer our assistance in support of your efforts.

This project continues to generate a great deal of interest in the academic and publishing communities. We thank the parent company of Thomson Learning for wholeheartedly and enthusiastically accepting and supporting the project.

Finally, each of us would like to thank our families, friends, and colleagues for their support. Writing a text is a time-consuming experience that often takes us away from those who mean the most in our lives. Thank you for your understanding, patience, and encouragement.

AUTHOR TEAM ACKNOWLEDGMENTS

PART ONE—INTRODUCTION—THE MARKETING ENVIRONMENT   **1**

Chapter One—Introduction to Strategic Marketing   2
Peter R. Dickson, Florida International University

Chapter Two—Marketing and Social Responsibility   30
Peter R. Dickson, Florida International University

Chapter Three—International Marketing   60
Michael R. Czinkota, Georgetown University
Ilkka A. Ronkainen, Georgetown University

PART TWO—UNDERSTANDING THE MARKET   **97**

Chapter Four—Marketing Research and Information Systems   98
Peter R. Dickson, Florida International University

Chapter Five—Consumer Behavior   136
Jagdish N. Sheth, Emory University
Balaji C. Krishnan, University of Memphis

Chapter Six—Business-to-Business Marketing   162
Michael D. Hutt, Arizona State University
Thomas W. Speh, Miami University, Ohio

Chapter Seven—Market Segmentation and Target Markets   196
Penny M. Simpson, Southeastern Oklahoma State University

PART THREE—PRODUCT   **235**

Chapter Eight—Marketing's Role in New Product Development
and Product Decisions   236
Abbie Griffin, University of Illinois, Urbana-Champaign

Chapter Nine—Services Marketing   278
K. Douglas Hoffman, Colorado State University

PART FOUR—DISTRIBUTION   **323**

Chapter Ten—Marketing Channels and Distribution   324
Bert Rosenbloom, Drexel University

Chapter Eleven—Retailing and Wholesaling   370
Patrick Dunne, Texas Tech University
Robert F. Lusch, Texas Christian University

PART FIVE—INTEGRATED MARKETING COMMUNICATIONS   **409**

Chapter Twelve—Integrated Marketing Communications:
Advertising, Promotions, and Other MarCom Tools   410
Terence A. Shimp, University of South Carolina

Chapter Thirteen—Personal Selling and Sales Management   456
Judy A. Siguaw, Cornell University

PART SIX—PRICING   **493**

Chapter Fourteen—Pricing Strategies and Determination   494
Joel E. Urbany, University of Notre Dame

PART SEVEN—THE FUTURE OF MARKETING   **535**

Chapter Fifteen—E-Marketing   536
John (Jack) H. Lindgren, Jr., University of Virginia

Appendix: Planning for Marketing Decisions   567
Video Cases   583
Glossary   608
Credits   618
Name Index   000
Company Index   000
Subject Index   000

CONTENTS IN BRIEF

CONTENTS

PART ONE—INTRODUCTION—THE MARKETING ENVIRONMENT   1

Chapter One—Introduction to Strategic Marketing   2
Peter R. Dickson, Florida International University

The Evolution of Markets via Spontaneous Economic Combustion   4
     Spontaneous Economic Combustion   4
The Evolution of Marketing into a Trading Relationship
Exchange Process   6
     The Traditional View of Marketing's Evolution   6
     An Alternative to the Traditional View of Marketing   8
     Marketing as an Exchange Process   9
Marketing as an Organizational Process   10
     The Marketing Concept   10
     The Fundamentals of Marketing Strategy   11
The Marketing Environment   16
Marketing Technologies: The Future of Electronic Shopping   17
     The Internal Marketing Environment   17
     The External Marketing Environment   18
Marketing Strategy in Action: Best/Worst Practices   22
     Boeing versus Airbus   22
     IBM's Revitalization Effort   23
     Webvan's Demise   24
     Cemex Online   24
Chapter Summary   25
Chapter Case: Amazon.com and Barnes & Noble   29

Chapter Two—Marketing and Social Responsibility   30
Peter R. Dickson, Florida International University

Marketing's First Social Responsibility:
Be Ever More Efficient and Effective   33
     Too Many Unneeded Products Are Marketed That Fail   33
     Too Many Unneeded Products Are Marketed That Succeed   33
     Market Distribution Systems Are Inefficient   34
Marketing Technologies: What to Do with Old Technology   35
     A Lot of Advertising Is Wasteful Expenditure   36
     Marketers' Self-Interested, Unintended Consequences on Supply   37
     Marketers' Self-Interested, Unintended Consequences on Demand   39
Marketing's Second Social Responsibility: Behave Ethically   40
     I Was Only Following Orders   41
     Theories of Marketing Ethics   43
     Where Do Our Basic Values Come From?   46
     Recognizing Ethical Issues   47
Marketing's Third Social Responsibility: Obey the Law   49
Marketing's Fourth Social Responsibility: Help Market Good Causes   51
     Cause-Related Marketing   51
Careers in Marketing: The Case of Development Organizations   53
     The National High Blood Pressure Education Program (NHBPEP)   53
Chapter Summary   54
Chapter Case: Gambling and the Internet   59

Chapter Three—International Marketing   60
Michael R. Czinkota, Georgetown University
Ilkka A. Ronkainen, Georgetown University

What International Marketing Is   62
Opportunities and Challenges in International Marketing   63
The International Marketing Environment   66
     Cultural Environment   66
     Socioeconomic Environment   67
     Legal and Political Environment   69
International Market Selection   70
     Identification and Screening   70

Marketing Technologies: Bringing the New Economy to New Markets   72
     Concentration versus Diversification Strategies   73
The Internationalization Process   73
     The Role of Management   73
     Motivations to Go Abroad   73
Alternative Entry Strategies   75
     Indirect Exporting and Importing   75
     Direct Exporting and Importing   76
     International Intermediaries   76
     Licensing   76
     Foreign Direct Investment   78
A Comprehensive View of International Expansion   81
     Adjusting the Marketing Mix   82
Implementing Marketing Programs Worldwide   86
     Management Process   86
     Organization Structure   87
Careers in Marketing: Global Experience Leads to the Top   88
Chapter Summary   89
Chapter Case: Lakewood Forest Products   94

PART TWO—UNDERSTANDING THE MARKET   97

Chapter Four—Marketing Research and Information Systems   98
Peter R. Dickson, Florida International University

The Competitive Importance of Market Research   100
Consumer Research   100
Marketing Technologies: A Dumb Study of a Smart Product
or a Smart Study of a Dumb Product?   101
     Secondary Data Analysis   101
Careers in Marketing: From "On Wisconsin" to "Advance Australia Fair"   103
     Qualitative Consumer Research   104
     Customer Visits in Business-to-Business Marketing   105
     Focus Group Research   106
     Consumer Survey Research   107
     Sampling   109
     Question Design   111
     Electronic Observational Research   114
     Decision Support Systems   116
Competitor Research   117
     Researching the History of the Market   119
     Auditing Current Competitors   120
Channel Research   124
     Researching Individual Trade Customers   125
Chapter Summary   127
Chapter Case: Online Marketing Research   134

Chapter Five—Consumer Behavior   136
Jagdish N. Sheth, Emory University
Balaji C. Krishnan, University of Memphis

The Scope of Consumer Behavior   138
     Three Consumer Roles   138
     Consumer Needs and Wants   139
Psychological Bases of Consumer Behavior   140
     Perception   140
     Learning   140
     Motivation   140
Careers in Marketing: Why Study Consumer Behavior?   141

Psychographics: Describing Consumer Behavior	145
Values	145
Self-Concept	146
Lifestyle	147
Values and Lifestyles (VALS)	147
Attitude: Definition and Characteristics	149
Individual Consumer Decision Making	149
Step 1: Problem Recognition	150
Step 2: Information Search	151
Step 3: Alternative Evaluation	152
Step 4: Purchase	153
Marketing Technologies: Self-Service at the Point of Sale	154
Step 5: Postpurchase Evaluations	154
Household Decision Making	155
Families and Households	155
Steps in Family Buying Decisions	156
Children's Influence in the Family Decision Making	156
Conflict in Family Decisions	156
Chapter Summary	157
Chapter Case: Teaching Kids to Charge	161

Chapter Six—Business-to-Business Marketing   162

Michael D. Hutt, Arizona State University
Thomas W. Speh, Miami University, Ohio

The Business Market: Size and Scope	164
Types of Customers: An Illustration	164
Commercial Enterprises as Customers	166
Governmental Units as Customers	167
Institutions as Customers	168
International Customers	169
Classifying Business Customers	170
Characteristics of Business Markets	171
Demand Issues	171
Close Buyer-Seller Relationships	173
Careers in Marketing: Delivering Service Solutions to IBM Customers	174
Supply-Chain Management	174
The Organizational Buying Process	176
Marketing Technologies: The Supply Chain Is Wired	177
The Search Process	178
Supplier Selection and Performance Review	178
Buying Situations Analyzed	178
How Organizational Buyers Evaluate Potential Suppliers	181
Evaluating Supplier Performance	182
Major Influences on Organizational Buyers	183
Environmental Forces	183
Organizational Forces	184
Group Forces: The Buying Center	185
Individual Forces	187
Chapter Summary	188
Chapter Case: The Segway Company: Reinventing the Wheel	194

Chapter Seven—Market Segmentation and Target Markets   196

Penny M. Simpson, Southeastern Oklahoma State University

Markets and Target Marketing	198
Mass Market versus the Individual	199

Careers in Marketing: Retirement: The End for Some,
the Beginning for One   200
Segmentation and Target Marketing   201
    Advantages   201
    Disadvantages   202
The Target Market Selection Process   204
    Identify the Total Market   204
    Determine Need for Segmentation   205
    Criteria for Successful Segmentation   206
    Determine Bases for Segmentation   208
    Collect Segmentation Data   212
    Profile Each Selected Segment   213
    Assess Potential Profitability of Each Segment and
    Select Segments for Targeting   214
    Select Positioning Strategy   215
    Develop and Implement Appropriate Marketing Mix and Monitor,
    Evaluate, and Control   222
Segmenting Business Markets   222
    Demographics   223
    Operating Characteristics   223
    Purchasing Approaches   223
    Product Use or Usage Situation   223
    Situational Factors   224
    Buyers' Personal Characteristics   224
Segmenting Global Markets   224
Marketing Technologies: Speaking the Language   225
    Economic Factors   226
    Legal/Political Factors   226
    Cultural Factors   226
Chapter Summary   228
Chapter Case: Targeting Credit Card Customers by Mail:
What Next?   233

PART THREE—PRODUCT   **235**

Chapter Eight—Marketing's Role in New Product
Development and Product Decisions   236
Abbie Griffin, University of Illinois, Urbana-Champaign

Types of Products   238
    Consumer Products   238
    Business-to-Business Products   238
Setting the Stage for Successful New Product Development   240
    Defining Products: Newness, Success, and Failure 240
    Requirements for Developing Successful New Products 244
Marketing Technologies: Information Acceleration:
Using Technology to Forecast the Future for Really New Products   247
Careers in Marketing: Careers in New Product Development—
Getting Cross-Functional   250
    Developing a Competitively Advantaged Product   252
    Shepherding Products through the Firm   259
Making Product Decisions: Branding, Packaging, and Labeling   261
    Branding Decisions   261
    Packaging Decisions   263
    Labeling Decisions   264
Product Management: Managing Products through Their
Life Cycles   264
    Introduction Strategies   264
    Growth Strategies   267

Maturity Strategies   267
Decline Strategies   268
Managing the Product Portfolio   **268**
Product Mix Decisions   268
Product Growth Opportunities   269
Chapter Summary   **271**
Chapter Case: Developing a New Degree Offering at Midwestern U. 276

Chapter Nine—Services Marketing   **278**
K. Douglas Hoffman, Colorado State University

The Fundamentals of Services Marketing   **280**
What Is a Service?   281
The Scale of Market Entities   282
Careers in Marketing: On the Road Again with Shomotion   283
Unique Differences between Goods and Services   284
Marketing Technologies: Meet Mya—The Virtual Service Provider   286
Understanding the Service Experience   289
Creating Compelling Experiences   294
The Quest for Customer Satisfaction   **295**
What Is Customer Satisfaction?   296
The Importance of Customer Satisfaction   297
The Benefits of Customer Satisfaction   297
Customer Satisfaction as It Relates to Customer
Relationship Management   299
Service Quality   **302**
What Is Service Quality?   302
The Gap Model   303
Customer Retention   **306**
Customer Retention Tactics   307
Chapter Summary   **311**
Chapter Case: Emmy's and Maddy's First Service Encounter   317

PART FOUR—DISTRIBUTION   **323**
Chapter Ten—Marketing Channels and Distribution   **324**
Bert Rosenbloom, Drexel University

Marketing Channel Defined   **326**
Marketing Channel Structure   **327**
Length of Channel Structure   328
Intensity of Channel Structure   328
Types of Intermediaries in the Channel Structure   330
Determinants of Channel Structure   **330**
Distribution Tasks   330
Marketing Technologies: Music Distribution:
Who Needs CDs and Stores When Electrons Will Do   331
The Economics of Performing Distribution Tasks   332
Management's Desire for Control of Distribution   334
Flows in Marketing Channels   **335**
Marketing Channels as Social Systems   **337**
Power in Marketing Channels   337
Conflict in Marketing Channels   337
Marketing Channel Management   **338**
Perspectives for Channel Management   **338**
Decision Areas of Channel Management   **339**
Formulating Channel Strategy   339
Careers in Marketing: Using Her Degree in Direct Relation
to the Fourth P   341
Designing the Channel Structure   342

Selecting Channel Members   344
Motivating Channel Members   346
Coordinating Channel Strategy in the Marketing Mix   349
Evaluating Channel Member Performance   350
Logistics in Marketing Channels   351
The Role of Logistics   351
Logistics Systems, Costs, and Components   352
The Output of the Logistics System: Customer Service   357
Chapter Summary   358
Chapter Case: Dell Computer Corporation:
Which Channels Will Keep Growth Going?   366

Chapter Eleven—Retailing and Wholesaling   **370**
Patrick Dunne, Texas Tech University
Robert F. Lusch, Texas Christian University

The Role of Retailing in the U.S. Economy   372
Reaching the Consumer   373
Current Retail Trends   373
Differentiating the Retail Experience   379
Evolution of Retail Competition   380
Major Types of Retail Formats   383
Store-Based Retailers   383
The Inside Story: All Laws Governing Retailing Are Not the Same   384
Nonstore-Based Retailers   388
Managing the Retail Mix   391
Atmospherics   392
Careers in Marketing: Charlie Hamilton: Making Retailing Fun   394
Category Management   394
Wholesaling in the U.S. Economy   395
Types of Wholesalers   396
Selecting and Working with Wholesalers   399
Chapter Summary   401
Chapter Case: Cycle South   406

PART FIVE—INTEGRATED MARKETING COMMUNICATIONS   **409**
Chapter Twelve—Integrated Marketing Communications:
Advertising, Promotions, and Other MarCom Tools   410
Terence A. Shimp, University of South Carolina

The Tools of Marketing Communications   413
Personal Selling   413
Advertising   413
Public Relations   413
Sales Promotion   414
Sponsorship Marketing   414
Point-of-Purchase Communications   414
Key Participants in Marketing Communications   415
The Philosophy and Practice of Integrated Marketing
Communications   415
Careers in Marketing: From Consumer Packaged Goods to High Tech:
Skills Will Travel   416
Key Aspects of Integrated Marketing Communications   417
Key Changes in MarCom Practice Resulting from the IMC Thrust   419
The MarCom Challenge: Enhance Brand Equity   419
Brand Awareness   420
The Inside Story: Mountain Dew—Staying True to the Brand   421
Brand Image   422

Determining an Appropriate Mix of IMC Tools   423
   Who Is the Intended Market?   423
   What Objectives Must the MarCom Initiative Achieve?   423
   What Is the Nature of the Product?   425
   What Is the Product Life-Cycle Stage?   425
   What Are Competitors Doing?   425
   What Is the Available Budget?   425
   Will a Push or Pull Strategy Be More Effective?   426
Managing the MarCom Process   426
   Selecting Target Markets   426
   Establishing Objectives   426
   Formulating a Positioning Strategy   427
   Setting the Budget   427
   Formulating and Implementing Message and Media Strategies   427
   Evaluating Program Effectiveness   428
Advertising   428
   Setting Advertising Objectives   429
   Budgeting for Advertising   429
   Establishing the Brand Positioning   430
   Creating Advertising Messages   430
   Selecting Advertising Media   432
   Assessing Advertising Effectiveness   434
   Direct Advertising   436
Sales Promotion   437
   The Shift from Advertising to Sales Promotion   437
   Sales Promotion: Roles and Objectives   439
   Trade Promotions: Roles and Objectives   440
   Consumer Sales Promotions: Roles and Objectives   441
Public Relations   442
   Proactive MPR   442
   Reactive MPR   443
Sponsorship Marketing   443
   Event Marketing   444
   Cause-Related Marketing   444
Point-of-Purchase Communications   444
Chapter Summary   445
Chapter Case: Getting American Consumers to Accept and Use
Recycling Kiosks   454

Chapter Thirteen—Personal Selling and Sales Management   **456**

Judy A. Siguaw, Cornell University

Sales and Marketing in the 21st Century   459
   The Strategic Importance of Personal Selling   459
Careers in Marketing: Radical Selling: The Cure All   460
   The Evolution of Personal Selling and the Changing Face of Sales   461
   The Sales Professions: Rewards and Drawbacks   462
Selling Environments and Types of Salespeople   464
   Telemarketing   464
   Over-the-Counter Selling   465
   Field Selling   465
Careers in Marketing: Best Practices in a Sales Career:
Harvesting the Fruits of the Vine   466
   Sales Certification   467
The Sales Process   467
The Inside Story: Team Selling Drives Revenues   468
   Prospecting   469

Preapproach and Planning   470
Approaching the Client   470
Identifying Client Needs   471
The Inside Story: Question Formats in Sales: Open versus Closed   472
Presenting the Product   472
Handling Objections   473
Gaining Commitment   475
Following Up and Keeping Promises   475
Building and Managing the Sales Force   475
Recruiting   475
Sales Force Training   476
Marketing Technologies: Will the Internet Eliminate Salespeople?   477
Motivating the Sales Force   478
Compensating the Sales Force   479
Evaluating Salespeople's Performance   480
Organizing and Managing Sales Territories   481
Legal and Ethical Responsibilities in Selling and Sales Management   482
Sales Representative's Legal Responsibilities   482
The Firm's Legal Responsibilities   482
Unethical/Illegal Behaviors   482
Sexual Harassment   483
Chapter Summary   483
Chapter Case: Selling the Big Apple: Avero, Inc.   491

PART SIX—PRICING   **493**

Chapter Fourteen—Pricing Strategies and Determination   **494**
Joel E. Urbany, University of Notre Dame

What Is Price? What Determines Base Price?   497
Cost-Plus Pricing: The Natural (but Sometimes Wrong) Way to Set Base Prices   497
Demand Considerations: The Relationship between Price and Sales   501
Break-Even Analysis   501
The Demand Schedule   502
Elasticity of Demand   502
Profit Maximization   504
Pricing Strategies: Price Drivers   508
Positioning Strategy/Competition   508
Objectives   509
New Product Pricing   511
Explaining Adjustments to Base Price over Time   512
Variations in Objectives over the Product Life Cycle   513
Competitive Price Moves   514
Price Flexing: Different Prices for Different Buyers   514
Careers in Marketing: Edwin L. Artzt and the EDLP Solution   518
Marketing Technologies: Price Shopping Dream   521
Legal and Ethical Issues in Pricing   521
Price Fixing   522
Price Discrimination   522
Resale Price Maintenance   522
Predatory Pricing   523
Exaggerated Comparative Price Advertising   523
Ethical Concerns   523
Chapter Summary   525
Chapter Case: Grocery Pricing: The Ourstore Company Case   532

PART SEVEN—THE FUTURE OF MARKETING   **535**

   Chapter Fifteen—E-Marketing   536
   Dr. John (Jack) H. Lindgren, Jr., University of Virginia

   The E-Marketing Landscape   538
      History of the Internet   538
      A Primer of Internet Terms and Markets   538
      Markets   538
      Types of Internet Sites   539
   Marketing Technologies: Victoria's Secret   544
   The Growth of Internet Marketing   545
      Electronic Commerce   545
      Improving Business Practices Using the Internet   549
   Profit Models   551
      Advertising   551
      Subscriptions   552
   Marketing Technologies: Napster   553
      Online Product Vending   554
      Electronic Intermediary Commissions   554
   E-Marketing and the Marketing Mix   556
      Product   556
      Price   556
      Place   556
      Promotion   556
   Careers in Marketing: E-Marketing: A Different Game   558
   Costs and Benefits of E-Marketing   558
      Drawbacks   558
      Benefits of E-Marketing   560
   Chapter Summary   561
   Chapter Case: A Different Kind of Résumé   566

   Appendix: Planning for Marketing Decisions   567

   Video Cases   583

   Glossary   608

   Credits   618

   Name Index   000

   Company Index   000

   Subject Index   000

PART one

Introduction

The Marketing Environment

CHAPTER 1

Introduction to Strategic Marketing

CHAPTER 2

Marketing and Social Responsibility

CHAPTER 3

International Marketing

Peter R. Dickson, Florida International University

Dr. Dickson earned his undergraduate degrees at the University of Otago, New Zealand. He has published over 70 papers in journals and proceedings and served on the editorial board of several publications, including *Journal of Business Research*, *Journal of Marketing*, and *Marketing Letters*. He is the author of *Marketing Management*, published by the Dryden Press, and a coauthor of a logistics strategic planning guide. He has also worked in the real world, marketing several new products.

Dr. Dickson helped found the Business School at the University of Waikato, where he taught for seven years. After receiving a Fulbright-Hays Bicentennial scholarship and completing his Ph.D. at the University of Florida, he taught for 14 years at The Ohio State University, where he became the Crane Professor of Strategic Marketing and a professor of industrial design, and for 5 years at the University of Wisconsin–Madison, where he was the Arthur C. Nielsen Jr. Chair of Marketing Research. He is currently Knight-Ridder Eminent Scholar in Global Marketing at Florida International University.

Introduction to Strategic Marketing

In its most basic form, marketing is about identifying customer needs, developing products that satisfy those needs, and working with trading partners to deliver and sell the product to customers. All of this has to be done better than one's competitors, which can be very hard to sustain over time.

Motorola Inc. is a great company. Led by Christopher Galvin, grandson of the founder, Motorola generates global sales of $35 billion and operates its own Motorola University. The company has invented and marketed numerous products, including the first portable two-way FM radios and the first pager. In addition, Motorola is a past recipient of the prestigious Malcolm Baldrige Quality Award. Overall, Motorola has been an exemplary representative of the high-technology firms that have helped grow the prosperity and quality of life of the modern capitalist economy.

In addition to its many successes, Motorola has made profound marketing mistakes over the last 5 to 10 years. These mistakes have cost thousands of employees their well-paid jobs, and the value of Motorola stock has plummeted from $60 to $15. One of the company's more recent mistakes involved the development and launch of a global wireless satellite venture called Iridium. Ultimately, the venture failed because it simply was not competitive. The phone was a "gee whiz" invention that connected directly to the satellite, but the cost of the phone and its associated services was 10 times greater than that of the competition. Moreover, Iridium's primary competitive advantage benefited few—it offered unique services for *National Geographic* explorers in the middle of the Gobi desert. Meanwhile, the frequent global business travelers simply solved the problem of "staying in touch" by purchasing or renting wireless phones in the countries they visited. Mistakes at the front end of the project were compounded by a back-end reluctance to terminate the project. No one in marketing wanted to be the bearer of bad news. Instead of wasting billions on this project, Motorola should have spent the money and management time switching from analog to digital phone technology.

In the early years of the wireless industry, Motorola was a dominant force, commanding as much as 26 percent market share in 1996. However, by 2000, Motorola had lost half of its market share to companies with better marketing, such as Nokia, the Finnish telecommunications company (ironically, Nokia started as a forest products company). As the mass market for wireless phones developed in the 1990s, Nokia understood that the emerging major market segment was the teen and young adult market. The primary use of wireless technology for this market was social networking—keeping in touch with friends and family. Product adoption frequently spawned further adoptions by friends and family. Key features the market desired included inexpensive digital quality and reliability, simplicity, and sleek and attractive design features. Unfortunately, Motorola wireless phones were more expensive, less reliable (because of their complex features), often cumbersome, and unattractive in appearance. Time and again senior management asked marketing whether the market data supported the company's designs, and they were told "absolutely." This was despite the fact that its major marketing partners, the phone service companies, were repeatedly warning Motorola that companies like Nokia, Siemens, and Samsung were producing more attractive, better value-for-money phones. After a while these major trading partners gave up on Motorola and switched most of their business to other suppliers who would listen to them. Ultimately, Motorola's trading partners had no choice: They had to switch suppliers to stay competitive themselves.

The shortcomings of the marketing function at Motorola were matched by poor design features and production inefficiencies. Motorola offered 120 different varieties of phones compared with Nokia's 10. In addition, Motorola's phones lacked the benefit of interchangeable components and parts, driving the price of Motorola's most basic phone far higher than Nokia's comparable offerings. Furthermore, since 1997, Motorola's $13 billion wireless division has undergone three major overhauls that have continuously disrupted the company's ability to focus on the external competition and rapidly expanding market. The result has been a bureaucratic nightmare. In 2001, Motorola finally announced the launch of a new line of phones, featuring candy-colored face plates and FM radio, that were targeted to teenagers. This could have been done 10 years ago by Motorola, and if it had done so, it probably would have gained rather than lost market share. Today, it is too little, too late. The "cool" global brand is Nokia; meanwhile, Motorola has most likely alienated enough wireless service providers that it has little chance of gaining back any of its former vendors. A great business legacy—a Malcolm Baldridge Award and its own business university—could not save Motorola from making the most basic of marketing mistakes: not properly identifying customer needs, not developing products that satisfy those needs, and not working closely with trading partners to deliver and sell the product to customers.

Developing and sustaining the ability to make and market goods and services that consumers want and prefer over rivals' goods and services is clearly not as simple as it would seem. It is readily apparent that when it actually comes time to implement a marketing strategy, it is much easier to talk the talk than to walk the walk. And Motorola is not alone. It now appears that the whole "new economy" Internet fiasco had a lot to do with the same sets of issues: arrogant technologists, investors, and marketers not paying

(Continued)

After you have completed this chapter, you should be able to:

1. Understand the historical origins of marketing and why markets have evolved.
2. Specify how marketing has evolved into a trading relationship exchange process.
3. Show how marketing as an organizational process revolves around the marketing process, and note the fundamental concepts that comprise marketing strategy.
4. Understand how the marketing environment affects strategic decisions.
5. Describe and identify best practices in marketing strategy.

attention to how consumers were really using the Internet. Instead, fantastic scenarios about future Internet usage were developed and promoted. Unfortunately, these fictions (successfully marketed to investors rather than consumers) had nothing to do with the emerging reality of consumer Internet usage. The same is happening today with the marketing of the next generation of broadband technology that will allow video to be streamed to wireless phones. Communications companies are spending tens of billions of dollars purchasing the rights to broadband radio wave spectrums around the world to be the market leaders of the next generation of wireless use. These companies are betting that watching movies or a caller's face on a two-inch wireless phone screen is going to generate hundreds of billions of dollars of additional revenue. Time will tell.[1]

Welcome to the second edition of *Marketing: Best Practices*. The first three chapters of this text, which comprise Part 1, titled "Introduction—The Marketing Environment," lay the foundation for the remainder of the text. Chapter 1 begins by providing a historical perspective on how markets and marketing have evolved via spontaneous economic combustion. In its most basic form, marketing is based on the principle of exchange. Marketers facilitate the exchange process by engaging in a variety of marketing activities that are presented herein. The chapter concludes its introduction of marketing by acquainting readers with the core marketing terminology that comprises marketing strategy and by providing a variety of best practice examples of marketing strategy in action.

THE EVOLUTION OF MARKETS VIA SPONTANEOUS ECONOMIC COMBUSTION

LEARNING OBJECTIVE   1

Raw material scarcity
occurs when valuable raw material resources are geographically concentrated in some locations and not in others, resulting in resource scarcity in some locations.

Labor specialization
occurs when labor and management undertake specific activities and processes, the repetition and focus increase the effectiveness, efficiency, and learning of labor and management.

Consumption satiation
is what occurs when the more units of a product that are consumed in a short period of time, the less the added value of consuming another unit of the same product and the greater the variety-seeking behavior.

Spontaneous Economic Combustion

To understand why marketing is such a fascinating economic and sociological activity, we have to first understand the fundamental reason why markets developed and how marketing adds value. Markets exist because of three primary conditions—raw material scarcity, labor specialization, and consumption satiation. Simply stated, markets exist because valuable raw material resources are geographically concentrated in some locations and not in others (**raw material scarcity**); we get better at doing things the more we do them (**labor specialization**); and beyond some level of normal consumption, we tend to become less interested in consuming things the more we consume them (**consumption satiation**). Put raw material scarcity, labor specialization, and consumption satiation together in any human society and markets, marketing, and trade will be created spontaneously. Let us walk slowly through the logic of this theory of spontaneous economic combustion.

Raw Material Scarcity
Throughout history, tribes of humans have flourished in very different geographical locations. Each location provided very different access to raw material resources, for example, flint, turtles, wheat, water buffalo, potatoes, whale blubber, iron ore, gold, and salt. The most fundamental reason for the spontaneous creation of markets, marketing, and trade was varying access to important raw material resources. Making the best of what they had on hand, different tribes survived and flourished by becoming skilled at hunting, gathering, growing, and processing these raw material resources. This created the second reason for the spontaneous creation of markets, marketing, and trade between clans, tribes, and nations: the development of differential skills in inventing new products out of raw materials, producing them, and then distributing them. How did tribes become skilled at marketing and trading? They did so through labor specialization.

Labor Specialization
The simple notion that we get better at doing things the more we do them provides the basis for labor specialization. As people specialize in a particular activity, they learn to become better, more efficient, and more skilled at that particular activity. Of course, there are setbacks to learning, and some individuals are more motivated to learn than

others. As a general principle, however, the benefits of labor specialization were established and made famous in the 1700s by the pioneering economist Adam Smith. His consulting report to the British government on how to compete in the new global marketplace being created by the industrial revolution (particularly cotton manufacture) was later published in book form as *The Wealth of Nations*.[2] The principles Adam Smith wrote about some 200 years ago are still relevant today. Think about your own early work experiences. Even when working as a dishwasher or when mowing neighborhood lawns as a child to earn spending money, you learned over time how to do the job faster and better. Your hand–eye coordination required to perform tasks improved, but you also thought of better or easier ways of accomplishing the tasks at hand. The same learning process makes brain surgeons better, runners faster, and golf professionals more accurate. Management scientists and economists have observed that the same learning occurs at the organizational level. This learning process has been studied by economists who analyze it in terms of learning curves.[3] In general, as a company's experience increases, the cost of production and distribution decreases and the potential for its knowledge, learning, and ability to lead to the invention of new goods and services around its expertise increases.

Consumption Satiation

The third necessary ingredient to generate spontaneous economic combustion is consumption satiation. In essence, the basic reason why trading occurs on the demand side is that we like to acquire and use a variety of goods and services rather than live an isolated existence in which we consume only what we produce. When we consume only what we produce, we produce only enough to satisfy our own needs, because to produce more would create a glut or an excess that is not used and is subsequently wasted. This is called consumption satiation. Consumption satiation also leads us to want to swap what we have an excess of for something we are short of. It is based on the idea that beyond some normal level of consumption, the more we consume the same product over time, the less interested we are in consuming another unit of that same product. Hence, the marginal added value of consuming another unit is less than the marginal utility of the unit preceding it. For example, the marginal utility of a customer's third bowl of Ben & Jerry's

ice cream is less than the marginal utility of the second bowl, which is less than the marginal utility of the first bowl. The bottom line is that humans tend to become satiated even when consuming the products they enjoy the most. Consequently, trading will spontaneously occur and thrive because of customer needs, wants, desires, and preferences for a variety of products. Furthermore, trading eliminates the impracticality and inefficiency associated with each individual inventing and making distinct products for his or her own personal use. Thus, raw material scarcity, labor specialization, and consumer satiation are the major forces behind spontaneous economic combustion and the field of marketing itself. These forces have raised the skill of trading and marketing to an economic, social, and political imperative.

THE EVOLUTION OF MARKETING INTO A TRADING RELATIONSHIP EXCHANGE PROCESS

LEARNING OBJECTIVE 2

The Traditional View of Marketing's Evolution

Most introductory marketing textbooks present the historical and philosophical development of marketing by discussing the distinct stages that businesses purportedly moved through during specific time periods. The most frequently noted eras are the production era, the sales era, the marketing era, and the relationship marketing era. (See Figure 1.1.) The production era is identified with the years before 1925; the sales era covers the period between 1925 and the early 1950s; the marketing era spans the next 30 years; and the relationship marketing era began in the 1990s.

Production Era

The *production era* was based on the philosophical attitude that "good products" would sell themselves. Perhaps a takeoff of the line from the movie *Field of Dreams* typifies the prevailing beliefs of the production era—"If we build it, they will come." The production era is said to be characterized by companies that focused on developing mass production skills in the belief that if good products were made affordable and widely available, the

| The Evolution of Marketing | Figure 1.1 |

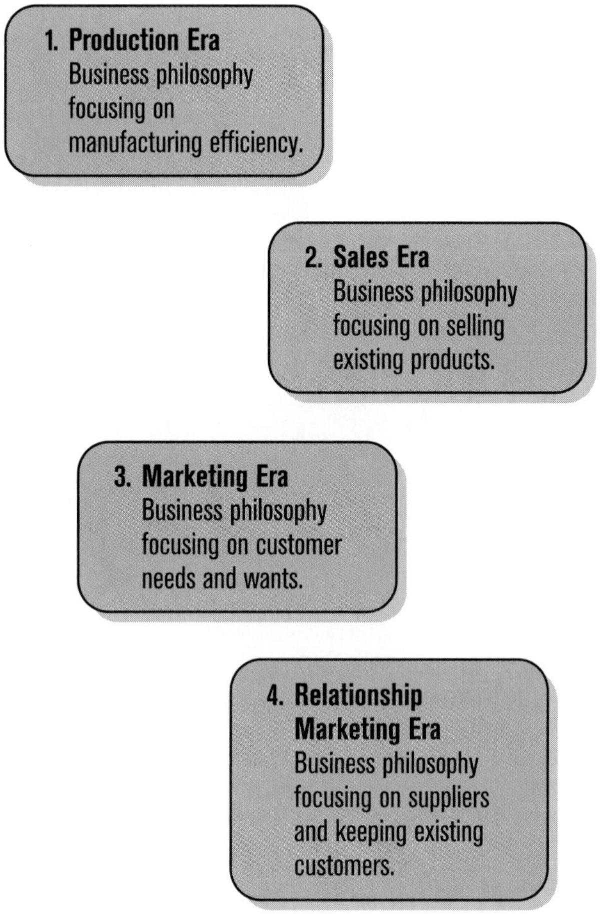

1. Production Era
Business philosophy focusing on manufacturing efficiency.

2. Sales Era
Business philosophy focusing on selling existing products.

3. Marketing Era
Business philosophy focusing on customer needs and wants.

4. Relationship Marketing Era
Business philosophy focusing on suppliers and keeping existing customers.

consuming public would "beat a pathway to the doors" of the manufacturers of these products. Henry Ford's Model T automobile and the development of the production line assembly plant are often noted as prime examples of the production era. Throughout the production era, marketing is said to have played a secondary role to production.

Sales Era

The proposed consequences of the production era were piles of unsold inventory built up because a product did not sell itself. The prevailing philosophy of the *sales era* was to find customers for inventories that went unsold. Advertising campaigns were developed to convince customers to buy products that they otherwise would not have purchased. In essence, during the sales era, companies were trying to sell what they produced as opposed to producing what they could sell. Marketing continued to play a secondary role during the sales era to other functional areas, such as engineering, production, and finance. Throughout the sales era, the head of the marketing department was frequently given the title sales manager.

Marketing Era

Based on the knowledge gained by the mistakes made during the production and sales eras, business organizations began to appreciate the value of market information prior to making plans for production. As a result, the *marketing era* was characterized by a great deal of importance placed on identifying customer needs and wants prior to producing the product. The rationale was that the company would produce what the customer

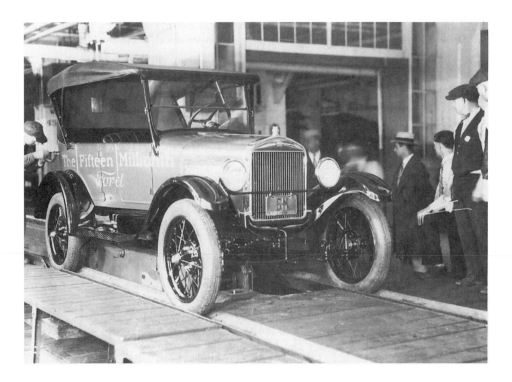

actually wanted, and the customer would then purchase the product. During the marketing era, marketing moved to the forefront of business strategy, and satisfying customer needs became the responsibility of everyone in the organization, regardless of whether employees were engineers, production specialists, financial analysts, or sales personnel.

Relationship Marketing Era

The driving philosophical approach of the *relationship marketing era* is to reinforce and broaden the scope of the customer-oriented focus of the marketing era. In the past, businesses focused on conquest marketing activities, which emphasized the sale itself rather than the parties to the sale. In contrast, the relationship marketing era recognizes the value and profit potential of customer retention: creating long-term trading relationships by providing reasons to keep existing customers. The relationship marketing era is also characterized by a broadening of the definition of customers to include suppliers. Hence, the guiding emphasis is to develop long-term, mutually satisfying relationships with the firm's customers and suppliers.

An Alternative to the Traditional View of Marketing

The primary problem with the traditional view of marketing eras as described above is that it does not fit the facts. In reality, the idea of inventing and marketing products that customers need and want, then supplying them, has been fundamental to the development of free-market economies from prehistory on, not something that has been implemented in recent times. The history of global trade and economic development has involved bringing new, attractive products, such as flint arrowheads, bone needles, fertility figurines, chocolate, and spices, to market and creating long-term trading relationships between tribes, countries, companies, and wealthy customers.[4] Ancient economies that were very good at such relationship marketing flourished and came to dominate other economies. Eventually, these traders became targets for raiders. Military forces were subsequently formed to protect their trade, trade routes, and the fruits of their trade. Thus, there never was a production era or a sales era. In reality, what there have been are companies that become too production-oriented or too sales-oriented, at the expense of listening to the voice of the customer. Eventually, these companies are forced by the competition (with more of a marketing orientation) to become more customer-oriented, or they are driven out of the market. Motorola's misfortunes described in the opening vignette provide ample evidence of the costs to be paid for not listening to the customer and other trading partners.

http://www.motorola.com

What, then, has been the real history of the development of market economies and marketing? It is the history of the development of well over 10,000 product markets, each with its own unique evolutionary story.[5] Marketing scholars have attempted to draw further general conclusions about the evolution of such diverse markets and their marketing traditions and practices by focusing on the exchange process.

Marketing as an Exchange Process

According to the most widely accepted definition provided by the American Marketing Association, **marketing** is ultimately an exchange process:

> *Marketing is the process of planning and executing the conception, pricing, promotion, and distribution of ideas, goods, and services to create exchanges that satisfy individual and organizational goals.*[6]

To illustrate the fundamental concept of added value associated with the exchange process, consider the following scenario. The grower of beef would rather exchange a steak for a watermelon because he is tired of eating steak (consumption satiation) and it costs him a lot less to produce an additional steak (labor specialization) than to grow a watermelon. Similarly, the grower of watermelons also would like to exchange one of her watermelons for a steak because she is sick of eating watermelons and it costs her a lot less to produce a watermelon than a steak. Therefore, if they meet, an exchange is likely to occur between the beef farmer and the watermelon grower. When both benefit, added value has been created by the exchange. Hence, the fundamental benefit of the **exchange principle** (the law or truth underlying exchange) is added-value creation: By the simple act of exchanging goods and services for other goods and services (or for money), added value is created.

Marketing exchanges exist because they are beneficial to both parties. They are beneficial to both parties because of the principles of raw material scarcity, labor specialization, and consumption satiation. **Comparative advantage** in the cost of producing various goods has long been understood to underlay the benefits of trading. But production-based comparative advantage does not, by itself, lead to production surpluses that create trade and markets. The satiation principle is also necessary. In other words, if the more the farmer ate steak, the more he liked it and wanted more of it to eat, then he would be very happy producing more beef at an ever lower cost and eating more of it than ever. In essence, the farmer would have an ever increasing interest in eating his cattle, rather than exchanging them for other products in the marketplace. Consequently, the fundamental principle of exchange is based on the principles of production-based comparative advantage (which is itself based on resource scarcity and labor specialization) and consumption satiation.

Marketing facilitates exchange by performing a variety of activities that benefit consumers, producers, and resellers alike. Marketing exchange activities include the following:

- *Buying:* Marketers, besides being skilled manufacturers, are often skilled buyers of other products from many different manufacturers that are then resold to customers under one roof. When you shop at Wal-Mart, for example, you are taking advantage of this marketer's considerable expertise in assessing quality and its volume-buying power that enables it to promise the lowest prices.
- *Selling:* By making a variety of products available under one roof, marketers sell to numerous customers in a single location, thereby alleviating the need for individual customers to deal with individual manufacturers for each and every product they desire to purchase. Selling also includes the skills of understanding, educating, and persuading customers, all much needed in a world of rapidly improving technology and increased competition.
- *Transporting:* Marketers facilitate the transportation of products by providing the products customers want, where and when they want them. Improvements in transportation, from wagon to sailboat to steamboat to jumbo jets and containerization, have made markets global, to the benefit of billions of people.

Marketing
is the process of planning and executing the conception, pricing, promotion, and distribution of ideas, goods, and services to create exchanges that satisfy individual and organizational goals.

The exchange principle
maintains that when an exchange benefits both trading partners, the exchange adds value. This principle is derived from the raw material scarcity, labor specialization, and consumption satiation principles.

Comparative advantage
results when a strategic advantage is held relative to the competition.

- *Storing:* Marketers store products, for example, at a grocery store, so that customers do not have to and so that manufacturers do not have to keep everything that they produce in their own inventories until each product is sold. Today, distribution logistics (sometimes called supply-chain management) combines the management of buying, transporting, and storing into a single system. Innovations in these systems have helped to reduce the cost of distribution in the U.S. economy from around 12 percent of gross domestic product (GOP) to 6 percent over the last 20 years.
- *Financing:* Marketers offer special paying (e.g., 90 days, same as cash) and leasing agreements that enable more customers access to the products they desire to purchase. Innovations in household financial services in the mid-20th-century U.S. economy led to an enormous increase in the purchase of homes and automobiles and the formation of household debt. These innovations are now taken for granted, but from the early 1930s through the early 1960s, there were many marketing departments in university business schools that taught entire courses on managing consumer credit.
- *Risk taking:* By purchasing products from manufacturers before they are sold to customers, marketers assume the risk that the products may not sell in the marketplace. This diversification of financial risk encourages manufacturer invention, innovation, and entrepreneurship that benefits everyone.
- *Standardization and grading:* Marketers play a role in standardizing and grading the quality and quantity of products made available to customers (e.g., eggs). Such standards are also often mandated by regulation but increasingly are determined by the quality of rivals' goods and services. Standards increase buyer confidence in the quality and performance of what is purchased.
- *Obtaining market information:* Marketers collect information about buyers and suppliers (1) to increase the efficiency and effectiveness of the exchange process (e.g., by suggesting changes in what is exchanged or how it is exchanged to increase the resulting satisfaction of both parties and thus the total value of the exchange) and (2) to increase the returns from a firm's deployment of assets and resources.
- *Fostering trust with trading partners:* Marketers are important boundary spanners whose goal is to build and foster trust with trading partners that ensures that the terms of trade are implemented. Trust also leads to cooperative innovations in trading processes and expansion of the relationship into new ventures, product categories, and types of services exchanged, and acts as a goodwill buffer in economic hard times or when new rivals enter the market.

LEARNING OBJECTIVE   3

MARKETING AS AN ORGANIZATIONAL PROCESS

The Marketing Concept

Initially, the teaching of marketing covered two main topics: (1) how and why the unique marketing and trading institutions in different markets evolved and (2) the many and diverse ways that marketing activities (particularly undertaken in agriculture and processed foods markets) added value to the exchange process. From 50 years of such case study research and teaching emerged a consensus belief that the keys to business success were to achieve organizational goals by identifying the needs and wants of customers and delivering products that satisfy customers more effectively than competitors could. This prescription for success became known as the **marketing concept**. The marketing concept consists of three fundamental principles:[7]

Marketing concept
refers to how organizational goals are achieved by identifying the needs and wants of customers and delivering products that satisfy customers more effectively than competitors could.

1. The organization exists to identify and to satisfy the needs and wants of its potential and existing customers.
2. Satisfying customer needs is accomplished through an integrative effort throughout the organization.
3. The organizational focus should be on long-term cooperative trading relationships with customers as opposed to short-term exploitation of customers.

The marketing concept has its roots in customer orientation founded on the philosophy that production and selling efforts must be based on understanding and serving customers' needs and wants. The marketing concept puts companies and managers on notice that neither production nor sales nor customers exist in a vacuum: They exist in a competitive marketplace that is becoming increasingly more competitive. It is this competitiveness that ultimately drives the marketing concept. The problem with the marketing concept, however, is that it is too simplistic. There is a great deal more to a firm's **marketing strategy** (the planning and directing of a firm's marketing efforts) than taking the long-term perspective, focusing on the customer, and diffusing such beliefs across the organization.

The Fundamentals of Marketing Strategy

How is marketing strategy, the deployment of the resources and skills described in Table 1.1, actually implemented? Markets consist of **market segments**—homogeneous groups of customers who have similar product usage wants and needs (see Chapter 7). For example, the soft drink market consists of a regular cola segment, a diet cola segment, and a caffeine-free segment, among others. As a business strategy, market segmentation allows the firm to focus its marketing efforts on narrowly defined markets. Many firms lack the resources to efficiently and effectively appeal to every segment in a market; therefore, they often choose to focus on specific segments called **target markets**. The **marketing mix**, composed of product, pricing, distribution (place), and promotion decisions, is then tailored to meet the needs and wants of specific target markets and to carve out a position in the marketplace. **Product positioning** refers to how customers perceive a product's position in the marketplace relative to the competition. Ultimately, marketing strategy directs the product positioning of the firm and directs and develops a

Marketing strategy
refers to using vision and planning to create and deploy a company's assets and capabilities most profitably.

Market segments
are those segments of the market or submarkets that seek similar benefits from product usage, and that shop and buy in similar ways that are different from other market segments and submarkets.

Target markets
are those market segments whose needs and demands a company seeks to serve and satisfy.

Marketing mix
is composed of product, price, place (distribution), and promotion decisions and programs that the company decides to pursue in implementing its marketing strategy.

Product positioning
refers to how customers perceive a product's position in the marketplace relative to the competition.

Marketing Strategy	Table 1.1

Deploying Assets and Capabilities

Marketing strategy involves deploying major financial and human capital resources, such as building an Internet presence or a sales force, to develop a superior, distinctive, and difficult to imitate competitive advantage that the company can claim as its own based on the following dimensions:

1. Superior product design and technology as measured by sales growth, performance in use (not on paper), and customer satisfaction. How does the company rate compared to its major and high-growth competition? More importantly, how is this comparison changing? Who has new product development momentum?

2. Superior distribution system alliances, technology, and sales forces as measured by sales growth, service quality effectiveness, efficiency, and distributor satisfaction. How does the company rate compared to its major and high-growth competition? More importantly, how is this comparison changing? Who has distribution system momentum?

3. Superior cost structure, which leads to lower prices and the potential for significantly lower prices as sales grow. How is the company rated compared to its major and high-growth competition? More importantly, how is this comparison changing? Who has cost reduction momentum?

4. Superior brand reputation based on a history of superior product and distribution strategy (not just a heavy advertising campaign that produces top-of-mind audience name awareness). How does the company rate compared to its major and high-growth competition? More importantly, how is this comparison changing? Who has brand reputation momentum?

(Continued)

Table 1.1	Marketing Strategy (continued)

Using Superior Vision

The competitive positioning advantages listed are achieved and cleverly deployed through superior vision (seeing evolutionary market trends into the future) and using the following:

1. Superior market scanning and tracking systems involving the sales force and customer and trade satisfaction tracking services. How is consumer behavior changing?

2. Superior processes that link the highest levels of company decision making (the board and executive committees) to the knowledge and market insights of the company's boundary spanners (sales force, customer service support, and market researchers).

3. Research and development that tracks trends in new emergent technology used in product and distribution system design. The company learns by imitating as well as by innovating.

4. Information technology systems that measure what is being managed and that allow real-time communication of new knowledge across cross-functional teams and sister operations in other countries.

5. Superior targeting of products and services to market segments.

6. Superior assessment of the growth potential of markets and the company's competitiveness in each market.

7. Superior marketing planning and improvisation processes that act on the above information.

---

http://www.pepsico.com

http://www.drpepper.com

mix of other marketing activities, processes, and practices that are specifically tailored to effectively and profitably serve the needs of a target market. For example, Pepsi's product positioning strategy is to be thought of as a product targeted to "the younger generation." Similarly, Dr. Pepper is positioned to those who want to be considered "individuals" or "original," and Mountain Dew is positioned as the drink of "active Generation Xers" (see Figure 1.2). These various positioning strategies are developed through creative adjustments to the components of the marketing mix.

Marketing Mix

The conventional way of thinking about marketing mix is to categorize marketing decisions and activities as being related to product, pricing, distribution (place), and promotion decisions. (See Figure 1.3.) We will take a brief look at each of these marketing mix elements. An in-depth discussion on each of these elements is given in later chapters.

Product Decisions and Activities

Product decisions and activities encompass a wide array of processes, such as new product development, branding, packaging, labeling, and the strategic management of products throughout their technological life cycle. Materials relating to product decisions are presented in Chapters 8 and 9.

Form utility
is achieved by the conversion of raw and component materials into finished products that are desired by the marketplace.

Products provide **form utility**—the transformation of raw materials or labor into a finished good or service that the consumer desires. However, we would like you to think of products as more than just tangible goods. Throughout this text, unless otherwise specifically stated, the term *product* refers to *goods* (e.g., appliances, automobiles, and clothing), *services* (e.g., legal, health care, and financial), *people* (e.g., political candidates, religious leaders, and students looking for their first job), *places* (e.g., tourism destinations, shopping centers, and countries seeking economic development), and *ideas* (e.g.,

Figure 1.2

Figure 1.3	A Marketing Strategy Framework

HIV protection, Mothers Against Drunk Driving, and antidrug campaigns). Similarly, the term *customer* includes both business customers and household consumers. No one would dispute that product markets vary greatly in large part because of differences in the types of customers who make a market. A customer can be a government, a corporation, a family business, a household, or an individual. Clearly, any firm that seeks to satisfy its customers must possess a deep understanding of how customers derive satisfaction from a purchase. In particular, it must strive to have a better understanding than its rivals. Marketing to businesses is so different from marketing to households that it is best to study them separately. That is why Chapter 5 is dedicated to household consumers and Chapter 6 examines marketing to business-to-business customers.

Pricing Decisions

Pricing decisions should satisfy multiple objectives. At the very least, a firm's pricing strategy should

1. support a product's marketing strategy
2. achieve the financial goals of the organization
3. fit the realities of the marketing environment

Despite decades of study by economists and market researchers, price setting is still often determined by a best-guess decision that is quickly revised when the guess turns out to be wrong. For example, when Procter & Gamble (P&G) first marketed Pampers, it priced the diapers at 10 cents apiece. The product bombed, because consumers thought that disposable diapers cost more than buying and washing cloth diapers. The convenience advantage of disposable diapers did not compensate for their higher cost. Therefore, P&G developed a new design for the product and its packaging. It cut material costs and lowered production time, thereby decreasing production costs. P&G relaunched the product at a price of 6 cents per unit, and Pampers became a great success and highly profitable. Pricing decisions are discussed in detail in Chapter 14.

http://www.pg.com

Distribution (Place) Decisions

Distribution decisions reflect the marketer's ability to create time, place, and possession utilities for customers. *Time utility* and *place utility* reflect the marketer's ability to provide products when and where customers would like to purchase them. *Possession utility* facilitates the transfer of ownership of the product from the producer to the customer through marketing channels. A typical *marketing channel* would consist of the following channel members: the *manufacturer*, who produces the product and sells it to a wholesaler; the *wholesaler*, who resells the product to a retailer; and the *retailer*, who sells the product to the *final consumer*.

The importance of distribution's role in the marketing mix cannot be overstated. By far the greatest achievement of the ancient Romans was the construction of 50,000 miles of highways, some of which are still used today. By comparison, there are 42,000 miles of federal highways in the United States. These Roman roads were the first interstate highways in the world and contributed greatly to the Pax Romana, the peace that Rome brought to the Mediterranean region for several hundred years. The Romans did so by reducing the cost of trading, which increased the likely returns and therefore increased trading.

Similarly, the history of the development of markets and marketing in the United States is best understood by thinking about it in terms of two periods: the period before the railway and the period from 1840 to 1900, when the railway network came to dominate trade and commerce in the United States. Before the railway, both markets and economies were local. A few luxury goods made their way across the country, but even the wealthiest had to wait months for items to arrive at their front door. As the tentacles of the railway lines spanned the country, the economy changed. Goods could travel thousands, rather than tens, of miles in a few days. Markets went from local to regional almost overnight. Eventually, isolated markets became mass markets through the web of the railway system. Mass markets provided the incentive for producers to manufacture on a larger scale, which led to innovations and advances in manufacturing.[8] These innovations led to even lower costs of manufacturing, which, combined with still lower distribution costs, led to even lower prices and further market growth.

Yet even as the railway network dominated the U.S. economy, the new road network was evolving. Road transportation really took off with the construction of the interstate highway system in the 1950s. Air transportation's network of hubs and spokes rapidly developed during the 1970s as a result of deregulation. Companies such as Federal Express (FedEx) and United Parcel Service (UPS) continue to thrive on this once innovative distribution system. An important aspect of modern marketing is about learning to harness new and improved transportation and distribution networks. Materials related to distribution decisions are presented in Chapters 10 and 11.

http://www.fedex.com

http://www.ups.com

Promotion Decisions

Promotion decisions communicate the firm's marketing strategy to customers and channel members who assist in the product's distribution to the market. Every firm has choices to make as to how to communicate with the market. Communication is accomplished by managing the firm's promotion mix. Elements of this mix include personal selling, advertising, publicity, and sales promotion. Each element has its advantages and disadvantages, as will be discussed in Chapters 12 and 13.

Promotion elements that are used simultaneously are termed integrated marketing communications (IMC). For example, when the Disney/Pixar movie *A Bug's Life* was released, it was frequently advertised on television. In addition, sales promotions such as the "Find Flik and Win Instantly" game that was printed on cans of Dr. Pepper also promoted the movie, and fast-food restaurants included *A Bug's Life* toys in their children's meals. Integrated marketing communications support one another and reinforce the customer's awareness of the product being promoted. Recently, we have seen similar IMC campaigns for *Harry Potter, Monsters, Inc., Lord of the Rings: The Fellowship of the Ring,* and the 20th-anniversary release of *E.T.*

http://disney.go.com

Ultimately, promotion is a form of communication. The evolution of communication technology has been a major force in the development of human relations, and has greatly reduced the costs of buyers and sellers communicating with each other. For thousands of years, trading and communication required personal travel by land and sea. It was very slow, dangerous, and costly. The Romans greatly improved the transportation of both goods and information. The Roman highway system, for example, allowed couriers to travel faster and even led to the invention of billboards (first used by roadside inns), which were the first forms of advertising. The irony was that the original purpose of the Roman highway system was to serve as a strategic defense initiative, built to move troops around the empire. It worked so well that the roads were converted to a peaceful purpose, increasing communication and trading between people.

If you have grown up with cable television, which allows you to watch what is happening anywhere in the world as if you are actually there, then it is hard to appreciate

how isolated people were 200 years ago. They could not communicate easily with anyone more than 50 miles away. Today, we can use the Internet to trade with anyone in the world in real time, most likely in the emerging language of world trade, which is English.

This split-second communication with anyone, anywhere, has come about through the invention and creation of a whole series of communication technologies and networks. The invention of printing, which first made the Bible available for ordinary folks to read, also led to the introduction of advertising fliers. But it was the invention of the telegraph and telephone that led to a great step forward in marketing: Orders could now be placed, tracked, and delivered. It created two-way communication between buyers and sellers that took minutes or hours rather than days or weeks. This greatly reduced order-delivery cycle time (both its average time and its variance in time taken), which greatly increased the amount and efficiency of trading.

Radio and television further enabled buyers and sellers to communicate as never before. These communication technologies led to the tremendous growth of advertising that has become a separate profession often taught in journalism rather than in business schools. Marketing success is about learning to master ever new and improved one- and two-way communication technologies. It has evolved into management of communication networks that themselves are evolving through technological innovation. Mastering the use of the Internet in marketing is today's exciting challenge and why Chapter 15 is dedicated to marketing on the Internet.

LEARNING OBJECTIVE 4

THE MARKETING ENVIRONMENT

Marketing environment
involves the micro- and macroenvironmental influences, including the company's own objectives and resources, the sociocultural environment, the competitive environment, the economic environment, the technological environment, and the political and legal environment.

Environmental scanning
identifies important trends in the micro- and macroenvironments, then considers the potential impact of these changes on a firm's existing marketing strategy.

Businesses do not operate in a vacuum. Environmental forces surround a firm and often change the rules of engagement. Consequently, a firm's marketing strategy must adapt to changes in the **marketing environment** if the firm is to survive and thrive. In general, a marketing environment comprises six elements. First, the firm's internal marketing environment (the *microenvironment*) consists of *objectives and resources*. The external marketing environment (the *macroenvironment*) consists of the *socio-cultural environment, economic environment, legal/political environment, competitive environment*, and *technological environment*.

Figure 1.4 provides a framework that incorporates these environmental forces. The model illustrates that these forces impinge on and influence the likely successful fit of all elements of the marketing mix to the internal and external marketing environment and to the target market. Successful firms track changes in the marketing environment via environmental scanning. **Environmental scanning** identifies important trends in the micro- and macroenvironments, then considers the potential impact of these changes on a firm's existing marketing strategy.

The Future of Electronic Shopping

The Internet has already become the backbone of commercial communication between businesses, involving trillions of dollars of trading each year. It will ultimately kill business-to-business snail mail and faxes and do much more to increase system control over business-to-business supply chains.

The less certain question is how big home electronic shopping will become. In 1995, forecasts of Internet sales ranged from $5 billion to $300 billion by 2000. In 2000, home electronic shopping was around $50 billion, at the low end of earlier estimates, and about half of this was travel and accommodation business. Experts predicted that the Internet will take over traditional marketing and selling channels for many products. The Internet market reduces prices by cutting selling and marketing costs and by providing more quality information to buyers than traditional markets. That, at least, was the argument.

The stock market is a case in point. In early of 1999, five million Americans were buying and selling stocks on the Internet, and the number was increasing by 15,000 a week. Consumers were attracted by services such as Etrade.com that offered low trading fees and a great deal of information about companies. This is virtually the same information that traditional brokers access to give expensive advice to clients (advice that often also favors the stocks that the brokerage house is pushing). But are these shoppers behaving the way that the marketing experts expected? Are these Internet shoppers carefully appraising the long-term prospects of the companies whose stock they are buying? Not always, maybe not at all. Most of the shoppers may be following the tips on the message boards and chase the stocks that are in high demand. Some examples of their buying tactics are:

My philosophy is to buy high and sell higher and not be afraid to take risks. I use no research tools or software. I just surf the message boards and look for volume.

My philosophy is don't marry your stocks and, above all, take your profits and run. . . . I pay no attention to P/Es [price to earnings ratios]. They don't matter.

The traditional way of assessing a stock is to use its price to earnings ratio. Traditionally, the P/E for the stock market has been around 15 to 20. In the late 1990s, it shot up to around 30, and for some Internet stocks it is infinite because the company has yet to generate any earnings. The traditional safe way of creating a nest egg is to invest for the long term. That way, you weather the short-term runs up and down, and gain through the long-term trend in stock prices. According to *The Economist* (30 January 1999, p. 17):

The casino capitalists who spend 7 or 8 hours a day at their PCs trading Internet shares appear to be stark, staring mad.

Fast-forward to fall 2001. The Internet bubble driven by the above behavior burst, and online day trading collapsed. Today, many technology stocks are priced at 10 to 20 percent of what they were in 1999. Now the big stock market companies are advising clients to weather the storm of the economic recession and the effects of the terrorist attacks and to pay attention to P/E ratios. They are also being investigated for issuing far more buy recommendations than sell recommendations during the stock market bubble (in many cases 10 buy recommendations for every sell recommendation), which fed the buying boom. Part of the reason for this discrepancy is that they were selling many of the stocks that they were recommending as buys.

Sources: Joseph Alba et al., "Interactive Home Shopping: Consumer, Retailer, and Manufacturer Incentives to Participate in Electronic Marketplaces," *Journal of Marketing* 61 (July 1997): 38–53; Mathew Schifrin and Om Malik, "Amateur Hour on Wall Street," *Forbes*, 25 January 1999, 82–85; "Why Internet Shares Will Fall," *The Economist*, 30 January 1999, 17.

The Internal Marketing Environment

Objectives and Resources

Top-level corporate executives formulate annual and long-term objectives that affect marketing decision making.[9] For example, a corporate objective to increase profits by 15 percent over the previous year has implications for current marketing actions. Objectives are critical to any company's success. Without objectives, a company has no direction. If no objectives are set, a company will waste a great amount of time, money, and effort in pursuing what may prove to be unprofitable or unrealistic strategies. A company must know where it is going if it is to be successful. It needs an overall set of objectives to guide its efforts. Each functional area in the company (e.g., operations, finance, and marketing) also has its own objectives, but its goals must fit into or be guided by the company's overall objectives. It is imperative that the entire company works together toward

Figure 1.4	Marketing Mix Fit

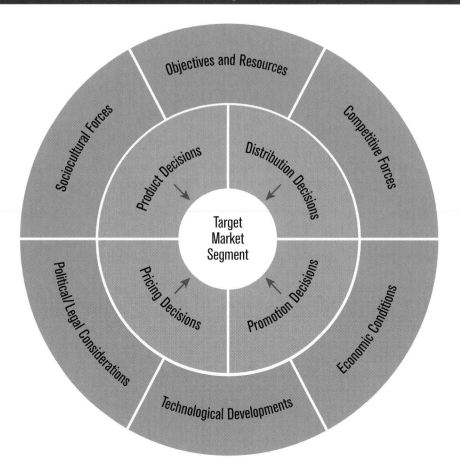

The marketing mix is targeted to a market segment. The marketing mix must also fit within the larger marketing environment.

the same goals. Thus, marketing strategy is influenced by, and is to some extent constrained by, overall corporate objectives.

Marketing strategy is also constrained by available resources. A firm's resources include finances, technological and production capabilities, and managerial talent. Resource constraints prevent marketing managers from pursuing every available opportunity. For example, financial restrictions can prevent a firm from running a prime-time television campaign for a new product introduction. Instead, it may be able to afford a national radio campaign. Or a firm's current production line may not be equipped to package a trial size of an existing product. New equipment may be needed, but perhaps finances will not allow it at this time. If a firm is fully aware of its limitations, strategies can be developed and opportunities pursued that are within the company's limits.

The External Marketing Environment

Sociocultural Environment

Changes in the sociocultural environment reflect the reshaping of the world's population in terms of numbers, characteristics, behavior, and growth projections. In 1960, three billion people inhabited the planet; in 1984, this number increased to five billion; by 2025, the world population is expected to exceed eight billion. The sociocultural environment also includes age categories within populations. The median age of Americans is increasing. In 1970, the median age was 28; in 1980, it was 30; and in 1990, 33. It was expected to rise to 36 by the year 2000. Nearly 55 million U.S. citizens are over age 55, represent-

We're Not Just Yuppies Anymore	Table 1.2

In the 1980s, yuppies, the nickname for young, upwardly mobile, urban professionals, represented a market frequently targeted by marketers. In the 1990s, markets changed and became increasingly fragmented. The new terms below describe some of the changes that took place in the sociocultural environment.

SKIPPIES	School kids with purchasing power
MOBYS	Mother older, baby younger (reflects the trend that women are waiting until they are older to start a family)
DINKS	Double income families, no kids
DEWKS	Dual earner families, with kids
PUPPIES	Poor urban professionals
GUPPIES	Gay urban professionals
WOOFS	Well-off older folks

ing approximately 21 percent of the total population. This group alone accounts for over $7 trillion of the country's wealth. Some major advertisers who have recognized the importance of marketing to this segment have begun using seniors in cross-generational ads.

Customer attitudes and behavior also impact the sociocultural environment and the way marketers perceive the market. Even marketing vocabulary is changing, as seen in Table 1.2. As changes in the sociocultural environment occur, so do customer needs and wants, and so should marketers' attempts at fulfilling customer requests. For example, consider these statistics about today's women.

- Seventy percent of women between the ages of 25 and 54 are in the labor force.[10]
- Women head nearly one in three households compared to one in seven in 1950.[11]
- A larger share of women are remaining single into their 30s because of disenchantment with marriage and more educational and employment opportunities.[12]

Marketers must consider the changing roles of women both in marketing their products and in reaching target markets. A traditional medium such as daytime television is no longer effective in reaching working women. Direct mail, magazines, and radio are proving to be more effective in reaching this group.

Cultural and age diversity, between and within countries, also affects the sociocultural environment. Marketers are now targeting the specific needs of ethnic markets such as African Americans, Asians, and Latinos. This change in marketing strategy reflects the growing purchasing power of ethnic groups, their increasing rate of population growth relative to the slower growth rate of Caucasian populations, and cultural differences in how different groups purchase and use products. By 2010, minorities will represent one-third of the U.S. population.

The Americanization of world culture through science, entertainment, and business has helped to reduce cultural differences, particularly among countries with highly educated populations. This opens up the possibility for global segmentation and positioning, where segmentation spreads across rather than within cultures. In short, cultures no longer follow national, political, or cultural borders as much as they did even 50 years ago.

However, many countries still have different consumer wealth, buying power, price elasticity, experience with the product category, and competitive behavior. Consequently, relatively few products can be positioned exactly the same way across the global marketplace. Those products that can be positioned usually have a strong symbolic or intangible image that transcends cultural, technological, and economic differences. (Coca-Cola has

such an image.) Additional materials relating to international marketing are discussed in Chapter 3.

Economic Environment

Marketers must also monitor changes in the economic environment.[13] The economic environment includes factors such as the purchasing power of markets, per capita expenditures, employment rates, general consumer confidence, and the cost of capital that may be necessary to produce products. The mere size of markets is not enough to make a market profitable. Customers within those markets must have, in addition to the willingness to purchase products, the ability to purchase (purchasing power). For example, although there are three billion people in Asia, half of them are under age 25 and do not have much purchasing power. However, many of these countries have a growing middle class that outnumbers the middle classes of industrialized countries. India, for example, has a middle class of approximately 250 million consumers. Marketers such as Coca-Cola, Frito-Lay, KFC, Motorola, and Walt Disney have recently started operations in India, which they consider to be one of the largest untapped markets in the world.

http://www.fritolay.com

http://www.kfc.com

Legal/Political Environment

The legal and political environment poses another external force for the marketer. It is the job of the government to establish the rules and regulations to which businesses must conform. These rules and regulations affect each element in the marketing mix. Marketers must therefore be aware of and conform to all laws affecting their business.

As citizens, our behavior is constrained by the law and by our individual views of right and wrong. It is no different for firms that compete in domestic and international markets. Marketplaces are full of rules. Many are written into law, some are outlined in professional codes of ethics, and others are stated in company rules of good conduct. While the legal/political environment can frustrate initiative, in general it is positive for business. For example, many of the laws that affect marketing practice are in place to encourage competition and to protect consumers. A much broader discussion relating to the legal/political environment, business ethics, and marketing's social responsibility is presented in Chapter 2.

Competitive Environment

Competitiveness reflects how effective and efficient a firm is, relative to its rivals, at serving customers. *Effectiveness* pertains to the quality of products, market share, and profitability, while *efficiency* reflects response speed and low costs. Both effectiveness and efficiency ultimately depend on the strength of the firm's competitive drive and its decision-making skills.

Businesses are constantly exhorted by almost everyone—government agencies, associates oversees, and industry insiders, among others—to become more competitive. But becoming more competitive is like losing weight: It is easy to talk about, but it is not easy to do. The task is almost impossible if it is not based on a thorough competitive situation analysis (see Chapter 4). The analysis should start with a general overview of the competitive structure and dynamics of the market. This includes market share analysis, a review of the history of the market, and a search for emerging competitors that threatens to drive existing firms and their products into extinction. The analysis should then focus on major rivals and their likely behavior.

Technological Environment

Successful firms must also monitor changes in the technological environment. Technology is advancing at an incredible rate. Technological advances primarily influence marketing practice in two ways. First, they enable firms to develop new products and to compete in new markets. For example, a new process that allows flat screens for computers and televisions to be produced at a price much lower than the current technology must be considered in any technological environment analysis of existing flat-screen customers and suppliers. Have you wondered when you will be able to afford a high-quality flat-screen monitor? The answer is that it may be sooner than you think. The price of high-end liquid crystal displays (LCDs) halved in 2001, but researchers at Penn State University and Kent State University have developed a process that will produce lighter, more flexible, more durable, and higher quality LCDs at a cost that will reduce the price by 90 percent. When new technology results in an order of magnitude reduction in

cost—that is, by 10 times—or an increase in quality, firms using the old technology need all the advance warning they can get to switch to the new technology or risk extinction.

Technological advances also help marketers improve the way business trading is conducted on a day-to-day basis. For example, UPS handles more than 3 billion packages and 5.5 percent of the United States' GDP annually.[14] Jim Kelley, the chief executive officer of UPS, attributed much of his firm's success to technology:

> *We have 12 mainframes capable of computing 5 billion bits of information every second. We have 90,000 PCs [personal computers], 80,000 handheld computers to record driver deliveries, the nation's largest private cellular network and the world's largest DB-2 database designed for package tracking and other customer shipping information. To give you an idea of how valuable information [technology] has become to our company, the database actually has more storage capacity than the repositories of the U.S. Census Bureau.*

Clearly, monitoring the environment is critical to any firm's survival. To avoid failures, a company has to pay attention to what is going on in the marketing environment while implementing marketing strategy. It is that simple, yet many companies do not pay attention to what their sales force, sales figures, costs, and market research say is happening with regards to changes in the marketing environment. The reasons for not paying attention and acting on information are many. It may be that the firm does not conduct environmental screening analysis at all, or it collects information that is biased, or information is not passed on to the right decision makers, or the information is not timely enough. Today's senior management is often faced with numerous distractions, such as take-over attempts, lobbying efforts directed toward the government, involvement in major litigation, internal management succession battles, and labor disputes.

Reacting to changes in the marketing environment is often a challenging process. Companies often talk about valuing market research and market scanning systems, but the reality is that these activities are undertaken several layers of management away from boards of directors and executives who are making most of the marketing strategy decisions. For example, information technology companies such as Cisco, Oracle, and Lucent Technologies were caught by surprise by the suddenness of the technology spending downturn in late 2000. They talked about their new-economy skills at serving customer demand, yet their customer scanning systems gave them no warning of the declining economic health of their business customers and the collapse in demand. In contrast, more traditional companies such as DuPont and automobile manufacturers were much better prepared for the downturn because of their superior marketing scanning systems and economic indicators, developed over many economic cycles.[15] The lesson is that a major responsibility of the marketing function in any firm is to ensure that tracking measures that monitor the marketing environment get into the hands of the most senior management of the company.

MARKETING STRATEGY IN ACTION: BEST/WORST PRACTICES

LEARNING OBJECTIVE 5

http://www.boeing.com

http://www.airbus.com

Strategic marketing concept
is a company's mission to identify, generate, and sustain competitive advantage through superior positioning and vision.

Boeing versus Airbus

During the business boom of the 1960s and 1970s, the marketplace became increasingly crowded with companies serving the same groups of customers. This problem is evident in countries such as the United States that protect and promote strong competition in markets. To combat this competitive threat, the marketing concept has evolved into the **strategic marketing concept**, defined as a company's mission to identify, generate, and sustain competitive advantage through superior positioning and vision. (See Table 1.1.)

One example of competitive positioning is the contrast between the marketing strategies of Boeing and Airbus. Airbus, which is subsidized by several European governments, now has an order backlog bigger than Boeing's, but what of the future? Airbus plans to build a 550-seat superjumbo jet for long-haul flights. Just how security and customs clearance at already crowded airports will support such a jet is a concern, but Airbus has the market for super size alone because Boeing has chosen a different strategic plan and direction: It is developing a smaller sonic cruiser to fly across the Pacific at half the current flying time. Airbus is pursuing a strategy of offering business customers (the airlines) economies of scale and lower costs per passenger mile. Boeing is pursuing a strategy of offering airlines a higher quality, higher profit margin service. Which will be the most profitable strategy depends on whether the business for premium service air travel grows faster than traditional coach "cattle class" demand. Boeing's vision is that premium service air travel will grow faster. Airbus's vision is that the global air travel support infrastructure will be able to cope with ever larger jumbo jets whose per passenger mile operating cost is significantly lower than today's 747 jumbos.

IBM's Revitalization Effort

http://www.ibm.com

IBM is going through a quiet but massive competitive repositioning, from being a supplier of computers and systems to the world's largest computer services company. Ten years ago, IBM recognized that the future of computing was not in selling hardware boxes but in selling computer services to customers, and it started to change direction. The hardware business was too competitive and cutthroat, and the technology advances were outpacing the skills of its customers, making traditional sales support a very costly service. IBM has quietly positioned itself in two important market domains. The first is in developing grid computing—delivering computer power like an energy utility—which brings supercomputer capability to the desktop. With grid computing services, customers no longer need to staff expensive in-house computer centers operating at less than capacity and economic efficiency and subject to continual technology obsolescence. With on-demand computing, IBM can get the most out of its hardware that it uses to supply a market that has been estimated to grow to $30 billion in annual sales by 2010.[16] It can also seamlessly introduce new and more efficient hardware into the grid system to supply ever cheaper on-demand computing power without facing the cost of extensive customer education and usage training.

The second marketing domain is Web-based system control services. The services are designed around a customer's key added-value processes and manage the company's systems, such as purchasing, inventory warehousing, and shipping processes. IBM is

betting that many companies will continue to outsource accounting, supply-chain, and other process control systems to third parties whose vastly greater experience in successfully installing new technologies and systems (compared to the company's own limited and often negative experience) and focused expertise deliver competitive advantages that could never be achieved by any in-house system.

IBM Global Services is already the largest computer services customer in the world ($33 billion in sales in 2000), with every intention of becoming even larger. IBM is no longer positioned as the leading computer manufacturer but as the future leader in supplying computing power on demand and full-service management systems and control processes. Companies such as Electronic Data Systems ($19 billion sales in 2000) and Fujitsu ($13 billion in sales) are IBM's major current rivals, with consulting companies such as Accenture and other computer companies such as Sun Microsystems, Hewlett-Packard, Compaq, and SAP scrambling to compete in lucrative segments of the computer services market. But IBM, a company that looked as if it had lost its competitive position and vision 10 years ago has, through clever, customer-oriented, marketing strategy, emerged again as a high-profit, high-growth market leader—more correctly, a high-profit, high-growth market *maker*.

Webvan's Demise

A classic problem in marketing positioning is balancing investment in superior customer service with superior cost structure. Webvan, the Internet grocery retailer that went bankrupt, was led by the former chief executive of one of the world's leading management consulting firms, Anderson Consulting, and attracted hundreds of millions of dollars in initial investment capital. But it overinvested in huge warehouse capacity in major U.S. cities, which meant that it could not possibly be profitable because of its high fixed costs. When it needed to cut costs, it switched to offering lower quality produce, which is the grocery category most households use to judge the quality of a supermarket (along with meats). The better decision would have been to hire the ex-chief executive of a major supermarket chain and undertake a joint venture whereby the groceries and produce were picked and packed from the warehouses and supermarket shelves of an existing supermarket chain, thus greatly reducing costs and making the cost structure competitive. The British grocery chain Tesco PLC has successfully pursued such a strategy. The marketing strategy mistake of many dotcoms was to forget to make their purchasing and delivery fulfillment cost structure competitive and to not understand what made traditional brick-and-mortar rivals competitive in attracting and satisfying customers.

http://www.tesco.co.uk
↗

http://www.cemexusa.com
↗

Cemex Online

The Mexican cement manufacturer Cemex is an excellent example of a company that has strategically invested in information technology to reduce its costs and to increase the quality of its product (through automated production and quality control monitoring) and its customer service.[17] For 10 years Cemex executives have had access to online information, from sales to kiln temperatures, for all of the company's production plants. Such real-time knowledge has been used to create competition between divisions and regions to improve performance. Cemex has also put computers and global positioning systems in its cement trucks. Dispatchers use a computer scheduling program to direct and even redirect trucks en route. The system has dramatically increased customer service, for example, by cutting estimated delivery time from three hours to 20 minutes, even in traffic-snarled Mexico City.

Marketing strategy is about investing in technology and human capital in ways that increase the competitive position of the firm. Examples of successful marketing strategy that uses the Internet can be found in the most basic of commodity products, such as cement, in traditional technology industries, such as the after-market for auto parts, and in the financial services industry, such as Schwab's inexpensive on-line trading. The key is to see the opportunity to use the Internet to create new customers and increase existing customer satisfaction in a way that reduces the cost of doing business and is hard for rivals to imitate. Ultimately, marketing strategy is about developing decision-making and planning processes that adapt a firm to changing market conditions. The Market Planning Appendix at the end of this book offers an in-depth discussion of the formal planning processes for marketing decisions.

CHAPTER SUMMARY

- Markets came into being and trading developed as a result of the spontaneous economic combustion between resource scarcity, labor specialization, and consumption satiation.

- In essence, markets and marketing exist because of consumers' desire for a variety of ever improving products and because of the impracticality and inefficiency of each individual developing distinct products for his or her personal use.

- Marketing is based on the principle that exchange adds value and marketing facilitates the exchange process by performing a variety of activities. The completion of these marketing activities facilitates the flow of products along the supply chain from producers to customers. In doing so, marketing can have profound societal implications and is often closely related to the success of political and economic systems.

- Effective and efficient markets and marketing practices can help everyone, including poorer countries. But as we will discuss in Chapter 2, there is a price to this success: Greater prosperity as a result of trading integration and superior marketing systems places strains on the earth's ecology.

- Fifty years ago, the study of marketing developed a more managerial emphasis on earning profits through customer satisfaction, which became known as the marketing concept. This gave birth to the field of consumer research, which has developed a reputation for scholarship that is the equal of other social sciences. It also led to a more managerial emphasis on segmenting the market, targeting and serving segments with especially designed products, and carefully designing a marketing mix.

- As an organizational process, marketing develops and implements the marketing mix, consisting of product, distribution (place), promotion, and pricing decisions and activities specifically tailored to meet the needs of intended target markets. The marketing mix elements help firms develop positioning strategies that differentiate their products and brands from competitive offerings.

- Because businesses do not operate in a vacuum, successful firms regularly modify their marketing mix decisions to adapt to the changing internal and external environment, particularly to new types and forms of competition. Macroenvironmental forces include sociocultural, technological, economic, competitive, and legal/political influences. The microenvironment is comprised of organizational objectives and resources. An important role of marketing is to prepare situation analyses and reports on changes in these market environments.

- This chapter presents a best-practices view of marketing strategy. There appear to exist opportunities for tomorrow's graduates to improve the quality of firms' marketing planning and implementation. We hope that you find the other best practices discussed throughout this book thought-provoking and that they increase your interest in what the study of marketing has to offer in terms of careers and practical business strategy.

KEY TERMS

Comparative advantage results when a strategic advantage is held relative to the competition.

Consumption satiation is what occurs when the more units of a product that are consumed in a short period of time, the less the added value of consuming another unit of the same product and the greater the variety-seeking behavior.

Environmental scanning identifies important trends in the micro- and macroenvironments, then considers the potential impact of these changes on a firm's existing marketing strategy.

The **exchange principle** maintains that when an exchange benefits both trading partners, the exchange adds value. This principle is derived from the raw material scarcity, labor specialization, and consumption satiation principles.

Form utility is achieved by the conversion of raw and component materials into finished products that are desired by the marketplace.

Labor specialization occurs when labor and management undertake specific activities and processes, the repetition and focus increase the effectiveness, efficiency, and learning of labor and management.

Market segments are those segments of the market or submarkets that seek similar benefits from product usage, and that shop and buy in similar ways that are different from other market segments and submarkets.

Marketing is the process of planning and executing the conception, pricing, promotion, and distribution of ideas, goods, and services to create exchanges that satisfy individual and organizational goals.

Marketing concept refers to how organizational goals are achieved by identifying the needs and wants of customers and delivering products that satisfy customers more effectively than competitors could.

Marketing environment involves the micro- and macroenvironmental influences, including the company's own objectives and resources, the sociocultural environment, the competitive environment, the economic environment, the technological environment, and the political and legal environment.

Marketing mix is composed of product, price, place (distribution), and promotion decisions and programs that the company decides to pursue in implementing its marketing strategy.

Marketing strategy refers to using vision and planning to create and deploy a company's assets and capabilities most profitably.

Product positioning refers to how customers perceive a product's position in the marketplace relative to the competition.

Raw material scarcity occurs when valuable raw material resources are geographically concentrated in some locations and not in others, resulting in resource scarcity in some locations.

Strategic marketing concept is a company's mission to identify, generate, and sustain competitive advantage through superior positioning and vision.

Target markets are those market segments whose needs and demands a company seeks to serve and satisfy.

QUESTIONS FOR DISCUSSION

1. What is wrong with the statement "Trade came about because of labor specialization"?

2. What are historically considered the four marketing eras? Discuss the different characteristics of each era.

3. For thousands of years a market was a marketplace, a physical place where buyers and sellers gathered to trade goods and services. Why is it so difficult to define what a market is today?

4. While R.D., a frequent flyer, is waiting in line at the gate for an American Airlines flight, he is paged. The ticket agent invites him to sit in an empty seat in first class. What type of focus or approach to business does American have toward business if this is a deliberate program? How have computers and Internet communication helped in creating such a program? What other invention does this program depend on?

5. Marketing is based on what principle? Explain this principle.

6. According to the information provided in this chapter, is Motorola production-oriented or market-oriented? Please explain.

7. Marketing facilitates the exchange process by engaging in a number of activities. Briefly describe each of these activities.

8. Discuss the significance of the marketing environment to marketing strategy.

9. If you had to write a report to your boss on how to organize the digital files/directory for storing information about the market environment, what general headings might you consider? Why would you make them more specific in the real world?

10. Discuss marketing strategy utilizing the terms *market segments, target markets, marketing mix,* and *product positioning*.

INTERNET QUESTIONS

1. By 2010, shopping will very likely benefit from the invention and marketing of a useful new product. For example, price search engine software will be packaged with personal computers and notepads. The software can be used to search for the lowest price within a requested delivery time of a particular product (e.g., a book). The search can be undertaken while the user is asleep or doing other tasks on the computer. The software will identify the best deals; all the user has to do is click the mouse, and the book is ordered, paid for by credit card, and on its way that day. How will this change the marketing strategy of Internet marketing companies? Is the price search engine software likely to be sold by Microsoft or America Online (AOL)? Why may these companies be reluctant to market such software?

2. Internet marketers may come and go; some of the new companies may become huge, while others may disappear, as did some of the first personal computer manufacturers. But there are some companies in the added-value chain that are surely going to benefit greatly from the growth of Internet shopping and become larger and more profitable. Who are they?

ENDNOTES

[1] Roger O. Crockett, "Motorola: Can Chris Galvin Save His Family's Legacy?" *Business Week,* 16 July 2001, 73–78; "Chris Galvin Shakes Things Up—Again," *Business Week,* 28 May 2001, 38–39; Andy Reinhardt, "Wireless Web Woes," *Business Week,* 4 June 2001, eb22–eb25.

[2] Adam Smith, *The Wealth of Nations* (New York: Random House, 1937).

[3] See Frank J. Andress, "The Learning Curve as a Production Tool," *Harvard Business Review* (January–February 1954): 16–19; Kenneth Arrow, "The Economic Implications of Learning by Doing," *Review of Economic Studies* (April 1962): 166–170; Winfred B. Hirschmann, "Profit from the Learning Curve," *Harvard Business Review* (January–February 1964): 125–139; George S. Day and David B. Montgomery, "Diagnosing the Experience Curve," *Journal of Marketing* 47 (Spring 1983): 44–58.

[4] David S. Landes, *The Wealth and Poverty of Nations* (New York: W.W. Norton & Company, 1988); Joel Mokyr, *The Lever of Riches* (Oxford: Oxford University Press, 1990).

[5] A superb history of the development of the global market for clocks and watches is presented in David S. Landes, *Revolution in Time* (Cambridge, MA: Harvard University Press, 1983).

[6] Peter D. Bennet, ed., *Dictionary of Marketing Terms* (Chicago: American Marketing Association, 1988), 54.

[7] Adapted from William O. Bearden, Thomas N. Ingram, and Raymond W. LaForge, *Marketing*, 2d ed. (Boston: Irwin McGraw-Hill, 1998), 8.

[8] Alfred D. Chandler, Jr., *The Visible Hand* (Cambridge, MA: Harvard University Press, 1977).

[9] This section adopted from John H. Lindgren, Jr., and Terence A. Shimp, *Marketing: An Interactive Learning System* (Fort Worth, TX: The Dryden Press, 1996), 58.

[10] Susan E. Shank, "Women and the Labor Market: The Link Grows Stronger," *Monthly Labor Review* 111 (March 1988): 3–8.

[11] Daphne Spain and Suzanne M. Bianchi, "How Women Have Changed," *American Demographics* (May 1983): 18–25.

[12] Ibid.

[13] This section was adapted from John Ward Anderson, "Thundering Herd," *The Louisville Courier-Journal*, 2 January 1994, A8; John E. G. Bateson and K. Douglas Hoffman, *Managing Services Marketing* (Fort Worth, TX: The Dryden Press, 1999), XI, 6.

[14] Jim Kelly, "From Lip Service to Real Service: Reversing America's Downward Service Spiral," *Vital Speeches of the Day* 64, no. 10 (1998): 302.

[15] Joseph Weber, "Management Lessons from the Bust," *Business Week*, 27 August 2001, 104–110.

[16] Spencer E. Ante, "Big Blue's Tech on Tap," *Business Week*, 27 August 2001, 52.

[17] "The Cemex Way," *The Economist*, 16 June 2001, 75.

[18] Robert Hof, Debra Sparks, Ellen Neuborne, and Wendy Zellner, "Can Amazon Make It," *Business Week*, 10 July 2000, 38–43; and Peter Dickson, Paul W. Farris, and Willem J. M. I. Verbeke, "Dynamic Strategic Thinking," *Journal of the Academy of Marketing Science* (29 March 2000): 216–237.

AMAZON.COM AND BARNES & NOBLE[18]

Over the last six years Amazon.com, the flagship of the new Internet retailing age, lost billions of dollars, but in the last quarter of 2001 it finally announced a small profit. The reason why its business model was flawed has had much to do with the fact that the sale of its books and music CDs did not earn high margins and the company found that to maintain sales it needed to continue to run an expensive advertising campaign that gives the company prominence on AOL. Amazon also has invested in warehouses and distribution centers and is now offering these facilities to other e-retailers. Meanwhile, Barnes & Noble was purchased by Bertelsmann, a major European publisher and whole-sale distributor.

Both companies are attempting to develop long-term relationships with their customers by using what is called collaborative filtering software. This software interacts with the customer at the point of purchase selection and suggests the customer consider other books or music. It does this by comparing the history of a customer's purchases with thousands of other customer histories, then recommending as incremental purchases books or music selected by other customers with similar interests and tastes. The recommendations become more targeted and fine-tuned as the company learns more about the customer, which increases the likelihood of a further sale. It also creates a Web site shopping experience that is unique for each shopper: No two shoppers experience the exact same interchange.

Before answering the following questions, please visit http://www.amazon.com and http://www.barnesandnoble.com. Compare the feel of their sites and their prices.

Discussion Questions

1. What long-term advantage over Barnes & Noble is Amazon.com creating by spending so much more on its America Online advertising?

2. Which user interface has the better feel? What are the best features of each?

3. How different are their prices? Did Amazon.com make a strategic mistake by not merging with a major brick-and-mortar bookstore chain? What effect will its recent marketing alliance with a major bookstore chain (Borders) have on the long-term success of Amazon.com's book selling?

4. What should Barnes & Noble do to make its current stores more competitive with electronic book shopping? Think about the competitive advantages of shopping for a book at a current Barnes & Noble store.

5. How does the use of collaborative filtering software help the company? How does it help the customer? How does it compare with a friendly sales clerk you get to know?

CHAPTER CASE

CHAPTER two

Peter R. Dickson, Florida International University

Dr. Dickson earned his undergraduate degrees at the University of Otago, New Zealand. He has published over 70 papers in journals and proceedings and served on the editorial board of several publications, including *Journal of Business Research*, *Journal of Marketing*, and *Marketing Letters*. He is the author of *Marketing Management*, published by the Dryden Press, and a coauthor of a logistics strategic planning guide. He has also worked in the real world, marketing several new products.

Dr. Dickson helped found the Business School at the University of Waikato, where he taught for seven years. After receiving a Fulbright-Hays Bicentennial scholarship and completing his Ph.D. at the University of Florida, he taught for 14 years at The Ohio State University, where he became the Crane Professor of Strategic Marketing and a professor of industrial design, and for 5 years at the University of Wisconsin–Madison, where he was the Arthur C. Nielsen Jr. Chair of Marketing Research. He is currently Knight-Ridder Eminent Scholar in Global Marketing at Florida International University.

Marketing and Social Responsibility

Is it fair if companies insert messages such as "Drink Coke" and "Eat Popcorn" into single frames of a motion picture and through such subliminal messages (messages we cannot detect) lead moviegoers like sheep to the theater's overpriced concession counter? Such behavior would seem to be outrageous manipulation and very unethical. Vance Packard, the popular sociologist, used this marketing practice as the central premise of his book *The Hidden Persuaders* (1957), which took modern marketing practices to task for their unethical behavior and lack of social responsibility. The book sold millions of copies and damaged the reputation of the marketing profession. Its sweeping condemnation of marketing was picked up uncritically by the popular press and mass media and led several states to pass laws against subliminal persuasion. This manifesto of the manipulative sneakiness used by marketers and the capitalist system is still being taught in high school classrooms.

There is just one small problem: The practice of such subliminal persuasion has absolutely no basis in fact. When challenged, Packard and his publisher were never able to document where and when such practices occurred, and cognitive psychologists, in search of fame and fortune, have not been able to create such effects in controlled experiments.[1] Vance Packard and his publisher made millions out of libeling the marketing profession. The image of all-powerful marketing tactics manipulating a vulnerable and gullible customer was indelibly burned into the folklore of American culture. Was that fair and socially responsible? Vance Packard becomes a rich folk hero, and modern marketing, despite all the wonderful products that it has helped bring to the modern world, is vilified. The fact is that the vast majority of marketing practices are socially responsible, aimed at honestly and competitively serving customers. Indeed, the concept of serving, respecting, satisfying, even delighting customers in a long-term relationship is the long-term goal of most marketing practices. Of course, as with any profession, there are the bad eggs. For example, there are the jackals who prey on the elderly, sometimes charging thousands of dollars for inspecting and repairing a chimney that "is about to burn your house down," or suckering them into ridiculous get-rich schemes and stealing all of their savings.

Very occasionally a whole industry goes bad, as we have witnessed with the cigarette manufacturers. Thirty years ago, the manufacturers' own scientists were informing them that tobacco was addictive and caused lung cancer and other fatal illnesses. But that did not stop the industry from publicly challenging and dismissing every published study that came to the same conclusion. The industry fought against the health warnings on tobacco packaging and then, 10 years later, used the presence of these warnings as an excuse for not being liable to consumers. Why? Because consumers had been warned on the packaging that smoking was not good for their health! The CEOs of the industry testified under oath at congressional hearings that tobacco was not addictive, when they knew it to be so. They all lied and they all knew they were lying (on the advice of their corporate lawyers). Officials swore that they never targeted children with their marketing campaigns, such as Joe Camel. Yet independent market research revealed that 90 percent of children 8 to 13 years old could recognize Joe Camel.[2] Court documents obtained from these companies' own research and marketing departments later revealed that children indeed had been targeted.

The American tobacco companies have begun to pay for their actions, but are they apologetic? Some are, but most are not. They have worked hard with their bought politicians to torpedo controlling legislation and are spending their marketing budgets expanding overseas sales. The World Heath Organization estimates that 200 million to 300 million children and young people under the age of 20 today will eventually be killed by tobacco. It is hard to understand how a whole industry could go so bad. Perhaps the cigarette manufacturers slipped so slowly into the slime, they did not notice where they ended up. Maybe they were very ill advised by their lawyers. Whatever the reason, the lesson is chilling. Whole industries can go bad and get away with it for decades.

As a profession, marketing can try to counter these negative images with stories about socially responsible companies that are working to care for people and the environment. For example, professional marketers have developed highly successful antismoking campaigns in states such as California and Florida. These marketing campaigns have helped cut smoking rates by over 20 percent among teens. These campaigns would be even more successful, though, if politicians spent the money received from the tobacco settlement on what it was designated for—antismoking public health marketing campaigns.

Such stories, however, are unlikely to have a significant impact on the impression of the popular press or to influence those people who already view marketing practices in a very negative light. Because of such critical attention, members of the marketing profession must therefore be ever vigilant that they are behaving responsibly. They must be willing to pull the plug on bad schemes and openly identify those who disgrace the discipline. This, after all, is what being a member of a profession is about. Furthermore, they must be responsive to the media and the general public and be able to counter some of the currently popular, yet perhaps quite unreasonable and poorly reasoned, criticisms of marketing.

After you have completed this chapter, you should be able to:

1. Recognize that marketing's first social responsibility is to be ever more efficient and effective, and understand the charges made against the marketing role in this regard.
2. Understand that marketing's second social responsibility is to behave ethically and honestly with customers, colleagues, and ourselves as marketers.
3. Observe how marketers must obey the letter of the law and spirit of various laws as a third social responsibility.
4. Appreciate how marketing exercises its fourth responibility via cause-related marketing.

In Chapter 1, we learned how successful firms adapt to changes in the marketing environment by adjusting one or more of their marketing mix elements (product, place, promotion, and price). Firms that are successful in the long term respond to these challenges and opportunities in a socially responsive manner. Failure to do so puts an industry or an individual company at risk. The thought that cigarette manufacturers, for example, launched marketing plans and campaigns directed at children and teenagers to get them addicted to a particular brand of cigarette (knowing what they were condemning the children to) is particularly troublesome. These same men and women went home at night to their own children. The fact that the manufacturers and marketers of cigarettes are even now admitting the evils of their product to Americans while launching marketing plans and campaigns directed at young Chinese to get them addicted is even more troublesome. Phillip Morris looked for and found a replacement vulnerable demographic group of consumers somewhere else in the world to victimize.

On a much smaller scale (but the fiery consequences were much more vivid), some Firestone executives put company short-term profits ahead of human lives and telling the truth. Firestone quality control systems tracking the reported accidents-from-tire-failure statistics failed to alert the senior management of the company early enough, and senior management did not respond fast enough. The result was more accidents, deaths, and injuries that could have been prevented. Can Firestone, which weathered a similar tire design flaw a generation ago, survive as a brand with a reputation for quality and safety? Probably not. New product safety regulations have also been passed requiring new cars to have dashboard lights that warn when tire pressure is too low. In this instance, the federal government has had to take on the role of product innovator because the tire and automobile companies were not prepared to develop and market such a feature in the competitive marketplace.

The **social responsibility** of marketing has several sides. Marketing activities must be efficient and effective and not squander scarce resources. Marketing executives must be mindful of the unintended social consequences of their efforts on culture and subcultures. Marketing executives, along with all other executives in a firm have to obey the law and participate responsibly in the making of laws. But simply abiding by the law is only a first step, and marketing executives are expected to have a strong moral compass that guides their behavior. In short, they are expected to behave according to the canons of ordinary or common decency. Finally, professional marketers are expected, as public citizens, to use their skills in promoting societal causes and in other ways that benefit humankind, such as helping the International Red Cross develop a more efficient global distribution system for the aid it sends to disaster areas. In the following sections we discuss each of these dimensions of social responsibility.

Social responsiblity
is the collection of marketing philosophies, policies, procedures, and actions intended primarily to enhance society's welfare.

MARKETING'S FIRST SOCIAL RESPONSIBILITY: BE EVER MORE EFFICIENT AND EFFECTIVE

Marketing's first responsibility to society is to advance life, liberty, and the general happiness through the creation of exchanges, markets, product innovations, and trading innovations that increase the efficiency and effectiveness of the economic process. In short, the first responsibility of marketers is to keep learning to do their job ever more efficiently and effectively. This is undertaken in the selfish pursuit of profit. But as 18th-century economist Adam Smith pointed out over 200 years ago, such self-improvement also makes markets more competitive, makes our lives as workers and customers more productive, and wastes less of the scarce resources on earth that need to be preserved for future generations. Many people believe that marketing is not fulfilling this first social responsibility very well. They believe a lot of products that are marketed are not needed and that a lot of marketing effort, particularly advertising, is wasteful and not becoming more efficient and effective. In the following sections, we address such criticisms.

Too Many Unneeded Products Are Marketed That Fail

Although it is almost impossible to assess what percentage of new products succeed, it has been estimated that about half of the resources earmarked for developing and marketing new products is spent on failures.[3] It is very probable that better marketing research and marketing planning could increase the success rate, but it must always be appreciated that success often comes as a result of lessons learned through failures. Babe Ruth, during his time, hit more home runs than any baseball player in history. He also struck out more times than any baseball player in history. In other words, new product development and marketing is always risky, and the price of occasional great success is frequent failure. Each year tens of thousands of new products fail. But do you think, before the fact, that the marketers of these products believed they would be unwanted and unneeded? Did they purposefully and deliberately intend to waste all of their money and effort in such ways? Presumably not. Such wastage of money, blood, sweat, and tears is an argument for *better marketing, not less marketing*. But even the best marketing efforts often fall short. Companies can misunderstand customer preferences, fail to anticipate competitors' lowering prices, or miss the clues that foreshadow the unveiling of a product even better than their own. The responsibility of marketers is to keep learning how to improve their market research, new product development, and marketing processes. Whether the art of marketing is getting better as fast as it could is perhaps an open question. In this sense, marketing may not score very highly on its first responsibility, which is to strive as hard as it can to become ever more efficient and effective in its many and varied activities.

Too Many Unneeded Products Are Marketed That Succeed

The role of research and development in marketing is to invent, design, manufacture, and market new products that customers prefer over their currently used products. That is part of the natural evolution of markets where ever better products replace inferior alternatives. Who would argue against the marketing of better painkillers, cancer treatments, and safer, more fuel-efficient cars? There are also several reasonable and rational answers to the criticism that other successful products are just not needed and are a waste of the earth's dwindling resources and poor people's meager earnings.

The first answer is that care must be taken in making judgments for other people as to whether they should need or want a particular product. The individual freedom to pursue life, liberty, and happiness is one of the most noble principles and "rights" of the age of enlightenment that started in the 18th century and continues through today. Millions of men and women have given their lives to defend this "right" and extend it to peoples who have not possessed such freedom. *Freedom and free choice* does not simply mean the right to choose the political leadership of a society. It is freedom to pursue a desired education, freedom to pursue a vocation and career in a free labor market, and freedom to spend one's earnings and savings as one chooses. If we believe in such freedoms, then we must allow the expression of this freedom in other people's choices of products. For example, it is a slippery slope to criticize disposable diapers as a waste of trees that could be better used in producing books on enlightened thinking. The slope ends in a managed

economy where the powerful elite prescribes what is good and what is bad for everyone else. Again and again such a system of top-down dictatorship, no matter how well meaning, has been tested and has failed, most recently in communist economies. History is also a long and tragic litany of religious fanatics closing the minds of their followers, removing freedoms and rights, and viciously exterminating any threats to their tyranny. In the United States, consumers live with the fact that every supermarket has a full aisle of pet foods containing hundreds of choices. Is it wrong that many families spend more on their pets than on donations to feed starving children in other parts of the world? Perhaps. Do these same families have the right to choose to spend their money this way and to respond more positively to pet food marketing campaigns than charities' marketing campaigns? We may not agree with their choices and priorities, but, yes, they have this right, and it is a right that again many have died for.

An extension of the "do we need this product" criticism is that marketing encourages **planned obsolescence** by coming out with new, "improved" models too often (e.g., Microsoft 2000 or XP). But consumers do not need to buy the new model, and they often do not. Women do not always buy into the latest spring or fall fashions. If consumers are concerned about the rapid obsolescence of their purchase, they often postpone their purchase. Such a concern also creates a marketing opportunity for an enterprising seller to introduce an innovative leasing scheme that enables consumers to easily trade in and upgrade to the latest technology. This is precisely what Gateway did with its "Your:) ware" marketing campaign in the late 1990s. If this leasing solution proves that obsolescence is a real concern to personal computer buyers, then all sellers will offer similar leasing programs, and the obsolescence concern will be addressed.

Sometimes products are criticized for being too shoddy, with built-in components that fail too quickly. The answer to this is that quality always wins out when it is desired. The big three domestic automobile manufacturers learned this lesson the hard way in the 1980s. Should they have learned this lesson at the expense of their customers and shareholders? No, but such behavior always catches up with companies in free markets. The reputation of the offending firm is hurt for years, sometimes decades. On the other hand, many critics of the modern market economy complain that product parts last too long and that manufacturers should be required to dispose of their products at the customer's request and recycle the materials. The free market answer to this criticism is the creation of a new service market where firms compete to dispose of and recycle such products.

Market Distribution Systems Are Inefficient

There has been a long tradition of criticizing the inefficiency of distribution systems. It has its roots in the complaints of farmers who, for example, calculate that they are paid only 20 cents for the corn that is finally sold by the supermarkets as cornflakes for $3 or

Planned obsolescence
is the design of a product with features that the company knows will soon be superseded, thus making the model obsolete.

http://www.gateway.com

What to Do with Old Technology

About 15 million computers were sent to the landfill in the United States in 1999. Since then, this number has increased by at least 10 percent each year. While this represents a small portion of the total solid waste stream (less than one-half of 1 percent), computers contain a variety of hazardous materials that can adversely impact the environment. For instance, monitors and televisions with cathode ray tubes (CRTs) possess significant amounts of lead, an element that can damage the nervous system, especially in children. The U.S. Environmental Protection Agency reported that 24 percent of all lead in the municipal waste stream is attributable to CRTs. Other computer components that contain hazardous materials include mercury switches, cadmium batteries, and lead solder.

As a result of the rapid obsolescence of computers and worries about their environmental impact, governments around the world are crafting regulations to keep electronic equipment out of landfills. As of July 1, 1999, the Commonwealth of Massachusetts, for example, banned businesses and households from putting CRTs into local landfills. European countries are also pursuing far-reaching "take back" legislation that requires manufacturers to bear the full cost and responsibility of unwanted electronic equipment disposal.

Driven by this environmental concern and by government regulation, a whole new industry of electronic recycling has emerged. The largest such firm is Aurora Electronics of California. In 1995 it posted revenues of $95 million: $52 million from the resale of spare computer parts and $43 million from recycling and refurbishing. Envirocycle of Pennsylvania recycled over 500,000 monitors in 1996, and its full-service demanu-

facturing operation is growing at more than 40 percent each year. Additionally, hundreds of small firms have been formed in recent years around the world to refurbish, demanufacture, and recycle electronic waste. These companies succeed by regularly forming strategic alliances with the original equipment manufacturers (OEMs) to process their surplus inventory, warranty returns, and off-spec products, and by offering full-service asset management disposition to businesses and municipalities that generate electronic waste.

Electronic asset recovery programs excel in the marketplace for two reasons. First, they satisfy the growing demand by consumers for more environmentally friendly products. Second, they provide services that result in cost savings and avoid liability claims to OEMs and other waste generators. These issues propelled Xerox to institute its own asset recovery and remanufacturing program. "The switch to asset recovery was not done primarily because of environmental considerations, although we realized that would be a benefit," notes Jack Azar, manager of environmental design and resource conservation for Xerox. "We saw competitive advantage coming from this program." From 1991 to 1995, Xerox reaped $200 million in raw material and parts savings, and reduced its landfill and potential liability costs by more than $450,000 annually. These cost savings are shared with the customers.

Electronics recycling firms are finding treasure in other people's electronic trash. By responding to a market demand created by the growth of a "waste" product, new government regulations, consumers' environmental concerns, and operational cost reduction projects at OEMs, these businesses are able to earn a profit while providing a beneficial service to the environment.

---

more. Does this seem fair? Who is making all the profits in the added-value process from the farm to the breakfast table, and how much "added value" are they really adding?

It is hard not to have sympathy for the average farmer, particularly if you come from a farming heritage. But to ask whether each player in the chain deserves its margins, and to try to calculate some efficiency measure, is to ask completely the wrong question. The right question is, have the distribution systems evolved as a result of the forces of free-market competition? If they have, then, by the laws of competition, the existing distribution systems are efficient. A further very important truth is that a great deal of innovation and learning has occurred in physical distribution in the United States over the last 30 years, so much so that the percentage of the gross domestic product spent on the cost of physical distribution (order processing, transportation, and inventory storage) has dropped from 12 percent to about 6 percent. At the same time, the reliability and quality of these services have greatly increased. This came about because deregulation of the transportation and communication industries in the late 1970s led to an incredible burst of competition and innovation that reduced the cost of transportation and communication services and increased their quality. The cost of distribution has also benefited from stable and low interest rates and fuel costs. No other major sector has increased its efficiency, as measured by its reduced share of the gross domestic product, by anything like physical distribution's 50 percent improvement. It puts the increased costs of health care and education to shame. No other country has as efficient a physical distribution system as the United States. Has enough innovation occurred in physical distribution to make it "efficient"? Again, this is a silly question because it cannot be answered. What is clear is that competitive forces are forcing supermarkets, mass merchandisers, and department stores to adopt the new technologies of distribution. If they do not, then fierce competitors who are trendsetters in innovation of new, more efficient distribution processes such as Wal-Mart and Home Depot will take away their business.

The current distribution system will last only as long as a more competitive system is not invented and developed. The current system replaced an earlier system, which replaced an even earlier system, and so on back to primitive distribution systems. As long as we see that this evolution is occurring in distribution, we know that distribution is becoming more efficient. We see this occurring everywhere: Cars are being marketed by super-dealerships; vacations are being booked using travel agents identified by Web searches; books are being purchased through online stores on the Web. We see an increase in mail-order catalog sales. We saw Kmart replace Sears as *the* mass merchandiser, and now Wal-Mart has replaced Kmart. But stores such as Meijer and Target are now challenging Wal-Mart. We see major new airports being built, major container ports being expanded, and trains stacking containers two high.

Of course, some intermediaries will stubbornly remain inefficient relative to best practices, and they can be viewed as betraying the first social responsibility of marketing, which is to strive to improve and become more efficient. They are a blight on marketing, just as doctors who refuse to improve their practices and teachers who refuse to improve their teaching are a blight on their profession. But how long will the inefficient distributor survive before a new, more efficient, competitor enters the marketplace? Not as long as the inefficient doctor or teacher who is protected from competition. If marketing is socially irresponsible because it does not try hard enough to improve the efficiency of its distribution systems, then the medical and teaching professions presumably face much greater condemnation because their comparative improvement in performance over the last 30 years to some has seemed pitiful. The reason is also clear: Doctors and teachers have too little competition to force better customer service at lower cost. So let's give at least two cheers for marketing's role in distribution rather than complaining about the cost of distribution.

A Lot of Advertising Is Wasteful Expenditure

Perhaps what is underlying a lot of the criticism of marketing is identified with mass advertising, because mass advertising is inherently inefficient in reaching interested customers. This inefficiency leads to a lot of people being exposed to advertising of products or brands that they are not the least interested in, and hence is viewed as intrusive and wasteful, even alien to their values.[4]

http://www.walmart.com

http://www.homedepot.com

http://www.meijer.com

http://www.target.com

For example, let us consider a typical commercial break that consists of a flight of six 30-second television commercials. Even if the advertiser has targeted a program that has a high percentage of its target customers as viewers, it is unlikely that more than 20 percent of the viewing audience are *potential buyers* (that is, they are current satisfied users of the brand or are open to switching to the brand). What percentage of such a viewing audience will be interested in three or more of the advertisements in the flight of six commercials? The answer is less than 10 percent. No wonder so many people say that television advertising, junk mail, and telephone marketing waste money and intrude on their privacy. It is because advertising and marketing use **inefficient targeting** to identify interested audiences, not because they are too efficient, skilled, and manipulative.

In fact, the phrase "being turned off" by advertising may not simply describe a negative attitude. It may actually describe the psychological mechanism that customers in a "high consumption" materialistic society develop, from an early age, to cope with the irrelevance and inefficiency of advertising and sales pitches. It is very evident that we learn to develop attention mechanisms that allow us to tune out advertising, just as we tune out so many other stimuli that are competing for our attention day in and day out.

How do advertisers cope with the increased tuning out of customers? They increase their efforts to try to get us to tune in, through more powerful attention-grabbing mechanisms. This explains why television advertisements have become ever more expensive and elaborate productions, crafted to gain and keep our attention, often by using popular celebrities or zany humor. It also explains why direct marketing has developed more devious ways of getting us to open the mail: A common ruse is to disguise the mail as coming from a friend or from the Internal Revenue Service. It is also likely that we are not fooled for long. In response, consumers have developed ever more powerful and selective tuning out mechanisms to cope with these increasingly attention-grabbing mechanisms. Thus, the cost of creating advertising that gains our attention is spiraling upward with little or no long-term increase in its effectiveness. It is not just that mass advertising is becoming more expensive. A greater percentage of the money is being spent on gaining our attention than on explaining why the product is better than other alternative products.

A development that may save the image and cost efficiency of advertising is the evolution of very specialized digital TV channels and specialized electronic and print magazines aimed at particular demographic (age, income, gender, ethnic, education, lifestyle) groups. If this results in a much better overlap of the product target market and the audience, the average ratings of advertising would become more positive. If the overlap were strong enough that an average of 50 percent of the viewing audience would be interested in any particular advertisement, then this would result in two-thirds of the audience reporting interest in three or more of the ads in a flight of six 30-second commercials. The audience would also learn to pay more attention to such advertising because it is of interest. In short, a major answer to the criticism of advertising's social value is better targeting of interested audiences, which requires the invention of communication channels that are better targeted to the "interested" audience.

Marketers have both a self-interest and a social responsibility to keep learning to undertake their functions more effectively, but there is more to this responsibility than increased efficiency and effectiveness. Marketers have to learn to consider the full consequences of their collective actions. Making marketing practices ever more efficient and effective is of no help if it leads to the destruction of resources that are vital to humankind or to a corruption of values that are considered fundamental to a civil society.

Marketers' Self-Interested, Unintended Consequences on Supply

In a free market, the individual activities of sellers can have an accumulative effect that is often not intended and can lead to harmful effects on others or society at large. This is called the **tragedy of the commons** because it was first described in the context of the common grazing area (sort of equivalent to the modern public park) that villages in England used to make available for local residents to graze their sheep. To each village household, it did not seem unreasonable to increase its small flock of sheep, but across a hundred households, this pursuit of individual self-interest led to such severe overgrazing that all of the grass on the commons died. Now no one was able to graze sheep on the

Inefficient targeting
results when advertising and distribution reach too broad an audience, most of whom are not interested in the product.

Tragedy of the commons
is the name given to the process in which individuals, pursuing their own self-interest, overuse a common good to such an extent that the common good is destroyed.

commons, and everyone's sheep starved and died. Modern examples of "the tragedy of the commons" are everywhere. The world's fish resources are running out because fishermen have used modern technology to increase their fishing capabilities, and each individual fisherman does not believe that his individual behavior will ruin fishing for everyone. But when accumulated, such behavior has led to such a destruction of supply that many varieties of fish have fallen below a sustainable breeding population. This is a prime example of **supply-side market failure**. The incremental self-interested behavior of millions of businesses and consumers around the world is threatening the very supply of trees, fresh water, and fresh air. Normally, as Adam Smith famously pointed out, the individual pursuit of self-interest benefits the collective interest of society, but not in today's worldwide fisheries.

Supply-side market failure results when the individual activities of a supplier inadvertently lead to destructive effects on the overall supply.

Yet how do you tell a family in China not to burn coal to heat their house, or a utility not to burn coal to generate electricity, when families and utilities in Europe and North America have done so for hundreds of years, creating much of the ozone problem? It is not easy. Table 2.1 presents earth's three *socioecological* classes. As the economies of China, India, and other countries experience very rapid growth over the next 20 years, a billion "sustainers" will become "overconsumers," and the stresses on the earth's environment resources will be tremendous. Markets will have to be regulated, and marketers will have to obey these regulations. If the abilities and resources of marketing are spent on fighting (or finding ways around) regulation, then we will face a "tragedy of the commons" of global proportions. The responsibility of marketers is to promote conservation, recycling, and product innovations that save energy, air, water, trees, fish, and other scarce resources (see Figure 2.1). They can be helped by government programs and policies that encourage sellers to market more earth-friendly products. Such efforts make everyone more environmentally conscious, and consciousness raising is what is needed. But note it is not just marketers' responsibility but everyone's responsibility to save the supply of scarce resources for the hundreds of generations of our descendants.

Not all is doom and gloom. Between 1980 and 1995, water use in the United States dropped by 9 percent even with a population growth of 16 percent.[5] Using innovative recycling programs, industry water use dropped by 35 percent during the same period.

Table 2.1	Earth's Three Socioecological Classes		
	Overconsumers **1.1 Billion** **> US $7,500 per capita** **(cars, meat, disposables)**	**Sustainers** **3.3 Billion** **US $7,500 per capita** **(living lightly)**	**Marginals** **1.1 Billion** **< US $700 per capita** **(absolute deprivation)**
	Travel by car and air	Travel by bicycle and public surface transport	Travel by foot, maybe donkey
	Eat high-fat, high-calorie, meat-based diets	Eat healthy diets of grains, vegetables, and some meat	Eat nutritionally inadequate diets
	Drink bottled water and soft drinks	Drink clean water, plus some tea and coffee	Drink contaminated water
	Use throwaway products and discard substantial waste	Use unpackaged goods and durables and recycle wastes	Use local biomass and produce negligible wastes
	Live in spacious, climate-controlled, single-family residences	Live in modest, naturally ventilated residences with extended/multiple families	Live in rudimentary shelters or in the open; usually lack secure tenure
	Maintain image-conscious wardrobe	Wear functional clothing	Wear secondhand clothing or scraps

Source: Based on Alan Durning, *How Much Is Enough,* Worldwatch Institute, 1993.

Ford Motor Company Promotion of Recycling Efforts | **Figure 2.1**

Water use for farm irrigation dropped by 11 percent primarily because farmers switched from rotary sprayers (which waste a lot of water) to underground systems that water the roots. Household use stayed steady, but innovations such as the short-flush toilet began to make a difference. The answer to gloom and doom is, again, the invention and marketing of clever new innovations. When the market fails to be "sufficiently" inventive, however, the federal government has to step in, for example, by requiring washing machine manufacturers to invent, manufacture, and market new models that use 35 percent less energy, all of this to be done by 2007.

Marketers' Self-Interested, Unintended Consequences on Demand

Other self-destructive forces exist in free markets. Over the last two decades in the United States, market research tools such as focus groups and continuous political polling have been used to target voter concerns and issues and market political candidates. But instead of being used to guide the creation of innovative new programs and policies, the resulting customer insights have been mostly used to create negative advertising that attacks the values and character of political opponents. Today voters get most of their information about candidates running for election from TV ads, yet more than 90 percent of adults believe that the claims made in these ads are mostly (or at least partially) false.[6] The result has been to greatly reduce voters' respect for politicians and the electoral process: "I'm so sick of these ads . . . because nine out of 10 are negative," is a typical response. Such turn-off has resulted in **demand-side market failure**, whereby participation in the fundamental democratic process has been dramatically reduced. The participative democracy market is in danger of failing because of the marketing practices

Demand-side market failure is the cumulative effect of the marketing practices of many thousands of advertising campaigns that has a residual negative impact on the values of buyers and the demand for various products (e.g., voting).

of candidates and political parties. Short-term self-interest is literally destroying long-term public interest.

More generally, the cumulative effect of the marketing practices of many thousands of advertising campaigns has been claimed to have a residual negative impact on the values of certain demographic groups. This surfaces in T-shirts worn by women that read "There are 9 supermodels and 3 billion other women on this earth." The point, which is immediately understandable to tens of millions of women (if not men), is that the extensive use of these supermodels in advertising sets impossible standards for girls and women to aspire to in their appearances. The result is lower self-esteem and self-confidence. A quite reasonable reaction is for women to be turned off by fashion and "lookism," and to turn to other self-esteem boosting activities. Demand is again being killed by the accumulated negative impact of advertising. The problem is that marketers have found that using supermodels sells. Consumers, both men and women, respond to such marketing: We find such models very appealing. If this were not true, then marketers would not spend billions of dollars on marketing campaigns using such models. Should we then limit the opportunities of people to make a living off their beauty? Should we limit the ability of advertisers to use beauty to sell, because it makes ordinary folks feel more ordinary? Again, this is a slippery-slope question. What if great writers, painters, composers, athletes, and heroes inspire us, enrich our dreams, and lift the human spirit, but they also make our own achievements seem very ordinary? Should their works be banned? This at least raises an issue of whether critics of marketing apply the same ethical standards and codes to marketing as they do to other fields of human achievement and activity. This brings us to the second major social responsibility of marketing.

MARKETING'S SECOND SOCIAL RESPONSIBILITY: BEHAVE ETHICALLY

The second major social responsibility of marketing is to conduct business in an ethical manner. Most companies do live up to this responsibility. Despite the well-publicized exceptions that the media have used to help create an image that business is unethical (e.g., Enron and Arthur Andersen), many companies in the United States today are moral enterprises, led by men and women of impeccable character. The moral rudder of most enterprises is under the very solid control of senior executives, particularly the chief executive officer and senior vice presidents of sales and marketing, who lead by example and encourage a corporate culture of honesty and decency. Such enterprises often have written codes of ethics. It has been estimated that about 60 percent of U.S. companies have written codes of ethics that all employees agree to abide by. They are commonly accepted as a "given" across all employees.[7] Some larger companies have appointed an ethics officer, or ombudsperson, to further promote ethical behavior. These individuals help executives in tough decisions, and provide a safe haven (and source of support) for whistle-blowers. Table 2.2 presents a summary of the business conduct guidelines of

Business Conduct Guidelines for IBM and Guides for Procter & Gamble	Table 2.2

IBM	Procter & Gamble
Do not make misrepresentations to anyone you deal with.	To provide customers with superior benefits.
Do not use IBM's size unfairly to intimidate or threaten.	To listen and respond to customer opinions.
Treat all buyers and sellers equitably.	To ensure products are safe for intended use and anticipate accidental misuse.
Do not engage in reciprocal dealing.	To strive for fair and open business relationships with suppliers and retailers.
Do not disparage competitors.	To help business partners improve performance.
Do not prematurely disclose an unannounced offering.	To reject illegal or deceptive activities anywhere in the world.
Do no further selling after competitor has the firm offer.	To safeguard the environment.
Keep contact with the competition minimal.	To encourage employees to participate in community activities.
Do not illegally use confidential information.	To be a good neighbor in communities in which business is done.
Do not steal or obtain information by willful deceit.	To provide employees a safe workplace.
Do not violate patents or copyrights.	To show concern for the well-being of all employees.
Do not give or accept bribes, gifts, or entertainment that might be seen as creating an obligation.	To create opportunities for employee achievement, creativity, and personal reward.
	To provide a fair annual return to the owners.
	To build for the future to maintain growth.

Sources: Gene R. Laczniak and Patrick E. Murphy, *Marketing Ethics* (Lexington, MA: Lexington Books, 1985), 117–123; and Jan Willem Bol, Charles T. Crespy, James M. Stearns, and John R. Walton, *The Integration of Ethics into the Marketing Curriculum* (Needham Heights, MA: Ginn Press, 1991), 27.

IBM and Procter & Gamble (P&G). The guidelines reflect concern about treating customers (and everyone in the marketplace) in a fair and decent way, but they also express more general concerns, such as respecting the intellectual property rights of others, caring about the environment, and encouraging community service. Notice that the IBM code focuses more on trading ethics, whereas the P&G code is a more general social contract.

Figure 2.2 summarizes the content of some two hundred company ethics statements. United States companies are more concerned about intellectual property rights (such as not stealing patents, copyrighted material, and confidential information) and about ethical purchasing practices. Does this mean that some companies are more concerned about making sure that their buyers do not take bribes and indulge in other unethical behavior, and less concerned about the ethical behavior of their own marketing practices (such as offering bribes)? Whatever your opinion, this figure reminds us that ethical trading requires both the seller and the buyer to behave ethically. European companies seem to address purchasing and marketing ethical issues in about the same proportion. Canadian companies are somewhat more concerned about environmental issues, suggesting that concern over the environment is a more important part of the "social contract" and culture in Canada.

I Was Only Following Orders

As was seen in Table 2.2, company codes of ethics are often stated in general terms, leaving specific interpretation up to the individual salesperson or marketing executive. However, ethical dilemmas often arise during the implementation of marketing strategy. When this happens, decisions must be made without an opportunity to consult superiors. Such situations throw heavy responsibility on the marketing manager, product manager, and sales force. This ethical stress on the marketing executive can be greatly heightened by the presence of a company double standard. A company must make clear what action it will take against unethical behavior and establish credibility by following through. It

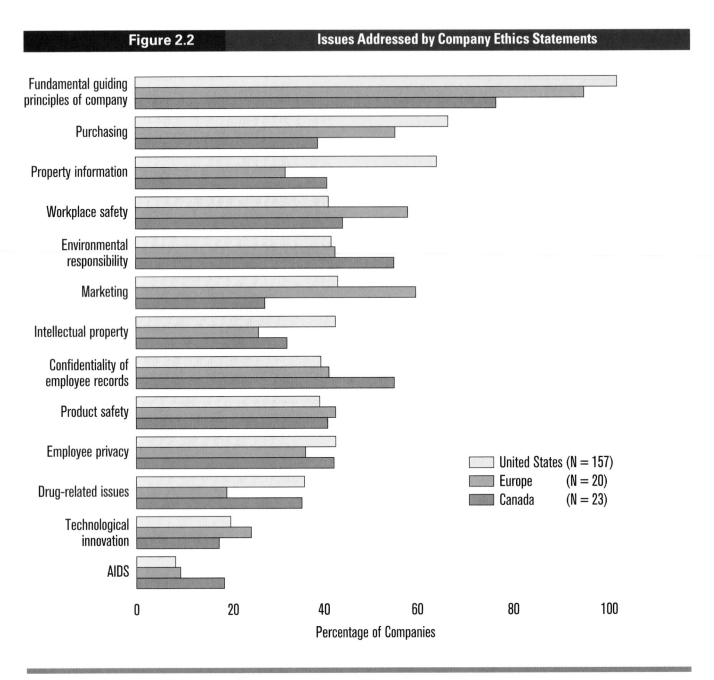

Figure 2.2   **Issues Addressed by Company Ethics Statements**

It seems that Canadian companies are more concerned that their purchasing is ethical than that their marketing is ethical. In comparison, U.S. firms are more frequently concerned about proprietary information, Canadian firms are more frequently concerned about environmental responsibility, and European firms are more frequently concerned about workplace safety.

Source: Permission from Ronald E. Berenheim, *Corporate Ethics Practices* (New York: The Conference Board, 1992).

must walk the walk. If actions are taken only when a company's unethical behavior is discovered and publicly challenged, then the company sends the worst signals to its marketing executives. What it says is that the company does not really mind what an executive does to achieve financial goals, as long as someone from outside does not find out. If the misconduct becomes public, the executive in question will take the fall, and the company will deny any knowledge of his or her actions. Unfortunately, many marketing decision makers face this conflict to varying degrees. It places great demand on their personal code of ethics. It also greatly undermines their respect for senior executives.

The famous Nuremberg trials of Nazi subordinates at the end of World War II established a new principle of ethical accountability. All of the evil could not be blamed on

Adolf Hitler, nor was the excuse "If I did not obey orders, then I would have been punished" found acceptable. We are all accountable for the lawfulness and decency of our trading decisions and behavior. Subordinates are responsible for their own behavior, even if following orders or under the threat of dismissal. Advertising agencies are accountable for the honesty of the messages they create for their clients. Ignorance is no excuse. No one gets an easy way out. To take a stand may put a promotion, a business contract, a trading relationship, or even a job at risk. To not take a stand is to sell out one's values, self-respect, and soul. To pass the responsibility on to senior executives may be construed as weakness, or worse, setting up the boss. When orders and ethics collide, a trusted mentor in the organization can be invaluable. That is why ethics ombudsmen and women have been created.

The American Marketing Association also has developed a code of ethics (see Figure 2.3) that marketing professionals can turn to for guidance and direction. The emphasis is on ethical trading behavior, and approximately half of the points mentioned are associated with honesty and disclosure. The code can help bolster an executive's belief that the stand that he or she is taking is ethical and socially responsible. However, the American Marketing Association, unlike some other "professional" organizations, is not in a position to provide legal support to its members who face a conflict between their personal ethics and what they are being asked to do. This places a great deal of responsibility on the individual marketing executive. Exercising this responsibility requires an understanding of what is prescribed as right and wrong. It requires an understanding of where such values and rules originate, as well as the issues and moral philosophy that underlie personal and organizational ethics.

Theories of Marketing Ethics

It is no accident that both primitive and advanced civilizations have ethical and moral codes that constrain group and individual behavior and attempt to maintain the social fabric of the culture. The enlightenment of a civilization is often measured by its underlying ethics. When ethical codes break down, societies cease to function and ultimately collapse from within (for example, the decline and fall of the Roman Empire, the collapse of communist systems) or under external pressures (for example, the defeat of the Third Reich in World War II).

The great philosophers of the Enlightenment, Jean-Jacques Rousseau and Thomas Hobbes, argued that society needs a set of ethical rules, a morality accepted by all, called

Figure 2.3	American Marketing Association Code of Ethics

American Marketing Association Code of Ethics

Members of the American Marketing Association are committed to ethical professional conduct. They have joined together in subscribing to this Code of Ethics embracing the following topics:

Responsibilities of the Marketer
Marketers must accept responsibility for the consequences of their activities and make every effort to ensure that their decisions, recommendations, and actions function to identify, serve, and satisfy all relevant publics: customers, organizations, and society.

Marketers' Professional Conduct must be guided by:
1. The basic rule of professional ethics: not knowingly to do harm
2. The adherence to all applicable laws and regulations
3. The accurate representation of their education, training, and experience
4. The active support, practice, and promotion of this Code of Ethics

Honesty and Fairness
Marketers shall uphold and advance the integrity, honor, and dignity of the marketing profession by:
1. Being honest in serving consumers, clients, employees, suppliers, distributors, and the public
2. Not knowingly participate in conflict of interest without prior notice to all parties involved
3. Establishing equitable fee schedules including the payment or receipt of usual, customary, and/or legal compensation for marketing exchanges

Rights and Duties of Parties in the Marketing Exchange Process
Participants in the marketing exchange process should be able to expect that
1. Products and services offered are safe and fit their intended uses
2. Communications about offered products and services are not deceptive
3. All parties intend to discharge their obligations, financial and otherwise, in good faith
4. Appropriate internal methods exist for equitable adjustment and/or redress of grievances concerning purchases

It is understood that the above would include, but is not limited to, the following responsibilities of the marketer:

In the area of product development and management:

Disclosure of all substantial risks associated with product or service usage
Identification of any product component substitution that might materially change the product or impact on the buyer's purchase decision
Identification of extra cost-added features

In the area of promotions:
Avoidance of false and misleading advertising
Rejection of high-pressure manipulations, or misleading sales tactics
Avoidance of sales promotions that use deception or manipulation

In the area of distribution:
Not manipulating the availability of a product for the purpose of exploitation
Not using coercion in the marketing channel
Not exerting undue influence over the reseller's choice to handle a product

In the area of pricing:
Not engaging in price fixing
Not practicing predatory pricing
Disclosing the full price associated with any purchase

In the area of marketing research:
Prohibiting selling or fund-raising under the guise of conducting research
Maintaining research integrity by avoiding misrepresentation and omission of pertinent research data
Treating outside clients and suppliers fairly

Organizational Relationships
Marketers should be aware of how their behavior may influence or impact the behavior of others in organizational relationships. They should not demand, encourage, or apply coercion to obtain unethical behavior in their relationships with others, such as employees, suppliers, or customers.

1. Apply confidentiality and anonymity in professional relationships with regard to privileged information
2. Meet their obligations and responsibilities in contracts and mutual agreements in a timely manner
3. Avoid taking the work of others, in whole or in part, and representing this work as their own or directly benefiting from it without compensation or consent of the originator or owner
4. Avoid manipulation to take advantage of situations to maximize personal welfare in a way that unfairly deprives or damages the organization or others

Any AMA member found to be in violation of any provision of this Code of Ethics may have his or her Association membership suspended or revoked.

a *social contract,* for it to function effectively. If you want to be part of society, you obey the rules. If entrepreneurs and firms wish to trade in a society and profit from such trade, then they have a social and moral obligation to accept the general ethical rules of the society, and not undermine them with unacceptable trading practices. So what are some of these rules?

Choose to Do the Most Good for the Most People.

The famous philosophers David Hume, Jeremy Bentham, and John Stuart Mill developed the principle of utility. The *principle of utility* is that "ethical behavior" is the behavior that produces the most good for the most people in a specific situation. At first glance, this sounds like a very good rule. But in practice this ethical principle is hard to apply. First, how do you calculate the most good for the most people? How do you add up all of the good and bad? Can you measure *good* by adding up all the positive outcomes, then subtracting all the negative outcomes? For example, is it allowable to have 1 out of 10,000,000 consumers die from the side effects of a new drug, if the drug is twice as effective at relieving the headache pain for the other 9,999,999 users?

And how do you keep your perspective and independence in making such judgments? How do people avoid underemphasizing what is good for others and overemphasizing what is good for themselves? How does a decision maker avoid overweighing the benefit that he or she is likely to receive personally? In our personal lives we have all experienced how hard it is to separate our desires and goals from the judgment of what is right. Furthermore, no less than Adam Smith pointed out that pursuing your own self-interest over the interests of others promotes the overall good. This sounds like ethical permission to overemphasize the good you will receive over the good and bad outcomes for others.

The utility principle can be twisted into some interesting interpretations. It can lead an otherwise ethical company to decide that it must sink to the lowest ethical standards among a group of competitors. "If we were to be more ethical," a company might argue, "we, as a good guy, might go out of business, and what good would be gained from that? It is in the interest of our employees, our customers, and society (that is, the total good) that we, who are basically an ethical firm, stay in business even if it means that we have to stoop to the unethical practices of our rivals." This kind of thinking can become moral quicksand. It can mean being dragged down to the ethics of the most desperate competitor. How common is this dilemma? It is as common as the occurrence of paying off government officials in many markets around the world, which is still quite common. It is as common as competing against companies that have lower costs because they are not using scrubbers or other technology to reduce pollution, again another common event.

Another harsh reality is that the more desperate the company or personal situation is, the lower the applied ethical standards will be, and the more the decision maker will be fixated by how his or her company will benefit. Again, the rationalization is that behaving unethically is for the total good, and that the means justifies the ends, such as saving the jobs of employees. Sometimes it seems that only successful companies and executives can afford a conscience. In economic terms, marketing ethics is a *normal good* because demand for ethical behavior in a firm increases as the net income of a company increases.

What If Everyone Did It?

The philosopher Immanuel Kant's famous categorical imperative offers an alternative to the utility principle. The *categorical imperative* asks whether the proposed action would be right if everyone did it. What would happen to the social fabric? This view of ethics asks us to think about the social destructiveness of trading practices that, if only we do it, seem hardly serious violations. For example, consider the trading practice of including puffery (exaggerated claims) in advertising. If only done occasionally by a few, it does not seem so serious, but if everyone did it all the time, then advertising would lose its integrity, its credibility, and end up destroying the usefulness of a major marketing tool. It would also greatly reduce the efficiency of markets, because markets rely on advertising to transmit information to everyone about prices, availability, new innovations, and quality. Some would say that this is precisely what has happened to advertising. What would happen if the one million plus companies in the United States each made several hundred unsolicited phone calls each evening? Would that be socially responsible and fair? What would happen if you were constantly on the receiving end of such ethics? At a global marketing level, many companies lobby their government to erect trade barriers to protect them from foreign competitors. But what happens if all countries were to erect such barriers? It would kill global trade, and the world would be plunged into a depression such as occurred in the 1930s.

This approach takes most of the situation or context out of the ethical evaluation and, in that sense, is more explicit than the utilitarian principle. It also has elements of "do unto others what you would have them do unto you." But the categorical imperative still requires the decision maker to *see* the universal wrong or evil in the act if everyone did it, including doing it to them. Depraved individuals, caring nothing for society or even their family, may answer that, yes, it would be fine for society and that others are welcome to act in the same way toward them, their children, and their grandmothers. Both **situational ethics** and the categorical imperative still require a basic set of values. Whose responsibility is it to instill such values in marketing decision makers?

Where Do Our Basic Values Come From?

Basic decency and morality are taught on or across a father or mother's knee, with grandmothers, grandfathers, uncles, aunts, or other surrogate parents helping out. If not taught by extended family members, such basic values are taught to us as children by teachers and coaches and through organizations such as the YMCA, Boy Scouts, and Girl Scouts. Finally, ethical teachings are provided to us at our church, synagogue, mosque, or other sources of our spiritual and religious beliefs. But what if, somehow as adults, some of us seem to have missed these lessons? Some say it is too late to teach adults about the basic ethics of honesty, decency, and consideration for others. Others seem to expect companies to take on this impossible task for their employees. But is that really a company's responsibility? Are parents, schools, and the world's great religions becoming lax in living up to their side of the social contract to teach children decency, honesty, and consideration for others?

One of the distinguishing characteristics of different civilizations, countries, societies, and tribes is their dominant religion. It often has great impact. For example, the predominant religion of the United States is Christianity. The Judeo-Christian creed, along with "enlightenment thinking" (some of which can be traced to the Islamic enlightenment of 900–1300) has greatly influenced the Constitution, common law, and the system of justice in the United States. Thus, it can be argued that marketers in the United States fulfill the social contract by adopting a code of marketing ethics based on Judeo-Christian religious beliefs that have defined our society's law and morality.

But what happens to those who believe in some other religion's ethical code, such as the seven million Americans who are believers in Islam? It is to be expected in a free society that a believer of another religion will apply his or her religious ethics to all situations, including marketing decision making. This exercise of different religious beliefs and values increases the variability in ethics that we are likely to observe in the marketplace. One economic reason we should use the "predominant religion" values as the common core for our society's ethics, even if we are not followers of that religion, is that the universal acceptance of its code enables us to anticipate the likely behavior of other parties in the market. This anticipation leads to an increase in certainty and a sense of confidence and control that the market is orderly and fair, and thus reduces the costs of doing business. Notice that this creates a fundamental ethical dilemma: a trade-off between freedom of religion, beliefs in different ethical codes, and the efficiency of the market. An example of this problem has occurred in diamond trading around the world. For years, a fundamental sect of Jews dominated the global trading of these precious gems. The ethical behavior of these diamond traders in their trading between themselves was very high for centuries. A trader's word was his bond. But now the sect's religious ethics do not have the same hold on some younger generations of traders, and new traders from Russia and Asia have entered the market. The result is that there is much less trust in the diamond-trading business than there used to be, and this has increased the risk and cost of diamond trading.

If the clearly dominant and underlying religious creed in a society or among a group of specialized traders is not to be used as the foundation for a generally accepted code of business ethics, then what should be used? It would be extraordinarily difficult to argue that some other religious or moral philosophy should be substituted. More generally, a serious and unresolved situational ethics problem often occurs in global marketing.

Situational ethics is that societal condition where "right" and "wrong" are determined by the specific situation, rather than by universal moral principles.

http://www.ymca.net

No international code of business ethics exists because each society's ethics vary, some slightly and others greatly. Fortunately, most of the world's major religions and cultures share common norms and ethics and would answer the questions on an ethical checklist similarly. In some countries, though, bribery, kickbacks, and dishonesty in advertising, selling, and dealing are much more acceptable than in others. How should American firms behave in such markets? If they do not tolerate such standard practices, they risk not doing business, and furthermore, may be hated for arrogantly imposing their values where they are not wanted. For example, should American garment manufacturers be concerned about the working conditions in the offshore factories that produce many of their clothing lines? Liz Claiborne makes unscheduled visits to its suppliers to ensure they meet the company's standards and attempts to work with those suppliers that provide the best working conditions. Presumably, other companies are less particular, only caring about price and output quality. But just how much American companies should be held responsible for the human rights abuses of their suppliers is unclear, particularly if caring puts the American company at a competitive cost disadvantage.

http://www.lizclaiborne.com

The quick and easy answer, "When in Rome, do as the Romans do," is no real answer for at least two reasons. First, international business is carried out in two places at once, for example, between a seller in New York and a buyer in Rome. What is the social contract in this situation? Is it determined by the accepted norms of the American or the Italian trading partner's political economy? Regulating the Internet is tied up in this very knot. An international body called the Hague Convention is trying to decide who has jurisdiction and how a common law is ultimately developed across 200 countries. It has been working for 10 years and has gotten nowhere. Second, this philosophy suggests abandoning one's own "moral compass," and replacing it with the ethical standards of a trading partner—not a comfortable or natural position to be in. With the increase in global marketing comes a pressing need to adopt an international code of ethics. Unethical behavior will always exist, but it can be defined the same way and condemned by every society. Even if this occurs some time in the future, international marketing decision makers still will have to reconcile their personal moral compass with situational issues and trade-offs among interest groups and stakeholders they are paid to serve. All of the above issues make it very difficult to prescribe answers to the ethical questions and dilemmas that surround marketing and trading practices.

Recognizing Ethical Issues

The set of general questions in Table 2.3 can be asked by the decision maker or decision-making team seeking to develop its own ethical standards. Although most questions are self-explanatory, others need some brief justification or raise issues worth exploring.[8] It seems that the least society should require of marketing executives is that they ask such

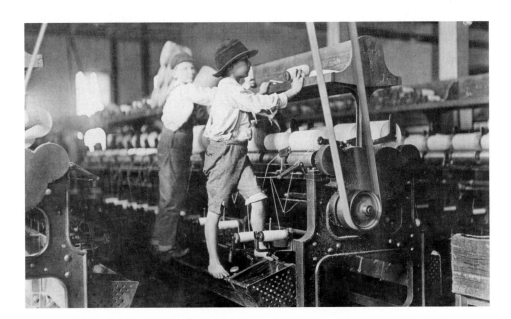

Table 2.3	A Personal Ethics Checklist for Marketers

☐ Am I violating the law? If yes, why?

☐ Are the values and ethics that I am applying in business lower than those I use to guide my personal life? If yes, why?

☐ Am I doing to others as I would have them do to me? If not, why not?

☐ Would it be wrong if everyone did what I propose to do? Why?

☐ Am I willfully risking the life and limb of consumers and others by my actions? If yes, why?

☐ Am I willfully exploiting or putting at risk children, the elderly, the illiterate, the mentally incompetent, the naive, the poor, or the environment? If yes, why?

☐ Am I keeping my promises? If not, why not?

☐ Am I telling the truth, all the truth? If not, why not?

☐ Am I exploiting a confidence or a trust? If yes, why?

☐ Am I misrepresenting my true intentions to others? If yes, why?

☐ Am I loyal to those who have been loyal to me? If not, why not?

☐ Have I set up others to take responsibility for any negative consequences of my actions? If yes, why?

☐ Am I prepared to redress wrongs and fairly compensate for damages? If not, why not?

☐ Are my values and ethics as expressed in my strategy offensive to certain groups? If yes, why?

☐ Am I being as efficient in my use of scarce resources as I can be? If not, why not?

This set of questions can be used as the basis for a team's or an individual's mental model to perceive and recognize an ethical issue associated with a proposed goal, strategy, program, or tactic.

Ethical vigilance
means paying constant attention to whether one's actions are "right" or "wrong," and if ethically "wrong," asking why one is behaving in that manner.

questions. Sometimes not asking a question can be as wrong as asking and giving a poor answer. For example, not considering the safety of a toy being marketed seems to be as irresponsible as considering the safety and deciding to sell the toy anyway. The effects are the same. One of the most common situations in which marketing executives suffer a lapse of ethics is when they have to make a quick decision because they are preoccupied with other concerns. The ethical sufficiency of the decision is simply not examined. **Ethical vigilance** means, in practice, asking hard questions. It is important to confront excuses and reasons for violating personal ethics. Avoiding or shelving the answers to such questions is no solution. Decision makers who ask why they do or do not behave in certain ways are more honest with themselves about their true intentions. This is the essence of executive responsibility, and it also can be the first step down the path of change. Such questions lead people to recognize that most of us have at least two codes of ethics: (1) the set we espouse and want others to apply in their behavior toward us and (2) the code of ethics that, for whatever rationalizations, we actually live up to. The more we recognize the differences between them, the closer we come to understanding how easy it is to talk about ethics in black and white, while practicing them in shades of gray.

The list of questions shown in Table 2.3 is organized in approximate order of importance and by the nature of the ethical or moral principles involved. The first question in the table is the first and last question the ethical minimalist will ask. The second question addresses the application of a double standard and the basis for such a double standard. The third question addresses the extent to which marketers apply the Golden Rule: "Do unto others as you will have them do unto you." A prominent British chief executive officer has suggested that a better way of posing the question is to look at oneself and ask, "What would I think of someone who has my business ethics or took the action that I propose to take?"[9]

MARKETING'S THIRD SOCIAL RESPONSIBILITY: OBEY THE LAW

LEARNING OBJECTIVE 3

As discussed in the previous chapter, the legal and political environment is a reality to which the marketer must adapt. It is the job of the government to establish the rules and regulations to which businesses must conform. These rules and regulations affect each element in the marketing mix. Marketers must therefore be aware of and conform to all laws affecting their business. This often involves getting lawyers to review marketing mix plans.

As individual citizens, our behavior is constrained by the law and by our individual views of right and wrong. It is no different for firms and marketing decision makers that compete in domestic and international markets. Marketplaces are full of rules. Many are written into law, some are stated in professional codes of ethics, and others are stated in company rules of good conduct. This section does not list all of the possible laws that might apply to a marketing decision. There are whole courses and majors in business law that are meant to provide such an understanding. Instead, this section asks you to think about some of the legal issues that affect marketers, in order to lay a foundation or framework for your understanding of marketing law. Such considerations may seldom be specifically stated in actual written marketing plans or decisions, but they are important.

Despite the fact that the U.S. marketplace is one of the most open and free in the world, federal, state, and local laws and agencies impose numerous constraints. The great surge of consumerism that occurred in the 1960s resulted in several new agencies, including the Product Safety Commission, and numerous new laws. More regulation means more restrictions, and more crusading regulators mean higher legal expenses and the risk of a company losing its reputation if a case is tried in the press. The Library of Congress has calculated that the annual cost of completing, filing, and handling an estimated 15,000 different government forms is $40 billion, well over the national expenditure for all research and development. Clearly, some of this paperwork is worth the cost, but much is not.

While the legal/political environment can frustrate initiative, in general it is positive for business. For example, in the United States, many of the laws that affect marketing practice are in place to encourage competition and protect consumers (see Table 2.4). Moreover, the current plague of lobbyists, who buy the influence and the votes of local, state, and national politicians in many and various ways, exists because thousands of companies and industries are trying to have law passed and law interpreted to favor the competitiveness of their particular firm or industry. In other words, if it is your law that is passed, then regulation is good; if it is someone else's law, then it is bad.

Table 2.4	Sampling of Major Laws That Affect Marketing
Acts	**Prohibitions**
Major Laws That Protect Consumers	
Child Protection Act of 1966	Prohibits the sales of hazardous toys.
Fair Packaging and Labeling Act of 1967	Requires certain information be listed on all labels and packages, including product identification, manufacturer or distributor mailing address, and the quantity of contents.
Consumer Credit Protection Act of 1968	Requires the full disclosure of annual interest rates on loans and credit purchases.
National Environmental Policy Act of 1970	Established the Environmental Protection Agency to deal with organizations that create pollution.
Consumer Product Safety Act of 1972	Created the Consumer Product Safety Commission and empowered it to specify safety standards for consumer products.
Nutritional Labeling and Education Act of 1990	Prohibits exaggerated health claims and requires all processed foods to provide nutritional information.
Americans with Disabilities Act (ADA) of 1991	Protects the rights of people with disabilities; prohibits discrimination against the disabled (illegal in public accommodations, transportation, and telecommunications).
Brady Law of 1993	Imposes a five-day waiting period and a background check before a customer can take possession of a purchased gun.
Laws That Encourage Competition	
Sherman Antitrust Act of 1890	Prohibits restraint of trade and monopolization; delineates a competitive marketing system as a national policy.
Clayton Act of 1914	Strengthens the Sherman Act by restricting such practices as race discrimination, exclusive dealing, tying contracts, and interlocking boards of directors where the effect may be to substantially lessen competition or tend to create a monopoly.
Federal Trade Commission Act of 1914	Prohibits unfair methods of competition; establishes the Federal Trade Commission, an administrative agency that investigates business practices and enforces the FTC Act.
Robinson-Patman Act of 1936	Prohibits price discrimination in sales to wholesalers, retailers, or other producers. Also prohibits selling at unreasonably low prices to eliminate competition.
Miller-Tydings Resale Price Maintenance Act of 1937	Exempts interstate fair trade contracts from compliance with antitrust requirements.
Wheeler-Lea Act of 1938	Amended the FTC Act to further outlaw unfair practices and give the FTC jurisdiction over false and misleading advertising.
Celler-Kefauver Antimerger Act of 1950	Amended the Clayton Act to include major asset purchases that decrease competition in an industry.
American Automobile Labeling Act of 1992	Requires a vehicle's manufacturer to provide a label informing consumers of where the vehicle was assembled and where its components originated.
North American Free Trade Agreement (NAFTA) of 1993	International trade agreement existing between Canada, Mexico, and the United States. Encourages trade by removing tariffs and other trade barriers among these three countries.

The point is that marketers can be just as shortsighted about changes in the legal/political environment as they can about changing customer needs and technological innovations. A hostile attitude toward the legal/political environment that is generalized into a hostile attitude toward public policy is unreasonable, and if it encourages a marketing strategy that willfully frustrates the letter or intent of the law, it can be disastrous.

For example, Toys "R" Us lost market share after the Federal Trade Commission pressed charges that the toy giant was violating antitrust regulations.[10] Bill Gates and Microsoft are facing similar backlash effects as the government pursues its antitrust campaign against the computer software monolith.

http://help.toysrus.com

Companies also have to be farsighted in their promotion of self-interest and in their lobbying for special regulation to protect their interests. Indeed, even the original Sherman Antitrust Act, the granddaddy of all market competition law (see Table 2.4), was initially supported by the "robber barons" of the day because it was deliberately vaguely worded so as to be uninterpretable and, hence, unconstitutional.[11] They did not expect a future Supreme Court to come along and interpret the vagueness as an invitation to make law from the bench designed to serve the needs of the time. They created a monster that ultimately broke up their giant monopolistic trusts. The lesson is that self-interested lawmaking often comes back to haunt the original sponsor through unintended and unanticipated consequences.

MARKETING'S FOURTH SOCIAL RESPONSIBILITY: HELP MARKET GOOD CAUSES

LEARNING OBJECTIVE 4

The fourth important dimension of marketing's social responsibility is to encourage its use in the promotion of worthy public causes. Today's marketers have come to recognize, as has been confirmed in a recent Roper poll, that in many markets a company's media expression of social responsibility influences consumer behavior more than advertising.[12] You do well by doing good; for example, see Budweiser's stand on drunk driving in Figure 2.4. It also helps if your "do-gooding" can be associated with your product. Clothing designer Ralph Lauren donated $13 million to restore the 184-year-old "Old Glory" American flag that flew in the rockets' red glare and inspired the national anthem. Kimberly-Clark sells disposable diapers and builds children's parks and playgrounds. McDonald's works with environment groups to increase its recycling. Shell Oil TV advertising features conservationists it employs to protect the environment that surrounds its drilling operations.

http://www.kimberly-clark.com

Some companies have started up their own nonprofit organizations, and these are not always cynical efforts to buy public relations. They are mostly initiatives suggested by their workforce and welcomed by management, who recognize that they will build company morale and are a positive expression of a company's ethics. They are a way of expressing what should be done by a socially responsible organization rather than what should not be done.

Cause-Related Marketing

Cause-related marketing includes those activities that governments, public service organizations, companies, and individuals undertake in an effort to encourage target customer participation in socially redeeming programs. These efforts are usually delivered through educational campaigns and provide free or low-priced services at convenient times and places. The following are examples of cause-related marketing:

1. How should future societies deal with the issue of using inexpensive genetic testing to reduce genetic disabilities? Genetic disabilities create very high medical care costs that are carried by everyone participating in health insurance pools and great anguish to families, not to speak of the misery of those afflicted with such disabilities. Education campaigns might inform and persuade individuals to take the tests, and might then target those with the flagged genetic markers with further education about the value of choosing not to have children. Marketing campaigns would be more proactive, setting up testing sites at convenient times and locations, providing professional counseling on test results, and, as an alternative, offering special adoption priority programs coupled with voluntary sterilization.[13]

2. Advertising campaigns sponsored by public service organizations and liquor companies are undertaken around holiday seasons to discourage drinking and driving. Over the years these campaigns have become much

Figure 2.4   **Budweiser Helps Market Good Causes**

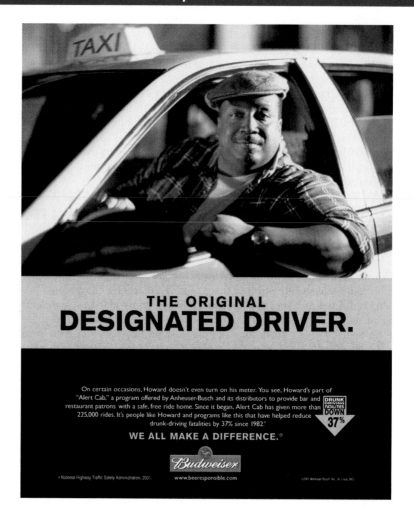

more aggressive, targeted at the friends of problem drinkers, suggesting appropriate behaviors such as taking the keys away from those at risk and creating a designated driver in a group. Market research found that targeting the problem drinker had no effect. What sort of products might be invented to support such communication campaigns? Some communities have sponsored free taxi services and encouraged bars to offer more recreational activities, such as providing pool tables and dancing to reduce the amount of liquor consumption in an evening. Other "social marketers" have encouraged the invention of devices that can be installed in problem drinkers' vehicles that require a "breath test" to start the engine.

The challenge for social marketing is coming up with alternative products that can be marketed to those at risk. Some suggestions, based on experts' extended study of the problem, are designed to lessen the evil, but are still considered too controversial. Examples of such products are providing free, less addictive drugs or clean needles for drug addicts and free birth control pills or abortions to teenagers. Marketing such products to reduce the problem is often argued to promote or encourage, rather than reduce, the socially undesirable behavior. The problem is that the critics do not have good alternative solutions, or their solutions are draconian new laws and punishment. On the other hand, there have been many successful social marketing programs that can be used as benchmarks of best practice for marketing professionals interested in using their talents for good causes. The next section, which pertains to the National High Blood Pressure Education Program, is an example of one such case.

The Case of Development Organizations

Rosemary aced her graduate degree in marketing, but what motivated her was not money but idealism. This led her to work for a not-for-profit nongovernmental organization (NGO) in New York that worked closely with the United Nations. The mission of this organization was to promote information, communications, and networking with the objective of women's advancement worldwide and achieving equality between men and women in all spheres of activity, using the analytic and policy frameworks developed under international agreements.

Rosemary worked for a specific project, which marketed information pertaining to the involvement of women as decision makers and beneficiaries in development programs, addressing a wide range of topics, ranging from women's rights to women in science and information technology, to gender analysis in economics. The project distributed books and literature on such topics not only from established publishers in "developed" countries but also from indigenous publishers and grassroots activist groups in developing countries. While the job was poorly paid, it was fascinating and opened up new horizons for Rosemary. She traveled to many international conferences and book fairs to locate publishers and target audiences for the literature, making connections with networks of small groups and publishers worldwide. After several years working for this organization, Rosemary was hired by the United Nations Development Program (UNDP) to work on information management around its gender programs in over 130 different countries and to liaise with related initiatives of other UN agencies and nongovernmental organizations.

Pursuing cause-related marketing careers poses a number of formidable challenges. Not-for-profit organizations, especially those focused on economic and social development in developing countries, often vary widely in staff competencies, geographic and subject focus, and organizational structures and incentives. Nongovernmental organizations are typically small, focus on a single issue or few issues, and offer low pay but attract highly motivated staff with specific skills. UN agencies, in contrast, are extremely large, bureaucratic, and address a whole slew of development topics. Because all these organizations tend to work together for common causes through continuous networking and partnership building, they offer ample scope for application of marketing concepts and skills. However, there is less competitive pressure to innovate and learn new improved ways of doing things than there is in profit-driven organizations, and efficiency and effectiveness often have to be sacrificed to address the needs or interests of specific constituencies. On the other hand, helping marketing human rights, health care, and environmental protection can be so much more rewarding than marketing toothpaste. Indeed, many retired marketing executives continue to work on causes that they feel deeply about.

The Internet is also revolutionizing cause marketing. Cause marketing depends on small groups working together, and the Internet enables communication as never before. It is also able to provide a great deal more information literally at the fingertips of not-for-profit organizations and people out in the field. Finally, despite the naysayers, young people today, particularly college students, are giving more of their time to working on charitable causes than they ever have before. The idealism of younger generations and their comfort level and skill with new technology suggest that cause marketing has an exciting future.

The National High Blood Pressure Education Program (NHBPEP)[14]

When the NHBPEP started in 1972, about 60 million Americans had blood pressure over 140/90 or were taking hypertensive medication. Less than 30 percent of the public knew that high blood pressure greatly increases the risks of strokes and heart disease. The initial goal of the campaign was to raise awareness of the risks and encourage tens of millions who were at risk to have their blood pressure checked. A social marketing consulting company coordinated a national advertising/education campaign that involved sponsored television advertising, public service announcements, publicity events, posters, and magazine and newspaper advertising. A partnership with over 40 public health organizations and charitable foundations was created. These organizations acted as channels of distribution for the campaign materials and for staging blood pressure monitoring events. The service was brought to as many people at risk as possible rather than just trying to persuade people to visit a doctor.

After 10 years, over 70 percent of the public knew about the link to specific diseases, and 92 percent understood that, in general, high blood pressure cannot be cured and a hypertensive person must always stay on a treatment program. By 1985, over 90 percent of the population knew what their blood pressure was, but half of the hypertensives had still not taken any action to treat their chronic condition. At this time the goal of this social marketing campaign shifted from general public awareness to a focus on those who had done nothing about it. Again, an education campaign was launched directed at doctors and nurses in contact with those at risk, supported by a targeted campaign mainly directed at the loved ones of those at risk and getting them to use their influence. By 1991, 73 percent of hypertensives were under medical treatment. Of this group, over 80 percent dieted and exercised. In the late 1990s, the focus has become targeted on African-American males over the age of 45 who have a high incidence of hypertension and who live in the southeastern United States, where the incidence of strokes among hypertensives is 10 percent higher than in any other region.

CHAPTER SUMMARY

- Marketing has a social responsibility to be efficient and effective, to behave decently and obey the law, and to help market worthy social causes.

- As marketers respond to the marketing environment, they must do so in a manner that reflects their concern for the welfare of others. This has been termed the social contract.

- A "free market" does not mean that suppliers and customers are free to do whatever they like, whenever they like. What it means is that they are free to pursue their own self-interests, but they are also free to suffer the economic and moral consequences of such behavior. For instance, competition forces sellers to serve the interests of customers. It is in the self-interest of a firm to serve the interests of the consumer and others who help the firm achieve its goals.

- The paradox of free markets is that sellers are free to blindly and naively pursue their own self-interest at the expense of customers and facilitators, but if they do so, they will very soon no longer have customers or any help from anyone else. Consequently, it is simply not true, as claimed by Adam Smith 225 years ago and by the influential *Economist* magazine today, that the unfettered pursuit of self-interest can be justified within the free-market, capitalist system because it collectively serves the public good.

- Ethical, lawful behavior, particularly honesty, is required to make markets work efficiently and to keep them from failing. Marketers must not cheat and steal because, when this becomes the norm, markets collapse and marketing ceases. Failed economies such as those that exist in Africa today provide ample evidence of the consequences of unethical and unlawful business practices.

- Marketers' decisions as to what to offer the marketplace and how to offer it also have an impact on the prevailing values and ethics of a society. Some products and marketing practices are ethically questionable. This heavy responsibility cannot be simply shrugged off. The enlightened leadership that marketing planners are expected to display is most put to the test when they are faced with ethical dilemmas created by conflicts of interests among customers, employees, and owners. How they choose to resolve such dilemmas tells them a lot about themselves.

- A lot of the criticisms of marketing that are popular among modern socialists simply have no basis in fact, reflecting, instead, the ideological prejudices of the critics. The collapse of the corrupt and hopelessly inefficient communist systems has not muted the shrillness of the critics of the capitalist market. It also has not increased their insights. Despite the unreasonableness of much of the criticism of marketing, the fact is that the world faces several potential "tragedy of the commons" effects on clean air, fresh water, trees, fish, participatory democracy, and young women's self-esteem and happiness with themselves. All functions of a firm, including marketing, have to be sensitive to such effects.

- This chapter was full of "on the other hand" statements, reflecting the complexity of the issues associated with the ethics and social responsibility of marketing. It also posed a lot of questions rather than offering a lot of answers. This is because there are a lot of questions that have to be confronted by marketers, and there are not a lot of definitive answers. Like any marketing skill, the skill of behaving ethically and socially responsibly develops with practice: the practice of asking the right questions, answering them honestly, and resolving dilemmas by balancing short- and long-term interests.

KEY TERMS

Demand-side market failure is the cumulative effect of the marketing practices of many thousands of advertising campaigns that has a residual negative impact on the values of buyers and the demand for various products (e.g., voting).

Ethical vigilance means paying constant attention to whether one's actions are "right" or "wrong," and if ethically "wrong," asking why one is behaving in that manner.

Inefficient targeting results when advertising and distribution reach too broad an audience, most of whom are not interested in the product.

Planned obsolescence is the design of a product with features that the company knows will soon be superseded, thus making the model obsolete.

Situational ethics is that societal condition where "right" and "wrong" are determined by the specific situation, rather than by universal moral principles.

Social responsiblity is the collection of marketing philosophies, policies, procedures, and actions intended primarily to enhance society's welfare.

Supply-side market failure results when the individual activities of a supplier inadvertently lead to destructive effects on the overall supply.

Tragedy of the commons is the name given to the process in which individuals, pursuing their own self-interest, overuse a common good to such an extent that the common good is destroyed.

QUESTIONS FOR DISCUSSION

1. In 1999, recycled disposable medical equipment had sales of $40 million out of a total $60 billion market for medical disposables. Recyclers buy, chemically wash, rinse, dry, sterilize, pack, and resell instruments like used catheters for $250 (half the cost of new ones). The Federal Drug Administration (FDA) regulates the new drug and equipment markets by setting standards and putting its stamp of approval on production and marketing practices. Normally, entrepreneurs hate government regulators who add millions of dollars of expense to business processes, but entrepreneurs in the recycled disposable medical equipment market begged the FDA to hold hearings about regulating their industry. The hearings began in December 1999 and resulted in an August 2000 announcement that the FDA would regulate the industry. The larger disposable medical equipment recyclers celebrated the FDA decision to regulate, and they had good reason to celebrate. Why would these sellers welcome such government regulation?

2. A competitor's disgruntled employee has just mailed you plans for what looks like a promising new product. Should you throw the plans away? Send them to your R&D people for analysis? Notify your competitor about what is going on? Call the Federal Bureau of Investigation?

3. All-terrain vehicles were involved in 1,500 deaths and 400,000 serious injuries during the 1980s—20 percent of these affecting children 12 and under. The automobile industry stopped selling the three-wheel version and notified dealers to instruct buyers that the vehicles should not be driven by children under 16. However, many dealers have ignored the direction. The industry view is that because state laws allow children to

use the vehicle, it is the parents' responsibility to supervise their children's use. Should the product be banned?

4. In the late 1970s, credit card interest rates rose to between 18 and 20 percent because of inflation. Through the 1980s and 1990s, many credit card interest rates remained at around 18 to 20 percent, long after inflation had cooled and the cost of money had dropped to under 7 percent. Many banks have argued that the cost of servicing credit card debt is high, but some banks charge only 10 percent on their cards. The merchant is charged a fee (2 to 5 percent) for each purchase made on a card. This covers the cost of the transaction and some of the risk of card theft and bad debt. Is still charging 18 to 20 percent ethical?

5. Increasingly, prescription drugs are being marketed directly to consumers, as if they were soap powder. How might such marketing be socially responsible? How might it be socially irresponsible?

6. A supermarket serving a low-income African-American market charges higher prices for its staples (such as bread and milk) than do supermarkets in the suburbs. Consumer groups have complained that this practice exploits the poor. The store argues that suburban shoppers buy more profitable luxuries, allowing suburban stores to lower their prices on staples. The store's management also can prove that there is a greater incidence of shoplifting and vandalism in its store, resulting in hardly any profit, even at the higher prices. Should the store lower its prices? Should it simply close down, if it would lose money by lowering its prices? What other creative options does the store have?

7. A Save the Children Fund (SCF) ad features little Pedro with the sad eyes and Joanne Woodward saying, "Imagine, the cost of a cup of coffee, 52 cents a day, can help save a child." But SCF has not been in the business of directly sponsoring children for many years. It is involved in community development work, such as building playgrounds and providing start-up loans for small businesses. The problem is that community development does not pull cash donations the way that little Pedro does. Only about 35 percent of the funds raised are actually spent on charitable projects; the rest is spent on marketing and overhead.[15] Was SCF's behavior ethical? Should SCF be held to a higher or lower standard than would be applied to a for-profit organization?

8. You are in a foreign country where bribing government officials and businesspeople is essential to doing business, and bribery is not outlawed as it is in the United States. Officials from the country approach you, saying that there are many buyers for your products and you could make good profits in their country. Would you do business and pay the bribes? Would you hide the practice, hoping that no one in the United States would find out? Would you pay a distributor in the country a set fee to take care of everything for you, pretending not to know what "taking care of everything" means?

9. A major U.S. bank in Chicago has been approached by an Arab sheik who wishes to make a major investment in its New Ventures Mutual Fund that has been brilliantly managed by a 35-year-old female executive. The bank is very keen to make the sale, but the sheik will only do business with men. Normally, the female mutual funds manager would travel to meet such a client. Should the bank send her anyway? What if a major commission is involved in making the sale? Would it make any difference if the sheik was visiting the United States and refused to meet the female executive?

10. Every February, audiences for the major networks' programs are measured. These ratings are used to compute audience size and what advertisers will be charged for advertisements placed within these programs. During "Sweeps Week," all of the networks advertise new episodes to boost their audiences. Before and after Sweeps Week, however, the net-

works present reruns of shows or episodes, sometimes out of sequence. How ethical is the Sweeps Week practices of the networks? How should audience measurement be undertaken?

INTERNET QUESTIONS

1. Pornography, one of the biggest businesses on the Web, naturally attracts the interest of children. Banning such sites is very difficult because it would require enforceable international laws and would not be popular. The most sensible solution is for parents and teachers to monitor the sites that children visit. A survey undertaken by *Family PC* found that 71 percent of parents say they monitor their children's use of the Internet, but only 26 percent say they use either built-in or commercial filtering or monitoring software. Imagine you have an easy-to-use monitoring software and operating system that operates on any PC and that tracks the sites that your PC visits. It could be sold on a disk for $3 per unit in bulk to a distributor. How might you use several nonprofit organizations to distribute this product to families with young children for under $10? The alliance has to be consistent with the goals of the organization and would earn badly needed income. It also has to avoid unnecessary controversy.

2. A major social responsibility of marketing is to make trading more efficient. One way the Internet can do this is by creating inexpensive auction markets that bring buyers and sellers together at low cost to exchange goods. Which of the following auction sites is easiest and least expensive to use: http://www.collectiblesgoantiques.com, http://collectoronline.com, http://www.ebay.com, http://www.icollector.com? What sorts of product markets are likely to be made more efficient by such Internet trading sites?

3. A problem with the Internet is that it is very good at spreading rumors very fast. For example, a rumor started by a "Nancy Markle" accused the artificial sweetener aspartame of causing Alzheimer's disease, birth defects, brain cancer, diabetes, Gulf War syndrome, lupus, multiple sclerosis, and seizures.[16] The site http://urbanlegends.miningco.com presents many other socially irresponsible slanders on the products we use. Reliable health sites such as http://mayoclinic.com, http://www.medhelp.org, http://www.oncolink.org, http://cancer.gov, and http://navigator.tufts.edu give excellent information on nutrition and illnesses. They are required to back up their advice and information with credible scientific research. How can the spread of false or unsubstantiated health claims that create great fear and distress be controlled on the Web? What long-term effect might such rumor mongering have on Internet use?

ENDNOTES

[1] For a review of the lack of evidence, see Timothy E. Moore, "Subliminal Advertising: What You See Is What You Get," *Journal of Marketing* 46 (Spring 1982): 38–47. For an interesting discussion of how the media persists in believing in subliminal messages in advertising and music, see John R. Vokey and J. Don Read, "Subliminal Messages: Between the Devil and the Media," *American Psychologist* (November 1985): 1231–1239.

[2] Richard W. Pollay et al., "The Last Straw? Cigarette Advertising and Realized Market Shares among Youths and Adults, 1979–1993," *Journal of Marketing* 60 (April 1996): 1–16.

[3] Booz-Allen & Hamilton, *New Product Management for the 1980s* (New York: Booz-Allen & Hamilton Inc., 1982).

[4] Steven H. Star, "Marketing and Its Discontents," *Harvard Business Review* (November–December 1989): 148–154.

[5] See "Turning Off the Tap," *The Economist*, 14 November 1998, 29.

[6] From the results of a survey of 511 Wisconsin adults surveyed two weeks before the 1998 elections, reported in the *Wisconsin State Journal*, 31 October 1998, 1.

[7] "Good Grief," *The Economist*, 8 April 1995, 57.

[8] Some of the questions are based on the thinking of Gene R. Laczniak, "Framework for Analyzing Marketing Ethics," *Journal of Macromarketing* (Spring 1983): 7–18; and William David Ross, *The Right and the Good* (Oxford: Clarendon Press, 1930).

[9] Sir Adrian Cadbury, "Ethical Managers Make Their Own Rules," *Harvard Business Review* 87, no. 5 (September/October 1987): 69–75.

[10] Kate Fitzgerald, "Antitrust Case Threatens the Image of Toys "R" Us," *Advertising Age*, 27 May 1996, 6.

[11] Peter R. Dickson and Philippa K. Wells, "The Dubious Origins of the Sherman Antitrust Act: The Mouse That Roared," *Journal of Public Policy and Marketing: Special Issue on Competition* (Spring 2001): 1–12.

[12] Claudia Gaines, "Next Step in Cause Marketing: Business Start Own Nonprofits," *Marketing News*, 12 October 1998, 4.

[13] See Michael L. Rothschild, "Promises, Carrots, and Sticks: A Conceptual Framework for the Management of Public Health and Social Issue Behaviors," *Journal of Marketing* 63, no. 4 (1999): 24–37, for an excellent review of contemporary social marketing issues and practices.

[14] The following examples are drawn from Alan R. Andreasen, *Marketing Social Change* (San Francisco: Jossey-Bass Publishers, 1995).

[15] See Richard Behar, "SCF's Little Secret," *Forbes*, 21 April 1986, 106–107.

[16] See Christine Gorman, "A Web of Deceit," *Time*, 9 February 1999, 76.

[17] Philip P. McGuigan, "Stakes Are High in Battle to Bar Internet Gambling," *The National Law Journal*, 3 November 1997, B8.

[18] Source: Greenfield Online, Wilton, CT. Results were presented in *Marketing News*, 12 February 2001, 12.

GAMBLING AND THE INTERNET

One in $10 of all the money spent in the United States on recreation is spent on gambling: about $47 billion a year in total. Gambling is very big business. Las Vegas is booming, and Native American tribes are building casinos around the country. As a form of "compensation" for the theft of their tribal lands in the 1800s, small regional tribes have become rich off their "right" to run casinos. According to surveys by respected market research firms, over 90 percent of adult Americans find casino gambling acceptable, particularly those local residents who benefit from the employment and entertainment that casinos create.[17] The typical casino gambler has a slightly higher income than the national norm, but otherwise is very average.

Why, then, is there so much objection to gambling on the Internet? Such gambling might ultimately require prepayment using a credit card that would make it difficult for children to participate. It is not even that clear that children would find gambling more attractive than video games. Providing the gambling Web sites were audited by government agencies for the fairness and integrity of their games, as casinos are now, the risk of widespread corruption and fraud would be very low. Currently, thirty-six states run their own lotteries, so it is hard for state legislators to object to Web-based gambling on moral grounds. Given that, why has the National Association of Attorney Generals created a special committee to draw up federal regulation to make Internet gambling illegal? Why has the state of Nevada already passed legislation banning Internet gambling? The reason seems simple: Internet gambling would pose a long-term serious competitive threat to existing gambling products marketed by casino companies and by state governments. It is banned to restrict competition. How long will such a ban last?

Legitimate and respectable Internet gambling companies operating from the Caribbean, as well as from other countries, that allow such businesses and regulate them appropriately cannot be prevented from offering the excitement of their gaming sites to Americans, and for that matter to the rest of the world. Furthermore, there is no way that governments anywhere can stop their citizens from using credit cards to purchase such entertainment. When this happens, the major casino companies and their software suppliers will be more than ready to enter the market, and the federal and state regulations will fade into the sunset. In a recent survey, only 15 percent of online gamblers indicated that online casinos are more fun than traditional Vegas casinos, and almost a third were dissatisfied with the online gambling experiences they have had.[18] When they play for money, 60 percent think that the online gambling sites are fixed. The most frequently visited gambling sites are http://www.freelotto.com, http://www.gamesvillelycos.com, http://www.prizecentral.com, http://www.goldenpalace.com, and http://www.virtualvegas.com.

Discussion Questions

1. Surveys show that people believe casinos should be responsible for offering programs to help problem casino gamblers. What unique problems exist in requiring Internet gambling services to be responsible for offering programs for problem Internet gamblers?

2. Do you think those who are attempting to restrict gambling on the Internet are behaving ethically? When do you think that the traditional casino gambling companies such as Harrah's will change sides and lobby for the legalizing of online casino gambling? What advantages do well-known names such as Harrah's have in setting up online gambling sites?

3. Do you think gambling on the Internet is an unethical product? Is it more or less ethical than the purveying of pornography on the Web? Is it more or less ethical than the selling of violent video games on the Web?

CHAPTER three

Michael R. Czinkota
Georgetown University

Dr. Czinkota has earned his doctorate degree in logistics and international business from The Ohio State University. He has received honorary degrees from Universidad Pontificia Madre y Maestra in the Dominican Republic and Universidad del Pacifico in Lima, Peru. Dr. Czinkota is a former U.S. deputy assistant secretary of commerce, former head of the U.S. delegation to the OECD Industry Committee in Paris, and a member of the Board of Governors of the Academy of Marketing Science. He is also a former board member and vice president of the American Marketing Association.

He has authored *International Marketing*, 6th edition, *International Business*, 6th edition, and *Global Business*, 3rd edition, all from South-Western.

Ilkka A. Ronkainen
Georgetown University

Dr. Ronkainen has earned his doctorate and master's degrees from the University of South Carolina and an additional master's degree from the Helsinki School of Economics. He has served on the review board of the *Journal of Business Research*, *International Marketing Review*, and the *Journal of International Business Studies*. He is a former North American coordinator for the European Marketing Academy and also a former board member of the Washington International Trade Association.

Dr. Ronkainen serves as a docent of international marketing at the Helsinki School of Economics. He has served as a consultant to IBM, the Rank Organization, and the Organization of American States. In addition, he maintains close ties with a number of Finnish companies and their internationalization and educational efforts.

International Marketing

LEARNING OBJECTIVES

Films made in the United States continue to sweep the globe. Most U.S. releases record at least half of their total box office revenues abroad; *Pearl Harbor* (56 percent), *The Mummy Returns* (52 percent), *Hannibal* (53 percent), and *Bridget Jones's Diary* (72 percent) are recent examples. In a poll of 60,000 British moviegoers for the top 100 films of all time, a full 90 percent of choices were U.S.-made. The top British entrants were *The Full Monty* (10th), *Zulu* (18th), and *Trainspotting* (25th). Consequently, British movies' market share has fallen to 14 percent of the home market, while the respective figures for French films are 27 percent in France and 10 percent for German films in Germany. The European Union's trade deficit with the United States in films and television is annually between $5 billion and $6 billion.

After you have completed this chapter, you should be able to:

1. Understand the importance of international marketing.
2. Appreciate the opportunities and challenges offered by international marketing.
3. Recognize the effect of the global environment on international marketing activities.
4. Understand the process of market selection.
5. Recognize the process of internationalization.
6. Appreciate the different forms of market entry.
7. Comprehend the international adjustment of the marketing mix.
8. Understand the steps necessary for the implementation of an international marketing strategy.

A number of developments seem to conspire to favor U.S. films. Multiplex cinemas have spread throughout Europe, with attendance increasing dramatically. However, multiplexes tend to show more U.S. movies. Along with the multiplexes has come the return of the blockbuster, such as *Titanic* and *Star Wars: The Phantom Menace*. These movies are made with budgets beyond most European producers' wildest dreams. At the same time, studios' spending on marketing has increased dramatically. Marketing campaigns start typically six months before the release, and spending has increased to an average of $3.2 million, up twofold from the mid-1990s' number. Finally, U.S. studios are becoming increasingly dependent on overseas revenues and are therefore keen on investing more in developing those markets. Currently, foreign revenues are equal to domestic revenues; 15 years ago, they were half as large.

(Continued)

Europeans have found a powerful ally in Canada, which has long been concerned about being overly influenced by its closest neighbor. Of the films shown on Canadian screens, 96 percent are foreign, primarily U.S. In 2000, a Molson beer advertisement in which the spokesperson ("Joe Canada") extolled the virtues of being a Canadian ("I have a prime minister, not a president; I speak English and French, not American. . . . I believe in peace-keeping, not policing; diversity, not assimilation. . . . Canada is the second-largest land mass, and the first nation of hockey, and the best part of North America") became a cult phenomenon (http://www.adcritic.com).

A strong case can be made on the dominance of the United States in the film industry. It does not make the most feature films, but its movies reach and are sought out by every market in the world. In contrast, movies made in India and Hong Kong, although numerous, seldom travel outside their regions. However, many arguments can also be made to negate the threat. The nature of U.S. films is increasingly not just "American." From its earliest days, Hollywood has been open to overseas talent and money. Some of the great U.S. film figures—Charlie Chaplin and Alfred Hitchcock, for example— were imports. Today, two of the most powerful Hollywood studios (Columbia Tristar and Fox) are owned by media conglomerates from abroad (Japan's Sony and Australia's News Corporation).

Several of Hollywood's most successful movies have drawn from international resources. *Three Men and a Baby*, for example, was a remake of a French comedy. *Total Recall* was made partly by French money, directed by a Dutchman, and starred an Austrian. *The English Patient* was directed by a Briton, shot in Italy, and starred French and British talent. The quest for new ideas and fresh talent has led studios to develop subsidiaries in Europe: Sony's Bridge in London, Miramax in Berlin, and Warner Brothers, in both Berlin and Paris.

One could conclude that it is less a matter of Hollywood corrupting the world than the world corrupting Hollywood. The more Hollywood becomes dependent on the world market, the more it produces generic blockbusters made to play from Pisa to Peoria to Penang. One could argue that because these films are more likely to be driven by special effects (which can be appreciated by people with minimal grasp of English rather than by dialogue and plot) and subjects that anyone can identify with, there is something inherently objectionable in them. The moviegoer is the final arbiter in this consumption situation.[1]

International marketing takes place all around us every day, has a major effect on our lives, and offers new opportunities and challenges. International marketing is necessary because economic isolationism has become impossible. Failure to participate in the global marketplace assures firms and nations of declining economic capability and consumers of a decrease in their standard of living. Successful international marketing, however, holds the promise of higher profits, an improved quality of life, a better society, and perhaps, due to increased linkages between people, even a more peaceful world.

The objective of this chapter is twofold. First, we discuss the opportunities and challenges that face marketers as they expand into international markets. This chapter is presented early in this text as recognition of the importance of international marketing in today's business world. Secondly, this chapter provides a glimpse of "marketing strategy in action." Thus far, Chapters 1 and 2 have provided the fundamental building blocks of marketing strategy. This chapter illustrates the importance of modifying marketing strategy to meet the needs of new markets.

International marketing
is the process of planning and conducting transactions across national borders to create exchanges that satisfy the objectives of individuals and organizations.

WHAT INTERNATIONAL MARKETING IS

International marketing is the process of planning and conducting transactions across national borders to create exchanges that satisfy the objectives of individuals and organizations. International marketing has forms ranging from export-import trade to licensing, franchising, joint ventures, wholly owned subsidiaries, and management contracts.

As this definition indicates, international marketing retains the basic marketing tenets of "satisfaction" and "exchange." The fact that a transaction takes place "across national borders" causes the international marketer to be subject to new sets of macro environmental factors, to different constraints, and quite frequently to conflicts resulting from different laws, cultures, and societies. The basic principles of marketing strategy still apply, but their implementation, complexity, and intensity may vary substantially. It is in the international marketing field that one can observe most closely the role of marketing as a societal process and as an instrument for the development of socially responsive business strategy. One look at the emerging market economies of central Europe shows some of the many new challenges that confront international marketers. How does the marketing concept fit into these societies? How should distribution systems be organized? How can one get the price mechanism to work? Similarly, in the international areas of social responsibility and ethics, the international marketer is faced with a multicultural environment with differing expectations and often inconsistent legal systems when it comes to monitoring environmental pollution, maintaining safe working conditions, copying technology, or paying bribes.[2] The capability to master these challenges successfully affords a company the potential for new opportunities and high rewards.

The definition also focuses on international transactions. Marketing internationally is an activity that needs to be aggressively pursued. Those who do not actively participate in the transactions are still subject to the changing influences of international marketing. The international marketer is part of the exchange, recognizes the changing nature of transactions, adjusts to a constantly moving target, and reacts to shifts in the business environment. This need for adjustment, for comprehending change, and, in spite of it all, for successfully carrying out transactions highlights the fact that international marketing is as much art as science.

To achieve success in the art of international marketing, it is necessary to be firmly grounded in its scientific aspects. Only then will consumers, policymakers, and business executives be able to incorporate international marketing considerations into their thinking and planning and make decisions based on the answers to such questions as these:

1. How will my product fit into the international market?
2. What marketing adjustments are or will be necessary?
3. What threats from global competition should I expect?
4. How can these threats be turned into opportunities?

The integration of international dimensions into each decision made by individuals and by firms can make international markets a source of growth, profit, and needs satisfaction, and can also lead to a higher quality of life.

OPPORTUNITIES AND CHALLENGES IN INTERNATIONAL MARKETING

LEARNING OBJECTIVE **2**

To prosper in a world of abrupt changes, of newly emerging forces and dangers, and of unforeseen influences from abroad, firms need to prepare themselves and develop active responses. New strategies need to be envisioned, new plans need to be made, and the way of doing business needs to be changed. To remain players in the world economy, governments, firms, and individuals need to respond aggressively with innovation, process improvements, and creativity.[3]

The growth of international marketing activities offers increased opportunities. By integrating knowledge from around the globe, an international firm can build and strengthen its competitive position. Firms that depend heavily on long production runs can expand their activities far beyond their domestic markets and benefit from reaching many more customers. Market saturation can be avoided by lengthening or rejuvenating product life cycles in other countries. Plants can be shifted from one country to another, and suppliers can be found on every continent, as illustrated in Figure 3.1. Cooperative agreements can be formed that enable all parties to bring their major strengths to the table and emerge with better products than they could produce on their own. In addition, research has found that firms that export grow faster, are more productive, and, equally important, have employees who tend to earn more.[4] At the same time, international marketing enables customers all over the world to find greater varieties of products at lower prices and to improve their lifestyles and comfort.

| Figure 3.1 | The Global Components of a Big Mac in Ukraine |

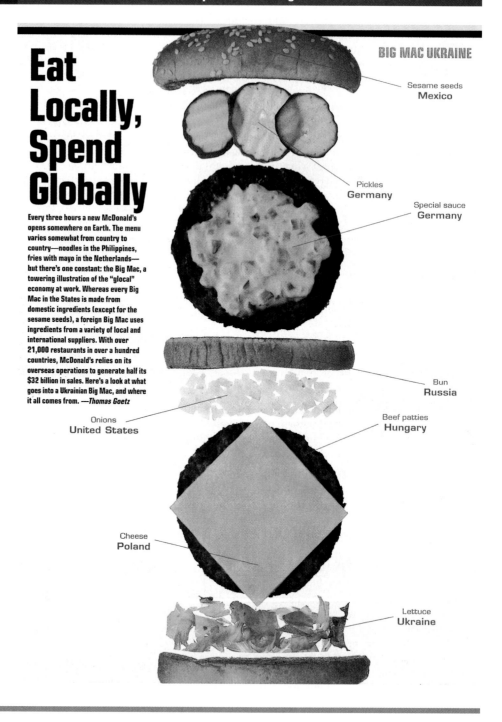

BIG MAC UKRAINE

Eat Locally, Spend Globally

Every three hours a new McDonald's opens somewhere on Earth. The menu varies somewhat from country to country—noodles in the Philippines, fries with mayo in the Netherlands—but there's one constant: the Big Mac, a towering illustration of the "glocal" economy at work. Whereas every Big Mac in the States is made from domestic ingredients (except for the sesame seeds), a foreign Big Mac uses ingredients from a variety of local and international suppliers. With over 21,000 restaurants in over a hundred countries, McDonald's relies on its overseas operations to generate half its $32 billion in sales. Here's a look at what goes into a Ukrainian Big Mac, and where it all comes from. —*Thomas Goetz*

Sesame seeds
Mexico

Pickles
Germany

Special sauce
Germany

Bun
Russia

Onions
United States

Beef patties
Hungary

Cheese
Poland

Lettuce
Ukraine

International opportunities require careful exploration. What are needed are an awareness of global developments, an understanding of their meaning, and a development of the capability to adjust to change. Firms must adapt to their international markets if they are to be successful.

Many firms do not participate in the global market. Often, managers believe that international marketing should only be carried out by large multinational corporations. It is true that there are some very large players from many countries active in the world market, as Table 3.1 shows. But smaller firms are major players, too. For example, 50 percent of German exports are created by firms with 19 or fewer employees.[5]

| The Top 25 Multinational Firms from Developing Economies, Ranked by Foreign Assets (millions of dollars, number of employees) | | | | Table 3.1 | | | |

				Sales		Employment	
Ranking by Foreign Assets	Corporation	Home Country	Industry	Total	Intl. Share (%)	Total	Intl. Share (%)
1.	Petróleos de Venezuela S.A.	Venezuela	Petroleum expl./ref./distr.	$25,659	42	50,821	12
2.	Daewoo Corporation	Republic of Korea	Trade	30,547	—	15,000	—
3.	Jardine Matheson Holdings, Limited	Hong Kong (China)/Bermuda	Diversified	11,230	71	160,000	—
4.	Cemex, S.A.	Mexico	Construction	4,315	54	19,761	49
5.	PETRONAS—Petroliam Nasional Berhad	Malaysia	Petroleum expl./ref./distr.	11,133	34	18,578	15
6.	Sappi Limited	South Africa	Pulp and paper	4,308	75	23,640	45
7.	Hutchison Whampoa, Limited	Hong Kong (China)	Diversified	6,639	33	39,860	52
8.	First Pacific Company Limited	Hong Kong (China)	Other	2,894	87	30,673	49
9.	Sunkyong Group	Republic of Korea	Diversified	38,274	31	29,000	8
10.	Petroleo Brasileiro S.A.—Petrobras	Brazil	Petroleum expl./ref./distr.	15,520	8	42,137	1
11.	New World Development Co., Limited	Hong Kong (China)	Construction	2,628	14	16,512	0
12.	China State Construction Engineering Corporation	China	Construction	5,890	33	239,102	2
13.	YPF Sociedad Anonima	Argentina	Petroleum expl./ref./distr.	5,500	16	9,486	18
14.	LG Electronics, Incorporated	Republic of Korea	Electronics and electrical equipment	12,213	40	60,753	46
15.	China National Chemicals Import & Export Corporation	China	Trade	13,800	57	8,415	6
16.	Keppel Corporation Limited	Singapore	Diversified	2,127	18	11,900	14
17.	Companhia Vale do Rio Doce	Brazil	Transportation	4,321	70	40,334	18
18.	Hyundai Engineering & Construction Co.	Republic of Korea	Construction	3,815	—	22,787	—
19.	Citic Pacific, Limited	Hong Kong (China)	Diversified	1,755	52	11,871	64
20.	Enersis, S.A.	Chile	Electric utilities or services	3,406	9	14,336	65
21.	Guangdong Investment Limited	Hong Kong (China)	Diversified	812	76	17,330	92
22.	San Miguel Corporation	Philippines	Food and beverages	1,811	16	15,923	27
23.	Samsung Electronics Co., Limited	Republic of Korea	Electronics and electrical equipment	16,640	—	42,154	—
24.	Shougang Group	China	Steel and iron	4,270	19	212,027	1
25.	Barlow Limited	South Africa	Diversified equipment	3,769	46	27,804	—
				2,921	—	19,719	—

Source: UNCTAD/Erasmus University database, http://www.UNCTAD.org, accessed 8 February 2001.

Those firms and industries that do not participate in the world market have to recognize that in today's trade environment, isolation has become impossible. Today, most firms and individuals are affected directly or indirectly by economic and political developments that occur in the international marketplace. Those firms that refuse to participate are relegated to react to the global marketplace, and therefore are unprepared for harsh competition from abroad.

LEARNING OBJECTIVE 3

THE INTERNATIONAL MARKETING ENVIRONMENT

International environmental forces will have similar, but most likely more powerful, impacts on the development of international marketing strategies when compared to purely domestic ones. Not only are these international environments different from the domestic ones, but they usually differ considerably between individual country markets as well. Key international environments are the cultural, socioeconomic, and legal/political environments.

Cultural Environment

The challenge for the marketing manager is how to handle the differences in languages (both spoken and nonverbal), values and attitudes, and subsequent behavior at two levels: first, as they relate to customer behavior, and second, with regard to their impact on the implementation of marketing programs within individual markets and across markets. After conducting market research throughout Europe, Whirlpool entered the fastest growing appliance market for microwaves with a product clearly targeted at the Euroconsumer, but one that offered various product features with different appeal in different countries.[6]

The international marketer is a **change agent** trying to impress on a local consumer the need to adopt a new product. The propensity to change will be a function of (1) customers' cultural lifestyles in terms of how deeply held their traditional beliefs and attitudes are, and also which elements of culture are dominant, (2) the power of opinion leaders and change agents themselves, and (3) communication about new concepts from sources ranging from reference groups and government to commercial media.[7]

It has been argued that differences in cultural lifestyle can be accounted for by four dimensions of culture. These dimensions consist of the **degree of individualism** in a culture (as compared to submitting to group decision making), the **level of equality** in a society (e.g., the presence of class differences and possessions), **uncertainty avoidance** (e.g., need for formal rules and regulations, risk taking), and attitudes toward **material achievement**.[8] For example, northern Europe features very high individualism, high equality, low uncertainty avoidance, and low focus on material achievement. For a marketing manager, this means there will be relatively low resistance to new products, strong consumer desire for novelty and variety, and high consumer regard for environmentally friendly and socially conscious solutions.[9] Similar analyses can and should be performed for markets and regions targeted for marketing action.

To foster cultural sensitivity and acceptance of new ways of doing things within the organization, management must institute internal training programs. These programs may include (1) culture-specific information (e.g., data in the form of videopacks or culturegrams covering other countries), (2) general cultural information (e.g., values, practices, and assumptions in countries other than one's own), and (3) self-specific information that involves finding out one's own cultural paradigm, including values, assumptions, and perceptions about others.[10] The Internet can also play a role in preparing marketing people for the international marketplace. While it cannot replace real-life interaction as an experiential tool, Web-based training can provide materials such as detailed scenarios and relevant exercises tied to the learner's background.[11]

These cultural dimensions can be looked at not only as a challenge but also as an opportunity to make the marketer's efforts more effective not only in one market but throughout the world. For example, when 3M's designers in Singapore discovered consumers wanted to use 3M's Nomad household floormats in their cars, the designers spread the word to their counterparts in Malaysia and Thailand. Today, the specially made car mats with easy-to-clean vinyl loops are best sellers across Southeast Asia.[12] Specifics are shown in Figure 3.2.

---

http://www.whirlpool.com

Change agent
is a person or institution that facilitates change in a firm or in a host country.

Degree of individualism
is the extent to which individual interests prevail over group interests.

Level of equality
is the extent to which less powerful members accept that power is distributed unequally.

Uncertainty avoidance
is the extent to which people feel threatened by ambiguous situations and have created beliefs and institutions to try to avoid these feelings.

Material achievement
is the extent to which the dominant values in society are success, money, and things.

http://www.3m.com

| Making Culture Work for You | Figure 3.2 |

Few companies have had as much experience—or success—as the 3M company. The maker of everything from heart-lung machines to Scotch tape, the company's revenues for 1996 from international sales reached $7.6 billion (54 percent of total), with $900 million coming from Asia-Pacific. At the root of the company's success are certain rules that allow it both to adjust to and exploit cultural differences.

- **Embrace Local Culture**—3M's new plant near Bangkok, Thailand, features a gleaming Buddhist shrine, wreathed in flowers, that pays homage to the spirits Thais believe took care of the land prior to the plant's arrival. Showing sensitivity to local customs helps sales, builds employee morale, and keeps the company from inadvertently alienating people.

- **Employ Locals to Gain Cultural Knowledge**—The best way to understand a market is to have grown up in it. Of the 7,500 3M employees in Asia, fewer than 10 are Americans. The rest are locals who know the customs and buying habits of their compatriots. 3M also makes grants of up to $50,000 available to its Asian employees to study product innovations, making them equals with their U.S. counterparts.

- **Build Relationships**—3M executives started preparing for the Chinese market soon after President Richard Nixon's historic visit in 1972. For 10 years, company officials visited Beijing and invited Chinese leaders to 3M headquarters in St. Paul, Minnesota, building contacts and trust along the way. Such efforts paid off when, in 1984, the government made 3M the first wholly owned foreign venture on Chinese soil. 3Mers call the process FIDO ("first in defeats other"), a credo built on patience and long-term perspective.

- **Adapt Products to Local Markets**—Examples of how 3M adapts its products read like insightful lessons on culture. When sales of 3M's famous Scotchbrite cleaning pads were languishing, company technicians interviewed maids and housewives to determine why. The answer: Fillipinos traditionally scrub floors by pushing a rough coconut shell around with their feet. 3M responded by making the pads brown and shaping them like the foot.

- **Help Employees Understand You**—At any given time, more than 30 Asian technicians are in the United States, where they learn the latest product advances while gaining new insights into how the company works. At the same time, they are able to contribute by infusing their insight into company plans and operations.

- **Coordinate by Region**—The company encourages its product managers from different Asian countries to hold regular meetings and share insights and strategies. The goal is to come up with regional programs and "Asianize" a product more quickly.

Source: John R. Engen, "Far Eastern Front," *World Trade* (December 1994): 20–24.

Socioeconomic Environment

The main socioeconomic variables of concern to the international marketer relate to population and its various characteristics, such as age distribution, income, and infrastructure. The global economy has witnessed unprecedented growth and change in the last 10 years. It is worthwhile to analyze population projections in the geographic areas of interest and focus on their possible implications. Industrialized countries (such as the European Union [EU] countries, Japan, and the United States) may be showing very low population growth and aging of the population, but the news is good for marketers: Consumers in the 45- to 55-year-old age group are among the most affluent consumers of all, having reached the peak of their personal earnings potential. Emerging markets (such as

Brazil, China, and India) will have the majority of their huge populations in prime working age, driving both economic and consumption growth. For example, the Coca-Cola Company now derives 37 percent of its revenue from Africa, Asia, and Latin America, and these markets contribute 49 percent of its operating profits. Similarly, according to a Gallup survey in China, 30 percent of the population intends to buy a color TV in the next two years and 22 percent a washing machine, and 10 percent are planning for a purchase of a personal computer.[13] Another key factor in consumer markets has always been the number of women in the paid workforce. Women who work outside the home create a demand for labor-saving devices, packaged and prepared foods, and household services. Working women typically have smaller households and greater disposable income. Infrastructure will also determine market opportunity for marketers. The diffusion of Internet technology into the lifestyles of consumers has been rapid, with the number of users evening out around the globe. Computers priced at less than $500 will boost ownership and subsequent online potential. Developments in television, cable, phone, and wireless technologies not only will make the market broader but will also allow for more services to be delivered more efficiently. For example, with the advent of third-generation mobile communications technology, systems will have a 100-fold increase in data transfer, allowing the viewing of videos on mobile phones.

A significant factor influencing international marketing is economic integration. This relates to an increasing tendency among nation states to cooperate in using their respective resources more effectively and to provide larger markets for their member-country companies. The forms these efforts have taken vary from bilateral trade agreements (such as between Chile and Canada) to free-trade areas (such as North American Free Trade Agreement [NAFTA]), to common markets (such as the Southern Cone Common Market [MERCOSUR]), and to economic unions (such as the European Union [EU]). Membership in such agreements provides marketers opportunity by lowering barriers and increasing access to new markets; lack of membership may hinder such endeavors.

http://www.nafta-sec-alena.org

↗

http://www.mercosur.com

↗

http://www.europa.eu.int

↗

For example, U.S. telecommunications marketers have lost deals in Chile to their Canadian counterparts due to an 11 percent tariff Americans have to pay, but which Canadians are exempted from as a result of the bilateral trade treaty between Chile and Canada. Overall, in the more advanced stages of economic integration, marketing environments are being standardized in terms of regulations and even currencies, as evidenced by the rollout of the euro currency in 12 EU countries in 2002. This makes marketers' operations easier, but at the same time competitively more challenging.

Legal and Political Environment

Legal and political factors often play a critical role in international marketing activities. Even the best business plans can go awry as a result of unexpected legal or political influences, and the failure to anticipate these factors can be the undoing of an otherwise successful business venture.

Of course, a single international legal and political environment does not exist. The business executive must be aware of legal and political factors on a variety of levels. For example, although it is useful to understand the complexities of the host country legal system, such knowledge does not protect against a home country's imposed export embargo.

Many laws and regulations, not designed specifically to address international marketing issues, can have a major impact on a firm's opportunities abroad. Minimum wage legislation, for example, affects the international competitive position of a firm using production processes that are highly labor intensive. Other legal and regulatory measures, however, are clearly aimed at international marketing activities. Some may be designed to assist firms in their international efforts, others may protect the international marketer from adverse activity in another country. For example, the U.S. government is quite concerned about the lack of safeguards of **intellectual property rights** in China. Counterfeiting results in inferior products being sold under fake logos, which damages the reputation of the company. It also reduces the chances that an innovative firm can recoup its investment in research and development through the sale of newly spawned products. With China's joining of the **World Trade Organization (WTO)** in 2002, the country became a signatory to many existing agreements honoring such property rights. It is therefore expected that the problem of imitation and theft will decrease.

Countries differ in their laws as well as in their use of these laws. For example, in the United States, institutions and individuals are quick to take a case to court. As a result, court battles are often protracted and costly, and simply the threat of a court case can reduce marketing opportunities. In contrast, Japan's legal tradition tends to minimize the role of the law and lawyers.

From an international business perspective, the two major legal systems worldwide can be categorized into common law and code law. **Common law** is based on tradition and depends less on written statutes and codes than on precedent and custom. Common law originated in England and is the system of law found today in the United States.

On the other hand, **code law** is based on a comprehensive set of written statutes. Countries with code law try to spell out all possible legal rules explicitly. Code law is based on Roman law and is found in the majority of the nations of the world. In general, countries with the code law system have much more rigid laws than those with the common law system. In the latter, courts adopt precedents and customs to fit the cases, allowing the marketer a better idea of the basic judgment likely to be rendered in new situations.

Although wide in theory, the differences between code law and common law, and their impact on the international marketer, are not always as broad in practice. For example, many common law countries, including the United States, have adopted commercial codes to govern the conduct of business.

Host countries may adopt a number of laws that affect a company's ability to market. There can be laws affecting the entry of goods, such as tariffs and quotas. Also in this category are **antidumping laws**, which prohibit below-cost sales of products, and laws that require export and import licensing. In addition, many countries have health and safety standards that may, by design or by accident, restrict the entry of foreign goods.

Other laws may be designed to protect domestic industries. For example, some governments restrict foreign investment for projects that are not in line with national economic development goals. For example, the Egyptian government places limits on foreign equity in construction, insurance, and transport services. In addition, the employment of nonnationals is restricted to 10 percent of the personnel employed by a company. Foreign

Intellectual property rights
is the protection provided by patents, copyrights, and trademarks.

World Trade Organization (WTO)
is the institution that administers international trade and investment accords. It supplanted the General Agreement on Tariffs and Trade (GATT) in 1995.

Common law
is law based on tradition and depending less on written statutes and codes than on precedent and custom.

Code law
is law based on a comprehensive set of written statutes.

Antidumping laws
are laws designed to help domestic industries that are injured by unfair competition from abroad due to imports being sold at less than fair value.

motion pictures are subject to a screen quota, and a distributor may import only five prints of a foreign film.[14]

Very specific legislation may also exist to regulate where a firm can advertise or what constitutes deceptive advertising. Many countries prohibit specific claims by marketers comparing their product to that of the competition and restrict the use of promotional devices. Some countries regulate the names of companies or the foreign language content of a product's label.

International law plays an important role in the conduct of international business. Although no enforceable body of international law exists, certain treaties and agreements, respected by a number of countries, profoundly influence international business operations. The World Trade Organization defines internationally acceptable economic practices for its member nations. Although it does not directly affect individual firms, it does influence them indirectly by providing a more stable and predictable international market environment.

http://www.wto.org

LEARNING OBJECTIVE   **4**

INTERNATIONAL MARKET SELECTION

The process of target market selection involves narrowing down potential country markets to a feasible number of countries and market segments within them. Rather than try to appeal to everyone, marketers utilize their resources best by (1) identifying potential markets for entry and (2) expanding selectively over time to those markets deemed attractive.

Identification and Screening

A four-stage process for screening and analyzing markets internationally is presented in Figure 3.3. It begins with general criteria and ends with product-specific analyses. The process is typically supported by data. Initially, secondary data will be able to provide most answers, while the more specific questions that emerge later on in the process are likely to require primary data collection. The collection of secondary and primary data are discussed more fully in Chapter 4.

The preliminary screening process must rely chiefly on existing data for country-specific factors as well as product- and industry-specific dimensions. Country-specific factors typically include those that indicate the market's overall buying power: for example, population, gross national product in total and per capita, and total exports and imports. Product-specific factors narrow the analysis to the marketer's operations. A company such as Motorola, manufacturing for the automobile aftermarket, is interested in the number of passenger cars, trucks, and buses in use. The statistical analyses must be accompanied by qualitative assessments of the impact of cultural elements and the overall climate for foreign firms and products. Internally, the marketer must decide on the strategic fit of a market as well. In some cases, an individual market may not be attractive in its own right but may have some other significance, such as being the home market of the most demanding customers (thereby aiding in product development) or being the home market of a significant competitor (presenting a preemptive rationale for entry). Furthermore, the time dimension will have to be incorporated into the analysis. An insignificant market may turn into an emerging market, and those with a foothold may reap the benefits.

Market potential
is the level of sales that might be available to all marketers in an industry in a given market.

Total **market potential** is the sales, in physical units or in monetary terms, that might be available to all marketers in an industry. The marketing manager needs to assess the size of existing markets and forecast their future growth. Two general approaches are used. Analytical techniques based on the use of existing data include using indexes to measure potential through proxy variables that have been shown (by research or by intuition) to correlate closely with the demand of a product. For example, an index for consumer goods might involve population, disposable personal income, and retail sales in the market concerned. In addition to quantitative techniques, marketers use various survey techniques. These are especially useful when marketing new technologies. A survey of end-user interest and responses may provide a relatively clear picture of the possibilities in a new market. A second commonly used approach to assess the size of existing markets is estimating by analogy—where demand patterns in one market are expected to repeat themselves in other markets as function of indicators such as disposable income.

The Screening Process in Target Market Choice Figure 3.3

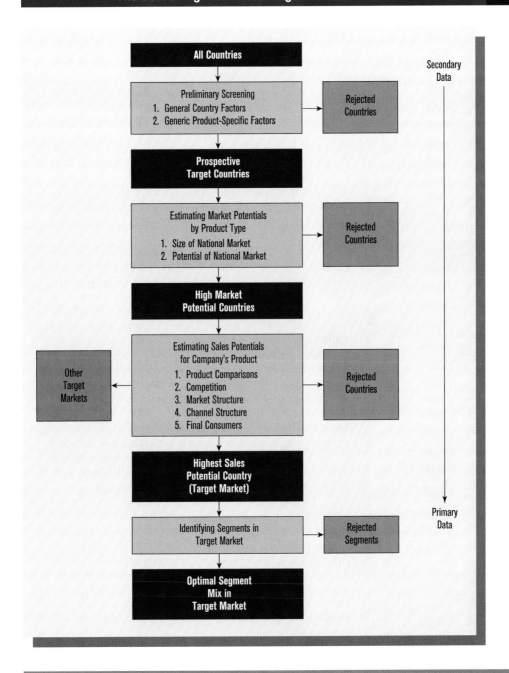

Source: Adapted from Franklin R. Root, *Entry Strategies for International Markets* (Lexington, MA: D.C. Heath & Co., 1994), 56.

Even when the international marketer has gained an understanding of overall demand conditions, the potential of the marketer's own efforts may not be known. **Sales potential** is the share of the market potential that the marketer can reasonably expect to gain over the long term. To arrive at an estimate, the marketer needs to collect data on perceptions of the product (as far as its relative advantage, compatibility, ease of use, trialability, and the extent to which it lends itself to word-of-mouth communication), competition (its strength and likely responses), market factors (such as barriers to entry), channel structure (including access and support of intermediaries such as wholesalers

Sales potential
is the share of the market potential that a particular marketer may hope to gain over the long term.

Bringing the New Economy to New Markets

With the U.S. market crowded with competitors, Yahoo!, Excite, Lycos, and America Online (AOL) are expediting their plans to establish their brands in Asia, Europe, and Latin America before local competitors can create dominant positions of their own. With the non-U.S. share of users increasing, the fastest growth can be secured abroad.

The battle in Europe is the hottest among the portals that serve as starting points for Web surfers looking for news, shopping, and search services. One significant reason for the growth is falling costs. At present, Internet users pay telephone charges on top of Internet access fees to use the Web. Increasingly, however, operators are offering free monthly access, and phone charges are dropping across the board.

Yahoo! and Lycos both operate about two dozen foreign sites, most with native-language news, shopping links, and other content custom-tailored to the local population. AOL has 12 international ventures, followed by Excite with 9. Lycos's German site features tips on brewing beer at home and a program for calculating auto speeding fines. Yahoo's Singapore site offers real-time information on haze and smog in Southeast Asia.

The top U.S. players face tough domestic competitors that often have a better sense of the local culture and Internet styles. In many countries, the dominant telephone companies offer portals, giving them a signifi-

cant competitive advantage with customers who are automatically sent to their home pages when they log on. Germany's leading portal, T-online, is run by Deutsche Telekom, while the leading French portal, Wanadoo, is run by France Telecom.

The danger for U.S. portals is that they might be viewed as "digital colonialists" trying to flex their muscles around the world. In Brazil, AOL was accused by its local competitor, Universo Online, of using a misleading slogan: "We're the biggest because we're the best." The operation has also been hurt because 500 of the 5 million of AOL's installation disks were mistakenly loaded with music and some of the other disks altered the user's hard drive. Local newspapers, some owned by the parent of Universo Online, publicized the incidents.

Market challenges may lead to a desire to form partnerships with local outfits that would also help in understanding the local culture. Joint ventures partners often front much of the capital needed to get the service off the ground, while AOL, for example, provides its technology and established brand name. In regional expansion, care has to be taken in choosing a partner that can provide support across countries. AOL ran into difficulties in Brazil because its Latin American partner was from Venezuela and had its relationships and influence built mostly in Spanish-speaking countries, whereas Brazil's official language is Portuguese. In some cases, partners may be chosen for their influence in the local market; in Japan, Lycos teamed up with Sumitomo, an ultra-traditional trading company with a 250-year history, while in Korea it teamed up with Mirae, a machinery and electronics company.

If a portal is late to a market, such as Lycos for the China market, the only approach is to differentiate. Not only are the leading U.S. portals well established in China, but local players, such as sina.com and sohu.com, are similar to their overseas rivals and promise to know best where locals eat, shop, trade, or get news. One area where Lycos hopes to distinguish itself is wireless Internet. In China, mobile phone penetration stands at 3 percent, while personal computers are owned by only 1 percent of the population.

Sources: "Yahoo Japan Learns from Parent's Achievements and Errors," *Wall Street Journal*, 11 December 2000, A28; "The Word at Yahoo! Yikes!" *Business Week*, 30 October 2000, 63; "Yahoo! Makes Grass-Roots Push in Asia," *Wall Street Journal*, 1 August 2000, B9; "AOL's Big Assault on Latin America Hits Snags in Brazil," *Wall Street Journal*, 11 July 2000, A1, A16; "Lycos Belatedly Scales Great Wall," *Wall Street Journal*, 23 May 2000, A21; "For U.S. Internet Portals, the Next Big Battleground Is Overseas," *Wall Street Journal*, 23 March 2000, B1, B4; and "Shopping Around the Web," *The Economist*, 26 February 2000, S-54. See also http://www.yahoo.com; http://www.excite.com; http://www.lycos.com; and http://www.aol.com.

and retailers), and final consumers (their ability and willingness to buy something new and nonlocal). The marketer's questions can never be fully answered until the commitment has been made to enter the market and operations have commenced. The mode of entry has special significance in determining the final level of sales potential.

Within the markets selected, final consumers and business users will vary in their wants, resources, geographical locations, attitudes, and buying practices. Initially, the decision may be made to enter one or only a few segments (e.g., major coastal cities in China, the government market, or the premium-priced segment) and later expand to others.

Concentration versus Diversification Strategies

Choosing a market expansion policy involves the allocation of effort among various markets. The major alternatives include a **concentration strategy** that focuses on a small number of markets or a **diversification strategy** that is characterized by growth in a relatively large number of markets.[15] The decision to concentrate or diversify is driven by market factors (e.g., market growth, sales stability, competitive lead time, and extent of restraints), marketing-mix related factors (i.e., the extent to which the same mix can be used across borders), and company factors (e.g., resources available and the level of direct control the marketer wants to exert on local operations).

Either concentration or diversification is applicable to market segments or to mass markets, depending on the marketer's resource commitment. One option is a dual-concentration strategy, in which efforts are focused on a specific segment in a limited number of countries. Another is a dual-diversification strategy, in which entry is to most segments in most available markets. The first is likely for small firms or firms that market specialized products to clearly defined markets, such as ocean-capable sailing boats. The second is typical for the large consumer-products companies that have sufficient resources for broad coverage.

THE INTERNATIONALIZATION PROCESS

LEARNING OBJECTIVE 5

The Role of Management

The type and quality of a firm's management are key to whether and how it will enter the international marketplace. Management dynamism and commitment are crucial in the first steps toward international operations.[16] Conversely, the managers of firms that are unsuccessful or inactive internationally usually exhibit a lack of determination or devotion to international marketing. The issue of **managerial commitment** is a critical one because foreign market penetration requires a vast amount of market development activity, sensitivity toward foreign environments, research, and innovation. Regardless of what the firm produces or where it does business internationally, managerial commitment is crucial for enduring occasional setbacks and failures.[17]

Initiating international marketing activities takes the firm in an entirely new direction, quite different from adding a product line or hiring a few more people. Going international means that a fundamental strategic change is taking place. The first step in developing international commitment is to become aware of international marketing opportunities. Management may then decide to enter the international marketplace on a limited basis and evaluate the results of the initial activities. An international business orientation develops over time.

Motivations to Go Abroad

A variety of motivations can push and pull individuals and firms along the international path. An overview of the major motivations that have been found to make firms go international is provided in Table 3.2. Proactive motivations represent firm-initiated strategic change. Reactive motivations describe actions that result in a firm's response and adaptation to changes imposed by the outside environment. In other words, firms with proactive motivations go international because they want to; those with reactive motivations do so because they have to.

Concentration strategy
is the market development strategy that involves focusing on a smaller number of markets.

Diversification strategy
is the market development strategy that involves expansion to a relatively large number of markets.

Managerial commitment
is the desire and drive on the part of management to act on an idea and support it in the long run.

Table 3.2	**Major Motivations to Internationalize Small and Medium-Sized Firms**

Proactive	**Reactive**
Profit advantage	Competitive pressures
Unique products	Overproduction
Technological advantage	Declining domestic sales
Exclusive information	Excess capacity
Tax benefit	Saturated domestic markets
Economies of scale	Proximity to customers and ports

Source: Michael R. Czinkota, Ilkka A. Ronkainen, and Michael H. Moffett, *Update 2003 International Business* (Mason, OH: South-Western, 2003), 279.

Proactive Motivations

Profits are the major proactive motivation for international marketing. Management may perceive international sales as a potential source of higher profit margins or of more added-on profits. Of course, the profitability perceived when planning to go international is often quite different from the profitability actually obtained. In international start-up operations, initial profitability may be quite low, particularly since unexpected influences, such as shifts in exchange rates, can change the profit picture substantially.[18]

Unique products or a technological advantage can be another major stimulus. A firm may produce products that are not widely available from international competitors. Special knowledge about foreign customers or market situations may be another proactive stimulus. Such knowledge may result from particular insights by a firm, special contacts an individual may have, in-depth research, or simply from being in the right place at the right time (for example, recognizing a good business situation during a vacation trip). Tax benefits can also play a major motivating role. Many governments use preferential tax treatment to encourage exports. Such tax mechanisms provide firms with certain tax deferrals and make international business activities more profitable.

A final major proactive motivation involves economies of scale. International activities may enable the firm to increase its output and therefore ride more rapidly on the learning curve. The Boston Consulting Group has shown that the doubling of output can reduce production costs up to 30 percent. Increased production for international markets can therefore help to reduce the cost of production for domestic sales and make the firm more competitive domestically as well.[19]

http://www.bcg.com

Reactive Motivations

Here firms respond to environmental changes and pressures rather than attempt to blaze new trails. Competitive pressures are one example. A company may fear losing domestic market share to competing firms that benefit from the economies of scale gained through international marketing activities.

Overproduction can result in international activities. During downturns in the domestic business cycle, foreign markets have historically provided an ideal outlet for excess inventories. International expansion motivated by overproduction usually does not represent full commitment by management, but rather a safety valve activity. As soon as domestic demand returns to previous levels, international activities are curtailed or even terminated.

Declining domestic sales or a saturated domestic market have a similar motivating effect. Firms may attempt to prolong the product life cycle by expanding the market. Excess capacity can also be a powerful motivator. If equipment for production is not fully utilized, firms may see expansion abroad as an ideal way to achieve broader distribution of fixed costs.

Physical and psychological closeness to the international market can often play a major role in the international marketing activities of the firm. For example, a firm established near a border may not even perceive itself as going abroad if it does business in

the neighboring country. Except for some firms close to the Canadian or Mexican border, however, this factor is much less prevalent in the United States than in many other nations. Most European firms automatically go abroad simply because their neighbors are so close.

In general, firms that are most successful in international markets tend to be motivated by proactive—that is, firm internal—factors. Proactive firms are also frequently more service oriented than reactive firms. Furthermore, proactive firms are more marketing-strategy oriented than reactive firms, which have as their major concern operational issues.

ALTERNATIVE ENTRY STRATEGIES

LEARNING OBJECTIVE 6

The key entry strategies used by the majority of firms to initiate international business activities are indirect exporting and importing, direct exporting and importing, licensing, and franchising.[20] Once firms are established in the international market, other modes of expansion are used, such as direct foreign investment, joint ventures, and contract manufacturing.

Indirect Exporting and Importing

Indirect involvement means that the firm participates in international marketing through an **international intermediary** and does not deal directly with foreign customers or firms. While such indirect activities represent a form of international market entry, they are unlikely to result in growing management commitment to international markets or increased capabilities in serving them.

Many firms are indirect exporters and importers without their knowledge. As an example, merchandise can be sold to a domestic firm that in turn sells it abroad. This is most frequently the case when smaller suppliers deliver products to large multinational corporations, which use them as input to their international sales. Foreign buyers may

International intermediaries are marketing institutions that facilitate the movement of goods and services between the originator and customer.

purchase products locally and send them to their home country. At the same time, many firms that perceive themselves as buying domestically may in reality buy imported products. They may have long-standing relations with a domestic supplier who, because of cost and competitive pressures, has begun to source products from abroad rather than produce them domestically. In this case, the buying firm has become an indirect importer.

Direct Exporting and Importing

Firms that opt to export or import directly have more opportunities ahead of them. They learn more quickly the competitive advantages of their products and can therefore expand more rapidly. They also have the ability to control their international activities better and can forge relationships with their trading partners, which can lead to further international growth and success.

However, these firms are faced with obstacles that those who indirectly access international markets avoid. These hurdles include identifying and targeting foreign suppliers and/or customers and finding retail space, processes that can be very costly and time-consuming. Some firms are overcoming such barriers through the use of intermediaries or "storeless" distribution networks (such as mail-order catalogs and Web sites on the Internet).

International Intermediaries

Both direct and indirect importers and exporters frequently make use of intermediaries who can assist with troublesome yet important details such as documentation, financing, and transportation. Intermediaries also can identify foreign suppliers and customers and help the firm with long- or short-term market penetration efforts. Two major types of international intermediaries are export management companies and trading companies.

Export management companies (EMCs) specialize in performing international business services as commission representatives or as distributors. EMCs have two primary forms of operation: They take title to goods and operate internationally on their own account, or they perform services as agents. They often serve a variety of clients; thus their mode of operation may vary from client to client and from transaction to transaction. An EMC may act as an agent for one client and as a distributor for another. It may even act as both for the same client on different occasions.

When working as an **agent**, the EMC is primarily responsible for developing foreign business and sales strategies and establishing contacts abroad. Because the EMC does not share in the profits from a sale, it depends heavily on a high sales volume, on which it charges commission. EMCs that have specific expertise in selecting markets because of language capabilities, previous exposure, or specialized contacts appear to be the ones most successful and useful in aiding client firms in their international marketing efforts.

When operating as a **distributor**, the EMC purchases products from the domestic firm, takes title, and assumes the trading risk. Selling in its own name, it has the opportunity to reap greater profits than when acting as an agent. The potential for greater profit is appropriate, because the EMC has drastically reduced the risk for the domestic firm while increasing its own risk. The domestic firm selling to the EMC is in the comfortable position of having sold its merchandise without having to deal with the complexities of the international market, but it is less likely to gather much international expertise.

A second major intermediary is the **trading company**. Today, the most famous trading companies are the **sogoshosha** of Japan. Names such as Mitsubishi, Mitsui, and C. Itoh have become household words around the world. A trading company engages in a wider variety of activities than an EMC. It can purchase products, act as a distributor abroad, or offer services. It can provide information on distribution costs, handle domestic and international distribution and transportation, book space on ocean or air carriers, and handle shipping contracts.

Licensing

Under a **licensing agreement**, one firm permits another to use its intellectual property for compensation, designated as **royalty**. The recipient firm is the licensee. The property

---

Export management companies (EMCs) specialize in performing international services as commissioned representatives or as distributors.

Agent is a marketing intermediary who does not take title to the products but develops marketing strategy and establishes contacts abroad.

Distributor is a marketing intermediary that purchases products from the domestic firm and assumes the trading risk.

Trading company is a marketing intermediary that undertakes exporting, importing, countertrading, investing, and manufacturing.

Sogoshosha are the trading companies of Japan, including firms such as Sumitomo, Mitsubishi, and Mitsui.

http://www.mitsui.co.jp

Licensing agreement is an arrangement in which one firm permits another to use its intellectual property in exchange for compensation, typically a royalty.

Royalty is the compensation paid by one firm to another under licensing and franchising agreements.

licensed might include patents, trademarks, copyrights, technology, technical know-how, or specific business skills. For example, a firm that has developed a bag-in-the-box packaging process for milk can permit other firms abroad to use the same process. Licensing therefore amounts to exporting intangibles.

Licensing has intuitive appeal to many would-be international managers. As an entry strategy, it requires neither capital investment nor detailed involvement with foreign customers. By generating royalty income, licensing provides an opportunity to earn income from research and development investments already made. After initial costs, the licensor can reap benefits until the end of the license contract period. Licensing also reduces the risk of **expropriation** because the licensee is a local company that can provide leverage against government action. Licensing also may provide a means by which foreign markets can be tested without major involvement of capital or management time.

Licensing is not without disadvantages. It is a very limited form of foreign market participation and does not guarantee a basis for future expansion. Quite the opposite may take place. In exchange for the royalty, the licensor may create its own competitor not only in the market for which the agreement was made but in third-country markets as well.

Franchising is the granting of the right by a parent company (the franchisor) to another independent entity (the franchisee) to do business in a prescribed manner. The right can take the form of selling the franchisor's products; using its name, production, and marketing techniques; or using its general business approach.[21] The major forms of franchising are manufacturer–retailer systems (such as car dealerships), manufacturer–wholesaler systems (such as soft drink companies), and service firm–retailer systems (such as lodging services and fast-food outlets).

Expropriation
is a government takeover of a company's operations frequently at a level lower than the value of the assets.

Franchising
is a form of licensing that grants a wholesaler or a retailer exclusive rights to sell a product or a service in a specified area.

To be successful in international franchising, the firm must be able to offer unique products or unique selling propositions. With its uniqueness, a franchisee must offer a high degree of standardization. In most cases, standardization does not require 100 percent uniformity, but rather, international recognizability. Concurrent with this recognizability, the franchisor can and should adapt to local circumstances. Food franchisors, for example, will vary the products and product lines offered depending on local market conditions and tastes. The need to do so, however, has to be researched. TGIFriday's assumed that Korean customers would expect to see kimchi (a kind of pickled cabbage that is a staple in Korean restaurants) on TGIF menus as well. They quickly found out that customers in American restaurants want only American food.[22]

Foreign Direct Investment

All types of firms, large or small, can carry out global market expansion through foreign direct investment or management contracts, and they are doing so at an increasing pace. Key to the decision to invest abroad is the existence of specific advantages that outweigh the disadvantages and risks of operating so far from home. Because foreign direct investment often requires substantial capital and a firm's ability to absorb risk, the most visible players in the area are large **multinational corporations**, which are defined by the United Nations as "enterprises which own or control production or service facilities outside the country in which they are based."[23] They come from a wide variety of countries, depend heavily on their international sales, and in terms of sales generate revenues that exceed the gross domestic products of many nations.

Many of the large multinationals operate in well over 100 countries. For some, their original home market accounts for only a fraction of their sales. For example, Nestlé's sales in Switzerland are only 2 percent of total sales. Through their investment, multinational corporations create economic vitality and jobs in their host countries, but also cause **displacement** in some economies.[24]

Reasons for Foreign Direct Investment

Marketing considerations and the corporate desire for growth are major causes of **foreign direct investment**. Today's competitive demands require companies to operate simultaneously in the "triad" of the United States, Western Europe, and Japan. Corporations therefore need to seek wider market access in order to maintain and increase their sales. This objective can be achieved most quickly through the acquisition of foreign firms. Through such expansion, the corporation also gains ownership advantages consisting of political know-how and expertise.

Foreign direct investment permits corporations to circumvent current barriers to trade and operate abroad as a domestic firm, unaffected by duties, tariffs, or other import restrictions. Furthermore, local buyers may wish to buy from sources that they perceive to be reliable in their supply, which means buying from local producers. Another incentive is the cost factor, with corporations attempting to obtain low-cost resources and ensure their sources of supply. Finally, once the decision is made to invest internationally, the investment climate plays a major role. Corporations will seek to invest in those geographic areas where their investment is most protected and has the best chance to flourish. Often, government incentives also play a role in guiding the investment location of firms.

As large multinational corporations move abroad, they are quite interested in maintaining their established business relationships with other firms. Therefore, they frequently encourage their suppliers to follow them and continue to supply them from a foreign location. Many Japanese automakers have urged their suppliers in Japan to begin production in the United States in order for the new U.S. plants to have access to their products. As a result, a few direct investments can gradually form an important investment preference for subsequent investment flows.

A Perspective on Foreign Direct Investors

All foreign direct investors, and particularly multinational corporations, are viewed with a mixture of awe and dismay. Governments and individuals praise them for bringing capital, economic activity, and employment, as investors are seen as key transferers of technology and managerial skills. Through these transfers, competition, market choice, and competitiveness are enhanced.

Multinational corporations
are companies that have production operations in at least one country in addition to their domestic base.

http://www.nestle.com

Displacement
is the act of moving employment opportunities from the country of origin to host countries.

Foreign direct investment
is an international entry strategy that is achieved through the acquisition of foreign firms.

At the same time, the dependence on multinational corporations is seen negatively by many. International direct investors are accused of actually draining resources from their host countries. By employing the best and the brightest, they are said to deprive domestic firms of talent, thus causing a brain drain. Once they have hired locals, multinational firms are accused of not promoting them high enough and of imposing many new rules on their employees abroad. By bringing in foreign technology, they are viewed either as discouraging local technology development or as perhaps transferring only outmoded knowledge. By increasing competition, they are declared the enemy of domestic firms. There are concerns about foreign investors' economic and political loyalty toward their host government. And, of course, their sheer size, which sometimes exceeds the financial assets that the government controls, makes foreign investors suspect. Clearly, a love–hate relationship exists between governments and the foreign direct investor. As the firm's size and investment volume grow, the benefits it brings to the economy increase. At the same time, the dependence of the economy on the firm increases as well.

Types of Ownership

A corporation has a wide variety of ownership choices, ranging from 100 percent ownership to a minority interest. The different levels of ownership will result in varying degrees of flexibility for the corporation, a changing ability to control business plans and strategy, and differences in the level of risk assumed. Often, the ownership decision is either a strategic response to corporate capabilities and needs or a necessary result of government regulations.

Full ownership.   Full ownership may be a desirable, but not a necessary, prerequisite for international success. At other times, it may be a necessity, particularly when strong linkages exist within the corporation. Interdependencies between and among local operations and headquarters may be so strong that anything short of total coordination will result in a benefit to the firm as a whole that is less than acceptable. This may be the case if centralized product design, pricing, or advertising is needed. Yet, increasingly, the international environment is growing hostile to full ownership by multinational firms. Many governments exert political pressure to obtain national control of foreign operations. Ownership options are limited either through outright legal restrictions or through measures designed to make foreign ownership less attractive—such as **profit repatriation limitations**. The international marketer is therefore frequently faced with the choice either of abiding by existing restraints and accepting a reduction in control or losing the opportunity to operate in the country.

Joint ventures.   **Joint ventures** are a collaboration of two or more organizations for more than a transitory period.[25] The participating partners share assets, risks, and profits. Equality of partners is not necessary. The partners' contributions to the joint venture can also vary widely and may consist of capital, technology, know-how, sales organizations, or plant and equipment. Joint ventures can help overcome existing market access restrictions and open up or maintain market opportunities that otherwise would not be available. If a corporation can identify a partner with a common goal, joint ventures may represent the most viable vehicle for international expansion. Joint ventures are valuable when the pooling of resources results in a better outcome for each partner than if each attempted to carry out its activities individually. This is particularly the case when each partner has a specialized advantage in areas that benefit the joint venture. For example, a firm may have new technology available, yet lack sufficient capital to carry out foreign direct investment on its own. By joining forces with a partner, the technology can be used more quickly and market penetration is easier. Similarly, one of the partners may have a distribution system already established or have better access to local suppliers, either of which permits a greater volume of sales in a shorter period of time. Greater experience with the culture and environment of the local partner may enable the joint venture to be more aware of cultural sensitivities and to benefit from greater insights into changing market conditions and needs.

Joint ventures also permit better relationships with local organizations—government, local authorities, or labor unions. Particularly if the local partner can bring political influence to the undertaking, the new venture may be eligible for tax incentives, grants, and government support and may be less vulnerable to political risk. Negotiations

Profit repatriation limitations
are restrictions set up by host governments in terms of a company's ability to pay dividends from its operations back to its home base.

Joint ventures
result from the participation of two or more companies in an enterprise in which each party contributes assets, owns the new entity to some degree, and shares risk.

for certifications or licenses may be easier because authorities may not perceive themselves as dealing with a foreign firm.

Problem areas in joint ventures, as in all partnerships, involve implementing the concept and maintaining the relationship. Seven out of 10 joint ventures have been found to fall short of expectations and/or are disbanded.[26] The reasons typically relate to conflicts of interest, problems with disclosure of sensitive information, and disagreement over how profits are to be shared. In some cases, managers dispatched to the joint venture by the partners may feel differing degrees of loyalty to the venture and its partners. Reconciling such conflicts of loyalty is one of the greatest human resource challenges for joint ventures.[27]

Strategic alliances
are informal or formal arrangements between two or more companies with a common business objective.

Strategic alliances.   Strategic alliances are informal or formal arrangements between two or more companies with a common business objective. They are more than the traditional customer–vendor relationship but less than an outright acquisition. The great advantage of such alliances is their ongoing flexibility since their formation, although stable at any given point in time, is subject to adjustment and change in response to environmental shifts.[28] In essence, strategic alliances are networks of companies that collaborate in the achievement of a given project or objective. However, partners for one project may well be fierce competitors in another situation.

Companies must carefully evaluate the effects of entering such a coalition. The most successful alliances are those that match the complementary strengths of partners to satisfy a joint objective. Often the partners have different product, geographic, or functional strengths, which the alliance can build on in order to achieve success with a new strategy or in a new market. Figure 3.4 shows how some firms have combined their individual strengths to achieve their joint objective. In light of growing international competition and the rising cost of technology, strategic alliances are likely to continue their growth in the future.

Contractual arrangements.   Firms have found contractual arrangements to be a useful alternative or complement to other international options, since they permit the

Figure 3.4	Complementary Strengths Create Value	
Partner *Strength . . .*	**+ Partner** *Strength . . .*	**= Joint Objective**
Pepsico *marketing clout for canned beverages*	**Lipton** *recognized tea brand and customer franchise*	*To sell canned iced tea beverages jointly*
Philips *consumer electronics innovation and leadership*	**Levi Strauss** *fashion design and distribution*	*Outdoor wear with integrated electronic equipment for fashion-conscious consumers*
Ford *automotive design and distribution*	**Qualcomm** *digital wireless communication*	*Phone, Internet, safety, navigation, and entertainment services for vehicles*
KFC *established brand and store format and operations skills*	**Mitsubishi** *real estate and site-selection skills in Japan*	*To establish a KFC chain in Japan*
Siemens *presence in range of telecommunications markets worldwide and cable-manufacturing technology*	**Corning** *technological strength in optical fibers and glass*	*To create a fiber-optic-cable business*
Ericsson *technological strength in public telecommunications networks*	**Hewlett-Packard** *computers, software, and access to electronics channels*	*To create and market network management systems*

Sources: "Portable Technology Takes the Next Step: Electronics You Can Wear," *Wall Street Journal,* 31 July 2000, A3, A14; Joel Bleeke and David Ernst, "Is Your Strategic Alliance Really a Sale?" *Harvard Business Review* 73 (January–February 1995): 97–105; and Melanie Wells, "Coca-Cola Proclaims Nestea Time for CAA," *Advertising Age,* 30 January 1995, 2. See also http://www.pepsico.com; http://www.lipton.com; http://www.kfc.com; http://www.corningcablesystems.com; http://www.ericsson.com; and http://www.hp.com.

Complementary marketing
is a contractual arrangement where participating parties carry out different but complementary activities.

Outsourcing
is using another firm for the manufacture of needed components or products or delivery of a service.

Contract manufacturing
is using another firm for the manufacture of goods so that the marketer may concentrate on the research and development as well as marketing aspects of the operation.

http://www.GeneralMills.com

international use of corporate resources and can also be an acceptable response to government ownership restrictions.

One form such an arrangement may take is that of **complementary marketing**, where the contracting parties carry out different activities. For example, Nestlé and General Mills have an agreement whereby Honey Nut Cheerios and Golden Grahams are made in General Mills' U.S. plants, shipped in bulk to Europe for packaging at a Nestlé plant, and are then marketed in France, Spain, and Portugal by Nestlé.[29] Other contractual arrangements exist for **outsourcing**, in which a firm enters into long-term arrangements with its suppliers. For example, General Motors buys cars and components from South Korea's Daewoo, and Siemens buys computers from Fujitsu. As corporations look for ways to grow and focus simultaneously on their competitive advantage, outsourcing has becomes a powerful new tool for achieving these goals. Firms increasingly also develop arrangements for **contract manufacturing** that allow the corporation to separate the physical production of goods from the research, development, and marketing stages, especially if the latter are the core competencies of the firm. Such contracting has become particularly popular in the footwear and garment industries. For example, Nike, the footwear company based in Beaverton, Oregon, has 100 percent of its footwear produced by subcontractors, most of them outside the United States. Nike's own people focus on the services part of the production process, including design, product development, marketing, and distribution.[30]

http://www.nike.com

A COMPREHENSIVE VIEW OF INTERNATIONAL EXPANSION

LEARNING OBJECTIVE 7

The central driver of internationalization is the level of managerial commitment. This commitment will grow gradually from an awareness of international potential to the adaptation of an international strategic direction. It will be influenced by the information, experience, and perception of management, which in turn are shaped by motivations and concerns of the firm.

Management's commitment and its view of the capabilities of the firm will then trigger various international marketing activities, which can range from indirect exporting and importing to a more direct involvement in the global market. Eventually, the firm may expand further through foreign direct investment measures such as joint ventures or strategic alliances. All of the developments, processes, and factors involved in the overall process of going international are linked to each other. A comprehensive view of these linkages is presented schematically in Figure 3.5.

| Figure 3.5 | A Comprehensive Model of International Market Entry and Development |

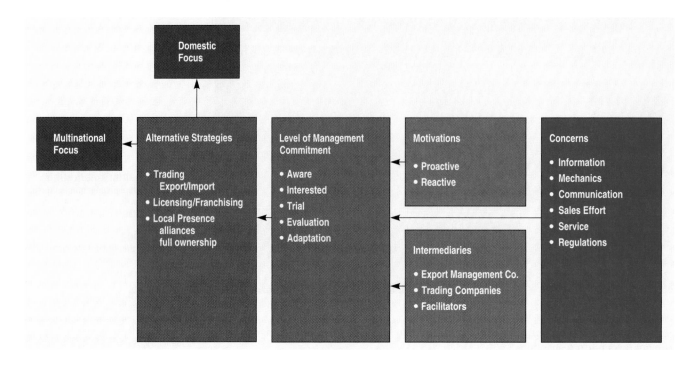

Adjusting the Marketing Mix

The choice of target markets and entry modes has to be accompanied by decisions relating to the marketing mix and the degree to which its elements should be standardized or localized. Three basic alternatives in approaching international markets are available:

- Make no special provisions for the international marketplace, but, rather, identify potential target markets, then choose products that can easily be marketed with little or no modification (**standardized approach**).
- Adapt to local conditions in each and every target market (the **multidomestic approach**).
- Incorporate differences into a regional or global strategy that will allow for local differences in implementation (**globalization approach**).

Ideally, the marketing manager should "think globally and act locally," not by focusing on the extremes of full standardization or full localization, but rather on exploiting good ideas, strategies, and products on a wider regional basis. Three sets of influences shape the final form of and the adjustments to be made in the marketing mix: (1) company policies and resources, (2) market-specific considerations, and (3) the product itself in terms of how it is to be marketed (as shown in Figure 3.6).

Company Decisions
Before launching a product or a program in the international marketplace, marketing managers need to consider organizational capabilities as well as the level of the endeavor needed to succeed. The issue of adaptation often climaxes in the question Is it worth it? The answer depends on the company's ability to control costs, correctly estimate market potential, and, finally, secure profitability in the long term.

Macroenvironmental Influences
Typically, as presented in Chapter 1, macroenvironmental influences often mandate a variety of marketing-mix adjustments. Among them, government regulations present the most stringent requirements. Some regulations may serve no purpose other than a politi-

Standardized approach
is the approach to international marketing in which products are marketed with little or no modification.

Multidomestic approach
is the approach to international marketing in which local conditions are adapted to in each and every target market.

Globalization approach
is the approach to international marketing in which differences are incorporated into a regional or global strategy that will allow for differences in implementation.

Factors Affecting Marketing-Mix Adjustments		Figure 3.6
Company Considerations	**Regional, Country, or Local Characteristics**	**Product Characteristics**
Profitability	Government regulations	Product constituents
Market opportunity	Customer characteristics, expectations, and preferences	Brand
Policies	Purchase patterns	Positioning
	Stage of economic development	Packaging
	Competitive offerings	Country of origin
	Climate and geography	Maintenance/after-sales service

Source: Adapted from V. Yorio, *Adapting Products for Export* (New York: The Conference Board, 1983), 7.

cal one, such as protection of domestic industry or response to constituent pressure. Because of the sovereignty of nations, marketers need to comply, but can influence the situation by lobbying, directly or through their industry associations, for an issue to be raised during trade negotiations. Government regulations may be spelled out, but marketers need to be vigilant in terms of changes and exceptions.

Standards often present the marketing manager with a set of adaptation challenges. For example, France requires the use of the French language in any offer, presentation, or advertisement whether written or spoken; in instructions for use; in specification or guarantee terms; and on invoices and receipts. This includes Web sites. Increasingly, quality standards may be imposed on marketers, especially in business marketing. The EU has chosen the **International Organization for Standardization (ISO) 9000** as a basis to harmonize varying technical norms of its member states, thereby making it necessary for all marketers interested in the EU to comply.[31] Increasing environmental concern is leading some governments to require marketers to take responsibility for their packaging waste, thereby resulting in attempts to redesign products and their packaging, reducing the waste generated, recycling it, and reusing it. At the Geneva auto show in 1998, Toyota introduced a concept car that is predominantly recyclable.

Product Decisions

While there are arguments for an increasing amount of product standardization from an economies of scale perspective, international marketing managers will have to balance these considerations against factors that may call for adaptation. In many cases, the marketing manager has no choice but to make the adaptations. For example, Murray Ohio Manufacturing has had to make its lawn mowers quieter for the European market because of the noise standards imposed by the European Union.[32] In some cases, the choice is based on customer preferences (e.g., Chrysler making available, in 1996 for the first time, right-hand drive vehicles for the Japanese market).

Design considerations. Climate and geography of international markets can have an impact on product design. For example, the marketing of chocolate products is challenging in hot climates and has led three companies to take different approaches to their marketing-mix adaptation. Nestlé's solution was to produce a slightly different Kit Kat wafer for Asia with reduced fat content to raise the chocolate's melting point. Cadbury Schweppes has its own display cases in the retail outlets to reject the heat and humidity, while Toblerone has confined its distribution to air-conditioned outlets.

The international marketer must also make sure products do not contain ingredients or features that might be in violation of legal requirements or religious or social customs. In Islamic countries, for example, animal fats have to be replaced by ingredients such as vegetable shortening.

Branding considerations. The use of standardization in branding is strongest in culturally similar markets; for U.S. marketers this means Canada and the United Kingdom. Standardization of product and brand do not necessarily move hand in hand; a global or regional brand may well have local features (such as Ford's Escort), or a highly standardized product may have local brand names (e.g., Snuggle, Cajoline, Kuschelweich,

International Organization for Standardization (ISO)
is a nongovernmental organization that promotes the development of standardization to facilitate the international exchange of goods and services.

http://www.iso.ch

http://www.toyota.com

Mimosin, and Yumos). While the same brand name may be used, additional dimensions may have to be considered. Chinese consumers expect more in terms of how the names are spelled, written, and styled, and whether they are considered lucky. Chee-tos are marketed in China under the Chinese name *qi duo* (roughly pronounced "chee-do") that translates as "Many Surprises." Segmentation decisions will affect branding as well.[33] At Whirlpool, the Whirlpool brand name will be used as the global brand name to serve the broad middle market segment, while regional and local brands will cover the others. Throughout Europe, the Bauknecht brand is targeted at the upper end of the market seeking a reputable German brand. Ignis and Laden are positioned as price-value brands—Ignis Europe-wide, Laden in France.[34]

Packaging considerations.   With packaging, marketers will have to worry about the protective, promotional, and user convenience dimensions of the function. Packaging will have to vary as a function of the transportation mode, transit conditions, and transit time. Promotional features take into consideration regulations and customer preferences, while package sizes take into account purchase patterns and market conditions.

Labeling considerations.   Country-of-origin has considerable influence on the quality perceptions of a product. For example, when Canon changed its supply of copiers to the Russian market from their Japanese production facilities to their newly opened China plant, sales slumped and Canon's dealers started importing Canon copiers from around the world that displayed the "made in Japan" label. This **gray marketing** of its copiers forced Canon to switch its procurement for Russia back to the Japanese source.

Promotion Decisions

Positioning considerations.   The most important category of adaptations is based on local behavior, tastes, attitudes, and traditions—all reflecting the marketer's need to gain customers' approval. The product itself may not change at all, only its positioning may need to be adjusted. For example, Coca-Cola launched Diet Coke in Japan by changing its name to Coke Light and shifted the promotion theme from "weight loss" to "figure maintenance." Japanese women do not like to admit that they are dieting by drinking something clearly labeled *diet*. Examples of such adjustments are provided in Figure 3.7. While the ads share common graphic elements, separate approaches in adjustment are evident. Past advertisements provided by Marriott from the United States and Saudi Arabia employed a relatively standard approach given the similarity in target audiences (i.e., the business traveler) and in the competitive conditions in the markets. Another set of ads from Latin America and German-speaking Europe were quite different. While the Latin advertisement stressed comfort, the German version focused on results.

Copy considerations.   While positioning strategy tends to be decided on a broader basis, the actual copy of the advertisement by market may well have to be adjusted. American Express, for example, with its "places you want to go, people you want to be" campaign, wanted to give traveling card holders the same campaign they see at home but one that would also look like a domestic effort to locals. This was achieved by having all spots around the world follow the same formula: Merchants expound on their business philosophies, then talk about the card. Featured were, among many, British designer and retailer Sir Terence Conran, Japanese innkeepers Koin and Emiko Horibe, and Toys "R" Us founder Charles Lazarus.[35]

Similarly, ads for cosmetic products marketed in countries such as Saudi Arabia have to take into account local moral standards. While a global creative approach can be used, it may have to be adjusted. For example, Guy Laroche's ad for Drakkar Noir shows a man's hand clutching the perfume bottle and a woman's hand seizing his bare forearm. This version used around the world was adjusted for Saudi Arabia to show the man's arm clothed in a dark suit sleeve, and the woman's hand merely brushing his hand.[36]

Distribution Decisions

While distribution decisions continue to be mostly tactical and made on a market-by-market basis, marketing managers have to be aware of the changes in the distribution function as well. Distribution formats are crossing borders, especially to newly emerging

http://www.canon.com

Gray marketing
is the marketing of authentic, legally trademarked goods through unauthorized channels.

http://www.coca-cola.com

http://www.marriott.com

http://www.americanexpress.com

Local Adjustments in a Global Advertising Campaign | **Figure 3.7**

http://www.marriott.com

markets. While supermarkets accounted for only 8 percent of consumer nondurable sales in Thailand in 1990, the figure today approaches 45 percent. The other trend is that intermediaries themselves have embarked on globalization efforts either independently or through strategic alliances. Entities such as Toys "R" Us from the United States, Galeries Lafayette from France, Marks & Spencer from the United Kingdom, and Takashimaya and Isetan from Japan have expanded worldwide.[37]

Some markets may require unique approaches to developing global products. At Gillette, timing is the only concession to local taste. Developing markets, such as China, eastern Europe, and Latin America, are first introduced to the older, cheaper products before the latest, state-of-the-art versions are sold. In a world economy where most of the growth is in developing markets, the global products' inevitable premium pricing may keep them out of the hands of the average consumer. As a result, Procter & Gamble

http://www.pg.com

figures out what consumers in various countries can afford, then develops products accordingly. In Brazil, the company launched a diaper called Pampers Uni, a less-expensive version of its mainstream product. The strategy is to create price tiers, hooking customers early, then encouraging them to trade up as their incomes and desire for better products grow.[38]

The monitoring of competitors' approaches—determining what has to be done to meet and beat them—is critical. In many markets, the international marketer is competing with local manufacturers and must overcome traditional purchasing relationships or face large multinational marketers that have considerable resources to commit. BBN Technologies, a marketer of interactive data-processing equipment and support services, is facing such competitors as Siemens and Philips and will have to prove not only that its products are competitive in price and quality but also that the company will honor its commitments and provide the necessary after-sales service.[39] This may mean that the marketer has to establish a sales office and employ its own personnel in selected target markets rather than being able to rely on independent distributors as is done at home.

Pricing Decisions

International competitiveness in price is a challenge for the marketing manager in two broad ways. First, exported products are threatened by price escalation—the combined effect of costs incurred in modifying products to the international marketplace, operational costs in exports (such as shipping), and market-entry costs (such as tariffs and taxes). Second, marketers may also face unfavorable foreign-exchange rates. The marketing manager has two options in making sure prices remain competitive: either to absorb the price increases, especially when customers are felt to be price elastic, or pass-through, which means that the customer bears the added costs but is still willing to buy the product due to its other attractive features. With the introduction of the euro, the common European Union currency, foreign-currency fluctuations will no longer present a challenge to marketers from the 12 member countries that have elected to utilize the common currency.

IMPLEMENTING MARKETING PROGRAMS WORLDWIDE

LEARNING OBJECTIVE 8

With world markets rapidly converging and merging, marketers have to make sure that their organizations are capable of taking advantage of the resulting opportunities. The necessary actions will relate to management processes, organization structure, and corporate culture, all of which should ensure the successful implementation of marketing programs both across borders and within individual markets.

The new realities of the global marketplace require, by design, a balance between sensitivity to local needs and deployment of technologies and concepts across borders. This means that neither headquarters nor country managers can alone call the shots. If decisions are not made in coordinated fashion, or if standard procedures are forced upon country operations, local resistance in the form of the not-invented-here syndrome may lead to the demise of potentially attractive innovation. Resistance may stem from opposition to any idea originating from the outside, from lack of involvement in strategy development, or from valid concerns about the applicability of a concept to that particular market. Without local commitment, no global marketing effort can survive.

Management Process

In the multidomestic approach, marketing managers at the country level had very little incentive to exchange ideas or coordinate activities with their counterparts. Globalization, however, requires transfer of information both between the headquarters and country organizations and within the country organizations themselves. By facilitating the flow of information and sharing best practices from around the world, whether through regular meetings or use of corporate intranets, ideas are exchanged and organizational values are strengthened.[40] IBM, for example, has a Worldwide Opportunity Council that sponsors

http://www.ibm.com

fellowships for employees to listen to business cases from around the world and to develop global platforms and solutions. At Levi Strauss, as with most successful global marketers, marketing personnel are supported through electronic networking capabilities and are encouraged to adopt ideas from other markets. Headquarters exercises its control only when necessary, for example, in protecting brand identity, image, and quality.

http://www.levi.com

Part of this global marketing readiness is personnel exchange. Many companies encourage (or even require) marketing managers to gain experience abroad during the early or middle levels of their careers. The more experience people have in working with others from different regions and ethnic backgrounds, the better a company's global philosophy, strategy, and actions will be integrated locally.

The role of headquarters staff should be that of coordinating and leveraging the resources of the corporation worldwide. This may mean activities focused on combining good ideas that come from different parts of the organization to be fed into global planning. Many companies employ world-class advertising and market research staffs whose role should be to consult country organizations in upgrading their technical skills and getting them to focus their attention not only on local issues but also on those with global impact.

Globalization calls for a substantial degree of centralization in marketing decision making, far beyond that in the multidomestic approach. Once a strategy has been jointly developed, headquarters may want to permit local managers to develop their own programs within specified decision-making boundaries. These programs could then be subject to headquarters' approval, rather than forcing local managers to adhere strictly to the formulated strategy. For tactical elements of the marketing mix, such as choice of distribution channels or sales promotional tools, decisions should be left to the country managers. Colgate-Palmolive allows local units to use their own ads, but only if they can beat the global "benchmark" version. With a properly managed approval process, effective control can be exerted without unduly dampening country managers' creativity and initiative.

http://www.colgate.com

Organization Structure

Various organizational structures have emerged to support global marketing efforts. Some companies have established global or regional product managers and their support groups at headquarters. Their task is to develop long-term strategies for product categories on a worldwide basis and to act as the support system for the country organiza-

Careers in Marketing

Global Experience Leads to the Top

E. V. Goings, president of Tupperware, took part in a total-immersion program in Spanish—his third language—but he hardly stands out on his company's executive committee. The eight other members of the group speak two to four languages each, and all can boast of international work experience.

International exposure has long been trumpeted as essential for middle managers in multinationals, but these days, even chief executives are going global. To keep up with the growing importance of foreign markets, more companies are requiring candidates for top management positions to have strong international resumes. Victor J. Menezes, a native of Puna, India, has worked for Citigroup since 1972—in Hong Kong, China, Brussels, Latin America, and Africa—and is now head of the corporate emerging markets planning group. During a trip to a recent acquisition in Poland, Menezes met with executives: several Poles, three Indians, an Englishman, an Argentinian, a Belgian, an Irishman, and a Chinese-Singaporean—and no Americans.

Executives who climbed the corporate ladder in the past typically ran successively bigger operations of a single product line or specialized in one discipline like finance. Leaving the United States for an overseas post was often perceived as dangerous, taking executives far from the center of power. Today, however, international experience is often a top priority for executive headhunters. Executive-search firms report that major corporations required candidates with international experience in 28 percent of senior-level searches [in 1995], up from 4 percent in 1990.

"It sends the most powerful signal you can send [to the employees] if the CEO has international experience or has been selected for that reason," says Jean-Pierre Rosso, the president and CEO of Case Corp. Rosso spent 12 years at Honeywell Inc. in France and Belgium. Dana Mead, the CEO of Tenneco Inc. and the person responsible for picking Rosso for the job, says that he "showed he could operate in both [American and French] cultures."

Combining high-profile roles abroad and at home seems to be the formula of success for many top management candidates. The Egyptian-born CEO of Goodyear Tire and Rubber, Samir Gibara, caught the eye of his predecessor Stanley Gault by turning around Goodyear's losses in its European operation in the early 1990s. Then Gibara took on several key U.S. jobs at the tire maker's Akron, Ohio, headquarters before becoming CEO.

Other types of foreign exposure can also offer executives the opportunity for great upward mobility. Expertise in the bigger and more challenging emerging markets such as Brazil, China, and India can often pave the way to success. A key reason why Andrea Jung was elected president of Avon Products Inc. was that she served the firm as president and COO of global marketing, with operating responsibility for all of Avon's global units.

Sources: Joann S. Lublin, "An Overseas Stint Can Be a Ticket to the Top," *Wall Street Journal*, 29 January 1996, B1; Paul Beckett, "To Fuel Its Growth, Citigroup Depends on Menezes' Work in Emerging Markets," *Wall Street Journal*, 21 February 2001, C1; http://www.avon.com.

tions. This matrix structure focused on customers, which has replaced the traditional country-by-country approach, is considered more effective in today's global marketplace by companies that have adopted it.

Whenever a product group has global potential, firms such as Procter & Gamble, 3M, and Henkel create strategic-planning units to work on the programs. These units, such as 3M's EMATs (European Marketing Action Teams), consist of members from the country organizations that will market the products, managers from both global and regional headquarters, and technical specialists.

Local marketing organizations are absorbing new roles as markets scan the world for ideas that can cross borders. The consensus among marketers is that many more countries, in addition to the strategic leaders, are now capable of developing products and solutions that can be applied on a worldwide basis. This realization has given birth to centers of excellence. Ford's centers of excellence have been established with two key goals in mind: to avoid duplicating efforts and to capitalize on the expertise of specialists on a worldwide basis. Located in several countries, the centers will work on key components for cars. For example, one will work on certain kinds of engines, while another may engineer and develop common platforms. Designers in each market will then style the exteriors and passenger compartments to appeal to local tastes.

CHAPTER SUMMARY

- International marketing offers new complexities, challenges, and opportunities to a firm.

- Managers need to understand and cope with a new set of macroenvironmental variables, which consist of varying cultural dimensions, different socioeconomic levels, and divergent and sometimes even conflicting legal and political approaches.

- In investigating global market opportunities, the firm must first identify and screen markets internationally based on general country factors and firm-specific criteria. After identifying specific desirable markets, management must then choose between a concentrated or diversified expansion approach to these markets.

- The initiation of internationalization depends very heavily on managerial commitment to the international strategy and on the firm's motivation for going international. Initial modes of entry are typically exporting or importing and licensing and franchising, and are often assisted by intermediaries. Over time and with growing experience, firms then expand through direct foreign investment, joint ventures, or contract manufacturing.

- As a next step, the firm needs to adjust its marketing mix in order to be responsive to differences in market, product, or company characteristics.

- Finally, managerial processes as well as the organizational structure need to be reviewed and adjusted in order to enable the worldwide implementation of marketing programs.

KEY TERMS

Agent is a marketing intermediary who does not take title to the products but develops marketing strategy and establishes contacts abroad.

Antidumping laws are laws designed to help domestic industries that are injured by unfair competition from abroad due to imports being sold at less than fair value.

Change agent is a person or institution that facilitates change in a firm or in a host country.

Code law is law based on a comprehensive set of written statutes.

Common law is law based on tradition and depending less on written statutes and codes than on precedent and custom.

Complementary marketing is a contractual arrangement where participating parties carry out different but complementary activities.

Concentration strategy is the market development strategy that involves focusing on a smaller number of markets.

Contract manufacturing is using another firm for the manufacture of goods so that the marketer may concentrate on the research and development as well as marketing aspects of the operation.

Degree of individualism is the extent to which individual interests prevail over group interests.

Displacement is the act of moving employment opportunities from the country of origin to host countries.

Distributor is a marketing intermediary that purchases products from the domestic firm and assumes the trading risk.

Diversification strategy is the market development strategy that involves expansion to a relatively large number of markets.

Export management companies (EMCs) specialize in performing international services as commissioned representatives or as distributors.

Expropriation is a government takeover of a company's operations frequently at a level lower than the value of the assets.

Foreign direct investment is an international entry strategy that is achieved through the acquisition of foreign firms.

Franchising is a form of licensing that grants a wholesaler or a retailer exclusive rights to sell a product or a service in a specified area.

Globalization approach is the approach to international marketing in which differences are incorporated into a regional or global strategy that will allow for differences in implementation.

Gray marketing is the marketing of authentic, legally trademarked goods through unauthorized channels.

Intellectual property rights is the protection provided by patents, copyrights, and trademarks.

International intermediaries are marketing institutions that facilitate the movement of goods and services between the originator and customer.

International marketing is the process of planning and conducting transactions across national borders to create exchanges that satisfy the objectives of individuals and organizations.

International Organization for Standardization (ISO) is a nongovernmental organization that promotes the development of standardization to facilitate the international exchange of goods and services.

Joint ventures result from the participation of two or more companies in an enterprise in which each party contributes assets, owns the new entity to some degree, and shares risk.

Level of equality is the extent to which less powerful members accept that power is distributed unequally.

Licensing agreement is an arrangement in which one firm permits another to use its intellectual property in exchange for compensation, typically a royalty.

Managerial commitment is the desire and drive on the part of management to act on an idea and support it in the long run.

Market potential is the level of sales that might be available to all marketers in an industry in a given market.

Material achievement is the extent to which the dominant values in society are success, money, and things.

Multidomestic approach is the approach to international marketing in which local conditions are adapted to in each and every target market.

Multinational corporations are companies that have production operations in at least one country in addition to their domestic base.

Outsourcing is using another firm for the manufacture of needed components or products or delivery of a service.

Profit repatriation limitations are restrictions set up by host governments in terms of a company's ability to pay dividends from its operations back to its home base.

Royalty is the compensation paid by one firm to another under licensing and franchising agreements.

Sales potential is the share of the market potential that a particular marketer may hope to gain over the long term.

Sogoshosha are the trading companies of Japan, including firms such as Sumitomo, Mitsubishi, and Mitsui.

Standardized approach is the approach to international marketing in which products are marketed with little or no modification.

Strategic alliances are informal or formal arrangements between two or more companies with a common business objective.

Trading company is a marketing intermediary that undertakes exporting, importing, countertrading, investing, and manufacturing.

Uncertainty avoidance is the extent to which people feel threatened by ambiguous situations and have created beliefs and institutions to try to avoid these feelings.

World Trade Organization (WTO) is the institution that administers international trade and investment accords. It supplanted the General Agreement on Tariffs and Trade (GATT) in 1995.

QUESTIONS FOR DISCUSSION

1. What are the principal differences between domestic and international marketing?

2. Is it beneficial for nations to become more dependent on each other?

3. Discuss the different effects that code law and common law can have on the international marketer.

4. Why is management commitment so important to export success?

5. What determines the mode of market entry of a firm?

6. What is the purpose of export intermediaries?

7. Suggest criteria on which international marketing managers can base their market choice.

8. Why are more marketers forming alliances with other companies to achieve their goals?

9. If there is a love–hate relationship between governments and foreign investors, what marketing approaches can be taken to present the investor as a contributor to its host country?

10. With more companies adopting global or regional marketing strategies, how can the participation of country-level marketers be ensured in the implementation of those strategies?

INTERNET QUESTIONS

1. Various companies, such as Wyndham International, are available to prepare and train international marketers for the cultural challenge. Using Wyndham's Web site (http://www.wyndham.com), assess their role in helping the international marketer.

2. Compare and contrast international marketers' home pages for presentation and content; for example, Coca-Cola (at http://www.coca-cola.com) and its Japanese version (http://cocacola.co.jp), as well as Ford Motor Company throughout the world (http://www.ford.com).

3. Imagine you are a marketer trying to enter the Asian market and have decided to use a sogoshosha as a facilitator. Using the Web site of the Sumitomo Corporation (http://www.sumitomocorp.co.jp), establish what information is available about the countries of your choice.

ENDNOTES

[1] Sources: "Worldwide Box Office Grosses" available at http://www.boxofficeguru.com/intl.htm; "BskyB's Millennium Movies," available at http://www.variety.com; "'Joe Canada' Crosses the Line," *The Washington Post*, 17 January 2001, A11; "Think Globally, Script Locally," *Fortune*, 9 November 1999, 156–160; "European Film Industry: Worrying Statistix," *The Economist*, 6 February 1999, 40–41; "If In Doubt, Bash the French," *The Economist*, 12 December 1998, 70–73; "Culture Wars," *The Economist*, 12 September 1998, 97–99; and "Does Canadian Culture Need This Much Protection?" *Business Week*, 8 June 1998.

[2] Robert W. Armstrong and Jill Sweeney, "Industrial Type, Culture, Mode of Entry, and Perceptions of International Marketing Ethics Problems: A Cross-Culture Comparison," *Journal of Business Ethics* 13 (1944): 775–785.

[3] Peter R. Dickson and Michael R. Czinkota, "How the U.S. Can Be Number One Again: Resurrecting the Industrial Policy Debate," *Columbia Journal of World Business* 31, 3 (Fall 1996): 76–87.

[4] J. David Richardson and Karin Rindal, *Why Exports Matter: More!* Washington, DC: Institute for International Economics and The Manufacturing Institute.

[5] Cognetics, Cambridge, MA, 1993.

[6] Warren Stugatch, "Make Way for the Euroconsumer," *World Trade*, February 1993, pp. 46–50.

[7] Jagdish N. Sheth and S. Prakash Sethi, "A Theory of Cross-Cultural Buying Behavior," in *Consumer and Industrial Buying Behavior*, eds. Arch G. Woodside, Jagdish N. Sheth, and Peter D. Bennett (New York: Elsevier North-Holland, 1977): pp. 369–386.

[8] Geert Hofstede, *Culture's Consequences: International Differences in Work-Related Values* (Beverly Hills, CA: Sage Publications, 1984). For ease of understanding, Hofstede's term for "power distance" was changed to "level of equality," and "masculinity" to "material achievement."

[9] Sudhir H. Kale, "Grouping Euroconsumers: A Culture-Based Clustering Approach," *Journal of International Marketing* 3 (number 3, 1995): pp. 35–48.

[10] W. Chan Kim and R. A. Mauborgne, "Cross-Cultural Strategies," *Journal of Business Strategy* 7 (Spring 1987): pp. 28–37.

[11] Peter T. Burgi and Brant R. Dykehouse, "On-line Cultural Training: The Next Phase," *International Insight* (Winter 2000): 7–10.

[12] "3M Operational Facts, Year-End 2000." John R. Engen, "Far Eastern Front," *World Trade* (December 1994): 20–24, accessible at http://www.3m.com.

[13] James A. Gingrich, "Five Rules for Winning Emerging Market Consumers," *Strategy and Business* (Second Quarter, 1999): 35–42; "In Search of the New China," *Fortune*, 11 October 1999, 230–232.

[14] *2001 National Trade Estimate Report on Foreign Trade Barriers* (Washington, DC: U.S. Government Printing Office, 2001), 94–95.

[15] Igal Ayal and Jehiel Zif, "Marketing Expansion Strategies in Multinational Marketing," *Journal of Marketing* 43 (Spring 1979): 84–94.

[16] Warren J. Bilkey and George Tesar, "The Export Behavior of Smaller Sized Wisconsin Manufacturing Firms," *Journal of International Business Studies* 8 (Spring–Summer 1977): 93–98.

[17] Finn Wiedersheim-Paul, H. C. Olson, and L. S. Welch, "Pre-Export Activity: The First Step in Internationalization," *Journal of International Business Studies* 9 (Spring–Summer 1978): 47–58.

[18] George Tesar and Jesse S. Tarleton, "Comparison of Wisconsin and Virginia Small and Medium-Sized Exporters: Aggressive and Passive Exporters," in *Export Management*, ed. Michael R. Czinkota and George Tesar (New York: Praeger, 1982), 85–112.

[19] Anthony C. Koh and James Chow, "An Empirical Investigation of the Variations in Success Factors in Exporting by Country Characteristics," *Midwest Review of International Business Research* (1993).

[20] S. Tamer Cavusgil, "Preparing for Export Marketing," *International Trade Forum* 2 (1993): 16–30.

[21] Donald W. Hackett, "The International Expansion of U.S. Franchise Systems," in *Multinational Product Management*, ed. Warren J. Keegan and Charles S. Mayer (Chicago: American Marketing Association, 1979), 61–81.

[22] Wallace Doolin, "Taking Your Business on the Road," *Wall Street Journal,* 25 July 1994, A14.

[23] United Nations, *Multinational Corporations in World Development* (New York: United Nations, 1973), 23.

[24] United Nations, *World Investment Report: Cross-border Mergers and Acquisitions, and Development* (New York: United Nations, 2000), Chapter 1.

[25] W. G Friedman and G. Kalmanoff, *Joint International Business Ventures* (New York: Columbia University Press, 1961).

[26] Yankelovich, Skelly and White, Inc., *Collaborative Ventures: A Pragmatic Approach to Business Expansion in the Eighties* (New York: Coopers and Lybrand, 1984), 10.

[27] Oded Shenkar and Shmuel Ellis, "Death of the 'Organization Man': Temporal Relations in Strategic Alliances," *The International Executive* 37, 6 (November/December 1995): 537–553.

[28] John Hageddoorn, "A Note on International Market Leaders and Networks of Strategic Technology Partnering," *Strategic Management Journal* 16 (1995): 241–250.

[29] Richard Gibson, "Cereal Venture Is Planning Honey of a Battle in Europe," *Wall Street Journal,* 14 November 1990, B1, B8.

[30] Dori Jones Yang, Michael Oneal, Charles Hoots, and Robert Neff, "Can Nike Just Do It?" *Business Week,* 18 April 1994, 86–90.

[31] Davis Goodman, "Thinking Export? Think ISO 9000," *World Trade* (August 1998): 48–49.

[32] Stephen C. Messner, "Adapting Products to Western Europe," *Export Today* 10 (March/April 1994): 16–18.

[33] "The Puff, the Magic, the Dragon," *Washington Post,* 2 September 1994, B1, B3.

[34] "Teach Me Shopping," *The Economist,* 18 December 1993, 64–65.

[35] "Don't Leave Home Without It, Wherever You Live," *Business Week,* 21 February 1994, 76–77.

[36] Michael Field, "Fragrance Marketers Sniff Out Rich Aroma," *Advertising Age,* 30 January 1986, 10.

[37] Rahul Jacob, "The Big Rise," *Fortune,* 30 May 1994, 74–90.

[38] "Divide and Conquer," *Export Today* 5 (February 1989): 10.

[39] Ilkka A. Ronkainen and Ivan Menezes, "Implementing Global Marketing Strategy," *International Marketing Review* 13, 3 (1996): 56–63.

[40] Ingo Theuerkaut, David Ernst, and Amir Mahini, "Think Local, Organize . . . ?" *International Marketing Review* 13, 3 (1996): 7–12.

[41] Source: This case was written by Michael R. Czinkota based on the following sources: Mark Clayton, "Minnesota Chopstick Maker Finds Japanese Eager to Import His Quality Waribashi," *Christian Science Monitor,* 16 October 1987, 11; Roger Worthington, "Improbable Chopstick Capital of the World," *Chicago Tribune,* 5 June 1988, 39; Mark Gill, "The Great American Chopstick Master," *American Way,* 1 August 1987, 34, 78–79; "Perpich of Croatia," *Economics,* 20 April 1991, 27; interview with Ian J. Ward, president, Lakewood Forest Products.

LAKEWOOD FOREST PRODUCTS[41]

Since the 1970s, the United States has had a merchandise trade deficit with the rest of the world. Up to 1982, this deficit mattered little because it was relatively small. As of 1983, however, the trade deficit increased rapidly and became, due to its size and future implications, an issue of major national concern. Suddenly, trade moved to the forefront of national debate. Concurrently, a debate ensued on the issue of the international competitiveness of U.S. firms. The onerous question here was whether U.S. firms could and would achieve sufficient improvements in areas such as productivity, quality, and price to remain successful international marketing players in the long term.

The U.S.-Japanese trade relation took on particular significance because it was between those two countries that the largest bilateral trade deficit existed. In spite of trade negotiations, market-opening measures, trade legislation, and other governmental efforts, it was clear that the impetus for a reversal of the deficit through more U.S. exports to Japan had to come from the private sector. Therefore, the activities of any U.S. firms that appeared successful in penetrating the Japanese market were widely hailed. One company whose effort to market in Japan aroused particular interest was Lakewood Forest Products in Hibbing, Minnesota.

Company Background

In 1983, Ian J. Ward was an export merchant in difficulty. Throughout the 1970s, his company, Ward, Bedas Canadian Ltd., had successfully sold Canadian lumber and salmon to countries in the Persian Gulf. Over time, the company had opened four offices worldwide. However, when the Iran–Iraq war erupted, most of Ward's long-term trading relationships disappeared within a matter of months. In addition, the international lumber market began to collapse. As a result, Ward, Bedas Canadian Ltd. went into a survivalist mode and sent employees all over the world to look for new markets and business opportunities. Late that year, the company received an interesting order. A firm in Korea urgently needed to purchase lumber for the production of chopsticks.

Learning about the Chopstick Market

In discussing the wood deal with the Koreans, Ward learned that in the production of good chopsticks, more than 60 percent of the wood fiber is wasted. Given the high transportation cost involved, the large degree of wasted materials, and his need for new business, Ward decided to explore the Korean and Japanese chopstick industry in more detail.

He quickly determined that chopstick making in the Far East is a fragmented industry, working with old technology and suffering from a lack of natural resources. In Asia, chopsticks are produced in very small quantities, often by family organizations. Even the largest of the 450 chopstick factories in Japan turns out only 5 million chopsticks a month. This compares with an overall market size of 130 million pairs of disposable chopsticks a day. In addition, chopsticks represent a growing market. With increased wealth in Asia, people eat out more often and therefore have a greater demand for disposable chopsticks. The fear of communicable diseases has greatly reduced the utilization of reusable chopsticks. Renewable plastic chopsticks have been attacked by many groups as too newfangled and as causing future ecological problems.

From his research, Ward concluded that a competitive niche existed in the world chopstick market. He believed that if he could use low-cost raw materials and ensure that the labor-cost component would remain small, he could successfully compete in the world market.

The Founding of Lakewood Forest Products

In exploring opportunities afforded by the newly identified international marketing niche for chopsticks, Ward set four criteria for plant location:

1. Access to suitable raw materials.
2. Proximity of other wood product users who could make use of the 60 percent waste for their production purposes.
3. Proximity to a port that would facilitate shipment to the Far East.
4. Availability of labor.

In addition, Ward was aware of the importance of product quality. Because people use chopsticks on a daily basis and are accustomed to products that are visually inspected one by one, he would have to live up to high-quality expectations in order to compete successfully. Chopsticks could not be bowed or misshapen, have blemishes in the wood, or splinter.

To implement his plan, Ward needed financing. Private lenders were skeptical and slow to provide funds. This skepticism resulted from the unusual direction of Ward's proposal. Far Eastern companies have generally held the cost advantage in a variety of industries, especially those as labor-intensive as chopstick manufacturing. U.S. companies rarely have an advantage in producing low-cost items. Furthermore, only a very small domestic market exists for chopsticks.

However, Ward found that the state of Minnesota was willing to participate in his new venture. Since the decline of the mining industry, regional unemployment had been rising rapidly in the state. In 1983, unemployment in Minnesota's Iron Range peaked at 22 percent. Therefore, state and local officials were eager to attract new industries that would be independent of mining activities. Of particular help was the enthusiasm of Governor Rudy Perpich. The governor had been boosting Minnesota business on the international scene by traveling abroad and receiving many foreign visitors. He was excited about Ward's plans, which called for the creation of over 100 new jobs within a year.

Hibbing, Minnesota, turned out to be an ideal location for Ward's project. The area had an abundance of aspen wood, which, because it grows in clay soil, tends to be unmarred. The fact that Hibbing was the hometown of the governor also did not hurt. In addition, Hibbing boasted an excellent labor pool, and both the city and the state were willing to make loans totaling $500,000. Furthermore, the Iron Range Resources Rehabilitation Board was willing to sell $3.4 million in industrial revenue bonds for the project. Together with jobs and training wage subsidies, enterprise zone credits, and tax increment financing benefits, the initial public support of the project added up to about 30 percent of its start-up costs. The potential benefit of the new venture to the region was quite clear. When Lakewood Forest Products advertised its first 30 jobs, more than 3,000 people showed up to apply.

The Production and Sale of Chopsticks

Ward insisted that in order to truly penetrate the international market, he would need to keep his labor cost low. As a result, he decided to automate as much of the production as possible. However, no equipment was readily available to produce chopsticks because no one had automated the process before.

After much searching, Ward identified a European equipment manufacturer that produced machinery for making popsicle sticks. He purchased equipment from this Danish firm in order to better carry out the sorting and finishing processes. However, because aspen wood was quite different from the wood the machine was designed for, as was the final product, substantial design adjustments had to be made. Sophisticated equipment was also purchased to strip the bark from the wood and peel it into long, thin sheets. Finally, a computer vision system was acquired to detect defects in the chopsticks. This system rejected over 20 percent of the production, and yet some of the chopsticks that passed inspection were splintering. However, Ward firmly believed that further fine-tuning of the equipment and training of the new workforce would gradually take care of the problem.

Given this fully automated process, Lakewood Forest Products was able to develop capacity for up to 7 million pairs of chopsticks a day. With a unit manufacturing cost of $0.03 per pair and an anticipated unit selling price of $0.057, Ward expected to earn a pretax profit of $4.7 million in 1988.

Due to intense marketing efforts in Japan and the fact that Japanese customers were struggling to obtain sufficient supplies of disposable chopsticks, Ward was able to presell the first five years of production quite quickly. By late 1987, Lakewood Forest Products was ready to enter the international market. With an ample supply of raw materials and an almost totally automated plant, Lakewood was positioned as the world's largest and least labor-intensive manufacturer of chopsticks. The first shipment of 6 containers with a load of 12 million pairs of chopsticks was sent to Japan in October 1987.

Discussion Questions

1. Is Lakewood Forest Products ready for exports? Using the export-readiness framework developed by the U.S. Department of Commerce and available through various sites such as http://www.tradeport.org (from "Trade Expert," go to "Getting Started" and finally to "Assess Your Export Readiness"), determine whether Lakewood's commitment, resources, and product warrant the action they have undertaken.

2. What are the environmental factors that are working for and against Lakewood Forest Products both at home in the United States and in the target market, Japan?

3. New-product success is a function of trial and repurchase. How do Lakewood's chances look along these two dimensions?

PART two

Understanding the Market

CHAPTER 4

Marketing Research and Information Systems

CHAPTER 5

Consumer Behavior

CHAPTER 6

Business-to-Business Marketing

CHAPTER 7

Market Segmentation and Target Markets

CHAPTER four

Peter R. Dickson, Florida International University

Dr. Dickson earned his undergraduate degrees at the University of Otago, New Zealand. He has published over 70 papers in journals and proceedings and served on the editorial board of several publications, including *Journal of Business Research*, *Journal of Marketing*, and *Marketing Letters*. He is the author of *Marketing Management*, published by the Dryden Press, and a coauthor of a logistics strategic planning guide. He has also worked in the real world, marketing several new products.

Dr. Dickson helped found the Business School at the University of Waikato, where he taught for seven years. After receiving a Fulbright-Hays Bicentennial scholarship and completing his Ph.D. at the University of Florida, he taught for 14 years at The Ohio State University, where he became the Crane Professor of Strategic Marketing and a professor of industrial design, and for 5 years at the University of Wisconsin–Madison, where he was the Arthur C. Nielsen Jr. Chair of Marketing Research. He is currently Knight-Ridder Eminent Scholar in Global Marketing at Florida International University.

Marketing Research and Information Systems

In the mid-1980s, R. G. Barry, the manufacturer of over half of the slippers sold in the United States, faced an unusual problem for such a dominant player: low profitability. Having gone public recently, the board of directors was asking questions. Although headquartered in Columbus, Ohio, most of the manufacturing was being undertaken in Mexico, so manufacturing cost was not the problem. The question that senior management confronted was whether its prices were too low. Recently, Isotoner, the glove manufacturer, had entered the slipper market with a line of attractive silk and velvet ballerina slippers targeted to the younger generation. They were priced between $10 and $15, approximately $5 above R. G. Barry's standard best-selling traditional Dearfoam slipper, and had grabbed about 20 percent of market sales. What would happen if R. G. Barry raised its prices? Would Isotoner grab another 20 percent of sales, or would it make no difference to sales and add a lot to the company's bottom line? How might market research provide some guidance?

The slipper market is very seasonal, with well over 60 percent of sales made through department and discount stores in the gift-giving season, mostly between Thanksgiving and Christmas. The CEO of R. G. Barry decided to undertake a pricing experiment, but insisted that it would have to be undertaken during the peak selling season. The Lazarus Department store chain, at that time also headquartered in Columbus, agreed to cooperate, and two very similar stores were chosen as sites for the experiment. Over four weeks the prices of all models of R. G. Barry slippers were set at normal, raised, returned to normal, and raised again over each of the four weeks. The price sensitivity of shoppers was measured and tested in three different ways:

1. Did sales volume, adjusted for total store sales, decrease when prices on slippers normally priced below $10 were raised 50 cents and slippers normally priced $10 or more were raised by $1?
2. Did sales volume on the lower-priced items in each line of slippers increase when prices were raised? A signal of price

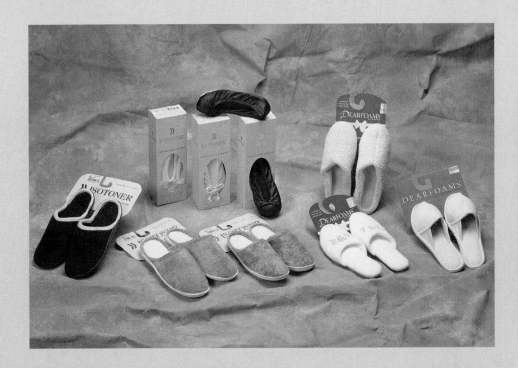

1. Understand how marketing research can contribute to a firm's competitive advantage.
2. Understand that market research includes consumer research, competitor research, and channel research, and explain how consumer research uses the basic marketing research process and various methods to study consumers and their choices.
3. Understand that an important part of market research is to study the history of competition, as well as examining current and potential competitors.
4. Understand how to research and analyze trading systems and distribution channels.

sensitivity is when consumers shift to lower priced items in a product line, when all of the prices in the product line are raised.

3. Does the number of shoppers who buy, compared to the number of shoppers who are observed to check the price of the slipper, decrease when prices are raised? This measure was called the purchase-inspection percentage (PI%) and measured the shoppers' observed reaction to price at the point of purchase. A lower PI% when prices were raised would indicate that shoppers were being turned off by the price of the slipper.

A temporary employment service was hired to supply observers who posed as inventory checkers and restockers, but whose job was to observe when shoppers checked price at the point of purchase. Store clerks were asked to keep the shelves stocked to make sure that no stock-outs occurred. Each Sunday night during the study, all of the inventory was changed and all of the shelves restocked because it was easier to replace the inventory than change the price tags. As with any field experiment, things could be expected to go wrong, and they did. A vicious winter storm closed one of the stores for two days, and Lazarus decided to run two unexpected chainwide sales because of slow Christmas sales. These unexpected events made it extremely important to adjust for total store sales and to focus on the second and third measures of price sensitivity.

The conclusion of the study was that the price increases had no impact on the sales of about 90 percent of R. G. Barry's line of slippers. In particular, Barry's line of ballerina slippers competing against Isotoner could be raised by $1 in price. The only slippers that showed any evidence of price sensitivity were Yak boot slippers that were already high-priced at $18. In the following year, R. G. Barry raised its prices, and its profit-to-sales ratio did increase. However, it also experienced a decline in sales. The experimental study serendipitously observed that too much shelf space in the department store slipper section was given over to poor-selling slipper styles and colors. Although this problem was reported to the company and to Lazarus, apparently this problem was not solved and continued to hurt category sales. Isotoner also continued to outdesign R. G. Barry and take away market share. The problem for R. G. Barry was not just its prices, it was also the attractiveness of its slippers.

THE COMPETITIVE IMPORTANCE OF MARKET RESEARCH

Firms that are able to adjust their marketing strategies to reflect changes in domestic and international markets more quickly than competitors are able to sustain a competitive advantage. Often the key to this advantage lies within the firm's ability to collect, organize, and act upon information that is gathered through market research and information systems. Market research can range from executive visits to a customer's manufacturing facility through to the rather complex and very rare market testing undertaken by R. G. Barry above.

http://www.shell.com

Whatever the research methodology, the competitive importance of market research and analysis was observed in Shell Oil's study of 30 companies that had survived in business for more than 75 years.[1] What impressed the Shell planners was the ability of these companies to learn about their changing marketplaces. Successful companies developed a shared way of thinking about consumers, competitors, distributors, and themselves. The managers in these companies were able to change their thinking about the marketplace faster than their competition. Such fast insight and learning also gave them more time to innovate, imitate, and avoid crisis management. Companies with such superior decision-making skills have a strategic competitive advantage over their rivals. Such skills start with a clear understanding about what market intelligence the firm needs to gather.

From a sociological and political economy perspective, a market is made up of many diverse players, each with its own distinct interests and behavior. Successful marketing decision-making teams obviously think a lot about how consumers will react to a new product or business tactic. But they also think about how other "players" in the marketplace will react to the firm's change in business strategy. It is like a game: You have to anticipate how the different players will react to your move. Some will welcome your moves, others will be indifferent to them, and yet others will contest your moves. Then you have to think about how consumers will react to your rivals' reactions, which are called second-order effects. A market typically contains four types of players: consumers, competitors, distribution channel members, and regulators: those that monitor the marketplace. Each of these groups can be further subdivided into segments, types, and individual entities. Consequently, it is generally recommended that the study of the market be divided into four topics: consumer research, competitor research, channel research, and public policy research. The point is that market research is not just consumer research; market research into changes in competitors, channels, and public policy is given far too little attention in market research practice and teaching.

Surprisingly little is known about what market information decision makers actually use when thinking about the market, but the analysis of the content of marketing plans described in the Market Planning Appendix suggests that it sometimes may be less than adequate. It is hoped that decision makers are briefed about changes in the marketplace in other ways than solely through the content of the marketing plan, such as during informal decision-making sessions by market researchers; otherwise, a great deal of market decision making is less informed than it could be. It is highly likely that many firms might benefit from rethinking how they use market research and what they learn from such analyses.[2] In the following sections, we highlight the different techniques that are used to research consumers, competitors, and distribution channels. How firms (and their lawyers) research the regulatory and policy environment is beyond the scope of this chapter.

CONSUMER RESEARCH

For many, market research means research that focuses on final consumers and users of the good or service. Such research can take many and varied forms, with arguments for and against the cost effectiveness of different practices. If there is one rule in consumer research, though, it is that it should always include firsthand observational research by the decision makers for whom the research is being undertaken. In short, decision makers should always undertake some of the market research themselves. A firm that does not require its marketing decision makers to be involved in some form of direct observa-

A Dumb Study of a Smart Product or a Smart Study of a Dumb Product?

In the fall of 1997 Henry Mundt, a vice president of MasterCard, said, "What we're doing today is launching a revolution. It will start here today and expand across the U.S." What he was referring to was the start of a major test market of plastic money, consumer smart cards containing a computer microchip that can store cash. What actually started was an example of how not to undertake a test market. Smart cards have been introduced successfully on military bases and college campuses, where they are used for multitudes of goods and service purchases. The four sponsors of the market test in New York City were MasterCard, Visa, Chase Manhattan, and Citibank. The card was issued to sixty thousand residents, but over the next year less than $20 was purchased in total on each card. On November 3, 1998, the plug was pulled on the whole test.

What went wrong with the test, and could it have been anticipated? First of all, unlike the bookstores, video stores, snack bars, restaurants, bars, and laundromats on or around campuses, getting the merchants in Manhattan to participate was a real problem for two understandable reasons. First, the test involved two different technologies, requiring each merchant to install two smart card readers on top of credit/debit card readers. Second, the smart card readers were unreliable. The result was that as the merchants discovered the smart cards were not catching on with consumers, they literally pulled the cords on the readers. By the end of the test, the number of participating merchants had shrunk from 600 to 200. As the number of merchants accepting the card shrank, consumers stopped carrying the smart card. Even at the beginning, though, the smart card offered very little benefit over and above the credit and debit cards that consumers already carry. Midtrial survey research of users discovered that consumers wanted to use the cards to ride the subways and for phone calls but could do neither.

The major sponsors should have undertaken survey research beforehand that would have established that there was no demand for the smart card that was tested. Several focus groups with merchants would have established that requiring merchants to use two readers, both of which were unreliable, was a really stupid idea. It might even be asked whether this experiment was ever needed. Smart cards have been very successful in Europe and Asia, but there the cards store much more than money. They are used to store medical histories and for security clearance. In short, the United States is not on the cutting edge of this technology. It can and should learn from the use of the product in foreign markets. Instead, it undertook a market test that made four otherwise great companies look as if they have no understanding of or skill at undertaking market research.

Source: Marcia Stepanek, "What Smart Cards Couldn't Figure Out," *Business Week*, 30 November 1998, 142.

tional research can hardly claim that it is customer-oriented. The excuse that executives are too busy doing other more important things simply says that the leadership is more focused on other issues than understanding its customers.

Figure 4.1 presents the conventional consumer research process. It indicates that in the real world consumer research often proceeds incrementally. The least costly source of answers to the perceived problem should be searched first. Major studies are undertaken only if satisfactory answers cannot be found from secondary sources, by studying other markets, or if the issue is of great importance and a precise answer is required. In the following sections we expand on the major stages presented in Figure 4.1. First, we search the secondary sources within and outside the firm for answers. This is often followed by fairly basic primary research, such as extensive customer visits, in-depth interviews with customers, and focus groups. This is often referred to as qualitative research because it does not generate data that can be quantitatively analyzed with much confidence. If the answer is not clear from qualitative research or if reassuring confirmation is sought, then more thorough survey research is likely to be undertaken that can provide quantitative answers.

Secondary Data Analysis

The U.S. Census Bureau, the biggest market research organization in the world, compiles masses of information about household trends. Almost every public library has the bureau's reports, and the bureau has offices in large cities with specialists whose job is to help businesspeople find out what they need to know. Data from any published source are termed *secondary data* because, in a sense, they are secondhand information. *American*

Figure 4.1	The Basic Market Research Process

1. **Problem recognition:**
   Basic questions are what happened and why?
   What is happening?
   Should we do it?

2. **Meet and define problem and determine how to solve it:**
   When is the answer needed? Limits research method that is used.
   How valuable is the answer to us? Limits research method that is used.
   How valuable is high accuracy? Limits research method that is used.

3. **Search secondary data sources and own databases:**
   Has it happened elsewhere? Check archives.
   Call outside experts for answers.
   How can syndicated research suppliers help?
   Does any published research on the problem exist? Search the Internet.
   Meet and review answers. *Stop if answers are satisfactory.*

4. **Undertake quick-and-dirty primary research:**
   Conduct an electronic voice-mail survey of the sales force.
   Call on or fax customers/distributors.
   Run focus groups. Meet and review answers. *Stop if answers are satisfactory.*

5. **Undertake thorough primary research:**
   Select sampling frame (random-sample national panel provided by market research
       firm).
   Choose survey technique (personal visit, mall intercept, telephone, mail). Design
       questionnaire.

6. **Analyze information:**
   Review descriptive statistics (such as percentages, means, standard deviations).
   Conduct relationship analyses (such as cross-tabs, chi-square, correlational
       analyses, structural equations modeling, logit, ANOVA, MANOVA, Conjoint).

7. **Present findings:**
   Offer progress briefings on important findings.
   Report the presentation.
   Archive findings and data under problem/topic key words.

This figure presents the conventional approach to research. Firms often undertake steps 1 through 4. If they require more formal primary research, they will likely hire a market research firm that will take a month or more to do the study at a cost of $10,000 to $30,000, sometimes much more.

Demographics magazine also presents analyses of census data, in addition to other analyses on population trends and changes in values, habits, hobbies, and entertainment. The Government Printing Office (Washington, DC 20402) has a subject bibliography index, which lists free government publications on some three hundred subjects. The Library of Congress (202–707–5000) also specializes in helping people find information. The U.S. government produces 3- to 30-page annual industry reports on more than 300 industries that cover both national and global trends in supply and competition. These *U.S. Industrial Outlook* reports provide references for further information, as well as the names and phone numbers of the government researchers who prepared the report. Other important government publications are *Statistical Abstract of the United States* and the transcripts of industry studies undertaken by the Federal Trade Commission, the Justice Department, and the U.S. International Trade Commission. The best free source of advice on obtaining secondary information is your local library.

Calling and asking for secondary information from an expert in government or working at an industry trade association is an important market intelligence skill. Some general contact process rules are listed here:

From "On Wisconsin" to "Advance Australia Fair"

Although Sara loved to travel, she never dreamed that she'd one day be working in destinational marketing. Sara initially completed a bachelor's degree in business management and marketing in 1985. During her studies, she was able to gain an internship in Turkey and work part time as a sales representative for a major truck leasing company. These positions gave a practical view of business to the academic work Sara was undertaking.

Following graduation, Sara worked for a major computer company as a sales representative covering southeastern Wisconsin. Although the position was challenging in that weekly sales quotas had to be achieved, the product category was not complex and provided limited opportunities for development. After achieving her first promotion in the company to account manager, Sara began looking for a position that provided more challenges. Although this position did not provide the long-term career options that Sara had envisioned, it did solidify her interest in marketing research. As a sales representative, customers were continually making suggestions on product enhancements or voicing complaints with various product attributes, and there did not seem to be formal mechanisms for collecting and encoding this information within the company.

Sara left this position to head overseas again, where she worked as a university lecturer. This position represented a significant deviation from Sara's main career aspirations, but it gave Sara the opportunity to develop her communication and presentation skills. However, after three years, the time had come to get back into the main game. Because the marketing research industry had progressed so significantly in the development of inexpensive personal computer systems and statistical software packages for data analysis, Sara decided to update her skills and knowledge by completing a master's degree in marketing research.

Following graduation and moving back to Australia, Sara accepted a position with one of Australia's larger research suppliers (A.G.B. McNair, subsequently purchased by A. C. Nielsen). Sara started as a senior researcher with the company, working with a variety of clients on research projects ranging from small qualitative studies of a few focus groups to large national household surveys. Working for a large research supplier, Sara honed and refined her research skills. In accepting the position with A.G.B. McNair, one of the main considerations was the caliber of other staff working within the organization. The company had established a reputation for doing sound, reliable quantitative research. A number of the research directors had been recruited from the Australian Bureau of Statistics and had advanced research skills, particularly in the areas of research design and sampling methods. Working alongside these individuals on major projects enabled Sara to operationalize her academic knowledge successfully.

As is frequently the case, clients often recruit individuals from their research suppliers. Sara was asked to apply for a position within one of her client's research units. Although the initial position offered represented a lateral move, the career advancement opportunities in both marketing research and marketing were significant. Furthermore, when working with a research supplier, one develops excellent research skills but is never able to become an expert in one subject area. Working on the client side provided Sara an opportunity to develop expertise in one subject area and in an area of personal interest: travel.

Sara started working as a market analyst with the Northern Territory Tourist Commission, which was responsible for the analysis of data from the Northern Territory Travel Monitor Surveys. Within six months, Sara was promoted to manager of the research unit and from there to the commission's senior management team as deputy general manager of marketing. Although Sara is still involved with the research unit, her current role is primarily managerial in focus.

- The hard part is the introduction. You should politely and cheerfully introduce yourself, give your name and the name of the person who recommended that you call, and state the purpose of your call. Credible compliments go a long way.
- Initially, ask specific, easy questions. Be open, enthusiastic, optimistic, humble, courteous, and grateful.
- Use a list of questions, but do not sound as if you are following a list. An apparent lack of structure encourages spontaneous insights and allows for bond-forming casual discussions of other icebreaking topics such as sports, world events, children, or hobbies.
- Send a thank-you note (you may wish to call again), and offer to return the favor.
- Be persistent. Keep generating leads. Calling a cooperative expert is by far the best $10 value for the money in market research and analysis. It may take 10 such calls before you find the "true" expert who is willing to share his or her expertise.[3]

The trade associations, journals, and newsletters associated with a particular industry can be located through a local library or by consulting the *Directory of Directories,* the *Encyclopedia of Associations,* the *Encyclopedia of Business Information Sources,* and the *Nelson Directory.* Trade associations often publish information on industry sales by geographical region, year, and product category. From time to time they also undertake general studies of consumer behavior that are published in trade magazines.

The World Wide Web has revolutionized the use of secondary data in market research because of its ability to search for relevant information at almost no, or at least very low, cost. Examples of important data sources on the Web are the Census Bureau site and STAT-USA, another comprehensive source of government statistics that focuses on trade and economic information. Other interesting sites of market research companies that provide information about consumer trends are: http://www.forrester.com, http://www.jup.com, http://www.yankelovich.com, http://www.gallup.com, http://www.nfow.com, and http://www.harrisblackintl.com.

Qualitative Consumer Research

Having cross-functional team members visit customers has emerged as one of the most important primary market research activities a firm can adopt. Talking directly to customers seems so obvious, yet some firms have lost themselves in sophisticated, arm's-length consumer research. The problem with survey research is that too many steps and interpretative judgments separate consumers and decision makers. The vivid impact of listening to customers' own words, of seeing how they use a product in their homes, in their offices, or on their production lines, is lost if customers are not visited at the point of use. Consequently, the importance of customers' concerns has less impact on decision making: Visits allow the **voice of the customer** to be heard, and they make this voice audible throughout the organization.[4]

Companies are often very creative in the ways that they observe customers. Fisher-Price, the toy manufacturer, has a special play laboratory and a waiting list of several years for children to participate in their new product testing, which is observed through one-way mirrors. Other toy manufacturers spend a lot of time visiting day-care facilities and watching how children play with toys. Day-care employees, who are "professional" observers, are great sources of ideas for product improvements. In general, there are millions of salespeople whose business it is to observe consumers and shoppers, who are great sources of information.

Japanese firms such as Panasonic and Sony for several decades have used **hands-on consumer research** that focuses on the way current customers use specific products and brands.[5] For example, one appliance manufacturer took hundreds of photos

---

http://www.census.gov

http://www.stat-usa.gov

Voice of the customer
is the expression of the preferences, opinions, and motivations of the customer that need to be listened to by managers.

http://www.fisherprice.com

http://www.panasonic.com

http://www.sony.com

Hands-on consumer research
is conducted by direct observation by managers of the way current customers use specific products and brands. The opposite is arm's-length research, which is undertaken by external suppliers.

of actual Japanese kitchens and concluded from the photos that the major problem that manufacturers have to address when designing new appliances is the extreme shortage of space in many kitchens. This observation might not have been made had researchers not visited the homes in person and taken the photographs. Such photos should be displayed on the walls of the room where the research team meets. They are a constant reminder of the customers' usage situation that can be "revisited" by simply looking up from the meeting table.

Other market researchers encourage consumers to take photos that describe how they use the product, then tell the story about the photo. This encourages consumers to reveal the deeper meaning and significance of the product in their lives. This in-depth technique, called **motivational research**, can sometimes be taken too far. It can lead management to attribute too much meaning and consumer involvement with a product or a brand because the rich and fanciful stories of a minority of consumers are highlighted in the research reports to management. An example is the research done in the 1950s that concluded that baking a cake was a surrogate for having a baby.

Motivational research is a research method directed at discovering the conscious or subconscious reasons that motivate a person's behavior.

A major camera company used observational research in a clever way to improve the design of its camera line. Research and development engineers searched through thousands of prints being processed at one-hour processing labs and counted the most common problems with the photos, such as poor focus adjustment, poor lighting, incorrect film speed, and double exposures because the film was not wound forward. From the situations that were captured in the photo, they could observe when and where these problems occurred. This led to design improvements in the cameras and better advice in the camera instruction manuals.

Customer Visits in Business-to-Business Marketing

The customer visit is particularly crucial for business-to-business marketing because a few key customers often account for 80 percent of a firm's business. DuPont's customer-oriented culture goes beyond having its cross-functional teams visit with its customers; its "Adopt a Customer" program encourages manufacturing process workers to visit a customer once a month and represent the customer's needs on the factory floor.[6]

If they can, marketing executives should also have firsthand experience of being a customer of competitors' products. For example, a team of Marriott executives spent six months on the road, staying in economy hotels and learning about competitors' strengths and weaknesses. The result was the $500 million launch of its Fairfield Inn chain that immediately achieved an occupancy rate 10 points higher than the industry average.[7] Japanese companies have been known to send up-and-coming executives to the United States for several years to do nothing but travel and study the market for their products firsthand. The importance of creating a company culture that encourages direct contact with the customer explains why the chief executive officer of United Airlines spends time at the ticket counter, and why senior executives at 3M spend several days a month visiting customers, and not just big accounts. Some process guidelines for such visits are listed here:

http://www.marriott.com

http://www.ual.com

http://www.3m.com

- Have customer visits arranged by the sales force: Cooperation between factory engineers and the sales force is crucial. No one likes someone else in a company doing anything behind his or her back, particularly a sales representative whose commissions depend on customer trust and goodwill.
- Visit 10 to 20 randomly chosen customers, as well as important customers who are leaders in adopting new technology. This reduces the impact of an extreme, atypical opinion in later decisions.
- Use jargon only if the customer uses the same jargon. Listen carefully, and note the way customers talk about the product. This gives you clues about the benefits they seek, how they think about the benefits, what problems they confront, and how to design the product to gain a competitive advantage. Rather than asking a customer to adopt your jargon, you should be adopting the customer's words and metaphors. This is how a team changes its thinking about the customer and related decisions. Do not talk in front of customers using jargon that makes them feel like outsiders.
- Learn to listen and observe; do not treat the visit as a sales call. This is something the sales representative will find hard to accept. Do not engage in disparaging the competition when the customer praises them. Instead, be open to ideas that can be quickly imitated.

- Define your research objectives in advance, and use a discussion guide based on these objectives. Write a report on the visit that addresses the research objectives. Report separately on the serendipitous information. "Report" means informing key people within your organization about what you saw or heard.
- Observe the product in use in every situation. Particularly, note and photograph how an innovative customer has adapted your product, package, or service to improve its performance in a particular usage situation. This may suggest a promising new design feature to better service a market niche.
- If possible, have two or three members of the team make the visit together. The time spent talking while traveling before and after the visit is invaluable. Shared expectations, perceptions, and insights are best when made close to the customer visit. Members of the team also discover what they did not see or hear and thus learn from each other how to become better observers and listeners.

Focus Group Research

Next to observation and in-depth discussions with consumers, the most common way of undertaking consumer research is to use a *focus group*. A focus group is a carefully recruited group of 6 to 12 people who participate in a freewheeling, one- to two-hour discussion that focuses on a particular subject, such as product usage, shopping habits, or warranty experiences. In recent years, it has been found that smaller focus groups are often more effective because individuals are more talkative, and they can be conducted in more casual locations, such as hotel suites. Young marketing executives often spend one or two weeks a year crisscrossing the country doing three or four focus groups a day. In more formal focus groups, a skilled, trained conversationalist called a *moderator* often conducts the session to encourage conversation and debate, and members of the cross-functional decision team watch the discussion through a one-way mirror or on closed-circuit television.

Focus groups can be used successfully by following these process suggestions:

- The random calling and screening of participants based on their product usage experience and target **demographics**, such as age and education, can be expensive, sometimes nearly $1,000 to find 30 to 50 willing participants. Consider spending more to create a longer list of willing, qualified participants that can be drawn from at fairly short notice. This will greatly speed up the process of running future focus groups. Take care to check how frequently they have participated in focus groups; avoid professional participants.
- Expect to pay at least $50 per participant to cover travel expenses and two to three hours of his or her time. Professionals such as doctors and architects may expect to be paid several hundred dollars for participating.
- Find a good moderator who can relate to your target group, and develop a long-term relationship with the moderator. Do not conduct focus groups yourself unless you have had professional training and can remain emotionally detached from the subject.
- Encourage the cross-functional team and senior management to watch the focus group. The focused attention and the discussion that ensues have an immediacy that will have a long-term impact on decision making. This also enables questions to be passed to the moderator during a break.
- Continue to run focus groups until no new, important insights are learned from the last focus group that is run. This often means only three or four focus groups need to be run.
- The concept of focus groups has been taken a step further in new product development, with experts recruited to participate.

Demographics
are measures such as age, gender, race, occupation, and income that are often used as a basis for selecting focus group members and market segments.

Although focus groups are great at surfacing issues, problems, and the range of services and features desired, they are seldom completely representative of the thoughts and opinions of a firm's total target market. Typically, focus groups are followed up with more formal survey research of a representative sample of the target market.

Consumer Survey Research

Survey research involves the sampling and surveying of a population of consumers using a carefully prepared set of questions. Surveys of individuals or households are normally taken to study and categorize the variation in buyer values, lifestyles, product usage, benefits sought, and beliefs about product performance (see Chapter 5). This categorization process helps marketers segment consumers into subgroups that share similar

Table 4.1			Major Survey Research Methods		
Criteria	**Direct/Cold Mailing**	**Mail Panels**	**Telephone**	**Personal In-Home**	**Mall Intercept**
Complexity and versatility	Not much	Not much	Substantial, but complex or lengthy scales difficult to use	Highly flexible	Most flexible
Quantity of data	Substantial	Substantial	Short, lasting typically between 15 and 30 minutes	Greatest quantity	Limited to 25 minutes or less
Sample control	Little	Substantial, but representativeness may be a question	Good, but nonlisted households can be a problem	In theory, provides greatest controls	Can be problematic; sample representativeness may be questionable
Quality of data	Better for sensitive or embarrassing questions; however, no interviewer is present to clarify what is being asked		Positive side, interviewer can clear up any ambiguities; negative side, may lead to socially accepted answers	The chance of cheating arises	Unnatural testing environment can lead to bias
Response rates	In general, low, as low as 10%	70%–80%	60%–80%	Greater than 80%	As high as 80%
Speed	Several weeks; completion time will increase with follow-up mailings	Several weeks with no follow-up mailings, longer with follow-up mailings	Large studies can be completed in 3 to 4 weeks	Faster than mail but typically slower than telephone surveys	Large studies can be completed in a few days
Cost	Inexpensive; as low as $2.50 per completed interview	Lowest	Not as low as mail; depends on incidence rate and length of questionnaire	Can be relatively expensive, but considerable variability	Less expensive than in-home but higher than telephone; again, length and incidence rates will determine cost
Uses	Executive, industrial, medical, and readership studies	All areas of marketing research, particularly useful in low-incidence categories	Particularly effective in studies that require national samples	Still prevalent in product testing and other studies that require visual cues or product prototypes	Pervasive-concept tests, name tests, package tests, copy tests

preferences and behavior (see Chapter 7). Table 4.1 compares the major survey research approaches.

These days survey research is mostly used to track customer satisfaction. In a competitive market, customer loyalty and satisfaction are leading indicators of future sales. If they begin to decrease, then it is likely future sales also will decrease. Therefore, in an effort to avoid losing customer sales, marketers are increasingly conducting surveys of customer satisfaction.[8] Table 4.2 presents an example of such an analysis. It categorizes customers by their past loyalty. A slip in satisfaction from a company's most loyal cus-

	Customer Satisfaction by Past Loyalty				Table 4.2

	Current Satisfaction				
Past Loyalty	Completely Satisfied	Somewhat Satisfied	Neutral	Dissatisfied	% of Sales
Firm friends	7%	3%	0%	0%	10%
Core loyal	10	5	5	5	25
Loyal switchers	10	10	10	10	40
Buy-on-price customers	0	5	10	10	25
Overall	27%	23%	25%	25%	100%

Just looking at the overall result, the situation seems rather grim. An analysis of the past loyalty figures, however, provides a little more assurance and explanation. Fortunately, the customers who are most loyal are generally still satisfied. The firm should be somewhat concerned with the 20% of core loyal customers who are currently dissatisfied. The customers who buy on price have a tendency to be less satisfied because they have not developed a continuous cooperative relationship, and they always will be dissatisfied if they think they could have gotten a better deal.

tomers is much more serious than a decline in satisfaction among customers who never have been very loyal. The most rigorous customer satisfaction index (CSI) counts the percentage of "happy" customers in a satisfaction survey. Happy customers say (1) they are completely satisfied, (2) they would definitely recommend the product to friends, and (3) they definitely plan to continue to be loyal customers. The two major issues in survey research are sampling and questionnaire design.

Sampling

To discover how representative the various opinions expressed in focus groups and in-depth interviews are, market researchers survey a sample of the group or population of interest whose attitudes, interests, beliefs, and behaviors they wish to better understand. Examples of such groups are heavy users, nonusers of the product, new Hispanic immigrants in Texas, and new entrepreneurial families in southern China. But how is a sample drawn, and what are the advantages of the different methods?

Random Sampling from a Complete List of the Population
Companies are often interested in finding out whether its current customers who buy a lot from the company are very satisfied, how the customer service they experienced could be improved, and what other goods or services might be sold to them. In this case, the company can randomly generate a sample from the consumers who have made $1,000 in purchases in the last year and are identified as such in the company customer account database. A **random sample** uses a random number generator to determine which consumers in the database will be selected to be part of the sample. A computer program can be designed to randomly draw a sample of 400 to 1,000 participants from a customer list of several hundred thousand. (This is a typical consumer survey sample size, although samples can involve tens of thousands of participants.) The company may track customer satisfaction over time by drawing a fresh sample monthly. The advantage of the random sample is that it greatly reduces the potential for a biasing error in the conclusion of the results. It also enables the confident estimation of the behavior and attitudes of the entire population of interest given the random sample result. For example, if the random sample survey of 400 heavy buyers indicates that 50 percent of those surveyed are satisfied, then the true incidence of satisfaction in the population of heavy buyers is almost certainly (at least 99 percent certain) to be between 42.5 and 57.5 percent.[9] With a larger random sample of 1,600 indicating 50 percent satisfaction, the true incidence of satisfaction in

Random sample
is a set of items that have been drawn from a population in such a way that each time an item was selected, every item in the population had an equal opportunity to appear in the sample.

the population of heavy buyers is almost certainly (99 percent certain) to be between 46 and 54 percent. A sample of 10,000 that reports 50 percent are satisfied brings the precision of the estimate down to 48.5 to 51.5 percent.[10]

Sampling with this sort of precision can be much more cost effective than surveying the whole population of heavy buyers and has the additional advantage of not constantly bothering customers for feedback. The problem with random sampling is that it is rare to obtain a list of the entire target population of interest. If you are very lucky, you may find friendly distributors who will allow you to study competitors' customers by sampling from their databases of customers who have recently purchased rival products. In this case, though, the results generalize only to customers of a particular distributor. If you wish to study why some consumers are product category nonusers, you will need to find a specific list of this population of interest. That is why convenience samples that risk not being representative are often used.

Convenience Samples of a Population

To get a sense of demand in different geographical regions of the United States for a premium brand of Columbian coffee called Grower Reserve, how might a marketer undertake taste tests against a premium supermarket brand? One approach might be to survey a sample of 100 adults intercepted in a shopping mall by a local market research firm that has a testing facility at the mall. Passersby would be recruited in the mall and offered $10 to $20 to participate in a taste test. Normally, people who are systematically too busy because they work long hours at white-collar jobs in offices (where they also drink a lot of premium coffee) would be underrepresented in such a survey, creating a **nonresponse or participation bias**. The design might involve three upscale malls in each of the seven regions of the country (New England and Northeast, South, Midwest, Mountain and High Prairies, Southwest, California, and Northwest), adding up to a total convenience sample of 2,100 ($7 \times 3 \times 100$). This constitutes a convenience sample because the malls chosen are not selected randomly from the population of all malls available, not all mall visitors are randomly sampled, and nonmall visitors are not included. Efforts would need to be made to choose malls that are targeted to the population of interest. The mall interceptors may be asked to fill quotas—say, 100 men and 100 women—to ensure that men are not underrepresented in the sample. This is called a **convenience quota sample**. The interceptors would also have to make sure that store employees were not overrepresented.

Many market research firms offer access to **panels of households** put together by themselves or third-party research suppliers, where each panel is already identified or qualified as possessing specific sociodemographic and buying behavior characteristics (e.g., representing the population of all households across the United States). The firm will then randomly sample from these panels or provide an entire panel of 5,000 that is already randomly selected to provide a demographic representation of the U.S. population. This is by far the most convenient and probably best way of undertaking sampling and survey research—a marketer can purchase answers to individual questions in **omnibus surveys** (several firms studying different product markets participate in the same survey).

The major problem with sampling is nonresponse error. For example, in an effort to study what Americans eat, the Environmental Protection Agency (EPA) hired the market research firm National Analysts. The firm scientifically selected 6,000 households of all incomes and 3,600 low-income households.[11] Accurate results were important because the EPA planned to use the results to measure the ingestion of pesticides through the consumption of different agricultural products (e.g., corn and potatoes) and, based on results, set agricultural pesticide regulations. Future government support of school lunch and food stamp programs also depended on the results. The questionnaire took up to three hours to complete, and respondents were paid $2 to participate. In the end, only 34 percent of those who initially agreed to be surveyed actually participated. The problem with this particular study was that households should have been paid more—$20 to $30—to encourage participation. For an additional cost of $250,000, the response rate would have been about 90 percent, particularly in the low-income sample.

A general problem with sampling is that many populations have been oversurveyed or taken in by bogus market research studies that are merely sophisticated sales pitches. The Council of American Survey Research Organizations estimates that about one-third of households now refuse to participate in telephone surveys because of inconvenience or

---

Nonresponse or participation bias
in responses is created by underrepresentation and overrepresentation in a sample of different groups. For example, most studies have an overrepresentation of consumers who are interested in the product and a nonresponse underrepresentation of consumers not interested in the product.

Convenience quota sample
is a sample of consumers that is not randomly sampled from a population (e.g., users of the product) but is obtained through approaching people in a mall to participate. Quotas are placed on how many men and women should be interviewed (e.g., 200 of each) or some other demographic categorization such as age, education, or income.

Panels of households
are groups of households (e.g., 5,000) recruited by market research firms and rewarded for participating in market research surveys. The firm creates a panel by carefully selecting the composition of the group so that it is representative of the general population in terms of demographics such as geographical location, income, education, and age of the heads of households.

Omnibus surveys
are a survey research service offered by a number of large marketing research companies where several companies' research studies and sets of questions are included in a single questionnaire sent to representative panels of households.

a suspicion that the call is really selling under the guise of research (called **sugging**), which has been made illegal by the Federal Trade Commission. In addition, Americans have less time to participate in such studies because they generally work longer hours today than in the past. As a result, it takes a lot of incentives to avoid the risk of non-response bias and the consequent accusations made by those who oppose the findings that the research was biased.

Question Design

Table 4.3 presents examples of various question types that are used to measure consumer beliefs and attitudes. Sometimes questions can be combined to create a new measure. In the example of a Likert agreement scale shown in Table 4.3, each respondent's ratings of Bank One on the seven-point semantic differential scale in the table can be weighted by the relative importance the respondent assigns to each feature, then summed to create an overall evaluation of Bank One. This overall evaluation measure has been found to be a good predictor of choice. The ratio scale presented was developed to track the changes in shoppers' price perceptions of supermarkets in their neighborhood and to study whether loyal customers of each store had different price perceptions. The difference between a **ratio scale** and an **interval scale** is that a ratio scale has a meaningful, natural zero point and is a continuous measure, rather than measured in discrete intervals. **Reliability** is a measure of the stability or consistency of consumer responses when the same question is asked again or when several similar questions are used to measure consumer response. A study of the reliability of survey measures did not find that any one of the types of measures presented in Table 4.3 was any better than any other but that reliability of the measure increased as the number of points in the scale increased.[12] Thus, a 10-point scale is more reliable than a 7-point scale, which is more reliable than a 5-point scale. This same study also found that it was better to use several measures, such as the three-item CSI scale mentioned earlier that tracks satisfaction, rather than just a single measure of a belief, behavior, or attitude. Using multiple measures of customer satisfaction increases the reliability of the responses and the **validity** of the result.

A useful follow-up question in satisfaction survey research is to ask the **open-ended question**, How can we improve? The answers to this question can then be used to increase the quality of the product and reduce dissatisfaction. For example, for several years United Parcel Service (UPS) questioned customers about their satisfaction with the speed and reliability of the shipping service. When the company asked how the service could be improved, it discovered that customers wanted more face-to-face contact with UPS drivers; they wanted a person to front the service whom they could get to know, ask

Sugging
refers to an illegal survey conducted under the guise of research but with the intent of selling.

A ratio scale
is a scale that measures length, weight, or income.

An interval scale
has intervals of measure that stay constant along the scale. For example, the interval between the measures of 1 and 3 on the scale is the same as the interval between 5 and 7.

Reliability
means the consistency of data. It is often tested by reexamining customer opinions using the same survey on a different occasion, or by another method of measurement.

Validity
in customer survey results refers to their accuracy in measuring what they are intended to measure.

Open-ended questions
allow respondents to determine the direction of the answer without being led by the question. They also prevent "yes" or "no" answers.

Table 4.3	Types of Survey Questions

Likert agreement scale that measures a bank's performance beliefs:

	Strongly Disagree	Disagree	Some- what Disagree	Neither Agree nor Disagree	Some- what Agree	Agree	Strongly Agree
Bank One offers courteous service	____	____	____	____	____	____	____
Bank One has conveniently located ATMs	____	____	____	____	____	____	____
Bank One offers low interest rates	____	____	____	____	____	____	____
Bank One has an easy-to-use Internet site	____	____	____	____	____	____	____

Semantic differential scale that measures a bank's performance beliefs:

Bank One is discourteous	:__:__:__:__:__:__:__:	Bank One is courteous
Bank One ATMs are inconveniently located	:__:__:__:__:__:__:__:	Bank One ATMs are conveniently located
Bank One has low interest rates	:__:__:__:__:__:__:__:	Bank One has high interest rates
Bank One's Internet site is not easy to use	:__:__:__:__:__:__:__:	Bank One's Internet site is easy to use

Importance scale:

Using a 10-point importance scale, where 1 = not important, 5 = moderately important, and 10 = very important, how important are the following to you in evaluating a bank?

Courteous service   ____

ATM location convenience ____

Interest rates   ____

Convenient Internet site ____

To indicate their relative importance in evaluating a bank, please allocate 100 points across the following four performance features: (e.g., 25, 25, 25, 25 would indicate equal importance):

Courteous service   ____

ATM location convenience ____

Interest rates   ____

Convenient Internet site ____

Total   100

Specialized ratio scales (a ratio scale has a natural zero point):

If a shopping basket full of groceries costs $100 at Publix, how much would that same basket of groceries cost at:

Kroger $____

Winn-Dixie $____

Kmart $____

Wal-Mart $____

for advice on shipping, and personally approach with problems and emergencies. As a result, the company is now giving its 62,000 drivers an additional 30 minutes a day to spend time with customers, as well as a small commission on any leads they generate.[13] The program initially cost about $6 million in extra drivers' hours and commissions but generated tens of millions in additional revenue.

Like samples, questions can be biased or subject to nonresponse (because a particular question cannot be answered or the respondent chooses not to answer). Consequently, survey questions have to be carefully designed to avoid "leading" respondents. For example, if a question starts with an explanation of how a company has recently spent $50 million on training its employees to be more friendly and responsive, then the answers are likely to overstate customer satisfaction because the respondents will have been led. Even top business schools are not above trying to destroy the objectivity of consumer survey research. The annual rankings of business schools, such as those by *Business Week*, has become big business. When a school's ranking rises dramatically, so do its applications. This has led some otherwise very respectable business schools to ask their graduates who are surveyed by such rating services to rate the school very high on customer satisfaction questions: High ratings increase the reputation of the school and hence the value of the alumni's degrees. Imagine the fuss that would be created if it were discovered that the validity of J. D. Power surveys of new car customer satisfaction were similarly corrupted by a car manufacturer asking all of its new car buyers to rate a particular model highly because this would increase the resale value of the car. The only sure way of detecting whether questions are confusing, hard to follow, unanswerable because respondents cannot remember their behavior, or not answered because they are too personal is to pretest the survey using a small sample from the population. The **pretest** is administered in the same way that the full survey will be administered. After the respondent has completed the survey, the market researcher interviews the respondent, talking through the survey and the responses item by item. This method can reveal problems with understanding, interpretation, and nonresponse. The fundamental issue is Do the questions consistently measure the true opinions and behavior of the respondent?

A commonsense approach should always be adopted in undertaking survey research. For example, before a firm undertakes regular surveys of customer satisfaction, it should develop a program to monitor customer dissatisfaction complaints registered with the company through letters and telephone calls. Unsolicited consumer complaints send red-alert signals about problems with product design or after-sales service. Tracking service

A pretest
may be undertaken before the major study to test the validity and reliability of measures and other components of the study's research methodology.

requests is another way of identifying customer dissatisfaction. The downtown Chicago Marriott hotel, for example, discovered that two-thirds of its guest calls to housekeeping were for an iron and ironing board. Instead of replacing the black-and-white televisions in the bathrooms of concierge-level guest rooms (housekeeping had received no calls requesting color televisions in the bathroom), the hotel spent $20,000 putting irons and ironing boards in all guest rooms.[14] In fact, many marketers are starting to question the conventional problem-oriented market research process described in Figure 4.1. In today's world of rapidly changing supply and demand, the conventional consumer research process, with its problem-solving emphasis, is being challenged by a process that emphasizes the continuous observation and tracking of consumer behavior. The reason is simple. Once a significant problem is detected, whose full understanding requires extensive study, it is too late to respond effectively. Continuous tracking, particularly electronic tracking, detects a problem almost immediately, allowing more time for an effective response.

Electronic Observational Research[15]

In the mid-1970s, consumer packaged goods companies and grocery retailers settled on a system of bar codes called the **Universal Product Code (UPC)** that is now on almost all items. These bar codes are read by scanners at the checkout and have greatly increased the efficiency and speed of checkout processes. Today, the UPC and the **European Article Numbering (EAN)** systems are used in stores and libraries in North America and Europe and are expected to be used worldwide in almost all product categories in the next 20 years.

A very important side benefit of this technology is that it allows companies to electronically track what is purchased. The data about sales are now purchased by two major market research companies, A. C. Nielsen and IRI, which combine all of the individual retailers' data into massive syndicated databases that can report on sales of tens of thousands of items in over 70 metro-markets. The top 100 packaged goods companies each spend an average of $5 million a year on market research information. As part of their service, Nielsen and IRI researchers work with clients to analyze buying trends on a week-to-week basis in product categories of interest to each client. For example, Quaker Oats spends about $4 million a year studying the supplement drink category created by its Gatorade brand, which generates over $1 billion in annual sales. Ultimately, almost all consumer retail sales will be tracked by such syndicated services, which already make up about 20 percent of all spending on market research.

Both IRI and A. C. Nielsen also collect other information that they combine with their scanner data. For example, the IRI BehaviorScan service that operates in over a dozen markets uses a device that attaches to a household's TV sets and controls which TV advertisements are shown in the household. This allows IRI to undertake field experiments that track the impact of advertising campaigns. The purchase behavior of a randomly chosen sample of households from the IRI household panel is compared against a random sample of households that is not exposed to the advertising campaign (the **control sample**). Hundreds of such field experiments have revealed that TV advertising campaigns are usually effective only for new products and do very little for established brands. A. C. Nielsen has household panels that track the total purchases of a household

Universal Product Code (UPC)
is a bar code on a product's package that provides information read by optical scanners.

European Article Numbering (EAN)
is the European version of the Universal Product Code located on a product's package that provides information read by optical scanners.

http://www.QuakerOats.com

http://www.gatorade.com

Control sample
is that part of a sample group that is left unchanged and receives no special treatment, and serves as a basis of comparison to allow analysis of the results of an experiment.

Geodemographic information
allows identification of customer segments based on geographical location and demographic information.

Census blocks
are geographical areas made up of several city blocks or part of a rural county identified as such by the U.S. Census Bureau.

Cluster analysis
is the geographical grouping and labeling of individuals based on their buying behavior, demographics, and lifestyles.

and its exposure to various marketing campaigns carried by TV, radio, magazines, newspapers, the Internet, and direct mailings. Such panel behavior can then be combined with **geodemographic information** to make predictions about the behavior of households in different parts of a city or a county called **census blocks**. Geodemographic analysis is based on two premises. The first is that any two people who live in the same neighborhood are more likely to share similar lifestyles and demographic characteristics than any two people who live far apart. The second is that a number of market research firms have used **cluster analysis** on household census data that has enabled them to "label" neighborhoods by their demographics and lifestyles. These names can be quite colorful, such as Blue Blood Estates, Pools and Patios, Shotguns and Pickups, and Family Ties. Table 4.4

	Applications of Geodemography	Table 4.4

Application	Description
Repositioning	A geodemographic system was used to determine if changing the title of a national magazine from *Apartment Life* to *Metropolitan Home* along with upscaling its format would induce a shift in readership. Subscriptions before and after the change were classified by geodemographic segment to track subscriber trends.
Recruiting	Branches of the U.S. armed forces classify their recruits by geodemographic segment in order to determine where to locate recruiting centers and to decide what media and appeals work well to attract young men and women into the military.
Locating	A national chain of boutiques analyzed its clientele by geodemographic segment in order to determine the type of shopping center in which to locate to maximize store traffic. Supplemental analyses were used to select within-center locations and a store format.
Linking Research and Strategy	A household appliance manufacturer interested in coordinating distribution and media coverage for a new product linked each positive response from a national telephone survey to the respondent's geodemographic segment. Program results focused the manufacturer's new product roll-out, media selection, and distribution decisions.
Qualifying Lists	Direct marketers classify current clientele by geodemographic segment. A marketer then identifies segments that contain particularly high concentrations of those clients exhibiting superior purchase volumes. The marketer then identifies new lists that target these geodemographic segments.
Fund-Raising	Organizations seeking funds to support medical research, literacy programs, or other causes classify previous givers by geodemographic segment. Mailing lists and telephone contact lists with high concentrations of sympathetic segments are used to expand the program's donor base.

lists ways that geodemographic market research has been used in marketing. Information from A. C. Nielsen panels combined with geodemographic analysis enable companies to better pinpoint what types of households are heavy buyers of certain product categories and specific brands.

Decision Support Systems

A *decision support system (DSS)* is a set of computer software programs built into a user-friendly interface package, such as Windows, that helps a manager make marketing mix decisions. It enables a user to answer state-of-the-market questions, undertake market forecasts, and create simulations showing what might happen if tactics were changed. Behind the interactive, user-friendly icons, frameworks, prompts, and pull-down guide screens are major online market and accounting databases full of millions of observations of individual consumer behavior provided by companies such as A. C. Nielsen and IRI, but also generated from a company's own records of customer trading exchanges. These databases are "mined" for insights by powerful spreadsheets, statistical programs, and mathematical models. Some companies use these systems to target individual customers with special promotions through direct marketing (see Figure 4.2).

Figure 4.2	Database Mining and Direct Marketing

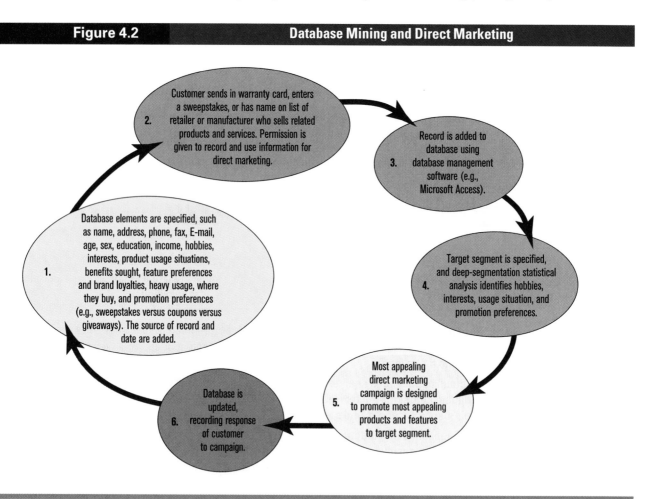

Direct database marketing is a tool for direct communication with target customers of a special product and promotion offer that has a high chance of appealing to customers. It combines the fundamentals of deep market segmentation with modern database technology and the implementation of microcommunication promotions offered to thousands of hot prospects, rather than millions of mostly indifferent customers. As the database records the history of interactions with each customer, customer segmentation can go beyond a deep understanding of heavy users and identify the sort of marketing interactions and trading relationships that groups of customers wish to have with the company.

Similarly, **Transaction-Based Information Systems (TBISs)** link, communicate, and process all of the transactions with a company's distributors/customers. The TBIS has evolved out of the **electronic data interchange (EDI)** among businesses. Examples are McKesson's ECONOMIST system for its drugstore customers and American Airline's Sabre reservation system for its travel agents. Transaction-based information systems are having a dramatic effect on channel and business-to-business customer relationships. By speeding up transaction communication and increasing the monitoring and control of sales and orders, TBISs have greatly reduced the working capital tied up in inventory and the risks of obsolete inventory. Beyond saving billions of dollars a year by reducing warehousing and inventory costs, they have enabled retailers and manufacturers to become much more responsive to market demand because a TBIS provides the manufacturer with online information about what is "hot" and what is not. This type of observational market research can immediately be used to change manufacturing schedules and the procurement of supplies.

Transaction-Based Information System (TBIS)
captures and analyzes all of the transactions between a company and its customers.

Electronic data interchange (EDI)
is the computer-to-computer exchange of invoices, orders, and other business documents.

COMPETITOR RESEARCH

LEARNING OBJECTIVE 3

The first question almost every company asks in its decision-making process is, Who are the major players in the market? That is, who has what share of market sales? *Market share* is measured as a percentage of total industry sales over a specified time period. Before determining the major players, we must define the term *market*. Clearly, problems exist in defining the market. A company's market share can change dramatically depending on whether the market is defined as global, a particular export market, the U.S. market, a region of the United States, a city, or a segment of users or usage. The scope of the market is normally specified by a realistic assessment of company resources and by company growth objectives. Often, the market is defined by the way market researchers are able to collect sales and market share information. This information is often supplied by government agencies, trade associations, or market research firms that survey all of the firms in a market.

Some of the different types of markets a product competes in are illustrated in Figure 4.3. The closest and most immediate competition comes from rivals' products targeted at the same segment that share similar, specific design features (e.g., a 12-ounce can of diet cola). The next level of product category competition comes from products that share some similar features (e.g., soft drinks). More general competition comes from products that satisfy a core benefit (e.g., thirst-quenching or pick-me-up drinks). The most distant competition is for consumers' discretionary spending. At this level, a new car may compete against a new deck for the house or an overseas trip.

The historical problem with research into competition has been too much focus on measuring the number of current competitors, the concentration of market share (the combined market share of the largest three competitors), and the current balance sheet assets of major competitors. The emphasis needs to be placed on market dynamics, such as who is introducing new manufacturing, distribution, and product development processes into the market. Competitive insight comes from explaining such drivers of success in the market, and not from knowing who has the largest market share. The acid test for such insight is whether an executive wants to know what company has the largest market share (*static thought*) or what company has experienced the largest change in market share (*dynamic thought*). Does the firm study the history of change in the industry to identify the trends in changing supply to further identify which paths the market will take in the future (i.e., production and distribution technological paths)? A dynamic analysis is thus able to identify what and who are the drivers of change in the market.[16]

Competitor research efforts are misspent on working out to the last share point (1 percent of market share) what the market share is, because defining the exact bounds of the market is seldom that precise. Such efforts are better spent on finding out which established competitor or new start-up is using radical new product or process technology to increase customer satisfaction and reduce costs. The history of technology suggests that small start-up companies often revolutionize a market.[17] For example, the typewriter was invented by Christopher Sholes, working in Milwaukee as a civil servant, and not for a printing or publishing company. The electric typewriter was developed and enhanced by IBM, and not by Remington or Underwood, the market leaders in manual

| **Figure 4.3** | **Examples of Levels of Competition** |

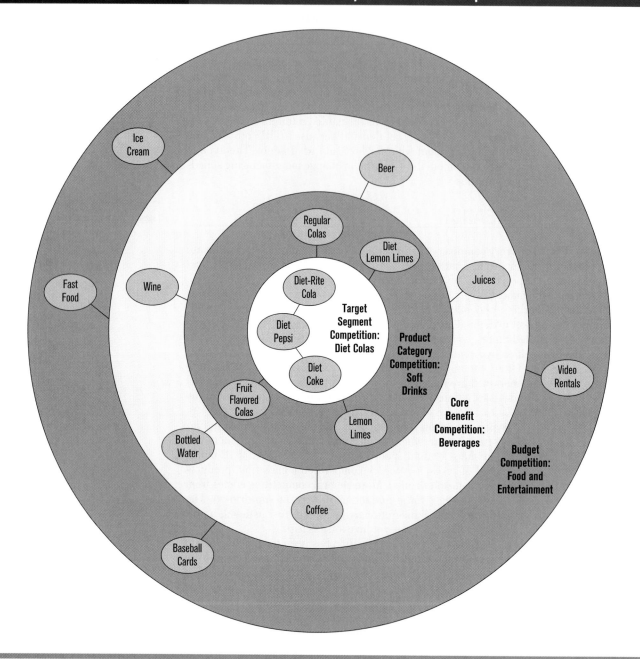

Most managers just consider their segment or product category competition and are sometimes blindsided by the success of less direct competition (e.g., bottled water and iced tea's effect on diet cola sales).

Source: Adapted from Donald R. Lehmann and Russell S. Winer, *Analysis for Marketing Planning* (Homewood, IL: Irwin, 1991), 22.

http://www.ibm.com

http://www.wang.com

http://www.apple.com

typewriters. In turn, it was Wang and Apple, rather than IBM, that developed the computer word processing and desktop publishing market. Amazon.com was started by a Wall Street analyst in 1994 working out of his home.

The change in market share over time is a vital indicator of the competitive environment. However, market share is not the only measure of competitiveness. The following measures are often used as leading indicators of a likely change in future sales and profits.

1. *Mind share:* The percentage of customers who name the brand when asked to name the first brand that comes to mind when they think about buying a particular type of product. This indicates the consumer's top-of-mind brand awareness and preferences. How is it changing among different segments?

2. *Voice share:* The percentage of media space or time a brand has of the total media share for that industry, often measured simply as dollars spent on advertising. This is likely to lead to a change in mind share (but not always, if the messages are weak). How and why is it changing?

3. *Research and development (R&D share):* A company's expenditure as a percentage of the total industry R&D expenditure. This is a long-term predictor of new product developments, improvements in quality, cost reductions, and hence market share. It is an important measure of future competitiveness in many high-technology markets. How is it changing, and what is it being spent on?

Researching the History of the Market

A study of the recent history of the product market identifies the marketing mix and product dimensions on which sellers have competed most strongly to serve the interests of the resellers and consumers. In some markets, this competition may have resulted in a price war. In others, sellers have competed with each other to improve product quality. Often, a technological improvement made by an innovator forces every competitor to respond. This occurred when Duracell introduced the alkaline battery. All of its competitors were forced to match the new technology. The history of the product market is seldom recorded. It is often carried around in the heads of experienced executives, and the invaluable insights they can provide are lost when they retire.

http://www.duracell.com

An industry often has standard marketing tactics and rules that are universally adopted. Examples are certain formulas for cost-plus pricing and spending a certain percentage of the previous year's sales on advertising in the next year. Sales force commissions and incentives are also often standardized in an industry. These rules of doing business make the market more predictable and stable. If the market "learns" and has moved toward more efficient ways of making and marketing its products, then these rules and processes should reflect such learning, and hence make sense. Knowing how and why standard industry practices and decision rules came about enables a firm to better understand whether the rules are based on continuous market learning or whether they have simply become established practice.[18] If they are based on market learning, then a

competitor can better understand what works and what does not in the marketplace and why. However, if the rules are based on old-fashioned agreements to restrain competition, then violating them represents an opportunity for the aggressive firm.

Michael Porter's pioneering text, *Competitive Strategy*, changed the way many companies think about their competition.[19] Porter identified five forces that shape competition: *current competitors, the threat of new entrants, the threat of new substitutes, the bargaining power of distributors (or business-to-business customers)*, and *the bargaining power of suppliers*. This structure can be reduced further to include simply current competitors and potential competitors and substitutes. The way distributors and suppliers behave determines the threat posed by immediate and potential competition. Distributors and suppliers are therefore not separate competitive elements but moderators or amplifiers of competition (see Figure 4.4). Generally, suppliers and distributors are used to gain competitive advantage and should be seen in this light. That is why distributor and channel research should be undertaken separately from competitor research. It is true that at times distributors and suppliers have to be directly considered in a competitive analysis, but only when they threaten to become a new direct competitor. A company must be on guard against new entrants and from others up and down the supply chain. This concern is best addressed in competitive research by asking and answering the questions presented in Table 4.5.

Auditing Current Competitors

For most companies, it is not possible to put all current competitors under the microscope and undertake an in-depth analysis of their competitive strengths and weaknesses. However, particular competitors are always worthy of such attention, either because they are attacking with a new product or because a firm has decided, in a previous plan, to attack them. The isolation of "aggressors" or "targets" usually requires a preliminary

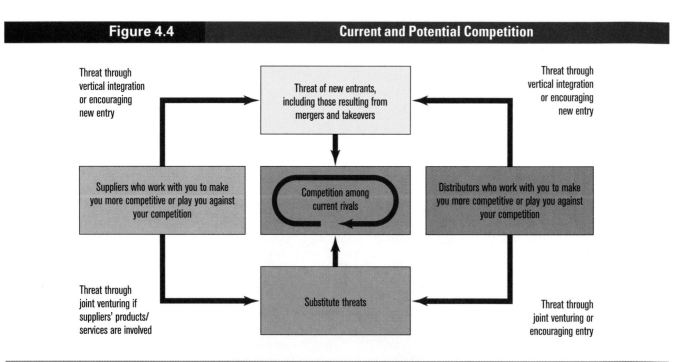

| Figure 4.4 | Current and Potential Competition |

Competition occurs among current rivals. Distributors and suppliers can help or hinder a firm's efforts to become more competitive. Sometimes, they even encourage a new entrant or the development of a new substitute. They seldom, if ever, discourage such entry or the development of a new technological substitute. However, distributors and suppliers are not competitors. In fact, the trading relationship a firm has with a supplier or distributor is a cooperative effort that competes with other trading relationships in the market.

New Competitive-Threats Audit	Table 4.5

The skill in identifying potential new competition is to ask a series of questions that narrows in on the most likely competitor and its situation.

New Technology—Converging Markets Threat

- What price changes in other technology markets appear to influence our sales? Is this effort changing?
- Which new technology or service is starting to be considered as a substitute for our product by consumers? Is this occurring in any particular usage situation or by any particular group of buyers? Are our existing channels encouraging such substitution?
- What is our closest new technological or service competition?
- Who is the major mover and shaker in this new industry?
- What appears to be its current objective and strategy?
- What is its growth rate?
- What has been its effect on our sales?
- What further threat does it pose?
- What constraints does it face?

Channel Integration Threat

- Which supplier is most likely to become a downstream direct competitor in the near future? Why? How would it do it? Is there any evidence of this occurring?
- Which customers are most likely to become upstream, do-it-themselves competitors in the near future? Why? How would they do it? Does any evidence of such plans exist?

Competitor Takeover—Merger Threat

- Which mergers, takeovers, or trading coalitions among competitors or from inside pose the greatest threat to our position? What evidence exists that this is likely to occur?

---

analysis that identifies from which rivals you are gaining business and to which competitors you are losing business. This is the way you identify your immediate current competition, which may or may not be using similar technology.[20] For example, many major U.S. cities now have only one daily newspaper, yet such monopolies have not inflated profits for the publisher. The reason is simple. Although other major newspapers may have died, competition for advertising has increased from the suburban weeklies, direct marketing, and other media. Television, radio, and local magazines also have become more competitive with their news and features. The mistake the newspaper publishers made was not identifying these competitors early on when they could have taken countermeasures.[21]

The initial investment in time, effort, and expense necessary to audit competitors may be very high (amounting to several weeks or even months of an executive's or consultant's time), but it should be treated as an investment. The results will produce a report that can be built on from year to year with constantly expanding details and insights. This file then becomes part of the collective memory of your organization to be passed on to successive managers.

Table 4.6 presents a competitor analysis template that a company can use as a basis for developing its own unique competitor analysis form. The competitive strategy

Table 4.6	A Competitor Analysis Template

Competitor _____ Analyst _____ Date _____

Summary of Competitor's Position

- Goals and major competitive strategy   _____
- Current success story   _____
- Current mistakes   _____
- Competitive advantages/disadvantages   _____

Benchmarking Analysis*

Financial Position
Cash flow, cost structure, access to capital, profits   _____

Market Position
Major geographical markets, target segments   _____

Product Position
Raw material, manufacturing, design quality, features   _____

Brand strength and image with target markets   _____

Price Position
How much above/below average, types of promotions   _____

Inbound Logistics Process
Sources of supply, purchasing skills, inventory flow   _____

Production Processes
Production capacity, adaptability, efficiency, quality, costs   _____

Labor adaptability, skill, and loyalty   _____

Outbound Logistics Processes
Order-delivery time, inventory flow, special services   _____

Trade Relations Processes
Major channels used, channel relationships   _____

Advertising and Promotion Processes
Message themes, media usage, campaign schedules   _____

Sales Force Processes
Sales force management, morale, training, incentives   _____
Use of technology, service quality, and efficiency   _____

*Comparative benchmarking rating, direction of change, what processes, technology, people are driving its performance improvement.

guru Michael Porter has argued that competitive advantage in product quality and costs can come from one or more of the following stages in the added-value chain:[22]

1. Inbound logistics processes
2. Operations processes
3. Outbound logistics processes
4. Marketing and sales processes
5. Service processes

The implication is that a rival's competitive standing at all stages of the added-value chain from inbound logistics to after-sales service must be studied. The analysis form presented in Table 4.6 addresses characteristics of these processes. This analysis should involve at least three types of information. The first type of information is a rating of the rival's performance compared or **benchmarked** against the very best in the industry. The second type of information is the direction this performance is moving (improving indicated by an up arrow and declining indicated by a down arrow beside the rating). The third type of information should be a detailed explanation as to what is unique and interesting about the rival's behavior or product, or at least the name and E-mail of someone who can provide such detail. This brings us to the question of how competitor research is undertaken. It is seldom gathered through James Bond methods of industrial espionage, using sources of doubtful reputation. Interestingly, the market research

Benchmarked
refers to when performance, cost, and price are compared to the most competitive alternatives.

| Competitor Intelligence | | Table 4.7 |

Most Useful Source of Information (by type of market)

Percent Distribution

	Total	Industrial Products	Consumer Products	Both Consumer and Industrial
Sales force	27%	35%	18%	23%
Publications, databases	16	13	15	22
Customers	14	13	11	17
Marketing research, tracking services	9	3	24	9
Financial reports	5	7	3	1
Distributors	3	4	1	1
Employees (unspecified)	2	2	6	—
Analysis of products	2	1	3	3
Other	8	6	8	13
No answer	14	16	11	11
	100%	100%	100%	100%
Number of responding companies	308	158	72	78

Most Useful Type of Information (by type of market)

Percent Distribution

	Total	Industrial Products	Consumer Products	Both Consumer and Industrial
Pricing	23%	26%	20%	19%
Strategy	19	20	15	22
Sales data	13	11	18	12
New products, product mix	11	13	8	10
Advertising/marketing activities	7	3	19	4
Costs	6	8	3	5
Key customers/markets	3	3	6	1
Research and development	2	2	1	3
Management style	2	1	3	1
Other	4	4	—	8
No answer	10	9	7	15
	100%	100%	100%	100%
Number of responding companies	308	158	72	78

Source: Howard Sutton, *Competitive Intelligence* (New York: The Conference Board, 1988).

company A. C. Nielsen started business in 1923 by doing competitive market research for machinery manufacturers. It was not until 1928 that it started to undertake consumer research. Table 4.7 reports on the most useful sources of competitor information and the most useful type of information. The following is a description of how many firms make sense of the information they gather about competitors:

> *We gather about 10 people in a room, twice a month, in long (think-tank) sessions, anything from three hours to a couple of days. The sessions have no formal structure. We examine and massage the latest competitor and industry information to determine where things are going and what we should be doing. There are a lot of people in the business unit who know something about a competitor. But it's almost like the three blind men and the elephant: Each one examines a small part of the whole. When you put them all together in a room, they are amazed about how much they know. That coalesces into one or two sheets of paper presenting all we know about a competitor's strengths and weaknesses, and our judgments with respect to a competitor's strategies and measures of success. That is the beginning of a competitor file.*[23]

LEARNING OBJECTIVE 4

CHANNEL RESEARCH

The first professional market researcher, Charles Parlin, started business in 1911 conducting distribution channel research and not consumer research. He studied the distribution channels for agricultural instruments and then for textiles. Interest in researching channels of distribution has greatly increased in the 1990s for at least two reasons. The first is that retailing has become much more competitive because the market is becoming overstored. Management Horizons, a retailing consulting company, estimates that in the 1990s the amount of retailing square footage increased from about 15 square feet for every person in the United States to 20 square feet. By comparison, for every person in the United Kingdom, it is estimated there is only two square feet of retail space per person. There is so much available retail space competing for consumer dollars that rivalry between retailers has become ferocious. The second reason for undertaking distribution market research is that in the next few years Web direct marketing is predicted by many to gain 10 to 30 percent of sales in certain product categories, such as computer software, computer hardware, recorded music, books, videos, and air travel. How are traditional distribution channels going to respond to this threat?

The suggested procedure for learning about distribution channels is to first address a number of questions about what are the drivers of change in the channel (see Table 4.8) and then to zero in on a detailed audit of some key resellers (sometimes called trade customers). Table 4.8 lists several questions that address the impact on the distribution channel of (1) changes in technology, (2) new entrants, (3) changes in established channel relations, and (4) changes in the way existing channel members do business. The recorded music market provides an excellent example of how such changes impact product marketing.

In the 1950s and early 1960s, record retailers allowed consumers to play new records in the store. This was an important way of exposing a new artist or title to the public because the enthusiasts and opinion leaders did most of this in-store sampling. But as popular music took off with rock and roll, and the spending power of the baby boomers increased, chain stores opened record bars that did not provide the sound booths for sampling but undercut the record stores in prices. Consumers would often listen to the music in the record store and buy at the chain store. To compete, the record stores dropped the sound booths but offered a generous return policy. Eventually, even the return policy was also dropped.

As a result of the termination of in-store sampling, popular radio stations became critical in marketing records. But radio was also going through a transition. Increased competition was forcing the stations into top 20 or top 40 formats, where the hit-parade music was played continuously at the expense of the new artists and songs. This program format kept the audiences and advertisers happy, but it forced the recording companies to buy airtime in order to advertise their new releases (where previously such exposure was free). This increased the cost of launching a new release, thus giving a major competitive advantage to the larger recording studios and distributors. MTV pulled the

Channel Change Audit	**Table 4.8**

- **Who are the latest new entrants in the reseller market?**
  What is their competitive advantage?
  Which existing resellers are being most affected?
  How has it affected us?

- **What new trading coalitions among resellers are occurring?**
  What will be their competitive advantage?
  How will it affect us?

- **What changes in order-processing technology are now occurring?**
  What impact will they have on the way business is done?
  What competitive advantage do they provide?

- **What changes in transportation technology are now occurring?**
  What impact will they have on the way business is done?
  What competitive advantage do they provide?

- **What changes in warehousing technology are now occurring?**
  What impact will they have on the way business is done?
  What competitive advantage do they provide?

- **What changes in payment technology are now occurring?**
  What impact will they have on the way business is done?
  What competitive advantage do they provide?

recording industry out of the doldrums in the early 1980s, but this new promotion channel also forced the studios into a whole new marketing activity: video production. The music video component has become an important new competitive element in selling compact discs and tapes and a further entrance barrier for new competition. But Web marketing is again revolutionizing the distribution of music. It is now possible for individual musicians to make their own digital recordings and distribute them directly from their own Web site to consumers who download the music for a small fee. What effect does this have on the traditional music distribution system? The role of distribution research is to find out what new forms music retailing is taking, undertake consumer research to assess their potential, then undertake further distribution research to assess the profitability and competitiveness of various types of Web-based music retailing. Big companies such as Time Warner AOL and Microsoft are betting a lot on the answers.

Researching Individual Trade Customers

Once the general channel change audit has been undertaken, important trade customers will have been identified for further study. Clearly, not all of these resellers can be studied, and some good managerial judgment is needed to make sure greater attention is paid to the major players and innovators. When a manufacturer's sales force uses an account management approach for its major retail trade accounts, it should be relatively easy to complete audits of such trade customers. However, care must be taken that day-to-day operating relations do not drive the evaluations of those who are in constant contact with representatives of suppliers and resellers. The reseller audits require the auditor to stand back, to assess the changes that have occurred over the past trading year, and to explain some of the basic reasons for predicting longer-term changes.

The reseller audit in Table 4.9 starts with a summary evaluation that can also be used as a short-form audit when the product team does not have the time or interest to fully evaluate particular resellers. A paragraph can be written to provide responses to the concerns listed. The evaluation can be updated on a regular basis (normally annually), so the major investment is in preparing the initial evaluation. The detailed evaluation questions have been categorized into those dealing with the reseller's trading

Table 4.9	Individual Distributor Audit

Company Name: _____   **Date:** _____

Summary Evaluation
- Image and reputation
- Geographical markets/customer segments served
- Major strength, unique value, and importance of this
- reseller
- Major weakness and failure of reseller
- Special personal relations with distributor

Detailed Evaluation
Trading Performance
- Annual sales
- Annual sales of our products
- Contribution earned from sales to this reseller
- Average stock-turn of our products
- Past average stock-turn of our products
- Profit performance

Competitive Selling Effort
- Quality of locations
- Quality of advertising
- Quality of premises
- Quality of sales staff
- Sales staff knowledge of our products
- Inventory management
- Extent we are treated as a preferred supplier
- Special marketing efforts and cooperation

Purchasing Behavior
- Recent ordering history
- Volume deals/discounts sought and given
- Other allowances and considerations sought and given:
  Freight
  Cooperative advertising
  Promotions
  Returns
  Push money and sales contests
  Special credit terms

performance, marketing position, competitive effort, and purchasing behavior. Understanding what is going right or wrong in a channel relationship almost always involves taking information and putting it together like a jigsaw puzzle. That is why it is important to add depth to the audit by answering as many questions as possible, using facts, good judgment, and best guesses. Trying to understand the reasons for a channel member's change in performance or behavior often means tracing back from its buying behavior, through trading and operating indicators, to its competitive effort and market position. Distribution market research also must forecast distributors' future competitive strengths and weaknesses.

CHAPTER SUMMARY

- Market research and analysis is a very large topic covering many topics and techniques. This explains why there are many advanced courses in marketing research that can be taken at the undergraduate and graduate level. It also explains why so much market research is contracted out by companies to research suppliers who, like advertising agencies, are specialists in their profession.

- Some people might argue that market research is only "research" when it involves complex scientific method and analysis borrowed from the social sciences and economics. But such research often costs tens of thousands of dollars, sometimes millions of dollars. In reality, how many firms undertake such research? Several hundred huge packaged-goods and service companies spend millions of dollars a year on market research, employing highly skilled researchers. A few thousand companies spend hundreds of thousands a year on marketing research, mainly using smaller market research firms whom they work with over many years. What sort of market research do the remaining hundreds of thousands of businesses undertake? Their managers spend a lot of time observing customers, competitors, and distributors firsthand. They are increasingly using secondary sources of information they obtain from the business press, government sources, or Web searches. The reason why this chapter emphasized simple methods such as observing customers, competitors, and distributors is because these are the methods that all firms should use, but that few actually employ.

- Over the last 100 years, a lot has been learned about how to practice market research, and some of that learning is presented in this chapter. The first general lesson that has been learned is that market research is about helping to improve managers' intuitive understanding of the behavior of customers, competitors, and distributors.

- The second lesson is that a firm should follow a process similar to that described in Figure 4.1. First gather, analyze, and discuss all the information that managers already have on hand from their own information systems, from their sales force, from secondary information, and from their own personal observation. As explained in Figure 4.1, a particular market research project needs to be defined in terms of the crucial questions that need to be answered. Ways of quickly and cheaply answering these questions need to be pursued, then a cost/benefit decision has to be made as to whether to pursue more expensive research. In the chapter opener, millions of dollars were at stake in the decision by R. G. Barry to raise its slipper prices. For about $40,000 the company was able to assure itself and its retail customers that it could raise its prices with little loss in sales. The research also provided other valuable information about product design and merchandising practices.

- The third lesson is that market research methods are evolving as new technologies are being used. Fifty years ago, computers did not exist, and all analyses had to be undertaken mechanically or by hand. Today, a personal computer can do sophisticated quantitative and qualitative analyses that were unheard of 30 years ago. Twenty years ago, scanner technology was invented and with it the ability to track company and competitor sales through specific distribution channels. Today, companies that specialize in Web-based market research are being invented. These companies may greatly increase the quality and decrease the cost of market research in the near future.

- The fourth and final lesson is that research needs to be reported in ways that make it easy for decision makers to understand what is going on. This is best achieved by developing digital files on consumer, competitor, and distributor behavior that can be readily consulted and analyzed, online, for changing patterns. These files can be used by marketing analysts and planners to provide heads-up situation reports for senior managers, sales management, research and development, and marketing planning. Companies with superior market research and analysis skills are able to change their thinking about the marketplace faster than their competition. Such fast insight and learning may give them more time to innovate, imitate, and avoid crisis management. A company with such superior decision-making skills has a clear competitive advantage over its rivals.

KEY TERMS

Benchmarked refers to when performance, cost, and price are compared to the most competitive alternatives.

Census blocks are geographical areas made up of several city blocks or part of a rural county identified as such by the U.S. Census Bureau.

Cluster analysis is the geographical grouping and labeling of individuals based on their buying behavior, demographics, and lifestyles.

Control sample is that part of a sample group that is left unchanged and receives no special treatment, and serves as a basis of comparison to allow analysis of the results of an experiment.

Convenience quota sample is a sample of consumers that is not randomly sampled from a population (e.g., users of the product) but is obtained through approaching people in a mall to participate. Quotas are placed on how many men and women should be interviewed (e.g., 200 of each) or some other demographic categorization such as age, education, or income.

Demographics are measures such as age, gender, race, occupation, and income that are often used as a basis for selecting focus group members and market segments.

Electronic data interchange (EDI) is the computer-to-computer exchange of invoices, orders, and other business documents.

European Article Numbering (EAN) is the European version of the Universal Product Code located on a product's package that provides information read by optical scanners.

Geodemographic information allows identification of customer segments based on geographical location and demographic information.

Hands-on consumer research is conducted by direct observation by managers of the way current customers use specific products and brands. The opposite is arm's-length research, which is undertaken by external suppliers.

An **interval scale** has intervals of measure that stay constant along the scale. For example, the interval between the measures of 1 and 3 on the scale is the same as the interval between 5 and 7.

Motivational research is a research method directed at discovering the conscious or subconscious reasons that motivate a person's behavior.

Nonresponse or participation bias in responses is created by underrepresentation and overrepresentation in a sample of different groups. For example, most studies have an overrepresentation of consumers who are interested in the product and a nonresponse underrepresentation of consumers not interested in the product.

Omnibus surveys are a survey research service offered by a number of large marketing research companies where several companies' research studies and sets of questions are included in a single questionnaire sent to representative panels of households.

Open-ended questions allow respondents to determine the direction of the answer without being led by the question. They also prevent "yes" or "no" answers.

Panels of households are groups of households (e.g., 5,000) recruited by market research firms and rewarded for participating in market research surveys. The firm creates a panel by carefully selecting the composition of the group so that it is representative of the general population in terms of demographics such as geographical location, income, education, and age of the heads of households.

A **pretest** may be undertaken before the major study to test the validity and reliability of measures and other components of the study's research methodology.

Random sample is a set of items that have been drawn from a population in such a way that each time an item was selected, every item in the population had an equal opportunity to appear in the sample.

A **ratio scale** is a scale that measures length, weight, or income.

Reliability means the consistency of data. It is often tested by reexamining customer opinions using the same survey on a different occasion, or by another method of measurement.

Sugging refers to an illegal survey conducted under the guise of research but with the intent of selling.

Transaction-Based Information System (TBIS) captures and analyzes all of the transactions between a company and its customers.

Universal Product Code (UPC) is a bar code on a product's package that provides information read by optical scanners.

Validity in customer survey results refers to their accuracy in measuring what they are intended to measure.

Voice of the customer (VOC) is the expression of the preferences, opinions, and motivations of the customer that need to be listened to by managers.

QUESTIONS FOR DISCUSSION

1. In the mid-1980s, Pepsi overtook Coke in supermarket sales with its highly successful "Take the Pepsi Challenge" marketing campaign. The challenge was to choose which cola you preferred in a blind taste test. In a blind taste test, a participant does not know what brand is being tested. Coke's response was to search for a new flavor that beat Pepsi in blind taste tests. After 200,000 taste tests, it settled on New Coke, a sweeter, smoother flavor that beat Pepsi and Old Coke in the blind taste tests. The result was a marketing disaster. In 1985, New Coke replaced Classic Coke on the shelves, and tens of thousands of angry Coke customers called Coke to complain. Coca-Cola brought back Classic Coke alongside New Coke and insisted that it had not made a mistake. Five years later, New Coke was dead. What mistake did Coca-Cola make in the market research it undertook? (Hint: Did it not do enough research, or did it do the wrong sort of research?)

2. Imagine that you were part of the cross-functional team developing the Depends adult disposable diaper. Several members of the team seem to have a problem understanding consumer complaints about the existing product in the market. What market intelligence–gathering activity might you suggest to raise their understanding?

3. When researching customer needs, would it be better for a product designer to visit customers personally or to read a survey research report on customer needs, beliefs, and behaviors? What biases are inherent in each approach that might lead to misunderstanding consumer behavior?

4. How would a company that combines a bar with a laundry service use geo-demographic analysis?

5. In the recent case brought against Microsoft charging that it monopolizes the PC software market, Microsoft claimed that 80 percent of software developers are happy with the situation as it is. This result was based on a yes/no question that followed a 350-word statement describing all of the

advantages of the current situation and none of the disadvantages. The dean of the business school of the Massachusetts Institute of Technology defended the question, saying that he saw nothing wrong with it. What is wrong with such a question?

6. Table 4.7 presents information about the usefulness of competitive intelligence and the most useful sources of such intelligence. Why is price information more important than strategy information? List several reasons. What do the results of the most useful sources tell us about how we should set up an intelligence-gathering operation?

7. The State Department is in charge of over a hundred U.S. embassies and consulates scattered around the globe. How is the U.S. diplomatic service and State Department likely to change if the predominant conflict between countries in the 21st century will be economic rather than ideological?

8. "To outguess them, [General George] Washington sought the best strategic advice and had no pride of ownership. The excellence and not the origin of the plan was decisive with him. He learned by listening well, or by observing and reflecting. During the greater part of the struggle, he had to be his own chief intelligence officer, and he did so with considerable success. Always he tried to learn what was not happening as well as what was, and he frequently undertook the careful analysis, in person, of conflicting intelligence reports."[24] If General George Washington could, with his "now you see it, now you don't" army, win a war and a nation's freedom against the world's superpower of the time by doing this, why is it that a CEO of a modern corporation does not lead in a similar way?

INTERNET QUESTIONS

1. The PC revolution has led to executives doing a lot of their own typing, letter writing, and report writing themselves rather than relying on an executive assistant or secretary to do the work. The Internet provides a huge source of information about markets, countries, consumers, products, and technologies that can be searched easily using key words. Schoolchildren learn from a very early age today how to search the Internet for research projects. How will this change the demand for market researchers and market analysts in the future? How will their jobs change?

2. An infamous bank robber, when asked why he robbed banks, said because that is where the money is. Some have argued that a similar but much more legal principle applies to Internet marketing. Those with wealth, who are prime targets for marketers, are online wired. The rich of the world are online, the poor are not and never will be. Starting wherever you wish, search Web sites so that you can participate in a class discussion of the following two questions:
   a. Are the world's rich, those with the top 10 percent of incomes, already connected to the Internet wherever they live in the world? Are the wealthy in India, Africa, China, Russia, and South America already connected to the Web? If they are, what impact will this have on the marketing of premium brands to the world's wealthy? (Hint: Start searching U.S. government or Internet company sites.)
   b. Which group of very wealthy Americans has the Internet and Internet shopping hardly penetrated yet? How will this change in the future?

3. Table 4.10 presents examples of different types of questions that can be used to learn about Internet usage. Identify any problems with the measures. If you were taking the survey, would you find the questions ambiguous, hard to answer, or biased toward a particular response?

Types of Questions	Table 4.10

Dichotomous Questions

Have you ever browsed the Internet?　　　　Yes　　　　No

Open-Ended Questions

Microsoft has been prosecuted for unfair business practices, such as trying to drive competitors out of business. What is your opinion of Microsoft's browser?

_____

_____

_____

_____

_____

"The most important consideration for me in choosing a browser is . . ."

_____

_____

_____

_____

_____

Multiple-Choice Questions

Which one of the following products have you purchased from a Web site:

Books	Software	Music CDs	Airline tickets
Clothing	X-rated material	Stocks	Computers and peripherals

Intention-to-Buy Scale

How likely is it that next Christmas Holiday Season you will buy a gift for a family member or a friend from a Web site:

Definitely will buy	Probably will buy	Maybe will buy
Not certain	Probably will not buy	Definitely will not buy

Rating Scales

Amazon.com's Web site is:

Excellent	Very good	Good	Fair	Poor

On a scale of 1 to 10, where 10 is excellent and 1 is a dog, how would you rate the Amazon.com Web site? _____

Table 4.10	Types of Questions (continued)

Semantic Differential Scale

Amazon.com's Web site is:

Easy to use	:___:___:___:___:___:___:___:	Hard to use
Fun	:___:___:___:___:___:___:___:	Boring
Modern	:___:___:___:___:___:___:___:	Old-fashioned
Friendly	:___:___:___:___:___:___:___:	Unfriendly
Laid back	:___:___:___:___:___:___:___:	Pushy
Soft sell	:___:___:___:___:___:___:___:	Hard sell
Helpful	:___:___:___:___:___:___:___:	Unhelpful
Cluttered	:___:___:___:___:___:___:___:	Uncluttered

Importance Scale

How important is it for you to pay a price in Web shopping that is less than regular retail?

Extremely important	Very important	Somewhat important
Not very important	Not important at all	

Likert Scales

"Amazon.com is very easy to learn to use compared with other shopping sites."

Strongly disagree	Disagree	Somewhat disagree	Neither agree nor disagree
Somewhat agree	Agree	Strongly agree	

"You learn more about products when you Web shop than when you shop in a regular store."

Strongly disagree	Disagree	Somewhat disagree	Neither agree nor disagree
Somewhat agree	Agree	Strongly agree	

ENDNOTES

[1] Arie P. DeGeus, "Planning as Learning," *Harvard Business Review* (March/April 1988): 70–74.

[2] See George S. Day and Prakash Nedungadi, "Managerial Representations of Competitive Advantage," *Journal of Marketing* 58 (April 1994): 31–44; George S. Day, *Learning about Markets* (Cambridge, MA: Marketing Science Institute, 1991): 91–117; and Jeffrey Pfeffer and Gerald R. Salancik, *The External Control of Organizations: A Resource Dependence Perspective* (New York: Harper, 1978).

[3] This list is based in part on advice from "The Art of Obtaining Information," Washington Researchers, Washington, DC.

[4] Edward F. McQuarrie and Shelby H. McIntyre, "The Customer Visit: An Emerging Practice in Business-to-Business Marketing" (Cambridge, MA: Marketing Science Institute, 1992), 92–114.

[5] Johny K. Johannson and Ikujiro Nonaka, "Market Research the Japanese Way," *Harvard Business Review* (May/June 1987): 16–22; Lance Ealey and Leif Soderberg, "How Honda Cures Design Amnesia," *The McKinsey Quarterly* (Spring 1990): 3–14; and Kenichi Ohmae, *The Borderless World* (New York: Harper Business, 1990).

[6] B. Dumaine, "Creating a New Company Culture," *Fortune,* 15 January 1990, 127–131.

[7] B. Dumaine, "Corporate Spies Snoop to Conquer," *Fortune,* 7 November 1988, 68–76.

[8] Robert A. Westbrook, "A Rating Scale for Measuring Product/Service Satisfaction," *Journal of Marketing* 44 (Fall 1980): 68–72; and Richard L. Oliver and John E. Swan, "Consumer Perceptions of Interpersonal Equity and Satisfaction in Transactions: A Field Survey Approach," *Journal of Marketing* 53 (April 1989): 21–35.

[9] The calculation is based on the statistic
$$p \pm 3 \times s.d._p = 50\% \pm (3 \times (0.5 \times 0.5/400)^{1/2}) \times 100\%.$$

[10] The calculation is $50\% \pm (3 \times (0.5 \times 0.5/10{,}000)^{1/2}) \times 100\%$.

[11] See Angelina Herrin (1991), "Food Survey Called Flawed," *Wisconsin State Journal,* September 11, 3A and Gilbert A. Churchill, Jr., *Marketing Research* (Fort Worth, TX: Dryden Press, 1995), 654.

[12] See Gilbert A. Churchill, Jr. and J. Paul Peter, "Research Design Effects on the Reliability of Rating Scales: A Meta-Analysis," *Journal of Marketing Research* 21 (November, 1984), 360–375.

[13] David Greising, "Quality: How to Make It Pay," *Business Week,* 8 August 1995, 54–59.

[14] The bad news is that it took the hotel 15 years to discover the ironing problem. See Leonard L. Berry, "Improving America's Service," *Marketing Management* 1, 3 (1992): 29–37.

[15] Much of the material in this section is drawn from the following book written by David J. Curry, which is an excellent review of the new high-tech use of scanner data: *The New Marketing Research Systems* (New York: John Wiley & Sons, 1993).

[16] See Peter R. Dickson, Paul W. Farris, and Willem J. M. I. Verbeke, "Dynamic Strategic Thinking," *Journal of the Academy of Marketing Science* 29, 3 (2001): 216–237.

[17] James M. Utterback, *Mastering the Dynamics of Innovation* (Cambridge, MA: Harvard Business School Press, 1994).

[18] Gloria P. Thomas and Gary F. Soldow, "A Rules-Based Approach to Competitive Interaction," *Journal of Marketing* 52 (April 1988): 63–74.

[19] Michael E. Porter, *Competitive Strategy* (New York: The Free Press, 1980).

[20] Thomas W. Dunfee, Louis Stern, and Frederick D. Sturdivant, "Bounding Markets in Merger Cases: Identifying Relevant Competitors," Northwestern University *Law Review* 78 (November 1983): 733–773.

[21] Subrata N. Chakravarty and Carolyn Torcellini, "Citizen Kane Meets Adam Smith," *Forbes,* 20 February 1989, 82–85.

[22] Michael E. Porter, *Competitive Advantage* (New York: The Free Press, 1985).

[23] Howard Sutton, *Competitive Intelligence* (New York: The Conference Board, 1988), 31, 37.

[24] Richard Harwell, *Washington* (New York: Collier Books, 1992), 511–512.

CHAPTER CASE

ONLINE MARKETING RESEARCH

Computers have been used to tabulate surveys and analyze relationships between responses since the late 1960s. They have greatly reduced the cost of survey research while greatly increasing its quality. As computers became increasingly accessible, the field of multivariate statistical analysis flourished. The next great advancement occurred in the 1970s with the birth of computer-assisted telephone interviewing (CATI), which allowed for survey automation. These systems prompted telephone interviewers with the questions to be asked and provided immediate data capture as a respondent's answers were recorded. Data analysis could be undertaken as soon as the last interview in the sample was completed.

However, it took the computer revolution until the mid-1990s for it to have its most dramatic and potentially revolutionary impact on survey research. In September 1995 America Online (AOL) and a prominent research firm called The M/A/R/C Group launched a joint venture called Digital Marketing Services (DMS). The goal was to activate the online medium for conducting marketing research. As development options were considered, a revelation occurred: Why not redesign the CATI software to allow respondents to enter their answers to questions directly? In many research applications, respondents are asked to fill out paper surveys. This self-administered surveying could be taken to a new level, characterized by a scientifically controlled computer experience. A new method of surveying was born.

This partnership opens the doors to millions of AOL subscribers as potential respondents via an area called Opinion Place, only two clicks away from the AOL Welcome Screen. As of 1999, AOL accounted for 60 to 70 percent of all household Internet traffic, and the composition of its members today looks more "mainstream America" than the entire Internet population. Given this tremendous volume of potential respondents, The M/A/R/C Group opened access to some of its traditional competitors in the best interests of growing the online research business. Within the first two years of existence, DMS had completed hundreds of surveys and over one million interviews.

The team of researchers at DMS had to solve some interesting problems in creating this business. How do you encourage online users to participate in 15-minute surveys? You create AOL Rewards, a frequent-flyer program for AOL subscribers, where points are earned for participating in surveys, as well as for buying products from merchants' AOL Web sites. The points can be redeemed for products from DMS's online catalog, but the vast majority of participants use their points to pay for their monthly AOL service fee.

In 1999, Opinion Place attracted hundreds of thousands of respondents per week, and participation has since grown. But does this violate the random sampling requirement of good survey research? DMS handles this by prequalifying whether a respondent is in the target population to be sampled. Upon entry to Opinion Place, a survey is randomly selected for a respondent, who is then put to the test of qualification. If they are qualified, they are sent into the survey. If they fail the qualification for the preselected survey, they are sent to a randomly chosen survey from those for which they qualified. Respondents do not select which survey they would "like" to respond to (which would create a serious self-selection bias). Instead, they are selected into a sample by their responses to the screening questions. Client companies have found that a major advantage to this approach is the ability to reach very specialized target populations, given AOL's wide reach across millions of consumers.

Major companies are finding that online market research increases the quality of survey data, reduces the data collection time, and reduces the cost of the study: It is a win-win-win situation. It enables companies to do survey research they could never do before: Low costs lead to more studies, and iterative research to refined ideas. Companies are using previously difficult (or impossible) techniques such as including colored graphics, photos, and multimedia stimuli. JCPenney tested 60 styles of women's swimsuits in a survey, allowing complex branching and asking of different follow-up questions depending on earlier answers (very difficult to handle with mail surveys). A study can take only days from start to finish, with all study materials sent to and from a client via E-mail. In fact, a major packaged goods manufacturer works with DMS to get feedback on concepts from thousands of consumers in less than 24 hours. They take the iterative approach to idea refinement, learning from each study. The velocity of this volume of information is unattainable in other research methods.

Finally, DMS claims that it charges 30 to 50 percent less for an equivalent survey undertaken in a mall or by mail. Proponents of online survey research point out that this capability is less than five years old and that it will have its greatest impact in the area of global market research. Companies are increasingly interested in the preferences and behavior of the emerging economic elite in countries such as China, where they can contact those who are highly educated, high tech, and wired. Companies as diverse as Coca-Cola, Avon, the Discovery Channel, Hewlett-Packard, Hickory Farms, Kodak, Sprint, Starbucks, and Warner Bros. are using DMS' services and the services of others offering online marketing research. For example, IntelliQuest specializes in doing online product development research for PC hardware and software companies.

The main argument against online marketing research is that participants are not representative of the entire population of U.S. households. For example, AOL's Opinion Place respondents are younger, more highly educated, and somewhat more affluent than the average U.S. adult. They appear more likely to buy brands, try new products, and influence the purchase decision of others. But the questions companies must ask themselves remain: Does the sample validly represent the desired marketing target? Can any method attract a sample representative of the U.S. population? Maybe the critics of online research (who are mostly research companies using telephone, mail, or mall intercept methods) are encountering their own problems as new technologies and changing attitudes impede interviews.

Discussion Questions

1. What types of target customers are most easily reached by online market research? What target customers are not able to be reached by online market research?

2. What are the greatest advantages of online market research?

3. Almost all orders between retailers and manufacturers and between businesses will be done on the Internet within 10 years. What invaluable market research information will this generate to complement online market research?

CHAPTER five

Jagdish N. Sheth,
Emory University

Dr. Jagdish (Jag) N. Sheth is the Charles H. Kellstadt Professor of Marketing in the Goizueta Business School and the founder of the Center for Relationship Marketing (CRM) at Emory University. He has also taught at the University of Southern California, the University of Illinois, Columbia University, and the Massachusetts Institute of Technology. Dr. Sheth is nationally and internationally known for his scholarly contribution in marketing, customer satisfaction, global competition, and strategic thinking.

Dr. Sheth has received numerous awards, including the Outstanding Marketing Educator award by the Academy of Marketing Science; the Outstanding Educator Award by the Sales and Marketing Executives International; and the P. D. Converse Award for outstanding contributions in marketing theory from the American Marketing Association. He has been recognized as a Distinguished Fellow of the Academy of Marketing Science, and a Distinguished Fellow of the International Engineering Consortium. Dr. Sheth is also a Fellow of the American Psychological Association (APA).

Professor Sheth has worked for numerous industries and companies in the United States, Europe, and Asia, both as an advisor and as a seminar leader. His clients include AT&T, BellSouth, Cox Communications, Delta, Ernst & Young, Ford, GE, Lucent Technologies, Motorola, Nortel, Pillsbury, Sprint, Square D, 3M, Whirlpool, and many others. He has offered more than 5,000 presentations in at least 20 countries.

Balaji C. Krishnan,
University of Memphis

Balaji C. Krishnan is an Assistant Professor of Marketing in the Fogelman College of Business and Economics at the University of Memphis, where he teaches in the undergraduate, graduate, international MBA, and executive MBA programs. His research interests are in the areas of pricing and price promotions, branding and brand equity, services marketing, and cross cultural issues in marketing. He has published in the *Journal of Public Policy and Marketing*, the *Journal of Business Research*, and the *Journal of Services Marketing*.

Consumer Behavior

Hailey McGuire likes rocks. If they're pretty, or oddly shaped, or contain interesting markings, she'll snag them and put them in her collection.

Seven-year-old Hailey, a student at Blair Elementary School in Traverse City, Michigan, started collecting rocks and mineral samples at a shop near her home, the Emerald Mountain Mining Company. Now, she picks them up anywhere, even in her driveway. Though she can't always tell rose quartz from feldspar, she thinks her collection is pretty cool.

"I have too many to count," she says. "All different kinds. I especially like the ones with neat things inside them, like fossils."

Collecting seems to be an almost universal human trait, and it starts very early in life. They may not have the relentlessness and greed of some adult collectors, but children seem to learn at a very young age how to gather, classify, and display their treasures.

Some young collectors are traditionalists, like 14-year-old Jessica Partridge of Acme, Michigan, who's been collecting postage stamps since she was "3 or 4." She is a regular customer at the local post office whenever the new commemoratives arrive.

Like Jessica, 12-year-old Matthew Dayton was inspired and guided by a parent when he began collecting insects two years ago. He already has already surpassed his father's modest bug collection with hundreds of his own specimens—all of them caught in Michigan.

Jessica and Matthew both followed the traditional path of the collector: learning the art of collecting from adults who shared and passed along their own passions and skills for finding stamps and stones, butterflies and bottle caps. But experienced collectors say it is hard to find youngsters with the patience and interest to pursue serious collecting. It doesn't help that many items are now priced beyond the reach of the average child. Comic books and sports cards, for example, are far more popular with adults than with the youngsters they were originally made for.

"I'd say the average age of our collectors is 27 or 28," says William West of Top of the Ninth, which deals mainly in collectible comics. "The kids just aren't interested anymore. They're busy on the Internet or playing their video games."

And for those who have the money (or generous friends and relatives), there are all those for-profit, fad-driven collectibles. Of course, today's hot item can sometimes become tomorrow's dim memory; only 7 or 8 years ago, kids fought and scuffled over Pogs (those highly decorated imitation milk-bottle tops), but hardly anyone mentions them anymore.

One child-accessible collectible that has been able to maintain its popularity for more than a year or two, in spite of marketing missteps and the greed of adult collectors, is the small and relatively inexpensive Beanie Baby. At about $5 per Beanie, those little bead-filled fabric animals remain a favorite among young collectors.

And there's a sign that at least one traditional collectible is making a comeback, thanks to the U.S. government: New mintings of U.S. coins—including the Sacagawea gold dollar and a series of quarters commemorating each of the 50 states—have resulted in a modest coin-collecting boom. Hallmark, a leader in the creation and marketing of collectibles, has packaged the new coins in special commemorative packages.

(Continued)

After you have completed this chapter, you should be able to:

1. Appreciate the wide scope of consumer behavior studies, including the three consumer roles and analysis of consumer wants and needs.
2. Describe the psychological bases of consumer behavior, including perception, learning, and motivation.
3. Explain how psychographics seeks to explain consumer behavior by discussing such aspects as values, lifestyles, and self-concepts.
4. Identify the steps in a typical consumer decision process.
5. Describe how households make group consumer decisions.

"We're promoting the coins very consciously because it's an intergenerational thing that can bring families closer together," says Bonnie Stephan of Bonnie's Hallmark in Cadillac, Michigan.[1]

Consumer behavior
is the process by which individuals or groups select, use, or dispose of goods, services, ideas, or experiences to satisfy needs and wants.

THE SCOPE OF CONSUMER BEHAVIOR

Consumer Behavior is the process by which individuals or groups select, use, or dispose of goods, services, ideas, or experiences to satisfy needs and wants. This definition of consumer behavior includes a variety of activities and a number of roles that people hold as consumers. In addition to the actual purchaser (*buyer*), our definition of *consumer* includes *payers* as consumers and *users* as consumers. For example, during Christmas people frequently purchase gifts—though they are the payers and the buyers, the users are the recipients of the gifts.

Consumer behavior deals with the buying behavior of consumers for both goods and services. However, since Chapter 9 deals with services marketing, in this chapter we focus mainly on consumer behavior as it relates to the marketing of goods. Similarly, though our definition of consumer behavior includes business consumers, the focus in this chapter is on household consumers as the behavior of business consumers is covered in Chapter 6.

Three Consumer Roles

In identifying and satisfying consumer needs and wants, it is important to recognize the significance of the various consumer roles. In each role we are concerned with a different facet of the product. As **users**, we are concerned with the product features and the uses they can be put to. As **payers**, we are concerned with the price of the product and the inherent financial considerations. It is the payer who is being targeted by ads claiming "0 down and 0% interest till 2004." As **buyers**, we are concerned with the logistics of procuring the product for either our own use or the use of others. For example, ads that claim consumers can order on a company's Web site as late as 10 February for products to be delivered on Valentine's Day are clearly targeted at the buyer.

To understand consumer behavior, we need to understand about consumers' *needs and wants*, their *perceptions*, how they *learn*, their *motivations and emotions*, how they form *attitudes* and how they make *purchase decisions*. This chapter addresses each of

Users
are the consumers who actually use the product.

Payers
are the consumers who actually pay for the product.

Buyers
are the consumers who actually purchase the product.

these issues. In the following section we discuss the differences between consumers' needs and wants, as well as the factors that influence needs and wants.

We will learn each of these concepts by following Mr. Howard Rock, who is a senior at the University of Utopia. He is 21 years old, has lots of friends, and has an active social life. Howard hopes to graduate in the spring and is fairly confident he will get a good job in sales and marketing in one of the local firms.

Consumer Needs and Wants

To understand consumer behavior, we need to understand how consumers perceive, learn, and make decisions to satisfy their needs and wants. It is important to understand what the needs and wants of users, payers, and buyers are. **Needs** are unsatisfactory conditions of the consumer that prompt him or her to an action that will make the condition better. **Wants** are desires to obtain more satisfaction than is absolutely necessary to improve an unsatisfactory condition. The difference between a need and a want is that need arousal is driven by discomfort in a person's physical and psychological conditions. For example, if Howard is hungry, he physically needs food; if he is stressed and cannot sleep, he is psychologically discomforted. Wants occur when humans desire to take their physical and psychological conditions beyond the state of minimal comfort. Thus for Howard food satisfies a need, whereas gourmet food satisfies a want. Similarly, just any car would satisfy Howard's need for transportation from his apartment to school, a Miata or a Porsche would satisfy his wants to feel the excitement of performance, or gain prestige among his peers, or project a particular self-image to his significant others. Only when needs are satisfied do wants surface.

Needs
are unsatisfactory conditions of the consumer that prompt him or her to an action that will make the condition better.

Wants
are desires to obtain more satisfaction than is absolutely necessary to improve an unsatisfactory condition.

LEARNING OBJECTIVE   2

PSYCHOLOGICAL BASES OF CONSUMER BEHAVIOR

Perception

Perception
is the process by which an individual senses, organizes, and interprets information received from the environment.

The objective reality of a product matters little; what does matter is the consumer's perception of a product or a brand. **Perception** is the process by which an individual *senses*, *organizes*, and *interprets* the information he or she receives from the environment. Marketers seek to understand the sources of consumer perceptions and to influence them. For example, cereals are made darker in color to make them appear more masculine while mouthwashes are colored green or blue to connote a clean, fresh feeling.

When Howard decides to eat at a restaurant, the smell, the ambience, and the taste of the food in the restaurant affect his senses. He organizes this information as being similar or dissimilar to his prior experiences. Having organized the information along different criteria like quality of the food, service, and ambience, he interprets this information as being either good or bad depending on whether he likes the experience.

http://www.tacobell.com

Taco Bell restaurants, for example, feature a bright purple and green color motif in their interiors, replacing a somewhat lackluster look of the past. When Taco Bell made this change some years ago, the new colors were so significantly different from before that most customers inevitably sensed the change. Moreover, given the prior associations most people have with bright neon colors, customers readily interpreted the new motif to signify youthfulness and an upbeat ambience.

Learning

Learning
is a change in the content of long-term memory. As consumers, we learn to adapt better to our environment.

Learning is a change in the content of long-term memory. Most consumer behavior is learned behavior. We learn consciously and subconsciously from a number of sources. We learn from our prior experiences, our peers, mass media, or family and friends. Learning helps us to respond better to our environment. A child who accidentally puts his hand on a hot electric bulb learns never again to touch anything resembling that object. Thus, human learning is directed at acquiring a potential for future adaptive behavior. Howard, for example, took advantage of a going-out-of-business sale and bought a substandard product. From this experience he learned about the futility of buying a nonreturnable product.

When Howard runs out of cereal, he knows he has to restock the next time he shops for groceries. He knows exactly where the cereal is located and picks up a box of his brand on his next trip. There is not a lot of explicit thought that goes into the decision making. However, if he decides to purchase a cellular phone, he will try to acquaint himself with the various offers and options available. Hence, the learning process is vastly different if a purchase involves merely the replenishment of existing goods or a specific problem that has to be solved.

Motivation

Motivation
is the state of drive or arousal that moves us toward a goal-object.

Motivation is what moves people—it is the driving force for all human behavior. More formally, **motivation** is defined as the state of drive or arousal that impels behavior toward a goal-object. Thus, motivation has two components: (1) *drive or arousal*, and (2) a *goal-object*. For example, the arousal or drive is akin to stepping on the gas pedal in an automobile, whereas the goal-object is analogous to the steering of the vehicle. Having the former without the latter is dangerous and having the latter without the former is useless.

Consumer Needs

The concept of needs and wants described earlier is closely aligned to the concept of motivation. Human beings have potentially infinite needs. To make sense of these various needs, psychologists have classified them. Among the most relevant classifications to marketers is Maslow's needs hierarchy.

Why Study Consumer Behavior?

As we begin the 21st century, understanding the consumer will be the key to business success. Companies are in business only to serve the customer. Those that do so efficiently and effectively are the ones that make a profit. The study of consumer behavior provides the basic knowledge necessary to make successful business decisions.

Studying and understanding consumer behavior opens several avenues for a student embarking on a career in the field of marketing. A person with a good knowledge of consumer behavior understands the underlying reasons why consumers are loyal to a brand. Knowledge about the psychology and sociology of consumers helps brand managers in preparing strategies for their business. Thus, studying consumer behavior can lead to a career in brand management.

Similarly, understanding the psychology of consumers can help one to secure a position as an account executive in an advertising agency. Knowing how consumers will react to certain types of cues should help determine the advertising strategy for different brands in different industries.

If a student has strong quantitative and analytical skills, a course in consumer behavior will be useful in conjunction with marketing research courses in securing a market research analyst position. As a market research analyst who understands consumer behavior, one is able to provide deeper insight into what the numbers mean. This helps provide better recommendations to top management.

Recently the concept of customer relationship management (CRM) has come to the forefront. A number of companies are interested in deploying some sort of CRM strategy in their firm. An understanding of consumer behavior is a prerequisite to employing a CRM strategy in a firm.

Some students become very fascinated by the field of consumer behavior and pursue a master's degree, or even a doctorate, in this field. Through their study, they develop the knowledge of the field and further our understanding of consumers.

Maslow's Hierarchy of Needs. Psychologist Abraham Maslow described motivation as a means of satisfying human needs. Higher level needs are dormant until lower level needs are satisfied. As shown in the Figure 5.1, **Maslow's hierarchy of needs** consists of (from lowest to highest):

Maslow's hierarchy of needs is a classification scheme of needs satisfaction where higher level needs are dormant until lower level needs are satisfied.

1. Physiological needs
2. Safety and security needs
3. Belongingness and love needs
4. Esteem and ego needs
5. Need for self-actualization

People "progress" to higher-level needs if their lower-level needs are satisfied; they "regress" back to lower-level needs when these needs become unsatisfied again. While Maslow does not distinguish between needs and wants, most contemporary books on marketing do. If we apply marketing concepts to Maslow's hierarchy, we find that the first two levels involve needs, while the three higher levels involve wants.

There are lots of examples of Maslow's needs. Physiological needs lead consumers to strive for, purchase, and use food, clothing, and shelter. For all humans, these needs are paramount. For many, such as those who live in poverty, these needs are never adequately met so they never progress to the next level of need. Howard typically makes sure that he buys his groceries and pays his rent and utility bills first. This is a reflection of the fact that his physiological needs have to be met first.

At the next level, safety and security are what is responsible for many people's fear of flying, especially since the attacks on the World Trade Center and the Pentagon. In marketing terms, automobile safety is becoming a major concern, reflected in the renewed emphasis on safety features by almost all carmakers. For example, Volvo appeals to this need in all its advertisements with the slogan "Drive Safely." Howard always visits his parents at Thanksgiving. Typically he flies the distance of 250 miles. However, since 9/11, he is unsure about airline safety and has decided to drive. Howard is being motivated by concerns of safety and security.

http://www.volvo.com

Figure 5.1	Maslow's Hierarchy of Needs

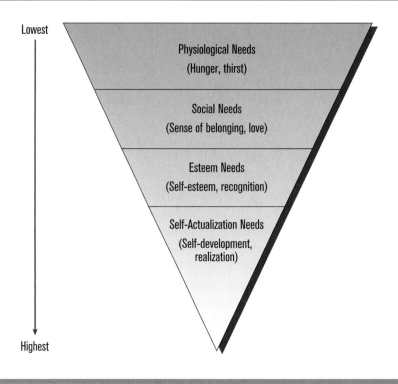

Once our safety needs are met, we crave love and belonging, according to Maslow. There are many manifestations of this need. Teenagers act and dress in a certain manner to fit in with their peer group. Some adults take up golf in order to be seen as belonging to the corporate world. Similarly, we want to be loved by others in our society. Toward this end, many products, such as greeting cards, flowers, and other kinds of gifts, are bought specifically to promote relationships between individuals. Marketers, especially greeting card manufacturers, have been credited with promoting, if not creating, Mother's Day, Father's Day, Boss's Day, Secretary's Day, and even Mother-in-Law Day. In such cases, companies hope to cash in on the consumers' desire to conform and belong.

Once accepted as part of a group, we begin to crave esteem and become conscious of our status. We want to be respected. We need to feel confident, important, and appreciated. We use self–gift giving as a way to motivate ourselves. For example, Howard may decide that if he makes an A grade in marketing, he will buy himself a new cell phone.

Finally, once these physiological, safety, social, and esteem needs are satisfied, people begin to explore and extend the bounds of their potential—that is, they seek self-actualization. This self-actualization motive is what is behind a person engaging in self-improvement activities, such as taking an adult education course or tenaciously pursuing a skill toward perfection. The U.S. Army's slogans of "Be All You That Can Be" and "An Army of One" are appeals to a person's need for self-actualization.

Consumer Emotions

Needs and emotions are closely related. **Emotions** are strong, relatively uncontrolled feelings that affect our behavior.[2] Emotions are often triggered by environmental factors or events. Many of us felt sad and insecure after the events of 9/11. Such emotions affect our consumption behavior. Some emotions may be internally generated too. Emotions are typically accompanied by physiological changes such as dilation of the pupils of the eyes, rapid breathing, or an increase in blood pressure. We all seek positive emotional experiences and avoid negative emotional experiences. Much of the consumption or use of products is driven by and immersed in emotions.

http://www.army.mil

Emotions
are strong, relatively uncontrolled feelings that affect our behavior.

We cuddle a baby because we feel affection and love for it. We swear at a rude driver who cuts in front of us because we feel anger and frustration. Although we have all experienced emotion, it is not easy to define. The reason is that emotion is a complex set of processes, occurring concurrently in multiple systems. Emotions have three response components: cognitive, emotional, and physiological. *Cognitive responses* are the thought processes of individuals and include beliefs, categorization, and symbolic meaning. *Emotional responses* do not involve thinking, they simply happen, often unexplainably and suddenly. Specific songs, for example, may make individuals feel happy, feel sad, or recreate other past feelings that were associated with the particular piece of music. In contrast to cognitive and emotional responses, *physiological responses* are often described in terms of physical pleasure or discomfort.

Consumer Moods

Do you recall the last time you really enjoyed shopping? Maybe you were in a bookstore such as Border's, and some especially mellow music was playing. You relaxed and lingered on, browsing through the books on the "new release" shelves. Maybe you ended up buying four books that day. That is the power of positive mood! This is the same reason many online storefronts have audio files attached, so that when you visit their Web site you hear music playing in the background.

When an emotion is less intense and transitory, it is termed a **mood**. We are in some mood all the time. We may be in a happy, sad, positive, negative, or introspective mood at any given point of time. Since we are in some mood or another at any given point of time, it is important for marketers to understand consumer moods.

Just like emotions, moods are induced both by external stimuli as well as internally by autistic thinking—that is, recalling some past incident or fantasizing about some event. The ambience of the store, demeanor of the salespeople, the tone and manner of advertising are all marketing stimuli that can affect a person's moods. For example, Howard may get into a good mood when a helpful saleswoman pays personal attention to him. His cheerful mood may induce him to buy products that he was ambivalent about when he entered the store.

Mood states have consequences in terms of favorable or unfavorable consumer response to marketing efforts. We generally do not buy anything from salespersons who put us in an unpleasant mood—for example, by not showing that they care about our business. Research studies indicate that consumers linger longer in positive mood

Moods
are emotions that are less intense and transitory.

environments, recall those advertisements more that had created good moods, and feel more positive toward brands based on advertising that created feelings of warmth.[3]

Involvement

Involvement
is the degree of personal relevance of a product to a consumer.

Involvement can be defined as the degree of personal relevance of an object or product to a consumer. Involvement is a matter of degree—how relevant or how central a product is. Accordingly, we can expand the notion of involvement to refer, beyond relevance, to the degree to which a consumer finds a product of interest. While both salt and cosmetics are relevant to people, it is quite likely that consumers would be more involved in a decision about cosmetics than salt.

Involvement, defined as the degree of interest, can be viewed as having two forms: enduring involvement and situational involvement. *Enduring involvement* is the degree of interest a consumer feels about a product on an ongoing basis. In contrast, *situational involvement* is the degree of interest in a specific situation or on a specific occasion, such as when buying a product or when consuming something in the presence of an important client or friend. Howard has no particular interest in vacuum cleaners. However, when his vacuum cleaner breaks down and has to be replaced he gets very involved in the decision to buy a vacuum cleaner. However, this involvement is temporary and ceases to exist once the problem is solved. Hence, Howard's involvement with the vacuum cleaner is situational. However, Howard is a techie and interested in knowing more about computers, regardless of whether he needs to purchase one. This kind of involvement does not depend on the situation but is enduring in nature.

PSYCHOGRAPHICS: DESCRIBING CONSUMER BEHAVIOR

Another facet of motivation is **psychographics**. These are characteristics of individuals that identify them in terms of their psychological and behavioral makeup—how people occupy themselves (behavior) and what psychological factors underlie their activity pattern. For example, Howard's need to seek affiliation or peer approval makes him engage, say, in becoming a member of a golf club or going to theaters. Theatergoing or playing golf thus becomes part of his psychographics. This psychographic in turn drives him to buy golf equipment or do whatever is needed to implement that particular psychographic. It thus becomes motivational. Psychographics have three components: values, self-concept, and lifestyles.

Psychographics
are characteristics of individuals that describe them in terms of their psychological and behavioral makeup.

Values

When you think about what is important to you in life, you are thinking about your values. **Values** are end-states of life, the goals one lives for. Psychologist Milton Rokeach has identified two groups of values: terminal and instrumental. *Terminal values* are the goals we seek in life (e.g., peace and happiness), whereas *instrumental values* are the means or behavioral standards by which we pursue our goals (e.g., honesty).

Consumer researchers felt a need to identify the values directly relevant to everyday consumer behavior. Toward this end, consumer researchers Lynn Kahle and his associates developed a list of values (LOV), consisting of nine terminal values:

1. Self-respect
2. Self-fulfillment

Values
are end-states or goals one lives for.

3. Security
4. Sense of belonging
5. Excitement
6. Sense of accomplishment
7. Fun and enjoyment
8. Being well respected
9. Warm relationships with others[4]

Consumers cluster into three groups depending on which of these values are more important to them. They are *internals,* if they value self-fulfillment, excitement, a sense of accomplishment, and self-respect. These people like to be in control of their lives. In marketing terms, internals take proactive steps such as looking at nutritional labels while buying products. The second group is *externals,* who value a sense of belonging, security, and being well respected. These people like to conform and hence are more likely to buy products that they think most people buy. Externals are brand-conscious people who buy a popular brand because everybody else is buying it. Finally, *interpersonals* value warm relationships with others, as well as fun and enjoyment.

Self-Concept

Self-concept
refers to a person's self-image.

Everyone has a self-image—a perception of who we are. This is called **self-concept.** Furthermore, self-concept includes an idea of what an individual currently is and what he or she would like to become. These two components of self-concept are called *actual self* and *ideal self,* respectively.

Self-concept deeply influences people's consumption, for people express their self-concept in large measure by what they consume. For example, in his senior year Howard may begin to think of himself as a professional and hence begins to dress like one, retiring his baseball caps and sneakers. Many Generation Xers, now well past their teen years, have begun to nurture a self-concept of being grown-up, responsible people, and consequently, they are flocking to dermatologists to take off their body tattoos—the same tattoos that they had proudly sported for many years.

Individuals' self-concepts vary according to which of the three consumer roles described earlier—users, payers, and buyers—they are playing. A user might have the self-concept of a very discerning connoisseur or a very involved user. The payer might

have the self-concept of being thrifty, financially prudent, or a nonchalant, money-is-no-object-to-me attitude. Finally, the buyer might have the self-concept of being a convenience seeker or service seeker or being very time conscious.

Lifestyle

To this point, we have looked at how we think of ourselves and what we value, now we will focus on the way we live—our *lifestyle*. A good way to determine the lifestyle of a person is to look at the products and brands that they consume. Lifestyle is a function of (1) a consumer's personal characteristics, namely, genetics, race, gender, age, and personality; (2) personal context, namely, culture, institutions, reference groups, and personal worth; and (3) needs and emotions. These three sets of factors together influence the pattern of our activities—how we spend time and money.

Values and Lifestyles (VALS)

One of the most widely used psychographic profiling schemes is called **VALS**™. Developed by SRI International and currently run by SRI Consulting Business Intelligence (SRIC-BI), its first version introduced in 1978 (VALS I) segmented the entire U.S. adult population into nine groups, based on the identities they seek and implement via marketplace behaviors. According to SRIC-BI, "People pursue and acquire [goods], services, and experiences that provide satisfaction and give shape, substance, and character to their identities."[5] In 1989, VALS 2 (see Figure 5.2), with eight groups, was introduced to reflect the changes that had taken place as well as to improve the segmentation principles for advertising and marketing applications.

VALS™
is a psychographic profiling scheme developed by SRI Consulting Business Intelligence.

Figure 5.2	VALS™ Network

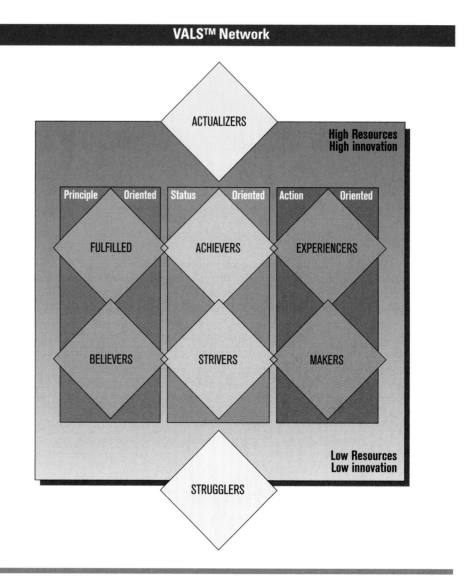

Source: SRI Consulting Business Intelligence Web site, http://www.sric-bi.com/VALS, accessed 24 April 2002.

Strugglers, who are at the bottom of Figure 5.2 are passive consumers who are generally not well educated and have limited resources. Typically they are more concerned with safety and security and represent a modest market for products. *Makers* are the do-it-yourself (DIY) category of consumers. They are value conscious and buy products that they can use to build things they would like to use. They are conservative and are suspicious of government intrusion. *Strivers* constantly seek approval of their peers and people around them. They are typically people of limited means and bemoan this fact. *Believers,* on the other hand, have limited but sufficient resources to meet their limited needs, and are conservative in their decision making. They value the church, family, and community very much and are more likely to buy American products. *Experiencers* are young, enthusiastic, and rebellious. They seek variety and excitement in the products they consume. They are more likely to spend a substantial amount of their money on clothing, fast food, movies, and videos. *Achievers* are successful career people who value stability and status quo. They are likely to be politically and economically conservative. Their lives revolve around their family and church. They are more likely to buy products that enhance their sense of prestige and exhibit their success to their peers. *Fulfilleds* are mature, successful consumers who are well educated and are in (or have recently retired from) professional jobs. They are fairly knowledgeable about world events and have social consciousness. They are practical consumers who look for durability and value in the products they purchase. *Actualizers* are the "take charge" people with high self-esteem and plentiful resources. While image is important to these consumers, it is not to impress others but as a reflection of their taste and character. They are established or emerging leaders of business or government and are open to new ideas and change. They are socially conscious and have a diverse and rich life.

You can take the VALS survey at the SRI Consulting Business Intelligence Web site to find out in which VALS category you belong. Consumers tend to be dynamic in that as their available resources as well as the pressures on these resources change, their VALS category may also change. However, the psychological motivations measured by VALS are enduring traits, lasting on the order of 15 years or more.

http://www.sric-bi.com

Attitude: Definition and Characteristics

Gordon Allport, the psychologist, defines, **attitudes** as "learned predispositions to respond to an object or class of objects in a consistently favorable or unfavorable way."[6]

The definition has several implications:

1. Attitudes are learned. That is, they get formed on the basis of some experience with or without information about the object.
2. Attitudes are predispositions. As such they reside in the mind.
3. Attitudes cause consistent response. They precede and produce behavior.

Attitudes
are learned predispositions to respond to an object or class of objects in a consistently favorable or unfavorable way.

Because attitudes precede and produce behavior, they can be used to predict behavior. For example, if we know that Howard's attitude toward George W. Bush in the presidential elections is positive, then we could predict that he is more likely to vote for him. Marketers use attitude measures before launching new products. Behavior also can be used to infer the underlying attitudes. In everyday life, we observe somebody's behavior toward us and use that observation to infer whether that person likes us; we then use that inferred attitude to predict how the person will behave toward us in the future. Marketers, too, often use this logic. When consumers buy a product, this purchase behavior is used to infer a favorable attitude toward the related product class, which is in turn deemed to be an indicator of the potential purchase of an item in the related product class.

Attitudes, then, are our evaluations of objects—people, places, brands, products, organizations, and so on. People evaluate objects in terms of their goodness, likability, or desirability. Consumers may hold attitudes toward salespersons in general (e.g., "Salespeople are basically all hucksters"), and about specific companies (e.g., "Company X makes good electronic appliances but not computers"). Attitudes do change with time and marketers strive to influence consumers' attitudes. Marketers try to change them if consumers have a negative attitude toward their brand and reinforce the attitude if they have a positive attitude toward their brand.

INDIVIDUAL CONSUMER DECISION MAKING

LEARNING OBJECTIVE 4

So far we have discussed *psychological concepts* that affect consumer behavior, including consumers *needs and wants, perception, learning, motivation,* and *attitude formation.* Consumers use some or all of these processes when they make decisions to buy (or not buy) a product. Purchase decisions are sometimes made by individuals in households; at other times they are made collectively by groups of people such as spouses and children.

As discussed earlier, consumers adopt three different roles in the decision-making scenario—buyer, payer, and user. In each of these roles, consumers constantly face choices—how much to spend, what product to acquire, and where to purchase it from. These choices call for **consumer decision making**. Typically, these decisions include *whether* to purchase, *what* to purchase, *when* to purchase, from *whom* to purchase, and *how* to pay for it. Consumers have finite resources in terms of money and time, so they have to constantly weigh the possibility of either postponing or forsaking the purchase of a product. For example, Howard may have to scrap his plan to attend tonight's game to study for the test. Similarly he may have to postpone buying a BMW until he has made enough money to afford it. Thus we constantly make decisions about whether to purchase and what to purchase at the product level.

Consumer decision making
is a process that typically involves whether to purchase, what to purchase, when to purchase, from whom to purchase, and how to pay for a purchase.

An important consumer behavior at this decision level is *mental budgeting*—how the budget consumers set for a product category guides their subsequent behavior as a consumer. The payer plays the most important role in mental budgeting as the user is

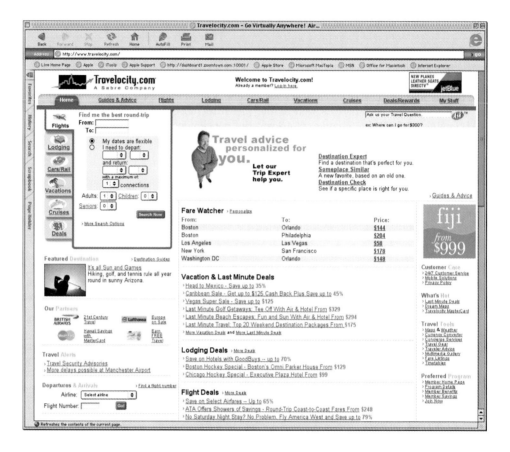

constrained by what the payer has budgeted and whether the product is within the budget. This occurs subconsciously, even when one consumer is playing both the payer and user roles. Travelocity.com appeals to this predisposition by allowing you to specify the amount you are willing to spend on a vacation and comes up with alternatives (vacation packages) from which you can choose. Similarly, priceline.com understands that consumers make mental budgets and lets you select the price you are willing to pay for airline tickets and hotel rooms.

Following the choice at the product level, the consumer makes another what-to-purchase decision—a choice among brands. For example, if the product category–level decision is to take a vacation, the next decision is which brand to purchase—that is, which travel destination to select, how to get there, and so on.

The process of consumer decision making consists of the steps shown in Figure 5.3.

Step 1: Problem Recognition

Consumers typically make purchase decisions to satisfy a particular need or a want. Howard, for example, could realize that he is hungry and hence has to buy some food, or that the leaking faucet needs to be fixed. A consumer problem can be any state of deprivation or discomfort felt by a consumer. **Problem recognition** occurs when consumers realize that they need to do something to get back to a normal state of comfort.

Problem recognition can occur due to either an internal stimulus or an external stimulus. *Internal stimuli* are perceived states of discomfort—physical or psychological (e.g., hunger or boredom, respectively). *External stimuli* are informational cues from the marketplace that lead the consumer to realize the problem.

Problem recognition can occur for each consumer role. A VCR was not considered a need until one was made available. There was no obvious problem that the VCR solved. However, once it was available, consumers could use it to view programs that they had missed and the need to be able to watch a program at one's convenience was recognized. Hence, though the need had existed, it was not recognized till the advent of a VCR. The same is true for products such as Post-it notes and the personal digital assistant (pda). These products serve the *latent needs* of the consumer in the user role.

http://www.travelocity.com

http://www.priceline.com

Problem recognition
is a consumer's realization that he or she needs to buy something to get back to a normal state of comfort.

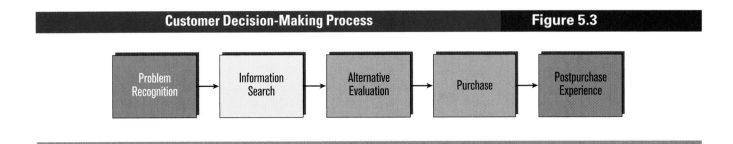

Customer Decision-Making Process — **Figure 5.3**

Problem Recognition → Information Search → Alternative Evaluation → Purchase → Postpurchase Experience

Consumers typically had to go to a store to buy their pizza before home delivery was made available. The convenience of being able to order the pizza from home is a solution to buying a pizza. This serves the needs of a consumer in the role of a buyer. For the payer, the availability of leasing automobiles has improved affordability. Also, availability of credit makes many consumers realize the need to buy a new car or furniture. Similarly, in order to "help" consumers identify these problems, marketers promote credit cards by sending preapproved cards.

Step 2: Information Search

The **information search** stage of the consumer decision process could be as simple as scanning one's memory to check what product/brand was bought when the last purchase decision occurred. This can be a subconscious search for information. However, more often than not, we specifically seek information to solve the problem that has been identified. This search rarely includes every brand in existence. Consumers consider only a select subset of brands, organized as follows:

- The *awareness set* consists of brands of which a consumer is aware.
- An *evoked set* consists of the brands in a product category that the consumer remembers at the time of decision making.
- Of the brands in the evoked set, not all are deemed to fit the need. Those considered unfit are eliminated right away. The remaining brands are termed the *consideration set*—the brands a consumer will consider buying.

Initially, consumers seek information about the consideration set of brands. New information can bring additional brands into the awareness, evoked, and consideration sets.

Different sources of information are used in the information search process. These sources of information may be categorized as marketer or nonmarketer. When the source of the information is the marketer/manufacturer, it is termed as *marketer source*. This information may be from advertising, packaging, in-store displays, or other product literature that is made available to consumers. Lately, most companies have set up Web sites in order to facilitate consumers' search for information.

Nonmarketer sources are those that are independent of the marketer's control. They include personal sources and independent sources, such as information provided by *Consumer Reports* and friends and acquaintances. Since these sources have no personal interest in biasing the information (unlike marketer sources), they are deemed to be more credible. The information provided by friends and acquaintances is also called word-of-mouth and plays a critical role in the selection of products.

The choice of information sources depends partly on a consumer's search strategy. A search strategy is the pattern of information acquisition consumers utilize to solve their decision problems. Since information acquisition has costs in terms of time, physical effort, and mental effort, consumers weigh the costs against the likely gains from information acquisition. That comparison helps them decide how much information they will acquire and from what sources.

Sometimes consumers may not go through such a long and conscious search strategy. They may use a contrasting search strategy called heuristics. *Heuristics* are quick rules of thumb and shortcuts used to make decisions. Heuristics can be implemented in a variety of ways:

- Broad inferences are quickly drawn from partial information (e.g., price may be used to judge quality).

Information search
is the stage in the consumer decision process when consumers collect information on only a select subset of brands.

- Past experiences are considered adequate.
- Others' judgments are sought and summarily adopted as final choice.
- Brand names are heavily relied on to the exclusion of seeking further attribute information.

Although these strategies are not systematic, they are also not irrational. They are rational to their users in terms of the cost versus benefit trade-offs they perceive. Given the paucity of time, more consumers are likely to use the heuristics route to guide them in their information search.

Step 3: Alternative Evaluation

Alternative evaluation
is the stage in the consumer decision process when consumers select one of the several alternatives (brands, dealers, and so on) available to them.

Once consumers have the necessary information, how do they use that information as they proceed through the **alternative evaluation** stage of the consumer decision process to arrive at a specific choice? Consumers select one of the several alternatives (brands, dealers, and so on) available to them. These specific processes and steps are referred to by researchers as *choice models*. For example, Howard is considering buying a new automobile. Let's say that he has four brands in his consideration set. He rates them on four different categories—price, mileage, power/speed, and aesthetics. His rating of these factors are given in Table 5.1.

There are two broad categories of choice models: compensatory and noncompensatory.

Compensatory Model

In the *compensatory model*, the consumer arrives at a choice by considering all of the attributes of a product (or benefits of a service) and mentally trading off the alternative's perceived weakness on one or more attributes for its perceived strength on other attributes. If Howard decides to assign weights for the criteria he is using as 40 percent to price, 30 percent to mileage, 20 percent to power/speed, and 10 percent to aesthetics, he will arrive at the following perceived values:

Brand A = 0.4 (6) + 0.3 (8) + 0.2(6) + 0.1(7) = 6.7

Brand B = 0.4 (7) + 0.3 (9) + 0.2(4) + 0.1(6) = 6.9

Brand C = 0.4 (8) + 0.3 (7) + 0.2(5) + 0.1(8) = 7.1

Brand D = 0.4 (5) + 0.3 (8) + 0.2(8) + 0.1(8) = 6.8

Using the compensatory model of evaluating alternatives, Howard would decide to buy Brand C, though it is worst brand as far as mileage is concerned.

Noncompensatory Models

While there are several *noncompensatory* models that have been identified, four are most common and useful. These are called conjunctive, disjunctive, lexicographic, and elimination by aspects.[7] In the *conjunctive model*, the consumer begins by setting the minimum cutoffs on all salient attributes. Each alternative is then examined on each attribute, and any alternative that meets the minimum cutoffs on all attributes can potentially be chosen.

If Howard uses a cutoff of 6, by examining Table 5.1 it is clear that the only brand that meets his cutoff on every criterion is Brand A. Hence Howard will choose Brand A, if he uses the conjunctive model to make the decision.

The *disjunctive model* entails trade-offs between aspects of choice alternatives. Sometimes the consumer is willing to trade off one feature for another. For example, a homebuyer might say that the house she is willing to consider buying should have either five bedrooms or, if it has only four bedrooms, a finished basement. Although similar trade-offs are made in the compensatory model, there are differences. First, the disjunctive model considers the sheer presence or absence of attributes, rather than the degree or amount to which these attributes are present. Second, in the compensatory model, the attributes traded off need not serve the same purpose, while they tend to in the disjunctive model.

Another model consumers use to make a choice is the *lexicographic model*. In this model, attributes of alternatives are rank ordered in terms of importance. Consumers examine all alternatives on the most important criterion and identify the ones that sur-

Howard's New Car Alternative Evaluation				Table 5.1

	Attribute			
Brands	**Price**	**Mileage**	**Power/Speed**	**Aesthetics**
A	6	8	6	7
B	7	9	4	6
C	8	7	5	8
D	5	8	8	8

Note: Each attribute is rated on a scale of 1 to 10; 10 represents the highest in that attribute except in the case of price, where the scale is reversed since the lowest price is the most desirable for the consumer.

pass a threshold level. If more than one alternative remains in the choice set, they then consider the second most important criterion and examine the remaining alternatives with respect to that criterion's threshold level. The process continues until only one alternative remains. Using this approach Howard would have decided on Brand C as it scores the highest (8) in the most important attribute—price.

The *elimination by aspects model* is similar to the lexicographic model but with one important difference: Consumers rate the attributes in order of importance and, in addition, define cutoff values. They then examine all alternatives first on the most important attribute, admitting for further consideration only those that satisfy the minimum cutoff level on this most important attribute. If more than one alternative meets the requirement, they go on to the next aspect, appraising the remaining alternatives on the second attribute. In our example, if Howard has a cutoff of 6 for the first attribute (price), Brand D would be eliminated because it does not meet the criterion. All the remaining brands meet the second criterion of mileage. Hence Howard would proceed to the third attribute where Brands B and C have scores less than the cutoff; hence, Brand A is selected.

It has been found that consumers may use any of these choice models independently or use a combination of the choice models. For some of the more important decisions, a consumer might first use a noncompensatory model and then, to further identify the choice, use a compensatory model. The noncompensatory model could be used to eliminate choices and narrow down the set of alternatives for closer comparisons.

Step 4: Purchase

Once Howard has evaluated the alternatives, he makes a **purchase**. This appears a straightforward step, but even here consumer behavior at times becomes intriguing. Howard, for example, may use one of the alternative evaluation techniques to determine the brand he is going to purchase. At this stage he arranges for the terms of the transaction, seeking and obtaining the transfer of title or ownership from the seller, paying for the automobile, and receiving possession of the product commitment from the seller. While the steps described here are automatic in the case of groceries, they become important in the case of purchases such as automobiles or homes. In case of rare artifacts, purchase implementation, including finding a seller, may be a long drawn-out process. The Internet auction retailer eBay attempts to make this simpler for consumers.

Sometimes the consumer purchase process may be derailed by a deviation from the identified choice. Several conditions account for this. First, the preferred brand may be out of stock, thus forcing the consumer to buy a brand different from the one identified. Second, new in-store information may reopen the evaluation process. Third, financing terms may render a purchase infeasible, forcing the consumer as payer either to abandon the purchase altogether or to substitute the intended brand with a lower-level model or another brand available on preferred terms. Fourth, unexpected situations may lead to a postponement of the purchase. For example, Howard might learn that there is a recruitment freeze in the company he is expecting to employ him, and hence he is not sure of where he is going to be employed.

Purchase
is the stage in the consumer decision process when transaction terms are arranged, title of ownership is transferred, the product is paid for, and the consumer takes possession of the product from the seller.

Marketing Technologies

Self Service at the Point of Sale

When it comes to making purchases, consumers love convenience at the point of sale (POS). From drive-up windows to pay-at-the-pump card readers, any advancement that allows consumers to complete their purchases faster and have greater control over the payment process is certain to be a winner.

For merchants, the primary benefits of such enhancements are greater customer throughput, which can lead to increased market share and lower operating costs by reducing the number of cashiers. For merchant acquirers, the payoff is the opportunity to capture more volume on credit and debit cards at the expense of checks and cash.

As a result, POS technology vendors are constantly pushing the envelope by developing new concepts or products that will bring a higher level of convenience to consumers. One of the latest developments in this trend is the self-checkout lane that allows consumers to scan items themselves and pay for their purchases without the aid of a clerk.

Retailers and grocers quietly began testing new versions of the technology in the late 1990s. It has spread rapidly to leading supermarket chains such as Kroger, Meijer, and Shaw's. Overall, about 20 percent of grocery chains have installed self-checkout lanes, according to the Food Marketing Institute, a Washington, D.C., industry group.

"Self-checkout is a compelling technology for merchants," says Will Ander, a consultant with McMillan

Doolittle, a Chicago retail consulting firm. "It helps merchants control labor costs, which is a huge benefit to high-volume stores, and gives consumers a greater sense of control over the transaction. Plus, it increases the likelihood consumers will pay with a credit or debit card because it is faster."

Self-checkout systems used by grocers and discounters feature a conveyor belt to move items automatically toward a bar-code reader, a scale to weigh produce, a bagging area, a POS terminal, and a slot to deposit cash and checks. The systems are menu driven and use both automated voice and visual prompts to guide consumers through each stage of the checkout process. Many of the systems are bilingual. Merchants typically assign about two employees to monitor the self-checkout area to help customers in need of assistance and to direct customers with fewer than 20 items in their cart to those lanes.

So far, merchants that have installed self-checkout technology report that between 20 percent and 40 percent of total transaction volume in the equipped stores is going through those lanes, according to Dayton, Ohio–based NCR Corporation, a leading vendor of self-checkout terminals.

"At some point, self-checkout will find its way into department stores, but right now adoption is going to be driven by multi-lane retailers," predicts NCR's Jennifer Nugent.

Source: Adapted from Peter Lucas, "Self Service at the Point of Sale," *Credit Card Management* 14 (March 2002).

Step 5: Postpurchase Evaluations

The purchase of the product is followed by a postpurchase evaluation stage. When consumers' expectations are not met by the performance of the product, they get dissatisfied. When performance meets the expectation level, consumers are satisfied, and when consumers' expectations are surpassed by performance, they are delighted. Hence, marketers should be concerned not only with the performance of their product but also must manage consumers' expectations, knowing that whether consumers are satisfied will affect future purchase decisions.

Postpurchase behavior
is the last stage in the consumer decision process, when the consumer experiences an intense need to confirm the wisdom of that decision.

After consumers make an important choice decision, they experience an intense need to confirm the wisdom of that decision. The flip side is that they want to avoid disconfirmation. One of the processes of this **postpurchase behavior** is *cognitive dissonance*: a postpurchase doubt the buyer experiences about the wisdom of the choice. One of the methods of reducing cognitive dissonance and confirming the soundness of one's decision is to seek further positive information about the chosen alternative and avoid negative information about the chosen alternative.

Following a satisfactory or dissatisfactory experience, consumers have three possible responses: *exit, voice,* or *loyalty*. If consumers are dissatisfied with their experience with a brand, they may decide never again to buy that brand. This places them back to the start of the decision process the next time the problem arises. Some dissatisfied consumers complain and then decide either to give the brand or marketer another chance or simply to exit. Following the complaint, negative word-of-mouth is less likely and repatronage more likely if the complaint is successfully redressed. If the complaint is not successfully redressed, the negative word-of-mouth might intensify beyond what it would have been had the consumer not made the complaint in the first place.

The third response is, of course, loyalty. Consumer loyalty means the consumer buys the same brand repeatedly. It is fair to assume that satisfied consumers are more likely to be loyal. However, the converse is not necessarily true as some researchers have found that not all satisfied consumers are loyal. Some consumers exhibit switching behavior despite being satisfied with the current brand.

HOUSEHOLD DECISION MAKING

Households are the basic unit of buying and consumption in a society despite the fact that what constitutes a household has changed vastly with the passage of time. A household is a consumption unit of one or more persons identified by a common location with an address. While a number of consumer decisions are no doubt made by individuals for personal consumption (e.g., buying food during office lunch hour), the more significant decisions are made by individuals jointly with other members of their household, and for joint use by the members of the household.

Household decision making is important to study as it is likely to be different from that of the individual decision-making process. The critical difference is that it is quite likely that in the individual decision-making process all three roles—buyer, user, and payer—are more likely to merge in one person, in the case of the household it is more likely that the three roles will be assumed by separate individuals. The separation of the three roles makes household buying behavior somewhat complex to track and influence. Moreover, these role allocations are dynamic. They vary from time to time, from one product to another, and from one family type to another.

Household decision making occurs when significant decisions are made by individuals jointly with other members of their household, and for joint use by the members of the household.

Families and Households

The composition of the family is dynamic and changes with time and place. Years ago, a typical U.S. household would have been described as the traditional nuclear family, with a husband, a wife, and 2.5 children. In 1970, married couples with children comprised 41 percent of all households in the United States. By 2000, such households had declined to 23.5 percent. On the other hand, the number of single-parent households rose from 6 percent in 1970 to 9.3 percent in 2000.[8]

Family size varies from culture to culture and from subculture to subculture. In some cultures, the family extends beyond the immediate nucleus to include grandparents, aunts, and uncles. Today, however, the "typical" family has changed dramatically, and households display much more diversity.

Steps in Family Buying Decisions

If you think back to a recent marketplace decision made in your family, you might recall that various members undertook different activities en route to the final decision. Based on research and observations, scholars have identified and described the family buying process as consisting of the following steps.[9]

1. Initiation of the purchase decision
2. Gathering and sharing of information
3. Evaluating and deciding
4. Shopping and buying
5. Conflict management

The first four steps are self-explanatory and are similar to those steps described in the case of the individual consumer. The fifth step is particularly salient in the context of family decision making. Regarding the first four steps, although their meaning is self-evident and their basic operation similar to that in individual decision making, the actual dynamics are more involved. Different members of the family play different roles in the decision process. One member might initiate the purchase decision by making a product request. Another member of the family might collect information. A third member might evaluate and decide. Yet another member might make the actual product purchase. Finally, someone might take the responsibility of resolving any differences of preference and conflicts that may arise. Such conflicts not only arise before the decision is made, but may continue or may arise anew after the purchase. Interspousal or intrafamily influence can vary from step to step.

Children's Influence in the Family Decision Making

In 2000, U.S. children between the ages of 8 and 14 spent about $155 billion a year and influenced another $300 billion in spending by their parents.[10] Children's influence increases with age. Children influence household buying in three ways. First, children influence household purchases by having individualistic preferences for products paid for and bought by parents. Second, children in their teen years begin to have their own money and become payers and buyers of items for self-use. Third, children influence their parents' choice of products that are meant for shared consumption (e.g., family vacation), or even products solely for parental consumption, by exerting expertise influence (e.g., high-tech products or the latest fashions in clothes).

Conflict in Family Decisions

Family decision making may give rise to conflict, whether the consumer roles are distributed among family members or shared by family members. Conflict among distributed roles arises when the user, payer, and buyer roles are played by different family members and different alternatives satisfy each person. Conflict also arises when a single role is shared by multiple family members and their goals diverge. For example, in the case of a family car, one parent may be interested in the high-performance of a turbo engine car, while the other parent may want a minivan that is safe and roomy enough for small children in the family.

Conflicts will inevitably arise if there is disagreement among family members either on goals or on perceptions. The nature of the conflict will differ according to whether there is a disagreement in one or both of these areas.

Four strategies of conflict resolution have been suggested by scholars: problem solving, persuasion, bargaining, and politicking. *Problem solving* entails members trying to gather more information or to add new alternatives. When motives/goals are congruent and only perceptions differ, obtaining and sharing information often suffices to resolve conflicts. *Persuasion* requires educating about the goal hierarchy; one parent might argue how a large, safe car is in the best interest of the whole family since the car is needed to transport children. *Bargaining* entails trading favors (wife gets to buy the house of her choice as long as the car that is being bought is one that the husband prefers). When goals and evaluations are so divergent that even bargaining is infeasible, families resort to *politicking*. Here, members form coalitions and subgroups within the family and by so doing simply impose their will on the minority coalition. Incidentally, it is not unusual for parents to find themselves a part of the minority coalition.

CHAPTER SUMMARY

- A consumer is a person who is party to a transaction with the marketer. Consumer behavior determines how we select, purchase, and dispose products to satisfy our needs and wants. The three roles a consumer plays are those of the user, the payer, and the buyer.

- Whether they are users, payers, or buyers, consumers have needs and wants. A need is an unsatisfactory physical condition of the consumer that leads him or her to an action that will satisfy or fulfill that condition. A want is a desire to obtain more satisfaction than is absolutely necessary to improve an unsatisfactory condition.

- Some of the underlying processes that consumers use to make product and brand choices are perception, learning, motivation, and attitude formation. The characteristics of the stimulus or incoming information, the context, and consumers themselves all influence the perceptual process.

- Consumer learning is directed at acquiring a potential for future adaptive behavior. Consumer motivations explain why consumers buy, pay for, and use specific products. This topic is organized in terms of needs, emotions, and psychographics. Needs are felt deprivations of desired states. Maslow's hierarchy is a useful classification scheme of needs. Human emotions also play a significant role in motivating human behavior. Psychographics describe consumers' profile of needs, emotions, and resulting behaviors, and as such explain much of consumer behavior. Psychographics include self-concept, personal values, and lifestyles. An important type of psychographics is VALS (values and lifestyles).

- Attitudes are consumers' likes and dislikes toward various products and their predispositions to respond to (approach or avoid) them.

- Consumer decision making is a five-step process: (1) problem recognition; (2) information search; (3) alternative evaluation; (4) purchase; and (5) post-purchase evaluation. The consumer decision process begins with problem recognition. The problem recognition occurs due to an internal cue which comes from one's motives being in a state of unfulfillment, or from external stimuli evoking these motives. Once problem recognition occurs, the consumer either (a) relies on prior knowledge and previously learned solutions, or (b) searches for new solutions through new information acquisition and its evaluation and integration.

- Evaluations of alternatives entail use of compensatory (trade-off) and non-compensatory (non-trade-off) decision models. The latter include conjunctive, disjunctive, lexicographic, and elimination-by-aspects models. The outcome of these evaluation processes is the identification of a preferred brand and the formation of purchase intent. Such purchase intent is then implemented by the actual purchase act, but the purchase act does not always occur as planned. Sometimes, substantial delays occur in purchase implementation, and other times, the brand actually bought is different from the one planned, because of stock-outs or new information at the time of purchase. In the postpurchase evaluation phase, the processes of decision confirmation, satisfaction/dissatisfaction, exit, complaining, and loyalty responses take place.

- In addition to making purchase decisions as individuals, consumers often make purchase decisions as members of households. These household decisions are complex because the user, payer, and buyer roles are often distributed among different household members. The family buying process is one in which different members of the family influence various stages of the decision process. Children influence parental choices of products that they use as well as those used only by parents.

KEY TERMS

Alternative evaluation is the stage in the consumer decision process when consumers select one of the several alternatives (brands, dealers, and so on) available to them.

Attitudes are learned predispositions to respond to an object or class of objects in a consistently favorable or unfavorable way.

Buyers are the consumers who actually purchase the product.

Consumer behavior is the process by which individuals or groups select, use, or dispose of goods, services, ideas, or experiences to satisfy needs and wants.

Consumer decision making is a process that typically involves whether to purchase, what to purchase, when to purchase, from whom to purchase, and how to pay for a purchase.

Emotions are strong, relatively uncontrolled feelings that affect our behavior.

Household decision making occurs when significant decisions are made by individuals jointly with other members of their household, and for joint use by the members of the household.

Information search is the stage in the consumer decision process when consumers collect information on only a select subset of brands.

Involvement is the degree of personal relevance of a product to a consumer.

Learning is a change in the content of long-term memory. As consumers, we learn to adapt better to our environment.

Maslow's hierarchy of needs is a classification scheme of needs satisfaction where higher level needs are dormant until lower level needs are satisfied.

Moods are emotions that are less intense and transitory.

Motivation is the state of drive or arousal that moves us toward a goal-object.

Needs are unsatisfactory conditions of the consumer that prompt them to an action that will make the condition better.

Payers are the consumers who actually pay for the product.

Perception is the process by which an individual senses, organizes, and interprets information received from the environment.

Postpurchase behavior is the last stage in the consumer decision process, when the consumer experiences an intense need to confirm the wisdom of that decision.

Problem recognition is a consumer's realization that he or she needs to buy something to get back to a normal state of comfort.

Psychographics are characteristics of individuals that describe them in terms of their psychological and behavioral makeup.

Purchase is the stage in the consumer decision process when transaction terms are arranged, title of ownership is transferred, the product is paid for, and the consumer takes possession of the product from the seller.

Self-concept refers to a person's self-image.

Users are the consumers who actually use the product.

VALS™ is a psychographic profiling scheme developed by SRI Consulting Business Intelligence.

Values are end-states or goals one lives for.

Wants are desires to obtain more satisfaction than is absolutely necessary to improve an unsatisfactory condition.

QUESTIONS FOR DISCUSSION

1. How do needs differ from wants? Are needs internally realized or can others (marketers) make us realize our needs?

2. What is Maslow's hierarchy of needs and how is it helpful to marketers?

3. What is VALS? What are the eight categories of people represented in VALS 2? Which of these profiles do you fit? Why?

4. What are the different sources of information that a consumer uses to make a purchase decision? Which of these is more important as a source of information? How do they differ from each other?

5. Describe compensatory and noncompensatory choice models. Give examples of each type.

6. Contrast individual consumer decision making and family buying decisions.

7. How can conflicts that arise from family buying decisions be resolved?

8. Marketers are often criticized for targeting children with their advertisements. Why do you think marketers like to target this segment?

9. If Howard buys groceries for his apartment that he shares with Bob, another student, would that be household buying or individual buying behavior? Why?

INTERNET QUESTIONS

1. Select a product that you are likely to buy in the near future. Go to Google (http://www.google.com) and search for the product. Visit three Web sites that carry information about this product. For each of the three sites, answer the following questions:
   a. How useful is the site for the information search stage of the decision making?
   b. Is the site useful for the evaluation of alternatives stage of the decision making?
   c. Does the site allow you to purchase the product?
   d. Is this site promoting the product category or promoting a specific brand?

2. In 1978, the research and consulting firm SRI Consulting Business Intelligence developed a psychographic segmentation system called VALS, which stands for values and lifestyles.
   a. Go to SRI's home page (http://www.sric-bi.com) and link to the VALS 2 survey.
   b. Complete the survey on this page to place yourself in a VALS segment.
   c. Do you agree with the results? Why or why not? What values and lifestyle issues are dominant for you as a consumer?
   d. How do companies use the VALS information to infer consumer behavior?

ENDNOTES

[1] This section is adapted from: Mike Norton, "These Kids Perfected Art of Collecting Early," *Marketing News*, 11 September 2000.

[2] Richard P. Bagozzi, Mahaesh Gopinath, and Prashant U. Nyer, "The Role of Emotions in Marketing," *Journal of the Academy of Marketing Science* 27 (Spring 1999): 184–206.

[3] Rajeev Batra and Douglas M. Stayman, "The Role of Mood in Advertising Effectiveness," *Journal of Consumer Research* 17, no. 2 (September 1990): 203–214.

[4] Lynn R. Kahle, Sharon E. Beatty, and Pamela Homer, "Alternative Measurement Approaches to Consumer Values: The List of Values (LOV) and Values and Lifestyle (VALS)," *Journal of Consumer Research* 13 (December 1986): 405–409.

[5] VALS description on the Internet, SRI Consulting Business Intelligence Web site, at http://www.sric-bi.com/VALS, accessed 24 April 2002.

[6] Gordon W. Allport, "Attitudes," in *A Handbook of Social Psychology*, ed. C. A. Muchinson (Worcester, MA: Clark University Press, 1935), 798–844.

[7] Hillel J. Einhorn, "Use of Nonlinear, Noncompensatory Models in Decision Making," *Psychological Bulletin* 73 (1970): 221–230.

[8] Based on U.S. government census estimates, obtained from the U.S. Census Bureau Web site, http://www.census.gov/main/www/cen2000.html, accessed 24 April 2002.

[9] Jagdish N. Sheth, "Models of Buyer Behavior: Conceptual, Quantitative, and Empirical," in *A Theory of Family Buying Decisions* (New York: Harper & Row, 1974), 17–33.

[10] Lisa Bertagnoli, "Continental Spendthrifts," *Marketing News*, 22 October 2001, 1.

TEACHING KIDS TO CHARGE

It seems like something an eighth-grader would dream up. An entrepreneur decides to tap the teenybopper market for financial services. He offers so-called "buying cards" to people as young as 13, calls the product Cobalt Card, with the tagline, "My money, my life, my card."

Randall M. Chesler, the 41-year-old president and chief executive officer of Cobalt Card, says the product's main goal is to "empower" this age group by enabling them to make their own spending choices. Chesler says Cobalt Card was not meant to ride on the tails of American Express's Blue Card, but that cobalt "is a base element that reflects power and passion," noting that the idea of an "explosion" comes to mind.

Offered on http://www.cobaltcard.com, children are told the product is "free to get, free to use, and free of debt." Also, there are no interest charges or fees. Unlike other new shopping schemes for children, Cobalt Card can be used in physical locations where Visa is accepted, as well as in cyberspace. In effect, it is a debit card, with funds drawn from the youngster's account immediately when the card is used.

Chesler says people 13 to 22 years old annually spend $150 billion, or between $3,000 and $4,500 each. Online purchases represent only 5 percent of the total. He declined to say how many cards he expects to issue, but added that "it's an untapped market, and it should be good business."

Cobalt Card expects to make money from commissions and interchange fees. Some credit card experts, however, predict that the product cannot be profitable on its own. Clearly, others disagree. Cobalt Card has raised more than $20 million in equity, according to Chesler. Among the investors are the National Broadcasting Company, Crosspoint Venture Partners, and Media Tech Ventures.

Discussion Questions

1. Do you think it is a good idea to target 13-year-olds with the Cobalt Card?

2. Do you think 13-year-olds will be interested in such a product offering? Will this idea succeed?

3. Do you think children under 13 years of age may be interested in such products? Will they be able to make judicious use of this card?

4. Can this concept be used to teach children to be responsible shoppers?

CHAPTER CASE

CHAPTER six

Michael D. Hutt,
Arizona State University

Michael D. Hutt (Ph.D., Michigan State University) is the Ford Motor Company Professor of Marketing at Arizona State University. He has also held faculty positions at Miami University (Ohio) and the University of Vermont.

Dr. Hutt's teaching and research interests are concentrated in the areas of business-to-business marketing and strategic marketing. His current research centers on the cross-functional role that marketing managers assume in the formation of strategy. Dr. Hutt's research has been published in the *Journal of Marketing, Journal of Marketing Research, Sloan Management Review, Journal of Retailing, Journal of the Academy of Marketing Science,* and other scholarly journals. He is the coauthor of *Business Marketing Management* (South-Western), now in its seventh edition, and of *Macro Marketing* (John Wiley & Sons).

Thomas W. Speh,
Miami University, Ohio

Thomas W. Speh is the James E. Rees Distinguished Professor of Marketing and Director of the Warehousing Research Center, Miami University, Ohio.

Dr. Speh earned his Ph.D. from Michigan State University. He is the recipient of several awards, including the Beta Gamma Sigma Distinguished Faculty award from Miami University's School of Business and the Effective Educator award from the Miami University Alumni Association. He is the past president of the Warehousing Education and Research Council and also the past president of the Council of Logistics Management.

Prior to his tenure at Miami University, Dr. Speh taught at the University of Alabama and Michigan State University. He is the coauthor of *Business Marketing Management* (South-Western), now in its seventh edition.

Business-to-Business Marketing

Cisco Systems Inc. provides the networking solutions that are the foundation of the Internet and of most corporate, education, and government networks on a global scale. Today, the Internet and computer networking are a fundamental part of business, education, personal communications, and entertainment. Virtually all messages or transactions passing over the Internet are carried efficiently and securely through Cisco equipment. Cisco provides the hardware and software solutions for transporting data, voice, and video within buildings, across campuses, or around the world.

Rather than serving individuals or household consumers, Cisco is a leading-edge business-to-business firm that markets its goods and services to organizations: commercial enterprises (e.g., corporations and telecommunications firms), governmental units, and institutions (e.g., universities and health care organizations). Marketing managers at Cisco give special attention to transforming complex technology goods and services into concrete solutions to meet customer requirements. For example, when Guess? Inc., the casual apparel retailer, wanted to launch a major Internet initiative to meet its aggressive sales goals, the firm turned to Cisco. The sales team from Cisco described how an efficient Internet strategy could be used to improve the way the company interacts with employees, suppliers, and customers. Paul Marciano, co-CEO of Guess?, observed: "Cisco made it easy for Guess?, a nontechnology business, to understand, absorb, and take on an Internet strategy. We walked out of the meeting believing it was something we could do."[1] Working with Cisco, the firm launched several e-commerce initiatives, including Guess?.com, a Web site that offers online shopping

After you have completed this chapter, you should be able to:

1. Understand the major types of customers that comprise the business market.
2. Understand the basic similarities and differences between household consumer and business-to-business markets, and the importance of close buyer-seller relationships in the business market.
3. Explain the decision process that organizational buyers apply as they confront different buying situations and explain how organizational buyers evaluate the performance of business marketers.
4. Understand the environmental, organizational, group, and individual factors that influence the buying decisions of organizations.

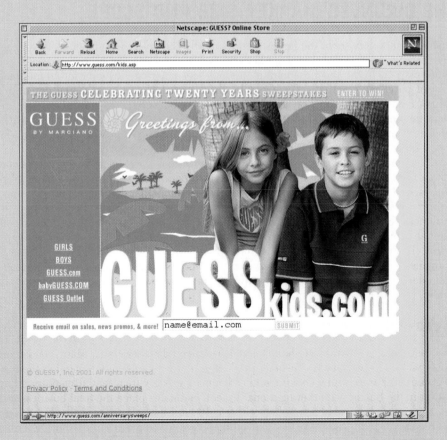

(Continued)

and a powerful way to offer new items quickly and easily to a market that eagerly pursues the latest trends in apparel.

In serving customers like Guess?, business marketers like Cisco attempt to define the customer's needs and goals, identify key buying influentials within the organization, and deliver a solution that responds to those requirements. Rather than an immediate sale, business marketers attempt to build long-term relationships with customers by delivering on their promises and responding to the customer's changing requirements over time.

Because business marketers like Cisco serve fewer but far larger customers than consumer product marketers (e.g., Coca-Cola), special attention must be given to monitoring customer satisfaction at important customer accounts. For example, John Chambers, Cisco's CEO, reviews the status of 15 to 20 of the firm's top customers each evening. To demonstrate the importance of putting the "customer first" throughout the organization, all employees at Cisco are rated and given bonuses based, in part, on customer satisfaction.[2] Moreover, every major initiative at the company is developed hand in hand with leading customers. For example, based on extensive customer feedback, Cisco developed and continuously refines its Web site to make it easier for customers to secure technical information, troubleshoot problems, receive extensive training, or order products. As a result, over 80 percent of Cisco's sales are now booked via the Internet.

This chapter explores the unique characteristics of the business market and the special opportunities and challenges that it presents for marketers. What are the different types of customers that comprise the business market? What are the distinguishing features of business markets? What types of buying decisions do business (organizational) buyers make? Who participates in the buying process? What factors influence the buying behavior of organizations?

THE BUSINESS MARKET: SIZE AND SCOPE

http://www.gm.com

Business market
consists of all organizations that buy goods and services for use in the production of other goods and services or for resale.

Business marketers serve the largest market of all: The dollar volume of goods and services purchased in the business market significantly exceeds that of the household consumer market. In the business market, a single customer can account for an enormous level of purchasing activity. For example, the General Motors purchasing department spends more than $85 billion annually on goods and services—more than the gross domestic product for countries such as Ireland and Greece.[3] Indeed, the business market consists of millions of organizations—large or small, public or private, profit or not-for-profit—that collectively buy trillions of dollars of goods and services.

The **business market** consists of all organizations that buy goods for use as component parts for the production of other goods, as operational supplies (e.g., paper clips, pencils, and janitorial supplies), or for resale. The factors that distinguish business marketing from household consumer marketing are the nature of the customer and how that customer uses the product. In business marketing, the customers are organizations: commercial enterprises, governments, and institutions (see Table 6.1). Commercial enterprises (businesses) buy products to form or facilitate the production process or as components for other goods and services. Government agencies and institutions (for example, hospitals) buy goods to maintain and deliver services to their own market: the public.

Types of Customers: An Illustration

The vast business market is characterized by tremendous diversity. Many goods commonly viewed as household consumer products generate significant demand in the business market. For example, cooking oil is a common grocery item that also enjoys a huge market in the business marketing arena. In fact, estimates place the total business market usage of cooking oil at somewhere close to 400 million gallons annually. Firms, such as Procter & Gamble that have established brands of cooking oil displayed on supermarket shelves for final consumers also serve the business market. Why?

http://www.pg.com

Selected Types of Organizational Buyers			Table 6.1
Commercial Customers	**Institutional Customers**	**Governmental Customers**	
Manufacturers	Schools, colleges, universities	Federal government General Services Administration Defense Supply Agency	
Construction companies	Health care organizations		
Service firms	Libraries	State government	
Transportation companies	Foundations	Local government Counties Townships	
	Art galleries		
Selected professional groups	Clinics		
Wholesalers			
Retailers			

Commercial Customers

Cooking oil is bought by *commercial firms*—manufacturers of food products (frozen foods, breaded fish, etc.), fast-food restaurant chains, airline meal preparation contractors, hotel restaurant operators, and business firms that furnish food for their employees. Collectively, these diverse commercial customers represent a huge opportunity for a firm like Procter & Gamble.

Institutional Customers

Other buyers of cooking oil include *institutions*—schools, hospitals, and universities. Educational institutions, including schools, colleges and universities, sell more than $17 billion of food annually, and health care institutions exceed $23 billion in annual food sales. Represented here are customers such as the University of Texas and the New York City school district that run sizable food service operations.

Governments and International Customers

Governments—federal, state, and local—are also significant customers for products such as cooking oil. For example, the U.S. Army is the single largest food service organization in the world, and various officer and noncommissioned officer clubs serve nearly $1 billion in food each year. Beyond the borders of the United States, international customers, such as food manufacturers, restaurant chains, and health care units, also represent a sizable market. The magnitude of the food service market and its importance to manufacturers of cooking oil is illustrated by its annual sales volume: over $300 billion.[4]

Organizational Buyers Have Diverse Requirements

Requirements for product quality are as diverse as the types of buyers in the food service market. For a small, elegant restaurant, how long the cooking oil lasts and its effect on the taste of the food will be critical factors, so the highest quality oil will be purchased. A school district will be responsive to cost and concentrate on finding the lowest priced oil. The Marriott Corporation, which operates a major in-flight meal preparation business for

http://www.hostmarriott.com

the airlines, will pay close attention to product availability (i.e., the reliability of delivery service) as well as the cost and quality. Each of the three types of business market customers—commercial firms, institutions, and governments—have unique characteristics and special needs that must be understood by the business marketer.

Commercial Enterprises as Customers

Commercial enterprises include manufacturers, construction companies, service firms (e.g., hotels), transportation companies (e.g., the airlines), selected professional groups (e.g., dentists), and resellers. *Resellers* include wholesalers and retailers. *Wholesalers* are businesses that purchase products to sell to organizational users and retailers. In turn, *retailers* are businesses that sell to household consumers. A detailed discussion of wholesalers and retailers is provided in Chapter 11.

A Concentration of Customers

Manufacturers are the most important commercial customers, spending more than $1.5 trillion on materials each year. A startling fact about manufacturers is that there are so few of them. There are approximately 360,000 manufacturing firms in the United States. And although only 10 percent of these manufacturers employ more than 100 workers each, this handful of firms ships more than 75 percent of all products manufactured in the United States.[5] Because of this concentration, the business marketer normally serves *far fewer but far larger* customers than a consumer-product marketer. For example, Intel sells microprocessors to a few manufacturers, such as Dell and Compaq, who, in turn, target millions of potential computer buyers. In addition to concentration by size, business markets are geographically concentrated. More than half of the manufacturers are concentrated in eight states: California, New York, Ohio, Illinois, Michigan, Texas, Pennsylvania, and New Jersey.

Significant Buying Power

Every firm, regardless of its organizational characteristics, must procure the materials, supplies, equipment, and services necessary to operate the business successfully. On average, more than half of every dollar earned from sales of manufactured products is

Commercial enterprises are the sector of the business market represented by manufacturers, construction companies, service firms, transportation companies, professional groups, and resellers that purchase goods and services.

http://www.dell.com

http://www.compaq.com

spent on materials, supplies, and equipment needed to produce the goods. The 250 largest industrial firms (from a purchasing standpoint) annually spend over $1.5 trillion on a wide array of goods and services.[6] The magnitude of expenditures by large corporations is staggering—in one year, Chrysler spent $2.1 billion on car seats alone, Intel doled out $960 million on production equipment, and Black & Decker spent $100 million on batteries.[7] When a customer buys a $24,000 sports utility vehicle from Ford, the automaker has already spent more than $12,000 to buy steel, paint, glass, fabric, aluminum, and electrical components to build that product.

http://www.blackanddecker.com

http://www.ford.com

The Purchasing Function

Rarely do individual departments within a corporation do their own buying. Procurement is usually administered by an individual whose title is manager of purchasing or director of purchasing. The purchasing manager is responsible for administering the purchasing process and managing relationships with suppliers. The day-to-day purchasing function is carried out by buyers, each of whom is responsible for a specific group of products (e.g., personal computers or office supplies). Organizing the purchasing function in this way permits buyers to acquire a high level of expertise on a limited number of items. The salesperson works closely with buyers and develops relationships with personnel from other departments who may influence purchase decisions.

e-Procurement. Like consumers who are shopping at Amazon.com, purchasing managers use the Internet to find new suppliers, communicate with current suppliers, or place an order. (See Chapter 15 for expanded treatment of e-commerce strategies.) The Boston Consulting Group projects business-to-business online purchasing will reach $4.8 trillion, or about 40 percent of total purchasing by 2004.[8] While providing a rich base of information, purchasing over the Internet is also very efficient: It is estimated that purchase orders processed over the Internet cost only $5, compared to the current average purchase order cost of $100. For example, IBM has moved all of its purchasing to the Web and has created a "private exchange" that links together its suppliers. A private exchange allows a company, such as IBM, to automate their purchases and collaborate in real time with a specially invited group of suppliers.[9] By handling nearly all its invoices electronically (some 400,000 e-invoices a month), IBM saves nearly $400 million per year using its more efficient Web purchasing strategy.

http://www.ibm.com

John Patterson, IBM's chief procurement officer, sees the Internet as a strategic tool that can be used to build closer relationships with important suppliers:

> *I believe that the Web creates the platform upon which strategic relationships can be built. It takes a lot of effort and energy to have meaningful strategic relationships with suppliers 12,000 miles away. But with the Web, you can have your engineers get together with supplier's engineers, you can have video-conferencing sessions, data exchanges, and engineering drawing exchanges. I don't think there is any future without the Web relationship with suppliers.*[10]

Purchasing managers are also using the Internet to conduct online reverse auctions. Rather than one seller and many buyers, a **reverse auction** involves one buyer who invites bids from several prequalified suppliers. For example, FreeMarkets Inc. offers an independently run auction site that enables buyers of industrial parts, raw materials, and services to find and screen suppliers and to negotiate with those suppliers through a dynamic, real-time competitive bidding process. To illustrate, Cooper Industries, a worldwide producer of electrical tools and hardware, recently used the site to solicit bids for its air freight service requirements.[11] During the event, 11 suppliers placed more than 50 bids, and the winning bid provided Cooper with cost savings of 26 percent. Reverse auctions are best suited for commodity-type items such as packaging materials, diesel fuel, metal parts, and motor freight.

A reverse auction involves one buyer who invites bids from several prequalified suppliers.

http://www.freemarkets.com

Governmental Units as Customers

Federal (1), state (50), and local (87,000) **governmental units** generate the greatest volume of purchases of any customer category in the United States. Collectively, these units spend over $1.3 trillion in goods and services each year—the federal government

Governmental units comprise the sector of the business market represented by federal, state, and local governmental units that purchase goods and services.

accounts for \$500 billion, and states and local government contribute the rest.[12] Governmental units purchase from virtually every category of goods and services—office supplies, personal computers, furniture, food, health care, and military equipment. Business marketing firms, large and small, serve the government market. In fact, 25 percent of the purchase contracts at the federal level are with small firms.[13]

Government Buying

The government uses two general purchasing strategies: formal advertising (also known as open bid) or negotiated contract. *Formal advertising* means the government will solicit bids from appropriate suppliers. This strategy is followed when the product is standardized and the specifications are straightforward (e.g., 20-pound bond paper or a personal computer with certain defined characteristics). Contracts are generally awarded to the lowest bidder; however, the government agency may select the next-to-lowest bidder if it can document that the lowest bidder would not responsibly fulfill the contract. Following the lead of the private sector, government buyers are using online reverse auctions in purchasing a range of products. For example, the Internal Revenue Service (IRS) held a reverse auction for 11,000 desktop PCs and 16,000 notebook PCs. The prebid pricing started at \$130 million; when the auction closed, the price was down to \$63.4 million.[14]

Negotiated Contract

A *negotiated contract* is used by the government to purchase goods and services that cannot be differentiated on the basis of price alone (such as complex scientific equipment or R&D projects) or when there are few potential suppliers. There may be some competition because the contracting office can conduct negotiations with competing suppliers simultaneously. The purchasing decision for the government is much like that of the large corporation. Which is the best possible product at the lowest price, and will the product meet performance expectations?

For example, Lockheed Martin Corporation emerged as the winner in a five-year battle with Boeing Company to manufacture the Joint Strike Fighter, an agile radar-evading aircraft intended as the standard fighter for the U.S. Air Force.[15] The competition included a flyoff where each of the firms demonstrated the performance of its plane. After the contest, the Pentagon conducted a thorough analysis of cost and performance data before picking Lockheed as the prime contractor for this lucrative contract—a project expected to total more than \$200 billion and involve the production of 3,000 fighters over the next four decades. (See Figure 6.1.)

Institutions as Customers

Institutional customers comprise the third sector of the business market. Institutional buyers make up a sizable market—total expenditures on public elementary and secondary schools alone exceed \$400 billion, and national health expenditures exceed \$850 billion.[16] Schools and health care organizations make up a sizable component of the institutional market, which also includes colleges and universities, libraries, foundations, art galleries, and clinics. On one hand, institutional purchasers are similar to governments in that the purchasing process is often constrained by political considerations and dictated by law. In fact, many institutions are administered by government units— schools, for example. On the other hand, other institutions are privately operated and managed like corporations; they may even have a broader range of purchase requirements than their large corporate counterparts. Like the commercial enterprise, institutions are ever cognizant of the value of efficient buying and are adopting sophisticated approaches to purchasing, such as e-procurement.

Institutional Buying

Many institutions are staffed with professionals—doctors, professors, researchers, and others. In most cases, depending on size, the institution will employ a purchasing agent and, in large institutions, a sizable purchasing department. Business marketing and sales personnel, in formulating their marketing and personal selling approaches, must understand the needs of the full range of participants in the buying process. Often, the salesperson must carefully cultivate the professional staff in terms of product benefits and service while developing a delivery timetable, maintenance contract, and price schedule to sat-

| Lockheed Martin Corporation's Joint Strike Fighter | Figure 6.1 |

isfy the purchasing department. Leading business marketers also use the Internet to provide added value to their customers. For example, General Electric Medical Systems has embraced the Internet as the centerpiece of its marketing strategy and provides an online catalog, daily Internet specials, and a host of services for its customers—purchasing managers at hospitals and health care facilities worldwide. (See Figure 6.2.)

http://www.gemedicalsystems.com

An important factor in institutional buying is group purchasing. Hospitals, schools, and universities may join cooperative purchasing associations to secure purchasing efficiencies. Group buying allows institutions to enjoy lower prices, improved quality (through improved testing and supplier selection), reduced administrative costs, and greater competition. Moreover, for-profit hospital chains, which are a growing force in health care, can achieve many of these economies by consolidating purchases through a centralized purchasing function. In addition to responding to the needs of individual institutions, the business marketer must be prepared to meet the special requirements of cooperative purchasing groups and large hospital chains.

International Customers

A complete picture of the business market must include a horizon that stretches beyond the boundaries of the United States. As introduced in Chapter 3, the demand for many industrial goods and services is growing more rapidly in many foreign countries than in the United States. Countries like Germany, Japan, Korea, and Brazil offer large and growing markets for many business marketers. Countless small firms and many large ones—such as General Electric (GE), 3M, Intel, Boeing, Dow Chemical, and Motorola—derive a significant portion of their sales and profits from international markets. For example,

http://www.motorola.com

| Figure 6.2 | GE Medical Systems |

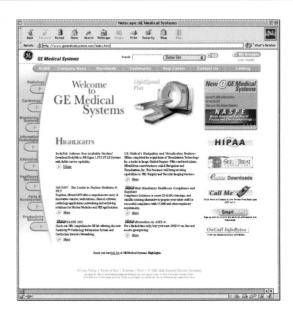

Motorola is helping China leapfrog one stage of industrial evolution for which Western nations have invested billions of dollars—the need to tie every home and business together with copper wire. Motorola's pagers and cell phones provide valuable solutions to customers in an unwired world, and the firm's sales in China and Hong Kong exceed $3 billion annually.[17] Going forward, the market potential is huge, but the competition will be fierce from rivals such as Finland's Nokia and Sweden's Ericsson.

Different Buying Procedures

The process of purchasing, including the formal procedures, negotiations, and personnel, may show marked differences from one country to another. To illustrate, decision making is often a slow and deliberate group process in many Asian countries. Frequently, these buyers will go to extraordinary lengths to avoid individual action on any decision and will work to achieve a group consensus. In this type of decision-making climate, patience and a low-pressure selling approach are the keys to success. Although similarities exist in the business marketing process across countries, the marketing strategy must be targeted to the culture, product usage, and buying procedures of the international buyers. However, when customers in different countries around the world want essentially the same type of product or service, the opportunity exists to market a global good or brand. Some research suggests that, compared to consumer goods, industrial and high-technology products (e.g., computers) may be more appropriate for global brand strategies.[18]

Classifying Business Customers

Marketers can gain valuable strategy insights by identifying the needs and requirements of different types of commercial enterprises or business customers. The *North American Industrial Classification System (NAICS)* organizes business activity into meaningful economic sectors and identifies groups of business firms that use similar production processes.[19] The NAICS is a result of the North American Free Trade Agreement (NAFTA); it provides for standardization among Canada, Mexico, and the United States in the way that economic data are reported. Every plant or business establishment is assigned a code that reflects the primary product produced at that location. The new system, which includes traditional industries while incorporating new and emerging technology industries, replaces the Standard Industrial Classification (SIC) system that was used for decades.

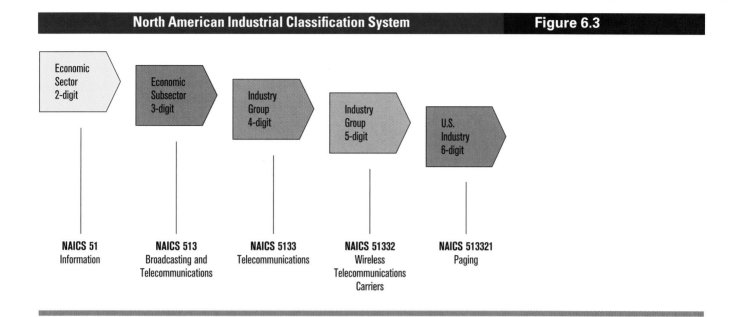

North American Industrial Classification System — **Figure 6.3**

Economic Sector 2-digit → Economic Subsector 3-digit → Industry Group 4-digit → Industry Group 5-digit → U.S. Industry 6-digit

NAICS 51 Information

NAICS 513 Broadcasting and Telecommunications

NAICS 5133 Telecommunications

NAICS 51332 Wireless Telecommunications Carriers

NAICS 513321 Paging

Figure 6.3 illustrates the building blocks of the system. Observe that the first two digits identify the economic sector and as more digits are added, the classification becomes finer. For example, all business establishments that create, disseminate, or provide the means to distribute information are included in the Information sector: NAICS Code 51. Nineteen other economic sectors are included in the system. More specifically, U.S. establishments that produce paging equipment are assigned an NAICS Code of 513321. The six-digit codes are customized for industry subdivisions in individual countries, but at the five-digit level they are standardized across the three countries.

Using the Classification System

If a manager understands the needs and requirements of a few firms within a classification category, requirements can be projected for others that share that category. Each group should be relatively homogeneous in terms of raw materials required, component parts used, and manufacturing processes employed. The NAICS provides a valuable tool for identifying new customers and for targeting profitable segments of business buyers.

CHARACTERISTICS OF BUSINESS MARKETS

LEARNING OBJECTIVE 2

The basic task of management cuts across both household consumer marketing and business marketing. Marketers serving both sectors succeed by implementing the strategic marketing concept—understanding the needs of customers and by satisfying those needs more effectively than competitors. However, business markets differ from consumer markets in several ways. See Table 6.2 for examples of the distinguishing characteristics of business market customers.

Demand Issues

Derived Demand

Derived demand refers to the direct link between the demand for an industrial product and the demand for consumer products: *The demand for industrial products is derived from the ultimate demand for consumer products.* Consider the materials and components that are used in a Harley-Davidson motorcycle. Some of the components are manufactured by Harley-Davidson, but the finished product reflects the efforts of over 200 suppliers or business marketers who deal directly with the firm. In purchasing a Harley-Davidson motorcycle, the customer is stimulating the demand for a diverse array of

Table 6.2	Characteristics of Business Market Customers
Characteristic	**Example**
• Business market customers are comprised of commercial enterprises, institutions, and governments	• Among Dell's customers are Boeing, Arizona State University, and numerous state and local government units
• A single purchase by a business customer is far larger than that of an individual consumer	• An individual may buy one unit of a software package upgrade from Microsoft, while Citigroup purchases 10,000
• Business market customers in some industries tend to be geographically concentrated	• Auto manufacturing in the United States is largely concentrated in Michigan, Ohio, and California
• Relationships between business marketers tend to be close and enduring	• IBM's relationships with some key customers span decades
• Business market customers are using the Internet to advance purchasing efficiency and effectiveness	• Purchasing managers are using the Internet to search for suppliers, conduct auctions, and communicate with suppliers
• While serving different types of customers, business marketers and consumer-goods marketers share the same job titles	• Job titles: marketing manager, product manager, sales manager, account manager

products manufactured by business marketing firms, such as tires, electrical components, coil springs, aluminum castings, and other items.

Fluctuating Demand

Because demand is derived, the business marketer must carefully monitor demand patterns and changing buying preferences in the household consumer market, often on a worldwide basis. For example, a decline in mortgage rates can spark an increase in new home construction and a corresponding increase in appliance sales. Retailers generally respond by increasing their stock of inventory. As appliance producers, such as Maytag, increase the rate of production to meet the demand, business marketers that supply these manufacturers with items such as motors, timers, and paint experience a surge in

sales. A downturn in the economy creates the opposite result. This explains why the demand for many industrial products tends to fluctuate more than the demand for consumer products.

Stimulating Demand

Some business marketers must not only monitor final consumer markets but also develop a marketing program that reaches the ultimate consumer directly. Aluminum producers use television and magazine ads to point out the convenience and recycling opportunities that aluminum containers offer to the consumer—the ultimate consumer influences aluminum demand by purchasing soft drinks in aluminum, rather than plastic, containers. Over four billion pounds of aluminum are used annually in the production of beverage containers. Since the events of September 2001, Boeing has promoted improved airport security and the convenience of air travel in a media campaign targeted to the consumer market to create a more favorable environment for longer-term demand for its planes. Similarly, DuPont advertises to ultimate consumers to stimulate the sales of carpeting, which incorporates its product.

Close Buyer-Seller Relationships

Relationships in the business market are often close and enduring. Rather than providing the end result, a sale in the business market signals the beginning of a relationship. By convincing a chain of sporting goods stores to use its computers, IBM initiates a potential long-term business relationship. More than ringing up a sale, IBM creates a customer. To maintain that relationship, the business marketer must develop an intimate knowledge of the customer's operations and contribute unique value to the customer's business.

Relationship Marketing

Relationship marketing centers on all marketing activities directed toward establishing, developing, and maintaining successful exchanges with customers.[20] Managing customer relationships is the heart of business marketing and an important strategy priority in most firms. Why? First, loyal customers are far more profitable to keep than those customers who are price sensitive and perceive little difference among competing offerings. Second, a firm that is successful in developing strong relationships with customers secures important and durable advantages that are hard for competitors to understand, copy, or displace.[21]

The search for improved quality and superior performance have spawned a significant shift in the purchasing practices of automakers such as Ford and Honda, as well as those of other leading-edge firms like Cisco Systems and Hewlett-Packard. To develop profitable relationships with business customers, business marketers must be attuned to these changes. Rather than relying on competitive bidding and dealing at arm's length with a large number of suppliers, a new approach to purchasing has been adopted in many industries. This approach is characterized by:

http://www.hp.com

- Longer-term and closer relationships with fewer suppliers (e.g., over the past decade, the numbers of suppliers used by Harley-Davidson, Xerox, and Ford have been reduced by 60 percent or more).
- Closer interactions among multiple functions—manufacturing, engineering, and logistics, as well as sales and purchasing—on both the buying and selling sides (e.g., through computer links with its suppliers, Intel can change specifications and delivery schedules).[22]

IBM spends 85 percent of its vast purchasing budget with just 50 suppliers.[23] Of particular importance to IBM is the quality of engineering support that it receives from suppliers. IBM actively seeks supplier partners that will contribute fresh ideas and leading-edge technologies to attract buyers of future IBM products. Long-term relationships are built on trust and demonstrated performance. Such relationships require open lines of communication between multiple layers of the buying and selling organizations. Long-term relationships also require delivering on promises. One purchasing executive observed that once a supplier is selected, "that supplier will have the business forever" as long as quality,

Careers in Marketing

Delivering Service Solutions to IBM Customers

After receiving a B.S. degree in business management from the University of Maryland, John R. Roope III began his career at IBM, working in field engineering. He then served in several management positions, becoming a national account customer executive, branch manager, and director of customer satisfaction. Following this leadership track, John is now vice president of IBM Global Services—Integrated Technology Services (ITS) for the Midwest. John is responsible for sales, service delivery, and customer satisfaction for the diverse business market customers that make up this region. The people to whom John reports include a sales executive, a service support manager, and service executives. His team is responsible for advancing IBM's services growth and customer loyalty in this region.

John observes that "successful customer relationships are forged by connecting real technical solutions to the needs and requirements of a particular customer's business." To that end, John's team is organized around five industry sectors: distribution, financial, industrial, public/government, and small-medium businesses. "A sector leader and a set of account principals give dedi-

cated attention to each segment and pursue this mission: build customer relationships, consult, continue to sell the entire ITS portfolio, and increase customer satisfaction with those delivered services."

IBM is embracing industry specialization to secure a deeper understanding of the customer's business. For example, supply-chain solutions for an industrial customer differ from those for a retailer. Deep industry and customer knowledge coupled with a rich understanding of IBM's services portfolio allow account managers to craft tailored customer solutions and build long-term relationships. By building this base of knowledge and a broad skill set, John asserts that "we become a strategy partner by using our technical solutions to directly advance the mission and goals of our customer. In delivering these service solutions, we are working not only with Information Technology specialists on the customer side, but also with the key strategists who are shaping the future of the customer organization."

Many business school students feel that you need a technical degree to succeed at IBM. "That's a myth," according to John. His successful career at IBM speaks for itself and proves his point.

Source: Interview with John R. Roope III, 18 February 2002.

---

cost, technology, and delivery requirements are met.[24] Because relationship management skills reside in people rather than in organizational structures or roles, marketing managers with these skills will become valuable assets to the organization.[25]

Supply-Chain Management

Figure 6.4 further illuminates the importance of a relationship perspective in business marketing by considering the chain of suppliers involved in the creation of an automobile. Consider Honda and Ford. At its Marysville, Ohio, auto assembly plant, Honda spends more than $5 billion annually for materials and components from some 300 North American suppliers.[26] These expenditures by the 300-member purchasing staff at Honda of America represent 80 percent of the firm's annual sales. Similarly, Ford relies on a vast supplier network, including firms such as TRW and Johnson Controls, to contribute half of the more than 10,000 parts of a typical Ford car. The relationships between these auto producers and their suppliers fall squarely into the business marketing domain. Similarly, business marketers such as TRW rely on a whole host of others farther back on the supply chain for raw materials, components, and other support. Each organization in this chain is involved in the creation of a product, marketing processes (including delivery), and support and service after the sale. In performing these value-creating activities, each also affects the quality level of the Honda Accord or Ford Explorer.

Supply-chain management
is a technique for linking a manufacturer's operations with those of all of its strategic suppliers and its key intermediaries and customers to enhance efficiency and effectiveness.

Supply-chain management is a technique for linking a manufacturer's operations with those of all of its strategic suppliers and its key intermediaries and customers to enhance efficiency and effectiveness. The Internet allows members of the supply chain all over the world to exchange timely information, exchange engineering drawings during new product development, and synchronize production and delivery schedules (see Fig-

The Supply Chain   Figure 6.4

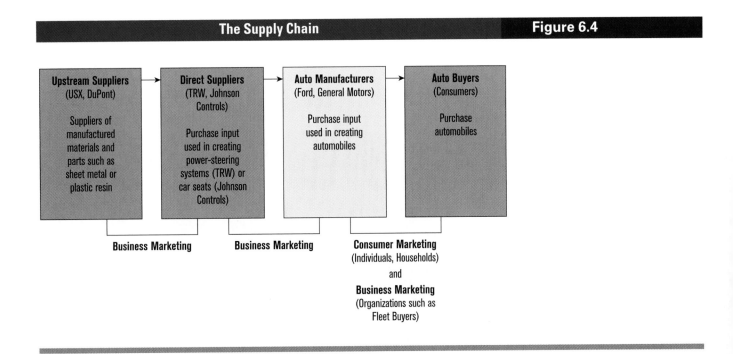

ure 6.5). A buyer, like Honda, following a supply-chain management strategy, will reach several tiers back in the supply chain to assist second-, third-, and fourth-tier suppliers in meeting cost, quality, and delivery requirements. The goal of a supply-chain strategy is to improve the speed, precision, and efficiency of manufacturing and delivery through strong supplier relationships.[27] This goal is achieved through information sharing, joint planning, shared technology, and shared benefits. If the business marketer can become a valued partner in a customer's supply chain, the rewards are substantial: a long-term profitable relationship in which the supplier is viewed as an extension of the customer's company. To achieve these results, the business marketer must demonstrate the ability to meet the precise quality, delivery, service, and information requirements of the customer.

Just-in-Time Systems

A strategy of purchasing, production, and inventory practiced in many manufacturing firms is referred to as *just-in-time* or *JIT*. The essence of the concept is to deliver defect-free parts and materials to the production process just at the moment they are needed. Consider Dell Computer Corporation's JIT system.[28] Most of Dell's suppliers have warehouses near the firm's manufacturing plants. When Dell receives an order for a personal computer, it transmits the requirements to suppliers, who pick the proper parts and pack them in reusable bins. Following a continuous loop between suppliers and Dell, trucks deliver the carefully sorted parts to the computer maker's plant for final assembly. The goals of JIT are to minimize inventory costs, improve product quality, maximize production efficiency, and provide optimal levels of customer service. To illustrate, JIT practices have allowed Dell to provide prompt service to its rapidly growing base of customers—a PC is shipped three days after the order is received.

JIT systems are built on trust, demonstrated performance, and a close supplier–customer relationship. To illustrate, Owens-Illinois is the primary supplier of glass containers to the J. M. Smucker Company, the jam and jelly manufacturer. To reduce container inventory costs, Smucker's maintains only enough glass containers to run the production line for a few hours. Production managers at Smucker's have learned that they can count on Owens-Illinois for deliveries that permit a seamless production process. Such consistent delivery performance to Smucker's standards has created a long-standing customer for Owens-Illinois.

Figure 6.5	A Supply Chain Is Built around Demand

ORDERS ARE ON TIME. EVERYONE'S IN THE LOOP. CUSTOMERS ARE HAPPY.

(AN ADAPTIVE SUPPLY CHAIN IS A BEAUTIFUL THING.)

A business is a jigsaw puzzle of people, products and processes. And because it's constantly in flux, it's hard to predict what, when. The mySAP™ Supply Chain Management Solution connects you with your customers, partners and suppliers, so you can adapt on the fly to shifts in supply and demand. It also offers higher visibility and covers all the bases – from planning and execution to networking and coordination. Which makes it the only adaptive SCM solution that can turn a supply chain into a profit center. To find out how you can optimize your supply chain, go to sap.com/scm

THE BEST-RUN E-BUSINESSES RUN SAP

THE ORGANIZATIONAL BUYING PROCESS

Organizational buying behavior is a process rather than an isolated act. Tracing the history of a procurement decision in an organization uncovers critical decision points and evolving information requirements. In fact, organizational buying involves several stages, each of which yields a decision.[29] Table 6.3 lists the eight major stages in the organizational buying process.

The Supply Chain Is Wired

The Internet is transforming the way in which firms are managing the supply chain. For example, Covisint is potentially the most important development in the automobile industry since the automatic transmission. A joint venture between Ford, General Motors (GM), DaimlerChrysler, Nissan, and others, Covisint is a public exchange or e-marketplace for the auto industry. Covisint allows the automakers to come together with suppliers from all over the world at the Covisint Web site, where they can buy and sell parts, collaborate on product design, and coordinate supply chain activities. Ultimately, the organizers of Covisint predict that over $250 billion worth of goods and services will be bought and sold through the e-marketplace each year. In essence, a global electronic marketplace like Covisint:

- Enables a firm, like GM, and its supply chain partners to transact business and share information in real time
- Simplifies purchasing processes and reduces purchasing costs
- Consolidates the buying power of the supply chain to reduce the cost of raw materials, products, and services

By using the exchange, Covisint expects auto manufacturers to achieve savings of $2,000 to $3,000 per vehicle. However, experts suggest that it may take several years for the concept to achieve its full potential.

Source: Rich Taylor, "Digital Design: Transparency," *New York Times*, 13 June 2001, DD4 (supplement).

	Major Stages of the Organizational Buying Process	Table 6.3

Stage	Description
1. Problem recognition	Managers at Pillsbury need new high-speed packaging equipment to support a new product launch.
2. General description of need	Production managers work with a purchasing manager to determine the characteristics needed in the new packaging system.
3. Product specifications	An experienced production manager assists a purchasing manager in developing a detailed and precise description of the needed equipment.
4. Supplier search	After conferring with production managers, a purchasing manager identifies a set of alternative suppliers that could satisfy Pillsbury's requirements.
5. Acquisition and analysis of proposals	Alternative proposals are evaluated by a purchasing manager and a number of members of the production department.
6. Supplier selection	Negotiations with the two finalists are conducted, and a supplier is chosen.
7. Selection of order routine	A delivery date is established for the production equipment.
8. Performance review	After equipment is installed, purchasing and production managers evaluate the performance of the equipment and the service support provided by the supplier.

http://www.pillsbury.com

Similar to the consumer decision-making process discussed in Chapter 5, the business-to-business purchasing process begins when someone in the organization recognizes a problem that can be solved or an opportunity that can be captured by acquiring a specific product. Problem recognition (Stage 1) can be triggered by internal or external forces. Internally, a firm, like Pillsbury may need new high-speed production equipment to support a new product launch. Or a purchasing manager may be unhappy with the price or service of an equipment supplier. Externally, a salesperson can precipitate the need for a product by demonstrating opportunities for improving the organization's performance. Likewise, business marketers also use advertising to alert customers to problems and demonstrate how a particular product may provide a solution (see Figure 6.6).

During the organizational buying process, many small or incremental decisions are made that ultimately translate into the final choice of a supplier. To illustrate, a production manager might unknowingly establish specifications for a new production system that only one supplier can meet (Stages 2 and 3). This type of decision early in the buying process will dramatically influence the favorable evaluation and ultimate selection of that supplier.

The Search Process

Once the organization has defined the product that will meet its requirements, attention turns to this question: Which of the many possible suppliers can be considered promising candidates? The organization will invest more time and energy in the supplier search when the proposed product has a strong bearing on organizational performance. When the information needs of the buying organization are low, Stages 4 and 5 occur simultaneously, especially when standardized items are under consideration. In this case, a purchasing manager may merely check a catalog or secure an updated price from the Internet. Stage 5 emerges as a distinct category only when the information needs of the organization are high. Here the process of acquiring and analyzing proposals may involve purchasing managers, engineers, users, and other organizational members.

Supplier Selection and Performance Review

After being selected as a chosen supplier (Stage 6) and agreeing to purchasing guidelines (Stage 7), such as required quantities and expected time of delivery, a marketer faces further tests. A performance review (Stage 8) is the final stage in the purchasing process. The performance review may lead the purchasing manager to continue, modify, or cancel the agreement. A review critical of the chosen supplier and supportive of rejected alternatives can lead members of the decision-making unit to reexamine their position. If the product fails to meet the needs of the using department, vendors screened earlier in the procurement process may be given further consideration. To retain a new customer, the marketer must ensure that the needs of the buying organization have been completely satisfied. Failure to follow through at this critical stage leaves the marketer vulnerable.

The flow of stages in this model of the procurement process may not progress sequentially and may vary with the complexity of the purchasing situation. For example, some of the stages are compressed or bypassed when organizations are making routine buying decisions. However, the model provides important insights into the organizational buying process. Certain stages may be completed concurrently; the process may be discontinued by a change in the external environment or in upper-management thinking. The organizational buying process is shaped by a host of internal and external forces such as changes in economic or competitive conditions or a basic shift in organizational priorities.

Buying Situations Analyzed

The same product may elicit markedly different purchasing patterns in various organizations with various levels of experience and information. Therefore, attention should center on buying situations rather than on products. Three types of buying situations have been identified: (1) new task, (2) modified rebuy, and (3) straight rebuy.[30]

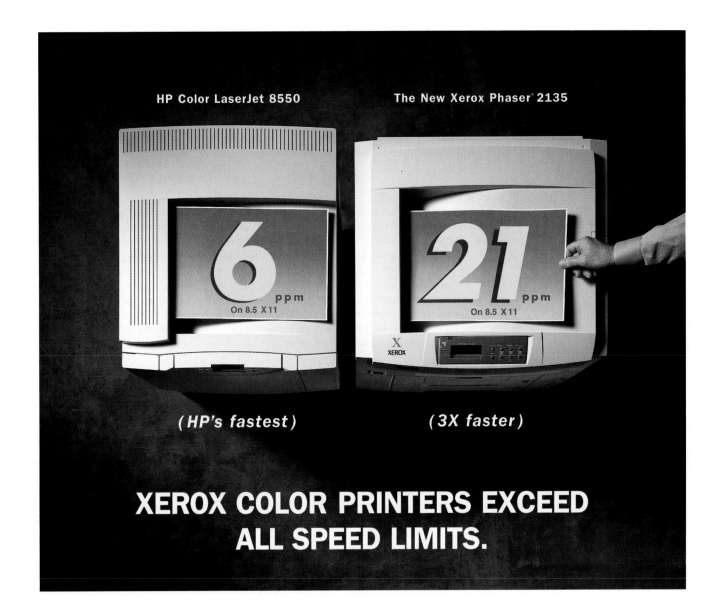

Xerox color just blew the competition out of the office. Our network-ready Phaser® 2135 color printer, from the combined expertise of Tektronix® and Xerox, offers brilliant 1200-dpi color at an incredible 21ppm and black at 26ppm. It's powered by a 500 MHz processor and offers a 2850-sheet capacity. Plus, it prints on a wide variety of media, up to 12x18 and 75lb cover stock. Now everything you create, you can print in-house. Let us help you exceed all speed limits in your office with this or other printers. Call 1-877-362-6567 ext. 1815 or visit us at **www.xerox.com/officeprinting/print1815.**

THE DOCUMENT COMPANY
XEROX

XEROX PRINTERS MAKE IT HAPPEN.

XEROX
NETWORK PRINTERS

New-task buying situation
is a purchase situation that results in an extensive search for information and a lengthy decision process.

New Task

In the **new-task buying situation**, the problem or need is perceived by organizational decision makers as totally different from previous experiences. Therefore, decision makers must explore many alternative ways of solving the problem, then search for appropriate suppliers. To illustrate, a large health insurance company placed a $600,000 order for workstation furniture. The long-term impact on the work environment shaped the six-month decision process and involved the active participation of personnel from several departments.[31] New-task buying decisions can be of extreme importance to the firm—strategically and financially.

When confronting a new-task buying situation, organizational buyers operate in a stage of *extended problem solving*.[32] The buying influentials and decision makers lack well-defined criteria for comparing alternative products and suppliers, but they also lack strong predispositions toward a particular solution. In the consumer market, this is the same type of problem solving an individual or household might follow in buying a first home.

Strategy Guidelines

The business marketer confronting a new-task buying situation can gain a differential advantage by participating actively in the initial stages of the procurement process. The marketer should gather information on the problems facing the buying organization, isolate specific requirements, and offer proposals to meet the requirements. Ideas that lead to new products often originate not with the marketer but with the customer.

Marketers who are presently supplying other items to the organization ("in" suppliers) have an edge over other firms; they can see problems unfolding and are familiar with the "personality" and behavior patterns of the organization. The successful business marketer carefully monitors the changing needs of organizations and is prepared to respond to the needs of new-task buyers.

Straight Rebuy

When there is a continuing or recurring requirement, buyers have substantial experience in dealing with the need, and they require little or no new information. Evaluation of new alternative solutions is unnecessary and unlikely to yield appreciable improvements. Therefore, the organization is likely to undertake a **straight rebuy**.

Straight rebuy
is routine reordering from the same supplier of a product that has been purchased in the past.

Routine problem solving is the decision process organizational buyers employ in the straight rebuy. Organizational buyers have well-developed choice criteria to apply to the purchase decision. The criteria have been refined over time, and the buyers have developed predispositions toward the offerings of one or a few carefully screened suppliers. This process is termed *routine problem solving*. In the consumer market, this is the same type of problem solving that a shopper might use in selecting 30 items in 20 minutes during a weekly trip to the supermarket.

Strategy guidelines. The purchasing department handles straight rebuy situations by routinely selecting a supplier from a list (formal or informal) of acceptable vendors, then placing an order. The marketing task appropriate in this situation depends on whether the marketer is an "in" supplier (on the list) or an "out" supplier (not among the chosen few). An "in" supplier must reinforce the buyer–seller relationship, meet the buying organization's expectations, and be alert and responsive to the changing needs of the organization.

The "out" supplier faces a number of obstacles and must convince the organization that significant benefits can be derived from breaking the routine. This can be difficult because organizational buyers perceive risk in shifting from the known to the unknown. The organizational spotlight shines directly on them if an untested supplier falters. Testing, evaluations, and approvals may be viewed by buyers as costly, time-consuming, and unnecessary.

The marketing effort of the "out" supplier rests on an understanding of the basic buying needs of the organization: information gathering is essential. The marketer must convince organizational buyers that their purchasing requirements have changed or that the requirements should be interpreted differently. The objective is to persuade decision makers to reexamine alternative solutions and to revise the preferred list to include the new supplier.

Modified Rebuy

In the **modified rebuy** situation, organizational decision makers feel that significant benefits may be derived from a reevaluation of alternatives. Several factors may trigger such a reassessment. Internal forces include the search for quality improvements or cost reductions. A marketer offering cost, quality, or service improvements can trigger the reassessment. The modified rebuy situation is most likely to occur when the firm is displeased with the performance of present suppliers (e.g., poor delivery service).

Limited problem solving best describes the decision-making process for the modified rebuy. Decision makers have well-defined criteria, but they are uncertain about which suppliers can best fit their needs. In the consumer market, college students buying their second computer might follow a limited problem-solving approach.

Strategy guidelines. In a modified rebuy, the direction of the marketing effort depends on whether the marketer is an "in" or an "out" supplier. An "in" supplier should make every effort to understand and satisfy the procurement need and to move decision makers into a straight rebuy. The buying organization perceives potential payoffs from a reexamination of alternatives. The "in" supplier should ask why, and act immediately to remedy any customer problems. The marketer may be out of touch with the buying organization's requirements.

The goal of the "out" supplier should be to hold the organization in modified rebuy status long enough for the buyer to evaluate an alternative offering. Knowing the factors that led decision makers to reexamine alternatives could be pivotal. A particularly effective strategy for an "out" supplier is to offer performance guarantees as part of the proposal.[33] To illustrate, the following guarantee prompted International Circuit Technology, a manufacturer of printed circuit boards, to change to a new supplier for plating chemicals: "Your plating costs will be no more than x cents per square foot, or we will make up the difference."[34] Pleased with the performance results, International Circuit Technology now routinely reorders from this new supplier.

How Organizational Buyers Evaluate Potential Suppliers

The business marketer must understand how organizational buyers measure value and evaluate supplier performance. To develop profitable relationships with organizational customers, the value offerings developed by the business marketer must be based on skills and resources that provide value *as perceived by customers.*

Total Cost of Ownership

To address the needs of business customers of all types, the marketer requires an understanding of the goals and priorities that occupy the attention of purchasing managers. Given rising competitive pressures, purchasing managers use rigorous cost modeling approaches to identify the factors that drive the total cost of ownership of purchased goods and services. The **total cost of ownership** considers not only the purchase price but also an array of other factors such as transportation and acquisition costs, as well as the quality, reliability, and other attributes of a product or service over its complete life cycle.[35] Based on this perspective, paying a premium price for a higher quality product could be justified because the initial purchase cost will be offset by fewer manufacturing defects, lower inventory requirements, and lower administrative costs. To illustrate:

> *Honda of America reduced the cost of the purchased content that goes into the Accord by setting cost targets for each component—engine, seats, chassis, and so on. Then purchasing managers worked with suppliers to understand the cost structure of each component, observe how it is manufactured, and then identified ways to reduce cost, add value, or do both. The result? Honda achieved a 20 percent cost reduction in the external purchases that are embodied in the current Accord.*[36]

Measuring Value

The accurate measurement of value is crucial to the purchasing function. The principles and tools of **value analysis** aid the professional buyer in approaching this task. For example, Ferro Corporation developed a new coating process that allows Maytag to paint a refrigerator cabinet in 10 minutes, compared to the old process that took three hours.[37]

Modified rebuy
is a purchase where the buyers have experience in satisfying the need but feel the situation warrants reevaluation of a limited set of alternatives before making a decision.

Total cost of ownership
considers not only the purchase price but also an array of other factors such as complete life cycle.

Value analysis
is a method of weighing the comparative value of materials, components, and manufacturing processes from the standpoint of their purpose, relative merit, and cost in order to uncover ways of improving products, lowering costs, or both.

Dramatic cost savings were achieved by Maytag. Value is achieved when the proper function is secured for the proper cost. Because functions can be accomplished in a number of different ways, the most cost-efficient way of fully accomplishing a function establishes its value.

Evaluating Supplier Performance

Once a contract is awarded to a supplier, the evaluation process takes a different form. Actual performance must be evaluated. Buyers rate supplier performance in assessing the quality of past decisions, in making future vendor selections, and as a negotiating tool to gain leverage in buyer–seller relationships. The *weighted-point plan* is a supplier rating system that is widely used by organizational buyers.

The Weighted-Point Plan

In the weighted-point plan, the buying organization weights each performance factor according to its relative importance. Quality might be given a weight of 40; service, 30; and price, 30. This system alerts the business marketer to the nature and importance of the evaluative criteria used by a particular organization. The marketer's total offering can then be adjusted to fit the organization's needs more precisely.

For example, DaimlerChrysler Corporation "grades" suppliers of electronic components. Under this program, suppliers can be awarded a total of 100 points, including up to 40 points for quality, 25 points for pricing, 25 points for delivery, and 10 points for technical assistance. Working with other departments, such as engineering and production control, purchasing calculates a performance score for each supplier. In the pricing area, DaimlerChrysler is giving increased attention to the cost savings plans submitted by the supplier.[38] Detailed records are kept of the number of proposals each supplier makes and the dollar savings that they generate. By focusing on continual improvement, suppliers can improve their profitability and increase the amount of sales they generate from DaimlerChrysler. Those scoring 91 points or higher make the preferred supplier list. It is important to note that only 300 of DaimlerChrysler's 1,000 electronics suppliers achieve this distinction, and they receive more than 80 percent of the firm's $350 million annual budget for electronic components. Suppliers scoring less than 70 points are usually dropped automatically. As this illustration demonstrates, customers in the business market are interested in the total capabilities of a supplier and how these capabilities might assist them in improving their competitive position—now and in the future.

MAJOR INFLUENCES ON ORGANIZATIONAL BUYERS

As illustrated in Figure 6.7, the buying decisions of organizations are influenced by environmental factors (e.g., the growth rate of the economy), organizational factors (e.g., the size of the buying organization), group factors (e.g., patterns of influence in the buying center), and individual factors (e.g., personal preferences).

Environmental Forces

A projected change in business conditions, a technological development, or a new piece of legislation can drastically alter organizational buying plans. Among the types of environmental forces that shape organizational buying behavior are economic, political, legal, and technological influences. Collectively, such environmental influences define the boundaries within which buyer–seller relationships develop in the business market. Particular attention will be given to selected economic and technological forces that influence buying decisions.

Economic Influences

Because of the derived nature of industrial demand, the marketer must also be sensitive to the strength of demand in the ultimate consumer market. The demand for many industrial products fluctuates more widely than the general economy. Firms that operate on a global scale must be sensitive to the economic conditions that prevail across regions. For example, as the U.S. economy moves out of a recession, the European economy may continue to sputter. A wealth of political and economic forces dictate the vitality and growth of an economy.

 The economic environment influences an organization's ability and, to a degree, its willingness to buy. However, shifts in general economic conditions do not affect all sectors of the market evenly. For example, a rise in interest rates may damage the housing industry (including lumber, cement, and insulation) but may have minimal effects on

---

Forces Influencing Organizational Buying Behavior — **Figure 6.7**

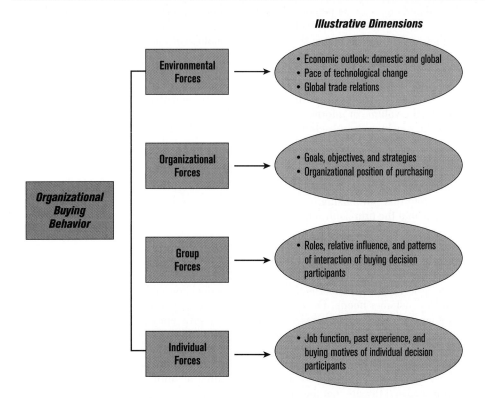

Illustrative Dimensions

Organizational Buying Behavior

Environmental Forces
- Economic outlook: domestic and global
- Pace of technological change
- Global trade relations

Organizational Forces
- Goals, objectives, and strategies
- Organizational position of purchasing

Group Forces
- Roles, relative influence, and patterns of interaction of buying decision participants

Individual Forces
- Job function, past experience, and buying motives of individual decision participants

industries such as paper, hospital supplies, office products, and soft drinks. Marketers that serve broad sectors of the business market must be particularly sensitive to the differential impact of selective economic shifts on buying behavior.

Technological Influences
The rate of technological change in an industry influences the composition of the decision-making unit in the buying organization. As the pace of technological change increases, the importance of the purchasing manager in the buying process declines. Technical and engineering personnel tend to be more important to organizational buying processes in which the rate of technological change is great. Recent research also suggests that buyers who perceive the pace of technological change to be more rapid will (1) conduct more intense search efforts and (2) spend less time on their overall search processes.[39] Why? "In cost-benefit terms, a fast pace of change implies that distinct benefits are associated with search effort, yet costs are associated with prolonging the process" because the acquired information is "time sensitive."[40] The Internet is also expanding the volume of information that is available to purchasing managers and transforming the way buyers and sellers come together (see Chapter 15).

Organizational Forces

An understanding of the buying organization is based on the strategic priorities of the firm, the role that purchasing occupies in the executive hierarchy, and the competitive challenges that the firm confronts.

Advancing the Customer's Goals
Organizational buying decisions are made to facilitate organizational activities and to support the firm's mission and strategies. A business marketer who understands the strategic priorities and concerns that occupy key decision makers is better equipped to respond to customer needs. For example, IBM centers attention on how its information technology and assorted services can improve the efficiency of a bank's operations or advance the customer service levels of a hotel chain. Alternatively, a supplier to Hewlett-Packard will strike a responsive chord with executives by offering a new component part that will increase the performance or lower the cost of its ink-jet printers. To provide such customer solutions, the business marketer requires an intimate understanding of the opportunities and threats that the customer confronts.

Strategic Role of Purchasing

In many firms, purchasing strategy is becoming more closely tied to corporate strategy. To illustrate, purchasing executives at Motorola have a clear understanding of the firm's objectives, markets, and competitive strategies. As purchasing assumes a more strategic role in the firm, the business marketer must understand the competitive realities of the customer's business and develop a **value proposition** unique to the customer. For example, Motorola is keenly interested in working with suppliers who can contribute technology or component parts that enhance the value of the firm's cellular handsets for customers and that strengthen its competitive position.

Value proposition
is a program of goods, services, ideas, and solutions that a business marketer offers to advance the performance goals of the customer organization.

Organizational Positioning of Purchasing

An organization that centralizes procurement decisions will approach purchasing differently than will a company where purchasing decisions are made at individual user locations. When purchasing is centralized, a separate organizational unit is given authority for purchases at a regional, divisional, or headquarters level. For example, Mead Corporation's centralized purchasing function directs the purchase of common materials used by Mead plants across the United States. Boeing, AT&T, 3M, Hewlett-Packard, and Xerox are among other corporations that emphasize centralized procurement. A marketer who is sensitive to organizational influences can more accurately map the decision-making process, isolate buying influentials, identify important buying criteria, and target marketing strategy for both centralized and decentralized organizations.[41]

Group Forces: The Buying Center

Buying decisions typically involve not one but several members of the organization, whether the decisions are made by commercial enterprises, institutions, or governmental organizations. The decision-making unit of a buying organization is called the **buying center**. The buying center consists of those individuals who participate in the purchasing decision and who share the goals and risks arising from the decision.[42] The size of the buying center varies, but an average buying center will include more than four persons per purchase; the number of people involved in all stages of one purchase may be as many as 20.[43]

Buying center
consists of those individuals who participate in the purchasing decision and who share the goals and risks arising from the decision.

The composition of the buying center may change from one purchasing situation to another and is not prescribed by the organizational chart. A buying group evolves during the purchasing process in response to the information requirements of the specific purchase situation. Because organizational buying is a process rather than an isolated act, different individuals are important to the process at different times.[44] A design engineer may exert significant influence early in the purchasing process when product specifications are being established; others may assume a more dominant role in later phases. Again, the composition of the buying center evolves during the purchasing process, varies from firm to firm, and varies from one purchasing situation to another. To be successful, the business marketer must identify the organizational members who comprise the buying center and understand each participant's *relative influence* and the *evaluative criteria* that are important to each member in reaching a decision.

Isolating the Buying Situation

Defining the buying situation and determining whether the firm is in the early or later stages of the procurement decision-making process are important first steps in defining the buying center. The buying center for a new-task buying situation in the not-for-profit market is presented in Table 6.4. The product, intensive-care monitoring systems, is a complex and costly purchase. Buying center members are drawn from five functional areas, each participating to varying degrees in the decision process. Moreover, each buying center member emphasizes different evaluation criteria. Administration and purchasing are concerned with price and cost issues, while physicians are concerned with product quality and service. A marketer who concentrated exclusively on the purchasing function would be overlooking key buying influentials.

Salespeople who frequently encounter new-task buying situations generally observe that

The buying center is large, slow to decide, uncertain about its needs and the appropriateness of the possible solutions, more concerned about finding a good

Table 6.4	The Involvement of Buying Center Participants at Different Stages of the Procurement Process

Stages of Procurement Process for a Medical Equipment Purchase

Buying Center Participants	Identification of Need	Establishment of Objectives	Identification and Evaluation of Buying Alternatives	Selection of Suppliers
Physicians	High	High	High	High
Nursing	Low	High	High	Low
Administration	Moderate	Moderate	Moderate	High
Engineering	Low	Moderate	Moderate	Low
Purchasing	Low	Low	Low	Moderate

solution than getting a low price or assured supply, more willing to entertain proposals from "out" suppliers and less willing to favor "in" suppliers, more influenced by technical personnel, [and] less influenced by purchasing agents.[45]

By contrast, salespeople facing more routine purchase situations (that is, straight and modified rebuys) frequently observe buying centers that are "small, quick to decide, confident in their appraisals of the problem and possible solutions, concerned about price and supply, satisfied with 'in' suppliers, and more influenced by purchasing agents."[46]

Buying Center Roles

Members of the buying center assume different roles throughout the purchasing process: users, influencers, buyers, deciders, and gatekeepers.[47] As the name implies, *users* are the personnel who will be using the product in question. Users may have anywhere from inconsequential to extremely important influence on the purchase decision. In some cases, the users initiate the purchase action by requesting the product. They may even develop the product specifications.

Consider Clark Equipment Company, which manufactures forklift trucks for the business market.[48] They found that equipment operators (users) assume an important role in the buying decision. Users spend a considerable part of their work day operating the equipment and often receive financial incentives that are tied to their performance. This means that driver comfort and equipment reliability (minimal equipment downtime) are central to the buying decision. In designing a new line of forklifts, Clark Equipment is giving an unprecedented level of attention to driver comfort, reduced engine noise level, and product reliability.

Gatekeepers control information to be reviewed by other members of the buying center. The control of information may be accomplished by disseminating printed information, such as advertisements, or by controlling which salesperson will speak to which individuals in the buying center. To illustrate, the purchasing agent or an administrative assistant might perform this screening role by opening the gate to the buying center for some sales personnel and closing it to others.

Influencers affect the purchasing decision by supplying information for the evaluation of alternatives or by setting buying specifications. Typically, those in technical departments, such as engineering, quality control, and R&D, are significant influences on the purchase decision. Sometimes, individuals outside the buying organization can assume this role. For high-tech purchases, technical consultants often assume an influential role in the decision process and broaden the set of alternatives being considered.[49]

Deciders are the individuals who actually make the buying decision, whether or not they have the formal authority to do so. The identity of the decider is the most difficult role to determine: Buyers may have formal authority to buy, but the president of the firm may actually make the decision. A decider could be a design engineer who develops a set of specifications that only one vendor can meet.

The *buyer* has formal authority to select a supplier and implement all procedures connected with securing the product. The power of the buyer is often usurped by more powerful members of the organization. The buyer's role is often assumed by the purchasing agent, who executes the administrative functions associated with a purchase order.

One person could assume all roles in a purchase situation or separate individuals could assume different buying roles. To illustrate, as users, personnel from marketing, accounting, purchasing, and production may all have a stake in which information technology system is selected.

Identifying Buying Influentials

Multiple buying influences and **key buying influentials** are critical in organizational buying decisions. A central challenge for the business marketer is to identify the patterns of influence within the buying center. Except for repetitive buying situations, key influencers are frequently located outside the purchasing department. However, research provides some valuable clues for identifying powerful buying center members.[50] To illustrate, organizational members tend to assume an active and influential role in the buying center when they

- Have an important personal stake in the decision.
- Possess expert knowledge concerning the choice at hand.
- Have direct access to top management.
- Are central to the flow of decision-related information.

Key buying influentials are those individuals in the buying organization who have the power to influence the buying decision.

Individual Forces

Individuals, not organizations, make buying decisions. Each member of the buying center has a unique personality, a particular set of learned experiences, a specified organizational function, and a perception of how best to achieve both personal and organizational goals.[51] Organizational members are influenced by both rational and emotional motives when choosing among competing offerings. *Rational motives* are usually economic, such as price, quality, and service. *Emotional motives* include such human factors as the desire for status within the organization, for salary increases, and for increased job security. For example, a purchasing manager may be intrigued by the quality or price offered by a newly created supplier firm but fear the personal consequences if the new supplier stumbles. A marketer concentrating exclusively on rational motives has an incomplete picture of the organizational buyer.

Differing Evaluative Criteria

Evaluative criteria are specifications that organizational buyers use to compare alternative goods and services; however, these may conflict. Organizational product users generally value prompt delivery and efficient servicing; engineering values product quality, standardization, and testing; and purchasing assigns importance to cost savings and delivery reliability.[52] Product perceptions and evaluation criteria differ among organizational decision makers as a result of differences in educational backgrounds, source and type of information exposure, interpretation and retention of relevant information, and level of satisfaction with past purchases.[53] Engineers have an educational background different from that of plant managers or purchasing agents; they are exposed to different journals, attend different conferences, and possess different professional goals and values. For example, engineers may be most interested in choosing a new piece of equipment that represents state-of-the-art technology, while purchasing managers are concerned with the price and operating costs. A sales presentation that is effective with purchasing may be entirely off the mark with engineering. Knowledge of the buying criteria that key buying influentials emphasize allows the business marketer to tailor marketing strategies to the needs of individual customers.

Evaluative criteria are specifications that organizational buyers use to compare alternative goods and services.

CHAPTER SUMMARY

- In business-to-business marketing, the customers are organizations. The business market can be divided into three major sectors: commercial enterprises, governments (federal, state, and local), and institutions. Many business marketers—for example, Intel, Boeing, and IBM—generate a significant proportion of their sales and profit by serving international customers. Indeed, the demand for many industrial products is growing more rapidly in many foreign countries than in the United States.

- Commercial enterprises include manufacturers, construction companies, service firms, transportation companies, selected professional groups, and resellers. Of these, manufacturers account for the largest dollar volume of purchases. Furthermore, although the majority of manufacturing firms are small, buying power is concentrated in the hands of relatively few manufacturers, which are also concentrated geographically. Governmental units also make substantial purchases of products. Two general purchasing strategies are used by government buyers: the formal advertising approach for standardized products and negotiated contracts for unique requirements. Institutional customers, such as health care organizations and universities, comprise the third sector of the business market. Depending on size, the institution will employ a purchasing agent and, in large institutions, a sizable purchasing department. Across business market sectors, purchasing managers are using the Internet to identify potential suppliers, conduct online reverse auctions, and communicate with suppliers.

- Business markets differ from household consumer markets in several ways. Because purchases made by business customers are linked to the goods and services that they sell, derived demand is an important, and often volatile, feature in the business market. Business market customers are developing closer relationships with fewer suppliers than they have used in the past, and they expect these suppliers to provide defect-free products at the moment they are needed. These trends place a premium on the relationship marketing and supply chain capabilities of the business marketer.

- Knowledge of the process that organizational buyers follow in making purchasing decisions is fundamental to responsive marketing strategy. As a buying organization moves from the problem recognition phase, in which a need is defined, to later phases, in which suppliers are screened and ultimately chosen, the marketer can play an active role. The nature of the buying process followed in a particular situation depends on the organization's level of experience with similar procurement problems. There are three types of buying situations: (1) new task, (2) modified rebuy, and (3) straight rebuy. Each requires a unique problem-solving approach, involves unique buying influentials, and demands a unique marketing response. Purchasing managers center on the total cost of ownership in evaluating products, rely on tools such as value analysis to make informed decisions, and use a weighted point plan to evaluate supplier performance. A wealth of factors—which can be classified as environmental, organizational, group, and individual—influence the buying decisions of an organization. A central challenge for the business marketer is to identify the organizational members who comprise the buying center.

KEY TERMS

Business market consists of all organizations that buy goods and services for use in the production of other goods and services or for resale.

Buying center consists of those individuals who participate in the purchasing decision and who share the goals and risks arising from the decision.

Commercial enterprises are the sector of the business market represented by manufacturers, construction companies, service firms, transportation companies, professional groups, and resellers that purchase goods and services.

Evaluative criteria are specifications that organizational buyers use to compare alternative goods and services.

Governmental units comprise the sector of the business market represented by federal, state, and local governmental units that purchase goods and services.

Institutional customers comprise the sector of the business market represented by health care organizations, colleges and universities, libraries, foundations, art galleries, and clinics that purchase goods and services.

Key buying influentials are those individuals in the buying organization who have the power to influence the buying decision.

Modified rebuy is a purchase where the buyers have experience in satisfying the need but feel the situation warrants reevaluation of a limited set of alternatives before making a decision.

New-task buying situation is a purchase situation that results in an extensive search for information and a lengthy decision process.

A **reverse auction** involves one buyer who invites bids from several prequalified suppliers.

Straight rebuy is routine reordering from the same supplier of a product that has been purchased in the past.

Supply-chain management is a technique for linking a manufacturer's operations with those of all of its strategic suppliers and its key intermediaries and customers to enhance efficiency and effectiveness.

Total cost of ownership considers not only the purchase price but also an array of other factors such as complete life cycle.

Value analysis is a method of weighing the comparative value of materials, components, and manufacturing processes from the standpoint of their purpose, relative merit, and cost in order to uncover ways of improving products, lowering costs, or both.

Value proposition is a program of goods, services, ideas, and solutions that a business marketer offers to advance the performance goals of the customer organization.

QUESTIONS FOR DISCUSSION

1. Describe the major categories of customers that comprise the business market.

2. Compare and contrast the two general procurement strategies employed by the federal government: (1) formal advertising and (2) negotiated contract.

3. DuPont, one of the largest industrial producers of chemicals and synthetic fibers, spends millions of dollars annually on advertising its products to final consumers. For example, DuPont invested more than $1 million in a TV advertising blitz that emphasized the comfort of jeans made of DuPont's stretch polyester-cotton blend. Because DuPont does not produce jeans or market them to final consumers, why are large expenditures made on consumer advertising?

4. The goal of a supply-chain strategy is to improve the speed, precision, and efficiency of manufacturing through strong supplier partnerships. Explain.

5. General Electric (GE) has embraced e-purchasing and has saved more than $500 million per year by conducting online reverse auctions in buying a range of goods including office, computer, and maintenance supplies. What new challenges and opportunities does this auctioning process present for business marketers who serve GE?

6. Mike Weber, the purchasing agent for Smith Manufacturing, views the purchase of widgets as a routine buying decision. What factors might lead him to alter this position? More important, what factors will determine whether a particular supplier, such as Albany Widget, will be considered by Mike?

7. Harley-Davidson, the U.S. motorcycle producer, recently purchased some sophisticated manufacturing equipment to enhance its position in a very competitive market. First, what environmental forces might have been important in spawning this capital investment? Second, which functional units were likely to have been represented in the buying center?

8. Millions of notebook computers are purchased each year by organizations. Identify several evaluative criteria that purchasing managers might use in choosing a particular brand. In your view, which criteria would be most decisive in the buying decision?

9. Describe the weighted-point plan and discuss how a purchasing manager at Xerox might use it in evaluating the performance of a supplier of component parts for the firm's high-speed photocopier.

10. Evaluate this statement: Both rational and emotional factors enter into the decisions that organizational buyers make.

INTERNET QUESTIONS

1. PeopleSoft is a high-growth company that seeks to deliver "outrageous customer service." Surveys suggest that nearly all of the firm's customers would recommend PeopleSoft to others. Go to the company's Web site— http://peoplesoft.com—and identify
   a. The goods and services that they sell.
   b. The types of customers in the business market that they serve.

2. Dell Computer has been wildly successful in selling its products over the Internet to customers of all types, including every category of customers in the business market: commercial enterprises, institutions, and government. Assume that the library at your university is planning the purchase of 25 new desktop computers. Go to http://www.dell.com and to the Dell Online Store for Higher Education and
   a. Identify the price and product dimensions of two desktop systems that might meet your university's needs.
   b. Provide a critique of the Web site and consider the degree to which it provided access to the information that a potential buyer might want.

3. FreeMarkets has conducted over 14,000 online auctions for more than $21 billion worth of goods and services and has helped over 100 billion customers, like United Technologies, save over $4 billion on purchases. Go to http://www.freemarkets.com and
   a. Identify the key services that the firm provides for its customers.
   b. Review a case history that describes a particular auction event for a customer.
   c. Decide whether you agree or disagree with one purchasing executive's observation: "Online auctioning is an appropriate way to buy some categories of products and services but it's entirely inappropriate for others." Provide support for your position.

ENDNOTES

[1] "Company Profile: Cisco Systems and Guess?" http://www.cisco.com, accessed 21 December 2001, 3.

[2] Scott Thurm, "How to Drive an Express Train," *Wall Street Journal,* 1 June 2001, B1, B4.

[3] Anne Millen Porter, "Big Companies Struggle to Act Their Size," *Purchasing Magazine Online,* 1 November 2001, 1–16.

[4] Michael Bartlett, "Restaurants and Institutions' 1996 Annual Forecasts," *Restaurants and Institutions,* 1 January 1996, 18.

[5] U.S. Department of Commerce, Bureau of the Census, *Statistical Abstract of the United States, Annual Survey of Manufacturers: 1999* (Washington, DC: Author, 2001).

[6] Porter, "Big Companies Struggle to Act Their Size," 1.

[7] Anne Millen Porter, "Big Spenders: The Top 250," *Purchasing*, 6 November 1997, 40–52.

[8] Carolyn Pye Sostrom, "The Next Step in E-Commerce," *Purchasing Today* (June 2001): 46.

[9] Nicole Harris, "'Private Exchanges' May Allow B-to-B Commerce to Thrive After All," *Wall Street Journal*, 16 March 2001, B4.

[10] James Carbone, "There's Lots More to the Web than Click and Buy," *Purchasing*, 21 October 1999, S76.

[11] Case Study: Cooper Industries, http://www.freemarkets.com, 9 January 2001.

[12] U.S. Department of Commerce, Bureau of the Census, *Statistical Abstract of the United States: 1995* (Washington, DC: Author, 1995), 297.

[13] Stephanie N. Mehta, "Small Firms Are Getting More Government Contracts," *Wall Street Journal*, 27 April 1995, B2.

[14] Richard Walker and Kevin McCaney, "Reverse Auctions Win a Bid of Acceptance," *Buyers.Gov* (December 2001).

[15] Laura M. Holson, "Pushing Limits, Finding None," *New York Times*, 1 November 2001, C1, C6.

[16] U.S. Department of Commerce, Bureau of the Census, *Statistical Abstract of the United States: 1995*, 109, 150.

[17] Melanie Warner, "Motorola Bets Big on China," *Fortune* 27 (May 1996): 116–124.

[18] Subhash C. Jain, "Standardization of International Marketing Strategy: Some Research Hypotheses," *Journal of Marketing* 53 (January 1989): 70–79.

[19] U.S. Census Bureau, "1997 Economic Census: What's New?" *The Official Statistics*, http://www.census.gov, 27 September 1996.

[20] Robert M. Morgan and Shelby D. Hunt, "The Commitment–Trust Theory of Relationship Marketing," *Journal of Marketing* 58 (July 1994): 20–38.

[21] George S. Day, "Managing Market Relationships," *Journal of the Academy of Marketing Science* 28 (Winter 2000): 24–30.

[22] Frank V. Cespedes, *Concurrent Marketing: Integrating Products, Sales, and Service* (Boston: Harvard Business School Press, 1995), 14–18.

[23] James Carbone, "Reinventing Purchasing Wins Medal for Big Blue," *Purchasing*, 16 September 1999, 45–46.

[24] "Chrysler Pushes Quality Down the Supply Chain," *Purchasing*, 13 July 1995, 126.

[25] Frederick E. Webster Jr., "The Changing Role of Marketing in the Corporation," *Journal of Marketing* 56 (October 1992): 14.

[26] Kevin R. Fitzgerald, "For Superb Supplier Development: Honda Wins!" *Purchasing*, 21 September 1995, 32–40.

[27] Rick Mullin, "Managing the Outsourced Enterprise," *Journal of Business Strategy* (July/August 1996): 32.

[28] Tim Minahan, "JIT: A Process with Many Faces," *Purchasing*, 4 September 1997, 42–48.

[29] Patrick J. Robinson, Charles W. Faris, and Yoram Wind, *Industrial Buying and Creative Marketing* (Boston: Allyn & Bacon, 1967), chapter 1.

[30] Robinson, Faris, and Wind, *Industrial Buying and Creative Marketing*, chapter 1; see also Erin Anderson, Wujin Chu, and Barton Weitz, "Industrial Purchasing: An Empirical Exploration of the Buyclass Framework," *Journal of Marketing* 51 (July 1987): 71–86; and Morry Ghingold, "Testing the 'Buygrid' Buying Process Model," *Journal of Purchasing and Materials Management* 22 (Winter 1986): 30–36.

[31] The discussion of buying decision approaches in this section is drawn from Michele D. Bunn, "Taxonomy of Buying Decision Approaches," *Journal of Marketing* 57 (January 1993): 38–56.

[32] The levels of decision making discussed in this section are drawn from John A. Howard and Jagdish N. Sheth, *The Theory of Buyer Behavior* (New York: John Wiley and Sons, 1969), chapter 2.

[33] Christopher P. Puto, Wesley E. Patton III, and Ronald H. King, "Risk Handling Strategies in Industrial Vendor Selection Decisions," *Journal of Marketing* 49 (Winter 1985): 89–98.

[34] Somerby Dowst, "CEO Report: Wanted: Suppliers Adept at Turning Corners," *Purchasing*, 29 January 1987, 71–72.

[35] Timothy M. Laseter, *Balanced Sourcing: Cooperation and Competition in Supplier Relationships* (San Francisco: Jossey-Bass Publishing, 1998), 224.

[36] Laseter, *Balanced Sourcing*, pp. 5–18.

[37] Matthew G. Anderson and Paul K. Katz, "Strategic Sourcing," *International Journal of Logistics Management* 9, 1 (1998): 1–13.

[38] Jeffrey A. Dyer, "How Chrysler Created an American Keiretsu," *Harvard Business Review* 74 (July/August 1996): 52–56; see also Lisa M. Ellram, "A Structured Method for Applying Purchasing Cost Management Tools," *International Journal of Purchasing and Materials Management* 32 (Winter 1996): 11–19.

[39] Allen M. Weiss and Jan B. Heide, "The Nature of Organizational Search in High Technology Markets," *Journal of Marketing Research* 30 (May 1993): 220–233; see also Jan B. Heide and Allen M. Weiss, "Vendor Consideration and Switching Behavior for Buyers in High-Technology Markets," *Journal of Marketing* 59 (July 1995): 30–43.

[40] Weiss and Heide, "The Nature of Organizational Search," 221.

[41] E. Raymond Corey, *The Organizational Context of Industrial Buyer Behavior* (Cambridge, MA: Marketing Science Institute, 1978), 99–112.

[42] For a comprehensive review of buying center research, see Wesley J. Johnston and Jeffrey E. Lewin, "Organizational Buying Behavior: Toward an Integrative Framework," *Journal of Business Research* 35 (January 1996): 1–15; and J. David Lichtenthal, "Group

Decision Making in Organizational Buying: A Role Structure Approach," in *Advances in Business Marketing*, vol. 3, ed. Arch G. Woodside (Greenwich, CT: JAI Press, 1988), 119–157.

[43] For example, see Robert D. McWilliams, Earl Naumann, and Stan Scott, "Determining Buying Center Size," *Industrial Marketing Management* 21 (February 1992): 43–49.

[44] Arch G. Woodside, "Conclusions on Mapping How Industry Buys," in *Advances in Business Marketing and Purchasing*, vol. 5, ed. Arch G. Woodside (Greenwich, CT: JAI Press, 1992), 283–300; see also Gary L. Lilien and M. Anthony Wong, "Exploratory Investigation of the Structure of the Buying Center in the Metalworking Industry," *Journal of Marketing Research* 21 (February 1984): 1–11.

[45] Anderson, Chu, and Weitz, "Industrial Purchasing," 82.

[46] Ibid.

[47] Frederick E. Webster Jr. and Yoram Wind, *Organizational Buying Behavior* (Englewood Cliffs, NJ: Prentice-Hall, 1972), 77. For a review of buying role research, see J. David Lichtenthal, "Group Decision Making in Organizational Buying," 119–157.

[48] B. G. Yovovich, *New Marketing Imperatives: Innovative Strategies for Today's Marketing Challenges* (Englewood Cliffs, NJ: Prentice-Hall, 1995), 4–5.

[49] Philip L. Dawes and Paul G. Patterson, "The Use of Technical Consultancy Services by Firms Making High-Technology Purchasing Decisions," in *Twenty-First Annual Conference of the European Marketing Academy*, ed. Klaus G. Grunert and Dorthe Fuglede (Aarhus, Denmark: Aarhus School of Business), 261–275.

[50] John R. Ronchetto, Michael D. Hutt, and Peter H. Reingen, "Embedded Influence Patterns in Organizational Buying Systems," *Journal of Marketing* 53 (October 1989): 51–62; see also Ajay Kohli, "Determinants of Influence in Organizational Buying: A Contingency Approach," *Journal of Marketing* 53 (July 1989): 50–65; and Daniel H. McQuiston and Peter R. Dickson, "The Effect of Perceived Personal Consequences on Participation and Influence in Organizational Buying," *Journal of Business Research* 23 (September 1991): 159–177.

[51] McQuiston and Dickson, "The Effect of Perceived Personal Consequences on Participation and Influence in Organizational Buying," 159–177.

[52] Jagdish N. Sheth, "A Model of Industrial Buyer Behavior," *Journal of Marketing* 37 (October 1973): 51; see also Sheth, "Organizational Buying Behavior: Past Performance and Future Expectations," *Journal of Business and Industrial Marketing* 11, 3/4 (1996): 7–24.

[53] Sheth, "A Model of Industrial Buyer Behavior," 52–54.

[54] Amy Harmon, "An Inventor Unveils His Mysterious Personal Transportation Device," *New York Times*, 3 December 2001, C1, C10.

[55] John Heilemann, "Reinventing the Wheel," *TIME.com*, 2 December 2001, 4.

[56] Ibid., 2.

[57] Ibid., 6.

THE SEGWAY COMPANY: REINVENTING THE WHEEL

After months of fevered speculation and a tidal wave of provocative clues and predictions that appeared in media reports around the world, Dean Kamen, an award-winning inventor, revealed his innovation: a two-wheeled battery-powered device designed for a single standing rider. The device, the Segway Human Transporter, better known by its code name, Ginger, can go up to 17 miles per hour depending on settings. The speed and direction of the Segway are controlled by the rider's shifting weight and a manual turning mechanism on one of the handlebars. Strikingly, a finely tuned gyroscopic balancing mechanism intuits where its rider wants to go.

Demonstrating the device, Kamen said, "Think forward," and inclined his head ever so slightly and zoomed ahead. "Think back," he continued, effortlessly reversing direction. You turn by twisting the handlebar mechanism and stop by simply thinking about stopping.[54] How does the Segway achieve this surprising effect? Kamen explains that when you use a Segway, "there's a gyroscope that acts like your inner ear, a computer that acts like your muscles, wheels that act like your feet. Suddenly, you feel like you have on a magic pair of sneakers. . . ."[55] Tilt sensors monitor the Segway rider's center of gravity more than 100 times a second, signaling to the electric motor and wheels which way to turn and how fast.

Kamen, a college dropout and self-taught physicist and mechanical engineer, has made millions of dollars creating new medical devices, including the first portable dialysis machine, the first insulin pump, and an array of widely used heart stents. The idea for the Segway grew out of his work on a novel motorized wheelchair that can climb stairs. Typically, Kamen—who wears blue jeans, a blue work shirt, and Timberland boots for every occasion—directs exclusive attention to research and development with his company, DEKA Research and Development. He then licenses his inventions for other firms, like Johnson & Johnson, to market. But given the dramatic potential that he believes the Segway presents, Kamen decided to form his own company to produce and market it. John Doerr, a partner in the Silicon Valley venture capital firm Kleiner Perkins Caufield & Byers, has invested $38 million in the project, the largest single investment in the firm's history. Interestingly, Doerr, a renowned technology expert, was also the lead investor in Netscape and Amazon.com. Other investors have also provided start-up funds to Kamen, who retains majority control of Segway.

The Segway was developed at a cost of more than $100 million. Kamen envisions many potential uses of his latest invention: "in parks and at Disneyland, on battlefields

http://www.segway.com

and factory floors, but especially on downtown sidewalks from Seattle to Shanghai."[56] The firm plans to concentrate initial attention on the business market, namely corporate and government customers, before rolling out a consumer version in late 2002. The 80-pound industrial version of the Segway is priced at $8,000, while the 65-pound consumer model will cost about $3,000. The first business market customers to test the Segway are the U.S. Postal Service, the City of Atlanta, General Electric, and Amazon.com. For example, mail carriers are using the Segway on mail routes in selected cities, and Amazon.com employees use them to navigate the warehouse while picking stock from shelves to fulfill particular customer orders. The Department of Defense is also intrigued about the possibility of equipping its special forces units with Segways.

While the business market offers huge potential, Kamen believes that the true promise for the Segway lies in the consumer market. For downtown transportation, he believes that the Segway can become the preferred mode of transportation within cities, particularly in the developing world. In short, by traveling three or four times faster than walking speed and turning what would have been a 30-minute walk into a 10-minute ride, Kamen contends, Segways will in effect shrink cities to the point where cars "will not only be undesirable but unnecessary."[57]

Discussion Questions

1. Evaluate the potential for the Segway Human Transporter in the business market. What evaluative criteria would organizational customers, such as Disneyland and Wal-Mart, use in considering the product?

2. Do you believe that the Human Transporter will be a success in the consumer market? Explain your position and consider key hurdles that must be scaled by the firm to achieve a deep market penetration.

CHAPTER seven

Penny M. Simpson,
Southeastern Oklahoma State University

Penny Simpson earned her D.B.A. in marketing from Louisiana Tech University and currently teaches at Southeastern Oklahoma State University. Dr. Simpson has received several teaching awards and was previously selected as the David D. Morgan United Teacher Associates Insurance Company Endowed Professor. She serves on the editorial board of *Teaching Business Ethics* and has reviewed articles and books for other journals including *Journal of Business Research* and the *Journal of the Academy of Marketing Science*. She has also published research in a number of journals including the *Journal of Marketing*, the *Journal of the Academy of Market Science, Journal of Marketing Channels, Journal of Business Research*, and the *Journal of Marketing Education*. Dr. Simpson has a wide area of research interests and publications, ranging from health care and tourism to promotion and channels of distribution, including the Internet. All of these research interests have focused on understanding targeted markets and the effects of various factors on their responses. Dr. Simpson also worked several years in management in the savings and loan industry and has consulted with a number of regional banks. Her primary consulting activities involve the development and success of small businesses in a competitive environment.

Market Segmentation and Target Markets

A deep understanding of a group of potential customers and a marketing plan specifically tailored for that group helps to ensure the success of a product. One notable example of this matching strategy comes from the relatively new product class: energy drinks. Though popular in Europe for over a decade, energy drinks were virtually unknown in the United States until 1997 when Red Bull first appeared and virtually created the energy drink market. By 2001, sales of energy drinks, popular with teens and young adults, reached $275 million. Since Red Bull's beginnings in the U. S. market, the company's sales have doubled each year, reaching over $130 million wholesale and a dominant 65 percent share of the energy drink market by 2000. In 2001, sales had increased to 10.5 million cases, a volume increase of 118.8 percent over the previous year, which landed Red Bull at eighth position of all beverage companies in the United States.

Beverages such as Red Bull are called energy drinks because they usually contain stimulants such as caffeine, sugar, taurine (an amino acid), and various herbs. Drinkers of the energy beverages believe the product gives them a burst of energy. Revitalization appeals especially to party goers to keep on partying (and to day-after-the party goers to get going), to students who stay up all night studying, to drivers who need to stay awake, and to athletes who need a performance boost.

A large number of these partiers, studiers, drivers, and athletes are in their late teens and early twenties. Known as Generation Y (a.k.a. the Millennium Generation, Gen Y, Echo Boomers), this group includes 60 million consumers born between 1979 and 1994. Gen Yers grew up surrounded by advertising and marketing and are not easily impressed by conventional marketing efforts. They generally prefer edgy entertainment such as extreme sports and being met on their own turf and on their own terms. This means that companies that want to reach Gen Yers must be perceived as "authentic" and go to them where they live and play, using values and lifestyles they understand, often with humor, irony, and irreverence. As such, Gen Yers represent the perfect match for the Red Bull product; but, then, how to reach them?

(Continued)

After you have completed this chapter, you should be able to:

1. Understand how target marketing depends upon the idea of heterogeneous demand among different market segments.
2. Note the advantages and disadvantages to segmentation and target markets.
3. Understand the process of target market selection.
4. Appreciate how segmenting business markets differs from segmenting consumer markets.
5. Understand the issues that arise when segmenting global markets.

Although Red Bull won't reveal its marketing strategies, the company has worked hard to bring the brand to Gen Y consumers where they live, in a way they understand, through several unique grassroots, customized, and credible methods. These methods include making the product available only at selected "in" places where young adults like to party or hang out. Red Bull also makes use of popular members of its targeted market by giving selected student "brand managers" free cases of the drink and asking them to party with their friends and spread the buzz about Red Bull. Another tactic involves the use of "consumer educators" who drive around in a silver, Red Bull off-road vehicle passing out free samples to anyone who looks like they need a boost of energy. To further identify with the edginess of Gen Yers, Red Bull routinely sponsors extreme sporting events such as snowboarding, skateboarding, street luge, and mountain biking, as well as sponsoring athletes in these events. All these efforts create a real sense of product-market match—that Red Bull belongs to Gen Yers.[1]

The Red Bull story illustrates the importance of understanding customers before defining a total marketing mix that will satisfy customers' needs and wants. After all, satisfying customer needs is at the very heart of the marketing concept. The first step to understanding the customer is identifying those customers who might actually buy a specific product. Once prospective customers are known, they can be analyzed in detail to better understand their needs and wants so that a marketing mix that meets those needs can be created. This process of identifying and analyzing prospective customers is key to target marketing, market segmentation, and positioning, and these activities are key to a successful marketing plan. The target marketing process for household consumer markets, for business markets, and for international markets are discussed in this chapter.

MARKETS AND TARGET MARKETING

A *market* is any individual, group of individuals, or organizations willing, able, and capable of purchasing a firm's product. For example, if you want to buy a new car, you are in the new car market. Before a firm can effectively market its products to you, or to any other member of the market for that matter, it must fully understand your needs and wants from that product. However, the needs and wants from a product are not the same for everyone in a market. For example, you and your mother may both want a new car, so you are both in the new car market; but chances are good that you each want a different type of car. You may want a small, fast, red sports car while your mother would like a large, safe, dependable, white car that gets good mileage.

Generally, different groups of customers have differing needs from specific products, or *heterogeneous demand*. For example, teens may want blue jeans that are stylish, construction workers want jeans that are durable, and older "gray" consumers want jeans that are comfortable. Real differences in product preferences exist. This means that a company wanting to reach these different groups of consumers must divide the market into distinct groups based on these differences, then analyze in detail each group it wants to reach, to truly understand what customers need and want from the products they buy.

As introduced in Chapter 1, the separation of markets into distinctive groups based on homogeneous (similar) characteristics is called *market segmentation*,[2] and is critical to reaching consumers who need different things from a product. Each of the divided markets, or **market segments**, that a company selects to reach with its marketing efforts is a target market. More formally, the specific group of customers toward which a firm directs its market efforts is the firm's *target market*. This process of matching a specialized marketing mix with the needs of a specific market segment is critical to the marketing success of a product and is called *target marketing*. To illustrate, just imagine the likely success (or failure) of cases where market needs do not match the marketing mix: Cadillac and Ensure diet supplement targeting young girls in *Teen* magazine, heavy metal music playing in upscale hotel lobbies, or mascara advertised in *GQ* magazine.

Market segments
consist of groups of consumers who are alike based on some characteristic(s).

http://www.cadillac.com

198

A firm will not generally want to try to appeal to *all* members of a total market in the same way, but rather may concentrate on selected groups of customers. Depending on many factors, firms may target any number of market segments, and each segment targeted may be as small as one consumer or as large as the total mass market. These targeting options are explained next.

Mass Market versus the Individual

Defining specific market segments to target with customized marketing mixes can create a distinctive competitive advantage for a company. As the continuum in Figure 7.1 illustrates, the options for the size of a market segment range from one mass market to one individual, or anywhere in between. For mass markets, the marketing mix is standardized to reach all customers in the same way. The smaller the size of the segments targeted, the more customized or individualized the marketing efforts toward the market can be. A firm choosing the mass market end of the continuum will choose to make one product and market that product in the same way to everyone who may want it.

Moving toward the middle of the continuum, firms may define a relatively small segment, or *niche,* within a large market for targeting, called **niche marketing**. A number of well-known companies illustrate the point: Old Navy and Gadzooks are specialty stores that appeal to teenagers, Estee makes sugar-free food products for diabetics, and Foot Joy makes shoes for golfers. Less well-known is a company called The Rolling Strong Gym. While health clubs appealing to health and fitness enthusiasts have been popular in the past few years, this Richardson, Texas–based gym identified a new market segment to target—interstate truck drivers. The gym has developed exercise programs for truckers to improve fitness and health, and the program now has the support

Niche marketing
is the process of targeting a relatively small market segment with a specific, specialized marketing mix.

http://www.gadzooks.com

Careers in Marketing

Retirement: The End for Some, the Beginning for One

For most people, retirement signals the end of a career, but for niche marketer David D. Morgan, "retired teachers" meant the beginning of a very successful business endeavor. After graduating from Northwestern State University of Louisiana and gaining 8 years of experience in insurance sales, David began selling insurance to a special "niche" interest market—retired teachers—from the trunk of his car in 1981. As David proudly states, "We work with one group of people who have many things in common." What made this niche strategy especially successful was the exclusive endorsement of this product and company by the Texas Retired Teachers Association. This meant information about his insurance products was mailed to all retired teachers in Texas—140,000 of them—on association letterhead, which gave the product instant credibility with association members. In return, membership in the association increased because the retired teachers were required to belong to the association in order to purchase the asso-

ciation group policy. This strategy worked especially well for both organizations. As David states, "It is really tough selling insurance, or just selling anything. You have to have a way to get in front of people." The Texas Retired Teachers Association provided the means for getting the product in front of interested prospects of the target market.

Did this niche marketing strategy pay off? The company, United Teachers Associates Insurance Company, has greatly expanded and now services new niches, such as government employees in Puerto Rico, and underwrites as well as sells insurance. In 1998, the company was one of the top 30 largest insurance companies with guaranteed renewal premiums, had 140 office employees, 2,000 agents, operations in 47 states and U.S. territories, and assets in excess of $205 million. David advises others interested in this type of success "to do something that you like to do, that's fun, work really hard, and do more than you are being paid to do."

Sources: Interview with David Morgan, 6 October 1998; Earl Golz, "Insurer Finds His 'Niche,'" *Austin American Statesman*, 29 July 1997, D1–D2.

Figure 7.1	Continuum of Market Segmentation Size

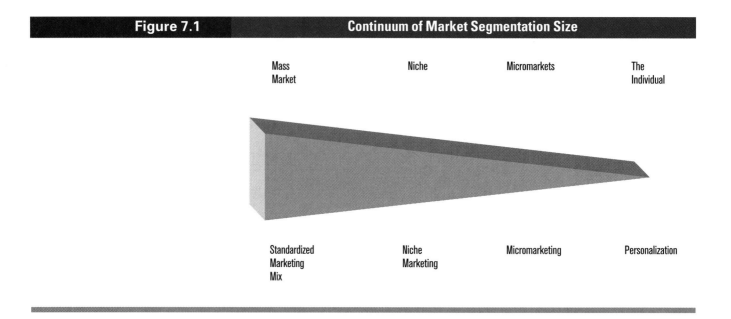

Mass Market   Niche   Micromarkets   The Individual

Standardized Marketing Mix   Niche Marketing   Micromarketing   Personalization

---

of the federal government and the trucking industry because physically fit drivers are safer drivers.[3]

Micromarkets are very small market segments, such as zip code areas or even neighborhoods.

Even smaller market segments are known as **micromarkets**, and marketing efforts aimed at these segments are called *micromarketing*. Micromarketing is the process of targeting these small, narrowly defined market segments. A large, upscale retail store, for example, may identify high-income neighborhoods within a city where the store's likely customers live. The retailer can then target those neighborhoods with announcements of special sales or store events.

On the individual consumer end of the continuum, a firm may decide to target individual consumers and personalize marketing efforts toward each. An example of personalization comes from Levi Strauss, which adopted this approach with its Levi's Personal Pair and Original Spin personalized women's blue jeans. These blue jeans are custom tailored to fit each individual's own size and fit requirements. You can visit Levi Strauss' home page to see how to purchase a unique pair of jeans customized to fit. Other common examples of delivering individual consumers with customized products are common in services: wedding planners, hairstylists, doctors, and even Burger King, which invites customers to "have it your way."

http://www.levi.com

A time-poor society and the increasing popularity of in-home, interactive shopping options, such as the Internet, are leading to greater personalization or customization in markets. Consider the choices. An individual consumer sees a mass-media advertisement, wants the product, runs out to a mass merchandiser to buy that product, and returns with a mass-produced version of that product identical to everyone else's. The consumer, on the other hand, sees the product, wants it, connects to the manufacturer's home page on the Internet, requests a customized version of the product, and has that personalized version delivered to his or her home.

This interactivity, combined with innovative technological capabilities, allows firms to create a complete picture of individual customers based on their individual characteristics and preferences, then customize marketing efforts, especially services and information, to fit individual customer needs. The current trend in targeting markets is clearly toward this individualization and personalization of markets. The day is coming when customers will be able to scan in their own image and "try on" clothing. In fact, Adidas is already testing a digital scanner that measures shoe size.[4] Soon, consumers may even be able to use simple computer-assisted design (CAD) programs to design their own clothes for manufacture.

http://www.adidas.com

SEGMENTATION AND TARGET MARKETING

LEARNING OBJECTIVE 2

Advantages

In general, the process of segmenting markets and targeting them accordingly is a widespread practice with numerous advantages. The target market selection process is essential to marketing strategy for the following reasons:[5]

1. Identification of the market allows a company to know whom to analyze in its efforts to better understand potential and actual consumers.
2. A detailed analysis and understanding of the market allows a firm to develop and implement a marketing mix tailored to the specific needs of the market. For example, after carefully analyzing the needs of its market, Honda was able to reduce the price of its cars by reducing the number of available options, making the total product better suited to the needs of the car's "reliable" target market.
3. Identification of the market allows a company to assess potential demand for its products. For example, the total market for a principles of marketing textbook can be determined by looking at the number of college students enrolled in college business programs. The textbook publisher can then forecast the percentage of the total market it is likely to acquire, based on a specific formula and/or past experience.
4. Knowing the market allows firms to identify competing products in their specific market, and develop responsive competitive positions. Certainly, Burger King and McDonald's recognize that they are direct competitors in the burger market, and each responds to changes in the other's marketing efforts.
5. Targeting market segments with a marketing mix customized for specific market needs increases the likelihood of sales effectiveness and cost efficiencies in reaching the market. Foot Joy, for example, could maximize cost efficiencies by advertising its golf shoes in *Golf Digest*

http://www.mcdonalds.com

instead of in *Teen* or *People* magazines where most of the readers are not golfers.

6. Defining and analyzing a target market allows a firm to position its products to the market based on assessed needs and preferences. For example, Toyota could create a marketing mix that emphasizes an image of dependability, reliability, and good value from its cars, after understanding that these are the characteristics its market segment most desires.

7. Defining a target market allows a firm to identify opportunities. For example, the aging of the 76 million baby boomers suggests the need for products in three major areas: leisure and entertainment, pharmaceuticals and health care, and annuities.[6]

Disadvantages

A number of disadvantages to target marketing have also been identified. These disadvantages center on ethical criticisms of the practice and the possibility of missed opportunities from targeting specific segments. Firms should carefully consider these disadvantages when developing a targeted marketing plan.

1. Targeting multiple markets generally increases marketing costs.

2. Efforts toward personalization and individualization of markets can lead to proliferation of products that becomes overly burdensome and costly to manage.

3. Efforts to overly segment markets into too small niches may be viewed cynically by the targeted individual, and negatively affect consumer response to marketing efforts. After seeing letters to all your friends from Publishers Clearing House, your letter arrives stating that: "Yes, you, Lucky W. Inner, from Muleshoe, Texas, have won $10 million, if . . ." You may be a little skeptical, or even immune to such personalized tactics, and come to resent companies that engage in the practice. One writer terms this practice "faux segmentation" and asks "Who do these guys think they're fooling?"[7]

4. Narrowly segmenting a market to target may actually prevent a product from developing brand loyalty. Ned Anschuetz argues that the only way to build a large, sustainable brand-loyal customer base is to build broad brand popularity. More to the point, he says:

> *It is very clear, however, that building loyal frequent buyers means broadening brand appeal to more and more different kinds of households rather than narrowing it through segmentation to a small, homogeneous group. One can go further to say that to successfully build a base of loyal frequent buyers a brand must also become broadly popular among category users. This is the opposite of segmentation. It is integration, building brand popularity.*[8]

5. Target marketers have been widely criticized for unethical or stereotypical activities.

The most public criticism of segmenting and target marketing comes from minority and consumer groups who claim that the practice of aiming potentially harmful products to disadvantaged or vulnerable markets is highly unethical. Popular examples of such practices include Camel cigarette's Joe Camel character, which was accused of targeting children; the widespread practice of using extremely thin, waif-like models in advertisements targeting the identity-seeking, vulnerable teenage-girl market; and beer companies targeting underage college students. The consumer perception of targeting potentially harmful products, such as cigarettes, alcohol, and lottery tickets, toward vulnerable consumers, such as children, poor, or uneducated consumers, may have negative effects on the marketing firms. Some research evidence suggests that consumer ethical judgment of such practices can lead to behavioral reactions such as negative word-of-mouth and boycotts. In fact, plans for PowerMaster malt liquor and Uptown cigarettes aimed toward African American males and Dakota cigarettes aimed at pink-collar workers (working-class females) were canceled before the products were marketed because of public outcry.

Finally, the process of segmenting and targeting markets is akin to stereotyping and has been criticized for that reason. For decades, women were unrealistically portrayed as submissive to men, domestic, or as sex objects in advertisements, and the 50-plus market was portrayed by advertisers as doddering old people sitting on a porch and rocking all day. Images such as these further proliferate stereotyping and may actually alienate potential customers.

These criticisms and potentially negative and positive effects of segmenting and targeting markets are important for firms to consider when developing marketing strategies. A summary of these advantages and disadvantages appears in Table 7.1. However, the practice of target marketing is widespread and will likely continue far into the future because firms must understand the needs of their markets and deliver an appropriate marketing mix to succeed. To do this, they must first define their market through the target market selection process.

Summary of Advantages and Disadvantages of Target Marketing	Table 7.1

Advantages	Disadvantages
Defines the market for further analysis	Increased costs
Allows creation of a customized marketing mix	Increased number of products
Aids in assessing potential demand	Faux segmentation
Aids identification of competitors	May decrease brand loyalty
Increases sales effectiveness and efficiency	Some practices considered unethical
Aids in positioning products	Proliferates stereotyping
Aids in identifying opportunities	

LEARNING OBJECTIVE **3**

THE TARGET MARKET SELECTION PROCESS

The process of selecting a potential market, segmenting, analyzing, and profiling the market to better target it with a customized marketing mix is the *target market selection process*. This process consists of the eight interrelated tasks shown in Figure 7.2. Although depicted as a series of sequential steps, in practice the ordering of tasks varies, with some tasks actually occurring simultaneously or in a completely different order. Moreover, the target market selection process is a continuous, ongoing process because markets are dynamic and constantly changing.[9] Consequently, firms may need to revise their marketing mix based on the segments' changing needs or identify new markets to replace shrinking ones.

Not only is the segmentation process continuous, it may either be a priori or post hoc. *A priori* segmentation occurs when variables for segmenting markets, such as age or income, are selected first, then customers are classified accordingly. For example, a car manufacturer could decide that there are a large number of consumers with incomes greater than $75,000 and develop a car aimed at that group of consumers. *Post hoc* segmentation involves the examination of existing customer data, then segmenting it to classify the customers into segments, or clusters, based on similarities of variables.[10] A bank may use post hoc segmentation to analyze its existing customer database and determine which customers have the largest savings and then develop special programs to reach these segments. Some evidence suggests that post hoc segmentation is more common than a priori among businesses, especially small businesses, which actually create and offer a product then examine their customers in efforts to revise and refine their marketing mix.[11]

Identify the Total Market

The first step in the target market selection process is to specifically define the total market of all potential customers for a product category. Purchase patterns of the market and whether the user of the product is the same person as the buyer are a few factors that should be considered when defining the total market.

Who actually buys a product is not always obvious. For decades, men's clothing manufacturers have targeted their marketing efforts toward men. However, a recent survey commissioned by the Haggar Clothing Company indicated that women influence the selection of or actually buy 89 percent of all men's clothing purchased in department

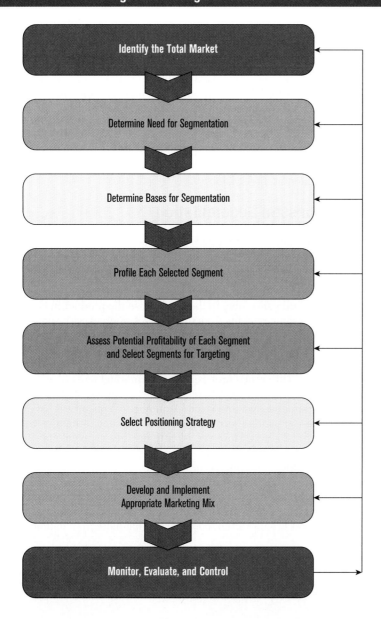

The Target Marketing Selection Process | **Figure 7.2**

Identify the Total Market

Determine Need for Segmentation

Determine Bases for Segmentation

Profile Each Selected Segment

Assess Potential Profitability of Each Segment and Select Segments for Targeting

Select Positioning Strategy

Develop and Implement Appropriate Marketing Mix

Monitor, Evaluate, and Control

stores. This finding suggests that the "market" for men's clothing is not men, but rather women. Haggar now intends to direct all of its advertising toward women.[12]

Determine Need for Segmentation

Another important task in the market segmentation process is determining whether the total market needs to be divided into segments for the purpose of targeting with special marketing programs; after all, not all markets need to be segmented. In general, for segmentation to be warranted, *there must be differences with respect to customer needs or demands, potential product variations must be cost-effective (profitable), and implemented product differences must be apparent to customers.*[13]

For example, the market for sugar is huge. Most kitchens stock sugar; but is there a need to segment markets when selling sugar? Probably not, because of the product's homogeneity of demand and little perceived differences in brands. Like the sugar market, the ready-to-eat (RTE) cereals market is huge: An amazing 95 percent of all American households purchase RTEs each year. Should the RTE market be divided into different segments for targeting? Consider this: Households with children ages 6 to 17 years old buy 75 percent more RTE cereal than average, while singles under 35 years spend 54 percent less than average on RTE cereal. However, these young singles spend 39 percent more than average on granola and natural cereal. Clearly, consumers have different demand preferences for RTE cereals, and they perceive real differences in brands. Some consumers prefer chocolate, rice, and a sweet taste for breakfast, while others prefer cereals that they believe promote good health.

Differences in demand preferences are only one criterion that firms must consider when deciding whether to segment a market. There are a total of five criteria for successful segmentation that should be considered along with various strategic and external factors in making the segmentation decision.

Criteria for Successful Segmentation

Criteria for successful segmentation
include target markets that are heterogeneous, measurable, substantial, actionable, and accessible.

Once a firm has identified potential market segments, the segments should be analyzed according to five **criteria for successful segmentation** before making the segmentation decision. In general, to successfully segment a market, the market must be:

1. Heterogeneous—Clear differences in consumer preferences for a product must exist. If all consumers in the market use the product in the same way and want the same benefits from the product, such as with sugar, there may be no added value from dividing the market into segments for special targeting. Clearly, however, there are differences in consumer preference, or heterogeneity of demand, for ready-to-eat cereals.

2. Measurable—Difference preferences for a product must be identifiable and capable of being related to measurable variables, such as age, gender, lifestyle, product usage, and so on. A number of consumers have larger than average feet and require large shoe sizes, such as men's size 20 or women's size 12 shoes. However, identifying these special consumers and associating them with specific variables, such as age, income, or geographic region, is virtually impossible.

3. Substantial—The proposed market segment must have enough size and purchasing power to be profitable. The benefits of alterations in the marketing mix must exceed the costs incurred from the changes. Obviously, the pet market is substantial, considering that more than half of U.S.

households have pets—a total of 58 million pets—and spend more than $5 billion dollars each year.[14] Segments within the pet market, such as all anaconda owners, may not be substantial enough to warrant specialized marketing efforts, however.

4. Actionable—Companies must be able to respond to difference preferences with an appropriate and profitable marketing mix. Although a marketing mix directed toward consumers with larger than average feet or toward all anaconda owners could be developed, the cost of marketing products only to those consumers may far outweigh the benefits derived from the revenue generated.

5. Accessible—The proposed market segment must be readily accessible and reachable with targeted programs. Consider the problems of reaching homeless consumers with information about discounted food and clothing or of inexpensively reaching only those male consumers who wear a size 20 shoe.[15]

Strategic Factors

Internally, a firm must consider the appropriate, viable segmentation strategy for reaching segments. Companies might develop one marketing mix strategy that is appropriate for all members of the total market, known as an *undifferentiated targeting strategy*. Generally, this strategy is effective when all members of the market have homogenous demand with respect to the product, as the case with sugar. This means that **differentiation** of the product by brand is difficult because, in general, all consumers derive the same benefits from different brands and there is little perceived difference between brands. Salt, flour, and fresh produce are examples of products where there is virtually no difference in brands or the benefits that consumers derive from those brands.

Differentiation
is the process of creating and sustaining a strong, consistent, and unique image about one product in comparison to others.

Where heterogeneity of demand exists, and thus multiple market segments, marketers may adopt either a concentrated strategy or a differentiated strategy. A *concentrated strategy* is where only one marketing mix is developed and directed toward a few, or perhaps one, profitable market segments. In contrast, a *differentiated strategy* exists when a firm develops different marketing mix plans specially tailored for each of two or more market segments. Each of the three types of segmentation strategies a firm might adopt are shown in Figure 7.3. Obviously, marketing costs increase as the number of market segments targeted increase. Considering the substantial costs of differentiated strategies, firms must examine the resource requirements for segmenting in light of available resources.

External Factors

Firms must also consider external factors that may affect the success of segmentation. The stage in the product life cycle, the competition, the product itself, and the market can each affect segmentation strategy. In response to strong competition and flat sales in a slow growth market, Coors Brewing Company implemented a differentiated strategy aiming new marketing efforts for its beer at the African American and Hispanic markets in the summer of 1998. Together with Asian Americans, these combined minority markets are expected to account for one-third of the U.S. population by 2010 and almost half by 2040.[16]

http://www.coors.com

Determine Bases for Segmentation

A number of different variables or descriptors can be used to characterize market segments and the data needed for the variables comes from a variety of sources. Specific variables used for segmenting consumer markets and descriptor information sources are discussed in this section.

Segmentation Variables

Segmenting means dividing markets into homogenous, or like, groups based on some related characteristic or trait. Any one or combination of a number of variables or descriptors of the market, such as astrological sign,[17] and attitudes toward the past,[18] can serve as a basis for segmenting markets. The most generally accepted bases for segmenting markets, however, are demographics, geographics, psychographics, benefits sought, situation, and behavior or usage patterns.

Demographic Segmentation. Age, income, occupation, level of education, race, gender, family life cycle, family size, religion, race, and nationality are demographic characteristics commonly used to segment markets for targeting. Most everyone is familiar with the descriptors associated with these important market segments, such as age, education level, and race.

Figure 7.3	Segmentation Strategies

Undifferentiated Strategy · **Concentrated Strategy** · **Differentiated Strategy**

Not as commonly known, but perhaps as important as these other segment variables, is the family life cycle. The *family life cycle (FLC)* describes the stages or evolution of the typical consumer over his or her lifetime. The FLC variable incorporates income and lifestyle to explain differences in expenditure patterns based on family role and transitions between roles.[19] Typically, consumers evolve from single, to married, then to married with children, to no children, to retired, and finally to single again. Quite obviously, consumers' needs for different products vary with each of these stages in the FLC. For example, singles buy canned vegetables in individual serving sizes and families with babies buy strained vegetables. Retired older persons may "buy" their vegetables by eating out in family-style restaurants. The family life cycle model is presented in Figure 7.4.

Geographic Segmentation. Geographic regions may be used to segment markets for specialized marketing efforts. Types of products and brands of products purchased vary greatly by regions of the world, country, state, city, or even neighborhood. Certainly snow sleds are common purchases in the northern sections of the United States, while outdoor furniture is popular in the South. Interestingly, one researcher has identified

Family Life Cycle	**Figure 7.4**

Bachelor I
Bachelor II
Newlywed
Single Parent (young and middle-aged)
Full Nest I (child < 6)
Delayed Full Nest (child < 6)
Full Nest II and III (youngest child ≥ 6)
Childless couple (no children home)
Older Couple
Bachelor III

Source: As shown in Charles M. Schaninger and William D. Danko, "A Conceptual and Empirical Comparison of Alternative Household Life Cycle Models," *Journal of Consumer Research* (March 1993): 580–594.

nine distinctively different regions of the United States, based on individual values called "nations of North America."[20] Regional differences are apparent in more than just values and purchase behavior—in speech and driving behavior, for example. While waiting in stop-and-go traffic, southern women are more likely to apply makeup than women from other regions of the United States, West Coast drivers are more likely to read while driving, and men with higher incomes are more likely to swear.[21]

Generally, geographic segmentation is used in conjunction with other segmentation descriptors. For example, companies may target teenagers in Dallas—which combines demographics with geographics and is called *geodemographics,* or they may target tennis-playing teenagers in New York City—which combines geodemographics and psychographics (lifestyle).

Geodemographics is a routinely used descriptor, and the data for demographically describing a geographic area is widely available from both private and public sources. For example, Business Information Solutions (formerly CACI Marketing Systems) and SRI Consulting Business Intelligence are private providers of descriptor information, and the U.S. Census Bureau serves as a public source of data. A summary of a sample profile from the CACI Web site for Austin, Texas 78701, is shown in Figure 7.5.

http://www.esribus.com

http://www.sric-bi.com

http://www.census.gov

Psychographic Segmentation. Segmenting markets by social class, lifestyles, and psychological characteristics, such as attitudes, interests, and opinions (AIO), and values, is increasingly popular and often creates a better picture of market segments than does demographics or geographics. These segmentation bases allow the marketer to truly understand the inner workings of potential consumers before developing a marketing mix aimed at those consumers. For example, a psychographic profile conducted for the automobile industry of the 11 percent of the U.S. population classified as *wealthy* indicates that there are three distinctive groups within the wealthy class, and that each must be targeted differently. Young wealthy individuals are active and are looking for adventure and thrills from driving, while safety and spaciousness are most important for wealthy baby boomers. Finally, the eldest group of the wealthy are looking for luxury and utility in their transportation.[22]

http://www.claritas.com

Claritas provides other psychographic tools, including the popular PRIZM analysis. PRIZM provides lifestyle segmentation analysis based on 62 distinct clusters throughout the United States. In fact, PRIZM was instrumental in developing the profile of Elvis fans shown in Figure 7.6.

Benefits-Sought Segmentation. Markets can also be segmented based on consumer preference for a specific product attribute or characteristic. Nowhere is this more apparent than the toothpaste aisle at your local grocery store. Various toothpastes not only help prevent cavities, they freshen breath, control tartar, contain baking soda or peroxide, provide gum care, are designed for consumers with sensitive teeth problems, and

Figure 7.5	Profile of Austin, Texas 78701

"This is the youngest and smallest consumer market, comprising the dormitories and student housing located around universities. Their budget goes to college expenses or an active social life. Top-ranked for take-out fast food, having ATM cards, and making long-distance calls using calling cards, their purchase decisions are based on price. They rank highest for watching sports on TV."

Total Population:	3,828
Male:	61.0%
Female:	38.9%
2000 Median Household Income:	$31,027
2000 Average Rent:	$493

Source: Business Information Solutions, http://www.infods.com/freedata, accessed 15 April 2002.

Profiling Elvis Fans	Figure 7.6

Most any market can be profiled for more efficient targeting. Take Elvis fans, for example. Though not a huge market, approximately 700,000 fans pay $15 each to visit his home in Memphis, Tennessee, each year. Using information, such as zip codes, from some 7,000 members of Elvis fan clubs across the nation and tying it to Claritas's PRIZM system, Bob Lunn profiled Elvis fans. The profile included a map of the United States showing attitudes toward Elvis by geographic area. For example, the highest concentration of Elvis fans in the nation is in Banks, Georgia, followed closely by Tupelo, Mississippi, Elvis' birthplace. A number of areas around major cities also contain a large number of Elvis fans, such as Washington County, Pennsylvania; Atlanta, Georgia; Austin, Texas; Kansas City, Missouri; and San Diego, California. Despite the fact that typical Elvis fans are white women between the ages of 40 and 50 with no college education, Elvis memorabilia shown on television is sold primarily to women in their 30s and men in their 20s. Lunn's profile also indicated that Elvis lovers typically purchase video cameras, malt liquor, menthol cigarettes, pickup trucks, Velveeta, *National Enquirer*, frozen dinners, and *Soldier of Fortune*. Get the picture?

Source: Brad Edmonson and Linda Jacobsen, "Elvis Lives Again," *American Demographic* (January 1998): 18–19.

they whiten teeth. There are even special toothpastes for children that have many of these same attributes including whitening and flavors. Recently, another toothpaste segment was identified: consumers who are concerned about deterioration of tooth enamel. This segment has led to the introduction of Enamelon, which is designed to strengthen tooth enamel. Other examples of product benefits that can serve as a basis for segmentation are airline systems divided into first, business, and coach classes; restaurant seating in smoking and nonsmoking sections; and mail delivery via regular service or express mail. Based on preferences for each of these items, customized marketing mixes can be developed.

Most segmentation strategies should include the benefits-sought variable. After all, marketers must understand the benefits their consumers want from a product before an appropriate marketing mix can be tailored to a specific segment. Then, consumers must understand how that product will solve their needs best before they will buy it. Many experts maintain that the benefits sought from a product are more predictive of consumer purchase behavior than any other segmentation variable.[23]

Situation Segmentation. The purchase situation or occasion can also serve as a basis for segmenting markets. Think, for example, about purchasing a meal and what might influence the purchase decision. A meal purchased by a busy student to eat in the 10 minutes between classes would likely be much different from a meal purchased for a much anticipated first date, or even a meal purchased for a night at home alone watching TV. Each of these situations or purchase occasions represents a different market segment potentially suitable for targeting.

There are five different situational characteristics that may each affect purchase behavior and serve as a descriptor for a market segment. These situational characteristics and examples are:

1. Physical Surroundings—Is the store or salesperson pleasant or offensive?
2. Social Surroundings—Are friends or parents watching the purchase?
3. Temporal Perspective—How much time is there to make the purchase?
4. Task Definition—Why is this product being purchased? Is it a gift? If so, is it a gift for a girlfriend? boyfriend? parent? boss?
6. Prepurchase Attitude—What is the purchaser's mood at the time of purchase, happy or sad?[24]

These situational variables can serve as the basis for a unique marketing mix. For example, in today's time-poor society, marketers can define segments based on the temporal perspective—consumers who are time conscious or pressed for time—and develop a marketing mix tailored toward them that emphasizes convenience and time savings.

Behavior or Usage Segmentation. Loyalty toward a product, the way a product is used, and usage patterns (heavy, medium, or light users) can also serve as a basis for segmenting markets. A major factor to consider here is the *80/20 principle*. This means, in general, that about 20 percent of a firm's customers are responsible for generating 80 percent of the firm's revenue. Firms must pay special attention to developing and maintaining close relations with this "best" 20 percent of their loyal customers. The Gerland's Food Fair example shown in Figure 7.7 illustrates how one company identified its best customers then developed promotions especially for them.

Another example of appealing to the heavy-users segment comes from the classic Miller Lite advertising campaign. The beer and its advertising campaign were designed to appeal to heavy beer drinkers who complained about wanting to drink more beer, but often couldn't because they were too full. The advertisements told consumers that Miller Lite tastes great and is less filling, effectively appealing to heavy beer drinkers. The successful campaign lasted over 20 years and resulted in sales as high as 22 percent of all beer sold.[25]

http://www.millerbeer.com

Collect Segmentation Data

Information for segmenting markets may be obtained from internal or external sources. Internally, most companies create and retain information about their existing and potential customers in a database. However, to expand their customer base, firms need to get new prospective customers into their database for targeting. This data must be obtained from external sources.

Internal Database Sources

http://www.mci.com

These customer and marketing databases can be tremendous in size: Fleet Financial Group, for example, has a 500 gigabyte marketing database and MCI WorldCom has about 2.5 terabytes (TB) of sales and marketing data.[26] Examples of customer information often collected in an internal database are date of birth (age), educational attainment, profession, credit rating, purchases, purchase patterns, and so forth. This information can be sorted and results used to classify customers into segments based on selected attributes or characteristics in an increasingly popular process called data mining.

http://www.americanexpress.com

Data mining is exploring data for patterns and relationships. These patterns can be used to target specific groups with special programs. For example, American Express could examine the data from all of its customers who purchased an airline ticket using their credit card in the last year. Their ticket purchase patterns—time of day, day of week, destination, frequency of travel, or even class of travel—and purchases made while traveling could be explored to determine patterns or segments. The company could then separate consumers with similar purchase patterns into segments for targeting with

Figure 7.7	Opportunities from Databases: The Gerland's Story

Gerland's Food Fair, Inc., based in Houston, Texas, is considered a leader in database marketing in the grocery industry. The company has created a 250,000-household database of its 20-store chain. The data comes from customers themselves. As customers check out, their "Advantage" card is scanned and each purchase is then recorded so the store knows what each customer buys, when they buy it, and how much they buy. The monitoring of individual customer purchases allows the firm to better use their marketing dollars by targeting their loyal shoppers: the ones who shop 2.98 times a week and spend over $35 during each visit. Gerland's has implemented a number of programs aimed at these loyal purchasers. One promotion gave free turkeys to customers who spent $500 during an 11-week period while another promotion continuously rewarded customers who spent $250 with a 5 percent gift over a 13-week period. After these customers spent $1,000, they were given a $100 gift certificate.

Source: Len Lewis, "Divided Loyalties," *Progressive Grocer* 76 (February 1997): 47–48.

special catalogs and direct mail about travel clubs and special products, such as luggage and vacation travel packages. Internal data are readily available to firms and can be extremely valuable in developing customized marketing mixes.

Results from data mining and databases have been used in a number of ways. American Express has helped restaurants identify their frequent, lunchtime-only customers to target with special promotions.[27] AT&T uses its database to send inquiries from the least profitable customers to automated answering systems, while the best customers hear human voices.[28] Federal Express uses its database to segment consumers according to their value and need, matching anticipated customer value with market-segment spending.[29]

http://www.att.com

http://www.fedex.com

External Data Sources

Databases have been shown to be extremely useful for firms profiling their *existing* customers. In order to grow, however, firms need to expand their customer base. A useful way to acquire these prospects is to buy mailing lists. There are a wide variety of lists such as magazine or catalog subscribers, association members, voters, and postal residents, and they are available for myriad consumer types and interests. For example, *The Lifestyle Market Analyst* published by Standard Rate & Data Service contains a section of consumer magazines and direct mail lists sorted by lifestyle. These consumer interest lists include everything imaginable—from consumers interested in art, casino gambling, or yachting to contributors to "Pete Wilson for Governor."

Lists of consumer e-mail addresses by demographic or geographic characteristics can also be obtained by using software that searches the Web with a technique called *spidering*. The software allows automated Web site searches for key variables. Possible search variables can include profession, state, city, or even countries. Personalized e-mail can then be sent to the individual names collected.

A large number of private organizations and magazines offer market research data and segmentation profiling. For example, among other publications, CACI publishes *The Sourcebook of Zip Code Demographics* and *The Sourcebook of County Demographics;* Standard Rate & Data Service publishes *The Lifestyle Market Analyst;* and Simmons Market Research Bureau, Inc., publishes an annual study of media and markets. Magazines such as *American Demographics* and *Sales & Marketing Management* often contain useful data about various types of markets.

Much useful information is in the public domain and available at no charge. One of the best sources of geodemographic information about market segments is the U.S. Census Bureau. The TIGER/Line Files with LandView Mapping capabilities can be used to access census data and is used by most profiling organizations. The TIGER/Line Files and other U.S. Census Bureau data are available online and at any U.S. Federal Repository Library.

Profile Each Selected Segment

Before a marketing program aimed at a specific market segment can be developed, the marketer must truly understand the typical customers in that market—their wants and needs, interests, attitudes, etc. A detailed picture of a market segment is called a *profile*. The profile should paint a clear picture of the typical customer for the company's product using all applicable segmentation variables discussed previously—demographic, geographic, psychographic, benefits sought, situation, and usage. Although this profile is a *generalized average* of the typical customer in the segment, it helps marketers discover and understand who the potential users of the product are, so that the best marketing mix for that customer can be developed. One way of profiling markets is to use a table such as that shown in Figure 7.8.

A now classic example of profiling comes from the "Don't Mess with Texas" antilitter campaign. Research had indicated that the typical deliberate litterer in Texas was a male between the ages of 18 to 34, drove a truck, liked sports, and did not typically respond to appeals to civic duty. The "Don't Mess with Texas" antilitter campaign developed from the profile of this Texas "Bubba" involved using sports celebrities and country music and rock stars in a macho appeal to these Texans' sense of pride in their state.

Figure 7.8   **Profile of Market Segments Form**

Profile of Market Segments Form

	Segment		
	A	B	C
Size			
Number of consumers			
Growth rate			
Profile			
Demographic characteristics			
Geographic characteristics			
Psychographic characteristics			
Benefits sought			
Product Usage			
Favorite brands			
Quantities consumed			
Occasions of use			
Etc.			
Communications Behavior			
Media used			
Frequency of media usage			
Etc.			
Purchasing Behavior			
Distribution channel preferred			
Outlet preference			
Purchase infrequency			
Price range			
Etc.			

Littering was reduced by an amazing 29 percent within 9 months after the campaign began.[30] The success of the campaign comes directly from a true understanding of the "typical litterer" and how to reach him. Another example of a profile, this time of teenagers, is presented in Figure 7.9.

Assess Potential Profitability of Each Segment and Select Segments for Targeting

Forecast Demand

Once segments have been identified and clearly distinguished, a firm must determine the profitability of customizing marketing efforts aimed at these segments. This involves first forecasting demand for the product within each segmented target market. For example, a company targeting college students in Louisiana would need to determine that there are 23 public colleges and community colleges and that the total enrollment in these schools in Spring 2001 was 162,602 students.[31] If the company expects a 50 percent share of the market, the sales forecast would be 81,301 units.

Firms must consider expected growth and competition in forecasting future sales. A large market share in a small, fast growth market may mean more long-term profits than a small market share in a crowded, stagnate, large market. Think about opening a new fast-food hamburger restaurant under slow growth, highly competitive market conditions with McDonald's as your competitor. Entering 2001, McDonald's owned a 43.1 percent share of the market and has a restaurant located within four minutes of most consumers.[32] Competitors' actions and other environmental factors that may affect future sales must also be carefully anticipated when forecasting potential demand.

| Teens: Can We Really Understand Them? | Figure 7.9 |

In 1997 there were about 29 million teenagers who spent, on average, 84 cents of every dollar they got, and they got about $64 each week. Not only do teens spend a lot of money, they influence the expenditures of others–about $58 each week on groceries–for a total exceeding $50 billion each year. They have the most influence on the purchases of sports drinks, breakfast bars, pretzels, tortilla chips, potato chips, sweet snacks, and desserts. Teens also heavily influence purchases of convenience type food items such as frozen foods.

The sheer numbers and purchasing power of teenagers in the United States makes this market attractive to many industries, including the restaurant industry. One research firm compiled a study of the teen market for restaurants and found the following:

- Peer acceptance, spending time with friends, and having fun are high priorities for teens.
- Teens recognize and resent fake attitudes and having others "talk down" to them. They want to be treated politely and with respect by a business.
- Teens value their music, so play "cool" music.
- Teens like to receive special treatment and like to be singled out as with teen-only cards or clubs.
- As for what makes a brand cool in the eyes of teens: 66 percent said quality, 47 percent said, "If it's for people my age," and 39 percent believed advertising made a brand cool.

This information about the teen market may help a new restaurant tailor its marketing mix to better attract those elusive teens.

Estimate Costs

The projected cost of developing and implementing specialized marketing efforts must also be determined. In the Louisiana college students example described earlier, the added costs of reaching this market might include revising the product to meet Louisiana college student needs, changing the price to fit the budgets of these college students, changing distribution channels by offering the product for sale in Louisiana college bookstores, and advertising in Louisiana college newspapers. Finally, the additional costs of the specialized marketing program must be weighed against the estimated revenue to be gained from the market segments and against company objectives and the resources required to generate those revenues.

Select Positioning Strategy

After the target markets have been selected and are fully understood, the marketing mix that best suits the target can be developed. Key to developing the appropriate marketing mix is the **positioning** strategy of the product. Creating and sustaining a strong, clear, and consistent customer image of the product in comparison with its competitors is key to *differentiating* the product, which is essential to developing a brand image that leads to customer loyalty. For example, take the PepsiCo product Mountain Dew. Sales rose an amazing 13 percent in 1997, placing the brand into the number four position in the carbonated drink market, ahead of Coca-Cola Company's Sprite, now ranked fifth. The success of Mountain Dew in the highly competitive soft drink market is attributed to a consistent, strong image that links teenagers, the major market segment, with outdoors, outrageousness, high energy, and the thirst-quenching ability of the drink. Although the messages change to fit the times, Mountain Dew has retained its strong position, packaging, and formula over the last 25 years.[33]

Effective positioning means determining (1) what consumers currently think about the product, especially in relation to competing products; (2) what the marketer wants consumers to think about the product; and (3) which positioning strategy will elevate the

Positioning
is the image that customers have about a product, especially in relation to the product's competitors.

http://www.coca-cola.com

consumers' current product image to the desired product image. In other words, where are we now, where do we want to go, and how do we best get there, bearing in mind the product position relative to competitors.

Determining what consumers think of a product often involves market research. A firm may want to survey its potential customers to determine what they think about the product based on several selected criteria, such as color, taste, freshness, etc. Criteria selected should be variables that are important to consumers and can be used to help the firm create a unique advantage or position for a product in the marketplace. A commonly used method for this is **perceptual mapping**. Interested students may want to visit http://www.surveysite.com/engine to view the perceptual mapping tutorial or create their own perceptual map using the demonstration of the Market Visioner tool at http://www.dssresearch.com.

An example of a perceptual map shown in Figure 7.10 was created from hypothetical data for pain relievers. In this example, consumers rated seven different brands of pain reliever according to how they believe each brand performs on the product characteristics: reasonably priced, hard to swallow, gentle, good for children, long lasting, and effectiveness. The perceptual map gives brand manufacturers a clear picture of how their product is perceived to perform on the selected characteristics, how each product performs on the attributes as compared to the competition, and gaps in the market that may need filling. The map of consumer perceptions of product characteristics helps answer the where-are-we-now question, and the gaps help provide possible answers to the where-we-want-to-go question. Figure 7.10 illustrates hypothetical consumer perceptions that Tylenol is the most gentle and competes closely with Motrin, private label brands are the hardest to swallow, and Anacin and Excedrin are the most effective. What would you do if you were the brand manager for Bayer or Panadol?

Not only does the positioning strategy determine where a company wants to go, it must also specify how to get there. Generally, products can be positioned by any one, or combination, of the following ways:

Perceptual mapping
is a commonly used, multidimensional scaling method of graphically depicting a product's performance on selected attributes or the "position" of a product against its competitors on selected product traits.

http://www.tylenol.com

| **Figure 7.10** | **Perceptual Map of Pain Relievers** |

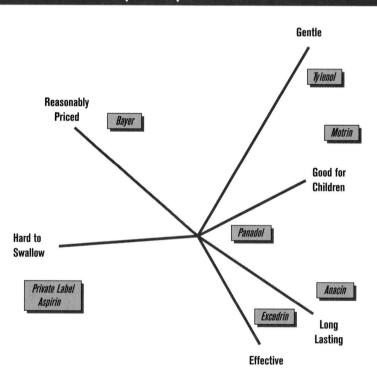

- Price/Quality—Positioning by price/quality emphasizes the value derived from the product, either in terms of its quality or price or both. Wal-Mart stores are positioned based on every day low pricing (EDLP) and good value, while Neiman Marcus stores offer unique, high quality products for sale. The advertisement for the Chevrolet Corvette, shown in Figure 7.11, is an example of positioning by quality.

Example of Positioning by Quality	Figure 7.11

- Product Attributes—The characteristics or attributes of a product may serve as the basis for positioning the product. Some Colgate-Palmolive toothpastes are positioned by their attributes: Colgate Tartar Control Plus Whitening has both an antitartar and whitening formula for "clean, white teeth," and Colgate Total toothpaste helps prevent cavities, gingivitis, plaque, and tartar and provides "long-lasting fresh breath protection." These toothpastes are clearly positioned in consumers' minds based on product attributes.
- Product User—The typical user of a product can also be used to position a product. Marlboro cigarettes, with their Marlboro man, appealed to the rugged individual, and the Motorola v60 phone, shown in Figure 7.12, is positioned to appeal to the successful, individualistic business leader.

Figure 7.12	Example of Positioning by User

- Product Usage—Products can be positioned based on the ways in which they are typically used. For example, the advertisement for Aquia Sanitizing System in Figure 7.13 shows different ways in which the Aquia may be used.

Example of Positioning by Product Usage   **Figure 7.13**

- Product Class—Some products are positioned against another type of product or product class. The advertisement in Figure 7.14 hints that the nutritional, low-calorie energy bar Pria is an alternative to a chocolate candy bar.

Figure 7.14	**Example of Positioning by Product Class**

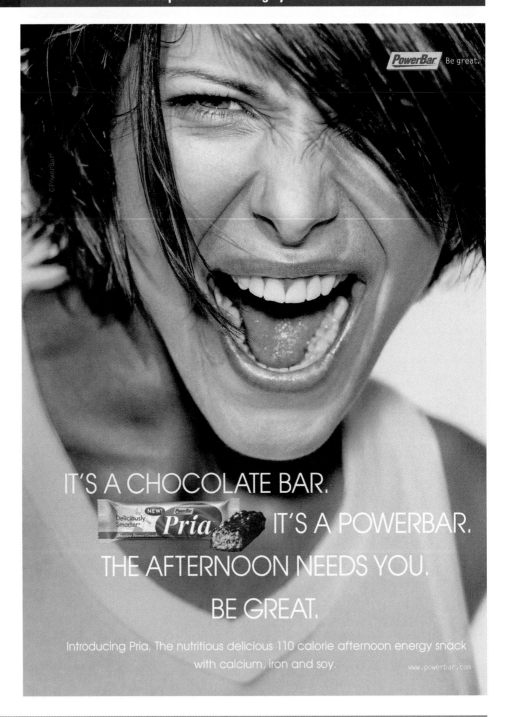

- Competition—Comparing a product to its competition, either directly or indirectly, is another form of product positioning. Burger King and McDonald's often compare their products to each other as do Ragu and Prego spaghetti sauces. Tide claims to "clean better" and Imodium AD is positioned against the "white stuff" and the "pink stuff." Product advertisements do not have to name a competitor, however, to be considered positioned based on competition. The ad shown in Figure 7.15, for example, positions Snyder's Bakery Pretzel Pieces against all other flavored pretzels.

Example of Positioning by Competition   **Figure 7.15**

- Symbol—Occasionally companies use a symbol or icon to position their product in the minds of consumers. Over time, the symbol can become synonymous with the company or product as with the Maytag Man, the golden arches of McDonald's (or Ronald McDonald), the Pillsbury Doughboy, the Jolly Green Giant, and, of course, the Nike swoosh. In each of these cases, most adult consumers have a clear image about the product or company by merely seeing the symbol.

http://www.nike.com

As companies', competitors', and consumers' needs evolve over time, brand positions may also need to change. This process of creating a new image about an existing product in consumers' minds is called *repositioning*. Repositioning involves changing existing attitudes and beliefs about a product, and is much more difficult and more costly than establishing a position for a new product. To illustrate the difficulty in repositioning, imagine Wal-Mart trying to convince you it is a high-priced, prestige store or that Neiman Marcus stores have clothing everyone can afford.

In one advertising campaign aimed at flat sales and a growing designer jeans market, Levi Strauss repositioned its brand of jeans as the brand that designers wore. The advertising campaign involved 20,000 billboards with slogans such as "Calvin wore them," "Tommy wore them," and "Ralph wore them." With this new positioning campaign, the company hopes to reassert Levi's as "America's authentic blue jeans," according to Mark Hogan, director of consumer marketing for Levi's.[34]

Also in a stagnate market with slow growth, Miller Brewing embarked on a repositioning strategy with its Genuine and Lite beer brands by returning to the old advertising slogan "It's Miller Time." The purpose of the repositioning strategy was to appeal to the 21-to-30-year-old market, while maintaining their existing beer drinking market. The revised strategy boosted sales revenues by 4.5 percent.[35]

Develop and Implement Appropriate Marketing Mix and Monitor, Evaluate, and Control

The final steps in the target market selection process are to develop and implement a marketing mix matched to the needs of the market segments selected for targeting and evaluating and controlling the plan. After putting the marketing mix into action, indicators of marketing effectiveness, such as sales and consumer perceptions, must be continually monitored and evaluated to determine effectiveness of the marketing mix in meeting desired plan objectives. New segments, new needs, and new opportunities may be identified through continual monitoring of target markets and changes in the mix made accordingly.

SEGMENTING BUSINESS MARKETS

Firms that sell products to other businesses rather than household consumers often need to segment their market, depending on heterogeneity of demand. For example, Weyerhaeuser makes wood products, such as particle board. It can sell this product to furniture manufacturers for use in building furniture, or it can sell the product directly to lumber yards for sale to household consumers. Each of these business customers has a different set of needs for the particle board product Weyerhaeuser sells. An understanding of each of the two markets will help Weyerhaeuser tailor an effective marketing mix that will satisfy each customer's needs.

Segmenting the business market can help a firm analyze the market, select the best markets for targeting, and manage marketing programs.[36] While the steps in the target market selection process are essentially the same for business markets as those shown in Figure 7.2, there are three major differences within the steps in segmenting business markets. Those differences include a thorough understanding of the purchase process—which differs greatly from the consumer market—differences in the bases for segmentation, and differences in how the segmentation is implemented. The business-to-business purchase process was discussed in detail in Chapter 6, so the discussion here is limited to segmentation descriptors:[37]

Demographics

The demographics components of the business market include the industry, the size and growth potential, and the location of the targeted firm operations. Although some firms sell products to companies in the same industries, as Nike sells shoes to Foot Locker or Footaction USA, some companies sell products to many different industries. Xerox, for example, sells its copiers to businesses in all industries, ranging from small independent restaurants to multinational heavy equipment manufacturers. By grouping segments into industry type, the selling firm can learn more about an industry to better develop a marketing mix that will help solve the markets' needs.

Selling firms may need to segment their business markets by company size and tailor their marketing efforts accordingly. For example, Xerox would certainly not devote the same resources to selling a copier to one restaurant in a small town as it would to selling thousands of machines to an international corporation. Finally, location is often an important descriptor for segmenting business markets. The proximity of the segment to sales offices or manufacturing facilities, or the geographic concentration of the market segment may substantially affect marketing efforts.

http://www.footlocker.com

http://www.footaction.com

http://www.xerox.com

Operating Characteristics

This descriptor is related to the operations of the targeted business and includes company technology, product and brand-user status, and customer capabilities. Obviously, the type and brand of product a customer business uses affects the way in which a selling firm will market the product to that business. Also, a supplying firm may want to approach loyal or heavy product users differently than it approaches infrequent product users. The business customer's technology and capabilities will also affect the types of products that a firm buys and its needs from supplying firms; and so may serve as a segmentation bases. For example, the computer needs of a large multinational firm with its own extensive, in-house computing specialists would differ greatly from those of a small-town restaurant. A firm selling computers to these two distinctively different markets would need to tailor the marketing mix to the specific needs of each.

Purchasing Approaches

Factors internal to the buying firm and its purchase process, such as what level in the organization products are purchased, purchasing policies, purchasing criteria, such as speed of delivery, size of order, and nature of the buyer-seller relationship, and so on, comprise the various purchasing approaches. A customer firm's purchase process, the policies and criteria for purchasing, and how formalized or centralized the process is can each affect a customer's special needs. For example, a large fast-food restaurant may purchase products at its main headquarters and disperse those products out to each individual member of the chain, or each store may buy certain products individually. Each of the two purchasing approaches requires different marketing tactics from suppliers. Different type of firms and specific policies for purchasing also require special marketing efforts. Some private firms and governmental agencies often require bids on all purchases over a set dollar figure or require that prices be based on supplier cost.

The stage in the purchase process can also serve as a bases for segmenting business markets. There are three distinctive stages that may each represent a different market segment, regardless of the industry. These stages are first-time prospects, novices or new users, and sophisticates or long-time users.[38] Buyers in each of these buying categories have a different set of needs from the supplying firm, so marketing mixes customized to the needs of each segment can be developed.

Product Use or Usage Situation

The way in which a product is used by a business and the level of service a customer needs can also determine the marketing efforts required to effectively reach that business market. Weyerhaeuser's sales of particle board to different markets mentioned at the beginning of this section is an example of product use segmentation. The Ryan's Family

Steakhouse chain has a service technician who visits each site and maintains equipment, such as ice makers, while a single, independent restaurant in a small town may need the seller of the equipment to maintain that equipment. Accordingly, selling firms can devise different marketing plans based on different needs for services from the supplying firm.[39]

Situational Factors

As with consumer market segmentation, a myriad of temporary, situational factors can affect purchasing needs of the business-to-business market. Most obviously, special product uses and special physical distribution requirements such as order size and urgency of delivery can affect the purchase process, and thus serve as bases for segmenting the market.

Buyers' Personal Characteristics

Finally, the individual personal characteristics of the participants in the purchase process can influence a buyer's needs. For example, some buyers are afraid to take risks and require a lot of time and information to make a decision, or a buyer could have a brother-in-law who also sells the needed product. In the first case, the supplier may need to develop a marketing mix that provides this type of buyer with testimonials and substantial support about product benefits to reassure the buyer, while in the second case, the supplier may not want to waste valuable resources targeting this buyer.

As with segmenting consumer markets, a combination of these segmentation variables are generally needed to draw a profile of business market segments. Once the potentially profitable segments are profiled, specialized marketing mix programs can be implemented to meet their special needs and the plan can be monitored, evaluated, and controlled.

LEARNING OBJECTIVE 5

SEGMENTING GLOBAL MARKETS

Increasingly, companies must reach out to foreign countries to prosper, as opportunities for domestic growth in many industries decline. After all, about two-thirds of the world's total purchasing power and 95 percent of the population lives outside the United States.[40] In the restaurant industry, international sales are growing faster than are domestic sales for the industry's top 100 companies.[41] McDonald's alone has over 10,000 restaurants

Speaking the Language

What would you think if you got a letter from a phone company that tells you "Con nosotros no habra sorpresas"? If you don't speak Spanish, you probably don't understand the message. What's more you may be irritated with this company that just can't seem to understand who you are.

Such mistakes from marketers trying to directly target market segments with personalized messages may increase unless they take extra care in monitoring their mailing lists. The 2000 census figures found at http://www.census.gov confirm the significance of diversity in the U.S. population. About 12.5 percent (35.3 million) of the population is Latino and 4.2 percent (11.9 million) is Asian, for example. This diversity makes the target marketing process even more difficult, since each of these significant consumer groups has diverse backgrounds that affect not only what they buy and how they think, but also determine the languages they speak. For example, the Asian population is in part made up of Korean, Japanese, Vietnamese, and Chinese, each group having a different native language. The Latino subculture is just as diverse with members descending from Mexico, Puerto Rico, and Central America, among others. That diversity is likely to continue, at least in the Latino market, as three-fourths of Latino youth are bilingual and 54 percent consider themselves "Hispanic only."

So what's a direct marketer to do? Companies such as Geoscape International and Ethnic Technologies have developed the technological capability of running mailing lists of customers' names through software to examine different consumer characteristics such as country of origin and time and place in residence to determine most probable language preference. Considering last and first names can provide a clue useful in determining language preference. For example, Jorge Sanchez and Sulema Martinez are more likely to speak Spanish than Michael Sanchez or Sue Martinez. Although helpful, using both names alone may not be enough to identify language preferences because married names, among other factors, can further cloud the issue. Information about automobile type, children at home, computer use, and so on may also be used to further focus on preferred markets. Finally, areas of a region, city, or even neighborhood can be examined for all of these same characteristics for direct targeting purposes.

This type of list-filtering technology allows firms to better determine language preference for appropriateness of mailings, as Verizon discovered in a promotional campaign it used when the firm launched its long-distance telephone service in New York state. Thanks at least in part to the multilingual direct marketing efforts, the firm gained 1.7 million customers in one year. Though not perfect, these methods help eliminate some mistargeting errors so that "there will be no surprises with us."

Sources: Rebecca Gardyn, "Habla English?" *American Demographics* (April 2001): 54–57; Sandra Yin, "Lesson in Linguistics," *American Demographics* (August 2001): 36–37.

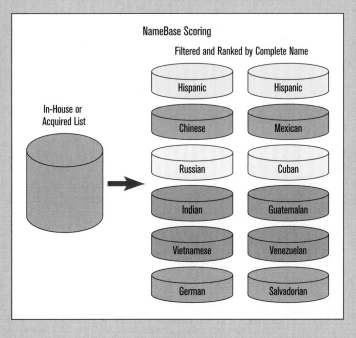

NameBase Scoring

Filtered and Ranked by Complete Name

In-House or Acquired List

Hispanic · Hispanic
Chinese · Mexican
Russian · Cuban
Indian · Guatemalan
Vietnamese · Venezuelan
German · Salvadorian

internationally, in over 105 countries with a new store opening, on average, every 4 hours.[42] Just as in domestic markets, firms must understand who their customers are through market segmentation and match the marketing mix they deliver with the needs of their customers before entering these new global markets.

In general, the target market selection process and the segmentation descriptors are the same for global markets as for household consumer markets. Like domestic consumer markets, global markets can be segmented based on demographics, geographics, psychographics, benefits sought, situation, and usage. A common approach is to segment international markets geographically by country combined with demographics or general lifestyle of the country, although some research indicates that combining geographics with consumer purchase behavior patterns is preferable.[43] Other variables that are generally considered in defining homogenous demand segments in international markets include economic, legal/political, and cultural factors.

Economic Factors

The stage of industrial development of the country may affect the ability, willingness and capability, and purchase patterns of individuals in the market. For example, consumers in poorer, developing countries spend proportionally more of their incomes on basic consumer goods and services, while more prosperous developing countries spend more on durable goods.

Legal/Political Factors

The political and legal environment of a country may affect the ability of a firm to market to its consumers so that specialized marketing programs must be revised to meet those requirements. For example, the French government requires that marketers get special permission from the Commission Nationale Informatique et Liberté before creating a customer database.[44] The stability and type of government must also be considered in defining segments and determining the way in which products are marketed in countries. The protectionist government in Mexico, for example, has hindered marketing practices in that country.[45]

Cultural Factors

Culture and language can pose real challenges to firms targeting consumers in different countries. Marketers targeting Canadians must consider the fact that both English and French are spoken in Quebec and that a law forbids making offers there in only one language.[46] Cultural and religious factors can also affect consumer needs for goods and services in ways that marketers must consider. The Islamic religion's proscriptions for

female dress would certainly affect a clothing firm's offerings in Muslim countries. Similarly, certain colors have different meanings in different countries. For example, white, a symbol of purity in America, is a symbol of death in Asian countries.

Despite these differences by country, some market segment lifestyle traits transcend country boundaries in what is known as *intermarket segmentation*. A profile of some intermarket "global consumers" is shown in figure 7.16.

As with household consumer markets and business markets, the best market segment profiles are derived from a combination of market descriptors. A summary of these descriptors is shown in Table 7.2. However, firms deciding to target international markets may have difficulty in finding data needed for defining segments. Many countries do not have a standardized, routine census of citizens to provide reliable demographic and geodemographic data about potential consumers. Also, data needed for some segmentation descriptors are very difficult to obtain or nonexistent. Finally, an effective target marketing program evaluates potential segments for profitability, then continuously monitors the effectiveness of both the marketing mix in meeting customer needs and the environment for opportunities and changes in the market.

The Global Consumer	Figure 7.16

Research has defined profiles of five homogeneous lifestyle segments that apply to consumers worldwide. Those groups are:

- *Rich around the World* – These consumers frequently travel, want quality, and will pay for it; they love new goods and services.

- *Older and Comfortable* – Members of this segment are 55 and older, have plenty of time on their hands and discretionary income to spend, although they are very value-oriented. They look for leisure products and new experiences, they like to buy gifts and to travel.

- *Indulged Kids* – The trend toward one-child families in many developing countries has created families that spend lavishly on things for their children. Typical items purchased by members of this segment include popular clothing, video games, electronics, and compact discs.

- *Emerging Middle Class* – In many developing countries, a growing middle class is now demanding basic goods and services widely available in the United States, such as household items, consumer electronics, and health and beauty aids. While this segment is value-oriented for these basic products, they will pay premium prices for high-quality, high-prestige items.

- *Women Employed Outside the Home* – In developed and some developing countries, a large percentage of women with families work. These women look for convenience and time-saving products and for services for the family, such as home maintenance and child care.

Summary of Segmentation Descriptors by Market Type	Table 7.2

Consumer Market	Business Market	Global Market Same as Consumer Market, Plus:
Demographic	Demographic	Economic
Geographic	Operating Characteristics	Legal/political
Psychographic	Buyer's Personal Characteristics	Cultural
Benefits Sought	Purchasing Approaches	
Situation	Situation	
Behavior/Usage	Product Use/Usage Situation	

CHAPTER SUMMARY

- Successful firms must truly understand the markets they serve and match their marketing mix to the needs of the market, in a process called target marketing. A market is an individual, group of individuals, or organizations willing and able to purchase a firm's product. A market may be subdivided into any number of smaller markets, called segments. The number and the size of markets a firm may select for targeting can vary greatly from a mass market to one individual.

- The target marketing process is extremely important to businesses because it allows firms to identify and analyze their customers, develop tailored market mixes to meet customer needs, identify market demand, identify competition, increase operating efficiencies, improve product positioning, and identify opportunities. Despite these advantages, there are some disadvantages to target marketing. Most notably, some firms have targeted disadvantaged, poor, or uneducated consumers with illegal or unethical products; others have portrayed some market segments stereotypically and offensively; and in doing so both groups have created cynicism toward target marketing practices. These firms may have actually inhibited brand popularity and loyalty, and wasted money and effort.

- Nevertheless, the target marketing process is important and begins with: (1) identifying the total market; (2) determining the need for segmentation based on criteria for segmentation, strategic factors, and external factors; and (3) determining the bases for segmentation using demographic, geographic, psychographic, benefits sought, situation, and behavior (usage) descriptors. The firm must then collect segmentation data. These sources may be internal (from the company's database) or external (from research, other firms, or the government). The target marketing process continues with the following steps: (4) profiling each selected segment; (5) assessing potential profitability of each segment and selecting segments for targeting; (6) selecting the positioning strategy on the basis of price/quality, product attributes, product user, product usage, product class, competition, or symbols; (7) developing and implementing an appropriate marketing mix; and (8) monitoring, evaluating, and controlling the selection process.

- Firms that target other businesses can segment their markets using the same process. However, the bases for segmentation for business markets include demographics, operating characteristics, purchasing approaches, product use or usage situations, situational factors, and buyers' personal characteristics. Targeting global markets also requires the same target market selection process but has slightly different segmentation descriptors. Along with the consumer markets segmentation descriptors, global segments should be profiled using economic, political/legal, and cultural factors.

KEY TERMS

Criteria for successful segmentation include target markets that are heterogeneous, measurable, substantial, actionable, and accessible.

Differentiation is the process of creating and sustaining a strong, consistent, and unique image about one product in comparison to others.

Market segments consist of groups of consumers who are alike based on some characteristic(s).

Micromarkets are very small market segments, such as zip code areas or even neighborhoods.

Niche marketing is the process of targeting a relatively small market segment with a specific, specialized marketing mix.

Perceptual mapping is a commonly used, multidimensional scaling method of graphically depicting a product's performance on selected attributes or the "position" of a product against its competitors on selected product traits.

Positioning is the image that customers have about a product, especially in relation to the product's competitors.

QUESTIONS FOR DISCUSSION

1. StrengthMaker, the maker of a creatine monohydrate product designed to help body builders build muscle mass, is considering targeting high school athletes for its product, even though some people consider the use of creatine risky because it has been associated with pulled muscles and kidney damage. Explain the advantages and disadvantages of this strategy and make a recommendation about targeting the teenage market segment.

2. Using Figure 7.2 as a guideline, select and profile a target market for LitTalk, an audiotape copy of great literature, such as *Great Expectations* and *War and Peace,* covered in popular college literature textbooks. Use as many bases of segmentation variables as possible.

3. Since everyone drinks water, explain why you would or would not segment the "water" market if you were selling Naya bottled water. What if you were selling prune juice? Justify your answers using the criteria for successful market segmentation.

4. Which segmentation variable(s) is most important? Why?

5. Find articles in the library that discuss the target market for a particular product, such as Guess jeans or Nike, and profile the market. Include as many of the segmentation bases as possible.

6. Understanding what consumers are looking for in a product, or benefits sought, is an important way of segmenting markets. Ask 10 friends what they most want from their shampoo, then identify possible benefits-sought market segments for shampoo.

7. Discuss sources of data for segmenting markets.

8. Find an advertisement that represents positioning based on each of the seven ways discussed in the chapter. Explain each selection.

9. Compare and contrast segmentation for consumer markets, business markets, and international markets.

INTERNET QUESTIONS

1. Profile your hometown by visiting the U.S. Census Bureau Web site at http://www.census.gov/main/www/access.html. First click on Map Stats, then click on your home state, and select your county or parish. Click to browse more data sets for your area. Under Geography QuickLinks, browse the TIGER map of your area to draw a map of your hometown area; under Other QuickLinks access the U.S. Counties General Profile for 1996 to obtain the latest census information about your county. Also access Business Patterns and Economic Profile for your area.

2. Visit http://www.visa.com and http://www.mastercard.com. How do these companies target college students? Explain your suggestions for improving their targeting efforts.

3. What is your Internet privacy IQ? Visit http://www.truste.org and take the TRUSTe Privacy Challenge.

ENDNOTES

[1] Kenneth Hein, "Red Bull Charging Ahead," *Brandweek,* 15 November 2001, 38–41; Ellen Neuborne and Kathleen Derwin, "Generation Y," *Businessweek Online,* 15 February 1999. Kelly Pate, "Denver Native's Energy-Drink Company Bolts Out of Gate," *Denver Post,* 1 March 2002. "Making the Grade: Generation Y Sends College Marketing to the Extreme," *Promo,* 1 August 2001, 19. Annie Layne Rodgers, "It's a (Red) Bull Market After All," *Fastcompany.com,* October 2001, http://www.fastcompany.com/build/ build_feature/redbull.html, accessed 27 March 2002. "Top-10 U.S. Soft Drink Companies and Brands for 2001," *Beverage Digest,* Special Issue, http://www.beverage-digest.com/ editorial/020228s.php, accessed 28 February 2002.

[2] Peter R. Dickson and James I. Ginter, "Market Segmentation, Product Differentiation, and Marketing Strategy," *Journal of Marketing* (April 1987): 1–10.

[3] "Health Club for Truckers," *Marketing News,* 5 January 1998, 1.

[4] David Pescovitz, "The Future of Clothing," *Wired,* at http://www.wired.com/wired/ archive/3.11/reality_check.html, accessed 17 June 1998.

[5] Adapted from Jock Bicker, "Cohorts II: A New Approach to Market Segmentation," *Journal of Consumer Marketing* (Fall–Winter 1997): 362–380.

[6] N. H. Dover, "Where There's Gray, There's Green," *Marketing News,* 22 June 1998, 2.

[7] Kevin Sheridan, "Segs and the Single Card," *Bank Marketing* (August 1997): 5.

[8] Ned Anschuetz, "Building Brand Popularity: The Myth of Segmenting to Brand Success," *Journal of Advertising Research* (January/February 1997): 63–67.

[9] Sally Dibb and Lyndon Simkin, "A Program of Implementing Market Segmentation," *Journal of Business & Industrial Marketing* (Winter 1997): 51–66.

[10] Yoram Wind, "Issues and Advances in Segmentation Research," *Journal of Marketing Research* (August 1978): 317–337.

[11] Erwin Daneels, "Market Segmentation: Normative Model Versus Reality," *European Journal of Marketing* (June 1996): 36–42.

[12] Carol Marie Cropper, "Haggar Men's Wear Turns to More Sophisticated Consumers: Women," *New York Times,* 6 October 1997, D12.

[13] Paul E. Green and Abba M. Krieger, "Segmenting Markets with Conjoint Analysis," *Journal of Marketing* (October, 1991): 20–31; Dickson and Ginter, "Market Segmentation, Product Differentiation, and Marketing Strategy," 1–10.

[14] Adapted from Green and Krieger, "Segmenting Markets with Conjoint Analysis," 20–31.

[15] Mary Brophy Marcus, "Target Market: Fido, Fluffy—You," *U.S. News & World Report,* 1 December 1997, 57.

[16] Maricris G. Briones, "Coors Turns Up the Heat," *Marketing News,* 22 June 1998, 1, 15.

[17] Vincent-Wayne Mitchell and Sarah Haggett, "Sun-Sign Astrology in Market Segmentation and Empirical Investigation," *Journal of Consumer Marketing* (Spring 1997): 113–132.

[18] See Morris B. Holbrook and Robert M. Schindler, "Market Segmentation Based on Age and Attitude Toward the Past: Concepts, Methods, and Findings Concerning Nostalgic Influences on Customer Tastes," *Journal of Business Research* (September 1996): 27–40.

[19] Charles M. Schaninger and William D. Danko, "A Conceptual and Empirical Comparison of Alternative Household Life Cycle Models," *Journal of Consumer Research* (March 1993): 580–594.

[20] Lynn R. Kahle, "The Nine Nations of North America and the Value Basis of Geographic Segmentation," *Journal of Marketing* (April 1986): 37–47.

[21] "Drivers' Habits Revealed," *Marketing News*, 22 June 1998, 2.

[22] "Profile: The Wealthy," *Automotive Marketing*, 3 April 1996, 5–28.

[23] Russell I. Haley, "Benefit Segmentation: A Decision-Oriented Research Tool," *Journal of Marketing* (Summer 1995): 59–62.

[24] Russell W. Belk, "Situational Variables and Consumer Behavior," *Journal of Consumer Research* (December 1975): 157–164.

[25] C. J. Mellor, "Though the Beer Is Lite, Campaign's a Heavyweight," *Back Stage*, 15 January 1988, 1–3.

[26] Craig Stedman, "Marketing Megamarts on the Rise," *Computerworld*, 22 September 1997, 65–66.

[27] Kate Fitzgerald, "Marketers Capture Prospects Using AmEx 'Closed Loop,'" *Advertising Age*, 9 October 1995, 18–19.

[28] Michael Schrage, "Sticky Times for Customer Service," *Computerworld*, 23 February 1998, 25.

[29] Laura Loro, "FedEx Mines Its Database to Drive New Sales," *Business Marketing* (March 1997): 4–6.

[30] "Real Men Don't Litter," *Time*, 19 January 1987, 25.

[31] "Statewide Student Profile System, Spring, 1995–96 Master File," http:\\www.regents.state.la.us/Reports/datapub.htm, accessed 29 March 2002.

[32] Bob Sperber, "As Wendy's Supersizes Growth, McD's, BK Lose Some Sizzle," *Brandweek*, 18 June 2001, 9.

[33] Louise Kramer, "Mountain Dew Stays True to Its Brand Positioning," *Advertising Age*, 18 May 1998, 26.

[34] Miles Socha, "Levi's New Ads Play the Name Game," *WWD*, 5 May 1998, 16.

[35] Greg W. Prince, "Time and Again: Miller Goes Straight to the Core and Likes the Results," *Beverage World*, 15 February 1998, 32–35.

[36] Benson P. Shapiro and Thomas V. Bonoma, "How to Segment Industrial Markets," *Harvard Business Review* (May/June 1984): 104–110.

[37] Section adapted from Shapiro and Bonoma, "How to Segment Industrial Markets," 104–110.

[38] Thomas S. Robertson and Howard Barich, "A Successful Approach to Segmenting Industrial Markets," *Planning Review* (November/December 1992): 4–12.

[39] For more detail, see Arun Sharma and Douglas M. Lambert, "Segmentation of Markets Based on Customer Service," *International Journal of Physical Distribution and Logistics Management* (May 1994): 50–58.

[40] Dom Del Prete, "Winning Strategies Lead to Global Marketing Success," *Marketing News*, 18 August 1997, 1–2.

[41] Kimberly D. Lowe, "Going Global; Operating a Restaurant in Familiar Territory Is Tough Enough: Some Companies Raise the Stakes by Going Overseas," *Restaurants & Institutions*, 1 November 1997, 65–70.

[42] Jolie Solomon and John McCormick, "A Really Big Mac: Bruised, Battered and Bashed, McDonald's Deserves a Break—Today," *Newsweek*, 17 November 1997, 56–58; Kimberly D. Lowe, "Going Global: Operating a Restaurant in Familiar Territory Is Tough Enough. Some Companies Raise the Stakes by Going Overseas," *Restaurants & Institutions*, 1 November 1997, 65–70.

[43] Peter G. P. Walters, "Global Market Segmentation: Methodologies and Challenges," *Journal of Marketing Management* (January/April 1997): 165–177.

[44] Hallie Mummert and Lisa Yorgey, "Selling Around the World," *Target Marketing* (January 1995): 28–32.

[45] Ibid.

[46] Ibid.

[47] Adapted from Jane Adler, "Suddenly Security," *Credit Card Management* 14 (January 2002): 30–37; "Anthrax Immunity?" *Chain Store Age* 77 (December), 110–111; "As Credit Card Mail Volume Soars Response Rates Reach New Low," *Direct Marketing* 64 (June 2001): 12; "A Red Light for Telemarketing," *Credit Card Management* 14 (8): 12; Burney Simpson, "How Rising Postage Could Change Card Marketing," *Credit Card Management* (September 2001): 78, 80–82; and Direct Marketing Association, "Economic Impact: U.S. Direct Marketing Today Executive Summary," report posted on the DMA Web site, http://www.the-dma.org/cgi/registered/research/libres-ecoimpact2.shtml, accessed 27 March 2002.

TARGETING CREDIT CARD CUSTOMERS BY MAIL: WHAT NEXT?[47]

Direct marketing consists of reaching consumers in a target market directly through telephone, mail, television, newspaper, magazine, radio, and "other" categories, including interactive and Internet marketing. In 2000, total spending on direct marketing efforts was $191.6 billion, more that half of the U.S. spending on all advertising. This expenditure resulted in total sales of $1.7 trillion, a figure expected to reach an incredible $2.7 trillion by 2005. A breakdown of direct marketing expenditures and resulting sales dollars for both consumer and business-to-business markets by media for year 2000 is shown in Table 7.3 below.

As this table shows, $44.6 billion was spent on direct mailings that generated $528.5 billion in sales. This expenditure on direct mail accounts for a significant 23 percent of the total direct marketing expenditures in the United States. Direct mail category spending is expected to continue its growth through 2005 at a rate of 6.4 percent each year.

A major player in the direct mail game is the credit card industry. In 2000 alone, 3.5 billion direct mail pieces from credit card companies were mailed, meaning that the average household received three mailings each month. At a U.S. Postal Service best rate of 24.3 cents, that means the mailings cost credit card companies over $850 million. This expenditure is huge considering that only about 6 of every 1,000 people who receive these credit card mailings actually respond, though not too surprising considering that about 75 percent of all households already have a credit card. So why do credit card companies continue to use direct mail, despite the low response rate? Direct mail accounts for 68 percent of the new credit card applications and is the most preferred way of hearing about credit card offers.

Two new major challenges face the direct mail industry. First, in September 2001, anthrax-tainted mail was discovered to have passed through the U.S. Postal Service and terrorists struck the World Trade Center in New York City. Many worried that these terrorist events would make consumers fearful of opening mail from unknowns, including businesses they have never used. The immediate effects on mailings, however, appeared fairly limited in time and scope. Estimated sales from direct marketing efforts dropped by only 2.4 percent below predictions. While the direct effects of the anthrax-tainted mailings and 9/11 appear short-term, consumer cautiousness may linger as a result of a heightened sense of concern for the future—a fear of what's next. The second, potentially more harmful effect on direct mail efforts may be the stream of increases in postal rates that will likely continue into the future, considering the financial condition of the U.S. Postal Service. With both the increasing cost of postage and the new costs companies now incur to ensure customer (and company employees') mailings safety, direct marketers will likely change the way they reach targeted customers.

Many direct marketers, including credit card companies, are implementing new direct mail practices. Examples include clearly labeling the outside of the envelope with

CHAPTER CASE

Expenditures and Resulting Sales of Direct Marketing by Media Category for Year 2000, in Billions of Dollars		Table 7.3

Media	Expenditure	Sales
Telephone	$73.2	$611.7
Direct Mail	$44.6	$528.5
Direct Response TV	$21.9	$117.6
Newspaper	$18.4	$239.0
Other (including interactive marketing)	$16.0	$ 92.0
Magazine Direct Response Advertising	$ 9.8	$ 91.3
Radio Direct Response	$ 7.7	$ 50.4

the brand name, putting "teaser" messages on the outside of the envelope, using new envelopes with windows that wrap around the bottom or have tamper proof seals, and even e-mailing customers telling them to expect a mailing. Some firms are also responding to the new challenges by reducing direct mailing efforts in favor of TV advertising, e-mailing, encouraging online bill paying, and telemarketing. Some of these alternatives to direct mail present challenges as well, for example, the passage of an increasing number of state and federal laws that regulate spam (unsolicited e-mails) and telemarketing, consumer resentment of firms that use telemarketing and spam which they consider an invasion of privacy, and limited e-mail lists.

Nevertheless, these limitations may mean that direct mail is likely to stay around for a long time. As marketers have noted: "The U.S. Postal Service goes to every home in the country. E-mail doesn't have nearly that level of market penetration" (*Chain Store Age*, 111).

Discussion Questions

1. Should credit card companies continue to use direct mail as a major means of finding new customers? If not, which methods should they use? Why?

2. Should credit card companies use different methods of customer contact for different market segments? Explain.

3. Keeping in mind the threats that face direct mail, suggest new ways for credit card companies to modify their mailings to ensure consumer privacy and safety.

PART three

Product

CHAPTER 8

Marketing's Role in New Product Development and Product Decisions

CHAPTER 9

Services Marketing

CHAPTER eight

Abbie Griffin,
University of Illinois,
Urbana-Champaign

Dr. Griffin earned her Ph.D. in management from the Massachusetts Institute of Technology, her M.B.A. from Harvard University and her B.S.ChE from Purdue University. She is editor of the *Journal of Product Innovation Management*, and serves as director of the Product Development and Management Association. She has received the 1997 Marketing Science Institute Best Paper Award, the 1993 John D. C. Little Best Paper Award, and the 1994 Frank M. Bass Dissertation Paper Award for "Voice of the Customer." Dr. Griffin teaches product development and business-to-business marketing.

Her research interests include measuring and improving new product development processes, obtaining customer inputs into new product development, decreasing time to commercialize products, and management of technology.

Dr. Griffin's professional experience includes consulting in marketing, strategic planning, and technology management to technology dependent firms. She is on the Board of Directors of International Truck and Engine (formerly Navistar).

Marketing's Role in New Product Development and Product Decisions

The Newton personal digital assistant (PDA) was conceived by the advanced research group at Apple, evolving out of their development effort to eliminate keyboard entry into computers. The Newton's core benefit proposition (CBP) was to capture, organize, and communicate ideas and data, without requiring keyboard entry.[1] The advanced research group and Apple management defined Newton's form and features without first asking how people in the target market were capturing information and what unsolved problems remained. In the end, Apple found that $800 bought a lot of pens, Post-It Notes, paper, calendars, and even electronic address books. Newton did not solve peoples' remaining information-use problems in a cost-effective way. Newton sales were dismal, and the product was ultimately withdrawn from the market.

Contrast Newton's failure to the runaway success of the Palm Pilot, another PDA. The Palm Pilot's CBP is also to capture, organize, and communicate ideas. However, Palm Pilots provide value to customers not only by replacing paper or electronic address books and calendars, but also by replacing computer-based time management systems. Individuals are therefore willing to pay the $200 to $400 purchase price. The product is so successful that it has spawned a whole host of look-alike competitors.

Why was the Palm Pilot successful while the Newton was a dismal failure? There are three major differences between the Newton and the Palm Pilot, each of which contributed to the Palm Pilot's success. First, the Palm team obtained input from potential customers while developing the design. For example, they obtained size and carrying reactions from one of their own employees in the business development group because he wore Brooks Brothers shirts, which have the smallest pockets of any major shirtmaker. Additionally, the Palm Pilot's buttons that allow users to switch instantly from one application to another, say from the calendar to the to-do list, are arranged according to information about the frequency of use for each application gathered from customers.

Second, the handwriting recognition technology in the Palm Pilot, although less sophisticated than Newton's, works much more effectively. Palm Pilot users must learn a simple, but rather intuitive, alphabet (called "Graffiti") to make written inputs. For example, writing "⌐" with the stylus produces a "t". Palm created a product from proven technologies that require users to modify writing behavior to conform to a standard form, but works reliably when they do so.

The third success contributor is the way the Palm Pilot seamlessly integrates with other standard products, including both computers and software. The development team thought through solutions to peripheral details of information management problems, rather than just thinking of the PDA as the total answer. The PDA itself was one piece in a full system that solved the set of problems surrounding capturing, organizing, and communicating information. The data exchange cradle and desktop software included with the PDA create a system that functions effectively, both when a user is in the office and away from the office. Overall, by soliciting customer input to guide the design, using proven technology to deliver the design, and ensuring seamless integration with other already available products, the Palm Pilot was quickly accepted by customers (with sales of over a million units by year three) in a way the Newton never achieved.

Palm not only designed an effective and useful new product, it supported the positioning of the product in the market through its branding and packaging strategies—some of the product management decisions marketing makes. Palm used the brand, the "Palm Pilot," which is evocative of the product's purpose and size (packaging)—it would pilot you through your day, while fitting in the palm of your hand.

But the Palm team didn't stop there. The original Palm used a simple yet effective design philosophy with intuitive interfaces to deliver a clearly defined and somewhat narrowly focused set of benefits to their target market—business professionals with complex schedules, networks, and lives. While the original Palm Pilot has been retired, the product line has expanded over time to reach other segments with slightly different needs, which has allowed the Palm portfolio of products to continue to grow sales over the product life cycle. For example, the Palm IIIx targets those with higher performance (more storage, more interactivity) needs. The Palm V is more aesthetically streamlined, with increased screen contrasts. Its more sophisticated packaging of the functions appeals to more mature and upscale business professionals. Business professionals requiring continual wireless contact are targeted by the Palm VII, which is positioned between two-way pagers and wireless Internet–accessing laptops. Finally, the M100 and M105 are recent, "cooler" Palm models with functions, features, and prices that are more appropriate for teenagers and college students—whose lives seem to be more complicated than ever.

The Palm story is an excellent example of a business unit that set the stage for product success by first uncovering customer needs, and then developing a competitively advantaged product that delivered effective, obvious answers to those needs. The company followed up by creating a brand name and package that appeals to the target market and captures the essence of the purpose of the product. Finally, Palm has developed a portfolio of products over time that spread the brand's appeal from their initial target market to many others, which has allowed the division to grow, profit, and prosper over the life cycle of the product, even in the face of numerous entering competitors.

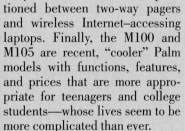

After you have completed this chapter, you should be able to:

1. Categorize products by type.
2. Define new product success and newness, and learn how to set the stage for creating success.
3. Describe strategies, processes, and organizational structures by which products are developed.
4. Discuss the importance of branding, packaging, and labeling decisions.
5. Understand how to manage products through their life cycles.
6. Identify issues associated with managing across the multiple projects in the portfolio.

http://www.palm.com

This chapter provides information about new product development and product management decisions. It begins with information about different kinds of products, and definitions of product newness and new product success. The chapter then discusses how to set the stage for achieving new product success and the steps necessary for developing competitively advantaged products. Marketing decisions about product branding, packaging, and labeling are also presented. The chapter ends with discussions of managing products through their life cycle and managing product portfolios.

TYPES OF PRODUCTS

Products[2] are the core of every organization. Whether it be a good, service, person, place, or idea, organizations need a product to offer. In general, products offer customers a bundle of attributes that address a set of needs. The attributes may include the product's **features**, its package and **brand** name, the service that supports product performance, on-time delivery, courteous and effective customer relations, an adequate warranty, and so on. Over time, customers choose products with the set of features that delivers the maximum benefit for them. Based on differences in markets, buyer attitudes and motivations, purchase patterns, and product characteristics, products can be categorized into several groups with important implications for marketing mix decisions.

In general, products can be classified as either consumer or business-to-business products, depending on *who the buyer is* and *for what purpose the product is being bought*. If a consumer purchases a product for his or her own household use, the product is called a *consumer product*. Consumer products are classified further into categories based on how the consumer views and shops for the product. Products purchased by organizations to be used in producing other products or in operating their businesses are classified as *business-to-business products*. Business-to-business products are further divided into categories based on how the products will be used.

Consumer Products

Examples and the marketing mix implications of the four kinds of consumer products are summarized in Table 8.1.

- *Convenience products* are typically inexpensive items consumers purchase with little effort, which are used on a frequent basis. Consumers spend little time shopping for convenience products.
- *Shopping products* are more expensive than convenience products, so the decision to purchase them is more important. The consumer will spend more time searching for information before selecting a particular brand, and compare prices and benefits among brands offering similar features.
- *Specialty products* are high-involvement consumer purchases, where the product reflects the consumer's personality or self-image. Thus, consumers are willing to spend a great deal of time to acquire one particular brand. Substitutes are not an option.
- *Unsought products* are either unknown to the buyer or are known, but not actively being sought at this point in time. Consumers do not search for unsought products until they need or are made aware of the products.

Business-to-Business Products

The five categories of business-to-business products vary in how they are used, as well as the closeness, or strength, of the relationship between the buyer and seller (see Chapter 6).

- *Raw materials* are unprocessed products that become part of a company's finished goods. Almost all raw materials are commodities. Farm products such as milk, eggs, corn, wheat, and processed sugar are considered raw materials for the food industry, as are oil and gas for the chemical and petroleum industries. Because there is little or no differentiation between sellers, buyer-seller transactions are conducted at arm's length.
- *Supplies* are used in support of business operations but are not part of the finished product. Supplies are standardized, purchased often, and are

Classifications and Marketing Mix Considerations for Consumer Products				Table 8.1
Marketing Mix Considerations	**Consumer Product Type**			
	Convenience	**Shopping**	**Specialty**	**Unsought**
Product Examples	Soda and other soft drinks, milk, toothpaste, soap	Clothing, computers, appliances, furniture	Luxury items: Rolex watch, Jaguar cars	Insurance, medical trauma services
Consumer Attitudes	Low involvement, minimize time and decision effort, feature and price focus	Moderate to high involvement, balance between image and features/functionality	Very high involvement, image (brand) far more important than features	Unaware, possibly avoiding learning about category
Consumer Purchase Behavior	Frequent purchases, no planning, routine decisions	Less frequent purchases, planned shopping, compare along multiple dimensions	Infrequent purchases, special purchase effort, little brand comparison	Infrequent purchases, comparison shopping (features and brand) when made aware of need to purchase
Place (Distribution)	Widespread, with convenient locations	A large number of more selective outlets	Limited and exclusive, few outlets per market	More selective outlets, from few to many
Price	Inexpensive, low price	More expensive, moderate price	Very expensive, high price	Varies
Promotion	Mass communication, focus on price, availability, awareness	Mass communication and personal selling, focus on features, differentiation	Targeted communication, stress brand and status	Aggressive ads to create awareness, personal selling to close sale

inexpensive compared to other product categories. Examples include pens, paper, Post-It Notes, cleaning solutions, and lubricating oil. Buyer-seller interactions for supplies are arm's length, with little or no ongoing relationship between the firms.

- *Accessories* are usually standardized pieces of equipment that support the overall running of factories and businesses. They are purchased more frequently than installations, but far less frequently than supplies. Examples include printers, copiers, retail display cases, and delivery trucks. While accessories are frequently bought through arm's-length transactions, some firms have developed stronger relationships with one or two suppliers to try to reduce overall costs. For example, USX (formerly US Steel) has a long-term supply relationship with Compaq for all the firm's PCs.

- *Component parts and materials* are products that are partly assembled or already processed to be ready for assembly into the finished product. Hamburger patties, buns, ketchup, onions, and pickles are all component parts/materials for both McDonald's and Burger King. Tires, seats, and engines are components used in manufacturing new automobiles. Firms are trending toward closer buyer-seller relationships with their suppliers of components and materials, using relationship marketing to try to capture competitive advantages through differentiation and product design efficiencies.

- *Installations* are major capital goods. Usually, installations are customized, expensive, and purchased infrequently. Products such as buildings, laboratories, and major computer systems are all considered installations. The

http://www.mcdonalds.com

selling process is typically longer, more complex, and more challenging than for any other type of business-to-business product. The practices of relationship marketing are the norm for installations.

Without a product, there is no firm. Thus, the long-term basis for the success of a firm relies on its ability not only to market one product well, but also to continue to grow and prosper by developing new products for the marketplace. As we saw in the previous section, firms have many types of products that they can choose to develop. The next section of this chapter outlines issues associated with understanding developing potentially successful products, by providing information that sets the stage for successful development.

SETTING THE STAGE FOR SUCCESSFUL NEW PRODUCT DEVELOPMENT

This section covers the three underpinnings for managing successful new product development programs: information that helps firms define and evaluate products under development, requirements for developing successful new products, and definitions of and methods for uncovering unmet needs.

Defining Products: Newness, Success, and Failure

Defining What We Mean by New

The next time you go through the grocery store, go to the cereal section and count the number of cereals that you do not recognize. Some of these products will be totally new types of cereals. Others are variants, or **line extensions**, of current products, as Honey

Line extensions are new products that are developed as variations of existing products.

Nut Cheerios is a line extension of Cheerios. Walk around the store and look at the packages that declare a product is "New and Improved." One dimension of newness is how new a product is in the eyes of the market. This ranges from small, incremental changes to improve one aspect of performance or to provide choice variety, to totally new types of products that solve problems never before solved for consumers.

http://www.cheerios.com

A second dimension of newness is how new the product is to the firm. Theme parks are familiar products for consumers, but a theme park based on cars would be a very new product for Ford Motor Company to produce. It would require much more effort for Ford to develop a new theme park than for Disney, which has built them before, just as it would require much more effort for Disney to develop a new car than it would for Ford. While it may not make strategic sense for Ford to develop a new theme park, it might make sense for Ford to diversify beyond cars and trucks into the motorcycle market. Again, motorcycles are not new to consumers, but they would be new to Ford, and likely would require more time, effort, and risk for the company to develop than a new car.

http://www.ford.com

http://disney.go.com

Overall, "newness" is thus a combination of newness to the market and newness to the firm. Products that are newer on either dimension are riskier to develop and commercialize. "New-to-the-world" products—products that create an entirely new market—are the riskiest of all, but present enormous profit potential, because they represent monopoly opportunities, at least in the short term. On average, only 10 percent of the products commercialized by firms are new-to-the-world. As shown in Figure 8.1, most of the projects in firm portfolios are improvements to products already on the market or additions to existing lines (line extensions), and products that are new to the firm but already manufactured by competitors (new product lines).[3] Fully 70 percent of the average firm's products focus on changing or adding to current products.[4] Ultimately, however, a new product is any product a firm spends money on to change, improve or reduce cost.

Firms do not commercialize a product, and then just reap ongoing profits. Once a product is developed and introduced to the market, competitors introduce products that improve on the initial product's performance. New technologies also become available over time that solve additional customer problems not addressed by the first-generation product. Both events require that firms manage products and product development as an ongoing spiral, as shown in Figure 8.2.[5] Thus, product development does not take place just once, but must be repeated over and over for a firm to stay in business in the long run. Some cycles of the spiral may only be small, incremental changes in the product. For example, in each of the two years after Ford introduced the Taurus, they made small changes in a number of components. Some changes were made to reduce costs, while others were to improve quality and performance. In other cycles, more radical changes were made, as when Ford totally redesigned the Taurus for its 1996 reintroduction. The target market for the Taurus remained unchanged, as did its **core benefit proposition (CBP)**.

Core benefit proposition (CBP) is the primary benefit or purpose for which a customer buys a product. The CBP may reside in the physical good or service performance, or it may come from augmented dimensions of the product.

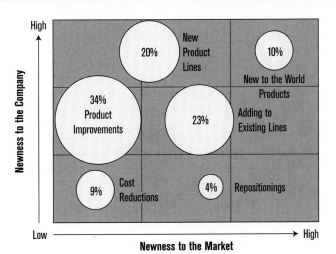

The Average Project Portfolio   **Figure 8.1**

| Figure 8.2 | The New Product Development Spiral |

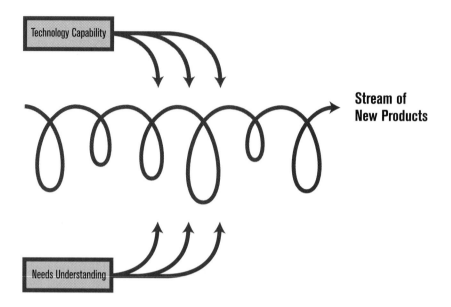

However, both the styling and many components and subsystems were updated, some with newly available technology or materials. These design changes in turn caused manufacturing changes. Just keeping pace with competitors requires repeatedly reinvigorating products to make them new in the eyes of customers.

Defining What We Mean by Success

Developing new products is time- and resource-consuming, as great care must be taken to ensure the best decisions are made *before* the product reaches channel members and final consumers. Much of this chapter looks closely at the process and management of product development. However, before discussing methods for new product development (NPD), it is first important to consider what firms are actually attempting to achieve by introducing new products to the market. Quite frankly, new product development success is difficult to define. Whereas most firms' ultimate objective is financial success, some product development projects have goals that are more than just financial. The Ford Taurus, for example, achieved a high market share though it had the lowest long-run quality of any Ford car or truck in 20 years, and did not break even on recovering development expenses for many years. However, in Ford's eyes, and in the eyes of many customers, the Taurus was very successful. How, then, should product success be measured?

NPD managers recommend that *NPD project success* be measured using four items that span three dimensions.[6] One item is a measure of *financial success*, most frequently the project's profitability. A second item assesses *technical performance success*, often measuring the product's competitive advantage from a technical (performance) point of view. For example, a new Intel processor may be 20 percent faster than the competitor's current processor. The specific performance measure used depends on which features and specifications are important to consumers. The third dimension consists of two measurements that evaluate *success from the customer's perspective*—most frequently, *market share* and *customer satisfaction*. A new product in the ready-to-eat cereal category is considered a success if it achieves only a 1 percent share of this highly fragmented market. On the other hand, in more concentrated industries such as pickup trucks, firms look for a new truck to obtain a 20 to 25 percent share.

Achieving product success along one dimension does not necessarily mean the product will achieve success along another. For example, superior technical performance levels may not lead to a significant market share or customer satisfaction. As the Taurus example shows, a product can even achieve high levels of customer satisfaction without achieving profitability, if either development spending or product cost is not controlled.

Unfortunately, the perfect product development project that achieves high levels of success on all three dimensions, known as the *silver bullet*, rarely exists. Firms frequently sacrifice some level of success on one dimension to achieve success on another. For instance, the objective of one project may be to increase customer satisfaction; another may be to raise the technical performance bar for the product category. Though profits need not be the primary goal of any particular project, the firm does need to generate a profit across the portfolio of products that comprise its **product mix**.

Product mix
is the full set of a firm's products across all markets served.

Why Products Fail

Achieving product success is difficult. Even though firms over the last 20 year have improved the probability that a project which starts the new product development process will succeed, it still takes almost five projects to create one market success,[7] as Figure 8.3 illustrates. Projects are abandoned during development for a number of reasons. Sometimes available technology is unable to meet desired performance specifications or a desired price point. At other times, a firm's strategy changes, rendering the product no longer interesting, or a competitor beats the firm to the market. A firm may uncover information that suggests the product as conceived would not solve customer problems, and thus they would not purchase it. Sometimes the development team is unable to interest marketing or management in commercializing the product.

Even if a product makes it to market, it can be a failure. On average, only about 55 percent of products that are launched are categorized as successes by the commercializing firms.[8] Products can fail due to either strategic or development process factors, or some combination of the two. Strategic reasons that products fail in the marketplace include:

- Failure to provide an advantage or performance improvement to customers over products already available in the market
- Lack of synergy with the technologies and manufacturing processes of the firm, requiring that the firm learn about how to design and make new technologies
- Marketing synergies lack necessary distribution channels, promotion and selling practices, or pricing policies, often because the product targets a group to whom the firm has never before marketed a product.

Additionally, products may not be successful in the marketplace because different aspects of the new product development process were not executed effectively. The most important aspects to manage effectively in the process are the predevelopment stages (idea generation and screening, preliminary investigation, and detailed investigation) and the proficiencies of both the technological and marketing-related activities within them. Failure also results when a firm fails to develop a well-thought-out **project strategy** at the outset of the process. Lack of strategy can lead to a mistargeted product, or one that lacks benefit. Finally, projects that have not garnered upper management support

Project strategy,
sometimes called a protocol, is a statement of the attributes the project is expected to have, the market at which it is targeted, and the purpose behind commercializing the product.

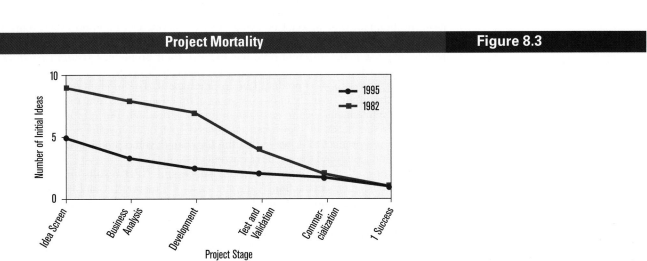

Project Mortality   **Figure 8.3**

throughout the development process are more likely to be failures in the marketplace. Lack of management support can lead to performance that is not quite high enough to win sales, or inadequate marketing expenditures to create adequate awareness and trial when the product is launched.

The next sections of the chapter provide insights into how to prevent most of these failures.

Requirements for Developing Successful New Products

The objective for marketing professionals and new product development teams is to create a series of Palm Pilots for their firm. The key is to do this not just once, but systematically and repeatedly. Actually, effective product development only requires that a firm successfully complete three activities:

1. Uncover unmet needs and problems
2. Develop a **competitively advantaged product**
3. Shepherd products through the firm

These three activities are simple enough in concept. Unfortunately, none of them is easy to complete. Further, if any one activity is not fully completed, the product is unlikely to succeed in the marketplace. Each activity requires that the firm master a different set of complex issues. Each issue must also be addressed across functional lines. Marketing cannot address the issues alone; neither can engineering or any other functional area. For example, developing a competitively advantaged product requires: (1) input from customers on unmet needs; (2) input from marketing as to what the competition is doing to address the need; (3) input from manufacturing about what the firm can currently build to satisfy the need; (4) input from engineering as to what additional technologies are available; (5) input from R&D about new ways of potentially addressing the need; and (6) input from finance about costs. Excelling at each NPD activity requires cooperation across multiple departments, which is still difficult to achieve in many corporations.

Another difficulty in implementing these activities arises because firms do not undertake product development solely for one purpose. Growing a business over time requires a continual process of repeatedly recommercializing old products to maintain (or grow) the firm's presence in current markets and commercializing new products to expand the firm's market presence. The activities required for sustaining current business through NPD, however, may differ from those needed for expanding market presence.

A product development team working on the next generation Palm Pilot product, for example, starts from an already available base of features, software, and manufacturing assets. All of these must be taken into account in developing a new version so that already obtained economies are not lost. Their task for the next cycle may be to gather more in-depth information, but in a narrower area of function or use, as they already have a great deal of knowledge concerning the needs of all potential customers—both existing and unrealized. *Potential customers* are the population of people or organizations who have the problem your product is trying to solve. If you are the Palm Pilot group, your potential customers are people who need to keep their complex lives organized. These people may use many different products to solve their problem. *Existing customers* are the subset of potential customers who already use your firm's products. They are already satisfied enough with your product line to purchase it. The product development team gathers further input, usually in narrow areas of function or use, from existing customers to produce refinements for the next generation of a product. But it is not until the firm understands the needs of *unrealized customers*—potential customers who are not yet using the firm's product offerings—that the firm can develop products that truly expand its market and go beyond the needs of current customers.

Fulfilling all three requirements for successful NPD results in profits, market share, and customer satisfaction. Take the case of Procter & Gamble's Pert+™. The product's core benefit proposition—to simultaneously clean and condition hair—originally targeted women away from home, either traveling, or those showering after a workout at a health club, for example, because it allowed them to eliminate carrying multiple bottles of products. While other products previously had tried to fulfill this CBP, none had. One firm's failed attempt consisted of supplying both conditioner and shampoo in one bottle, like an oil and vinegar salad dressing. Using it required shaking vigorously to

---

Competitively advantaged product is a product that solves a set of customer problems better than any competitor's product. This product is made possible due to this firm's unique technical, manufacturing, managerial, or marketing capabilities, which are not easily copied by others.

http://www.pg.com

http://www.pert.com

mix the two parts into one consistent fluid. Unfortunately, like oil and vinegar dressings, the first few uses of a new bottle usually contained a lot more shampoo than conditioner, and the last few uses had more conditioner than shampoo. Although the need was well known, achieving cleaning *and* conditioning had been an unsolvable technical problem. Indeed, it took researchers at Procter & Gamble nearly 10 years to discover a technical solution—a radically different surfactant system (wetting agent) than had ever been considered. Once the technical problem was solved, the project management system at Procter & Gamble moved the product to market. This very different technology has provided Procter & Gamble with a sustainable competitive advantage and has resulted in a successful entry in the shampoo category, both in terms of share and profits.

Uncovering Unmet Needs and Problems

Defining customer needs. Customer needs are the problems that a person or firm would like to have solved. They describe what products let you do, not how they let you do it. Customers have general problems they want solved that relate to overall product performance. These needs are readily obvious. For example, people need to "be able to communicate with others when we are not together."

Products deliver solutions to customers' problems. Telephone service solves the problem of communicating with others when we are far away, as long as the other person also has a telephone and you know the phone number (or can get it). Every competitor knows that they must develop a way to transport voices from one location to another. The traditional telephone systems' wires deliver the general function of "transporting my voice from here to there." New services may use satellites.

Customers also have very specific needs or details of the overall function that a product must solve to be truly successful. These detailed needs can be more difficult to learn, because most detailed needs are specific to particular contexts in which the product is used. For example, telephones are used in many different situations. Some of the detailed needs include "let me talk to someone when I'm in the kitchen," ". . . in the bedroom," ". . . in the living room," and ". . . outside sitting on my porch." Features provide the ways in which products function. Wiring multiple rooms in the house for telephone service and installing multiple phones solve these problems. Or one can talk in all of these places (and many more) by purchasing a cordless phone rather than multiple wall phones. Consider the detailed need of "let multiple people here participate in the conversation." Again, this can be delivered though multiple extensions, or alternatively, by using a speakerphone. Different sets of features are better for each of these detailed needs.

Customer problems are complex, and frequently, different needs conflict. For example, while I want to be able to talk on the phone from any room in the house, my teenager may want to ensure that his conversations are private. Yet, with extensions everywhere in the house, anyone can pick up a phone and listen. Alternative solutions to this problem include installing another phone line or getting the teen his own mobile phone. Yet, because both of these solutions are rather expensive, they directly conflict with the need to talk cheaply with others.

As this example shows, no product is perfect. Each product is a compromise, in that it only partially solves a complex set of customer problems. Ultimately, products are sets of features that deliver extremely well against some needs, adequately against others, and do not deliver at all against others. Over time, customers choose products with the set of features that delivers the maximum benefit for them. Although technologies and competitors evolve, customer needs tend to be more stable than product features.

As an example, think about how communications have evolved. Grandmothers separated from grandchildren emigrating west in America in the early 1800s, before the telephone, wanted to talk with their grandchildren just as much as grandmothers today. Back then, they were limited to exchanging letters rather than speaking with someone far away. Letters have certain disadvantages over talking. Letter conversations take place serially, with long periods of time between responses. Also, nuances of meaning usually conveyed by tone of voice are more difficult to convey.

Through telephones, people can talk easily when separated by a great distance, and sometimes even more cheaply than writing. People are now more likely to pick up a phone to talk to someone rather than take the time to write. However, with the Internet, people are moving back from verbal (phones) to written communication by sending e-mail messages. In doing so, customers give up a richer understanding for convenience. For example, I can e-mail a message at 3:00 A.M., when I think of something in the middle of the night, whereas I would be reluctant to phone someone unless it was an emergency.

The lessons gleaned from these examples are threefold. First, customer needs are complex. Second, developing successful products requires understanding the details of needs. Finally, while needs are rather stable, potential features and technologies change over time. Firms must repeatedly return to the drawing board to understand which new set of compromises customers prefer. Providing product development teams with a rich understanding of complex and detailed customer needs and problems prepares them to select the best technology and feature compromises to continue delivering successful products in the future.

Methods for Understanding Customer Needs. Realistically, customers cannot tell firms exactly what products to develop. Customers are unlikely to have the technical understanding necessary to describe new features or technologies a product should have or forecast what features will best serve those needs in the future. They also cannot provide reliable information about anything with which they are not personally familiar or with which they have no experience. By definition, then, customers are not familiar with a new product a firm may be thinking of developing, and cannot provide fully reliable information when asked to react to a **concept** or **prototype**.

Does that mean that firms should not try to understand customer needs and problems? Not at all. Customers can indeed provide reliable information about products they have used and situations they have experienced. They will readily talk about problems they have had and product uses that are relevant to them. They can discuss which products and features they currently use to meet their needs—where these products fall short, where they excel, and why.

Customer needs are often ascertained initially through qualitative market research. As discussed in Chapter 4, qualitative market research is often conducted with a small number of customers. Three methods are especially useful for gathering customer needs qualitatively: *becoming the people with the problems* the firm wants to solve, *critically observing those with the problems* of interest, and *talking to (interviewing) people in depth about their problems.* Each method produces slightly different kinds of information. No one technique is sufficient to produce a full understanding of needs. The best results are obtained when a product development team uses multiple methods to understand people's problems in great detail. Once a full set of needs has been gathered, then a number of different quantitative market research techniques can be used to predict which needs are more important.

Becoming the Customer: Discovering Problems. An enormous amount of customer knowledge and understanding can be gained by putting development team members into situations where they "become" customers and experience the problems firsthand that the firm is trying to solve. This method encourages team members to use the firm's products, and all competitors' products, in everyday as well as extraordinary situations.

For example, the product development team for a feminine hygiene pad product at one company is known for the extent to which they try to fully understand and identify with customer problems. The entire team—both men and women—personally tests relevant products both from their own firm and the competition. Both male and female team members wear pads underneath armpits and in shoes to test chafing and odor elimination. They also wear pads in the anatomically appropriate area to simulate normal use. Team members are also sent on expeditions to purchase the product.

This technique applies not just to consumer products, but with a bit of creativity is useful for many firms selling business-to-business products. For instance, team members at firms that supply McDonald's with cooking equipment are encouraged to work in the kitchens, both on current equipment and with development prototypes. McDonald's readily assigns the development people shifts because they hope to get improved products. Of course, all kitchen equipment firms have test kitchens in which they operate their equipment during development. However, operating a system in a laboratory setting simply does not provide the same breadth of operating experience as working in a real McDonald's—crammed in a kitchen full of teenagers flipping burgers on a Friday night after the local high school football game has ended, with hordes of other teenagers

Concept
is a written description or visual depiction of a new product idea. A concept includes the product's primary features and benefits.

Prototype
is a product concept in physical form. A prototype may be a full working model that has been produced by hand or a nonworking physical representation of the final product. It is used to gather customer reaction to the physical form (aesthetics and ergonomics) or to initial operating capability. It is also used in internal performance tests to ensure that performance goals have been met.

Information Acceleration: Using Technology to Forecast the Future for Really New Products

One of the more difficult marketing tasks in new product development is forecasting future sales. Accurate forecasts are needed to ensure an adequate return on investment for a project, obtain funding from corporate, and make decisions regarding manufacturing strategy. Early projections frequently are made based on customer "intent to buy" reactions to one- to two-sentence, text-based concept statements. More refined information may then be obtained from one-page concept statements, which are sometimes accompanied by pictures or additional technical documentation or marketing support materials. Still more accurate information may be obtained from prototypes and pilot production models that allow customers to gain actual experience with the product under development. As the materials presented to customers more realistically, accurately, and completely reproduce the final product and use experience, customers are able to provide more accurate information about their eventual market response to the product, which translates directly to more accurate forecasts of purchase intent.

Forecast accuracy is particularly problematic for really new products—ones that look very different or deliver very different benefits from those currently on the market. Customers find it especially difficult to imagine how they might actually use products that provide new benefits. One new method to provide vastly greater quantities of more realistic information to customers before prototype development is through a multimedia "information accelerator" that combines images, audio, and text stored on videodisk or CD-ROM to provide full-motion, realistic, computer-based simulations of the product and its use. This system provides photorealistic product simulations that customers can rotate, walk around, and even run demonstrations of how various parts operate. The system also provides access to simulated marketing materials (product brochures, print and TV advertisements), videotaped word-of-mouth (customer reactions to using the product, mentioning specific features and benefits), shopping visits to virtual stores, and personal selling videos. It allows customers to interact with the materials presented and choose which information they want to access. Information accelerators provide greater realism at earlier stages of the product development process, and faster access to larger amounts of information, through linking computer-based engineering design and visualization tools with multimedia technologies.

Source: Glen Urban, John R. Hauser, William J. Qualls, Bruce D. Weinberg, Jonathan D. Bohlmann, and Roberta A. Chicos, "Information Acceleration: Validation and Lessons from the Field," *Journal of Marketing Research* 34, no. 1 (1997): 143–152.

demanding to be fed quickly. By working full shifts during different time periods, development personnel learn about shift startup and cleanup, and the effects of different volume levels on operation, breakage, and fatigue. They are exposed to a random day's worth of the strange things that can happen in a fast-food kitchen that affect both the operator and the equipment.

Having employees become actively involved customers is the best way, sometimes the only way, to transfer **tacit knowledge** to the product development team. Becoming a routine customer for all the different products in a category may also be the most efficient way to expose development teams to the trade-offs others have made in their products and the effects these decisions have had on product function. While this technique brings rich data to the product development team, it has several inherent problems:

Tacit knowledge is knowledge that is implied by or inferred from actions or statements.

- The firm must learn how to transfer one person's experience and tacit knowledge to another.
- If experiences are not recorded, retaining personal knowledge becomes a critical issue if team members frequently shift jobs or leave the firm.
- Project management must take steps to ensure that team members understand that their own needs differ from needs of the "average" customer in unexpected ways.
- Being a customer takes time, money, and personal team member effort.

While personally gathering customer information is not possible in all product areas, with a little imagination it is more feasible than many firms currently realize.

Anthropological Excursions: Live with and Critically Observe Customers. Product developers who cannot become customers may be able to "live with" their customers,

observing and questioning them as they use products to solve problems. Developers of new medical devices for doctors cannot act as doctors and personally test devices in patient situations. However, they can observe operations, even videotape them, and then debrief doctors about what happened and why.

Sometimes observing customers in their natural settings leads directly to new products or features. Developers at Chrysler observed that many pickup truck owners had built holders for 32-ounce drinks into their cabs, so starting in 1995 Ram trucks featured cupholders appropriate for 32-ounce drinks. In other instances, observation points out a problem. The team must determine whether the problem is specific to a particular individual or applies generally across the target market, and if so, develop an appropriate solution. Another Chrysler engineer watched the difficulty his petite wife had wrestling childrens' car seats around in the family minivan. It took him several years to convince management that his innovative solution—integrating children's car seats into the car's seating system—would solve a major problem for a large number of customers.

Critical observation, rather than just casual viewing, is a major key to obtaining information by watching customers. Critical observation involves questioning *why* people are performing each action rather than just accepting what they are doing. The best results are achieved when team members spend significant time with enough different customers to be exposed to the full breadth of problems people encounter. They must spend enough time observing customers to uncover both normal and abnormal operating conditions. Using team members responsible for different functions is important because people with different training and expertise "see" and pay attention to different things.

Anthropological excursions identify tacit information and expose team members to customer language. It is the most effective means for gathering workflow or process-related information. These customer needs are particularly important for firms marketing products to other firms. Products they develop must fit into the workflow of those firms, which means the workflows must be fully understood. Even when questioned in detail, people frequently forget steps in a process or skip over them. Although forgotten in the course of the interviews, these steps may be crucial to product design trade-offs.

Observing and living with customers is not especially efficient. Its problems include:

- Significant team member time and expense. Events and actions unfold slowly in real time, and there are no shortcuts.
- "Natural" actions may not be captured. Videotaping or observation, no matter how well designed and intentioned, is intrusive by nature and may change behavior.

http://www.chrysler.com

http://www.dodge.com

- Observations must be interpreted through the filter of team members' own experiences. It is a challenge for the team to turn observed actions into words that reliably capture customer needs.

Being customers and critically observing customers are powerful techniques for gathering rich, detailed data on customer problems. However, both activities require significant amounts of time that may not be available in every product development project. These techniques are best used in an ongoing way to continually expand a group's knowledge of customer problems. When time is short, the only means to rapidly gather customer needs is to talk to customers and get them to tell you their problems.

Talk to Customers to Get Needs and Problems. By talking to customers, NPD teams can gather needs faster and more efficiently than by being or observing customers. A structured, in-depth, probing, one-on-one, situational interview technique called **voice of the customer (VOC)** can uncover both general and very detailed customer needs.[9] This method differs from standard qualitative techniques in the way questions are asked. Rather than asking customers "what do you want" directly, VOC uses indirect questions to discover wants and needs by leading customers through the ways they currently solve particular problems. VOC asks questions about functions rather than about products.

For example, one study asked customers *what* they would use to transport food that they had prepared at home to be consumed at another location, especially if the food would have to be stored for some period of time before it was eaten. Picnic baskets, coolers, and ice chests most frequently were the items suggested to fulfill this general function. However, asking *how* they fulfilled the function, rather than about a particular product, yielded information about many different and unexpected products customers used—including knapsacks, luggage, and grocery store bags with handles—and the reasons *why* they used them. Detailed probing reveals specific features, drawbacks, and benefits of each product. Most important are questions delving into why various features of products are good and bad. What problem does each feature solve, and does a particular feature cause any other problems? Probing *why* uncovers needs.

One advantage of interviewing is that many different use situations can be investigated in a short period of time, including a range of both normal and abnormal situations. Each different use situation provides information about additional dimensions of functional performance. A good way to start an interview is to ask customers to tell about the last time they found themselves in a particular situation. The food transportation study began, "Please tell me about the most recent time you prepared food in your home, to be shared by you and others, then took the food outside your home and ate it somewhere else

Voice of the customer (VOC) is a one-on-one interviewing process to elicit an in-depth set of customer needs.

Careers in New Product Development— Getting Cross-Functional

International Truck and Engine Corporation is a leading North American producer of heavy-duty trucks (Class 8 or semis, where the tractor is separate from the trailer), medium-duty trucks (Class 5–7, where the cab is integrated into the body of the truck, as in beverage and parcel delivery trucks), severe service trucks (dump trucks and interstate snow plows), and school buses. In the 1980s, International (originally named International Harvester and then Navistar) focused management efforts on attaining operational excellence in truck manufacturing. These actions took cost out of the product and radically improved manufactured truck quality, putting the firm onto a solid performance track. By the early 1990s, the firm was mean and lean, but hadn't commercialized a new medium product since 1978.

Enter Mark Stasell, a freshly minted Indiana University MBA marketing major. In 1991, he joined a new product program to refresh the interiors of International's reliable, but aging, medium-duty trucks. Mark had started his career in the functional area of engineering, but after 6 years decided he "wanted to get more cross-functional." The MBA was a perfect way to supplement his engineering expertise with additional functional capabilities. He moved into project management program at International, initially managing all the functional inputs into the new interior program for medium-duty trucks (International's 4000 series), including marketing, engineering, manufacturing, purchasing, quality, and finance.

While the refresh program helped sustain the business, International considered this just a scrimmage for the real goal—developing an entirely new product line. The firm knew they needed to design and develop a whole new truck platform that delivered significant additional customer benefits to better meet their needs, while taking advantage of platform economies of scale to truly grow the business.

Mark had been successful enough at managing across functions in the interior development project that he got assigned to the product planning role for the new product line—a completely new truck that would launch initially in the medium truck line, but ultimately would become the base platform across all four product lines. Mark and his cross-functional team collected customer input, created the line's value proposition, constructed modularity strategies, estimated development expenses and product manufacturing costs, and participated in all the other tasks associated with a major product development planning effort. Along the way, Mark picked up a commercial license to operate medium and Class 8 trucks, increasing his customer needs knowledge by "being a customer."

The team got formal broad approval in October 1997 for this "bet the firm" endeavor to produce a new truck. International formed a new center, called the Next Generation Product Center, to develop this platform that wold apply across its four product lines. Mark was chosen to lead the new center and became project manager of the project.

The new medium-duty truck launched successfully and on time in February 2001, increasing International's share in this part of the market. Mark is now vice president for product development at the truck division of International, responsible for NPD across all four truck businesses, as well as for International's new joint venture with Ford. "I'm one of the first VPs of a process, rather than a function, at International. It lets me interact with all the businesses and functional areas of the firm. I never get bored." As this book goes to press, he's moving the new platform into the severe service, bus, and Class 8 product lines.

later." By asking customers to relate specifics—what they did, why they did what they did, what worked well, and what did not work—both detailed and general customer needs are obtained indirectly.

After customers relate their most recent experiences, they are asked about the specifics of how they fulfilled the function in a series of other potential use situations. These use situations are constructed by the team to attempt to cover all the performance dimensions across which customers may expect a product to function. In the food transportation example, customers were asked about the last time they took food with them:

- On a car trip
- To the beach
- To a football or baseball game
- On a romantic picnic
- On a bike trip
- Canoeing or fishing
- Hiking or backpacking

They also related the most disastrous and marvelous times they ever took food with them. The set of situations constructed varies the different dimensions of expected performance as widely as possible. In the food study, the amount, types, and temperatures of the food taken varies, the outside temperature varies, and different aesthetics are covered, as is a large range of ease of mobility and transportability. While no customer experiences all situations, the food transporting and storage needs resulting from each situation were uncovered fully by interviewing 20 to 30 people.

Buried in the stories customers tell about specific use instances are the nuggets of needs. Through indirect questioning, customer needs that relate to technical design aspects can be obtained, even from nontechnical customers. For example, by relating how their car behaves in various driving situations—flooring the accelerator at a stop sign, traveling at city speeds around 35 mph, and traveling at interstate speeds—senior citizens can provide information that determines the gear ratios governing the speeds at which an automatic transmission shifts gears, even though they may have no idea how their transmission works.

While VOC is not difficult, it gathers needs differently than other qualitative market research techniques. It results in a much larger list of very detailed and context- or situation-specific customer needs. This is because the objective of VOC is to obtain a level of detail that enables teams to make engineering trade-offs during product development.

There are several keys to successfully obtaining the voice of the customer. First, it is critical to ask about functions (what customers want to do), not features (how it is done). Continually probing about why a feature is wanted or works well reveals underlying needs. Only by understanding functional needs can teams make appropriate technology and feature trade-offs in the future. A second key is that VOC only covers reality. People who have never been on one cannot accurately tell you what they would like on a romantic picnic because they really do not know. Anything they say is conjecture. The final key to success is to ask detailed questions about specific use instances. General questions (tell me about going on picnics) elicit general needs. General needs are not as useful to the development team for designing products as are details of needs, which are obtained through using specific questions (tell me about the last time you went on a romantic picnic). Customers can provide tremendous levels of detail when asked to relate the story of a specific situation that occurred in the last year.

While VOC provides numerous verbal details about problems directly usable by the team, it has several drawbacks:

- The development team obtains a better understanding of a fuller set of detailed needs if the team interviews customers, but this adds to the team's development tasks.
- Interviewing customers is a nontraditional task for many team members (e.g., engineers, accountants).
- Extreme care must be taken to maintain the words of the customer and not translate individual problems into solutions before understanding the full set of customer needs.
- Tacit and process-related needs may not be complete.

No one technique easily provides all the customer needs knowledge that product development teams seek. Tacit needs are best discovered by being a customer. Process-related needs are identified most easily by critically observing customers. In-depth interviewing is the most efficient means to obtain masses of detailed needs, but may not provide tacit and process-related information. Unfortunately, few projects can afford the time and expense of fully using all these processes. Development teams need to use the most appropriate one(s), given the project's informational requirements, budget, and time frame. Once needs have been gathered, the team can turn to developing a competitively advantaged product that fully solves customers' problems.

LEARNING OBJECTIVE 3

Developing a Competitively Advantaged Product

Developing competitively advantaged products consistently over time is aided by having a strategy for what will be done and a process for how it will be accomplished. Firms with both a new product development strategy and a formal process for doing so demonstrate superior performance in terms of percentage of sales by new products, success rates, and meeting sales and profit objectives.[10]

Product Development Strategy

"If you don't know where you are going, any road will get you there." New product strategy provides the long-term destination for where the firm is going. Effective strategies for product development flow from the overall business strategy of the firm. For example, if the firm's stated strategy is to be a low-cost manufacturer, then an effective new product strategy for the business unit probably is not to develop a continuous stream of technologically leading-edge products. A more effective new product strategy might be to continually improve the cost-effectiveness of the manufacturing processes.

Effective strategies consist of a set of clear new product goals that derive directly from the overall business strategy. Areas of strategic focus can be defined in a number of ways, including:

- Markets or market segments
- Product types or categories (such as by newness categories)
- Product lines
- Technologies or technology platforms

http://www.fordvehicles.com/
cars/taurus

Areas of strategic focus are then selected and prioritized, and a plan for how to attack each area is developed. A plan of attack defines the way in which the firm will compete in each strategic arena. For example, in the 1980s, Ford Motor Company's plan of attack for the family sedan market was to be the industry design and styling innovator. Thus, successive generations of Taurus styling have been radically different from other family sedans on the market. However, different plans of attack may be adopted across different strategic arenas of a firm. In the minivan product category, Ford has chosen more of a fast-follower strategy behind Chrysler. Here they have allowed Chrysler to innovate and have chosen to compete using a "second but better" design.

Project Strategy

Even after the new product development strategy for the business unit is set, a strategy for each individual product development project must be developed. A project strategy is the specific plan of how this project will proceed and why. An effective project strategy states the reasons the firm is undertaking a project and identifies specific business goals for the product. For example, it outlines whether the firm is undertaking this project to meet a previously unmet customer need, to update performance in a current product, or to counteract share losses from a newly commercialized competitive product. Each project's goals will depend, in part, on why the project is being undertaken. For example, the goal for a performance-improvement project may be increased share or customer satisfaction while maintaining profitability.

Customer prototypes are the detailed pictures and descriptions of individuals or firms in the target market for a product. Creating these descriptions helps firms envision how products and the marketing mix might best be combined to maximize profits.

The strategy also describes the target market and CBP for the product. It details the firms or individuals who are expected to purchase the new product. Some project teams draw pictures or create collages of people in the target market, **customer prototypes,** and hang them on the walls to remind themselves who the target market is as the project moves forward.

Finally, successful strategies require a schedule to establish key milestones, including the planned market introduction date. The schedule helps keep the team task-focused, and helps managers across the company identify key resources and activities that will be required to achieve success. Once the team and management agree on the project purposes, goals, timing, and required resources, it is ready to proceed to development.

A Framework for Managing Product Development: Stage-Gate Processes

A formal **product development process**, such as that illustrated in Figure 8.4, outlines the normal way NPD proceeds at the firm. It defines which functions (i.e., marketing or engineering) are responsible for performing what tasks, in what order, and in conjunction with what other tasks and functions. A formalized process institutionalizes learning about what works and does not work, and how interdependent steps must be completed. Projects that follow a formalized product development process are more successful, and firms that are the best at new product development are more likely to use formalized processes for new product development.[11] Firms without formalized NPD processes depend on one or a few product development "craftsmen" who "just know how to do it." If they leave the firm, NPD knowledge leaves with them.

Most firms use a formal **Stage-Gate process** to organize the tasks for developing new products (see Figure 8.5). Stage-Gate processes are organized and consistent, and can be understood by and deployed across all those involved in NPD projects at a firm. Personnel responsible for each function complete tasks that are related to that function at each stage. The process acknowledges that different functions require a different expertise in each stage, all of which are necessary to successfully complete the stage. Thus, it encourages cross-functional teamwork and problem solving. As the goals for each stage are completed, management reviews progress at a gate meeting, determines whether the criteria necessary to move forward have been met, approves the tasks and resources for the next stage (go), asks for more information (recycle), or stops the project (kill). A well-designed process ensures that senior management participates in the NPD process where there is a significant jump in risk or cost.

Product development process consists of a clearly defined set of tasks and steps that describes the normal means by which product development proceeds. The process outlines the order and sequence of the tasks and indicates who is responsible for each.

Stage-Gate process is a common new product development process that divides the repeatable portion of product development into a time-sequenced series of stages, each of which is separated by a management decision gate. In each stage, a team completes a set of tasks that span the functions involved in product development. At the end of each stage, management reviews the results obtained and, based on the team's ability to meet the objectives in that stage, provides the resources to continue to the next stage ("go"), requests additional work ("recycle"), or stops the project ("kill").

NPD Process Tasks and Road Map	Figure 8.4

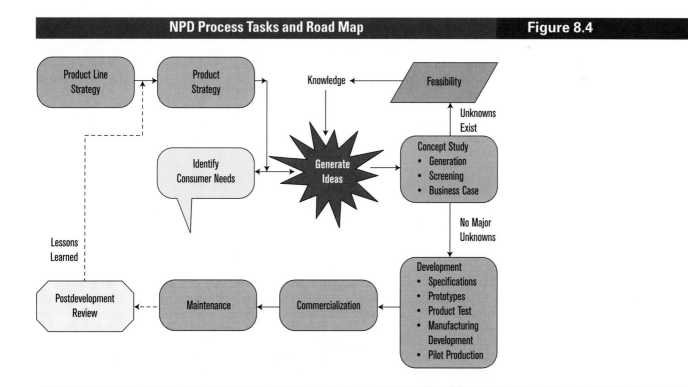

Figure 8.5	A Stage-Gate Approach to NPD

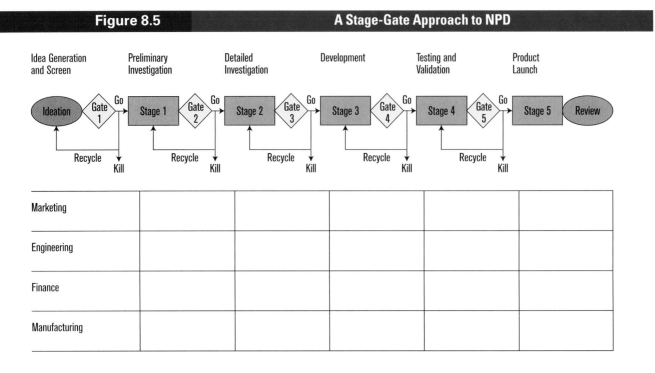

Individual firms implement the Stage-Gate process differently, personalizing it to meet the needs of their corporation. Table 8.2 shows four actual NPD processes. For example, CalComp uses a 9-stage process that does not include idea generation or postintroduction review. In contrast, the other three firms all use different 7-stage processes. Traditionally, the most common tasks and stages that may be included in the firm's NPD process include the following activities.[12]

Generate and Screen Ideas. The objective of this stage is to create one or more "interesting" new product ideas. An interesting idea solves customer problems, fits the business unit's strategy and capabilities, and presents a profit-making opportunity at reasonable risk, given the size of the profit potential. In this step, ideas are first generated and then screened against a set of criteria to determine which provide the greatest opportunity for the firm. At the end of this stage, a small number of ideas that have been screened for fit and potential reward will be ready to move forward into the next stage of development.

Ideas come from many sources. Customers may ask directly for a new product or feature. Competitors may introduce a new product that sparks an idea to counteract their effort. Employees frequently have new product ideas they are eager to suggest. Alternatively, creativity sessions can be held specifically to generate new ideas. Frequently, the problem is not generating ideas but gathering ideas from a wide variety of sources so they can be evaluated. Some firms use a database or construct a new product idea bulletin board on their intranet to collect and retain ideas over time.

The objective of idea screening is to evaluate new product ideas rationally and consistently over time, and to maintain the integrity of the process as product development team membership evolves. Initial idea screening is done based on what management already knows, rather than on information specifically developed for the project. Many firms develop a standard set of criteria that managers can use to consistently evaluate ideas. Table 8.3 lists AT&T's idea-screening criteria. Other firms numerically rate each idea against objectives, as illustrated in Table 8.4, where a larger number indicates a better rating. Ideas proceed to the next phase based either on their absolute overall rating or their rating relative to the other ideas considered.

Idea generation and screening can be completed relatively quickly, sometimes in days or hours. The resources required are usually minimal, consisting predominantly of

Stage	CalComp	Xerox	Exxon Chemical	Keithley Instrument
Generate ideas		Pre-concept	Idea	Concept
Preliminary investigation	Market requirement Specification Design	Concept	Preliminary assessment	Study
Detailed investigation			Detailed assessment	Definition
Development	Engineering model Prototype	Design	Development	Design
Test and validate	System verification Manufacturing verification	Demonstration Production	Validation	Prototype Pilot
Launch	Production	Launch	Commercial launch	Introduction
Maintenance Review	End of life	Maintenance	Postreview	

Table 8.2 — Stages Used by Firms

Sources: Public presentations and brochures.

Table 8.3 — Potential Idea Evaluation Criteria

- **Will the market care?**
  How will consumers benefit?
  What is the total market potential?

- **Will it be important to this firm?**
  Does it fit with our strategy and goals?
  Will it create shareholder value?
  Can we obtain sufficient market share?
  Will it provide us with a comparative advantage?

- **Does it fit with our firm's capabilities?**
  Does it match our technology infrastructure?
  Does it match our marketing capabilities?
  Can we produce at a cost that will provide profits?

Table 8.4 — Evaluating Ideas by Rating Them against Objectives

	Idea 1	Idea 2	Idea 3	Idea 4
Meets customer needs	3	5	3	1
Fits manufacturing capability	1	3	5	1
Fits our strategy	5	3	1	3
Large market size	5	5	1	3
Noncyclical market	3	1	3	1
Fits distribution	5	5	1	1
Sum	**22**	**22**	**14**	**10**

management time, the cost of developing and maintaining an idea database, and the cost of running creativity sessions.

Preliminary Investigation. This stage develops preliminary market assessments, technical feasibility assessments, and financial assessments. This is the up-front homework necessary before detailed design work can start. Typically a small, focused, multifunctional core team of marketing and technical specialists performs this step using available resources and knowledge. At the end of the preliminary investigation, the team will know whether unknowns exist, and thus whether the project must be routed back through a research step to demonstrate feasibility, or whether the project can proceed to a detailed investigation that builds a business case based on new and more detailed information.

The preliminary market assessment is a quick-and-dirty market study using data that can be quickly assembled to answer several questions: market attractiveness and potential, probable customer acceptance of the concept, and competitive intensity. The preliminary technical assessment identifies the key technical risks and how each might be overcome. The firm's technical staff—R&D, engineering, and manufacturing—develop rough initial technical and performance specifications and pinpoint specific technical risks in both product and manufacturing process design. Regulatory issues and competitors' patent situations also are reviewed. The preliminary financial assessment is an initial check that the project has enough revenue and profit potential to warrant continuation. At this point, potential volume, revenue and cost per item, and total development cost are extremely speculative, so these estimates are no more than ballpark figures.

Because the information used in the analyses is only that which is readily available within the firm, preliminary investigation can be completed relatively quickly, generally within a few weeks. However, completing this step requires inputs from manufacturing, technologists, marketers, and financial analysts. Thus, a lack of support by management, or from any of these functional units, can delay completion. Research has repeatedly shown that the quality of the up-front homework in preliminary investigation and business case development is strongly associated with increased new product success. A major objective, then, is to obtain functional support for each task in this stage so that high-quality answers are generated.

Detailed Investigation. Detailed investigation builds a business case for the project that provides enough solid information to upper management so that they can approve the resources necessary for product development. The business case defines and justifies the project, and details the plan for completing the project. The cross-functional team that develops the business case becomes the core of the team that will take the project through development and into the marketplace. At the end of this stage, management has all the information it needs to make a go or kill decision on the project, and the team will be poised to move rapidly into the more expensive phases of development.

Justification requires completing a *market analysis, technical assessment, concept test, competitive analysis,* and a *detailed financial analysis.* The market analysis quantifies market size and growth and analyzes market segments and buyer behavior. A competitive analysis identifies competitors and competing products, including details of product strengths and deficiencies. The team analyzes competitor strategies, position in the market, and performance. These serve as inputs for developing the marketing strategy for product commercialization. The financial analysis includes a cash flow analysis that takes into account the required timing and level of investment. This is possible because the team now has a much more detailed definition of the product specifications.

The difference between the preliminary investigation and this stage is that detailed investigation requires gathering and generating new information, rather than relying on what a firm already knows. That is, a product is defined based on the combination of a user needs study and a detailed technical assessment. A needs study may use any of the market research techniques covered earlier in this chapter. This information is gathered from potential customers in the target market. It cannot be developed just through internal knowledge. Additional quantitative market research (see Chapter 4) may be done to understand the relative importance of different needs, preferred trade-offs between requirements, and to assess competitive product performance. The development team then translates market inputs into a technically feasible product by determining what aspects of performance deliver each customer need, developing performance specifications, and assuring feasibility of achieving those specifications. Assuring feasibility may require some laboratory work. The technologists map out the technical solutions to achieving performance and develop the route that will get them to that technical solution. Concept manufacturability is investigated simultaneously to ensure that the product can be made.

The final component of the business case is the plan of action. This includes a go/kill recommendation and a detailed plan for how physical development, testing, and manufacturing development will proceed. The plan also specifies the intended launch date for the product.

The detailed investigation stage has high levels of interdependency across tasks (see Figure 8.6), and is the first stage that requires a reasonable investment of time,

Task Interdependencies in Building a Business Case   Figure 8.6

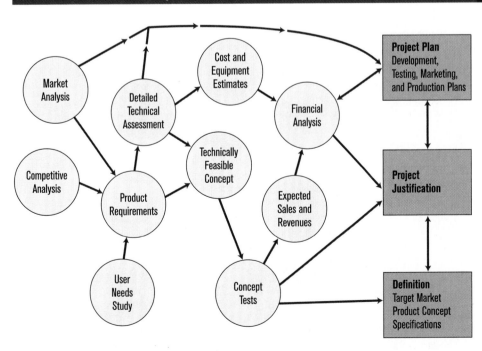

money, and people to provide quality results. The resources required will depend on the size, complexity, and degree of uniqueness of the project. A firm can expect that even the smallest projects may require a team of three to five individuals (because each function must be represented), working at least half-time over a period of 1 to 4 months. Larger, more complex projects, however, may require four to six people working full-time for up to 6 months to a year. Spending enough time, money, and personnel resources during this stage, in order to produce high quality definitions, justifications, and plans, saves a much larger amount of spending later to fix problems that arise because they were not dealt with in the initial phases of the project.

Development. The actual design and physical development of the product takes place during the development stage. The outputs of this stage are:

- A prototype that has been tested in-house for performance and in a limited way with customers for preliminary reaction
- A mapped-out manufacturing process, with critical aspects pilot tested
- A marketing launch plan
- A test and validation plan

In development, team size and resource consumption peak. Different parts of the project move forward in parallel, completed by different subgroups of the team. While some tasks can be completed by one function relatively independently, many others still require extensive interaction across functions. At the heart of a successful development stage is a plan that drives the process by organizing the efforts of all of those involved. It includes a chronological listing of tasks and the individuals responsible for completing them, with expected stop and start dates. Successful project leaders expect team members to adhere to the time lines and milestones, and proactively manage the project based on them. Project management plans can only be followed when the unknowns have been eliminated from the project prior to development.

Development time increases with the size and complexity of a project. Additionally, the relative newness of a project impacts development time. New-to-the-world projects average about 3.5 years to complete, new-to-the-firm projects take just over 2 years, major revisions of current projects require 1.5 years, line extensions 1 year, and incremental improvements take about 9 months.[13] Team size ranges from two to three people for incremental improvements to relatively simple projects such as shampoos or other customer packaged goods to hundreds, or even thousands, of people when a large and complex new-to-the-firm or new-to-the world project is undertaken. Boeing assembled

http://www.boeing.com/
commercial/777family

an entire hierarchy of teams in developing the 777 airplane, with the total staff involved numbering in the thousands.

Testing and Validation. This stage provides final project validation. The product, production process, and marketing strategy plan are all put through verification tests. The objectives are to provide management with final proof that expectations for the project in terms of performance, volume, and profit will be met, and to eliminate any final bugs in the product, process, and marketing plan. The product typically undergoes customer field trials for performance verification, and test marketing or limited rollout for testing the marketing plan. Pilot or trial production of the manufacturing process is used to produce the products tested with customers to ensure that the process operates as designed. Finally, based on the results from the field and plant trials, the expected financial outcomes are updated. Results from the field, plant, and financial analyses are presented to management for a final go/kill decision, and to obtain the investment for a full market launch.

The time and effort required in testing and validation varies greatly with the size, complexity, and newness of the project. Field-testing with customers can require as little as a week for a limited test with a few customers to as much as a year for a full test market. The expense can be as little as the cost of producing one or two products, or run as much as 5 percent of the estimated expense of going to market.

Commercialization and Launch. The final activity in new product development is commercialization, the beginning of full production and commercial selling. Some of the team members on the project may change as the marketing and sales functions ramp up activities to implement the communications plan, marketing launch plan, and sales plan. Manufacturing also may add people to the team as they deploy production to one or more plants. However, to counterbalance these additions, some of the technical development team may move to a more limited role. While large amounts of money may be spent on advertising and communications at this stage, the project finally starts generating income.

Shepherding Products through the Firm

Even if a firm has uncovered a customer problem and developed a competitively advantaged product that solves the problem, it still may not be able to profit from that effort if the firm cannot bring the product to market through its own corporate infrastructure. Shepherding products through the firm is done by putting in place appropriate organizational processes, which includes developing project leaders to lead the NPD process and navigate the politics of the organization, providing appropriate organizational structures within which to manage projects, and ensuring upper management support.

Leading NPD Projects

NPD project leaders fulfill a number of roles. The leader ensures that the NPD process is followed, that tasks are assigned to those who can complete them, and that those tasks are completed in a timely manner. The leader may help protect the team from external interference and may ensure that necessary resources are available to the team. Generally, the leader represents the team in formal meetings and reviews with management. Leaders can also play other roles including coaching and developing team personnel.

Project leadership can take several forms including: project leaders, champions, and more recently, NPD process owners. These leadership types differ in the ways in which they fulfill leadership roles. Studies of NPD projects have found that multiple types of leadership are used during development, with no one type leading to higher performance.

Project leaders, the most frequently used leadership type in NPD, are appointed by upper management and given formal power and authority to complete the project. They guard the project's objectives, continuously communicate with team members, serve as a translator across different functions, and are the primary management contact point. The project leader manages the efforts of team members from the different functions. In a "lightweight" team, the leader coordinates work through liaison functional representatives but has little influence over the work. In a "heavyweight" team, the leader exerts a strong, direct, integrating influence across all functions. Shifting to heavyweight teams has been credited with reducing NPD cycle time and increasing development productivity in the automotive industry.[14]

Champions generally work outside official roles and processes to informally influence others' actions, taking an acute interest in seeing that a particular project is pursued. The role may vary from little more than stimulating awareness of the opportunity to extreme cases where the champion tries to force a project past strongly entrenched internal resistance. The champion's role in new product development has been a topic of discussion for over 30 years, with champion use reported by over 40 percent of firms. While some specific NPD successes may be due to the efforts of a particular champion, using a champion does not raise the probability that any particular project will be a success.[15]

Process owners administer the formal NPD process across business groups within the firm.[16] Process owners build and maintain expertise in the NPD process, facilitating NPD process use for all projects in the firm, and in some projects additionally serve in leadership roles. Process owners may not be responsible for the success outcome of a project, just for the implementation quality of the NPD process used. Even though this leadership type is a relatively recent development, about 12 percent of reporting firms claim that process owners lead NPD projects.

Mustering Management Support for NPD

A consistent finding for producing successful new products is tangible and visible top management commitment to NPD. While top managers formally control the budgets and plans of NPD groups only loosely, they exert considerably tighter control over them informally in the way they allocate top management attention and contact. The NPD team's goal, then, is to obtain and retain top management commitment to the project by maintaining their attention.

Getting a project favored and approved over others requires managing more than just a rational decision-making process. It requires managing the personalities and politics of the upper managers supporting NPD at a firm to convince them that the value of a particular project warrants the necessary resources they must provide. The NPD team thus needs to continually communicate with top management about the project. Firms usually have mechanisms for formally communicating with management through gate meetings and design reviews, and during the annual budgeting process. However, communication also needs to occur informally between the team and management. Some strategies include:

- Interview specific managers for their view of project expectations or customer needs
- Send out brief (one to two paragraphs), weekly e-mail updates
- Invite managers with particular areas of expertise to participate as consultants to the project
- Request management presence in the laboratory as new prototypes are unveiled
- Use one or more managers as subjects in various phases of testing
- Create a weekly or monthly project lunch and invite managers to attend
- Invite managers to after-hours team functions, such as project picnics and parties

The objectives of some interactions are to exchange information, such as informing management about the status of the project, obstacles that are creating roadblocks, or small successes such as beating completion time to a milestone. At other times, the objectives of an interaction will be more persuasive in nature. Examples include when the team is interacting to sell the project either to a potential project sponsor, is bargaining for different or additional resources, or is defending the project from criticism by another group within the firm.

Successful product development is a multifunctional effort. Marketing has an important role to play in this effort, but by themselves marketing staff cannot ensure success. Indeed, marketing will not even lead many product development efforts. However, there are other product-related decisions over which marketing does exert control. The remainder of the chapter covers types of product-related decisions that are solely marketing's responsibility.

MAKING PRODUCT DECISIONS: BRANDING, PACKAGING, AND LABELING[17]

Prior to the commercialization and launch stage of new product development, marketing is responsible for making a number of decisions that will help reinforce a product's competitive position in the minds of consumers.[18] These include decisions about branding, packaging, and labeling.

Branding Decisions

Customers handle an enormous amount of information in the course of their daily activities. Consequently, they develop efficient ways of processing information in order to make purchasing decisions. Brands are one of the most fundamental pieces of information customers use to simplify choices and reduce purchase risk. Brand names assure customers that they will receive the same quality with their next purchase as they did with their last. Consequently, buyers are willing to pay a premium for quality and assurance. For this reason, branding has become an essential element of product strategy.

Brands serve important communication functions and, in doing so, establish beliefs among customers about the attributes and general image of a product. After a brand has been established, the brand name (letters or numbers used to vocalize the brand), logo (symbols such as McDonald's golden arches and Prudential's rock), and trademark (brand name and/or logo that is legally protected) serve to remind and reinforce the beliefs that have been formed. To arrive at this point, the firm must have made good on its promises. The case for a new brand, however, is different. A good brand name, logo, or trademark has four important characteristics. It should

1. attract attention
2. be memorable
3. help communicate the positioning of the product
4. distinguish the product from competing brands

Brand Equity

Successful brands develop **brand equity**. The financial value of brand equity is enormous. For example, Kohlberg Kravis Roberts purchased RJR Nabisco for $25 billion (double its book value); Philip Morris paid $12.9 billion for Kraft (four times book value) and $5.7 billion for General Foods (over four times book value). Even under the generous notion that the tangible assets of these companies were undervalued by 50 percent, this still means that the reputation and goodwill of their brand names—their brand equity—were worth billions.

In addition to the financial value, brand equity also has a very important strategic value. Manufacturers have become increasingly interested in marketing new products under the umbrella of well-established brand names that are already familiar to consumers. Several of these are presented in Figure 8.7. New products marketed under

Brand equity
is the marketplace value of a brand based on reputation and goodwill.

Figure 8.7	Successful and Unsuccessful Brand Extensions

Successful Brand Extensions to New Product Categories

BIC disposable shavers	BIC disposable lighters
Kodak film	Kodak cameras and batteries
Coleman camping lamps	Coleman stoves, tents, sleeping bags
Winnebago campers	Winnebago tents, sleeping bags
Ivory soap	Ivory shampoo, dishwashing liquid
Woolite detergent	Woolite carpet cleaner
Jell-O gelatin	Jell-O pudding pops
Rubbermaid housewares	Rubbermaid farm food bins
Barbie dolls	Barbie games, furniture, clothes, magazines
Odor-Eater foot pads	Odor-Eater socks
Dr. Scholl's foot pads	Dr. Scholl's shoes, socks, wart remover
Bausch & Lomb optics	Bausch & Lomb contact lenses, sunglasses
Minolta cameras	Minolta copiers
Honda bikes	Honda cars, lawnmowers, rototillers, generators
Fisher-Price toys	Fisher-Price playwear
Lipton tea	Lipton soup mixes

Unsuccessful Brand Extensions to New Product Categories

Jack Daniel's bourbon	Jack Daniel's charcoal briquets
Dunkin' Donuts	Dunkin' Donuts cereal
Jacuzzi baths	Jacuzzi bath toiletries
Harley-Davidson bikes	Harley-Davidson cigarettes
Rubbermaid housewares	Rubbermaid computer tables
Stetson hats	Stetson shirts, umbrellas
Levi jeans	Levi business wear
Certs candy	Certs gum
Mr. Coffee coffeemakers	Mr. Coffee coffee

well-established brand names are more likely to be accepted by channel members (e.g., wholesalers and retailers) due to the proven track record of the brand and disenchantment with the risks involved in launching new brands. Strong brand equity is not only used to roll out new products, but it also helps companies break into new markets. For example, Kodak used its film brand equity to break into the camera market, and Lipton tea used its brand equity to launch soup mixes. Finally, brand equity can be strategically utilized as an effective barrier to entry, making it difficult for competitors to enter or expand in the market.

Branding Strategies: Individual versus Family Branding

When selecting branding strategies, marketers essentially have two options. The first option is to pursue an *individual brand name strategy* where each product in a company's product mix is given a specific brand name. Procter & Gamble and General Mills are often cited as prime examples of companies that employ an individual brand name strategy. The advantage of an individual brand name strategy is that it allows a firm to develop the best brand name possible for every product. In addition, an individual brand name strategy diversifies the firm's risk by not allowing individual product failures to tarnish the reputation and image of the company's other products. The downside of an individual brand name strategy is that the firm is not taking advantage of the brand equity of existing brands that may facilitate channel and consumer acceptance of new products.

The other branding option is to use a *family brand name strategy* where all, or a significant portion, of a company's products are associated with a family brand name. The

http://www.GeneralMills.com

primary advantage of a family brand name strategy is that it can be used to launch new products. Firms typically extend their family brand names in two ways:

1. The family brand is extended into product categories that are used in the same situation as the original branded product or used by the consumers of the original branded product (e.g., Coke, Diet-Coke, and Caffeine Free-Coke).
2. The family brand is extended to help the company introduce products into new product categories (e.g., Fisher-Price toys introduces Fisher-Price playwear).

Over the years, variations of the family branding strategy have evolved. The three most common include:

1. Blanket family name for all products; this strategy is followed by General Electric and Heinz.
2. Separate family names for types of products; this strategy is followed by Sears Roebuck which markets Kenmore appliances, Craftsman tools, and DieHard batteries.
3. Family names combined with individual brand names: this strategy is pursued by Kellogg's (e.g., Kellogg's Raisin Bran and Kellogg's Corn Flakes).

A strong family brand name will grab the customer's attention and may lead to product trial. It provides a foot in the door. Family branding is most effective when it is applied to a product that is complementary in usage to the original branded product, an approach evidenced by the successful brand extensions presented in Figure 8.7.

Packaging Decisions

Each year, companies spend more on packaging than on advertising. As markets have matured and competitive differentiation has narrowed, packaging has become a very important component of marketing strategy. Sometimes a firm forgets that it's the packaged product, and not the product alone, that is sold and purchased. A product's package is often its most distinctive marketing effort. Packaging performs a number of essential functions.

- *Protection:* A package must protect the product in several different situations: in the manufacturer's warehouse, during shipment to the wholesaler and retailer, in the seller's warehouse, and in transporting the product from the seller's store to the consumer's final point of consumption.
- *Identification:* A product's package, particularly one that is distinctive, helps customers identify the product in a crowded marketplace. The classic case of an eye-catching display was the L'Eggs point-of-purchase stand with hundreds of plastic eggs in different colors.
- *Information:* The package provides another means of communicating with the customer. An informed customer gets the very best performance out of a product.
- *Packaging to enhance usage:* Several very innovative packages have added real convenience to product use. For example, when Beech-Nut apple juice switched from cans to bottles (onto which plastic nipples for babies could be attached), sales quadrupled. Another example involved Chesebrough-Ponds who put nail polish in a special type of felt tip pen. The new packaging helped increase sales by over 20 percent.
- *Packaging to enhance disposal:* A package that is biodegradable, or made from recycled materials, will appeal to environmentally conscious market segments. Downy's (fabric softener) change to milk carton refills for fabric softener was to minimize plastic waste.
- *Packaging to enhance channel acceptance:* New shipping and warehouse technology may require standard package dimensions. *Cubic efficiency* is a term that describes how efficiently a package occupies storage, transportation, and display space. Boxes are more cubic efficient than cans, and cans are more efficient than most bottles. Packaging that suits the needs of

channel members is more apt to be adopted over competitive packaging that does not.

Ultimately, effective packaging adds to the value of a product. For instance, opening and resealing, pouring, mixing, processing, and cooking may all be enhanced or made easier by creative packaging. A package also continues to communicate on the kitchen shelf, workshop bench, and, most importantly, during product use. Firms that underestimate the power of a product's packaging are making a major tactical mistake.

Labeling Decisions

A customer can tell a lot about a company by the labels it places on its products. If the label appears to be an afterthought, and contains only what is legally required, then the customer will likely conclude that the company doesn't care. On the other hand, a customer-oriented label is likely to serve the following six functions:

1. Identify the manufacturer, country of origin, and ingredients or materials comprising the product.
2. Report the expiration date and the contents' grading based on a prescribed government standard (as on cartons of eggs).
3. Explain how to use the product.
4. Warn about potential misuse.
5. Provide easy-to-understand care instructions.
6. Serve as an important communication link between the users, eventual buyers, and the company.

A quality label signals a quality product. Often the label must also be designed for a particular market segment. For example, seniors need labels with large lettering. Furthermore, because many customers toss instructions and packaging away, often the only way a customer can reach a manufacturer is through the information provided on the label.

PRODUCT MANAGEMENT: MANAGING PRODUCTS THROUGH THEIR LIFE CYCLES

Product life cycle
is the cycle of stages that a product goes through from birth to death: introduction, growth, maturity, and decline.

A product now has been designed, developed, and tested; brand, label, and package decisions have been made. As product development nears completion, product management is just beginning. The product must now be introduced to the market, and strategies for generating profit over the life of the *product category* (all brands that satisfy a particular need) must be developed and implemented. Figure 8.8 shows the general pattern of expected sales and profit over the **product life cycle.** *Innovators* and *early adopters,* customers generally willing to take more risk, buy the product shortly after introduction. During growth, product purchase begins to spread to the *early majority* of the mass market, with full penetration and adoption by the *late majority* occurring primarily in the maturity stage. Near the product's decline, only *laggards* are left purchasing the product. Marketing strategy and tactics must be adapted to meet the special opportunities and challenges presented by each stage of the life cycle as illustrated in Table 8.5.

Introduction Strategies

The introduction stage starts when a new product is presented to the market. Initial sales are slow, as potential customers must go through a learning process about the new product and its benefits before they purchase. Creating customer learning requires heavy expenditures in advertising, sampling, promotion, distribution, and personal selling, all of which contribute to profit losses at this stage. The set of marketing tactics employed must work together to make customers aware of the product and encourage them to try it.

The Individual Adoption Process

Customers go through several distinct stages of learning before purchasing a new product. Ideally, a firm's marketing program helps customers move through these stages,

The Product Life Cycle — Figure 8.8

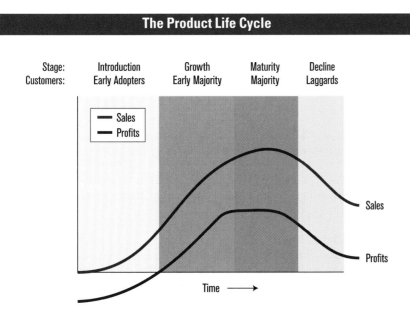

Stage:	Introduction	Growth	Maturity	Decline
Customers:	Early Adopters	Early Majority	Majority	Laggards

Marketing Tactics and Outcomes through the Product Life Cycle — Table 8.5

Outcomes	Introduction	Growth	Maturity	Decline
Sales	Low	Fast growth	Slow growth	Decline
Profits	Negligible	Positive to flat	Flat to declining	Low or zero
Cash flow	Negative	Moderate	High	Low
Customers	Innovative	Mass market	Mass market	Laggards
Competitors	Few	Growing	Many rivals	Declining number

Tactics	Introduction	Growth	Maturity	Decline
Strategic focus	Expanded market	Market penetration	Defend share	Productivity
Expenditures	High	High (declining %)	Falling	Low
Emphasis	Product awareness	Brand preference	Brand loyalty	Selective
Distribution	Patchy	Intensive	Intensive	Selective
Price	High	Lowest	Lowest	Rising
Product	Basic	Differentiated	Differentiated	Rationalized

thereby decreasing their risk in purchasing a new product. The stages customers generally go through in the *adoption process* include:

- *Awareness:* Realizing that a new product exists
- *Knowledge:* Building an understanding of what the product does, what benefits it provides, and how it works
- *Liking:* Developing positive feelings toward the product
- *Preference:* Coming to prefer this product over any other, if one were to buy
- *Purchase:* Making the decision to buy and acting upon it

To encourage adoption of a new product, firms use their marketing programs to lead potential customers through each successive stage. Before customers can develop knowledge about what a new product does, they must first have become aware that it exists. Frequently product introductions are accompanied by large initial advertising campaigns designed specifically to create awareness. Only after people develop knowledge about a product can they come to a conclusion as to whether they like it. Preference can only develop for products a person likes, which may lead to eventual purchase. The time frame required for new product acceptance varies widely from product to product. Some of the factors that influence this rate of adoption are listed in Figure 8.9.

The elements of the marketing program in the introduction stage of a new product's life cycle are designed to move more innovative customers (early adopters) swiftly through the learning process to purchase. Customers will be slower to adopt products that are more radically innovative, such as microwave ovens when they were first introduced in the 1970s, and products that are expensive, such as the Apple Newton. More innovative and expensive products require higher marketing effort, especially in the introduction stage.

http://www.apple.com

The Diffusion Process

Broad *product diffusion* into the mass market results from three processes. First, a firm's marketing program induces innovators and early adopters to purchase and try the product, as outlined above. Then, if the design team has developed a product that meets the needs of these customers, they will be satisfied with their purchase and tell other potential customers, generating free word-of-mouth product advertising. Finally, positive word-of-mouth endorsements work in concert with the firm's marketing program to help provide less innovative (more imitative) customers, who make up the bulk of most markets, with enough understanding of and confidence in the product to purchase it. For a more complete understanding of the profiles of the various types of customers that together create the market, see Figure 8.10.

Word-of-mouth approvals from customers reinforce the messages sent by the firm, giving them credibility. Hearing one's neighbors rave about their new Palm Pilot and how it changed the way they organize their life is much more powerful for many people than reading about what the product does in a print ad. Of course, if the product does not live up to expectations, negative word-of-mouth will be generated. This will almost certainly guarantee market failure, regardless of the quality of the marketing program used to launch the product. When Apple's Newton routinely failed to recognize the handwriting of early customers, negative word-of-mouth spread rapidly. Some small articles and cartoons poking fun at the problem were even published in the business press that further contributed to market failure.

Diffusion is only partly under the control of a firm. Diffusion is aided early in the development process by ensuring that the product solves the problems customers want solved, and by getting the details of the product right. Once launched, the firm can

Figure 8.9	Factors Influencing the Rate of New Product Adoption

- **Relative Advantage:** The greater the relative advantage—lower price, ease of use, savings in time—the faster the adoption process.

- **Compatibility:** The greater the compatibility—consistent with values, needs, and experiences of potential users—the faster the adoption process.

- **Complexity:** The more difficult a new product is to understand and use, the longer it will take to be adopted.

- **Trialability:** The greater the degree that the new product can be used on a trial basis, the faster the adoption process.

- **Observability:** The greater the degree to which the results of using a product are visible to others, the faster the adoption process.

Customer Profiles	**Figure 8.10**

- **Innovators:** Innovators, 2.5 percent of all potential adopters, tend to be younger, higher in social status, more cosmopolitan, and better educated than later adopter groups.

- **Early adopters:** Early adopters, 13.5 percent of potential adopters, enjoy the prestige and respect that comes with owning new products, but are less venturesome and more concerned with group norms and values than innovators.

- **Early majority:** The early majority, 34 percent of potential adopters, spends more time deciding whether to try new products and seeks the opinions of the innovators and early adopters.

- **Late majority:** The late majority, 34 percent of potential adopters, is less cosmopolitan and responsive to change than any of the previous groups.

- **Laggards:** 16 percent of all potential adopters, laggards tend to be conservative, older, low socioeconomic status, and suspicious of change.

speed diffusion by developing a marketing program that maximizes the number of people who become early adopters. More early adopters mean that there are more users who can spread positive word-of-mouth endorsements to more potential customers early in the marketing cycle. Finally, a firm can encourage mechanisms to spread word-of-mouth endorsements throughout the target market. For example, Amazon.com allows readers to write and post book reviews that other Amazon.com customers can access. Whatever mechanisms the firm develops must work in concert with the rest of the marketing program surrounding the product launch.

Growth Strategies

The growth stage of the product life cycle is initially characterized by rapidly increasing product demand, new competitors entering the market in response, and rapidly increasing profits for the product varieties that customers decide best meet their needs. The firm's emphasis shifts to building and holding a set of loyal customers and distribution channel members, and sustaining sales growth as long as possible. To do this, they may invest in product improvements and expanding and strengthening distribution channels. As overall spending increases to offset competitive pressures, profits begin to level off as the product category leaves the growth stage and enters the maturity stage.

Maturity Strategies

Most product categories can be assigned to the maturity stage; therefore, marketing managers are most often dealing with mature products. During the maturity stage, sales initially increase but at a slower rate as the market becomes saturated and as competitive pressures reach their peak. Sales and profits typically decline in the latter half of the maturity stage.

Using the marketing program to maintain customer loyalty and satisfaction is important to maintaining profitability throughout the maturity stage. Airline frequent flyer programs, hotel honored guest programs, and grocery store frequent shopper programs all were developed to maintain customer loyalty and improve profits. The objective is to take the pressure off price reductions as a way to keep customers by using other tactics in the marketing mix. Several strategies can be used, even in maturity, to attempt to grow the market. For example, a firm can find new users (*market development*) or increase the usage rate per user (*market penetration*). Another mechanism for growth in the mature stage is to offer significant improvements on a routine basis (*product development*). Each of these strategies are discussed in more detail in the following pages.

Decline Strategies

Even if new users are found and usage rates are increased, product sales may eventually start a long-term decline, as when a substitute product that offers a superior set of benefits displaces the "old" product. Products based on new technologies frequently lead to a current product's demise. For example, 35 years ago nearly every student going to college brought along a typewriter. First the electric typewriter caused the decline of manual typewriter sales. Then word-processing machines started making inroads into the electric typewriter market. But the real death blow to typewriter sales was dealt by the advent of the PC and easy-to-use word-processing programs like Write, WordPerfect, and Word. A few forms in some offices still require a typewriter. However, the majority of offices and even students now depend on PCs and word-processing programs for producing easily readable written communication.

Reduced sales do not necessarily mean that a firm should exit from the business immediately. The higher a firm's competitive strength in an industry, the longer they will want to stay in the market to reap returns from previous investments. However, the marketing tactics used at this stage will again have to be modified to maintain acceptable profitability levels. Marketing expenses, and promotion expenses in particular, will need to be reduced. IBM divested its typewriter division in the 1990s so that the business could continue operations without being burdened with the large overhead costs associated with IBM's traditional business structures. Products in decline continue to sell, but customer satisfaction (and thus loyalty) and word-of-mouth will become more important generators of sales than marketing campaigns.

http://www.ibm.com

LEARNING OBJECTIVE 6

MANAGING THE PRODUCT PORTFOLIO

Product Mix Decisions[19]

Few companies are successful by relying on a single product. Most companies manufacture and market a variety of products. All of the products a company markets can be thought of as its product mix. The mixture of products typically includes various items that are related in terms of the raw materials used to create them or the products' end-uses. A group of related items in a company's product portfolio constitutes a **product line**. The following example illustrates the number of product mix decisions marketers must make.

The Purex Corporation had a relatively small product mix when it opened its doors. The company primarily manufactured bleach and a few powdered laundry detergents. Over the years, through new product development and acquisitions, Purex extended its product mix (see Figure 8.11) by offering fabric softeners (StaPuff), fabric softener sheets (Toss'n Soft), Brillo Soap Pads, Sweetheart soaps, Sweetheart Dish Liquid, Mildew Stain Remover, and sponge products (Dobie Pads). These products all relate to household cleaning.

The *product mix width* is the number of different product lines a company offers. The width of Purex's product mix includes detergents, fabric softeners, cleansers, scouring pads, bleach, dish liquids, soaps, ammonia, and toilet bowl cleaners. The *product mix depth* refers to the number of brands within each product line. The depth of Purex's detergent product line includes Purex Powdered, Purex Liquid with Fabric Softener, Trend Powdered, Trend Liquid, Dutch Powdered, and Dutch Liquid.

Any company limits its growth potential if it chooses to concentrate on a single product line. Companies that offer multiple product lines enjoy numerous benefits:

- *Protection against competition:* If a company relies on one product for success, a competitor can enter the market, undercut price, and steal market share. A company with more than one product line will not be devastated by the effects of a competitor's actions in any one particular area.
- *Increase growth and profits:* Companies offer more than one product line to boost market growth and company profits. If a product category is mature with little to no growth, a company may find it difficult to increase its share

Product line
is the set of products a firm targets to one general market. These products are likely to share some common features and technology characteristics or be complementary products. They also are likely to share several elements of the marketing mix, such as distribution channels.

Purex Corporation Product Mix									Figure 8.11
	Width of the Product Mix								
	Detergents	**Fabric Softeners**	**Cleansers**	**Scour Pads**	**Bleach**	**Dish Liquids**	**Soaps**	**Ammonia**	**Bowl Cleaners**
Depth of Product Lines	Purex Powdered	StaPuf Liquid	Old Dutch BabO	Brillo Dobie	Purex	Sweet-heart	Sweet-heart	Bo-Peep	SnoBol
	Purex Liquid	StaPuf Sheets		Brillo Lane		Trend			
	Purex Liquid with Fabric Softener	Toss'n Soft				Lemon Trend			
	Trend Powdered								
	Trend Liquid								
	Dutch Liquid								

and profits unless it is willing to spend more to take market share away from a competitor.

- *Offset sales fluctuations:* Companies that offer products with seasonal variations find that multiple product lines help to offset these fluctuations in sales.
- *Achieve greater impact:* Multiple product lines allow a company to achieve greater market impact. A company with multiple lines of products often is more important to both consumers and channel members.
- *Enable economical resource usage:* Multiple product lines enable the economical use of resources. Spreading operational costs over a series of products enables a manufacturer to reduce the average production and marketing costs for all its products; this results in lower prices to customers.
- *Avoid obsolescence:* Companies offering more than one product line avoid becoming obsolete when one product line reaches the end of its life cycle.

Product Growth Opportunities[20]

Established products are the lifeblood of most companies. But a company that depends solely on its current stable of products may be headed for trouble. Aggressive competitive activity or a major change in technology can cause a rapid decline in sales even for the most successful product. Growth is fundamental to the long-term success of any organization.

Growth opens up new sales and profit opportunities for a firm while reducing dependence on existing products for its success. Companies can pursue a number of growth options. Figure 8.12 presents four such options. A firm might attempt to grow its business through *market penetration* by selling more of its existing products to existing markets. The main objective of this strategy is to convince existing customers to purchase and use more of the firm's product. In other words, the firm is attempting to increase its current market share. Typical market penetration tactics include aggressive promotion campaigns and price discounts. Airlines, soft drink companies, and fast-food chains are examples of firms that actively pursue a market penetration strategy.

Firms that find new uses for existing products are pursuing *market development*. In this scenario, a firm attempts to grow its business by selling more of its existing products to new markets. Baking soda is the classic example. Although its original use was for baking, it is now marketed as a deodorizer, carpet cleaner, and toothpaste among other

http://www.armhammer.com

Figure 8.12 — Growth Strategies

	Markets	
Products	**Existing**	**New**
Existing	Market Penetration	Market Development
New	Product Development	Product Diversification

---

http://www.jnj.com

uses. These new uses have attracted new markets and have increased the overall sales of the product. Other examples include Johnson & Johnson baby shampoo and Tony the Tiger Frosted Flakes, which are now being marketed to adults. In addition, the hair loss remedy Rogaine that was originally targeted to men is now being targeted to women with thinning hair.

Firms that develop new products that they feel will appeal to existing markets are pursuing a *product development strategy*. In this scenario, a firm seeks to provide its existing market with a variety of new choices. For example, Procter & Gamble markets Tide, Cheer, and Bold detergents; Wendy's added pita bread sandwiches and salads to its menu; Bacardi, the rum distiller, markets premixed cocktail ingredients such as piña colada and daiquiri mixes.

http://www.wendys.com

The most risky growth option is *product diversification*. Under this option, firms pursue a growth strategy by developing new products that appeal to new markets. Chrysler's introduction of the Neon in 1994 represented a diversification move to appeal to the relatively unserved group of Generation Xers. Similarly, the Toyota Motor Corporation recently unveiled the Echo (see Figure 8.13) at the 1999 Detroit auto show. The Echo features low emissions and a low price, and is targeted directly at Generation Y (the "Echo" Boom). Product diversification enables a company to be less dependent on any one product or product line.

http://www.toyota.com

Figure 8.13 — Toyota's Echo: A New Product Aimed at the "Echo" Boom

CHAPTER SUMMARY

- Products are the lifeblood of every organization whether they are goods, services, people, places, or ideas. In general, products can be either classified as consumer or business-to-business products. Consumer products include convenience, shopping, specialty, and unsought products that are characterized based on how the consumer views and shops for the product. Business-to-business products include installations, accessories, raw materials, component parts/materials, and supplies and are classified based on how the products will be used.

- Few companies are successful by relying on a single product. Marketing's role in successfully accomplishing new product development requires firms to continually: understand customer needs and problems; match technological capabilities to solving those problems; and move projects through the corporation and into the market. Unless all three tasks are performed well, product development is unlikely to be successful.

- Understanding customer needs requires performing qualitative market research and making the details available to the development team. No one technique will easily provide a list of *all* the customer needs. Actually being a customer best conveys tacit needs. Process-related needs are identified most easily by critically observing customers. In-depth interviewing is the most efficient means to obtain masses of detailed needs, but may not provide tacit and process-related information. Few projects can afford the time and expense of fully implementing all these processes. Development teams must use the most appropriate customer need–generating technique(s), given the informational requirements, budget, and time frame for their project.

- Effectively using technological capabilities to solve problems requires implementing a strategy for the NPD program overall, strategies for each project, and a product development process. Commercializing new products consists of repeatable tasks and less repeatable tasks. Firms that use a formalized new product process to help complete the more repeatable tasks in a consistent manner tend to have greater NPD success. Formalized processes are personalized to meet the needs of each firm.

- Shepherding products through the firm requires implementing effective leadership, providing an organizational structure that allows projects to move forward efficiently, and developing mechanisms to maintain management support over the life of projects. Project leaders, champions, and process owners all have been used to lead projects effectively. NPD in firms is organized through two different structures, each providing better ways to organize depending on the "newness to the organization" of the project being developed. No one structure seems to be associated with consistently higher performance. A number of different influence strategies, both formal and informal and affecting both rational and political decision-making processes, are used to obtain and maintain management support for projects.

- Product mix decisions must be made regarding the width and depth of product lines to be marketed. Additional product decisions must be made in the areas of branding, packaging, and labeling.

- Once launched, marketing must manage profitability throughout the product life cycle by modifying marketing mix elements to achieve the objectives of different life cycle stages. The objective in the introduction stage is to make potential early adopters aware of the product and persuade them to try it. During growth, the objective is achieving maximum market share. Profitability is the primary objective during both maturity and decline.

- Still more product decisions must be made with regard to the sustaining growth. Established products are the mainstay of most companies. But a company that depends solely on its current stable of products may be headed for trouble. Growth opportunities exist in the form of market penetration, market development, product development, and product diversification strategies.

- Long-term corporate success depends upon executing new product development effectively and efficiently. Managing product development is one of the most complex tasks of the organization, in part, because of the cooperation needed between different departments. Marketing is crucial in achieving successful new product development and making product decisions.

KEY TERMS

Brand equity is the marketplace value of a brand based on reputation and goodwill.

Brands are the name, representative symbol or design, or any other feature that identifies one firm's product as distinct from another firm's. Trademark is the legal term for a brand. Brands may be associated with one product, a family of products, or with all of the products sold by a firm.

Competitively advantaged product is a product that solves a set of customer problems better than any competitor's product. This product is made possible due to this firm's unique technical, manufacturing, managerial, or marketing capabilities, which are not easily copied by others.

Core benefit proposition (CBP) is the primary benefit or purpose for which a customer buys a product. The CBP may reside in the physical good or service performance, or it may come from augmented dimensions of the product.

Concept is a written description or visual depiction of a new product idea. A concept includes the product's primary features and benefits.

Customer prototypes are the detailed pictures and descriptions of individuals or firms in the target market for a product. Creating these descriptions helps firms envision how products and the marketing mix might best be combined to maximize profits.

Features are the way that benefits are delivered to customers. Features provide the solution to customer problems.

Line extensions are new products that are developed as variations of existing products.

Product development process consists of a clearly defined set of tasks and steps that describes the normal means by which product development proceeds. The process outlines the order and sequence of the tasks and indicates who is responsible for each.

Product life cycle is the cycle of stages that a product goes through from birth to death: introduction, growth, maturity, and decline.

Product line is the set of products a firm targets to one general market. These products are likely to share some common features and technology characteristics or be complementary products. They also are likely to share several elements of the marketing mix, such as distribution channels.

Product mix is the full set of a firm's products across all markets served.

Products are the set of features, functions, and benefits that customers purchase. Products may consist primarily of tangible (physical) attributes or intangibles, such as those associated with services or some combination of tangible and intangible.

Project strategy, sometimes called a protocol, is a statement of the attributes the project is expected to have, the market at which it is targeted, and the purpose behind commercializing the product.

Prototype is a product concept in physical form. A prototype may be a full working model that has been produced by hand or a nonworking physical representation of the final product. It is used to gather customer reaction to the physical form (aesthetics and ergonomics) or to initial operating capability. It is also used in internal performance tests to ensure that performance goals have been met.

Stage-Gate process is a common new product development process that divides the repeatable portion of product development into a time-sequenced series of stages, each of which is separated by a management decision gate. In each stage, a team completes a set of tasks that span the functions involved in product development. At the end of each stage, management reviews the results obtained and, based on the team's ability to meet the objectives in that stage, provides the resources to continue to the next stage ("go"), requests additional work ("recycle"), or stops the project ("kill").

Tacit knowledge is knowledge that is implied by or inferred from actions or statements.

Voice of the customer (VOC) is a one-on-one interviewing process to elicit an in-depth set of customer needs.

QUESTIONS FOR DISCUSSION

1. How do the differences between consumer products and business-to-business products impact the way new product development is managed and organized?

2. Several examples were given in the chapter of products that were successful on one dimension of success, but not on another. What are some other examples, and on what dimensions were they less successful? Why did the companies undertake these projects?

3. NPD teams always seem to want to include every feature possible in a new product. The restraint shown by the Palm Pilot team in not adding infrared technology to the first-generation product is unusual. What steps can be taken to keep NPD teams from "over-featuring" the product?

4. Why do NPD processes need to be "personalized" for each firm? What are the factors that will contribute to the way in which a firm personalizes the process for its use?

5. What is the weakest aspect in our understanding about how to manage NPD?

6. In which types of NPD projects might a heavyweight project manager not be successful? A champion?

7. What are your options if you just cannot garner management support for a proposed NPD project?

8. Hewlett-Packard started as a firm that developed and sold scientific measurement equipment like oscilloscopes. Over the years they have increased the width of their product mix to include computer equipment and medical equipment. Name three other companies that have increased their product mix width, and name the sets of product lines they sell.

9. Since Procter & Gamble is such a highly revered company and strong marketer, why do they follow an individual branding strategy rather than take advantage of a family brand name?

10. In what stage of the product life cycle are family sedans? Station wagons? Minivans? If these are all segments of the car market, how is it possible for them to be at different stages of the product life cycle?

INTERNET QUESTIONS

1. Using your favorite search engine, type in the search string "product development." How do you sort through the enormous number of hits obtained to find something useful?

2. Go to the Web site http://www.pdma.org. This is the Web site for the Product Development and Management Association, a nonprofit association whose mission is to seek out, develop, organize, and disseminate leading-edge information on the theory and practice of product development and product development processes. How does their Web site, and the associated hotlinks, help fulfill that mission?

3. Go to http://www.amazon.com. What is the best-selling book on new product development? What other books have been written by that author?

4. The Internet is changing the way some firms gather customer information. See if you can find a company that is using the Internet to gather information on customer needs. What evidence on their site suggests that they are using the information gathered to aid in developing new products? What are the benefits of gathering customer needs from the Web? What are the drawbacks? For what kinds of industries might this information be most useful or appropriate to use? Least useful or appropriate?

5. What information about innovation can be obtained from the following Web sites: http://www.inside.com, http://www.creativemag.com, http://www.fastcompany.com, http://www.idsa.org, http://www.pachamber.org? How would you use this information in developing a new product?

ENDNOTES

[1] Markos Kounalakis, *Defying Gravity: The Making of Newton* (Hillsboro, OR: Beyond Words Publishing, 1993).

[2] *Product* refers to both physical goods such as cars and shampoos and to services such as banking, dining, and consulting, as well as to ideas and people. For example, graduates are a college "product." Developing new services frequently requires developing both a physical good as well as the intangible benefits. For example, a new hotel chain requires developing the physical building, including the room layout, the software and hardware infrastructure to handle reservations and billing, and ancillary physical spaces such as outdoor recreation and parking facilities. Chapter 9 presents additional information about the marketing impacts of the special aspects of services.

[3] The section "Managing the Product Portfolio," also in this chapter, presents more on this topic.

[4] Abbie Griffin, "PDMA Research on New Product Development Practices: Updating Trends and Benchmarking Best Practices," *Journal of Product Innovation Management* 14, no. 6 (1997): 429–458.

[5] The section "Managing Products through Their Life Cycle," also in this chapter, presents more on this topic.

[6] Abbie Griffin and Albert L. Page, "The PDMA Success Measurement Project: Recommended Measures for Product Development Success and Failure," *Journal of Product Innovation Management* 13 (November 1996): 478–496.

[7] Abbie Griffin, "PDMA Research on New Product Development Practices," 429–458.

[8] Ibid.

[9] Abbie Griffin and John R. Hauser, "The Voice of the Customer," *Marketing Science* 12, no. 1 (1993): 1–27; Gerald Zaltman and Robin A. Higgie, "Seeing the Voice of the Customer: The Zaltman Elicitation Technique," Working Paper 9–114, Cambridge, MA: Marketing Science Institute.

[10] Griffin, "PDMA Research on New Product Development Practices," 429–458.

[11] Ibid.

[12] A fuller explanation of each of these may be found in Chapters 6 and 8 of Robert G. Cooper, *Winning at New Products*, 2nd edition (Reading, MA: Addison Wesley, 1993).

[13] Griffin, "PDMA Research on New Product Development Practices," 429–458.

[14] Kim B. Clark and Steven C. Wheelwright, *Managing New Product and Process Development* (New York: Free Press, 1993).

[15] Stephen Markham and Abbie Griffin, "The Breakfast of Champions: Associations between Champions and Product Development Environments, Practices and Performance," *Journal of Product Innovation Management* 14, no. 6 (1998): 436–454.

[16] Michael E. McGrath, Michael T. Anthony, and Amram R. Shapiro, *Product Development: Success through Product and Cycle-Time Excellence* (Boston: Butterworth-Heinemann, 1992).

[17] This section is adapted from Peter R. Dickson, *Marketing Management* (Fort Worth, The Dryden Press, 1994), 310–322.

[18] See Chapter 7 of this book for additional information on product positioning.

[19] This section is adapted from John H. Lindgren, Jr. and Terry Shimp, *Marketing: An Interactive Learning System* (Fort Worth: The Dryden Press, 1996), 227–235.

[20] This section is adapted from Lindgren and Shimp, *Marketing: An Interactive Learning System*, 262–264.

CHAPTER CASE

DEVELOPING A NEW DEGREE
OFFERING AT MIDWESTERN U.

Sam Stanza, Associate Dean for Teaching at Midwestern University's School of Business, a leading business school in a large city in the Midwest, was contemplating the possibilities for offering an additional degree in business at the school. The university trustees were looking to the business school to provide additional financial contributions to offset large deficits in other departments. They had indicated that he would have free rein to develop any program he proposed, as long as it provided a net positive contribution to the school within the first 2 years of introduction, and a net positive contribution to the university within the first 3 years of operation.

The business school currently offered several degree programs. As did all major business schools, it offered a full-time master's in business administration (MBA) to 400 students/class that generally required 2 years to complete a set of 20 classes. Students competed fiercely to attend this program, which cost $30,000 per year in tuition. The MBA program was a world leader for its marketing curriculum, and very highly thought of in terms of its finance program. Its general management capabilities were not as highly regarded.

The school also offered a part-time MBA program, conferring an identical degree to the full-time program. These students paid the same per-class tuition ($3,000/class), and completed the program in 4 years. At any given time, about 1,500 part-time students were enrolled in the degree program. These students were drawn primarily from local businesses. Because the curriculum was identical to the full-time program, and the same professors taught in both programs, there was great competition to be accepted into this program as well. The difference between full-time and part-time students lay predominantly in an unwillingness (or inability) to sacrifice 2 years of full-time salary for the sake of further education.

The business school also offered an executive MBA (EMBA) degree, which differed significantly from the cachet of an MBA degree. EMBAs were executives who had been out of school for at least 20 years, and whose firms had sent them back to this program on a part-time basis. Each class of the 65 company-sponsored executives attended a full-day session each week of the school year—Friday one week, and Saturday the next—for 2 years. Four 90-minute classes were offered each day. Additionally, the students spent 2 weeks overseas in the summer between the school years, wrote a summer paper on some aspect of change needed in their firm, and spent spring break of the second year of the program on a U.S. study tour. Tuition (including the study trips) came to $100,000 for the 2-year program. Firms sent executives to the program for a number of reasons:

- To provide a technical manager with business education.
- To indicate within the firm that a manager had top management potential.
- To provide a business refresher to a manager changing functional areas (from finance to marketing, for example).
- As a reward for service.

While the part-time program was at capacity (which was a classroom and facilities limitation issue due to the evening class schedules), there was capacity within the resources of the full-time program for offering additional daytime classes in terms of both teaching manpower as well as facilities. Dean Stanza considered several concept options that fit into this constraint before narrowing the list to one. Options that did not seem to be as interesting in terms of potential profitability for the effort and risk included:

1. Creating an undergraduate (bachelor's) degree program. This would require an enormous infrastructure much different from that currently in place for the school's graduate programs. Payback would require too long a time period to warrant this.
2. Offering a series of management short courses during the summer only, when few students attended class. While from a facilities point of view, these courses would greatly increase the use of underutilized space, this would require an enormous amount of time investment as each course would have to be individually developed, with a specific target market

identified that could find benefit from it. Each 1- to 4-week course would have to be individually marketed to the appropriate target market, creating little marketing synergy across the potential set of courses offered.

The concept most favored by Dean Stanza at this stage of the development process was to offer a 12-month, full-time master's of management (MM). The focus of the curricula would be to provide a general management master's degree, but with advanced marketing expertise overlaid on the general management studies. The program would start in June with classes in business fundamentals. At the end of the summer, students would take the first of two study trips to a consumer marketing powerhouse. During spring break, students would take a study trip to a business-to-business marketing firm. The target market would be low- to mid-level (10 years out) managers with top management potential who currently worked in marketing positions or in other functional areas but needed marketing experience. Dean Stanza believed that 75 percent of the students would be supported by their firms during their matriculation. Tuition for the year would be $50,000, including both study trips.

Discussion Questions

1. How might Dean Stanza determine if his proposed program would meet the needs of his target market?

2. If the university decides to proceed with this program, list some of the preliminary steps to be completed before opening the program to students. Discuss the relevance of each of these steps to the ultimate success of the program.

3. If early response to the program proved to be sluggish, what marketing techniques could be used to increase interest and enrollment? What would be the costs and benefits of each technique?

CHAPTER nine

K. Douglas Hoffman,
Colorado State University

Dr. Hoffman earned his master's and doctorate degrees from the University of Kentucky and his bachelor's degree from The Ohio State University. He has been formally recognized for teaching excellence and has served as past education coordinator for the Services Marketing Special Interest Group of the American Marketing Association.

Dr. Hoffman currently is a professor of marketing and has taught such courses as Principles of Marketing, Services Marketing, E-Marketing, Retail Management, and Marketing Management. His primary teaching and research passion is services marketing. He launched the first services marketing classes at Mississippi State University, the University of North Carolina at Wilmington, and Colorado State University.

Prior to his academic career, Dr. Hoffman was actively involved in his family-owned golf course business, served as a distribution analyst for Volkswagen of America, and worked as a research analyst for the Parker Hannifin Corp. His current research and consulting activities are primarily in the areas of customer service/satisfaction and services marketing education. Dr. Hoffman has coauthored two other South-Western/Thomson Learning texts: *Essentials of Services Marketing* and *Managing Services Marketing*, both with John E. G. Bateson.

Services Marketing

"Okay, everyone knows that the Net is changing everything . . . that's old news. The savvy companies are already asking themselves: what comes next? Chapter Two of the Internet will be about the mass proliferation of e-services."

—The Hewlett-Packard Company

One of the most profound changes driving the growth of the service economy has been the phenomenal advance in technology and in particular—the Internet. Let's recap the growth of the Internet in a nutshell. Sometime around 1996, the obsession with the Internet began. Thousands of businesses, customers, employees, and partners got wired to one another and began conducting business processes online (a.k.a., e-business). Eventually, more and more customers (businesses and final consumers) became wired and formed a critical mass. Through repeated usage, customer trust dramatically increased, and the Net became a viable means for revenue production and economic growth (a.k.a., e-commerce). Hewlett-Packard (http://www.hp.com) refers to this period as "Chapter One of the Internet."

It was during Chapter One that the foundation of the Internet was laid, providing the infrastructure that enabled the evolution of the Net to follow. Chapter One required users to:

- do it yourself
- at your desk
- on a PC
- tapping into Web storefronts
- using monolithic applications
- where IT (Internet technology) is viewed as an asset

Chapter One is old news. According to the experts, Chapter Two will be about the mass proliferation of e-services. In comparison to Chapter One, which required users to work the Web, Chapter Two is about the Internet working for the user. Now the Internet helps users to:

- do it for me
- while I am living my life
- on PCs, devices, and things
- through the use of automated e-services
- using modular e-services
- where IT is viewed as a *service*

Chapter Two will require companies to rethink their Web site strategy. In an e-service world, driving thousands of users to your Web site is no longer the best Internet strategy. E-service users will access the Internet using a multitude of appliances, including mobile phones, watches, VCRs, heart monitors, and automobiles. Users will no longer need traditional Web sites because these appliances will connect them directly to Internet-based e-services to solve problems, perform specific tasks, or complete transactions.

Hewlett-Packard's Web site provides several intriguing scenarios of how e-services will reshape our daily activities. In one such scenario titled "Anticipating the Unforeseeable," a traveler experiences difficulty as she drives to the airport.

There's nothing like leaving on a business trip the day before Thanksgiving. The hapless executive heads for the airport. While she's en route, all hell breaks loose in Salt Lake City. A blizzard grounds her connecting flight to LaGuardia. All other flights to New York City are overbooked. And by the way, NYC's taxi drivers have just gone on strike. Not to worry, by the time the executive gets to the airport, several different e-services have gone to work, turning a near disaster into a minor delay.

- First, the airline's flight information service notifies the executive's travel service that her flight has been canceled.
- Next, the executive's travel service sends out a request for bids to five other airline flight information services.
- Since the executive is holding a full-fare ticket and her frequent flyer status is higher than other people's, the executive is awarded the best available seat on the next plane going to the nearest airport—Newark.
- The travel service automatically checks with ground transportation services and learns of the taxi strike.
- As a result, the travel service contacts a rental car service, books a rental car at Newark Airport, and requests directions, provided by the car's GPS system, to the hotel in New York City.
- Noting the executive will arrive later than anticipated, the travel service notifies the hotel's reservation service of the delay and guarantees payment.
- All of this information is transmitted to the executive through her pager or PDA (e.g., Palm Pilot) as she walks through the terminal.

All in all, it's an exciting time to live as new technological developments and e-services become the next big thing on the Net.[1]

After you have completed this chapter, you should be able to:

1. Understand the fundamental differences between the marketing of goods and services.
2. Appreciate the benefits of customer satisfaction and evaluate the pros and cons of various customer relationship management practices.
3. Understand the managerial significance of the gap model of service quality.
4. Discuss why customer retention is so important and identify tactics that help firms retain customers.

THE FUNDAMENTALS OF SERVICES MARKETING

Services are everywhere we turn, whether we are visiting the doctor, responding to e-mail messages, eating at a favorite restaurant, or studying at school. Simply put, the global service economy is booming. More and more, the so-called industrialized countries are discovering that their service sector is generating the majority of their gross national product. However, the growth of the service sector does not just arise within traditional service industries such as business services, the hospitality industry, health care, and other professional services. Traditional goods producers such as automotive, computer, and numerous other manufacturers are now turning to the service aspects of their operations to establish a competitive advantage in the marketplace. These previously unexplored service aspects also generate additional sources of revenue for their firms. In essence, these companies, which used to compete by marketing "boxes" (tangible goods), have now switched their competitive focus to providing unmatched, unparalleled customer services (Figure 9.1). Hewlett-Packard has embodied this idea through an ad saying "A Box without Service Is Just a Box."

| **Figure 9.1** | **Service Is Expanding Beyond These Traditional Customer Services** |

Turning to Services As a Competitive Advantage   **Figure 9.2**

Ample evidence documents this transition from selling boxes to service competition.[2] For example, the traditional goods-producing automotive industry now emphasizes the service aspects of its businesses: low APR financing, attractive lease arrangements, bumper-to-bumper factory warranties, low maintenance guarantees, and free shuttle services for customers (Figure 9.2). Simultaneously, automotive firms are saying less about the tangible aspects of vehicles such as gas mileage, acceleration, and leather seats in their marketing communications. Similarly, the personal computer industry promotes in-home repairs, 24-hour customer service, and leasing arrangements, and the satellite television industry now touts the benefits of digital service, pay-per-view alternatives, and security options to prevent children from viewing certain programming.

The service boom looks set to continue into the near future. It seems likely that no business will succeed unless it makes service the foundation of its competitive strategy. The growing importance of services is also reflected in the changing role of the service department within organizations. In the not-so-distant past, the service department tended to be viewed as a necessary evil—it was the place that fixed the box and made good on failed production promises. As service has evolved to become a primary source of competitive advantage, the service department has grown in importance as well.

What Is a Service?

Services include a vast array of businesses ranging from profit to nonprofit services, private to government services, and unskilled to professional services (Table 9.1). However, the distinction between goods and services is not always perfectly clear. In fact, providing

Table 9.1	Types of Services		
Government Services	**Nonprofit Services**	**For-Profit Services**	**Professional Services**
Police and fire protection	Community hospitals	Car rental	Legal
IRS	United Way	Movie theater	Medical
Social Security	American Red Cross	Car wash	Insurance
Social services	Credit unions	Dry cleaning	Financial
Public transportation	Civic organizations	Landscaping	Architectural
U.S. Postal Service	Humane societies	Taxi service	Accounting
Department of Motor Vehicles		Airlines	Consulting
		Salon	

an example of a pure good or a pure service is very difficult in today's market economies. A pure good implies that any benefits received by the consumer contain no elements supplied by service. Similarly, a pure service would contain no benefits provide by tangible elements.

In reality, many services contain at least some "goods," or tangible elements, such as the menu selections at an Outback Steakhouse, a MasterCard statement from MBNA, or the written life insurance policy that State Farm Insurance issues. Also, most goods at least offer "services," or intangible elements. For example, table salt is delivered to the grocery store, but a company such as Morton Salt that sells it to thousands of retailers may offer innovative invoicing services that further differentiate it from competitors. The distinction between goods and services is blurred even further because a number of firms conduct business on both sides of the goods/services fence. For example, General Motors, the goods manufacturing giant, generates 20 percent of its revenue from its financial and insurance businesses, and the car maker's biggest supplier is Blue Cross and Blue Shield, not a parts supplier of steel, tires, or glass as most people would have thought.[3]

Despite the confusion, the following definitions should provide a sound starting point in developing an understanding of the differences between goods and services. In general, **goods** are objects, devices, or things, whereas **services** are deeds, efforts, or performances.[4] Ultimately, the primary difference between goods and services is the property of **intangibility**—lacking physical substance. Because of intangibility, a host of marketing problems for services arise that are not always adequately solved by traditional goods-related marketing solutions. For example, how would you (1) advertise a service that no one can see; (2) price a service that has no cost of goods sold; (3) inventory a service that cannot be stored; or (4) mass-produce a service that needs to be performed by an individual (e.g., dentist, lawyer, physician)? Clearly, managing a service operation seems much more complicated than managing a firm that primarily produces and markets goods.

The Scale of Market Entities

One helpful approach to looking at the differences between goods and services is provided by the **scale of market entities**.[5] This scale, presented in Figure 9.3, displays a range of products based on their tangibility and illustrates that there is really no such thing as a pure good or a pure service. All products have some tangible and some intangible aspects. Goods are *tangible dominant*. As such, goods possess physical properties called **search attributes** that customers can feel, taste, and see prior to their purchase decisions. For example, when purchasing a car, the consumer can kick the tires, look at the engine, listen to the stereo, smell that "new-car smell," and take the car for a test drive before making the actual purchase. In contrast, services are *intangible dominant*.

Goods
are objects, devices, or things.

Services
are deeds, efforts, or performances.

Intangibility
is a distinguishing characteristic of services that makes them unable to be touched or sensed in the same manner as physical goods.

Scale of market entities
displays a range of products along a continuum based on their tangibility.

Search attributes
are physical properties that customers can evaluate prior to their purchase decisions.

On the Road Again with Shomotion

One of the great pleasures in teaching a Principles of Marketing class is that it offers students from a variety of majors insights into the business world that may profoundly affect them the rest of their lives. Such was the case for Michael Scherkenbach, a Natural Resource and Tourism major at Colorado State University.

Upon graduation from CSU, Michael left the friendly scenic confines of Fort Collins, Colorado, to work for a family-owned company in Chicago, Illinois. Although the overall experience was great, Michael found it difficult to work with family members on a day-to-day basis. Within a year, Michael set out on his own and created Shomotion—a service-based transportation company specializing in mobile marketing campaigns and entertainment transportation. With a lot of hard work and some incredible luck, Shomotion has assisted in the transportation service needs of the Dave Matthews Band (2000 and 2001 tours), Blink 182, Destiny's Child, and various other national touring acts. Shomotion was selected as the exclusive transporter for the fall 2001 Discover Card/ESPN Tailgate Tour and was contracted to handle several similar marketing tours for *Lucky Magazine* and Jolly Rancher in 2002.

Shomotion provides users with a number of unique services. Ultimately, the company specializes in the transportation and repositioning of mobile marketing campaigns and entertainment transportation. This is accomplished through a wide variety of transportation and driver services. Shomotion's competitive edge is its abil-ity to provide customized solutions to meet the needs of individual customers. For instance, customers can personally select drivers from a pool of over 100 professionals and Shomotion's entire fleet of vehicles is equipped with state-of-the-art Qualcom satellite tracking and communications. All trailers feature air-ride suspension to ensure the safe transport of sensitive cargo and are outfitted with E-track load-securing systems.

Shomotion can handle human cargo in style as well. Shomotion's full-service coach leasing company offers services such as state-of-the-art entertainment systems, "In-Motion" satellite TV and Internet access, sleeping quarters from 6 to 12 bunks, fiber-optic interior lighting, full-size refrigerators, exterior perimeter lighting, granite floors, and marble countertops. Shomotion reports that many of its clients have found coach leasing to be a cost-effective substitute for rising hotel rates.

In addition to its transportation services, Shomotion offers a network of warehouses and storage facilities that greatly enhance the company's ability to accommodate sudden changes in tour schedules and down periods during mobile marketing campaigns. Michael notes, "When the Backstreet Boys had to suddenly postpone the remaining half of their 2001 summer tour, Shomotion was able to provide secure storage for 22 equipment trailers until the tour resumed." As a result, Shomotion has been able to position itself as the company to call when customers find themselves in a logistical jam.

Source: Interview with Michael Scherkenbach, November 2001, and http://www.shomotion.com.

Scale of Market Entities — Figure 9.3

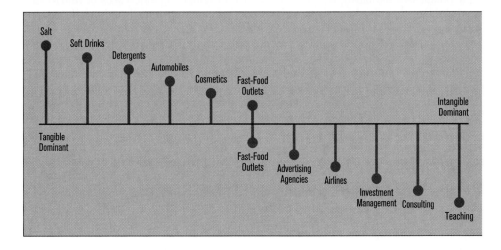

Source: Adapted from G. Lynn Shostack, "Breaking Free from Product Marketing," *Journal of Marketing* (April 1997): 77.

Experience attributes
can be evaluated only during and after consumption.

Credence attributes
cannot be evaluated confidently even immediately after consumption.

Marketing myopia
is too narrowly defining one's business.

As such, services are primarily characterized by **experience attributes** and **credence attributes**. Experience attributes can be evaluated only during and after consumption, such as a meal at a restaurant or the quality of a haircut. Credence attributes cannot be evaluated with certainty even after consumption of the product, such as a minister's counseling or a financial advisor's retirement investment advice. Finally, businesses such as fast-food restaurants, whose products contain both a goods and services component, fall in the middle of the continuum and are characterized by a combination of search, experience, and credence attributes.

The scale of market entities affirms that companies that manufacture tangible goods and ignore, or at least forget about, the intangible service elements of their business may be overlooking a vital differential advantage in the marketplace. By defining their businesses too narrowly, these firms have developed classic cases of **marketing myopia**. For example, the typical family pizza parlor may myopically view itself as being solely in the pizza business. However, a broader view recognizes that the business provides consumers with a convenient, reasonably priced food product in a unique atmosphere that the firm has created for its customers. Interestingly, adding service aspects to a product often transforms the product from a commodity into a compelling experience, and by doing so dramatically increases the revenue-producing opportunities of the product. For example, Build-a-Bear Workshops offer an experience-based business model where customers and their children or grandchildren can build and accessorize their own teddy bears. Given the option of going to a store to purchase a bear for a child versus taking the child to a Build-a-Bear Workshop where they can be personally involved in producing the bear, many customers are enthusiastically opting for the latter choice.

Unique Differences between Goods and Services

Initially, the field of services marketing was slow to develop within the academic community. Many marketing educators felt the marketing of services did not differ significantly from the marketing of goods. It was still necessary to segment markets, identify target markets, and develop marketing mixes that cater to the needs of a firm's intended target market. However, since those early days, a great deal has been written regarding the specific differences between goods and services and their corresponding marketing implications. The majority of these differences are attributed to four unique characteristics—intangibility, inseparability, heterogeneity, and perishability.[6]

Intangibility

Of the four unique characteristics that distinguish goods from services, *intangibility* is the primary source from which the other three characteristics emerge. As a result of their intangibility, services cannot be seen, felt, tasted, or touched in the same manner that goods can be sensed. For example, compare the differences between purchasing a movie ticket and a pair of shoes. The shoes are tangible goods, so the shoes can be objectively evaluated prior to purchase. The customer can pick up the shoes, feel the quality of materials from which they are constructed, view their specific style and color, and actually sample the shoe for comfort and fit. After purchasing the shoes, the customer takes them, claiming physical possession and ownership of a tangible product.

In comparison, the purchase of a movie ticket buys the customer an experience. Since the movie experience is intangible, the movie is subjectively evaluated. For example, the customer must rely on the judgments of others (e.g., friends, movie critics, etc.) who have previously experienced the service for *prepurchase information*. Because the information provided by others is based on their own sets of expectations and perceptions, opinions will differ regarding the value of the experience. After the movie is over, the customer returns home with a memory of the experience, retaining physical ownership of only a ticket stub. In addition, the customer's evaluation of the movie will extend beyond what was seen on the screen to include the treatment by theater employees, the behavior of other customers, and the condition of the theater's physical environment.

Inseparability

One of the most intriguing characteristics of the service experience involves the concept of **inseparability**. Inseparability refers to (1) the service provider's physical connection to the service being provided; (2) the customer's involvement in the service production process; and (3) the involvement of other customers in the service production process.

Inseparability
is a distinguishing characteristic of services that reflects the interconnection among the service provider, the customer receiving the service, and other customers sharing the service experience.

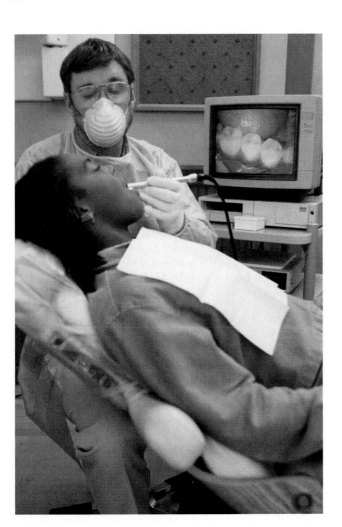

Meet Mya—The Virtual Service Provider

In an attempt to expand sales, many traditional PC manufacturers are looking for new product development ideas that involve mobile methods of using the Internet. For example, Motorola has recognized that many consumers are away from their computer when they would most like to use it. Motorola's response to this consumer need is Mya, a mobile platform that integrates voice and data. According to Motorola, Mya is essentially a voice-enabled browser that eliminates the middleman—the computer.

Mya has been designed specifically to act as a sort of digital secretary. Subscribers to Mya's services are given an 800 number and PIN that provides 24-hour access to the Net, 7 days a week. Theoretically, a subscriber can call Mya and ask for a list of Italian restaurants within a specified location. If a restaurant's Web site has been designed to take reservations, Mya can book the reservation. The limitation is that Mya can only access what is on the Internet. So, if a restaurant does not have a Web site, Mya has no way of knowing that it exists. Other services that Mya can provide include checking subscribers' e-mail and reminding them of upcoming appointments, birthdays, and anniversaries.

Although Mya is virtual, she has been given a human voice and physical appearance in order to assist in Motorola's marketing efforts. Mya's voice is that of Gabrielle Carteras, an actress who played Andrea on Fox television's *Beverly Hills 90210*. Mya's physical appearance is digitally animated—she is a tall, thin blonde with spiked hair, wearing a silver pantsuit. She was created by the same firm that generated the special effects for *Terminator 2* and *Titanic*. Mya's services are currently available to BellSouth subscribers. Other networks have yet to be finalized.

Source: Tobey Grumet, "Mya Desires Your Attention," *Revolution* 1, no. 5, (2000): 25.

Unlike the manufacturer, who may seldom see an actual customer while producing goods in a factory, service providers are often in constant contact with their customers and must construct their service operations with the customer's physical presence in mind.

Service Provider Involvement. For many services to occur, the provider must be physically present to deliver the service. For example, dental services require the physical presence of a dentist or hygienist, medical surgery requires a surgeon, and in-home services such as carpet cleaning require an actual individual to complete the work. Because of the intangibility of services, the service provider becomes part of the physical evidence upon which the customer's evaluation of the service experience is at least partly based.

Face-to-face interactions with customers make employee satisfaction crucial. Without a doubt, *employee satisfaction and customer satisfaction are directly related.* The interaction of dissatisfied employees with customers will lower consumers' perceptions of the firm's performance. The importance of employee satisfaction within service firms cannot be overemphasized. Customers will never be the number one priority in a company where employees are treated poorly. In fact, employees should be viewed and treated as "internal customers" of the firm.

Customer Involvement. Unlike goods, which are produced, sold, and then consumed, services are first sold and then produced and consumed simultaneously. For example, a box of breakfast cereal is produced in a factory, shipped to a store where it is sold, and then consumed by customers at a place and time of the customer's choosing. In contrast, services are produced and consumed simultaneously (e.g., surgery, a haircut, an amusement park ride, etc.), so consumption takes place inside the service factory. As a result, service firms must design their operations to accommodate the customer's presence. Inseparability makes the service factory another piece of physical evidence that consumers consider when making service quality evaluations.

Interestingly, as customer contact increases, the efficiency of an operation may decrease. This happens because the customers' involvement in the production process creates uncertainties in the scheduling of production and directly impacts the type of service desired, the length of the service delivery process, and the cycle of service demand. The attempt to balance consumer needs with efficient operating procedures is a delicate art. For example, imagine attempting to staff the emergency department of a hospital with exactly the right number of personnel, who have exactly the right qualifications, on any given night.

Other Customer Involvement. The presence of other customers during the service encounter is the third defining aspect of inseparability. Because production and consumption occur simultaneously, several customers often share a common service experience. For example, other students share your learning experience in the classroom, and other customers share your entertainment experience at a Six Flags Theme Park (Figure 9.4). The marketing challenges presented by having other customers involved in the production process generally reflect the negative aspects of their involvement. For example, the popular press has been full of stories about incidents of "air rage" or "passenger-induced turbulence." Factors known to contribute to this disruptive behavior include alcohol abuse, sexual misconduct, smoking in nonsmoking areas, failure to follow boarding instructions, violating carry-on baggage restrictions, and a variety of other conditions that arise from lapses in creature comforts, crew training, and food quality. In fact, the number of incidents involving passengers interfering with flight crews has more than tripled over the last 10 years. The policing of customer misconduct aboard planes is a tricky issue. According to one flight attendant, "At 37,000 feet, you don't have the option of throwing people out like you can in a cocktail lounge."[7]

The impact of other customers is not always negative. On the positive side, audience reaction in the form of laughter or screams of terror often enhances the moviegoer's experience. Similarly, a crowded pub may facilitate social interaction, and a happy crowd may make a concert an even more pleasurable event. As social creatures, humans tend to frequent places of business, and feel more comfortable in those places, that have other customers in them. In fact, the lack of other customers can act as a tangible clue that the impending service experience may be less than satisfactory. For example, would you eat at an unfamiliar restaurant that had no cars in the parking lot, or would you choose to eat at the restaurant down the street with a full parking lot? In the absence of other information, at which restaurant would potential customers expect to receive the better dining experience?

The Influence of "Other Customers" on the Service Experience   Figure 9.4

Heterogeneity

One of the most frequently stressed differences between goods and services is the lack of ability to control service quality before it reaches the consumer. Service encounters occur in real time, and consumers are often physically present, so if something goes wrong during the service process, it is too late to institute quality-control measures before the service reaches the customer. Indeed, the customer (and other customers who share the service experience) may be part of the quality problem. If something goes wrong during a meal in a restaurant, the service experience for a customer is bound to be affected; the manager cannot logically ask the customer to leave the restaurant, reenter, and start the meal again.

Heterogeneity, almost by definition, makes it impossible for a service operation to achieve 100 percent perfect quality on an ongoing basis. Manufacturing operations may also have problems achieving this sort of target, but they can isolate mistakes and correct them over time because mistakes tend to reoccur at the same points in the process. In contrast, many errors in service operations are one-time events; the waiter who drops a plate of food in a customer's lap creates a service failure that can be neither foreseen nor corrected ahead of time.

Another challenge heterogeneity presents is that not only does the consistency of service vary from firm to firm and among personnel within a single firm, it also varies when interacting with the same service provider on a daily basis. For example, one Enterprise rental car franchise can have helpful and pleasant employees, while another franchise might employ individuals who conduct their daily interactions with customers like robots. Not only can this be true among different franchises, the same can be true within a single franchise on a day-to-day basis because of the mood swings of employees.

Perishability

Perishability also distinguishes goods from services. It refers to the fact that services cannot be inventoried in the traditional sense. Unlike goods that can be stored and sold at a later date, services that are not sold when they become available cease to exist. For example, hotel rooms that go unoccupied for the evening cannot be stored; airline seats that are not sold cannot be inventoried and added to another aircraft during the holiday season when airline seats are scarce; and service providers such as dentists, lawyers, and hairstylists cannot regain the time lost from an empty appointment book.

The inability to inventory creates profound difficulties for marketing services. In a manufacturing setting, the ability to create an inventory of goods means that their production and consumption can be separated by time and space. In other words, a good can be produced in one location and transported for sale in another, or a good can be produced in January and not released into the channels of distribution until June. Most services, however, are consumed at the point of production.

The existence of inventory also facilitates statistical quality control in goods-producing organizations. A representative sample of the inventory can be easily inspected for variations in quality. In contrast, when you spend the night at a hotel, you are likely to experience a wide range of factors that influence your good night's sleep. Finally, having inventory enables a business to separate the production and marketing departments. In service firms, however, marketing and operations constantly interact with each other and must be in synch to deliver services effectively.

Because of the effects of intangibility, inseparability, heterogeneity, and perishability, marketing plays a very different role in service-oriented organizations than it does in pure goods organizations. Clearly, the different components of the service organization are closely interwoven. The invisible and visible parts of the organization, the contact personnel and the environment in which the service is provided, the organization and its customers, and, indeed, the customers themselves are all bound together by a complex network of relationships. Consequently, the marketing department must maintain a much closer relationship with the rest of the service organization than is customary in many goods-producing businesses. The concept of operations being responsible for producing the product and marketing being responsible for selling the product cannot work in a service firm.

Heterogeneity
is a distinguishing characteristic of services that reflects the variation in consistency from one service transaction to the next.

http://www.enterprise.com

Perishability
is a distinguishing characteristic of services in that they cannot be saved, their unused capacity cannot be reserved, and they cannot be inventoried.

Understanding the Service Experience

All products, be they goods or services, deliver a bundle of benefits to the consumer.[8] The **benefit concept** is the encapsulation of these benefits in the consumer's mind. For a tangible-dominant product such as Tide laundry detergent, the benefit concept for some consumers might simply be clean clothes. However, for other consumers the benefit concept might also include attributes ascribed to the product that go beyond the mere powder or liquid, such as cleanliness, whiteness, and/or being a good parent.

In contrast to goods, services deliver a bundle of benefits through the experience that is created for the consumer. For example, most Tide customers will never see the inside of the manufacturing plant where Tide is produced; they will most likely never interact with the factory workers who produce the detergent or with the management staff who direct the workers; and they will also generally not use Tide in the presence of other customers. In comparison, Taco Bell's dine-in customers are physically present in the "factory" where the food is produced, and these customers *do* interact with the workers who prepare and serve the food as well as with the management staff who run the restaurant. Moreover, Taco Bell customers consume the service in the presence of other customers who may influence one another's service experience.

Figure 9.5 illustrates the key factors that create the service experience for the consumer. The service experience itself creates the benefit concept for the consumer. The most profound implication of the service experience is this: It demonstrates that consumers are an integral part of the service process. Their participation may be active or passive, but consumers are always involved in the service delivery process. Factors that influence the customer's service experience include dimensions that are visible and invisible to the customer:

- Servicescape (visible)
- Service providers (visible)
- Other customers (visible)
- Organizations and systems (invisible)

The Servicescape

The term **servicescape** refers to the use of physical evidence to design service environments (Table 9.2).[9] Due to the intangibility of services, customers often have trouble evaluating the quality of service objectively. As a result, consumers rely on the physical evidence that surrounds the service to help them form their evaluations (Figure 9.6).

Benefit concept
is the encapsulation of the benefits of a product in the customer's mind.

Servicescapes
refers to the use of physical evidence to design service environments.

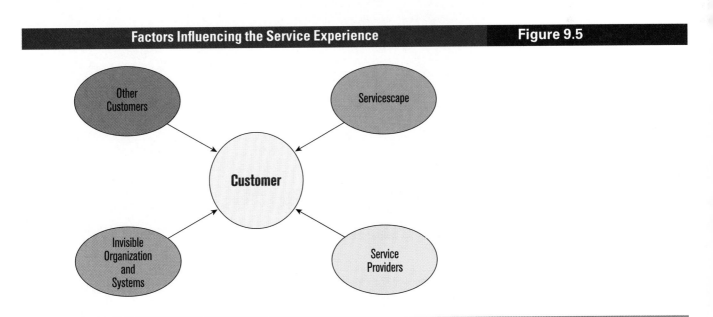

Factors Influencing the Service Experience   **Figure 9.5**

Table 9.2	Servicescape Dimensions		
	Ambient Conditions	**Space/Function**	**Signs, Symbols, and Artifacts**
	Temperature	Layout	Signage
	Air Quality	Equipment	Personal Artifacts
	Noise Level	Furnishings	Decor
	Music		Uniforms
	Odors		Award Plaques

Figure 9.6	Physical Evidence Is Often Used to Market Travel Destinations

For the time of your life, live it up in Singapore! Feast on local treats at a hawker center, then shop the world along Orchard Road. Play with friendly dolphins and dive off exotic islands. Marvel at a breathtaking collection of art, then check out our colorful nightlife. Come to Singapore and catch the buzz and excitement of Asia's most vibrant city. **For a free mini-CD video tour of Singapore call (800) 944-8778** or contact Singapore Tourism Board, 4929 Wilshire Boulevard, Suite 510, Los Angeles, CA 90010.

Hence, the servicescape consists of *ambient conditions* such as room temperature and music; *inanimate objects* that assist the firm in completing its tasks, such as furnishings and business equipment; and *other physical evidence* such as signs, symbols, and personal artifacts such as family pictures and personal collections.

The extensive use of physical evidence varies by the type of service firm. Service firms such as hospitals, resorts, and child-care centers often use physical evidence extensively as they design facilities and other tangibles associated with the service. In contrast, service firms such as insurance agencies and express mail drop-off locations use limited physical evidence. Regardless of the variation in usage, all service firms need to recognize the importance of managing their physical evidence because of its role in:

- packaging the service
- facilitating the service delivery process
- socializing customers and employees
- differentiating the firm from its competitors[10]

Packaging the Service. A firm's physical evidence plays a major role in packaging its service. The service itself is intangible and therefore does not require a package for purely functional reasons. However, the firm's physical evidence does send quality cues to consumers and adds value to the service when it helps customers develop positive images of the service. The firm's exterior and interior elements and other tangibles create the package that surrounds the service. The firm's physical environment forms the customer's initial impression of the type and quality of the service provided. For example, Mexican and Chinese restaurants often utilize specific architectural designs that communicate to customers about their firms' offerings. Physical evidence also conveys expectations to consumers. Consumers will have one set of expectations for a restaurant with dimly lit dining rooms, soft music, and linen tablecloths and napkins; they will form quite a different set of expectations for a restaurant that has picnic tables and peanut shells covering the floor.

Facilitating the Service Process. Another use of a firm's physical evidence is to facilitate the flow of activities that produce the service. Physical evidence can provide information to customers on how the service production process works. Examples include signage that specifically instructs customers; menus and brochures that explain the firm's offerings and facilitate the ordering process for consumers and providers; physical structures that direct the flow of consumers while waiting; and barriers, such as counters at a dry cleaners, that separate the technical core of the business from the customer contact areas where customers are actively involved in the production process.

Socializing Employees and Customers. **Organizational socialization** is the process by which an individual adapts to and comes to appreciate the values, norms, and required behavior patterns of an organization.[11] The firm's physical evidence plays an important part in this socialization process by conveying expected roles, behaviors, and relationships among employees and between employees and customers. Physical evidence, such as the use of uniforms, helps to socialize employees toward accepting organizational goals and affects consumer perceptions of the caliber of service provided. Studies have shown that the use of uniforms:

Organizational socialization is the process by which an individual adapts to and comes to appreciate the values, norms, and required behavior patterns of an organization.

- aids in identifying the firm's personnel
- presents a physical symbol that embodies the group's ideals and attributes
- implies a coherent group structure
- facilitates the perceived consistency of performance
- provides a tangible symbol of an employee's change in status (e.g., military uniforms change as personnel move through the ranks)
- assists in controlling the behavior of errant employees

One classic example of how tangible evidence affects the socialization process of employees involves women in the military. Pregnant military personnel were originally permitted to wear civilian clothing in lieu of their traditional military uniforms. However, the military soon noticed discipline and morale problems among these servicewomen as they began to lose their identification with their roles as soldiers. "Maternity uniforms are now standard issue in the Air Force, Army, and Navy, as well as at US Air, Hertz, Safeway, McDonald's, and the National Park Service."[12]

A Means of Differentiation. The effective management of the servicescape can also be a source of differentiation. For example, several airlines such as American Airlines, United Airlines, and British Airways are now expanding the amount of leg room available for passengers. British Airways differentiates itself further by featuring the first fully flat bed for passengers traveling business class (Figure 9.7).[13] In addition, the appearance of personnel and facilities often directly impact how consumers perceive the way that the firm will handle the service aspects of its business. Numerous studies have shown that well-dressed individuals are perceived as more intelligent, better workers, and more pleasant to engage in interactions.[14] Similarly, well-designed facilities are going to be perceived as better than their poorly designed counterparts.

Differentiation can also be achieved by utilizing physical evidence to reposition a service firm in the eyes of its customers. Upgrading the firm's facilities often upgrades the

Figure 9.7	The Servicescape Can Provide an Effective Means of Differentiation

image of the firm in the minds of consumers and may lead to attracting more desirable market segments, which further aids in differentiating the firm from its competitors. On the other hand, note that elaborate facility upgrades may alienate some customers who believe that the firm will pass on the costs of the upgrade to consumers through higher prices. This is precisely why many offices are decorated professionally, but not lavishly.

Service Providers

The second component of the service experience involves the personnel who provide the service. Simply stated, the public face of a service firm is its service providers.[15] Unlike the consumption of goods, the consumption of services often takes place where the service is produced (e.g., hair salon, dentist office, restaurant). Even when the service is provided at the consumer's residence or workplace (e.g., lawn care, housekeeping, professional massage), interactions between consumers and service providers are commonplace. As a result, service providers have a dramatic impact on the service experience. For example, when asked what irritated them most about service providers, customers have noted seven categories of complaints:

- *Apathy:* What comedian George Carlin refers to as DILLIGAD—Do I look like I give a damn?
- *Brush-off:* Attempts to get rid of the customer by dismissing the customer completely . . . the "I want you to go away" syndrome
- *Coldness:* Indifferent service providers who could not care less what the customer really wants
- *Condescension:* The "you are the client/patient, so you must be stupid" approach
- *Robotism:* When the customers are treated simply as inputs into a system that must be processed
- *Rulebook:* Providers who live by the rules of the organization even when those rules do not make good sense
- *Runaround:* Passing the customer off to another provider, who will simply pass them off to yet another provider[16]

Service personnel perform the dual functions of interacting with customers and reporting back to the internal organization. Strategically, service personnel are an important source of product differentiation. It is often challenging for a service organization to differentiate itself from other similar organizations in terms of the benefit bundle it offers or its delivery system. For example, many airlines offer similar bundles of benefits and fly the same types of aircraft from the same airports to the same destinations. Therefore, their only hope of a competitive advantage is from the service level—the way things are done. Hence, the factor that often distinguishes one airline from another is the poise and attitude of its service providers. Singapore Airlines, for example, enjoys an excellent reputation due in large part to the beauty and grace of its flight attendants. Other firms that hold a differential advantage over competitors based on personnel include the Ritz Carlton, IBM, and Disney Enterprises.[17]

http://www.singaporeair.com

http://www.ritzcarlton.com

http://www.ibm.com

Other Customers

Ultimately, the success of many service encounters depends on how effectively the service firm manages its clientele. A wide range of service establishments such as restaurants, hotels, airlines, and physicians' offices serve multiple customers simultaneously. Hence, other customers can have a profound impact on an individual's service experience. Research has shown that the presence of other customers can enhance or detract from an individual's service experience.[18] The influence of other customers can be *active* or *passive*. For instance, examples of other customers actively detracting from one's service experience include unruly customers in a restaurant or a night club, children crying during a church service, or theatergoers carrying on a conversation during a play. Some passive examples include customers who show up late for appointments, thereby delaying each subsequent appointment; an exceptionally tall individual who sits directly in front of another customer at a movie theater; or the impact of being part of a crowd, which increases the waiting time for everyone in the group.

Though many customer actions that enhance or detract from the service experience are difficult to predict, service organizations can attempt to manage the behavior of customers so that they coexist peacefully. For example, firms can manage waiting times so that customers who arrive earlier than others get first priority, clearly target specific age segments to minimize potential conflicts between younger and older customers, and provide separate dining facilities for smokers and customers with children.

Organization and Systems

The invisible component of the service experience, the organization and its systems, can also profoundly affect the consumer's service experience. For example, throughout the last two decades, the distribution center of L.L. Bean has been a required stop for companies engaging in benchmarking exercises.[19] Many companies, including Nike, Disney, Gillette, and DaimlerChrysler, have come to see how L.L. Bean fills orders so effectively. In fact, the center they visited is no more; it has been replaced by a completely new approach—one driven by an ever-expanding volume of orders, an increasingly global market, and a growing variety of customized products. L.L. Bean's old system built orders from the telephone operations, issuing them every 12 hours to pickers. The pickers assembled the orders from around the center and then delivered them to packers, who prepared the orders for shipment.

The new system, referred to as Wave Pick Technology, operates differently. Orders come directly from the telephone operators and are immediately allocated to pickers based on available capacity. Moreover, the orders are broken down by item and assigned to different pickers, who are themselves assigned to different parts of the warehouse. Order items are placed on a conveyor belt and bar-coded. Scanners then automatically assemble the orders for packing. As a result, 100 percent of orders can be serviced within 24 hours; from order to delivery to the on-site Federal Express depot only takes 2 hours.

A firm's organization and systems also involve a human component. The behind-the-scenes activities of hiring, training, and rewarding employees are directly related to how well customers are served. The United Parcel Service (UPS) believes in building trust and teamwork and making employees loyal to the company's mission.[20] UPS spends over $300 million a year on training, it pays full-time drivers more than $50,000 a year on average, and it surveys its employees for suggestions. The company is virtually 100 percent employee-owned.

Creating Compelling Experiences

Service firms that are able to effectively mold the customer's experience via the effective management of the servicescape, service providers, other customers, and the invisible organization and system have the means to develop *compelling experiences*.[21] The development of compelling experiences is the latest competitive weapon in the war against service commodification. For example, when priced as a *commodity*, coffee is worth little more than $1 per pound. When processed, packaged, and sold in the grocery store as a *good*, the price of coffee jumps to between 5 and 25 cents a cup. When that same cup is sold in a local restaurant, the coffee takes on more *service* aspects and sells for 50 cents to $1 per cup. However, in the ultimate act of added value, when that same cup of coffee is sold within the compelling experience of a five-star restaurant or the unique environment of a Starbucks, the customer gladly pays $2 to $5 per cup. In this instance, the whole process of ordering, creating, and consuming becomes a pleasurable, even theatrical, experience. Economic value, like the coffee bean, progresses from commodities to goods to services to experiences. In this example, coffee was transformed from a raw commodity valued at approximately $1 per pound to $2 to $5 per cup—a markup of as much as 5,000 percent.

Creating compelling experiences for customers is not a new idea. The entertainment industry and venues such as those operated by Disney have been doing it for years. Other types of businesses have picked up on the idea and introduced "experience" concepts, including the Hard Rock Cafe, Build-a-Bear Workshops, and a variety of theme hotels located in Las Vegas such as New York–New York, the Venetian, and Caesars Palace. The question facing many other service providers is how to transform their own operations into memorable experiences for the customer. One unique example involves a computer repair firm based in Minneapolis, Minnesota. This company's team of crack technicians, formally called the "Geek Squad," intentionally dress in white shirts and sport thin black ties, pocket protectors, and badges. This firm has successfully transformed a mundane service into a memorable event that's fun for the customer.

http://www.llbean.com

http://www.chrysler.com

http://www.hardrock.com

http://www.buildabear.com

http://www.caesarspalace.com

THE QUEST FOR CUSTOMER SATISFACTION

LEARNING OBJECTIVE 2

To market services effectively, marketing managers need to understand customers' thought processes as they assess their satisfaction with services provided (see Figure 9.8). Customer satisfaction is one of the most studied areas in marketing.[22] Over the past 20 years, more than 15,000 academic and trade articles have been published on the topic. Tracking customer satisfaction in the United States is a highly complex task that is currently undertaken through the joint efforts of the American Society for Quality and the University of Michigan's business school. The two groups have developed the American Customer Satisfaction Index (ACSI), which is based on 3,900 products representing more than two dozen manufacturing and service industries. Companies included in the study are selected based on size and U.S. market share, and together represent about 40 percent of the U.S. gross domestic product (GDP). Government services are also included in the index.

http://www.asq.org

    An overview of the best and worst companies included in the ACSI and their satisfaction ratings is presented in Table 9.3. DaimlerChrysler earned top honors, while the Internal Revenue Service (IRS) brought up the bottom (although its performance is improving). Unicom and McDonald's are the IRS's closest competitors, with several U.S. airlines not far behind. Perhaps the most disturbing finding of the ACSI results is that the 10 companies at the top of the list produce goods, while the 10 at the bottom, firms such as the Wells Fargo & Company, Kentucky Fried Chicken, Taco Bell, and the police, are service organizations.

    From a historical perspective, a great deal of the work in the customer satisfaction area began in the 1970s, when consumerism was on the rise. The rise of the consumer movement was directly related to the decline in service felt by many consumers. The decline in customer service and resulting customer dissatisfaction can be attributed to a number of sources. First, skyrocketing inflation during this period forced many firms to slash service in an effort to keep prices down. In some industries, deregulation led to fierce competition among firms that had never had to compete before. Price competition quickly became the main means of differentiation, and price wars quickly broke out. Here again, firms slashed costs associated with customer service to cut operating expenses.

    As time went on, labor shortages also contributed to the decline in customer service. Motivated service workers were difficult to find, and who could blame them? The typical service job meant low pay, no career path, no sense of pride, and no training in customer relations. Automation also contributed to the problem. Replacing human labor with machines indeed increased the efficiency of many operating systems, but often at the expense of distancing consumers from the firm and leaving customers to fend for themselves. Finally, over the years, customers have become tougher to please. They are more informed than ever, their expectations have increased, and they are more particular about where they spend their discretionary dollars.

Is It Always Worthwhile to Keep a Customer?

Figure 9.8

Although saving every customer at any cost is a controversial topic and opinions are divided, some experts believe that the customer is no longer worth saving under the following conditions:

- The account is no longer profitable.
- Conditions specified in the sales contract are no longer being met.
- Customers are abusive to the point that it lowers employee morale.
- Customer demands are beyond reasonable, and fulfilling those demands would result in poor service for the remaining customer base.
- The customer's reputation is so poor that associating with the customer tarnishes the image and reputation of the selling firm.

Table 9.3	Customer Satisfaction Ratings

The American Customer Satisfaction Index (ACSI), which measures customer satisfaction across a variety of sectors, demonstrates the added complexity of managing a service firm. All of the Top Companies are traditional goods manufacturers. In contrast, those scoring lowest on the ACSI are service firms. Scores are out of a possible 100.

Top Companies		Bottom Companies	
Company	**Score**	**Company**	**Score**
DaimlerChrysler	87	Wells Fargo & Company	65
Maytag	87	KFC	64
Colgate-Palmolive	86	Police service (metro)	64
GM-Buick	86	Taco Bell	64
GM-Cadillac	86	US West Inc.	64
Hershey Foods Corporation	86	American Airlines	63
Whirlpool Corporation	86	Continental Airlines	62
Cadbury Schweppes	86	Northwest Airlines	62
Ford-Lincoln-Mercury	85	United Airlines	62
H.J. Heinz Company	85	USAirways Group, Inc.	62
Kenmore	85	McDonald's	61
		Unicom	59
		Internal Revenue Service	51

Source: http://www.theacsi.org, accessed 10 March 2001.

What Is Customer Satisfaction?

Customer satisfaction
is a short-term, transaction-specific measure of whether customer perceptions meet or exceed customer expectations.

Ultimately firms achieve **customer satisfaction** through the effective management of customer *perceptions* and *expectations*. If the perceived service is better than or equal to the expected service, then customers are satisfied. Because of this, firms can increase customer satisfaction by either lowering expectations or by enhancing perceptions. Note that this entire process of comparing expectations to perceptions takes place in the minds of customers. Hence, it is the *perceived* service that matters, not the *actual* service. One of the best examples to illustrate this concept involves a high-rise hotel. The hotel was receiving numerous complaints concerning the time guests had to wait for elevator service in the lobby. Realizing that from an operational viewpoint, the speed of the elevators could not be increased, and that attempting to schedule the guest's elevator usage was futile, the hotel's management installed mirrors in the lobby next to the elevator bays. Guest complaints were reduced immediately—the mirrors provided a means for guests to occupy their waiting time. Guests were observed using the mirrors to observe their own appearance and that of others around them. In reality, the speed of the elevators had not changed; however, the customer's perception of time had changed.

Companies can also manage expectations in order to produce customer satisfaction, without in any way altering the quality of the actual service delivered. For example, Motel 6 downplayed its service in a clever advertising campaign to increase consumer satisfaction by lowering customer expectations prior to purchase. The firm's advertising informs consumers of both what to expect and what not to expect: "A good clean room for $39.99 . . . a little more in some places . . . a little less in some others . . . and remember . . . we'll leave the light on for you." Many customers simply do not use services such as swimming pools, health clubs, and full-service restaurants that are associated with higher-priced hotels. Economy-minded hotels, such as Motel 6, are carving out a niche in the market by providing the basics. The result is that customers know exactly what they will get ahead of time and are happy not only with the quality of the service received but also with the cost savings.

The Importance of Customer Satisfaction

The importance of customer satisfaction cannot be overstated. Without customers, the service firm has no reason to exist. Every service business needs to proactively define and measure customer satisfaction. Waiting for customers to complain in order to identify problems in the service delivery system, or gauging the firm's progress in achieving customer satisfaction based on the number of complaints received, is naive. Consider the following findings gathered by the Technical Assistance Research Program (TARP):[23]

- The average business does not hear from 96 percent of its unhappy customers.
- For every complaint received, 26 other customers actually have the same problem.
- The average person with a problem tells 9 or 10 people. Thirteen percent of dissatisfied customers tell more than 20 people.
- Customers who have their complaints satisfactorily resolved tell an average of five people about the treatment they received.
- Complainers are more likely to do business with you again than noncomplainers: 54 to 70 percent if their problem was resolved at all, and 95 percent if it was handled quickly.

The TARP figures demonstrate that customers do not actively complain to the source of the failure. Instead, consumers voice their dissatisfaction with their feet, by defecting to competitors, and with their mouths, by telling existing and potential customers exactly how they were mistreated by the offending firm. The impact of dissatisfied customers on future business operations is astounding. Based on the figures, a firm that serves 100 customers per week, and boasts a 90 percent customer satisfaction rating, will be the object of thousands of negative stories by the end of the year. For example, if 10 dissatisfied customers per week tell 10 friends about the poor service they received, by the end of the year (52 weeks), 5,200 negative word-of-mouth communications have been generated.

The TARP figures are not all bad news, however. Firms that effectively respond to customer complaints are the objects of positive word-of-mouth communications. Although positive news travels at half the rate of negative news, the positive stories can ultimately translate into customer loyalty and new customers. Businesses should also learn from the TARP figures that complainers are a firm's friends. Complainers are a free source of market information, and the complaints themselves should be viewed as opportunities for the firm to improve its delivery systems, not as a source of irritation. As evidence, the International Customer Service Association found that of customers who had experienced a problem and complained, 54 percent continued to do business with the firm on a long-term basis. In comparison, only 9 percent of customers who experienced problems and did not complain continued to do business with the offending firm.[24] Remember, too, that less than 5 percent of consumers with problems actually complain to companies.

The Benefits of Customer Satisfaction

Although some may argue that customers are unreasonable at times, little evidence can be found of extravagant consumer expectations.[25] Consequently, satisfying consumers is not an impossible task. In fact, meeting and exceeding customer expectations creates several valuable benefits for service firms. Positive word-of-mouth from existing customers often translates into new customers. In addition, satisfied customers purchase products more frequently and are less likely to be lost to competitors than are dissatisfied customers.

Companies who command high customer satisfaction ratings also seem to be able to insulate themselves from competitive pressures—particularly price competition. Customers are often willing to pay more and stay with a firm that meets their needs than to risk moving to a lower-priced service. Finally, firms that pride themselves on their customer satisfaction efforts generally provide better environments in which to work, and therefore have increased their chances to attract and retain the best and brightest employees. These positive work environments produce organizational cultures that challenge

http://www.microsoft.com

employees to perform and reward them for their efforts. Some companies even use their positive work environments to encourage employee applications. Microsoft, for example, is known for providing a remarkably challenging atmosphere for the "brainy." "Everybody gets stock options, and most professionals hired before 1992 have thus become millionaires; six became billionaires."[26]

In and of themselves, customer satisfaction surveys also provide several worthwhile benefits. Such surveys provide a formal means of customer feedback to the firm, which may identify existing and potential problems. Satisfaction surveys also convey the message to customers that the firm cares about their well-being and values customer input concerning its service delivery process.

Other benefits are directly derived from the results of the satisfaction surveys. Satisfaction results are often incorporated into employee performance evaluations for merit and compensation reviews. As we discuss in Chapter 13, sales managers use such results to develop sales training programs. Survey results are also useful for comparison purposes to determine how a firm stacks up against its competition. When ratings are favorable, many firms utilize the results in their corporate advertising (Figure 9.9).

Figure 9.9	Awards Enhance a Firm's Advertising Effects

Customer Satisfaction as It Relates to Customer Relationship Management

One of the most recent business practices affecting customer satisfaction levels (both positively and negatively) is customer relationship management.[27] **Customer relationship management (CRM)** is the process of identifying, attracting, differentiating, and retaining customers. CRM allows a firm to focus its efforts disproportionately on its most lucrative clients. CRM is based on the adage that 80 percent of a company's profits come from 20 percent of its customers; therefore, the 20 percent should receive better service than the 80 percent. For example, when a plastics manufacturer focused on its most profitable customers, it cut the company's customer base from 800 to 90 and increased revenue by 400 percent.

The increased use of CRM practices, where high-value customers are treated superior to low-value customers, can be attributed to several trends. First, some believe that customers have created the situation themselves by opting for price, choice, and convenience over high-quality service. However, trade-offs arise with this focus on price and other factors over service concerns. For example, although priceline.com offers discounted tickets at significant savings, the customer trade-offs include forfeiting the right to any refund, flying on whatever brand airline is available, and being forced on connecting flights in many instances. In addition, according to one state investigation, an additional trade-off is that priceline.com is inappropriately prepared to handle customer complaints.

Another reason CRM is currently fashionable is that labor costs have risen, while competitive pressures have kept prices low. The end result is that gross margins have been reduced to 5 to 10 percent in many industries. With these kinds of margins, companies simply cannot afford to treat all of their customers equally. Consider the plight of Fidelity Investments. Ten years ago, the company received 97,000 calls a day. Half of those calls were handled by an automated telephone system. Today, Fidelity receives 700,000 calls as well as 550,000 Web site visits a day. Three-quarters of the phone calls are now handled by automated systems, which cost the company less than $1 per call. Live customer service personnel handle the remaining calls at $13 per call. This is just one of the reasons the company contacted 25,000 of its customers to request that they use its Web site or automated phone system.

Finally, firms are expanding CRM efforts because markets are increasingly fragmented and promotional costs are on the rise. Six Continents, the owner of Holiday Inn and Inter-Continental Hotels, recently learned a valuable lesson about not treating customers equally. The company now sends its promotional mailings only to those who have "bit" on earlier mailings. The end result is that company has reduced mailing costs by 50 percent, while response rates have increased by 20 percent.

CRM Outcomes

Typical outcomes of CRM practices include **coding**, **routing**, **targeting**, and **sharing**. Each practice is typically associated with both positive and negative consequences for customers.

Coding. Firms grade customers based on how profitable the customer's business is. Service staff are instructed to handle customers differently based on their category code. Compare the following examples.

- A New York customer travels to New Jersey to buy a table from an Ikea store. After returning home, he discovers that the table is missing necessary brackets and screws. The store refuses to mail him the missing parts and insists that he must return to the store. The customer does not own a car.
- A Platinum customer of Starwood Hotels & Resorts Worldwide wants to propose to his girlfriend in India. Starwood arranges entry into the Taj Mahal after hours so that he can propose in private. Starwood also provides a horse-driven carriage, flowers, a special meal, an upgraded suite, and a reception led by the hotel's general manager.
- Sears Roebuck and Company's most profitable credit card customers get to choose a preferred 2-hour time window for repair appointments. Regular customers are given a 4-hour time window.

Customer relationship management
is the process of identifying, attracting, differentiating, and retaining customers.

http://www400.fidelity.com

http://www.sixcontinents.com

Coding
is categorizing customers based on how profitable their past business has been.

Routing
is the process of directing incoming calls to customer service representatives in which more profitable customers are more likely to receive faster and better customer service.

Targeting
involves offering the firm's most profitable customers special deals and incentives.

Sharing
involves making key customer information accessible to all parts of the organization and in some cases selling that information to other firms.

http://www.ikea.com

http://www.sears.com

Routing. Call centers route incoming calls based on the customer's code. Customers in profitable code categories get to speak to live customer service representatives. Less profitable customers are inventoried in automated telephone queues. For example:

- Call this particular electric utility company and depending on your status, you may have to stay on the line for quite awhile. The top 350 business clients are served by six people. The next tier, consisting of the next 700 most profitable customers, are handled by six more people. The next 30,000 customers are served by two customer service representatives. The final group, consisting of 300,000 customers, are routed to an automated telephone system (Figure 9.10).

- Charles Schwab and Company's top-rated Signature clients, consisting of customers who maintain $100,000 in assets or trade at least 12 times a year, never wait more than 15 seconds to have their calls personally answered by a customer service representative. Regular customers can wait up to 10 minutes or more.

Figure 9.10   **CRM Routing Often Leaves Customers Far Less Than Satisfied**

Targeting. Profitable customers have fees waived and are targeted for special promotions. Less profitable customers may never hear of the special deals. Consider these examples:

- Centura Bank, Inc. of Raleigh, North Carolina, ranks its 2 million customers on a profitability scale from 1 to 5. The most profitable customers are called several times a year for what the bank terms "friendly chats," and the CEO calls these same customers once a year with season's holiday greetings. Since the "friendly chats" program was implemented, the retention rate of the most profitable group has increased by 50 percent. In comparison, the most unprofitable group has decreased from 27 percent to 21 percent.
- First Bank of Baltimore, Maryland, provides its most profitable customers with a Web option that its regular customers never see. The option allows preferred customers to click a special icon that connects them with live service agents for phone conversations.
- First Union codes its credit card customers with colored squares that flash on customer service representatives' computer screens. A green square indicates that the customer is profitable and should be granted fee waivers and given the "white glove" treatment.

Sharing. Customer information is shared with other parts of the organization, and information is sold to other companies. Although the customer may be new to the organization, his or her purchase history and buying potential are well-known to insiders. For example:

- A United Airlines passenger was shocked when a ticketing agent told him: "Wow, somebody doesn't like you." Apparently the passenger was involved in an argument with another United employee several months earlier. The argument became part of the passenger's permanent record that follows him wherever he flies with United. The passenger, who is a Premier Executive account holder, feels that the airline has been less than accommodating following the incident.
- Continental Airlines has introduced a Customer Information System where every one of Continental's 43,000 gate, reservation, and service employees has access to the history and value of each customer. The system also suggests specific service recovery remedies and perks such as coupons for delays and automatic upgrades. The system is designed to provide more consistent staff behavior and service delivery.

Limitations of CRM Practices

Technology greatly enhances CRM processes by identifying current and potential customers, differentiating among high-value and low-value customers, and customizing offers to meet the needs of individual high-value customers. However, there are limitations. First, customers do not like hearing that some customers are valued more than others, especially where they are not the ones receiving the white glove treatment. Many companies are well aware of potential customer ill will and are fairly tight-lipped about the outcomes of their respective CRM practices. In a *Business Week* lead story pertaining to CRM issues, companies such as GE Capital, Sprint Corporation, and World-Com, Inc., declined repeated requests to speak about their service discrimination practices.[28] Meanwhile, in service operations where service discrimination is common such as airlines, banks, retail stores, hotels, and telecommunication companies, customer satisfaction is taking a nosedive and customer complaints are on the rise (see Figure 9.11).

Another concern relating to CRM practices involves privacy issues. How much should a company really know about its customers? When discussing its new Customer Information System, the vice president of Continental Airlines boasted, "We even know if they [the customers] put their eyeshades on and go to sleep."[29] Ironically, in this day and age of high-tech CRM systems, experts are now suggesting that if customers want better service, they should protect their privacy. In doing so, it is recommended that customers avoid filling out surveys and be protective about credit card and Social Security information. The less companies know about customers, the less they will be able to categorize them, and the less likely customers will be treated as low-value.

Figure 9.11	Satisfaction Takes a Nosedive

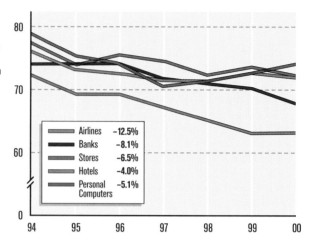

Satisfaction Takes a Nosedive . . .

Based on annual poll of more than 50,000 customers, measuring overall satisfaction with goods and services. Scale 1–100

Data: University of Michigan Business School's American Customer Satisfaction Index

Airlines	−12.5%
Banks	−8.1%
Stores	−6.5%
Hotels	−4.0%
Personal Computers	−5.1%

Source: Diane Brady, "Why Service Stinks," *Business Week,* 23 October 2000, 120–121.

CRM is also limited by its focus on past purchase patterns. In reality, what customers spend today is not necessarily a good predictor of what their behavior will be tomorrow. How many potential profitable customers are being eliminated today because their current purchasing behavior has them slotted and treated as "commoners"? Spurned by such treatment, how many of these customers defect to another provider that appreciates their potential and treats them appropriately? Life situations and spending habits do change over time.

Service discrimination also leads to some interesting ethical questions. Should only the wealthy be recipients of quality service? Is this a form of **red-lining**—the practice of identifying and avoiding unprofitable types of neighborhoods or people?

Red-lining
is the practice of identifying and avoiding unprofitable types of neighborhoods or people.

LEARNING OBJECTIVE 3

Service quality
is an attitude formed by a long-term, overall evaluation of performance.

SERVICE QUALITY

Service quality researchers agree on one issue: **Service quality** is an elusive and abstract concept that is difficult to define and measure.[30] The productivity of education and government services is notoriously difficult to measure. Increases in quality, such as improving the quality of education and training governmental employees to be more pleasant throughout their daily interactions with the public, do not show up in productivity measures. In contrast, providing poor quality can ironically increase the country's gross national product (GNP).[31] If a mail-order company sends a customer the wrong product, the dollars spent on phone calls and return mailings to correct the mistake will actually add to the country's GNP. However, it is readily apparent that increases in quality can have a dramatic impact on a firm's or industry's survival. As evidence, Japan did not simply bulldoze its way into U.S. markets by offering lower prices alone—superior quality relative to the competition at that time ultimately won customers over.

What Is Service Quality?

Perhaps the best way to begin a discussion of service quality is to first attempt to distinguish service quality from customer satisfaction. Most experts agree that customer satisfaction is a short-term, transaction-specific measure, whereas service quality is an attitude formed by a long-term, comprehensive evaluation of performance. Service quality offers a way for competing services to achieve success. In particular, where a small number of firms, such as banks, offer nearly identical services competing within a small area, establishing service quality may be the only way for a firm to differentiate itself. Service quality differentiation can generate increased market share and ultimately mean the difference between financial success and failure.

Goods manufacturers have already learned this lesson and over the past decade have made producing quality goods a priority issue. Improving the quality of manufactured goods has become a major strategy for both establishing efficient, smoothly running operations and increasing consumer market share in an atmosphere of increasing customer demand for higher quality. Goods quality improvement measures have focused largely on the quality of the products themselves, and specifically on eliminating product failure. Initially, these measures were based on rigorous checking of all finished products before they came into contact with the customer. More recently, quality control has focused on the principle of ensuring quality during the manufacturing process, on "getting it right the first time," and on reducing end-of-production line failures to zero. The final evolution in goods manufacturing has been to define quality as delivering the right product to the right customer at the right time, thus extending quality beyond the good itself and using external as well as internal measures to assess overall quality.

Service quality cannot be understood in quite the same way. The service experience depends on the customer as a participant in the production process, so normal quality-control measures that depend on eliminating defects before the consumer sees the product are not applicable. Service quality is not a specific goal or program that can be achieved or completed before the final product reaches the customer. Consequently, while manufacturers of goods aim for *zero defects*, the primary goal of service firms is *zero defections*. This often entails handling problems in real time as they unfold throughout the service delivery process.

The Gap Model

Service quality can be examined in terms of gaps that exist between expectations and perceptions on the part of management, employees, and customers (see Figure 9.12).[32] The most important gap—the **service gap**—is between customers' expectations of service and their perception of the service actually delivered. Ultimately, the goal of a service firm is to close the service gap or at least narrow it as much as possible. Before the firm can close the service gap, it must close or attempt to narrow four other gaps:

> The *knowledge gap*—the difference between what consumers expect of a service and what management perceives the consumers expect.

> The *standards gap*—the difference between what management perceives consumers expect and the standards set for service delivery.

> The *delivery gap*—the difference between the standards set for service delivery and the actual quality of service delivery. For example, do employees perform the service as they were trained?

> The *communications gap*—the difference between the actual quality of service delivered and the quality of service described in the firm's external communications such as brochures and mass media advertising.

Hence, the service gap is a function of the knowledge gap, the standards gap, the delivery gap, and the communications gap. As each of these gaps increases or decreases, the service gap responds in a similar manner.

The Knowledge Gap
The most immediate and obvious gap is usually between what customers want and what managers think customers want. Briefly, many managers think they know what their customers want but are, in fact, mistaken. Banking customers may prefer security to a good interest rate. Some restaurant customers prefer quality and taste of food over an attractive arrangement of the tables or a good view from the window. A hotel may feel that its customers prefer comfortable rooms, though the majority of them spend little time in their rooms and are more interested in on-site amenities.

When a knowledge gap occurs, a variety of other mistakes tend to follow. The wrong facilities may be provided, the wrong staff may be hired, and the wrong training may be undertaken. Services may be provided that customers have no use for, while the services they do desire are not offered. Closing this gap requires minutely detailed knowledge of what customers desire and then building responses to customer needs into the service operating system.

The service gap
is the gap between customers' expectations of service and their perception of the service actually delivered, which is a function of the knowledge gap, the standards gap, the delivery gap, and the communications gap.

Figure 9.12	Service Quality Gap Model

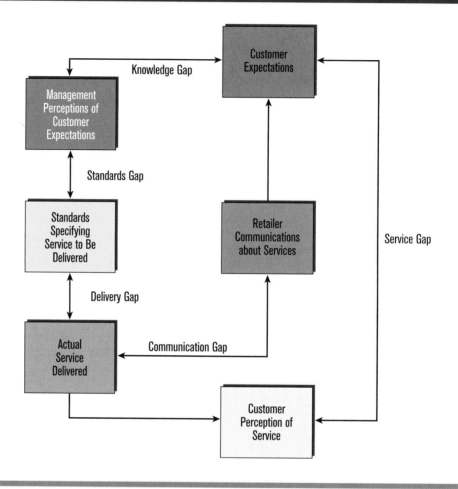

Source: Adapted from A. Parasuraman, Valerie Zeithaml, and Leonard Berry, "A Conceptual Model of Service Quality and Its Implications for Future Research," *Journal of Marketing* 49 (Fall 1985): 41–50.

The Standards Gap

Even if customer expectations have been accurately determined, a standards gap may open between management's perception of customer expectations and the actual standards set for service delivery, such as order processing speed, the way cloth napkins are folded, or the way customers are greeted. Simply stated, standards comprise the blueprint of the service operation—they dictate how the service delivery process is to be implemented. When developing standards, the firm should develop a flowchart of its operations to identify all points of contact with its customers. Detailed standards can then be written for (1) the way the system should operate, and (2) the behavior of contact personnel at each point in the system. For example, front-desk personnel of Marriott hotels may be trained to perform to specification in such areas as acknowledging the customer on arrival, establishing eye contact, smiling, completing the proper paperwork, reviewing available amenities with the customer, and providing the customer with keys to the room.

In some cases a standards gap exists because management does not believe it can or should meet customer requirements for service. For example, overnight delivery of mail used to be thought of as an absurd possibility before CEO Fred Smith and FedEx proved that, in fact, it could be done (Figure 9.13). Sometimes management has no commitment to the delivery of service quality. Corporate leadership may set other priorities that interfere with standards that lead to good service. For example, a company's empha-

Closing the Standards Gap   **Figure 9.13**

sis on cost-reduction strategies that maximize short-term profits is often cited as a misguided priority that impedes the firm's progress in delivering quality services. Personal computer companies whose automated service hotlines reduce the number of customer service employees are typical examples. In some instances, customers have been forced to remain on hold for hours before they could actually speak to a real person. *Hotlines* were originally named to reflect the speed with which customers could talk with manufacturers. Now the name more appropriately reflects the customer's temper by the time he or she talks to someone who can actually help.

The Delivery Gap

The delivery gap is the difference between how a service is actually delivered compared to the standards set by management. The existence of a delivery gap depends on both the willingness and the ability of employees to provide the service according to specification. For example, do employees wear their name tags, do they establish eye contact, and do they thank the customer when the transaction is completed? One factor that influences the size of the delivery gap is the employees' willingness to perform the service. Obviously, willingness to provide a service can vary greatly from employee to employee and for the same employee over time. Many employees who start off working to their full potential become less willing to do so over time because of frustration and dissatisfaction with the organization. Furthermore, a considerable range exists between what employees are actually capable of accomplishing and the minimum the employees must do in order to keep their jobs. Most service managers find it difficult to keep employees working at their full potential all the time.

Other employees, no matter how willing, may simply not be able to perform the service to specification. Individuals may have been hired for jobs they are not qualified to handle or to which they are temperamentally unsuited. Some employees do not receive sufficient training for the roles expected of them. Generally, employees who are not capable of performing assigned roles are less willing to keep trying.

Finally, a delivery gap may expand due to inadequate support, such as when employees do not receive the technological and other resources necessary for them to perform their jobs in the best possible manner. Even the best employees can be discouraged if they are forced to work with out-of-date or faulty equipment, especially if the employees of competing firms have superior resources and are able to provide the same or superior levels of service with far less effort. Failure to properly support employees leads to wasted effort, poor employee productivity, unsatisfied customers, and an increase in the size of the delivery gap.

The Communications Gap

The communications gap is the difference between the service the firm promises it will deliver through its external communications (e.g., brochures, advertising, etc.) and the service it actually delivers to its customers. If the firm's advertising or sales promotions promise one level of service and the consumer receives a different level of service, the communications gap widens. External communications are essentially promises the firm makes to its customers. When the communications gap is wide, the firm has broken its promises, resulting in a lack of future customer trust. A customer who orders a bottle of wine from a menu only to be told it is out of stock may feel that the offer held out on the menu has not been fulfilled. Similarly, customers who are promised delivery in 3 days but then wait a week to receive their order will lower their perceptions of service quality.

http://www.e-satisfy.com

Unfortunately, the communications gap appears to be burgeoning among firms conducting business online. Findings from a study conducted by the International Customer Service Association and TARP indicate that only 36 percent of the 50,000 e-shoppers surveyed report satisfaction with electronic commerce service. Customers report that they typically expect a reply to their e-mail requests within one hour; however, only 12 percent receive such a response, and only 42 percent of respondents were replied to within 24 hours. In many instances, simply getting companies to respond to their e-mails is a real problem. A Rainer-Web index study of the Fortune 100 and the Financial Times Security Exchange (FTSE) 100 found that more than two in five U.S. and U.K. companies failed to reply promptly to e-mail requests. In fact, 29 FTSE companies and 21 Fortune 100 could not be contacted from their Web sites, including Marks & Spencer, Thames Water, GTE, and Intel. Of the companies contacted by e-mail, 15 FTSE and 20 Fortune 100 never replied. Such results led the chairman of Rainer to comment, "all too often, companies focus on the content and look and feel of the [Web] site without considering its integration with existing customer contact systems. The result is [that these types of sites end up being] little more than corporate wallpaper."[33]

LEARNING OBJECTIVE 4

CUSTOMER RETENTION

The value of retaining existing customers is critical in these days of saturated markets and rising marketing costs. In fact, some experts believe that customer retention has a more powerful effect on profits than market share, economies of scale, and other variables commonly associated with competitive advantage. Studies have indicated that as much as 95 percent of profits come from long-term customers via profits derived from sales, referrals, and reduced operating costs.[34]

Simply stated, **customer retention** refers to focusing a firm's marketing efforts toward the existing customer base. Customer retention is the opposite of **conquest marketing**, which focuses on discounts and markdowns and developing promotional campaigns that will attract new customers from competing firms. Conquest marketing is consistent with a number of other marketing strategies that are designed to replace "disloyal" customers—termed the **leaky bucket theory** (see Figure 9.14). In contrast to conquest marketing, firms engaged in customer retention efforts work to satisfy existing customers with the intent of developing long-term relationships between the firm and its current clientele. However, it should be noted that expecting 100 percent loyalty from customers is unrealistic. Previous studies have shown that only about 10 percent of buyers are truly loyal to a particular brand over a 1-year period. In addition, buyers who are 100 percent loyal tend to be light purchasers. In reality, customer loyalty tends to be divided among a number of brands. **Polygamous loyalty** is apparent in a number of markets including car rentals, restaurants, and airlines. For example, 80 percent of European business travelers are members of more than one frequent flyer program.[35]

Customer Retention Tactics

Two-thirds of customers who defect to competitors do so because they feel that companies are not genuinely concerned about their well-being. Because of the lack of consistent customer service that customers often experience, firms that effectively communicate

Customer retention
refers to focusing a firm's marketing efforts toward the existing customer base.

Conquest marketing
is a strategy for constantly seeking new customers by offering discounts and markdowns and developing promotions that encourage new business.

Leaky bucket theory
is traditionally associated with conquest marketing where new customers replace disloyal customers at the same rate; hence, the firm never grows.

Polygamous loyalty
reflects the notion that customer loyalty tends to be divided among a number of providing firms.

| The Leaky Bucket Theory | Figure 9.14 |

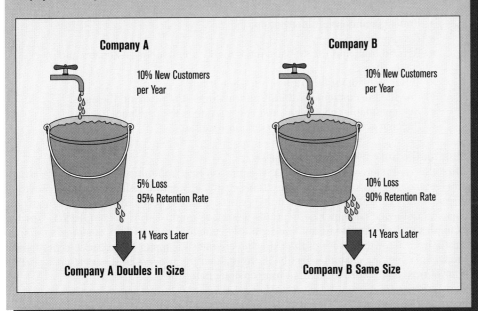

Cost of New versus Old Customers: The Leaky Bucket

The leaky bucket depicted below portrays two companies. Each company is working hard to generate new customers each year and has managed to generate 10 percent more new customers per year, perhaps by developing new services or targeting new segments. However, not all of the new customers acquired by the firm in a given year stay with the firm. The retention rate is not 100 percent; there is a "hole in the bucket." For company A, the "hole" is small and the company loses only 5 percent of its customers each year. As a result, after 14 years company A has doubled the number of its customers. Company B has a bigger problem, because retention is 90 percent and the "hole in the bucket" is 10 percent. As a result, company B loses and gains customers at the same rate.

Source: K. Douglas Hoffman and John E. G. Bateson, *Essentials of Services Marketing: Concepts, Strategies, and Cases,* 2nd ed. (Mason, Ohio: South-Western, 2002), 235.

customer retention as a primary goal are noticed. Consequently, a firm's customer retention efforts should serve to successfully differentiate the firm from its competitors. Methods for retaining customers through the use of effective customer retention tactics include maintaining the proper perspective, remembering customers between sales, building trusting relationships, monitoring the service delivery process, focusing on proper installation and training, standing behind the product, providing discretionary effort, offering service guarantees, and practicing the art of service recovery.

Maintain the Proper Perspective

Managers and employees need to remember that the company exists to meet the needs and desires of its customers. Processing customers like raw materials on an assembly line or being rude to customers is incredibly short-sighted. Companies such as US Airways employ slogans such as, "The U in US Airways starts with U the passenger." Credos such as this influence customer expectations and reinforce the firm's priorities to employees.

Interacting with the public is not an easy task and, unfortunately, employees occasionally fail to maintain the proper perspective. Different customers may ask the same questions of employees over and over, and not every customer is polite. Maintaining the proper perspective involves a customer-oriented frame of mind and a commitment to service. Employees need to remember that every customer has his or her own personal set of needs, and that the customer's, not the employee's, expectations define performance.

Remember Customers between Sales

Contacting customers between sales transactions is a useful approach in building relationships with the firm. The key is in making customer contact sincere and personal. Typical approaches include sending birthday, get-well, and/or anniversary cards; writing personal notes congratulating customers for their personal successes; and keeping in touch with customers concerning past services rendered and offering assistance if necessary. The goal of this tactic is to communicate to customers that the firm genuinely cares for their well-being and values the ongoing relationship.

Build Trusting Relationships

Trust is defined as a firm belief or confidence in the honesty, integrity, and the reliability of another person. In the service environment, three major components of trust are: (1) the service provider's expertise; (2) the service provider's reliability; and (3) the service provider's concern for the customer (see Figure 9.15). Strategies for building trust include:

- Protect confidential information.
- Keep promises.
- Refrain from making disparaging remarks about other customers and competitors.
- Tell the customer the truth, even when it hurts.
- Provide the customer with full information—the pros and the cons.
- Be dependable, courteous, and considerate with customers.
- Become actively involved in community affairs.

Monitor the Service Delivery Process

After the customer has requested a specific service, monitoring the service delivery process should be a key tactic in the firm's customer retention efforts. Service providers that are able to monitor the service delivery process are able to correct service inadequacies and influence customer perceptions of service quality prior to completion. Obvious examples include the restaurant that regularly communicates with its customers throughout their meal, or the owner of the firm who contacts customers about recent purchases. Proactively seeking customer feedback throughout the process builds customer perceptions of trust and facilitates maintaining customers for life.

Focus on Proper Installation and Training

Proper installation of products and training customers how to use what they have purchased saves a lot of headaches. Customers should not become frustrated over not understanding how to use something or, worse, improperly using the product, which may result in damage and further dissatisfaction. Simply dropping off a product such as a refrigera-

Programs Like State Farm's Good Neighbor Teaching Award Signal That the Company Is Concerned with More Than Just Making a Sale

Figure 9.15

If you're in Mr. Garwick's class, you're going to pay.

The good news is that Mr. Garwick pays students to attend class. The bad news is that everything – chairs, desks, even trips to the water fountain – must be purchased.

It's his ingenious way of making math fun for sixth graders while teaching them the concepts of saving, spending, banking and supply & demand.

For selling kids on the importance of math, State Farm is pleased to present Ken Garwick with our Good Neighbor Teacher Award™ and to donate $10,000 to Marlatt Elementary School in Manhattan, Kansas.

Good Neighbor Teacher Award™

STATE FARM INSURANCE COMPANIES
Home Offices: Bloomington, Illinois

statefarm.com

The Good Neighbor Teacher Award was developed in cooperation with the National Council of Teachers of Mathematics.

tor with an automatic ice cube maker, and leaving customers to fend for themselves reinforces the idea that the company is not genuinely concerned for the customer's well-being. It leaves the impression that the company is more interested in short-term profits than in building long-term relationships.

Stand Behind the Product

When a customer returns a product that is in need of service or repair is no time to hide. Every firm should stand behind what it sells, and ensure that every transaction is handled to the customer's satisfaction. Most customers are realistic and understand that nothing lasts forever. Many times customers are simply looking for advice and alternative solutions to problems, and are not looking for someone to blame. Expressing a sincere concern for the customer's situation reinforces the firm's customer retention efforts.

Provide Discretionary Effort

Discretionary effort is behavior beyond the call of duty. It is the Procter & Gamble salesperson who voluntarily bags groceries at the grand opening of a new grocery store. It is the hotel that sends items misplaced by customers to their homes at no charge. It is the oil company that recognizes the special needs of its customers during weather-related disasters. Discretionary effort involves countless personal touches, little things that distinguish a one-time business transaction from an ongoing relationship.

Offer Service Guarantees

One of the most intriguing customer retention strategies to be developed in recent years is the service guarantee.[36] Service guarantees appear to facilitate three worthwhile goals: (1) reinforce customer loyalty; (2) build market share; and (3) force the firm offering the guarantee to improve its overall service quality. The Hampton Inn offers an unconditional guarantee to its customers: Any guest who has a problem and is not satisfied by the end of the stay will receive one night's stay free of charge. The guarantee is paid out when the guest settles his or her account and is not a voucher for a future stay. The impact of the guarantee has been overwhelmingly positive. Employees took notice and responsibility for correcting potential service problems. Moreover, quality standards in the company's hotels have noticeably changed. During the guarantee's first 2 years, 7,000 guests representing $350,000 in sales had invoked the guarantee. Of these 7,000 guests, 86 percent said they will return to Hampton Inn, and 45 percent have already done so.

In general, successful guarantees are unrestrictive, stated in specific and clear terms, meaningful and hassle-free when invoked, and quick to be paid out. On the other hand, mistakes to avoid when constructing a guarantee include: (1) promising something that is trivial and normally expected; (2) specifying an inordinate number of conditions as part of the guarantee; and (3) making the guarantee so mild that it is never invoked.

Practice the Art of Service Recovery

Service recovery
is a firm's reaction to a complaint that results in customer satisfaction and goodwill.

When the service is provided incorrectly, an important but often overlooked management tool is the art of **service recovery**.[37] While some companies are great at delivering service until something goes wrong, other companies thrive on recovering from service failures and impressing customers in the process. Customers of service organizations often allow the firm one mistake. Consequently, when a failure occurs, the customer generally provides the business with an opportunity to make amends. Unfortunately, many companies still drop the ball and further aggravate the customer by failing to take the opportunity to recover.

The customer's perception of whether the recovery strategy is just includes evaluations of the recovery process itself; the outcomes connected to the recovery strategy; and the interpersonal behaviors enacted during the recovery process. Accordingly, perceived justice consists of three components: **distributive justice**, **procedural justice**, and **interactional justice**.

Distributive justice
focuses on the specific outcome of a firm's recovery efforts.

Procedural justice
examines the process a customer is required to travel in order to arrive at a final outcome.

Interactional justice
refers to the human interaction during service recovery efforts.

- Distributive justice focuses on the specific outcome of a firm's recovery effort. In other words, what specifically did the offending firm offer the customer to recover from the service failure, and did this outcome (output) offset the costs (inputs) of the service failure? Typical distributive outcomes include compensation (e.g., gratis, discounts, coupons, free upgrades, and free ancillary services); offers to mend or totally replace/reperform; and apologies.
- Procedural justice examines the process that is undertaken to arrive at the final outcome. Hence, even though a customer may be satisfied with the type of recovery strategy offered, recovery evaluation may be poor due to the process endured to obtain the recovery outcome. For example, research has indicated that when implementing identical recovery strategies, those that are implemented promptly are much more likely to be associated with

higher consumer effectiveness ratings and retention rates than when restitution is delayed.

- Interactional justice refers to the manner in which the service recovery process is implemented and how recovery outcomes are presented. In other words, interactional justice involves the courtesy and politeness exhibited by personnel; empathy; effort observed in resolving the situation; and the firm's willingness to provide an explanation for why the situation occurred.

A limited amount of research exists that specifically examines the influence of perceived justice on recovery strategy effectiveness. However, the bottom line is that the three components of perceived justice should be considered when formulating effective service recovery strategies. Deploying recovery efforts that satisfy distributive justice without considering customer procedural and interactional justice needs may still result in customer defections. If service firms are truly committed to the recovery process and retaining customers for life, all three aspects of perceived justice must be integrated into the service recovery process.

CHAPTER SUMMARY

- This chapter focuses on the marketing of services. Service consumers purchase a bundle of benefits that are provided by the service experience that is created for consumers. The four primary factors that influence the customer's service experience are the service providers, the servicescape, other customers, and the invisible organization and systems. Service firms that are able to effectively mold the customer's experience have mastered the means to develop "compelling experiences"—the latest competitive weapon in the war against service commoditization.

- The major differences between the marketing of goods and services are often attributed to four unique service characteristics: intangibility, inseparability, heterogeneity, and perishability. Of the four unique characteristics that distinguish goods from services, intangibility is the primary source from which the other three characteristics emerge.

- A goal for all marketers is to strive for customer satisfaction. Customers typically assess satisfaction by comparing expectations to perceptions. If perceptions meet or exceed expectations, then customers are satisfied. As such, customer satisfaction can be increased by lowering expectations or by enhancing perceptions. It is crucial to remember that this entire process of comparing expectations to perceptions takes place in the minds of customers. Hence, it is the perceived service that matters, not the actual service. One of the most recent business practices affecting customer satisfaction levels (both positively and negatively) is customer relationship management (CRM)—the process of identifying, attracting, differentiating, and retaining customers. CRM allows a firm to focus its efforts disproportionately on its most lucrative clients.

- Service quality can be examined in terms of gaps that exist between expectations and perceptions on the part of management, employees, and customers. The most important gap—the service gap—is between customers' expectations of service and their perception of the service actually delivered. Ultimately, the service gap is a function of the knowledge gap, the standards gap, the delivery gap, and the communications gap. As each of these gaps increases or decreases, the service gap responds in a similar manner.

- The value of retaining existing customers is critical in these days of saturated markets and rising marketing costs. In fact, some experts believe that customer retention has a more powerful effect on profits than market share, economies of scale, and other variables commonly associated with competitive advantage. Firms that excel at customer retention maintain a proper perspective, remember customers between sales transactions, build trusting relationships with customers, monitor the service delivery process, ensure proper product installation, and train customers how to use products that they have purchased. Customer service-oriented firms also are available when needed most, provide discretionary effort to assist customers, offer service guarantees, and anticipate needs for recovery.

KEY TERMS

Benefit concept is the encapsulation of the benefits of a product in the customer's mind.

Coding is categorizing customers based on how profitable their past business has been.

Conquest marketing is a strategy for constantly seeking new customers by offering discounts and markdowns and developing promotions that encourage new business.

Credence attributes cannot be evaluated confidently even immediately after consumption.

Customer relationship management is the process of identifying, attracting, differentiating, and retaining customers.

Customer retention refers to focusing a firm's marketing efforts toward the existing customer base.

Customer satisfaction is a short-term, transaction-specific measure of whether customer perceptions meet or exceed customer expectations.

Distributive justice focuses on the specific outcome of a firm's recovery efforts.

Experience attributes can be evaluated only during and after consumption.

Goods are objects, devices, or things.

Heterogeneity is a distinguishing characteristic of services that reflects the variation in consistency from one service transaction to the next.

Inseparability is a distinguishing characteristic of services that reflects the interconnection among the service provider, the customer receiving the service, and other customers sharing the service experience.

Intangibility is a distinguishing characteristic of services that makes them unable to be touched or sensed in the same manner as physical goods.

Interactional justice refers to the human interaction during service recovery efforts.

Leaky bucket theory is traditionally associated with conquest marketing where new customers replace disloyal customers at the same rate; hence, the firm never grows.

Marketing myopia is too narrowly defining one's business.

Organizational socialization is the process by which an individual adapts to and comes to appreciate the values, norms, and required behavior patterns of an organization.

Perishability is a distinguishing characteristic of services in that they cannot be saved, their unused capacity cannot be reserved, and they cannot be inventoried.

Polygamous loyalty reflects the notion that customer loyalty tends to be divided among a number of providing firms.

Procedural justice examines the process a customer is required to travel in order to arrive at a final outcome.

Red-lining is the practice of identifying and avoiding unprofitable types of neighborhoods or people.

Routing is the process of directing incoming calls to customer service representatives in which more profitable customers are more likely to receive faster and better customer service.

Scale of market entities displays a range of products along a continuum based on their tangibility.

Search attributes are physical properties that customers can evaluate prior to their purchase decisions.

The **service gap** is the gap between customers' expectations of service and their perception of the service actually delivered, which is a function of the knowledge gap, the standards gap, the delivery gap, and the communications gap.

Service quality is an attitude formed by a long-term, overall evaluation of performance.

Service recovery is a firm's reaction to a complaint that results in customer satisfaction and goodwill.

Services are deeds, efforts, or performances.

Servicescapes refers to the use of physical evidence to design service environments.

Sharing involves making key customer information accessible to all parts of the organization and in some cases selling that information to other firms.

Targeting involves offering the firm's most profitable customers special deals and incentives.

QUESTIONS FOR DISCUSSION

1. What is a service? Is there a clear distinction between goods and services? Please explain.

2. The growth of the service sector has not occurred solely within traditional service industries such as hospitality, health care, financial services, and insurance. Traditional goods producers such as automotive, computer, and numerous other manufacturers are now turning to service as a differential advantage. Please explain.

3. Discuss the benefit concept and its relationship to factors involved in creating service experiences.

4. Service firms that are able to effectively mold the customer's experience have the means to develop compelling experiences, the latest competitive weapon in the war against service commoditization. Please explain the economic value of transforming products from commodities to goods to services to experiences.

5. Define the concepts of intangibility, inseparability, heterogeneity, and perishability.

6. To market services effectively, marketing managers need to understand the thought processes customers use to assess their satisfaction with services. Define customer satisfaction. Provide examples of how satisfaction can be managed by altering consumer perceptions and expectations.

7. Customer relationship management (CRM) is the process of identifying, attracting, differentiating, and retaining customers. Discuss the motives behind CRM. What are the pros and cons associated with the customer relationship management outcomes of coding, routing, targeting, and sharing?

8. According to the service quality gap model, the service gap is a function of the knowledge gap, the standards gap, the delivery gap, and the communications gap. Please explain each of these five gaps.

9. Discuss the differences between conquest marketing and customer retention. Which is more important under saturated market conditions? Please explain.

10. While some companies are great at delivering service until something goes wrong, other companies thrive on recovering from service failures and impressing customers in the process. Discuss the three main components of an effective recovery strategy.

INTERNET QUESTIONS

1. Visit Hewlett-Packard's e-service homepage at http://www.hp.com/solutions1/e-services/index.html.
   a. What is an e-service?
   b. Go to http://www.cooltown.hp.com/mpulse/backissues/0601/0601-cooltown.asp. How are e-services being used to created Cooltown ecosystems?

2. Investigate http://www.LivePerson.com.
   a. What products does LivePerson.com offer to its corporate customers?
   b. As a corporate customer, what benefits would your firm obtain from outsourcing your customer contact duties to LivePerson.com?
   c. If you are the owner of a business in the travel industry, what customer contact solutions does LivePerson.com recommend for your type of business?

3. Investigate http://www.mysimon.com.
   a. Discuss the purpose of this Web site. What service does it offer the customer?
   b. How do the sponsors of the Web site make their money?
   c. When would it make sense for a company to sign-up and be listed on the Web site? Under what conditions would it not make much sense? Would these same reasons hold true for customers using the Web site? Please explain.

ENDNOTES

[1] This section adapted from Hewlett-Packard http://www.hp.com/solutions1/e-services/understanding/transform, and http://www.hp.com/solutions1/e-services/understanding/scenarios/scenario1pop, accessed 31 August 2001; http://www.hp.com, accessed 10 March 2001.

[2] K. Douglas Hoffman and John E. G. Bateson, *Essentials of Services Marketing: Concepts, Strategies, and Cases*, 2nd ed. (Mason, OH: South-Western, 2002), 3.

[3] "The Final Frontier," *The Economist*, 20 February 1993, 63.

[4] G. Lyn Shostack, "Breaking Free from Product Marketing," *Journal of Marketing* 41 (April 1977): 73–80.

[5] Ibid.

[6] This section adopted from Hoffman and Bateson, *Essentials of Services Marketing*, 2nd ed., 26–51; and Valerie A. Zeithaml, A. Parasuraman, and Leonard L. Berry, "Problems and Strategies in Services Marketing," *Journal of Marketing* 49 (Spring 1985): 33–46.

[7] Asra Q. Nomani, "In the Skies Today, A Weird New Worry: Sexual Misconduct," *Wall Street Journal*, 10 June 1998, A1; Frances Fiorino, "Passengers Who Carry Surly Bonds of Earth Aloft," *Aviation Week and Space Technology* 149, no. 5 (28 December 1998): 123.

[8] This section adopted from Hoffman and Bateson, *Essentials of Services Marketing*, 2nd ed., 4–16; and E. Langeard, J. Bateson, C. Lovelock, and P. Eigler, *Marketing of Services: New Insights from Consumers and Managers*, Report No. 81-104 (Cambridge, MA: Marketing Science Institute, 1981).

[9] Mary Jo Bitner, "Servicescapes: The Impact of Physical Surroundings on Customers and Employees," *Journal of Marketing* 56 (April 1992): 57–71.

[10] Michael R. Solomon, "Packaging the Service Provider," in *Managing Services Marketing, Operations, and Human Resources*, ed. Christopher H. Lovelock (Englewood Cliffs, NJ: Prentice-Hall, 1988), 318–324.

[11] Alan J. Dubinsky, Roy D. Howell, Thomas N. Ingram, and Danny N. Bellenger, "Salesforce Socialization," *Journal of Marketing* 50, no. 4 (1986): 192–207.

[12] Solomon, "Packaging the Service Provider," 318–324.

[13] "Plane Seats Get Bigger, Cost More: Airlines Betting Fliers Will Pay Extra for Added Legroom," *Denver Rocky Mountain News*, 28 February 2000, 2A, 31A.

[14] Solomon, "Packaging the Service Provider," 318–324.

[15] For more information, see Hoffman and Bateson, *Essentials of Services Marketing*, 2nd ed., 247–269.

[16] Ron Zemke and Kristen Anderson, "Customers from Hell," *Training* (February 1990): 25–29.

[17] John E. G. Bateson and K. Douglas Hoffman, *Managing Services Marketing*, 4th ed. (Fort Worth, TX: Harcourt College Publishers, 1999).

[18] For more information, see Charles L. Martin, "Consumer-to-Consumer Relationships: Satisfaction with Other Consumers' Public Behavior," *Journal of Consumer Affairs* 30, no. 1 (1996): 146–148; and Stephen J. Grove and Raymond P. Fisk, "The Impact of Other Customers on Service Experiences: A Critical Incident Examination of Getting Along," *Journal of Retailing* 73, no. 1 (1997): 63–85.

[19] Bateson and Hoffman, *Managing Services Marketing*, 4e.

[20] Jim Kelly, "From Lip Service to Real Service: Reversing America's Downward Service Spiral," *Vital Speeches of the Day* 64, no. 10 (1998): 301–304.

[21] Joseph B. Pine II and James H. Gilmore, *The Experience Economy* (Boston, MA: Harvard School Press, 1998).

[22] This section adopted from Hoffman and Bateson, *Essentials of Services Marketing*, 2nd ed., 293–322.

[23] Karl Albrecht and Ron Zemke, *Service America! Doing Business in the New Economy* (Homewood, IL: Business One Irwin, 1985), 6.

[24] Bob Romano and Barbara Sanfilippo, "A Total Approach: Measure Sales and Service," *Texas Banking* 85, no. 8 (1996): 16–17.

[25] Leonard L. Berry, A. Parasuraman, and Valerie A. Zeithaml, "Improving Service Quality in America: Lessons Learned," *Academy of Management Executive* 8, no. 2 (1994): 36.

[26] Robert Levering and Milton Moskowitz, "The 100 Best Companies to Work For in America," *Fortune* 137, (12 January 1998), 84.

[27] This section developed from Diane Brady, "Why Service Stinks," *Business Week*, 23 October 2000, 118–128.

[28] Ibid, 124.

[29] Ibid.

[30] J. Joseph Cronin, Jr., and Steven A. Taylor, "Measuring Service Quality: A Reexamination and Extension," *Journal of Marketing* 56 (July 1992): 55.

[31] Thomas A. Stewart, "After All You've Done for Your Customers, Why Are They Still NOT HAPPY," *Fortune*, 11 December 1995, 178–182.

[32] A. Parasuraman, Valerie A. Zeithaml, and Leonard L. Berry, "A Conceptual Model of Service Quality and Its Implications for Future Research," *Journal of Marketing* 49, (Fall 1985), 41–50.

[33] C. Brune, "E-business Misses the Mark on Customer Service," *Internal Auditor* 57, no. 3 (June 2000): 13–15; "Rainer: Top Companies Lax in Replying to Email," http://www.nua.ie/surveys, accessed 3 August 2000.

[34] Frederick F. Reichheld and W. Earl Sasser, Jr., "Zero Defections: Quality Comes to Services," *Harvard Business Review* (September–October 1990): 105–111.

[35] Grahame R. Dowling and Mark Uncles, "Do Customer Loyalty Programs Really Work?" *Sloan Management Review* 38, no. 4 (September 1997): 71–82.

[36] Christopher W. L. Hart, Leonard A. Schlesinger, and Don Maher, "Guarantees Come to Professional Service Firms," *Sloan Management Review* (Spring 1992): 19–29.

[37] Adapted from Christopher W. L. Hart, James L. Heskett, and W. Earl Sasser, "The Profitable Art of Service Recovery," *Harvard Business Review* (July–August 1990): 148–156; and K. Douglas Hoffman and Scott W. Kelley, "Perceived Justice Needs and Recovery Evaluation: A Contingency Approach," *European Journal of Marketing* 34, no. ¾ (2000): 418–432.

EMMY'S AND MADDY'S FIRST SERVICE ENCOUNTER

Our day began at 5:20 A.M. Hurricane Felix was predicted to hit the Carolina coast by the end of the afternoon, and I, like most of the other folks in southeastern North Carolina had spent much of the previous day preparing the house for the upcoming storm. However, my wife and I had one extra concern that the others did not. My wife was 6 months pregnant with twins, and the prospect of spending lots of time in the car in the attempt to remove ourselves from harm's way was not particularly attractive. We had decided to wait until after my wife's doctor appointment at 9:00 A.M. to make a decision on whether we should leave or stay at home and ride out the storm. We never made it to the doctor's appointment.

At 5:20 A.M., I was awakened by the fear in my wife's voice. Her water had broken, and the twins that were due on November 16 had apparently made up their collective minds that they were going to be born 13 weeks early. As first-time parents, we understood that our next move would be to go to the hospital; however, we were unsure as to the best mode of transportation given our particular situation. We had been informed by doctors that multiple-birth pregnancies were high-risk pregnancies and that every precaution should be taken. We quickly called the hospital and asked for advice. The hospital suggested that my wife take a shower, shave her legs, and pack some essentials and that it would be appropriate for us to drive ourselves to the hospital. Too stressed out to take any chances, we passed on the shower advice, quickly threw some things together, and drove to the hospital immediately.

The Emergency Department

Upon our arrival at the hospital, we drove to the emergency entrance, and I quickly exited the car to find a wheelchair. I was immediately confronted by a security guard who had been previously engaged in a casual conversation with another gentleman. I was informed that I could not leave my car in its current position. In response, I informed the security guard that I needed a wheelchair and would move the car after I was able to move my wife inside. The security guard pointed his finger in the direction of the wheelchairs. I grabbed the first wheelchair I could get my hands on and headed back out the sliding doors to assist my wife. At this point, the security guard informed me that I had grabbed a juvenile-sized wheelchair. I headed back inside and grabbed a much larger wheelchair. I returned to the car, assisted my wife into the wheelchair, and headed back inside. The security guard, while continuing with his other conversation, instructed me to leave my wife with the triage nurse in the emergency department so that I could move my vehicle. I said goodbye to my wife and went to move the vehicle. When I returned, the security guard informed me that they had taken my wife to the maternity ward, located on the third floor.

My wife's encounter with the triage nurse was apparently short and sweet. The triage nurse had called for an orderly to move my wife to the maternity ward. On her way to the third floor, the orderly asked my wife whether she was excited about having the baby. She responded that she was scared to death because she was only 6 months pregnant. The orderly replied that there was "no way [she was] having a baby that early that [would] survive."

The Maternity Ward

As I exited the elevator on the third floor, I headed for the nurses' station to inquire about my wife's current location. I was greeted by several smiling nurses who escorted me to my wife's room. On my way to the room, I met another nurse who had just exited my wife's room. This nurse pulled me aside and informed me of the orderly's remarks. She continued on to assure me that what he said was not only inappropriate, but more importantly, inaccurate. She also informed me that my wife was very upset and that we needed to work together to help keep her calm. This particular nurse also informed us that she herself had given birth to a premature child, who was approximately the same gestational age as ours, a couple of years earlier.

By this time, it was between 6:00 and 6:30 A.M. The resident on duty entered the room and introduced himself as Dr. Baker. My wife gave me this puzzled and bewildered look. The clinic where my wife is a patient consists of five physicians who rotate their various duty assignments. Dr. Baker is one of the five. However, Dr. Baker was 30 to 40 years older than the resident who had just introduced himself as Dr. Baker. What had happened was that the resident was nervous and had introduced himself as Dr. Baker rather than as Dr. Baker's assistant. Realizing his mistake, he embarrassingly reintroduced himself and informed us that Dr. Baker was the physician on call and that he was being contacted and kept informed of my wife's condition.

The resident left the room and soon reappeared with an ultrasound cart to check the positions of the babies. This time he was accompanied by a person I assumed to be the senior resident on duty. For the next 30 minutes or so, I watched the junior resident attempt to learn how to use the ultrasound equipment. He consistently reported his findings to us in sentences that began with, "I think. . . ." Several times during this period my wife voiced her concern over the babies' conditions, and the location of Dr. Baker. We were reassured by the residents that Dr. Baker was being kept informed and were told that being upset was not going to help the babies' conditions. After about 30 minutes, I informed both residents that despite their advice for us to stay calm, they were not exactly instilling a lot of confidence in either one of us. The senior resident took over the ultrasound exam at this time.

Dr. Baker arrived at the hospital somewhere between 7:00 and 7:30 A.M. He apologized for not being there earlier and mentioned that he was trying to help his wife prepare for the ensuing hurricane. Sometime during this same time period, it was shift-change time for the nurses and also for Dr. Baker. New nurses were now entering the room, and now Dr. Johnson was taking over for Dr. Baker. By approximately 8:00 A.M., Dr. Baker had pulled me aside and informed me that after conferring with Dr. Johnson, they had decided that if my wife's labor subsided, she would remain in the hospital for 7 to 10 days, flat on her back, before they would deliver the babies. It was explained that with each passing day, the babies would benefit from further development. The lungs were of particular concern.

Upon being admitted to the maternity floor, my wife had immediately been hooked up to an EKG to monitor contractions. Due to the small size of the babies, the contractions were not severe. However, as far as my wife and I could tell, the interval between contractions was definitely getting shorter. Being first-time parents, we were not overly alarmed by this since we figured we were in the hospital and surrounded by health care providers.

Between 8:00 and 8:30 A.M., two other nurses entered the room with lots of forms for us to complete. Since we were having twins, we needed duplicates of every form. The forms covered the basics: names, addresses, phone numbers, Social Security numbers, and insurance information. All the same questions that the hospital had sent to us weeks earlier, which we had completed and returned. The nurses asked us the questions, we supplied the information, and they wrote the responses.

By 8:30 A.M., Dr. Baker was informing me that due to one of the baby's breach position, they would deliver the babies by caesarean section. Wondering whether the schedule had been moved up from a week to 10 days, I asked when he thought this would be happening. He replied: "In the next hour or so." He then commented that labor had not subsided and that Dr. Johnson would be delivering the babies.

As my wife was being prepared for the operating room, I stood in the hallway outside her room. I noticed another physician limping down the hall with one foot in a cast and a crutch underneath one arm. He stopped outside my wife's room and began to examine her medical charts. He introduced himself as Dr. Arthur (he had broken his foot while attempting to change a tire). Dr. Arthur was the neonatologist, which meant nothing to me at the time. I eventually figured out that my wife had her set of doctors and that my unborn children had their own set of health care providers. Dr. Arthur asked to speak to my wife and me together. This is when he told us that 90 percent of babies such as ours survive and that 90 percent of those survivors develop normally. He was a calm, pragmatic individual who encouraged us to ask questions. He continued to explain that the babies would spend their next few months in the hospital's Neonatal Intensive Care Unit (NICU) and that if all went well, we could expect to take them home within 2 weeks of their due date (November 16th).

By 9:00 A.M., all hell had broken loose. My wife had dilated at a quicker pace than had been anticipated . . . the contractions had indeed been occurring at more frequent intervals. Some orderlies and nurses grabbed my wife's bed and quickly rolled her down the hall to the delivery room. I was thrown a pair of scrubs and told to put them on. I was further told that they would come back and get me if they were able. For 10 to 12 very long minutes, I sat on a stool in an empty hospital room by myself, watching the Weather Channel track Hurricane Felix. The volume on the television had been muted, and the only thing I could hear was a woman screaming from labor in the next room. Suddenly, a nurse popped her head in the door and said that a space had been prepared for me in the delivery room.

The Delivery Room

As I entered the delivery room, I was overwhelmed by the number of people involved in the process. Myself included, I counted 12 "very busy" people. I was seated next to my wife's head. She had requested to stay awake during the procedure. My wife asked me whether the man assisting Dr. Johnson was the junior resident. Sure enough, I looked up to see the junior resident wearing a surgical gown and mask with a scalpel in his hand. I lied and told her, "No."

Suddenly, we realized that we had not finalized our choices for names. Somehow, what we couldn't decide despite months of discussion, we decided in 30 seconds. Our first baby girl, Emma Lewis (Emmy), was born at 9:15 A.M. Emmy weighed 2 pounds and was 14.5 inches long. Our second baby girl, Madeline Stuart (Maddy), was born at 9:16 A.M. and weighed 2 pounds, 2 ounces, and also measured 14.5 inches long. Both babies were very active at birth, and their faint cries reassured my wife and I that they had at least made it this far.

Upon being delivered from their mother, the babies were immediately handed to Dr. Arthur and his staff, who had set up examination stations in the delivery room. Each baby had her own team of medical personnel, and I was encouraged by Dr. Arthur, who hopped on one foot across the delivery room, as I watched him examine the girls. The neonatal staff examining the girls "ooohed and aaahed," and almost in a competitive manner compared measurements about which baby had better vitals in various areas. Dr. Arthur then suggested that I follow the girls to the NICU to watch further examinations. He also made sure that my wife got a good look at both babies before they were wheeled out of the delivery room in their respective incubators. My wife and I said our goodbyes, and I was told I could see her again in the recovery room in about 20 to 30 minutes.

The Recovery Room

The recovery room and the delivery room are contained within the maternity ward on the third floor of the hospital. The NICU is located on the fourth floor, which is designated as the gynecological floor. The staff on the third floor is geared for moms and babies. The staff on the fourth floor, outside the NICU, is geared for women with gynecological problems.

After receiving the "so far, so good" signals from both my wife's and my babies' doctors, I was permitted to rejoin my wife in the recovery room. It was a basic hospital room with the exception that a nurse was assigned to the room on a full-time basis. One of the hospital volunteers from the maternity floor had taken pictures of each of the babies and taped them to the rails of my wife's hospital bed. The nurses of the third floor maternity ward asked my wife whether she would like a room on the fourth floor so that she could be closer to her babies when she was ready to start walking again. She agreed and spent the next four days in a room on the fourth floor.

Hurricane Felix stayed out to sea and moved up the coastline, missing us completely.

The Fourth Floor

My wife's private room on the fourth floor was small, dingy, and dirty. From an emotional standpoint, the staff on the fourth floor were not prepared to deal with our situation. In fact, one nurse, after discussing the situation with my wife, asked whether we were going to have the babies transported to a major university medical center 3 hours away.

My wife's quality of care on the fourth floor was sporadic. Some of the nurses were good and some were inattentive . . . slow to respond to the patient's call button and blaming nurses on other shifts when medications and other scheduled or promised care (e.g., providing the patient with a breast pump) were not provided on a timely basis. Although it might seem trivial to many, the breast pump represented my wife's primary contribution to the care of her babies. It was the only thing she could control. Everything else was out of her hands. My wife was instructed to begin pumping as soon as she felt able, yet due to her location away from the maternity ward, obtaining a breast pump was difficult and became a sore point for my wife.

After receiving a courtesy call by the hospital's patient representative, my wife expressed her concerns. Shortly thereafter, personnel were changed, the quality of care improved, and we were moved to a much larger room on the third afternoon.

The Neonatal Intensive Care Unit

The NICU (pronounced "nick-u") is located in an isolated area of the fourth floor. The primary purpose of the NICU is to provide care for premature babies and for full-term babies requiring special care. The number of babies cared for each day throughout our stay typically averaged 12.

Emmy and Maddy spent approximately 7 weeks in the NICU. The staff made every effort to explain the purpose of every piece of machinery and every tube that seemed to cover the babies' bodies. I was repeatedly told that I could and should ask questions at any time and that the staff understood that it was an overwhelming amount of information. Hence, it was understandable and acceptable to ask the same questions day after day. The staff had made signs welcoming each of the babies in bright neon colors and taped them above each of their stations. For ease of access, the girls had not yet been placed in incubators. They laid in what looked like large in/out baskets with raised borders. We celebrated weeks later when they finally had enough tubes removed so that they could be moved into incubators . . . what we called "big-girl beds."

During the first 3 days, I walked into the NICU to find baby quilts at each of the girls' stations. A local group called Quilters by the Sea had sewn the quilts; apparently they regularly provide the quilts for infants admitted to the NICU. For some reason that I still cannot explain today, the fact that someone outside the hospital who I did not know cared about my girls touched me deeply. The signs the staff had made and the babies' patchwork quilts humanized all the machines and tubes. Somehow, I was no longer looking at two premature infants . . . I was looking at Emmy and Maddy.

Throughout the girls' stay in the NICU, the quality of care delivered was primarily exceptional. The staff not only excelled at the technical aspects of their jobs but also were very good in dealing with parents. Some of the personal touches included numerous pictures of each of the girls for us to take home, homemade birthday cards with pictures from the girls for Mom and Dad on their birthdays, baby stickers on their incubators, and notes of encouragement from staff when a milestone, such as when weighing 3 pounds, was achieved. We arrived one day and found pink bows in the girls' hair. The nurses even signed Emmy's and Maddy's names on the foot cast worn by the baby boy in the next incubator.

Parental involvement in the care of all the infants was encouraged, almost demanded. I had somehow managed to never change a diaper in my life (I was 35 years old). I was threatened, I think jokingly, that the girls would not be allowed to leave the NICU until I demonstrated some form of competency with diaper changes, feedings, and baths. The primarily female staff made me feel at times that my manhood was at stake if I was not able to perform these duties. Personally, I think they all wished they'd had the same chance to train their husbands when they'd had their own babies. I am now an expert in the aforementioned activities.

As for the babies' progress, some days were better than others. We celebrated weight gains and endured a collapsed lung, blood transfusions, respirators, alarms caused by bouts with apnea and bradycardia, and minor operations. Throughout the seven weeks, many of the staff and three neonatologists became our friends. We knew where one another lived, we knew about husbands, wives, boyfriends, and kids. We also heard a lot about the staff's other primary concern . . . scheduling.

The Grower Room

Sometime after the 7th week, we "graduated" from the NICU and were sent to the Grower Room. The Grower Room acts as a staging area and provides the transition between the NICU and sending the babies home with their parents. Babies who are transferred to the Grower Room no longer require the intensive care provided by the NICU but still require full-time observation. As the name indicates, the Grower Room is for feeding and diaper changing, administering medications, and recording vital statistics . . . basic activities essential for the growth and development of infants. The Grower Room held a maximum of four infants at any one time.

The Grower Room was located in a converted patient room located in the back corner of the second floor, which is designated as the pediatric floor of the hospital. In general, the Grower Room was staffed by one pediatric nurse and visited by the neonatologists during rounds. As parents who were involved in the care of their babies, being transferred to the Grower Room meant that we had to establish new relationships with another set of health care providers all over again.

Compared with the "nurturing" culture we had experienced in the NICU, the Grower Room was a big letdown. One of the first nurses we were exposed to informed us that the nurses on the second floor referred to the Grower Room as "The Hole," and that sooner or later they all had to take their turn in "The Hole." We asked the reasons for such a name, and the nurse explained that because the room was stuck back in the corner, the rest of the staff seldom allowed the "grower nurse" to take a break, and because of the constant duties involved, the grower nurse could never leave the room unattended. It was also explained that some of the nurses simply did not feel comfortable caring "for such small little babies." We quickly found that this attitude had manifested itself in a lack of supplies specifically needed for smaller babies, such as premature-sized diapers and sheepskin rugs inside the incubators.

Furthermore, it became quickly apparent that friction existed between the NICU and the Grower Room. The Grower Room was very hesitant to request supplies from the NICU and on several occasions would delay informing NICU that an occupancy existed in the Grower Room. The reason for delay was so that the Grower Room nurse could catch up on other duties and avoid having to undertake the additional duties involved in admitting new patients. The "successful delay" would pass on these activities to the nurse taking the next shift. Apparently, the friction was mutual, since one of the nurses in the NICU commented to us on the way out of the NICU, "Don't let them push you around down there. If you don't think they're doing what they should, you tell them what you want them to do."

When the Grower Room was in need of supplies for our babies and others, I (on more than one occasion) volunteered to ask for supplies from the NICU. Although my foraging attempts were successful, I definitely got the feeling that there was some reluctance on both sides for me to do this. I suspected that the Grower Room nurses did not want to ask for any favors, and the NICU staff felt that it was not their job to keep the Grower Room stocked with supplies. Moreover, I suspect that the NICU and the Grower Room operate from different budgets. Stocking the Grower Room is not one of the objectives of the NICU's budget. However, from my side, my babies needed supplies, and I did not care about either department's budget.

After a few dark days, we established new relationships with the Grower Room personnel and became very involved with the care of our babies. After spending seven weeks in the NICU, we felt more familiar with each baby's personal needs than some of the Grower Room staff were. Recognizing our level of involvement, most of the staff looked forward to our visits since it meant less work for them. By now, we had learned to ask lots of questions, to double-check that medications had been provided, and to develop a working relationship with Grower Room personnel. Looking back, it was almost as if we and the Grower Room staff trained each other. At the conclusion of our Grower Room experience, my wife and I felt that we had met some good people, but also that the quality of the experience was far lower than what we had grown accustomed to in the NICU.

Nesting

Once the babies had "graduated" from the Grower Room, our last night in the hospital was spent "nesting." Friends of ours joked that this must have involved searching for twigs, grass, and mud. The nesting rooms were located on the second floor of the hospital, in the same general location as the Grower Room. Nesting allows the parents and the babies to spend a night or two together in the hospital before they go home. During the nesting period, parents are solely responsible for all medications, feedings, and general care of the infants. The nesting period allows the parents to ask any last-minute questions and to smooth the transition from, in our case, 9 weeks of hospital care to multiple infant care at home.

The nesting room itself was a small patient room that consisted of one single bed and a fold-out lounge chair. By now, the babies had been moved from their incubators to open, plastic bassinets that were wheeled into the room with us. Each baby remained attached to a monitor that measured heart and breathing rates. To say the least, space was limited, but for the first time in 9 weeks, the four of us were alone as a family.

Throughout the 22 hours we nested, we were frequently visited by neonatologists, nurses who continued to take the babies' vital signs, the babies' eye doctor, social workers who were assigned to all premature baby cases, hospital insurance personnel, and a wonderful discharge nurse who was in charge of putting everything together so that we could get out the door. Nine weeks to the day after we had entered the hospital, we took our two 4-pound babies home.

Discussion Questions

1. Where does health care fall along the Scale of Market Entities continuum? Please explain your answer.

2. Using the four key factors presented in Figure 9.5, categorize the factors that influenced this service encounter.

3. How do the concepts of inseparability, intangibility, heterogeneity, and perishability apply to this case?

4. Discuss corrective actions that need to be taken to ensure that subsequent encounters run more smoothly.

5. How would you go about measuring customer satisfaction in this situation?

Epilogue

One year later, Emmy and Maddy both weighed approximately 18 pounds and appeared to be in good overall health. One of the NICU nurses we met at the hospital helped us out in our home on a regular basis, and we have kept in touch with many of the NICU staff as well as with Dr. Arthur. The charges for our hospital stay were more than $250,000. This bill did not include any of the physicians' (e.g., neonatologists, eye doctors, surgeons, or radiologists) charges. Emmy recently returned to the hospital for a cranial ultrasound, which is an outpatient service (the results were negative for brain bleeds, and Emmy is fine). Despite her previous lengthy stay in NICU, we once again had to provide the hospital with all the insurance information one more time. Ironically, the only information the outpatient service had about Emmy was that her "responsible party" was Maddy. In terms of our overall experience, we are thankful for the lives of our babies and for the health of their mother. We are particularly grateful to the staff of the NICU and to Dr. Arthur.

Source: Originally printed as: K. Douglas Hoffman, "Rude Awakening," *Journal of Health Care Marketing* 16, no. 2 (Summer 1996): 14–22.

PART four

Distribution

CHAPTER 10

Marketing Channels and Distribution

CHAPTER 11

Retailing and Wholesaling

CHAPTER ten

Bert Rosenbloom,
Drexel University

Dr. Rosenbloom earned his Ph.D. at Temple University. He currently is a professor of marketing and Rauth Chair in Electronic Commerce in the LeBow College of Business, Drexel University, and editor of the *Journal of Marketing Channels*. He has served on the editorial boards of several publications including the *Journal of Consumer Marketing, Journal of the Academy of Marketing Science*, and *Journal of International Consumer Marketing*. Dr. Rosenbloom also serves on the ad hoc review boards of the *Journal of Marketing Research, Journal of Marketing*, and *Journal of Retailing*. He is former president of the International Management Development Association and former vice president of the Philadelphia Chapter of the American Marketing Association. Dr. Rosenbloom is a past member of the Board of Governors of the Academy of Marketing Science.

Dr. Rosenbloom is a leading expert on the management of marketing channels and distribution systems and the author of 10 books and more than 100 articles. His book *Marketing Channels: A Management View*, now in its sixth edition, has been the leading college textbook on marketing channels for over two decades. His book *Marketing Functions and the Wholesale Distributor* has been acclaimed in the wholesaling sector for providing the industry with new concepts and analytical methods to increase productivity in wholesale marketing channels.

Dr. Rosenbloom has consulted for a broad range of industries in manufacturing, wholesaling, retailing, communications, services, and real estate in the United States and abroad. He has won two teaching awards.

Marketing Channels and Distribution

Marketing channel strategy (place) along with the other three Ps of the marketing mix—product, pricing, promotion—must be developed and then blended together to meet the demands of an organization's target markets. Consider, for example, the situation faced by the small boutique beer brewery that produces St. Stan's Ale. The company was founded by Californian Garith Helm after buying a used book entitled *Brew It Yourself* for 10 cents at a garage sale. After trying his hand at brewing the traditional German brown ale described in the book, he found it to be far superior to big name national brands. When the boutique-beer/microbrewery craze came along in the 1990s, Garith Helm was eager to cash in on the growing market. He quit his job and went into beer brewing full-time.[1]

The first three Ps of Helm's marketing mix came together quickly: The formula for a superior product already existed, the market would support a premium price, and word-of-mouth advertising took care of much of the promotion as young, affluent consumers talked up St. Stan's Ale at parties and social gatherings. The fourth P, establishing marketing channels for the ale, was more challenging because Helm had to convince beer wholesalers all over California to carry and aggressively sell his product to retail stores, restaurants, and taverns. A hard-slogging effort, coupled with a quality product offering high profit potential, convinced enough beer wholesalers to carry the product. Eventually, St. Stan's was selling over $300,000 per month throughout California with prospects for distribution into other states on the horizon.

But by the late 1990s, clouds began to appear on that horizon—clouds caused by problems in St. Stan's marketing channels. Anheuser-Busch Company, which controls 44 percent of the beer market and produces the world's leading beer, Budweiser, decided it did not like having competition, even from such little guys as St. Stan's Ale. So, Anheuser-Busch initiated a campaign to discourage beer wholesalers from carrying microbrews. Using its tremendous marketing channel power, Anheuser-Busch could both reward and punish the beer wholesalers by giving them special discounts on its own products and at least implying that it would stop selling profitable products to those beer wholesalers that continued to sell boutique beers such as St. Stan's. Within a month, five of St. Stan's key beer wholesalers stopped carrying the product and sales fell almost by half. St. Stan's very existence was threatened by this decimation of its marketing channels.

This example points out how important marketing channels can be as a component of the marketing mix and in the overall success of a firm. The struggle to maintain space on distributors' shelves, as exemplified in the case of St. Stan's Ale, is one of the most common challenges in marketing channel management for all kinds of firms, both large and small.[2] In fact, even firms with great strength in the three Ps of products, price, and promotion may find, as did St. Stan's, that sometimes the greatest challenges they face in managing the marketing mix is in the fourth P—marketing channels.

http://www.gap.com

Whether the product is music, a Palm Pilot, an automobile, a bottle of Mike's Hard Lemonade, or any of a host of other possibilities, somehow this vast array of products must be made available to literally billions of people, as well as millions of industrial firms, businesses, institutions, and other organizations all over the world. Somehow, these millions of products and billions of customers around the globe must be matched up so that consumers can get the products they demand when and where they are needed. This may involve a consumer going to a retail store such as The Gap to buy a sweater, ordering a pair of Prada sunglasses over the telephone, or using the Internet to order a Harry Potter book from Amazon.com.[3] In the business-to-business sector, industrial distributors, manufacturer's representatives, and sales agents may be needed to make everything from sophisticated electronic components to paper towels available to organizational customers in a broad spectrum of different industries.[4]

Most customers are unaware of the enormous effort involved in making such a vast range of products so conveniently available. Indeed, most take it for granted.[5] A virtually limitless array of products can be purchased by simply taking a drive to the mall, picking up the telephone and ordering from a catalog, or clicking the mouse on a PC to buy online.[6] In fact, the availability of so many products from so many sources has become a given—a routine fact of everyday life for millions of consumers and organizations. But behind this seemingly routine process is an extraordinary combination of businesses, people, and technologies, comprising the marketing channels that have made such effective and efficient distribution possible.[7]

In this chapter we go "backstage" to examine marketing channels more closely. We take a look at the concept of modern marketing channels—their structure, strategy, design, and management. As we peer behind the scenes to look at marketing channels in this chapter, an important and exciting part of marketing is revealed.

LEARNING OBJECTIVE 1

MARKETING CHANNEL DEFINED

Marketing channel
is the network of organizations that creates time, place, and possession utilities.

A **marketing channel**, also referred to as a *distribution channel* or *channel of distribution*, is the network of organizations that creates time, place, and possession utilities for consumers and business users.

An example will help to clarify this definition. The updated Volkswagen Beetle, inspired by nostalgia for the Beetles of the 1950s and 60s, is a product that captured the public's imagination. Though Volkswagen is a German company, the retro Beetle is actually manufactured in Mexico. As these cars roll off the assembly line and out the factory door they appear to be totally complete. But are they? Actually, they are complete only to the extent of having *form utility*, which has been provided through the manufacturing process. But as exciting and cute as these cars may be, to be of use to consumers, they must be available when and where customers want them, and arrangements must be made so consumers can actually take possession of the cars through purchasing or leasing. In other words, **time, place, and possession utilities** still need to be added to make these cars complete from the standpoint of meeting customer needs. Clearly, a Beetle sitting on the factory lot in Mexico is of little use to a consumer in San Francisco who wants one to traverse the hilly streets of that city. Marketing channels are what create these other utilities not just for Volkswagen Beetles but for millions of other products as well.

Time, place, and possession utilities
are conditions that enable consumers and business users to have products available for use when and where they want them and to actually take possession of them.

The creation of time, place, and possession utilities may result from marketing channels that are simple or complex. In the case of the Volkswagen Beetle, the channel is fairly simple. The cars are sold by the manufacturer to retail dealers, who in turn sell the cars to consumers. The cars are transported from the factory to dealer showrooms by independent railroad or truck carriers who charge a fee for their services. Thus, the participants in this marketing channel are the manufacturers, retailers, consumers, and transportation companies. Only the first three, however, are what is referred to as the *sales channel*, which is that part of the channel involved in buying, selling, and transferring title. The rail or trucking firms, which do not buy, sell, or transfer the title to the cars, are part of the *facilitating channel*. Public storage firms, insurance companies, finance companies, market research firms, and several other types of firms also frequently participate as facilitating organizations in various marketing channels.

http://www.vw.com

Some marketing channels are more complex than that used for the Volkswagen Beetle. Beer, for example, which goes from manufacturers to wholesalers to retailers and then to consumers, has an extra organization (the wholesaler) in its sales channel.[8]

The simplest sales channels go directly from producers to customers, as in the case of Dell Computer Corporation, which sells all of its products directly from its manufacturing plants to customers. Dell's facilitating channel, however, which uses telephone, mail, and the Internet for order placement as well as United Parcel Service (UPS), Federal Express, and other transportation firms to deliver its computers to customers, is more complex than its sales channel.

Both the sales and facilitating channels are usually needed to create time, place, and possession utilities. But it has become a customary practice in marketing to describe and illustrate marketing channels only in terms of the sales channel, because it is the relationship involving the functions of buying, selling, and transferring of title where most of the strategic marketing issues emerge. For example, when setting up its sales channel, Volkswagen faced such marketing strategy issues as identifying and selecting the appropriate kinds of dealers to sell the new Beetles, convincing them to carry sufficient numbers of the cars, motivating the dealers to do an effective job of promoting and selling the cars, as well as making sure that they provided good servicing and warranty support. Moreover, Volkswagen also needed to make provisions for numerous other issues as part of its continuing relationship with independent dealers, such as future inventory levels expected of dealers, training of sales and service people, credit terms, evaluation of dealer performance, and numerous others. In contrast, Volkswagen's efforts to arrange for transportation, storage, insurance, and similar matters, while important, are usually not considered strategic marketing issues.

http://www.dell.com

http://www.ups.com

http://www.fedex.com

MARKETING CHANNEL STRUCTURE

The form or shape that a marketing channel takes to perform the tasks necessary to make products available to consumers is usually referred to as **channel structure**. Firms such as transportation companies, warehousing firms, insurance companies, and the like are usually referred to as *facilitating agencies*, because they are not involved in buying, selling, or transferring title and hence, as we mentioned earlier, are not considered to be part of the channel structure.

Marketing channel structure has three basic dimensions:

1. Length of the channel
2. Intensity at various levels
3. The types of intermediaries involved

Channel structure
consists of all of the businesses and institutions (including producers or manufacturers and final customers) who are involved in performing the functions of buying, selling, or transferring title.

Length of Channel Structure

Channel length
is the number of levels in a marketing channel.

Channel length can range from 2 levels, where the producer or manufacturer sells directly to consumers (direct distribution), to as many as 10 levels, where eight intermediary institutions exist between the producer and consumers. With the exception of Japan, such long channels of distribution are quite rare in industrialized countries. Much more common are channel structure lengths ranging from two levels up to five levels. Figure 10.1 provides an illustration of typical channel structure lengths for consumer products in developed countries.

Many customer-based factors influence the length of the channel structure, such as the size of the customer base, their geographical dispersion, and their particular behavior patterns. The nature of the product, such as its bulk and weight, perishability, value, and technical complexity, can also be very important. For example, technically complex products such as X-ray machines often require short channels because of the high degree of technical support and liaison needed by customers, which may only be available directly from the manufacturer. Moreover, length can also be affected by the size of the manufacturer, its financial capacity, and its desire for control. In general, larger and more well-financed manufacturers have a greater capability to bypass intermediaries and use shorter channel structures.[9] Manufacturers desiring to exercise a high degree of control over the distribution of their products are also more likely to use shorter channel structures because the shorter the channel, the higher the degree of control. Polo, by Ralph Lauren apparel, for example, sells only through upscale department and specialty retailers as well as its own Web site to protect the fashion image of its products.

Intensity of Channel Structure

Channel intensity
refers to the number of intermediaries at each level of the marketing channel.

Intensive distribution
occurs when all possible intermediaries at a particular level of the channel are used.

Selective distribution
means that a carefully chosen group of intermediaries is used at a particular level in the marketing channel.

Channel intensity is usually described in terms of intensive distribution, selective distribution, or exclusive distribution. **Intensive distribution** means that all possible intermediaries at the particular level of the channel are used. **Selective distribution**

Figure 10.1	Examples of the Length of Dimensions of Marketing Channel Structure for Consumer Products

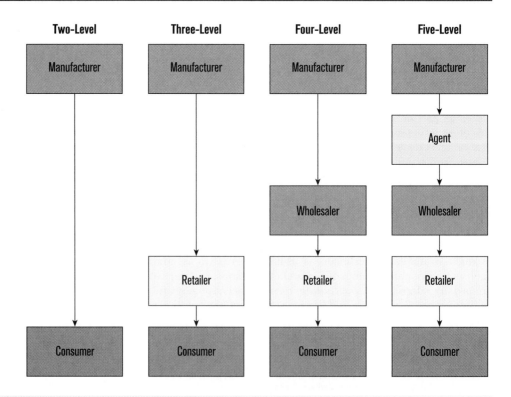

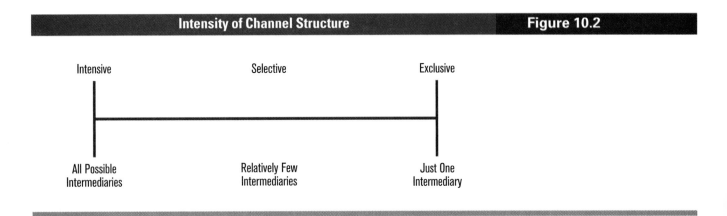

Intensity of Channel Structure — Figure 10.2

Intensive — Selective — Exclusive

All Possible Intermediaries — Relatively Few Intermediaries — Just One Intermediary

means that a smaller number of intermediaries are used, while **exclusive distribution** refers to only one intermediary used at the particular level of the channel to cover a defined territory. The intensity dimension of channel structure can be portrayed as a continuum as shown in Figure 10.2. Although there are many exceptions, in general, intensive distribution is associated with the distribution of convenience goods, selective distribution with shopping goods, and exclusive distribution with specialty goods. Thus, inexpensive Bic pens, Gillette razor blades, and Hallmark greeting cards (convenience goods) tend to be carried by large numbers of intermediaries, particularly at the retail level; while home appliances such as Whirlpool refrigerators and apparel such as Levi's jeans (shopping goods) are handled by relatively fewer retailers; and specialty goods such as Rolex watches or Rolls-Royce automobiles are featured by only one dealer in a specified geographical area (territory).

Exclusive distribution
occurs when only one intermediary is used at a particular level in the marketing channel.

http://www.bicworld.com
http://www.gillette.com
http://www.hallmark.com
http://www.whirlpool.com

http://www.snickers.com

Types of Intermediaries in the Channel Structure

This third dimension of channel structure refers to the different kinds of intermediary institutions that can be used at the various levels of the channel. At the retail level, there may be many possibilities for some products. For example, a Snickers candy bar can be sold through many different types of retailers such as candy stores, grocery stores, drugstores, supermarkets, mass merchandisers, discount department stores, and many others. For other products, such as automobiles, the choice is more limited. We should point out, however, that in recent years with the growth of *scrambled merchandising,* where all kinds of products are sold in stores not traditionally associated with those products, the types of stores that sell various products have broadened considerably. Motor oil, for example, is now regularly available in supermarkets, while hardware items are frequently found in drugstores. Consequently, manufacturers today need to be broadminded when considering the types of intermediaries to use in their channel structures. The conventional wisdom of particular products being distributed only through certain types of wholesalers or retailers may no longer hold. The largest U.S. seller of Dom Perignon champagne, for example, is Costco, a wholesale club usually known for selling bulk packs of basic groceries and general merchandise.[10]

DETERMINANTS OF CHANNEL STRUCTURE

The structure of marketing channels, in terms of their length, intensity, and types of participating intermediaries, is determined basically by three factors:

1. The distribution tasks that need to be performed
2. The economics of performing distribution tasks
3. Management's desire for control of distribution

Distribution Tasks

Distribution tasks, also often referred to as *marketing functions* or sometimes *channel functions,* have been described by various lists for many years. Such functions as buying, selling, risk taking, transportation, storage, order processing, and financing are commonly mentioned. More generalized terms can also be used to describe these tasks, such as *concentration, equalization,* and *dispersion*—whereby the main tasks of marketing channels are grouped together in familial relationships—bringing products together from many manufacturers (concentration), adjusting the quantities to balance supply and demand (equalization), and delivering them to final customers (dispersion). Others describe distribution tasks in terms of a sorting process: *accumulating* products from many producers, *sorting* them to correspond to designated target markets, and *assorting* them into conveniently associated groups to ease the shopping burden of customers. Distribution tasks have also been described in much more detailed terms where specific activities sometimes unique to the particular industry are cited.[11]

Regardless of the particular list of distribution tasks presented, the rationale is the same for all of them: Distribution functions must be performed in order to consummate transactions between buyers and sellers. The reason is that discrepancies exist between buyers and sellers that must be overcome through the performance of distribution tasks. The channel structure the firm chooses to perform these tasks reflects how the tasks are to be allocated to various marketing institutions such as wholesalers, retailers, agents, brokers, or others. The **discrepancies between production and consumption** can be separated into four basic groups:[12]

1. Discrepancies in quantity
2. Discrepancies in assortment
3. Discrepancies in time
4. Discrepancies in place

Discrepancies between production and consumption are differences in quantity, assortment, time, and place that must be overcome to make goods available to final customers.

Discrepancies in Quantity

The quantities in which products are manufactured to achieve low average costs are usually too large for any individual customer to use immediately. Wrigley's chewing gum,

Music Distribution: Who Needs CDs and Stores When Electrons Will Do

It wasn't so long ago that the CD was hailed as a great technological breakthrough in the world of music. An album of music that used to be a 12-inch plastic platter could now be put on a 4-inch minidisc. CDs are more durable and produce far better sound. Moreover, they take up much less shelf space in stores and are easier to send through the mail than the old LP records.

But as convenient and space efficient a technology as CDs are for delivering music, there's something even better—electrons traveling over the Internet. Instead of music being stored on and distributed from a physical disc it is now available on demand from the "thin air" of cyberspace.

It didn't take long for entrepreneurs and the public to catch on to this new music distribution technology. Napster, the best known of the free Internet-based music distribution services, led the way in providing hundreds of thousands of music titles to millions of users. Of course, the major record manufacturers, such as Sony, EMI, Capitol, Universal, and Warner, still in the business of selling music via CDs, were able to shut down Napster and similar sites after launching lawsuits based on copyright infringement.

The record companies, as well as many of the artists producing the music, argue that new technologies should not change the rules—pirating music is pirating whether it takes place using an LP, a CD, or the Internet. Eventually, a system will have to be worked out for distributing music over the Internet that is acceptable to all parties—the artists, record companies, and listeners. Clear Channel Communications, Inc., a major radio broadcasting conglomerate based in San Antonio, Texas, thinks it has a solution. Clear Channel is offering a subscription service it calls FullAudio for which listeners pay $10.00 a month to hear a certain number of songs over the Internet. The major record companies have also been experimenting with similar types of online music subscription services. In addition, many other independent entrepreneurs are trying to figure out how to use the Net to deliver music fairly, legally, and profitably.

So, while electrons moving over the Internet is a great technology for distributing music, it's going to take a lot of old-fashioned human thought and effort to keep those musical electrons flowing in a way that makes for harmony instead of discord.

---

for example, produces literally millions of packages of gum each day. Even the most ardent gum chewer could not possibly use that much gum every day! Thus, institutions in the channel structure, such as wholesalers and retailers, provide a buffer to absorb the vast output of manufacturers and provide the smaller quantities desired by individual customers.

Discrepancies in Assortment

Products are grouped for manufacturing purposes based on efficiencies of production, while customers group products based on convenience of shopping and consuming. In most cases, the production and consumption groupings are not inherently matched. For example, the thousands of items a consumer finds grouped so conveniently together in a supermarket are not, of course, produced by one manufacturer. Hundreds of relatively specialized manufacturers have made those products. The supermarket and many other intermediaries in marketing channels have performed the distribution tasks necessary to regroup this conglomeration of products, thereby overcoming the discrepancy in assortment. This enables particular manufacturers to concentrate on producing a relatively limited range of products, which when combined through marketing channels with the products of many other manufacturers, allows consumers to have wide and convenient assortments of products that greatly simplify shopping and consumption. Consumers need only stroll down the aisles, and place the chosen items in their shopping cart.

Discrepancies in Time

Most products are not manufactured for immediate consumption or use. Hence, some mechanism must be available to hold products between the time they are produced and needed by final customers. A bottle of Snapple iced tea, a Tommy Hilfiger shirt, or a pair of Rollerblade in-line skates are not desired by consumers at the instant they roll off the production line. So intermediaries in marketing channels, particularly merchant wholesalers and retailers, who take title to and physically hold goods until they are needed by consumers, are crucial in overcoming this discrepancy in time.

Discrepancies in Place

The location of manufacturing facilities for products is determined by such factors as raw material availability, labor costs, expertise, historical considerations, and numerous other factors that may have little to do with where the ultimate consumers of those products are located.[13] Thus, the production and consumption of products can literally take place half a world apart from each other. In fact, today it is more likely than ever that the products we buy are made in China, Singapore, Japan, Brazil, India, or some other faraway country than in some nearby factory. Channel structures evolve or are consciously designed to connect distant manufacturers and consumers by eliminating place discrepancies.

The Economics of Performing Distribution Tasks

Given that distribution tasks must be performed to overcome the four discrepancies discussed earlier, the channel structure needs to be organized to perform tasks as efficiently as possible. The development of efficient marketing channel structures is based on two principles: specialization or division of labor and transaction efficiency.[14]

Specialization or Division of Labor

The principle of **specialization or division of labor** underlies most modern production processes. Each worker in a factory focuses on performing particular manufacturing tasks and thereby develops specialized expertise and skills in performing those tasks. Such specialization results in much greater efficiency and higher output than if each worker were to perform all or most of the tasks necessary to manufacture the product him- or herself.

This 200-year-old principle which is illustrated in Figure 10.3 shows that it applies as much to distribution as it does to production. The various intermediaries in marketing

Specialization or division of labor
occurs when each participant in the marketing channel focuses on performing those activities at which it is most efficient.

channels are analogous to production workers or stations in a factory, but instead of performing production tasks, they are performing distribution tasks. These intermediaries—whether they are wholesalers, retailers, agents, or brokers—develop expertise in distribution that manufacturers would find uneconomical to match. Moreover, many large intermediaries, such as mass merchandisers, enjoy **economies of scale and economies of scope** that would be impossible for most manufacturers to match. Home Depot, for instance, with over 800 giant warehouse stores enjoys great economies of scale and scope, because it is able to spread its operating costs over a vast quantity and variety of products.

Economies of scale and economies of scope
are obtained by spreading the costs of distribution over a large quantity of products (scale) or over a wide variety of products (scope).

Specialization and Division of Labor Principle: Production versus Distribution for an Electric Guitar Manufacturer	Figure 10.3

Production

Production Tasks

1. Thicknessing the Wood
2. Shaping the Body and the Neck
3. Gluing and Clamping the Parts
4. Sanding and Assembly
5. Applying the Finish
6. Installing the Electric Components
7. Attaching the Machine Heads and Strings
8. Adjusting the Action and Pickups

Distribution

Distribution Tasks

1. Buying
2. Selling
3. Transferring the Title
4. Transportation
5. Storage
6. Processing Orders
7. Providing Information

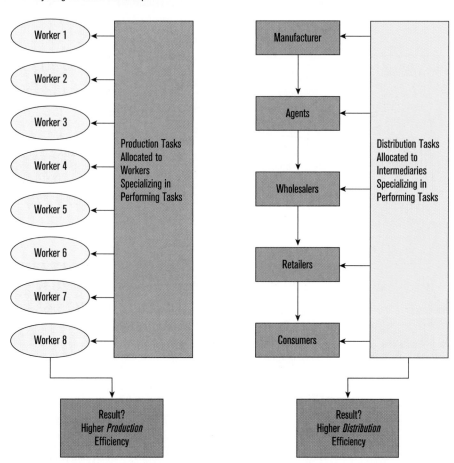

Source: Bert Rosenbloom, *Marketing Channels: A Management View*, 6th ed. (Fort Worth, TX: The Dryden Press, 1999), 20.

Transaction efficiency
refers to designing marketing channels to minimize the number of contacts between producers and consumers.

Transaction Efficiency

Transaction efficiency refers to the effort to reduce the number of transactions between producers and consumers. If many producers attempt to deal directly with large numbers of consumers, the number of transactions can be enormous. Paradoxically, by lengthening the channel structure through the addition of intermediaries, the number of transactions can actually be reduced. Consequently, transaction efficiency is increased. This is illustrated in Figure 10.4. As shown in the figure, the number of transactions has been cut in half as a result of the introduction of the retailer into the channel structure. Given that the costs of transactions can be very high, especially if personal face-to-face meetings are necessary to consummate transactions, the reduction in contacts through the use of intermediaries in the channel structure is in many cases absolutely vital for economical distribution.

Management's Desire for Control of Distribution

Even though the economics of the performance of distribution tasks may seem to call for a particular type of marketing channel structure, a firm's desire for control of the marketing channel may outweigh the economic considerations.[15] In general, the shorter the channel structure, the higher the degree of control, and vice versa. Further, the lower the intensity of distribution, the higher the degree of control, and vice versa. For example, suppose an economic analysis, based on specialization/division of labor and transaction efficiencies, calls for a long marketing channel structure with a fairly high degree of intensity at the various levels. However, management in the manufacturing firm feels a

| Figure 10.4 | How the Introduction of an Intermediary Reduces the Number of Transactions |

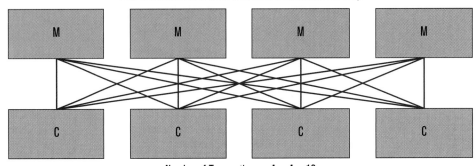

Four Manufacturers Deal with Four Consumers Directly

Number of Transactions = 4 × 4 = 16

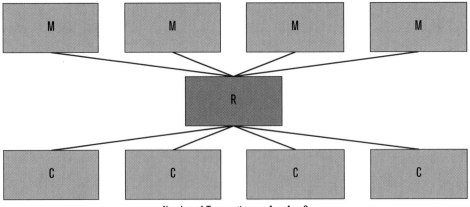

Four Manufacturers Use One Retailer to Deal with Four Consumers

Number of Transactions = 4 + 4 = 8

need to protect the image of the product and also believes it is necessary to provide high levels of customer service. To do so, the manufacturer is convinced that it needs a high degree of control, and so it may opt for only one level of intermediary, with a very high degree of selectivity in appointing them as channel members, based on their willingness to take direction from the manufacturer. This is exactly the situation Gucci, the Italian maker of world-famous luxury goods, found itself in. Focusing mainly on gaining distribution efficiency, Gucci ended up selling its products through several thousand retailers. This proliferation of retailers—many of whom were not of the highest stature—although providing economies of scale in the distribution of Gucci products, adversely affected the exclusive image of Gucci. Realizing the problem, Gucci restructured its marketing channels by drastically reducing the number of retailers selling its products to less than 500 worldwide. Moreover, all of these retailers were of the highest quality, and were willing to take close direction from Gucci to project a world-class quality image vital to the long-term success of Gucci. In contrast, a brand such as Fruit of the Loom underwear, which uses intensive distribution would have far less concern about control of the channel than Gucci.

FLOWS IN MARKETING CHANNELS

LEARNING OBJECTIVE 2

When a marketing channel is developed, a series of *channel flows* emerge. These flows provide the links that tie channel members and other agencies together in the distribution of goods and services. The most important of these flows are the (1) product flow, (2) negotiation flow, (3) ownership flow, (4) information flow, and (5) promotion flow. These flows are illustrated for Coors beer in Figure 10.5.

The *product flow* refers to the actual physical movement of the product from the manufacturer (Coors) through all of the parties who take physical possession of the product, from its point of production to consumers. In the case of Coors beer, the product comes from breweries and packaging plants in Colorado, Tennessee, and Virginia by way of company trucks or common carriers (transportation companies) to beer distributors (wholesalers), who in turn ship the product (usually in their own trucks) to liquor stores, supermarkets, convenience stores, restaurants, and bars (retailers), where it is finally purchased by consumers.

Flows in the Marketing Channels for Coors Beer | **Figure 10.5**

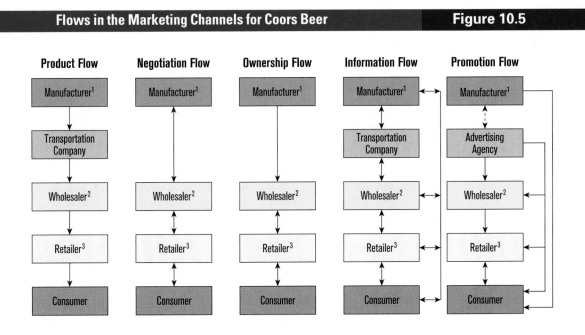

[1]Brewers and packaging plants.
[2]Beer distributors.
[3]Liquor stores, supermarkets, convenience stores, restaurants, and bars.

The *negotiation flow* represents the interplay of the buying and selling tasks associated with the transfer of title to Coors products. Notice in Figure 10.5 that the transportation firm is not included in this flow because it does not participate in the negotiation tasks of buying, selling, and transferring title. Notice also that the arrows flow in *both* directions, indicating that negotiations involve a mutual exchange between buyers and sellers at all levels of the channel.

The *ownership flow* shows the movement of the title to the product as it is passed along from the manufacturer to final consumers. Here again, the transportation firm is not involved because it does not take title to the product, nor is it actively involved in facilitating its transfer. It is only engaged in the transportation of the physical product itself.

Turning now to the *information flow*, we see that the transportation firm has reappeared, since all parties participate in the exchange of information. We also see that all of the arrows showing the flow from the manufacturer to consumers are two-directional, as the flow of information can be either up or down. For example, Coors may obtain information from the transportation company about its shipping schedule and rates, and the transportation company may in turn seek information from Coors about when and in what quantities it plans to ship the product. The flow of information sometimes bypasses the transportation firm, as shown by the arrow leading from the manufacturer (at the right-hand side of the box) directly to the wholesalers, retailers, and consumers. This route of information flow occurs when the information sought does not concern the transportation company, such as details associated with the buying, selling, or promotion of Coors products.[16] For example, if the manufacturer makes available to beer distributors a special reduced price on particular beer varieties, such as Coors Zima Clear Brew or Coors Extra Gold beer, this information would be passed directly to the beer distributors, and would not be of concern to the transportation firm.

Finally, the *promotion flow* refers to the flow of persuasive communication in the form of advertising, personal selling, sales promotion, and public relations. Here, a new party, the advertising agency, is included in the flow because the agency is actively involved in providing and maintaining the promotion flow, especially the advertising component of promotion. The two-directional arrow connected by a broken line between the manufacturer and advertising agency is meant to show that the manufacturer and advertising agency work together closely to develop promotional strategies. All other arrows are one-directional from the advertising agency, or directly from the manufacturer to the other parties in the marketing channel.

The concept of channel flows help us to understand the scope and complexity of marketing channels. By thinking in terms of the five flows, it becomes obvious that marketing channels involve much more than just the physical flow of the product through the channel. The other flows (negotiation, ownership, information, and promotion) must also be coordinated to make products conveniently available to customers. Moreover, the concept of **flows in marketing channels** captures the dynamic nature of marketing channels. The word *flow* suggests movement or a fluid state, and in fact this is the nature of marketing channels. New forms of distribution emerge, different types of intermediaries appear in the channel while others drop out, and unusual competitive structures close off some avenues of distribution and open up others. Changing patterns of buyer behavior and new forms of technology such as the Internet add yet another dimension of change. Channel flows need to be adapted and managed to meet such changes.[17]

Flows in marketing channels
are the movement of products, negotiation, ownership, information, and promotion through each participant in the marketing channel.

MARKETING CHANNELS AS SOCIAL SYSTEMS

LEARNING OBJECTIVE 3

Once viewed only as economic systems, marketing channels are now seen as social systems as well because they involve people interacting with each other in different organizations and institutions. Consequently, the rules that govern channel relationships are not only a matter of economics. In the broader social systems perspective, marketing channels are subject to the same behavioral processes associated with all social systems.[18] The behavioral processes of most significance in marketing channels are power and conflict.

Power in Marketing Channels

Marketing channel power refers to the capacity of one channel member to influence the behavior of another channel member. McDonald's, for example, as the franchiser of the world's largest chain of fast-food restaurants has been able to exercise tremendous power over its franchisees. Indeed, it is probably not an exaggeration to say that no king or queen ever had any more power over their subjects than McDonald's enjoys over its franchisees. McDonald's operates what is known as a business format franchise. Under this arrangement, not only the products the franchisees sell, but also virtually all aspects of their operations from the design of the restaurants to the smallest details of operating procedures, such as how long french fries should be cooked, are controlled by McDonald's. All of these provisions are included in minute detail in a franchise contract which, once signed by the franchisees, means that they are legally bound to abide by all of the provisions spelled out in the contract. Thus, the social system in which McDonald's and its thousands of affiliated franchisees operate is probably closer to being a dictatorship than a democracy because McDonald's has most of the power.

For decades, most McDonald's franchisees were delighted with this unequal power relationship because a major source of McDonald's power came from its ability to reward the franchisees in the form of fat profits that turned thousands of them into millionaires. So, as long as most of the franchisees were making plenty of money, they were not very vocal about McDonald's dictatorial tactics. Recently though, some franchisees are no longer content to let McDonald's rule the roost. These franchisees are especially concerned about McDonald's opening too many restaurants that takes sales away from existing franchisees. Some franchisees have even initiated lawsuits in the hope of using the legal system to gain countervailing power to offset McDonald's power over them.[19]

Marketing channel power
is the capacity of one channel member to influence the behavior of another channel member.

Conflict in Marketing Channels

Conflict in marketing channels is usually defined as goal-impeding behavior by one or more channel members. In other words, when one channel member takes actions that another channel member perceives as reducing its ability to achieve its goals, conflict

Conflict in marketing channels
occurs when one channel member believes that another channel member is impeding the attainment of its goals.

can result. In the McDonald's case just mentioned, for example, McDonald's behavior in the form of opening so many new restaurants near existing ones was seen as goal-impeding behavior by franchisees who owned established restaurants in the same territories. They believed that McDonald's attempt to enhance its own bottom line by setting up so many new restaurants was hurting the franchisees' ability to reach their profit goals. Some of these conflicts have become so intense that lawsuits have been initiated by the franchisees.

Conflicts can also arise between producers of products and other channel members when the producer attempts to force channel members to buy a particular product as a condition for access to another product. Such tying arrangements were allegedly practiced by Microsoft when it forced computer makers such as Compaq and Dell to install its Internet Explorer browser software instead of rival Netscape's Navagator browser as a condition of the computer maker receiving the Windows operating system.[20] Since virtually all personal computers rely on Microsoft Windows, the computer makers had little choice but to use Microsoft's Internet Explorer. The U.S. Justice Department found Microsoft's behavior to be illegal because it violated the Sherman Antitrust Act by creating a monopoly position for Microsoft.[21]

Other marketing channel strategies that can create conflicts among channel members include exclusive dealing whereby a manufacturer requires channel members to carry only its brand, price discrimination where a producer or manufacturer charges different prices to the same class of channel member for the same products, and territorial restrictions where a producer or manufacturer dictates where a channel member such as a wholesaler can sell its products.[22]

MARKETING CHANNEL MANAGEMENT

Marketing channel management
refers to the analysis, planning, organizing, and controlling of a firm's marketing channels.

Interorganizational context
refers to channel management that extends beyond a firm's own organization into independent businesses.

Marketing channel management, frequently shortened to the term *channel management*, refers to the analysis, planning, organizing, and controlling of a firm's marketing channels.[23] Channel management can be a challenging and complex process, not only because many aspects are involved, but also because of the difficulties arising from the **interorganizational context** of the channel structure. That is, marketing channels are made up of independent business organizations such as manufacturers, wholesalers, and retailers as well as agents and brokers who, although linked together in a relationship to form a marketing channel, are still independent businesses. As such, these firms have their own objectives, policies, strategies, and operating procedures, which may or may not be congruent with those of the other members of the channel. Indeed, as mentioned earlier in this chapter, sometimes they come into outright conflict. Moreover, in marketing channels, usually there are no clear superior/subordinate relationships, or lines of authority, so typical of management in single-firm intraorganizational settings. Hence, managing marketing channels is frequently more challenging than managing within the intraorganizational setting of a single firm.

PERSPECTIVES FOR CHANNEL MANAGEMENT

Channel management can be viewed from two basic vantage points:

1. From that of the producer or manufacturer looking "down the channel" toward the market
2. From that of the retailer (or other final reseller) looking "up the channel" back to the producer or manufacturer

Although either of these perspectives is valid for examining the subject of channel management, the first one (the producer or manufacturer looking down the channel toward the market) is by far the most commonly used perspective. Indeed, virtually all modern analysis and research on the subject is from this vantage point. This is probably because channel management is regarded as a part of the larger field of marketing management, which has almost universally been treated from the perspective of the producer or manufacturer. Consequently, our discussion of channel management will be from the producer/manufacturer perspective.

DECISION AREAS OF CHANNEL MANAGEMENT

LEARNING OBJECTIVE **4**

Channel management viewed from the perspective of the producer or manufacturer looking down the channel toward the market can be divided into six basic decision areas:

1. Formulating channel strategy
2. Designing the channel structure
3. Selecting the channel members
4. Motivating the channel members
5. Coordinating channel strategy with the marketing mix
6. Evaluating channel member performance

Figure 10.6 provides an overview of these decision areas. The rest of this section of the chapter is organized around a discussion of each of these areas of channel management.

Formulating Channel Strategy

Channel strategy refers to the broad set of principles by which a firm seeks to achieve its distribution objectives to satisfy its customers. The Saturn Division of General Motors, for example, developed an innovative channel strategy to meet the needs of a large segment of customers who were dissatisfied with the car buying experience available through existing automobile marketing channels. These customers did not want the high-pressure, sales gimmicks, and price haggling so common in traditional auto dealerships. Thus, Saturn's channel strategy provided a revolutionary way of selling cars through dealerships that would not pressure customers to buy, that would provide them with detailed product information, charge one price, and offer a 30-day return policy.[24]

Channel strategy
is the broad set of principles by which a firm seeks to achieve its distribution objectives to satisfy its customers.

http://www.saturnbp.com

Major Decision Areas of Channel Management — **Figure 10.6**

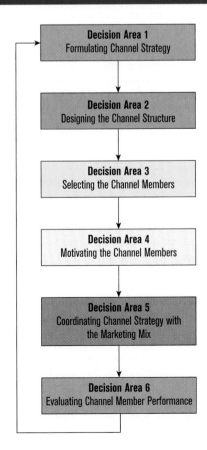

Sustainable competitive advantage
is a competitive edge that cannot be easily or quickly copied by competitors in the short run.

http://www.chrysler.com

http://www.wd40.com

http://www.3M.com

http://www.dupont.com

http://www.ge.com

This channel strategy involved a huge investment and commitment by Saturn, because the new General Motors division had to plan and organize for the selection and training of dealers to create an entirely new marketing channel structure and culture for selling cars, which previously had not existed in automobile marketing channels. Saturn felt that such an effort was worthwhile because the firm hoped to achieve a **sustainable competitive advantage** through its innovative marketing channel strategy—believing that Ford and Chrysler would find it much more difficult and time-consuming to develop their own new marketing channels comparable to Saturn's than it would be to imitate a new product feature, price incentive, or advertising campaign that Saturn might offer.

In recent years, more firms are discovering the value of innovative channel strategy for creating a sustainable competitive advantage.[25] These firms realize that of the four Ps of the marketing mix—product, pricing, promotion, place—only place (marketing channels) provides shelter from quick imitation by competitors. Why? Simply because rapid technology transfer has made it difficult, if not impossible, to hold on to a competitive advantage based on the P of superior products; competitors, domestic or foreign, can quickly match virtually any product innovation. Holding on to the P of a pricing advantage is even more difficult, because global competition ensures that a competitor somewhere in the world will match or beat the price. The other P, promotion, also does not provide for much sustainability, because there is simply too much advertising from literally thousands of promotional messages knocking each other out of the box in short order.

So channel strategy has moved to the center stage of marketing strategy as firms seek to gain a leg up on the competition that they can hold onto for awhile. The range of firms using this approach cuts across many products and industries: WD-40, for example, the lubricating product that is present in 75 percent of U.S. homes, has used channel strategy to beat back such giants as 3M, DuPont, and General Electric who for years have tried to replace WD-40 with competing products. By paying extraordinary attention to keeping retailers happy with high-profit deals and special merchandise campaigns, WD-40 created a kind of big happy family between itself and tens of thousands of

Using Her Degree in Direct Relation to the Fourth P

During her time at Texas A&M University, it was not difficult for Eleanor Shaw to decide on a major. She knew all along that she wanted to study business; but the difficulty came at graduation when she was clueless as to what she actually wanted to do with this degree.

I would stroll the halls of the career fair and nothing seemed to spark my interest. Fortunately, I was forced to make a quick decision and accepted the position as a marketing analyst for Chef America, Inc., the makers of HOT POCKETS® Brand stuffed sandwiches.

As a marketing analyst for Chef America, I am exposed to many aspects of the marketing mix. I was lucky to find an entry-level marketing position that incorporates many aspects of the business, so that while learning and "paying my dues" I do not go mad staring at a computer screen all day. As the club analyst, I focus primarily on the warehouse club business for Sam's Clubs and Costco. HOT POCKETS® Brand stuffed sandwiches reach final consumers through many different channels: traditional retail, institutional food service, and warehouse clubs. Selling the product through the clubs requires a different combination of the marketing mix compared to more traditional retailers, because of the differences in the structure of the channels and the unique buying patterns of the customers.

Although the product sold in clubs is essentially the same as that sold in grocery stores, the other Ps of the marketing mix are quite different. Promotion is very limited in the clubs. I am responsible for coordinating graphic changes to packaging. The packaging must be enough to entice the consumer to purchase the product, because little else is used for promotional purposes. Of course the price usually adds value, but the club consumer must be willing to buy in bulk.

The biggest difference between selling in clubs and traditional retailers is place. *By selling to the clubs, we are reaching a different consumer than that found in the grocery store. Understanding this unique channel can determine the success of our products reaching consumers through the clubs. Coordination and timing are crucial to the introduction of a new item, and the channel structure can greatly affect the timing. Even within an individual club chain there are different types of structures to be considered. For example, Sam's Clubs use both cross-docking and traditional warehousing. Club buyers typically have more power than grocery store chains and are able to influence which items are sold. This makes it more important to exchange information to ensure that customers receive the products they desire and distribution objectives are met. Wal-Mart/Sam's provides a unique and extremely helpful information system to its vendors called Retail Link. I am always gathering sales and inventory information from this system to feed back through the channel. By understanding this information, we are better able to control this aspect of the marketing mix. We might be able to create a great product, but it must reach the consumer to be a successful product.*

Retail and trade marketing analysts at Chef America focus on other aspects of the marketing mix that more strongly influence the success of HOT POCKETS® Brand stuffed sandwiches in other areas. For example, some analysts direct much attention to the success and failure of specific promotions. But, as the club analyst, much of my time is devoted to understanding the unique channel structure in which the warehouse clubs work.

retailers. The Coca-Cola company has run circles around PepsiCo all over the world through superior channel strategy, not only by focusing on giant distributors and retailers, but by paying attention to the little channel members as well.[26] In Japan, for example, Coca-Cola publishes trade magazines and holds special seminars for owners of *sakayas* (mom-and-pop stores) on how to operate more efficiently and compete with more modern outlets. In Paris, Coke uses 5-foot inflatable Coca-Cola cans to help hundreds of tiny street corner shops. Heavy earth-moving equipment manufacturer Caterpillar has emphasized channel strategy to gain a sustainable competitive advantage by building a superior dealer organization that guarantees critical parts delivery anywhere in the world within 48 hours. This emphasis came in handy not very long ago when fierce product competition from Japanese companies threatened Caterpillar's very existence. And of course, Amazon.com turned the book industry on its head with its strategy of using Internet-based marketing channels to sell books. Barnes & Noble, Borders, and other competitors are scratching their heads trying to copy Amazon.com's channel strategy but so far with limited success.[27]

http://www.caterpillar.com

Designing the Channel Structure

Having considered the overall strategic role of channel strategy in the firm, management needs to turn its attention to the job of designing the firm's marketing channels. Channel design is the process of developing new channels where none had existed before, or making significant modifications to existing channels. The process of channel design can be broken down into four basic phases:

1. Setting distribution objectives
2. Specifying the distribution tasks that need to be performed by the channel
3. Considering alternative channel structures
4. Choosing an optimal channel structure

These phases are depicted in Figure 10.7.

Setting Distribution Objectives

Distribution objectives refer to what the firm would like its channel strategy to accomplish in terms of meeting the needs of its customers. At this stage of channel design then, distribution objectives need to be stated from the point of view of the customer. This is sometimes referred to as the bottom up or backward approach to channel design because the starting point for designing the channel is also the end point of the channel—the customer. This is precisely the approach taken by Saturn discussed earlier. Saturn asked the question: "What do our customers want when they go out to buy automobiles?" The company then formulated its distribution objectives in terms of developing auto dealerships that could provide the friendly, helpful, no-haggle environment sought by customers.

Dell Computer provides another example of setting distribution objectives from the bottom up, so as to design marketing channels that meet the needs of customers better than the competition. Michael Dell founded the company after experiencing frustration when trying to buy computers from dealers who knew less about computers than he did. This frustration is what led Dell to develop a direct channel using the telephone and then the Internet. When customers called or logged in, they were able to get information and advice of much better quality than they had received from computer stores, because the people staffing the phones or responding to e-mail were knowledgeable computer sales-

| **Figure 10.7** | **Phases of the Channel Design Process** |

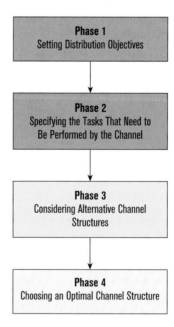

people rather than minimum-wage store clerks. The person-to-person interaction available in this channel enabled Dell to provide customized high-performance computers, technical support, and other value-added services to a segment of sophisticated personal computer users who wanted more than what was available from existing retail computer channels. Dell's innovative channel design of direct sales to customers via telephone has proved to be spectacularly successful, making Michael Dell a multibillionaire in the process.

Specifying the Distribution Tasks

Making products available to final consumers—how, when, and where they want them—calls for the performance of numerous distribution tasks such as storage, inventory control, order processing, transportation, order tracking, and many others.[28]

Firms often make the mistake of underestimating the level of detail and subtlety involved in particular industries. Consider, for example, what happened to the Snapple Beverage Corporation soon after it was purchased by Quaker Oats Company. By tying Snapple in with its highly successful Gatorade, Quaker hoped to gain tremendous synergy for the two drinks. So, Quaker designed a channel for Snapple that paralleled the channel for Gatorade, which was from factory to retailers' warehouses, from which individual stores then ordered what they needed to keep their shelves stocked. Quaker knew this pattern well and was comfortable with it. But Quaker failed to realize that unlike Gatorade, which was treated in the channel as a consumer packaged product such as cereal, Snapple had to compete in the soft-drink market. The channel for soft drinks places a much heavier burden on the producer and/or distributors, because individual stores do not usually place orders for soft drinks on an as-needed basis and then stock their own shelves. Instead, they rely on bottlers and distributors to perform these distribution tasks for them. Quaker had not arranged with these intermediaries to perform these tasks for retailers, and hence Quaker was totally out of step with industry practice. Quaker's failure to understand this distribution task performance requirement deprived Snapple of the retail shelf space it needed to compete in the intensely competitive soft-drink market. Within a couple of years, Quaker gave up and sold Snapple at a huge loss.

http://www.snapple.com

Considering Alternative Channel Structures

As discussed earlier in this chapter, the form or shape the channel takes to perform the distribution tasks is referred to as the channel structure. Also recall that the channel structure has three dimensions: (1) length, (2) intensity, and (3) the types of intermediaries used.

In terms of *length,* the number of alternatives available to a firm is usually limited to three or four at a maximum. These may range from using a direct structure from manufacturer to final customer as in the case of Dell Computer; one level of intermediaries as used by Saturn (auto retailers); two levels as used by Coors beer (wholesalers and retailers); or three levels of intermediaries, where an agent or broker may appear in the channel structure, which is common for many imported products.

The number of alternatives in the *intensity* dimension is even more limited, because intensity is so closely related to the nature of the product in question. Thus, the only realistic alternative for products intended for mass markets, such as Gillette razor blades, is intensive distribution in order to provide adequate market coverage. At the other end of the spectrum, expensive or prestigious products, such as BMW automobiles, require highly selective or even exclusive distribution to help maintain the aura and quality image of the product.

http://www.bmw.com

Management's range of alternatives for the third dimension of channel structure, the *types of intermediaries* to use, is usually broader than for the first two. Within reason, management is limited only by its imagination in deciding what kinds of distributors it wants to include in its channel structure.[29] Supermarkets, for example, now sell all kinds of products besides groceries. Schnucks Markets Inc. of St. Louis sells furniture, exercise equipment, bed linens, TVs, and VCRs. HyVee, a supermarket chain based in Des Moines, has gone a step further with upscale merchandise such as $200 clocks, $250 tea sets, and $270 humidors.[30] So-called drug stores now sell almost every kind of product in addition to drugs. And it is now possible to buy virtually anything from all types of firms operating on the Internet.[31]

http://www.schnucks.com

Choosing an Optimal Structure

Many different approaches have been suggested over the years for choosing an optimal channel structure. Formal management science approaches, financial capital budgeting methods, and distribution cost analysis techniques have all been offered as a means for choosing channel structure. For the most part, these methods have not found much use in the real world. Much more common are approaches that rely on managerial judgment accompanied by some data on distribution costs and profit potentials. Judgment approaches can be made more formal through explicit identification of criteria to be used in choosing the channel structure. The most basic of these are:

- *Market variables:* The location of final customers, the numbers of customers and their density, together with their patterns of buying behavior are the key market variables to consider.
- *Product variables:* Such factors as bulk and weight, unit value, newness, technical versus nontechnical, and perishability are product variables that are frequently important.
- *Company variables:* The financial capacity of the firm, its size, expertise, and desire for managerial control are some of the most important company variables.
- *Intermediary variables:* Cost, availability, and services provided are indicative of intermediary variables that management needs to consider.
- *Behavioral variables:* Factors such as the potential of particular channel structures to reduce conflict, while maximizing power, are key behavioral variables for management to consider.
- *External environmental variables:* Finally, variables such as economic conditions, sociocultural changes, competitive structure, technology, and government regulations are all important environmental variables to consider when choosing channel structure.

Apple Computer considered all of these variables in deciding to establish a new channel consisting of a chain of its own retail stores. Market variables were considered via Apple's belief that existing independent retailers and Apple's own Web site were not covering the market sufficiently to reach Apple's target market. Product variables were of major concern because Apple felt that its highly innovative products needed a special "showcase" in the form of upscale company-owned stores staffed by knowledgeable Apple salespeople. The crucial company variable that Apple weighed was its desire for control of how its products were marketed. The company-owned stores channel would provide such control.

Intermediary variables were examined in terms of a lack of existing computer retailers that could meet Apple's desired standards for representing its products. The power to control its own destiny was the behavioral variable Apple focused on in establishing its own stores. Rather then face power struggles with giant retailers, Apple hoped to outflank them with its own stores.

Finally, at least two environmental variables played a role in Apple's decision to establish its new channel: competitive structure and sociocultural changes. Apple wanted to avoid going head-to-head in the mass market for home computers so it chose to deemphasize distribution through mass retail merchandisers where competition would be most intense. From a sociocultural perspective, Apple's vision of the computer as having unlimited possibilities for enhancing peoples' lives as they work and play called for a channel that could spark the public's imagination every time a customer set foot in one of its exciting retail stores.[32]

Selecting Channel Members

The selection of channel members, the last phase of channel design, consists of four steps:

1. Developing selection criteria
2. Finding prospective channel members
3. Evaluating prospective channel members against certain criteria
4. Converting prospective members into actual members

Developing Selection Criteria

Although general lists of **selection criteria**, such as those shown in Figure 10.8, can provide a framework, each firm needs to develop criteria for selecting channel members that are consistent with its own distribution objectives and strategies. Thus, the list of criteria for a firm practicing highly selective distribution, such as Polo by Ralph Lauren, might include such factors as the prospective channel member's reputation and the competing product lines it carries. A firm using very intensive distribution, such as Bic pens, might use little more than one criterion consisting of the ability of the prospective channel members to pay the manufacturer for the products it ships to them.

Selection criteria are the factors that a firm uses to choose which intermediaries will become members of its marketing channel.

Finding Prospective Channel Members

The search for prospective channel members can utilize a number of sources. If the manufacturer has its own outside field sales force, this is generally regarded as the best prospect source because of the sales personnel's knowledge of prospective channel members in their territories. Other useful sources include customers, advertising, trade shows, and the Internet. Usually, a combination of several of these sources is used to find prospective channel members at both the wholesale and retail levels.[33]

Evaluating Prospective Channel Members

Once prospective channel members have been identified, they need to be assessed against certain criteria to determine those who will actually be selected. This can be done by an individual manager (such as the sales manager) or by a committee. Depending on the importance of the selection decision, such a committee might well include top management, up to and including the chairman of the board, if the selection decision is of great strategic importance. For example, when Goodyear Tire and Rubber Company selected Sears Roebuck and Company to sell its tires, Goodyear's CEO was involved in the decision because it had long-term strategic implications for Goodyear.

General Criteria for Selecting Channel Members	Figure 10.8

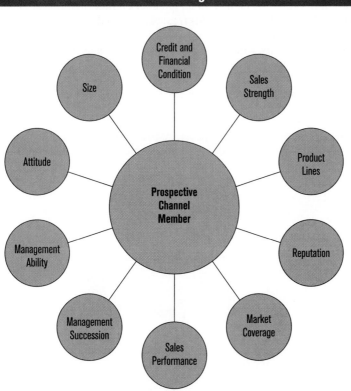

Converting Prospective Members into Actual Members

It is important to remember that the selection process is a two-way street. Not only do producers and manufacturers select retailers, wholesalers, or various agents and brokers, and franchisers select franchisees, but these intermediaries also select manufacturers and franchisers. Indeed, quite often it is the intermediaries, especially large and powerful retailers and wholesalers, who are in the driver's seat when it comes to selection. Wal-Mart for example can pick and choose virtually any manufacturers it wants. Consequently, the manufacturers or franchisers seeking to secure the services of quality channel members have to make a convincing case that selling their products will be profitable for the channel members.

Motivating Channel Members

Motivating channel members
is the action taken by a manufacturer or franchiser to get channel members to implement its channel strategies.

Motivating channel members refers to the actions taken by manufacturers (or franchisers) to get channel members to implement their channel strategy. Because efforts to motivate channel members take place in the interorganizational setting of the marketing channel, the process is usually more difficult than motivation in the intraorganizational setting of a single firm. Motivation in the marketing channel can be viewed as a sequence of phases:

1. Learning about the needs and problems of channel members
2. Offering support to channel members to help meet their needs and solve their problems
3. Providing ongoing leadership

Although the stages in the motivation process are sequential, the process repeats itself because of the continuous feedback from steps 2 and 3. This is illustrated in Figure 10.9.

Learning about Channel Members' Needs and Problems

If manufacturers or franchisers expect strong cooperation from channel members, their channel strategies should meet channel members' needs and help solve their problems. But this is easier said than done, because it is all too easy for manufacturers or franchisers to project their own views onto channel members rather than investigate the channel members' views. McDonald's fell into this trap when it tried to gain franchisee support for its ill-fated Campaign 55 strategy. Campaign 55 was introduced by McDonald's in the late 1990s and then hastily withdrawn after dismal customer response and even worse reactions by most McDonald's franchisees. The Campaign 55 promotion consisted of a special price deal on the famous Big Mac, which sold for 55 cents during the promotion in honor of the founding of McDonald's in 1955. But to get the 55-cent price, consumers

Figure 10.9	**The Motivation Process in Marketing Channels**

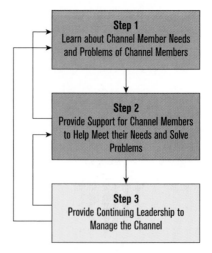

had to buy a drink and fries along with the Big Mac. Consumers balked at the strings-attached promotion, while competitors like Burger King and Wendy's jumped on McDonald's in their advertisements by offering special deals with no strings. The franchisees were furious with McDonald's because they were not consulted and hence felt that the program was rammed down their throats. Had the franchisees been asked, most would have rejected the Campaign 55 promotion because they believed that it would be a big money loser for them. But what was most troubling was that many franchisees viewed this strategy as akin to using a "Bandaid to cure cancer." Campaign 55 was seen as a superficial, quick-fix gimmick that ignored more fundamental underlying needs and problems that franchisees were experiencing, including lack of exciting new products to sell, pricing pressures, and franchisee proliferation.

McDonald's could have foreseen the problem if they had done a better job of learning about the real needs and problems of channel members. They should have avoided the tendency to project their own views and biases onto their channel members by taking a proactive approach to learning about channel member needs and problems.[34] This could have been accomplished through such approaches as: (1) researching channel members using in-house research teams, (2) investigating channel members using outside researchers, and (3) using channel member advisory committees.

In-house research consists of taking the same research methods used to gather information about final customers, and applying them to channel members in order to learn about their needs and problems. Outside research can be used by firms who do not have an in-house research capability, or by those firms that want to avoid the possible bias that can creep into in-house research. A channel member advisory committee consists of channel member representatives and key executives from the manufacturer or franchiser who meet on a regular basis in some neutral location. This type of close interaction can foster the kind of candid dialogue needed to uncover channel member needs and problems, which may not emerge in the normal course of business.

Offering Support for Channel Members

Providing support for channel members can be done in a variety of ways, from an informal hit-or-miss approach to carefully planned strategic alliances.[35]

Informal support approaches are the most common in traditional channels. Advertising dollars, promotional support, incentives, contests, and increasingly in recent years slotting fees (cash payments to channel members to gain shelf space) are frequently offered by manufacturers to jump-start the channel members' efforts to push the manufacturer's products. But these are often no more than cases of throwing money at a particular need or problem without thinking too deeply about it.

Strategic alliances or *channel partnerships*, however, represent a more substantial and continuous commitment between the manufacturer and channel members. Support provided by the manufacturer is based on extensive knowledge of the needs and problems of the channel members and is carried out on a long-term basis. There are often specific performance expectations that have been worked out by the manufacturer in conjunction with the channel members. Procter & Gamble and Wal-Mart, for example, have built one of the strongest strategic alliances in the consumer packaged-goods industry. This partnership emphasizes close working relationships, including stationing P&G executives permanently on-site at Wal-Mart's headquarters to stay in close touch with Wal-Mart's top management. A sophisticated EDI system also provides a super efficient means for assuring availability of P&G products in all 2,800 Wal-Mart stores.

Vertical marketing systems (VMSs) provide another means through which support can be provided for channel members. VMSs have been defined as "professionally managed or centrally programmed networks, preengineered to achieve operating economies and maximum impact."[36] There are three basic types of VMSs: (1) administered, (2) contractual, and (3) corporate.[37]

An *administered VMS* is characterized by a careful and comprehensive program developed by one of the channel members to support the efforts of other channel members. Ethan Allen Interiors Inc., a furniture maker, is a good example of an administered VMS. Ethan Allen sells its furniture through more than 300 independent retailers. These retailers, called Ethan Allen Galleries, carry no competing products from other manufacturers. The appearance of the store from architecture to lighting and display is controlled by Ethan Allen, as is the method of selling. Rather than use retail salespeople, the stores have "designers" who help customers select furniture according to the designer's decorating plan. Advertising, special events, promotions, and sales are also developed and run by Ethan Allen rather than by the independent retailers. How successful is this administered VMS? At least for Ethan Allen and its retail channel members the payoff has been better than average profits by competing on quality, service, and customer assistance rather than price as is so common in conventional marketing channels for furniture.

Contractual VMSs consist mainly of retail cooperatives, wholesaler-sponsored voluntary chains, and franchise systems. Retail cooperatives are created when a group of retailers unites and agrees to pool its buying power and contribute to the operation of the cooperative by collectively supporting its own professionally managed advertising, store design, information systems, and other major management tasks. The cooperative thus operates similarly to a large corporate chain store organization even though each retailer in the cooperative retains its independent status. With over 5,000 independent hardware stores, Servistar is one of the best-known retail cooperatives. The support provided by the cooperative to each of the independent retailers has enabled them to stay in business even in the face of competition from giant hardware chains such as Home Depot and Lowe's.

Wholesaler-sponsored voluntary chains are similar to retail cooperatives except that it is a wholesaler that gets large numbers of retailers to work together. By agreeing to buy a major portion of their inventories from the sponsoring wholesaler, buying power increases and the combined association has the resources to hire professional managers to increase the operating efficiency of the voluntary association. Wholesaler-sponsored voluntary chains are most prominent in the grocery trade. Independent Grocers Alliance (IGA), Spartan, and Supervalu are some of the best-known names.

Franchising, or what in more recent years has been referred to as business format franchising, is characterized by a close business relationship between franchiser and franchisee that includes not only the product, service, and trademark, but the entire business format itself, including marketing strategy, training, merchandise management, operating procedures and quality control. Consequently, it is a comprehensive method for distributing goods and services based on a continuous contractual relationship between franchiser and franchisee that covers virtually all phases of the business. The best-known business format franchisers are in the fast-food market with McDonald's

being the most recognized of all, but this type of franchising is also very popular among hotels (Holiday Inn), convenience stores (7-Elevens), business services (Kinko's), and real estate agencies (Century 21). Such franchise systems combine the advantages of the large-scale and professional management of the franchiser with the entrepreneurial drive of the independent business people who are the franchisees.

A *corporate VMS* exists when a firm owns and operates the organization at other levels in the marketing channel. The firm owning and operating the other units may be a manufacturer, wholesaler, or retailer. When it is a manufacturer that owns and operates wholesale and/or retail units, the system is usually described as forwardly integrated. When retailers or wholesalers own and operate their own manufacturing units, backwardly integrated marketing channels exists. Examples of firms operating forwardly integrated marketing channels include Goodyear Tire and Sherwin-Williams Company, while well-known firms operating backwardly integrated channels include Sears, The Limited, and Safeway. The most important advantage of corporate VMSs, whether forwardly or backwardly integrated, is the high degree of control they provide to the corporate channel leader because the other units in the marketing channel are owned rather than operated as independent businesses.

Providing Continuing Leadership

Even well-conceived motivation programs, based on a thorough attempt to understand the channel members' needs and problems coupled with a carefully targeted support program, still require leadership on a continuing basis to achieve effective motivation of channel members.[38] In other words, someone has to be in charge. Ethan Allen Interiors, cited earlier as an administered VMS, provides a good example of a firm that takes a leadership role in motivating its 300 domestic and foreign independent retailers. Not only does this furniture maker provide continuing direction and advice on all aspects of the business from inventory control to store design, it also sends all of the retailers' salespeople to the company's training school, called Ethan Allen College. At the school, salespeople learn about home decorating techniques and, even more importantly, about the Ethan Allen way of doing things. The curriculum is designed to build teamwork and inspire confidence in the retailers to look to Ethan Allen for leadership in helping them to compete successfully in the fiercely competitive home furnishing business.[39]

Coordinating Channel Strategy in the Marketing Mix

Channel strategy is not formulated in a vacuum. The other three Ps of the marketing mix—product, price, and promotion—must all be considered as well. What is especially important is to recognize the interrelationships among these marketing mix components, and to try to achieve synergy rather than conflict among the four Ps. Thus, channel strategy should enhance rather than detract from the firm's product, price, and promotion strategies.[40]

Product Strategy and Channel Strategy

Product strategy is often dependent on channel strategy because some key product strategies interface with channel strategy in ways that can mean the difference between success or failure. As presented in Chapter 1, *product positioning strategy*, which seeks to present products to customers in a way that gives them a certain image relative to competitive products, illustrates the relationship between product strategy and channel strategy. Consider, for example, a product such as Gargoyles Performance Eye Wear, which makes numerous high-end sunglasses ranging in price from $85 to $200. The sunglasses are aimed at skiers, bikers, water-sports enthusiasts, basketball players, and other sports aficionados. The large range of target customers and the relatively high prices reflect a product positioning strategy aimed at transforming sunglasses from a utilitarian product to an important fashion item associated with upscale, sports-oriented, glamorous lifestyles. Retailers play a crucial role in establishing the positioning strategy of these products. To position sunglasses as such an exciting and glamorous product with the high prices to match, retailers must create the kind of atmosphere that supports the image.[41] If retailers simply piled up these pricey sunglasses in a bin or stuck them on pegboard, the special aura associated with these products would be drastically undermined. So store atmosphere, display fixturing, and attentive personal selling at the retail level are crucial to the success of this product positioning strategy.

http://www.hyperski.com

Pricing Strategy and Channel Strategy

Pricing strategy is closely related to channel management, because pricing decisions need to take into account channel issues if the manufacturer expects strong cooperation from the channel members. Clearly, such factors as the profit margins available to channel members, the different prices charged to various classes of channel members, prices of competitive products carried, special pricing deals, changing pricing policies, and the use of price incentives are all factors of major concern to many channel members. Thus, the manufacturer needs to make sure that it knows something about the expectations of channel members for these and other relevant pricing issues before embarking on any pricing strategy.

A channel pricing miscue experienced by the Chrysler Corporation provides a case in point of why it is necessary to take into account channel members' views on pricing strategies. Introduced in the mid-1990s, the Neon subcompact car was touted as an automobile that could compete successfully in the under $10,000 market. With a base price advertised at just $8,975, Plymouth and Dodge dealers thought the Neons would move off their lots by the truckload. But a large gap occurred between the price that was advertised and what actually was available to consumers in dealer showrooms. Potential customers asking to "see the new $9,000 car" were quickly turned off when they found out that a decently equipped Neon cost several thousand more. So, instead of a $9,000 car, the customer was looking at a $12,000 to $14,000 car. At these prices, Neons piled up on dealers' lots. As it had done over a decade earlier with the introduction of the K-car, Chrysler had erred in formulating its pricing for the Neon. The low advertised price was essentially used as a gimmick to build showroom traffic. It was then up to the dealers to convince customers to actually purchase the higher-priced and more profitable versions of the car, which in most cases were the only models available. But this pricing strategy had not worked for the K-car and did not work for the Neon. Dealers found it too difficult to undo the low-price expectations of customers. Needless to say, numerous dealers were seething at Chrysler for not asking for their input about this pricing strategy.

Promotion Strategy and Channel Strategy

http://www.imac.com

Promotion interfaces extensively with channel strategy, because many promotions undertaken by a manufacturer require strong channel member support and follow-through to work successfully. For example, major advertising campaigns frequently require point-of-purchase displays in stores, special deals and merchandising campaigns require channel members to stock up on extra inventory, and contests and incentives call for participation from retailers and wholesalers. When Apple launched the iMac, it spent over $100 million on the advertising campaign for the new computer—the largest advertising expenditure for a product launch in Apple's history. But in order for this massive advertising expenditure to be successful, retailers had to be willing to inventory tens of thousands of iMacs well in advance of the release date, provide space for extensive point-of-purchase displays, and participate in special promotional events such as contests and T-shirt giveaways. Retailers also had to prep their salespeople so that they could show off the new iMac to its best advantage and respond to sales objections, such as the lack of disk drives on the iMac.[42]

Evaluating Channel Member Performance

http://www.7-eleven.com

The evaluation of channel member performance is necessary to assess how successful the channel members have been in implementing the manufacturer's channel strategies and achieving distribution objectives. Evaluations require the manufacturer to gather information on the channel members. But the manufacturer's ability to do this will be affected by its degree of control of channel members. Usually, the higher the degree of control, the more information the manufacturer (or franchiser) can gather, and vice versa.[43]

Southland Corporation, the franchiser of 7-Eleven stores in the United States, is an organization that enjoys substantial control of its franchisees. It has therefore been able to develop and implement a sophisticated channel member evaluation system that enables Southland to monitor the performance of each of its 5,500 stores down to the smallest detail. By using a point-of-sale (POS) computer linked to headquarters, the home office can track the sales of thousands of individual products in each store. But what especially sets this channel member performance evaluation system apart from

other similar POS performance monitoring systems is the monitoring it enables Southland to maintain on the actions of individual store managers. Headquarters can keep track of how much time each store manager spends using the analytical tools contained in the system, which store managers are expected to use to analyze sales data, demographic trends, and even local weather conditions in order to maximize sales opportunities and minimize inventory costs.[44]

LOGISTICS IN MARKETING CHANNELS

LEARNING OBJECTIVE 5

Logistics, also often referred to as **physical distribution** (PD), is commonly defined as "planning, implementing, and controlling the physical flows of materials and final products from points of origin to points of use to meet customers' needs at a profit."[45] In more recent years, the term **supply-chain management** has been used to describe logistical systems that emphasize close cooperation and comprehensive interorganizational management to integrate the logistical operations of the different firms in the channel.[46] Although a detailed discussion of the differences between what might be referred to as the "traditional" approach to logistics and the supply chain management approach is beyond the scope of this chapter, Table 10.1 provides an overview of the key distinctions. In any case, whether one chooses to use the term physical distribution, logistics, or supply chain management, the underlying principle is the building of strong cooperation among channel members through effective interorganizational management.

Logistics (or physical distribution)
is the planning, implementing, and controlling of the physical flows of materials and final products from points of origin to points of use to meet customers' needs at a profit.

Supply-chain management
is managing logistical systems to achieve close cooperation and comprehensive interorganizational management so as to integrate the logistical operations of different firms in the marketing channel.

The Role of Logistics

Even the most carefully designed and managed marketing channel must rely on logistics to actually make products available to customers. The creation of time and place utilities, essential for customer satisfaction, is therefore dependent on logistics. The movement of the right amount of the right products to the right place at the right time is a commonly heard description of what logistics is supposed to do. But achieving this goal is no simple job. On the contrary, mass markets, with their great diversity of customer segments spread over vast geographic areas, can make the task of logistics complex and expensive. Thus, logistics has become a gigantic industry that pervades virtually all firms, from the largest to the smallest.[47]

Table 10.1	Comparison of Traditional and Supply Chain Approaches to the Management of Logistics	
	Approach	
Element	**Traditional**	**Supply Chain**
Inventory management approach	Independent efforts	Joint reduction in channel inventories
Total cost approach	Minimize firm costs	Channel-wide cost efficiencies
Time horizon	Short-term	Long-term
Amount of information sharing and monitoring	Limited to needs of current transaction	As required for planning and monitoring processes
Amount of coordination of multiple levels in the channel	Single contact for the transaction between channel pairs	Multiple contacts between levels in firms and levels in channels
Joint planning	Transaction-based	Ongoing
Compatibility of corporate philosophies	Not relevant	Compatible at least for key relationships
Breadth of supplier base	Large to increase competition and spread risk	Small to increase coordination
Channel leadership	Not needed	Needed for coordination focus
Amount of sharing risks and rewards	Each on its own	Risks and rewards shared over the long term
Speed of operations, information, and inventory flows	"Warehouse" orientation (storage, safety stock) interrupted by barriers to flows; localized to channel pairs	"Distribution center" orientation (inventory velocity) interconnecting flows, JIT quick response

Logistics Systems, Costs, and Components

Systems concept of logistics
entails viewing all components of a logistical system together and understanding the relationships among them.

For many years, logistics was equated mainly with transportation. Hence the field was narrowly defined in terms of the activities involved in shipping and receiving products and was given relatively little management attention. But in recent decades, a broader perspective referred to as the **systems concept of logistics** has emerged. Rather than being thought of as separate and distinct from one another, logistical factors as diverse as transportation, materials handling, inventory control, warehousing, and packaging of goods are now recognized as interrelated components of a system. Decisions or actions affecting one component have implications for other components of the logistical system. For example, a faster mode of transportation for moving a quantity of iMacs from California to New York could result in a lower level of inventory needed in New York, which in turn could result in a smaller warehouse being required. Conversely, slower transportation for shipping iMacs from California to New York might well mean that a larger inventory and a larger warehouse would be needed in New York because of the slower rate of resupply.

The concept of logistics as a system has served as the foundation of modern logistics management. In essence, those in charge of managing logistics seek to find the optimum combination of logistics components (transportation, materials handling, order processing, inventory control, warehousing, and packaging) to meet customer service demands.

Total cost approach
is calculating the cost of a logistical system by addressing all of the costs of logistics together rather than individual costs taken separately, so as to minimize the total cost of logistics.

The logistics manager also attempts to achieve the desired level of customer service at the lowest cost by applying the **total cost approach**. This concept is a logical extension of the systems concept, because it addresses all of the costs of logistics taken together, rather than the cost of individual components taken separately, and seeks to minimize the total cost. Consequently, when designing a logistics system, a company must examine the cost of each component and how it affects other components. For instance, a faster mode of transport used to ship the iMacs mentioned earlier might increase transportation costs. But, because the inventory levels and warehouse space needed in New York would be smaller (faster transportation allows for quicker resupply), the inventory carrying costs and warehouse costs will be lower. These savings in costs may be more than enough to offset the higher transportation costs. So, from the standpoint of the total cost of the logistics system, the increase in transportation costs for the faster mode of transport may well result in a *lower* total cost for logistics.

The use of the systems concept and the total cost approach to manage logistics is shown in Figure 10.10. This figure suggests not only that all the basic components of a system are related, but also that the systems concept and the total cost approach provide the guiding principles for blending the components. This blending helps ensure that the types and levels of services desired by customers will be provided at the lowest total cost for the logistics system as a whole.

The basic components of a logistics system are transportation, materials handling, order processing, inventory control, warehousing, and packaging.

Transportation

Transportation is the most obviously necessary component of any logistics system, because in virtually all cases products must be physically moved from one location to another if a transaction is to be completed. Transportation is also often the component accounting for the highest percentage of the total cost of logistics. The five major modes of transportation are truck, rail, water, pipeline, and air. Table 10.2 shows the expenditures on each mode of transportation from 1980 to 1997. Truck transportation has been the most dominant mode, with its share growing to 73.7 percent from 63.3 percent between 1980 and 1997. But by far the most spectacular growth has occurred for airfreight, however, with expenditures increasing by 467 percent from 1980 to 1997.

From a logistics management standpoint, the overriding issue facing a firm is choosing the optimum mode of transportation to meet customer service demands. This can be a complex task because there are so many considerations. A few of these are: Should the firm use its own carriers or common carriers? What are the different rates available? What specific transportation services are offered? How reliable are various

View of Logistics Management Based on the Systems Concept and the Total Cost Approach	Figure 10.10

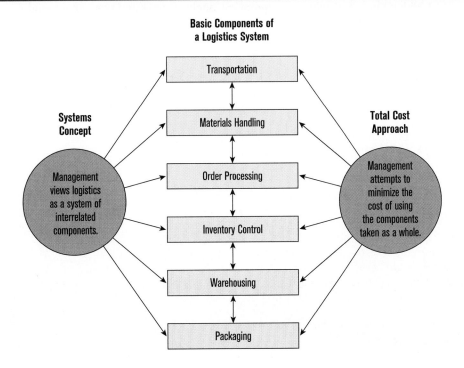

| Table 10.2 | **Total Expenditures for Various Modes of U.S. Freight Transportation in Billions of Dollars, 1980 and 1997** | | | | |

	1980		1997		Growth
Transportation Mode	**Dollar**	**Percentage of Total**	**Dollar**	**Percentage of Total**	**1980–1997**
Truck[1]	94.6	66.3	257.8	73.7	173%
Rail	27.9	18.6	35.3	10.0	26%
Water	15.5	10.4	25.3	7.2	63%
Pipeline	7.5	5.0	8.7	2.5	16%
Air	4.0	2.7	22.7	6.6	467%
Total	149.5	100%	349.8	100%	

[1]Intercity.

Source: U.S. Census Bureau, *Statistical Abstract of the United States: 2000*, 120th ed. (Washington, D.C.: U.S. Government Printing Office, 2000).

common carriers? What modes of transport are competitors using? Moreover, if the systems concept and total cost approach are applied, the logistics manager must think in terms of how the transportation component interacts with and affects the total cost of logistics. Such decisions require specialized knowledge and expertise—not only of logistics systems, but also of the specialized needs of the industry involved and of the latest technologies available.[48]

Materials Handling

Materials handling encompasses the range of activities and equipment involved in the placement and movement of products in storage areas. Questions that must be addressed when designing materials handling systems include:

- How can the distances products are moved within the warehouse during the course of receiving, storage, and shipping be minimized?
- What kinds of mechanical equipment (such as conveyor belts, cranes, and forklifts) should be used?

- How can the firm make the best use of the labor involved in receiving, handling, and shipping products?

For example, the growing use of *cross-docking* (sometimes referred to as *flow-through distribution*) has significantly enhanced materials handling efficiency.[49] In cross-docking, products from an arriving truck are not stored in a warehouse and then resorted later to fill orders. Rather, the merchandise is simply moved across the receiving dock to other trucks for immediate delivery to stores. This eliminates the need to pick stored products at a later time. In short, products are moved directly from shipping to receiving.

Order Processing

The importance of order processing in logistics lies in its relationships with *order cycle time*, which is the time between when an order is placed and when it is received by the customer. If order processing is cumbersome and inefficient, it can slow down the order cycle time considerably. It may even increase transportation costs if a faster mode of transportation must be used to make up for the slow order processing time.

Order processing often appears to be routine but is actually the result of a great deal of planning, capital investment, and training of people. When many thousands of orders are received on a daily basis, filling orders quickly and accurately is a challenging task. Indeed, in the hospital supply industry where medical and surgical supplies account for some 750,000 different products, developing a modern order processing system is a nightmarish challenge, because there is no standard nomenclature for all these different products. Hence, confusion and costly mix-ups have caused large numbers of errors and hundreds of thousands of returns for credit. The industry is just now beginning to grapple with order processing problems, but it will take years to attain the level of efficiency found in consumer product industries.[50]

Inventory Control

Inventory control refers to a firm's attempt to hold the lowest level of inventory that will still enable it to meet customer demand. This is a never-ending battle that all firms face. It is a critically important one as well. Inventory carrying costs—including the costs of financing; insurance; storage; and lost, damaged, and stolen goods—on average can amount to approximately 25 percent of the value of the inventory per year. For some types of merchandise, such as perishable goods or fashion merchandise, carrying costs can be considerably higher. Yet without inventory to meet customer demand on a regular and timely basis, a firm could not stay in business for very long.

Ideally, a firm always wants to be in the position of keeping inventory at the lowest possible level while at the same time placing orders for goods in large quantities, because holding the number of its own orders to the fewest possible enables the firm to minimize ordering costs. Unfortunately, there is a conflict between these two objectives. Average inventory carrying costs rise in direct proportion to the level of the inventory, while average ordering costs decrease in rough proportion to the size of the order. Thus, a trade-off must be made between these two costs to find the optimum levels for both. This point, usually referred to as the *economic order quantity (EOQ)*, occurs at the point at which total costs (inventory carrying cost plus ordering costs) are lowest. As Figure 10.11 shows, the logistics manager strives to achieve the lowest total cost by balancing inventory carrying and ordering costs.

One firm that has done a good job of controlling its inventory is Corning Consumer Products Company, a unit of Corning Inc. Having the right quantities of each Corelle dinnerware design pattern had become a huge problem, because it is so difficult to predict consumer buying patterns, especially around Christmas. To solve the problem, Corning developed a sophisticated inventory control system. A key feature of the system is the requirement that Corning keep a major portion of its Corelle dinnerware undecorated until it gets up-to-the-minute sales data from retailers. Soon after the system had been installed, it saved the company from a disastrous mistake. A week after a giant retail chain launched a special on 12-piece dinnerware sets, the computer-based forecasting model (a critical part of the inventory control system) predicted that the promotion would be a flop. Corning quickly warned another retailer to cancel its own order for 160,000 of these sets and replace it with an order for a more popular design. The unfinished dishes were completed with the newly selected design and shipped out in less than 2 weeks.[51]

http://www.corning.com

| Figure 10.11 | Economic Order Quantity (EOQ) Model |

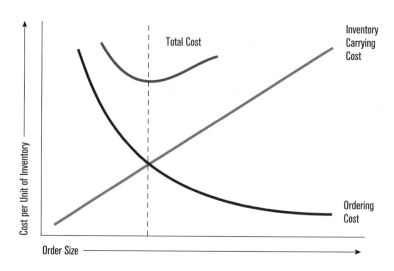

Warehousing

The warehousing or storage component of a logistics system is concerned with the holding of products until they are ready to be sold. Warehousing can actually be one of the more complex components of a logistics system.[52] Quite often, when considering options for warehousing, the firm faces several key decisions, each of which can be difficult and complex. These decisions might include (1) the location of warehouse facilities, (2) the number of warehousing units, (3) the size of the units, (4) the design of the units including layout and internal systems, and (5) the question of ownership. Successful decisions in each of the areas require careful planning and may require input from experts in such fields as location analysis, real estate, operations research, and industrial engineering, in addition to logistics management.

Warehousing is closely linked to the ability of firms to provide high levels of customer service. For example, with the growth of the Internet as a mode of consumer shopping, far more shipments of *eaches*—single items as opposed to product lots—will create massive numbers of *onesie transactions* in which only a single item is purchased.[53] Moreover, consumers will expect these single items to be delivered very quickly. Experts in the warehousing industry believe such demands by Internet shoppers will increase rather than decrease the need for warehousing, because most Internet retailers will be storefronts with no inventory on hand. They will instead rely on numerous, well-located, and efficient warehouses—either their own or third parties'—to provide the level of product availability demanded by Internet shoppers.[54]

Packaging

Packaging and the costs associated with the packaging of products are relevant as a component of the logistics system because packaging can affect the other components of the system, and vice versa. For example, the type of transport used can affect packaging and packaging costs; in the case of airfreight, for instance, packaging costs are generally reduced because risks of damage are generally lower than if rail or truck transportation are used. Materials handling and order processing procedures and costs can also be affected by packaging because well-designed packaging can help to increase efficiencies in these components of the logistics system. Effective packaging can also help control inventory carrying costs by reducing product damage. Further, warehouse space, and thus costs, can be saved if packaging is designed to be space efficient. Therefore, packaging is far more than just a promotional device for fostering product differentiation and attracting consumer attention. Packaging has an important logistical dimension that can make a significant difference in the effectiveness and efficiency of the logistics system. Indeed, a product in distinctive and attractive packaging will have even more appeal if it is also easy to handle, conveniently stackable, and shelf-space efficient.

THE OUTPUT OF THE LOGISTICS SYSTEM: CUSTOMER SERVICE

Good customer service is the desired end result of virtually all business activities, and logistics is an extremely important part of these efforts. This is particularly true for those aspects of customer service that are a direct function of the logistics system, including:

- Time from order receipt to order shipment
- Order size and assortment constraints
- Percentage of items out of stock
- Percentage of orders filled accurately
- Percentage of orders filled within a given number of days from receipt of the order
- Percentage of orders filled
- Percentage of customer orders that arrive in good condition
- Order cycle time (time from order placement to order delivery)
- Ease and flexibility of order placement

These logistics services and many others (see Table 10.3) are often quantified and utilized as **logistical service standards**, against which the manufacturer's actual performance is then measured.[55] For example, the first standard shown in the list—time from order receipt to order shipment—might be set at 24 hours for 90 percent of all orders received. So, for every 100 orders received, the manufacturer must have 90 of the orders processed and shipped within 24 hours to meet the standard. The second service standard in the list—order size and assortment constraints—might be set in terms of some minimum quantity of products, and certain restrictions might be placed on mixing the various products unless specified minimum quantities of each item are ordered. A steel producer, for example, might set the minimum order for various gauges of sheet metal at 2 tons, and the inclusion of several gauges in a single order might require a certain combined minimum tonnage. The third standard—percentage of items out of stock,

Logistical service standards are the kinds of quantifiable distribution services performed by a logistical system to meet the needs of customers.

Table 10.3	Inventory of Logistical Aspects of Customer Service

1. Order processing time
2. Order assembly time
3. Delivery time
4. Inventory reliability
5. Order size constraints
6. Consolidation allowed
7. Consistency
8. Frequency of sales visits
9. Ordering convenience
10. Order progress information
11. Inventory backup during promotions
12. Invoice format
13. Physical condition of goods
14. Claims response
15. Billing procedures
16. Average order cycle time
17. Order cycle time variability
18. Rush service
19. Availability
20. Competent technical representatives
21. Equipment demonstrations
22. Availability of published material
23. Accuracy in filling orders
24. Terms of sale
25. Protective packaging
26. Cooperation

or stockouts—is almost always set in terms of a percentage of the items ordered during a given period that cannot be filled from inventory. Thus, if a manufacturer wants to fill 95 percent of the items ordered, its stockout percentage can be no higher than 5 percent to meet the standard. The other six service standards in the list can be quantified and used in a similar fashion.

In general, the higher the service standards offered, the higher the costs will be. While well-designed logistics systems and modern technology can keep these costs under control, it is usually not possible to completely escape the trade-off of higher costs for higher service standards.

A manufacturer must cover these costs either indirectly in the price it charges for products, or by passing them along to channel members in the form of service charges. In either case, there is little point in offering logistics services that channel members do not want or higher levels of service than they desire. Types and levels of logistics service that go beyond real channel member demands simply increase costs for channel members without providing them with any desired benefits. Thus the key issue in defining logistics service standards is to determine precisely the types and levels of logistics service desired by the channel members.

CHAPTER SUMMARY

- Marketing channels, the networks of organizations that create time, place, and possession utilities, allow hundreds of millions of customers to gain convenient access to a vast array of goods and services.

- As one of the four Ps of the marketing mix—product, price, promotion, and place—marketing channels, place is a key part of any firm's marketing strategy.

- Channel structure is the form or shape taken by the marketing channel, which consists of three dimensions: (1) length, (2) intensity, and (3) types of intermediaries.

- Channel structure is determined by three major factors: (1) the distribution tasks that need to be performed, (2) the economics of performing the distribution tasks, and (3) management's desire for control of the channel.

- Marketing channels create five flows: (1) product flow, (2) negotiation flow, (3) ownership flow, (4) information flow, and (5) promotion flow. All of these flows need to be managed to achieve effective and efficient marketing channels.

- Marketing channels are social systems as well as economic systems, so power and conflict play an important role.

- Marketing channel management consists of analyzing, planning, organizing, and controlling a firm's marketing channels. Six areas are involved: (1) formulating channel strategy, (2) designing channel structure, (3) selecting channel members, (4) motivating channel members, (5) coordinating channel strategy, and (6) evaluating channel member performance.

- The planning, implementation, and control of the physical flows of materials and final goods from points of production to points of use is referred to as logistics, physical distribution (PD), or supply chain management.

- A logistics system consists of six major components: (1) transportation, (2) materials handling, (3) order processing, (4) inventory control, (5) warehousing, and (6) packaging.

- Logistics managers need to employ the systems concept to understand the relationships among the components and the total cost approach to determine and account for all of the costs of the logistical systems.

KEY TERMS

Channel intensity refers to the number of intermediaries at each level of the marketing channel.

Channel length is the number of levels in a marketing channel.

Channel strategy is the broad set of principles by which a firm seeks to achieve its distribution objectives to satisfy its customers.

Channel structure consists of all of the businesses and institutions (including producers or manufacturers and final customers) who are involved in performing the functions of buying, selling, or transferring title.

Conflict in marketing channels occurs when one channel member believes that another channel member is impeding the attainment of its goals.

Discrepancies between production and consumption are differences in quantity, assortment, time, and place that must be overcome to make goods available to final customers.

Economies of scale and economies of scope are obtained by spreading the costs of distribution over a large quantity of products (scale) or over a wide variety of products (scope).

Exclusive distribution occurs when only one intermediary is used at a particular level in the marketing channel.

Flows in marketing channels are the movement of products, negotiation, ownership, information, and promotion through each participant in the marketing channel.

Intensive distribution occurs when all possible intermediaries at a particular level of the channel are used.

Interorganizational context refers to channel management that extends beyond a firm's own organization into independent businesses.

Logistical service standards are the kinds of quantifiable distribution services performed by a logistical system to meet the needs of customers.

Logistics (or physical distribution) is the planning, implementing, and controlling of the physical flows of materials and final products from points of origin to points of use to meet customers' needs at a profit.

Marketing channel is the network of organizations that creates time, place, and possession utilities.

Marketing channel management refers to the analysis, planning, organizing, and controlling of a firm's marketing channels.

Motivating channel members is the action taken by a manufacturer or franchiser to get channel members to implement its channel strategies.

Marketing channel power is the capacity of one channel member to influence the behavior of another channel member.

Selection criteria are the factors that a firm uses to choose which intermediaries will become members of its marketing channel.

Selective distribution means that a carefully chosen group of intermediaries is used at a particular level in the marketing channel.

Specialization or division of labor occurs when each participant in the marketing channel focuses on performing those activities at which it is most efficient.

Supply-chain management is managing logistical systems to achieve close cooperation and comprehensive interorganizational management so as to integrate the logistical operations of different firms in the marketing channel.

Sustainable competitive advantage is a competitive edge that cannot be easily or quickly copied by competitors in the short run.

Systems concept of logistics entails viewing all components of a logistical system together and understanding the relationships among them.

Time, place, and possession utilities are conditions that enable consumers and business users to have products available for use when and where they want them and to actually take possession of them.

Total cost approach is calculating the cost of a logistical system by addressing all of the costs of logistics together rather than individual costs taken separately, so as to minimize the total cost of logistics.

Transaction efficiency refers to designing marketing channels to minimize the number of contacts between producers and consumers.

QUESTIONS FOR DISCUSSION

1. The opening of this chapter talks about the need for billions of customers around the globe to somehow be matched up with millions of products. How do marketing channels fit into this matching up process? Explain?

2. Is the marketing channel always the most important component of the marketing mix or does it depend on the particular set of circumstance involved? Discuss.

3. What are the determinants of channel structure? Explain.

4. Why do distribution tasks need to be performed? Explain in terms of the various discrepancies.

5. Why is it important to view marketing channels as social systems as well as economic systems?

6. Define *marketing channel management* and what is meant by the *interorganizational context* of channel management.

7. Successful motivation of channel members is dependent upon a process that involves several steps. What are these steps and why is it important to follow them when attempting to motivate channel members?

8. The text states that "channel strategy should enhance rather than detract from the firm's product, price, and promotion strategies." What does this have to do with coordinating channel strategy in the marketing mix? Discuss.

9. Define *logistics* or *physical distribution*. In the age of electronic commerce via the Internet, is this concept still valid? Discuss.

10. What is meant by the *systems concept* and *total cost approach*?

INTERNET QUESTIONS

Internet Exercise #1

Electronic commerce or e-commerce, in which goods and services are bought or sold via the Internet, may well revolutionize marketing channels in this new millennium. Internet sales are expected to grow significantly in the future so that within a few years into the new millennium, hundreds of billions in sales will occur and account for as much as 10 percent of total retail sales by 2005. Of course, no one knows for sure that this will happen, but if growth continues at its present pace, electronic marketing channels will be a major force in the distribution of goods and services.

Question: *What is it about Internet shopping that makes it appealing to consumers?*

Provide your answer to this question by doing the following:

1. Visit the Web sites of five different Internet sellers.

2. Make sure that you vary the product categories of the five sellers. Do not, for example, pick five booksellers or five CD sellers.

3. Click through each Web site and rate each on the following 10-point scales that compare the Internet channel with conventional channels. One is the lowest rating and 10 is the highest.
   a. How would you rate the *convenience* provided by the Internet channel compared with a conventional one? (circle your answers)

   Internet Channel vs. Conventional Channels

   ```
   | ---- | ---- | ---- | ---- | ---- | ---- | ---- | ---- | ---- |
     1      2      3      4      5      6      7      8      9     10
   ```

   b. How would you rate the *selection* provided by the Internet channel compared with a conventional one? (circle your answers)

   Internet Channel vs. Conventional Channels

   ```
   | ---- | ---- | ---- | ---- | ---- | ---- | ---- | ---- | ---- |
     1      2      3      4      5      6      7      8      9     10
   ```

   c. How would you rate the Internet channel versus conventional channels in offering *low prices?* (circle your answers)

   Internet Channel vs. Conventional Channels

   ```
   | ---- | ---- | ---- | ---- | ---- | ---- | ---- | ---- | ---- |
     1      2      3      4      5      6      7      8      9     10
   ```

   d. How would you rate the *fun* provided of shopping on the Internet channel compared with conventional channels? (circle your answers)

   Internet Channel vs. Conventional Channels

   ```
   | ---- | ---- | ---- | ---- | ---- | ---- | ---- | ---- | ---- |
     1      2      3      4      5      6      7      8      9     10
   ```

   e. How *secure* do you feel if you were to use your credit card to make a purchase on the Internet channel versus conventional channels? (circle your answers)

   Internet Channel vs. Conventional Channels

   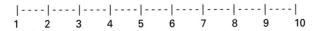
   ```
   | ---- | ---- | ---- | ---- | ---- | ---- | ---- | ---- | ---- |
     1      2      3      4      5      6      7      8      9     10
   ```

4. Now, for each Web site that you visited, add up the scores for the five questions comparing the Internet channel to conventional channels.

5. What is your reaction to the scores?

Internet Exercise #2

1. Pick one of your favorite conventional retailers. This can be a small or large retailer in any product category, a department store, or a mass merchandiser. Visit the store in your normal fashion but be sure to do the following:
   a. Write down the time you spent getting to and from the store and the total distance traveled.
   b. Make note of any parking problems or, if public transportation was used, any hassles that stand out.
   c. After you entered the store, note how hard or easy it was to navigate the aisles and pick out the product(s) you were looking for.
   d. Jot down your thoughts on availability and helpfulness of salespeople.
   e. Record how long it took you to get through the checkout line.

2. Go online to the Web site of the same store you just shopped at. Or if no Web site for that store exists, find the Web site for another retailer that is comparable to the retailer you visited. Then do the following:
   a. Write down the time it took you to boot-up your computer and locate the Web site.
   b. Navigate (click) through the site and make notes of any problems you experience.
   c. If you are actually going to buy a product(s), jot down your thoughts on the ease or difficulty of doing so. If you are just shopping, write down your thoughts on the ease or difficulty of the selection process up to the point before actual purchase.
   d. Record how long the online shopping process took from the time you booted-up the computer until shut-down.
   e. If you made a purchase online, record how long it takes before you actually receive the product.

3. Compare your two sets of notes on conventional shopping and Internet shopping and answer the following questions:
   a. What do you see as the advantages (if any) of shopping via the Internet versus conventional shopping?
   b. What do you see as the disadvantages (if any) of shopping on the Internet versus conventional shopping?
   c. Do you see yourself doing more shopping online in the future? Why or why not?

Internet Exercise #3

Check ads from newspapers, magazines, or TV and pick out any five firms that ask you to visit their Web sites and who provide their Web addresses in the ads. Now, visit those Web sites and answer the following questions:

1. Are you impressed with the Web site? Why or why not?

2. What information has been provided by the Web sites that was not offered in the ads?

3. Do you think that visiting these Web sites after seeing the advertisements was worth the extra time and effort involved? Why or why not?

4. If you were in the market for the products or services in question, would the material provided by your online visit make it easier for you to make a purchase? Explain.

ENDNOTES

[1] Mike France, "Are Corporate Predators on the Loose?" *Business Week,* 23 February 1998, 124–126.

[2] Bert Rosenbloom, *Marketing Channels: A Management View,* 6th ed. (Fort Worth, TX: The Dryden Press 1999).

[3] Jeanette Brown, Heather Green, and Wendy Zellner, "Shoppers Are Beating a Path to the Web," *Business Week,* 24 December 2001, 41.

[4] Evantheia Schibsted, "Ab Rockers, Ginsu Knives, E320s," *Business 2.0,* 29 May 2001, 26–49.

[5] Rosenbloom, *Marketing Channels,* 4–6.

[6] Jason Fry, "Why Shoppers' Loyalty to Familiar Web Sites Isn't So Crazy After All," *Wall Street Journal,* 13 August 2001, B1.

[7] Rosenbloom, *Marketing Channels,* 7–10.

[8] Bob Ortega, "How Big Brewers Are Sidling into Retail," *Wall Street Journal,* 18 May 1998, B1, B6.

[9] Gary L. Frazier and Kersi D. Antia, "Exchange Relationships and Interfirm Power in Channels of Distribution," *Journal of the Academy of Marketing Science* (Fall 1995): 21–26.

[10] Ann Zimmerman, "Taking Aim at Costco, Sam's Club, Marshal's, Diamonds and Pearls," *Wall Street Journal,* 9 August 2001, A1, A4.

[11] Bert Rosenbloom and Trina Larsen, "A Functional Approach to International Channel Structure and the Role of Independent Wholesalers," *Journal of Marketing Channels* (Summer 1993): 65–82.

[12] Wroe Alderson, *Marketing Behavior and Executive Action* (Homewood, IL: Richard D. Irwin, 1957).

[13] John W. Cebrowski, "Global Success Tied to Key Management Considerations," *Marketing News,* 20 July 1998, 14–16.

[14] Rosenbloom, *Marketing Channels,* 19–22.

[15] Donald V. Fites, "Make Your Dealers Your Partners," *Harvard Business Review* (March–April 1996): 84–95.

[16] Rekha Balu, "Big Brewers Find Price War Seems to Have No End," *Wall Street Journal,* 2 July 1998, B6.

[17] John O'Dell, "Land Rover's Mini-SUV Relies on Internet Marketing," *Philadelphia Inquirer,* 9 September 2001, F27.

[18] Louis W. Stern and Jay W. Brown, "Distribution Channels: A Social Systems Approach," in *Distribution Channels: Behavioral Dimensions,* ed. Louis W. Stern (New York: Houghton Mifflin, 1969), 6–19.

[19] Richard Gibson, "McDonalds Finds Angry Customers on Its Menu," *Wall Street Journal,* 16 July 2001, A14.

[20] John R. Wilke, "Microsoft Antitrust Case Heads Back to Trial Court," *Wall Street Journal* (3 August 2001), A3.

[21] John R. Wilke, Rebecca Buskman, and Gary McWilliams, "Microsoft Lets PC Firms Remove Browser," *Wall Street Journal,* 12 July 2001, A3, A8.

[22] Bert Rosenbloom, "Conflict and Channel Efficiency: Some Conceptual Models for the Decision Maker," *Journal of Marketing* (July 1973): 26–30.

[23] Bert Rosenbloom, "Channel Management," in *Encyclopedia of Marketing,* ed. Michael J. Baker (London: Routledge, 1995), 551–570.

[24] Douglas Levin and Krystal Miller, "Goodbye to Haggling: Savvy Consumers Are Buying Their Cars Like Refrigerators," *Wall Street Journal,* 20 August 1993, B1, B3.

[25] Fites, "Make Your Dealers Your Partners," 85–87.

[26] Nikhil Deogun, "PepsiCo Chief's Stand on Exclusive Pacts Adds to Cola Wars Charged Atmosphere," *Wall Street Journal,* 15 May 1998, A4.

[27] Robert D. Hof and Ellen Neuborne, "Amazon.com, the Wild World of E-Commerce," *Business Week,* 14 December 1998, 106–112.

[28] Debbie Howell, "Fleming Takes Distribution Service to Next Level," *DSN Retailing Today,* 2 November 2001, 3.

[29] Michael Krantz, "Virtual Shopping Is Better Than the Real Thing," *Time,* 20 July 1998, 36–41.

[30] Calmetta Y. Coleman, "Selling Jewelry, Dolls, and TVs Next to Corn Flakes," *Wall Street Journal,* 19 November 1997, B1, B2.

[31] "Click 'Til You Drop," *U.S. News and World Report,* 7 December 1998, 42–45.

[32] Pui-Wing Tam and Gary McWilliams, "Apple Is Mulling Own Store Chain to Expand Sales," *Wall Street Journal,* 29 September 2000, B1, B2.

[33] Angelo B. Henderson, "GM's Saturn Division Plans to Add 125 Dealerships," *Wall Street Journal,* 20 February 1998, B9.

[34] Richard C. Munn, "Marketers Must Align Themselves with Sales," *Marketing News,* 9 November 1998, 12.

[35] Kathleen Kerwin, "GM Brings Its Dealers Up to Speed," *Business World,* 23 February 1998, 82–84.

[36] Bert C. McCammon, Jr., "Perspectives for Distribution Programming," in *Vertical Marketing Systems,* ed. Louis P. Bucklin (Glenview, IL: Scott, Foresman, 1970), 43.

[37] Bert Rosenbloom, *Marketing Channels,* 485–503.

[38] Nirmalya Kumar, "The Power of Trust in Manufacturer-Retailer Relationships," *Harvard Business Review* (November–December 1996): 92–106.

[39] Rosenbloom, *Marketing Channels,* 305.

[40] Kenneth Leung, "Beyond Web Pages: Integrating the Internet," *Marketing News,* 22 June 1998, 9.

[41] Stephanie N. Mehta, "For Everything Under the Sun, Specialized Sunglasses," *Wall Street Journal*, 5 February 1996, B1.

[42] Jim Carlton, "From Apple, A New Marketing Blitz," *Wall Street Journal*, 14 August 1998, B1, B4.

[43] Frederick F. Reichheld and Phil Schefter, "E-Loyalty: Your Secret Weapon on the Web," *Harvard Business Review* (July–August 2000): 105–113.

[44] Norihiko Shirouzu and John Bigness, "7-Eleven Operators Resist System to Monitor Managers," *Wall Street Journal*, 16 June 1997, B1, B3.

[45] Philip Kotler, *Marketing Management, Analysis, Planning, Implementation, and Control*, 9th ed. (Upper Saddle River, NJ: Prentice-Hall, 1997).

[46] Donald J. Bowersox and David J. Closs, *Logistics Management: An Integrated Supply Chain Process* (New York: McGraw-Hill, 1996).

[47] Neil Gross, "Leapfrogging a Few Links," *Business Week*, 22 June 1998, 140–142.

[48] "Transportation Upgrade Boosts Productivity," *Grocery Distribution* (September/October 1997): 28–32.

[49] Carol Casper, "Flow-Through: Mirage or Reality?" *Food Logistics* (October/November 1997): 44–58.

[50] Rhonda L. Rundle, "Hospital Cost Cutters Push Use of Scanners to Track Inventories," *Wall Street Journal*, 10 June 1997, A1, A8.

[51] Michael M. Phillips, "Retailers Rely on High-Tech Distribution," *Wall Street Journal*, 19 December 1996, A2, A6.

[52] Ray A. Smith and Sheila Muto, "Dot-Coms' New Dilemma: Vacant Warehouses," *Wall Street Journal*, 22 August 2001, B10.

[53] James Aaron Cooke, "The Retail Revolution Is Coming!" *Logistics Management* (April 1996): 48–51.

[54] Steven E. Salkin, "Debunking the Myths of the Internet," *Warehousing Management* (October 1997): 29–32.

[55] Carol C. Bienstock, John T. Mentzer, and Monroe Murphy Bird, "Measuring Physical Distribution Service Quality," *Journal of the Academy of Marketing Science* (Winter 1997): 31–44

CHAPTER CASE

DELL COMPUTER CORPORATION: WHICH CHANNELS WILL KEEP GROWTH GOING?

History

In 1983, during his first year in college, Michael Dell took his interest in tinkering with computers to a new level. During his first semester, as the now legendary story goes, Dell began to purchase outmoded IBM PCs from local retailers, upgrade them, and resell them not just to other students but to local law firms and small businesses. Dell's sales method was simple door-to-door direct sales, bypassing the dealers and retail outlets through which virtually all computers were sold. The idea was so successful that during the summer after his first year of college, Dell sold $180,000 worth of PCs in only his first month! Shortly after his initial success, Dell modified his business. Instead of continuing to purchase older machines and upgrade them, Dell recognized that he could purchase new computer components, assemble them himself, and sell them directly to customers. This strategy enabled him to bypass the traditional channels of distribution adhered to by the established computer makers and offer PCs to his customers at a 15 percent discount. Dell's direct contact with customers allowed him to build products to order instead of maintaining an inventory. Dell's innovative concept of custom design and direct sales took off right from the start, and demand was overwhelming, so much so that Michael Dell never returned to college.

Dell continued to grow throughout the 1980s at an astounding rate, enabling Michael Dell to fund growth internally. Dell's sales grew to a level that enabled him to secure bank financing using only his receivables as collateral, avoiding the need for venture capital.

It was not until 1987 that Dell offered stock, and the company did not go public until 1988. Thirty million dollars was raised in its initial public offering, netting Michael Dell $18 million.

By 1991, with Michael Dell just 26 years old, sales reached $800 million and then more than doubled to $2 billion in 1992. This high rate of growth, however, was too rapid for Dell to handle. Flaws in the design of Dell's notebook computers began to emerge, and managers were too young and inexperienced to handle many of the new problems often associated with companies attempting the transition from entrepreneurial start-up to large public company. In 1992, despite its enormous sales increases, Dell reported a $36 million loss for the year. Many industry experts felt that Dell had made its run and could not return to profitability.

Michael Dell did not listen to the skeptics and instead bulked up his management team by bringing in experienced managers to add much-needed maturity and knowledge. Dell recruited Mort Topfer from Motorola to handle day-to-day operations. Topfer, an experienced executive, understood the purchasing and manufacturing of high-tech components and helped Dell set up a manufacturing facility in Asia. In addition to Topfer, Dell also recruited several key Apple executives, who were working on the Apple Power-Book laptop computer, to fix Dell's notebook computer problems. The results were astonishing. Within 12 months, many of the problems were worked out, and the following year Dell saw its profits hit $149 million. Despite the turnaround, skeptics abounded, consistently underestimating customer demand for direct sale computers. Many still had questions as to whether the growth could continue at such an exceedingly high rate, and whether Michael Dell had the skills to guide his company's growth in this highly competitive business.

Dell's Initial Attempt at Traditional Retailing

Not everything Michael Dell did turned to gold. In fact there were some serious mistakes, such as an initial attempt in 1993 to sell computers via traditional retail channels in an attempt to target the consumer market. By selling computers via this channel, Dell faced new problems that the company had never before encountered. The competitive advantage that Dell had gained by selling computers direct to customers evaporated when placed in traditional retail distribution channels. Dell could no longer adjust its supply to fit customers' specialized demands, but instead had to create an inventory for resellers to stock. Further, since most of Dell's sales were to businesses, its computers faced a brand recognition problem when placed in retail stores, and invariably fierce price competition became a factor for Dell. Since retailers were now selling the computers, Dell could no longer avoid the increased costs associated with this traditional channel structure. This experiment at selling computers via retail channels turned out to be unsuccessful and short-lived; Dell discontinued sales though traditional retailers within the year.

Dell's Order Processing System

Continuing to retain the direct selling concept that Michael Dell utilized from the start, today's Dell computer has come a long way in the level of sophistication and technology it uses to meet its customers' needs, to drive revenue growth, and to keep operating costs at a minimum.

Virtually all of Dell's customer orders are placed via a toll-free number, a dedicated internal company sales representative, or Dell's Web site. Recently, Dell has been experimenting with accepting customer orders via cable shopping channels and through salespersons located in shopping mall kiosks. However, one constant remains: Regardless of the medium by which a customer order is taken, virtually all of Dell's PCs are still made to order, thereby consistently eliminating inventory buildup and excessive lag times. The entire process from initial order to loading for delivery can take as little 36 hours. Dell's larger customers can even get their computers shipped via Dell's quick-ship program within as little as 12 hours after manufacture.

Currently, customer orders are immediately relayed to one of Dell's three plants in Austin, Texas, Penang, Malaysia, or Limerick, Ireland. Next, suppliers are notified. Dell's Austin plant manager says that all the suppliers know that components must be delivered to the plant within an hour of a request. Once the components arrive, they are taken from the trucks and placed on the assembly lines, so there is no component inventory or finished goods inventory in Dell's system.

The efficiency in the order processing system continues to help keep Dell's operating expenses low, by accounting for only 10.2 percent of Dell's revenue. Dell continues to find ways to improve its order processing efficiency while reducing costs. For example, much of Dell's call center work has been shifted to call centers in India in order to take advantage of a low cost, English-speaking workforce, while maintaining the same type of order processing efficiency.

Virtual Integration

The direct sales model that Dell continues to use provides other benefits besides customization. As founder Michael Dell said in an interview several years ago, the direct sales model allows Dell to build relationships with its customers. The relationship generates valuable information that in turn allows Dell to leverage its relationships with both suppliers and customers. When you add the advancements in data sharing, just-in-time-manufacturing, and the Internet to the mix, the traditional functions of each member of the supply chain become blurred, thus creating virtual integration. Operating under this model, Dell can maintain a tightly coordinated supply chain, yet still concentrate on customization and specialization found in virtual corporations.

Technology continues to be the key to Michael Dell's continued vision for virtual integration, enabling real time data exchange to track everything from product orders to service calls. The consistent real-time exchange of information enables suppliers, component manufacturers, customers, and others to become an integral part of Dell's business, almost as if they worked inside the company. Although virtual integration exists in theory, and many of the now defunct dot-com companies were touting the Internet as the key to its implementation, it still remains to be seen whether Dell can implement virtual integration successfully. And, if it does implement virtual integration, whether it will be the key further growth and profitability, or whether it will simply be a small part of Dell's overall strategy.

The Internet

Throughout the late 1990s and into 2000, virtually every new and existing company embraced the Internet as the ultimate channel by which to sell their respective products. Many companies even saw the Internet as far more than simply another channel through which their respective products could be sold, but instead viewed it an entirely new means of doing business. To many of these companies, traditional methods of conducting business no longer mattered, and the Internet was now the only way to do business. Most of the companies that embraced this concept, that is, the dot-coms, have disappeared over the past 2 years almost as quickly as they were founded.

Despite the precipitous decline and collapse of many of these companies that touted the Internet as the new paradigm by which all businesses would operate, Dell continues to drive its revenues by using the Internet as one of its key channels for selling computers directly to customers. Unlike other channels, the Internet provides an instantaneous global sales network. Michael Dell has referred to it as the ultimate direct model. Through its Web site, customers may place orders for Dell products, ask questions via e-mail, and even obtain customized computer systems and technical solutions. Instead of calling the company on the phone, customers can simply log onto the Web site. As a result, Dell continues to have to hire fewer employees to take orders and provide technical support, thereby further reducing the company's operating expenses. The sales numbers for Dell's Web site continue to grow at a staggering pace. As of March 1997, Dell was already selling $1 million per day via the Web site, and by January 1999, this number had grown spectacularly to $10 million in sales per day. Today, sales from the Web site have been estimated as high as $14 million per day.

As a result of the on-going success of Dell's Web-based sales, its corporate strategy continues to focus on increasing the use of the company's Web site. Dell envisions all of its customers conducting virtually all of their business through the Dell Web site. Currently Dell's large corporate customers, which account for more than 35 percent of the company's revenues, and its Asian and European customers, do not use the Internet for their transactions.

Dell is not alone, however, in its use of the Internet. Several other companies continue to use the Internet successfully as extensions of their traditional channels. Despite recent slowdowns in sales and lower stock prices, both Cisco Systems and PC manufacturer Gateway Computer continue to use the Internet successfully to drive sales. Gateway continues to operate under a business model similar to Dell's by taking orders from customers before building the machines. Many other PC manufacturers have followed with their own versions of Dell's Internet-based, direct, built-to-order manufacturing systems, including IBM and Compaq.

Given these other competitors, Dell continues to face new challenges that it has not encountered before. Indeed, for much of Dell's existence, it was the only computer manufacturer that could produce built-to-order computers at competitive prices. With increasing competition, falling component prices, shrinking margins in build-to-order computers, and as of the time of this publication the proposed merger between Hewlett-Packard and Compaq, Dell faces new challenges. Despite the failure of most of the companies that relied solely on the Internet as a means of conducting business, the Internet still remains an effective part of an overall channel strategy which other competitors could use to potentially attempt chip away at Dell's dominance. Similar to Dell, by increasingly using the Internet, other computer manufacturers also can avoid the increased costs associated with traditional channels of distribution, allowing them to lower prices and inventory, thereby eliminating Dell's price advantage. Other computer manufacturers could also use the Internet in an attempt to attract large customers, and the Asian and European customers that Dell has not yet fully integrated into its Internet services.

Focusing on Consumers

From its inception, Dell has consistently focused on selling its products to the business market, and has focused little on the consumer and education markets. Although Dell currently maintains annual sales of approximately $32 billion, recent predictions estimate a potential drop in annual PC sales of as much as 21 percent in 2002. Thus, Dell is searching for another method by which it can continue to drive its sales and revenue growth. The consumer and education market appears to be its new focus. Dell's current sales to the home and education market represent only 15 percent of its annual sales, while the average of its competitors is approximately 24 percent. While the corporate computer market was booming in the late 1990s and into 2000, Dell remained better positioned than its competitors to take advantage of the increased demand, since it was primarily focused on sales to businesses. However, with many experts predicting that the corporate computer market will be weak for the foreseeable future, Dell appears to have shifted some of its focus to the consumer market in an attempt to boost sales and revenues.

Dell's recent foray into the consumer and education market has included television advertising and selling PCs though a particular cable television shopping network, on which Dell's computers were said to be the most popular item on a particular day with the network setting a record one-day total of $80 million in sales. In addition to cable television, and for the first time since 1993, Dell has made a very conservative entrance into traditional retailing. Dell recently opened Dell Direct Store kiosks in malls located in Franklin, Tennessee, and Frisco, Texas, each of which is staffed by several Dell salespersons who are there to take orders for built-to-order systems.

Perhaps more significantly, Dell has even broken from its built-to-order business model to produce its first premade, off-the-shelf Dell system. The premade system is geared specifically to the low-end consumer market, is manufactured in Taiwan, and retails for $599. Although it remains to be seen whether this low-cost computer will attract more of the consumer market, initial reports indicate that sales of the machines are meeting Dell's expectations.

Possibly learning from its first unsuccessful venture into the consumer and retail markets in 1993, John Hamlin, Dell's current vice president of consumer products, says that Dell has no intention of engaging in a massive rollout of company stores, similar to those currently operated by Gateway and Apple, and intends to proceed into any type of traditional retailing store strategy very cautiously.

While it still remains to be seen how successful Dell's entrance into the consumer market will ultimately be, as of the third quarter of 2001, Dell's revenue from consumer sales rose 17 percent over the same period one year earlier. Also, Dell's overall share of the U.S. home PC market increased to 16.6 percent at the end of the third quarter of 2001, just barely behind Hewlett-Packard's 17.7 percent share.

Dell's initial entry into the consumer and education PC market has been successful in the short term, but how successful will they be in the future? The players in the consumer PC market continually face cutthroat price wars and constant pressure to provide more product to consumers for less money. Dell, however, believes itself to be better positioned than many of its competitors to keep prices low in the consumer and education markets. Theoretically, its built-to-order method of manufacturing its computers enables Dell to keep inventory at a minimum, thereby allowing it to purchase components, which consistently fall in price, on an as-needed basis. In contrast, Dell's competitors who utilize the traditional model are often stuck with larger inventories, which were manufactured with higher cost components, thereby forcing them to charge customers more for their product in order to maintain profitability. It remains to be seen whether Dell's approach is sounder.

Discussion Questions

1. Is the Internet channel still the ideal means for sustaining Dell's strategy of made-to-order computers and direct sales to customers?

2. Should Dell continue to focus on the consumer market as a new addition to its overall channel strategy?

CHAPTER eleven

Patrick Dunne,
Texas Tech University

Patrick Dunne, an Associate Professor of Marketing at the Jerry Rawls School of Business at Texas Tech University, received his MBA and Ph.D. from Michigan State University and his BSBA from Xavier University.

In over 30 years of years of university teaching at Michigan State, Drake, Oklahoma, and Texas Tech, Dr. Dunne has taught a wide variety of marketing and retailing courses at both the undergraduate and graduate levels. In addition to authoring over a dozen retailing textbooks, he has published articles in many of the leading academic journals.

Professor Dunne has been honored with several university teaching awards and has an active involvement in professional training programs. He is also an active consultant to a variety of retailers and wholesalers.

Robert F. Lusch,
Texas Christian University

Robert F. Lusch is Distinguished University Professor and Dean of the M. J. Neeley School of Business at Texas Christian University. Previously he served on the faculty of the University of Oklahoma for 24 years, where he held the Helen Robson Walton Chair in Marketing Strategy and was George Lynn Cross Research Professor. A prolific author, he has published 16 books and over 150 articles and is best recognized for his work in marketing and retailing strategy. In 1996 he received the Harold Maynard Award for Theoretical Contributions to the Marketing Literature, and in 1997 was named the Distinguished Marketing Educator of the Year by the Academy of Marketing Science. He is also the past editor of the *Journal of Marketing*, which is the oldest academic journal in marketing (founded in 1936), and past chairperson of the American Marketing Association, the largest professional association of marketing educators and practitioners in North America.

Retailing and Wholesaling

Many consumers think that the success of the world's largest retailer, Wal-Mart, is merely the result of the chain's ability to perform the wholesaling functions discussed in the previous chapter better than the competition. They believe that by squeezing out inefficient and ineffective middlemen, Wal-Mart has been able to offer lower prices and forever changed the way retailers do business. In fact, by seizing upon the new opportunities offered by free trade and exploiting its massive buying power and distribution network, Wal-Mart, is seeking to replicate its U.S. success around the world.

After you have completed this chapter, you should be able to:

1. Describe the role retailing plays in the U.S. economy.
2. Explain the differences in the major types of retail formats used today.
3. Discuss how a retailer manages in today's environment.
4. Describe the role wholesaling plays in the U.S. economy.

However, what these consumers overlook is the fact that Wal-Mart has not only reengineered its marketing channel, but that the chain has done an outstanding job of attracting consumers to its stores. In addition, Wal-Mart offers more than low prices, which can be copied by competitors—at least over the short run—to generate this store traffic.

Consider, for example, how Wal-Mart has made use of the parking lots at its 3,200 Wal-Mart and Sam's Club outlets across the United States (even those with precious little greenery) by turning them into campgrounds for trailers and recreational vehicles.

Since the stores are open all night and they sell gear, groceries, auto supplies, and souvenirs, these locations are more appealing than other traditional "spaces for rent" campgrounds outside town. Besides Wal-Mart does not require reservations to use its parking lots. At the same time, so as to not offend either campground owners or townspeople, who are in all likelihood customers, Wal-Mart does not advertise its "open invitation" to campers, neither does it provide hookups for water, power, or sewage disposal on its parking lots. The retailer also asks campers not to stay more than 3 nights. Thus, after a few days visitors are going to need to go to a real "for rent" campsite.

By catering to campers and RVers in not-so-subtle ways, the retailer shows it understands the value of getting customers to its stores. Similarly, Sam's and its main competitor, Costco, recently improved their fresh fruit and grocery selections in an effort to generate more traffic. By stocking more fresh items, the average customer now visits a wholesale club store every 2 to 4 weeks, compared to the average 4 to 8 weeks in the past when customers would only shop to purchase the bulk nonperishable supplies. Using the same idea, the customized Rand McNally road atlas sold at all Wal-Marts includes the address of each store, its map coordinates, and the availability of RV accessories. RV

(Continued)

campers, after all, are profitable customers, so Wal-Mart stores in heavily traveled areas of the country stock extensive recreational vehicle and camping supplies, which have higher profits as a percentage of sales.

Trade association data shows that there over 32 million RV enthusiasts in the United States and many expect the number to grow as baby boomers begin to retire. These people like to travel, like the comforts of their own home, and best of all have money to spend. Thus, it seems that Wal-Mart will continue to be not only a general merchandise retailer, but a service retailer as well.

Retailing
consists of the final activity and steps needed to place merchandise made elsewhere into the hands of the consumer or to provide services to the consumer.

Retailing consists of the final activity and steps needed to place merchandise made elsewhere into the hands of the consumer or to provide services to the consumer. Quite simply, any firm that sells merchandise or provides services to the ultimate consumer for personal or household consumption is performing the retailing function. Regardless of whether the firm sells to the ultimate consumer in a store, through the mail, over the telephone, through a television infomercial, over the Internet, door to door, or through a vending machine, it is involved in retailing. Thus, while everybody realizes that fast-food establishments, discount stores, and florists are retailers, they often fail to recognize that a bank is also a retailer. Some experts point out the importance of retailing by noting that retailers are the marketing channel's "gatekeepers" since they are the final foot, or 12 inches, in a channel that may stretch thousands of miles. After all, if the consumers do not buy the retailer's offering, there is no need for a manufacturer to have a marketing channel.

Wholesalers
are persons or establishments that sell to retailers and/or other organizational buyers for industrial, institutional, and commercial use, but do not sell in significant amounts to ultimate consumers.

Wholesalers are those persons or establishments that sell to retailers and/or other organizational buyers for industrial, institutional, and commercial use, but do not sell in significant amounts to ultimate consumers. For example, a Costco outlet, even though it sells to consumers, would be considered a wholesaler since a majority of its sales are to small business operators. As a result, the government classifies all such sales as wholesale transactions.

These channel partners—retailers and wholesalers—in conjunction with the manufacturers, have made a significant contribution to this country's economic prosperity by having the goods/services readily available in an efficient, low-cost manner. In fact, the nations that have enjoyed the greatest economic and social progress have been those with strong retail and wholesale sectors. These channel partners have become valued and necessary members of society.

In the remainder of this chapter, we show the size and importance of retail marketing—the type of marketing you observe most frequently in your daily activities. We discuss the most popular types of retailing in the United States, and how retailers make their business decisions. In addition, this chapter looks at wholesale marketing. We describe the structure of wholesaling in our economy and discuss how manufacturers can market their products more effectively through wholesalers.

LEARNING OBJECTIVE 1

THE ROLE OF RETAILING IN THE U.S. ECONOMY

Currently, there are approximately 2.7 million retail establishments in the United States with total annual sales of nearly $2.6 trillion, or nearly $11,000 per capita.[1] The retail sector of the U.S. economy accounts for one out of every five jobs. In addition, there are 25 retail establishments for every 1,000 households, with each establishment averaging annual sales of nearly $1 million. Most retailers, however, are smaller and many have annual sales of less than $500,000 annually.

These figures, however, do not adequately reflect the changes that have occurred as a result of the number of new retail formats that developed during the last two decades of the 20th century. Most of these businesses have actually been new institutional forms, such as retailing on the Internet, warehouse club retailing, and supercenters. Change is truly the major cause of growth in retailing today. Remember, retailers are not obliged to conform to traditional ways of selling to consumers. Retailers and would-be retailers are free to forge new retailing approaches that capitalize on emerging market opportunities. This is all the more evident when we consider the fact that fashion trends, which in the past would have lasted for years, now may last only a few months.

Reaching the Consumer

When most people think of retailing, they usually think of the various types of fixed-based physical stores. After all, the overwhelming majority of retail sales occur in these stores. Today, however, retailing is much broader than simply thinking about a physical store. Retailers are finding alternatives to having the customer travel to a fixed-based store to purchase goods and services. For example, Dell Computer sells its computers and peripherals to households via the Internet, through the mail, or over the phone and still delivers within 2 days of the receipt of the order. Saks Fifth Avenue sells merchandise not only in its high fashion stores, but also through its Web site on the Internet. And Avon, Tupperware, and other direct sellers, while selling most of their goods via in-home parties, are also now using the Internet to reach their target customers. Therefore, it is important to remember that when discussing the various types of retailers, one must first consider if they are selling from a fixed physical location or not.

http://www.dell.com

http://www.saks.com

http://www.avon.com

http://www.tupperware.com

Current Retail Trends

Today retailers come in many different forms and classifications. After reviewing these classifications of retailers, which are usually expressed in terms of number of outlets, margin versus inventory turnover, and location, one will have a better appreciation of the diversity in retailing and the reasons why retailers behave as they do.

Number of Outlets and the Growth of Chain Stores

As a rule, retailers with several units are a stronger competitive threat because they can spread their fixed costs, such as advertising and top management salaries, over a larger number of stores and can achieve economies of scale in purchasing. However, single-unit retailers, such as your neighborhood IGA grocery store, do have several advantages when competing with larger chains. These single-unit retailers are generally owner- and family-operated and tend to have harder-working, more motivated employees. Also, they can focus all their efforts on one trade area and tailor their merchandise to that area. A strength for these stores is that in the past they were usually able to spot emerging customer desires sooner and respond to them faster than the larger multiunit retailers operating in many diverse markets.

http://www.iga.com

Any retail organization that operates more than one unit is technically a chain, but this is really not a very practical definition. The U.S. Census Bureau classifies chain stores into two size categories: 2 to 10 stores and 11 or more. We will use the 11 or more units when we use the term *chain stores*.

Figure 11.1 shows the importance of sales by chain stores, those retail operations with 11 or more units, as a percentage of total U.S. sales for some of the different merchandise lines. The statistics in Figure 11.1 reveal that chain stores account for 41 percent of all retail sales (including 99 percent of all department store sales and 63 percent of all grocery store sales). Though large chain operations account for 57 percent of nondurable goods sales, they only account for 16 percent of durable goods sales, such as autos and furniture.

Not all chain operations enjoy the same advantages. Small chains are local in nature and may enjoy some economies in buying and in having the merchandise tailored to their market needs. Large chains are generally regional or national and can take full advantage of the economies of scale that centralized buying, accounting, training, and information systems and a standard stock list can achieve. (A standard stock list requires that all stores in a retail chain stock the same merchandise.) Some national chains, such as Sears and Wal-Mart, recognizing the variations of regional tastes, use an optional stock list approach that gives each store the flexibility to adjust its merchandise mix to local tastes and demands. Sears, for example, has found that stores in the Rio Grande Valley in Texas sell a preponderance of smalls and mediums in men's shirts, while in Minnesota the chain sells a preponderance of larger sizes. Wal-Mart has gone so far as sell cans of Spamouflage—Spam in camouflage design cans—next to hunting rifles and fishing rods in its 760 rural Wal-Marts.[2]

Both standard and optional stock lists provide scale advantages in other retailing activities. For example, promotional savings occur when more than one store operates in an area and can utilize the same advertisements, even while tailoring specific merchandise to specific stores.

Chain stores have long been aware of the benefits of taking a leadership role in managing the marketing channel. When a chain store retailer is able to achieve critical mass in purchasing, it can get other channel members—wholesalers and manufacturers—to engage in activities they might not otherwise engage in and is thus referred to as the *channel captain*. Some of these activities include direct to store deliveries, increased promotional allowances, extended payment terms, and special package sizes. This action will allow the entire channel to operate in the most efficient manner.

In recent years, chains have relied on their high level of consumer recognition to engage in *private label branding*. Private label branding, sometimes called store branding, occurs when a retailer develops its own brand name and contracts with a manufacturer to produce the product with the retailer's brand on it. For example, Marks &

Figure 11.1	Importance of Large Chain Operations

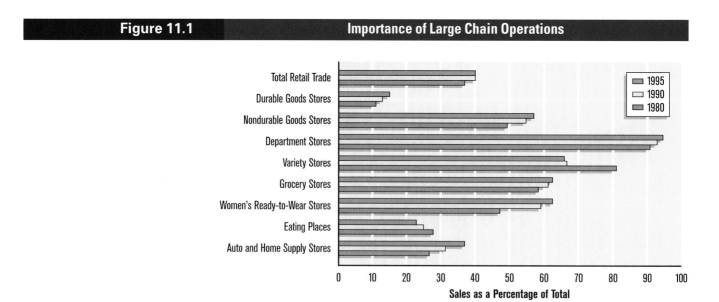

Source: U.S. Bureau of the Census, *Statistical Abstract of the United States: 1996*, 116th ed., Washington, D.C., 1996. Table No. 1259. *Retail Trade Sales of Multiunit Organizations, by Kind of Business: 1980–1995*, 766.

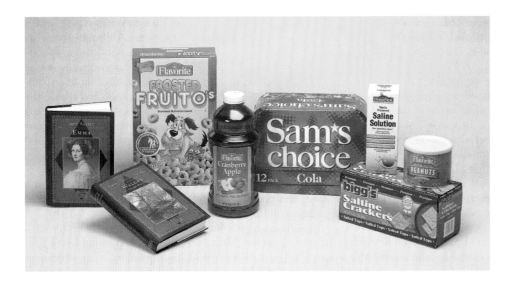

Spencer, the English retailing giant, first used the St. Michael private brand in 1928. The success of the St. Michael brand has enabled the firm to grow to more than 700 stores worldwide through a value orientation. Overall, private branding now accounts for almost 40 percent of department store sales and over 20 percent of total grocery units sold, and is expected to surpass 30 percent of grocery sales by the year 2005. Other retailers have borrowed from the success of the supermarkets and department stores with their private labels. Barnes & Noble now sells deluxe hardcover editions of many of the classics with its own publishing house imprint. Private labels usually have lower acquisition costs, thus producing savings that can be passed on to the consumer in the form of lower prices, thereby increasing demand. But while private brands have no national advertising costs, the retailer must spend more to develop local demand for the brand. As a result, retailers today are now competing with the national brand manufacturers, as well as the store across the street.

The major shortcoming of using the number of outlets to classify retailers is that it only addresses those retailers operating in a traditional brick-and-mortar space. As such, this scheme ignores many nontraditional retailers such as catalog-only operators and online retailers. How many outlets does Amazon.com have? One could argue that each new online computer is a potential retail outlet for the e-tailing giant.

Margins versus Inventory Turnover

Retailers can be classified in terms of their gross margin percent and rate of inventory turnover as shown in Figure 11.2. The **gross margin percentage** shows how much

Gross margin percentage shows how much gross margin a retailer makes as a percentage of sales.

Retailers Listed by Margin and Turnover **Figure 11.2**

High Margin

High-Margin/Low-Turnover Retailers	High-Margin/High-Turnover Retailers
Low-Margin/Low-Turnover Retailers	Low-Margin/High-Turnover Retailers

Low Turnover (left)   High Turnover (right)

Low Margin

Gross margin
equals net sales minus the cost of goods sold.

Operating expenses
are the costs a retailer incurs in running a business, other than the cost of merchandise.

Inventory turnover
refers to the number of times per year, on average, that a firm sells its inventory.

gross margin (net sales minus the cost of goods sold) the retailer makes as a percentage of sales; this is also referred to as the gross margin return on sales. A 40 percent gross margin indicates that on each dollar of sales the retailer generates 40 cents in gross margin dollars. This gross margin will be used to pay the retailer's **operating expenses** (the expenses the retailer incurs in running the business, other than the cost of the merchandise, e.g., rent, wages, utilities, depreciation, insurance, etc.). **Inventory turnover** refers to the number of times per year, on average, that a retailer sells its inventory. Thus an inventory turnover of 12 times indicates that, on average, the retailer turns over or sells its average inventory once a month. Likewise, an average inventory of $40,000 (retail) and annual sales of $240,000 means the retailer has turned over its inventory six times in one year ($240,000 divided by $40,000) or every 2 months.

Highly successful retailers have long recognized the relationship between gross margin percent, inventory turnover, and profit. One can classify retailers into four basic types by using the concepts of margin and turnover.

Typically, the low-margin/low-turnover retailer will not be able to generate sufficient profits to remain competitive and survive. Thus there are no good examples of successful retailers using this approach. On the other hand, the low-margin/high-turnover retailer is common in the United States. Perhaps the best brick-and-mortar example is the discount department stores such as Target, the warehouse clubs such as Sam's and Costco, and the category killers, which will be discussed in detail later in the chapter, such as Toys "R" Us. Toys "R" Us.com and Amazon.com are probably the best-known examples of low-margin/high-turnover e-tailers.

High-margin/low-turnover brick-and-mortar retailers are also quite common in the United States. Furniture stores, jewelry stores, gift shops, funeral homes, and most of the mom-and-pop stores located in small towns across the country are generally good examples of high-margin/low-turnover operations. Some clicks-and-mortar retailers using this approach include Coach and Sharper Image. Finally, some retailers are able to operate as a high-margin/high-turnover operation. As you might expect, this strategy can be very profitable. Probably the most popular examples are convenience food stores such as 7-Eleven, Circle K, Stop&Shop, or Quick Mart. However, because most retailers are trying to achieve a high turnover rate in these early stages of Internet retailing, there are no examples of e-tailers using this strategy.

A low-margin/low-turnover retailer is the least able of the four to withstand a competitive attack because this retailer is usually unprofitable or barely profitable, and when competitive intensity increases, profits are driven even lower. On the other hand, the high-margin/high-turnover retailer is in an excellent position to withstand and counter competitive threats because profit margins enable it to finance competitive price wars.

While the margin/turnover scheme provides an encompassing classification, it fails to capture the complete array of retailers operating in today's marketplace. For example, service retailers, such as those discussed in Chapter 9, and even some e-tailers, such as eBay and priceline.com, have no inventory to turnover. As such, while this scheme provides a good way to analyze retail competition, it neglects several important types of retailing.

Location

Location can be a key element in a retailer's success. In fact, one retailing axiom is that "the three major decisions in retailing are location, location, and location." After all, all retail stores attract customers from a limited geographic area. For example, a convenience store attracts most customers from within a 1.5-mile radius, a drug store from within a 3-mile radius, and a discount department store from within an 8-mile radius. Even retailers selling services must pay particular attention to location. A movie theater, dry cleaner, and barbershop will attract most of their customers from within a 3-mile area. As shown in Figure 11.3, there are four basic types of locations from which a store-based retailer can select: business districts, shopping centers/malls, freestanding units, and nontraditional locations.

As a rule, retailers selling convenience goods or services will have a smaller trade area than retailers of shopping or specialty goods and services. A physician specializing in cardiovascular diseases can attract patients from beyond his/her local community, but a general practitioner will only attract patients from his/her local community.

Types of Store-Based Retail Locations | Figure 11.3

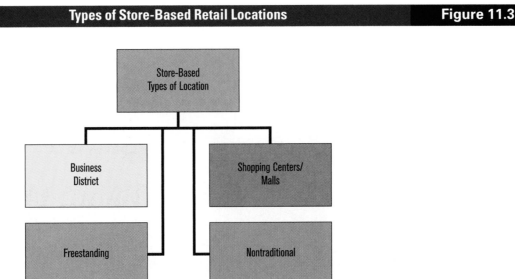

Business Districts. Historically, most retailers were located in their community's *central business district* (CBD), which was usually an unplanned shopping area that sprang up around the geographic point where public transportation systems converged. Many of the traditional department stores were located in the central business district along with a selection of specialty stores. Stores located here drew their clientele from the entire metropolitan area and even from nonresidents visiting the city.

The central business district has several strengths and weaknesses. Among its strengths are easy access to public transportation; wide product assortment; variety in images, prices, and services; and proximity to commercial and cultural activities. Some weaknesses are inadequate (and usually expensive) parking, older stores, high rents and taxes, traffic and delivery congestion, potentially high crime rate, and the general decaying conditions of many inner cities. Staples, the office supply superstore chain that began life as a freestanding suburban operation, has found success in the business district location and now operates over two dozen Staples Express stores in downtown locations. These Express stores are only a third the size of a regular Staples, but they are successful because they satisfy the customers' "immediate" needs.

In larger cities, secondary business districts and neighborhood business districts have developed. A *secondary business district* (SBD) is a shopping area that is smaller than the CBD and that revolves around at least one department or variety store at the intersection of two major streets. A *neighborhood business district* (NBD) is a shopping area that evolve to satisfy the convenience-oriented shopping needs of a neighborhood and generally contains several small stores, with the major retailer being either a supermarket or a variety store. An increasing number of national retail chains are finding these smaller districts an attractive location for new stores. This includes retailers such as Ann Taylor, The Body Shop, Starbucks, Crate & Barrel, Williams Sonoma, and Pottery Barn.

Shopping Centers/Malls. Ever since 1956 when Dayton's, now a part of Target, opened the country's first fully enclosed shopping center, Southdale Center, in Edina, Minnesota, America has had a love affair with the shopping center. Today, over 80 percent of Americans visit a shopping center three or more times a month. The key difference between shopping centers and a business district is that the shopping center, or mall, is a centrally owned and/or managed shopping district which is planned to have a **balanced tenancy** (the stores complement each other in merchandise offerings), and is surrounded by parking facilities. In addition, a shopping center has one or more **anchor stores** (a dominant large-scale store that is expected to draw customers to the center) and a variety of smaller stores.

Balanced tenancy
occurs where the stores complement each other in merchandise offerings.

Anchor stores
are dominant, large-scale stores that are expected to draw customers to a shopping center.

Figure 11.4 lists some of the advantages and disadvantages of locating in a shopping center/mall.

Freestanding Retailer. As the name implies, a freestanding retailer is not physically connected to other retailers, but instead has an individual building and parking area. Freestanding retailers generally locate along major traffic arteries. The difficulties involved in drawing, and then holding, customers to an isolated, freestanding store are the reason that only large, well-known retailers should attempt it. Small retailers may be unable to develop a loyal customer base because customers may not be willing to travel to a freestanding store that does not have a wide assortment of products and a local or national reputation. Kmart, Target, and Wal-Mart, as well as many convenience stores and gasoline stations, have used a freestanding location strategy successfully in the past. Discount appliance stores such as Best Buy and wholesale clubs such as Costco are successfully using freestanding locations today. However, when these large national chains

Figure 11.4	Advantages and Disadvantages of Locating in a Shopping Center/Mall

Advantages
1. Heavy traffic resulting from the wide range of product offerings
2. Nearness to the population
3. Cooperative planning and sharing of common costs
4. Access to highway and availability of parking
5. Lower crime rate
6. Clean, neat environment
7. More than adequate parking space

Disadvantages
1. Inflexible store hours (the retailer must stay open the hours of the center and can't be open at other times)
2. High rents
3. Restrictions as to the merchandise that the retailer may sell
4. Inflexible operations and required membership in the center's merchant organization
5. Possibility of too much competition and the fact that much of the traffic is not interested in a particular product offering
6. Dominance of the smaller stores by the anchor tenant

acquire land for a freestanding store, they often acquire more land than they need and then "out-parcel," or sell, the remaining land to smaller retailers. Some astute local retailers, as well as small regional chains, have found it quite attractive to buy excess land and build stores, even at a premium price, because of the traffic a large discounter generates.

Nontraditional Locations. Increasingly retailers are identifying nontraditional locations that offer more place utility or locational convenience. Recognizing, for example, that a significant number of travelers spend several hours in airports and can use this time to purchase merchandise they might otherwise purchase in their local community, retailers are experimenting with airport malls. One of the most unique airport malls is located within the confines of the Philadelphia International Airport. The mall's 33 shops include many well-known retailers (The Gap/Gap Kids, Godiva Chocolatier, and Sunglass Hut), as well as local favorites (Philly's Finest, the Philadelphia Museum Store, and Dinardo's). Similar to other malls, it is organized around a food court.[3]

On college campuses there are an increasing number of food courts in student unions, and truck and travel stops along interstate highways also are incorporating food courts. Some franchises such as Taco Bell and Dunkin' Donuts are putting in small food service units in convenience stores. Georgia Tech has a supermarket on its campus.[4] Hospitals are building emergency care clinics near where people live in the suburbs and away from the hospital, lawyers are opening storefront offices wherever there is high pedestrian traffic, and copying services such as Kinko's are locating in major office buildings.

Differentiating the Retail Experience

In today's highly competitive marketplace, retailers must develop marketing strategies that separate them from their competition. Wal-Mart's management, as the opening vignette illustrates, is keenly aware that not only must their marketing channel be superior to their competition, but that they must also make the "sale." They are aware of the three most basic tasks facing every retailer:

1. Attract consumers from their trading area into their store.
2. Convert these consumers into paying customers.
3. Operate in the most efficient manner, so as to reduce costs.

While these three tasks may seem too simple to be operational, they actually summarize the strategies that every retailer must perform. All retailers must try to differentiate themselves from the competition in order to accomplish these three tasks.

Perhaps, one of the greatest failings in retailing today is that too many retailers have concentrated on just one means of differentiation—price. Price promotions usually attract, but rarely hold, customers. The customers that the retailers gain with these promotions are just as apt to switch to another retailer when that retailer cuts its prices. As a result, retailers have taught consumers that if they wait, and in many cases this wait is only a matter of days, the merchandise they desire will go on sale. Unless a retailer has substantially lower operating costs, lowering prices is a very dangerous strategy to use because it can easily be copied by the competition and will usually result in reduced profits, or even a loss. Some better forms of differentiation for retailers to use in attracting customers include:

- *Physical differentiation of the product,* such as Target's brilliant and innovative "upscale" merchandise that really catches trends before other mass merchandisers. Little wonder that Target is the discount store for many shoppers, "who do not want to be seen in a discount store." Another retailer using this strategy is Lane Bryant, the women's plus size clothier. Lane Bryant, which was recently acquired by Charming Shoppes (which also operates the Fashion Bug and Catherine's Plus retail chains), has dropped its dowdy, baggy styles and refocused on body-hugging fashions that were only previously marketed to smaller sized women.
- *Selling process,* such as the way Saturn auto dealers use their excellent customer service to connect with their target customers.
- *After-purchase satisfaction,* which some of the major retailers, such as Lands' End and L.L. Bean, achieve with their "satisfaction guaranteed" programs that enable customers to return clothing even after years of wear for a new item.

- *Locational*, which Wal-Mart used with its parking lots in our opening vignette. Another retailer, Family Dollar, has tried to use its locational advantage to lure customers away from Wal-Mart. Family Dollar, with over 3,000 small stores that are usually located in strip centers en route to a nearby supercenter on the outskirts of a city, hopes to intercept shoppers who would rather pick up that toothpaste and motor oil in a convenient manner instead of having to walk through a cavernous building offering tires and tomatoes; shirts and soup; and bananas and car batteries. In addition, the small size of their stores also gives the retailer advantages in negotiating leases, thus reducing their operating costs in comparison to other chains.
- *Never being out-of-stock*, which means being in stock with regard to the sizes, colors, and styles that the target market expects the retailer to carry. Nordstrom, for example, offers a free shirt if it is out-of-stock on basic sizes.

These nonmonetary means of differentiation not only attract more customers, but also result in increased sales. Note also that in all these examples, the retailers are able to develop their own unique niches in the minds of the consumer and avoid price wars.

Evolution of Retail Competition

Since it is relatively easier to open a retail store, as opposed to a manufacturing plant, in terms of entry barriers (skill, expertise, and money), new retail institutions appear continuously. Marketing scholars have developed several theories to explain and describe the evolution of competition in retailing. We will review two of them briefly.

Wheel of Retailing

Wheel of retailing theory
is a pattern of competitive development in retailing which states that new types of retailers enter the market as low-status, low-margin, low-price operators. However, as they meet with success, these new retailers gradually acquire more sophisticated and elaborate facilities, thereby becoming less efficient and vulnerable to new types of low-margin retail competitors who progress through the same pattern.

The **wheel of retailing theory**, illustrated in Figure 11.5, is one of the oldest descriptions of the patterns of competitive development in retailing.[5] This theory states that new types of retailers enter the market as low-status, low-margin, and low-price operators. This is the entry phase and allows these retailers to compete effectively and take market share away from the more traditional retailers. However, as they meet with success, these new retailers gradually acquire more sophisticated and elaborate facilities, thereby becoming less efficient, in the trading-up phase. This creates both a higher investment and a subsequent rise in operating costs. Predictably, these retailers will enter the vulnerability phase and must raise prices and margins, becoming vulnerable to new types of low-margin retail competitors who progress through the same pattern. This appears to be the case today with outlet malls. Once bare-bones warehouses for manufacturers' imperfect or excess merchandise, outlet malls have quickly evolved into fancy, almost upscale

Figure 11.5	The Wheel of Retailing

Moderate to High Prices
Elaborate Facilities
Increase in Skills

Trading-up Phase

Vulnerability Phase

Entry Phase

Low Prices
Limited Facilities
Limited Service

High Prices
Excellent Facilities
Excellent Service
Declining ROI

malls where retailers try to outdo each other's accent lighting, private dressing rooms, and generous return policies. As a result, with the operating costs at such locations increasing and with regular department stores becoming more competitive, there is now little difference in the outlets' prices and the department stores' sale prices.

Holiday Hospitality Corporation, which is owned by Six Continents, recognizing that it could become vulnerable by constantly upgrading its lodging units, developed four distinct hotel/motel formats, Holiday Inn Express, Holiday Inn Select, Holiday Inn, and Holiday Inn Crowne Plaza (see Figure 11.6). Holiday Inn Express is targeted at the in-and-out businessperson or traveler who is willing to forgo some amenities for a lower price. Holiday Inn Select is similar to the Express but is aimed at the business traveler

Different Retail Formats of Holiday Hospitality Corporation   **Figure 11.6**

staying for a longer period of time who desires a few more amenities, such as dataport connections and conference rooms. The traditional Holiday Inn is targeted at the middle-class market and provides higher cost features such as a restaurant, lounge, conference rooms, and a swimming pool. The Holiday Inn Crowne Plaza is targeted at the more upscale or executive business traveler and features luxurious furnishings and restaurants, health spas, and a variety of business services, conference rooms, and other amenities. Realizing that consumers may have different lodging needs depending on the circumstances, Holiday Hospitality has tied these four different formats together with the same loyalty program—the Priority Club.

Retail Life Cycle

Retail life cycle

is a description of competitive development in retailing that assumes that retail institutions pass through an identifiable cycle that includes four distinct stages: (1) introduction, (2) growth, (3) maturity, and (4) decline.

Much like the product life cycle discussed in Chapter 8, the **retail life cycle** assumes that retail institutions pass through an identifiable cycle. This cycle includes four distinct stages:

1. introduction
2. growth
3. maturity
4. decline

Figure 11.7 lists the various stages of the retail life cycle for many of our current retail institutions.

Introduction. The process begins with an entrepreneur who is willing and able to develop a new approach that offers increased value to the customer. In other words, a new type of retail institution is developed at this stage. During the introduction stage profits are low, despite the increasing sales level, due to amortizing development costs.

Growth. During the growth stage, sales, and usually profits, explode. Many others begin to copy the idea. Toward the end of this period cost pressures that arise from the need for

Figure 11.7	**The Retail Life Cycle**

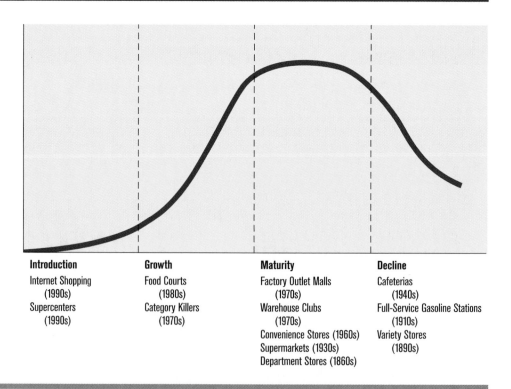

Introduction	Growth	Maturity	Decline
Internet Shopping (1990s)	Food Courts (1980s)	Factory Outlet Malls (1970s)	Cafeterias (1940s)
Supercenters (1990s)	Category Killers (1970s)	Warehouse Clubs (1970s)	Full-Service Gasoline Stations (1910s)
		Convenience Stores (1960s)	Variety Stores (1890s)
		Supermarkets (1930s)	
		Department Stores (1860s)	

a larger staff, more complex internal systems, increased management controls, and other requirements of operating large, multiunit organizations overtake some of the favorable results. Consequently, late in this stage both market share and profitability tend to approach their maximum level.

Maturity. In the maturity stage, market share stabilizes and severe profit declines are experienced for several reasons. First, managers have become accustomed to managing a high-growth firm that was simple and small, but now they must manage a large, complex firm in a nongrowing market. Second, the industry has typically overexpanded. Third, competitive assaults will be made on mature firms by new retailing formats (a bold entrepreneur offering a new value proposition, thus beginning a retail life cycle for yet another type of retail institution).

Decline. Although all types of retail institutions will inevitably reach the decline stage, retail managers will try to postpone it by changing their offerings. These attempts can stave off the decline stage, but a return to earlier, attractive levels of operating performance is not likely. Sooner or later a major loss of market share will occur, profits fall, and the once promising idea is no longer needed in the marketplace.

Three primary implications can be derived from the discussion of the retail life cycle:

1. Retailers should remain flexible so that they are able to adapt their strategies to the various stages of the life cycle.
2. Since profits vary by stage in the retail life cycle, retailers need to carefully analyze the risks and profits of entering the various life cycle stages or expanding their outlets at various stages in life cycle.
3. Retailers need to extend the maturity stage. Since they will have substantial investments in a particular form of retailing by the time maturity stage arrives, they will have a strong interest in trying to work that investment as long as possible.

The importance of these three points is reinforced by the fact that the retail life cycle is accelerating today. New retail concepts now move quickly from introduction to maturity because the leading operators have aggressive growth goals and their investors demand a quick return on investment. Larger retailers with the capital and expertise in concept rollout will acquire many smaller entrepreneurs with new ideas.

MAJOR TYPES OF RETAIL FORMATS

LEARNING OBJECTIVE 2

As pointed out in Chapter 1, once marketing managers identify a target market they must identify the most effective way to reach this market. The same is true with retailers. (See Inside Story box.) Essentially there are two types: store-based and nonstore-based formats. *Store-based retailers* operate from a fixed location that requires customers to travel to the store to view and select merchandise and/or services. Essentially, the retailer requires that the consumer perform part of the transporting activity. *Nonstore-based retailers* attempt to reach the customer at home, work, or any place other than a store where they might be susceptible to purchasing. Today, many retailers are trying to reach customers on the Internet.

There are many examples of retailers operating successfully in more than one type of format by using different marketing strategies, each making use of a unique blend of product, price, promotion, and place. Saks Incorporated, which owns 62 Saks Fifth Avenue stores and the Saks Web site, also owns 50 Saks Off 5th stores, 250 department stores under the names of Parisian Proffitt's, McRae's, Younkers, Herberger's, Carson Pirie Scott, and Bergner's. Each operation is tailored to meet the needs of a local market.

Store-Based Retailers

The six retailers using the store-based format today are department stores, specialty stores, supermarkets, supercenters, category killers, and convenience stores (see Figure 11.8).

All Laws Governing Retailing Are Not the Same

Each nation's regulations reflect and reinforce its brand of capitalism—predatory in the United States, paternal in Germany, and protected in Japan—and its social values. As a result, sometimes government regulations in foreign nations can drive retailers crazy.

As a result of these different philosophies, here are some of the "unusual" laws regulating retailers around the world.

In Germany, comparative advertising is banned, also local authorities can—and do—bar new stores if they believe existing stores will be hurt. Germany's paternal approach to protect existing firms impacted Lands' End in 1999 when the retailer tried to use its trademarked "Money Back Guarantee, No Matter What." It seems that the Center for the Fight Against Unfair Competition felt this guarantee would be unfair to traditional German retailers. The German courts ruled that the American retailer could honor the guarantee, just not advertise the fact. Lands' End got around this by having its German Web site not mention the guarantee, but instead link to a separate Web site that did.

Retailers in Germany are also restricted in the number of hours they may be open. The law allows retail stores to stay open until 8:00 P.M. on weekdays, until 4:00 P.M. on Saturday and, with the exception of bakeries which can open for three hours, cannot open on Sunday. However, certain transportation terminals are permitted to be open longer hours during the week and on Sunday for the convenience of travelers.

In addition, the sale of any item in Germany costing over 300 Euros ($300 U.S.) requires the registration of the customer's name and address. One German law that many Americans consumers might appreciate is that mail carriers have to obey "no advertising" (i.e., junk mail) stickers that many Germans attach to their mailboxes. However, such a law may be disheartening for retailers.

In Japan, local merchants can legally demand concessions when a new store opens nearby. This can often delay construction for years. Japan also has a law, designed to protect small retailers, stating that giant retailers can stay open until 8:00 P.M. but are required to close their stores at least 20 days a year for "holidays." In addition, self-service gas stations, and any discounter that wants to introduce them, are banned in Japan on the ground that they are a fire hazard.

Still, while it is more difficult to open and operate retail outlets in these two countries than in the United States, it is easier to open a bank branch in those countries than it is to open one in all but a few U.S. states. However, this is rapidly changing as more and more banks are merging, thus creating the need for branch banking.

Quebec, a Canadian province that is 80 percent French-speaking, allows English on commercial signs only if French words dominate.

In Italy, retailers may operate 44 hours per week provided that they close on Sunday.

In Mexico, the clock on cash discounts, discounts given to retailers by vendors for early payment, does not start ticking until the retailers receive the bill and determine it is acceptable.

In Australia, store hours are regulated separately by each state, resulting in confusion across the country. Also, supermarkets in Australia that use conveyor belts on their checkouts must pay an annual $25 "weights and scaffolding" fee for each one.

The Netherlands sets minimum selling prices for goods produced within the country, but none for imported items.

The size of a store in France is limited to 1,000 square meters if it is located in a city with a population of less than 40,000. If the city is larger, the store size may increase to 1,500 square meters. Also, in France, the funeral business was treated as a utility until recently. Funeral operators had to bid for the right to operate in a certain city at fixed prices.

Retailers in the United Kingdom, the country from which U.S. "blue laws" were copied, have to cope with laws that make it legal to buy food for a mule on Sunday, but not for your baby. Also, pornographic material may be sold on Sunday, but not a Bible to take to church. British retailers do get around these laws. One British furniture dealer, for example, sells a box of matches for 1,000 British pounds ($1,650), then gives the customer a "free" suite of furniture.

Norway, also, bans all Sunday retailing, except for filling stations less than 150 square meters, grocery stores less than 100 square meters, and certain transportation terminals.

China has backtracked from a blanket ban on all direct door-to-door selling to allow direct sales companies that invest at least $10 million in China (e.g., Amway), to sell door-to-door.

However, an international retailer seeking to open a store in the United States must be prepared for some of our unusual local laws. For example, a law in Kansas City prohibits the sale of capguns to children, but not shotguns.

Six Basic Types of Store-Based Retailers	Figure 11.8

Department stores are large-scale operations that contain a broad product mix consisting of many different product lines with above-average depth in each of them.

Specialty stores are relatively small-scale stores offering a great deal of depth in a narrow range of product lines.

Supermarkets are retailers that sell groceries and some general merchandise products through large-scale physical facilities with self-service and self-selection displays that enable the retailer to shift the performance of some marketing functions to the consumer.

Supercenters are cavernous, one-stop combinations of supermarkets and discount department stores, which range in size from 120,000 to 160,000 square feet, and carry between 80,000 to 100,000 products ranging from televisions to peanut butter to fax machines.

Category killers get their name from their marketing strategy of carrying such a large amount of merchandise in a single category at such good prices that they make it impossible for customers to walk out without purchasing what they need, thus "killing" the competition.

Convenience stores stock frequently purchased products such as gasoline, bread, tobacco, and milk that tend to be consumed within 30 minutes of purchase, as well as offering services such as ATMs and car washes.

Department Stores

Department stores were first introduced in the mid-1800s, about the time of the Civil War. Today Sears, May Company, Marshall Field, JCPenney, Federated Stores, and Dillard's are just some of the well-known traditional department stores operating in the United States. These stores generally have 120,000 to 300,000 square feet of selling space. The various related product lines carried in the store's product mix are merchandised in separate departments (including menswear, womenswear, jewelry, toys, sporting goods, home furnishings, and furniture). Department stores offer many customer services, such as knowledgeable and helpful sales clerks, delivery and wrapping services, liberal return policies, and store credit cards.

Despite its past successes, the future of the traditional department store is clouded. Squeezed by discounters at the low end of the price spectrum and specialty stores at the high end of the selection spectrum, today's department stores are only managing to achieve a low rate of sales growth. However, as consumers turn to alternative formats that are more convenient or offer a stronger value or lifestyle appeal, department stores are beginning to fight back by using technology to better manage their marketing channels in order to lower prices.

Discount department stores, commonly called *discounters*, are an outgrowth of the traditional department store. These stores first appeared in the mid-1940s, just after World War II, and featured low prices. Like traditional department stores, discounters carry a variety of product lines, and use departmental merchandising techniques. However, they do so at lower prices than traditional department stores. Their lower prices are the result of offering fewer customer services, having less upscale facilities, and using self-service to reduce operating expenses. Examples include Target, Kohl's, Wal-Mart, and Kmart. These stores usually range in size from 40,000 to 100,000 square feet. Most communities with a population over 10,000 have either a traditional department store or a discount department store. Strong growth is forecasted for this format as the discounters open new stores, add new product categories, and utilize their scale efficiencies to lower prices.

Specialty Stores

Specialty stores are relatively small-scale stores offering a great deal of product depth within a narrow range of product lines. Specialty stores are common in womenswear, menswear, jewelry, footwear, electronics, furniture, sporting goods, automotive, painting supplies, flowers, liquor, pets, bridal wear, and fabrics. Many specialty stores range from 3,000 to 7,500 square feet, although some are much smaller and others, such as furniture stores which can occupy over 100,000 square feet, are much larger. Some popular specialty stores are The Gap (leisure wear), Hickory Farms (specialty cheeses and snacks), Walgreens (drugstores), and Foot Locker (jogging and athletic shoes).

Most successful specialty stores pursue a strong store positioning strategy. Here all the elements of the store's marketing mix are aimed at a well-defined target market, which is segmented from the total market based on some specific demographic or lifestyle variable. Chico's, for example, is a specialty retailer of exclusively designed, private label, sophisticated, casual-to-dressy clothing, complementary accessories, and other nonclothing gift items that flatters baby boomer women with personal attention, special promotions, and discounts. dELiA, on the other hand, caters to the special whims of teenage girls through its retail stores, catalogs, and Web site.

Given the continued aging of the U.S population, the record introductions of new remedies and drugs, as well as the record number of Americans with health insurance, drugstores are one of the types of specialty stores for which sales volume is expected to surge over the next decade.

Supermarkets

The *supermarket* concept of retailing developed in the 1930s, when the Great Depression forced many grocers to replace their small, inefficient, traditional, mom-and-pop corner stores in order to offer consumers lower prices. Selling groceries and some general merchandise products through large-scale physical facilities with self-service and self-selection displays enabled the supermarket retailer to shift the performance of some distribution functions to consumers. Today, most grocery retailing is still done through supermarkets such as Safeway, Albertson's, and Kroger, although supercenters are rapidly gaining market share. Wal-Mart, however, with its new neighborhood stores as well as its supercenters (discussed later), is now the nation's volume leader in grocery sales.

The supermarket concept involves five basic principles directed at improving retail productivity and reducing the cost of distribution:

1. Self-service and self-selection displays
2. Centralization of customer services at the checkout counter/desk
3. Large-scale, low-cost physical facilities
4. A strong price emphasis
5. A broad assortment of merchandise to facilitate multiple-item purchases

Recently, the supermarket retailing concept has been used in developing two new types of nonfood retailing, which are discussed later: the supercenter and the category killer. In addition to expanding the supermarket concept to include new types of stores, the traditional food supermarket's product mix is being expanded to include prepared, or ready-to-eat, foods. For example, many supermarkets now offer HMRs (home-meal-replacements) to compete with fast-food operators, as well as nonfood items such as clothing, small appliances, automotive supplies, nonprescription drugs, cosmetics, and fragrances. This phenomenon is referred to as **scrambled merchandising**. This results in unrelated lines of merchandise being carried by a single retailer. For example, convenience stores today sell gasoline, bread, milk, beer, cigarettes, magazines, and even fast food. The effects of scrambled merchandising can be easily seen in Figure 11.9, which shows the various formats in which consumers can purchase different products.

Over the next decade, as more supercenters are opened and Americans eat out more often, thereby lowering their need for groceries, the growth in supermarket sales is expected to just match the level of inflation. This lower level of sales growth should foster industry consolidation as the remaining players seek to become more competitive.

Supercenters

One of the newest competitive retail types within the store-based format is the *supercenter*. These cavernous, one-stop combination supermarkets and discount department stores, which range in size from 120,000 to 160,000 square feet, carry between 80,000 to 100,000 products ranging from televisions to peanut butter to fax machines. In addition, these retailers provide services, such as in-store banks, hair stylists, restaurants, and eye-care specialists. Cross-shopping is a major appeal of supercenters as they offer the customer the availability of general merchandise, as well as prescriptions and gas, at the same location. The availability of such one-stop shopping draws customers from a 30- to 50-mile radius in some rural areas and lower the customer's total cost of purchasing in terms of time and stores visited without sacrificing service and variety.

Wal-Mart, Kmart, and Target are banking their future on this new format. Yet, while they are adding a combined 500 new supercenters a year, some retail analysts question if

Scrambled merchandising is the handling of merchandise lines based solely on the profitability criterion and without regard to the consistency of the product or merchandise mix.

| | The Effects of Scrambled Merchandising | | | | | | | Figure 11.9 |

Store	Loaf Bread	Hamburger	Dog Food	Candy	Paper Towels	Ice Cream	Motor Oil
Fast Food Outlet		●		●		●	
Supermarket	●	●	●	●	●	●	●
Convenience Store	●	●	●	●	●	●	●
Supercenter	●	●	●	●	●	●	●
Club Store	●	●	●	●	●	●	●
Pet Food Store			●				
Drug Store	●		●	●	●	●	●
Home Improvement		●		●	●		●

older consumers can get around in these stores, if the younger ones will take the time to shop these mammoth stores, or if folks will buy tires, apparel, and tomatoes on the same shopping trip. Nevertheless, since the country's major retailers are using supercenters as their vehicle for growth over the next decade, it is difficult to predict failure. Some retailers are prepared for customer dissatisfaction with supercenters. For example, Dollar General revamped its numerous small-sized discount stores to handle more paper goods and other frequently purchased general merchandise.[6] In addition, supermarkets who have always operated with paper-thin net profit margins are seeking to match, if not beat, the supercenters' prices.

Category Killers

Essentially the ultimate in specialty stores, the **category killer** got its name from its marketing strategy: carry such a large amount of merchandise in a single category at such good prices that it makes it impossible for customers to walk out without purchasing what they needed; thus "killing" the competition.

Toys "R" Us, which began operations in the 1950s, has the distinction of being the first category killer. Today, Toys "R" Us operates over 700 toy stores in the United States and over 500 additional stores around the globe. The company also operates 200 Kids "R"

Category killers
get their name from their marketing strategy of carrying such a large amount of merchandise in a single category at such good prices that they make it impossible for customers to walk out without purchasing what they needed, thus "killing" the competition.

Us children's clothing stores in the United States, 150 Babies "R" Us stores featuring infant-toddler apparel, and 37 educational specialty stores under the name Imaginarium.

Beginning in the 1980s, the category killer retail format exploded. Some other well-known category killers include: Best Buy, Home Depot, Lowe's, Blockbuster Video, Circuit City, Office Depot, Office Max, PetsMart, Bed Bath & Beyond, AutoZone, Barnes & Noble, and Sports Authority. Many category killers are also diverting business away from traditional wholesale supply houses. For example, Home Depot and Lowe's appeal to professional contractors and Office Depot and Office Max to business owners who traditionally purchased supplies from hardware wholesalers and office supply and equipment wholesalers.

Convenience Stores

Convenience stores (c-stores) are generally small (2,000 to 4,000 square feet) and offer products such as fast food, beverages, household staples, and gasoline. C-stores serve the neighborhood within 1.5 miles of the store. Because these stores offer greater time, place, and possession utility to the consumer, while operating with a lower inventory turnover rate than do larger grocery stores, c-stores often charge higher prices on comparable items. 7-Eleven, the originator of the c-store concept, is still this country's largest c-store chain. Unit growth of this format is coming from the major oil companies, such as ChevronTexaco and Conoco, who have been rapidly converting conventional gasoline stations into modern convenience stores. In addition, sales of lottery tickets, beverages, candy, and snacks, as well as food services, should offset the loss of tobacco sales and the uncertainty of future gasoline prices.

Nonstore-Based Retailers

Several industry analysts contend that changes in nonstore-based operators will lead to the next revolution in retailing. The mechanics for such a revolution are already in place as a variety of established selling techniques permit consumers to purchase goods and services without having to leave home. With accelerated communications technology and changing consumer lifestyles, the growth potential for nonstore retailing is explosive. Five types of nonstore retailing will be discussed: street peddling, direct selling, mail order, automatic merchandising machine operators, and electronic shopping.

In addition, the move into multiformat retailing has accelerated over the past few years. Catalog retailers, such as previously mentioned dELiA, have successfully expanded into the Internet by leveraging their direct marketing skills and established distribution network. Other Internet operators, such as the nation's number one online stockbroker Charles Schwab, are adding physical outlets to generate additional traffic for their sites. (Interestingly enough, while Schwab does 80 percent of their transactions electronically, they open 70 percent of their new accounts face-to-face in branch offices.[7] Many store-based retailers, such as Dillard's and JCPenney, are not only continuing to build traditional stores but are developing and enhancing their Web sites. This latter group has found that their Internet sites not only generate online sales, but they also increase sales in their traditional store-based outlets. According to one study, consumers who visit a retailer's Web site before shopping in the store spend 33 percent more on an annual basis than regular in-store shoppers.[8]

Street Peddling

Retailing has changed drastically throughout the history of this country. The United States has evolved from a nation dependent on *street peddlers* selling their products in the streets, open markets, or via covered wagons, to small stores near the geographic center of the town, to neighborhood shopping strips, and today to massive supercenters and indoor shopping malls in the suburbs.

Street peddling is still common in many parts of the world. To this day, peddlers sell their merchandise from pushcarts or temporary stalls set up on a street. Even today, in the United States, street peddlers are commonly seen on street corners in major metropolitan areas. Here they sell inexpensive items such as T-shirts, watches, books, magazines, tobacco, candy, and hot dogs, or provide a service as do streetside sketch artists and musicians. The increase in the number of street peddlers is an outgrowth of the increase in the number of pedestrians with disposable income.

Many cities view the presence of street peddlers as positive. It gives an area a distinctive flavor not unlike that of New Orleans' French Quarter. Other cities, due to pressure from store-based retailers who pay higher taxes and support many community activities, are considering a ban on this retail format.

Direct Selling

Direct sellers are primarily engaged in the retail sale of merchandise on a personal basis, through party plans (Discovery Toys, Artistic Impressions, and Kids Only Clothing Club) or one-on-one contact in the home or workplace (Avon, Amway, and Electrolux), away from a fixed place of business.[9] Other direct sellers, such as Tupperware, Regal Ware, and Jafra Cosmetics, use a combination of both plans. In the United States today, sales from direct selling total over $25 billion annually and are made by over 10 million individuals who are not employed by the organization they represent but are independent contractors. Worldwide direct selling sales are $68 billion, with Japan being the largest direct selling country. Major products sold in the United States include personal care items (Mary Kay Cosmetics), decorative home products (Princess House, Home Interiors and Gifts), cookware (West Bend, CUTCO), and encyclopedias (World Book).

Today, with women increasingly out of the home, little "cold canvassing" is done. Many companies now telephone to make appointments to show their merchandise. In addition, traditional direct selling techniques are being merged with newer marketing channels, such as mail order and the Internet. Merchandise is being shown and sold anywhere people gather, such as at state fairs, in shopping malls, and at airports. Although the time and place of direct selling have changed, the major attributes of direct selling remain the same: support from the parent organization for the independent contractor; knowledge and demonstration of the product by a salesperson; excellent warranties and guarantees; and the person-to-person component.

Mail Order

Mail order houses, which generate annual sales of $67 billion,[10] are primarily engaged in the retail sale of products by catalog and mail order. Included are book and music clubs, jewelry firms, novelty merchandise firms, and specialty merchandisers, such as sporting goods (L.L. Bean), children's apparel retailers (Right Start), and kitchenware (Williams-Sonoma). While mail order retailers continue to offer their merchandise via print catalogs, which produce a profit of $2.20 per mailed catalog,[11] almost all have also begun to offer their merchandise online.

While mail order houses have done a great job of segmenting the overall market for their particular offerings, increasing postal and paper costs may negatively impact the future of this retail format. To combat these cost increases, many catalog operations are relying on the use of new printing strategies that lower the overall cost of printing.

Automatic Merchandising Machine Operators

Automatic merchandising machine operators are primarily engaged in the retail sale of products by means of automatic merchandising units, or vending machines. Surprisingly, such machines have been with us since about 215 B.C., when Egyptians devised a coin-operated water dispenser for places of worship.[12] To be designated a vending machine, a machine must dispense a product in exchange for money, and operate unattended, except for refills and repairs. Therefore, sales made by coin-operated service machines, such as amusements, videos, and game machines, are not included.

Because laws in every state prohibit the sale of tobacco products to persons under the age of 18, retailers or owners of businesses that sell cigarettes or other tobacco products are required to post a conspicuous sign stating that tobacco sales to minors are illegal and that proof of age is required to purchase tobacco products. Such requirements are expected to limit the use of vending machines for cigarette sales, which will negatively impact total vending machine sales in the future.

Electronic Shopping

The general belief among retail experts at the beginning of the millennium was that *electronic shopping* would soon take off. Every major player in the retail industry, computer industry, telecommunications industry, and the transaction processing industry was committed to this growth engine of the so-called new economy. However, just as the Y2K problem was overrated, so were these early predictions about the Internet. Yes, consumers are using the Internet, but not to shop. So far, the Internet has been a revolution in communications, not distribution. E-tailers have found out that it is more difficult than

they planned to turn viewership of a Web site into a sales transaction.[13] Maybe consumers find it too difficult getting from the e-tailer's home page to its sales confirmation window. Another possible problem may be that some consumers might not like paying both a sales tax and shipping costs. Still others may not believe that their credit card numbers are really secure. Whatever the problem, and with the possible exception of books, music, and travel products, consumers have not used the Internet for retail purchases as expected.

Many e-tailers may have forgotten an important marketing lesson from the past. Being first into a market does not guarantee success. After all, Diet RC Cola, and not Diet Coke or Diet Pepsi, was the first diet cola on the market, and there were already 41 publicly held discount stores and another 2 dozen privately owned discounters already in business when Sam Walton opened his first Wal-Mart in 1962.[14] Most of the early entrants into e-tailing had a problem with their marketing plan: They believed that market share was more important than profits. As a result, they not only gave away cameras in an attempt to sell film, they also gave away the film, free developing, and postage. Their marketing plan forgot one of the simple rules of any business: Cash in must exceed cash out. Little wonder that between January 2000 and September 2001, 677 Internet firms failed.[15]

Still, as we will point out in Chapter 15, out of these failures will come businesses that will truly introduce a "new economy." As the Internet grows to allow real-time, fully immersive, three-dimensional video, Americans will spend more of their time in cyberspace. This in turn will create a whole new shopping experience. Future shoppers will opt for the convenience and heightened experience of virtual shopping. Browsing will be even easier and the choices more extensive. As a result conversion rates, the percentage of shoppers who actually make a purchase, will increase to the rates enjoyed by brick-and-mortar retailers.

Consumers will still want social activity and connections outside the home; however, e-tailing will likely evolve beyond shopping to include real entertainment, such as attending a sporting event or concert where, incidentally, a lot of merchandise and food will be offered for sale. The Internet will allow consumers to shop with family and friends, even if they live half the world away. However, before conceding that e-tailing will replace the traditional store, it may be advisable to consider several key facts.

1. The Internet will not increase overall consumer demand. In terms of overall consumer spending, online sales will definitely impact store and catalog sales. This cannibalization of sales will vary across product categories. Online shopping, which in 2001 accounted for less than 1 percent of retail sales, will be big for airline tickets, PCs, hotel reservations, books, music, and video.[16] However, online shopping will remain a minor player for all other categories, at least until technology dramatically improves.
2. Clicks-and-mortar strategies that integrate a single message will be more powerful than a pure e-tailing strategy. This will be especially true once clicks-and-mortar retailers, who operate both online and from traditional stores, learn the importance of reinforcing their Internet presence with in-store kiosks.
3. E-tailers must pay better attention to customer service. Most e-tailers tend to do a good job during busy seasons, such as Christmas. However, in an effort to reduce operating costs, they reduce their service standards at other times. Customers are demanding such basic services as e-mail confirmation of orders, availability of real-time inventory, and more product information, including the ability to view close-up product images online.

MANAGING THE RETAIL MIX

LEARNING OBJECTIVE 3

Like all marketers, retailers must first identify their target market and then determine the specific **retail mix** to appeal to this target market in order to perform the first two retailing tasks discussed earlier in this chapter: (1) attract consumers to come inside their store, and (2) turn these consumers into loyal customers by enticing them to make a purchase. A retail mix is a combination of merchandise, price, advertising and promotion, customer services and selling, and store layout and design.

Retail mix
is a retailer's combination of merchandise, prices, advertising, location, customer services, selling, and store layout and design that is used attract customers.

Atmospherics

When developing their retail mix, retailers must begin by realizing that the store (or Web site) is a major part of their offering. After all, the retailer must create a positive image for the store/Web site. Brick-and-mortar retailers, for example, need to be concerned with how customers perceive the in-store environment and whether they are comfortable in it. Customers are more likely to make larger and more frequent purchases if a store's total environment is comfortable and welcoming, and encourages browsing. Factors that influence customers' perceptions include the merchandise, level of service offered by employees, fixtures, floor layout, sound, and odor.

Attracting Consumers

The quality, style, and presentation of the merchandise lines carried by a store affect the store's status in the eyes of the consumer. Furniture retailers that want to project a high-status image will carry Heritage, Henredon, and other upscale furniture lines. Austrian crystal and Irish linen are not likely to be found in the same housewares department as plastic glasses and oilcloth table coverings. Customers select where to shop for particular items according to their overall perception of the available stores. Mothers might well go first to Target or Wal-Mart for children's playwear, but would probably skip over these stores in favor of Dillard's, or Bloomingdale's, or a specialty store when shopping for their daughter's prom gown.

Store fixtures must be consistent with the overall image that the retailer wishes to project. Suits crowded together on plastic coat hangers do not reflect the image of quality that similar suits project when hung on wooden hangers with ample space on the rack to facilitate customer browsing. If a retailer wants the store to project a quality image, the display units themselves must be adequately spaced and accessible. The aisles must be uncongested and well laid out, and related products should be placed close enough to promote ancillary purchases (e.g., a handbag to complement a newly purchased pair of shoes).

Effective store design must appeal to the human senses of sight, sound, smell, and touch. Obviously, the majority of design activity in a retail store is focused on affecting sight, but research has shown that the other senses can also be very important. Since smell is believed to be the most closely linked of all the senses to memory and emotions, retailers hope that its use as an in-store marketing tool will put consumers in the "mood." Victoria's Secret has deployed potpourri caches throughout its stores, and in fact now sells them, to create the ambiance of a lingerie closet. Disney uses the smell of fresh

baked cookies on Main Street in the Magic Kingdom to relax customers and provide a feeling of warmth.

Retailers have piped music, for example, Muzak, into their stores for generations, believing that a musical backdrop will create a more relaxing environment and encourage customers to stay longer.[17] However, the music must match the merchandise being offered. For example, a jeans retailer might play hip-hop over baggies and classic rock over the Dockers. Also, while soothing classical music has been shown to encourage customers to shop longer[18] and select more expensive merchandise,[19] it may be inconsistent with the desired ambiance of a trendy fashion store catering to college-age women. Today, some retailers are experimenting with placing advertisements in background music. Other retailers have found a different use for canned music: A shopping mall in Australia plays Bing Crosby music to drive out kids who want to hang out after school. In addition, the mall uses pink fluorescent lights, which supposedly highlight pimples, to keep teenagers from cruising the mall on Friday nights.[20]

Turning Consumers into Loyal Customers

It is not enough to simply attract store/Web site customers; the retailer must also convince them to make a purchase. Successful retailers recognize that they can differentiate themselves from the competition not only by having the right merchandise, but also by encouraging their employees to do a better job of satisfying the needs of their customers. There is general agreement that one of the most basic retailing strategies for creating competitive advantage is the delivery of high-quality service. As discussed in Chapter 9, good service must meet or exceed the customer's expectations. Retailers have come to realize that offering good customer service is a major demand-generator for their merchandise. Retailers must remember that not having properly trained employees to aid customers will lower the customer's satisfaction with the retailer, often irreparably.

Operating in the Most Efficient Manner

A store's environment must maximize its space productivity, a goal that is summarized in a simple but powerful truism in retailing: The more merchandise customers are exposed to, that is presented in an orderly manner, the more they tend to buy. The typical shopper in a department store goes into only two or three shopping areas per trip. Through careful planning of the store environment, the retailer can encourage customers to flow through the entire store, or at least more shopping areas, and see a wider variety of merchandise. The proper use of in-store advertising and displays will let customers know what is happening in other shopping areas and encourage visits to those areas. Conversely, however, the store does not want to push merchandise into every conceivable nook and cranny of the store so that customers cannot get to it.

Many retailers are focusing more attention on in-store marketing, based on the theory that marketing dollars spent inside the store, in the form of store design, merchandise presentation, visual displays, or in-store promotions, should lead to significantly greater sales and profit increases than marketing dollars spent in advertising and out-of-store public relations and promotions. After all, it is easier to get a consumer who is already in a store to buy more merchandise than planned, than to get a new consumer to come into a store.

One factor that hurts a store's productivity is shrinkage, or the loss of merchandise through theft, loss, and damage. It is called **shrinkage** because you usually do not know what happened to the missing items, only that the inventory level in the store has somehow shrunk. Even stores that move customers through the entire space and effectively use in-store marketing techniques to maximize sales can fall victim to high shrinkage. Remember, when a store sells an item for $1.29, it earns only a small percentage of that sale, perhaps ranging from 15 to 60 cents. When an item is stolen, lost, or damaged, however, the store loses the cost of that item (e.g., 69 cents in the case of the $1.29 item), and this loss is deducted from the store's overall sales. Shrinkage ranges from 1 to 4 percent of retail sales. While this may seem like a small number, consider that many retailers' after-tax profit is little more than 4 percent, so high shrinkage alone can make the difference between a profit and a loss.

Successful retailers manage their costs. Wal-Mart's founder, Sam Walton, was ahead of the curve and forever changed the face of retailing, when he realized that most of any product's cost gets added after the item is produced and moves from the factory to retailer's shelf and finally to the consumer. Therefore, Walton began enlisting suppliers to help him reduce these costs and increase the efficiency of product movement. Walton,

Shrinkage
refers to reduction of merchandise through theft, loss, and damage.

Charlie Hamilton: Making Retailing Fun

In 1985, at the young age of 12, Charlie Hamilton started his first fireworks stand in Lubbock, Texas, with nothing more than some inventory, a storage shed, and a fishing tackle box to hold change. Since his stand was near a busy intersection just outside the city limits, Charlie had five fierce competitors within 200 yards of his stand. Within 4 years, all but one competitor was left.

Charlie understood he was not selling fireworks, he was selling fun. He used many creative and colorful promotions to complete his mission of selling fun. For example, he dyed an adult sheep red and her lamb blue, while her other lamb remained white. Then he would dress up his little sister in a cowgirl outfit to ride the red sheep in front of the stand, as the blue and white lambs followed. The red, white, and blue sheep were a huge hit during Independence Day celebrations and received coverage from the local TV stations and newspaper.

Other interesting promotions included an Elvis impersonator, a 20-foot floating blimp, and an amusement ride. The goal of all these promotions was to attract attention to Discount City Fireworks and make it a fun and unique place to shop. He implemented a "No Dud" guarantee, which allowed customers to return any merchandise that did not perform properly. By the time that Charlie graduated from high school, he had eight stands and 45 employees. Charlie continued to operate the fireworks business until he graduated in 1995 from Texas Tech University with a degree in business management.

After graduation from college, along with three other partners, Charlie opened Boomer Book Company, a collegiate textbook store, at the University of Oklahoma. At 23, he was one of the youngest owners of a college bookstore in the country. Having purchased textbooks during college, Charlie was acutely aware of the poor customer service and depressing atmosphere of college bookstores. He wanted to change the way college text-

books were bought and sold. His first goal was to make the appearance of the store and the buying process fun.

One of the major problems in college bookstores is that students have difficulty locating the books they need. Charlie solved this problem by having clerks pull the books for students. Also, he placed a basketball net in the store so that customers could shoot baskets while they waited for their book order. Like the fireworks business, he developed creative ways to attract customers. For example, he would give each book customer a free Papa John's pizza. On busy days, a local band played and the store gave out free snow cones. The store staff would ask customers Trivia Pursuit questions, and the person with the correct answer would win a T-shirt or another prize. The store motto was "Students Serving Students," and customers appreciated having salespeople who understood the problems and lifestyle of college students.

Within 2 years, Charlie opened a second bookstore, Rocky Top Books, at the University of Tennessee (UT). He used the same promotions and customer service strategies that were successful at Boomer. One creative promotion occurred when UT's football team played their arch rival, the University of Florida (UF). During the 1998 season, UT won a close game in overtime. The fans stormed the field and tore down the goalposts. Seeing a marketing opportunity, Charlie negotiated with students to take one of the goalposts to his store. This idea proved extremely successful because it attracted the attention of regional radio, television, and newspapers. Rocky Top donated a piece of the goalpost to the local United Way for a statewide auction. UT continued their winning streak and eventually won the national championship. This goalpost still hangs in Rocky Top today.

In May 2000, Charlie sold his stores to a national bookstore chain that was very impressed with his innovative model for college bookstores. Still in his twenties, Charlie and his wife, Kathleen, are today active in retail consulting.

---

who never operated a computer in his life, also made a major commitment in the 1980s to computerizing Wal-Mart operation as a means to reduce these expenses. As a result of the introduction of the computer to retail management, Wal-Mart's selling, general, and administrative costs as a percentage of sales fell to less than 16 percent, while all of its competitors' operating expenses were still 2 to 4 percent higher. Simply put, Wal-Mart became the world's largest retailer by relentlessly cutting unnecessary costs and demanding that its suppliers do the same.

Category Management

One of the ways to reduce costs is the use of category management. Because of the increasing cost of carrying inventory, the shortening of retail life cycles, the more rapid turning of the wheel of retailing, and the rapid growth of hypercompetitive retailers (especially category killers, supercenters, and Internet-based competitors), retailers have turned their attention to category management as the best way to reduce unnecessary costs. **Category management** is a process of managing and planning all SKUs within a product category as a distinct business. An **SKU**, or stock keeping unit, refers to

egory management
process of managing and planning all s within a product category as a dis- business.

U
stock keeping unit and refers to a dis- merchandise item in the retailer's handise assortment.

a distinct merchandise item in the retailer's merchandise assortment. When all SKUs in a category are managed as a business unit, every store has the proper assortment to match its customers' preferences. The end result is an increased ability to get consumers from the retailer's trading area into their store, converting these consumers into paying customers, while operating in the most efficient manner, so as to reduce operating costs.

Because retailers handle thousands of SKUs, they have found category management to be an extremely effective marketing tool. For example, a grocery store chain, which may stock up to 35,000 SKUs, may decide to have a category manager for laundry products. This category manager would first need to define this category, perhaps as detergent and soap products. Next, it would be important to determine where customers purchased detergent/soap products. Although in the past consumers may have primarily purchased these items at grocery stores, the category manager would now find that detergent/soap products are also frequently purchased at discounters, supercenters, and warehouse clubs. The category manager would also be interested in the major brands and their share of market. For example, within this category, Proctor & Gamble alone manufacturers seven products—Bold, Cheer, Dreft, Era, Gain, Ivory, and Tide. It would be helpful to know if these brands have different penetration levels in different marketing channels as well.

Each of the brands would have certain attributes that influence purchases; attributes such as price, added softening agents, whitening/brightening powers, stain-removal power, and whether the product is color-safe. With this knowledge and a knowledge of the store's target market and its competition, the category manager would develop a coordinated retail mix for the detergent/soap category, including which brands to stock, price points and price lines to establish, in-store display and shelf space allocation, and advertising expenditures and promotional activities such as couponing.

But how does a category manager make these marketing decisions?[21] The major goal of the category manager is to achieve a certain level of profit per square foot of space (allocated to the product category) and profit per dollar or linear foot of inventory investment (in the product category). These two measures of financial performance guide all marketing decisions. The category manager quickly realizes that he or she cannot infinitely increase the number of SKUs to better serve customers. This would require more inventory and space resources that are extremely valuable and constrained. There are approximately 300 different detergent/soap SKUs; by stocking all these SKUs, the retailer would certainly increase the likelihood of serving its customers. However, that might not be very profitable. More likely, the category manager may determine that 40 to 50 SKUs will serve 80 to 90 percent of the retailer's customer base or target market. Therefore, determining the retailer's target market, which will be a particular socioeconomic class, will help to determine the most popular detergent/soap SKUs that should be stocked and promoted.

A key advantage of category management is that it allows the retailer to concentrate its purchases with a more limited number of suppliers. This provides the retailer with more channel power. For example, the retailer may determine that by stocking only Tide, Cheer, and Wisk, which is manufactured by Lever Brothers, that it can gain promotional and price concessions from these manufacturers. Such concessions can be used to support the retailer's marketing efforts and help it to better serve customers.

Category managers have fully embraced information technology to help them better manage their category. Each SKU has a distinct product identification code that is recorded at the cash register when a product is sold. This data, when combined with other information, can provide valuable insights into how to better merchandise a category. For example, a category manager may find that detergent/soap products are most likely to be purchased with fabric softeners or other cleaning fluids. This can lead to ideas for cross-merchandising or cross-promotions between product categories.

WHOLESALING IN THE U.S. ECONOMY

As noted at the beginning of this chapter, **wholesaling** is a larger sector of the U.S. economy than retailing. Total wholesale sales by the nation's 453,000 wholesalers are almost $4.1 trillion,[22] compared to retailing's $2.6 trillion. Why are wholesale sales greater than retail sales? The answer lies in the fact that wholesalers sell not only to retailers, but also to manufacturers and other wholesalers. In fact, wholesalers can and do operate differently in the various types of marketing channels discussed in the previous chapter.

Wholesaling
involves the activities of persons or establishments that sell to retailers and/or other organizational buyers for industrial, institutional, and commercial use, but do not sell in significant amounts to final consumers.

Types of Wholesalers

Some wholesalers provide a wide ranges of services or handle broad lines of goods, others specialize in selling only to other wholesalers or manufacturers, and still others never take title to or possession of merchandise they are selling. As shown in Figure 11.10, wholesalers can be grouped into three broad categories: manufacturer's sales branches, merchant wholesalers, and agent/brokers.

Figure 11.11 shows the state of wholesaling today. Three facts and trends are apparent from this figure:

1. Manufacturer sales branches have the highest sales per establishment.
2. Merchant wholesalers now account for about 50 percent of sales.
3. Agents and brokers are the smallest when considering both total sales and establishments.

Manufacturer's Sales Branches

Manufacturer's sales branches is in the left margin:

> **Manufacturer's sales branches** are sales outlets owned by the manufacturer.

Manufacturer's sales branches actually include both sales outlets (which carry full inventory) and sales offices (which do not carry inventory) that are owned by the manufacturer. The reasons why a manufacturer might choose to distribute its goods directly through company-owned facilities include:

- Some perishable goods need rigid control of distribution to avoid spoilage.
- The goods have a high value per unit causing other middlemen not to want to handle the line.
- The goods require complex installation or servicing.
- The goods need aggressive promotion.

When inventory is carried at these outlets, the manufacturer is essentially performing most, if not all, of the wholesaling function. Predictably, the operating expenses of these manufacturer's outlets increase as the value of the inventory carried in stock increases. Black & Decker is an example of a manufacturer that uses its own sales branches and sales force to strengthen customer relations with key accounts, such as Home Depot and Lowes. In addition, these branch outlets provide service and display merchandise for other local dealers.

As Figure 11.11 points out, manufacturers' sales branches comprise less than 7 percent of wholesale establishments—but these operations account for nearly a third of all wholesale sales. A major reason for the high sales per branch outlet is that they are usually placed in the largest metropolitan markets and serve as a base of operation for the manufacturer's sales staff when calling on a large customer base.

Merchant Wholesalers

> **Merchant wholesalers** are independent firms that purchase a product from a manufacturer and resell it to other manufacturers, wholesalers, or retailers, but not to the final consumer.

Some manufacturers have found that it is more profitable to use merchant wholesalers than their own outlets to sell directly to retailers or other business firms. **Merchant wholesalers**, which are independent firms, purchase a product from a manufacturer, take title to that product, and resell it to other manufacturers, wholesalers, or retailers,

---

Figure 11.10	**Types of Wholesalers**

Manufacturer's sales branches actually include both sales outlets (which carry inventory) and sales offices (which don't carry inventory) that are owned by the manufacturer.

Merchant wholesalers are independent firms that purchase a product from the manufacturer and resell it to other manufacturers, wholesalers, or retailers, but not to the final consumer. Merchant wholesalers can be categorized as full-service or limited-service wholesalers.

> *Full-service merchant wholesalers* provide a wide range of services for retailers and business purchasers.
> *Limited-service merchant wholesalers* perform only a few services for manufacturers or their customers or perform all of them on a more restricted basis than do full-service wholesalers.

Agents/brokers never take title to the merchandise. Their key function is to help bring potential buyers and sellers together.

Percent of Sales and Establishments by Type of Wholesaler, 1929–1992 Figure 11.11

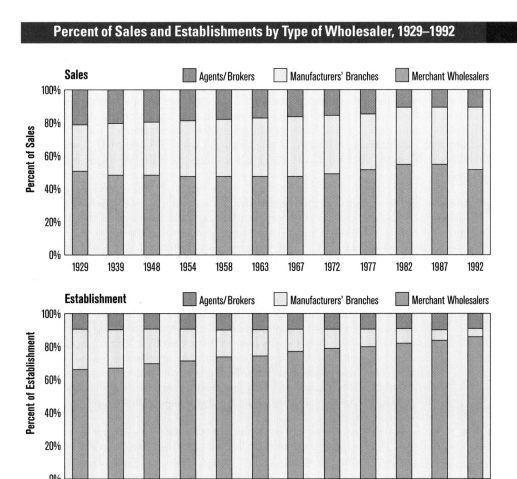

but not to the final consumer. These middlemen are used when it is not economical for the manufacturer's salespeople to call directly on its users or to send them separate shipments. Thus, the merchant wholesaler provides economies of scale to the manufacturer. For example, if each merchant wholesaler has 200 accounts, the manufacturer can reach 2,000 customers by selling to only 10 wholesalers, thereby reducing selling and distribution costs. Merchant wholesalers can be categorized as full-service or limited-service wholesalers.

A **full-service merchant wholesaler** provides a wide range of services for retailers and business purchasers, such as storing merchandise in a convenient location and allowing customers to make purchases on short notice, thus minimizing their inventory costs. The full-service wholesaler typically maintains a sales force to call on retailers, make deliveries, and extend credit to qualified buyers. The three most common full-service wholesalers are:

1. *General merchandise wholesalers*, who carry a complete line of nonperishable items such as hardware, drugs, and plumbing supplies. McLane Company, which supplies convenience stores with a wide variety of products in smaller quantities, is an example of this type of wholesaler.
2. *Single-line wholesalers*, who carry a particular line of goods. For example, Alpine Lace distributes and markets low-salt and low-fat cheeses through 45,000 retail outlets including supermarkets and specialty food stores.
3. *Specialty wholesalers*, who carry a rather limited range of items. McKesson, for example, distributes and markets ethical and proprietary drugs and health and beauty care products to 17,000 retail outlets; in addition they sell to hospitals and HMOs.

Full-service merchant wholesalers
provide a wide range of services for retailers and business purchasers.

In the industrial-goods market, full-function merchant wholesalers are often called *industrial distributors*. Products handled by these distributors, which were also discussed in Chapter 8, include machinery, inexpensive accessory equipment, and supplies. Industrial distributors can handle either a broad line of products or a narrow one. Bearings, Inc., for example, handles a broad line of over 100,000 different (SKUs) industrial bearings primarily to original equipment manufacturers and to the repair and maintenance industry. W.W. Grainger, which handles a narrow line, is a nationwide industrial distributor of maintenance, repair, and operating supplies to commercial, industrial, contractor, and institutional customers. Grainger stocks over 500,000 SKUs through 340 branches in 50 states. As a rule, full-service wholesalers generally have a gross margin of 15 percent.

Limited-service
merchant wholesalers
perform only a few services for manufacturers or other customers, or they perform all of them on a more restricted basis than do full-service wholesalers.

Limited-service merchant wholesalers perform only a few services for manufacturers or their customers, or they perform all of them on a more restricted basis than do full-service wholesalers. Limited-service wholesalers avoid some of the marketing functions by eliminating them entirely or passing them on to another marketing channel member or to the customer. Clearly, the fewer services performed by the wholesaler, the lower will be the markup it can charge on the merchandise it sells. Some of the more popular types of limited-service wholesalers are:

- *Drop-shipper (desk jobber),* who pass on customer orders with instructions that the manufacturer ship directly to a location specified by the customer. They have no warehouse or inventory and do not come in physical possession of the goods. They usually contact customers by telephone, so a sales force may not be necessary. In addition, they may be much less active in generating promotion. These limited-service wholesalers are particularly useful in handling bulky goods and where merchandise typically moves in car-lot quantities; in fact, they are sometimes called "car-lot wholesalers."
- *Cash and carry wholesalers,* who do not provide customers with credit or delivery. The customer must pick up the merchandise from the wholesaler and pay for it with cash or check. This type of wholesaler typically does not have a sales force. Customers are usually small retailers or small industrial accounts. An example of a cash and carry wholesaler is Smart & Final, Inc., which distributes foodservice supplies through over 150 outlets primarily located in the western United States. Smart & Final primarily supplies small restaurants, schools, and churches.
- *Truck jobbers (wagon jobbers),* who use their truck as a warehouse. Usually self-employed with little capital, they generally do not extend credit to customers. Truck jobbers may own their own goods, but usually get their merchandise on consignment from a large full-service wholesaler. They travel to customers and sell directly from the back of their truck. An example of a truck jobber that many students are familiar with is Snap-on, Inc. Snap-on distributes hand and power tools, diagnostic and shop equipment, and tool storage products to automotive service centers and repair shops. Sales are through a dealer van (truck) system that operates in over 100 countries.
- *Rack jobbers,* who maintain racks stocked with merchandise at the retailer's location. Rack jobbers assume heavy risk since the jobber holds title and the retailer holds goods sold from the rack. The retailer's only investment is in the space allotted to the rack. Most consumers are only aware of this type of limited-service wholesaler because they see rack jobbers filling the bread rack at grocery stores or the newspaper rack at convenience stores. Handleman Company, for example, is a rack jobber of prerecorded music, video, hardcover and paperback books, and personal computer software primarily to mass merchandisers in the United States, Canada, and Mexico.

Limited-service wholesalers generally have a gross margin of between 4 and 6 percent of sales. However, it is important to remember that when a manufacturer chooses to use a limited-service wholesaler, he is not saving 10 percent. After all, the manufacturer must now assume responsibility for those services not performed by the wholesaler.

Agents/Brokers

The key difference between agents/brokers and merchant wholesalers is that **agents/brokers** never take title to the merchandise. Their key function is helping to bring potential buyers and sellers together. Like merchant wholesalers, they may or may not take possession of the merchandise they handle or provide all the services a full-service wholesaler performs. As was shown in Figure 11.11, agents and brokers today account for just over 10 percent of wholesale sales.

Manufacturer's agents are independent middlemen who handle a manufacturer's marketing functions by selling part or all of a manufacturer's product line in an assigned geographic area. They are paid on commission but have little or no control over prices and terms of sale and may work for a number of firms that produce related, noncompeting products. Agents can earn between 2 and 20 percent on sales, depending on industry norms and how costly it is for them to perform the selling function. Manufacturer's agents are most likely to be used by manufacturers desiring to enter a new geographic market area, those with a limited product line, those with insufficient resources to develop their own sales force, and those seeking to enter a new market with a product unrelated to their existing product line.

Brokers are independent middlemen who bring buyers and sellers together and provide market information to one or the other parties. While most brokers work for the seller, some do work for buyers. Brokers, who normally earn less than 5 percent of sales, simply negotiate a sale and are paid a fee only if the transaction is completed. Most brokers today operate in the food industry, however, they are also common in the industrial equipment industry. Many students are familiar with mortgage brokers. Most home mortgages are initiated and then brokered into mortgage-backed securities. The mortgage broker receives some of the points or pre-paids as a fee.

Selecting and Working with Wholesalers

A major decision in designing any channel is selecting the right wholesalers for the tasks to be performed and determining how to manage the wholesalers chosen.

Selecting Wholesalers

To help assess the management skills wholesalers need to effectively and efficiently manage the resources at their disposal and the manufacturer's products, manufacturers need screening devices to help assess the quality of potential wholesalers on at least five broad dimensions:

1. Management skills—Wholesalers should be screened on such points as their record and reputation, their planning and management systems, procedures used, cooperation and helpfulness, and receptiveness to constructive management suggestions.
2. Financial characteristics—The wholesaler's financial strength, integrity, history, and future prospects must also be considered. For example, wholesalers in a poor financial position may not be able to perform the necessary marketing functions and services. Therefore, it is important to assess financial characteristics such as whether the wholesaler is making a profit, if it is sufficiently capitalized, if credit is adequate, and whether it can afford to keep adequate stocks on hand.
3. Physical facilities—The wholesaler's equipment and facilities should be assessed carefully. Considerable variation exists among wholesalers on this dimension. Here, it is necessary to know if the wholesaler has the needed facilities and equipment to handle a product, the age and condition of the facilities and equipment, the maintenance schedule, the wholesaler's reputation regarding service standards, and whether the office setup is adequate to handle the manufacturer's business.
4. Objectives and policies—To what extent are the wholesaler's objectives and policies compatible with the manufacturer's marketing channel? In evaluating this dimension, the wholesaler's managerial objectives and policies must be assessed with respect to growth, the stability and reliability of the organization, and the possibility of conflicts.

Agents/brokers
are independent middlemen who bring buyers and sellers together, provide market information to one or the other parties, but never take title to the merchandise. While most agents/brokers work for the seller, some do work for buyers.

Manufacturer's agents
are independent middlemen who handle a manufacturer's marketing functions by selling part or all of a manufacturer's product line in an assigned geographic area.

5. Marketing skills/strengths—Wholesalers need to have the marketing expertise and stamina to successfully market and distribute the manufacturer's product line. Therefore, the wholesaler's marketing know-how and the size, reputation, credibility, and attitude of its sales force must be assessed.

By carefully assessing wholesalers on these five dimensions, the manufacturer should be able to maximize the chances of selecting the best wholesalers. Unfortunately, the best available wholesalers may not always be willing to handle the manufacturer's product line. Consequently, it is important for the manufacturer to know how to properly manage wholesalers in order to obtain their commitment to the manufacturer's products.

Managing Wholesalers

As pointed out earlier, manufacturers who operate through wholesalers typically do so because they find it more efficient and less expensive than doing the wholesaling activities themselves. However, manufacturers can only use wholesalers successfully if they get the wholesalers' cooperation in marketing their products. To accomplish this, manufacturers must obtain some degree of control over wholesalers.

If manufacturers want the cooperation and commitment of wholesalers, they must offer them financial, promotional, training, and general management aids. Depending on the line of trade, some or all of these may be offered. The most important financial assistance that manufacturers can offer wholesalers is the planned gross margin, which must be large enough so that wholesalers can achieve an adequate profit after performing all the activities desired by manufacturers. Other important forms of financial assistance include inventory financing through liberal purchase terms, rebates, bonuses if quotas are achieved, seasonal dating to get wholesalers to stock up early in the season, and extra discounts for performing special services such as product recall or warranty services.

Frequently offered forms of promotional assistance include national or regional advertising that mentions the wholesaler's name; advertising allowances for local advertising; brochures, pamphlets, and other sales material to be distributed to potential customers; suggested advertising layouts or content for local advertising (i.e., prepared advertising mats); and salespeople employed by manufacturers to generate new accounts for the wholesaler.

If the wholesaler has neither the human nor financial resources to properly train salespeople, the manufacturer may offer a sales training program. A good training program will help the wholesaler to service the manufacturer's merchandise line by informing sales representatives about the strengths and weaknesses of the manufacturer's products and those of competing products, and by teaching them how to make effective sales presentations. Training of service personnel may also be advantageous, especially if the manufacturer's product line is technically complex and needs pre-installation or post-installation service.

Wholesalers are becoming more concerned about internal operating problems, including problems of credit and collection, inventory control, finance, planning, and personnel. Consequently, some manufacturers are designing management development programs to help wholesalers solve their operating problems. By offering such programs, manufacturers are recognizing the fact that their marketing efforts can only be successful if the wholesaler survives and prospers.

Finally, all wholesale distributors should be given a sales goal based on the market potential and competitive intensity in the geographic territory the wholesaler serves. The manufacturer and wholesaler must discuss this goal and arrive at some agreement on its reasonableness. Once wholesale distributors are selected and offered the proper mix of assistance, they should be expected to meet their targeted goals. To assess their performance, an objective annual evaluation should be conducted.

CHAPTER SUMMARY

- This chapter acquaints the reader with the major types and functions of retailing and wholesaling institutions.
- Retailing is a diverse business activity. There are several ways to categorize retailers on a variety of dimensions that explain the reasons why retailers behave as they do. These dimensions are number of outlets, margin versus turnover, and location.
- Since it is relatively easy to open a retail store, new retail institutions appear continuously. Scholars studying retailing have developed several theories to explain and describe the evolution of competition in retailing. Two of the most popular theories include the wheel of retailing and the retail life cycle.
- When discussing the various types of retailers, it is first necessary to determine if the retailer is selling from a fixed physical location. There are six basic types of store-based retailers: department stores, specialty stores, supermarkets, supercenters, category killers, and convenience stores. There are five types of nonstore-based retailing: street peddling, direct selling, mail order, automatic merchandising machines, and electronic shopping. Many experts believe that nonstore retailing is where the next revolution in retailing will occur.
- Like all marketers, retailers identify their target market and make marketing decisions to satisfy the needs of that market. When doing this retailers must realize that the store and the image it projects is a major part of their offering. A positive store image (the overall feeling or mood projected by a store through its aesthetic appeal to human senses) depends on its retail mix—that combination of merchandise, prices, advertising, location, customer services, selling, and store layout and design.
- Due to intensified retail competition, retailers have been increasingly employing category management. This is where all of the SKUs in a merchandise category are managed as a distinct business. Category managers are guided by the twin goals of increasing space and inventory productivity because space and inventory resources are constrained in retailing. Often the net result of category management is for the retailer to deal with fewer suppliers, which in turn can provide the retailer with more channel power.
- Wholesaling involves the activities of those persons or establishments that sell to retailers and/or other organizational buyers for industrial, institutional, and commercial use, but do not sell in significant amounts to final consumers. Wholesalers can be grouped into three broad categories: manufacturer's sales branches, merchant wholesalers, and agent/brokers.
- For manufacturers to operate successfully through wholesalers, they must be able to select and work with the chosen wholesalers. To select the best wholesalers, manufacturers need a screening device that assesses the quality of potential wholesalers on at least five broad dimensions: management skills, financial characteristics, physical facilities, objectives and policies, and marketing skills/strengths.
- Manufacturers who want their wholesalers' cooperation and commitment must offer them financial, promotional, training, and general management aids. Once the wholesale distributors are selected and offered the proper mix of assistance, they should be expected to meet targeted goals. To assess their performance, an objective annual evaluation should be conducted.

KEY TERMS

Agents/brokers are independent middlemen who bring buyers and sellers together, provide market information to one or the other parties, but never take title to the merchandise. While most agents/brokers work for the seller, some do work for buyers.

Anchor stores are dominant, large-scale stores that are expected to draw customers to a shopping center.

Balanced tenancy occurs where the stores complement each other in merchandise offerings.

Category killers get their name from their marketing strategy of carrying such a large amount of merchandise in a single category at such good prices that they make it impossible for customers to walk out without purchasing what they needed, thus "killing" the competition.

Category management is a process of managing and planning all SKUs within a product category as a distinct business.

Full-service merchant wholesalers provide a wide range of services for retailers and business purchasers.

Gross margin equals net sales minus the cost of goods sold.

Gross margin percentage shows how much gross margin a retailer makes as a percentage of sales.

Inventory turnover refers to the number of times per year, on average, that a firm sells its inventory.

Limited-service merchant wholesalers perform only a few services for manufacturers or other customers, or they perform all of them on a more restricted basis than do full-service wholesalers.

Manufacturer's agents are independent middlemen who handle a manufacturer's marketing functions by selling part or all of a manufacturer's product line in an assigned geographic area.

Manufacturer's sales branches are sales outlets owned by the manufacturer.

Merchant wholesalers are independent firms that purchase a product from a manufacturer and resell it to other manufacturers, wholesalers, or retailers, but not to the final consumer.

Operating expenses are the costs a retailer incurs in running a business, other than the cost of merchandise.

Retailing consists of the final activity and steps needed to place merchandise made elsewhere into the hands of the consumer or to provide services to the consumer.

Retail life cycle is a description of competitive development in retailing that assumes that retail institutions pass through an identifiable cycle that includes four distinct stages: (1) introduction, (2) growth, (3) maturity, and (4) decline.

Retail mix is a retailer's combination of merchandise, prices, advertising, location, customer services, selling, and store layout and design that is used attract customers.

Scrambled merchandising is the handling of merchandise lines based solely on the profitability criterion and without regard to the consistency of the product or merchandise mix.

Shrinkage refers to reduction of merchandise through theft, loss, and damage.

SKU is a stock keeping unit and refers to a distinct merchandise item in the retailer's merchandise assortment.

Wheel of retailing theory is a pattern of competitive development in retailing which states that new types of retailers enter the market as low-status, low-margin, low-price operators. However, as they meet with success, these new retailers gradually acquire more sophisticated and elaborate facilities, thereby becoming less efficient and vulnerable to new types of low-margin retail competitors who progress through the same pattern.

Wholesalers are persons or establishments that sell to retailers and/or other organizational buyers for industrial, institutional, and commercial use, but do not sell in significant amounts to ultimate consumers.

Wholesaling involves the activities of persons or establishments that sell to retailers and/or other organizational buyers for industrial, institutional, and commercial use, but do not sell in significant amounts to final consumers.

QUESTIONS FOR DISCUSSION

1. Would each of the following transactions be considered a retailing transaction according to the text's definition?
   a. A student buying a desk from a membership warehouse club, such as Sam's or Costco
   b. A homeowner purchasing fertilizer for her lawn
   c. A student buying a Valentine's Day card for a "special" friend
   d. A homemaker buying eggs and fresh fruit at a farmer's roadside stand
   e. An appliance repairperson coming to your home to fix a dishwasher

2. Can small independent retailers survive against large chains operators such as Target, Kroger, Kohl's, Dillard's, and Wal-Mart? What can small retailers do in order to strengthen their competitive position against large chains?

3. How can a retailer operate with a high-margin/high-turnover strategy? Won't customers avoid this type of retailer and shop at a low-margin store?

4. What are retailing's three basic tasks? Provide an example of a retailer in your local area who does an excellent job at each of these tasks. (You may use a different retailer for each task.)

5. According to the wheel of retailing theory of competitive evolution in retailing, what new type(s) of retail operation might be seen in the future?

6. Agree or disagree with the following statement: "Scrambled merchandising is really a very inefficient way of retailing. Retailers should specialize in the line(s) of merchandise they carry, otherwise they tend to confuse their customers. Therefore, the use of scrambled merchandising should decrease over the remainder of this decade." Support your position.

7. Why has category management become more important in retailing?

8. Which of the following transactions is considered a wholesale transaction according to the text's definition?
   a. A student buying a computer for personal use at a membership warehouse club
   b. Your university purchasing 10 reams of typing paper at a membership warehouse club
   c. Wal-Mart purchasing a carload of Maxwell House Coffee from General Foods
   d. A local television repairperson purchasing parts from a manufacturer's agent

9. If wholesalers sell to retailers and retailers sell to final consumers, why are total wholesaler sales $4.1 trillion when total retail sales are only $2.6 trillion? Should not retail sales be the larger number, since retailers mark up merchandise after they purchase it from wholesalers?

10. What are the key differences between a limited-service merchant wholesaler and a full-service merchant wholesaler?

INTERNET QUESTIONS

1. Using either a hard copy of the current *Statistical Abstract of the United States*, or its online version which can be found at http://www.census.gov, go to the table labeled "Retail Trade—Sales by Kind of Business." Using that table, determine what percent of total retail sales for the most recent year available were generated by automotive dealers, sporting goods and bicycle dealers, jewelry stores, department stores, grocery stores, and restaurants. Which type had the highest growth rate over the last 5 years? The lowest growth rate? What were the factors that caused differences in the various growth rates you found?

2. Go to the home page for the U.S. Census Bureau (http://www.census.gov). On this page you will find a link to the Census of Retailing. Access this site and locate the summary retail statistics (sales and number of stores) for your state. Identify the line of retail trade in your state that had the most rapid sales growth over the most recent 5 years of available data and the one that had the slowest growth. Why do you believe the fastest growing line of retail trade grew faster than the slowest line of retail trade? Try to develop several hypotheses or explanations.

3. Go to the home page for the U.S. Census Bureau (http://www.census.gov). On this page you will find a link to the Census of Wholesaling. Access this site and locate the summary statistics (sales and number of establishments) for your state. Identify the line of wholesale trade in your state that had the most rapid sales growth over the most recent 5 years of available data and the one that had the slowest growth. Why do you believe the fastest growing line of wholesale trade grew faster than the slowest line of wholesale trade? Try to develop several hypotheses or explanations.

ENDNOTES

[1] U.S. Bureau of the Census, *Statistical Abstract of the United States: 2000,* Tables nos. 1271 and 1274.

[2] "Spamouflage and Cajun Crawtators," *Fortune,* 29 October 2001, 85.

[3] "Streamlined Airport Retailing Takes Off in Philadelphia," *Shopping Centers Today* (December 1998): 48.

[4] "Retailing 101," *Progressive Grocer* (January 2000): 50–56.

[5] Malcolm P. McNair, "Significant Trends and Developments in the Postwar Period," in *Competitive Distribution in a Free High-Level Economy and Its Implications for the University,* ed. A. B. Smith (Pittsburgh: University of Pittsburgh Press, 1958).

[6] "The Buck Stops Here," *Advertising Age,* 6 November 2000: 3, 100.

[7] Based on sections of *Clicks and Mortar: Passion Driven Growth in an Internet Driven World,* by David S. Pottruck and Terry Pearce (San Francisco: Jossey-Bass, 2000) and the authors' experiences with Schwab.

[8] "E-tailers Channel Sales Effort," *The Globe and Mail* (Internet edition), 17 November 2000, 2.

[9] The information in this section was provided by the Direct Selling Association, Washington, D.C.

[10] U.S. Bureau of the Census, *Statistical Abstract of the United States: 2000,* Table no. 1275.

[11] Information supplied by John Schulte, Chairman of the National Mail Order Association, 30 June 2001.

[12] Fact Sheet from the National Automated Merchandising Association, Chicago.

[13] For a more complete discussion of this problem, see Soyeon Shim, Mary Ann Eastlick, Sherry Lotz, and Patricia Warrington, "An Online Prepurchase Intentions Model: The Role of Intention to Search," *Journal of Retailing* (Fall 2001): 397–416.

[14] From a list compiled by the late Robert Kahn.

[15] Based on information supplied by Webmergers.com.

[16] "By the Numbers," *Wall Street Journal,* 24 September 2001, R2; and U.S. Bureau of the Census, *Statistical Abstract of the United States: 2000,* Table no. 1286.

[17] Charles Areni and David Kim, "The Influence of Background Music on Shopping Behavior: Classical versus Top-Forty Music in a Wine Store," *Advances in Consumer Research* (1993): 336–340.

[18] Ronald E. Milliman, "Using Background Music to Affect Behavior of Supermarket Shoppers," *Journal of Marketing* (Summer 1982): 86–91.

[19] Areni and Kim, "The Influence of Background Music."

[20] Based on information supplied by Charles Areni, University of Sydney, July 2001.

[21] For a more detailed discussion of this topic, see Sanjay K. Dhar, Stephen J. Hock, and Nanda Kumar, "Effective Category Management Depends on the Role of the Category," *Journal of Retailing* (Summer 2001): 165–184.

[22] U.S. Bureau of the Census, *1997 Economic Census,* Wholesale Trade Sector, Table 6, 1545, 1571, 1597, 1620, and calculations by the authors.

CYCLE SOUTH

For the past four years you have worked part-time, while going to school, at your uncle Fred's bicycle shop. Cycle South is located in a community shopping center just inside the city limits of Mansfield, Ohio, near a major highway intersection. Mansfield is located in north-central Ohio and has a population of 65,000.

Within the last year, two major chains, Wal-Mart and Target, have replaced discount stores with supercenters in Mansfield. Each of these supercenters carries a limited assortment of bikes and offers no repair services. Also, two small bike shops have closed since you started working for your uncle, leaving only three competitors in Mansfield.

Early in September of your final year of college, your uncle called you into his office. Fred wanted you to be the first to know that he was planning on closing the shop in early January, right after the busy Christmas season. Even though the business was still profitable, he was afraid it would begin to slow. Besides, he did not want to have to compete with those "out-of-town chain 'superstores' selling those 'cheap' bikes that did not last."

Over the next 3 weeks, you think about your uncle's situation. You wonder if the business should be run differently. After all, since the supercenters do not offer repair service, your uncle's real competition is Mansfield's three other bike shops.

You remember learning in your Introduction to Marketing class that the three most basic tasks facing every retailer are:

1. Getting consumers from their trading area into their store.
2. Converting these consumers into paying customers.
3. Operating in the most efficient manner, so as to reduce costs, and thereby having lower prices.

Maybe, you can come up with a plan that would help your uncle do a better job performing these tasks, so that he can remain in business. Soon you are busy developing a marketing plan for your uncle based on these three tasks.

Two weeks later, you present your uncle with the following memo.

EIGHT WAYS TO IMPROVE
CYCLE SOUTH'S MARKETING PERFORMANCE

Ways to get people into our store:

1. Since the supercenters sell inexpensive bikes, promote the fact that Cycle South has the best bike repair shop in Mansfield.
2. Advertise that Cycle South has a 90-Day Price Protection Plan. The advertisement will state that if any customer finds the identical bike at a lower price at another Mansfield area retailer within 90 days of purchase, you will refund the difference plus 10 percent.
3. Offer a lifetime parts warranty on all Cycle South bikes.
4. Offer lifetime free service on any bike purchased at Cycle South.

Ways to get these consumers to make a purchase:

5. Never charge the customer for any item under $1.
6. Increase the shop's size by renting that small vacant store next door. Utilize this additional space by putting in a coffee bar and children's play area. This way customers won't feel rushed and will spend more time in the store.

Ways to reduce our costs and offer low prices:

7. Drop any line of bicycles that has high levels of warranty work. Even though the manufacturer will cover the cost of parts, we are obliged to provide free labor. However, given the lower gross margins we will realize with our price protection plan, we cannot afford the additional labor costs.

8. Install a better point-of-sale computer system that will enable us to track customers more effectively and do more targeted marketing.

After looking over your memo, your uncle questions the value of a college education and says, "You cannot make money when you are giving everything away. Free means my sales go down and I lose money. Didn't they teach you anything in college?"

Discussion Questions

1. Was your uncle right about not being able to make money when you are giving everything away?

2. How could he afford to undertake such a plan?

CHAPTER 12

Integrated Marketing Communications: Advertising, Promotions, and Other MarCom Tools

CHAPTER 13

Personal Selling and Sales Management

CHAPTER twelve

Terence A. Shimp,
University of South Carolina

Terence A. Shimp is Professor of Marketing, W.W. Johnson Distinguished Foundation Fellow, and Chair of the Marketing Department at the University of South Carolina. Dr. Shimp holds a doctorate in business administration from the University of Maryland. He is an award-winning teacher, having won the AMOCO teaching award in 1990 that is presented annually to a single faculty member at the University of South Carolina. In 2001, the American Academy of Advertising honored Dr. Shimp with a Lifetime Contributions to Advertising Award. He also has been recognized for outstanding articles in the *Journal of Consumer Research* and *Journal of Advertising*. He is past president of the Association for Consumer Research and president of the *Journal of Consumer Research* policy board. Dr. Shimp serves on the editorial review boards for the *Journal of Consumer Research, Journal of Consumer Psychology, Journal of Marketing, Journal of Public Policy and Marketing, Marketing Letters,* and the *Journal of Marketing Communications.*

After serving on the faculty at Kent State University for 4 years, Dr. Shimp has been a faculty member at the University of South Carolina for 25 years. He teaches marketing communications at undergraduate and graduate levels and research methods to Ph.D. students. His primary areas of research are the study of consumer learning, persuasion, and response to marketing and advertising communications. He is the author of *Advertising, Promotion, and Supplemental Aspects of Integrated Marketing Communications,* sixth edition, from South-Western.

Integrated Marketing Communications: Advertising, Promotions, and Other MarCom Tools

Dairy milk has been a favorite beverage among generations of Americans and consumers elsewhere around the world. It is regarded for its nutritional content, health benefits, and natural ability to complement cereal, cookies, and other (typically) dessert items. Despite an appealing and effective milk-moustache advertising campaign by the industry trade association (America's Dairy Farmers and Milk Processors), milk consumption has barely kept pace with the population growth rate. One problem faced by the dairy industry is that many consumers perceive milk as too high in fat content and thus unhealthy. This negative perception has opened the barn door, so to speak, for competition from an alternative source of "milk" that only a decade ago would have been considered unacceptable—soymilk. Please read on.

Whereas annual grocery sales of dairy milk in the United States is estimated at around $10 billion, soymilk and other nondairy milk substitutes command revenue of less than 3 percent of this amount (approximately $250 million). Yet, there appears to be considerable growth potential for soymilk products, which are touted as healthier than traditional dairy milk. Leading the way in this upstart category is the Boulder, Colorado-based company White Wave, with its Silk brand of refrigerated soymilk. Silk dominates

After you have completed this chapter, you should be able to:

1. Appreciate the variety of marketing communications tools, and how they work together to accomplish communication objectives.
2. Understand the nature, importance, and features of integrated marketing communications.
3. Describe the concept of brand-equity enhancement and the role of marketing communications in facilitating this objective.
4. Comprehend the factors that determine how different marketing communications elements are effectively combined.
5. Discuss the primary decision spheres involved in managing the marketing communications process.
6. Know the major activities involved in formulating advertising strategy.
7. Recognize the role of sales promotion, appreciate the reasons why this form of marketing communications has experienced rapid growth, and know the tasks that it can and cannot accomplish.
8. Evaluate the nature and function of public relations.
9. Appreciate sponsorship marketing and the practices of event marketing and cause-related marketing.
10. Understand the role, importance, and growth of point-of-purchase communications.

(Continued)

http://www.whitewave.com

the refrigerated soymilk category with a market share exceeding 70 percent. White Wave's products are sold through thousands of natural food and grocery stores across the United States and Canada. White Wave's business philosophy is captured succinctly in this quote from its president, Steve Demos: "Our interest is in promoting the use of foods we consider the world better off with, rather than without."

In late 2001, the company undertook an aggressive advertising campaign that was designed to increase overall sales in the product category (i.e., build primary demand) and especially to increase sales of its own soymilk contender, Silk, by enhancing brand awareness and boosting the brand's image—the two activities together represent efforts to augment Silk's brand equity. Toward this end, White Wave employed the services of Arnold Worldwide, a huge Boston-based advertising agency with billings exceeding $1 billion. White Wave chose this agency because of its reputation for enhancing the equity of brands that compete in novel and unique product categories, which surely is the case with soymilk.

White Wave invested $18 million in an integrated marketing communications campaign for Silk. The campaign was directed at health-conscious consumers by positioning the brand as hip and irreverent. Ads in magazines such as *People, Rolling Stone,* and *US* dared skeptics to try soymilk—including the tag line, "Don't be so stubborn." This approach is an obvious attempt to convert disbelievers to the category, to get prospective consumers to think more positively about soymilk and to at least give it a try. In addition to a captivating advertising campaign, trial purchasing was stimulated with the distribution of more than 3 million product samples at various cultural and sporting events. It will be interesting to observe whether soymilk ever becomes a major competitor to conventional dairy milk. However, one thing *is* certain: concerted advertising, promotions, and other marketing communications efforts are absolutely key to the category-development and brand-building efforts of Silk and other soymilk brands.[1]

Out of the thousands of brands on store shelves today, the odds are slim that a consumer will *see* any one particular item, much less buy it. Consumers are rushed for time; their lives are pressured; they are not often inclined to leisurely walk up and down every aisle, perusing every stock-keeping unit (SKU) available on the shelves. A brand may be of high quality and fairly valued, but it will fail to achieve sales and profit objectives if potential customers are unaware of it or do not perceive it favorably. Effective advertising and other forms of marketing communications are absolutely crucial to creating brand awareness, establishing positive brand identities, and moving products off store shelves. The Silk soymilk story in the opening vignette illustrates the crucial role played by advertising, promotions, and other marketing communications tools.

Marketing communications also are critical to the success of business-to-business (B2B) marketers in their efforts to achieve market share and profit objectives. Many, if not most, B2B products share similarities from one supplier to the next. Product quality generally is not that different among competitors, and prices often are near equal. The real distinctions among B2B competitors frequently amount to created differences achieved through effective advertising and, more importantly, via superior service and personal selling efforts.

Regardless of the nature of the product category or type of business, marketing communications are key to a company's overall marketing mission and represent a major determinant of its success; indeed, it has been claimed that marketing and marketing communications are inseparable: "[M]arketing . . . is communication and communication is marketing."[2]

This chapter first overviews the tools of marketing communications, which hereafter is abbreviated as "MarCom" and used interchangeably with marketing communications. A second major section describes the key MarCom participants. The two following sections discuss the nature of integrated marketing communications and the challenge of enhancing brand equity. Section five describes the factors that influence the choice of which MarCom tools are most appropriate for a particular brand-marketing situation. Managing the MarCom process is the focus of the sixth section. The sections thereafter are devoted, in turn, to the major MarCom tools: advertising, sales promotion, public relations, sponsorship marketing, and point-of-purchase communications.

THE TOOLS OF MARKETING COMMUNICATIONS

This section provides an overview of each of the MarCom elements. First, however, it will be useful to draw an analogy between getting the most out of the players on a basketball team and the challenge of mixing the MarCom tools to achieve maximum success.

In brief (and simplistically), a basketball team includes 10 to 12 players, 5 of whom play as a unit at any time. The players differ in the roles expected of them and the strengths they offer. One player, the point guard, has primary responsibility for dribbling, controlling the tempo of the offense, and setting up plays. Another guard, the shooting guard, has a greater scoring responsibility. Yet, both guards play defense as well as offense. The center, who typically is the tallest player on the team, has major responsibility for both inside scoring (i.e., close to the basket), rebounding, and defending against the opposing center. Two other players, the forwards, score from intermediate range and also have responsibility for rebounding and defending. The quality of a basketball team depends on all players working together as a unit. Offense is important, but so is defense. Players who can score points quickly and in spurts are important, but so are those who are steady and dependable rather than erratic. A basketball team would not be a very good team it if consisted only of five Shaquille O'Neals, or five Allan Iversons, or five Kobe Bryants, or five of any single type of player. An outstanding team requires players representing contrasting dimensions—different height, weight, speed, quickness, shooting skill, rebounding savvy, shot-blocking ability, and so on.

So it is with the MarCom mix and the various elements that comprise the mix. Personal selling, in a sense, is like a basketball team's point guard. It sets the tempo for all other MarCom elements. Advertising is more flamboyant—the Allan Iverson of marketing communications. Public relations (PR) is a great adjunct to advertising, working together, assisting, and augmenting advertising to accomplish mutual goals. PR also is great when the need for defense is especially important—such as when a firm or one of its brands is surrounded with negative publicity. Sales promotion is like the player who scores a lot of points quickly; it can achieve sales results in a shorter period than can other MarCom elements.

There is no need to strain the analogy further. The point should be clear: The MarCom mix is like a team consisting of players who provide distinct abilities and perform different but mutually reinforcing roles. Now we will briefly describe each MarCom tool and reserve detailed discussion for later sections.

Personal Selling

B2B marketers rely especially heavily on **personal selling**. In the consumer market, products such as insurance, automobiles, and real estate are sold mainly through personal selling efforts. Historically, personal selling involved face-to-face interactions between salesperson and prospect, but telephone sales and other forms of electronic communications are increasingly being used. Chapter 13 focuses exclusively on personal selling and sales management, so the present chapter will emphasize the other MarCom elements.

Personal selling
is person-to-person communication in which a seller informs and educates prospective customers and attempts to influence their purchase choices.

Advertising

The purpose of **advertising** is to inform the end consumer or the B2B customer about the advertiser's products and brand benefits and ultimately to influence brand choice. Advertising is paid for by an identified sponsor, the advertiser, but is considered to be *nonpersonal* because the sponsoring firm is simultaneously communicating with multiple receivers, perhaps millions, rather than talking with a specific person or small group. Advertising—such as White Wave's effort with Silk in the opening vignette—attempts to keep both the brand's name and image in the customer's mind over a long period of time.

Advertising
is nonpersonal communication that is paid for by an identified sponsor, and involves either mass communication via newspapers, magazines, radio, television, and other media (e.g., billboards, bus stop signage) or direct-to-consumer communication via direct mail.

Public Relations

Publicity, which is the major PR tool, usually comes in the form of news items or editorial comments about a company's products. These items or comments receive free print space or broadcast time because media representatives consider the information

Publicity,
like advertising, is nonpersonal communication to a mass audience, but unlike advertising, publicity is not directly paid for by the company that enjoys the publicity.

pertinent and newsworthy for their reading or listening audiences. It is the job of a firm's public relations personnel to garner positive publicity for the company and its brands. These personnel also face the challenge of overcoming negative publicity when a company is faced with a product disaster (e.g., Perrier bottled water contaminated with benzene) or confronted with claims of unfavorable business practices (e.g., Denny's restaurants accused of racial discrimination).

Sales Promotion

Sales promotion
consists of all marketing activities that attempt to stimulate quick buyer action, or, in other words, attempt to promote immediate sales of a product (thereby yielding the name *sales promotion*).

Sales promotion is directed both at the trade (i.e., wholesalers and retailers) and at consumers. It is intended to create an immediate response (a need to acquire the product right now); by comparison, advertising and publicity are designed more to favorably influence consumer/customer expectations and attitudes over the long-term. *Trade-oriented sales promotions* include the use of various types of allowances and merchandise assistance that activate wholesaler and retailer response. *Consumer-oriented sales promotions* include coupons, premiums, free samples, contests/sweepstakes, rebates, and other devices.

Sponsorship Marketing

Sponsorship marketing
is the practice of promoting the interests of a company and its brands by associating the company with a specific event (e.g., a golf tournament) or a charitable cause (e.g., the Leukemia Society).

In general, **sponsorship marketing** represents an opportunity for a company and its brands to directly target communications toward narrow, but highly desirable, audiences. This is accomplished by associating a brand with a charitable cause, a high-profile event, or a cultural affair. The use of sponsorship marketing generally is not expected to substitute for more traditional forms of marketing communications such as advertising, but rather to complement these activities. Silk soymilk, for example, uses traditional advertising but then supplements the gains from advertising with a brand presence at events where samples are distributed.

Point-of-Purchase Communications

Point-of-purchase communications
include all signage—displays, posters, signs, shelf cards, and a variety of other visual materials—that are designed to influence buying decisions at the point of sale.

Point-of-purchase communications are a final effort by the manufacturer to motivate consumers and encourage purchase of the manufacturer's brands. Research has shown that perhaps as many as three out of four buying decisions are made at the point of purchase. It is for this reason that various types of signs, mobiles, plaques, banners, shelf talkers, mechanical mannequins, lights, mirrors, plastic reproductions of products, checkout units, and various types of product displays are used extensively in retail outlets.

KEY PARTICIPANTS IN MARKETING COMMUNICATIONS

A general marketing manager—perhaps with the title, vice president of marketing—has overall responsibility for all aspects of a firm's marketing programs. However, most day-to-day, or tactical, marketing decisions occur at the product- or brand-management levels. Product managers for a business to business (B2B) company and brand managers for a consumer-goods company (business to consumer or B2C) have profit-and-loss responsibility for the particular product or brand that they manage. Product and brand managers also are responsible for long-term (*strategic*) and short-term (*tactical*) decisions relating to the product or brand they manage.

However, the various MarCom decisions are not the sole responsibility of the product/brand manager. Instead, in most corporations there are managers of departments who are responsible for the planning and implementation of individual elements. Sales management, for example, is responsible for the personal selling function. Advertising managers have authority over the entire advertising function, much of which is farmed out to independent advertising agencies such as White Wave's selection of Arnold Worldwide as its advertising agency of record for Silk soymilk. These agencies create advertising copy, schedule media, and assess advertising effectiveness. Public relations managers provide news media with positive messages about the company and its activities. As with advertising, in many instances public relations are delegated to independent PR agencies. Likewise, sales promotion managers carry out various trade- and consumer-oriented promotions. Again, outside vendors that specialize in specific forms of promotions (e.g., premium offers, sweepstakes, and contests) oftentimes are contracted to perform these specialized services.

Regardless of the number of managers or independent agencies involved in the MarCom process, product and brand managers must oversee the entire program and monitor its progress. One individual needs to have the big picture of the program at all times in order to ensure success of the program, as well as the brand itself. Advocates of integrated marketing communications, which is described in the following section, recommend that corporations reorganize by setting up an organizational unit headed by someone with a title such as marketing communications director.[3] This MarCom director would ensure that all aspects of marketing communications are indeed integrated. Most companies have not gone to this extreme, but some outside vendors have integrated their services to form full-service marketing communication operations. Many agencies that historically just provided advertising services have expanded their operations to include direct-marketing services, public relations, and sales-promotion assistance. Product and brand managers turn to these agencies and engage in one-stop shopping much in the same way that consumers do when shopping at department stores and other full-service retail outlets.

THE PHILOSOPHY AND PRACTICE OF INTEGRATED MARKETING COMMUNICATIONS

LEARNING OBJECTIVE 2

Companies in the past often treated MarCom elements as virtually separate activities, whereas current philosophy holds that integration of all elements is absolutely imperative for success. (Recalling the earlier basketball analogy, MarCom must be managed as a team rather than as a collection of individual players.) One of the significant marketing trends of recent years is a move toward fully integrating all business practices that communicate something about a company's brands to present or prospective customers. This development is known as **integrated marketing communications (IMC)**.

Companies traditionally have resisted integration because managers of individual MarCom elements (advertising, sales promotions, etc.) have feared that change might lead to reduced budgets, authority, and power. The IMC process becomes easier to understand and less intimidating when its premises receive closer inspection. Some skeptics have suggested that IMC is little more than a short-lived management fashion,[4] but evidence to the contrary suggests that IMC, rather than fleeting, has become a permanent feature of the marketing communications landscape around the world and in many

Integrated marketing communications (IMC)
is a system of management and integration of marketing communication elements—advertising, publicity, sales promotion, sponsorship marketing, and point-of-purchase communications—with the result that all elements adhere to the same message.

From Consumer Packaged Goods to High Tech: Skills Will Travel

Rajan Shah was always a high achiever. At the University of South Carolina he graduated with honors while pursuing a dual major in marketing and finance and also serving as president of the student senate. This Phi Beta Kappa honoree joined the ranks of Andersen Consulting (now Accenture) shortly after graduating from Carolina in 1991. He excelled as a consultant during his 2-year tenure at Anderson, where he ranked within the top 10 percent of his cohort and was promoted on an accelerated basis to team leader. This inaugural business experience was invaluable, but he knew an MBA degree was essential to achieving his long-term professional and personal goals.

Rajan entered the MBA program at Northwestern University's Kellogg Graduate School of Management in 1993. There he again excelled as a student, as leader in forming an international study course on business in India, and as vice president of Kellogg's student government. His first intensive marketing experience came when he interned in brand management at General Mills' cereal division. His abilities were quickly noted, and he was chosen to lead a cross-functional team that developed and executed a new packaging and pricing strategy for the Lucky Charms brand. Having completed a very successful internship, Rajan returned to Northwestern to complete the second year of his MBA program.

He was hired out of the Northwestern MBA program into the USA Division of the Coca-Cola Company in Atlanta. As associate brand manager for Diet Coke, he led the brand into its first foray into interactive marketing, managing cross-marketing with the then-new TV series *Friends* and assisting in developing the brand's new positioning, packaging, and advertising programs. His talents caught the eye of upper management, and he was promoted to a brand manager position for the company's lead brand, Coca-Cola Classic. In this post he was responsible for planning, developing, and implementing the brand's $250 million U.S. advertising plan, in particular its ethnic, promotional, and partnership advertising—such as with NASCAR—while also managing research that evaluated advertising effectiveness. During his time as brand manager, Rajan was eventually asked to lead a corporate effort to test the company's growth viability in the urban market through a new bottom up, grassroots integrated marketing approach.

In 1998, after only 3 years at the Coca-Cola Company, Rajan was promoted to the challenging and prestigious position of U.S. senior brand manager for Coca-Cola Classic—one of only two such positions. In this role he managed U.S. consumer marketing for the brand with responsibility for growth across existing and new consumer markets. This position afforded him a high-level opportunity to help steward one of the most respected brands in the world and to develop integrated marketing communication strategies that served to enhance the brand's equity, grow sales, and increase profits while leading a team of 12 assistant and associate brand managers.

Recognizing the far-reaching impact and relevance of technology, Rajan left the Coca-Cola Company in 2000 and became director of marketing for the Internet Capital Group, a 600-employee B2B technology goods and services company. In this position he was responsible for brand positioning, advertising, public relations, and overall efforts to enhance the company's brand equity. He led a national marketing launch of the ICG Commerce brand as well as assisted in forming marketing partnerships with notable firms such as Andersen Consulting, IBM, and Compaq.

Then in 2001, Rajan continued to explore and expand his perspective of the world of technology. He accepted a position as director of brand marketing for Earthlink, Inc., the third largest Internet service provider in the United States with $1 billion in annual revenues. At Earthlink he directs the marketing strategy for EarthLink Everywhere, the group responsible for EarthLink's fast-growing wireless and Internet appliance brands and one of the company's four business units. In the potentially huge growth area of wireless communications, Rajan once again is leading the growth of brands, building consumer demand, and driving increased revenue.

One could look at this synopsis of Rajan Shah's career and entertain the notion that he is a marketing vagabond who skips from job to job. This would be an erroneous impression. Rather, he is a skilled brand marketer who has developed a marketing tool set that is increasingly sought by companies that recognize the importance of sustained brand building. Rajan's experience and marketing insight allow him to build brands by intelligently applying advertising, promotions, and other forms of integrated marketing communications, all of which serve to build bridges between brands and consumers. His career trajectory is not unlike that of other well-educated and talented marketing practitioners. Rajan Shah is a risk taker who seeks to challenge himself with new opportunities that offer intellectual and financial rewards and the prospect for further learning. The first decade of his career has been extremely successful, and the future promises additional challenges and opportunities for personal and professional growth. What more could one want in a career?

different types of marketing organizations.[5] As one IMC pioneer puts it, "Integration just plain makes sense for those planning to succeed in the 21st-century marketplace. Marketers, communicators, and brand organizations simply have no choice."[6] In the final analysis, the key to successfully implementing IMC is that brand managers, who represent the client side, must closely link their efforts with outside suppliers of marketing communications services (such as ad agencies), and both parties must be committed to ensuring that all communication tools are carefully and finely integrated.[7]

Key Aspects of Integrated Marketing Communications

The philosophy and practice of IMC includes five features. These features are listed in Table 12.1 and discussed hereafter. It is important to note that these features are interdependent and that there is no particular sequence of importance attached to the ordering in Table 12.1.

Start with the Customer or Prospect

The initial key feature of IMC is that the process should start with the customer or prospect and then work back to the brand communicator in determining the most appropriate messages and media for informing, persuading, and inducing customers and prospects to act favorably toward the communicator's brand. The IMC approach avoids an "inside-out" (from company to customer) approach in identifying how best to reach, or contact, customers. It instead starts with the customer ("outside-in") to determine those communication methods that will best serve customers' information needs and motivate them to purchase the brand. The next IMC feature is a natural extension of being customer focused.

Use Any Form of Relevant Contact

IMC uses all forms of communication and all sources of appropriate contacts as potential message delivery channels. The term *contact* is used here to mean any message medium that is capable of reaching target customers and presenting the brand in a favorable light. The key feature of this second IMC element is that it reflects a willingness on the part of the brand communicator to use any communication outlets (contacts) that are appropriate for reaching the target audience. Marketing communicators who practice this principle do not have a prior commitment to any single medium or subset of media. Rather, their objective is to surround customers/prospects with the brand message at every possible opportunity, allowing them to use whatever information about the brand they deem most useful.[8] An established advertising practitioner has referred to this as "360-degree branding," an apt phrase indeed.[9]

IMC adherents are not tied to any single communication method (such as mass-media advertising) but instead use whatever media and methods of contact best enable the communicator to deliver the brand message to the targeted audience. Direct-mail advertising, promotions at sporting and entertainment events, advertisements on packages of other brands, slogans on T-shirts, in-store displays, and Internet banner ads are just some of the contact methods for reaching present and prospective customers. The IMC objective is to reach the target audience efficiently and effectively using whatever contact methods are appropriate. Television advertising, for example, may be the best medium for contacting the audience for some brands, while less traditional (and even unconventional) contact methods may best serve other brands' communication and financial needs.

Five Key Features of IMC	Table 12.1

1. Start with the customer or prospect.
2. Use any form of relevant contact.
3. Achieve synergy (speak with a single voice).
4. Build relationships.
5. Affect behavior.

Achieve Synergy

Inherent in the definition of IMC is the need for *synergy*. A brand's assorted communication elements (advertisements, point-of-purchase signage, sales promotions, event sponsorships, and so on) must all strive to present the same brand message and convey that message consistently across diverse message channels, or points of contact. Marketing communications for a brand must, in other words, *speak with a single voice*. Coordination of messages and media is absolutely critical to achieving a strong and unified brand image and moving consumers to action. The failure to closely coordinate all communication elements can result in duplicated efforts or, worse yet, contradictory brand messages. A vice president of marketing at Nabisco fully recognized the value of speaking with a single voice when describing her intention to integrate all of the marketing communication contacts for Nabisco's Oreo brand of cookies. This executive captured the essential quality of synergy when stating that under her leadership, "Whenever consumers see Oreo, they'll be seeing the same message."[10] A general manager at Mars Inc., maker of candy products, expressed a similar sentiment when stating: "We used to look at advertising, PR, promotion plans, each piece as separate. Now every piece of communication from package to Internet has to reflect the same message."[11]

http://www.oreo.com

Build Relationships

A fourth characteristic of IMC is the belief that successful marketing communications require building a relationship between the brand and the customer. In fact, it can be argued that relationship building is the key to modern marketing and that IMC is the key to relationship building.[12] A relationship is an enduring link between a brand and its customers.[13] Successful relationships between customers and brands lead to repeat purchasing and perhaps even loyalty toward a brand.

There are myriad ways to build brand/customer relationships. One, perhaps overused, method is the use of frequent-flyer and other so-called frequency, loyalty, or ambassador programs. All of these programs are dedicated to retaining existing customers and encouraging them to satisfy most of their product or service needs from offering organizations. Airlines, hotels, supermarkets, and many other businesses provide customers with bonus points for their continued patronage. Relationships between brand and customer also are nurtured by creating compelling brand experiences (see Chapter 9) that make positive and lasting impressions. This is done with the creation of special events, sometimes called *experiential programs*, that attempt to create the feeling that a sponsoring brand is relevant to the consumer's life and lifestyle. Companies such as Saturn automobiles and Harley-Davidson motorcycles, for example, have held retreats where they invite current customers to celebrate the brand, learn about new product offerings, and to generally enjoy the occasion in a festival-like atmosphere.

http://www.saturnbp.com

http://www.harley-davidson.com

Affect Behavior

The primary goal of the fifth IMC feature is to affect the behavior of the target audience. This means that marketing communications must do more than just influence brand awareness or enhance consumer attitudes toward a brand. Instead, successful IMC requires that communication efforts be directed at encouraging some form of behavioral response. The objective, in other words, is to move people to action. We must be careful not to misconstrue this point. An integrated marketing communications program ultimately must be judged in terms of whether it *influences behavior;* but it would be simplistic and unrealistic to expect an action to result from every communication effort. Prior to purchasing a new brand, consumers generally must be *made aware* of the brand and its benefits, and influenced to have a *favorable attitude* toward it. Communication efforts directed at accomplishing these three intermediate, or prebehavioral, goals are fully justified. Yet eventually—and preferably sooner rather than later—a successful marketing communications program must do more than encourage consumers to like a brand or, worse yet, merely familiarize them with its existence. This partially explains why sales promotions and direct-to-consumer advertising are used so extensively—both practices yield quicker results than other forms of marketing communications.

Key Changes in MarCom Practice Resulting from the IMC Thrust

The adoption of an IMC mind-set necessitates some fundamental changes in the way marketing communications have traditionally been practiced. The following changes are particularly prominent:[14]

1. *Reduced Dependence on Mass-Media Advertising.* Many marketing communicators now realize that communication methods other than mass-media advertising often better serve the needs of their brands. Media advertising is not always the most effective or financially efficient medium for contacting customers and prospects. This is not to say that mass-media advertising is fading away, nevertheless, MarCom professionals and brand managers are increasingly turning to alternative methods for contacting present or prospective customers.

2. *Increased Reliance on Highly Targeted Communication Methods.* Direct mail, special-interest magazines, cable TV, event sponsorships, and e-mail messaging (so-called permission, or opt-in, e-mailing) are just some of the contact methods that enable communications pinpointed to specific target groups rather than blanketed on the masses. The use of database marketing is a key aspect of targeted communications. Almost all sophisticated B2B and consumer-oriented companies maintain large, up-to-date databases of present and prospective customers.

3. *Expanded Efforts to Assess Communications' Return on Investment.* A final key feature of IMC is its insistence on systematic efforts to determine whether marketing communications yield a reasonable return on investment. All managers, and marketing communicators are no exception, must be held financially responsible for their actions.[15] Marketing communicators, perhaps especially advertisers, long held onto the assumption that advertising's influence on sales and profits cannot be adequately measured, but in a world where financial accountability is the watchword of business efficiency, advertisers have been forced to justify their efforts.

THE MARCOM CHALLENGE: ENHANCE BRAND EQUITY

LEARNING OBJECTIVE 3

We live in a world of brands. It just so happens that some brands are better known and more respected than others. A brand (as introduced in Chapter 8) comes into existence when a good, retail outlet, or service receives its own name, term, sign, symbol, design, or any particular combination of these elements. Coca-Cola, Levi's, Lexus, Sony, Adidas, the New York Yankees, and the *Wall Street Journal* exemplify well-known and respected

http://newyork.yankees.mlb.com

brand names. Silk soymilk, which was introduced in the opening vignette, is a relatively unknown brand. All organizations and their products can be considered brands. Some brands, however, have greater equity than others. Looked at from the consumer's perspective, a brand possesses equity to the extent that consumers are familiar with the brand and have stored in memory favorable, strong, and unique brand associations.[16] That is, *brand equity* from the consumer's perspective consists of two forms of knowledge: *brand awareness* and *brand image.* Figure 12.1 graphically portrays these two dimensions of brand knowledge, and subsequent discussion will fill in the details.[17]

Consider, for example, the Adidas brand of athletic shoes, which in a recent year substantially increased its advertising budget by a whopping 25 percent over the previous year's ad budget. Adidas' director of sales and marketing explained that the purpose of this increase was to (1) raise consumer awareness of the Adidas name, and (2) pound home the message that Adidas is an authentic and high-performance athletic shoe.[18] You will note that he does not refer to brand equity per se, but this is precisely what he's talking about in reference to raising awareness and conveying a desired performance image for the Adidas brand.

Brand Awareness

Brand awareness is an issue of whether a brand name comes to mind when consumers think about a particular product category and the ease with which the name is evoked. It is the basic dimension of brand equity, in that from the vantage point of an individual consumer, a brand has no equity unless the consumer is at least aware of it. Thus, achieving brand awareness is the initial challenge for new brands, and maintaining high levels of brand awareness is the task faced continuously by all established brands. Marketing

Figure 12.1	A Model of Brand Equity

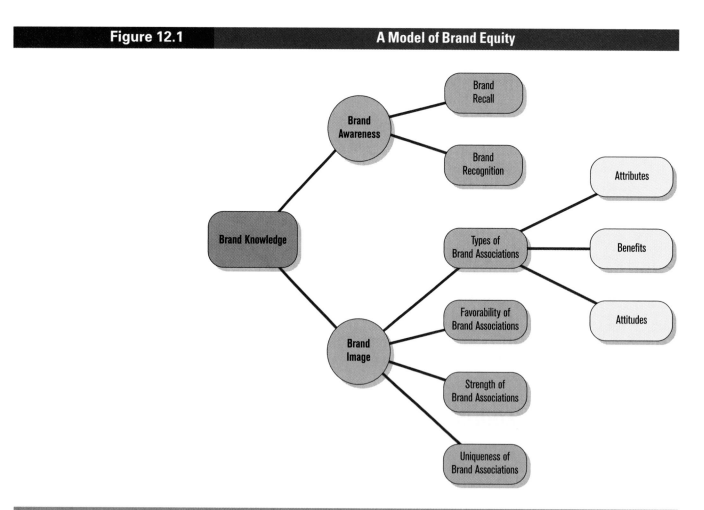

Mountain Dew—Staying True to the Brand

Consider this dilemma: Mountain Dew is often thought of as a fringe brand consumed only by teenagers who participate in skateboarding and other "alternative" sports. In actuality, Mountain Dew, or Dew for short, is the number three selling soft drink beverage in the United States with a market share exceeding 7 percent. Though teenagers do in fact represent the brand's primary market, 20- to 39-year olds make up a substantial secondary market for the brand. And the dilemma: How do the managers of Dew continue to increase the brand's revenues and share without alienating the core market that considers the brand to be theirs alone? In other words, how can the brand continue to grow and at the same time remain hip among its primary market without appearing to have "sold out," only to become just another Coke or Pepsi for the masses?

As a matter of fact, Dew's managers have masterfully handled this delicate balance by effectively integrating Mountain Dew's marketing communications program and staying true to the brand's heritage and positioning. On the market for more than 30 years, Dew remains positioned as a brand that stands for fun, exhilaration, and energy—FEE for short. Brand managers have been consistent over time and across communication media in maintaining the FEE theme that represents the brand's core meaning, its positioning. Various advertising media, event sponsorships, and consumer promotions have been recruited to trumpet and preserve the brand's core meaning. The holiday-like excitement of Super Bowl advertising reaches millions of viewers around the world. Heralding the brand's exciting and high-energy image, one Super Bowl commercial depicted a young man racing against a cheetah to retrieve a can of Dew from inside the animal's mouth. Local TV and radio spots are used to appeal to the brand's primary and secondary targets as well as to reach African American and Latino consumers who represent a major growth opportunity for the brand.

Event sponsorships provide a major communication medium for Mountain Dew, which sponsors two of the leading extreme sports competitions: ESPN's X Games and NBC's Gravity Games. In addition to these prominent sponsorships, Mountain Dew also hosts a variety of smaller events that draw audiences as small as 5,000 people. Appealing giveaway items (T-shirts, videos, branded snowboards and mountain bikes, etc.) are distributed at these events to generate excitement and to foster positive connections between the Dew brand and its loyal consumers.

Urban marketing techniques also are employed in the quest for more African American and Latino consumers. Vans and trucks loaded with 20-ounce bottles of Mountain Dew have toured major American cities and the schools, parks, and basketball courts where inner-city youth often congregate. Disk jockeys play hip-hop music and workers distribute free bottles of Mountain Dew with under-the-cap offers for another free bottle. Dew's brand managers have effectively implemented integrated marketing communications. IMC has accomplished FEE!

Sources: Adapted from Theresa Howard, "Being True to Dew," *Brandweek*, 24 April 2000, 28–31; Kate MacArthur and Hillary Chura, "Urban Warfare," *Advertising Age*, 4 September 2000, 16–17.

The Inside Story

---

communications is instrumental in confronting both these challenges. As described in the opening vignette, a major challenge facing White Wave's Silk soymilk was to increase brand awareness. Advertising was crucially important for this purpose.

Figure 12.1 shows two levels of awareness: brand recognition and brand recall. *Brand recognition* reflects a relatively superficial level of awareness, whereas *brand recall* reflects a deeper form of awareness. Consumers may be able to identify a brand if it is presented to them on a list or if hints/cues are provided. However, fewer consumers are able to retrieve a brand name from memory without any reminders or cues. It is this deeper level of brand awareness—recall—to which marketers aspire. Through effective and consistent MarCom efforts, some brands are so well known that virtually every living person can recall the brand. For example, asked to name brands of athletic footwear, most people would mention Nike, Reebok, and perhaps Adidas. The MarCom imperative is thus to move brands from a state of unawareness, to recognition, on to recall, and ultimately to top-of-mind awareness (TOMA). This pinnacle of brand-name awareness (i.e., TOMA status) exists when a brand is the first recalled when consumers think of the available options in a particular product category.

It is important to note that it is not just consumer-oriented B2C firms that must be concerned with building brand awareness. Most B2B practitioners also consider the major goal of their advertising efforts is to create awareness of their new products. These same practitioners also believe that building brand image is another goal of B2B MarCom efforts.[19]

Brand Image

The second dimension of consumer-based brand knowledge is a brand's image. *Brand image* can be thought of in terms of the types of associations that come to the consumer's mind when contemplating a particular brand. A *brand association* is simply the particular thoughts and feelings that a consumer has about a brand, much in the same fashion that we have thoughts and feelings about other people. For example, what thoughts/ feelings come immediately to mind when you think of your best friend? You undoubtedly associate your friend with certain physical characteristics, features, strengths, and perhaps frailties. Likewise, brands are linked in our memories with specific thought-and-feeling associations. As was shown in Figure 12.1, these associations can be conceptualized in terms of (1) type, (2) favorability, (3) strength, and (4) uniqueness.

Efforts to enhance a brand's equity are initially accomplished through the careful choice of positive brand identity (that is, the selection of a good brand name or logo). But they must be reinforced by MarCom programs that forge favorable, strong, and unique associations in the consumer's mind between a brand and its attributes/benefits. It is impossible to overstate the importance of efforts to enhance a brand's equity. Products that are high in quality and represent a good value potentially possess high brand equity. But effective and consistent marketing communication efforts are needed to build upon and maintain brand equity. A favorable brand image does not happen automatically. Sustained marketing communications are generally required. For example, it could be claimed that one of the world's greatest brands, Coca-Cola, is little more than colored sugar water. This brand nevertheless possesses immense brand equity because its managers are ever mindful of the need for continuous advertising executions that sustain the Coca-Cola story and build the image around the world. In the United States alone, the Coca-Cola Company commands over a 40 percent share of the carbonated soft drink

http://www.coca-cola.com

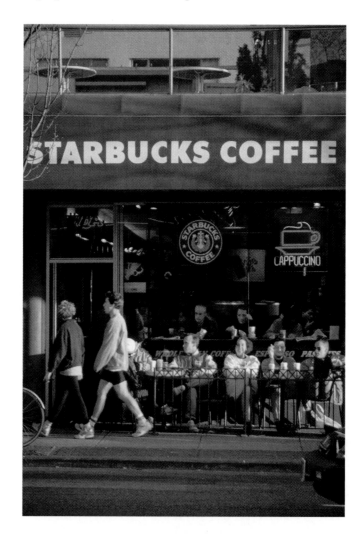

business, which exceeds $50 billion in sales revenue.[20] Consumers don't buy this "colored sugar water" merely for its taste; they purchase a lifestyle and an image when selecting Coca-Cola over other available brands. It is effective advertising, exciting sales promotions, creative sponsorships, and other forms of marketing communications that are responsible for Coca-Cola's positive image and massive market share.

Research has shown that when firms communicate unique and positive messages via advertising, personal selling, sales promotion, and other means, they are able to effectively differentiate their brands from competitive offerings and insulate themselves from future price competition.[21] Marketing communications play an essential role in creating positive brand equity and building strong brand loyalty. However, this is not always accomplished with traditional advertising or other conventional forms of marketing communications. For example, Starbucks, the virtual icon for upscale coffee, does very little advertising, yet this brand has a near cultlike following. The average Starbucks consumer visits a Starbucks outlet an estimated 18 times a month, a situation of nearly unparalleled brand loyalty.[22]

http://www.starbucks.com

DETERMINING AN APPROPRIATE MIX OF IMC TOOLS

LEARNING OBJECTIVE 4

In determining an appropriate mix of MarCom elements for a specific brand in a particular product category, a product or brand manager must weigh a variety of factors related to the category, the brand, and the market. The marketing manager typically has considerable discretion in determining which elements to use and how much relative emphasis each should receive. Should the entire budget go toward supporting the sales force, or should some be allocated to mass-media advertising? Are point-of-purchase materials needed at retail? Will coupons or bonus packs help move more product? There is no absolute formula a manager can use to determine an optimum blend of elements. The manager must thoroughly analyze the product, the competition, the brand's strengths and weaknesses, and the target market to determine the brand's MarCom needs and opportunities. The decision is guided by addressing each of the following issues:

- Who is the intended market?
- What objectives must the MarCom initiative achieve?
- What is the nature of the product?
- What is the product life-cycle stage?
- What are competitors doing?
- What is the available budget for marketing communications?
- Will a push strategy or pull strategy be more effective?

Who Is the Intended Market?

The blend of MarCom activities will differ considerably depending on the character of the intended market. Chapter 6 established that in the B2B market the number of organizational buyers are fewer, decisions are often made in groups, and buyers are more geographically concentrated. The marketing budget would be more effectively used in personal selling to reach this target market. However, to reach buyers in the consumer market—where individual buyers oftentimes number in the millions, where decisions are made by each consumer individually or in small groups, and where consumers are widely dispersed—the marketing budget is more effectively spent on advertising, sales promotion, and other communication approaches that are able to reach the masses. Hence, a clear understanding of the product's target market is vital in determining how best to allocate the MarCom budget.

What Objectives Must the MarCom Initiative Achieve?

Figure 12.2 presents a framework, called the *hierarchy of effects*, that provides a useful way of thinking about the objectives that marketing communications can accomplish. The hierarchy framework captures the idea that marketing communications are designed to advance B2B customers or B2C consumers from an initial stage of brand awareness, to learning about the brand (i.e., beliefs and knowledge), to forming a positive attitude toward the brand, to intending to purchase it, and ultimately to making a purchase decision that favors "our" brand versus competitive offerings.

Figure 12.2	The Hierarchy of Effects

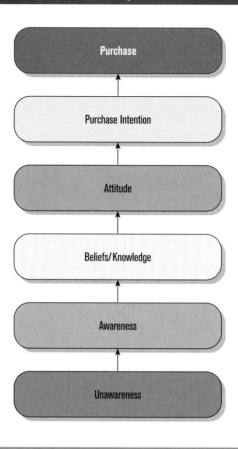

http://www.aflac.com

The different stages in the hierarchy are best understood by examining an actual MarCom situation. Have you ever heard of a company called American Family Life Insurance Company? I'll bet you haven't. Have you ever heard of a company called AFLAC? Perhaps you have. (AFLAC is, of course, the acronym for American Family Life Insurance Company.) Do you recall seeing a TV commercial with a talking, white duck that seems to go unnoticed by the participants *in* the commercial but not to viewers of the commercial who see the duck and repeatedly hear it exclaim, "AFLAAAAC!" Let's now appraise what the advertiser is attempting to accomplish.

First, most consumers are not all that interested in thinking about insurance or learning about different companies that compete in this industry. AFLAC, though a huge company in the so-called supplemental insurance business—the business that sells insurance policies to people to augment their inadequate health, life, and disability coverage from employer-funded insurance programs—generates annual revenues of $10 billion or more, yet most consumers were unaware of AFLAC prior to its commencing the "duck" advertising campaign.[23] The campaign was designed accordingly to familiarize consumers initially with the AFLAC name, to create brand awareness. Interestingly, the ad agency responsible for the campaign came up with the idea of using a duck after one of its creative people observed that when spoken "AFLAC" sounds like a squawking duck. Second, the campaign intended to make consumers knowledgeable of situations when supplemental insurance might be necessary, to build brand knowledge. For example, in one advertisement, a couple is shown riding in the front of a roller coaster. The duck in the car behind the couple reassures them about their own supplemental insurance coverage in the event the coaster has a disaster. Third, the reassuring advertising should have the effect of influencing consumers to like AFLAC's advertising and thus the company itself, creating positive attitude formation. Fourth, having now learned about supplemental insurance and recognizing that their own employer-based insurance coverage is inadequate, many consumers could be expected to contemplate the possibility of acquiring supplemental insurance, perhaps from AFLAC, thereby generating purchase intention. Finally, some consumers will act upon the intention by meeting with an AFLAC sales representative and purchase a supplemental insurance policy. AFLAC's duck campaign apparently accomplished its goal of moving consumers up the hierarchy of effects insofar as sales increased by a whopping 27 percent within 18 months of commencing the advertising campaign.[24]

What Is the Nature of the Product?

The nature of the product itself will influence the proper mixture of MarCom elements. For example, an industrial machine that is marketed to a small segment of B2B customers will utilize different elements than will a brand of toothpaste, deodorant, snack food, or other convenience goods. Although the industrial machine marketer might use some advertising and sales promotions, personal selling would provide the primary means for reaching prospective customers for the machine. In this case, the marketer's budget might be divided as follows: 70 percent to personal selling, 20 percent to trade-oriented media advertising, and the remaining 10 percent to direct-mail advertisements, an Internet Web site, and telemarketing efforts.

In promoting consumer goods, especially convenience items, other forms of marketing communications take on added importance. In this case, the marketer's budget might be distributed as such: 20 percent to trade-oriented personal selling to gain product distribution from wholesalers and retailers, 30 percent to trade-oriented sales promotions to achieve favorable shelf space, 25 percent to consumer-oriented sales promotions to encourage product trial and repeat purchasing, and 5 percent to point-of-purchase materials to encourage impulse buying. In both the B2B or B2C scenarios, no one element within the mix will be omitted completely from the marketing budgets. The focus on each element will change, though, depending on the nature of the product.

What Is the Product Life-Cycle Stage?

Is the brand well established and in the maturity stage of the product life cycle, or is it a new brand in the introduction stage? In the introduction stage, advertising is especially critical to create awareness and to inform consumers about the brand and its benefits (i.e., influence beliefs/knowledge). Trade-oriented sales promotions are essential for gaining wholesaler and retailer support, and consumer sales promotions (such as coupons and cents-off deals) are important for achieving consumer trial, especially when marketing packaged goods. Later on, as the product reaches the maturity stage, advertising and sales promotions both remain crucial, but both undergo qualitative changes. Advertising now is needed to maintain a positive brand image and differentiate the brand from competitive offerings, whereas sales promotions are used to encourage repeat purchase behavior.

What Are Competitors Doing?

Competitive action generally dictates what can or must be done. For example, in the deodorant category, if Soft N Dri offers a trade allowance that reduces the retail price to $1.99, and then offers a 75¢ coupon, consumers are able to buy this brand for only $1.24. Ban, Lady Speed Stick, and Secret cannot ignore this activity or they may see an erosion of their market shares, even if it's only on a temporary basis. These companies may be forced to take action to offset Soft N Dri's competitive push.

What Is the Available Budget?

The MarCom budget will determine what elements can be emphasized. In the B2B market, a marketer may emphasize personal selling and forgo advertising if the total MarCom budget is limited by poor performance the previous year or because the economic forecast for the coming year is unattractive. The sales force is a relatively fixed expense, whereas advertising can be increased or decreased depending on the situation and financial circumstances. (During the economic slowdown of 2000–2001, many marketers, B2C as well as B2B, substantially reduced their advertising budgets.) In the consumer market, on the other hand, a nationally distributed brand is forced by the competition to devote some funds to advertising and sales promotions. The actual amount varies depending on the product category and the economic situation, but most brands invest anywhere from 1 to 15 percent of sales revenue on advertising and an equal or greater amount to trade- and consumer-oriented sales promotions, collectively.

Will a Push or Pull Strategy Be More Effective?

The terms *push strategy* and *pull strategy* are metaphors that characterize the promotional activities marketers undertake to encourage channel members to handle products. A **push strategy** involves investing proportionately more of the MarCom budget toward the trade market as opposed to the consumers market, whereas with a **pull strategy** proportionately more is invested in encouraging consumer acceptance and purchase of the brand. It is important to realize, however, that both strategies utilize personal selling, advertising, sales promotion, and so on, though each strategy requires a different emphasis on the individual MarCom elements. Personal selling is much more important in the push strategy, whereas advertising is more important in the pull strategy. Most manufacturers use a combination of push and pull techniques. These techniques complement one another rather than representing perfect substitutes.

LEARNING OBJECTIVE 5

MANAGING THE MARCOM PROCESS

As the previous sections illustrate, many factors must be considered in creating an effective mixture of MarCom elements. Marketing communications—like any other business process—must be managed. MarCom management involves six primary areas

1. Selecting target markets
2. Establishing objectives
3. Formulating a positioning strategy
4. Setting the budget
5. Formulating and implementing message and media strategies
6. Evaluating program effectiveness

Selecting Target Markets

Selection of target markets is the critical first step toward effective and efficient marketing communications. Targeting allows marketing communicators to pinpoint a product's potential audience and to more precisely deliver messages to this group. Targeting attempts to avoid wasting valuable promotional dollars on those consumers outside the target market. As discussed in Chapter 7, companies identify potential target markets in terms of a combination of characteristics—demographics, lifestyles, product usage patterns, geographical location—that will cause these consumers to act in a similar fashion. For example, the target market for White Wave's Silk soymilk probably consists predominantly of younger to middle-aged women (18–49), who are slightly above average in educational achievement and income, are health conscious, and who live active lifestyles. The target market for AFLAC likely consists predominantly of younger families, with heads of households who generally are in the age range of 25 to 39 years, are of average socioeconomic status, are somewhat risk adverse, and who believe in the importance of insurance.

Establishing Objectives

As discussed earlier in the chapter, it is important for marketing communicators to establish clear and achievable objectives as a prelude to designing messages and executing communication programs. Marketing communication objectives must fit within a company's overall corporate and marketing objectives. The objectives must also be realistic and stated in quantitative terms with the amount of projected change and the time duration specified. For example, the objective "to increase brand awareness" is too general to be of much value. A much better objective would be "to increase brand awareness by 20 percent within the next 6 months."

Push strategy
involves aggressive trade allowances and personal selling efforts to obtain distribution for a new brand through wholesalers and retailers. The brand is "pushed" through the channel system in the sense that there is a forward thrust from the manufacturer to the trade

Pull strategy
involves a relatively heavy emphasis on consumer-oriented advertising to encourage consumer demand for a new brand and thereby obtain retail distribution. The brand is "pulled" through the channel system in the sense that there is a backward tug from the consumer to the retailer.

Formulating a Positioning Strategy

Brand positioning is an essential activity in developing successful MarCom programs. It is only by having a clear positioning statement that marketers define to whom a brand should be targeted, what they should say about the brand, and what media and message vehicles should be selected for contacting target customers.

Positioning is both a useful conceptual notion and an invaluable strategic tool. Conceptually, the term *positioning* suggests two interrelated ideas: first, that the marketing communicator wishes to create a specific meaning for the brand and to have that meaning clearly lodged in the consumer's memory (think of this as "positioned in"). The second aspect of positioning is that the brand's meaning in consumers' memories stands in comparison to what they know and think about competitive brands in the product category (think of this as "positioned against").

Strategically and tactically, positioning is a short statement—even a word—that represents the message marketers want to "imprint in the minds of customers and prospects."[25] This statement tells how a brand differs from and is superior to competitive brands. It gives a reason why consumers should buy the brand rather than a competitor's and promises a solution to the customer's needs or wants. A good positioning statement should satisfy two requirements: (1) reflect a brand's competitive advantage and (2) motivate customers to action.[26] Ultimately, a *positioning statement* for a brand represents how marketing communicators want customers and prospects to think and feel about their brand. These thoughts and feelings should stand out in comparison to competitive offerings and motivate the customers/prospects to want to try the brand.

Setting the Budget

An organization's financial resources are budgeted to specific MarCom elements in order to accomplish the sales and profit objectives established for its various brands. The amount of resources allocated to specific MarCom elements is typically the result, in most sophisticated corporations, of an involved process. Companies use different budgeting processes in allocating funds to brand managers. At one extreme is *top-down budgeting (TD)*, in which senior management decides how much each subunit receives. At the other extreme is *bottom-up budgeting (BU)*, in which managers of subunits (such as brand managers) determine how much is needed to achieve their objectives; these amounts are then combined to establish the total marketing budget.

Most budgeting practices involve a combination of top-down and bottom-up budgeting. For example, in the bottom-up/top-down process (BUTD), brand managers submit budget requests to a chief marketing officer (e.g., a vice president of marketing), who coordinates the various requests and then submits an overall budget to top management for approval. The top-down/bottom-up process (TDBU) reverses the flow of influence by having top managers first establish the total size of the budget and then divide it among the various brand managers. Research has shown that combination budgeting methods (BUTD and TDBU) are used more often than the extreme methods (TD or BU). The BUTD process is by far the most frequently used, especially in more sophisticated firms where marketing-department influence is high compared to finance-department influence.[27]

Formulating and Implementing Message and Media Strategies

Decisions must be made regarding the message to be communicated and the media within which the message will be sent. The message is a critical component of marketing communication effectiveness. Marketers must decide how best to present their ideas to achieve the established objectives. In creating a message, a marketer may choose from a variety of message alternatives including what image to create, how to position the brand, and what types of appeals to employ such as humor, nostalgia, and so on.

Marketing communications need also consider various **media strategies**. Media typically connotes a mode of advertising such as via television, radio, or magazines. But the term *media* can be applied to every MarCom element. Point-of-purchase materials, for example, can be a simple cardboard shelf talker, a take-one pad, or a sophisticated display. A sales promotion can range from a simple coupon distributed via freestanding insert to a more involved sweepstakes offer. Each of these alternatives is a different medium that has a unique rate of effectiveness as well as cost. Brand managers must

Media strategy
consists of four sets of interrelated activities: (1) selecting the target audience, (2) specifying media objectives, (3) selecting media categories and vehicles, and (4) buying media.

determine which message and media will be most effective—from both a communications as well as cost standpoint—in delivering the desired message.

Evaluating Program Effectiveness

Once a MarCom program is in place and being implemented, the program must be evaluated for its effectiveness. Only through evaluation can one learn what works, what does not work, and why. This information is critical in creating future programs and taking corrective action when necessary.

A program is evaluated by measuring its results against the objectives established in the planning stage. For some elements it is relatively simple to assess effectiveness, because the results generated are easily attributable to just that element. Consider a direct-mail campaign where the measure of effectiveness is the actual response rate, or the number of orders received as a percentage of the number of mailings, say, a 2 percent response rate. Effectiveness is evaluated by comparing the actual response rate with the objective established in the form of a projected response rate. For a premium offer, the total number of consumers sending in proofs of purchase can be compared against the number of submissions contained in the original objective. In either event, corrective action is called for if the actual response rate falls significantly below that which was projected.

Other promotional elements such as advertising are more difficult to evaluate inasmuch as objective outcomes—such as the amount of sales generated in a period—are not directly or exclusively attributable to the ads per se. In other words, sales are the result of all marketing mix variables, not just advertising. Moreover, current sales are due to past marketing efforts, and are not solely attributable to current advertising; that is, the advertising and sales relation is typically lagged, with advertising in the current period influencing sales at later times, as well as in the current period. Due to these complications, advertisers typically assess advertising effectiveness in terms of so-called *communication outcomes* such as changes in consumers' awareness of the advertised brand, knowledge of copy points, or attitudes toward the brand. All of these factors, if measured and known before an advertising campaign begins, can be measured again at the end of the campaign and compared to objectives to determine effectiveness.

Now that we have introduced the nature and management of marketing communications, subsequent sections—starting with advertising and ending with point-of-purchase communications—will examine each MarCom element in some detail.

LEARNING OBJECTIVE   6

ADVERTISING

There are three basic ways by which companies can add value to their offerings: by *innovating*, by *improving quality*, or by *altering consumer perceptions*. These three value-added components are completely interdependent. Advertising adds value to brands by influencing consumers' perceptions. Effective advertising causes brands to be viewed as more elegant, more stylish, more prestigious, perhaps superior to competitive offerings, and, in general, of higher perceived quality and/or value. When advertising is done effectively, brands are perceived as being higher quality or of better value, which in turn can lead to increased market share and greater profitability. It is little wonder that Procter & Gamble, perhaps the leading consumer-goods firm in the world, fully appreciates advertising's value-adding role. Indeed, a P&G vice president of worldwide advertising has characterized strong advertising as "a deposit in the brand equity bank."[28]

http://www.pg.com

Advertising also can be considered an economic investment, an investment regarded favorably by numerous businesses throughout the United States and the world. In recognition of advertising's invaluable role, U.S. companies invested approximately $250 billion on advertising in 2001.[29] This amounts to approximately $900 in advertising for each of the nearly 280 million men, women, and children in the United States as of 2001. Advertising spending is also considerable in other major industrialized countries, but not nearly to the same magnitude as U.S. spending. The biggest advertising spenders following the United States are Japan, Germany, the United Kingdom, France, and Canada. However, advertising expenditures in these countries are small compared to those in the United States.

Some American companies alone invest over $1 billion annually on domestic advertising. In a recent year, for example, the top five advertising spenders in the United States were General Motors, which spent slightly over $4 billion; Procter & Gamble, $2.61 billion; Philip Morris, $2.2 billion; Pfizer, $2.14 billion; and AT&T, $1.95 billion.[30] Even the U.S. government advertises to the tune of $998 million.[31] The government's advertising goes to efforts such as military recruiting, the U.S. Postal Service, Amtrak rail services, the U.S. Mint (e.g., commemorative coins), and AIDS awareness.

The actual advertising process for a particular brand can be thought of as the development and implementation of an advertising strategy. *Advertising strategy* entails five major activities: *objective setting, budgeting, positioning, planning message strategy, developing media strategy,* and *assessing advertising effectiveness.* The first three activities—objective setting, budgeting, and positioning—were described earlier in context of the overall MarCom process and are discussed only briefly in the present advertising situation. Suffice it to say that the objective-setting, budgeting, and positioning processes are fundamentally the same regardless of which MarCom element is involved.

Setting Advertising Objectives

Advertising objectives provide the foundation for all remaining advertising decisions. There are three major reasons for setting advertising objectives:

1. The process of setting objectives literally forces top marketing and advertising management to agree on the course advertising is to take for the following planning period, as well as the tasks it is intended to accomplish for a brand.
2. Objective setting guides the budgeting, message creation, and media selection aspects of advertising strategy.
3. Advertising objectives provide standards against which results can be measured.[32]

Advertisements are created to accomplish goals such as (1) making the target market aware of a new brand, (2) facilitating consumer understanding of a brand's attributes, (3) creating expectations about a brand's benefits, (4) enhancing attitudes toward the brand, (5) influencing purchase intentions, and (6) encouraging product trial.

Budgeting for Advertising

The advertising budgeting decision is, in many respects, the most important decision advertisers make. If too little money is spent on advertising, sales volume will not be as high as it could be, and profits will be lost. If too much money is spent, expenses will be higher than they need to be, and profits will be reduced.

Budgeting is also one of the most difficult advertising decisions. This difficulty arises because it is hard to determine precisely how effective advertising has been or might be in the future. The sales response to advertising is influenced by a multitude of factors (quality of advertising execution, intensity of competitive advertising efforts, customer taste, and other considerations), thereby making it difficult, if not impossible, to know with any certainty what amount of sales a particular advertising effort will generate.

Companies ordinarily set budgets by using judgment, applying experience with analogous situations, and using simple rules of thumb, or *heuristics.* Although criticized because they do not provide a basis for advertising budget setting that is directly related to the profitability of the advertised brand, these heuristics continue to be widely used.[33] The two most pervasive heuristics, in use by both industrial and consumer-goods advertisers, are the percentage-of-sales and objective-and-task methods.[34] The *percentage-of-sales method* involves allocating a fixed percentage of past or anticipated sales revenue to advertising. For example, a company may allocate 5 percent of the next fiscal period's anticipated sales to advertising. If sales are estimated to be $100 million for the upcoming year, the advertising budget will be $5 million. The *objective-and-task method* involves the following three-step procedure: (1) specifying the objectives that a particular advertisement or entire ad campaign is intended to accomplish; (2) identifying the specific tasks that must be accomplished in order to reach those objectives; and (3) accumulating anticipated costs to achieve the specified tasks. The outcome of this systematic, three-step process is an advertising budget that should be sufficient to achieve critical objectives.

Establishing the Brand Positioning

Brand managers work with their advertising agencies to formulate specific meaning for their brands. This meaning, or positioning, establishes how the brand is to be thought of by members of the target market and how the brand is to be perceived relative to competitive brands in the product category. Some illustrative positioning strategies include Volvo, which is basically synonymous with safety; Absolut (vodka), which has built a reputation for being cosmopolitan and hip (see Figure 12.3); Godiva chocolate, which represents in the minds of many consumers pleasurable indulgence; and Nike, which is *the* brand for serious athletes.

Creating Advertising Messages

Advertisers use a vast array of techniques to present their brands in the most favorable light and persuade customers to contemplate purchasing these brands. Frequently employed techniques include:

- Informational ads (such as automobile ads in the classified pages of a newspaper)

Figure 12.3	A Positioning Strategy That Works

- Humorous executions (e.g., most Budweiser advertisements; Holiday Inn's advertising campaign with the thirty-something slacker who lives at home with his parents and grandmother)
- Sex appeal (e.g., the attention-getting advertisement for Emporio Armani's fragrance shown in Figure 12.4).
- Celebrity endorsements (e.g., the McDonald's advertisement featuring Kobe Bryant).
- Various emotional appeals (nostalgia, romance, excitement, etc.).

The techniques to persuasively advertise products are limited only by advertisers' creativity and ingenuity. It is beyond the scope of this text to go into detail concerning these and other advertising techniques. Rather, we pose a more straightforward question: What makes an advertisement good or effective? Although it is impractical to provide a single, all-purpose definition of what constitutes effective advertising, it is useful to talk about general characteristics.[35] At a minimum, good or effective advertising satisfies the following six considerations:

1. *It extends from sound marketing strategy.* Advertising can be effective only if it is compatible with other elements of an integrated and well-orchestrated MarCom strategy.
2. *It takes the consumer's view.* Consumers buy product benefits, not attributes. Therefore, advertising must be stated in a way that relates to the consumer's needs, wants, and values and not strictly in terms of product characteristics.

Sex Appeal Campaign	**Figure 12.4**

3. *It is persuasive.* Persuasion usually occurs when there is a benefit for the consumer, and not just for the marketer.

4. *It finds a unique way to break through competitive clutter.* Advertisers continuously vie with competitors for the consumer's attention. This is no small task considering the massive number of print advertisements, broadcast commercials, and other sources of information available daily to consumers. Indeed, the situation in television advertising has been characterized as audiovisual wallpaper, which implies sarcastically that consumers pay just about as much attention to commercials as they do to the detail in their own wallpaper after it has been on the walls for awhile.[36]

5. *It never promises more than it can deliver.* This point speaks for itself, both in terms of ethics and in terms of smart business sense. Consumers learn quickly when they have been deceived and resent it.

6. *It prevents the creative idea from overwhelming the strategy.* The purpose of advertising is to persuade and influence; the purpose is not to be cute for cute's sake or humorous for humor's sake. The ineffective use of humor, for example, results in people remembering the humor but forgetting the selling message.

Effective advertising is usually *creative*. That is, it differentiates itself from the mass of mediocre advertisements; it is somehow different and out of the ordinary. Advertising that is the same as most other advertising is unable to break through the competitive clutter and fails to grab the consumer's attention. It is easier to give examples of creative advertising than to define exactly what it is. Here are three examples of what many advertising practitioners would consider effective, creative advertising:

1. The "Intel Inside" application of ingredient branding whereby this chip manufacturer convinced many computer purchasers that Intel chips substantially enhanced computer quality.

2. Absolut vodka's continuing magazine campaign that focuses on this brand's "hip" image by portraying the brand's unique bottle shape in trendy situations.

3. The milk-mustache campaign that associates drinking milk with a wide variety of interesting and respected celebrities. (For example, see Figure 12.5.)

Selecting Advertising Media

Outstanding message execution is to no avail unless messages are delivered to the right customers at the right time, and with sufficient frequency. In other words, advertising messages stand a chance of being effective only if the media strategy itself is effective. Good messages and good media go hand in hand; they are inseparable—a true marriage. Improper media selection can doom an otherwise promising advertising campaign.

Creative advertisements are more effective when placed in media whose characteristics enhance the value of the advertising message and reach the advertiser's targeted customers at the right time. A variety of decisions must be made when choosing media. In addition to determining which media to use (television, radio, magazines, etc.), the media planner must also pick *vehicles* within each medium (e.g., specific magazines or TV programs), and decide how to allocate the available budget among the various media and vehicle alternatives. Additional decisions involve determining when to advertise, choosing specific geographical locations, and deciding how to distribute the budget over time and across geographic locations.

A successful media strategy requires, first, that the target audience be clearly pinpointed. Failure to precisely define the audience results in wasted exposures; that is, some nonpurchase candidates are exposed to advertisements while some prime candidates are missed. Target audiences are usually selected based on geographic factors (e.g., ads are aimed at people residing in urban centers), demographic considerations (e.g., ads are directed to women aged 18 to 49), product-usage concerns (e.g., ads are focused on heavy product users), and lifestyle/psychographic characteristics (e.g., ads are directed to people with active, outdoor lifestyles).

The Effective Milk Moustache Campaign | Figure 12.5

Which is better for growing bones?

Here's a clue. Both chocolate milk and regular milk have the same good stuff to help your bones grow strong.

got milk?

Wanna race? Milk has nine essential nutrients active bodies need. It can't be beat. And neither can I.

got milk?

A second aspect of media strategy is establishing specific objectives. Four objectives are fundamental to media planning: reach, frequency, continuity, and cost. Media planners seek answers to the following types of questions:

1. What portion of the target audience do we want to see (or read, or hear) the advertising message? (*reach*)
2. How often should the target audience be exposed to the advertisement? (*frequency*)
3. When are the best times to reach the target audience? (*continuity*)
4. What is the least expensive way to accomplish the other objectives? (*cost*)

Advertisers work with statistics such as ratings, gross rating points (GRPs), and cost per thousand (CPM), to compare different vehicles within the same medium and to make intelligent selections. For example, an advertiser might consider advertising its brand on *The West Wing,* a TV program that appeals to a wide audience and produces a rating of about 18 percentage points at a cost of approximately $400,000 per 30-second commercial. The 18 rating means that of approximately 100 million households in the United States, on average, 18 percent, or 18 million, are tuned in to this program. Theoretically, then, the advertiser would reach 18 million households every time it places a commercial on *The West Wing.* If, say, during a 4-week period the advertiser placed a total of 8 commercials on this program (i.e., two ads during each episode), it would accumulate a total of 144 **gross rating points (GRPs)**. GRPs simply represent the mathematical product of individual ratings times the number of times that an advertisement is

Gross rating points (GRPs) are the accumulation of rating points including all vehicles in a media purchase over the span of a particular campaign.

Cost per thousand (CPM)
is calculated by dividing the cost of an ad placed in a particular ad vehicle (e.g., certain magazine) by the number of people (expressed in thousands) who are exposed to that vehicle.

http://www.sportsillustrated.
cnn.com

aired on a TV program (or placed in a magazine). In equation form, GRPs = R × F, where R equals ratings (or reach) and F equals frequency of ad placement.

Cost per thousand (CPM) (M is the Roman numeral for 1,000) is a useful statistic for comparing the cost efficiency of vehicles in the same medium. For example, in 2000 a single four-color, full-page advertisement placed in *Sports Illustrated* cost an advertiser about $180,000 and reached approximately 24 million readers. The cost of the ad per 1,000 readers is calculated as follows: CPM = Cost of ad placement divided by the size of audience expressed in thousands; therefore, $180,000 ÷ 24,000 = $7.50.

The advertiser would compare this value with the CPM to advertise in alternative vehicles. For example, in 2000 a full-page, four-color ad placed in *Sport* magazine cost approximately $50,000 and reached about 4.5 million readers. Its CPM is $11.11 (i.e., $50,000 ÷ 4,500). *Sports Illustrated* is a less expensive vehicle on a per-thousand basis than *Sport* and on a cost-basis alone is the obvious better buy. However, the choice of which magazine to select is based on considerations other than mere cost comparisons. Also crucial in the decision are considerations such as how closely a vehicle's readers/viewers match the brand's target audience and the fit between the image of the vehicle and the brand's desired image.

Advertisers have four major mass media from which to choose: television, radio, magazines, and newspapers. Each medium possesses various strengths and weaknesses. Some of the most prominent of these are summarized in Figure 12.6. One additional advertising medium that deserves mention is the Internet. Internet usage is growing rather dramatically throughout the world. Many advertisers have used the Internet for placing banner advertisements, for posting e-mail messages (so-called permission or opt-in emailing), and for conveying company and brand information via the creation of home pages. It has been estimated that the average Internet user will be exposed to over 900 banner ads daily by 2005.[37] The vast majority of these ads never receive our attention, however. According to Nielsen/NetRatings, the average click rate in 2001 was a paltry 0.49 percent; in other words, online users pay attention and solicit information from only a small percentage of all the Internet banner ads to which they are exposed. Internet advertisers, like advertisers in all other media, have to fight through the clutter to find ways to attract the online user's attention. Bigger ads, ads that pop up, and ads that offer sound and visuals are just some of the ways that have been devised to attract and hold the Internet user's attention.

The Internet is a potentially invaluable advertising medium for advertisers. Compared to other media, the Internet is an *interactive medium* in that consumers seek out information and devote their time to a particular home page, banner ad, or e-mail advertisement if it offers informational, educational, or recreational value. In a sense, the Internet is the modern version of the *Yellow Pages*—"Let your mouse do the walking," so to speak. Both media are successful only to the extent that they are easy to access and provide useful and/or interesting information. Creative advertisements on the Net are potentially capable of drawing and holding consumers' attention and serving to build relations between consumers and advertised brands. Second, Internet advertising provides advertisers with a medium to reach audiences (predominantly relatively well-educated and young people) who are difficult to access via other media. Third, it is estimated that in a few years the Internet will offer video quality on a par with TV and voice quality as good as telephone. This prospect will greatly expand the advertising value of this medium. Finally, the cost of advertising on the Net is relatively low compared to established media. On the downside, there are not yet (as of 2001) any syndicated services that are comparable in stature to Nielsen (of TV ratings fame) that measure the effectiveness of advertising on the Internet. Needless to say, various companies have developed methods for this purpose, but the effectiveness of these methods is yet to be determined.

Assessing Advertising Effectiveness

Assessing advertising effectiveness is a final critical aspect of advertising strategy, inasmuch as only by evaluating results is it possible to determine whether advertising objectives have been accomplished. This often requires that baseline measures be taken before an advertising campaign begins (to determine, for example, what percentage of the target audience is aware of the brand name), and then afterwards to determine whether the objective was achieved. Because, as earlier noted, billions of dollars are invested on

Comparative Strengths and Weaknesses of Major Advertising Media		Figure 12.6

Medium	Strengths	Weaknesses
Television	• Dramatic Presentation and Demonstration Ability • High Reach Potential • Attain Rapid Awareness • Relatively Efficient • Intrusive and Impactual • Ability to Integrate Messages with Other Media Such As Radio	• Relatively Downscale Audience Profile • Network Audience Erosion • Growing Commercial Clutter • High Out-of-Pocket Cost • High Production Costs • Long Lead Time to Purchase Network Time • Volatile Cost Structure
Radio	• Target Selectivity • High Frequency • Efficient • Able to Transfer Image from TV • Portable, Personal Medium • Low Production Cost • Use of Local Personalities • Ability to Integrate Messages with Other Media Such As TV	• Commercial Clutter • Some Station Formats Relatively Uninvolving for Listeners • Relatively Small Audiences • High Out-of-Pocket Cost to Attain Significant Reach • Audience Fractionalization
Magazines	• Efficient Reach of Selective Audiences • Ability to Match Advertising with Compatible Editorial Content • High Quality Graphics • Reach Light TV Viewers • Opportunity to Repeat Ad Exposure • Flexibility in Target Market Coverage • Can Deliver Complex Copy • Readership Is Not Seasonal	• Not Intrusive; Reader Controls Ad Exposure • Slow Audience Accumulation • Significant Slippage from Reader Audience to Ad-Exposure Audience • Clutter Can Be High • Long Lead Times to Purchase Magazine Space • Somewhat Limited Geographic Options • Uneven Market-by-Market Circulation Patterns
Newspapers	• Rapid Audience Accumulation • Timeliness • High Single Day Reach Attainable • Short Lead Times to Purchase Newspaper Space • Excellent Geographic Flexibility • Can Convey Detailed Copy • Strong Retail Trade Support • Good for Merchandising and Promotion • Low Production Cost • Excellent Local Market Penetration	• Limited Target Selectivity • High Out-of-Pocket Costs for National Buys • Significant Differential Between National and Local Rates • Not Intrusive • Cluttered Ad Environment • Generally Mediocre Reproduction Quality

advertising, advertisers go to great lengths to measure the effectiveness of their advertisements. There literally is an entire industry of companies that are in business to measure advertising effectiveness. Companies have developed services to measure magazine readership—Simmons Market Research Bureau (SMRB) and Mediamark Research, Inc. (MRI), for example. Other companies measure television audience size, most notably Nielsen. Then there are services to assess consumer recognition and recall of magazine ads (Starch Readership Service) and of television commercials (Burke Day-After Recall), and measures of the persuasive and emotional impact of TV commercials.

Perhaps the most notable development in advertising-effectiveness measurement is the advent of so-called **single-source systems.** Single-source systems became possible with the advent of two electronic-monitoring tools: television meters and optical

Single-source systems
are a measurement of the effectiveness of advertising (whether it leads to increased sales activity). They are unique in that all the relevant data is collected by a single source, processed, and then made available in a readily usable format to retailers and manufacturers.

laser scanning of universal product codes (UPC symbols) at the point of purchase. Single-source systems gather purchase data from panels of households using optical scanning equipment and merge it with household demographic characteristics. Most importantly, it is then combined with information about other marketing variables that influence household purchases (e.g., TV commercials, coupons, in-store displays, trade promotions, etc.).

Information Resource Inc. (IRI) pioneered single-source data collection in 1979 with its *BehaviorScan* system. BehaviorScan operates panel households in select markets around the United States, with approximately 2,500 panel members in each market. Ten thousand BehaviorScan households are installed with electronic television meters.[38] Panel members provide IRI with information about the size of their families, their income, number of televisions owned, the types of newspapers and magazines they read, and who in the household does most of the shopping.[39] IRI then combines all of these data into a single source, and thereby determines which households purchase what products/brands and how responsive they are to advertising and other purchase-causing variables.

Direct Advertising

Database marketing
involves collecting and electronically storing (in a database) information about present, past, and prospective customers.

In contrast to mass-media advertising, which is aimed at thousands or even millions of prospective customers, direct advertising typically is targeted to a single business or an individual consumer. The growth of direct advertising and its growing sophistication is due in large part to the advent of **database marketing**. Typical databases include purchase data and other types of relevant customer information, such as demographic details and geographic information. The information is used to profile customers and to develop effective and efficient marketing programs by communicating with individual customers and by establishing long-term communication relationships.[40]

Major advances in computer technology and database management have made it possible for companies to maintain huge databases containing millions of prospects/customers. *Niche marketing* can be fully realized by targeting promotional efforts to a company's best prospects (based on past product-category purchasing behavior), and who can be identified in terms of specific geographic, demographic, and psychographic characteristics. Growing numbers of marketers are making heavy investments in database marketing. For example, in an interesting use of its database, Saab mailed all past owners an invitation to a sneak preview of its totally redesigned Saab 900. Thousands of people attended this unique promotion in twenty-one cities throughout the United States. Saab also uses its database to maintain relations with its customers by publishing

a magazine called *Saab Soundings*.[41] Database marketing offers companies four distinct "abilities":[42]

1. *Addressability*—being able to identify every customer and reach each one on an individual basis. This could also be referred to as *targetability*.
2. *Measurability*—knowing whether customers purchased something; exactly what they purchased; and how, where, and when they purchased along with their purchase history.
3. *Flexibility*—having the opportunity to appeal to different customers in different ways at different times.
4. *Accountability*—having precise figures on the gross profitability of any marketing event, and qualitative data showing the type of customers who participated in each particular event.

All types of marketers use direct mail as a strategically important advertising medium. *Business Week* magazine claims, albeit with some hyperbole, that consumer-goods marketers "are turning from the TV box to the mailbox."[43] Some automobile manufacturers, for example, are budgeting as much as 10 percent of their advertising expenditures to direct mail.

At least four factors account for the widespread use of direct-mail advertising. First, the rising expense of television advertising, along with increased audience fragmentation, has led many advertisers to reduce investments in television advertising. Second, direct mail enables unparalleled targeting of messages to desired prospects—according to one expert, it is "a lot better to talk to 20,000 prospects than 2 million suspects."[44] Third, there is increased emphasis on measurable advertising results, and direct mail is the advertising medium that best lends itself to a clear identification of how many prospects have purchased the advertised product. Finally, surveys indicate that Americans like mail advertisements.

SALES PROMOTION

LEARNING OBJECTIVE 7

Sales promotions are the use of any incentive by a manufacturer to induce the trade (wholesalers and retailers), and/or consumers, to buy a brand and to encourage the sales force to aggressively sell it. Retailers also use promotions to encourage greater purchasing from their customers. The incentive is in addition to the basic benefits provided by the brand and temporarily changes its perceived price or value.[45] These features require further comment. First, by definition, sales promotions involve **incentives** that are additions to, not substitutes for, the basic benefits a purchaser typically acquires when buying a particular good or service. Second, the target of the incentive may be the trade, final consumers, the sales force, or all three parties. Finally, the incentive changes a brand's perceived price/value, but only temporarily. This is to say that a sales-promotion incentive for a particular brand applies to a single purchase or perhaps several purchases during a period, but not to every purchase a consumer would make over an extended period.

Incentives
are bonuses or rewards (sweepstakes, coupons, premiums, display allowances, etc.) for purchasing one brand rather than another.

The Shift from Advertising to Sales Promotion

Historically, the promotional emphasis in many consumer-goods firms was on creating promotional pull. Manufacturers advertised heavily, especially on network television, literally forcing retailers to handle their products by virtue of the fact that consumers demanded heavily advertised brands. However, over the past two decades, pull-oriented marketing has become less effective. Along with this reduced effectiveness has come an increase in the use of push-oriented sales promotion practices.[46]

The result of these developments is that advertising expenditures in mass media (television, radio, magazines, newspaper, and outdoor) have declined in most firms as a percentage of their total MarCom expenditures. On the other hand, expenditures on sales promotions, direct marketing, sponsorships, and point-of-purchase items have steadily increased. In fact, annual studies have shown that media advertising expenditures as a proportion of companies' total MarCom spending have declined steadily for over a decade. Whereas media advertising used to average over 40 percent of companies' MarCom budgets, now media advertising's portion of the total budget has fallen to about 25 percent.

Comparatively, consumer promotions (coupons, bonus packs, premiums, etc.) represent approximately 25 percent of the total promotional budget, and trade promotions constitute the remaining 50 percent.[47] These statistics make it clear that *the biggest shift in MarCom expenditures has been away from media advertising toward expenditures to support the trade.* The major form of trade promotions are deals, or discounts in the form of **trade allowances**, that encourage wholesalers and retailers to purchase larger quantities of promoted brands during the period when the manufacturer places them on promotion.

Increased investment in sales promotions, especially trade-oriented promotions, has gone hand-in-hand with the trend toward greater push-oriented marketing. The six factors listed below account for the shift in the allocation of promotion budgets away from advertising toward sales promotion and other forms of marketing communications. These are summarized in Table 12.2.

Trade allowances,
or trade deals, come in a variety of forms and are offered to retailers simply for purchasing the manufacturer's brand or for performing activities in support of the manufacturer's brand.

1. *Balance of Power Transfer.* Until recently, national manufacturers of consumer goods generally were more powerful and influential than the supermarkets, drug stores, and mass merchandisers that carried the manufacturers' brands. However, the balance of power began shifting when network television dipped in effectiveness as an advertising medium and, especially, with the advent of optical scanning equipment, which allowed retailers to attain as much "informational market power" as previously had been possessed only by manufacturers. The consequence for manufacturers is that for every promotional dollar used to support retailers' advertising or merchandising programs, one less dollar is available for the manufacturer's own advertising.

2. *Increased Brand Parity and Price Sensitivity.* In earlier years when truly new products were being offered to the marketplace, manufacturers could effectively advertise unique advantages over competitive offerings. As product categories have matured, however, most new offerings represent slight changes from existing products, resulting in more similarities between competitive brands than differences. With fewer distinct product differences, consumers have grown more reliant on price and price incentives (coupons, cents-off deals, refunds, etc.) as a way of differentiating alternative parity brands. Because real, concrete advantages are often difficult to obtain, firms have turned increasingly to sales promotion as a means of achieving at least temporary advantages over competitors.

3. *Reduced Brand Loyalty.* Consumers have become less loyal to brands than they once were. This is partly due to the fact that brands have grown increasingly similar, thereby making it easier for consumers to switch among brands. Also, marketers have effectively trained consumers to expect that at least one brand in a product category will always be on deal with a coupon, cents-off offer, or refund; hence, many consumers rarely purchase brands other than those on deal. The upshot of all of this dealing activity is that marketers' extensive use of sales promotions has reduced brand loyalty and increased switching behavior, thereby requiring ever-more dealing activity to feed consumers' insatiable desire for deals.

Table 12.2	Factors Giving Rise to the Growth of Sales Promotions

1. Balance of power transfer
2. Increased brand parity and price sensitivity
3. Reduced brand loyalty
4. Splintering of the mass market and reduced media effectiveness
5. Short-term orientation and corporate reward structures
6. Trade and consumer responsiveness

4. *Splintering of the Mass Market and Reduced Media Effectiveness.* Advertising efficiency is directly related to the degree of homogeneity in consumers' consumption needs and media habits. The more homogeneous are these needs and habits, the less costly it is for mass advertising to reach target audiences. However, as consumer lifestyles have become more diverse and advertising media have narrowed in their appeal, mass-media advertising is no longer as efficient as it once was. On top of this, advertising effectiveness has declined with simultaneous increases in ad clutter and escalating media costs. These combined forces have influenced many brand managers to devote proportionately larger budgets to sales promotions.

5. *Short-Term Orientation and Corporate Reward Structures.* The brand-management system and sales promotion are perfect partners. The reward structure in firms organized along brand-manager lines emphasizes short-term sales response rather than slow, long-term growth, and sales promotion is incomparable when it comes to generating quick sales response. In fact, for many brands of packaged goods, the majority of their sales are associated with some kind of promotional deal.[48]

6. *Trade and Consumer Responsiveness.* A final force that explains the shift toward sales promotion at the expense of advertising is that retailers/wholesalers (the trade) and consumers respond favorably to money-saving opportunities.

Sales Promotion: Roles and Objectives

Sales promotion is well suited for accomplishing the following 10 tasks,[49] which are summarized in Table 12.3.

1. *Facilitating the Introduction of New Products to the Trade.* Sales promotions to wholesalers and retailers are often necessary to encourage the trade to handle new products. In fact, many retailers refuse to carry new products unless they receive extra compensation in the form of trade allowances, display allowances, and other forms of allowances.

2. *Obtaining Trial Purchases from Consumers.* Marketers depend on free samples, coupons, and other sales promotions to encourage trial purchases of new products. Many consumers would never try new products without these promotional inducements.

3. *Stimulating Sales Force Enthusiasm for New, Improved, or Mature Brands.* Exciting sales promotions give salespeople extra ammunition to use when interacting with buyers; they revive enthusiasm and make the salesperson's job easier and more enjoyable.

4. *Invigorating Sales of a Mature Brand.* Sales promotion can stimulate sales of a mature brand that requires a shot in the arm.

Sales Promotion's Capabilities	Table 12.3

1. Facilitate the introduction of new products to the trade
2. Obtain trial purchases from consumers
3. Stimulate sales force enthusiasm
4. Invigorate sales of mature brand
5. Increase merchandise space
6. Neutralize competitive advertising and sales promotions
7. Hold current users by encouraging repeat purchasing
8. Increase product usage by loading consumers
9. Preempt competition by loading consumers
10. Reinforce advertising

5. *Increasing On- and Off-Shelf Merchandising Space.* Trade-oriented sales promotions enable a manufacturer to obtain extra shelf space for a temporary period. This space may be in the form of extra facing (i.e., rows of shelf space) or off-shelf space in, say, an end-aisle display.

6. *Neutralizing Competitive Advertising and Sales Promotion.* Sales promotions can be used to offset competitors' advertising and sales-promotion efforts. For example, one company's 50 cents-off coupon loses much of its appeal when a competitor simultaneously comes out with a $1 coupon.

7. *Holding Current Users by Encouraging Repeat Purchases.* Brand switching is a fact of life faced by all brand managers. The strategic use of certain forms of sales promotion can encourage at least short-run repetitive purchasing. Premium programs, refunds, and various other devices are used to encourage repeat purchasing.

8. *Increasing Brand Usage by Loading Consumers.* Consumers tend to use more of certain products (e.g., snack foods and soft drinks) when they have more of them available in their homes. Thus, sales-promotion efforts that load consumers with greater quantities than they normally would buy on a particular purchase occasion generate temporary increases in brand usage. Bonus packs and two-for-the-price-of-one deals are particularly effective loading devices.

9. *Preempting Competition by Loading Consumers.* When consumers are loaded with one company's brand, they are temporarily out of the marketplace for competitive brands. Hence, one brand's sales promotion serves to preempt sales of competitive brands.

10. *Reinforcing Advertising.* A final can-do capability of sales promotion is to reinforce advertising. An advertising campaign can be strengthened greatly by a well-coordinated sales promotion effort.

Sales promotions clearly are capable of performing important tasks. There are, however, distinct limitations that are beyond the capability of sales promotion. In particular, sales promotions cannot (1) compensate for a poorly trained sales force, (2) give the trade or consumers any compelling long-term reason to continue purchasing a brand, or (3) permanently stop an established brand's declining sales trend, or change the basic nonacceptance of an undesired brand.

Trade Promotions: Roles and Objectives

As earlier noted, manufacturers use some combination of push and pull strategies to accomplish both retail distribution and consumer purchasing. *Trade promotions*, which are directed at wholesalers, retailers, and other marketing intermediaries, represent the first step in any promotional effort. Consumer promotions are likely to fail unless trade-promotion efforts have succeeded in getting wholesalers to distribute the product, and retailers to stock adequate quantities. The special incentives offered by manufacturers to their distribution channel members are expected to be passed through to consumers in the form of price discounts offered by retailers and often stimulated by advertising support and special displays.[50] As we will see later, this does not always occur.

A manufacturer has various objectives for using trade-oriented sales promotions: (1) to introduce new or revised products, (2) to increase distribution of new packages or sizes, (3) to build retail inventories, (4) to maintain or increase the manufacturer's share of shelf space, (5) to obtain displays outside normal shelf locations, (6) to reduce excess inventories and increase turnover, (7) to achieve feature space in retailers' advertisements, (8) to counter competitive activity, and, ultimately, (9) to sell as much as possible to final consumers.[51]

Manufacturers employ a variety of trade-oriented promotional inducements, most of which are some form of trade allowance. These allowances/deals are needed to encourage retailers to stock the manufacturer's brand, discount the brand's price to consumers, feature it in advertising, or provide special display or other point-of-purchase support.[52] The most frequently used allowance is an **off-invoice allowance**. By using off-invoice allowances, manufacturers hope to increase retailers' purchasing of the manufacturer's brand and increase consumers' purchasing from retailers. This latter objective is based

Off-invoice allowance
are deals offered periodically to the trade that allow wholesalers and retailers to simply deduct a fixed amount, say 15 percent, from the full price at the time the order is placed.

on the expectation that retailers will in fact pass along to consumers the discounts they receive from manufacturers, which unfortunately does not always happen.

Off-invoice trade allowances create notable problems for the manufacturers that use them. One major problem is that off-invoice allowances often induce the trade to stockpile products in order to take advantage of the temporary price reduction. This merely shifts business from the future to the present. Two prevalent practices are **forward buying** and **diverting**, both of which represent efforts on the part of wholesalers and retailers to earn money from buying on deal rather than from selling merchandise at a profit.

Manufacturers' off-invoice allowances typically are available every 4 weeks of each business quarter (which translates to about 30 percent of the year), and a number of manufacturers sell upward of 80 to 90 percent of their volume at less than full price. When a manufacturer marks down a product's price by, say, 10 percent, wholesalers and retailers commonly stock up (i.e., forward buy) with a 10- to 12-week supply. Wholesalers and retailers are rationale businesspeople: they take advantage of deals!

A related buying practice, diverting, occurs when a manufacturer offers an off-invoice allowance in a particular geographical region rather than nationwide. What happens under this circumstance is that some retailers forward buy larger quantities than needed in just that region and ship out (transship) quantities to retailers in other geographical regions. The transshipping retailer earns a small profit on each item when engaging in this practice. It is estimated that the volume of merchandise involved in diverting amounts to at least $5 billion a year.[53] Interestingly, this practice of diverting in a marketing context is equivalent to what is known as *arbitrage* in finance circles, whereby financiers simultaneously buy and sell securities or foreign exchange in different markets to profit from unequal prices.

Consumer Sales Promotions: Roles and Objectives

A variety of sales promotion methods are used to encourage consumers to purchase one brand over another, to purchase a particular brand more often, and to purchase in larger quantities. *Consumer promotions* include such activities as sampling, couponing, refunding, rebating, and offering premiums, sweepstakes, and contests.

Consumers would not be responsive to sales promotions unless there was something in it for them—and, in fact, there is. All sales-promotion techniques provide consumers with incentives or inducements that encourage certain forms of behavior desired by brand marketers and/or retailers. Rewards are typically in the form of cash savings or free gifts. Sometimes rewards are immediate, while other times they are delayed. An *immediate reward* is one that delivers the savings or gift as soon as the consumer performs a marketer-specified behavior. For example, you receive cash savings at the time you redeem a coupon; pleasure is obtained immediately when you try, say, a free product while shopping in a grocery store. *Delayed rewards* are those that follow the behavior by a period of days, weeks, or even longer. For example, you may have to wait weeks before a free-in-the-mail premium object can be enjoyed. Generally speaking, consumers are more responsive to immediate rather than delayed rewards. Of course, this is in line with the natural human tendency to seek immediate rather than delayed gratification.

Manufacturers use sales promotions to accomplish three general categories of objectives: **trial impact, franchise holding/loading,** and **image reinforcement.** Figure 12.7 classifies a variety of sales promotion techniques by the specific objective each is primarily responsible for accomplishing, and by the type of reward, either immediate or delayed, provided consumers.[54] It is important to recognize that most forms of sales promotions perform more than a single objective. For example, refunds and rebates are classified as franchise holding/loading techniques but on some occasions they may also encourage trial purchasing. Note also that two techniques, coupons and premiums, have multiple entries. This is because these techniques achieve different objectives depending on the specific form of delivery vehicle. The choice of which sales promotion tool to use depends on the specific objectives that must be accomplished for a brand at a particular point in time, and an evaluation of the relative expense of using different tools. Coupons, for example, are widely used because types of coupons (e.g., shelf-delivered versus media-delivered) are capable of achieving different objectives, and the cost typically is not prohibitive.

Forward buying,
or bridge buying, is when retailers purchase enough product during a manufacturer's off-invoice allowance period to carry the retailers over until the manufacturer's next regularly scheduled deal.

Diverting
occurs when a manufacturer restricts an off-invoice allowance to a limited geographical area, resulting in some wholesalers and retailers buying abnormally large quantities at the deal price and then transshipping the excess quantities to other geographical areas.

Trial impact
refers to inducing nonusers to try a brand for the first time, or encouraging retrial by consumers who have not purchased the brand for an extended period.

Franchise holding/loading
includes manufacturers' efforts to hold on to their franchise of current users by rewarding them for continuing to purchase the promoted brand, or to load them so they have no need to switch to another brand.

Image reinforcement
involves the careful selection of the right premium object, or appropriate sweepstakes prize, to reinforce a brand's desired image.

Figure 12.7		Major Consumer-Oriented Forms of Sales Promotions	

Marketer's Objective

Consumer Reward	Trial Impact	Customer Holding/Loading	Image Reinforcement
Immediate	(1) • Sampling • Instant Coupons • Shelf-Delivered Coupons	(3) • Price-Offs • Bonus Packs • In-, On-, and Near-Pack Premiums	(5)
Delayed	(2) • Media- and Mail-Delivered Coupons • Free-in-the-Mail Premiums • Scanner-Delivered Coupons	(4) • In- and On-Pack Coupons • Refunds and Rebates • Phone Cards	(6) • Self-Liquidating Premiums • Contests and Sweepstakes

---

LEARNING OBJECTIVE 8

PUBLIC RELATIONS

Public relations, or PR, is the MarCom tool that is uniquely suited to fostering goodwill between a company and its various publics. When effectively integrated with advertising, personal selling, and sales promotion, public relations is capable of accomplishing objectives other than goodwill. It can also increase brand awareness, build favorable attitudes toward a company and its products, and encourage purchase behavior. PR is similar to advertising because both are forms of mass communication; the difference is that the publicity generated by PR receives free news space or broadcast time in comparison to the space and time purchased in the case of advertising. The public-relations department serves as the prime source of an organization's contact with the news media.

PR efforts are aimed at various publics, primarily the following: consumers, employees, suppliers, stockholders, governments, the general public, labor groups, and citizen action groups. Our concern, however, is only with the more narrow aspect of public relations involving an organization's interactions with customers. This marketing-oriented aspect of public relations is called *marketing PR*, or *MPR* for short. Marketing PR can be further delineated as involving either proactive or reactive public relations.[55]

Proactive MPR

Proactive marketing public relations (proactive MPR)
is offensively rather than defensively oriented, and opportunity-seeking rather than problem-solving. The major role of proactive MPR is in the area of product introductions or product revisions.

Proactive marketing public relations (proactive MPR) is another MarCom tool in addition to advertising and sales promotion that can give a brand additional exposure, newsworthiness, and credibility. This last factor, credibility, largely accounts for the effectiveness of proactive MPR. Whereas sales and advertising claims are sometimes suspect—because customers question salespeople's and advertisers' motives, knowing they have a personal stake in persuading us—product announcements by a newspaper editor or television broadcaster are notably more believable. Customers are less likely to question the motivation underlying an editorial-type endorsement.

Publicity is the major tool of proactive MPR. Like advertising and personal selling, the fundamental purposes of marketing-oriented publicity are to engender brand awareness, enhance attitudes toward a company and its brands, and possibly influence purchase behavior. Companies obtain publicity using various forms of news releases, press conferences, and other types of information dissemination. News releases concerning new products, modifications in old products, and other newsworthy topics are delivered to editors of newspapers and magazines, to managers of television and radio stations, and are disseminated en masse to Internet Web sites such as Yahoo! Finance. Press conferences announce major news events of interest to the public. Photographs, tapes, and films are useful for illustrating product improvements, new products, advanced produc-

tion techniques, and so forth. Of course, all forms of publicity are subject to the control and whims of the media. However, by disseminating a large volume of publicity materials and by preparing materials that fit the media's needs, a company increases its chances of obtaining beneficial publicity.

Reactive MPR

Reactive MPR is undertaken as a result of external pressures and challenges brought by competitive actions, changes in consumer attitudes, changes in government policy, or other external influences. Product defects and failures are the most dramatic factors underlying the need for reactive MPR. A number of negative publicity cases have received widespread media attention in recent years. For example, Audi of America experienced an irreversible loss in sales after news reports were disseminated claiming that the Audi 5000-S sometimes lunged out of control when shifted into drive or reverse gears. Food Lion, a regional supermarket chain, suffered grave losses and was forced to close some stores after news reports charged that Food Lion stores are unsanitary and that they sell meat, fish, and poultry products that are past their sell/use-by date. Cans of Pepsi Cola were rumored to be contaminated with hypodermic needles, but skillfully designed public relations quickly dispelled this hoax. Intel, the huge computer-chip manufacturer, was embarrassed by reports that its new Pentium chip failed to correctly perform some mathematical calculations. Although corrective technical alterations were made, Intel was slow in reacting to this negative publicity and suffered a temporary loss of credibility. Both Ford Motor Company and Bridgestone/Firestone, particularly the latter company, suffered considerable financial and reputational damage after numerous rollover accidents involving Ford Explorers equipped with Firestone tires.

Reactive MPR
is a form of defensively oriented public relations that deals with developments (such as product defects or flaws) having negative consequences for the organization. Reactive MPR attempts to repair a company's reputation, prevent market erosion, and regain lost sales.

SPONSORSHIP MARKETING

LEARNING OBJECTIVE 9

One of the fastest growing aspects of marketing and marketing communications is the practice of **corporate sponsorships**. Sponsorships range from supporting athletic events (golf and tennis tournaments, college football bowl games, etc.), to underwriting rock concerts, to throwing corporate weight behind worthy causes such as efforts to generate funds for cancer research.

Corporate sponsorships
involve investments in events or causes for the purpose of achieving various corporate objectives, such as increasing sales volume, enhancing a company's reputation or a brand's image, and increasing brand awareness.

At least four factors account for the growth in sponsorships.[56] First, by attaching their names to special events and causes, companies are able to avoid the clutter inherent in advertising media. Second, sponsorships help companies respond to consumers' changing media habits. For example, with the decline in network television viewing, sponsorships offer a potentially effective and cost-efficient way to reach customers. Third, sponsorships help companies gain the approval of various constituencies, including stockholders, employees, and society at large. Finally, the sponsorship of special events and causes enables marketers to target their communication and promotional efforts to specific geographic regions and/or to specific lifestyle groups. For example, the marketers of Fleischmann's margarine aligned that brand with health-conscious baby boomers by sponsoring a 22-city Beach Boys concert tour. Philip Morris reached 800,000 bowlers, many of whom smoke, by sponsoring the Merit brand bowling competition. Many companies in the apparel and casual footwear business sponsor alternative sports events to appeal to younger consumers who are difficult to reach via advertising media.

Event Marketing

Event-related marketing (ERM) is a form of brand promotion that ties a brand to a meaningful cultural, social, athletic, or other type of high-interest public activity.

http://www.phillipmorris.com

Thousands of companies invest in some form of **event-related marketing (ERM)** sponsorship. Event marketing is separate from advertising, sales promotion, point-of-purchase merchandising, or public relations, but it generally incorporates elements from all of these promotional tools. It is growing rapidly because these sponsorships provide companies with alternatives to the cluttered mass media, an ability to segment on a local or regional basis, and opportunities for reaching narrow lifestyle groups whose consumption behavior can be linked with the local event. Events are effective because they reach people when they are in a relaxed atmosphere and receptive to marketing messages.

As with every other MarCom decision, the starting point for effective event sponsorship is to clearly specify the objectives that an event is designed to accomplish. Event marketing has no value unless it accomplishes these objectives. For example, to create a fun and exciting image for Cool Mint Listerine mouthwash, Warner-Lambert literally pitched tents at ski resorts. Product samples and Cool Mint headbands were distributed from the tents. The event was further tied in to retail displays that offered lift-ticket discounts to consumers who appeared at ski resorts with a Cool Mint proof of purchase.

http://oral-care.com

Cause-Related Marketing

Cause-related marketing is a form of corporate philanthropy that links a company's contributions (usually monetary) to a predesignated worthy cause with the purchasing behavior of consumers.

Cause-related marketing is a relatively narrow aspect of overall sponsorship. It involves an amalgam of public relations, sales promotion, and corporate philanthropy; however, the distinctive feature of cause-related marketing is that a company's contribution to a designated cause is linked to customers engaging in revenue-producing exchanges with the firm.[57] The contribution is contingent on the customer performing a behavior (such as buying a product or redeeming a coupon) that benefits the firm.

The following examples illustrate how cause-related marketing operates. For each Heinz baby-food label mailed in by consumers, H. J. Heinz Company contributed 6 cents to a hospital near the consumer's home. Nabisco Brands donated $1 to the Juvenile Diabetes Foundation for each dollar donation certificate that was redeemed with a Ritz brand proof of purchase. Hershey Foods donated 25 cents to local hospitals for children for each redeemed Hershey coupon. Dutch Boy paint contributed 25 cents to Healthy Families America for each gallon of paint it sold during a designated period. Stride Rite made a donation to Save the Children in the amount of 3 to 4 percent of the retail price of each pair of specially designed footwear sold.

LEARNING OBJECTIVE **10**

POINT-OF-PURCHASE COMMUNICATIONS

Marketers use a variety of items at the point of purchase to draw attention to their brands and activate consumer purchases. These include various types of signs, mobiles, plaques, banners, shelf tapes, mechanical mannequins, lights, mirrors, plastic product reproductions, checkout units, full-line merchandisers, wall posters, motion displays, and other materials. Many of these materials are temporary items, with useful life spans of only weeks or months. Others are relatively permanent fixtures that can be used for years. Whereas temporary signs and displays are particularly effective for promoting impulse purchasing, permanent P-O-P units compartmentalize and departmentalize a store area to achieve high product visibility, facilitate customer self-service, prevent stock-outs, and help control inventory.

Brand managers recognize the value of point-of-purchase (P-O-P) advertising; indeed, Point of Purchase Advertising International (POPAI), the trade association for this form of advertising, estimates that in 2000 marketers in the United States spent $17 billion on P-O-P advertising.[58] This level of expenditure can be justified by the fact that point-of-purchase materials provide a useful service for all participants in the marketing process.

- Point-of-purchase materials and displays provide value to *consumers* by delivering useful information, identifying sale items, and simplifying the shopping process by setting products apart from similar items.
- P-O-P serves *retailers* by attracting the consumers' attention, increasing their interest in shopping, and extending the amount of time spent in the store—all of which mean increased sales. P-O-P helps retailers utilize available space to the best advantage by displaying several manufacturers' products in the same unit (e.g., many varieties of vitamins and other medicinal items all in one well-organized unit). It enables retailers to better organize shelf space and to improve inventory control, volume, stock turnover, and profitability.
- For *manufacturers*, who are the marketers of branded products, P-O-P keeps the company's name and the brand name before the consumer and both reactivates and reinforces brand information the consumer has previously received through advertising. P-O-P calls attention to special offers such as sales promotions and stimulates impulse purchasing. P-O-P serves to complement the job already performed by advertising before the consumer enters a store.[59] Indeed, it represents the capstone for an integrated MarCom program.

Because many product- and brand-choice decisions are made while the consumer is in the store, rather than before he or she arrives at the store, point-of-purchase materials play a role, perhaps the major role, in influencing unplanned purchasing. Indeed, the Point-of-Purchase Advertising Institute performed a major study based on a national sample of supermarkets and mass merchandise outlets (e.g., Wal-Mart) and determined that 70 to 74 percent of purchase decisions for items carried in these types of retail outlets are made by shoppers while in the store.[60]

CHAPTER SUMMARY

- A brand and its attributes/benefits must be communicated to customers through marketing communications. In today's highly competitive and dynamic marketing world, effective communications are critical to a company's success. Marketing managers have considerable discretion in determining which MarCom elements to use and how much relative emphasis each should receive. Various factors such as the target market, product life-cycle stage, objectives, competitive activity, budget, and nature of the product all affect the appropriate mix of MarCom elements.

- Whereas historically many marketing communication decisions were treated as rather disparate and managed by independent departments that failed to carefully coordinate their activities, there has been a trend toward integrated marketing communications, or IMC. Some key elements of IMC are that all marketing communication decisions start with the customer, which reflects the adoption of an outside-in mentality versus an inside-out position that historically has dominated this field. Another fundamental feature is that all communication elements must achieve synergy, or speak with a single voice. The belief that successful marketing communications must build a relationship between the brand and the customer is another key IMC feature.

- Advertising is a critical component of marketing communications, especially in the United States, where annual expenditures in 2000 alone were approximately $250 billion. The process of developing advertising strategy consists of the following major activities: setting objectives, formulating a budget, establishing a positioning statement, developing a message strategy, designing a media strategy, and assessing advertising effectiveness.

- Sales promotion—the use of any incentive by a manufacturer to induce the trade (wholesalers and retailers) and/or final consumers to buy a brand and to encourage the sales force to aggressively sell it—is another key MarCom element. Consumer promotions (such as coupons, cents-off deals, premiums, and sweepstakes) and trade-oriented promotions (primarily off-invoice allowances to wholesalers and retailers) constitute, on average, approximately three-fourths of businesses' MarCom budgets. Sales promotions are particularly useful for purposes of introducing new or revised products to the trade, obtaining trial purchases from consumers, and enhancing repeat purchasing. However, sales promotions cannot compensate for inadequate personal selling or advertising, give the trade or consumers any long-term reason for buying a brand, or permanently stop an established brand's declining sales trend.

- Public relations, or PR, is that aspect of promotion management uniquely suited to fostering goodwill between a company and its various publics. Public relations involves interactions with multiple publics (government, stockholders, etc.), but emphasis in this chapter is limited to the more narrow aspect of public relations involving an organization's interactions with customers. This marketing-oriented aspect of public relations is called marketing PR, or MPR for short.

- Marketing PR can be further delineated as involving either proactive or reactive public relations. Proactive MPR is another tool in addition to advertising and sales promotion for enhancing a brand's equity. Its major role is for disseminating information about brand introductions or revisions. Reactive MPR is undertaken as a result of external pressures and challenges brought by competitive actions, changes in consumer attitudes, changes in government policy, or other external influences. Reactive MPR typically deals with changes that have negative consequences for the organization, such as instances of product defects or failures.

- One of the fastest growing aspects of marketing and marketing communications is the practice of corporate sponsorships. Sponsorships take two forms: event sponsorships (such as athletic and entertainment events) and cause-oriented sponsorships. Event marketing is growing rapidly because it provides companies alternatives to the cluttered mass media, an ability to segment on a local or regional basis, and opportunities for reaching narrow lifestyle groups whose consumption behavior can be linked with the local event. Cause-related marketing, a form of corporate philanthropy with benefits accruing to the sponsoring company, is based on the idea that a company will contribute to a cause every time the customer undertakes some action. In addition to helping worthy causes, corporations satisfy their own tactical and strategic objectives when undertaking cause-related efforts. By supporting a deserving cause, a company can enhance its corporate or brand image, generate incremental sales, increase brand awareness, broaden its customer base, and reach new market segments.

- Communications at the point of purchase is another major growth area in marketing. This is due to the fact that point-of-purchase materials provide a useful service for all participants in the marketing process. P-O-P communications also serve as the capstone for an integrated MarCom program.

KEY TERMS

Advertising is nonpersonal communication that is paid for by an identified sponsor, and involves either mass communication via newspapers, magazines, radio, television, and other media (e.g., billboards, bus stop signage) or direct-to-consumer communication via direct mail.

Cause-related marketing is a form of corporate philanthropy that links a company's contributions (usually monetary) to a predesignated worthy cause with the purchasing behavior of consumers.

Corporate sponsorships involve investments in events or causes for the purpose of achieving various corporate objectives, such as increasing sales volume, enhancing a company's reputation or a brand's image, and increasing brand awareness.

Cost per thousand (CPM) is calculated by dividing the cost of an ad placed in a particular ad vehicle (e.g., certain magazine) by the number of people (expressed in thousands) who are exposed to that vehicle.

Database marketing involves collecting and electronically storing (in a database) information about present, past, and prospective customers.

Diverting occurs when a manufacturer restricts an off-invoice allowance to a limited geographical area, resulting in some wholesalers and retailers buying abnormally large quantities at the deal price and then transshipping the excess quantities to other geographical areas.

Event-related marketing (ERM) is a form of brand promotion that ties a brand to a meaningful cultural, social, athletic, or other type of high-interest public activity.

Forward buying, or bridge buying, is when retailers purchase enough product during a manufacturer's off-invoice allowance period to carry the retailers over until the manufacturer's next regularly scheduled deal.

Franchise holding/loading includes manufacturers' efforts to hold on to their franchise of current users by rewarding them for continuing to purchase the promoted brand, or to load them so they have no need to switch to another brand.

Gross rating points (GRPs) are the accumulation of rating points including all vehicles in a media purchase over the span of a particular campaign.

Image reinforcement involves the careful selection of the right premium object, or appropriate sweepstakes prize, to reinforce a brand's desired image.

Incentives are bonuses or rewards (sweepstakes, coupons, premiums, display allowances, etc.) for purchasing one brand rather than another.

Integrated marketing communications (IMC) is a system of management and integration of marketing communication elements—advertising, publicity, sales promotion, sponsorship marketing, and point-of-purchase communications—with the result that all elements adhere to the same message.

Media strategy consists of four sets of interrelated activities: (1) selecting the target audience, (2) specifying media objectives, (3) selecting media categories and vehicles, and (4) buying media.

Off-invoice allowance are deals offered periodically to the trade that allow wholesalers and retailers to simply deduct a fixed amount, say 15 percent, from the full price at the time the order is placed.

Personal selling is person-to-person communication in which a seller informs and educates prospective customers and attempts to influence their purchase choices.

Point-of-purchase communications include all signage—displays, posters, signs, shelf cards, and a variety of other visual materials—that are designed to influence buying decisions at the point of sale.

Proactive marketing public relations (proactive MPR) is offensively rather than defensively oriented, and opportunity-seeking rather than problem-solving. The major role of proactive MPR is in the area of product introductions or product revisions.

Publicity, like advertising, is nonpersonal communication to a mass audience, but unlike advertising, publicity is not directly paid for by the company that enjoys the publicity.

Pull strategy involves a relatively heavy emphasis on consumer-oriented advertising to encourage consumer demand for a new brand and thereby obtain retail distribution. The brand is "pulled" through the channel system in the sense that there is a backward tug from the consumer to the retailer.

Push strategy involves aggressive trade allowances and personal selling efforts to obtain distribution for a new brand through wholesalers and retailers. The brand is "pushed" through the channel system in the sense that there is a forward thrust from the manufacturer to the trade.

Reactive MPR is a form of defensively oriented public relations that deals with developments (such as product defects or flaws) having negative consequences for the organization. Reactive MPR attempts to repair a company's reputation, prevent market erosion, and regain lost sales.

Sales promotion consists of all marketing activities that attempt to stimulate quick buyer action, or, in other words, attempt to promote immediate sales of a product (thereby yielding the name *sales promotion*).

Single-source systems are a measurement of the effectiveness of advertising (whether it leads to increased sales activity). They are unique in that all the relevant data is collected by a single source, processed, and then made available in a readily usable format to retailers and manufacturers.

Sponsorship marketing is the practice of promoting the interests of a company and its brands by associating the company with a specific event (e.g., a golf tournament) or a charitable cause (e.g., the Leukemia Society).

Trade allowances, or trade deals, come in a variety of forms and are offered to retailers simply for purchasing the manufacturer's brand or for performing activities in support of the manufacturer's brand.

Trial impact refers to inducing nonusers to try a brand for the first time, or encouraging retrial by consumers who have not purchased the brand for an extended period.

QUESTIONS FOR DISCUSSION

1. One key feature of integrated marketing communications (IMC) is that the IMC process should start with the customer. Compare this perspective with "the marketing concept," which you studied in Chapter 1.

2. Assume that you are head of marketing communications for a sorority, fraternity, or other campus organization. Your responsibility is to recruit 25 percent more members than you presently have. Explain how "starting with the customer" would apply to your choice of ways to recruit new members.

3. List your mental associations for each of the following "brands" and prepare to share them in class: (1) Britney Spears, (2) Wrangler jeans, (3) Osama bin Laden, (4) Silk soymilk, (5) Harvard University, and (6) the *Wall Street Journal*.

4. Compare and contrast the brand-equity model (Figure 12.1) with the hierarchy-of-effects framework (Figure 12.2). What specifically are the similarities and differences between these models?

5. Explain the meaning of "push" and "pull" efforts in marketing communications. Comment on the following statement: "A brand manager chooses between either pushing or pulling a brand through a distribution channel."

6. Locate two magazine advertisements that you consider good illustrations of creative advertising, and explain precisely why you regard each to be especially creative.

7. **a.** Assume that a one-page, four-color advertisement in *Ebony* magazine cost $55,000 in 2001. A syndicated service that measures magazine readership estimated that *Ebony's* total readership that year was approximately 12 million adults. What was *Ebony's* CPM in 2001?

   b. Advertisements for a particular brand are run on each of four television programs on a Thursday evening. Designating these programs as P1, P2, P3, P4, let us assume that the ratings for each program are: P1 = 13.5, P2 = 15.3, P3 = 17.4, and P4 = 19.8. How many gross rating points (GRPs) would this advertiser accumulate on this one evening of advertising?

8. Several examples of negative publicity were listed in the Reactive MPR section of the chapter. Are you familiar with any other examples of companies that have suffered such negative press? Discuss the effectiveness of the companies' reactive MPR. Provide your views on how well Firestone and Ford Motors handled the Ford Explorer rollover problem.

9. Go to a local supermarket and pay careful attention to the point-of-purchase materials in use. Provide examples of three POP practices in this store that you consider particularly effective. In your opinion, why are these practices effective?

10. Hundreds of millions of coupons are distributed annually in the United States. Why do you think that brand managers use coupons so frequently? Because coupons represent a form of price reduction, wouldn't it make more sense for brand managers to directly reduce prices rather than requiring consumers to redeem coupons? Do you think consumers are most likely to redeem coupons for the brands they regularly purchase or to switch to brands that they purchase infrequently?

ENDNOTES

[1] Sources: Sonia Reyes, "White Wave's $18M Smooth as Silk Push," *Brandweek*, 3 September 2001, 3; http://www.arn.com/OurStory/PressReleases/whitewave.html; http://www.hoovers.com; http://www.bcbr.com/feb2500/soy2.htm; http://www.whitewave.com/asp, accessed 15 September 2001.

[2] Don E. Schultz, Stanley I. Tannenbaum, and Robert F. Lauterborn, *Integrated Marketing Communications* (Lincolnwood, IL: NTC Publishing Group, 1993), 46.

[3] Schultz, Tannenbaum, and Lauterborn, *Integrated Marketing Communications*.

[4] Joep P. Cornelissen and Andrew R. Lock, "Theoretical Concept or Management Fashion? Examining the Significance of IMC," *Journal of Advertising Research* 40 (September/October 2000): 7–15. For counter positions, see Don E. Schultz and Philip J. Kitchen, "A Response to 'Theoretical Concept or Management Fashion'," *Journal of Advertising Research* 40 (September/October 2000): 17–21; Stephen J. Gould, "The State of IMC Research and Applications," *Journal of Advertising Research* 40 (September/October 2000): 22–23.

[5] Don E. Schultz and Philip J. Kitchen, "Integrated Marketing Communications in U.S. Advertising Agencies: An Exploratory Study," *Journal of Advertising Research* 37 (September/October 1997): 7–18; Philip J. Kitchen and Don E. Schultz, "A Multi-Country Comparison of the Drive for IMC," *Journal of Advertising Research* 39 (January/February 1999): 21–38.

[6] Don E. Schultz, "Integration Is Critical for Success in 21st Century," *Marketing News*, 15 September 1997, 26.

[7] Stephen J. Gould, Andreas F. Grein, and Dawn B. Lernan, "The Role of Agency-Client Integration in Integrated Marketing Communications: A Complementary Agency Theory-Interorganizational Perspective," *Journal of Current Issues and Research in Advertising* 21 (Spring 1999): 1–12.

[8] David Sable, "We're Surrounded," *Agency* (Spring 2000): 50–51.

[9] The practitioner is Shelly Lazarus, whose career at Ogilvy & Mather advertising agency has extended over a quarter century. Lazarus was quoted by Laurie Freeman, "Internet Fundamentally Changes Definition," *Marketing News*, 6 December 1999, 15.

[10] Judann Pollack, "Nabisco's Marketing VP Expects 'Great Things,'" *Advertising Age*, 2 December 1996, 40.

[11] Stephanie Thompson, "Busy Lifestyles Force Change," *Advertising Age*, 9 October 2000, s8.

[12] See Schultz, Tannenbaum, and Lauterborn, *Integrated Marketing Communications*, 52–53.

[13] For an insightful discussion of different forms of consumer-brand relationships, see Susan Fournier, "Consumers and Their Brands: Developing Relationship Theory in Consumer Research," *Journal of Consumer Research* 24 (March 1998): 343–373.

[14] Glen J. Nowak and Joseph Phelps, "Conceptualizing the Integrated Marketing Communications' Phenomenon: An Examination of Its Impact on Advertising Practices and Its Implications for Advertising Research," *Journal of Current Issues and Research in Advertising* 16 (Spring 1994): 49–66.

[15] Don E. Schultz, "Trying to Determine ROI for IMC," *Marketing News*, 3 January 1994, 18; Don E. Schultz, "Spreadsheet Approach to Measuring ROI for IMC," *Marketing News*, 28 February 1994, 12.

[16] The following discussion borrows liberally from Kevin Lane Keller, *Strategic Brand Management* (Upper Saddle River, NJ: Prentice Hall, 1998), chap. 2; and Kevin Lane Keller, "Conceptualizing, Measuring, and Managing Customer-Based Brand Equity," *Journal of Marketing* 57 (January 1993): 1–22.

[17] This figure is from Keller, "Conceptualizing, Measuring, and Managing Customer-Based Brand Equity," 7.

[18] Terry Lefton, "Adidas Goes to Image Pitch with '98 $$ Boost," *Brandweek*, 26 January 1998, 37.

[19] Matthew Martinez, "Reed Study Sees Where Ad Dollars Go," *Advertising Age's Business Marketing*, October 1997, 46.

[20] "Coke's Market Share Rises to 43.9% as PepsiCo Slips," *Wall Street Journal Interactive Edition*, http://online.wsj.com, accessed 13 February 1998.

[21] William Boulding, Eunkyu Lee, and Richard Staelin, "Mastering the Mix: Do Advertising, Promotion, and Sales Force Activities Lead to Differentiation?" *Journal of Marketing Research* 31 (May 1994): 159–172.

[22] Bill McDowell, "Starbucks Is Ground Zero in Today's Coffee Culture," *Advertising Age,* 9 December 1996, 1, 49.

[23] Lisa Bertagnoli, "Duck Campaign Is Firm's Extra Insurance," *Marketing News,* 27 August 2001, 5–6.

[24] Ibid., 6.

[25] Kevin J. Clancy and Peter C. Krieg, *Counter-Intuitive Marketing: Achieve Great Results Using Uncommon Sense* (New York: The Free Press, 2000), 110.

[26] Ibid., 111.

[27] Nigel F. Piercy, "The Marketing Budgeting Process: Marketing Management Implications," *Journal of Marketing* 51 (October 1987): 45–59.

[28] John Sinisi, "Love: EDLP Equals Ad Investment," *Brandweek,* 16 November 1992.

[29] Suzanne Vranica, "Industry Forecaster Cuts Projections for U.S. Ad-Spending Growth to 2.5%," *Wall Street Journal Interactive Edition,* http://online.wsj.com/articles/SB992539885127595971.htm, accessed 15 June 2001.

[30] "100 Leaders by U.S. Advertising Spending," *Advertising Age,* 25 September 2000, s2.

[31] Ibid.

[32] Charles H. Patti and Charles F. Frazer, *Advertising: A Decision-Making Approach* (Hinsdale, IL: The Dryden Press, 1988), 236.

[33] Fred S. Zufryden, "How Much Should Be Spent for Advertising a Brand?" *Journal of Advertising Research* (April/May 1989): 24–34.

[34] Gary L. Lilien, Alvin J. Silk, Jean-Marie Choffray, and Murlidhar Rao, "Industrial Advertising Effects and Budgeting Practices," *Journal of Marketing* 40 (January 1976): 21; and Kent M. Lancaster and Judith A. Stern, "Computer-Based Advertising Budgeting Practices of Leading U.S. Consumer Advertisers," *Journal of Advertising* 12, no. 4 (1983): 6.

[35] Adapted from A. Jerome Jewler, *Creative Strategy in Advertising* (Belmont, CA: Wadsworth Publishing, 1985), 7–8; and Don E. Schultz and Stanley I. Tannenbaum, *Essentials of Advertising Strategy* (Lincolnwood, IL: NTC Business Books, 1988), 9–10.

[36] Stan Freberg, "Irtnog Revisited," *Advertising Age,* 1 August 1988, 32.

[37] Dana Blankenhorn, "Bigger, Richer Ads Go Online," *Advertising Age,* 18 June 2001, T10.

[38] Joe Schwartz, "Back to the Source," *American Demographics* (January 1989): 22–26.

[39] "What the Scanner Knows about You," *Fortune,* 3 December 1990, 51–52.

[40] Description adapted from Don E. Schultz, "The Direct/Database Marketing Challenge to Fixed-Location Retailers," in *The Future of U.S. Retailing: An Agenda for the 21st Century,* ed. Robert A. Peterson (New York: Quorum Books, 1992), 165–184.

[41] "Car Maker Uses Direct to Drive Loyalty," *Promo* (January 1994): 21.

[42] Terry G. Vavra, *Aftermarketing* (Homewood, IL: Business One Irwin, 1992), 32.

[43] "What Happened to Advertising," *Business Week,* 23 September 1991, 69.

[44] Don Schultz as quoted in Gary Levin, "Going Direct Route," *Advertising Age,* 18 November 1991, 37.

[45] Terence A. Shimp, *Advertising, Promotion, and Supplemental Aspects of Integrated Marketing Communications,* 5th ed. (Fort Worth, TX: The Dryden Press, 2000).

[46] Alvin A. Achenbaum and F. Kent Mitchel, "Pulling Away from Push Marketing," *Harvard Business Review* 65 (May-June 1987): 38–40; and Robert J. Kopp and Stephen A. Greyser, "Packaged Goods Marketing—'Pull' Companies Look to Improved 'Push'," *Journal of Consumer Marketing* 4 (Spring 1987): 13–22.

[47] *Cox Direct 20th Annual Survey of Promotional Practices* (Largo, FL: Cox Direct, 1998), 40.

[48] Robert C. Blattberg and Scott A. Neslin, "Sales Promotion: The Long and the Short of It," *Marketing Letters* 1, no. 1 (1989): 81–97.

[49] This discussion is guided by Charles Fredericks, Jr., "What Ogilvy & Mather Has Learned about Sales Promotion," *The Tools of Promotion* (New York: Association of National Advertisers, 1975); and Don E. Schultz and William A. Robinson, *Sales Promotion Management* (Lincolnwood, IL: NTC Business Books, 1986), chap. 3.

[50] Robert C. Blattberg and Alan Levin, "Modeling the Effectiveness and Profitability of Trade Promotions," *Marketing Science* 6 (Spring 1987): 125.

[51] See Chakravarthi Narasimhan, "Managerial Perspectives on Trade and Consumer Promotions," *Marketing Letters* 1, no. 3 (1989): 239–251.

[52] Rajiv Lal, "Manufacturer Trade Deals and Retail Price Promotions," *Journal of Marketing Research* 27 (November 1990): 428–444; and Ronald C. Curhan and Robert J. Kopp, "Obtaining Retailer Support for Trade Deals: Key Success Factors," *Journal of Advertising Research* 27 (December 1987/January 1988): 51–60.

[53] Howard Schlossberg, "Exposed: Retailing's Dirty Little Secret," *Promo* (April 1994): 50–55, and Patricia Sellers, "The Dumbest Marketing Ploy," *Fortune,* 5 October 1992, 88–94.

[54] For further discussion, see Shimp, *Advertisisng, Promotion, and Supplemental Aspects of Integrated Marketing Communications,* chap. 18.

[55] Jordan Goldman, *Public Relations in the Marketing Mix* (Lincolnwood, IL: NTC Business Books, 1984).

[56] Meryl Paula Gardner and Phillip Joel Shuman, "Sponsorship: An Important Component of the Promotions Mix," *Journal of Advertising* 16, no. 1 (1987): 11–17.

[57] P. Rajan Varadarajan and Anil Menon, "Cause-Related Marketing: A Coalignment of Marketing Strategy and Corporate Philanthropy," *Journal of Marketing* 52 (July 1988): 58–74.

[58] Cara Beardi, "POP Ups Sales Results," *Advertising Age,* 23 July 2001, 27.

[59] Kevin Lane Keller, "Cue Compatibility and Framing in Advertising," *Journal of Marketing Research* 28 (February 1991): 42–57.

[60] *Measuring the In-Store Decision Making of Supermarket and Mass Merchandise Store Shoppers* (Englewood, NJ: Point-of-Purchase Advertising Institute, 1995). Please note that POPAI recently changed its name from the Point-of-Purchase Advertising Institute to Point-of-Purchase Advertising International.

[61] Adapted from Jim Carlton, "Norway's Tomra Redefines Recycling with Bright, Clean, Accessible Kiosks," *Wall Street Journal Interactive Edition,* http://online.wsj.com/, accessed 6 March 2001.

CHAPTER CASE

GETTING AMERICAN CONSUMERS TO ACCEPT AND USE RECYLING KIOSKS[61]

Tomra Systems is a Norwegian company that specializes in recycling. After conducting an intensive analysis of American recycling practices, Tomra launched a chain of 200 recycling kiosks in a test market in southern California. Tomra has ambitious plans to expand its "rePlanet" kiosks across the United States. The rePlanet kiosks have several features that should appeal to Americans: They are clean, conveniently located in supermarket parking lots, and brightly lit to provide users with a sense of safety. Plus, the recycler gets paid for depositing used recyclable cans and bottles. Attendants are available during daytime hours and are trained to be friendly, accommodating, and efficient. But even when daytime attendants are not available, a "reverse" vending machine accepts containers and issues a machine-printed receipt the recycler can later redeem for cash.

Tomra has its sights on a huge recycling market in the United States. Fewer than half of all Americans have access to curbside recycling services. The consequence of this is that bottles and cans end up in landfills, which creates a huge environmental problem both in occupying landfill space and requiring energy expenditures to produce replacement containers. Tomra plans on converting millions of people into enthusiastic recyclers, people who now deposit cans and bottles in their curbside trash. This can be accomplished, according to Tomra's business plan, by rewarding consumers with anywhere from 2-to-10 cents per recycled container and by providing convenient, efficient, and safe recycling services.

What will it take for Tomra to succeed? The basic business model requires annual revenue from each kiosk of approximately $100,000. The rePlanet kiosks cost the company about $50,000 each to install and another $25,000 annually for payroll and pickup expenses. Tomra's plan is to process about 150,000 containers per month at each kiosk. This volume is essential for achieving reasonable profitable goals. In addition to its California kiosks, Tomra has also tested the viability of the concept in metropolitan areas such as Atlanta, Orlando, and Tampa.

An executive of Tomra's North American operation claims that the company hopes to market recycling as an "experience" rather than an unpleasant chore. "We want to be the Starbucks of the recycling business." Though perhaps a bit idealistic, this nonetheless represents a worthwhile goal both in terms of environmental benefits and profit opportunities for the company. The challenge, however, is one of convincing the American masses to change their recycling attitudes and behavior. Will Tomra's attractive and convenient kiosks provide people with sufficient reason to slightly complicate their lives in return for environmental enrichment and a relatively small economic incentive? Indeed, will the rePlanet kiosks become the Starbucks of recycling?

Discussion Questions

1. Table 12.1 and the surrounding text identified five key features of an integrated marketing communications program. Assume that rePlanet kiosks have just recently opened in your home state or province. Also assume that you are in charge of marketing communications for Tomra's marketing efforts in your home state/province. Apply the five key IMC features in proposing an integrated marketing communications program that would help produce rapid success for Tomra's rePlanet kiosks.

2. A good brand name generally must satisfy several criteria, including (1) distinguishing the brand from competitive offerings, (2) describing the brand and its attributes/benefits, (3) providing compatibility with the brand's desired image, and (4) achieving memorability and being easy to pronounce. With these considerations in mind, evaluate the rePlanet name for Tomra's recycling kiosks.

3. Develop a precise positioning statement in advertising and other forms of marketing communications for rePlanet kiosks.

4. Recommend a specific promotion to generate trial usage of the rePlanet kiosks. Similarly, recommend a promotion that would serve to influence repeat usage of kiosks.

5. Identify an event you would sponsor as a means to enhance the brand equity of the rePlanet kiosks. Justify the choice of this particular event.

CHAPTER thirteen

Judy A. Siguaw,
Cornell University

Dr. Siguaw earned her master's and doctorate degrees from Louisiana Tech University and her bachelor's degree from Lamar University. She has been awarded the Chancellor's Excellence in Teaching Award from the University of North Carolina at Wilmington; research grants from the Marketing Science Institute, American Express, and the American Hotel Foundation; and research awards from the Chartered Institute of Marketing, Cornell University, and the Academy of Marketing Science. She serves as the faculty advisor for the Cornell student chapter of the Hotel Sales and Marketing Association International and also as a trustee of the Hotel Sales and Marketing Association International Foundation Board.

Dr. Siguaw's research interests include sales/sales management, channels of distribution, market orientation, and innovation. She has published in *Journal of Marketing, Journal of Marketing Research, Journal of the Academy of Marketing Science, Journal of Business Research, Journal of Marketing Education, Industrial Marketing Management*, and others. She is a coauthor of *American Lodging Excellence: The Key to Best Practices in the Lodging Industry* and *Introducing LISREL*.

Prior to entering academia, Dr. Siguaw spent 10 years in the corporate environment, including a sales position with General Foods Corporation, now a division of Philip Morris known as Kraft Foods. Today, Dr. Siguaw provides executive education and consulting in the area of sales.

Personal Selling and Sales Management

Commercial real estate sales is a male-dominated, highly competitive industry. When Catherine Thompson and Kathleen Doyle started their own Boston-based commercial real estate firm in 1990, competitors and prospective customers alike did not give them much of a chance of staying in business. Time has proven the naysayers wrong, however. The firm, now known as Thompson Doyle Hennessey & Everest (TDH&E), currently employs 24 people and has proven to be very successful—in large part by employing key sales management tactics.

Commercial real estate firms face some unique challenges. The overall goal of the sales force is to assist owners in finding tenants for their empty buildings, and help companies find the best locations for their businesses. While the process sounds simple enough, a commercial real estate broker averages 75 calls in order to obtain one appointment. Eight or nine contacts are generally needed to close the sale, and the overall sales cycle requires 14 to 24 months. In addition, real estate, as the second or third largest line item in any company's budget, represents a significant investment. Consequently, chief executive officers and chief financial officers are the primary customer contacts and key decision makers that the sales force must reach—not an easy task. Overcoming these difficulties, however, has it rewards; on average, a successful close results in $400,000 to $500,000 in revenues for the real estate firm.

Thompson and Doyle originally developed and honed their sales skills while employed within other industries that underscored solid sales training. However, both women recognized that real estate firms in general did not focus on sales training. New hires were given little guidance—just routinely shown to a desk and told to get to work. Thompson and Doyle wanted their real estate firm to be different.

First, to ensure their firm's viability in a very competitive market, Thompson and Doyle hire only employees who would best fit with the firm's culture and work ethic. To be considered in the hiring process, candidates must have a college degree and possess

(Continued)

LEARNING OBJECTIVES

After you have completed this chapter, you should be able to:

1. Identify and understand the factors that make sales and marketing such critical components of promotion in the 21st century.
2. Describe the selling environments and types of salespeople.
3. Understand and explain the sales process.
4. Comprehend the diverse tasks and functions performed by the sales manager.
5. Recognize the legal and ethical issues confronting the salesperson and the sales organization.

457

some form of sales experience, although the experience does not have to be in the area of real estate. Generally, four to five job candidates are interviewed and then given a personality profile test for each position available. Ms. Doyle feels the personality test, as a quantitative measure, adds substantially to the more qualitative interview process in guiding the firm in its hiring process.

Because of the long sales cycle and the time needed to progress along the experience curve, new hires at TDH&E spend the first 18 months shadowing experienced brokers. In this role the recruits handle some administrative tasks, such as preparing sales presentations or conducting client tours, while learning valuable knowledge and skills. During this early training period, the employees receive a straight salary, but after the training period, these brokers can readily earn over $100,000 in commissions in their first year.

Not only are pains taken to hire and train the right candidates, but Thompson and Doyle also recognize the importance of continuous sales training in ensuring a successful business venture. One of the first things Thompson and Doyle did was to establish mandatory, weekly sales training, with an emphasis on a consultative selling approach, for all its employees. One hour of every week is dedicated to training on presentation or technical skills. The training is heavily focused on role-playing and the trainer and other participants critique each role-play. For the most part, Ms. Doyle administers the in-house training but outside trainers are also utilized.

In addition to weekly training sessions, weekly staff meetings are also conducted. During this meeting the previous week's successes are celebrated, future goals are discussed, scheduling is set, and activity reports are submitted. The activity reports identify how many cold calls were made, how many decision makers were reached, how many appointments were set, and because of the TDH&E training emphasis, how many educational events were attended by each broker. Finally, to keep its hard-working sales force and support staff motivated, the company sponsors fun activities. As a group, the TDH&E employees have participated in sky-diving, skiing, and kayaking.

The adept, progressive style of sales management employed by TDH&E has yielded an educational, motivating work environment. In turn, a customer-oriented competitive advantage has been created which now makes the company one of the preferred commercial real estate firms in the greater Boston area. Thompson and Doyle have definitely beat the odds!

Sources: Thompson Doyle Hennessey & Everest Web site, http://www.gvaboston.com; interview with Kathleen Doyle, 9 May 2001.

Everyone sells. If you have ever interviewed for a job, you were "selling" yourself by trying to persuade the interviewer that you would be the best person for the job. If you have ever tried to persuade a friend to do some activity that you wanted to do, you were "selling" your idea. When you were younger, you were "selling" every time you tried to persuade Mom or Dad to buy you something you wanted, and you were probably quite persistent in order to obtain what you desired. As an adult, you will find that you must "sell" regardless of what your job title is—whether it is selling your ideas to your boss, convincing your supervisor that you deserve a raise or promotion, or persuading customers to purchase your products. Not only do salespeople sell, so do accountants, engineers, financial analysts, insurance agents, stockbrokers, computer programmers, scientists, and nearly all other professions.

In the everyday selling situations mentioned previously, you have probably been successful in achieving your goals sometimes, but at other times have not been as successful. How can you improve your success rate? By learning to excel in sales through the acquisition of good selling skills. The material in this chapter provides you with a good start in that direction. First, we define personal selling and explain its importance in the promotion mix. Next, we discuss the evolution of personal selling and the pros and cons of the selling profession. We then present the various types of personal selling and selling environments, and the sales process. An explanation of the growing professionalism of selling through certification follows. We then discuss the sales management function, including the characteristics and duties of a good sales manager. We conclude by discussing sales force technology, and legal and ethical issues.

SALES AND MARKETING IN THE 21ST CENTURY

LEARNING OBJECTIVE 1

Personal selling is one of the most important elements of the promotional mix and a critical activity of marketing management; it is also the most expensive form of promotion that a firm can undertake. Recent figures indicate that the average sales call—factoring in compensation, benefits, and travel and entertainment expenses—costs the organization $169.64.[1] For firms emphasizing **consultative selling**, the average price of a sales call is even higher, $211.56.[2] Furthermore, across all industries, only one sales call in three is successful. Why then would a firm choose to utilize personal selling and incur the associated costs?

The Strategic Importance of Personal Selling

There are three primary reasons why personal selling is such an important component of a promotional strategy. First, because personal selling involves direct communication between a sales representative and a prospective customer, it is the only form of promotion that allows a firm to immediately respond to the needs of the prospect. That is, as the salesperson makes his or her presentation, the salesperson can continuously adapt the

Personal selling
is direct oral communication designed to explain how an individual's or firm's goods, services, or ideas fit the needs of one or more prospective customers.

Consultative selling
is the process of helping customers reach their strategic goals by using the products and expertise of the sales organization.

Radical Selling: The Cure All

Mark Cuban is the charismatic, controversial owner of the Dallas Mavericks (http://www.nba.com/mavericks/). His antics on the sidelines (and sometimes on the court) resulted in fines in excess of $500,000 for the 2000–2001 basketball season. But Cuban has always been a little remarkable.

At the age of 30, Cuban was a self-made millionaire and at the age of 40, a billionaire. He grew up in a middle-class, blue-collar neighborhood in Pittsburgh and as a youngster sold garbage bags and magazines door-to-door. In 1983, after earning a business degree from Indiana University, Cuban founded MicroSolutions and sold it 7 years later to CompuServe (http://web center.compuserve.com). Cuban then retired at the age of 31—at least for a short time. In 1995, he and a friend founded Broadcast.com, which allowed people to listen to live radio and TV stations via personal computers. Four years later Broadcast.com was sold to Yahoo! (http://www.broadcast.yahoo.com), making Cuban a multibillionaire. In March of 2000, Cuban purchased the Dallas Mavericks, a team that had not made the playoffs in 10 years, and whose revenues were dismal.

One of Cuban's early goals for the Mavs was to dramatically increase ticket sales and sponsorships. Cuban believes that "a business can't succeed without sales; it's the lifeblood of any company." His motto: "Sales cures all." While Cuban's sometimes outlandish behavior has garnered headlines for himself and the team, much of the Mavs newfound success is owed to Cuban's aggressive sales philosophy. Marketing, Cuban notes, requires that a company wait around to see if its prospective customers will respond to an ad and then show up, but sales means the company goes to the customer—no waiting around to see if the customer *might* respond. "In my experience, the biggest bang for the buck comes from using your sales force as your marketing arm. Having them on the phone and in the field gives far more impression than just taking out ads, or going to trade shows."

Cuban first increased the Mavericks' sales force from 5 to 30, then created a culture of enthusiasm that drives the sales force to succeed. Huge signs decorate the walls of the sales office: "12,000 Season Tickets or Bust," "Our #1 Priority Is Selling Season Tickets," and "Your Best Opportunity Is Today. Yesterday Has Already Passed." The vending machine dispenses sodas and juice for free, and a car wash service regularly arrives to wash the sale force's cars. The sales staff is rewarded not only for the number of tickets or sponsorships sold, but also how many phone calls are made. Anyone making more than 100 phone calls in one day receives a bonus. Cash incentives are routinely awarded along with special, surprise rewards. The result: a highly motivated, enthusiastic sales force that is helping Cuban reach his goals. Attendance at Mavericks games has increased more than 60 percent and television ratings have doubled—radical selling and radical results at their best!

Sources: E-mail from Mark Cuban (mark.Cuban@dallasmavs.com), 11 May 2001; Andy Cohen, "Is This Guy for Real?" *Sales & Marketing Management* 153 (May 2001): 36–44; http://www.abcnews.go.com/onair/2020/2020_000504_markcuban_chat.html, accessed 5 January 2001 and 8 February 2001; http://www.broadcast.yahoo.com/home.html; and http://www.foxsport.lycos.com.

presentation to the needs of the prospect. The ability to constantly adapt to the prospective customer, in turn results in a greater number of sales. Second, personal selling allows for immediate customer feedback, so a firm has timely information regarding customer satisfaction with its offerings. Other forms of promotion, such as advertising, are company-sponsored communications directed toward the target market, but direct, *immediate* feedback from customers is not usually possible. Finally, personal selling results in an actual sale—the salesperson can leave a customer's office with an order in hand. Thus, personal selling is one of the few forms of promotion to which the sale of a specific product can be *directly* traced. Consequently, successful companies truly value their sales forces.

Due to the costs associated with personal selling, this form of promotion is not used as often for consumer markets where there are many, geographically dispersed buyers whose individual purchases will not support the average cost of a sales call. Personal selling, however, is often a must in the business-to-business market, and may be used in consumer markets where buyers tend to be fewer in number, more geographically concentrated, and more inclined to purchase in larger quantities and dollar amounts. Additionally, personal selling is usually a necessity for complex products, high-involvement buying situations, and transactions involving trade-ins.

The Evolution of Personal Selling and the Changing Face of Sales

At one time, sales companies believed customers had to be forced into making a purchase. Salespeople utilizing the **hard sell** sought to make an immediate sale without being concerned about meeting the needs of the customer; this type of selling attitude resulted in singular transactional exchanges. That is, when customers purchased from these "hard sell" representatives, and learned that the products truly did not meet the customers' needs, they recognized that the salespersons were not working to satisfy their customers. Consequently, these customers would not purchase from those salespersons again, so these representatives gained only a one-time transaction. Additionally, the hard sell sometimes bordered on the unethical or even illegal.

Today, many businesses are experimenting with approaches other than the hard sell; thus, personal selling has begun to focus on the important concept of **relationship selling**. That is, the salesperson focuses on meeting customer needs, not just selling his or her product. When the salesperson clearly identifies customer needs and seeks to provide the best product to meet those needs, the salesperson is able to develop a long-term relationship with the customer. Not only does the customer benefit from this relationship, but the salesperson also benefits by way of the many future sales that are yielded from this relationship over time. In today's business environment, the goal is to develop long-term relationships with customers. However, to assist firms in identifying the best customers on which to focus their sales efforts, companies are adopting **customer relationship management (CRM)** strategies and applications.

Similar to the way in which sales has evolved from a hard sell to a relationship selling approach, the face of the sales force has also changed. In 1983, men represented the majority of the U.S. sales force, but women have made strong inroads (see Figure 13.1). Today, females comprise approximately half of all those employed in sales occupations.[3] Furthermore, African Americans now represent 8.8 percent of the total U.S. sales force, up 4.1 percent from 1983, while Hispanics constitute 8.5 percent, up 4.8 percent since 1983.[4] In addition, 40.3 percent of sales manager positions are now held by women, an increase of approximately 12 percent over the past two decades.[5]

Hard sell
involves trying every means to get the prospective customer to buy, regardless of whether it is in the prospect's best interest.

Relationship selling
requires the development of a trusting partnership in which the salesperson seeks to provide long-term customer satisfaction by listening, gathering information, educating, and adding value for the customer.

Customer relationship management (CRM)
relies on systematized processes to profile key segments so that marketing and retention strategies can be customized for these customers.

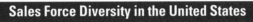

Sales Force Diversity in the United States — Figure 13.1

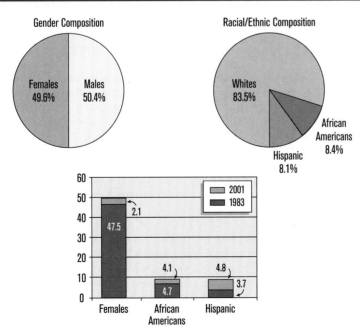

Source: U.S. Bureau of Labor Statistics, *Employment and Earnings*, January 2001.

The Sales Professions: Rewards and Drawbacks

Several studies suggest college students are not interested in pursuing a career in the sales profession.[6] Unfortunately, the all too frequent portrayal of salespeople as fast-talking, glad-handing, slick characters with highly questionable ethics has tainted the sales profession, so that many people think of selling as an undesirable profession. They fail to realize how highly dependent large and small companies are on the revenues that salespeople generate. If you do not think this is true, try staying in business without selling something. Further, salespeople provide expertise in the field to customers seeking product information. Salespeople also spot and report potential competitive and market trends, so their companies can respond appropriately.[7] Consequently, salespeople are truly vital to the business world.

The future for sales professionals looks great! Employment in sales occupations continues to grow. Today, approximately 16 million people hold sales-related jobs.[8] By the year 2005, the U.S. Department of Labor expects the number of people employed in sales positions to increase by 24 percent, placing sales as a growth profession 4 percent higher than any other profession.[9] Thus, in the next decade, the profession of selling probably offers more employment opportunities than any other career choice.

Sales positions also offer many advantages, which are summarized in Figure 13.2. There is great flexibility in sales activities, so no two workdays are alike.[10] There are intrinsic rewards gained in meeting the needs of customers and feeling that you have helped someone else. There are also extrinsic rewards. First, potential compensation is quite high. Sales representatives average $53,293, plus $31,441 in commissions—a

Benefits of Sales Occupations

Figure 13.2

- Flexibility in Day-to-Day Activities
- Intrinsic Reward from Helping Customers
- Good Compensation
- Travel Opportunities
- Limited Supervision
- Increasing Responsibilities
- High-Visibility Career Track
- Promotion Potential

total compensation package of $84,004.[11] Frequently, the compensation includes a company car, laptop computer, and cellular telephone to make the total compensation package even more valuable. For top-performing sales representatives, salaries average $74,000 to $172,000 per year.[12] Further, sales positions frequently offer travel opportunities, increasing responsibility, and limited supervision. Finally, it is also a great career track because of its high visibility. For example, a survey of 50 presidents and chief operating officers of privately owned apparel companies noted that 57 percent of these top executives had started their careers in sales.[13] Moreover, the average yearly sales growth for companies whose chief executives officers (CEOs) have sales backgrounds are higher, at 18.70 percent, than the average sales growth for all other companies.[14]

Sales, like all professions, also presents a few drawbacks. The hours can be long, and it is not unusual for salespeople to experience **role conflict** (e.g., the firm demands

Role conflict
is the anxiety caused by conflicting job demands.

Figure 13.3 — Desirable Salesperson Traits

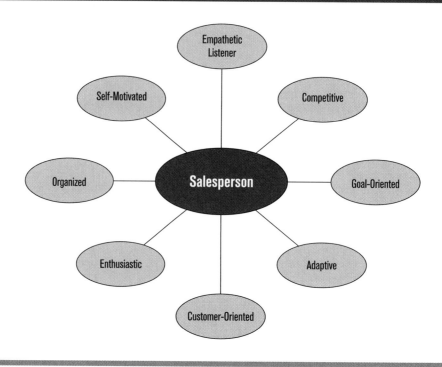

Role ambiguity
is anxiety caused by inadequate information about job responsibilities and performance-related goals.

Job anxiety
is tension caused by the pressures of the job.

Customer-oriented
means the salesperson seeks to elicit customer needs/problems and then takes the necessary steps to meet those needs or solve the problem in a manner that is in the best interest of the customer.

LEARNING OBJECTIVE 2

that the salesperson obtain a high price for the firm's product, while the customer demands a low price), **role ambiguity** (e.g., many organizational departments—billing, shipping, production, marketing, public relations—may influence the salesperson's activities and create uncertainty about what is expected of the salesperson), and **job anxiety** (e.g., the salesperson must perform, often simultaneously, many tasks: meeting sales objectives, servicing old accounts and producing new accounts, developing and conducting effective sales presentations, developing product and competitor knowledge, submitting timely reports to the company, and controlling sales expenses).[15]

Desirable Salesperson Traits

Good salespeople must be self-motivated, organized, enthusiastic, adaptive, competitive, goal-oriented, empathetic, and most importantly, **customer-oriented**, as shown in Figure 13.3. This last trait has been found to be the most significant differentiating factor between successful and mediocre salespeople.

SELLING ENVIRONMENTS AND TYPES OF SALESPEOPLE

Personal selling occurs in different environments, and each environment determines which types of selling are utilized. The three environments in which personal selling may occur are telemarketing, over-the-counter selling, and field selling (see Figure 13.4).

Telemarketing

Telemarketing utilizes the telephone for prospecting, selling, and/or following up with customers. Two types of salespeople are generally found in this environment. *Outbound telemarketers* are salespersons who use the telephone to call customers and close deals. *Inbound telemarketers,* on the other hand, are those salespeople who answer telephone calls from customers and help them place orders. Firms that employ inbound telemarketers often have toll-free phone numbers as a convenience for their customers. Of the

| **Selling Environments and Types of Salespeople** | **Figure 13.4** |

Selling Environments	**Selling Types**
Telemarketing	Outbound Telemarketers
	Inbound Telemarketers
Over-the-Counter	Order Takers
	Order Getters
Field Selling	Professional Salespeople
	National Account Managers
	Missionary Salespeople
	Support Salespeople

three selling environments, telemarketing, in general, tends to rely less on relationship development with customers.

Over-the-Counter Selling

Over-the-counter selling is usually conducted in retail outlets. As a consumer, you choose to enter a store where you may be greeted by a retail salesperson. If the store you have selected is heavily oriented toward self-service, your only interaction with a salesperson may be when you have to track one down to obtain an answer to a specific question you have regarding the merchandise. In this type of store, the over-the-counter salesperson will usually act only as an **order taker**, ringing up and appropriately packaging what you wish to purchase without imparting any product-specific knowledge. On the other hand, if the store is oriented toward personal service, the salesperson is likely to try to identify what it is you are seeking and to help you with merchandise selection. The salesperson may even practice **suggestion selling**. For example, if you go into a store with the intention of purchasing a business suit, the salesperson may make suggestions regarding styles and colors. After your selection is made, the salesperson may suggest a tie or blouse that will match the suit. In these situations, the salesperson is acting as an **order getter**.

Field Selling

As in over-the-counter selling environments, salespeople involved in **field selling** may act as order takers, such as in the food industry, or as order getters, such as in the encyclopedia business. Many salespersons in the field selling environment, however, are categorized as professional salespeople, national account managers, missionary salespeople, or support salespeople.

Professional Salespeople
Professional salespeople may be found in all industries, but especially in industries where products are adapted to individual customer needs, such as high-tech computers. The companies for which they work may assign professional salespeople a variety of job titles, including account executive, sales consultant, or sales representative.

National Account Managers
National account managers are highly skilled salespersons who call on key customers' headquarters sites, develop strategic plans for the accounts, make formal presentations to top-level executives, and assist with all the product decisions at that level.[16] Consequently, important customers associate one key person—the national account manager—with the vendor company, and the vendor company does not need to have its other salespeople call on all the local branches of a large, diverse customer. For example, the

Order taker
is a salesperson who only processes the purchase that the customer has already selected.

Suggestion selling
occurs when the salesperson points out available complementary items in line with the selected item(s), in order to encourage an additional purchase.

Order getter
is a salesperson who seeks to actively provide information to prospects, persuade prospective customers, and close sales.

Field selling
involves calling on prospective customers in either their business or home locations.

Best Practices in a Sales Career: Harvesting the Fruits of the Vine

In 1996, Erica Gantner was approaching graduation from Cornell University's College of Agriculture and Life Sciences with a degree in food industry management. Erica had narrowed her job search to either consumer-goods companies or supermarket chains. While she was not particularly interested in a sales career and found the prospect of selling a little frightening, she quickly realized that entry-level positions within consumer-goods companies routinely began in sales, so new recruits could learn the business from the ground up.

As part of the campus interviewing process, Erica met with General Mills, Black & Decker, and Procter & Gamble, but her interest level peaked when she interviewed with E. & J. Gallo Winery. She was extremely impressed by how Gallo clearly defined early career paths for new recruits via its management development program. Erica also liked the fact that Gallo pushed new hires along rapidly and regularly increased their responsibilities. Finally, Erica felt there was a good fit between her style and Gallo's corporate culture. Overall, she thought the company seemed energetic and motivated.

Erica participated in three interviews with Gallo recruiters within a single week while they were visiting the Cornell campus. Following that round of successful interviews, Erica and the other candidates from the northeast area were invited to a regional recruiting conference with Gallo upper management in attendance. On the first day, candidates rotated through three or four different interviews conducted by multiple interviewers. The point was to place each interviewee in front of as many Gallo managers as possible. Dinner, along with presentations and tastings of the various Gallo brands, followed these interviews. On the second day, candidates accompanied district managers to various retail outlets for demonstrations of a new hire's duties. Afterwards everyone met back at the hotel to recap the day's events and to go through a case study that helped illustrate the consultative sales role the candidates would assume as they move through management positions with Gallo. Finally, Gallo made its hiring decisions and the hand-picked recruits, including Erica, then spent half a day on a ride-along accompanying a sales representative and district manager in their prospective starting sales territory, prior to receiving a formal job offer.

Right after graduation, Erica began her training program in the Manchester, New Hampshire, area—her first assigned territory. Gallo provides a sound training process. The first 8 weeks on the job are designed to help recruits understand the wine industry and to get established in their assigned territory. The first few days on the job, Erica spent reading the sales manual that covers everything from wine-making processes and the history of the Gallo brands to consultative selling approaches, shelving and display standards, and merchan-

dising tactics. After gaining a basic knowledge of the Gallo products, Erica was then paired with the district manager and other experienced sales representatives each day for the next 3 weeks. During this period she received valuable sales training and her knowledge of Gallo's shelving standards, competitive products, and pricing was reinforced. In the 4th week, Erica began making sales calls on her own, but she remained in almost constant touch with her district manager as she struggled to figure out her new job and to learn her territory. Erica also had to adjust to life on her own in New Hampshire. She had grown up in Ohio, and gone to college in New York, so she knew no one in New Hampshire. To feel at ease in her new surroundings, she made an effort to develop friends and learn the area as quickly as possible.

In her first sales position, Erica recognized that there were "a lot of different balls that had to be juggled"—selling, servicing, merchandising, managing time efficiently, and completing administrative tasks. Before she knew it, though, Erica had gained a firm grasp of the wine business and was achieving a stellar sales performance. Within a year after being hired with Gallo, she was promoted to district manager, responsible for overseeing and developing the sales representatives in western New Hampshire. Nine short months later, Erica was promoted again—this time to field marketing manager—and transferred to the Pittsburgh area. As a field marketing manager, Erica served as a link between the winery and its distributors, and she had to gain a firm understanding of distributor operations, local market conditions, and winery initiatives. With territory consisting of western Pennsylvania, she called on the malt distributors, those middlemen distributing Bartles & James and Boone's Farm products. From Pittsburgh, Erica was relocated to Maine. As a field marketing manager there, she called on two full-portfolio distributors, which handled all Gallo products, and the liquor control board. After two years as field marketing manager, Erica was promoted to New Hampshire state manager, making her responsible for the entire sales force in that state. Recently, Erica received another promotion—her sixth one in 5 years. In this new position as regional sales coordinator, Erica serves as financial analyst for 10 states and reports directly to the regional manager for the Northeast. Each promotion has brought a pay increase, so that Erica has doubled her original, generous starting salary.

Erica feels Gallo management has been good at reading her and assessing her skills and interests. Consequently, her promotions and increased responsibilities have been rapid. She strongly encourages other graduating seniors to pursue a career in sales and especially urges students to check out career possibilities with E. & J. Gallo Winery.

Source: Interview with Erica Gantner, 11 May 2001.

Procter & Gamble national account manager for Wal-Mart conducts sales presentations at the Arkansas headquarters site, and any decisions made pertaining to Procter & Gamble products at the headquarters level will then be passed down to all of Wal-Mart's retail outlets. Procter & Gamble does not have to have individual salespeople calling on every Wal-Mart store to try to influence decision makers at that level.

National account managers are expected to know their customers' businesses intimately; consequently, national account managers call on very few accounts. Indeed, it is not unusual for a national account manager to be responsible for just one customer, if the customer is a very large one. Customers who are assigned national account managers have enormous sales potential and more complex buying behaviors, due to their multiple locations and various operating units. The national account manager's job is to provide these special accounts with greater attention and service to ensure that a partnership develops between the two organizations.

Missionary Salespeople

Missionary salespeople differ from other sales professionals in that they do not seek to obtain a direct order from their customers. Although they are charged with providing product information to customers, their primary goal is to persuade customers to place orders with distributors or wholesalers. For example, the goal of Kraft Foods salespeople is to convince the managers of grocery stores to place orders with food wholesalers for Kraft products. Pharmaceutical representatives are also missionary salespeople. Their job is to provide detailed information to physicians, so that the physicians will prescribe the drug to patients. These patients, in turn, will purchase the prescription from one of the pharmaceutical firm's resellers, such as a drug store.

Support Salespeople

Support salespeople do not actually perform all the steps in the sales process; instead, their job is to support the sales force in a number of ways. Technical support salespeople serve as technical advisors to the sales force, and prospective customers, on complex products such as data networking systems. They are often teamed with a sales representative to assist with the technical aspects of sales presentations. Other support salespeople, sometimes known as merchandisers, set up product displays in the customer's business after the sales representative has obtained the customer's permission to do so. Still other types of support salespeople complete and follow up on order processing, and do other related administrative tasks in order to free the salesperson to spend more time with customers.

Sales Certification

As selling evolves into the development of strategic partnerships with customers, salespeople are heralding a new level of professionalism through sales certification. Several organizations now offer certification programs that are designed to increase the professionalism and expertise of salespeople. Applicants for sales certification must meet a specified point criterion based on a combination of education and sales experience; pass a challenging written exam; provide professional references; and agree to adhere to a code of ethics.[17] They are also encouraged to participate in continuing education programs to maintain certification. Three organizations that offer salesperson certification programs are the Hospitality Sales and Marketing Association International (HSMAI), the National Association of Sales Professionals (NASP), and the Sales and Marketing Executives International (SMEI).[18] These certification programs are designed to increase the credibility and professionalism of the salesperson, and earn the public's respect for the sales profession.

THE SALES PROCESS

LEARNING OBJECTIVE 3

There are eight basic steps in the sales process: prospecting, the preapproach, the approach, need identification, presentation, handling objections, gaining commitment, and follow-up (see Figure 13.5). In the *traditional selling method*, little time is spent on the early stages of the process—especially the approach and need identification. Consequently, the prospective buyer is not usually convinced that he or she really needs the

http://www.pg.com

http://www.walmart.com

http://www.kraft.com

http://www.hsmai.org

http://www.nasp.com

http://www.smei.org

Team Selling Drives Revenues

As products and competitive environments have become increasingly complicated, the somewhat controversial use of selling teams has become more commonplace, especially in business-to-business contexts. Selling teams usually consist of a salesperson who is responsible for managing the sales cycle, and a technical expert who provides subject matter credibility for the customer. However, selling teams may take other forms as well. For example, a sales team may consist of all company representatives that will have any effect on a customer, or the sales team may be comprised of sales representatives who are responsible for the same territory but different products.

Why use selling teams? Salespeople often do not have the extensive technical knowledge necessary to understand customer requirements for highly complex products; engineers and technicians usually lack the skills necessary for guiding the customer through the sales process. In combination, however, salespeople and technical experts can form a powerful team that serves to better address customer needs and ensures that the sales team can speak the technical language of some of the key players in the buying decision process. Consequently, selling teams are most likely to be used when the customer is purchasing a complex product for the first time,

when the customer warrants special treatment, or when several people are involved in the purchasing decision.

The implementation of team selling within an organization, however, can be problematic. Sales representatives may want total control over the sales process and feel uncomfortable having to involve a technical expert. Similarly, technicians and engineers may resent being forced to participate in the more "earthy" business of sales. Consequently, sales teams are not always as productive as they should be. One study reported that only 13 percent of the selling teams of Fortune 1000 companies are perceived as highly effective. For companies that have formulated winning strategies for their sales teams, however, the payoffs can be huge. One company reported a 45 percent reduction in sales management costs and a significant increase in sales generated per dollar spent.

Sources: "How Teaming Can Reinvigorate Sales Performance," *Supervisory Management* (February 1995): 13; Jeff Baker, "Team Selling Is the Ticket to Winning the 'Revenue Bowl'," *Computer Reseller News*, 4 January 1999, 54; Dave Downey, Mike Jackson, and Marilyn Holschuh, "Strategic Selling: Team Selling=Greater Success with Key Accounts," *Agri Marketing* (September 2000): 18–19; Donald W. Jackson, Jr., Scott M. Widmier, Ralph Giacobbe, and Janet E. Keith, "Examining the Use of Team Selling by Manufacturers' Representatives: A Situational Approach," *Industrial Marketing Management* (March 1999): 155–164; Michele Marchetti, "Why Teams Fail" *Sales and Marketing Management* (June 1997): 91–92; "How Teaming Can Reinvigorate Sales Performance," 13.

Figure 13.5	The Sales Process

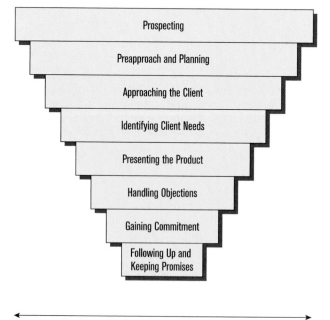

Prospecting

Preapproach and Planning

Approaching the Client

Identifying Client Needs

Presenting the Product

Handling Objections

Gaining Commitment

Following Up and Keeping Promises

Time Invested by Professional Salesperson at Each Stage

product, so gaining commitment from the buyer is difficult, tedious, and time-consuming. In the *professional selling method*, a great deal of time is spent in the early stages—prospecting, preapproach, approach, and need identification phases, so that commitment is gained as a very natural, or logical, next step. Essentially, customers are convinced that the product will solve their problem, or meet their need, because early in the sales process care has been taken to establish that need and link it to the benefits of the product. In the following sections, each of the eight steps in the sales process is discussed.

Prospecting

Prospecting involves finding **qualified sales leads**. There are many ways to find sales leads: cold calling, working trade shows, networking through industry associations or social organizations, offering educational seminars, and reading trade journals and newspaper business pages. One of the better means of finding leads, though, is through **referrals**. Generating just one referral is as effective as making 12 cold calls.[19] Prior to asking for referrals, a salesperson should ensure that the current customer is satisfied. But once a strong relationship has been established, the salesperson should not hesitate to ask for a referral. Referred leads usually mean faster closings, shorter sales cycles, and larger initial transactions.[20] Unfortunately, few salespeople ask for referrals, although over 80 percent of customers report they would gladly provide them.[21]

Although most salespeople dislike making cold calls, nearly all salespeople must conduct some **cold-calling** at some point in their careers. Some cold calling is done by phoning prospects. When utilizing the telephone for cold calls, most salespeople attempt

Qualified sales leads
are potential customers who have a need for the salesperson's product, and are able to buy; that is, they have the financial means to purchase the product and the authority to make the buying decision.

Referrals
are usually obtained by the salesperson asking current customers if they know of someone else, or another company, who might need the salesperson's product.

Cold calling
means contacting prospective customers without a prior appointment.

THE WAR IS OVER

And you've won. Just log on to salesforce.com. It's a powerful online customer relationship management service; a fully integrated sales, marketing, and customer support solution. Acquire, grow, and retain more customers immediately. No software. No start-up costs. No risk. No need to wait. And now for a limited time there's another reason to celebrate. Sign up online and your first five users are FREE for 12 months. Call us at 1-800-NO-SOFTWARE or better yet, visit us online at www.salesforce.com.

salesforce.com
Point. Click. Close.

only to secure a definite appointment with the prospect, although other salespeople will attempt to complete the sale over the phone. Cold calling may also involve stopping by the customer's business or home location without a prearranged appointment. While this face-to-face interaction can be quite effective, some customers may have strict rules concerning when salespeople are allowed to see their employees for solicitation purposes. Salespeople should familiarize themselves with the company policies before dropping in to visit.

Many salespeople have a fear of cold calling because they fear rejection. On average, a salesperson has to make 3 to 5 sales calls for every one sale; however, for some industries, this ratio may be 1 in 10 or 1 in 25 calls. Consequently, salespeople should not become discouraged. They can remain motivated by remembering that sales is a numbers game—sales representatives will likely hear many "nos" before they hear a "yes." Tom Hopkins, author of *How to Master the Art of Selling*, suggests recognizing that if each sale provides you with $100 in commission, and you average five calls per sale, then each "no" you hear is worth $20.[22]

Once prospects have been identified, these potential buyers should be incorporated into a customer relationship management database that will help salespeople have the right information, including the most effective contact method, at the right time.[23]

Preapproach and Planning

The preapproach is the collection of information about the potential customer and the customer's company prior to the initial visit. In very much the same way that job candidates should research any firm with whom they are going to interview, salespeople should also research any prospective client and the client's company.[24] A salesperson should seek answers to the following questions:

- Who will make the purchase decisions?
- What are that person's interests?
- What is that person's job title?
- What does the company do?
- Who are their primary competitors?
- Which direct competitors are currently doing business with the customer?
- What rules does the prospective customer have regarding salespeople?

In other words, the sales representative should want to obtain as much information as possible about the prospect and their company. One quick source for this information may be the local library or the Internet. Many firms have Web sites that provide useful company information. Researching the prospect and the prospect's company will indicate that the salesperson is serious about earning the prospect's business. This information also assists the salesperson in planning the initial presentation to the prospective customer.

Approaching the Client

The approach is the development of rapport with the customer. Using the information the salesperson has already gathered, the salesperson begins developing a relationship with the customer. The salesperson wants to illustrate that he or she is working to understand and assist in meeting the prospective customer's needs. In this stage, it is important that the salesperson adapt to the potential customer's social style.

Social Styles
There are four basic social style categories,[25] which are depicted in Figure 13.6.

1. The *driver* is action- and goal-oriented, and makes quick decisions. To adapt to this social style, the salesperson should provide the bottom-line information first, and then work backward to fill in essential details. The driver will want only the basic facts and will not want to socialize a great deal.
2. The *analytical* is fact- and detail-oriented. This individual will require time to make decisions, while carefully weighing all the facts. To adapt to this social style, the salesperson should inundate the analytical prospect

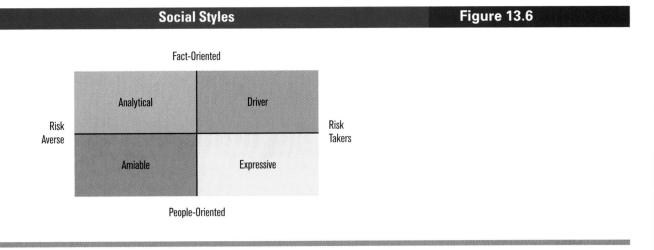

Social Styles — **Figure 13.6**

with facts and figures that can be supported with documentation. Like the driver, the analytical is not very interested in developing a personal relationship with the salesperson.

3. The *expressive* loves to socialize and will frequently base the purchase decision on the relationship with the salesperson. To adapt to this social style, the salesperson should be prepared to establish a personal relationship with the expressive prospect by telling anecdotal stories, by socializing outside the office, and by relating personal information.

4. The *amiable* tends to be a visionary with big ideas for the future, but is not a detail-oriented individual. The amiable prospect is hesitant to make quick decisions and will seek consensus from others before reaching a purchase decision. The amiable also seeks to have a personal relationship with the salesperson, as this relationship helps reduce some of the anxiety that is felt about making a decision. To adapt to this social style, the salesperson should establish a personal relationship and provide assurances that will reduce the amiable's feeling of risk. Further, the sales representative should present the product based on what it will do for the customer in the "big picture," and avoid getting into discussions of minute details.

Other factors must be considered in the approach stage. This is the salesperson's chance to make a good first impression. Consequently, the salesperson should dress neatly and professionally. Prospects should be greeted with a firm handshake and direct eye contact. Throughout the sales interview, the salesperson should maintain an open body posture to indicate interest and openness to the customer; that is, the salesperson should keep feet flat on the floor, body leaning slightly forward, direct eye contact, arms open (uncrossed), and hands open, palms slightly upward. The salesperson should also let the customer know that he or she is actively listening, by rephrasing or summarizing important points the customer has made.

Identifying Client Needs

Probing Questions

Success at the need-identification stage of the sales process requires asking probing questions of the prospective customer to determine needs. These needs may be organizational and/or personal. Organizational needs may involve finance, image, or performance issues, whereas personal needs may involve the ego or self-image. To obtain information about the prospect's needs, the salesperson should ask open-ended questions. Such questions are designed to elicit a true expression of the prospect's opinions and feelings, regardless of whether these opinions are favorable or unfavorable in the salesperson's view. The salesperson should use open-ended, or probing, questions frequently throughout the sales presentation to ensure that the customer's needs and potential concerns are

Question Formats in Sales: Open versus Closed

Whenever possible salespeople should use open-ended questions, rather than close-ended questions, to obtain the maximum information from customers and to get them to reveal and elaborate on their motives for purchase. The following illustrates the difference between open and closed questions:

Open-Ended		**Close-Ended**	
Salesperson:	What are you looking for in a new car?	Salesperson:	Do you want to look at our full-size, four-wheel drive vehicles?
Buyer:	I want an economic car that is easy to park, but handles well on icy roads. I don't want a big four-wheel drive vehicle, though. I also want to keep my monthly payments down.	Buyer:	No, I'm not interested in that.
Salesperson:	Excellent! I think you will find our new Subaru model is exactly what you are seeking. Let me show it to you.		

addressed. The key here is to learn what prospective customers want, not just to try to sell whatever the salesperson has to offer.[26] After needs have been identified, the salesperson should gain the prospect's permission to begin the presentation.

Presenting the Product

Features versus Benefits

Customers buy products not because of the features they offer, but because of the needs these features satisfy. Therefore, the focus of the sales presentation is the salesperson's explanation of how a product's features provide "benefits" that specifically address the prospect's previously identified needs or problems. These benefits should answer the buyer's often unvocalized question, "What's in it for me?" For example, rather than simply telling buyers that a shampoo contains special conditioners (feature), the marketer must tell the buyers that their hair will be softer and shinier (benefit) because of these special conditioners. Or, as Marriott has learned: "the guest end-benefit is a successful trip; the hotel's role is to enable this success."[27]

http://www.marriott.com

Types of Presentations

Presentations may be flexible or memorized (see Figure 13.7). *Flexible presentations* allow the salesperson to identify the customer's needs and customize the presentation

Figure 13.7	**Presentation Styles**

Flexible Presentations
- Identify customer needs
- Customize presentation

Memorized Presentations
- Does not address specific needs of customer
- Script features key benefits and selling points

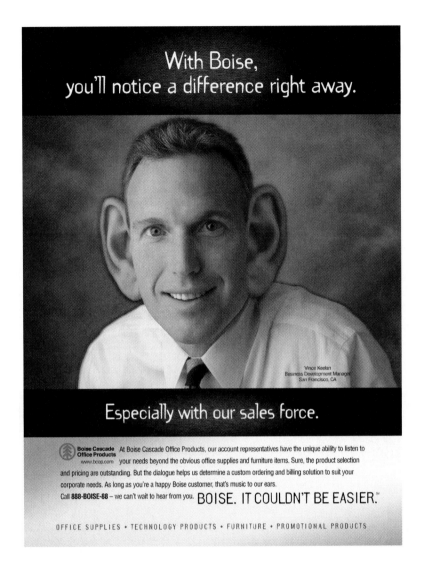

specifically for the individual customer. This type of presentation is sometimes called a *need-satisfaction presentation,* and is the preferred method for professional salespeople. *Memorized presentations* require that the salesperson commit a scripted presentation to memory. This type of presentation, sometimes called a *canned presentation,* does not address the specific needs of each customer; however, the script has been built around the best key benefits and selling points of the company and the product. Salespeople who sell to consumers in their homes may employ this method of presentation. For example, book companies that sell door-to-door often have their sales representatives use memorized presentations with successful results. This approach should be used with caution since it may create a perception of unoriginality, thereby making customers feel as if they are not special or important.

To improve the effectiveness of their presentations, many salespeople now incorporate the latest technology via laptop computers. Thus, sales representatives may employ computer graphics and/or Web sites in their sales presentations to generate increased attention and interest from prospective customers.

Handling Objections

Prospective buyers frequently raise objections as to why they should buy a particular product. However, these objections do not necessarily mean that the prospect is uninterested in the product. Instead, objections likely indicate the salesperson has failed to provide adequate information to the buyer, or has not demonstrated how the product meets the needs of the prospect. Consequently, the prospective customer is afraid that he or she

may be making a mistake in purchasing the product.[28] When faced with objections, the salesperson should approach the objection as a sign of interest on the part of the prospect, and provide information that will ensure the prospect's confidence in making the purchase. As a salesperson becomes more experienced, he will recognize that certain objections occur on a regular basis. After discerning what these common objections are, the salesperson should work to provide information early in the presentation that will counter these objections. For example, if the salesperson routinely hears prospective buyers say, "The price is too high," the salesperson should strive to emphasize the higher quality or special attributes offered by the product. Consequently, the prospect will recognize that added features/higher quality compensate for the higher price; thus, good value is still offered.

Providing Supporting Evidence

During the presentation, the salesperson should be prepared to document any statements of fact that are made. This documentation can come from a variety of sources, including letters of testimony from satisfied customers, independent reports, newspaper or magazine articles, company brochures or other literature, and product demonstrations. For example, a hotel sales manager might explain to a potential client that numerous companies have used the hotel's facilities to hold their annual meetings and have been quite satisfied. The salesperson should then produce letters of testimony from various companies that support the claim of satisfied corporate clientele.

Gaining Commitment

Commitment is gained when the prospect agrees to take the action sought by the sales-person. Usually, this means the buyer purchases the product, or at least signs a purchase agreement. However, prospects will not usually come right out and say they want to buy what the salesperson is offering; the salesperson must ask for commitment. In other words, *the salesperson must ask for the order,* just as the interviewee should ask for the job.[29] Failure to ask for an order frequently is the cause of a salesperson's unsuccessful presentation. Indeed, salespeople do not ask customers to buy in approximately 70 percent of all sales calls! Yet, the sales profession recognizes the importance of this stage of the sales process as evidenced by the numerous books written on gaining commitment.[30]

Following Up and Keeping Promises

The last step in the sales process, follow-up, requires that the salesperson complete any agreed upon actions. Unfortunately, while salespeople may work very hard to get a customer, they frequently fail to follow through on their promises, so they cannot keep these customers. As noted in previous chapters, it is much more expensive to obtain a new customer than it is to keep an old one; consequently, it is imperative that salespeople keep any promises they make to customers.

Additionally, salespeople should stay in touch after a sale by writing thank-you notes, clipping and mailing newspaper articles of interest to the prospect, and occasionally calling on customers just to ensure that they are still happy with their purchase decisions.

BUILDING AND MANAGING THE SALES FORCE

LEARNING OBJECTIVE 4

Selling is the revenue stream of the corporation. Managing this vital function requires strong skills so that the sales force will continue to generate the money to fund the rest of the organization. Sales management is the process of planning, directing, controlling, and implementing the personal selling function of the organization.

Sales managers must be good leaders who can recruit, train, motivate, and evaluate their sales representatives; manage territories; and develop sales plans and sales forecasts, while accomplishing the goals of the organization (see Figure 13.8).[31] They also need to be able to identify business opportunities and to create appropriate strategies. They must constantly encourage the sales team to exceed customer expectations, develop long-term relationships, and create added value for the customer.[32]

Recruiting

Sales managers must recruit the right individuals for any open sales positions. A sales force composed of the right people makes a big difference in how large a company can grow. The individuals the sales manager hires should possess the attributes previously discussed: empathy, competitiveness, goal orientation, customer orientation, enthusiasm, organization, and self-motivation. In addition, the sales manager should recruit individuals whose values and goals match those of the firm. This congruency will facilitate greater job satisfaction among new recruits.

Sales Manager's Tasks	Figure 13.8

- Recruiting
- Training
- Motivating
- Compensating
- Evaluating
- Territory Organization

To hire the best salespeople, the sales manager should not rely solely on résumés, but should pay close attention to how candidates conduct themselves throughout the interview process. For example, if the first contact is by telephone, the candidate should ask for an appointment. Candidates who do not ask are unlikely to ask for orders from prospective customers. Candidates should also demonstrate persistence by staying in touch with the sales manager, and not just waiting for the sales manager to call back. Additionally, candidates should be good listeners. Candidates who talk more than 50 percent of the time may not be effective at listening to prospects and customers. Finally, candidates should ask for the job. Candidates who do not ask for the job will probably be too timid to ask for commitment from prospective customers.[33]

Many sales organizations have resorted to objective tests to assist them in selecting the best sales candidates. Some companies, such as The Breakers, and Ramada Franchise Systems, have determined that certain personality types perform better in their industries; therefore, after passing initial screening interviews, candidates are subjected to personality tests. Only those candidates who fit a certain personality profile move on to the next level in the selection process. Other companies, such as Procter & Gamble, General Mills, and PricewaterhouseCoopers, test for certain sales skills such as critical thinking, adaptability, or intellect. Candidates who do not obtain an adequate score are dropped from the pool of eligible candidates. Still other organizations, such as McKinsey & Company, subject their job candidates to role-playing early in the selection process. Those candidates who perform well in the role-play progress to the next step. These somewhat more objective methods for selecting sales recruits are designed to reduce some of the difficulty firms have in finding the best candidates for their sales forces.

http://www.thebreakers.com

http://www.ramada.com

http://www.GeneralMills.com

http://www.pwcglobal.com

http://www.mckinsey.com

Sales Force Training

Corporate Culture

After hiring the best candidates, sales managers must orient recruits to the company culture. Additionally, sales managers must train new sales representatives on product and customer knowledge and selling skills. Although sales training is expensive—many companies invest between $22,500 to upwards of $100,000 to train a new sales representative—the payoff is worth it.[34] Indeed, experts suggest the return on investment for sales training is as high as $273 for every dollar spent.[35] Others note that employees achieve a 30 percent increase in productivity following effective training.[36] Further, training is essential to the success of the sales force. Consequently, all sales representatives, regardless of how long they have been selling, should periodically receive training to stay up-to-date and to keep their skills honed.

Product Knowledge and Sales Skills

The focus of training should be on product knowledge and sales skills. Good product knowledge is essential for making presentations and handling objections; whereas the acquisition of good sales skills is necessary for moving effectively through the sales process. Sales representatives should be taught to identify the social styles of customers and alter their presentations for each customer type. In other words, sales representatives should know and practice *adaptive selling*. In addition, the sales force should learn to develop attention-getting openings and good listening skills, focus on customer needs, handle objections, and be able to close the sale. More advanced salespeople should be trained in strategic account management and the development of long-term customer relationships. They should understand the importance of identifying the organizational structure, key decision makers, and decision influencers in their customers' organizations. They must learn more about their customers' businesses and how they can help customers be more profitable. Finally, all salespeople should be trained in how to utilize the latest technology to improve their ability to serve customers.

Sales Force Technology

The use of technology among sales forces is growing. Many companies are mandating that their sales forces operate from "virtual offices" equipped with laptop computers, cell phones, and portable printer-copier-fax machines, rather than driving to corporate headquarters each day.[37] These virtual offices allow a sales force to spend more time in the

Will the Internet Eliminate Salespeople?

Currently, online sales represent only 1 percent of total retail spending worldwide. However, this percentage is expected to grow as shoppers become more accustomed to purchasing products over the Internet. Companies that may have relied heavily on their sales forces and the sales forces of their distributors for revenues have now recognized that they can add customers, increase market share, and decrease sales expenses by using the Internet as an additional sales channel. E-sales, however, do not necessarily mean a shrinking sales force. Industries in which the sales force provides customized products and services, especially for large corporate clients, recognize that customers cannot obtain those same benefits by surfing the Net.

On the other hand, the Internet is being used to reduce operating expenses and provide salespeople with more selling time. Major accounts still receive high levels of personalized service, while small accounts or individuals who ate up valuable sales time, but did not purchase in sufficient quantities to warrant personalized sales service, can now be tactfully directed to the Web. Further, the Internet assists a sales force in efficiently communicating with its customers by making contracts, designs, and blueprints available to customers on the Web. In turn, the sales force saves hours of driving time. These time savings can be used to pursue new business and to develop stronger relationships with current customers.

Sources: Alastair Ray, "How to Encourage Internet Shopping," *Marketing*, 3 May 2001, 41–42; Rochelle Garner, "Mad As Hell," *Sales & Marketing Management* (June 1999): 54–61.

field with customers. Salespeople use the laptop computers to electronically communicate with their corporate office several times a day. Indeed, sales data are now routinely processed electronically for faster service to the customer. Computers are also used to prepare sales presentations to customers, receive continuous updates on products and pricing, and as noted earlier, may be a vehicle for sales training.[38] Cell phones are also standard equipment for most sales forces, and those phones with advanced features, such as Internet capabilities, are becoming increasingly popular.

A few companies, such as Compaq Computer Corporation, are pioneering the use of Web-based technology not only to prepare sales presentations, but also as a way to deliver presentations to customers. The greatest benefit cited is speed; using Web-based communications shortens the sales cycle.[39]

Sales representatives must be knowledgeable regarding spreadsheet software and other sophisticated software applications specific to their industry. Also, sales managers want to ensure that their representatives have a competitive edge by using a customer relationship management (CRM) database that maintains customer information and tracks customer purchase behaviors.[40] As introduced in Chapter 9, CRM systems allow a sales force to match customers with a customized marketing plan, identify customers at risk of defecting to competitors, track changing customer preferences, and determine a customer's profitability to the firm.[41] Rapidly advancing technology is allowing sales forces to access real-time customer data through wireless platform applications. As a result, sales can be closed faster and more often because sales representatives have all the information they need right at their fingertips.[42]

Finally, some sales managers are also suggesting their sales forces use a software program that allows sales representatives to enter their geographical location and immediately receive a listing and location of all current and potential accounts in the area. Such a program allows sales representatives to use their time more efficiently.

Frequently, sales training requires travel to a distant location and overnight stays in a hotel. For companies with large sales forces, the cost of such training can run into the millions of dollars, which precludes conducting frequent training. In today's high-tech world, though, many companies are training their sales forces with online or Web-based learning. The salespeople involved are able to use their own computers to link into a training session from their homes or hotel rooms if they are on the road visiting clients. This technology allows the sales force to come together in a virtual classroom where they can interact with classmates and the instructor.[43] Other companies are more flexible, allowing their sales forces to tap into the Internet whenever the need arises to become informed about new offerings or to refresh themselves on a particular product.[44]

Consequently, firms are now able to offer their salespeople more frequent training, without requiring that the representatives leave their sales territories and their customers.

Motivating the Sales Force

Sales representatives are individuals, and what motivates one may not motivate the other.[45] Sales managers have to employ a variety of methods for keeping all of these diverse individuals motivated, or incited, to put forth maximum effort. After all, the sales profession can be a high-pressure job that involves frequent rejection. For some salespeople, working to beat the set quota and winning sales contests is a great motivator. Winning builds confidence and reinforces the notion that the individual is a great sales representative. Other salespeople are motivated by extra training sessions that challenge them and groom them for upper management positions. Sales managers may also find some top-performing individuals are motivated by acting as a mentor to newer sales representatives, or by being sought for their advice and wisdom. Some salespeople are most motivated when their strong customer service efforts are recognized throughout the company, such as printing a letter from a grateful client in the company newsletter.[46] Finally, sales forces may be driven to perform at a high level when they are having fun at work. Several companies—Southwest Airlines, LEGO Systems, and Auto Glass Plus—ensure that their sales staff's morale is routinely boosted by theme days, games, and humor.[47] In summary, sales managers must identify what best motivates each of their sales representatives and then strive to motivate and reward them accordingly.

http://www.iflyswa.com

http://www.lego.com

http://www.autoglass-plus.com

Sales Force Quotas

Sales force quotas are used throughout the sales industry to further motivate salespeople and to encourage them to focus on company priorities. Basically, the sales manager provides each sales representative with a reward when the sales representative, or in some cases, the sales team, reaches a prespecified performance level called the *quota*.[48] The quota should be high enough to encourage the sales force to put forth greater effort, yet low enough to appear obtainable. Otherwise, the quotas that the sales manager sets may serve to discourage rather than motivate the sales force. Similarly, the reward offered for meeting or exceeding the quota should be of sufficient value. If it is too low, the sales force may deem that it is not worth their extra effort to achieve.

Sales Coaching

Coaching involves regular praising of salespeople to let them know their efforts are appreciated. It also involves rapport-building, open communication, and modeling behavior. The goal of the sales coach is to develop a relationship of mutual trust and respect with the sales force, which in turn encourages the sales force to listen to and follow directives from the sales manager. Good sales management feedback has also been found to reduce the role conflict and role ambiguity often associated with the sales profession. Finally, the sales manager serves as a model to the sales force so they know what behavior and actions to emulate. Sales manager coaching has consistently been found to motivate salespeople to improve their performance.[49]

As part of the coaching function, sales managers should assist sales representatives in overcoming **sales call anxiety** (SCA).[50] Most often sales call anxiety surfaces during the prospecting or closing phases of the sales process, and can be quite debilitating to the success of the salesperson. Sales managers should familiarize themselves with the various strategies that exist for overcoming SCA and work with sales representatives who may be avoiding initiating customer contact or gaining customer commitment.[51]

Sales call anxiety
is a fear of negative evaluation and rejection by customers.

Compensating the Sales Force

Continuum: Straight Salary to Straight Commission

Sales managers may also be responsible for determining how the sales force will be compensated for their efforts. The level of compensation may be established anywhere on a continuum from straight salary on one end to straight commission on the other (see Figure 13.9). That is, the sales manager may choose to pay the sales force a *straight salary*, in which pay is based on units of time (year, month, week, or hour). This form of compensation provides the sales force with greater security, but may reduce their desire to put forth extra efforts, because they will not receive a direct reward for this effort. The sales manager may choose to compensate the sales force on the basis of *straight commission*, in which pay is based on units of results. In this case, the sales representatives' pay is based solely on how much they sell. For many companies this has been the traditional means of rewarding the sales force. Straight commission, however, can create a great deal of insecurity in sales representatives since some factors not in their control, like an economic recession, may cause a downturn in their sales, and hence a reduction in their salary. The third method by which the sales manager may compensate the sales force is through a combination of the previous two, *salary plus commission*. Accordingly, the sales manager pays the sales force a sufficient base salary that provides just enough money for a basic standard of living, but also pays a commission on sales that is high enough to serve as an

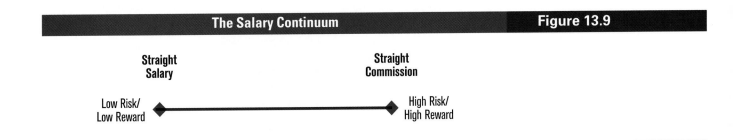

| The Salary Continuum | Figure 13.9 |

Straight Salary   Straight Commission

Low Risk/ ◆━━━━━━━━━━━━━━━━━◆ High Risk/
Low Reward   High Reward

incentive for extra sales efforts. This base salary plus high commission can allow a motivated salesperson to earn a six-figure income. A variation on this latter method of compensation is the *profit-center approach* which requires that sales revenues be used to cover the sales force's corporate expenses and contribute toward the corporation's predefined level of profitability, beyond which all remaining funds are retained by the sales force. Supporters of this approach indicate that such a compensation plan allows the sales force to earn unlimited incomes, but also guarantees profitability for the organization (see Figure 13.10).[52]

In today's environment where the focus is on long-term relationships and where e-commerce is altering the sales landscape, many companies are finding it necessary to adapt their method of compensating the sales force. The use of compensation plans that incorporate high commissions on sales units encourages the sales force to make quick sales without regard to actual customer needs; it does not encourage the sales force to take the time to establish relationships with their customers. Furthermore, customers are determining the sales channel (i.e., Internet, telemarketing, face-to-face) most appropriate for their particular needs. Consequently, some companies have set up different types of compensation plans in which a portion of commission money may be tied to customer satisfaction, customer retention rates, share of customer's business, or other nonrevenue objectives, and only a small portion is linked directly to sales dollars.[53] At the same time, other incentives encourage the sales force to integrate their efforts with e-commerce and support rapid, continuous corporate change.[54] Such a compensation plan facilitates long-term relationships between the salesperson and the customer, and in the long run, will better benefit the company.

Evaluating Salespeople's Performance

Another task of the sales manager is the evaluation of the sales force's performance. Evaluation of the sales force should not be performed only once a year. In conjunction with sales coaching guidelines, sales managers should provide continual guidance and feedback.

Qualitative and Quantitative Factors

The sales manager may choose to evaluate, or assess, the sales force on a combination of quantitative or qualitative factors. However, past studies have found that sales managers weight subjective, qualitative factors more heavily than quantitative variables when assessing salesperson performance. The most popular qualitative factors used for evaluation are communication skills, product knowledge, attitude, selling skills, initiative/aggressiveness, appearance/manner, and knowledge of the competition. The most commonly used quantitative factors are sales volume in dollars, sales volume to previous

Figure 13.10	Comparison of Compensation Plans

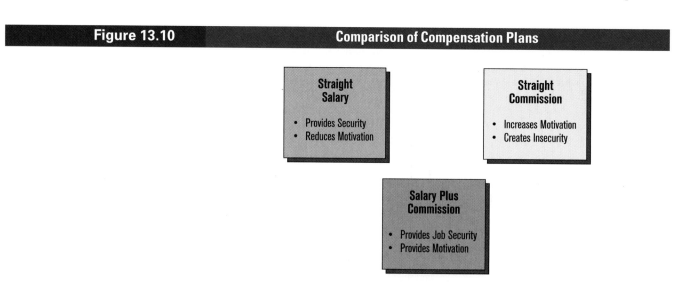

year's sales, number of new accounts, net dollar profits, and sales volume by dollar quota. Although qualitative measures of employee appraisals have value, experts suggest that sales managers should use more quantitative methods of evaluation to reduce bias in the evaluation process.[55] A promising metric that assesses a salesperson's ability to focus on both customer satisfaction and revenue maximization appears to be *RevPASH* (revenue per available salesperson hour).[56] RevPASH evaluation encourages salespeople to focus their sales efforts on customer segments that will generate the highest income, while accounting for customer expectations regarding sales force time.

Organizing and Managing Sales Territories

Geographical and Product Line Organization

Sales managers have a number of options when it comes to organizing the sales territories of their salespeople. Sales territories organized by product line or by geographical area are the more traditional means of organizing sales forces. Under geographical and product line territory organization, salespeople are often required to sell to *all* customers within a geographic area, although their product line may be somewhat limited. In either case, though, they call on customers who represent dozens of different industries.

Today, however, more and more sales managers are organizing sales territories around customers.[57] In this case, the salesperson is asked to call on customers in one or two specific industries, regardless of where the customer is located geographically. This allows the salesperson to become an expert in the particular industry to which he or she is assigned. Consequently, the salesperson can develop a better understanding of the customer's problems, which facilitates the development of a close, long-term relationship between the sales representative and the customer.

Territory Allocation

After deciding by which method to organize the territories, the sales manager must then divide up the territories among the company's salespeople. There are two criteria that should guide territory allocation: (1) all salespersons should feel that their territory offers as much potential as their colleagues' territory, and (2) all should feel the territory division does not require that they work harder than any other salesperson. To achieve these goals, the sales manager must determine the *revenue potential* of each account (regardless of whether the account is a current or potential customer), and how much of the sales representative's time is required to service each account.[58] Then, individual sales territories can be allocated to sales representatives in an equitable manner.

Territory Potential

The sales manager should also help the sales force maximize their territories' potential. The sales manager can accomplish this by encouraging sales representatives to devote their time and efforts to profitable accounts, and not waste efforts on accounts that are not potentially profitable to the company. Sales managers need to ensure that sales representatives get the maximum potential from all their accounts, and not just meet their quotas because of the large purchases of one key buyer. Finally, sales managers need to utilize market research to ensure no potential accounts are overlooked in any given territory.[59]

Review of Territory Allocations

Once territories are established, the sales manager should review them on a quarterly basis. This will not only assist the sales manager with the sales budget, but may also indicate where realignment of territories needs to occur. Key areas to check are those territories where the salesperson consistently exceeds, or fails to make, his/her quota. When a salesperson regularly exceeds the set quota, the sales manager should ensure that this is not due to the territory potential being so large that the sales representative has to make virtually no effort to reach quota. If this is the case, the quota should be raised, or if the territory potential warrants it, a new representative should be added to the area. In the case of the salesperson who never makes quota, the sales manager must determine if this is a function of a person's lack of sales ability or of a territory with truly poor potential. In the latter situation, the representative's territory should be expanded to include new accounts.[60]

LEARNING OBJECTIVE 5

LEGAL AND ETHICAL RESPONSIBILITIES IN SELLING AND SALES MANAGEMENT

Sales Representative's Legal Responsibilities

A sales representative has certain legal obligations to his or her employer.

- The salesperson is required to obey the instructions of the company.
- The salesperson must act with "due diligence."
- The salesperson is responsible and accountable for the company's property.
- The salesperson is expected to exhibit loyalty.
- The salesperson must relay information to the company that is relevant.[61]

Failure to meet these duties subjects the salesperson to termination, forfeiture of compensation, and liability for damages to the company.

The Firm's Legal Responsibilities

At the same time, the company has legal responsibilities to the salesperson.

- The company must comply with any agreement it makes with the salesperson.
- The company must act in good faith.
- The company must reimburse the salesperson for reasonable expenses incurred while carrying out company business.
- The company is required to warn the salesperson of any risks associated with carrying out the company's business.
- The company must protect the salesperson against legal liability for any damage, loss, or injury that occurs in the course of business.[62]

Unethical/Illegal Behaviors

Selling, like numerous other professions, offers many opportunities for unethical and illegal behaviors, and unfortunately, ethical issues are often closely tied to the type of relationships which sales representatives have with their customers and sales managers.[63] Common unethical, and sometimes illegal, practices found in the sales arena include: price discrimination and unfair pricing; gifts, gratuities, and bribes; misleading advertising; unfair competitive practices; defrauding customers; unfair credit practices; and price collusion with competitive firms.[64]

Prudent Claims

Salespersons must be especially prudent in making claims to customers about the performance, capabilities, or qualities of the salespersons' products. That is, sales representatives need to guard against overzealousness in their efforts to "make the sale." They must ensure that their presentations do not contain any false or misleading statements or promises about the products under consideration. Sales misrepresentation, which has recently come under heavy scrutiny from the courts, can result in large fines for the salesperson's company, and the salesperson's expulsion from professional organizations.[65]

Codes of Conduct

Sales management can reduce unethical or illegal behaviors and the ethical conflicts often experienced by sales representatives, by communicating clear, unambiguous messages concerning appropriate behaviors in various situations likely to be encountered by salespeople. These messages should be strongly supported by company codes of conduct. Sales managers can further reduce unethical behavior by appropriately reprimanding sales representatives who conduct themselves improperly.[66]

Sexual Harassment

An issue of special concern for salespeople and sales managers is sexual harassment. Because salespeople serve as boundary spanners between their own company and the companies of their customers, they can be especially vulnerable targets for sexual harassment by people outside of their own organization (e.g., customers). That is, the relationships and social interaction necessary for the sales profession may make sales representatives especially susceptible to sexual harassment. Furthermore, sexual harassment affects both males and females.[67]

Sexual harassment may take the form of sexual favors, unwanted sexual advances, or other behaviors of a sexual nature, when submission to these behaviors becomes a condition of employment, affects employment decisions such as promotions, and substantially interferes with an individual's work performance, or creates a hostile work environment.[68] Sexual harassment results in reduced job performance, and physiological and emotional health problems for the person who is harassed, which in turn affects the bottom line of the company. Consequently, sales managers should provide training on the nature and consequences of sexual harassment to prevent sexual harassment from occurring within the company or a client's company.[69]

Sales managers must take timely action if they are aware of occurrences of sexual harassment; otherwise the sales organization can be held legally responsible.[70] If the alleged harasser is a customer, the sales manager must protect the salesperson, even if such an action means losing the customer's business.[71] Such protection may necessitate reassigning the salesperson, or providing supervision for the salesperson when he or she calls on that customer. In any event, the sales manager should not make it appear the salesperson is being punished for reporting sexual harassment.[72]

CHAPTER SUMMARY

- Personal selling involves direct communication between the sales representative and the customer.

- Personal selling is one of the most important elements of the promotion mix and a critical element of marketing, but it is also the most expensive form of promotion a firm can undertake.

- Personal selling offers several advantages: salespersons can adapt their presentations to suit the needs of individual customers, immediate feedback from the customer can be responded to during sales presentations, and the effectiveness of personal selling can be more easily measured.

- Personal selling provides exciting and challenging career opportunities with a focus on relationship selling and the development of partnerships based on the long-term satisfaction of customers' needs.

- Personal selling occurs in different environments, and each environment determines which types of salespeople are utilized. The three environments in which personal selling may occur are telemarketing, over-the-counter selling, and field selling.

- Types of salespeople include inbound or outbound telemarketers, order getters, order takers, professional salespeople, national account managers, missionary salespeople, and support salespeople.

- The sales process is composed of prospecting, preapproach and planning, approaching the client, identifying client needs, presenting the product, handling objections, gaining commitment, and following up on and keeping promises.

- Sales management requires the skills of planning, directing, controlling, and implementing the personal selling function.

- Sales managers are responsible for many tasks including recruiting, training, motivating, compensating, and evaluating the sales force, as well as organizing and allocating territories, and updating the sales force's technological capabilities.

- Sales managers must be aware of potential ethical issues with which the sales force may struggle, and set appropriate guidelines to prevent and control these issues.

KEY TERMS

Cold calling means contacting prospective customers without a prior appointment.

Consultative selling is the process of helping customers reach their strategic goals by using the products and expertise of the sales organization.

Customer-oriented means the salesperson seeks to elicit customer needs/problems and then take the necessary steps to meet those needs or solve the problem in a manner that is in the best interest of the customer.

Customer relationship management (CRM) relies on systematized processes to profile key segments so that marketing and retention strategies can be customized for these customers.

Field selling involves calling on prospective customers in either their business or home locations.

Hard sell involves trying every means to get the prospective customer to buy, regardless of whether it is in the prospect's best interest.

Job anxiety is tension caused by the pressures of the job (e.g., the salesperson must perform, often simultaneously, many tasks: meeting sales objectives, servicing old accounts and producing new accounts, developing and conducting effective sales presentations, developing product and competitor knowledge, submitting timely reports to the company, and controlling sales expenses).

Order getter is a salesperson who seeks to actively provide information to prospects, persuade prospective customers, and close sales.

Order taker is a salesperson who only processes the purchase that the customer has already selected.

Personal selling is direct oral communication designed to explain how an individual's or firm's goods, services, or ideas fit the needs of one or more prospective customers.

Qualified sales leads are potential customers who have a need for the salesperson's product, and are able to buy; that is, they have the financial means to purchase the product and the authority to make the buying decision.

Referrals are usually obtained by the salesperson asking current customers if they know of someone else, or another company, who might need the salesperson's product.

Relationship selling requires the development of a trusting partnership in which the salesperson seeks to provide long-term customer satisfaction by listening, gathering information, educating, and adding value for the customer.

Role ambiguity is anxiety caused by inadequate information about job responsibilities and performance-related goals (e.g., many organizational departments—billing, shipping, production, marketing, public relations—may influence the salesperson's activities and create uncertainty about what is expected of the salesperson).

Role conflict is the anxiety caused by conflicting job demands (e.g., the firm demands that the salesperson obtain a high price for the firm's product, while the customer demands a low price).

Sales call anxiety is a fear of negative evaluation and rejection by customers.

Suggestion selling occurs when the salesperson points out available complementary items in line with the selected item(s), in order to encourage an additional purchase.

QUESTIONS FOR DISCUSSION

1. In your day-to-day routine, identify situations in which you have had to persuade someone to accept your ideas or suggestions. What did you do? Were you successful or unsuccessful? Can you identify other ways that might have worked better?

2. As regional sales manager for a large consumer goods company, you are interested in attracting college graduates to your sales force. Develop a marketing plan to do so. Determine why students are often not interested in sales as a profession and then develop the benefits of the sales position that will overcome these objections. What steps should be taken by your company to encourage more students to seek jobs in sales?

3. Think about the best salesperson you have ever met. What did you like about this individual? What traits did he or she possess? What made this salesperson better than others you have met? Describe the worst salesperson you have ever met. What did this individual do that you disliked? What made him or her the worst?

4. There are many methods of prospecting, that is, finding qualified individuals who may become customers. A few methods are listed in this chapter; however, do a little brainstorming and see how many more methods you can identify.

5. Pretend you want to convince a friend to join a school organization with which you are affiliated. What might you say? Using the steps in the sales process, outline your presentation to your friend. Next, role-play with a classmate to see if you can present a valid argument based on the classmate's needs.

6. Assume the president of your firm, a life insurance company, still believes in pushing his agents to use the hard sell. As the sales manager, how could you convince him that relationship selling is a better way of doing business? Compare the two methods of selling and write convincing arguments to support the use of relationship selling.

7. As vice president of sales and marketing for a large hotel chain, you are reviewing the current compensation plan for the national sales force. Sales representatives are presently hired in at a low base pay of $21,000. After 3 months of training, these representatives are eligible for 20 percent commission on their sales, but their base pay disappears. Quotas are also set for each representative; those who fail to achieve at least 80 percent of their quota objective for three of four quarters are terminated. What do you think of this plan? Should you support it or should you develop a new one? If you choose to create a new compensation plan, what arguments will you make to the president of your hotel chain to persuade her to accept it?

8. As a good salesperson, you should prepare responses to objections that you expect will be forthcoming from potential customers. Two of the most common objections heard in sales are "Your price is too high," and "I need to think about it." Assume you sell cellular telephones, prepare a brief list of responses for each objection that will assist you in moving the customer toward commitment.

9. Automation and the Internet are rapidly changing the way selling is conducted. As this trend continues, do you think salespeople will be phased out of business? Why or why not?

10. A female sales representative, Carol, has been working for you less than 6 months. During this time, as part of an overall training program, you

have placed her in the field for month-long stints with different, experienced sales representatives. Last night Carol called your home and requested an immediate meeting with you. You agreed to meet with her first thing in the morning. At the meeting, she informs you that one of the sales representatives you had assigned her to work with has made sexually explicit suggestions to her. You are surprised as this particular representative, Jim, has always been one of your top salespeople, and has a reputation for being a solid family man. He is also at least 20 years older than Carol. What should you do now?

INTERNET QUESTIONS

1. Visit http://www.sellingpower.com. This Web site supports the popular sales magazine *Selling Power* and is chock full of helpful advice for experienced and novice salespeople. Scan the readers' contributions by clicking on Memorable Sale or Reader Tip. What was most interesting to you? Examine the free leads option. How might these leads help a company that was just starting out? Take time to play a sales game as part of a contest to win a trip. Also, check out these other top sales sites:

   - Sales Biz at http://www.salesbiz.com

   - Just Sell at http://www.justsell.com

   - Guerilla Marketing Online at http://www.gmarketing.com

   - Sales Dog at http://www.salesdog.com

2. Visit http://www.accessalesjobs.com, http://www.monster.com, http://www.hotjobs.com, or http://www.jobs.com, which contain hundreds of thousands of job listings for the United States and several other countries. Select sales entry jobs that may be of interest to you. What type of salesperson is needed for each job? What qualifications are being sought in job candidates? What do you need to do to prepare yourself for these employment positions?

3. Just for fun, go to the LifeSavers Candystand Web site at http://www.candystand.com. The site, which attracts more than 300,000 visitors a month, is loaded with interactive games designed for children and teenagers, yet it also serves to convey product information. Further, LifeSavers obtains valuable verbatim comments and suggestions directly from its customers through the site's What Do You Think? feature. How might a Web site for an organization use a similar feature to increase its sales?

ENDNOTES

[1] Michelle Marchetti, "What a Sales Call Costs," *Sales & Marketing Management* (September 2000): 80.

[2] Ibid., 80.

[3] Bureau of Labor Statistics, *Employment and Earnings* (January 2001).

[4] U.S. Census Bureau, *Statistical Abstract of the United States*, Labor Force Employment and Earnings; Bureau of Labor Statistics, *Employment and Earnings* (January 2001).

[5] Bureau of Labor Statistics, *Employment and Earnings*.

[6] Charles Butler, "Why the Bad Rap?" *Sales & Marketing Management* (June 1996): 58–66; Andy Cohen, "Leading Edge: Sales Strikes Out on Campus," *Sales & Marketing Management* (November 1997): 13; Earl D. Honeycutt, Jr., John B. Ford, Michael J.

Swenson, and William R. Swinyard, "Student Preferences for Sales Careers around the Pacific Rim," *Industrial Marketing Management* (January 1999): 27–36; Michelle Marchetti, "Sales Reps to Go," *Sales & Marketing Management* (January 1999): 14; Erika Rasmusson, "Does Your Sales Force Need a New Look?" *Sales & Marketing Management* (May 2000): 13.

[7] Butler, "Why the Bad Rap?" 58–66.

[8] Bureau of Labor Statistics, *Employment and Earnings*.

[9] Caryne Brown, "Have I Got a Career for You," *Black Enterprise* 23 (February 1993): 145–152.

[10] Ibid.

[11] Andy Cohen, "2001 Salary Survey" *Sales & Marketing Management* (May 2001): 47.

[12] Marchetti, "What a Sales Call Costs," 80; Nancy Smith, "Waking Up to Your Dreams," *Black Collegian* (October 2000): 61–63.

[13] Bill Seitchik, "Hired Hands: The Big Payoff," *Bobbin* 33 (June 1992): 86–89.

[14] From April 1998 study by Sales & Marketing Executives International with results compiled by the Alexander Group. Study results are available through Sales & Marketing Executives International or at http://www.smei.org.

[15] Many articles and books have been published regarding the effects of role conflict, role ambiguity, and job anxiety. See, for example, Douglas N. Behrman and William D. Perreault, Jr., "A Role Stress Model of the Performance and Satisfaction of Industrial Salespersons," *Journal of Marketing* 48 (Fall 1984): 9–21; Jean-Charles Chebat and Paul Kollias, "The Impact of Empowerment on Customer Contact Employees' Role in Service Organizations," *Journal of Service Research* (August): 66–81; Gilbert A. Churchill, Neil M. Ford, and Orville C. Walker, *Sales Force Management* (Homewood, IL: Richard D. Iwin, 1990); Theresa B. Flaherty, Robert Dahlstrom, and Steven J. Skinner, "Organizational Values and Role Stress As Determinants of Customer-Oriented Selling Performance," *Journal of Personal Selling & Sales Management* (Spring 1999): 1–18; Eli Jones, Donna Massey Kantak, Charles M. Futrell, and Mark W. Johnston, "Leader Behavior, Work-Attitudes, and Turnover of Salespeople: An Integrative Study," *Journal of Personal Selling & Sales Management* (Spring 1996): 13–23.

[16] Thomas R. Wotruba and Stephen B. Castleberry, "Job Analysis and Hiring Practices for National Account Marketing Positions," *Journal of Personal Selling & Sales Management* 13 (Summer 1993): 49–65.

[17] For more information on sales certification programs see Rolph E. Anderson "Personal Selling and Sales Management in the New Millennium" *Journal of Personal Selling & Sales Management* (Fall 1996): 17–32; Earl D. Honeycutt, Jr., Ashraf M. Attia, and Angela R. D'Auria, "Sales Certification Programs," *Journal of Personal Selling & Sales Management* (Summer 1996): 59–65.

[18] These organizations can be contacted as follows: Hospitality Sales & Marketing Association International, 1300 L Street, NW, Suite 1020, Washington, DC 20005, 202–789-0089; National Association of Sales Professionals, 8300 N. Hayden Rd., Scottsdale, AZ 85288–2458, 602–951-4311; Sales & Marketing Executives International, 5500 Interstate North Parkway #545, Atlanta, GA 30328.

[19] Sarah Lorge, "Selling 101: The Best Way to Prospect," *Sales and Marketing Management* (January 1998): 80.

[20] Ibid.

[21] Ibid.

[22] Tom Hopkins, *How to Master the Art of Selling* (New York: Warner Books, 1994).

[23] Wendy O'Connell, "The E-vangelist: Prospective Customer Relationship Management," *Sales and Marketing Management* (March 2001): 29.

[24] Brian Tracy, *Advanced Selling Strategies* (New York: Simon & Schuster, 1995).

[25] David Merrill and Roger Reid, *Personal Styles and Effective Performance* (Radnor, PA: Chilton, 1981).

[26] Richard Hanks, Vice President, Mariott Corporation, from presentation made at the Hospitality Sales and Marketing Association International Summit Conference, 3 April 1998, Anaheim, CA.

[27] Ibid.

[28] Dan Sherman, *You Can Be a Peak Performer* (San Francisco, CA: Million Dollar Press, 1996).

[29] Sarah Lorge, "How to Close the Deal," *Sales & Marketing Management* 150 (April 1998): 84.

[30] For example, see Thomas J. Stanley, *Selling to the Affluent: The Professional's Guide to Closing the Sales That Count* (New York: McGraw-Hill, 1997).

[31] Rolph Anderson, Rajiv Mehta, and James Strong, "An Empirical Investigation of Sales Management Training Programs for Sales Managers," *Journal of Personal Selling & Sales Management* 17 (Summer 1997): 53–66.

[32] Anderson, "Personal Selling and Sales Management in the New Millennium," 17–32.

[33] *Entrepreneur* Small Business Square, "*Entrepreneur*'s Special Report: Super Sales Tips," http://www.entrepreneur.com/Your_Business/YB_SegArticle/0,4621,299184,00.html.

[34] "Average Costs of Sales Training per Salesperson," *Sales & Marketing Management* 142 (February 1990): 23; Churchill, et al., *Sales Force Management*.

[35] R. R. Donnelley & Sons study cited by Anthony R. Montebello and Maureen Haga, "To Justify Training, Test, Test, Again," *Personnel Journal* (January 1994): 83–87.

[36] Malcolm Campbell, "Training on Track," *Selling Power* (March 2000): 84–86.

[37] Olivia Thetgyi, "Radical Makeovers," *Sales & Marketing Management* (April 2000): 78–88.

[38] Melinda Ligos, "Point, Click, Sell," *Sales & Marketing Management* (May 1999): 50–56.

[39] Ibid.

[40] Don Peppers and Martha Rogers, "The Money Trap," *Sales & Marketing Management* (May 1997): 58–60.

[41] James H. Drew, D. R. Mani, Andrew L. Betz, and Piew Datta, "Targeting Customers with Statistical and Data-Mining Techniques," *Journal of Service Research* (February

2001): 205–219; Owen P. Hall, Jr., "Mining the Store," *Journal of Business Strategy* (March/April 2001): 24–27.

[42] Phat X. Chiem, "Wireless CRM Starting to Support Sales Forces," *B to B*, 19 February 2001, 29.

[43] Melanie Berger, "Technology Update: On-the-Job Training," *Sales & Marketing Management* (February 1998): 122–125.

[44] Julie Hill, "E-Briefings Change Training for a Firm in Transition," *Presentations* (February 2001): 20; Ligos, "Point, Click, Sell," 50–56.

[45] Vincent Alonzo, "Motivating Matters: The Case for Trophies," *Sales & Marketing Management* (February 1998): 34–35.

[46] Chad Kaydo, "Motivating Call Center Reps," *Sales & Marketing Management* 150 (April 1998): 82; Chad Kaydo, "How to Motivate Sales Stars," *Sales & Marketing Management* (May 1994): 89–92.

[47] Julie Sturgeon, "Fun Sells," *Selling Power* (20 March 2000): 56–65.

[48] For a detailed discussion of sales quotas, see Rene Y. Darmon, "Selecting Appropriate Sales Quota Plan Structures and Quota-Setting Procedures," *Journal of Personal Selling & Sales Management* 17 (Winter 1997): 1–16; Charles M. Futrell, John E. Swan, and John T. Todd, "Job Performance Related to Management Control Systems for Pharmaceutical Salesmen," *Journal of Marketing Research* 13 (February 1976), 25–33; Leon Winer, "The Effect of Product Sales Quota on Sales Force Productivity," *Journal of Marketing Research* 10 (May 1973): 180–183; Thomas R. Wotruba, "The Effect of Goal Setting on the Performance of Independent Sales Agents in Direct Selling," *Journal of Personal Selling & Sales Management* 9 (Spring 1989): 22–29.

[49] For a review of sales coaching, see Gregory A. Rich, "The Constructs of Sales Coaching: Supervisory Feedback, Role Modeling, and Trust," *Journal of Personal Selling & Sales Management* 18 (Winter 1998): 53–63.

[50] Willem Verbeke and Richard P. Bagozzi, "Sales Call Anxiety: Exploring What It Means When Fear Rules a Sales Encounter," *Journal of Marketing* (July 2000): 88–101.

[51] Pamela Yellen, "How to Blast through Call Reluctance and Fear of Rejection," *Insurance Sales* (May/June 1998): 14–18.

[52] David J. Cocks and Dennis Gould, "Sales Compensation: A New Technology-Enabled Strategy," *Compensation & Benefits Review* (January/February 2001): 27–31.

[53] Geoffrey Brewer, "Brain Power," *Sales & Marketing Management* (May 1997): 38–48; Peppers and Rogers, "The Money Trap," 58–60.

[54] Bill Weeks, "Setting Sales Force Compensation in the Internet Age," *Compensation & Benefits Review* (March/April 2000): 25–34.

[55] For a review of evaluation factors, see Donald W. Jackson, John L. Schlacter, and William G. Wolfe, "Examining the Bases Utilized for Evaluating Salespeoples' Performance," *Journal of Personal Selling & Sales Management* 15 (Fall 1995): 57–65.

[56] Judy A. Siguaw, Sheryl E. Kimes, and Jule B. Gassenheimer, "Sales Force Productivity: The Application of Revenue Management Strategies to Sales Management," Working Paper Series 2001, Cornell University, School of Hotel Administration.

[57] Brewer, "Brain Power," 39–42, 46–48.

[58] Michelle Marchetti, "Covering Your Turf," *Sales & Marketing Management* (May 1997): 51–57.

[59] Ibid.

[60] Erika Rasmusson, "Protecting Your Turf," *Sales & Marketing Management* (March 1998): 90.

[61] Leslie M. Fine and Janice R. Franke, "Legal Aspects of Salesperson Commission Payments: Implications for the Implementation of Commission Sales Programs," *Journal of Personal Selling and Sales Management* 15 (Winter 1995): 53–68.

[62] Ibid.

[63] Edmund L. Pincoffs, *Quandaries and Virtues: Against Reductivism in Ethics* (Lawrence: University of Kansas Press, 1986).

[64] Lawrence B. Chonko, John F. Tanner Jr., and William A. Weeks, "Ethics in Salesperson Decision Making: A Synthesis of Research Approaches and an Extension of the Scenario Method," *Journal of Personal Selling and Sales Management* 16 (Winter 1996): 35–52.

[65] "Misrepresentation," *Supply Management* 3 (15 January 1998): 44; Amy S. Friedman, "Chubb among Latest to be Served with Sales Lawsuit," *National Underwriter* 100 (2 September 1996): 3, 65.

[66] Chonko et al., "Ethics in Salesperson Decision Making," 35–52.

[67] Cathy Owens Swift and Russell L. Kent, "Selling and Sales Management in Action—Sexual Harassment: Ramifications for Sales Managers," *Journal of Personal Selling and Sales Management* 14 (Winter 1994): 77–87.

[68] Leslie M. Fine, C. David Shepherd, and Susan L. Josephs, "Sexual Harassment in the Sales Force: The Customer Is NOT Always Right," *Journal of Personal Selling and Sales Management* 14 (Fall 1994): 15–30; Swift and Kent, "Selling and Sales Management in Action—Sexual Harassment," 77–87.

[69] Swift and Kent, "Selling and Sales Management in Action—Sexual Harassment," 77–87.

[70] Barbara Lindemann and David Kadue, *Sexual Harrasment in Employment Law* (Washington, DC: Bureau of National Affairs, 1992).

[71] Fine et al., "Sexual Harassment in the Sales Force," 15–30; Swift and Kent, "Selling and Sales Management in Action—Sexual Harassment," 77–87.

[72] Swift and Kent, "Selling and Sales Management in Action—Sexual Harassment," 77–87.

SELLING THE BIG APPLE: AVERO, INC.

Christine is a new sales representative for Avero, Inc., formerly called RestaurantTrade, in New York City. Founded in September 1999, Avero, Inc. is a software company with products directed toward the food service industry, primarily independent restaurateurs and their suppliers. The Web-based software consists of three functionalities. One functionality is the procurement operating system which allows restaurateurs to order and receive inventory from their suppliers in a timely and more efficient manner; the second functionality offers inventory management tools and the third functionality integrates with the restaurateur's point-of-sales system to create customized managerial/operating reports.

Christine's job is to sell the software product. However, selling such a product requires that Christine first educate the independent restaurateur on what the software does and highlight the benefits. The sales presentation must be creative because the utilization of Avero, Inc.'s software requires a cultural change in the way the food service industry operates. The norm for restaurant procurement has been for various employees of each restaurant to place their orders through phone or fax with their suppliers. With Avero, Inc.'s software, the restaurateurs order online to streamline and concentrate their ordering with a one-stop shopping solution. Further, independent restaurateurs extract information to assess their operation's performance and productivity.

Christine is also to seek out new restaurants, and attempt to persuade the restaurateurs to use her company's services. Avero, Inc. targets Zagat's top 200 restaurants, such as Tavern on the Green, the Russian Tearoom, and Gramercy Tavern, which generally generate revenues above $4 million. These restaurants are considered good prospects because they tend to have an innovative and futuristic approach toward their operation and seek to increase efficiency through technology.

Christine has learned that a local restaurateur, James Simon, is opening an Italian restaurant in Manhattan. This restaurant will bring the total number of restaurants owned by Mr. Simon's firm to three. Currently, Mr. Simon's restaurant group aggregates a limited amount of the purchasing for the three restaurants to take advantage of quantity discounts. However, because the restaurants offer different cuisines—French, American and now Italian—certain specialty items, like produce and seafood, are purchased by each individual restaurant. With so many orders being placed and reports generated from his different restaurants as well as the central office, Mr. Simon has had some difficulty in tracking inventory and productivity and ensuring that the restaurant group stays within budget.

Christine has scheduled an appointment with Mr. Simon. From the information she has gathered, Christine believes the services offered by Avero, Inc. would be perfect for Mr. Simon's small group of restaurants. Essentially, Avero, Inc.'s software would allow employees at all three restaurants to log into the system, send all the orders to a centralized purchaser, who in turn would be able to rapidly send one order to each of the respective suppliers. By using Avero Inc.'s software, the restaurants and managers could track and conduct side-by-side comparison and generate managerial reports to aid in tracking and budgeting. In addition, the system would be basically immune to all the transmission failures that can occur with fax or answering machines. Furthermore, the system would create managerial reports to aid in tracking and budgeting. Although Mr. Simon insists on maintaining tight control of his restaurants, Christine is hoping she can convince him to try Avero, Inc.'s software for a 45-day trial period.

Lior Sekler, Avero, Inc.'s senior manager of business development and finance, has helped Christine identify some facets of the business that may elicit objections from prospective clients. First, because Avero, Inc. integrates with each client's point-of-sale system, Avero, Inc. has access to the restaurant's financial information, recipes and menus, all very sensitive information. Second, the hospitality industry has traditionally focused on "high touch" not "high tech." Thus, restaurateurs like to maintain personal relationships, even with their suppliers. Finally, the software requires that whoever will be ordering be trained on the system. In restaurants, though, the manager, chef, sous chef, and steward may all place their own orders for the items they need.

Lior Sekler has asked Christine to outline her sales presentation to Mr. Simon. He is especially interested in how Christine will explain the benefits Avero, Inc. provides. Lior also wants Christine to prepare a list of possible objections that she may hear from

CHAPTER CASE

http://www.averoinc.com

http://www.zagat.com

http://web.tavernonthegreen.com

http://web.russiantearoom.com

http://www.gramercytavern.com

Mr. Simon, and for each objection, she is to prepare a suitable response. Finally, Lior asks Christine to write out several ways to ask for commitment from Mr. Simon; the goal is to get Mr. Simon's signature on a letter of intent. Lior knows from experience that actually closing the sale is often the hardest thing for new sales representatives to do. This groundwork will help ensure Christine is well prepared for her meeting with this prospect.

Discussion Questions

1. Is Mr. Simon a good prospect? Why?

2. Prepare at least three statements that tie together a feature of the service and the specific benefit it provides to Mr. Simon.

3. From the information given, what are some possible objections Christine may hear from Mr. Simon? How should Christine respond to these objections?

4. How should Christine ask for Mr. Simon's business? Provide at least two statements Christine could use to ask for commitment.

Source: Interview with Lior Sekler, Senior Manager, Business Development & Finance, *RestaurantTrade*, March 2001; and http://www.averoinc.com, accessed 9 May 2001.

PART six

Pricing

CHAPTER 14

**Pricing Strategies
and Determination**

CHAPTER fourteen

Joel E. Urbany, University of Notre Dame

Dr. Urbany earned his Ph.D. from The Ohio State University. In 1998, he was awarded *Business Week*'s Most Popular Professor Rating for the MBA program at the University of Notre Dame. In 1993, he received the Outstanding Second Year Professor award for an MBA program from the University of South Carolina, and in 1988 he won the Alfred G. Smith Award for Teaching Excellence from the University of South Carolina. Dr. Urbany is a member of the editorial review boards of the *Journal of Consumer Research* and *Marketing Letters*, and serves as an invited reviewer for several publications, including *Marketing Science, Journal of Marketing, Journal of Marketing Research*, and *Journal of Retailing*.

Dr. Urbany's research focuses on information economics, managerial decision making, and buyer behavior. He has consulted with and conducted executive education programs for a wide variety of companies, including Bayer, Flagstar, Inc., Donnelly Corp., Milliken, Marsh Supermarkets, and Ambac International.

Pricing Strategies and Determination

Dell Computer Corporation is world-renowned for its business model and is creating a pricing firestorm in the personal computer industry.[1]

> *Dell's strategy is collapsing profit margins throughout the PC market, a dire development for rivals who can't keep up. Dell is pricing its machines not so much like lucrative hightech products, but more like airline tickets and other low-margin commodities.* (Wall Street Journal, *8 June 2001*)

Since early 2001, Dell has begun reducing prices by as much as 20 percent, aiming to take sales away from competitors. Results for Dell's aggressive and flexible pricing strategy have been remarkable. For example, in what had been a soft market, shipments for the industry grew 852,000 units to 31.6 million in the first quarter of 2001. Dell's shipments grew *957,000 units*. How could Dell's sales go up by *more than* the total of the industry's sales? The answer is that not only did Dell account for most of the new sales in the market, it also took market share from its competitors. Dell's U.S. market share in 2001 was 24.5 percent, up from 6.8 percent in 1996. Overall growth in the combined PC market has slowed substantially, but in 2001 Dell was poised to earn over $1.7 billion in 2001, accounting for almost every dollar of profit among makers of Windows-based PCs. Dell has expanded its selling effort into the consumer market with its ad campaign featuring the likable retail dude "Steven," but the aggressive pricing strategy has been responsible for the bulk of its share gains.

Dell's model is a "direct sales" model in which business customers or consumers order their computers directly from the company via catalogs, telephone, or the Web. The company is an assembler. It keeps a small inventory of component parts but relies on close relationships with suppliers who provide real-time order-supply capability. Its expertise is in developing systems and technology that allow it to take a customer's order and assemble and ship a made-to-spec product within a few days. (See the Chapter Case in Chapter 10 for more detail on this background.)

What are the key elements of Dell's business model and what do they have to do with pricing? There are three key themes: cost, flexibility, and competitive position.

Cost. Dell's business model affords it the lowest cost position in the market. One recent story holds that Michael Dell gave a hard time to a supplier who brought cinnamon rolls to a meeting with Dell employees, telling the supplier that he ought to save the money to keep his own prices down. The direct sales model eliminates the costs of dealing with retailers and is based on a quick turnover of inventory. Dell's inventory turns over 79.7 times per year, compared to 23.9 for Compaq, 30.5 for Gateway, and 8.6 for Hewlett-Packard. The *Wall Street Journal* reports that Dell's overhead costs were just 11.5 percent of every sales dollar, versus an average of 19.8 for these other competitors. Dell has no retailers to deal with and has developed a forecasting system and information-sharing routines (with suppliers) that allow the company to carefully focus on current and future costs. The company constantly directs everyone's attention on driving down costs to allow lower prices. Dell can immediately capitalize on cost savings and pass them on to its customers. In addition, the pricing gap between Intel's preferred customers and its channel customers has grown. Although it has been the norm for chip makers to offer bigger discounts to their high-volume customers, the gap was even wider than usual in 2001.

Flexibility. The real-time cost information systems that the company has developed, along with its close supplier relationships, has produced great flexibility in its ability to adjust prices in response to changes in costs and customer demand. The company is pushing hard to adapt quickly to changes in costs, passing them along in the form of lower prices to customers. In fact, prices are so flexible that one can often find the same product at different prices within Dell's own Web site! One story holds that a Dell telephone sales representative actually quoted a PC price $50 lower than the price which had been advertised in the *New York Times* that same morning.

Competitive Position: Standing in the Deep Water. Dell is the industry's cost leader. The innovative dimensions of its business model are the source of this strong competitive position. The cost leader position creates a clear advantage—you can withstand a price war longer than your competitors because you have a lower cost floor. A simple analogy illustrates this. If a price war is analogous to wading out into the deep end of the pool, then Dell can hold its head out of the water the longest, while competitors are likely to run out of oxygen. Dell maintained the price pressure through all of 2001. By the end of the year, Dell's average PC price had fallen $50 in less than 3 months.

(Continued)

After you have completed this chapter, you should be able to:

1. Define price and explain why cost-based pricing methods are used so widely, despite their drawbacks.
2. Incorporate demand considerations into pricing and determine a short-term profit-maximizing price.
3. Identify and explain strategic drivers of prices.
4. Explain and evaluate reasons why base prices change over time in both business and consumer markets.
5. Explain basic legal and ethical constraints on pricing behavior.

Strategy and Pricing

The developing industry wisdom is that the personal computer industry is taking on the classic characteristics of a mature business. The market, which grew at 15 percent a year for much of the 1990s, has now flattened out. Customers are less motivated to replace machines, most significantly because they see what the analysts see—that the market has become increasingly "commoditized." As J. William Gurley notes in *Fortune:* "'commodity' is typically used to describe a product . . . with no differentiation from the competition's, leaving price as the sole factor in the customer's purchase decision." PC products have become increasingly similar over time, as the industry has reduced research and development expenditures over the past decade. Deloitte Consulting reports that that industry spent half as much on research and development (as a percentage of sales) as it did 10 years ago.

Why has the industry invested less in innovation? The answer is simple: Dell. In a commodity market, the cost leader pushes relentlessly on price. Dell's emphasis on pricing has forced competitors to pay attention to prices, either by attempting to copy Dell's business model or by continually reducing costs out of their manufacturing systems. As a result, the focus has been less on creating new personal computing innovations and more on building cost- and price-competitive matching. In late 2000, then, Dell began slashing prices as the market was showing significant signs of sales growth decline. HP, Compaq, and Gateway all lost market share in the year ending 30 September 2001. In contrast, Dell's market share rose by almost one-third.

Conventional Wisdom. The price-cutting strategy flies in the face of conventional wisdom about how a firm should compete in a mature market. Dell has been called "irrational" by analysts and competitors. Yet, is there a sneaky logic to this strategy? First, in recessionary times, customers (particularly business customers), respond to better economic value that comes in the form of lower prices. Second, the tough economy makes it more difficult for Dell's competitors to react. Third, as noted, Dell's cost leadership position makes it very difficult for competitors to survive a price war if they do choose to follow.

In all, Dell's current pricing strategy reflects a focus on sound business fundamentals: a lower cost basis driven by flexibility based upon good information, attention to market demand, and close relationships with suppliers, resulting in a strong, unique competitive position.

Of the traditional marketing mix variables, the development of effective pricing strategies remains perhaps the most elusive. Consider the following sample of opinions expressed about pricing practices over the last 50 years:

> . . . pricing policy is the last stronghold of medievalism in modern management. . . . [Pricing] is still largely intuitive and even mystical in the sense that the intuition is often the province of the big boss.[2]

> . . . for marketers of industrial goods and construction companies, pricing is the single judgment that translates potential business into reality. Yet pricing is the least rational of all decisions made in this specialized field.[3]

> . . . pricing is approached in Britain like Russian roulette to be indulged in mainly by those contemplating suicide.[4]

> Perhaps it is reasonable that marketers have only recently begun to focus seriously on effective pricing. Only after managers have mastered the techniques of creating value do the techniques of capturing value become important.[5]

Pricing decisions are complex, driven by many different factors. What factors influenced Dell to cut prices? They include the shrinking of the overall PC market, a desire to exploit and reinforce its strong cost leadership position, the increasing commodity-status of personal computers, and a declining economy. In this chapter, we explore the complex array of factors that influence pricing decisions and consider the role of price in a company's marketing mix. The first half of the chapter examines the basics behind setting base prices, the usual approaches that firms take, and how those approaches can be improved. The second half focuses on the factors that determine why base prices change over time. We begin, though, with a definition of price.

WHAT IS PRICE? WHAT DETERMINES BASE PRICE?

So what is **price**? It is not just the number on the price tag in the store (although that is clearly what most customers think of). In general terms, any exchange involves a price, and it is not always monetary. As such, price can be or incorporate rent, tuition, wages, salary, fees, fare, lease payment, interest rate, or time donated. In short, price is an exchange rate—it defines the sacrifice that one party pays another to receive something in exchange.[6] Our specific focus will be on *price as a monetary value charged by an organization for the sales of its products.* In this chapter, we will distinguish between two general categories of pricing decisions: (1) setting a base price for a product, and (2) making adjustments to that product's price over time (see Figure 14.1).

Classic economics holds some important insights about how prices should be determined. Figure 14.2 illustrates simple tools that help explain the interaction between buyer and seller behavior. Consider a new college student named Andrew who is thinking about the purchase of one or more pairs of jeans for the coming school year. Figure 14.2 shows varying prices on the vertical axis and quantities on the horizontal axis. The curve labeled D illustrates the number of pairs of jeans Andrew is willing to purchase at a given price. So, at a price of $50, he would be willing to buy 3 pairs. If the jeans cost $75, he is only willing to buy 2 pairs. (This willingness to buy is determined by many factors, including Andrew's income and tastes, and the cost of other types of clothing.) However, market prices are determined by both the buyer's choice behavior and the seller's willingness to supply the product. The curve labeled S in Figure 14.2 captures this. It's called a supply curve and it indicates how many pairs of jeans a seller (say, Levi's) would be willing to supply at a given price. Over time, the market price would be determined by the intersection of supply and demand. In this case, demand and supply are matched up at $50.[7]

Cost-Plus Pricing: The Natural (but Sometimes Wrong) Way to Set Base Prices

There are many factors that influence pricing decisions, but the one that businesspeople most naturally think about is cost. Research conducted on pricing in large corporations concluded:

> . . . *the easiest way to think about a price is first to think like an accountant: price equals costs plus overhead plus a fair profit.* Cost-plus pricing, *furthermore, is a useful ritual, with great public-relations advantages . . . a smart, prudent businessman . . . admits only to wanting a "fair" return.*[8]

LEARNING OBJECTIVE **1**

Price
is some unit of value given up by one party in return for something from another party.

http://www.levi.com

Basic Pricing Decisions and Primary Driver: Cost	**Figure 14.1**

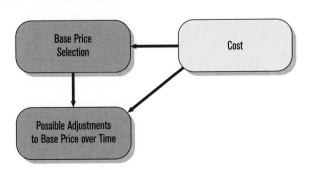

Figure 14.2   Demand and Supply Curves: Jeans

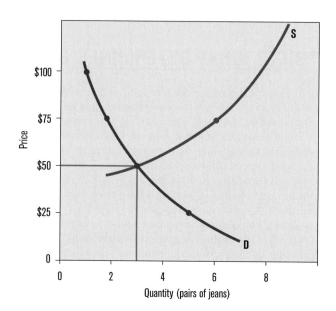

It is no surprise that costs come into play quite significantly in setting *base prices*. Managers are generally (although not always) aware of their costs of doing business. As a result, the practice of setting prices based on costs has become firmly entrenched in the American marketplace. Both early and fairly recent studies of managerial pricing have found cost to be a dominant consideration in pricing decisions.[9] Below, we illustrate cost-plus pricing and evaluate its advantages and drawbacks. We then use the following example as a springboard to discuss other pricing methods and factors that influence pricing.

The Symphony

Let's say you're a manager for a symphony orchestra.[10] The symphony season is just starting, and you've been hired as marketing director. One of your early assignments is to figure out a ticket price for a new concert series in the coming months. You have information about demand in the past (for several programs, the symphony sold about 950 of its 1,100 seats). In addition, the following costs have been identified:

Fixed Overhead	$1,500
Rehearsal Costs	$4,500
Performance Costs	$2,000
Variable Costs per Patron (programs, tickets)	$1 per patron

Note that some of these costs are fixed and some are variable. *Fixed costs* are costs that have no relationship to volume. They are, by definition, fixed. They do not change if more customers come to the show. The first three cost categories in our example (fixed overhead, rehearsal costs, and performance costs), totaling $8,000, are all fixed. *Variable costs,* on the other hand, are costs that are incurred for each customer. In this case, they are fairly small—only $1 per customer for tickets and programs.

To determine a price per patron using a cost-plus rule, you need to evenly spread all costs over each patron. Again, past history suggests an average attendance of 950 people. *Average total cost* can be calculated simply by adding an "average" fixed cost figure to variable cost.

$$\text{Average Total Cost} = \text{Variable Cost} + \frac{\text{Fixed Cost}}{\text{Unit Sales}}$$

In the current case, average total cost would be:

$$\$1 + \frac{(\$1,500 + 4,500 + 2,000)}{950} = \$9.42$$

So, for every "unit" you sell (in this case, each of the 950 seats), the orchestra incurs a cost of $9.42, accounting for both fixed and variable costs.

Cost-Based Pricing Approaches

Many companies use one of two common approaches to setting prices based upon cost. One is to use a standard rule of thumb markup. The second is to build up the price by adding together both cost per unit and desired profit.

Standard Markup. Let's say that the orchestra has always used a rule of thumb in the past: mark up costs by 20 percent. This is effectively saying that, "for every unit we sell, we want 20 percent of the selling price to represent profit—an extra incremental profit over and above costs." The price can be easily calculated as follows:

$$\text{Selling Price} = \frac{\text{Unit Cost}}{(1 - \text{Markup \%})} = \frac{\$9.42}{(1 - .20)} = 11.775$$

So, you might charge a price of $11.75 (rounded off to the nearest quarter). Keep in mind that all this means is the profit we get from each ticket ($11.75 − $9.42 = $2.33) is 20 percent of the selling price ($2.33 ÷ $11.75). In fact, the 20 percent in this case refers to *markup on retail price* (it's simply the "markup" as a percentage of the retail price). For the sake of clarity, it is important to distinguish this from *markup on cost*. You may have heard at times that the common rule for some retailers is to determine the retail price by "doubling costs" (i.e., multiply them by 2). This reflects a simple 100 percent markup *on cost*. In the orchestra example, such a 100 percent markup rule would produce a ticket price of $18.84. Using the example we've already calculated—a retail ticket price of

$11.75—we calculate the markup on cost to be 24.7 percent (i.e., $2.33 ÷ $9.42 = 24.7 percent).

Target Return Pricing. A similar approach would be for the orchestra to add a target profit to the unit cost figure (to cover both cost and profit):

$$\text{Selling Price} = \text{Unit Cost} + \text{Desired Profit per Unit}$$

The desired profit figure could come from a couple of places. First, there may be a rule of thumb that "we'd like to earn $2 a head coming in" (which would make the price $9.42 + $2.00 = $11.42). Alternatively, the desired profit per unit may be determined based on the company's desired return on investment.[11]

Let's say you apply the standard markup (as many retailers do, for example), and you set your price at $11.75. Have you done a good job? Well, yes and no.

- You have been smart in accounting for your costs, both fixed and variable.
- The pricing method is fair—it is steeped in tradition and is a widely accepted business practice.

For these reasons, no one could argue with your approach. However, there are some drawbacks:

- The fundamental flaw of this approach to pricing is that it *ignores demand.* This approach assumes a certain demand level as given, independent of price. This, as we shall see, is at odds with one of the most fundamental relationships in all of business: quantity sold is a function of price. Generally speaking, as price goes up, demand goes down (and vice versa). Yet, you're assuming that 950 seats will be sold no matter what the price! Note what happens if different demand levels are assumed. The average unit cost would be much higher if we assumed sales of only 850 tickets (in fact, in this case, average unit cost would be $1 + [$8,000 ÷ 850] = $10.41 rather than $9.42). This means that the $11.75 price would not be high enough to produce the 20 percent profit markup you desired. Alternatively, if ticket sales were 1,050, your unit cost would actually end up being lower ($1 + [$8,000 ÷ 1,050] = $8.62), and your price could be lower than $11.75 and still produce the desired markup return on sales. In the marketplace, because price influences customer perception of value, demand is a function of price. In other words, price determines demand, not the other way around.
- In addition, a cost-plus pricing rule *fails to account for competition.* Competitors' prices have a significant impact on sales and profit outcomes as well, because consumers make choices from competitive sets of alternatives rather than a single one. So, for example, if a new symphony was started in a nearby city, it might well compete for the dollars that patrons might normally spend on our symphony. As such, this would have implications for how high we set our price relative to competing alternatives. In fact, failing to consider these issues can have devastating consequences. Wang Laboratory developed and introduced the world's first word-processing software in 1976. The product was a great success and Wang came to dominate the market. Competition eventually increased and growth slowed, yet the company did not bring down prices to maintain the value position of its software. The reason? Their pricing was basically cost-driven. Wang managers constantly recalculated unit costs and prices to capture increasing overhead cost allocations. Prices remained high and customers made their way to less expensive alternatives.[12]

As you can see, cost-plus pricing takes into account neither price sensitivity nor competition, both of which are essential considerations in setting prices effectively. Further, as noted earlier, cost-plus pricing generally involves allocating fixed costs on a per-unit basis—that is, treating them as variable costs—even though fixed costs do not change with the number of units sold.

The next sections provide some detail on the factors that can and should be considered in pricing. They review additional techniques and considerations for setting an initial base price for a product. We discuss next the most fundamental of all pricing concepts.

DEMAND CONSIDERATIONS: THE RELATIONSHIP BETWEEN PRICE AND SALES

Our price of $11.75 is designed to cover average total costs for the projected 950 seats sold, and produce a 20 percent profit markup on costs. Yet, as discussed earlier, in setting price this way you have failed to consider one of the fundamental principles of economics—that price causes demand, not the other way around. If your price is lower, demand usually is higher, and vice versa. Economists have made this concrete for us by articulating a simple concept called **elasticity of demand**, which helps us better understand the relationship between price and sales.

Elasticity of demand
is the relationship between changes in price and quantity sold.

As will soon be discussed, elasticity of demand may be difficult to estimate. However, first few steps of thinking in terms of market response are very important and always helpful, even without precise knowledge of it. In fact, let's start with the assumption that you know very little about how much demand you'll get at different prices. Even under these circumstances, there is one brief analysis you can and should do before anything else, because it will help you frame good questions about potential demand. This is break-even analysis.

Break-Even Analysis

Break-even analysis (BEA) is a standard analysis technique that should be performed for nearly every business decision, particularly those for new products. BEA doesn't tell you what your demand will be at a given price point, but it does tell the very important tale of what sales level you *need* for a particular price to be profitable. The key question in this analysis is "at a price of $11.75, how many units (seats) do we need to sell to break even?"

The calculation for the **break-even point** is straightforward:

Break-even point
literally means "to have zero profit." It is that point at which total cost and total revenue are equal.

$$\text{Break-Even Sales} = \frac{\text{Fixed Costs}}{\text{Selling Price} - \text{Variable Costs}}$$

In the BEA, we treat fixed and variable costs separately (as we generally should). The numerator of the equation includes all fixed costs, which we have to pay regardless of how many seats we fill. In the denominator, we have our *contribution margin*. For each seat, we make $11.75 – $1.00 = $10.75, which captures the contribution of each ticket sold to covering fixed costs and producing a profit. At the $11.75 price, our break-even sales are:

$$\text{Break-Even Sales} = \$8,000 \div (\$11.75 - \$1.00) = 744.2 \text{ tickets}$$

If we sell 745 tickets at a price of $11.75, we will just break even—that is, our total costs will equal our total revenue. Note that we can vary price and see how BE sales change. In Table 14.1, the break-even sales figures at various prices appear in column E. If we go with the highest price under consideration ($15), we need to sell 571 seats at a minimum—just to have zero profit at the end. At $8 per ticket, you would have to sell more seats than the auditorium's capacity (which is 1,100) just to break even. You may have anticipated the next step. Since we clearly do not want to just break even, how can we account for profit in this analysis? Let's say the symphony board views this series as the group's big moneymaker and would like to bring in a profit of $2,000 per show. How many tickets do you have to sell at each price to cover fixed costs and produce a $2,000 profit? To determine this, you simply add the $2,000 profit figure to the fixed costs and again divide by the contribution margin. So, at a price of $10, you would need to have "standing room only" (sales of 1,111 seats) to cover fixed cost and meet the profit goal, while at a price of $11.00, you would need to sell 1,000 seats.

Some very important information emerges from the figures in column G of Table 14.1. Again, since the auditorium has only 1,100 seats, it is clear that a price of $10 or less is not feasible. The price of $11.75 determined earlier could cover fixed costs and produce the desired total profit if 930 tickets can be sold ($10,000 ÷ [$11.75 – $1.00]). At a $15 price, we would need to sell 714 tickets to meet the profit objective.

Table 14.1				Break-Even Analysis for the Symphony		
A	**B**	**C**	**D**	**E**	**F**	**G**
Price	Variable Cost	Contribution Margin	Fixed Costs	Units Needed to Break Even	Fixed Costs plus $2,000 Profit Goal	Units Needed to Cover FC and Profit Goal
$ 8	1	7	$8,000	**1,143**	$10,000	**1,429**
$ 9	1	8	$8,000	**1,000**	$10,000	**1,250**
$10	1	9	$8,000	**889**	$10,000	**1,111**
$11	1	10	$8,000	**800**	$10,000	**1,000**
$12	1	11	$8,000	**727**	$10,000	**909**
$13	1	12	$8,000	**667**	$10,000	**833**
$14	1	13	$8,000	**615**	$10,000	**769**
$15	1	14	$8,000	**571**	$10,000	**714**

At this point, we simply know what sales will be required at each price to cover costs and meet the profit objective. But the analysis also forces us to face an extremely important question: For a given price, can we sell the requisite number of tickets? (Can we sell at least 933 tickets at a price of $11.75?) In other words, what will demand be at each price point? To consider this question in more detail, let's take a short side road here and introduce the concepts of the demand schedule and elasticity of demand.

The Demand Schedule

Demand schedules provide a systematic look at the relationship between price and quantity sold.

Generally, we know that as price goes up, fewer people will buy a product. As price goes down, the opposite usually happens. Tables 14.2, 14.3, and 14.4 present hypothetical **demand schedules** for wheat, automobiles (back in the Model T era), and movies.[13] The first three columns of each of these tables show what quantity (B) is projected to be sold at each price (A), and then the resulting total revenue (C = A * B). Figures 14.3, 14.4, and 14.5 graphically depict the three demand schedules. Consider the demand schedule for wheat (Table 14.2). If wheat is priced at $5, 9 million bushels per month will be demanded by customers. If the price drops to $4, demand jumps up, but only to 10 million bushels and total revenue actually drops. Total revenue drops for every lower price point in this table.

In contrast, Table 14.3 illustrates Henry Ford's belief that consumers would be very responsive to the lowering of automobile prices. Dropping price from $2,500 to $2,000 increases sales by a factor of six (10,000 cars demanded jumps to 60,000). For nearly every price point reduction, the total revenue in column C increases.

Finally, Table 14.4 indicates that the demand for movies changes at the exact same rate as does price. When this happens, total revenue is the same regardless of the price charged.

Elasticity of Demand

Economists quantify the relationship between price and quantity sold using a concept called elasticity. The *elasticity coefficient* is simply the absolute value of the percentage change in quantity divided by the percentage change in price.

$$\text{Elasticity Coefficient } E = \frac{\text{Percentage Change in Q}}{\text{Percentage Change in P}}$$

Inelastic demand is reflected by an elasticity coefficient of less than 1. Take a look again at Table 14.2. Columns D, E, and F calculate these percentage changes (using the higher

			Table 14.2		
Demand Schedule for Wheat					

A	B	C	D	E	F
Price per Bushel	**Quantity Demanded (million bushels per month)**	**Total Revenue (mil. \$) (A * B)**	**Percentage Change in Price**	**Percentage Change in Quantity**	**Elasticity (E)**
\$1	20	\$20	−50.0%	25.0%	−0.5
\$2	15	\$30	−33.3%	20.0%	−0.6
\$3	12	\$36	−25.0%	16.7%	−0.7
\$4	10	\$40	−20.0%	10.0%	−0.5
\$5	9	\$45	0	0	0

Note: In calculating the percentage changes, we use the bigger number of the pair as the "base." Alternatively, the base could be the average of the two Ps or the two Qs being compared. This produces similar results.

	Figure 14.3
Demand Curve for Wheat	

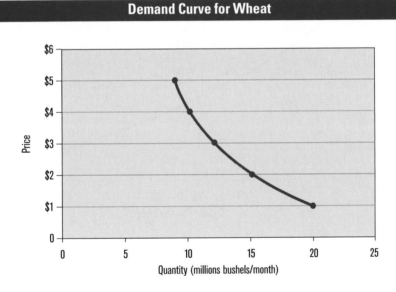

price point as the base for the calculations[14]) as well as the elasticity. The demand for wheat is inelastic; that is, the absolute values of the elasticity coefficients are less than 1. If the price of wheat were to drop, total revenue would drop. Note that the other side of this equation is that if price increases from a market price of \$1, for example, then total revenue increases. If you're looking only at total revenue, then *higher prices are favored when demand is inelastic.*

Elastic demand is reflected by an elasticity coefficient of greater than 1. Demand is elastic in the automobile example for price changes, except the change from \$1,000 to \$500 (Table 14.3). Generally speaking, *when demand is elastic, lower prices are favored* (again, when considering total revenue). An excellent current day illustration of highly elastic demand is seen in the number of new customers entering the computer market with the advent of sub-\$1,000 personal computers. By the end of 1997, sub-\$1,000 PCs accounted for 30 percent of all U.S. computer sales, and one-third of those sales were to consumers who had never purchased a PC before.[15]

Table 14.3		Demand Schedule for Model T Automobiles				
A	**B**	**C**	**D**	**E**	**F**	
Price per Auto	**Quantity Demanded (thousands per year)**	**Total Revenue (A * B)**	**Percentage Change in Price**	**Percentage Change in Quantity**	**Elasticity (E)**	
$500	300	$150,000	−50.0%	33.3%	−0.7
$1,000	200	$200,000	−33.3%	40.0%	−1.2
$1,500	120	$180,000	−25.0%	50.0%	−2.0
$2,000	60	$120,000	−20.0%	83.3%	−4.2
$2,500	10	$25,000	0	0	0

Figure 14.4	Demand Curve for Model T Automobiles

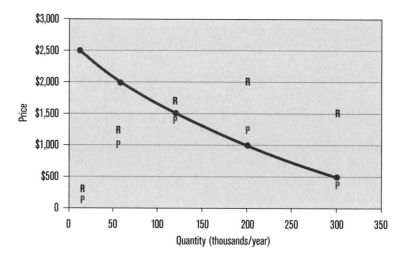

NOTES:
Add (00) to the y axis for total and total contribution.
R = Total revenue.
P = Total Contribution (profit before fixed costs).

Unitary elasticity means that the coefficient is exactly equal to 1. Table 14.4 shows that movies have unitary elasticity. In these cases, quantity demands changes at the same rate as does price.

Profit Maximization

Given the information contained in a demand curve, a firm can determine the *profit-maximizing price* by simply calculating the profit at each price point and determining which price produces the highest profit. To illustrate, see Table 14.5, which extends the Model T example from Table 14.2 by factoring in a variable cost per car of $350. With this additional information, the price that produces the maximum profit can be easily determined by identifying which price produces the largest *total contribution* (which equals [column C] Total Revenue minus [column D] Total Variable Cost). Given this demand schedule, the company would maximize profit for the car by pricing it at $1,500,

| | | Demand Schedule for Movies | | | | Table 14.4 |

A	B	C	D	E	F
Price per Ticket	Quantity Demanded per Day	Total Revenue per Day (A * B)	Percentage Change in Price	Percentage Change in Quantity	Elasticity (E)
$1	1,200	$1,200	−50.0%	50.0%	−1.0
$2	600	$1,200	−33.3%	33.3%	−1.0
$3	400	$1,200	−25.0%	25.0%	−1.0
$4	300	$1,200	−20.0%	20.0%	−1.0
$5	240	$1,200	0	0	0

| Demand Curve for Movies | Figure 14.5 |

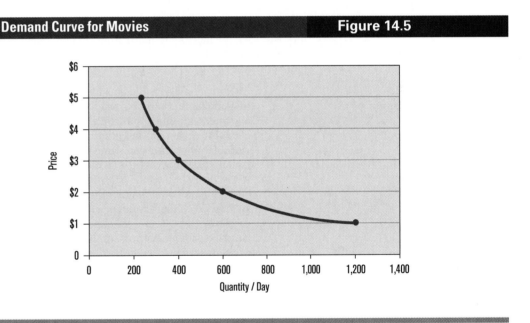

which produces a total contribution of $138,000.[16] You can verify this by looking at **marginal revenue** and **marginal cost** (columns F and G in Table 14.5). These reflect the changes in total revenue and total cost from price to price. Lowering price from $2,500 to $2,000 is good: revenue jumps $95,000 while costs jump only $17,500—marginal revenue (MR) exceeds marginal cost (MC). The same goes for dropping price from $2,000 to $1,500 (MR = $60,000, MC = $21,000). But, when you drop to a price of $1,000, the marginal revenue generated is just $20,000, and is exceeded by marginal cost ($28,000), indicating that this would not be a profitable move. Figure 14.4 provides a graphic representation of total revenue (R) and total contribution (P), illustrating that while a price of $2,000 produces maximum revenue, $1,500 produces the most profit.

If calculating maximum profit is this easy, why don't more companies set prices this way? In reality, other pricing goals—like meeting competition or achieving market share goals (discussed later)—tend to be used more frequently than profit maximization. This is partly because demand curves are difficult to estimate. While managers are likely to apply their own intuitive sense of market price response in their pricing, it is rare that

Marginal revenues
are the change in a firm's total revenue per-unit change in its sales level.

Marginal costs
are the change in a firm's total costs per-unit change in its output level.

Table 14.5			Calculating Maximum Profits for the Model T			
A	**B**	**C**	**D**	**E**	**F**	**G**
Price per Auto	Quantity Demanded (thousands per year)	Total Revenue (A * B)	Total Variable Cost (B * $350)	Total Contribution	Marginal Revenue	Marginal Cost
$500	300	$150,000	$105,000	$45,000	($50,000)	$35,000
$1,000	200	$200,000	$70,000	$130,000	$20,000	$28,000
$1,500	120	$180,000	$42,000	$138,000	$60,000	$21,000
$2,000	60	$120,000	$21,000	$99,000	$95,000	$17,500
$2,500	10	$25,000	$3,500	$21,500	0	0

Variable cost: $350

they will have the nice, neat information about demand provided in Table 14.2. There are so many variables that affect sales in a given market that isolating the effect of price is quite difficult. However, it can be done several ways:

1. *Analytic Modeling.* The most sophisticated approach is to develop a statistical model that predicts sales based on historical observations of sales, and such variables as the firm's price, advertising, and sales force levels, competitive tactics, and other variables that may influence demand (e.g., variables capturing economic conditions). This approach allows one to isolate the effect of price on demand.
2. *Experiments.* Firms might run experiments where they change prices in certain markets but not in others, allowing them to see more precisely how such price changes influence sales.
3. *Customer Surveys.* Another approach to identifying a demand curve is to survey customers or present them with purchase scenarios in which they evaluate the product and indicate their intention to purchase at various prices. One has to be careful about interpreting these results, as customers may overstate intentions. However, such an approach can be helpful in estimating price response.[17]
4. *Managerial Judgment.* Often, managers have good insight into sales response in a market. Although there may be some error in assessment, obtaining consensus estimates of demand across several managers who are familiar with a market can provide a useful picture of the demand curve.

Let's return to our symphony pricing problem. Assume that you ask a convenience sample of target symphony customers to evaluate the likelihood that they would go to the symphony at different prices. You present the symphony as an alternative against other activities (e.g., baseball games, going out to eat, going to the art museum, going to a movie). Projecting your results to the larger population, you are able to estimate demand at each price point (see Table 14.6, columns A and B).

Note that we have dropped the prices under $11 from consideration because the break-even analysis showed them to be infeasible. You ask a few local experts in the industry to look your estimates over, and everyone concurs that they are reasonable. The elasticities calculated between price points (columns C–E in Table 14.6) clearly indicate that demand is inelastic (i.e., since the absolute value of all of the elasticity coefficients are less than 1). As in the wheat example earlier, this suggests that customers are not highly responsive to price. Demand does not drop off significantly when price is raised, nor does it increase substantially when price is cut. Note that total revenue only drops as you go from higher to lower prices.

					Table 14.6

Elasticity and Total Revenue: Symphony Problem

A	B	C	D	E	F
Price	Estimated Demand	Percent Change in Price*	Percent Change in Quantity	Elasticity	Total Revenue (A * B)
$11	1,129	−8.3%	2.6%	−0.31	$12,419
$12	1,100	−7.7%	3.2%	−0.41	$13,200
$13	1,065	−7.1%	5.0%	−0.70	$13,845
$14	1,012	−6.7%	3.9%	−0.58	$14,168
$15	973	0	0	0	$14,595

*Uses the higher price numbers as base for calculating percentage changes.

However, we are not seeking to maximize total revenue. Instead we are seeking to maximize profit. As you know, variable cost is $1.00 and fixed costs are $8,000. What price produces the maximum profit? (Don't read ahead or look at Table 14.7 until you figure this out.)

The answer, perhaps not surprisingly, is the highest price ($15), which produces a total contribution of $13,622 compared to the next highest, $13,156, when price is $14 (see column E of Table 14.7). The table also provides fixed costs in column F and a total profit calculation in column G to confirm that the same price point ($15) is selected as profit-maximizing whether fixed costs are included or not. Incorporating fixed costs here is equivalent to subtracting a constant, which illustrates why fixed costs are not relevant to determining the profit-maximizing price in this example.

So, the profit-maximizing approach would have you setting price at $15,[18] selling approximately 975 tickets, and earning substantially more than the $2,000 profit goal.

How do you like the $15 price? Some further consideration illustrates why pricing is a little bit science and a little bit art. There actually are other considerations to be taken into account, which suggest that the short-term profit-maximizing price would not be the "right" price. In this case, the issue is auditorium capacity. The symphony board may be willing to give up some profit (as long as we've reached the $2,000 goal) in order to fill up the auditorium. Filling up the auditorium would be a public relations victory, allowing us to promote the fact that the performances are "sold out" and improving the symphony's outcomes in the longer term. Hence, other strategic considerations or objectives come into play. Figure 14.6 displays a larger set of factors, which may influence the selection of a base price. We examine these factors next.

						Table 14.7

Total Contribution and Total Profit: Symphony Problem

A	B	C	D	E	F	G
Price	Estimated Demand	Total Revenue (A * B)	Total Variable Cost (B * $1)	Total Contribution	Fixed Costs	Total Profit
$11	1,129	$12,419	$1,129	$11,290	$8,000	$3,290
$12	1,100	$13,200	$1,100	$12,100	$8,000	$4,100
$13	1,065	$13,845	$1,065	$12,780	$8,000	$4,780
$14	1,012	$14,168	$1,012	$13,156	$8,000	$5,156
$15	973	$14,595	$973	$13,622	$8,000	$5,622

Variable Cost: $1.00

| Figure 14.6 | Determinants of Price |

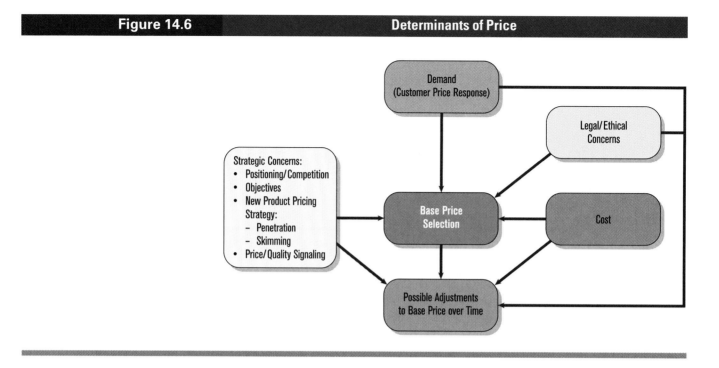

PRICING STRATEGIES: PRICE DRIVERS

Important strategic factors that play a role in setting base prices include positioning strategy, objectives, specific new product pricing strategies, and price-quality inferences.

Positioning Strategy/Competition

Envision two different home furnishing stores in Atchison, Kansas (population 11,000). One store has reasonably inexpensive household goods (e.g., dishes, glasses, towels, bedding, and decorating items) and small pieces of furniture, many from national manufacturers. The store is neat and clean. It has something of a "warehouse" feel to it, with wire shelving and wide aisles and bright lighting. Employees make a little above minimum wage, and management makes every effort to keep costs low to maintain low prices to consumers. In contrast, consider another local store called Neil Hill's, which is set in a turn-of-the-century bank building in the downtown area and is run by an entrepreneur named Mary Carol Garrity. Inside, the store looks like a home, with high walls and many different rooms with carpeted floors. It doesn't have shelves. Instead, it has merchandise hanging from walls and ceilings, ranging from $2 candle holders to $7,000 French antiques. It sells the same kinds of products as the first store (home furnishings), but the merchandise is all very unique. Products come from large city markets and are hand-selected by the owner, who has an unusual knack for being able to identify and buy merchandise that will become popular before it becomes trendy. She changes the merchandise frequently, and regularly redecorates the store, often repainting the walls and changing the look of every room. The owner greets many of her customers by name, and works closely with them (many times after hours) on decorating ideas. Incredibly, 95 percent of this store's sales are made to people who live more than 50 miles away, primarily in Kansas City.

The two stores represent opposite ends of a *competitive strategy positioning continuum* anchored by "low cost leadership" on one end and "differentiation" on the other.[19] The first store might be any local, regional, or national competitor that competes by maintaining very low costs of purchasing and operation. Neil Hill's, however, seeks to create an absolutely unique (if not peculiar) shopping experience for customers. As a result, the two stores have very different pricing policies. The first store would likely attempt to

maintain everyday low prices and have frequent sales. Neil Hill's, on the other hand, would have much higher prices, in part, because the cost of its unique merchandise is higher, but also because customers are far less sensitive to price than they would be at the more mundane price-oriented store.[20] One can find this strategic distinction between brands in almost any product category (e.g., Timex versus Rolex, Honda versus Harley Davidson, private label cookies versus Pepperidge Farm). With uniqueness comes a price premium.

Returning to our symphony example, it is not likely, given the nature of the product category and the audience, that a cost leadership strategy would generally be effective. Differentiation, though, might involve positioning the symphony experience as distinct and prestigious, making it fun and unique—perhaps by offering dinner and wine with performances, an opportunity to meet with members of the orchestra or special guest stars, or rotating concert locations between very unique, attractive locations. Such efforts would merit higher prices in part because costs would be higher, but also because of the higher value being returned to patrons.

A concrete illustration of how these different strategies capture value is provided in Table 14.8, which contrasts estimated income statements for Suave and Vidal Sassoon. Suave's high volume compensates for its very low price and margin. Vidal Sassoon, in contrast, offers a more distinctive and higher quality shampoo (along with a more intensive advertising campaign to support it), and as such charges retailers a price per ounce more than *four times* that of Suave's. Interestingly, Sassoon has only one-tenth the volume that Suave does, yet is estimated to be more profitable (as measured by return on sales) because of its substantially higher prices and margin. Each brand is profitable, but they travel different routes to profitability: one through volume and one through margin. Clearly, competitive positioning strategy is an important determinant of base price level.

Objectives

We saw in our symphony example that $15 was the profit-maximizing price. Yet, management may have another goal in mind: Fill up the auditorium (i.e., maximize sales). *Goal-setting*, or *objective-setting*, is an important part of a firm's strategic planning process. Plans occur at both the corporate and business levels, and the objectives for a particular brand or business (like Suave) are in part a function of the corporation's objectives (Helene-Curtis). In a classic work on pricing in large corporations conducted by the Brookings Institution, four predominant objectives in pricing were identified: to achieve a target **ROI**, to create stabilization of price and margin, to reach a market share target, and to meet or prevent competition. We address each of those individually and then consider two other commonly discussed objectives—profit maximization and survival.

http://www.vidalsassoon.com

ROI
stands for "return on investment."

Table 14.8	Contrasting Prices, Volumes, and Margins: Suave (Low Cost Leader) vs. Vidal Sassoon (Differentiator), 1984		
Price, Cost, Volume		**Suave**	**Vidal Sassoon**
Unit Price (to retailers, per ounce)		.063	.266
Unit Cost		.036	0.72 (est.)
Volume (million ounces)		1,161	133
Income Statement (all $ figures in millions)			
Total Revenue		$73.1	$35.4
Total Variable Cost		$ 2.8	$ 9.6
Total Contribution to Fixed Costs		$31.3	$25.8
Advertising		$ 6.0	$13.5
Promotion		$17.9	$ 5.8 (est.)
Operating Profit		$10.7	$ 6.5
Return on Sales		14.6%	18.4%

Theory of dual entitlement
holds that consumers believe there are terms in a transaction to which both consumers and sellers are "entitled" to over time. Cost-driven price increases are believed to be fair because they allow sellers to maintain their profit entitlement. Demand-driven price increases are not believed to be fair, however, since they allow sellers to increase per-unit profit, while buyers receive nothing in return.

http://www.danone.com

Pricing to Achieve a Target ROI

This was found to be the most common approach to pricing in the Brookings' study. Assuming a standard volume, firms add a particular margin to standard cost, which is expected to produce a target profit rate on investment. Across 20 firms, the target return figure averaged 14 percent, ranging between 8 and 20 percent.

Pricing to Create Stabilization of Price and Margin

Generally, this approach reflects the goal of avoiding the fluctuations in prices that are characteristic of a commodity market. Managers in the Brookings' study reflected a desire to "refrain from upping the price as high as the traffic will bear in prosperity." This motive raises questions about the fairness of frequent price changes (particularly increases), a point which has been raised more recently in an economic theory labeled dual entitlement.[21] The **theory of dual entitlement**, in fact, argues similarly that concerns about fairness may constrain price increases. Fairness may be an issue even when companies do not openly increase prices. In response to electricity rationing in May 2001, some Brazilian companies reduced the amount of product in their packaging without changing price (e.g., the Danone Group reduced cookie packages by near 1 ounce and relaunched them under a new brand name). Consumer protection groups have been quite vocal in their opposition to such practices, leading to government investigations.[22]

Pricing to Reach a Market Share Target

Particularly when there is no patent protection on a product, firms may pursue a market share target. In most cases, firms will seek a significant share upon entry into the market. For example, 3M's Scotch Brite Never Rust soap pad was priced aggressively enough to gain a 15.4 percent market share upon introduction, taking significant share from SOS and Brillo.

Pricing to Meet or Prevent Competition

The logic behind meeting competitors' prices is straightforward. Meeting price cuts will eliminate a competitive disadvantage, while meeting price increases (although less likely) can fatten margins. This reflects a classic tit-for-tat strategy, which has been found to be effective in promoting higher profits for all players.[23] An additional benefit is that a consistent pattern of matching competitors' price moves sends rivals the signal that "undercutting price is not a good idea because we will simply match you." In the 1980s, following a horrific price war in a regional soft drink market, Brian Dyson of Coca-Cola Enterprises (a major Coke bottler in Atlanta) made it clear in an interview in *Bever-*

age World that CCE would not tolerate further aggressive pricing from rivals, noting that ". . . if somebody attempts to lowball the price on us, we will meet that. We insist on a level playing field."

Pricing for Profit Maximization

As noted, the pursuit of this objective requires substantial cost and demand information. It has rarely been articulated as a goal by executives being interviewed about their pricing.

Pricing for Survival

A company experiencing trouble may seek to produce an acceptable cash flow, to cover marginal costs, and simply survive. This may result when competition is especially intense, when consumer needs are changing, and/or when substantial excess capacity exists. Chip maker Advanced Micro Devices reported a loss of $64.6 million in the second quarter of 1998 in the face of price cutting by rival Intel, a slowdown in demand for personal computers, and downturns in its other semiconductor businesses. In order to hang on in the face of competing with Intel's value, the company dropped average microprocessor prices from $105 to $86 in the second quarter, significantly cutting into margins.[24]

http://www.amd.com

http://www.intel.com

New Product Pricing

Two classic pricing strategies are commonly discussed for new products: skimming versus penetration.

Price Skimming

The strategy of **market (price) skimming** requires that a large enough segment of the customer market (innovators, see Chapter 8) is willing to pay the high price for the unique value that a product provides, and that competitors cannot quickly enter with similar products at lower prices. For example, VCRs were initially priced as high as $800 to $900, but have gradually come down to around $200. Other products that followed similar price patterns are CD players, cellular phones, and multimedia computers. Intel is well known for this strategy, pricing its microprocessors for up to $1,000 per chip, but then dropping that price as new superior chips are developed. Skimming is a strategy that obviously would be more likely followed by a firm pursuing a clear differentiation strategy. In addition, a skimming strategy would tend to be pursued in the introduction phase of the product life cycle (see Chapter 8).

Market (price) skimming is a strategy of pricing the new product at a relatively high level and then gradually reducing it over time.

Price Penetration

By pursuing a **penetration strategy** in the face of a retail book marketplace dominated by large chains such as Borders and Barnes & Noble (together having 13 superstores in Atlanta alone), a small bookseller called Chapter 11 thrives with price cutting.[25] The

Penetration strategy requires that the firm enter the market at a relatively low price in an attempt to obtain market share and expand demand for its product.

http://www.bordersgroupinc.com

http://www.barnesandnobleinc.com

http://www.chapter11books.com

http://www.iflyswa.com

http://www.dell.com

store's slogan is "Prices So Low, You'd Think We Were Going Bankrupt" and it prices aggressively, discounting best-sellers 30 percent and all books at least 11 percent. Its new stores are small, in low-cost locations, and designed for quick shopping, all tactics quite different from the larger competitors. Such a "penetration" strategy is the opposite of a skimming strategy. Firms following such a strategy sometimes even enter a market at a loss, hoping to make up initial losses with longer term repeat purchases. This strategy makes sense when competitive imitation will occur quickly, costs are likely to drop a good deal with increases in volume, and target consumers are relatively price sensitive. Southwest Airlines has been able to obtain 75 percent of Florida's intrastate air traffic, while simultaneously increasing the size of the market through its low pricing.[26] As noted at the outset of the chapter, Dell is another good example of a price penetrator. Penetration pricing is the standard strategy followed by low cost leaders.

Price-Quality Judgments. One of the downsides of penetration pricing is that customers may infer low quality from low price. This is most likely to happen under the following circumstances:

1. *When customers are uncertain about brand quality prior to purchase.* The quality of some products is difficult to judge because of their complexity (e.g., computers and cameras), while other products are difficult to assess simply because one cannot "try them out" prior to buying them (e.g., many consumer package goods like food products). For example, a new household cleaner called Pathmark Premium was introduced at a price of $0.89. Pathmark had the same cleaning formula as market leader Fantastik, which was priced at $1.79. Despite aggressive in-store promotion of the new product, it failed because its price could not convince consumers (who would have to buy it to truly assess its quality) that it would be effective.[27] Similarly, Omega destroyed a brand name, more prestigious than Rolex in the 1970s, by pursuing a penetration pricing strategy with a series of lower priced products.[28] The latter case is a particularly frightening scenario in that the negative perceptions created by the low price overpowered a great brand name.

2. *When the risk to customers of a bad decision is high.* When the risk of a bad choice is high, customers will often rely on price to suggest quality. Risk may vary across product categories (e.g., in general, the perceived risk associated with service purchases is higher than that for goods), perceived variance among products within the category (e.g., risk is low if all refrigerators are perceived to provide roughly the same performance), and consumption situations (e.g., higher risk when a disposable camera is used to take pictures at a wedding or on the first day of first grade).

Although there continues to be a debate about how frequently (and when) customers use price as a signal of quality, it is fairly safe to assume that customer uncertainty about quality of a new brand is often very high, so that price-quality inference is a concern. It is also clear that firms pursuing differentiation strategies should maintain relatively high prices, for an additional reason beyond those discussed earlier: to credibly communicate their high quality to customers who may have uncertain quality assessments.

LEARNING OBJECTIVE   4

EXPLAINING ADJUSTMENTS TO BASE PRICE OVER TIME

Most of the pricing decisions that are made for a product in its lifetime are *price change decisions*. Base price may change as a natural function of different objectives over the product life cycle, in response to specific *competitive price moves,* or as a function of special pricing tactics that may create a "schedule" of prices or even unique prices for different customers. In addition, prices may change for short periods of time as a result of the ever-popular practice of price promotion. Figure 14.7 summarizes each of these factors. We examine them in turn.

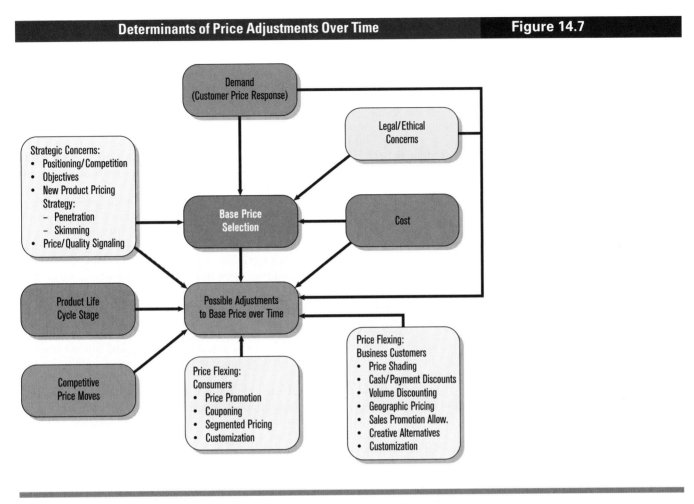

Determinants of Price Adjustments Over Time — **Figure 14.7**

Source: Adapted from Peter R. Dickson, *Marketing Management* (Fort Worth: The Dryden Press, 1996).

Variation in Objectives over the Product Life Cycle

As discussed in Chapter 8, the firm's objectives in pricing and other elements of the marketing mix will vary over the product life cycle. DuPont's classic strategy is described as follows:

> DuPont's strategy for the best part of 50 years was to develop "proprietary" products and to charge all it could get for them as long as the getting was good. So were the giants in data processing, pharmaceuticals, machine tools, and other high technologies. But these proprietary profits inevitably fire up competition, which invades the market with innovations of its own. Thus, the story of Western industrial progress is the story of the progressive liquidation of proprietary positions.[29]

In the introductory phase, paying attention to costs is important, and the firm may choose to pursue a skimming or penetration strategy (see earlier sections). In the growth phase, the firm is faced with the opposing forces of growing demand, yet increasing competition. This necessitates aggressive pricing if the firm cannot hold on to a unique product advantage. Maturity is likely to bring either stable, competitive prices or price wars if some rival attempts to get aggressive (again, this assumes no unique advantage of any rival). The firm should do its best to maintain stable prices and not rock the boat in maturity. Alternatively, some firms will attempt to innovate to break out of the commodity trap. In decline, the firm should try to keep prices up if the decision has been made to harvest

http://www.dupont.com

the brand. The DuPont example illustrates that there is likely to be a declining trend in prices over time, as an industry matures. Predicting when and how much to cut prices is an important task.

Competitive Price Moves

Very often, one firm's price change prompts a reaction from another. This is particularly true today as markets move quickly into maturity and face commodity status. Even brands as strong as Rubbermaid are affected by such competitive forces. Once a Wall Street darling and able to charge a price premium for its innovative new products, Rubbermaid has more recently had to lower prices in the face of growing competition and increasing retailer pressure to discount.[30] Similarly, Nucor Corporation faced record steel imports coming from Russia and Japan (among others), in some cases leading to deep price cuts.[31] When competitors enter and improve products as an industry moves into the growth phase of its life cycle, the incumbent almost always has to respond with price and/or innovation. This is dramatically illustrated in the case of Johnson & Johnson who, after 7 years of R&D, completed a workable stent. A stent is a unique device that cardiologists use to keep arteries propped open following an angioplasty procedure. Incredibly, in just 37 months following introduction, J&J had 1996 sales of $1 billion and a 91 percent share of this market it had created. Yet, J&J's pricing remained quite high, and it was initially reluctant to give hospitals—even those accounting for a substantial volume of stents—breaks on price. As competitors (Guidant and Arterial Vascular Engineering) entered the market with equivalent or superior products, J&J did not respond quickly enough with product innovation or pricing, and its market share went into a free fall. Analysts projected it would be *8 percent* by the end of 1998.[32]

It has been found that of all the marketing mix decisions, price is the one most likely to motivate a response from competitors.[33] Companies tend to keep a sharp eye on competitors' prices, especially in mature markets where overall demand is price inelastic. More recently, it has been found that management's decision to follow a competitor's price change is affected by the decision maker's perception of product price elasticity, as well as the behavior of other competitors.[34]

Price Flexing: Different Prices for Different Buyers

A naive look at pricing would lead to the assumption that once price is set, it then remains constant and is the same for all buyers. In fact, however, we have seen that prices are not static—they may change in response to changes in the firm's objectives over the product life cycle and in response to competitive price moves. Yet, even more variation in prices is introduced by both established promotion and discount practices, and innovative pricing practices related primarily to new information technology. We discuss each of these in turn.

Price Flexing to Business Customers

Although the Robinson-Patman Act places constraints on manufacturers' ability to charge business customers different prices, there is a tremendous amount of price flexing that takes place in the form of a wide variety of discounts and allowances. For example, *Computerworld* has reported that instead of using fixed pricing, "IBM will negotiate software charges on a case-by-case basis in emerging application areas such as electronic commerce and enterprise resource planning."[35] To IBM, this policy may have some appeal because potential customers view it as an opportunity to save money and as an incentive to try new applications. The cost to IBM, though, is the hassle of negotiating every deal and then managing nonstandard bid licenses. There are many other ways that a supplier may end up selling to different buyers for different prices. Traditional approaches that result in flexible prices include the following:

Price Shading. This occurs when, during a negotiation, a salesperson reduces the base price of a product. This may occur for a variety of reasons but is most likely due to the attractiveness of obtaining the business of the particular customer being pursued (e.g., a large customer or one who promises a potentially profitable long-term relationship). It may be common for some haggling to take place and may, in fact, be a badge of honor

http://www.nucor.com

among purchasing agents to achieve some discount off-list price. For companies attempting to pursue a strategy of differentiation, though, price shading is not desirable. Booklet Binding, Inc. is a company who, through sales training, reinvented their sales culture to get the sales force (and customers) focused more on value-added products and less on price shading.[36]

Cash or Payment Discounts. These are discounts the buyer receives for either paying in cash or paying promptly. A standard payment term is "two-ten, net thirty," meaning that the buyer gets a 2 percent discount for paying in less than 10 days (otherwise, they pay the total net cost within the 30-day term). This practice effectively price discriminates between slow- and fast-paying customers.

Volume Discounting. Customers who buy in larger volumes are often given more favorable terms. In fact, this is one of the key justifications for price discrimination in the eyes of the Robinson-Patman Act: total handling, shipping, and clerical expenses are lower (per unit) for larger volumes sold. Providing such discounts also encourages customers to purchase in large volumes, which has the added benefit of reducing the customer's probability of doing business with competitive firms.

Geographic Pricing. It is common for business customers in different regions to receive different prices since transportation costs may be accounted for in pricing. Sellers deal with freight charges in different ways. **Free on board (FOB) pricing** requires the customer to pay for all costs of transportation. This simplifies things for the seller, but also creates a disadvantage in that her products become increasingly expensive to buyers who are geographically further away. An alternative to FOB pricing is **uniform delivered pricing**, where, in effect, the seller averages the costs of transportation across all customers. A good example of this is postage stamp pricing—it costs 34 cents to send a letter anywhere in the United States.

Sales Promotion Allowances. These are discounts that business customers (like retailers) receive for putting the manufacturer's product on sale to consumers for a particular period of time. As discussed in Chapter 12, such allowances have become a staple in business today, particularly in consumer package goods.

http://www.bookletbinding.com

Free on board (FOB) pricing leaves the cost and responsibility of transportation to the customer.

Uniform delivered pricing means that the seller charges all customers the same transportation cost regardless of their location.

Creative Alternatives to Discounting.[37] Consider the following scenario:

Peregrine Inc., a Southfield (Mich.) auto-parts maker, is about to close a big contract with a paint supplier. In the old days, it would be pushing for an up-front price discount. But today, the company is getting very different concessions: a multiyear contract with guaranteed on-time deliveries, low reject rates, and no down-the-road price hikes.

Suppliers are getting very creative today with their price flexing, such that list price appears to stay fairly constant, but other tactics provide the flex. A few examples:

1. Some manufacturers provide generous financing for buyers. For example, Lucent Technologies, Inc. will sell equipment to startups in return for some negotiated share of the startup's (sometimes shaky) revenue.
2. Some customers are requiring long-term contracts with suppliers that guarantee no price increases for the life of the deal.
3. Suppliers may provide services (e.g., repairs) at no cost.
4. An increasing number of customers are demanding promises of quality improvement over the course of a contract at the same or lower price.

Similarly, economist Alan Blinder found in a series of interviews with executives in the 1980s that the most plausible explanation of why list prices often don't change very much is that, instead of changing prices, sellers adjust delivery lags or service.[38]

Price Customization. While price shading, discounting, and the creative approaches to price flexing we've discussed clearly reflect some degree of "customizing" price for customers, new technology may make it possible for prices to be customized literally on a transaction-by-transaction basis, depending on the conditions of supply and demand at the moment. In the free market, prices are determined by the interplay of supply and demand. Prices will be higher when demand exceeds supply and they will drop as more suppliers (or more supply) enter the market. Traditionally, supply and demand adjustments have taken days, weeks, or months to occur, as information about current supply and demand slowly found its way to buyers and sellers. However, new technology has made the sharing of supply and demand information nearly instantaneous, as "the Internet, corporate networks, and wireless setups are linking people, machines, and companies around the globe—and connecting sellers and buyers as never before."[39] Consider the following examples:

http://www.ebay.com

- In some cases, this new, more customized pricing comes in the form of *online auctions*. *CRN* reports that "Once known as the epicenter of the Beanie Baby and baseball card online trading world, eBay has emerged as a force to be reckoned with in B2B IT sales." eBay's access and ratings capability, along with its ability to provide access to hard-to-find equipment and "storefronts" for IBM, Compaq, and Sun Microsystems, make it a very attractive supply option. Solution provider Sherlock Systems, for example, does 150 transactions and spends $25,000 a month on computer products and parts on eBay.[40]
- Enermetrix creates an online market for buying and selling energy. The company's Web site provides an auction forum for sellers of energy to link up with (primarily large) buyers, who can lock very good rates into contracts. Buyers have the ability to post secure buy orders for real-time, competitive bidding, as well as the ability to digitally sign electronic contracts with counter parties.[41] The company's service went live in January of 1998 and in the ensuing year and a half produced contracts worth better than $70 million.[42]
- Arbitrage Networks has developed the technology—currently available in carrier-to-carrier exchanges—that will allow every long distance call to be instantaneously placed on the carrier that has the lowest price. This is accomplished by having carriers supply moment-to-moment information about their network availability and price, and then accessing computers and switching networks powerful enough to match incoming calls with lowest-cost carriers at any given time.[43]

In short, new technology presents the capability to bring supply and demand together in real time, producing highly efficient markets and, potentially placing significant downward pressure on price. Such customization has become increasingly available in consumer markets as well.

Price Flexing to Consumers

While there are some circumstances in which consumers negotiate pricing (e.g., new or used automobiles), you may think that retailers use a "one-price" approach almost exclusively. With a few exceptions—particularly smaller local shops, antiques, and used goods—sellers do appear to charge fixed prices for products. Even the automobile industry is seeing a trend toward *single-pricing*, both with Saturn's innovative sales approach and the online car vendors (e.g., Auto-By-Tel, AutoVantage, or Microsoft's CarPoint), which each sell products at no-haggle prices.[44]

Interestingly, though, there is more price flexing taking place in consumer markets than meets the eye. It takes the form of price promotion, couponing, segmented pricing, and, as we saw earlier with the business market, an increasing trend toward customization. We review each of these below.

***Price Promotion.* Price promotion** is a ubiquitous and effective practice in many situations, particularly early in a product's life, where the objective would be to encourage trial and to allow the seller to maintain a higher list price. The dangers of price promotion in more mature markets can be illustrated with a simple example.

Let's say that you and your competitor sell widgets to the consumer market, and you each have a reasonable market share and comfortable profit of $20 million per period. Your competitor, though, decides to try a 10 percent temporary price reduction and boosts profit to $27 million for the period. This is fine for your rival, but you lost market share and your profit dropped to $13 million for that same period, since that competitor stole some of your market share. So, what do you do? You retaliate with a price promotion

Price promotions
are short-term price reductions designed to create an incentive for consumers to buy now rather than later and/or stock up on the specially priced product.

Edwin L. Artzt and the EDLP Solution

Edwin Artzt is a tough manager. His ability to carry out tough decisions brought about big changes at Procter & Gamble. One big change occurred in the early 1990s, a time when—like many consumer product manufacturers—Procter had gotten "hooked" on price promotions.

The Problem

Consider a situation in which a manufacturer gives a retailer a reduced price every so often, which allows the retailer to sell that product on special to its customers. In response to such promotions, retailers and end consumers show their appreciation by making purchases in large quantities. Competitors notice the success of price promotions and begin to offer them as well. Once all manufacturers begin offering price promotions, the deals begin to look the same to consumers. Because of this, some firms get more aggressive by having more frequent (or deeper) promotions.

Such aggressiveness (reinforced by retailers' and consumers' positive reactions) led to an increasing reliance on price promotion in the 1970s and 1980s. While Procter & Gamble had internal rules that limited promotional money to 5 percent of the sales of any business, this soon gave way to a new promotional reality. As Ed Artzt explained in the trade press:

> Somewhere along the line, and I don't know where, we argued that 5 percent was impractical, so let's raise it to 10 percent. Sooner or later the policy goes away . . . you've lost control. And you don't even know what it's costing you.

Amazingly, the company found that at one time 17 percent of product sales were made on deal, including some categories in which deals accounted for *100 percent* of sales.

The costs, P&G discovered, were substantial. Production schedules often swung wildly when a promotion was run. Factories would run overtime at the end of the quarter (when promotions were used to help managers meet their quarterly goals), but then would be underutilized for weeks. The volume of paperwork on promotional deals exploded and retailers disputed more invoices as billing became less accurate. At one point, P&G was making *55 daily price* changes on 80 different brands. On top of this, retailers began to develop warehouse and logistics capacity to enable them to load up on (i.e., forward buy) products offered by manufacturers at discounted prices. Alternatively, retailers might sell the extra product they purchased on promotion to retailers in other regions that did not have access to the manufacturer's deal (diverting).

The EDLP Solution

Procter & Gamble was the first company to have the courage to cut back on promotions in an effort to improve the efficiency of promotional spending. In 1991, the company adopted a "value pricing," or every day low price (EDLP), strategy to lower list prices and slash discounts across most of its U.S. product line to try to stem some of its problems. For example, rather than charge a regular price of $4.65 per jar of coffee, and an occasional promotional price of $3.90, the EDLP or value price of the coffee might be $4.39. In 1992 and 1993, P&G twice cut the prices of Tide and Cheer, the second time by 15 percent. In that span, the price of Pampers diapers also was reduced three times, 17 percent in all. This reduced the price gap between Pampers and store brands (private labels) from 40 percent to 25 percent.

With the new policy, these "everyday" prices would be available all the time, allowing both P&G and its retailers to plan future sales with more accuracy and to avoid the dramatic up and down swings in sales attributable to price promotions. A growing number of big-volume retailers who themselves used EDLP policies (such as Wal-Mart) quickly warmed to P&G's policy. At the same time, there were numerous roadblocks. For example, many conventional grocery retailers who had become accustomed to profiting from the ups and downs of promotional pricing were not happy, and some dropped P&G products. In addition, the company soon came to the realization that every day low pricing would work only when a firm has "every day low costs."

Mr. Artzt pushed company management to identify major sources for potential cost reductions. Eleven teams were assigned to evaluate every inch of the company. In their analysis of 41 work processes, one team assigned to benchmark the costs of the sales organization found that Procter & Gamble had the highest overhead in the industry. The teams developed many cost-reduction strategies, including methods that better coordinated orders across salespeople and a continuous replenishment system with retailers, whereby information at a given retailer's checkout was immediately transferred to P&G's computers, which allowed orders for product replenishment to be generated automatically.

Through Ed Artzt's leadership and persistence, Procter & Gamble stuck to its guns and, by 1993, the strategy began to pay off. The company's measure of factory efficiency increased from 55 percent to over 80 percent. The number of price changes dropped to almost zero and inventories in North American markets were down significantly. Although profits were down 31 percent in the year ending March 1994 as a result of charges due to plant closings and layoffs, P&G grew its profitability substantially, with year-ending profits of $3.4 and $3.8 billion in 1997 and 1998, respectively. A more recent assessment found that P&G's EDLP initiative has paid off over a longer period of time. Ailawadi, Lehmann, and Neslin (2001) found that Procter & Gamble lost 18 percent market share across 24 categories examined following the implementation of EDLP, but estimated that P&G's gross margin in the United States increased by $1.35 billion as a function of value pricing and that this more than covered the $260 million increase in advertising.

Sources: Jack W. Lindgren and Terence A. Shimp, *Marketing* (Fort Worth: The Dryden Press, 1996), 20–22; Dan Moreau and Joan Goldwasser, "New and Improved P&G Cleans Up," *Kiplinger's Personal Finance Magazine* 47 (September 1993): 26; Silvia Sansoni and Zachary Schiller, "Is That Ed Artzt Pushing Pasta?" *Business Week*, 15 April 1996, 102; Bill Saporito and Ani Hadjian, "Behind the Tumult at P&G," *Fortune*, 7 March 1994, 74+; Kusum L. Ailawadi, Donald R. Lehmann, and Scott A. Neslin, "Market Response to a Major Policy Change in the Marketing Mix: Learning from Procter & Gamble's Value Pricing Strategy," *Journal of Marketing* (January 2001): 44–61.

of your own! You and your competitor go back and forth like this a few times, and you find that you're both promoting at 10 percent off most of the time and that you're now each making $18 million each period, instead of the $20 million that you were making before the price promotions were initiated!

This is a version of the famous *prisoner's dilemma* from game theory, which poses the paradox of a joint decision-making situation in which the players do best by cooperating (not promoting), but each player has an individual incentive to "defect" (in our case, to do a price promotion). If both players defect, both are worse off. Once promotions get started, it may become clear to the firms that their profitability is lower, but they have a hard time raising prices back up again. Why is this so?

The reason is that consumers respond well to promotions, which encourages manufacturers to do more of them. As consumers grow accustomed to such price specials, any firm that does not price promote is likely to lose sales. So, promotions tend to increase over time, leading consumers to be more sensitive to price.[45] As this happens, retailers adapt to promotions by forward buying or diverting product as described in Chapter 12. All in all, everyone's attention goes to price, when price is highlighted through increasing promotion. As a response to this vicious cycle of competitive promotions—and its related inefficiency—Procter & Gamble instituted **every day low pricing (EDLP)** in the early 1990s (also known as *value pricing*). This pricing initiative was spearheaded by Procter & Gamble leader Edwin Artzt.

Every day low pricing (EDLP) refers to the pricing strategy in which a firm charges the same low price every day.

Couponing. Couponing provides another means of price discrimination in that it gives some consumers—those who wish to take the time and effort to clip coupons—the capability of paying lower prices. Most coupons come from *free-standing inserts (FSIs)* in the weekend newspaper but, increasingly, coupons are available at point-of-purchase and printed on grocery register tapes. Into the early 1990s, manufacturers were following a trend of continuously increasing the number of coupons distributed per year. A significant change has occurred more recently in that consumer package goods firms, led again by Procter & Gamble, are looking into cutting back many incentives, including coupons.[46] *Advertising Age* reported that coupon distribution declined 10 percent to 276 billion coupons in 1997, attributing the change to a shifting of funds into frequent-shopper cards and electronic discounts. Note that coupon redemption fell 18 percent to 4.8 billion in 1997, reflecting an overall paltry 1.7 percent redemption rate.[47] More recently, and in spite of significant past increases in coupon distribution during recessionary periods, leading promotional firms see continued softness in the $5 billion industry.[48]

http://www.adage.com

Pricing for Different Segments. Marketers very often have different marketing programs for different consumer segments.

- *Geographic Segments.* It is possible that price sensitivity varies across geographic regions. For example, some grocery retailers have different price zones and prices are likely to vary across those zones. Competition and consumer profiles may differ between geographic segments. To generate interest among potential patrons in outlying areas, the symphony (discussed earlier) might plan smaller, fun ensemble concerts at performance halls or public places in other locales priced at or below variable cost.

- *Usage Segments.* It is common for marketers to recognize high-volume users and reward them with different prices. For example, regular customers at a particular grocery store who carry the stores' frequent shopper card receive discounts at checkout that other shoppers do not receive. Where capacity is an issue for the manufacturer or service provider, the heaviest users may actually pay more. IBM applied this strategy to its Internet service, charging accounts that exceed a threshold level of usage an hourly fee in addition to the basic monthly rate. In contrast, symphonies and theaters often have packages that charge patrons who commit to attending a certain number of events receive a reduced price.

- *Demographic Segments.* A symphony might provide special prices for students or children to encourage attendance, or give discounts to senior citizens. This is a common strategy used by museums, athletic events, and amusement parks.

- *Time Segments.* There are many examples of how "time" provides a relevant basis for segmenting markets for pricing. Resort hotels have on- and off-season rates, reflecting differences in demand for those seasons. Similarly, plumbers have regular and overtime, or weekend rates, capturing the same concept. A bakery might lower prices at the end of the day to move leftover merchandise. A symphony might have a Saturday morning or afternoon concert to reach new markets, accompanied by lower pricing. *Forbes* magazine reports that the cities of Singapore, San Diego, and Toronto all engage in "congestion pricing" on their toll roads. This is where higher toll rates charged during rush hours to reallocate traffic to less busy times.[49]

Customization. As discussed earlier for business markets, new technology may have a significant effect on the prices consumers pay for products and may lead to significant variation in the prices that consumers pay for the same item. Consumers can participate in the Internet auctions described earlier. Further, Arbinet's services (linking callers to the lowest cost long-distance provider) may be available for consumers in the near future. In fact, some envision a "smart" phone that automatically seeks the lowest cost carrier each time a long-distance call is placed. Beyond this, the Internet is affecting consumers' ability to search for and access low prices. For example, airlines today often send out e-mail alerts of last-minute fare specials to fill up empty seats on flights. Only consumers on the airline's e-mail list receive notice of these fares. Priceline.com allows consumers to specify their travel plans, and then "name their price" for the flight(s). Priceline acts as a go-between for participating airlines and consumers, forwarding bids to the airlines

www.arbinet.com

www.priceline.com

Price Shopping Dream

Imagine a marketplace where you can find exactly what you want and pay exactly what you can afford. Sound too good to be true? Well, you're right—for now anyway. But with the vast capabilities of the Internet, many Web sites are making strides toward just such a reality. Companies around the globe have seized the opportunity to provide instant information and feedback to consumers who never even have to leave their homes.

One such site is priceline.com, which began as a service offering consumers the chance to name their own price for airline tickets. From the consumer's end, priceline's process is relatively simple: Enter the Web site address in a Web browser, click an icon, and in only a few moments, you can be filling out the online form, specifying the dates of your flight, the cities you are traveling between, and a host of other specifics about the potential flight. Having submitted a bid, the consumer can expect to have e-mail confirmation of their bid almost instantaneously and hear back an acceptance or refusal in less than an hour.

Priceline utilizes a reverse auction model: given the consumer's bid, the company seeks out the best offer from vendors who have excess capacity. If the consumer's bid price is acceptable to a particular vendor, the consumer's credit card is charged and they are committed to the purchase. Priceline's auction model was deemed unique enough to be granted U.S. Patent number 5,794,207 in August 1998.

For all of priceline's advantages, there are many challenges in its environment. For example, competition has emerged in the form of online services that allow people to make their own travel arrangements, much as a travel agent would. These include services such as Microsoft's Expedia.com and Travelocity.com. While different from the priceline.com model in that these services do not have a bid capability, they still provide consumers with the capability to track and be notified of price changes so that they can seek the lowest prices.

Further, priceline.com's management has learned from its forays into many different businesses. Attempts were made over the past 2 years to extend the priceline model into the markets for life insurance, mortgages, cars, telephone service, and groceries. These efforts proved difficult because these categories do not have the same "perishability" as airline seats and hotel rooms. So, priceline has again redefined itself, returning to its original core business with airline seats, hotel rooms, and rental cars. All in all, there has never been a better time to be a price-shopping traveler.

Sources: Paul Davidson, "Web Site Lets You Set Price," *USA Today*, 16 September 1998; Alex Grove, "Priceline.com Sparks a Patent Controversy," *Red Herring* (December 1998); Rudy Maxa, "Make a Bid for Your Bed," MSNBC Web page, accessed 17 December 1998; Kent German, "Priceline on the Rise," *Upside*, (December 2001/January 2002): 16; Monica Roman, "Priceline Shocker: Black Inc.," *Business Week*, 13 August 2001, 40. Mary Ann Keller, "Opinion: Inside Priceline's Sausage Factory," *Fortune*, 3 September 2001, 42.

and relaying acceptances or refusals to consumers. The priceline Web site received more than 1 million visits in the week after it was launched, and within 2 months had sold 100,000 tickets.[50] While the company experienced challenges in 2000, Priceline reported record sales of $364.8 million in the second quarter 2001, and $2.8 million in profit.[51] *The Economist* recently argued that companies will continue to use new technology to manage customer relationships and track customer loyalty (as well as shape offers for loyal customers), and to use lower prices where appropriate as a tool to maintain loyalty. The publication notes that "in the future, 'good' customers will routinely expect to pay less for a service (or get more for their money) than the rest of us."[52]

LEGAL AND ETHICAL ISSUES IN PRICING

LEARNING OBJECTIVE 5

The laws of the land represent an additional set of considerations that influence the setting of base price. Prudent marketers must be attentive to legal and ethical concerns in pricing. As proof, consider a case involving John Taylor,[53] who in 1983 was an honest, hard-working division manager at Allegheny Pepsi, a large bottling company that controlled numerous Pepsi franchises. In late spring of that year, Taylor traveled to Norfolk, Virginia, at the request of his boss, George Goodwin, to meet with Bob Miller, the regional division manager for their competitor, Mid-Atlantic Coke. Taylor listened at the meeting as George Goodwin described the significant price cutting that had been taking place in the market and how it was hurting both firms' profit. Goodwin suggested ". . . let's forget all the problems we've had up to this point . . . let's just agree not to have it continue on." He then pulled out a notepad and wrote down prices for each size soda package, and these prices were agreed upon by both competitors.

Price-fixing
is a conspiracy to fix competitive prices.

Such **price-fixing** was fairly common in the soft-drink industry at the time. Yet, price-fixing is illegal because it restricts competition and leads to higher prices for customers. John Taylor did not design the price-fixing scheme, but he did help to implement it. On occasion, he would make sure his sales reps did not give customers any deals that would break the implicit agreement with Coke. When a disgruntled customer learned about the agreement, he contacted the police and the FBI. In the legal proceedings that followed, Taylor declined offers of immunity. Ironically, his boss George Goodwin—architect of the price-fixing plan—took an immunity offer and became a star witness in the federal government's case *against* John Taylor. In spite of recognizing Mr. Taylor's good character and the awkward situation in which the price-fixer received immunity, the judge was compelled to sentence Taylor to 3 years in prison and a $15,000 fine. Several others went to jail over this incident as well.[54]

This case illustrates the dramatic personal and professional consequences that can result from illegal pricing behavior. Ironically, Mr. Taylor did not benefit financially from the price-fixing arrangement, as he was just doing his job. A similar situation involved two of the most famous auction houses in the world. In this case, executives from Christie's and Sotheby's were alleged to have discussed and agreed to increasing buyers' fees before they announced these pricing policy changes for their respective companies. By setting identical commission rates they would effectively limit competition as well as increase the amount that buyers paid when they bought fine art and antiques from each auction house. The completion of a U.S. Justice Department investigation resulted in a guilty plea by Diana Brooks, Sotheby's chief executive officer.[55] Certain illicit practices can become commonplace in an industry and seem legitimate because "this is the way we've always done it." That's a slippery slope to walk, however. An understanding of the law will help inform pricing decisions. Several types of pricing behavior are illegal in the United States. We review some of them next.[56]

Price Fixing

Sherman Antitrust Act
prohibits any contract, combination, or conspiracy that restrains trade. It was passed by Congress in 1890 in an effort to prevent companies from controlling (monopolizing) an industry.

Price fixing is a violation of the **Sherman Antitrust Act**, which prohibits any contract, combination, or conspiracy that restrains trade. It is one of the key reasons that **cartels** exist. Archer Daniels Midland pleaded guilty in 1996 to criminal charges of price fixing in the distribution of lysine (an amino acid that speeds livestock growth). ADM paid $100 million in penalties. In their individual trials, the executives were found guilty in September 1998 and one executive is currently serving a 3-year sentence in a federal prison camp.[57]

Cartel
is an organization of firms in an industry where the central organization makes certain management decisions and functions (often regarding pricing, outputs, sales, advertising, and distribution) that would otherwise be performed within the individual firms.

Price Discrimination

Price discrimination
occurs when a seller offers a lower price to some buyers than to other buyers.

Price discrimination is *not* illegal when the buyers are consumers (who do not compete with one another). But, a manufacturer that offers different retailers different prices without economic justification is violating the Robinson-Patman Act (1936), which amended the 1914 Clayton Act. Price discrimination is legal when:

http://www.admworld.com

http://www.walmart.com

1. *It is cost-justified.* For example, there may be cost differences in selling to two different customers. Wal-Mart, for example, obtains more favorable prices than smaller retailers because of its sheer size, and the economies that manufacturers obtain in selling in such high volumes. Alternatively, if the manufacturer's costs go up, one customer may be charged a higher price than another customer who bought before the price increase.
2. *The seller is attempting to match a competitor's lower prices.* The Robinson-Patman Act has a "good-faith clause" that allows a seller to charge a lower price to Store X than to Store Y, if a competitor is already charging Store X a lower price.
3. *There is no apparent harm to competition.*

Resale Price Maintenance

If I'm a manufacturer and you're a retailer selling my product, we are in violation of the law if we get together and *agree upon* some minimum price to be charged to consumers at retail. I can, however, suggest retail price levels to you. Further, I can stop dealing with you if you do not follow my recommendation.[58] The primary concern regarding *resale price maintenance* is that retail price competition not be eliminated by manufacturers and retailers agreeing upon specific minimum prices.

Predatory Pricing

Predatory pricing has been alleged recently in the airline market. Spirit Airlines abandoned its Detroit-Philadelphia service when Northwest Airlines cut its one-way fares to $49 on all seats and added 30 percent more seats. Following Spirit's departure from the route in September of 1996, Northwest's one-way fare climbed to over $230 and the number of available seats dropped.[59] This is the classic pattern of predatory pricing in which an incumbent firm apparently attempts to drive out newer, smaller rivals with aggressive pricing. The practice of aggressive pricing and capacity expansion has come under intense scrutiny recently in the airline industry[60]—although no convictions have been made. It is quite difficult to prove predatory behavior, as federal law requires demonstrating that the alleged predator priced below an appropriate measure of its average cost and that it had a reasonable expectation that it would recoup its losses.[61] Northwest has argued that it is competing "fairly but aggressively" and that smaller airlines often survive in spite of these aggressive tactics. Predatory pricing continues to be "rarely tried and even more rarely successful."[62]

    Markup laws are a regulatory approach to prevent predatory pricing. Such laws require a certain markup above cost in particular industries. For example, Wal-Mart ran into significant regulatory trouble in several states in the spring and summer of 2001 when it opened up parking lot gas pumps to lure consumers to the store. Thirty-seven states have laws that either prohibit selling gas below cost or general fair marketing laws that apply more broadly. These laws are specifically designed to protect consumers and small businesses from predatory pricing. In many states, the laws prevented Wal-Mart from exploiting its natural cost advantage with aggressive pricing at levels that would be below the costs of other gasoline retailers. To this point, Wal-Mart has been unsuccessful in lobbying states to repeal the laws.[63]

Exaggerated Comparative Price Advertising

A very common price advertising tactic is to compare an advertised sale price to a former price; for example, "Was $49.99, Now $29.99." Adding a comparison price has been found to significantly improve consumers' perception of savings and value in an advertised offer.[64] If such a comparative price is bona fide and "was offered to the public on a regular basis for a reasonably substantial period of time," it is perfectly legal.[65] Yet, many retailers appear to stretch this guideline, using comparison prices of questionable validity. While such charges have been considered by many state attorneys-general, few cases have gone to trial. An exception was a case against May D&F, which resulted in a judgment against the retailer. May D&F had institutionalized a policy in which a profitable "intermediate markup" price was set for a product (e.g., $79.99 for a Krups coffee maker), but a much higher "promotional markup" price was also set (e.g., $119.99), which would be charged for as few as 10 days at the beginning of the 6-month selling season. After the initial 10 days, the company's stores would promote the item as "originally $119.99, now $79.99" for much of the remaining season. May D&F was found to be in violation of FTC standards for comparative price advertising.

Ethical Concerns

There are many questions raised by customers and public policy groups about pricing practices, primarily concerning what often appears to be exorbitant prices charged by firms. In the recent past, the cereal industry has been the target of such criticism, as has the pharmaceuticals industry and the banking industry (for excessive ATM fees). Consider these additional pricing scenarios:

- A hardware store raises its price for snow shovels on the morning after a big snowstorm.
- A supermarket chain charges higher prices in its inner-city stores than its suburban stores.

Predatory pricing
is a practice where one firm attempts to drive out rivals (usually smaller ones) by pricing at such a low level that the rival cannot make money.

http://www.spiritair.com

http://www.nwa.com

Markup laws
require a specified markup above cost in particular industries.

http://www.krups.com

- A microchip manufacturer initially charges very high prices for its new generation chip and then sharply reduce prices after the less price-sensitive buyers have purchased.
- A retailer prices dresses at 400 percent above cost.
- A consultant prices her services at $5,000 per day.
- A bank charges a $1.50 fee for ATM usage to customers who do not have an account with the bank.

Are these all ethical pricing practices? Are they all unethical? People from different backgrounds are likely to apply very different frameworks and standards in making their judgment. Further, we might judge them differently depending on whether we are buyers or sellers. All of the above behaviors can be justified from a business perspective in one of two ways: (1) demand exceeds supply, so equating the two (specifically, rationing demand) requires high prices; and/or (2) the value or return that the buyer receives from each transaction merits these higher prices. These are powerful arguments, yet it should be noted that customers do not always buy into them. Higher prices—even those justified on the basis of supply and demand—may be viewed as unfair by customers and may create resentment, which will affect long-term business. For example, a majority of consumers surveyed felt that the hardware store owner in the first example behaved unfairly.[66] Two-thirds of consumers surveyed about recent ATM fees said they changed their usage in response to the fees, with 11 percent saying they stopped using ATMs altogether.[67]

Regarding ethical standards, the law defines minimally acceptable behavior. In some states, there are *gouging laws,* which attempt to prevent substantial price increases in response to special circumstances.[68] In the wake of the September 11 terrorist attacks, panic-buying of consumers fearful of gas shortages led to prices as high as almost $6 a gallon in some locations. States of emergency were declared in Texas, Mississippi, and Florida to trigger emergency price-gouging laws and Michigan's attorney general accused several gas stations of charging prices "grossly in excess" of normal.[69]

Business common sense defines another standard: One does not want to alienate customers and lose them. There are also personal standards of ethics, which each of us needs to think about and develop:

> *Firms can facilitate ethical marketing behavior from their employees by suggesting that employees apply each of the following tests when faced with an ethical predicament: (1) act in a way that you would want others to act toward you (the Golden Rule), (2) take only actions which would be viewed as proper by an objective panel of your professional colleagues (the professional ethic), and (3) always ask, would I feel comfortable explaining this action on TV to the general public? (the TV test).[70]*

CHAPTER SUMMARY

- This chapter provided an overview of pricing behavior in firms, with a focus on factors that influence the setting of base prices, and the key reasons underlying why base prices are adjusted over time.

- We started by discussing how the natural starting point for pricing decisions is cost, and how cost-based methods of pricing seem to predominate in the marketplace. Yet, there are difficulties with such approaches, particularly when demand is uncertain.

- Pricing decisions must, then, take into account the relationship between price and demand. The transition from a cost-based approach to a more market-driven approach begins with a break-even analysis, which motivates the question, "Can we sell the number of units needed at this price to make the desired profit?" From here, estimates of a demand schedule provide important input into pricing decisions, as do consideration of the firm's strategic position, competitive prices, and legal and ethical considerations.

- It is also significant to remember that there are many reasons why firms change base prices over time. Prices change both because objectives change over the product life cycle, and because competitors likely change prices.

- Further, we discovered reasons for price flexing for both business users and household consumers. Some of these reasons for flexible pricing are due to traditional discounting and price promotional practices. But we also discussed the impact of new technology and the Internet. They are providing the possibility of aligning conditions of supply and demand almost instantaneously, leading to near-customized, or at least very efficient pricing.

KEY TERMS

Break-even point literally means "to have zero profit." It is that point at which total cost and total revenue are equal.

Cartel is an organization of firms in an industry where the central organization makes certain management decisions and functions (often regarding pricing, outputs, sales, advertising, and distribution) that would otherwise be performed within the individual firms.

Demand schedules provide a systematic look at the relationship between price and quantity sold.

Elasticity of demand is the relationship between changes in price and quantity sold.

Every day low pricing (EDLP) refers to the pricing strategy in which a firm charges the same low price every day.

Free on board (FOB) pricing leaves the cost and responsibility of transportation to the customer.

Marginal costs are the change in a firm's total costs per-unit change in its output level.

Marginal revenues are the change in a firm's total revenue per-unit change in its sales level.

Market (price) skimming is a strategy of pricing the new product at a relatively high level and then gradually reducing it over time.

Markup laws require a specified markup above cost in particular industries.

Penetration strategy requires that the firm enter the market at a relatively low price in an attempt to obtain market share and expand demand for its product.

Predatory pricing is a practice where one firm attempts to drive out rivals (usually smaller ones) by pricing at such a low level that the rival cannot make money.

Price is some unit of value given up by one party in return for something from another party.

Price discrimination occurs when a seller offers a lower price to some buyers than to other buyers.

Price-fixing is a conspiracy to fix competitive prices.

Price promotions are short-term price reductions designed to create an incentive for consumers to buy now rather than later and/or stock up on the specially priced product.

ROI stands for "return on investment."

Sherman Antitrust Act prohibits any contract, combination, or conspiracy that restrains trade. It was passed by Congress in 1890 in an effort to prevent companies from controlling (monopolizing) an industry.

Theory of dual entitlement holds that consumers believe there are terms in a transaction to which both consumers and sellers are "entitled" to over time. Cost-driven price increases are believed to be fair because they allow sellers to maintain their profit entitlement. Demand-driven price increases are not believed to be fair, however, since they allow sellers to increase per-unit profit, while buyers receive nothing in return.

Uniform delivered pricing means that the seller charges all customers the same transportation cost regardless of their location.

QUESTIONS FOR DISCUSSION

1. A manufacturer of golf equipment has developed a new driver call the Big Bomber. The company has $80 million invested in operating capital. The unit cost of producing this driver is $100 and the projected volume of product and sales is 1.5 million units. In the text, we discussed how an orchestra could set price by incorporating a desired figure for profit into its pricing calculation (we added $1 per customer to the price). In the case of the Big Bomber, we are looking to determine a per-unit cost for the product by accounting for a particular dollar amount that the company is seeking to earn on its investment. If the company's objective is to earn a 30 percent return on investment with this driver, what should the price be? How would you determine it?

2. If cost-plus pricing is used as a means to coordinate among oligopolistic rivals and is used consistently over time with adjustments made in markup levels as sales figures are studied, could it lead to profit-maximizing prices?

3. Answer the following questions, explaining the relationships among changes in price, demand (units sold), and profit. Explain whether demand appears to be elastic or inelastic in each case.
   a. Hewlett-Packard dropped prices on personal computers during 1997 by offering customers discounts of up to 50 percent. Unit sales shot up 70 percent during this period. Yet, the personal computer division *lost $50 million*. What would explain this odd combination of performance outcomes? (Note: There were no especially large accounting write-offs for the PC business during this period.)
   b. Heublein, Inc. raised prices 8 percent on its Popov brand of vodka to an average of $4.10 for a fifth of vodka. Popov lost 1 percent of its market share. What would determine whether Popov actually lost money?
   c. Scott Mt. Joy is cofounder of Nieto Computer Services, a 3-year old Houston computer and network-services company. In 1995, the company charged $35 to $50 an hour for its contract work. By 1998, those rates were $75 to $150. "We raised hourly rates (two years in a row) and lost one or two clients out of 130," says Mr. Mt. Joy. What would explain this inelastic demand?

4. Given the data below, at what price does this manufacturer of barbecue grills maximize profit?

Price	Estimated Quantity Sales	Variable Cost
$125	100,000	$70
$130	95,000	$70
$135	85,000	$70
$140	75,000	$70

5. Quaker Oats recently raised prices on several cold cereals by 3.6 percent. Quaker could defend the practice one of two ways:
  a. It could argue that it is only trying to regain some of its profitability lost as a result of a price war.
  b. It could argue that its price increases are meant to offset the rising cost of doing business. Labor and advertising costs are increasing, and the company also has higher costs due to product innovation (e.g., zip-pak closes on bagged cereals).

Which approach do you think would be perceived as more fair by consumers? Why?

6. Diamonds are a luxury. Water is an essential requirement for human life. Why are diamonds so much more expensive than water?

7. Consider your answer to question 6, then answer the following two questions:
  a. *Business Week*, 29 March 1998: "Step into a Kmart or Wal-Mart store these days and you can pick up a diamond bracelet for $29.99—about the same price as a toaster . . . prices of smaller diamonds are plunging." Why do you think this is happening?
  b. In contrast, water is more expensive (bottled water). What makes consumers willing to pay $1.09 for a 16-ounce bottle of water?

INTERNET QUESTIONS

1. Identify two services that sell automobiles via the Internet. How do they communicate price information? Why? What impact do you think these services will have on the cost of purchasing automobiles in the future?

2. Go to http://www.netgrocer.com. Sign up for the service (you don't need to give them a credit card number) and then go shopping for breakfast. How much would it cost you if you ordered a box of Wheaties, a box of Nutri-grain bars, and Orange Tang in the 31.70 ounce container? Compare this to the local grocery store and explain the differences in pricing.

3. Go shopping for a video copy of the following movies: *It's a Wonderful Life, Gone with the Wind, Good Will Hunting*, and the Beatles' *Yellow Submarine*. (Hint: *Yahoo!, Excite*, and *Junglee*.) What are your best prices for each of these items? What are the implications of this search capability for the pricing of products and services in the future?

ENDNOTES

[1] This section adapted from Disclosure's SEC databases, Pirahana Web (Thomson Financial), Gary McWilliams, "Dell Fine-Tunes Its PC Pricing to Gain an Edge in Slow Market," *Wall Street Journal*, 8 June 2001, A1; "As More Buyers Suffer from Upgrade Fatigue, PC Sales Are Falling," *Wall Street Journal*, 24 August 2001, A1; Chris Kraeuter, "Dell Dips with Market Despite Results," http://cbs.marketwatch.com, accessed 15 February 2002; J. William Gurley, "Why Dell's Wart Isn't Dumb," *Fortune*, 7 July 2001, 134; Bob Brewin, "Top PC Makers Preparing for Price War," *Computerworld*, 14 May 2001, 25.

[2] J. Dean, "Research Approach to Pricing," in *Planning the Price Structure*, Marketing Series No. 67 (New York: American Management Association, 1947), 4.

[3] A. W. Walker, "How to Price Industrial Products," *Harvard Business Review* 45 (1967): 8–45.

[4] "Finding the Right Price Is No Easy Game to Play," *Chief Executive* (September 1981): 16–18.

[5] Thomas T. Nagle and Reed K. Holden, *The Strategy and Tactics of Pricing,* 2nd ed. (Englewood Cliffs, NJ: Prentice Hall, 1995), 15.

[6] John H. Lindgren, Jr. and Terence A. Shimp, *Marketing: An Interactive Learning System* (Fort Worth, TX: The Dryden Press, 1996), 378.

[7] Example used with permission from Professor Kim Sosin, UNO Center for Economic Education, College of Business Administration, University of Nebraska at Omaha, NE 68182.

[8] Gilbert Burck, "The Myths and Realities of Corporate Pricing," *Fortune,* April 1972: 85. See also, Richard Thaler, "Mental Accounting and Consumer Choice," *Marketing Science* (Summer 1985): 199–214.

[9] R. Hall and C. Hitch, "Price Theory and Business Behavior," *Oxford Economic Papers,* 1939; and Thomas V. Bonoma, Victoria L. Crittenden, and Robert J. Dolan, "Can We Have Rigor and Relevance in Pricing Research?" in *Issues in Pricing: Theory and Research,* ed. T. DeVinney (Lexington, MA: Lexington Books, 1988).

[10] This example is adapted from Nagle and Holden, *The Strategy and Tactics of Pricing,* 19–22.

[11] For target ROI pricing, the desired profit per unit is calculated as follows:

$$\text{Desired Profit per Unit} = \frac{(\text{Target Return} + \text{Investment})}{\text{Projected Unit Sales}}$$

[12] Nagle and Holden, *The Strategy and Tactics of Pricing,* 3.

[13] Tables 14.2, 14.3, and 14.4 are taken from Paul A. Samuelson, *Economics: An Introductory Analysis,* 4th ed. (New York: McGraw-Hill, 1958), 370–374.

[14] For example, the percentage price change going from \$5 to \$4 in Table 14.2 is (\$4 − \$5)/\$5 = 20 percent. The percentage change in quantity sold is (10 − 9)/10 = 10 percent.

[15] "Cheap PCs," *Business Week,* 23 March 1998, 28.

[16] Note that there are no fixed costs included in Table 14.3, which may seem a bit odd. It is important to recognize that fixed costs do not help in determining the profit-maximizing price for one simple reason: They are the same no matter what price we charge. As such, the only fixed costs that would be relevant would be those that change as a function of pricing. For example, going with a very low price for a product may require extra investment in production capacity to make sure enough product is available. The fixed costs associated with additional production would then be relevant and should be accounted for.

[17] Simulated purchase tasks have been found to provide reasonably accurate assessments of consumer response to price. See John R. Nevin, "Laboratory Experiments for Estimating Consumer Demand: A Validation Study," *Journal of Marketing Research* (August 1974): 261–268; and Raymond R. Burke, Bari A. Harlam, Barbara E. Kahn, and Leonard M. Lodish, "Comparing Dynamic Consumer Choice in Real and Computer-Simulated Environments," *Journal of Consumer Research* (June 1992): 71–82.

[18] One could argue that the symphony consider an even higher price as profits show a continual upward trend as price gets higher.

[19] Michael Porter, *Competitive Strategy* (New York: Free Press, 1980).

[20] We should note that, although Neil Hill's prices are likely to be equal to or lower than a similar store in Kansas City because of the lower costs of doing business in Atchison, driving from Kansas City is part of the price of shopping Neil Hill's. The combination of

an absolutely unique shopping experience and fair prices (relative to Kansas City alternatives) is likely a strong draw. See Kevin Helliker, "Word of Mouth Makes Kansas Store a Star," *Wall Street Journal*, 7 November 1997, B1.

[21] See Daniel Kahneman, Jack L. Knetsch, and Richard H. Thaler, "Fairness as a Constraint on Profit Seeking: Entitlements in the Market," *American Economic Review* 70 (September 1986): 728–741.

[22] Miriam Jordan, "Brazilian Producers Economize, and Some Consumers Cry Foul," *Wall Street Journal*, 27 August 2001, A8.

[23] Robert Axelrod, *The Evolution of Cooperation* (New York: Basic Books, 1984).

[24] Dean Takahashi, "AMD Posts Loss Amid Price War, Sluggish Demand," *Wall Street Journal*, 9 July 1998, B3.

[25] Jeffrey Tannebaum, "Small Bookseller Beats the Giants at Their Own Game," *Wall Street Journal*, 4 November 1997, B1.

[26] Scott McCartney, "Southwest Airlines Lands Plenty of Florida Passengers," *Wall Street Journal*, 11 November 1997, B4.

[27] Peter R. Dickson, *Marketing Management* (Fort Worth, TX: The Dryden Press, 1996), 618.

[28] Reed K. Holden and Thomas T. Nagle, "Kamikaze Pricing," *Marketing Management* 7, no. 2 (1998): 30–40.

[29] Burck, "The Myths and Realities of Corporate Pricing," 87.

[30] Timothy Aeppel, "Rubbermaid Is on a Tear, Sweeping Away the Cobwebs," *Wall Street Journal*, 8 September 1998, B4.

[31] Chris Adams, "Nucor Cuts Steel Prices Amid Rush of Imports," *Wall Street Journal*, 11 September 1998, A2.

[32] Ron Winslow, "How a Breakthrough Quickly Broke Down for Johnson & Johnson," *Wall Street Journal*, 18 September 1998, A1.

[33] Venkataraman, Chen, and MacMillan, in a study of the airline industry, find that price moves produce a competitive reaction with 75 percent probability. The probability that a competitor would match a nonprice move was 17 percent. S. Venkataraman, Ming-Jer Chen, and Ian C. MacMillan, "Anticipating Reactions: Factors That Shape Competitor Responses," in *Wharton on Dynamic Competitive Strategy*, ed. George S. Day and David J. Reibstein (New York: John Wiley and Sons, 1997).

[34] Peter R. Dickson and Joel E. Urbany, "Retailer Reactions to a Competitor's Price Change," *Journal of Retailing* 70 (Spring 1994): 1–22; Joel E. Urbany and Peter R. Dickson, "Competitive Price-Cutting Momentum and Pricing Reactions," *Marketing Letters* 2, no. 4 (1991): 393–402.

[35] Jaikumar Vijayan, "IBM Proposes Flexible Software Pricing," *Computerworld*, 6 April 1998, 57.

[36] Joshua Hyatt, "Hot Commodity," *Inc.*, February 1996, 50–60.

[37] This short section is based on the article by Howard Gleckman and Gary McWilliams, "Ask and It Shall Be Discounted," *Business Week*, 6 October 1997, 116–120.

[38] Alan S. Blinder, "Why Are Prices Sticky? Preliminary Results from an Interview Study," *American Economic Association Papers and Proceedings* (May 1991): 89–96.

[39] Amy Cortese and Marcia Stepanek, "Good-Bye to Fixed Pricing?" *Business Week*, 4 May 1998, 71.

[40] Amy Rogers, "E-Bay: The New Kid in Town," *CRN*, 12 November 2001, 16–20.

[41] Clinton Wilder, "The Power of the Net," *Informationweek*, 23 August 1999, 63–64.

[42] "Energy & Utilities," *Forbes*, 17 July 2000, 136–138.

[43] Cortese and Stepanek, "Good-Bye to Fixed Pricing?"

[44] Jim O'Brien, "Hot Off the Wire," *Computer Shopper* (August 1998): 474; and Mary Connelly, "Philosophy of Car Pricing Is Clear: Cut Out Games," *Advertising Age*, 28 March 1994, S28–34.

[45] Carl F. Mela, Sunil Gupta, and Donald R. Lehmann, "The Long-Term Impact of Promotion and Advertising on Consumer Brand Choice," *Journal of Marketing Research* (May 1997): 248–261.

[46] Kenneth Hein and Vincent Alonzo, "P&G Scales Back Promotions," *Incentive* (April 1997): 15.

[47] "Distribution of Coupons Falls 10% to 276 Billion," *Advertising Age*, 23 March 1998, 32.

[48] Jack Neff, "Coupons Get Clipped," *Advertising Age*, 5 November 2001, 1.

[49] Peter Huber, "The Four-Hour Energy Crisis," *Forbes*, 17 September 2001, 88.

[50] David Leonhardt, "Make a Bid, but Don't Pack Your Bags," *Business Week*, 1 June 1998, 164.

[51] Kent German, "Priceline on the Rise," *Upside* (December 2001/January 2002): 16; Monica Roman, "Priceline Shocker: Black Inc.," *Business Week*, 13 August 2001, 40.

[52] McCarthy, FT, "Managing Customers: All Customers Are Important, But Some Are More Important Than Others," *The Economist*, 13 August 2001.

[53] These individuals' names have been changed.

[54] Andrew Galvin, "The Price of Fixing Prices," *Journal of Pricing Management* (Summer 1990): 46–51.

[55] Kathryn Kranhold, "Taubman Lawyers Seek Evidence He Didn't Know of Pricing Talks," *Wall Street Journal*, 20 August 2001, B2.

[56] See the Federal Trade Commission's publication, "Promoting Competition, Protecting Consumers: A Plain English Guide to Antitrust Laws," at the FTC's Web site: http://www.ftc.gov/bc/compguide/index.htm.

[57] Scott Kilman, "Federal Jury Convicts Ex-Executives in Archer-Daniels-Midland Lawsuit," *Wall Street Journal*, 18 September 1998; Scott Kilman, "ADM Says Ex-Chief Dwayne Andreas Will Leave Board," *Wall Street Journal*, 13 August 2001, A6.

[58] See, for example, *Ben Elfman & Son, Inc., et al. v. Criterion Mills, Inc., et al.*, CCH 69,611 (DC MA, October 1991); BNA ATRR No. 1538 (October 24, 1991), 507, summarized in the *Journal of Marketing* (July 1992): 100.

[59] Wendy Zellner, "How Northwest Gives Competition a Bad Name," *Business Week*, 16 March 1998, 34.

[60] In fact, the Department of Transportation has instituted a policy that defines "unfair exclusionary tactics" and penalizes any airline engaging in such tactics. See "Department of Transportation to Major Airlines: Forewarned Is Fair Warned," *Airline Financial News*, 13 April 1998.

[61] Joseph P. Guiltinan and Gregory T. Gundlach, "Aggressive and Predatory Pricing: A Framework for Analysis," *Journal of Marketing* (July 1996): 88.

[62] Zellner, "How Northwest Gives Competition a Bad Name"; "Majors Fault DOT for Ignoring Law, History, Real-World Economics," *Aviation Daily*, 30 July 1998, 180.

[63] Russell Gold and Ann Zimmerman, "Pumped Out: Wal-Mart's Defeat in Low-Cost Gas Game," *Wall Street Journal*, 13 August 2001, A14.

[64] Joel E. Urbany, William O. Bearden, and Dan C. Weilbaker, "The Effect of Plausible and Exaggerated Reference Prices on Consumer Perceptions and Price Search," *Journal of Consumer Research* (June 1988): 95–110; Kent B. Monroe, *Pricing: Making Profitable Decisions*, 2nd ed. (New York: McGraw-Hill, 1990).

[65] These are the Federal Trade Commission Guides, as cited in *The State of Colorado vs. The May Department Stores Company*, Case No. 89 CV 9274, District Court, City and County of Denver, Colorado, 1990.

[66] See Daniel Kahneman, Jack L. Knetsch, and Richard H. Thaler, "Fairness As a Constraint on Profit Seeking: Entitlements in the Market," *American Economic Review* 70 (September 1986): 728–741.

[67] Christine Dugas, "Consumers Walking Away from ATM Charges," *USA Today*, 16 August 1996, 1B.

[68] For example, the Georgia Legislature passed a price-gouging law in 1994 to prevent hotels and wholesalers from taking advantage of visitors to the Olympics in Atlanta in 1996. It is unclear how successful the law was, as many hotels were still observed to double or triple room rates. See Donna Rosato, "Some Room Rates Have Done a Triple Jump," *USA Today*, 15 July 1996, 1B.

[69] Alexei Barrionuevo, Gary McWilliams, and Russell Gold, "Gasoline Gouging Draws Ire of Officials," *Wall Street Journal*, 13 September 2001, A2; "Michigan Joins Attack on Gasoline Sellers Who Gouge Prices," *Wall Street Journal*, 14 September 2001, A2.

[70] Lindgren and Shimp, *Marketing: An Interactive Learning System*, 403.

Additional References

Backman, J. *Price Practices and Price Policies*. New York: Ronald Press, 1953.

Dean, J. "Research Approach to Pricing." In *Planning the Price Structure*. Marketing Series No. 67. New York: American Management Association, 1947.

"Finding the Right Price Is No Easy Game to Play." *Chief Executive* (September 1981): 16–18.

Marhall, A. *More Profitable Pricing*. London: McGraw-Hill, 1979.

Nagle, Thomas T., and Reed K. Holden. *The Strategy and Tactics of Pricing*. Englewood Cliffs, NJ: Prentice Hall, 1995.

Walker, A.W. "How to Price Industrial Products." *Harvard Business Review* 45 (1967): 38–45.

CHAPTER CASE

GROCERY PRICING: THE OURSTORE COMPANY CASE

This case study was designed to be a realistic representation of a retail grocery market. It is based on the author's experience and does not present specific retailers or city names. Case facts are presented briefly to keep the presentation simple and to make the important facts clear.

Tom Evans is the marketing area vice president of the Ourstore Company, a retail grocery chain. Currently, he is facing the company's pricing and advertising decisions for the coming week (the week of 29 June 2002) in the Anytown market (population 800,000). Ourstore's retail stores in Anytown are primarily superstore format, averaging 35,000 square feet. Tom must decide how to respond to the following changes in the competitive environment.

Ourstore's major competitor in Anytown is the Leader Company. Leader is a large national chain and has traditionally been the market share leader in the Anytown market. Both Ourstore and Leader stores are full-service operations. Two other full-service chains in the market are the Feisty Company and the Opponent Company. The latest market share figures (obtained from a research report dated 19 March 2002) are as follows:

Chain	Number of Stores	Share of the Anytown Market (based on total $ volume)
Leader	25	40%
Ourstore	16	23%
Opponent	16	22%
Feisty	6	10%
All others	—	5%

The New Competitive Environment

On 8 June 2002, the Feisty chain (with six stores and a 10 percent market share in Anytown) began an every day low price (EDLP) promotional blitz. Feisty now promotes "rock-bottom" EDLPs in all its print advertising and has cut prices dramatically on many of its products. There is no information yet available on overall market share changes that have occurred since Feisty began its EDLP campaign.

Price Surveys

The following table contains excerpts from prices surveys taken by a local market research firm in Anytown on 20 April 2002 (2 months *before* Feisty's EDLP campaign began) and on 22 June 2002 (2 week's *after* Feisty's EDLP campaign began). The price surveys show that Leader did not lower its prices to meet Feisty's new prices last week. The Opponent Company (16 stores, 22 percent market share) also did not lower its prices in response to Feisty's EDLP campaign.

Consumer Behavior in Anytown

Several recent research studies, coming from a major university and an industry organization (both located in Anytown) indicate that Anytown consumers do not comparison shop extensively. More specifically, the research indicates that:

1. Only 25 percent of Anytown consumers actively compare competitive stores' prices by shopping around and reading advertising.
2. Most Anytown consumers shop one grocery store all the time.

These results have been consistent over several recent research studies.

What Should Tom Do?

Tom has to set prices for the week of 29 June, determining whether to respond to Feisty's low-price challenge. To date, he has not changed pricing strategy. Tom is under no pressure from the home office to follow or not follow the new price competition. The decision has to be based on his evaluation of the current consumer and competitive situation. What prices would you recommend for the following items? Why?

Item	Ourstore's Wholesale Cost	Recommended Retail Price
Bananas (branded 1 lb.)	$0.25	
Kellogg's Corn Flakes (24 oz.)	$1.70	
Oscar Meyer Sliced Bologna (8 oz.)	$0.93	
Whole Milk (1 gal.)	$1.45	
Minute Maid Orange Juice (frozen 16 oz.)	$0.85	
Hellman's Mayonnaise (1 qt.)	$1.65	
Coke (2 liter)	$0.93	
Maxwell House Coffee (1 lb. regular grind)	$2.75	

Price Survey: Anytown Market
(Selected Products Carried by Major Competitors)

Product	20 April 2002 Store Prices			22 June 2002 Store Prices			
	Ourstore	Leader	Opponent	Ourstore	Leader	Opponent	Feisty
Bananas (branded 1 lb.)	0.49	0.49	0.49	0.49	0.49	0.49	0.39
Kellogg's Corn Flakes (24 oz.)	1.89	1.89	1.87	1.89	1.89	1.87	1.67
Oscar Meyer Sliced Bologna (8 oz.)	1.39	1.39	1.39	1.39	1.39	1.39	1.09
Whole Milk (1 gal.)	2.49	2.39	2.49	2.39	2.39	2.39	1.97
Minute Maid Orange Juice (frozen 1 oz.)	0.89	0.83	0.85	0.89	0.89	0.85	0.69
Hellman's Mayonnaise (1 qt.)	1.99	1.99	1.99	1.99	1.99	1.99	1.59
Coke (2 liter)	1.79	1.79	1.79	1.79	1.79	1.79	1.19
Maxwell House Coffee (1 lb. regular grind)	3.19	3.09	2.99	3.09	3.09	2.99	2.67

PART seven

The Future of Marketing

CHAPTER 15

E-Marketing

John (Jack) H. Lindgren, Jr.
University of Virginia

Dr. Lindgren is currently the Consumer Bankers Association Professor, Area Coordinator of the Marketing Group at the McIntire School of Commerce, the University of Virginia. He was appointed to the Consumer Bankers Association Chair in 1991. He previously served as Director of the PricewaterhouseCoopers Center for Innovation in Business Learning (1993–1999), Director of the Center for Financial Services Studies (1986–1990), Academic Director for the Ph.D. Institute (1983–1987), and Program Director for the Society of Marketing Professional Services Institute (1982–1984). He is a past Vice President of the American Marketing Association and served on the National AMA Board of Directors (1984–1986). He served as President and Board member for the Central Virginia Chapter of the American Marketing Association (1981–1986 and 1998–1999). He also served as the President of the Collegiate Activities Council for the American Marketing Association (1982–1983).

Professor Lindgren has published numerous articles and monographs in publications such as the *Journal for the Academy of Marketing Science, Journal of Services Marketing, Journal of Professional Services Marketing, Journal of Marketing Education, Journal of Retail Banking, Banker's Magazine, Cost and Management,* and the *Journal of Accounting, Auditing and Finance,* as well as numerous proceedings of national and regional professional associations. He has coauthored six books and monographs in the field of marketing and serves on the editorial boards of marketing publications. He has developed numerous CD-ROMs for use by faculty in the classroom. The most recent of these is titled *SuperBowl CD: Ads from Advertising's Premier Day.* In 1996, he published the first of its kind CD-ROM textbook titled *Marketing: An Integrated Learning System.*

With his expertise in multimedia learning and Web design, Dr. Lindgren has designed Web sites for institutions and has served as a consultant to the University of Virginia, U.S. Department of Commerce, Touche Ross and Company, Berman Technologies, International Auto, Star (Texaco) Enterprise, Crestar Bank, Jefferson National Bank, First Pennsylvania Bank, Hamilton Bank, and the Federal Reserve Banks for Atlanta and Chicago. He has served on the faculty of numerous executive education programs throughout the United States, including the McIntire Entrepreneurial Executive Institute (1989–1991), Graduate School of Retail Bank Management (1979–1990), Savings Institutions Advanced Marketing School (1982–1993), Virginia Bankers School of Bank Management (1979–present), Society for Marketing Professional Services (1982–1984), and the National Banking School (1980–present).

Dr. Lindgren was a Peace Corps volunteer from 1968 to 1970 in the Philippines. He was named outstanding young professor at the University of Virginia in 1983.

E-Marketing

One of the new e-marketing technologies that are emerging is "mass customization." A leader in this new segment is Poindexter Systems, formerly ru4; the company's central product is an engine that optimizes ads based on anonymous impression data and viewer behavioral response. As direct marketers have known for decades, all customers should not be treated the same way; customers and prospective customers have different needs and desires, and successful companies identify these differences and market to each customer by leveraging his or her individual wants and needs.

Poindexter is bringing these direct marketing tenets to online advertising. Its flagship product, Poindexter POE, uses statistical analysis to identify the shared characteristics of viewers who respond to ads in a similar manner, grouping similar viewers into clusters. Viewers that fall into a cluster are shown ads that are proven to perform best with that specific cluster. This has a great effect on improving ad performance and therefore driving profitability.

These clusters are further refined as the ad campaign continues and relevant data is gathered. Basically the Poindexter system learns, and as it does so it delivers higher performance boosts to the ad campaign.

Poindexter offers some ancillary services that also incorporate this concept of delivering the appropriate ad to each viewer. For example, Poindexter's dynamic ad generation feature permits online ads to automatically and intelligently adapt to individual consumers. This is quite similar to other technologies that pull regularly updated news stories from a newspaper database and allow dynamic price promotion within the banner for an airline. Poindexter has taken this process one step further by showing viewers up-to-date information that is relevant to them, based on the anonymous data that is collected about them, such as geography and network data. They are able, for example, to deliver ads for an airline company that display current flight information for trips departing from a viewer's home city. An electronics company could deliver ads for different product lines based on demographic information. An international company could deliver ads in the consumer's native language, by using Poindexter.[1]

Poindexter uses a fictional online bookseller to demonstrate the ultimate promotional piece, which uses anonymous information passed from the bookseller to adapt ads based on each viewer's prior behavior. If the viewer has been to the site and put items into the shopping cart but has not purchased them, the bookseller could deliver an ad featuring those items with an offer for 20 percent off. If the viewer has made a purchase, the system could suggest similar books.[2]

After you have completed this chapter, you should be able to:

1. Understand the e-marketing landscape, including the basic history of the Internet, basic Internet terms and markets, and types of Internet sites.
2. Identify factors responsible for the explosive growth of Internet marketing.
3. Know how Web sites earn money.
4. Describe how the marketing mix elements work together within the e-marketing context.
5. Examine the costs and benefits of e-marketing.

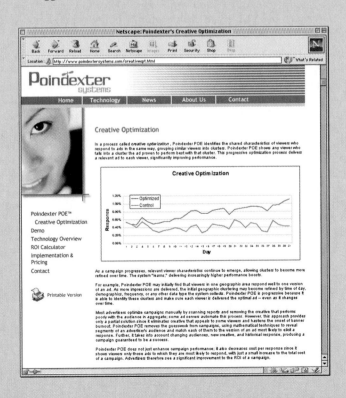

Internet
is a worldwide network of interconnected computer networks originally built by the U.S. government.

World Wide Web (Web)
is a data network system that allows users to interact with documents stored on computers across the Internet.

THE E-MARKETING LANDSCAPE

The **Internet** is a worldwide network of interconnected computers and computer networks that carry data and make information exchange possible. The **World Wide Web (Web)** is a subset of the Internet. It is a collection of hyperlinked documents or files, not computers. These documents include text, graphics, video, animation, and/or audio files. Thus, the Internet includes a number of computer networks set up by individuals, companies, and organizations, while the World Wide Web is the mechanism to link the documents available on those computers/computer networks. For purposes of this book, the terms *World Wide Web* and *Internet* will be used interchangeably.

The Internet has grown exponentially over the past few years because of two major developments. The first is the development of user-friendly interfaces such as Netscape's Navigator/Communicator and Microsoft's Explorer. The second reason for the explosion of the Internet is that these interfaces allow individuals, businesses, and organizations to use data, graphics, sound, and video with ease.

History of the Internet

The beginnings of the Internet can be traced back to World War II. At that time, the government and military establishment attempted to link together thousands of scientists to discover ways of applying their scientific knowledge and expertise to modern warfare.

In 1969, the U.S. Department of Defense established a program called the Advanced Research Projects Agency Network (ARPANET). The purpose of this network was to provide secure communications among organizations engaged in defense-related research. Shortly after the establishment of ARPANET, the National Science Foundation created a similar network for the academic community called NSFNet. NSFNet was established to enable researchers and academics in nondefense fields to make use of these methods of advanced communications. The NSFNet became the backbone of the Internet.

The original Internet was developed for military intelligence and as a mechanism for academic communications. Today's Internet bears little resemblance to these first efforts to link computers and scientific intelligence.

A Primer of Internet Terms and Markets

As technology is rapidly integrated into business practice and our everyday lives, a number of new terms have emerged. Each of these terms is described below and their relationships are graphically illustrated in Figure 15.1.

- Internet—The global network of interconnected computers and computer networks.
- World Wide Web (Web)—That portion of the Internet which includes hyperlinked documents and graphics, video, animation, and/or audio files. People use browsers such as Netscape and Internet Explorer to navigate the Web.
- Portals—The methods that people use to enter the Web. Examples include Yahoo! and Lycos. While commonly used for searching the Web, these types of sites have many stand-alone features such as shopping, news, etc.
- Extranets—Networks of computers that connect businesses or organizations with computers at other businesses or organizations.
- Intranet—A network of interconnected computers existing within a business or organization. Intranets are typically used for internal communications.

Markets

E-marketing
is the set of activities that bring customers and companies together using electronic means such as the Internet.

E-marketing is the set of activities that bring customers and companies together using electronic means such as the Internet. A number of markets comprise the e-marketing landscape. The typical markets include:

1. *Business-to-Business (B2B)*—Includes all the activities of business that occur between two business entities. B2B activities include purchasing, sales, service, support, and payments systems.

| Relationship of Various Internet Terms | Figure 15.1 |

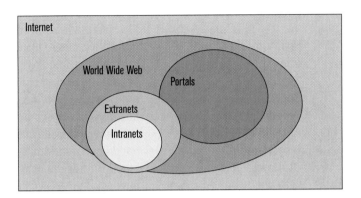

2. *Business-to-Consumer (B2C)*—Includes all activities of business that occur between a business and its ultimate consumers. We think of B2C transactions as retail customers purchasing from businesses via a company Web site. The activities include sales, service, customer information, and customer support.

3. *Consumer-to-Consumer (C2C)*—Includes all activities involving interactions between consumers. C2C activities include auctions between consumers that are facilitated by firms such as eBay, personals, classified advertising, and games.

4. *Business-to-Government (B2G)*—Includes all activities involving transactions between various businesses and government entities. B2G activities include sales to the government, purchasing support, product information, and service.

5. *Government-to-Consumer (G2C)*—Includes all activities involving interactions between consumers and government entities. G2C activities include mostly information exchange.

Organizations are not limited to one model or the other. Many organizations utilize multiple models simultaneously, selling their products to other businesses (B2B), to ultimate consumers (B2C), and to the government (B2G). This chapter will focus on the first three types of markets: B2B, B2C, and C2C.

Types of Internet Sites

As fast as the Internet is expanding, the number and type of Internet sites are increasing. Sites can be classified into four major categories: **company/brand sites**, **service sites**, **selling sites**, and **information sites**. Obviously, these categories are not mutually exclusive and collectively exhaustive, but this typology is presented to help the reader begin to see how companies are using the Internet for either cost savings or profit. Table 15.1 provides examples for each of these types of Internet sites. As you visit the sites, you should begin to think of how each company has positioned itself to maximize the benefits of its site.

Company/Brand Sites

A number of companies that do not currently expect to sell products online have developed Internet sites. The purpose of these sites is to provide users with information about the company and its brands. Visitors to these sites will find information about the company history, mission, financial statements, public relations efforts, news releases, and even up-to-the-minute stock quotes. Additionally, company/brand sites are packed with information on how to use their products, how they are made, and how they can be used with other products.

Company/brand sites
are Web sites that provide information about a company, such as history, mission, financial statements, etc.

Service sites
are Web sites that provide a customer service interface for a company.

Selling sites
are Web sites that provide products for purchase over the Internet.

Information sites
are Web sites that generate revenue through advertising or the subscription rates that are charged to members.

Table 15.1	Four Categories of Internet Web Sites		
Type of Sites	**Company**		**URL**
Company/	Coca-Cola Company		http://www.coca-cola.com
Brand Sites	Tide		http://www.tide.com
	Sunkist		http://www.sunkist.com
Service Sites	Wells Fargo		http://www.wellsfargo.com
	Federal Express		http://www.fedex.com
Selling Sites	Amazon.com		http://www.amazon.com
	Chrysler		http://www.daimlerchrysler.com
	L.L. Bean		http://www.llbean.com
Information Sites	CNN and *Sports Illustrated*		http://www.sportsillustrated.cnn.com
	Wall Street Journal		http://online.wsj.com
	Yahoo!		http://www.yahoo.com

http://www.coca-cola.com

http://www.tide.com

http://www.sunkist.com

The Coca-Cola Company Web site includes seven sections: Our Company, Features, Cool Links, Shop, Country Sites, Contact Us, and Site Map. Coca-Cola products are featured in Figure 15.2.

The Tide home page contains similar information as the Coca-Cola home page. The purpose of this site is not to sell Tide products from the manufacturer but to enhance the brand equity (see Chapter 12) of the product line. Because Procter & Gamble does not want to compete with regular retailers or e-tailers and thus create channel conflict (see Chapter 10), consumers visiting the site cannot purchase Tide products directly. While they do have a Products section of the site, visitors are directed to either online retailers or stores located in their geographic area. The site does sell some products that are not available in retail stores, such as Ricky Rudd (a Tide-sponsored race driver) collectibles.

Some companies also have Internet connections for their suppliers. Sunkist has a hyperlink on its site for Sunkist growers. Sunkist growers can access newsletters, citriculture tips, and related resources. Other visitors to the site can obtain information about the company, citrus products, news stories about Sunkist, recipes, and engineering breakthroughs; however, the site does not sell Sunkist products.

Service Sites

Customer service sites have developed rapidly on the Web because of the self-service nature of the Internet. The purpose of service sites is to provide customers a service interface to the company. Because this interface no longer needs to be a live person, the company is able to reduce its overhead labor costs as well.

Before the introduction of automatic teller machines (ATMs), the banking industry was plagued by limited hours and a reliance on human contact. Banks built more brick-and-mortar locations to get closer to their ultimate customers. They also extended their hours and provided telephone services to extend their market. These moves were extremely costly to the banks, but seemed necessary to improve customer satisfaction. The introduction of ATMs allowed banks to extend banking hours to 24 hours a day without the need for human contact. Additionally, locating ATMs in grocery stores and other retail establishments allowed banks to expand geographically without the necessity of building full-service branches. ATMs not only improved customer satisfaction, they saved the banks money by eliminating the need for new branches and reducing labor costs, which had a significant impact on the profitability of banks in the past decade.

Many companies have been able to provide enhanced customer access while increasing their overall customer satisfaction and retention by using the Internet. Wells Fargo first offered online services in 1989, and introduced retail banking over the Internet in 1995. It has been found that customers who bank online are 50 percent less likely to leave the bank. Web services to total online banking. Now through the Wells Fargo

http://www.wellsfargo.com

Coca-Cola Products   **Figure 15.2**

Web site, customers can access their account balances and transactions history, transfer funds between accounts, pay all of their bills, buy and sell securities, apply for consumer accounts and lines of credit, receive real-time decisions on applications for home equity loans/lines of credit, and order specialized checks or foreign currency (see Figure 15.3).

Perhaps the most dramatic savings produced by a service site involves the Federal Express Web site. FedEx built its own private network to track the millions of packages they ship each day. This combination of a private network and the Internet allows them to have a 99 percent on-time delivery rate while shipping over 3.1 million packages daily.[4] In 1994, FedEx was spending millions of dollars on telephone charges and for support personnel to answer customer questions about the whereabouts of their packages. By developing a Web site to help customers track their own packages online, FedEx saved a tremendous amount for the company. How *much* money does it save? FedEx's Webmaster at the time said that an average of 500,000 packages per month were tracked on the site over the first six months. She estimated that while half of those were "curiosity" tracks by people just checking out the feature for the fun of it, the other half of those checks would otherwise have been calls to the company's 800 number. Such telephone calls average 2 minutes each, she said. At an independently estimated cost to FedEx of about $0.50 per call, including personnel costs, that works out to about $125,000 in savings per month—due to just one simple feature. She said that the company spent only $50,000 developing the original site and $50,000 promoting it.[5]

http://www.fedex.com

Selling Sites

Selling sites are virtual stores that allow consumers to purchase products over the Internet. They typically represent a new distribution channel to the seller. While many companies who sell online have utilized direct marketing either through direct mail or catalogs, a few, such as Amazon.com, have started as a new venture using the Internet as their entry into the direct-selling industry.

Amazon.com is a company that started on the Web in July 1995 with a mission "to educate, inform, and inspire." Today it offers 4.7 million books, CDs, audiobooks, DVDs, computer games, and related products. Since its inception, Amazon.com has sold to over 6.2 million people from more than 160 countries around the world.[6]

http://www.amazon.com

| Figure 15.3 | Wells Fargo's Service Web Site |

At the Amazon.com site (see Figure 15.4), visitors can search for books or CDs by author, artist, title, subject, or keyword. Browsing pages allow visitors to gather information about titles, sections to get recommendations, and links to allow visitors to read reviews written either by the media or by other visitors.

While the purpose of the Amazon.com site is to sell directly to the ultimate consumer, some sites are designed much like sales promotional tools to aid consumers in the decision-making process. This kind of site allows visitors to screen themselves to see how they match up with the company's products. One might consider this the logical extension of market segmentation—consumers provide information about themselves and then the site attempts to match their individual needs and wants with the product offerings of the company.

http://www.daimlerchrysler.com

DaimlerChrysler's Web site moves customers closer to the buying decision by offering many ways for consumers to collect information about the company's vehicle. Each brand has its own page, so that consumers can click to the Jeep Grand Cherokee page and receive information about that make, or they can look at all the cars at once and then click on those of interest. If consumers want specific attributes, they can navigate the site based on types of cars or even types of incentives that are available. Information about prices, models, and options can aid consumers in their choice of a vehicle.

After visitors choose a make and model, they can actually get a quote on the price of their desired car from dealers. This price quote is available only from Daimler-Chrysler's five-star dealers. Additionally, the site has information about the history of the company, the technology awards won by the company, innovations in the auto industry, and even a page for Chrysler owners to post pictures and stories about their Chrysler products.

Amazon.com Is a Selling Web Site

Figure 15.4

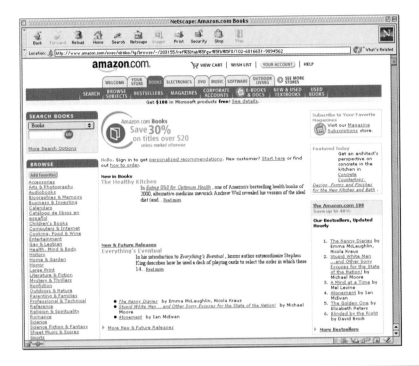

Many catalog marketers have logically developed Web sites because of the lower cost of presenting their catalog online versus the printing and mailing costs associated with direct distribution to consumers. While most of these marketers have not abandoned their printed catalogs, they are prepared for the next logical advance in direct marketing, that is, online selling. Online selling requires not only that companies sell but also that they provide information related to their product line.

An excellent example of an online vendor is L.L. Bean. The L.L. Bean site offers visitors the opportunity to receive any of their catalogs through the mail or allows visitors to shop online. One special feature of the L.L. Bean site is the section on outdoor activities. Visitors can receive information on the Outdoor Discovery Schools, state and national parks around the world, or on specific outdoor activities such as fly-fishing, camping, winter camping, backpacking, cycling, snowshoeing, or cross-country skiing. In addition, a compete history of the company and background material on L.L. Bean is available on the site. While L.L. Bean still does over 90 percent of its business via telephone, the company's Web site shows definite promise for cost savings and revenue generation in the future.[7]

http://www.llbean.com

Information Sites

A number of media outlets have developed Web sites to reinforce their presence in the marketplace. CNNSI.com is an example of two media firms—CNN and *Sports Illustrated*—that have joined to provide sports lovers with complete information on any sports topic (see Figure 15.5). This new media on the Internet allows the organizations that typically report the news daily and weekly to now report sports news almost up-to-the-minute. Sports enthusiasts not only get each week's *Sports Illustrated* magazine online but also can access past issues. If that is not enough, the sports fan can get information about games in progress, with actual play-by-play information. Additionally, a visitor to the site can get statistics, both daily and season-to-date, about the teams and the players. Finally, sports fans can subscribe to the magazine and purchase other sports-related products.

http://www.sportsillustrated.cnn.com

Victoria's Secret

Some business models are ideal for the Web. Take catalog retailers, for example. These business are able to make a smooth transition to the Internet, owing to the already rather independent shopping process.

Given this, it was no surprise when Victoria's Secret, a lingerie retail store and catalog vendor, took to the Internet. What came as a surprise to many, is how the company chose to promote its Web presence.

Seeking an alternative to the banner ads commonly used to promote Web sites, Victoria's Secret decided to get a little creative, in the form of a virtual fashion show of its products, modeled by some of the most famous supermodels of the time. The company heavily advertised its Webcast through traditional channels, including print ads in newspapers and even a 30-second commercial during the Superbowl.

The first fashion show took place in February of 1999, just in time for Valentine's Day shoppers. According to broadcast.com, the company providing technical support for the event, more than 1.5 million visitors were attracted to the site. This led to slowdowns and bottlenecks, as the site had not been constructed to handle that much traffic simultaneously.

Victoria's Secret was not discouraged by technical troubles during its first Webcast. The 2001 Victoria's Secret fashion show took place on 15 November, and was aired live both on the Web site and on the ABC television network. The result of the show was to double traffic to 423,000 visitors, up from 212,000 the previous week. Interestingly, men comprised 52 percent of the site's audience, while women made up the remaining 48 percent. More importantly, the average visitor spent 10 minutes at the site, giving them plenty of opportunity to check out the merchandise.

Source: Adapted from "Victoria's Secret Show Doubles Traffic to Site," http://64.12.50.249/2001/TECH/internet/11/26/netratings.victorias.secret.reut/, accessed 26 November 2001.

http://www.victoriassecret.com

| Figure 15.5 | CNN and *Sports Illustrated*'s Information Web site |

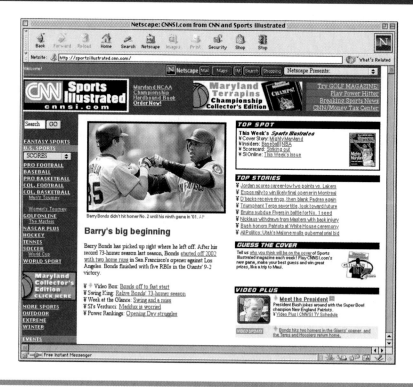

The *Wall Street Journal* Online is an example of an information site that has been able to generate revenues via subscriptions, as well as revenue from advertising. This method of operation is explored in more detail later in this chapter in the section on Profits Models.

Search engines represent another type of information site that people use to find information on other Web sites. Since the Internet is so vast and rich in information, surfers must have some mechanism to help them find what they are looking for. One of the most popular search engines on the Web is Yahoo!. In addition to the search feature on the Yahoo! site, visitors are able to get up-to-the-minute news from Reuters, purchase products at auctions, or even build a personal virtual store online by clicking on the Yahoo! Store. Another feature of the Yahoo! site is the Yahoo! Clubs that visitors can join. These are virtual communities of individuals with common interests that share information among members.[8]

THE GROWTH OF INTERNET MARKETING

The growth of the Internet required three separate developments in order for it to become an efficient marketing tool. First, businesses had to develop their electronic commerce **intranets** and **extranets** that connect to the Internet. Second, network server growth had to allow for fast connections. Finally, consumers (either at work or at home) had to have access to the Internet either through a PC or some kind of Web TV device. Let us look at growth in all three of these areas.

Electronic Commerce

Electronic commerce includes all the activities of a firm that use e-marketing to aid in the exchange of products. The term includes business activities between manufacturers, intermediaries, and ultimate customers. Electronic commerce, or e-commerce, originated over 20 years ago with the development of **electronic data interchange (EDI)** and *electronic funds transfer (EFT)* systems in the late 1970s and early 1980s. Other forms of e-commerce include credit cards, ATMs, and the activities of telephone banking.[9] These developments along with the expansion of the Internet have offered new opportunities to firms both large and small.

B2B Usage

Web sites that market or sell to other businesses online will experience tremendous growth in the next five years, rising to $8.5 trillion in 2005 from $433 billion in 2000, according to Gartner, Inc.[10] (See Figure 15.6.) Currently, B2B Web sites comprise the second largest industrial group, with 38 percent of the publicly listed domains on the English-language Web. Most B2B sites are designed to stimulate and support client relations, which are primarily fostered offline. Unlike B2C operations, where most products are prepriced, B2B operations are highly negotiable, and in-person customer assistance is highly valued. It is more important for a company to execute business well in the real world than to market effectively online.[11]

According to a report by ActivMedia Research, 33 percent of B2B sites market, but do not sell, products online; 25 percent offer professional services; and only 15 percent actually sell products on site.[12] Eighty percent of these companies are integrated, selling both online and offline. B2B commerce swelled from 3 percent to 42 percent of total B2B domestic trade within five years.[13]

Jupiter Research studied the trading activities of 12 major industries and concluded that aerospace and defense, chemicals, computer and telecommunications equipment, electronics, and motor vehicle and parts will be conducting half of their total business online by 2004. The computer and telecommunications space is expected to become the largest online B2B market with relation to sales, which will top $1 trillion in 2005 (see Figure 15.7).[14] Although sales among B2B sites are expected to increase in future years, revenue is not currently a top priority; only 32 percent of sites are profitable, with another third expected to be profitable someday.[15]

Figure 15.6   **Worldwide B2B E-Commerce Market**

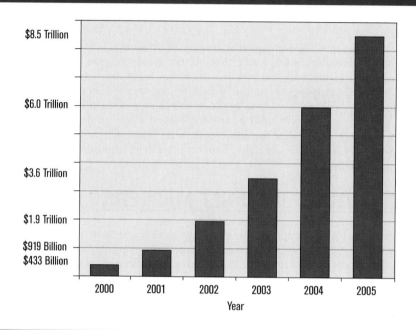

Source: Gartner, Inc.; CyberAtlas Web site, http://cyberatlas.internet.com/markets/b2b/article/0,,10091_719571,00.html.

Figure 15.7   **B2B Spending by Industry**

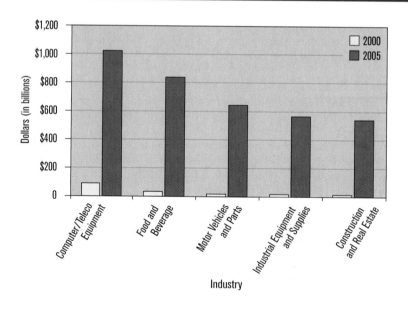

Of the current B2B companies, 60 percent are globalizing their Web sites; this figure is expected to grow to 80 percent by 2004. Global and nonglobal companies have approximately the same percentage of foreign visitors, but globalization makes it easier for these visitors to purchase online, which in turn has a massive impact on revenue. Those companies that are nonglobal planned for foreign revenue earnings of 10 percent in 2000 and 12 percent in 2001. However, global companies planned foreign revenue earnings of 25 percent and 30 percent during those same years, making evident the benefits that globalization provides.[16]

Internet Hosts

The second development that has allowed the Internet to become an efficient marketing tool was the expansion of high-speed connections to the Internet, which are called **Internet hosts**. These hosts are businesses' interface with the Internet. In 1990, there were only 1,000 Internet hosts;[17] however, by January 2001 this number had exploded to over 109 million. With a growth rate of 63 new hosts and 11 new domains per minute worldwide, there is no sign of growth slowdown at the present time.[18]

Dial-up Internet service providers (ISP) remain the most popular Internet access method, accounting for nearly 46.7 million customers (93 percent) (see Figure 15.8). The 10 percent growth among this segment in the first quarter of 2000, however, is incomparable to the growth in the emerging high-speed access market. Connections through cable modems increased by 44 percent with 2.3 million customers, while subscriptions to DSL service rocketed 183 percent, though with only 200,000 customers total. There was a minor decline to just over 1.1 million subscribers accessing the World Wide Web through Internet TV.[19]

According to a study by the media research firms Arbitron, Inc. and Coleman Insights, 31 percent of American Internet users now have broadband access at home, work, or school. A further study by Centris found that not only are broadband households 60 percent more likely to make a purchase online, but they spend an average of 38 percent more than dial-up households.[20]

Internet hosts
provide high-speed connections to the Web.

B2C: Consumers Using the Internet

While the growth of consumer Internet usage has lagged behind that of businesses and Internet hosts, its expansion is still significant. The Internet adds one new user every quarter-second. Currently, there are over 327 million Internet users and this number is expected to reach 1 billion by 2005. North America leads the geographic market in international Web use with 63 million online; following behind in order are Japan, the United Kingdom, Germany, and Canada.[21]

While females comprise 50.7 percent of Internet users, men use the Internet for longer periods of time. In 1999, the average age of users was 30; today it has reached 38 years, with those 55 and older representing the fastest growing age group. The number of seniors using the Internet is expected to triple from 11.1 million in 1999 to 34.1 million

Most Popular Internet Access Methods   Figure 15.8

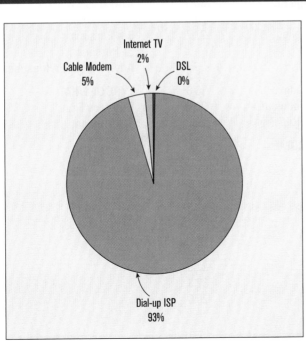

in 2004, accounting for 20 percent of all new users.[22] Currently, 60 percent of Internet users are married, 38 percent have graduated college plus had further education, and nearly 33 percent generate a household income between $75,000 and $149,000 per year. Table 15.2 summarizes U.S. online demographics.

On average, the U.S. home Internet user spends almost 10 hours online each month and visits 10 sites, viewing each Web page for an average of 51 seconds. Because searching the Web can be so overwhelming, half of the top 10 sites are search engines, with Yahoo!, MSN, America Online, Microsoft, and Passport being the top five (see Figure 15.9).[23]

What attracts an online shopper to a specific site? Studies have shown that there are several site characteristics that turn shoppers into buyers. It is understandable that search functions are the most popular site feature when choosing a retail site, but the availability of thorough product information doesn't fall far behind. Consumers like having zoom-in images, product reviews, and in-stock status at their fingertips. Other features on the list include customer service, personalization, and wish lists, which are used

Table 15.2	U.S. Online Demographics		
	Percent		**Percent**
GENDER		**JOB FUNCTION**	
Male	49.3	Accounting	13.7
Female	50.7	Banking	9.3
		Engr./Design/Research	10.9
AGE		Finance	10.3
Age 18–34	40.1	General Management	19.5
Age 35–54	7.2	International	2.0
Age 55+	12.7	MIS/EDP	2.8
		Manufacturing	5.0
MARITAL STATUS		Marketing	10.8
Single	27.9	Medical	6.8
Married	60.9	Sales	17.7
Other	11.2	Service	47.9
EDUCATION			
Graduated College Plus	38.3	**HOUSEHOLD SIZE**	
Attended College	34.0	1–2 Persons	39.9
Did Not Attend College	27.7	3–4 Persons	44.5
		5+ Persons	15.6
OCCUPATION		Any Children in Household	47.5
Professional	18.2		
Exec./Manager/Admin.	16.6	**TYPE OF FIRM**	
Clerical/Sales/Technical	26.7	Business Firm	45.1
Precision/Crafts/Repair	6.5	Government	15.5
		Other	20.8
HOUSEHOLD INCOME			
$150,000 or More	7.7		
$75,000–149,000	32.8		
$50,000–74,999	26.4		
Less Than $50,000	33.0		
CENSUS REGION			
Northeast	19.8		
North Central	22.9		
South	32.3		
West	25.0		

Source: IconoMap 2001, http://www.iconocast.com/iconomap/, accessed 2 April, 2002.

Most Popular Internet Sites   **Figure 15.9**

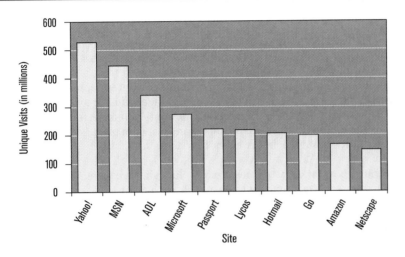

Source: Iconomap 2001, http://www.iconocast.com/pdf/ataglance1=01.pdf, accessed 7 May 2002.

by a smaller percentage of consumers and are therefore slightly less important when selecting an online shopping site.[24]

Improving Business Practices Using the Internet

Initially computer usage in business was confined to accounting tasks, payroll processing, and production planning. The 1980s saw expanded usage with the development of private networks in the distribution channel to handle purchase orders, shipping instructions, and reorder merchandise, using the EDI protocol. In addition to these EDI networks, firms began to develop internal networks to pass information from department to department at locations throughout the world. These intranets were extremely expensive to maintain and thus only the largest firms could afford to build and maintain this kind of private network.[25]

The Internet brought electronic commerce to all firms: small, medium, or large. Because the Internet requires only one server to be connected, even the smallest firms can use the Internet for internal communications as well as a connection for business-to-business relationships. A firm's private networks can also be connected to the Internet. These networks are typically accessed via some kind of password system.

Electronic commerce expanded on the Internet primarily because of four major areas of improvement to business practices.[26] These improvements in business practice include reduced costs, inventory reduction, improved customer service, and market/product development opportunities. Each of these benefits is discussed in the following sections.

Reduced Costs

Many firms have justified their investment in a Web site based on cost savings. Firms such as FedEx and Cisco Systems have saved millions of dollars through the implementation of a Web strategy. FedEx dramatically reduced their customer service costs with a minimal investment, while Cisco used the Web to provide their customers with the most up-to-date information on its products.

Other firms, such as General Electric, have reduced costs through the analysis of the supply chain. Identifying and evaluating suppliers of component parts and other materials can be an expensive and time-consuming process. Product specifications, delivery times, service schedules, pricing, and a multitude of other items must be continually evaluated. If a firm can identify suppliers and products that meet its procurement specifications, the firm will be able to potentially consolidate purchases and build close relationships with its suppliers.

Procurement costs
are those costs to a firm associated with the process of receiving customers' orders.

Storage costs
are those costs to a firm associated with the act of storing inventory.

Handling costs
are costs to a firm associated with the act of transferring inventory to customers.

Obsolescence costs
are those costs to a firm associated with holding inventory that is not selling due to a loss in demand for the product.

EDI networks evolved to allow firms to integrate their manufacturing processes and procurement processes. These networks reduced the overall costs of procurement by building relationships with suppliers and providing timely information on products, pricing, delivery times, and availability. Using the same principles on the Internet, a small firm could easily compete with larger firms in supplier procurement processes. In addition, the Internet has the potential to reduce overall **procurement costs** by automating manual systems of reorder and supplier identification.

Using online information instead of printed brochures represents another cost-saving aspect of the Internet. Obvious savings include printing and mailing costs, but less obvious savings result from the ability to present even more information and products. When this information is available online instead of in print, marketers do not need to republish costly color brochures every time there is a change in price and product information.

If a firm uses a market expansion strategy through direct contact with its customers, it must either increase the number of salespeople or the number of customer contact personnel to service the increased customer base. This type of expansion can increase costs dramatically. A market expansion strategy using the Internet, where customer self-service is the norm, allows a firm to add new customers at little or no additional cost.

Inventory Reduction

Holding excessive inventory can result in high costs to a firm. These costs include **storage costs**, **handling costs**, and **obsolescence costs**. Just-in-time production sys-

tems allow a firm to reduce its dependence on inventory and the storage costs associated with that inventory. The result of better management of inventory is not only lower inventory but also a better matching of that inventory to specific customer needs.

Amazon.com is an example of a firm that has been able to expand because of an efficient just-in-time delivery system. Amazon.com has differentiated itself by offering 4.7 million[27] books, music, and other titles online versus the typical bookstore that houses 175,000[28] books at one time. The typical bookstore's reliance on bricks, mortar, and people limits both their customer base and offerings.

Improved Customer Service

Customer service can be improved greatly using the Internet to automate the process to allow for customer self-service. Firms such Federal Express and Wells Fargo[29] have shown excellent savings and improved customer service by moving away from labor-intensive phone contact to customer-controlled information systems. As discussed earlier in the chapter, FedEx now sends over 3.1 million packages a day with a 99 percent on time rating and the tracking of those packages is now totally automated to a customer self-service system.[30]

Firms such as Cisco use the Internet as a communications tool to keep their customer contact employees and their customers informed about changes in products. In addition, the potential of the Internet as a delivery system for training is just now being explored. Delivering training programs to employees and/or customers can also result in substantial savings. Rather than take people off the job for training and incur the expenses of travel to bring together trainers and trainees, many companies today have developed virtual universities, delivered via the Internet, to keep their employees up-to-date. The benefits of this kind of just-in-time training can improve overall customer satisfaction by providing better-trained and informed employees and/or customers.

Market/Product Development Opportunities

Companies using the Internet can stay open for business 24 hours a day not only in the United States but also around the world. To maintain a customer contact organization that can serve customers in all countries of the world and do so in all time zones, without an automated system using the Internet, would be very costly.

The Internet allows a firm to market its products throughout the world and avoid the significant costs associated with face-to-face selling to customers. Even the smallest company can sell its products globally with little more than a Web page and the use of a delivery company such as FedEx or UPS, which will handle all of the export papers, as well as the shipping of the product.[31]

PROFIT MODELS

LEARNING OBJECTIVE 3

How do Web sites make money? This is a common question for businesses and investors. To answer this question, four basic profit models have emerged. Again, these categories are by no means mutually exclusive or collectively exhaustive, but they do provide a basic classification system. To generate profits firms use advertising, subscriptions, product vending, and intermediary commissions. Many web sites utilize a combination of these strategies, but we will examine them each individually.

Advertising

Companies can generate revenue by selling **banner ad** space on their Web sites. Banner ads are typically animated GIF graphics placed on the host site and hyperlinked to the URL of the advertiser. The price for banner ad space varies according to the size and popularity of the host.[32]

Search engines, such as Yahoo!, successfully generate revenue by selling banner advertising, especially to businesses that sell goods or services. Yahoo! segments advertising based on the type of information for which the user is searching. For example, try typing in any computer-related word in a Yahoo! search and you will probably see banner advertising for IBM.

Customer service
is the service a business provides to accommodate customers' questions and concerns.

A banner ad
is typically an animated GIF graphic placed on a host site and hyperlinked to the URL of the advertiser.

Click through
is a term that describes the act of clicking on an advertising banner located at a host site and being transported electronically to the advertiser's site.

Affiliate programs
have advertisers pay for each person who enters their Web site via a link on the host site or pays for each sale generated.

Another source of advertising revenue is the click through ad, or **click through**. The host earns a commission from the advertiser when a user clicks on a banner ad on the host site and is transported to the advertiser's site. There are two common commission arrangements or **affiliate programs** for this type of ad. The advertiser may pay the host for each person who enters their site via the link on the host site or just for each sale generated by a user who originated on the host site.

Web site owners who join the Amazon.com Associates Program can incorporate a link that recommends books, music, and other products available at Amazon.com on their sites. In return, they receive a referral fee for every sale generated. Since its inception in July 1996, the Associates Program has signed up over 100,000 members.[33]

According to eMarketer's eAdvertising Report, online advertising spending is expected to reach $7.6 billion by the end of 2001, a 7 percent increase from the $7.1 billion spent in 2000. Online advertising is expected to grow substantially in the next several years as well, escalating to $10.3 billion in 2002 and as high as $23 billion by 2005.[34] In addition, the eMarketer's also revealed that:

- The average Internet user is exposed to 610 ad impressions per day.
- Seventy-four percent of Web advertising space goes unsold.
- More than 99.7 percent of banner ads do not get clicked[35]

Data from Neilsen/NetRatings' AdSpectrum service revealed that lower exposure to ad campaigns combined with a higher reach resulted in higher click rates. "Through a low-reach, high-frequency model, dot-com advertisers have numbed Web surfers by exposing them to the same ads over and over again. This contributes to low click rates and ineffective branding," according to Allen Weiner, vice president of analytical services at NetRatings.[36] Such low click rates may have an effect on those sites reliant on click through ads in the future.

Subscriptions

Subscription
is a fee paid by users to be granted access to certain online information or services.

Web sites can also earn revenues with a subscription-based profit model. In this model, users pay a **subscription** to be granted access to certain online information or services. This type of model is common with publications such as newspapers and journals (see Figure 15.10).

| Figure 15.10 | *Wall Street Journal* Subscription Site |

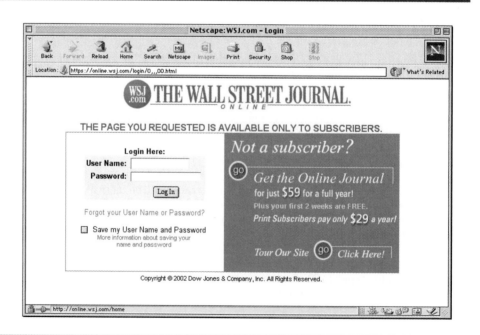

Napster

According to its Web site, "Napster is the world's leading file sharing community." The business model is not complex: The site brings together a network of people who trade computer files, most commonly MP3 music files. Simply log on and type in the name of a song or artist and presto!—A list of files to choose from appears for your downloading pleasure. And the cost? Nothing!

Well, nothing to those downloading the music. But the artists and record labels were (and are) losing royalties because so many people were going to the Web for their music needs. A study done by Forrester Research in September of 2000 estimates that within 5 years, the music industry could lose $3.1 billion due to this type of piracy.

Because of this, these record labels and artists decided to take action in the form of a class action lawsuit against Napster.

The results were inconclusive, but the pressure did bring about some changes. Napster voluntarily took itself offline to rework its business plan in July of 2001. The company is anticipating a relaunch of the new and improved site in early 2002. No longer will Napster's file-sharing community be free to the general public.

Instead, to have access to the products, users will have to subscribe to Napster's membership service. In fact, Napster has even come up with its own file format to protect songs.

But this does not mean the end of the battle for record labels. No sooner had Napster been disabled than a number of other Web services appeared. And unlike Napster, many of these, such as Morpheus, will be near impossible to stop because the files are transferred directly from one PC to another, with no central site to shut down.

The only solution for record labels is to take to the Web themselves. Two possible plans have surfaced. The first is for the record labels to start their own subscription service that allows users to listen to music for a monthly fee. The other solution is a pay-for-play model that charges a nominal fee each time a song is played. Time will tell which course of action the record labels take, but in the meantime, MP3s remain cheap and easy for consumers to get.

Sources: Adam Cohen, "Napster the Revolution, A Crisis of Conduct," *Time* http://www.cnn.com/ALLPOLITICS/time/2000/10/02/revolution.html, accessed 2 October 2000; and Dennis Michael, "Win or Lose, Napster Has Changed the Internet," http://www.cnn.com/2000/SHOWBIZ/Music/10/02/napster/index.html, accessed 2 October 2000.

An example of a subscription-based site that generates revenue from member subscription fees as well as banner advertising is the *Wall Street Journal* Interactive site. Similar to the *Sports Illustrated* site previously discussed, the *Wall Street Journal* Online provides up-to-the-minute information while incorporating the daily feature articles from the *Wall Street Journal*. The links on this site allow subscribers to get historical information on financial products, track markets and investments, follow special industries such as technology, and even do research on topics of interest to the subscriber. In addition, it has an affiliate program that allows other businesses to integrate the *Wall Street Journal* into their site. The *Wall Street Journal* Online pays these businesses for any subscriptions that come from click throughs. While many publications have failed in gathering subscribers on the Web, the *Wall Street Journal* has found a formula that seems to be working. In fact, the company was able to attract over 100,000 subscribers in its first year of operation.[37]

The Internet is an information-rich environment. When consumers visit a Web site, they are typically looking for in-depth specialized information. If valuable information is not provided it is unlikely that the company will get the consumer to return to the site. Financial news or sports information that might be integrated into a site, from organizations such as the *Wall Street Journal* Online or CNN/*Sports Illustrated*, could enhance the richness of a site.

Consumers are willing to provide information about themselves in exchange for the valuable information they are seeking. Many sites today request that visitors fill out brief questionnaires about themselves and their likes/dislikes. This information can be extremely valuable in designing a company's marketing plan. It may also be utilized to sell advertising on the company's site to other firms. The essential observation is that consumers are willing to exchange valuable information as long as they get valuable information and/or experiences in return.

Online Product Vending

According to the eCommercePulse online survey of 39,000 Web users, 1.2 million U.S. adults, or 48.2 percent of the U.S. adult population age 18 and over, have purchased online. In other words, more than 81.2 percent of all adults with Web access have made a purchase online since they started using the Internet.[38] By 2005, it is forecasted that shoppers will buy $269 billion worth of products online (see Table 15.3).[39] Most online merchants state that repeat buyers generate about half of their sales, and the number of items purchased increases with each visit. The most popular products consumers purchase are books (29 percent), music (20 percent), software (11 percent), and clothes (10 percent). Table 15.3 provides a list of the most popular categories in order of popularity, with forecasts for the next several years.

Dell Computer (see Figure 15.11) is a great example of a successful e-tailer site. Dell does more than $50 million a day in online sales worldwide. These sales account for about half of the company's total revenues.[40]

http://www.dell.com

Electronic Intermediary Commissions

Electronic intermediary is a profit model based on commissions received by bringing buyers and sellers together.

http://www.ebay.com

The fourth and final type of common profit model—the **electronic intermediary**—is based on commissions received by bringing buyers and sellers together. This can occur in a B2B, a B2C, or a C2C context. The host receives either a set fee for facilitating the transaction, a commission on the sale, or a combination of both.

A very popular example of a site that operates on this profit model is eBay (see Figure 15.12). eBay is a virtual auction house, where sellers can post their products online to be auctioned off to the highest bidder. For this service, eBay receives two fees, both from the seller. The first is an insertion fee for listing the item online. This fee can be anywhere from $.30 to $3.30 for basic service, depending on the minimum bid the seller declares he or she will accept for the item. Once a transaction has been finalized, eBay again receives payment, this time in the form of a final value fee.

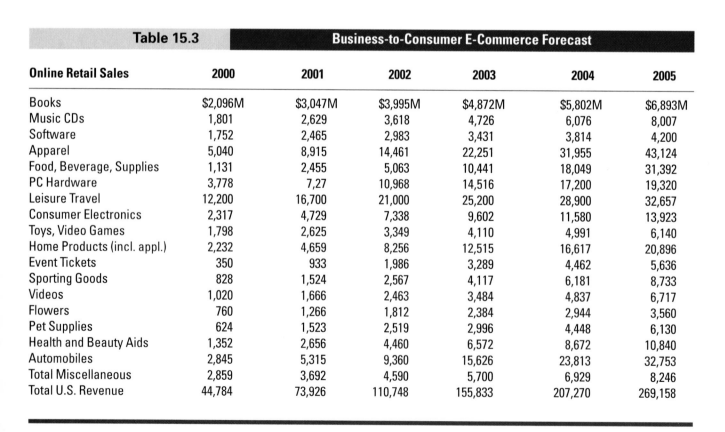

Table 15.3	Business-to-Consumer E-Commerce Forecast					
Online Retail Sales	**2000**	**2001**	**2002**	**2003**	**2004**	**2005**
Books	$2,096M	$3,047M	$3,995M	$4,872M	$5,802M	$6,893M
Music CDs	1,801	2,629	3,618	4,726	6,076	8,007
Software	1,752	2,465	2,983	3,431	3,814	4,200
Apparel	5,040	8,915	14,461	22,251	31,955	43,124
Food, Beverage, Supplies	1,131	2,455	5,063	10,441	18,049	31,392
PC Hardware	3,778	7,27	10,968	14,516	17,200	19,320
Leisure Travel	12,200	16,700	21,000	25,200	28,900	32,657
Consumer Electronics	2,317	4,729	7,338	9,602	11,580	13,923
Toys, Video Games	1,798	2,625	3,349	4,110	4,991	6,140
Home Products (incl. appl.)	2,232	4,659	8,256	12,515	16,617	20,896
Event Tickets	350	933	1,986	3,289	4,462	5,636
Sporting Goods	828	1,524	2,567	4,117	6,181	8,733
Videos	1,020	1,666	2,463	3,484	4,837	6,717
Flowers	760	1,266	1,812	2,384	2,944	3,560
Pet Supplies	624	1,523	2,519	2,996	4,448	6,130
Health and Beauty Aids	1,352	2,656	4,460	6,572	8,672	10,840
Automobiles	2,845	5,315	9,360	15,626	23,813	32,753
Total Miscellaneous	2,859	3,692	4,590	5,700	6,929	8,246
Total U.S. Revenue	44,784	73,926	110,748	155,833	207,270	269,158

Dell Computer Web Site   **Figure 15.11**

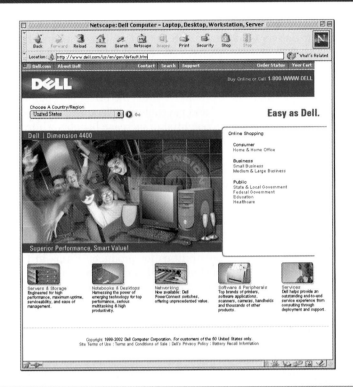

eBay Web Site   **Figure 15.12**

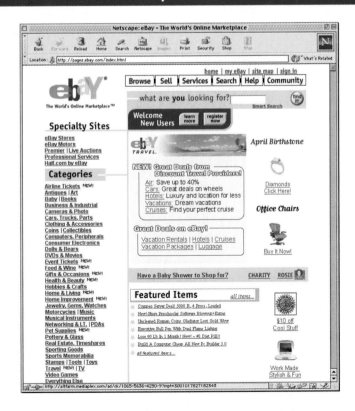

E-MARKETING AND THE MARKETING MIX

E-marketing is both the same and unique in comparison to other types of marketing. All marketers attempt to deliver value to ultimate customers (final consumers, business customers, or governmental customers). Value is determined by subtracting costs from benefits. This is true in any type of marketing, electronic or otherwise. Benefits are based on consumer perceptions of the product by evaluating attributes, brands, and after-the-sale services. The costs associated with a product include the price, plus other factors such as time invested in the purchase process and psychological factors.

Ultimately, the Internet has the potential to increase benefits while lowering costs. These benefits include mass customization, digital delivery of products, and/or one-stop shopping. Lower costs can result from direct selling, segmented pricing, and/or expanded delivery services via the Web. The potential increased benefits and/or decreased costs can be explored by looking at the product, price, place (distribution), and promotion components of the marketing mix.

Product

E-marketing opens a multitude of possibilities for products. Firms in touch with their customer base have the ability to constantly evaluate customer needs and match those needs with technological developments to create new and innovative products. Product life cycles have been shortened because competitors are now able to develop products on the fly. Firms that capitalize on these phenomena and introduce new products earlier than competitors have the potential for far greater profits.

Small businesses can be big on the Web and big businesses can be small on the Web. Even the smallest firm can compete globally by using the expertise of the transportation companies today. Transportation companies such as FedEx and UPS make it easy to export products, as well as deliver them worldwide. Even the largest firm can be "small" and focus on individual needs if it can automate its systems enough. In addition, larger firms can design the self-service systems on the Web that can perform many of the customer contact functions.

Price

Standard pricing models have limited use in electronic markets. Traditional pricing theory is based on the experience curve that has declining fixed costs as volume expands. While this theory still holds for electronic markets, the shortness of the product life cycle makes volume efficiencies less likely because of constant innovation.

Many firms have created market efficiencies by lowering costs associated with the final exchange of products marketed on the Web. Self-service Web sites offer potential for lower costs and thus lower pricing on the Web. In addition to self-service, the automation of order processing and payment adds to potential savings.

Place

E-marketers have expanded the ways they sell their products. Several new channels of distribution have evolved from the use of the Internet to market goods. E-tailers represent a new distribution channel for traditional brick-and-mortar firms, as well as for firms that exist only on the Internet such as Amazon.com.

E-marketers, also, have developed new ways to deliver goods and services including digital products, more efficient customer service, and new ways to sell directly to consumers. Innovative new intermediaries have emerged because of special needs associated with Internet marketing. These intermediaries and other innovations were presented in the profit models section earlier.

Promotion

In most circumstances when a company sells to consumers through traditional media, the consumer is passive in the communication process, that is, consumers typically do not interact with the company, instead they read advertisements, listen to radio ads, or view TV commercials. E-marketing is an active media where consumers must choose (click) to see something and can view it for as long or as short as they like. Additionally, even in the personal selling process, in which consumers are more active in the process, there are differences when one markets on the Web. Table 15.4 shows the steps in the personal selling process and suggests different techniques that can be used when marketing on the Web.

Obviously, having consumers actively participate in the process rather than be passive bystanders affords the marketer the ability not only to save money but also to provide a higher level of service. That means that sites can be used to identify needs and wants, discover preferences, provide information and service, develop loyalty, and position the firm for future sales from the prospect.

Firms promote themselves in different ways using the medium of the Internet. Negotiating hyperlinks with related products is a critical promotional tool on the Web. Banner advertising has become very popular in recent years and provides a way to hyperlink these sites together. Mass media typically push messages to consumers, while consumers on the Web must actually pull advertisements by clicking. Web sites must be designed in such a way that consumers can quickly see the value of their spending time at the site. Table 15.5 summarizes a number of important issues to consider when designing Web sites.

Steps in the Personal Selling Process Adapted to the Web		Table 15.4
	Personal Selling	**Web Selling**
Prospecting	Names from databases, referrals, past customers, other sources	Search engines, listserv(es), e-mail, links
Preapproach	Information gathering on needs, wants, preferences	Data collection online, site searches, screening links
Approach	Method of contact, atmospherics, initial impressions, cold call	URL, Opening Web screen, navigation
Presentation	Discussing the options, listening and replying to objections	Graphics, screen design, links to other products
Closing the Sale	Asking for the sale Filling out the order	Taking the order online, self-service
Follow-Up	Determining customer satisfaction	E-mail, other follow-up

Keys to Web Design	Table 15.5
Things to Do:	**Things to Avoid:**
Provide description of the firm Fast load times Consistent navigation Make the site interactive Provide ways to contact the firm Register with search engines Register the domain name Copyright the site Use trademarks appropriately Market the site in other materials	Scrolling Large graphic files Reliance on one browser Broken links Excessive use of plug-ins

E-Marketing: A Different Game

After receiving an international baccalaureate high school diploma from the International School of Paris, Stuart was accepted to the University of Virginia. His adjustment to Virginia took a little getting used to. Having come from a graduating class of 30 or so students, it was quite a shock for Stuart to sit in on the 300+ student chemistry lectures! Luckily, he had placed out of most of the math, science, English, and foreign language requirements, which freed up his schedule to explore other disciplines. Stuart knew he wanted to double major in French and something else.

"Toward the end of the first two years, I had really enjoyed a computer programming class and was interested in the business applications of technology. I knew that I did not want to be a pure programmer."

After his first 2 years, he applied for and was accepted to the McIntire School of Commerce. For the next two years, he studied management information systems (MIS), marketing, and French. He explains his choice, "The business grounding in accounting, finance, and the softer issues such as marketing and organizational management were all new to me. Not quite pure science, not quite social science . . . somewhere in between. I was much less comfortable with these subject matters than in pure sciences, but that was part of the challenge. I rooted myself in MIS and French, those were essentially my fallback subjects. . . . Both were

subjects that I didn't really think twice about. Marketing was a different game . . . more comprehensive in strategic outlook with a strong reliance on creative skills as well as analytical skills. The business frameworks provided different lenses from which to critique business problems."

To increase his technical skills after his undergraduate degree program, Stuart stayed at Virginia to get a master's degree in MIS. After graduation, Stuart accepted a position with Booz Allen Hamilton. He worked as a multimedia programmer, network administrator, and lab manager for the next 2 years. "At Booz Allen Hamilton I refined my technical skills and received a good deal of exposure to teamwork and project and client management. However, once the lab evolved from 4 people to 10 people, and the project pipeline was steady, it was time to move on. I was responsible for the running of the technical side of the lab and wanted greater exposure to the management side. I felt that I needed to develop those skills further, and decided to apply for an MBA program."

To further capitalize on his international background, Stuart attended INSEAD for his MBA program. Following his graduation, Stuart accepted a marketing information technology (IT) position with F. Hoffmann La Roche in Basel, Switzerland. He is excited to be working in B2B marketing in the company's vitamins division, along with data warehouse and enterprise planning systems projects.

Electronic brochures
are digital versions of a company's brochures.

http://www.wine.com

Placing a company's brochures online is a sure way to chase consumers from your site. **Electronic brochures**, that is, digitizing a company's print brochures and placing them on the Web as straight text, does not work! Consumers know this medium is interactive and expect to interact.

Web marketing also changes the other promotional activities of the firm. All future advertisements must contain the Web address for the company if the firm expects to grow its equity in the Web site.

Designers of Web sites need to be cognizant that their sites must do more than just sell. Web sites that offer other benefits to the ultimate consumer such as analysis of needs, assistance in product selection, information on usage with complimentary products, and meeting places for interested visitors can provide customers with reason to come back to a site over and over again. The wine.com site (see Figure 15.13) provides information on the types of wines, how they should be served, the use of wines in cooking, as well as a multitude of other information on wines and the wine industry. The success of this site comes from the fact that they do much more for customers than just sell wine.

LEARNING OBJECTIVE 5

COSTS AND BENEFITS OF E-MARKETING

Drawbacks

Although it is evident that there are numerous advantages for companies using e-marketing, there are two major drawbacks at this time: limited target audience and consumers' resistance to change. Both of these are likely to change as the Internet diffuses throughout our society.

Limited Audience

For those of us who use the Internet daily for information, e-mail, and as a mechanism to purchase products, it seems that everyone is using it. However, a very large segment of our society has yet to embrace the Internet (presently 73 million users in the United States). As stated earlier in this chapter, a majority of Internet users fit a definite profile. Although this profile is beginning to match the overall U.S. population and might match the target market of some companies, it does not match the profile of all companies (see Table 15.6).

There are still a number of underrepresented segments on the Web.[41] Most significant differences exist in higher income and higher percentages of 18- to 49-year-olds for Internet users versus the population as a whole. These numbers clearly indicate underrepresentation within certain segments of our society. Although Internet use is increasing and these numbers are changing at a rapid rate, until the demographics of Internet usage mirror society as a whole, companies must use caution in over emphasizing e-marketing in their total marketing mix.

wine.com Web Site	Figure 15.13

Internet Adoption by Gender, Age, and Income	Table 15.6

	1996 Online Population	2001 Online Population[a]	U.S. Population (2000 Census)
Male	62%	49%	49%
Female	38%	51%	51%
Household Income	$62,700	$49,800	$40,816[b]
Adults 18–49	88%	76%	63%
Adults 50+	12%	24%	37%

[a] InsightExpress sample.
[b] 1999 U.S. Census.
Source: InsightExpress

Resistance to Change

In general, people are resistant to change. This resistance was clearly demonstrated by the slow movement of people from retail stores to purchasing products via mail order catalogs. This same resistance is being demonstrated as people begin to purchase products over the Internet.

While many people think nothing of giving their credit card number to a customer service representative they don't know personally during a mail order telephone purchase, there is clear resistance among customers to typing their number into the computer and then clicking a Send button. Although someone educated in Internet security knows that decrypting a credit card number electronically is much more difficult than picking up a receipt with a number printed on it, the average user may not know this. Warranties, security measures, and other ways to augment the overall product offering to reduce the risk of consumers must be evaluated by companies to overcome consumers' resistance to change.

Benefits of E-Marketing

E-marketing can aid a company's overall marketing effort in a number of ways. First, e-marketing allows a company/brand to *increase its brand equity in the marketplace.* Company and brand sites give marketers an opportunity to communicate the overall of mission of the company/brand, provide information on the attributes and/or ratings of the company/brand, and can give information on the history of company/brand. In addition, firms can communicate information on the marketing mix offered.

Second, e-marketing allows a company to *develop prospective customers into buying customers.* Providing important information about the decision-making process can help the potential customer with external search processes. Information about a product's attributes and competitive products can aid in the decision-making process. In addition, a Web site can demonstrate a company's products in use. This kind of information can help build consumer interest in a company/brand.

E-marketing can move customers closer to purchasing a product/brand by allowing Web site visitors to match their needs with the offerings of the company. It is extremely important to remember that while traditional marketing techniques tend to be push oriented (see Chapter 12), that is, the marketer decides what consumers will see and where, e-marketing is a pull technique—consumers choose when they want to gather information and what and how much they want to know. This requires Web site designers to think differently about what should or should not be offered in the site.

Third, e-marketing can *improve customer service by allowing customers to serve themselves* when and where they choose. The self-service nature of Web sites can produce the cost savings that will ultimately pay for some sites. As more and more consumers begin to use the Internet, companies can serve these individuals without expensive distribution costs. The expansion of the number of customers served only requires that the organization have enough servers available.

The fourth benefit to marketers is that of *information transfer.* Traditionally, marketers gathered information via focus groups, mail surveys, telephone surveys, and personal interviews. These techniques can be quite expensive to implement. The Web offers a mechanism for companies to collect similar information at a fraction of the cost. It is important to recognize the potential bias that might exist in such a sample. However, as the number and demographics of Internet users begin more closely to represent a firm's target market, the collection of information on the Web might offer many benefits.

Not only can information be gathered from consumers, it also can be shared with consumers. The Web can be used to provide expensive or specialized material to consumers who request such information from the company. Annual reports are now a typical part of company Web sites. Rather than print the millions of copies that might be requested by consumers, the company now provides Web copies that consumers print out at their own expense. Other specialized material can also be provided for consumers to print out themselves. By fulfilling these types of information requests, the Web can offer substantial savings to companies.

The greatest potential for e-marketing is probably in direct marketing where catalogs can be offered online. Web-based catalogs can be changed with ease if prices and/or product offerings change. This alone can represent substantial savings for organizations that would normally print new catalogs and mail those catalogs to consumers.

CHAPTER SUMMARY

- Electronic commerce includes all the activities of a firm that use the Internet to aid in the exchange of products.

- As fast as the Internet is expanding, the number and type of Internet sites is increasing. Sites can be classified into four major categories: company/brand sites, service sites, selling sites, and information sites. These sites are obviously not mutually exclusive and collectively exhaustive.

- The growth of the Internet required three separate developments in order for it to become an efficient marketing tool. First, businesses had to develop their electronic commerce intranets and extranets that connect to the Internet. Second, network server growth, allowing fast connection, was necessary. Finally, consumers (either at work or at home) had to have access to the Internet.

- E-commerce expanded on the Internet primarily because of four major areas of improvement to business practices: reduced costs, inventory reduction, improved customer service, and market/product development opportunities.

- Web sites make money through the use of advertising, subscriptions, product vending, and intermediary commissions. Many Web sites utilize a combination of these strategies.

- E-marketing can aid a company's overall marketing effort in a number of ways. First, e-marketing allows a company/brand to increase its brand equity in the marketplace. Second, e-marketing allows marketers to develop a prospective customer into a buying customer. Third, e-marketing can improve customer service by allowing customers to serve themselves when and where they choose. The fourth benefit to marketers is information transfer. Traditionally, marketers gathered information via expensive focus groups, mail surveys, telephone surveys, and personal interviews. The Web offers a mechanism for companies to collect similar information at a fraction of the cost.

- Although there are numerous advantages for companies using e-marketing, there are two major drawbacks at this time: a limited target audience and consumers' resistance to change. Both of these are likely to change as the Internet diffuses throughout our society.

- The digital revolution is here and will have similar effects as any revolution would have on a society. A mere 10 years ago the Internet thrust itself upon society. As this innovation permeates society, it becomes increasingly important for businesses to make the Internet an integral component of their marketing strategy.

KEY TERMS

Affiliate programs have advertisers pay for each person who enters their Web site via a link on the host site or pays for each sale generated.

A **banner ad** is typically an animated GIF graphic placed on a host site and hyperlinked to the URL of the advertiser.

Click through is a term that describes the act of clicking on an advertising banner located at a host site and being transported electronically to the advertiser's site.

Company/brand sites are Web sites that provide information about a company, such as history, mission, financial statements, etc.

Customer service is the service a business provides to accommodate customers' questions and concerns.

E-marketing is the set of activities that bring customers and companies together using electronic means such as the Internet.

Electronic brochures are digital versions of a company's brochures.

Electronic data interchange (EDI) is a computer-to-computer communications protocol that allows basic information on purchases and invoices to be transferred.

Electronic intermediary is a profit model based on commissions received by bringing buyers and sellers together.

Extranet is a network of computers that connect a business or organization with computers outside of the intranet.

Handling costs are costs to a firm associated with the act of transferring inventory to customers.

Information sites are Web sites that generate revenue through advertising or the subscription rates that are charged to members.

Internet is a worldwide network of interconnected computer networks originally built by the U.S. government.

Internet hosts provide high-speed connections to the Web.

Intranet is a network of computers within a business or organization.

Obsolescence costs are those costs to a firm associated with holding inventory that is not selling due to a loss in demand for the product.

Procurement costs are those costs to a firm associated with the process of receiving customers' orders.

Search engines are mechanisms through which Internet users can automatically search Web sites to find desired information.

Selling sites are Web sites that provide products for purchase over the Internet.

Service sites are Web sites that provide a customer service interface for a company.

Storage costs are those costs to a firm associated with the act of storing inventory.

Subscription is a fee paid by users to be granted access to certain online information or services.

World Wide Web (Web) is a data network system that allows users to interact with documents stored on computers across the Internet.

QUESTIONS FOR DISCUSSION

1. Briefly, discuss the history of the Internet. How did it get started?

2. Thinking about the diffusion of computers throughout our society, what are some of the factors that will limit the expansion of the Internet?

3. Discuss the types of consumers on the Internet. How many are there? What do they do on the Internet? Are they purchasing products on the Web?

4. Discuss the size and potential for businesses utilizing the Internet. How fast is this area growing? What are the largest segments of business using the Internet?

5. Discuss the areas of improvement that businesses can achieve by using the Web. In what ways can firms either reduce costs or expand offerings?

6. What are the four types of Internet sites? How can we learn from knowing the various types?

7. How close are Internet users to the profile of all consumers?

8. Discuss the drawbacks to e-marketing, limited audience and resistance to change. Where are we in the diffusion process for this innovation?

9. How do Internet sites make money? What are some of the effective profit models they employ? Name some sites that use each of these models.

10. Discuss the ways that businesses can benefit from the use of e-marketing.

INTERNET QUESTIONS

1. Visit the Millward Brown IntelliQuest Web site at http://www.intelliquest. com. How does Millward Brown IntelliQuest aid technology companies in improving their marketing?

2. The Graphic, Visualization, and Usability Center at Georgia Tech conducts periodic surveys of WWW users. Visit http://www.gvu.gatech.edu/ user_surveys to obtain a basic demographic profile of Web users from the latest survey.

3. There are a number of discussion groups (Listservs) to aid Internet marketers such as the e-marketing sales discussion group at http://www. adventive.com/lists/isales/summary.html. Join this or a similar group and prepare a brief report on the benefits of belonging to such a group.

ENDNOTES

[1] Jeremy Lockhorn, "What's New Out There (Part 2)?" http://www.clickz.com/tech/ ad_tech/article.php/878221, accessed 5 September 2001.

[2] http://www.poindextersystems.com/, accessed 6 February 2002.

[3] Evan I. Schwartz, *Webonomics: Nine Essential Principles for Growing Your Business on the World Wide Web* (New York: Broadway Books, 1997), 128.

[4] Federal Express Web site, http://fedex.com/us/about/express/history.html, accessed 2 April 2002.

[5] Schwartz, *Webonomics*, 118.

[6] Amazon.com Web site, http://www.amazon.com/exec/obidos/subst/misc/company-info. html/, accessed 2 April 2002.

[7] L.L. Bean Web site, http://www.llbean.com/customerservice/aboutLLBean/today.html, accessed 2 April 2002.

[8] John Hagel, III, and Arthur G. Armstrong, *Net Gain: Expanding Markets through Virtual Communities* (Boston: Harvard Business School Press, 1997).

[9] Nabil R. Adam, et al., *Electronic Commerce: Technical, Business, and Legal Issues.* (Upper Saddle River, NJ: Prentice Hall, 1999), 1–3.

[10] http://www.emarketer.com/ereports/ecommerce_trade/welcome.html, accessed 2 April 2002.

[11] http://www.emarketer.com/ereports/ecommerce_trade/welcome.html, accessed 2 April 2002.

[12] http://cyberatlas.internet.com/markets/b2b/article/0,,10091_498621,00.html, accessed 2 April 2002.

[13] http://cyberatlas.internet.com/markets/b2b/article/0,,10091_498621,00.html, accessed 2 April 2002.

[14] http://cyberatlas.internet.com/markets/b2b/article/0,,10091_475401,00.html, accessed 2 April 2002.

[15] http://cyberatlas.internet.com/markets/b2b/article/0,,10091_439221,00.html, accessed 2 April 2002.

[16] http://cyberatlas.internet.com/markets/b2b/article/0,,10091_498621,00.html, accessed 2 April 2002.

[17] http://www.isc.org/ds/host-count-history.html, accessed 2 April 2002.

[18] Center for Next Generation Internet, http://www.ngi.org/trends/TrendsPR0102.txt, accessed April 2 2002.

[19] http://cyberatlas.internet.com/markets/b2b/article/0,,5911_3527611,00.html, accessed 2 April 2002.

[20] http://cyberatlas.internet.com/markets/b2b/article/0,,10091_790641,00.html, accessed 2 April 2002.

[21] http://www.iconocast.com/iconomap/, accessed 2 April 2002.

[22] http://www.iconocast.com/iconomap/, accessed 2 April 2002.

[23] Ibid.

[24] http://cyberatlas.internet.com/markets/b2b/article/0,,6061_706191,00.html, accessed 2 April 2002.

[25] U.S. Department of Commerce, *The Emerging Digital Economy* (Washington, D.C.: Author, April 1997).

[26] Ibid.

[27] Amazon.com, http://www.amazon.com/exec/obidos/subst/misc/company-info.html/, accessed 2 April 2002.

[28] Schwartz, *Webonomics*, 98.

[29] http://www.wellsfargo.com, accessed 2 April 2002.

[30] Federal Express, http://www.fedex.com/us/about/express.history, accessed 4 April 2002.

[31] Federal Express, http://www.fedex.com/us/; and United Parcel Service, at http://www.ups.com/bussol/logistics/customs.html, accessed 2 April 2002.

[32] http://www.wilsonweb.com/articles/bannerad.htm.

[33] Amazon.com, http://www.amazon.com/exec/obidos/subst/associates/join/associates.html/, accessed 2 April 2002.

[34] http://cyberatlas.internet.com/markets/b2b/article/0,,5941_757221,00.html, accessed 2 April 2001.

[35] Ibid.

[36] http://cyberatlas.internet.com/markets/b2b/article/0,,5941_757221,00.html, accessed 2 April 2002.

[37] Schwartz, *Webonomics*, 35.

[38] http://cyberatlas.internet.com/markets/b2b/article/0,,6061_751021,00.html, accessed 2 April 2002.

[39] Iconomap 2001, http://www.iconocast.com/iconomap/, accessed 2 April 2002.

[40] Dell Computer Corporation, http://www.dell.com/us/en/gen/corporate/press/pressoffice_us_2000-09-08-rr-000.htm, accessed 2 April 2002.

[41] CyberAtlas, http://www.cyberatlas.internet.com/big_picture/demographics/article/0,,5901_959421,00.html, accessed 2 April 2002.

A DIFFERENT KIND OF RÉSUMÉ

John Adams is just entering his final year at the state university. He has spent the past 3 years studying business and has a double major in management information systems and marketing. John enjoys management information systems because he has learned how to make a computer do what he wants it to do, especially through programming. However, he does not like the systems design aspects of MIS, that keep him behind his desk and away from his computer.

John enjoys marketing for the creative aspects of the field, especially the promotional components of marketing. He does not like the topics of distribution, logistics, or pricing. He loves to use the Internet in school and wants very much to get a position with a firm that allowed him to develop Web sites. John feels that this kind of position would allow him to bring together what he likes most about his two majors—programming and promotion.

The Office of Career Planning at the university requires that all students create a résumé before using the school's interview services. John struggled with writing his résumé because he was told it must be kept to one page. He thought it would be next to impossible to indicate all of his qualifications, including his education, experiences, and career aspirations. And he wanted to bring together both of his concentrations to demonstrate his background and qualifications for a Web designer's job. While he was able to complete the task for the Office of Career Planning, he did not feel that the single page provided enough information for him to succeed in the job-hunting process.

As he thought about the résumé writing task, he realized he had at his fingertips the ability to demonstrate his qualifications and not be limited to just one page. He would design his own Web site to demonstrate his qualifications to potential employers. As John thought about what to include in his Web page, he realized the importance of developing specific objectives, designing the site for ease of navigation, utilizing graphics appropriately, and a host of other Web design issues. He wanted to rush to the computer and begin programming but knew that some background and research work would increase the overall value of his site.

Discussion Questions

1. What are the overall objectives of the site and any major sections of the site?

2. What should the opening page of the site look like?

3. What should the major sections look like and what should be included in each?

4. What kind of navigation would he use?

5. What kinds of sites exist on the Web today that can help in the design?

6. What would the story boards for the site look like?

Appendix

Planning for Marketing Decisions[1]

LEARNING OBJECTIVES

After you have completed this appendix, you should be able to:

1. Appreciate the importance of the planning process.
2. Discuss the five fundamental elements of strategic planning and various models used to evaluate product successes.
3. List the components of a marketing plan.
4. Discuss current trends and issues that arise within marketing planning.

THE NATURE AND IMPORTANCE OF PLANNING

LEARNING OBJECTIVE 1

Planning is the basis for sound decision making in any situation in life. Whether you are planning a wedding, a vacation, or a multimillion dollar sponsorship program, numerous efforts pertaining to the particular activity must be coordinated and planned well in advance. Without planning, the activity may have disastrous results.

Consider, for example, a wedding. John and Susan get engaged, and then announce in March that they wish to marry in June because they simply can't wait any longer. The bride, groom, and their parents meet to discuss the wedding. In making a list of things to do, the top priorities are to secure the church and reception site for the desired date. Once those details are set, invitations, flowers, bride's and bridesmaids' dresses, and tuxedos must be ordered. Next, the music, menus, cake, and invitation list must be decided on. And finally, table seating, the rehearsal dinner, and the honeymoon must be planned.

If any of these elements are overlooked or not followed up on, John and Susan's wedding day will be ruined in their eyes. For example, if the responsibility of ordering the flowers is not assigned to a particular person, there is a risk that no flowers will be displayed at the church or on tables at the reception. If the responsibility of ordering and mailing invitations is not assigned to someone, there is a risk that no guests will attend the wedding. John and Susan want everything perfect for that day, so tasks are assigned to the bride, groom, and parents, and the group decides to meet in two days to discuss their progress.

When they next meet, John and Susan are very upset. The church and the reception sites are both booked on their desired date. John and Susan learn that most engaged couples have secured these details many months in advance. Susan also discovers that the dress she wants will take six months to order. And Susan's parents find that the cost of the reception with the desired number of guests far exceeds their budget. The group is forced to rethink their original plan and make the necessary modifications, allowing for these environmental factors.

This example demonstrates several elements that are key to any planning activity:

- *Timing.* Planning must occur well in advance of the activity. Planning postponed until the last minute will produce only negative results.
- *Tasks.* Every activity consists of a number of specific tasks. All details about each task must be planned in order for the entire activity to be successful.
- *Responsibility.* Every task needs a specific coordinator. If one person is not held accountable, the task may not get done.
- *Follow-up.* Even if responsibility for each task has been delegated, one individual must follow up on and coordinate the progress of the overall activity. Even the most responsible person can slip up and forget something.
- *Budgeting.* Budgeting is essential in planning. Plans that are too expensive for an individual or organization can have serious financial consequences. Through planning, costs are estimated and deemed acceptable or unacceptable.

These elements are critical in business planning. However, business planning has more far-reaching consequences than a wedding. Thousands of jobs and millions of dollars rely on solid planning efforts by management.

There are several levels of planning in any organization. The most important level is *strategic planning*, or the organization's overall game plan. This plan typically encompasses the firm's long-range goals and dictates direction for all departments in the firm. The means of achieving the company goals and the resources needed are detailed in full. The plan establishes goals and strategies, delineates activities, and assigns responsibility for every facet of the organization.

Marketing planning is the game plan for a particular product or product line. The marketing plan is the detailed scheme of the marketing strategies and activities associated with each product's marketing mix. Hence, the strategic plan is the company's overall plan, while the marketing plan details the marketing efforts and strategies as outlined in the strategic plan.

Tactical planning is another level of organizational planning. *Tactical planning* involves specifying details that pertain to the organization's activities for a certain period of time. For example, the scheduled dates for a radio or television campaign for the third quarter would be included in a tactical plan. So, too would the details regarding the fourth-quarter price deal offered to dealers. The production department's tactical plan may include the testing of a new quality control program on a packaging line. The tactical plan is a detailed account of the firm's short-term activities as outlined in the strategic plan.

Strategic planning is an effective way for an organization to coordinate efforts among various departments, analyze its competitive position within its environment, and allocate its resources. The strategic planning process causes all employees involved in the process to thoroughly think through the strategies that will prove most effective in achieving company goals. We will now turn to a discussion of the fundamental elements involved in strategic planning.

LEARNING OBJECTIVE 2

FUNDAMENTALS OF STRATEGIC PLANNING

Strategic planning comprises five fundamental elements as shown in Figure A.1.

Organization Mission

An organization's mission is the most important element in strategic planning. As part of the mission statement the organization must define its business, or what makes it different from competition. The entire strategic plan is built around this element. By focusing on its mission, management can concentrate their energies on making sound decisions, allocating resources, and generating profits in the long run. A mission statement is a guideline for the organization's decision making for both the short and long run. The mission provides direction to the strategic planning and marketing planning processes as is illustrated in the following mission statement of the Coca-Cola Company:

> *We exist to create value for our share owners on a long-term basis. . . . As the world's largest beverage company, we refresh that world. We do this by developing superior soft drinks, both carbonated and noncarbonated, and profitable nonalcoholic beverage systems that create value for our Company, our bottling partners, our customers, our share owners and the communities in which we do business.*
>
> *In creating value, we succeed or fail based on our ability to perform as worthy stewards of several key assets: (1) Coca-Cola, the world's most recognized trademark, and other highly valuable trademarks; (2) the world's most effective distribution system; (3) satisfied customers, who make a good profit selling our products; (4) our people, who are ultimately responsible for building this enterprise; (5) our abundant resources, which must be intelligently allocated; and (6) our strong global leadership in particular and in the business world in general.*[2]

Coca-Cola's mission statement has three characteristics that are typical of corporate mission statements. First, the statement is a vision: The chairman of the board views

Elements of Strategic Planning	**Figure A.1**

- Organization Mission
- Strategic Business Units
- Objectives
- Strategic Planning Tools
- Marketing Plans

the entire world as a potential target market with his company satisfying the needs of the entire target. Second, the statement is motivational both for employees and for stockholders. And third, the statement refers to certain philosophies or guidelines that will be followed: In the case of Coca-Cola, to refresh the world and to perform as stewards of the six noted key assets. Marketing plans can be developed supporting these elements.

Strategic Business Units

Large companies offering diverse product lines or operating in several countries create *strategic business units (SBUs)*, or smaller divisions, to facilitate planning and general operations. Smaller companies also use SBUs as a way to organize operations. Ultimately, an SBU can be one specific product, one product line, or a particular business. Each SBU establishes its own mission statement, objectives, and strategic and marketing plans independent of other SBUs in the organization. The SBU operates as a separate entity. Typically, the individual SBUs have their own management teams and operational goals, while maintaining common management and production facilities.

Intellvisions Software Limited (ISL) develops networks and markets goods and services to support the communications infrastructure required for Internet-based electronic commerce.[3] These include kiosk networks, VPNs, ISPs, enterprise-wide networks, and software to handle issues such as bandwidth management, e-mail, e-commerce, news, Web hosting, firewalls, and other products. The company is broken into three major strategic business units, as shown in Figure A.2. An organization's mission statement directs its objectives. All strategic and marketing plans are based on these objectives. Every department and SBU can have its own objectives, but these objectives must be guided by the organization's overall objectives.

http://www.intellvisions.com

Any objective must be clear, concise, and realistic. Objectives are typically based on profit, market share, growth, or diversity. For example, an objective for the marketing department may be "to obtain a 15 percent market share and maintain a profit margin of 20 percent by the end of the fiscal year" for a specific product or product line. An objective for the production department may be to "reduce the level of rework from packaging from 5 percent to 3 percent by the end of the fiscal year." An important part of any objective is the time frame assigned for achievement. A time frame is necessary to determine whether the objective has been met by the department or SBU. Many organizations base management bonuses on the achievement of objectives.

Strategic Planning Tools

Tools are available to help managers in their strategic and marketing planning efforts. Careful planning efforts are acutely important to most large organizations that are structured into multiple SBUs with many product offerings. The fundamental issue is one of resource allocation and prioritization. Which products (SBUs) are most, and least, deserving of additional investments? The situation faced by business planners can be compared to that which confronts medical personnel in times of war and medical crises, when these personnel are faced with the wrenching task of determining which of many injured people should receive immediate aid. *Triage* is the medical practice that is used in times of medical crisis. Patients are prioritized in terms of how badly they require immediate medical care, and how likely it is that their lives can be saved. Those patients who badly need care and are likely to survive are the top priority for assistance, whereas those who either are unlikely to survive or are not in desperate condition are lower in the priority scheme.

| Figure A.2 | The Strategic Business Units of Intellvisions Software Limited |

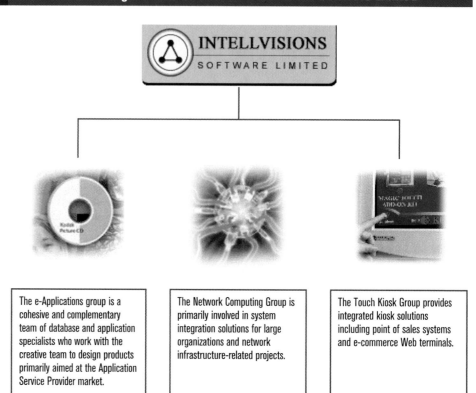

The e-Applications group is a cohesive and complementary team of database and application specialists who work with the creative team to design products primarily aimed at the Application Service Provider market.

The Network Computing Group is primarily involved in system integration solutions for large organizations and network infrastructure-related projects.

The Touch Kiosk Group provides integrated kiosk solutions including point of sales systems and e-commerce Web terminals.

Source: Intellvisions Software Limited, http://www.intellvisions.com.

The following sections examine three frameworks that are broadly analogous to the practice of triage. These models are the Growth Vector Model, Boston Consulting Group's (BCG) Product-Portfolio Analysis, and General Electric's Market Attractiveness-Business Position Model.

Growth Vector Model[4]

Established products are the lifeblood of most companies. But a company that depends solely on its current products is clearly not planning for the future. Growth is fundamental to the long-term success of any organization and an integral part of the planning process. But growth can only come in a limited number of ways:

1. Increasing the market share of existing products in existing markets
2. Expanding existing products into new markets
3. Developing new products

Opportunities for growth depend on a firm's ability to expand its operations in existing or untapped markets or to introduce innovative new products into existing or new markets. As shown in Figure A.3 and discussed in more detail in Chapter 8, firms can expand their sales growth in four ways.

Market Penetration. Market Penetration is a strategy that is used to increase sales and market share of existing products in their existing markets. This strategy is used most often for mature products in mature markets. Firms attempt to penetrate markets either by improving quality, dropping prices, increasing distribution, or engaging in aggressive advertising and other promotional activities.

Market Development. A market development strategy involves finding new markets and new users for existing products. This strategy is undertaken when (1) new uses are discovered for mature products, (2) new users are found due to a change in consumer behavior or demographics, or (3) new markets are entered with an existing product.

| The Growth Vector Market | Figure A.3 |

Present Products   New Products

	Present Products	**New Products**
Present Markets	Market Penetration	Product Development
New Markets	Market Development	Diversification

Product Development. A product development strategy introduces new products into established markets. The new product, sometimes, is the first entry in a particular marketplace.

Product Diversification. A product diversification strategy focuses on developing new products for new markets. Product diversification enables a company to be less dependent on any one product or product line.

BCG's Product-Portfolio Analysis

An organization's product mix can be viewed as a portfolio, with each product having a different growth rate and market share. Product-portfolio analysis offers suggestions for appropriate marketing strategies to best utilize an organization's scarce cash and other limited resources.[5]

The BCG model (illustrated in Figure A.4) classifies products from the perspective of a single company and its particular products or SBUs. Classification is based on two dimensions. The horizontal axis represents the relative market share that a particular product realizes, vis-à-vis the dominant brand in the category. This axis delineates relative share into "high" and "low" categories.

Consider, for example, a product category with four brands and the following market shares: Brand A, the industry leader, enjoys a relative market share that is twice as large as its nearest rival, Brand B. Comparatively, Brands B, C, and D realize relative shares of 0.5 (i.e., 25/50), 0.4 (20/50), and 0.1 (5/50), respectively. If the point of division between the right and left quadrants of the matrix is at a relative share of 1.0, Brand A has a relatively high market share, whereas Brands B, C, and D are all relatively low.

The vertical axis in the BCG matrix is based on the product, market, or industry growth rate. Here, the dividing point between upper and lower quadrants is traditionally set, albeit arbitrarily, at 10 percent. Realizing that the population growth rate in the United States is around 2 percent per annum, many staple products (e.g., milk, bread, industrial commodities) generally grow at a rate commensurate with the population, and, as such, are considered relatively low on the scale. It is in the area of new technologies and fads that growth rates are high. Innovative new products experience growth rates of 50 percent or higher in early years, and then eventually decrease over time.

With these distinctions in mind, Figure A.4 categorizes four general types of products, and gives each a metaphoric name, suggesting implications that each holds for a firm's marketing strategy: cash cows (to be milked), stars (to sustain their ascendancy), problem children (to treat with caution), and dogs (to avoid).

| Figure A.4 | The BCG Product-Portfolio Model |

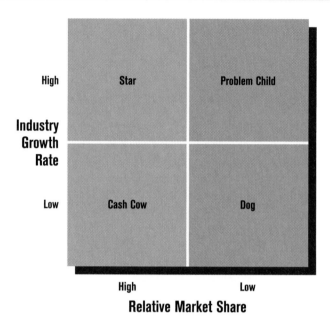

Cash Cows. Cash cows are products that enjoy high market share but show low levels of market growth. These are generally very profitable products that generate more cash than what is needed to maintain the market share. Strategically, corporate-wide efforts should be to manage cash cows by investing in improvements to maintain superiority, attempting to maintain price leadership, and using excess cash to support development of new products and growth elsewhere in the SBU.

Stars. Stars are products with high market growth rates and high market shares. Stars are market leaders with substantial profits. A large investment is required, though, to generate any growth. Strategically, effort must be made to protect existing share by obtaining a large share of new users and investing in product improvements, better market coverage, and perhaps price reductions.

Problem Children. Problem children are products that enjoy rapid growth but low market shares and poor profit margins. Problem children have enormous demand for cash, and risk becoming dogs, since growth inevitably will slow if cash is not forthcoming. Strategically, marketers of a problem child must either invest heavily to earn a disproportionate share of new sales or buy existing shares via acquisition of a competitor.

Dogs. Dogs are products with low market shares and low market growth rates. Dogs operate at a cost disadvantage and have few opportunities for growth inasmuch as the markets are not growing and there is little new business. Marketers of dog products can pursue several strategies: (1) focus on a particular segment of the market and attempt to outperform competitors in that segment; (2) harvest the product by cutting back to minimum levels all marketing support and other investments; (3) divest the product by selling the business to a competitor; or (4) eliminate the product from the product line.

Ideally, an organization should have a balance of products in its portfolio to be successful. Products that generate cash offset those products that require additional investment for growth. If a firm has too many cash cows or dogs, overall company growth is unlikely. Likewise, if it has disproportionate numbers of stars or problem children, the cash demands may be too excessive to provide sufficient support for these products. The logic underlying product portfolios is similar to financial investment logic: Don't place all your eggs in one basket! Having only a single type of security in one's investment portfolio can lead to disaster if the market for that one offering experiences a sudden decline.

General Electric's Attractiveness/Strength Model

General Electric has provided another model useful for strategically evaluating how a company's or SBU's products are faring and what changes might be needed. The GE model (see Figure A.5), like the BCG matrix, is a two-dimensional matrix that portrays the position of a company's products or SBUs. Unlike the BCG, however, which classifies products on the basis of only two considerations (relative market share and industry growth rate), the GE model employs several measurements and observations to classify products. *Market,* or *industry, attractiveness* is measured on the vertical dimension of the model. An attractiveness index is constructed for each of an organization's products or SBUs based on such factors as market growth rate, market size, seasonality of demand, economies of scale in the production of a product, extent and likelihood of competition, and the overall cost. More attractive products enjoy larger growth rates, less seasonal demand, less competition, and so on. The vertical axis of the matrix delineates three levels of attractiveness: low, medium, and high.

A product's *business position,* depicted on the horizontal axis, refers to an organization's strength or ability to take advantage of market opportunities. As with attractiveness, a product's or SBU's strength is indexed based on such considerations as product quality, adequacy of distribution channels, the company's relative market share, price

GE's Attractiveness/Strength Matrix	Figure A.5

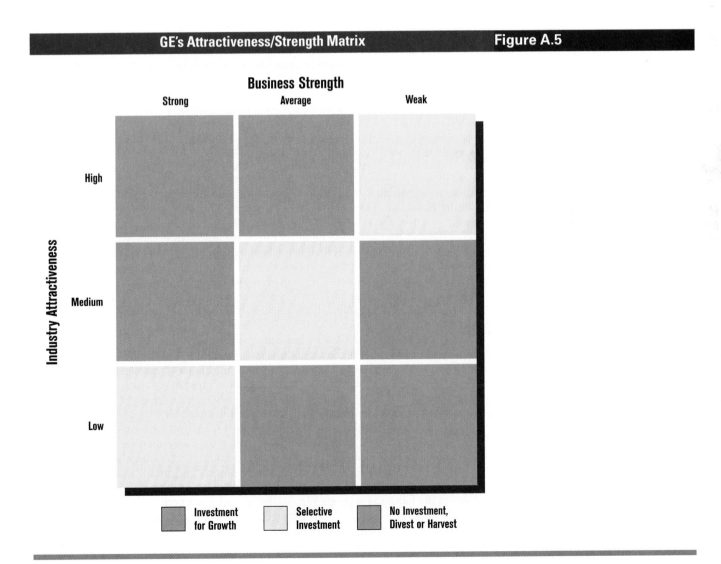

competitiveness, sales force quality, and so on. Business position is divided into three qualitative groupings: strong, medium, or weak.

Crossing the three attractiveness groupings with the three business-strength break-downs results in a matrix with nine cells. Individual products or SBUs are shown as circles in the matrix, with the circle's size representing a product's (or SBU's) dollar sales volume in relation to other products (SBUs) in the matrix. The ideal situation is for an organization to have products with high market attractiveness and strong business positions (the upper-left portion of the matrix). The worst situation is a product with low market attractiveness and weak business position (the lower-right corner).

The intention is to use the model to chart the status of products of SBUs and determine which products are the best candidates for investment and growth, and which are possible candidates for elimination. Resource-allocation decisions, in other words, are based on comparing each product or SBU against other company offerings. Products or SBUs in the upper-left portion of the matrix require investment and management attention; those in the bottom right are candidates for harvesting or divesting.

Marketing Plans

The final fundamental element of strategic planning is the marketing plan. As outlined earlier, the marketing plan is the detailed scheme of the marketing strategies and activities associated with each product's marketing mix. The marketing plans emanate from and are inspired by the overall strategic plan. Marketing plays an instrumental role in determining the strategic plan, and in turn, marketing plans are influenced and directed by the strategic plan.

Marketing plans can take many forms depending on the size of the company and the number of products within its portfolio. A marketing plan can be developed for the entire family of products, for each product line, or for each individual product. Most marketing plans are short-term, covering a 1-year period. Other marketing plans are much longer, encompassing a period of 2 to 10 years. A combination of the two, which pairs a 1-year operational plan with a section on long-range goals and plans, represents the best of both worlds.

LEARNING OBJECTIVE   3

MARKETING PLANNING

Once the strategic plan is developed and approved, marketing planning takes place. Marketing plans can be created for an entire product category or for specific brands, depending on the size of each. For example, Procter & Gamble's marketing plan for Pringle's Potato Chips probably includes the entire line: sour cream and onion, original, rippled, barbecue, and so on. There is no need to develop a complete marketing plan for each of these products. On the other hand, even though it is a product within the line, Diet Coke probably has a marketing plan of its own, separate from Coca-Cola.

Marketing plans vary in length. Some companies require only an outline of the overall plan, with details provided on a quarterly basis in a tactical plan. Other companies require a complete product history with a detailed plan covering the upcoming year.

Marketing plans also vary in formality. Some companies do not require a formal marketing plan. A marketing budget is assigned for a product, and the product manager submits proposals as potential promotions arise. In this case, management is taking a Band-Aid approach to marketing—competitive "fires" are put out with a quick-and-dirty promotional effort. These companies fail to realize, though, that many of these fires could be avoided if proper planning had taken place well in advance.

The most successful marketing efforts are driven by a formal marketing plan, which includes specific objectives, necessary resources, planned activities, and expected results. A detailed plan is critical in creating and coordinating effective marketing activities. Marketing plans take different forms and follow many formats. The seven major components of a typical marketing plan are listed in Figure A.6 and explored in the following sections.[6] In our discussion, a marketing plan will be simulated for the consumer product Rold Gold Pretzels.[7] The discussion includes facts about the product line, but the planned activities are purely conjectural. They are simply included to illustrate the salient points. Also, keep in mind that the actual plan will be much more detailed and greater in length.

Components of a Marketing Plan	Figure A.6

- Executive Summary
- Analysis of the Marketing Situation
- Assessment of Opportunities and Threats
- Specification of Marketing Objectives
- Formulation of Marketing Strategies
- Preparation of Action Programs and Budgets
- Development of Control Procedures

Executive Summary

The executive summary is a recapitulation of the entire marketing plan. Usually included in the summary are a recap of the previous 12 months, the objectives of the plan, a list of planned activities, and the resources required to support the plan. The executive summary is useful for those in upper management who need to be aware of these facts and figures, but who are not intimately involved with the implementation of the details. In its barest essentials, an executive summary statement for Rold Gold Pretzels would look something like this:

> *The Rold Gold Pretzel product line increased sales from $122 million in 2000 to $181 million in 2001, a jump of 48 percent over the prior year. The increase was achieved by the introduction of the brand's first national ad campaign, increased trade support, and line extensions. Sales for the next 12-month period are expected to be $208 million, an increase of 15 percent over the prior year. One trade promotion will be run in each quarter, supported by a coupon drop in freestanding inserts and a national ad campaign in two of the four quarters. The estimated budget to support these activities is $22 million, an increase of 12 percent over the prior year.*

Analysis of the Marketing Situation

The analysis of the marketing situation is a breakdown of the brand's current status in the marketplace. The prior year's activities are reviewed and analyzed. Actual sales results are compared to the stated objectives in the prior year's plan. Competitive activities that affected the brand are also included. This section acts as the "state of the union" for the brand. An analysis of Rold Gold's situation would be along the following lines:

> *Pretzels currently represent a $1 billion dollar industry. It is considered the salty snack industry's fastest growing category. The Rold Gold brand is the market leader with a market share of 18 percent. Sales increased 48 percent over the prior year. In 1997, the brand had no ad support. In 1998, a national ad campaign supported the brand with Jason Alexander, formerly of TV's Seinfeld, as the spokesperson. Four trade promotions were run, one per quarter. Coupons were distributed twice during the year. All of these factors contributed to the huge increase in sales and the brand's market dominance. Eagle brand pretzels matched the Rold Gold deal levels to the trade, but ran no supporting media or promotional efforts.*

Assessment of Opportunities and Threats

In this section, all opportunities regarding the brand are examined, as well as any threats. Threats may come in the form of production or quality control problems within the company, competitive activities that pose problems, or potential problems within the marketing environment. Opportunities may come in the form of increased distribution, new markets, additional line extensions, changes in consumer behavior that are conducive to a brand's success, and so on. Rold Gold's assessment, in simplified terms, may look something like the following:

> *Rold Gold enjoys an 85 ACV (all-commodity volume) level of distribution according to the latest Nielsen figures.[8] The objective for this coming year is to achieve a 90 ACV distribution level. Sales efforts will focus on the Southwest, where distribution is the lowest. Also, efforts in the Northeast will focus on cracking a major wholesaler who controls $50 million in sales of salty snack foods. A pretzel nugget is being pursued by R&D. Samples of several types are available and being tested in focus groups. Sales and marketing efforts will also focus on a major chain in the Midwest that has threatened to discontinue the Rold Gold line. Additional support will be given in the form of in-ad coupons. Eagle brand is being highly promoted in the Northwest and taking some Rold Gold share away. The Eagle trade allowances will be met by Rold Gold and the situation will be reviewed on a monthly basis.*
>
> *Inconsistent quality has been found in the pretzels produced at the XYZ site. Production and quality control are aware of the problems and new procedures have been established to prevent further inconsistencies. [This latter statement is hypothetical, not factual.]*

Specifications of Marketing Objectives

This section details the objectives on which the marketing plan is based. As stated earlier, objectives must be clear, concise, and realistic. Objectives are typically based on profit, market share, growth, or diversity. An important part of any objective is the time frame assigned for achievement. A time frame is necessary to determine whether the objective has been met by the plan, department, or SBU.

> *The objective of the Rold Gold marketing plan in the upcoming 12 months is to:*
>
> - *Increase sales of the line by 15 percent to $208 million*
> - *Increase market share from 18 percent to 21 percent*
> - *Achieve a 90 ACV for the line*
> - *Maintain a 19 percent profit margin on the line*

Formulation of Marketing Strategies

The formulation of the marketing strategies details how the marketing objectives will be accomplished. Target markets are outlined as are the marketing mixes that will be used to satisfy the needs of these target markets. All activities that are included in the plan and the budget are detailed in full. This section acts as the blueprint for the building process for the brand that will take place over the next 12 months. Rold Gold's strategy might appear in abbreviated form as follows:

> *The national ad campaign introduced in 2001 will continue. Ad flights will be scheduled twice a year, in June and December, the peak selling periods for salty snack foods. The ads will continue to use Jason Alexander as spokesperson, since he continues to have great appeal. We will continue to stress that the products are low in fat because they are baked; they are a good value; and they appeal to all age groups.*
>
> *Trade allowances at the current level of $1.20 per case will be continued once per quarter except in the Northwest where the Eagle's level of $1.80 per case will be met.*
>
> *Additional new product slotting allowances will be offered to those accounts who do not currently carry the line, in an effort to increase distribution. Two new line extensions will be added in the second quarter. The introduction will be supported by trade allowances only.*

Preparation of Action Programs and Budgets

This section of the marketing plan details any programs that are designed to result in some specific action, as well as the budget required to support the marketing activities created to achieve the company's objectives. This section is critical in that the entire year's budget is either approved, increased, or decreased based on the plan. If a mistake is made in the budgeting, the manager and the brand may have to live with the mistake for the entire year. All figures must be accurate and precise.

In total, Rold Gold's required budget for the upcoming 12 months is as follows:

	(in millions)
Ad campaign	*$ 5.5*
Trade allowances	*13.0*
Special slotting allowances	*1.0*
Introduction of line extensions	*1.5*
Regional in-ad coupon support	*1.0*
Total	*$22.0*

Special distribution programs as outlined above are scheduled for the first quarter. Heavier allowances in the Northwest are scheduled for the second quarter.

Development of Control Procedures

This final section of the marketing plan details how results of the plan will be measured on an ongoing basis. Management may require a monthly or quarterly update of sales measured against projections. If sales are far from projections, action can be taken to alleviate the situation. Ultimately, control procedures keep the marketing plan on course.

Sales of Rold Gold will be monitored on a monthly basis. Actual case sales for the month and cumulative year will be compared to the prior year same period and to objectives. Achievement of the market share and distribution figures will be reviewed semi-annually, when Nielsen figures are updated and available. Since Nielsen figures are a few months behind in reporting, final judgment as to the achievement of these goals will be delayed until the Nielsen figures for the entire year are released. Profit margin figures will be judged on the basis of total revenues less total costs for the brand.

LEARNING OBJECTIVE 4

Marketing Planning Trends

Ultimately, the marketing plan is a road map for running and monitoring the marketing mix. In addition to using the marketing plan to help fit the marketing mix to situation realities, the purpose of the plan is to communicate a team of managers' intentions to top management, to justify the budget request, and to provide points of reference for charting progress in executing the marketing mix programs, week by week and month by month.

Table A.1 presents the changing contents of large company market plans over the last 20 years. Information about company goals and top-down decisions made by senior management about choice of market segments, new product development, and market penetration strategy are commonly detailed in the plan, and Table A.1 indicates such top-down direction may be increasing. Table A.2 shows that although some marketing plans include some information about changing market conditions, what the company is actually doing is often left out of the formal written marketing plan (see also Table A.3).

As noted in Table A.2, the aspects of the market environment that are commonly described in detail are company goals, demand forecasts, market share, and customer segmentation analysis. In contrast, the profitability of customers and distributors, changes in distributor competitiveness, and in supply-chain technology are not commonly detailed in the plan. Furthermore, only about a third of the firms present a detailed SWOT analysis—a strengths-weaknesses (SW) analysis along with a detailed appraisal of opportunities-threats (OT). Hence, if the written marketing plan is indeed a road map, it more often than not is a pretty sketchy road map. Presumably a lot of the missing information is in stored e-mails, separate situation reports, or in the heads of individual executives. There is also the possibility that the information is completely missing and

Table A.1	Changes in Marketing Planning of Large U.S. Corporations 1980–2000

Who prepares and approves the marketing plan:

	Prepares			Approves		
	1980	**1990**	**2000**	**1980**	**1990**	**2000**
President/GM/CEO	2%	3%	4%	50%	53%	58%
Vice president marketing	49%	52%	34%	46%	42%	35%
Marketing director/manager	33%	34%	40%			
Product/brand manager	15%	10%	16%			
Product/market cross-functional team			6%			

Percent of plans including top-down instructions and directions from senior management on:

	1990	**2000**
Choice of target markets	42%	53%
New product/service development	39%	51%
Pricing strategy	45%	40%
Market penetration strategy	27%	39%
Distribution strategy	28%	34%
Advertising strategy	26%	34%

Percent of plans that presented a detailed analysis on the following environment topics/issues:

	1980	**1990**	**2000**
Demand forecasts	76%	65%	40%
Market segments	60%	75%	40%
Changing needs of customers	58%	59%	28%
Company/competition market share	66%	63%	47%
Changing competitor behavior	65%	48%	30%
Government regulatory issues	36%	27%	13%
Environment issues	30%	26%	9%

Responsibility for preparing and approving the marketing plan has not changed a lot. However, the chain-of-command distance between who prepares and who approves the plan has increased. Compared with a decade ago there is more top-down direction of the key elements of marketing strategy and the marketing mix. Less detailed situation analysis in the written marketing plan also appears to be more common today than a decade or 2 decades ago. Source: Peter Dickson, Tom Bodenberg, and Rebecca Slotegraaf, *The Marketing Plan 2000*, Working Paper, Florida International University.

important managers and teams in the firm do not know what is happening and what the firm is doing or going to do. Either way, the sketchier the marketing plan, the greater the potential breakdown in command and control. Other common problems associated with constructing marketing plans are described in the sections that follow.

Executive Summary Problems

The risk inherent in an executive summary is that it sometimes glosses over important details that senior executives need to know and comment on. The entire marketing plan is already a summary of the environment and a company's strategies and action plans. A summary of a summary can be dangerous. A related problem is whether, within the evolution of the management culture of a firm, the purpose of the summary and the plan has become to impress rather than honestly inform senior executives. When the summary and the plan become an advocacy or political document rather than a decision-making document, the usefulness of marketing planning as a decision process and the plan as a road map can be questioned.

Analysis of Market Environment Issues in Major Corporations' Marketing Plans	Table A.2		
	Not Applicable to Us	**Not Included in Our Plan**	**Described Only Briefly**	**Described in Detail**
Economic/market sales forecasts	2%	12%	46%	40%
Technological trends in product/service design	8%	29%	47%	16%
Product-market life cycle/growth analysis	12%	35%	39%	13%
Company goals and mission/vision	1%	12%	42%	45%
Customer segmentation analysis	2%	15%	43%	40%
Changes in consumer wants/needs/preferences	2%	20%	53%	26%
Changes in customer use of Internet/Web	8%	25%	52%	15%
Current customer profitability analysis	7%	48%	28%	17%
Trends in distribution logistics/technology	26%	35%	31%	8%
Changes in distributor's competitiveness	34%	29%	30%	7%
Current distributor profitability analysis	37%	44%	15%	5%
Market share of company and competitors	3%	9%	42%	47%
Changes in behavior of competitors	2%	15%	53%	30%
Benchmarking of rival products/services	3%	33%	44%	20%
Current product/service-line profitability analysis	8%	27%	33%	32%
Trends/changes in regulations, laws, and government support programs	11%	32%	44%	13%
Environment/safety issues and trends	25%	39%	27%	9%
SBU strengths/weaknesses analysis	9%	19%	39%	33%
Appraisal of opportunities and threats	2%	7%	42%	49%

The marketing plans of the sample of 200 major companies studied by *The Conference Board 2000 Study of Marketing Planning* more often present details about demand, market share, and customer segments but are weaker in their in-depth analysis of changing consumer behavior, changing competitor behavior, distribution, and the profitability of products, customers, and channels. At least half of the marketing plans have large gaps in their situation analysis. The environment aspects/issues that are detailed by at least a third of the sample are boldface. Source: Peter Dickson, Tom Bodenberg, and Rebecca Slotegraaf, *The Marketing Plan 2000*, Working Paper, Florida International University.

Market Analysis Problems

The marketing plan is an important due-diligence document in any company because it presents a record of how much attention decision makers are paying to the important changes in the market (how well informed they have made themselves), the logic behind their decision making and what major adaptations are being made (or at least planned) to strategies, tactics, programs, and procedures. Marketers need to develop the skill of extracting key facts about changes in the environment that provide real insight to decision makers. In practice, the market analysis section of the marketing plan is often a few PowerPoint slides with bulleted one-liners and slogans that omit and overlook key facts, details, issues, threats, and opportunities. It can also be too long, presenting page after page of market research results or sales reports on issues and topics where the key *need-to-know* facts are buried in a mass of *nice-to-know* facts.

With the development of knowledge management systems and sophisticated shared databases within firms, it can be expected that marketing executives will be assigned responsibility to maintain up-to-date digital files about market share, customer satisfaction, individual major account behavior, and other marketing environment topics. This information can be captured by scanning and routing the myriad relevant information being sent digitally within the firm. Files on a specific trade customer or the effect of a campaign can be accessed by other executives to allow fast, up-to-date situation analysis. With such an information system the preparation of a marketing plan that details a broad and deep environment scanning and analysis is a relatively easy task.

Table A.3	Major Corporation Marketing Plan Content			
	Not Applicable to Us	Not Included in Our Plan	Described Only Briefly	Described in Detail
New product or service development	2%	7%	42%	49%
New product or service launch	4%	7%	36%	53%
Product/service-line repositioning	10%	12%	41%	37%
Product quality programs (e.g., QFD)	16%	30%	40%	14%
New channels-of-distribution strategy	17%	12%	33%	38%
Distributor/dealer relationship programs	33%	14%	29%	24%
Joint campaigns with specific distributors	34%	26%	31%	10%
EDI and order-delivery logistics programs	33%	29%	32%	6%
Major customer relationship programs	7%	12%	40%	41%
Role of field sales force/sales reps	8%	24%	38%	31%
Customer after-sales service programs	12%	27%	42%	19%
Field sales force/reps education programs	10%	35%	42%	14%
Sales force/trade incentive programs	19%	29%	31%	22%
Regional sales campaigns	19%	35%	29%	17%
Integrated marketing communication program	6%	11%	40%	43%
Direct marketing/telemarketing programs	18%	13%	38%	31%
Data-based marketing programs	11%	17%	44%	28%
Ad agency's planned campaign	17%	20%	32%	31%
Web marketing campaign	14%	16%	47%	24%
Pricing policies/discounts/promotions	7%	21%	33%	39%
PR and promotion programs	5%	15%	51%	30%
Cross-functional team organization	9%	33%	43%	15%
Marketing research projects	3%	12%	60%	25%
Program performance tracking measures	3%	18%	49%	29%

The marketing plans of the sample of 200 major companies studied by *The Conference Board 2000 Study of Marketing Planning* present more details about the product aspects of the marketing mix but are weaker in their detailing of the distribution and sales programs that are part of the marketing mix. The programs that are described by more than a third of the sample in detail are boldface. Source: Peter Dickson, Tom Bodenberg, and Rebecca Slotegraaf, *The Marketing Plan 2000*, Working Paper, Florida International University.

Marketing Strategy and Action Plans Problems

Here again, this section of the plan often does not provide enough detail about plans for product development, customer satisfaction and quality improvement, and distribution system improvement, and the time-line activity sequences that identify who is responsible for undertaking each activity (see Table A.3). As a result, too many uncoordinated decisions may be made on the fly by different executives. A much rarer problem occurs when too much time and effort is spent on detailing action plans that are blindly executed without sensible improvisation and adaptation by the sales force, advertising agency, or product-development group, among others. The plan should not be treated as chiseled in stone but also not so fluid that no one takes its decisions and proposals seriously.

Forecasts and Budget Problems

The most common problem with forecasts and budgets is that they are put together quite separately from the rest of the plan. Problems can arise when forecasts are based on past performance history and anticipated economic conditions but are not related to the expected effectiveness of the new and adapted marketing programs and action plans, and when budgets are based on past spending but don't account for planned spending.

Another problem is that junior- and middle-level marketing executives often have minimal management and financial accounting skills and do not adequately understand the short- and long-term costs of what they are proposing in the plan. This can lead to mistakes that must be handled by senior executives who then lose confidence in the marketing plan and planners.

Clearly, "best practices" in marketing involve skilled planning and skilled improvisation. Both are essential processes within the command and control system of a firm. Just as importantly, they are a source of innovation and creativity from which will spring the next generation of products and services, as well as other new, more competitive marketing practices and tactics.

APPENDIX SUMMARY

- Planning is the basis for sound decision making in any situation in life. Strategic planning and forecasting are key activities that influence and direct the development of specific marketing strategies.

- The most important level of planning is strategic planning, or the organization's overall game plan. This plan typically encompasses the firm's long-range goals and dictates direction for all departments in the firm. Strategic planning differs from marketing planning, or the game plan, for a particular product or product line. The marketing plan is the detailed scheme of the marketing strategies and activities associated with each product's marketing mix—product, pricing, distribution, and promotional decisions. Tactical planning is another level of organizational planning that involves specifying details that pertain to the organization's activities during the current period.

- Strategic planning comprises five fundamental elements: (1) organization missions (how an organization defines its business or what makes it different from the competition); (2) strategic business units (smaller divisions created to facilitate planning and general operations); (3) objectives (clear, realistic goals based on measurable achievements such as sales or market share); (4) strategic planning tools (tools designed to help managers in their strategic and marketing planning efforts); and (5) marketing planning (which includes specific objectives, necessary resources, planned activities, and expected results).

- Marketing plans emanate from and are inspired by the overall strategic plan. Marketing plans vary in length and formality. A marketing plan can cover a specific product or an entire product line or category. A typical marketing plan includes an executive summary, an analysis of the marketing situation, an assessment of opportunities and threats, specification of marketing objectives, a formulation of marketing strategies, the preparation of action programs and budgets, and the development of control procedures.

ENDNOTES

[1] This appendix was adapted from Lindgren and Shimp, *Marketing: An Interactive Learning System* (Fort Worth: The Dryden Press, 1996).

[2] The Coca-Cola Company's 1997 Annual Report.

[3] Intellvisions Software Limited http://www.intellvisions.com.

[4] H. Igor Ansoff, "Strategies for Diversification," *Harvard Business Review* (September–October 1957): 113–114.

[5] This discussion is adapted from George S. Day, "Diagnosing the Product Portfolio," *Journal of Marketing* 41 (April 1977): 29–38.

[6] For further reading on marketing planning, see William A. Cohen, *The Marketing Plan* (New York: John Wiley & Sons, 1995); and Donald R. Lehmann and Russel S. Winer, *Analysis for Marketing Planning*, 2nd ed. (Homewood, IL: Irwin, 1991).

[7] Jennifer Lawrence, "The Marketing 100," *Advertising Age*, 4 July 1994, S8.

[8] *All-commodity volume (ACV)* is a term used by marketing and advertising practitioners to refer to total sales of a product. For example, an 85 ACV level for Rold Gold simply means that brand has obtained distribution in retail outlets that account for 85 percent of the total pretzel volume in the United States.

CASE 1

Neiman Marcus

You've probably never spent $3,000 for a suit, even if the label came from a designer and the quality was impeccable. But would you drive several hours to shop at a store that carried all the clothing brands and styles you loved? Maybe, if you were a diehard shopper and you felt a strong bond with the store. What if the store offered you a trip to Paris for your loyalty? It might happen if you're a Neiman Marcus shopper.

Neiman Marcus. The name tumbles off the tongue, conjuring up visions of affluence, high fashion, and an anxiously awaited annual catalog featuring exotic—and expensive—holiday gifts for the recipient whose closets and carports are already filled with clothing and cars most of us would die for. The specialty retailer that traces its beginnings to Dallas opened in the early part of the 20th century and has gradually expanded nationally to 15 states and more than 30 locations from Boston to Southern California. Neiman Marcus is known around the world as a specialty retailer offering high-end fashion, jewelry, gifts, and home furnishings. Billy Payton, vice president of marketing and customer programs, identifies Neiman's customers as consumers—mostly women—whose household income is $150,000 and above, who are between the ages of 35 and 55, and who like the one-to-one relationship that Neiman's tries to build with them. He says that the Neiman's customer "appreciates fashion and appreciates quality in merchandise and gifts and apparel." Burton Tanksy, president of the Neiman Marcus Group targets his customers this way: "Our customer wants designer clout. She wants something easily recognizable so that people will know she paid a lot for it." Payton further identifies two main categories of customer: long-term customers who have shopped with the store for years and occasional customers who visit the store for a specific need such as a wedding gift.

How does Neiman Marcus develop relationships with customers who could shop anywhere they want? First, by recognizing the very fact that these customers can afford to shop anywhere, then by looking for ways to create greater utilities for them. "Neiman Marcus is all about developing relationships with customers, through our sales associates, through our marketing efforts, through editing the selection of quality merchandise and fashion. So it's all about a one-to-one relationship," explains Payton. One important way of doing this is attracting customers to the InCircle Program, a frequent buyer program that was the first of its kind when it was launched in 1984. For every dollar a customer spends at Neiman Marcus, one point is added to the customer's InCircle account. Later, customers can redeem points for gifts and purchasing privileges—say, that trip to Paris. So a long drive to a Neiman's store becomes worthwhile to many customers. Neiman's has also upgraded the old-fashioned gift certificate, replacing it with a plastic card that looks like a credit card. The new card has a new name: the NM Gift Card.

To increase personal service even more, Neiman's sales associates develop exclusive relationships with particular customers. Pat Ames, a sales associate, notes that she often drops off a purchase at a customer's home or workplace or selects appropriate gifts for customers when they are short on time or ideas. Finally, there's Neiman's famous "The Book," a large, glossy fashion publication that is more idea book than catalog; customers are encouraged to sift through its pages, glean fashion and gift ideas, then visit the stores themselves for personal service. Customers treasure their copies as if they were first editions of literary classics.

Whereas Neiman's traditionally focused on developing long-term customer relationships, recently the company has broadened its marketing focus to include the occasional customer. Payton notes, "The new buzz term is *CRM*, continuous relationship management, meaning, are we serving the occasional customer—all of their needs? All of their shopping needs, or fashion needs, their gift needs, their accessory needs, their cosmetic needs? Are we maximizing the servicing and our selling opportunity to all of our customers? The NM Gift Card is a result of this thinking, and Payton notes that every holiday—or occasion—counts at Neiman's. In fact, he refers to the company's new focus on occasions as a "year-round business." Another new area of focus is "the whole culture of successful young Gen-Xers craving high fashion, high-quality merchandise who may not think of Neiman Marcus as a place for them," says Payton. The trick, he says, is to attract the younger shoppers without alienating the older ones.

1. Neiman Marcus
2. The Timberland Company
3. ESPN
4. Tower Records
5. FedEx Corporation
6. Furniture.com
7. Fisher Price
8. Fresh Samantha
9. Goya Foods, Inc.
10. UPS
11. Pfizer, Inc.
12. Hasbro, Inc.
13. RadioShack
14. Wine.com
15. Polaroid
16. Pizza Hut
17. Concept2
18. Cybex International
19. Learjet

Not willing to be left behind in the wake of Internet technology, Neiman Marcus has already launched its own online shopping site at http://www.neimanmarcus.com and has joined forces with other organizations on the Internet. Neiman's and several other retailers have signed up with a wedding registry site called http://www.dellajames.com, which allows wedding guests to buy gifts directly online from the group of retailers. As for the company's regular Web site, Billy Payton notes, "We definitely recognize and know that the Web will play a major part in our marketing in the future. . . . We're trying to reach a very sophisticated customer, who appreciates technology, who understands technology and responds to it." Will Neiman's be able to replicate its brick-and-mortar presence and also become a leading upscale Internet retailer? If its sales associates can still offer the personal touch, if customers still believe they are getting the best of the best, and if occasional customers like the idea of buying a wedding gift with the click of a mouse, the company could do very well online. Still, it is probably safe to predict that not a single Neiman's customer will give up that precious copy of "The Book."

Questions

1. In what ways does Neiman Marcus create time, place, and ownership utilities for its customers? In what ways does Neiman Marcus avoid marketing myopia?

2. Describe the typical Neiman Marcus customer. How well do you think Neiman Marcus meets the needs of this market?

3. In what ways might technology affect Neiman's marketing strategy?

4. Neiman's sales associates are known for providing excellent personal service for their customers. Describe how Neiman's Web site (http://www.neimanmarcus.com) attempts to integrate a "personal touch" for their customers.

Sources: Neiman Marcus company Web site, http://www.neimanmarcus.com, http://www.neimanmarcusgroup.com, accessed 15 February 2000; Bruce Horovitz, "Neiman Marcus Spins Own Webcast," *USA Today*, 30 August 1999, http://www.usatoday.com; "My Biggest Mistake: Stanley Marcus," *Inc.com*, 1 July 1999, http://www.inc.com; Wendy Bounds, "Retailers Say 'I Do' to Wedding Web," *Wall Street Journal*, 9 June 1999, B9.

CASE 2

The Timberland Company

Timberland makes boots—all kinds of boots, from work boots to hiking boots to mountain biking shoes. They come in all shapes, sizes, and colors. Timberland also churns out backpacks for school children, outerwear, and leather fashion boots for women. Most of these products come at a premium—a pair of hiking boots can cost more than $100. Consumers like the image that Timberland products evoke—love of the outdoors, rugged individuality, health consciousness, and fashion.

But Timberland has taken its product image a step farther, integrating the company with socially responsible activities. Touting the virtues of volunteerism, Timberland encourages both its customers and its employees to give their time and effort to create a better world. "With your boots and your beliefs, you will be able to interact responsibly and comfortably within the natural and social environments that all human beings share," says the company's Web site. In other words, Timberland boots aren't just boots, they are vehicles for good works.

Timberland doesn't just talk the talk; the company walks the walk, in its own boots. Through their Path of Service Program, all full-time Timberland employees receive 40 hours of paid time a year to volunteer within their community. By the year 2000, employees had performed over 80,000 hours of service. Timberland employees have renovated day care facilities, cleared hiking trails, cleaned streets, worked at animal shelters, installed playgrounds, and even assisted in hurricane relief efforts. Timberland gives employees a wide range of volunteer options to suit their skills and interests; or they can participate in City Year, a nationwide program designed to get young people more involved in restoring inner-city communities. In addition, Timberland keeps in close contact with various United Way organizations, matching employee volunteers to organizations that need help.

Some Timberland employees take the volunteer mandate even further and head up individual activities. Glenn Myers of New Hampshire spearheaded a fundraising effort that collected $18,000 in relief for the people of war-torn Kosovo. Timberland matched his efforts so that a check for $36,000 was presented to the Red Cross. Then Myers offered to temporarily house a Kosovo refugee in his home. When two entire families arrived instead, he and several Timberland coworkers arranged for the families to occupy an apartment. When winter arrived Myers conducted a clothing drive throughout the Timberland headquarters in Stratham, New Hampshire, and delivered boxes of warm clothing to the Kosovo families. "Timberland believes in the power of the individual," notes the company Web site. "That one voice can and must make a difference." Employees like Glenn Myers take this message to heart.

Timberland is well known for its corporate donations to socially responsible causes, ranging from local events such as a road race to benefit an elementary school parent-teachers organization to the expansion of a homeless shelter to its support of the City Year program, which has received over $10 million from Timberland.

What about Timberland's economic responsibilities? The company now earns over $800 million per year in revenues and continues to announce growth in revenues. Company president and CEO Jeffrey Swartz notes that the formula for social responsibility works just as well on the bottom line. "I am pleased to report Timberland's fourth consecutive year of record revenue and improved earnings," he stated in 2000. "Results in 1999 reflect Timberland's continued focus on developing a portfolio of businesses that are diversified by product, geography, and channel."

Timberland's careful balance between social responsibility and economic responsibility has earned the company a spot on *Fortune's* list of 100 best companies to work for. Timberland was number 30 in the January 2000 issue of the magazine. With roughly 4,000 employees worldwide, nearly 50 percent of whom are women and 25 percent of whom are minorities, the New Hampshire bootmaker needs to combine a cosmopolitan and local outlook in the way it presents itself to the public. In doing so, the company has managed to sell both its footwear and its social mission in one slogan: "Pull on your boots and make a difference."

Questions

1. How do Timberland's social responsibility activities fit the social-cultural marketing environment?

2. How does Timberland use social responsibility to promote its products? Is this ethical? Why or why not?

3. On the pyramid of social responsibility, how does Timberland balance its philanthropic actions with its economic responsibilities?

4. As stated in the chapter text, "Socially responsible marketing involves campaigns that encourage people to adopt socially beneficial behaviors." Explore Timberland's Web site (www.timberland.com). Does Timberland's site effectively work towards this goal? Explain your answer.

Sources: Timberland Web site, http://www.timberland.com, accessed 16 February 2000; Kate Barbera, "Reaching Out to the Homeless," *Portsmouth Herald*, 13 February 2000, http://www.seacoastonline.com; "Timberland Announces Record Fourth Quarter and Full Year Revenue and Earnings," *Business Wire*, 3 February 2000; "100 Best Companies to Work For," *Fortune*, 10 January 2000, http://www.fortune.com; "Here and Abroad, People Are Doing Wonders for Relief Effort," *Portsmouth Herald*, 18 November 1999, http://www.seacoastonline; Christine Gillette, "Agency Plans Center," *Portsmouth Herald*, 28 June 1999, http://www.seacoastonline.

CASE 3

ESPN

It began by mistake. Back in the late 1970s, Bill Rasmussen decided to launch a cable station to broadcast Connecticut-area sports. With the assistance of his partners, Rasmussen leased a building in Bristol from which to broadcast and then bought some satellite time. Only after signing the agreement did he learn that his satellite coverage was national—and his small-scale plan of New England sports coverage began to grow. Their early name for the channel—Entertainment and Sports Programming Network—proved too much of a tongue twister and, in 1985, they settled on the ESPN acronym as the corporate name. The letters now stand for nothing—except a sports phenomenon.

Since those early days during which the network scrambled to televise whatever it could—from a men's pro, slow-pitch softball game to its first NHL game in 1979—the organization has grown dramatically, filling what Will Burkhardt of ESPN says is now a saturated market for televised sports in the United States and rapidly moving overseas. "We reach 150 to 155 million households around the world [excluding the United States]; that encompasses about 180 markets and territories," says Burkhardt. ESPN reaches all 7 continents, including one of the scientific stations located in Antarctica. The expansion has taken place over the last 15 years, beginning when ESPN provided groundbreaking coverage of the America's Cup international sailing race from Australia in 1987. That race seemed to be a turning point not only for ESPN, but for cable broadcasting itself. From there, ESPN purchased a majority interest in the European Sports Network (called Eurosport) and began service to 25 Middle Eastern and North African nations. In addition to its Eurosport market, ESPN's largest international markets have become China, India, and Argentina.

Burkhardt notes that ESPN entered the international marketplace because of a "desire to grow outside of the U.S. borders and to take what we had learned in the United States in terms of people's passion for sport . . . and bring that to the international marketplace." This was around the same time that cable and satellite television were expanding around the world, so ESPN's timing seemed perfect.

However, marketing around the world isn't easy. For instance, although India has a huge middle-class population, middle class in that country means that a family might earn about $1,800 per year, as opposed to an American middle-class family's earnings of $35,000 per year. Thus, attracting viewers to pay for television is more difficult in India. In addition, the infrastructure for cable television is very different from that of the United States, which requires more effort for ESPN marketers. India has tens of thousands of cable entrepreneurs serving approximately 100 customers each, instead of a giant like AOL-Time Warner, which serves 13 million. Still, ESPN thinks that serving India is worth the effort and tailors its programming to the single most-watched sport in the nation: cricket.

In the burgeoning South American markets, where sports fanatics thrive, viewers can watch all kinds of programming—Argentine rugby, Argentine polo, Brazilian basketball, and Brazilian tennis, to name a few. But Burkhardt emphasizes that ESPN starts with a regional marketing strategy, "building a bed of programming from which you then start to localize." Currently, most broadcasts are in English or the local language, but dealing with some countries' multiple local dialects is extremely difficult. In addition, consumers in smaller markets want to see broadcasters of their own nationality instead of ESPN's standard crew of broadcasters. "There is no question that people in Mexico would prefer all of our commentators to be Mexican instead of some which are Argentine," remarks Burkhardt. ESPN simply can't afford to provide this degree of customization yet.

Ultimately, ESPN's goal is to reach as many households worldwide as possible, despite any difficulties in penetrating new markets. For example, the company landed a huge deal that gave it distribution rights in Latin America for all four rounds of the Masters Golf Tournament. ESPN Latin America alone is now distributed in more than 11 million households in 41 countries and territories, broadcasting in English, Spanish, and Portuguese.

In spite of victories like the Masters broadcast, perhaps one of the greatest challenges to ESPN is that the company must, in large part, make its pitch to cable and satellite television operators before its programming ever reaches the consumers themselves. Those operators conduct business in different ways, they lack rating systems, and some even replace ESPN programming with home grown shows. Then there are political challenges, such as when ESPN was thrown off Chinese cable after the United States mistakenly bombed its embassy in Eastern Europe. And there are legal tangles in each country that need to be dealt with, as well. But sports are an international language that tries to provide entertainment without political ramifications, and people everywhere love to watch. "We're obviously not trying to promote any kind of political message through the showing of an American baseball game," says Burkhardt. And perhaps that is the key to ESPN's success—its ability to bring sport to everyone, everywhere, anytime.

Questions

1. What questions might ESPN marketers ask themselves as they try to develop business in Asia or South America?

2. Why is it important for ESPN to global? What might be some barriers to trade for ESPN?

3. How would you describe ESPN's global marketing strategy?

4. Search ESPN's Web site at www.espn.com and summarize what they are currently doing in international markets.

Sources: Telephone interview with Will Burkhardt of ESPN, January 2000; "TV Listings," 8 February 2000, http://www.msn.espn.go.com; "ESPN International Lands Masters for Latin America," company press release, 11 November 1999, http://www.msn.espn.go.com; Michael Hiestand, "Did You Know? ESPN Is 20 Today," *USA Today*, 7 September 1999, http://www.usatoday.com; "Looking Back, Back, Back . . . ," company press release, 6 September 1999, http://www.msn.espn.go.com; Rudy Martzke, "ESPN at 20," *USA Today*, 18 August 1999, 2c.

CASE 4

Tower Records

E-commerce has struck the music industry, and the echoes are still reverberating. Today, musicians can record high quality music online from their homes, aficionados can download their favorite tunes or soundtracks, and, of course, consumers can order just about any tape or CD they can imagine with the click of a mouse. How does a company like Tower Records—the nationally known chain of music, book, and video stores—keep pace with the times?

Tower Records has survived in a tough industry where others have faltered. The company was founded in 1960 by Russ Solomon, who managed to coax his father, a drugstore owner, into a small loan. Today Tower operates 219 stores, including 39 franchise locations, and it has 7,400 employees worldwide. Although Tower offers books and videos at its stores, music still makes up 85 percent of the company's business. The company understands the need to establish a presence on the Internet, but Tower executives—including Russ Solomon himself—believe that they should do so cautiously. They have watched other companies jump headlong on to the Internet, sinking a lot of money into Web sites and ultimately losing millions because the move was made too quickly, without enough research. Indeed, Solomon says that he's not going to get caught up in the "hysteria about the Internet."

So Tower has taken its move to the Internet one step at a time, incorporating this effort with its overall marketing strategy, which includes developing more and larger stores, new markets, and a new product line—consumer electronics. Instead of concentrating solely on its Web site, Tower managers prefer to make the Internet part of an overall strategy so that the company doesn't lose "millions and millions," according to Michael Solomon, Russ Solomon's son and president and CEO of Tower. "We would like it to be profitable." Currently, Tower's online sales account for roughly 2 percent of the total, or "the equivalent of one of our good stores."

The Solomons believe that, although many consumers like to shop online, just as many like to visit Tower's stores. They also agree with experts who assert that online and traditional shopping can coexist peacefully, and even benefit each other. Jim Donio, spokesman for the National Association of Recording Merchandisers says, "For a lot of people there's nothing that can equate with the social experience" of visiting a store, talking with salespeople, picking up and handling the merchandise. So in addition to continually upgrading its Web site, Tower is building new, larger stores that will contain more inventory, more listening stations and all kinds of new electronic gadgets for consumers to play with.

What will you find on Tower's Web site? Consumers can log on and order music in six different languages, in 150 currencies, from 40 locations in Tower's global distribution network. In the United States, you can click on your favorite music, video/DVD titles, and books. You get store locators, chart lists—the works. If you log on to Tower Europe, you get great specials, a look at Tower's Music Magazine, a chance to play games, and a list of top chart titles in every category imaginable, from blues to movie soundtracks. Click over to the link for Japan, and you'll find much the same thing—presented in both English and Japanese. "Whether you are mad for Madonna in Mozambique or avid for ABBA in Alaska, Tower Record's range of over 600,000 entertainment titles . . . will be available at the end of your fingertips," says the company in a press release about the unveiling of its site. "We're in a competitive business," notes Tower board member Bob Lorber. "All of a sudden, we have lots more competition." Tower has no intention of being left behind the online competition.

Some Internet music marketers worry about the problem of people illegally downloading music from the Internet, but Michael Solomon is philosophical about it. "You can get music for free now," he observes. Indeed, music buffs have been taping songs from the radio or each other's collections for decades. "You can do it [download] and some people do, but I don't think it's a threat."

So Tower Records continues to rock to its own beat. "We're comfortable and secure, but we're never satisfied and complacent," says Michael Solomon. "You've got to be on edge all the time," adds his father, who in his seventies still holds the position of chairman of the company. It looks like this music company will be heard from for a long time.

Questions

1. What are the benefits to Tower Records in offering online shopping?

2. In what ways might Tower customize or personalize its Web site and online services for individual customers?

3. In what ways might Tower combine its marketing strategies for its brick-and-mortar stores and its e-commerce site?

Sources: Tower Europe Web site, http://uk.towerrecords.com, accessed 18 February 2000; Tower Japan Web site, http://www.towerrecords.co.jp, accessed 18 February 2000; Kelly Johnson, "Solomons Still Feel That Tower Power," *Sacramento Business Journal,* 19 April 1999, http://www.sacramento.bizjournals.com/sacramento; "Tower Records to Launch Online Sales," *Sacramento Business Journal,* 17 August 1998, http://www.sacramento.bizjournals.com/sacramento; "Tower Records Hangs Out Shingle on Internet," *Reuters News Service,* 19 April 1998.

CASE 5

FedEx Corporation

If you've ever ordered anything by phone or over the Internet, chances are you've received a package delivered by a purple, orange, and white FedEx truck. Millions of other customers, both consumers and businesses, received their packages on the same day. In fact, FedEx makes 3 to 4 million deliveries each day, in more than 200 countries, 24 to 48 hours after the shipping order was placed.

Shipping a package via FedEx costs more than shipping via UPS or Airborne. But FedEx maintains its competitive position by offering security and reliability—in other words, FedEx relies on the trusting relationship it builds with customers. FedEx claims that more than 99 percent of its deliveries arrive on time. And when there's a mistake, the company offers a two-way, money-back guarantee: First, the customer is given a refund if the delivery is late; second, the customer receives a refund if there is any difficulty in obtaining tracking information.

Technology is the foundation of FedEx's ability to build complex, integrated relationships with its customers. FedEx maintains a database that details every aspect of each shipping transaction. With FedEx's database, both the company and customer know where the package is during every moment of the transaction; if there is ever a gap in this information, the customer gets a refund. But FedEx's service goes much farther than tracking packages. Major customers, such as L.L. Bean, Dell Computer, or any of the major American automakers, can download FedEx software solutions right into their own desktop computers to customize the way they want to use the information that FedEx can provide. For instance, FedEx Ship API software allows business customers to customize the application to their own shipping needs, from generating shipping labels to tracking packages in real time.

Jeff Wyne, marketing manager for FedEx, notes that one of his organization's goals is to help other businesses be successful. One way to do this is to help a customer manage its supply chain. For instance, FedEx not only handles shipping but also owns warehouses throughout the world, where it holds inventories for companies that don't want to manage their own. FedEx has also become involved in handling international logistics for its customers, through its recently formed subsidiary, FedEx Trade Networks Inc. "We listened to our customers, and that's what they wanted," says G. Edmond Clark, head of the new subsidiary.

If you order an anorak or a pair of hiking boots from L.L. Bean in Maine, the FedEx truck will be at your house in two days. FedEx is an integral part of L.L. Bean's entire business, from the order system on down to the customer service system, where a representative locates a product number, fulfills the request, and generates a FedEx shipping label. Shipping personnel attach a label to the box and scan it, then place the box on the truck. Being part of the entire logistics process helps FedEx build a long-term relationship with customers like L.L. Bean—a relationship in which each company helps the other grow.

FedEx has the reputation of pulling out all the stops to get a package delivered on time, no matter what. The company has even been known to rent commercial jets when its own planes have suffered mechanical failures. If a delivery doesn't make it, not only is the customer's money refunded, a FedEx man will make a personal phone call or visit to apologize and try to find a solution to the problem. Then FedEx will study the situation to make sure it doesn't happen again. "We strive for 100 percent satisfaction guaranteed," says Jeff Wyne. And they'll do whatever it takes.

Questions

1. How does FedEx's use of technology help build relationships with its customers?

2. Go to FedEx's Web site at http://www.fedex.com, select "U.S.A." and then "eBusiness Tools." On that page, you'll see a link for "FedEx eCommerce Solutions" (currently found at http://www.fedex.com/us/ebusiness/ ecommerce/). Choose one of the e-commerce options described, click on its link, and read more about it. Do you think the solution is easy for customers to use? Why or why not?

3. How do FedEx and L.L. Bean benefit from the reciprocity of their relationship?

4. How does FedEx strengthen a relationship after making a mistake?

Sources: Alan Gersten, "FedEx Creates New Unit for Logistics Focus," *Reuter's Limited,* 17 February 2000; "FedEx Trade Networks to Offer Full Range of Global Trade Services," *Business Wire,* 17 February 2000; Brian O'Reilly, "They've Got Mail!" *Fortune,* 7 February 2000, http://www.fortune.com; "FedEx eShipping Tools," FedEx Web site, http://www.fedex.com, accessed 4 February 2000; Scott Kirsner, "Digital Competition—Laurie A. Tucker," *Fast Company,* December 1999, 166.

CASE 6

Furniture.com

"Decorating one's home is an extremely personal and information-intensive decision," says Andrew L. Brooks, president and CEO of Furniture.com. Decorating in general, and furniture shopping in particular, can be a frustrating, time-consuming, and intimidating experience for many people. Few people relish dragging spouses or kids from furniture store to furniture store to sit on sofas and order swatches. And many consumers are just plain afraid to make a decision—what if the color or style is "wrong"? What if the dining room table is too big for the room? Furniture.com is determined to change all that.

Unlike other Internet businesses, Furniture.com is not an online start-up company. The idea to sell furniture on the Web actually began with the owner of a brick-and-mortar furniture store called Empire Furniture Showroom in downtown Worcester, Massachusetts. Steven Rothschild and his partner, Misha Katz, launched the first version of the online company from the Worcester store in the late 1990s. Rothschild is now company chairman and Katz is vice president of new technology. Throughout the changes the company has undergone, however, it has maintained a clear mission, as articulated by Brooks: "to take a shopping experience in the traditional world, which is not particularly easy, to re-create it, and to make it fun, easy, and accessible to everybody."

Rothschild and Katz recognized an opportunity. "The traditional brick-and-mortar environment hasn't been very good to furniture consumers," explains Brooks. "The average consumer needs to go to five or six retail establishments. That potentially ruins five or six weekend days with kids in tow, trying to find the perfect place. That is often a frustrating exercise." With more and more consumers flocking to the Internet to do their shopping, Furniture.com took advantage of a strategic window to attract customers early and keep them coming back for more. The company offers over 50,000 items from 140 manufacturers through its site, and it provides free delivery and setup. Most brick-and-mortar stores offer only 4,000 to 10,000 items, and many charge for delivery beyond a few miles.

Connecting all these pieces of furniture with the right customers requires strategic and tactical planning. Perhaps the company's most important strategy is considering the impact every decision its managers make have on the consumer. "Examples of that include multiple ways to search," explains Brooks. "You can search on our site by room, by piece, and by very specific criteria. . . . What sets us apart is the extent to which we have identified real consumer needs. We then found technology that can provide solutions as opposed to technology for technology's sake." To that end, customers can build their own virtual showroom at the Web site, filled with their favorite pieces of furniture to see what the finished product will look like. The Room Planner, Style Guide, Furniture Finder, and Personal Shopper features of Furniture.com's site are all implementations of the overall strategy.

Furniture.com's strengths include the following:

- Its huge selection—as already mentioned, the company offers over 50,000 items, much more than competitors
- Its service—customer service is open around the clock, by phone, live Internet chat, or e-mail, and sales reps contact customers after delivery to make certain the right items arrived on time
- Its freedom from having to hold inventory—most items are shipped directly from manufacturers

Its one major weakness is the fact that currently the company does not offer cash refunds; instead, customers receive an exchange or store credit. Since furniture is a major purchase for most consumers, having $500 or $1,000 tied up in store credit could be a problem. However, Furniture.com does have a "no questions asked" return policy, and the company pays return shipping fees.

Looking toward future growth, Furniture.com has entered into several strategic alliances with other organizations. The company now has online advertising agreements with MSN Internet services, Yahoo!, and Lycos as part of a move to strengthen its position in the e-commerce marketplace. Indeed, Furniture.com's position is already at the head of its class. In review after review, the company receives high marks for selection and service. *Entertainment Weekly* calls the site "best of breed." *Access* rates the company with four stars, and *PC Magazine* reports, "The smartest furniture shoppers are heading to Furniture.com." That's a satisfying image for Furniture.com's founders: smart shoppers buying products from a smart company.

Questions

1. Do Furniture.com's strategic and tactical planning accurately reflect the company's overall mission? Why or why not?

2. Describe one or two strategies that Furniture.com might use to plan to expand into foreign countries.

3. Identify some potential threats to Furniture.com over the next few years.

4. Visit Furniture.com's Web site at http://www.furniture.com. What are the site's strengths? What are its weaknesses?

Sources: Furniture.com Web site, http://www.furniture.com, accessed 23 March 2000; Anne Stuart, "Furniture.com," *CIO Magazine*, 15 January 2000, http://www.cio.com; Karen Lake, "Creating an Internet Following," *Inc.com*, 10 November 1999, http://www.inc.com; Karen Lake, "Lead Your Industry to the Internet," *Inc.com*, 10 November 1999, http://www.inc.com; June Fletcher, "Internet Home Stores Grow, but Selection Stays Limited," *Wall Street Journal*, 15 October 1999, http://www.djreprints.com; "Furniture.com Announces Multimillion-Dollar Online Advertising Agreements with Lycos and MSN," press release, 27 July 1999, http://www.lycos.com; Timothy J. Mullaney and David Leonhardt, "A Hard Sell Online? Guess Again," *Businessweek.com*, 12 July 1999; Beth Cox, "Furniture.com Launches Multimillion-Dollar Brand Campaign," *InternetNews.com*, 30 June 1999, http://www.internetnews.com; "Furniture.com Offers Proactive, Live Online Assistance," *InternetNews.com*, 30 April 1999, http://www.internetnews.com; "Furniture.com and Amazon.com Team Up on Home Furnishing/Decorating 'Reading Room,'" press release, 8 March 1999.

CASE 7

Fisher-Price

The toy business isn't child's play. It's a marketing environment in which competition is tough, consumers are fickle, and truly new ideas are hard to come by. Shelly Glick Gryfe, director of marketing research at Fisher-Price, knows all that, yet she still enjoys searching for that perfect product, the one that children and their parents will buy—and buy again—with fierce loyalty. Gryfe and her colleagues at Fisher-Price believe in the value of marketing research to bring a new toy to store shelves. But they don't conduct research indiscriminately; they carefully choose which types will be most useful and stick to the budget.

Through exploratory research, Fisher-Price marketers discovered that there was a gap in toys available for preschool and early elementary school boys. Little boys liked the idea of action figures that their older brothers and friends played with, but those toys were difficult for them to understand and handle. And their moms clearly did not want their young children playing with toys that had violent overtones. The research caused Fisher-Price to coin the term KAGOY—Kids Are Getting Older Younger—meaning that younger children want more grown-up toys. Yet those toys must be designed for little hands and young imaginations. "So we were then looking for something that might move away from the [traditional Fisher-Price playset] and be more specifically action figure, but in a way that was more appropriate for preschool boys on many dimensions," explains Gryfe.

Fisher-Price marketers combined the idea of action figures with an age-appropriate context, and the idea for a new group of figures—Rescue Heroes was born. Fisher-Price used a combination of in-house and outside researchers to obtain primary data on their concept, and later the toy itself. First, marketers conducted in-house focus groups they called "mom talks." Gryfe explains, "A mom talk is basically a focus group that we do in-house. It's done very early in the process to see if we're on the right track. . . . We do this before we spend lots of money on out-of-house focus groups and prototypes." During the mom talks, marketers interviewed mothers to find out what they wanted—and didn't want—in a new toy. They learned quickly that mothers liked the idea of imaginative play but didn't want their children playing with aggressive or violent toys. Gryfe admits that these in-house focus groups tend to be subject to sampling bias, because the people who participate are those who want to have an impact on products; they aren't necessarily representative of the general buying public. She also believes that participants may edit their responses when they are on site, whereas they may be more candid when they participate in focus groups located elsewhere. Once they got some answers, Fisher-Price marketers refined their research and took it on the road. They hired outside moderators to conduct focus groups, often in shopping malls.

Once they had prototype Rescue Heroes, Fisher-Price marketers invited children to the on-site "play lab" to test the figures, each of whom represents an occupation in which a hero rescues people in need—such as firefighters Billy Blazes and Wendy Waters, emergency medical assistant Perry Medic, alpine guide Cliff Hanger, and scuba diver Gil Gripper. In the play labs, boys played with Rescue Heroes and other toys while researchers observed them through a one-way mirror. During these sessions, marketers learned that the figures needed to have oversized feet to stand on their own and not topple over. Similar studies were conducted off the premises to refine the products, including one at Simon Fraser University in British Columbia, Canada, which involved 28 families with boys aged 3 to 6. Later, Fisher-Price actually sent the toys home with children to play with for a week and then interviewed the mothers about their boys' activities. Finally, marketers interviewed parents about whether they would buy the toys and whether they were comfortable with the price.

One nagging theme that emerged from all this research was, "Who are the rescuers? Whom do they rescue? Are there stories behind them?" Marketers realized that they needed to create a scenario for the figures, so little synopses about the characters were developed and printed on the backs of the packages. Then CBS decided that the Rescue Heroes would make a terrific basis for a new children's animated series, and the Saturday morning show of the same name was launched. With careful marketing research behind them, it looks like the Rescue Heroes are going to stand on their own two feet after all.

Questions

1. Why was it important for Fisher-Price marketers to define their problem through exploratory research?

2. Do you think that Fisher-Price's methods for collecting primary data are effective? Why or why not? Describe other techniques that might be effective.

3. In what ways might Fisher-Price use secondary data in its research?

4. Go to the Fisher-Price Web site (http://www.fisherprice.com) and see what Rescue Heroes information and/or activities are available. Describe what you found at the Web site. Does the site contain any elements that would allow it to collect further research on this product?

Sources: Fisher-Price Web site, http://www.fisherprice.com/us/rescueheroes/products, accessed 28 February 2000; Karl Taro Greenfeld, "Mattel: Some (Re)Assembly Required," *Time Magazine*, 25 October 1999, http://www.time.com; "Rescue Hero Toys Offer Positive Influence," Simon Fraser University Web site, 31 May 1999, http://www.sfu.ca.

CASE 8

Fresh Samantha

A decade ago, Douglas Levin decided he wanted to live the good life: He quit his high stress advertising job in New York and moved to Maine with his wife to help his in-laws run their alfalfa sprout farm. While he was delivering sprouts to various stores around the region, Levin kept encountering another local product, a blended carrot juice aptly named 24 Carrot. He tried some of the juice and loved it so much, he bought the business. Levin and his wife renamed the juice business Fresh Samantha after their 2-year-old daughter. As Levin began producing the juice, his wife Abby designed a logo for the product. Then Levin took Fresh Samantha on the road to small grocery stores around rural Maine. No one wanted the juice.

"That wasn't our consumer," Levin now says of his first efforts. People living in rural Maine were not enthusiastic about paying 2 to 3 dollars for a 16-ounce bottle of juice when they could buy private label or name brand apple juice for $1.30 a gallon. No one was willing to spend the extra money for the luxury of premium juice. Levin knew his product, but he hadn't targeted his market accurately. That first year, he lost $20,000 from his own pocket.

Then a friend suggested that Levin try a certain age group: college students. So he drove to Tufts University in Boston and handed the university's food buyer a bottle of his juice. The buyer liked the taste and agreed to stock it throughout Tufts's eateries. Fresh Samantha clicked with the college kids: they loved the taste, they loved the idea of fresh juice, they even loved the names of the different blends that Levin was now producing, like Desperately Seeking C and Mango Mama. With success at Tufts, Levin was able to convince some of the regional supermarkets around New England to begin stocking Fresh Samantha. "Reception was suspicious at first, because no one on the East Coast had heard of a super-premium refrigerated juice," recalls Betta Stothart of Fresh Samantha. "Today, we have gained widespread acceptance in health food stores, whole food markets, bagel and coffee shops, as well as grocery store chains."

With more and more people searching for healthful foods, Fresh Samantha took off around New England. College students continued to be strong supporters of the juice, but adult consumers bought the juice as well. With its higher price, Fresh Samantha had to differentiate itself from those gallons of apple juice or orange juice, and even from the single serving juices marketed by such companies as Veryfine. So, the health benefits that consumers would get from drinking its juices became Fresh Samantha's calling card. Consumers could learn as much as they wanted about the ingredients and health benefits of Fresh Samantha's products by visiting the company's Web site, which has everything from a definition of the word *calorie* to a list of the natural ingredients in the juices and the way they work in the body, "to give your body the material it needs for energy and many nutrients essential to good health."

As consumers grew more sophisticated in their tastes, marketers had to refine further the position of Fresh Samantha products. So Levin and his colleagues developed more complex products, blending more fruits and adding nutraceuticals such as St. John's Wort into flavors like Oh Happy Day. By now, Fresh Samantha had its own refrigerator in many supermarkets, often placed near the health-food aisle.

Still, Fresh Samantha's target market included only consumers living in New England and down the eastern seaboard. It included college students and Generation Xers who were health conscious and who also had the income to spend on premium food products. Levin wanted more. "There's a place for this product in the mass market—I'm convinced of it," he noted. Several years after making that remark, Levin announced that Fresh Samantha would merge with Odwalla Inc., the leading brand of super-premium juice on the West Coast. "We are excited about bringing Fresh Samantha together with Odwalla," said Stephen Williamson, Odwalla's chairman and chief executive officer. "Since our respective inceptions, Odwalla and Fresh Samantha's spirit have been aligned in our visions of delivering great-tasting nourishment. Together, these two innovative brands have national leadership of this category."

Levin agreed. "We will go further in growing the super-premium refrigerated juice category together than by going at it alone." Odwalla and Fresh Samantha now hope to quench an entire nation's thirst for juice.

Questions

1. Based on what you've read, from which psychographic consumer segment(s) do you think Fresh Samantha drinkers come? Why?

2. Why was it so important for Fresh Samantha marketers to differentiate the product early on?

3. In what ways might the merger of Fresh Samantha and Odwalla change the positioning of each?

4. Find the Fresh Samantha Web site. Does it reflect the target market accurately? Why or why not?

Sources: Fresh Samantha Web site, http://www.freshsamantha.com, accessed 21 February 2000; "Odwalla Announces Purchase Agreement and Merger with Fresh Samantha," *Business Wire*, 2 February 2000; KellyAnn LaCascia, "Chilling the Organic and Natural Beverage Market," *Organic & Natural News*, November 1999, http://www.organicandnaturalnews.com; Leigh Gallagher, "Mango Mama Anyone?" *Forbes Global*, 6 April 1998, http://www.global.forbes.com.

CASE 9

Goya Foods, Inc.

Eighty years ago, Spanish immigrant Prudencio Unanue and his wife longed for the comfort foods of their home, so they started an import business to satisfy the need. However, a few years later, the Spanish Civil War broke out, and they could no longer obtain the foods they wanted for their business. So they began importing sardines from a cannery in Morocco. "He had to do something. He had four kids, and we had to eat," recalls his son, Joseph A. Unanue, now in his 70s. The elder Unanue bought the brand name, Goya, along with the sardines. The name cost an extra dollar. Throughout the years, Unanue added olive oil, olives, and other products the Hispanic community in America requested. During the 1960s, Goya began canning everything from beans to coconut juice. Today, Goya serves up entire menus of beans, rice, pasta, seasonings, beverages, and a variety of specialties.

On the surface, it might seem to be a simple matter to import and manufacture food products to serve what appears to be a niche community. But it isn't. First, the Hispanic population, including immigrants and descendants, now numbers more than 30 million in the United States. By 2050, Hispanics will make up about 25 percent of the population. Thus, Hispanic consumer tastes are becoming more and more a part of the mainstream, not to mention a huge segment of purchasing power. Second, there is no such thing as a single Hispanic population. Although Goya was founded originally to serve consumers of Spanish descent, American Hispanics come from a variety of countries, from Puerto Rico and Mexico to Nicaragua and Cuba. Their cultures, family structures, attitudes, and tastes in food are different. "Hispanics from different countries eat different foods," notes Andy Unanue, Joseph's son and likely successor as CEO. But Goya is ahead of other marketers in pinpointing the location of different populations. "Luckily, we have a big arm out in the field who acts as the census. We know which Hispanics are moving into what regions before anybody else," says Andy. For instance, Andy's sister Mary Ann moved to Chicago to run the Goya business for that location and focused on the growing Mexican community there. "We started thinking like Mexicans, deciding what they would like."

Of course, Goya often ends up serving different groups of Hispanic consumers within the same geographical region. But its marketers know that Cubans prefer black beans, while Nicaraguans want small chili beans, and Mexicans will buy pintos. So they provide all three—and more.

Changing roles in Hispanic families have also reflected a change in purchasing habits, and Goya has adeptly kept up with the times, serving both the young and the old. Hispanic seniors still want to create their own meals from scratch; they don't want packaged or prepared foods. So Goya offers a full complement of ingredients for this market. But "the younger people are busy, they are used to the microwave, and they want to eat those things they grew up on that they don't have time to make or can't make as well as their mothers," explains Mary Ann. So Goya provides a wide range of rice and bean mixes and other foods that can be prepared quickly by working mothers or fathers. The company Web site offers even more help for this new generation: a section with favorite recipes that includes menus for holiday celebrations and other occasions.

By being first to the grocery shelves decades ago, Goya established itself as the premiere Hispanic food brand, and it has been discovered by more and more non-Hispanic consumers whose food tastes are changing. Moreover, Goya has managed to ward off attempts by larger companies to tread on its turf by simply producing higher quality, more authentic products. "We firmly believe that Hispanics like buying things they consider their own, that are authentic," remarks Andy Unanue. "And we are. We're Hispanic and we give them authenticity." Not only do Hispanic consumers prefer Goya's authenticity, but so do non-Hispanics. Thus, after failed attempts to introduce their own Hispanic food lines, giants like Campbell's Soup are trying to compete by purchasing genuine Hispanic food businesses. Goya is watching carefully.

Goya remains a privately owned business steeped in strong family tradition, with no plans to change the way it operates. Although Goya products generally represent low involvement purchase decisions, consumers relate strongly to the traditions that these products represent. When they fill their shopping carts with Goya rice, olives, and salsa, they feel like members of a community.

Questions

1. On Maslow's hierarchy, which needs do Goya products fulfill for its consumers? How does the company's Web site (http://www.goya.com) appeal to those needs?

2. Why is it so important for Goya marketers to understand the different subgroups within the Hispanic community?

3. What might be some pros and cons of Goya's attracting more and more non-Hispanic consumers to its products?

Sources: Goya Foods Web site, http://www.goya.com, accessed 4 March 2000; "Venezuela's Flood Victims Desperately Waiting for Aid," *PR Newswire*, 3 January 2000; Bill Saporito, "Food Fight," *Corporate Board Member*, Autumn 1999, http://www.boardmember.com; "Goya Foods," *Hispanic Online*, January/February 1999, http://www.hispaniconline.com.

CASE 10

UPS

Nearly a century ago, United Parcel Service (UPS) drivers began delivering packages for Seattle department stores from Model T Fords and the backs of a few motorcycles. Today, UPS employees are easy to spot, in their crisp brown uniforms and lumbering brown trucks that have earned the company just one of its nicknames: the brown bear. Although everyone reading this has probably received a package delivered by UPS at one time or another, perhaps UPS's biggest impact is behind the scenes as it helps businesses and nonprofit organizations of all sizes get rolling.

UPS delivers about 12 million packages a day around the world for 2.5 million customers, using 225 jets and nearly 160,000 trucks. But UPS wants to do more for its business customers than just drop a box at the front desk. "We want to increase our global footprint across the entire supply chain," says CEO James Kelly. UPS has spent a whopping $11 billion on upgrading its technology in the last decade—on everything from mainframes, PCs, wireless communication devices, cellular networks, and 4,000 programmers and technicians, The reason? With this huge investment in technology, UPS is setting itself up to help its customers cope with different types of demand by assisting them in managing inventory, by offering warehouse services, and even by helping repair products. For instance, UPS has set up an "end of runway" facility near its air hub in Louisville, Kentucky. Computers and other electronic devices in need of repair are trucked from the airport to the facility close by, where technicians repair them on site for customers like Hewlett-Packard and then reship them quickly either to HP itself or to one of its customers. In addition, UPS has revived the old-fashioned COD service for large customers such as Gateway, but it is doing so in high tech fashion. UPS drivers collect payments from customers and deposit the funds directly into Gateway's bank through electronic funds transfer. No other shipping company currently offers that type of service.

UPS intends to be a major player in e-commerce, where it already dominates shipping by Internet retailers. UPS stocks shoes and other clothing for Nike.com in its Louisville warehouse and fulfills orders every hour. A UPS call center in San Antonio actually handles customer orders from Nike.com. In this way, UPS grows its own business by handling more of Nike.com's operations, while Nike.com reduces its overhead and reaps the benefits of reliability and quick turnaround from UPS. Still, this isn't enough for UPS, which launched UPS e-Ventures to act as the research and development division of the company's e-commerce initiatives. The first project, among many to come, is e-Logistics, which will be designed to provide end-to-end business logistics solutions for small- and medium-sized Web businesses. "UPS recognizes the power the Internet has to impact business-to-business and business-to-consumer commerce," notes Mark Rhoney, president of UPS e-Ventures.

To assist its business customers, UPS must communicate with them to get them to think about logistics on a larger scale. One challenge faced by UPS as it develops these B2B efforts has been to increase customers' awareness of ways that UPS can make them more successful. But UPS must reach more people within an organization than just those who are directly involved in the company's transportation or shipping. "We need to work deeper in our customers' organizations," notes Ed Buckley, vice president of marketing, Europe. "There are people [within an organization] who don't see any connection to shipping; we try to get them to think differently." For instance, the UPS product called Document Exchange provides a secure venue for executives to transmit information.

One way the company raises its profile is to team up with very visible sports organizations such as the Olympic Games and NASCAR, both of whom are customers of UPS. UPS has been a worldwide partner of the Olympic Games since 1994 and the official express delivery sponsor of the NFL since 1993. Most recently, the company sealed an agreement with NASCAR that includes customer promotions, hospitality events, a souvenir program, and a specially designed UPS package delivery car. If nothing else, affiliations like these might get other potential customers to think about UPS as more than a big brown truck.

Questions

1. How might derived demand affect UPS's business?

2. Choose a company or nonprofit organization that interests you—say, Holiday Inn, Kentucky Fried Chicken, Old Navy clothing, Hard Candy cosmetics, Harley Davidson motorcycles, or the Red Cross. In what ways could UPS serve the organization you've chosen?

3. The UPS Web site (http://www.ups.com) includes links to click for tracking, shipping, transit time, pick up, drop off, and supplies. If you were an entrepreneur starting a small business, in what ways would these be help-

ful to you? Are there any categories you would add to make the site more useful?

Sources: UPS Web site, http://www.ups.com, accessed 7 March 2000; "UPS Takes to the Track as Official Express Delivery Company of NASCAR," *Business Wire*, 17 February 2000; Jennifer Couzin, "UPS Tests Its Peddle's Mettle," *Industry Standard*, 7 February 2000; Sandeep Junnarkar, "UPS Delivers e-Commerce Unit," *CNet News*, 7 February 2000, http://www.cnet.com; Kelly Barron, "Logistics in Brown," "At Ground Level," and "Addicting the Customer," *Forbes*, 10 January 2000, http://www.forbes.com; "Out of the Box at UPS," *Business Week Online*, 10 January 2000, http://www.businessweek.com; Scott Kirsner, "Venture Vérité: United Parcel Service," *Wired*, 9 September 1999, http://www.wired.com.

CASE 11

Pfizer, Inc.

A few years ago, the most successful pharmaceutical product ever introduced to the marketplace was launched. In its first year, the drug had worldwide sales of over $1 billion. Was it a cure for the common cold? No. It was Pfizer's new product Viagra (sildenafil), approved for sale by the Food and Drug Administration (FDA) to relieve the male condition known as erectile dysfunction (ED).

Although Viagra may have appeared to be an overnight sensation, in reality the product had taken years just to reach the introductory stage in its life cycle. In general, pharmaceuticals require rigorous testing, clinical trials, and lengthy review procedures before being approved for sale by the FDA. A decade before Viagra hit the market, Pfizer researchers were researching potential drugs for heart patients. Sildenafil didn't work very well on heart symptoms, but during trials it became apparent that it worked on another problem. It was a relatively easy decision for Pfizer marketers and researchers to pursue a new direction: roughly 30 million American men suffer from erectile dysfunction, and only about 10 percent were being treated for the condition. Viagra was also easy to differentiate from treatments already on the market, which were invasive and sometimes difficult to use. Viagra was an easy pill to swallow that promised localized effects.

Despite its popularity, Viagra encountered technical difficulties during its introductory stage. Side effects included headaches, indigestion, and hazy vision. But the worst side effect received the most publicity: it could put some cardiac patients at risk for heart attack. In addition, says David Brinckley, director of marketing, Pfizer "had to contain misinformation about the condition [of erectile dysfunction] and the drug."

As Viagra entered the growth stage in its product life cycle, competing products began to arrive on the scene, including Uprima (from TAP Pharmaceuticals) and Vasomax (from Zonagen and Schering-Plough). Bayer and ICOS/Eli Lilly also had products in the works. It was clear that with these new competitors Pfizer needed to capitalize on its position as first in the marketplace. One way it did that was to be a force in raising awareness about the condition. David Brinckley describes former senator Bob Dole's awareness advertisements as a "natural" because Dole's image among older men—the greatest number of ED patients—is as someone with great courage. Brinckley calls Dole's advertisements "the second wave of the ED discussion," in which the situation was made more human and less clinical. Of course, Pfizer's hope was that consumers would associate Bob Dole's courage with their product.

Brinckley notes that Viagra "is like a lot of other pharmaceutical products," in that, because it is sold only by prescription, its relationship to the services of physicians and pharmacists is important to its success. "Our biggest job as marketers is to get guys to talk to their doctors and get doctors to talk to them," he notes. Of course, if doctors and patients don't talk about sexuality, thousands of bottles of Viagra could sit on the shelves.

Brinckley says that Viagra has recently settled into a "more traditional life cycle process," during which Pfizer plans to do further development to refine the product and investigate the potential of related products, such as a faster acting Viagra wafer and a similar product for women. However, because of the nature of the pharmaceutical business, all of these developments will take time and millions of dollars. Still, Brinckley is optimistic. As new products are developed, he says, "the winner is really the patient."

Questions

1. As a product like Viagra reaches the maturity stage of the life cycle, what steps can Pfizer take to maintain its product's position in the marketplace?

2. In what ways is the connection between goods and services important to the future success of a product like Viagra?

3. Visit Pfizer's main Web site (http://www.pfizer.com) and choose the "Health, Medicines & Lifestyle" link. At the "Diseases and Conditions" link select a condition and then view the products that Pfizer offers. How does the Web site enhance Pfizer's product line?

Sources: Viagra Web site, http://www.viagra.com, and Pfizer Web site, http://www.pfizer.com, accessed 3 March 2000; Alexandra Alger, "Viagra Falls," *Forbes*, 7 February 2000, 130, 132; Mindy Blodgett, "Prescription Strength," *CIO Magazine*, 1 February 2000, http://www.cio.com; "Move over Viagra: Competition Is on the Way," *Health Central*, 30 November 1999, http://www.healthcentral.com; David Friedman, "A Real Growth Stock," *Salon News Real*, April 1998, http://www.salon.com.

CASE 12

Hasbro, Inc.

How many of these names do you recall from childhood—Play-Doh, Tonka toys, Nerf balls, G.I. Joe, Risk, Monopoly, Trivial Pursuit? Chances are, you played with at least one or two of these toys and games, along with plenty of other products from Hasbro, Inc. Hasbro is the second largest toy manufacturer in the United States, after Mattel. And its brands are well known around the world. Even with such strong brands, company revenues began to founder during the late 1990s as both children and adults began to turn away from traditional toys and games toward electronic and interactive choices. So Hasbro marketers looked for ways to strengthen existing brands as well as develop products for these new media. According to the GartnerGroup, "Companies that have strong brand identities and popular time-tested products can leverage those corporate assets in cyberspace rather than fall over and die in the face of the threat presented by the new medium." Hasbro decided to trade on its strengths rather than fall over and die.

What came out of the crisis was a perfect blend of the old and the new: Monopoly for the new millennium. Since its introduction in 1935, the traditional Monopoly board game has sold more than 200 million copies, in 80 countries, translated into 26 languages. Monopoly has now been played by four generations of devoted fans, whether at camp on a rainy summer day or in formal tournaments. Although not everyone necessarily knows that the game was originally set in Atlantic City, almost everyone knows the streets Park Place and Boardwalk, not to mention the phrase "go directly to jail." All of these identifying features are part of Monopoly's brand recognition. So Hasbro marketers looked to its popular old standby to help attract a new generation of customers.

The company formed a subsidiary, Hasbro Interactive, to develop new interactive games and transform old favorites. In 1995, the division released its first Monopoly CD-ROM, which sold 1 million copies and became the fifth best-selling PC game of all time. Four years later an updated version hit the market. In the new version, players could customize the 3D board properties with streets and landmarks of their own choosing, even their own hometowns. They could choose from several game board options: 1930s Atlantic City, a custom-made town such as their own, or one of ten modern preprogrammed city boards, including Atlanta, New York, Boston, San Francisco, and Toronto. Still, the CD-ROM version wasn't all the company had in store. Hasbro decided to bring Monopoly and other favorite games to the Internet. "We're pioneering e-mail as a new online game platform," explained Tom Dusenberry, president of Hasbro Interactive. "We don't see board games disappearing, but we do see that there needs to be an alternative means of delivering games to customers in today's marketplace. . . . We've been in the interactive game business for [several] years now. Our primary focus has been taking our games into the computer world. But, that being said, the number one reason why people are buying computers is so they can get on the Internet. And the number one reason why they get on the Internet is e-mail. So we came up with the concept of making e-mail a computing game platform."

How does e-mail Monopoly work? Consumers can purchase the game at Hasbro's Web site or even at a retail store. They load the game into their computer, then e-mail a friend, asking if the friend wants to play. "They can play and send a message back to you at the same time," explains Dusenberry. Thus, the game hasn't changed at all—just the medium over which it is played. Players still get rich, go broke, go to jail. They just don't have to be in the same room with each other.

Hasbro's ability to adapt one of its strongest brands to new media and new marketplaces speaks volumes about its capacity to survive and grow as a company. Being able to transfer a brand from one generation to the next is perhaps the best test of brand loyalty. Even expert analysts are impressed by Hasbro's most recent move. "I haven't heard of anybody else doing this kind of thing to date," says Jim Browning, senior analyst with GartnerGroup. "Hasbro is taking advantage of the ubiquitous nature of e-mail to make it easy and fun for people to play games. Millions of people have e-mail, and users can play at their convenience." That's just what Hasbro has in mind: millions of consumers having fun playing Hasbro games.

Questions

1. Think of your favorite Hasbro toy or game—or any toy you remember well from childhood. Jot down everything you can remember about it, from its name to what it looked like, to what the packaging looked and felt like. Now look back at this toy as a marketer; what features most effectively made it a strong brand in your mind?

2. Do you think that Hasbro's move to put some of its games on the Internet will increase or decrease its brands' equity? Why?

3. Browse through the Monopoly Web site at http://www.monopoly.com. What are some characteristics you would use to describe the game's trade dress?

4. Again, go to the Monopoly Web site. What activities have Hasbro marketers been doing to strengthen its Monopoly brand?

Sources: Monopoly Web site, http://www.monopoly.com, accessed 7 March 2000; "Hasbro, Inc.," *Hoover's Online*, http://www.hoovers.com, accessed 7 March 2000; "Hasbro Interactive's New Monopoly CD-ROM Lets You Play Your Way," press release, Hasbro Web site, 15 November 1999, http://www.hasbro.com; Gene Koprowski, "Park Place in Cyberspace," *Executive Edge*, April–May 1999, http://www.ee-online.com.

CASE 13

RadioShack

"You've got questions? We've got answers." RadioShack's slogan permeates its ads, its 7,000 stores, its new corporate culture. When Leonard Roberts took over as CEO of RadioShack (formerly Tandy), in the mid-1990s, RadioShack was losing ground against competitors like Best Buy and Circuit City. RadioShack, then dubbed the "Technology Store," didn't have the selection or the low prices that the large discount stores offered. But Roberts discovered that RadioShack had something no one else did: answers to questions that consumers asked when they visited RadioShack's stores. So Roberts told his managers to tear up their job descriptions. "From now on, you have a new job description: either you serve our customers directly, or you serve someone who does." When Roberts was through reshaping RadioShack's mission and corporate culture, "We were no longer selling products, we were selling answers," he says.

Meanwhile, competition for all aspects of wireless communications was growing more and more intense. RadioShack had several suitors for partnerships in delivering communications goods and services, but it settled on Sprint. Roberts cites five reasons for doing so:

1. Within a few years, Sprint would have the largest wireless system in the United States.
2. The agreement would grant RadioShack exclusivity of the Sprint brand on its residential phone equipment.
3. Seventy percent of RadioShack's customers were actually AT&T users, so Roberts saw great potential for converting customers.
4. The Sprint management team was stable and shared many of the values held by RadioShack managers.
5. Sprint was the most technologically innovative company that RadioShack was dealing with.

Later, Roberts would cite number 4 as the most important reason for entering into a channel agreement with Sprint.

Sprint also benefited tremendously from the agreement. First, RadioShack literally has a store in every American neighborhood; most consumers have to drive no more than a few minutes to reach a RadioShack store. Second, Sprint gained access to RadioShack's 30,000 sales representatives. Third, RadioShack agreed not to sell competitors' goods and services. Fourth, RadioShack's ability to acquire customers for Sprint was tremendous.

RadioShack took the opportunity the agreement presented to remodel its outdated stores, constructing actual "Sprint stores" within all of its RadioShack stores. Customers now knew exactly where to go for Sprint products—and to get answers to questions concerning Sprint. The relationship has had some channel conflict, but for the most part it has worked well. The companies made a mutual agreement to advertise the Sprint stores, and Roberts laughs as he recalls the challenges of combining two different advertising agencies to get the job done. To help smooth over potential or actual conflicts, Sprint and RadioShack developed a joint steering committee, composed of three top executives below the rank of CEO from each company. The committee meets monthly on tactical and strategic issues.

Then Sprint and MCI merged. Did Roberts see this as a threat? No, he insisted, because the Sprint brand remained strong. Outside telecommunications industry analyst Dennis Telzrow predicted that "MCI-Sprint will give RadioShack the opportunity to leverage their marketing expertise with a much larger telecommunications entity." Meanwhile, Roberts intends to intensify RadioShack's presence in consumers' homes via Sprint's constantly connected Internet service (called ION) and a more recent agreement with Microsoft involving an e-commerce alliance. The ultimate goal? "We want to be known as the home connectivity store," says Roberts. In other words, Roberts wants RadioShack to deliver everything consumers need to integrate their Internet, cable or satellite TV, and local and long distance calling services. Delivering all this technology—and all these answers—to consumers' homes means actually dispatching fleets of service vans to neighborhoods to make installations and adjustments. Roberts has decided to franchise potentially half of this business to accomplish fast delivery of these services and to offset training costs with the franchise fees. This may mean that RadioShack loses some control over this part of the channel, but the company is willing to take that risk. Why? Because getting there first is critical to winning the market. "Everyone's building the big engines," notes Roberts, "but no one's building the tracks. We're building the tracks." That sounds like a good answer.

Questions

1. How does Leonard Roberts's retooling of his managers' job descriptions relate to RadioShack's partnership with Sprint?

2. Between RadioShack and Sprint, whom would you designate channel captain? Why?

3. Is exclusivity important in the agreement between RadioShack and Sprint? Why or why not?

4. Visit the RadioShack Web site at http://www.radioshack.com. Does the site itself reflect the company's slogan "You've got questions? We've got answers." Why or why not?

Sources: RadioShack Web site, http://www.radioshack.com, accessed March 2000; Edward C. Baig, "CEO of Tandy Tunes in on Fix for RadioShack," *USA Today*, 18 January 2000, 10B; Mike Ricciuti and Jim Hu, "Microsoft, RadioShack in Surprise Deal," *CNET News.com*, 11 November 1999, http://www.cnet.com; Andrea Ahels, "MCI-Sprint Merger Has Big Ties to Texas," *Fort Worth Star-Telegram*, 5 October 1999, http://www.dfw.com/mld/startelegram; Om Malik, "Going Digital," *Forbes*, 5 April 1999, http://www.forbes.com; "Cable, Phone, Internet: Just Call . . . RadioShack?" *BusinessWeek Online*, 1 March 1999, http://www.businessweek.com.

CASE 14

wine.com

"wine.com is a direct marketing company," states wine.com's Web site, under the section that describes the company's business model. "It sources directly from producers, markets directly to customers, and manages product delivery. This gives the company control over the execution of all aspects of the ordering process, thus ensuring quality." The description makes wine.com sound like a traditional organization engaged in traditional direct marketing—but it isn't. Nor are many other companies that operate exclusively online. In fact, these companies are practically changing the definition of direct marketing because of their ability to, as wine.com cofounder Peter Granoff puts it, "collapse geography." In other words, although wine.com's target market may be fairly narrow in that it encompasses adults who are interested in wine, the market encompasses wine lovers everywhere, not just in California or New York.

If you're over 21 and want to order a bottle of wine—expensive or inexpensive—you can click on to wine.com from anywhere and make your choice. If you're interested in good food or even the restaurant business, wine.com's Web site can offer you helpful information to educate you about wine. That's wine.com's major point—information. Yes, the company wants to sell eligible customers its wine products, but in doing so it wants to educate them about what they are buying. "Wine is the ideal product for the Internet," notes Granoff, because the Internet can overcome geographic obstacles and because of the amount of information that many consumers want about the products they are purchasing.

What does wine.com offer consumers that their local wine shop doesn't? First, a larger selection of wines that have been selected by experts. "We do the selecting for you," says Granoff. But it doesn't stop there. wine.com's site includes wine tasting charts and notes from tasters. If after making a purchase based on all this information a consumer isn't happy with a choice, wine.com offers a money-back guarantee. Of course, says Granoff, if a consumer is looking for a bottle of wine to have for dinner that evening, the place to shop is the local brick-and-mortar store. But for those who think ahead, want to stock up, or are planning for a special occasion, wine.com offers the widest range of choices backed by the most information, and it emphasizes customer service every step of the way.

When you visit the site, you can browse through red, white, bubbly, and rare wines; find out what's new; get suggestions for gifts; even e-mail questions to experts. Within the site, you can visit specialty shops such as the Rare Wine Shop. "We are dedicated to offering a quality selection of wines to meet the needs of a wide range of wine lovers, from novices to the more seasoned collectors," notes Bill Newlands, president and CEO of wine.com. "The Rare Wine Shop at wine.com offers us the opportunity to capitalize on the demand for world class, hard-to-find vintages." Your neighborhood wine store is unlikely to have much—if any—inventory of rare wines because they are so expensive to stock.

Selling wine over the Internet isn't necessarily complicated, but distributing it is, due to state laws regarding alcohol sales and distribution. So, although the company calls itself a direct marketer, and began as a direct shipper, wine.com now functions within a network of in-state wholesalers and retailers to deliver wine shipments within the United States. The delivery systems must be customized to meet the regulations of each state. International shipments can be made directly to the consumer.

Recently, wine.com has entered into a number of comarketing and cobranding agreements with such diverse companies as United Airlines, the Bloomberg Business Report, America Online, Amazon.com, and Microsoft. Granoff comments that the marketing budget is huge—upwards of $10 million per year. This hefty budget is targeted to one goal: making consumers aware of the site. Cobranding and comarketing alliances assist in boosting consumer awareness.

It's not surprising that Granoff sees wine.com's ultimate market in global terms—beyond simply shipping bottles of wine from the United States to another country. "I see a global business in the future, with global sourcing and distribution," he predicts. Undoubtedly, many of his customers would be willing to drink to that.

Questions

1. Why is customer service so important to a company like wine.com?

2. As a consumer, what do you see as the advantages to shopping for wine this way? Any disadvantages?

3. In addition to those mentioned, describe one or two other types of organizations that wine.com might benefit from establishing comarketing or cobranding agreements.

4. Browse through the wine.com Web site at http://www.wine.com. Do you find it to be as information-rich as Peter Granoff claims it to be? Why or why not?

Sources: wine.com Web site, http://www.wine.com, accessed March 2000; "wine.com Pulls the Cork on Remarkable Rare Wines," company press release, 24 February 2000, http://www.wine.com; Paul M. Sherer, "Thomas H. Lee Leads an Investment of $50 Million in Retailer wine.com," *Wall Street Journal*, 10 November 1999, http://www.djreprints.com; Sandeep Junnarker, "Growing Wine Rivals Pour It On," *CNet News.com*, 27 September 1999, http://www.cnet.com; "wine.com Announces Next Phase of Wine Portal," 24 September 1999, company press release, http://www.wine.com; Julie Landry, "Virtual Vineyard.com Goes wine.com Tasting," *Redherring.com*, 16 September 1999, http://www.redherring.com; Sandeep Junnarker, "Virtual Vineyards Harvests Venture Cash," *Cnet News.com*, 18 June 1999, http://www.cnet.com.

CASE 15

Polaroid

"Where will you stick it?" If you hear those words from a young teen brandishing a brightly colored camera, relax. You aren't being attacked or insulted. To the contrary, your friend probably just wants to take your picture. "Where will you stick it?" is Polaroid's slogan for its I-Zone pocket camera, the firm's first new consumer-product introduction in more than 20 years. It's also a new target market for Polaroid product: teens. Polaroid, famous for its instantly developing film, has come up with a new filmstrip with a sticky back that turns tiny photos into instant stickers. Kids can snap a photo, pull out the strip, wait a few seconds for the picture to develop, then peel it off the strip and stick it anywhere—on a notebook, on a jacket or hat, on a key chain, on a purse, or on a bicycle. Within months of its launch, the I-Zone became the No. 1-selling camera in the United States.

How did the I-Zone zoom to the top of the charts so quickly? Polaroid made a commitment to integrated marketing communications in researching the market, getting the product to the right consumers, and promoting it. First, they did the research, and discovered that teens now have more spending power than any other generation of teens before them. "Polaroid decided to enter the kids market because the kids market right now is the biggest it's ever been in history," says Mary Courville. Second, they divided the market further, into preteens—tweens—and older teenagers. Girls seem to be most interested in taking pictures, so the Polaroid team focused there. Third, they thought "outside the box" about different uses for a camera. For instance, the younger girls actually view the camera as a fashion accessory—so a sleek design in fashion bright colors was important. By thinking creatively, the team came up with whole new ways to use a camera. "It's not about taking pictures to put in a photo album," explains Courville. This is "a cool camera that allows kids to be creative and have fun. It's about play and doing what you want to do." The I-Zone's sticky film lets young photographers become artists. They can take their camera anywhere and stick their pictures anywhere.

Courville stresses that Polaroid couldn't have come up with either the product or the promotion that followed without integrated communications among the marketing, public relations, advertising, and promotion staff. "We're a very tight group," she says. "We're always together." They conducted focus groups and field tests together. They met with the advertising agency together. "We are just always talking to each other," she says. "Always, always, always." Not only does this increase the efficiency with which the product is launched it keeps the message to the consumer consistent. The consumer sees the same message through television commercials, magazine or Internet ads, and various promotions.

What exactly is the message? For Polaroid in general, says Courville, it's about instant gratification. "Only Polaroid can give you that photograph instantly. Only

Polaroid can enliven your time, your party, right then. Polaroid is the only one that allows you to capture the moment instantly." I-Zone takes it a step farther by giving kids instant pictures that they can use to transform and personalize something else—a backpack, a belt buckle, a baseball cap.

In addition to advertising in traditional media as well as the Internet, Polaroid decided to hook up with the popular teen group the Backstreet Boys, becoming a sponsor of their Into the Millennium tour. "Sponsorship allowed us wonderful promotional opportunities," comments Courville. Because the group's biggest fans are girls age 14 to 17, the match was perfect. The Backstreet Boys actually used the I-Zone cameras during their concerts, and girls were invited on stage to have their pictures taken with band members, with I-Zone cameras, of course. Polaroid distributed cameras to fans at concerts so they could take pictures of each other and the band. Results were so positive that Polaroid decided to sponsor another pop singer, Britney Spears, the following year. "This sponsorship is the perfect combination of music, fun, and friendship—all key aspects of our target consumers' lifestyle. Polaroid is committed to giving teens and tweens exactly what they want." Even the stars themselves seem hooked on I-Zone. "I'm psyched to be working with Polaroid," says Spears. "The I-Zone is the coolest way for me and my fans to have fun taking pictures. We can stick them everywhere." That's just what Polaroid has in mind.

Questions

1. In what ways does Polaroid link its promotional strategy to the process of communication?

2. What steps might Polaroid's IMC group take to market I-Zone overseas? Would it be successful? Why or why not?

3. Did the I-Zone promotion with the Backstreet Boys succeed according to standard objectives? Why or why not?

4. Visit the Polaroid Web site (http://www.polaroid.com) to find out more about I-Zone. Imagine that you are part of the IMC group, and write a slogan for the site with suggestions for more ways to use the I-Zone and more places to stick the photos. Where else besides the Web would you advertise or conduct a promotion?

Sources: Polaroid Web site, http://www.polaroid.com, accessed 10 March 2000; "Polaroid and Britney Spears Will Drive You Crazy," *PR Newswire*, 3 March 2000; Cara Beardi, "Targeting Teens Pays Off for Polaroid," *Advertising Age*, 6 March 2000, 16; "Polaroid's New I-Zone Pocket Camera #1 Selling Camera in the United States," *PR Newswire*, 2 December 1999.

CASE 16

Pizza Hut

Just about everyone loves pizza. And just about everyone has a favorite pizza joint, whether it's a local neighborhood spot or one of the big chains. If you're a pizza lover, maybe it's the cheese that makes your mouth water; or maybe it's the sauce, toppings, or crust. Whatever your favorite pizza is, Pizza Hut wants to serve it to you. Pizza Hut is the world's largest pizza chain, with more than 11,000 outlets in the United States and 85 countries around the world. Pizza Hut's Pan Pizza brand is its best-selling pizza, but pizza lovers can get everything from its Stuffed Crust brand to a line of dessert pizzas with fruit and other sweet toppings at its popular lunch buffet. The latest blockbuster, though, is called the Big New Yorker.

The Pizza Hut marketing team doesn't care whether you live in New York or Wisconsin, they don't care whether you've ever even been to New York. But they are betting that if you love pizza, you'll love the Big New Yorker. Initial ads and press releases for the new pizza were informative. After all, most people would ask, what is a Big New Yorker? Consumers learned that the Big New Yorker is big: 16 inches instead of 14 inches. The crust is thicker without losing a bit of crustiness. It's also cut into 8 slices instead of 12, so people can fold a slice. Then there's more cheese and a sweeter sauce. Those are the facts. But with all the pizzas out in the marketplace, Pizza Hut still needed to find a way to differentiate this specialty.

The company's marketers chose a series of celebrity testimonials, leading up to the Super Bowl—guys like Donald Trump and Spike Lee, whose images represent New York. "We picked larger-than-life celebrities because we wanted to make sure people understood that this pizza was huge," says Sean Gleason, director of advertising at Pizza Hut. "And it really doesn't get much more simple than that, quite honestly. We wanted to communicate the size and the value price of $9.99." Gleason points out that no other pizza chain uses celebrities the way the Big New Yorker ads did. "This is a statement that we are number one in pizza, and no one else could do this." Pizza Hut spent millions of dollars for the pre-game Super Bowl commercials, running one every 20 minutes in the hour leading up to the game. This made 200 million consumers aware of the new product.

The marketing team, including advertising, public relations, and promotion, chose television as the medium because they thought they could present the product in the best light—literally and figuratively. A television commercial showing a steaming hot pizza could send viewers to the phone quickly and more effectively than any other medium. It also reaches the most people.

In addition to the commercials, Pizza Hut mailed print coupons and other promotional materials to consumers. The public relations team also found a unique way to launch the actual product: a press conference attended by New York Mayor Rudolph Giuliani. Although the mayor couldn't endorse the pizza, he bit into a slice and said, "This pizza is great." The photo and caption ran nationally in ads. But one of the largest promotional programs Pizza Hut engaged in was a tie-in with *Star Wars: Episode I*. The Big New Yorker pizza is targeted at the same broad-based audience as *Star Wars*, including baby boomers and their children. The release of the new *Star Wars* movie was also a big media event. "Because of that kind of qualitative tie-in to our product of the Big New Yorker, we've really focused on size," explains Bill Ogle, director of promotions. "We felt there was some kind of neat intrinsic tie-in." Pizza Hut broadened the promotion even more, tying in the Big New Yorker and the movie with its sister brands, KFC and Taco Bell, with a game that consumers could play to win prizes. Subsequent tongue-in-cheek commercials focused on the size of outer space as it related to the size of the Big New Yorker.

To celebrate the Big New Yorker's huge success—70 million sold in its first year—Pizza Hut teamed up with CDNow in promotion that offered consumers a free, custom CD with every order of a Big New Yorker. CDNow is an e-commerce company that offers music and entertainment products, including custom CDs and music downloads. "We wanted to thank consumers in a big way," explained Randy Gier, chief marketing officer of Pizza Hut. "What better way to celebrate than by combining two of America's favorite tastes—pizza and music—with the same kind of value and variety that have made Pizza Hut famous." He's right: Consumers are eating it up in a big way.

Questions

1. Do you think that comparative advertising would have worked better than celebrity testimonials in Pizza Hut's launching of the Big New Yorker? Why or why not?

2. Would the U.S. advertising campaign automatically work overseas? Why or why not? If not, what changes might the marketing team make?

3. Pizza Hut chose a tie-in with *Star Wars: Episode I* as a sales promotion. Can you think of another tie-in that might be equally effective?

4. Visit the Pizza Hut Web site at http://www.pizzahut.com. Is the site effective as an interactive ad for the Big New Yorker and other products? Why or why not?

Sources: Pizza Hut Web site, http://www.pizzahut.com, accessed 15 February 2000; "Pizza Hut," company capsule, *Hoover's Online*, http://www.hoovers.com, accessed 15 February 2000; "Pizza Hut Predicts Big Win With Pizza Hut Big Game Day Ad Strategy," *PR Newswire*, 26 January 2000; "The Big New Yorker from Pizza Hut Celebrates 1st Anniversary and Offers Consumers a Free, Customized CD from CDNow," *PR Newswire*, 21 January 2000.

CASE 17

Concept2

Concept2 is the story of two brothers who turned their passion for a sport into a passion for a business, involving their wives, children, friends, and relatives. In 1976, Pete and Dick Dreissigacker, avid rowers, were training to make the final cut for the U.S. Olympic Team in rowing. During training, they started tinkering with a design for a new oar—Pete is a design engineer; Dick is a mechanical engineer. They didn't make the Olympic team, but they came up with an oar design that has since swept through the sport around the world. Made from synthetic materials instead of wood, the oars are stronger, lighter, and cheaper than their traditional counterparts, and rowers worldwide love them. Within a few years, the brothers, who had settled in Vermont, were kicking around ideas for an indoor rowing machine that would allow them to continue their beloved pastime during winter, when Vermont rivers and lakes were frozen. So they turned Pete's old bicycle upside down, nailed it to the floor, added a handle and seat that would slide, and presto—they had the first indoor rowing machine.

Twenty years later, the Concept2 Indoor Rower is still sold directly from the Dreissigacker's factory in Morrisville, Vermont. Customers can place orders via phone or the Web site, and although miles may separate Concept2 from its customers, the company has worked hard to develop relationship selling so that everyone who buys a Concept2 rower will feel like part of the Concept2 "family." Customer service is a top priority. "We aren't trying to sell a lot of machines," explains Judy Geer, wife of cofounder Dick Dreissigacker. "We're trying to have a lot of satisfied customers." Although the Web site has a section containing answers to most-asked questions, customers can contact someone at Concept2 for in-person answers anytime. Shawn Larose is a service technician who handles problems or warranty questions for customers who call: "When people call with what they think is a very serious problem and it turns out to be a 30-second answer, that's very rewarding."

Concept2 also has an on-staff "coach," Larry Gluckman, to help customers learn how to use the rower and improve their individual workouts. Concept2 publishes a semi-annual newsletter called Ergo Update, with product and company news, rowing stories from customers, and letters the company receives. "We get letters [that describe how] we've changed someone's life, we've really improved their health, and that definitely makes it," notes Judy Geer. To make the sport of indoor rowing a bit more interesting—and to keep customers connected with each other and the company—Concept2 started a world ranking system, in which rowers from anywhere in the world can send in their best times achieved rowing a virtual distance on their rower. Ergo Update publishes the rankings once a year. Finally, anyone can take a tour of the Concept2 factory. They just need to call or show up. All of these approaches help build continuous relationships with customers by keeping them connected to Concept2 in personal ways, no matter where they live.

Concept2 makes ordering a rower easy, but the company had to find ways to provide demonstrations to potential buyers to sell their product. After all, at roughly $800 plus shipping, an indoor rower is not a small purchase for most individuals, no matter how passionate they are about the sport. Once the questions are answered, people still want to see how the equipment works before making a purchase. So Concept2 has a 22-minute promotional video that shows how the machine functions—how it's built, how to assemble it, and how to use it. Anyone who watches the short film—narrated by Dick and Judy's 8-year-old daughter, Hannah—will pull out a credit card in a single stroke.

Questions

1. Concept2 focuses on relationship selling. As the company grows, in what ways might the company use consultative selling and telemarketing? If you think either of these approaches would be a poor choice for the company, explain why.

2. In what ways might Concept2 practice creative selling?

3. Why is demonstration an important part of the Concept2 sales process? Do you think that Concept2 handles this well? Why or why not?

4. Visit the Concept2 Web site at http://rowing.concept2.com. and browse through the site for ways that the company uses the site to develop its relationship with customers. Discuss your findings in class.

Sources: Concept2 Web site, http://rowing.concept2.com, accessed 23 March 2000; Concept2 video and promotional materials, 1999; Sean Thomas Langan, "The Big Blade," *Vermont Inc.*, February 2000, 22–23, 59; David Churbuck, "Virtual Racing," *Forbes.com*, 6 May 1996, http://www.forbes.com.

CASE 18

Cybex International

"Fitness reaches into every motion and emotion in our daily lives, whether at work, at home, or at play. It electrifies our every action and thought, from the most mundane tasks to the most dramatic achievements. The pursuit of fitness is about nothing less than the quality of our lives." Cybex's vision statement elevates the pursuit of fitness far beyond pumping iron and doing sit-ups. In fact, it sounds more like the philosophy of ancient Greek athletes, whose fitness was virtually deified.

Cybex International manufactures premium fitness equipment—cardiovascular systems, strength systems, and personal systems. More than 80 percent of the company's products are sold to commercial markets, including health and fitness clubs, hotels, and schools, with nearly 20 percent going to consumers through independent retailers. Cybex emphasizes quality, technology, and prestige, from the way it builds and markets its products to the way it prices them. Thus, fitness buffs who know the brand names of equipment used at their clubs or schools recognize Cybex as a top-flight name. Some gyms even advertise that they have Cybex treadmills, cycles, steppers, and hikers, along with its resistance machines and weights. Yet Cybex is careful to balance the image of the workout fanatic with the one of the average athlete who wants to keep fit. "Life is about finding the perfect balance," says the company's Web site. "Whether you're a club owner, a weekend warrior or a soccer mom, deep down, you know this is true. It's our goal, too. To offer superior technology that produces maximum results. With plenty of enjoyment."

Cybex assumes that its customers are serious about the good life—including the best workout equipment. "At Cybex, we continue to examine trends within the industry to develop new products that help improve human performance and address the daily needs of users," says Peter Haines, CEO and president of Cybex International. So, getting fit on a Cybex machine does cost more than slapping on a pair of running shoes and heading out the door for a quick jog. If you want a Personal Climber 400s stepper, it will cost you around $2,395, plus shipping. Your own commercial-quality personal gym system will run you $4,195. Strength systems come in components that can run anywhere from $500 to $1,000 each. If you purchase options at the time you buy your system, they'll cost less than if you wait to purchase them later. Cybex products, particularly the commercial-quality items, are manufactured to take a beating—they are designed using the latest technology and constructed of the strongest materials. Because of the premium construction and durability, Cybex customers expect to pay more for their workouts than those who purchase other machines.

Prestige pricing requires Cybex to seek out partnerships and alliances with other organizations that have similar images and objectives. One such organization is Fit-Care.com, an online integrated health source that specializes in sports, health, and fitness lifestyles, giving credence both to traditional and alternative approaches to health. "The Web site represents the best that all related philosophies have to offer and uniquely packages these choices for consumers and professionals to make educated decisions," states one press release. Cybex and FitCare.com have planned a partnership that includes such elements as articles on new developments in human performance and exercise science by Cybex training expert Tracy Morgan. Cybex will also offer an advanced personal training certification program online at FitCare.com. Again, Cybex and FitCare.com assume that Web site customers—both consumer and commercial—are looking for the best in health and fitness training resources.

Finally, Cybex launched a new site called eCybex.com, which allows consumers and trade partners to log in to a secure account where they can shop online and track their orders. "This new site is what we're all about at Cybex—a passion for human performance," says Peter Haines. "We intend for eCybex.com to be an easy, educational and fun tool for everyone from our dealers to club owners to fitness beginners and world-class athletes." Cybex wants all of its customers to feel as though they belong to an elite, virtual Cybex health club. The company even wants them to "feel like millionaires." As part of the site launch, the company held an online contest, "Who Wants to Feel Like a Millionaire," a takeoff on the popular television game show. For 8 weeks, a new health and fitness question was posted on the site each week. Contestants submitted their answers, and each correct answer was entered into the grand prize drawing. What was the grand prize? A vacation at an elite spa, where any millionaire can afford to go.

Questions

1. Suppose the economy went into a recession and the demand for premium exercise equipment fell. Toward which of the other pricing objectives might Cybex marketers be forced to shift? Explain your choice.

2. How does Cybex's current choice of pricing objectives reflect the company's vision, and vice versa?

3. How and where do you exercise? Is cost a consideration in your choice? Did image—of the sport you participate in, the club you belong to, and so forth—play a part in your decision? Why or why not?

4. Visit the new Cybex site at http://www.ecybex.com and browse through it to look for ways that Cybex uses the idea of prestige to market its products. Then, come up with your own slogan for a single product line, or for all of Cybex's products in general, emphasizing prestige.

Sources: Cybex Web sites, http://www.cybexintl.com and http://www.ecybex.com, accessed 5 April 2000; "Cybex International," company capsule, *Hoover's Online*, 5 April 2000, http://www.hoovers.com; "Cybex Introduces Products to Improve Human Performance; New Cardiovascular and Strength Products Make Exercise Functional and Easier," *Business Wire*, 23 March 2000; "Cybex Announces Strategic Partnership with FitCare.com," *Business Wire*, 20 March 2000; "Cybex's Passion for Human Performance Goes On-Line, New Web Site Launched with 'Who Wants to Feel Like a Millionaire' Contest," *Hoover's Online*, 28 February 2000, http://www.hoovers.com; "Cybex International, Inc. Launches eCybex.com for Online Shopping and Customer Support Services for Fitness Equipment," *Business Wire*, 3 February 2000.

CASE 19

Learjet

Bombardier Aerospace would be happy to sell you a sleek little Learjet so you can hop from customer to customer over a wide geographic area with ease and style. If you don't have $10 million but can come up with $1 million, Bombardier can still accommodate you. Here's how.

There's a brisk demand for business aircraft during a good economy, and Bombardier has been building more than usual. In 1994, the company built about 60 jets; 5 years later, it turned out 183. And while there is now more demand for these aircraft, industry executives also claim that they are building better planes, so that increased quality is also increasing demand. But Bombardier and other manufacturers have figured out a way to increase demand even further by spreading the price of a single plane among several owners. Called fractional ownership, the pricing program works like this: A business customer buys a share of a Learjet; a share of the model 60 would be about $1.4 million, with $300,000 a year in operating costs. The share comes with a guaranteed 100 hours of annual flying time. Bombardier maintains a fleet of 82 Learjets ready at all times so that each customer has access to a plane within 10 hours of a request. Since the $10 million price tag for a jet and roughly $1 million annually in running costs is more than many small businesses can afford—not to mention the fact that they are paying for the plane's down time—fractional ownership is becoming increasingly popular. When the fractional ownership business began in 1993, the aircraft industry sold three planes for the purpose. In 1999, more than 90 planes were sold into fractional ownership programs. "There is no sign of it leveling off in the next few years," predicts John Lawson, sales president of Bombardier.

Bombardier is also looking at other ways to manage the pricing function of its Learjets by managing supply chain costs. Recently, the company signed a contract with Optum, Inc. for Optum's supply chain software to improve logistics at Learjet's manufacturing facility in Wichita, Kansas. Optum will work through consulting firm Arthur Andersen. Optum's warehouse management software (WMS) will help Learjet manage its aircraft inventory levels as well as improve its receiving and shipping processes. The distribution software is intended to help Learjet track shipping in real time as well as detail individual aircraft parts as they move from the warehouse stock room to the assembly floor. Better logistics efficiency should help the company reduce the time it takes to assemble or repair an aircraft, reduce the cost of mistakes, and increase customer satisfaction. "Bombardier is looking to leverage supply chain automation and real-time inventory visibility to improve our manufacturing and service operations, and work more quickly and profitably," explains Alan Young, director of work and material planning for Bombardier Aerospace in Wichita. If the company can build more planes, more quickly—and reduce turnaround time on repairs—then it has the freedom either to invest the savings elsewhere in the business or to reduce the price of the Learjet.

If you purchase a Learjet what benefits do your millions buy you? First, Learjet offers what it calls a "strong warranty," which includes 5 years on major parts like airframe and structure and two years on smaller parts like windshields and paint. Second, the company offers several maintenance programs and says that operating costs are predictable because of the reliability of the plane's parts. Finally, there is a guaranteed trade-in value program. Of course, availability of some of these programs vary between outright ownership and fractional ownership, but Bombardier remains committed to customer support for all of its Learjets. "Our mission is to provide the finest support in the industry by understanding and fulfilling customer needs," notes the company Web site. That's a lofty goal, at any price.

Questions

1. If Bombardier could reduce its manufacturing and distribution costs and thus reduce the price of a Learjet, do you think that more or fewer of the planes would sell? Why?

2. Can you think of another high-priced product that would benefit from a fractional ownership program (excluding time-share apartments)? Describe your idea.

3. Visit the Learjet Web site at http://www.learjet.com and browse through the sections on Business Aircraft for some of the Learjet models, including the Ownership link, which provides information on operating cost, maintenance programs, and warranties. Does Bombardier appear to be practicing product line pricing with its Learjets? Why or why not?

Sources: Bombardier Web site, http://www.learjet.com, accessed 16 March 2000; "Learjet Flies High With Optum Supply Chain Software," *PR Newswire*, 6 March 2000; "Heady Days for Bizjet Makers," *Reuters Company News*, Reuters Limited, 27 February 2000; "Bombardier Aerospace Enjoys Record Growth in Asia-Pacific and Continues to Invest in Strategic Partnerships," *PR Newswire*, 22 February 2000; "Bombardier Provides an Update on Its Deliveries and Backlogs," *BusinessWire*, 16 February 2000.

A

Advertising is nonpersonal communication that is paid for by an identified sponsor, and involves either mass communication via newspapers, magazines, radio, television, and other media (e.g., billboards, bus stop signage) or direct-to-consumer communication via direct mail.

Affiliate programs have advertisers pay for each person who enters their Web site via a link on the host site or pays for each sale generated.

Agent is a marketing intermediary who does not take title to the products but develops marketing strategy and establishes contacts abroad.

Agents/brokers are independent middlemen who bring buyers and sellers together, provide market information to one or the other parties, but never take title to the merchandise. While most agents/brokers work for the seller, some do work for buyers.

Alternative evaluation is the stage in the consumer decision process when consumers select one of the several alternatives (brands, dealers, and so on) available to them.

Anchor stores are dominant, large-scale stores that are expected to draw customers to a shopping center.

Antidumping laws are laws designed to help domestic industries that are injured by unfair competition from abroad due to imports being sold at less than fair value.

Attitudes are learned predispositions to respond to an object or class of objects in a consistently favorable or unfavorable way.

B

Balanced tenancy occurs where the stores complement each other in merchandise offerings.

A **banner ad** is typically an animated GIF graphic placed on a host site and hyperlinked to the URL of the advertiser.

Benchmarked refers to when performance, cost, and price are compared to the most competitive alternatives.

Benefit concept is the encapsulation of the benefits of a product in the customer's mind.

Brand equity is the marketplace value of a brand based on reputation and goodwill.

Brands are the name, representative symbol or design, or any other feature that identifies one firm's product as distinct from another firm's. Trademark is the legal term for a brand. Brands may be associated with one product, a family of products, or with all of the products sold by a firm.

Break-even point literally means "to have zero profit." It is that point at which total cost and total revenue are equal.

Business market consists of all organizations that buy goods and services for use in the production of other goods and services or for resale.

Buyers are the consumers who actually purchase the product.

Buying center consists of those individuals who participate in the purchasing decision and who share the goals and risks arising from the decision.

C

Cartel is an organization of firms in an industry where the central organization makes certain management decisions and functions (often regarding pricing, outputs, sales, advertising, and distribution) that would otherwise be performed within the individual firms.

Category killers get their name from their marketing strategy of carrying such a large amount of merchandise in a single category at such good prices that they make it impossible for customers to walk out without purchasing what they needed, thus "killing" the competition.

Category management is a process of managing and planning all SKUs within a product category as a distinct business.

Cause-related marketing is a form of corporate philanthropy that links a company's contributions (usually monetary) to a predesignated worthy cause with the purchasing behavior of consumers.

Census blocks are geographical areas made up of several city blocks or part of a rural county identified as such by the U.S. Census Bureau.

Change agent is a person or institution that facilitates change in a firm or in a host country.

Channel intensity refers to the number of intermediaries at each level of the marketing channel.

Channel length is the number of levels in a marketing channel.

Channel strategy is the broad set of principles by which a firm seeks to achieve its distribution objectives to satisfy its customers.

Channel structure consists of all of the businesses and institutions (including producers or manufacturers and final customers) who are involved in performing the functions of buying, selling, or transferring title.

Click through is a term that describes the act of clicking on an advertising banner located at a host site and being transported electronically to the advertiser's site.

Cluster analysis is the geographical grouping and labeling of individuals based on their buying behavior, demographics, and lifestyles.

Code law is law based on a comprehensive set of written statutes.

Coding is categorizing customers based on how profitable their past business has been.

Cold calling means contacting prospective customers without a prior appointment.

Commercial enterprises are the sector of the business market represented by manufacturers, construction companies, service firms, transportation companies, professional groups, and resellers that purchase goods and services.

Common law is law based on tradition and depending less on written statutes and codes than on precedent and custom.

Company/brand sites are Web sites that provide information about a company, such as history, mission, financial statements, etc.

Comparative advantage results when a strategic advantage is held relative to the competition.

Competitively advantaged product is a product that solves a set of customer problems better than any competitor's product. This product is made possible due to this firm's unique technical, manufacturing, managerial, or marketing capabilities, which are not easily copied by others.

Complementary marketing is a contractual arrangement where participating parties carry out different but complementary activities.

Concentration strategy is the market development strategy that involves focusing on a smaller number of markets.

Concept is a written description or visual depiction of a new product idea. A concept includes the product's primary features and benefits.

Conflict in marketing channels occurs when one channel member believes that another channel member is impeding the attainment of its goals.

Conquest marketing is a strategy for constantly seeking new customers by offering discounts and markdowns and developing promotions that encourage new business.

Consultative selling is the process of helping customers reach their strategic goals by using the products and expertise of the sales organization.

Consumer behavior is the process by which individuals or groups select, use, or dispose of goods, services, ideas, or experiences to satisfy needs and wants.

Consumer decision making is a process that typically involves whether to purchase, what to purchase, when to purchase, from whom to purchase, and how to pay for a purchase.

Consumption satiation is what occurs when the more units of a product that are consumed in a short period of time, the less the added value of consuming another unit of the same product and the greater the variety-seeking behavior.

Contract manufacturing is using another firm for the manufacture of goods so that the marketer may concentrate on the research and development as well as marketing aspects of the operation.

Control sample is that part of a sample group that is left unchanged and receives no special treatment, and serves as a basis of comparison to allow analysis of the results of an experiment.

Convenience quota sample is a sample of consumers that is not randomly sampled from a population (e.g., users of the product) but is obtained through approaching people in a mall to participate. Quotas are placed on how many men and women should be interviewed (e.g., 200 of each) or some other demographic categorization such as age, education, or income.

Core benefit proposition (CBP) is the primary benefit or purpose for which a customer buys a product. The CBP may reside in the physical good or service performance, or it may come from augmented dimensions of the product.

Corporate sponsorships involve investments in events or causes for the purpose of achieving various corporate objectives, such as increasing sales volume, enhancing a company's reputation or a brand's image, and increasing brand awareness.

Cost per thousand (CPM) is calculated by dividing the cost of an ad placed in a particular ad vehicle (e.g., certain magazine) by the number of people (expressed in thousands) who are exposed to that vehicle.

Credence attributes cannot be evaluated confidently even immediately after consumption.

Criteria for successful segmentation include target markets that are heterogeneous, measurable, substantial, actionable, and accessible.

Customer-oriented means the salesperson seeks to elicit customer needs/problems and then takes the necessary steps to meet those needs or solve the problem in a manner that is in the best interest of the customer.

Customer prototypes are the detailed pictures and descriptions of individuals or firms in the target market for a product. Creating these descriptions helps firms envision how products and the marketing mix might best be combined to maximize profits.

Customer relationship management (CRM) is the process of identifying, attracting, differentiating, and retaining customers (Ch. 9); relies on systematized processes to profile key segments so that marketing and retention strategies can be customized for these customers (Ch. 13).

Customer retention refers to focusing a firm's marketing efforts toward the existing customer base.

Customer satisfaction is a short-term, transaction-specific measure of whether customer perceptions meet or exceed customer expectations.

Customer service is the service a business provides to accommodate customers' questions and concerns.

D

Database marketing involves collecting and electronically storing (in a database) information about present, past, and prospective customers.

Degree of individualism is the extent to which individual interests prevail over group interests.

Demand schedules provide a systematic look at the relationship between price and quantity sold.

Demand-side market failure is the cumulative effect of the marketing practices of many thousands of advertising campaigns that has a residual negative impact on the values of buyers and the demand for various products (e.g., voting).

Demographics are measures such as age, gender, race, occupation, and income that are often used as a basis for selecting focus group members and market segments.

Differentiation is the process of creating and sustaining a strong, consistent, and unique image about one product in comparison to others.

Discrepancies between production and consumption are differences in quantity, assortment, time, and place that must be overcome to make goods available to final customers.

Displacement is the act of moving employment opportunities from the country of origin to host countries.

Distributive justice focuses on the specific outcome of a firm's recovery efforts.

Distributor is a marketing intermediary that purchases products from the domestic firm and assumes the trading risk.

Diversification strategy is the market development strategy that involves expansion to a relatively large number of markets.

Diverting occurs when a manufacturer restricts an off-invoice allowance to a limited geographical area, resulting in some wholesalers and retailers buying abnormally large quantities at the deal price and then transshipping the excess quantities to other geographical areas.

E

Economies of scale and economies of scope are obtained by spreading the costs of distribution over a large quantity of products (scale) or over a wide variety of products (scope).

Elasticity of demand is the relationship between changes in price and quantity sold.

Electronic brochures are digital versions of a company's brochures.

Electronic data interchange (EDI) is the computer-to-computer exchange of invoices, orders, and other business documents (Ch. 4); a computer-to-computer communications protocol that allows basic information on purchases and invoices to be transferred (Ch. 15).

Electronic intermediary is a profit model based on commissions received by bringing buyers and sellers together.

E-marketing is the set of activities that bring customers and companies together using electronic means such as the Internet.

Emotions are strong, relatively uncontrolled feelings that affect our behavior.

Environmental scanning identifies important trends in the micro- and macroenvironments, then considers the potential impact of these changes on a firm's existing marketing strategy.

Ethical vigilance means paying constant attention to whether one's actions are "right" or "wrong," and if ethically "wrong," asking why one is behaving in that manner.

European Article Numbering (EAN) is the European version of the Universal Product Code located on a product's package that provides information read by optical scanners.

Evaluative criteria are specifications that organizational buyers use to compare alternative goods and services.

Event-related marketing (ERM) is a form of brand promotion that ties a brand to a meaningful cultural, social, athletic, or other type of high-interest public activity.

Every day low pricing (EDLP) refers to the pricing strategy in which a firm charges the same low price every day.

The **exchange principle** maintains that when an exchange benefits both trading partners, the exchange adds value. This principle is derived from the raw material scarcity, labor specialization, and consumption satiation principles.

Exclusive distribution occurs when only one intermediary is used at a particular level in the marketing channel.

Experience attributes can be evaluated only during and after consumption.

Export management companies (EMCs) specialize in performing international services as commissioned representatives or as distributors.

Expropriation is a government takeover of a company's operations frequently at a level lower than the value of the assets.

Extranet is a network of computers that connect a business or organization with computers outside of the intranet.

F

Features are the way that benefits are delivered to customers. Features provide the solution to customer problems.

Field selling involves calling on prospective customers in either their business or home locations.

Flows in marketing channels are the movement of products, negotiation, ownership, information, and promotion through each participant in the marketing channel.

Foreign direct investment is an international entry strategy that is achieved through the acquisition of foreign firms.

Form utility is achieved by the conversion of raw and component materials into finished products that are desired by the marketplace.

Forward buying, or bridge buying, is when retailers purchase enough product during a manufacturer's off-invoice allowance period to carry the retailers over until the manufacturer's next regularly scheduled deal.

Franchise holding/loading includes manufacturers' efforts to hold on to their franchise of current users by rewarding them for continuing to purchase the promoted brand, or to load them so they have no need to switch to another brand.

Franchising is a form of licensing that grants a wholesaler or a retailer exclusive rights to sell a product or a service in a specified area.

Free on board (FOB) pricing leaves the cost and responsibility of transportation to the customer.

Full-service merchant wholesalers provide a wide range of services for retailers and business purchasers.

G

Geodemographic information allows identification of customer segments based on geographical location and demographic information.

Globalization approach is the approach to international marketing in which differences are incorporated into a regional or global strategy that will allow for differences in implementation.

Goods are objects, devices, or things.

Governmental units comprise the sector of the business market represented by federal, state, and local governmental units that purchase goods and services.

Gray marketing is the marketing of authentic, legally trademarked goods through unauthorized channels.

Gross margin equals net sales minus the cost of goods sold.

Gross margin percentage shows how much gross margin a retailer makes as a percentage of sales.

Gross rating points (GRPs) are the accumulation of rating points including all vehicles in a media purchase over the span of a particular campaign.

H

Handling costs are costs to a firm associated with the act of transferring inventory to customers.

Hands-on consumer research is conducted by direct observation by managers of the way current customers use specific products and brands. The opposite is arm's-length research, which is undertaken by external suppliers.

Hard sell involves trying every means to get the prospective customer to buy, regardless of whether it is in the prospect's best interest.

Heterogeneity is a distinguishing characteristic of services that reflects the variation in consistency from one service transaction to the next.

Household decision making occurs when significant decisions are made by individuals jointly with other members of their household, and for joint use by the members of the household.

I

Image reinforcement involves the careful selection of the right premium object, or appropriate sweepstakes prize, to reinforce a brand's desired image.

Incentives are bonuses or rewards (sweepstakes, coupons, premiums, display allowances, etc.) for purchasing one brand rather than another.

Inefficient targeting results when advertising and distribution reach too broad an audience, most of whom are not interested in the product.

Information search is the stage in the consumer decision process when consumers collect information on only a select subset of brands.

Information sites are Web sites that generate revenue through advertising or the subscription rates that are charged to members.

Inseparability is a distinguishing characteristic of services that reflects the interconnection among the service provider, the customer receiving the service, and other customers sharing the service experience.

Institutional customers comprise the sector of the business market represented by health care organizations, colleges and universities, libraries, foundations, art galleries, and clinics that purchase goods and services.

Intangibility is a distinguishing characteristic of services that makes them unable to be touched or sensed in the same manner as physical goods.

Integrated marketing communications (IMC) is a system of management and integration of marketing communication elements—advertising, publicity, sales promotion, sponsorship marketing, and point-of-purchase communications—with the result that all elements adhere to the same message.

Intellectual property rights is the protection provided by patents, copyrights, and trademarks.

Intensive distribution occurs when all possible intermediaries at a particular level of the channel are used.

Interactional justice refers to the human interaction during service recovery efforts.

International intermediaries are marketing institutions that facilitate the movement of goods and services between the originator and customer.

International marketing is the process of planning and conducting transactions across national borders to create exchanges that satisfy the objectives of individuals and organizations.

International Organization for Standardization (ISO) is a nongovernmental organization that promotes the development of standardization to facilitate the international exchange of goods and services.

Internet is a worldwide network of interconnected computer networks originally built by the U.S. government.

Internet hosts provide high-speed connections to the Web.

Interorganizational context refers to channel management that extends beyond a firm's own organization into independent businesses.

An **interval scale** has intervals of measure that stay constant along the scale. For example, the interval between the measures of 1 and 3 on the scale is the same as the interval between 5 and 7.

Intranet is a network of computers within a business or organization.

Inventory turnover refers to the number of times per year, on average, that a firm sells its inventory.

Involvement is the degree of personal relevance of a product to a consumer.

J

Job anxiety is tension caused by the pressures of the job.

Joint ventures result from the participation of two or more companies in an enterprise in which each party contributes assets, owns the new entity to some degree, and shares risk.

K

Key buying influentials are those individuals in the buying organization who have the power to influence the buying decision.

L

Labor specialization occurs when labor and management undertake specific activities and processes, the repetition and focus increase the effectiveness, efficiency, and learning of labor and management.

Leaky bucket theory is traditionally associated with conquest marketing where new customers replace disloyal customers at the same rate; hence, the firm never grows.

Learning is a change in the content of long-term memory. As consumers, we learn to adapt better to our environment.

Level of equality is the extent to which less powerful members accept that power is distributed unequally.

Licensing agreement is an arrangement in which one firm permits another to use its intellectual property in exchange for compensation, typically a royalty.

Limited-service merchant wholesalers perform only a few services for manufacturers or other customers, or they perform all of them on a more restricted basis than do full-service wholesalers.

Line extensions are new products that are developed as variations of existing products.

Logistical service standards are the kinds of quantifiable distribution services performed by a logistical system to meet the needs of customers.

Logistics (or physical distribution) is the planning, implementing, and controlling of the physical flows of materials and final products from points of origin to points of use to meet customers' needs at a profit.

M

Managerial commitment is the desire and drive on the part of management to act on an idea and support it in the long run.

Manufacturer's agents are independent middlemen who handle a manufacturer's marketing functions by selling part or all of a manufacturer's product line in an assigned geographic area.

Manufacturer's sales branches are sales outlets owned by the manufacturer.

Marginal costs are the change in a firm's total costs-per-unit change in its output level.

Marginal revenues are the change in a firm's total revenue-per-unit change in its sales level.

Market potential is the level of sales that might be available to all marketers in an industry in a given market.

Market segments are those segments of the market or submarkets that seek similar benefits from product usage, and that shop and buy in similar ways that are different from other market segments and submarkets (Ch. 1); consist of groups of consumers who are alike based on some characteristic(s) (Ch. 7).

Market (price) skimming is a strategy of pricing the new product at a relatively high level and then gradually reducing it over time.

Marketing is the process of planning and executing the conception, pricing, promotion, and distribution of ideas, goods, and services to create exchanges that satisfy individual and organizational goals.

Marketing channel is the network of organizations that creates time, place, and possession utilities.

Marketing channel management refers to the analysis, planning, organizing, and controlling of a firm's marketing channels.

Marketing channel power is the capacity of one channel member to influence the behavior of another channel member.

Marketing concept refers to how organizational goals are achieved by identifying the needs and wants of customers and delivering products that satisfy customers more effectively than competitors could.

Marketing environment involves the micro- and macroenvironmental influences, including the company's own objectives and resources, the sociocultural environment, the competitive environment, the economic environment, the technological environment, and the political and legal environment.

Marketing mix is composed of product, price, place (distribution), and promotion decisions and programs that the company decides to pursue in implementing its marketing strategy.

Marketing myopia is too narrowly defining one's business.

Marketing strategy refers to using vision and planning to create and deploy a company's assets and capabilities most profitably.

Markup laws require a specified markup above cost in particular industries.

Maslow's hierarchy of needs is a classification scheme of needs satisfaction where higher level needs are dormant until lower level needs are satisfied.

Material achievement is the extent to which the dominant values in society are success, money, and things.

Media strategy consists of four sets of interrelated activities: (1) selecting the target audience, (2) specifying media objectives, (3) selecting media categories and vehicles, and (4) buying media.

Merchant wholesalers are independent firms that purchase a product from a manufacturer and resell it to other manufacturers, wholesalers, or retailers, but not to the final consumer.

Micromarkets are very small market segments, such as zip code areas or even neighborhoods.

Modified rebuy is a purchase where the buyers have experience in satisfying the need but feel the situation warrants reevaluation of a limited set of alternatives before making a decision.

Moods are emotions that are less intense and transitory.

Motivating channel members is the action taken by a manufacturer or franchiser to get channel members to implement its channel strategies.

Motivation is the state of drive or arousal that moves us toward a goal-object.

Motivational research is a research method directed at discovering the conscious or subconscious reasons that motivate a person's behavior.

Multidomestic approach is the approach to international marketing in which local conditions are adapted to in each and every target market.

Multinational corporations are companies that have production operations in at least one country in addition to their domestic base.

N

Needs are unsatisfactory conditions of the consumer that prompt him or her to an action that will make the condition better.

New-task buying situation is a purchase situation that results in an extensive search for information and a lengthy decision process.

Niche marketing is the process of targeting a relatively small market segment with a specific, specialized marketing mix.

Nonresponse or participation bias in responses is created by underrepresentation and overrepresentation in a sample of different groups. For example, most studies have an overrepresentation of consumers who are interested in the product and a nonresponse underrepresentation of consumers not interested in the product.

O

Obsolescence costs are those costs to a firm associated with holding inventory that is not selling due to a loss in demand for the product.

Off-invoice allowance are deals offered periodically to the trade that allow wholesalers and retailers to simply deduct a fixed amount, say 15 percent, from the full price at the time the order is placed.

Omnibus surveys are a survey research service offered by a number of large marketing research companies where several companies' research studies and sets of questions are included in a single questionnaire sent to representative panels of households.

Open-ended questions allow respondents to determine the direction of the answer without being led by the question. They also prevent "yes" or "no" answers.

Operating expenses are the costs a retailer incurs in running a business, other than the cost of merchandise.

Order getter is a salesperson who seeks to actively provide information to prospects, persuade prospective customers, and close sales.

Order taker is a salesperson who only processes the purchase that the customer has already selected.

Organizational socialization is the process by which an individual adapts to and comes to appreciate the values, norms, and required behavior patterns of an organization.

Outsourcing is using another firm for the manufacture of needed components or products or delivery of a service.

P

Panels of households are groups of households (e.g., 5,000) recruited by market research firms and rewarded for participating in market research surveys. The firm creates a panel by carefully selecting the composition of the group so that it is representative of the general population in terms of demographics such as geographical location, income, education, and age of the heads of households.

Payers are the consumers who actually pay for the product.

Penetration strategy requires that the firm enter the market at a relatively low price in an attempt to obtain market share and expand demand for its product.

Perception is the process by which an individual senses, organizes, and interprets information received from the environment.

Perceptual mapping is a commonly used, multidimensional scaling method of graphically depicting a product's performance on selected attributes or the "position" of a product against its competitors on selected product traits.

Perishability is a distinguishing characteristic of services in that they cannot be saved, their unused capacity cannot be reserved, and they cannot be inventoried.

Personal selling is person-to-person communication in which a seller informs and educates prospective customers and attempts to influence their purchase choices (Ch. 12); direct oral communication designed to explain how an individual's or firm's goods, services, or ideas fit the needs of one or more prospective customers (Ch. 13).

Planned obsolescence is the design of a product with features that the company knows will soon be superseded, thus making the model obsolete.

Point-of-purchase communications include all signage—displays, posters, signs, shelf cards, and a variety of other visual materials—that are designed to influence buying decisions at the point of sale.

Polygamous loyalty reflects the notion that customer loyalty tends to be divided among a number of providing firms.

Positioning is the image that customers have about a product, especially in relation to the product's competitors.

Postpurchase behavior is the last stage in the consumer decision process, when the consumer experiences an intense need to confirm the wisdom of that decision.

Predatory pricing is a practice where one firm attempts to drive out rivals (usually smaller ones) by pricing at such a low level that the rival cannot make money.

A **pretest** may be undertaken before the major study to test the validity and reliability of measures and other components of the study's research methodology.

Price is some unit of value given up by one party in return for something from another party.

Price discrimination occurs when a seller offers a lower price to some buyers than to other buyers.

Price-fixing is a conspiracy to fix competitive prices.

Price promotions are short-term price reductions designed to create an incentive for consumers to buy now rather than later and/or stock up on the specially priced product.

Proactive marketing public relations (proactive MPR) is offensively rather than defensively oriented, and opportunity-seeking rather than problem-solving. The major role of proactive MPR is in the area of product introductions or product revisions.

Problem recognition is a consumer's realization that he or she needs to buy something to get back to a normal state of comfort.

Procedural justice examines the process a customer is required to travel in order to arrive at a final outcome.

Procurement costs are those costs to a firm associated with the process of receiving customers' orders.

Product development process consists of a clearly defined set of tasks and steps that describes the normal means by which product development proceeds. The process outlines the order and sequence of the tasks and indicates who is responsible for each.

Product life cycle is the cycle of stages that a product goes through from birth to death: introduction, growth, maturity, and decline.

Product line is the set of products a firm targets to one general market. These products are likely to share some common features and technology characteristics or be complementary products. They also are likely to share several elements of the marketing mix, such as distribution channels.

Product mix is the full set of a firm's products across all markets served.

Product positioning refers to how customers perceive a product's position in the marketplace relative to the competition.

Products are the set of features, functions, and benefits that customers purchase. Products may consist primarily of tangible (physical) attributes or intangibles, such as those associated with services, or some combination of tangible and intangible.

Profit repatriation limitations are restrictions set up by host governments in terms of a company's ability to pay dividends from its operations back to its home base.

Project strategy, sometimes called a protocol, is a statement of the attributes the project is expected to have, the market at which it is targeted, and the purpose behind commercializing the product.

Prototype is a product concept in physical form. A prototype may be a full working model that has been produced by hand or a nonworking physical representation of the final product. It is used to gather customer reaction to the physical form (aesthetics and ergonomics) or to initial operating capability. It is also used in internal performance tests to ensure that performance goals have been met.

Psychographics are characteristics of individuals that describe them in terms of their psychological and behavioral makeup.

Publicity, like advertising, is nonpersonal communication to a mass audience, but unlike advertising, publicity is not directly paid for by the company that enjoys the publicity.

Pull strategy involves a relatively heavy emphasis on consumer-oriented advertising to encourage consumer demand for a new brand and thereby obtain retail distribution. The brand is "pulled" through the channel system in the sense that there is a backward tug from the consumer to the retailer.

Purchase is the stage in the consumer decision process when transaction terms are arranged, title of ownership is transferred, the product is paid for, and the consumer takes possession of the product from the seller.

Push strategy involves aggressive trade allowances and personal selling efforts to obtain distribution for a new brand through wholesalers and retailers. The brand is "pushed" through the channel system in the sense that there is a forward thrust from the manufacturer to the trade.

Q

Qualified sales leads are potential customers who have a need for the salesperson's product, and are able to buy; that is, they have the financial means to purchase the product and the authority to make the buying decision.

R

Random sample is a set of items that have been drawn from a population in such a way that each time an item was selected, every item in the population had an equal opportunity to appear in the sample.

A **ratio scale** is a scale that measures length, weight, or income.

Raw material scarcity occurs when valuable raw material resources are geographically concentrated in some locations and not in others, resulting in resource scarcity in some locations.

Reactive MPR is a form of defensively oriented public relations that deals with developments (such as product defects or flaws) having negative consequences for the organization. Reactive MPR attempts to repair a company's reputation, prevent market erosion, and regain lost sales.

Red-lining is the practice of identifying and avoiding unprofitable types of neighborhoods or people.

Referrals are usually obtained by the salesperson asking current customers if they know of someone else, or another company, who might need the salesperson's product.

Relationship selling requires the development of a trusting partnership in which the salesperson seeks to provide long-term customer satisfaction by listening, gathering information, educating, and adding value for the customer.

Reliability means the consistency of data. It is often tested by reexamining customer opinions using the same survey on a different occasion, or by another method of measurement.

Retailing consists of the final activity and steps needed to place merchandise made elsewhere into the hands of the consumer or to provide services to the consumer.

Retail life cycle is a description of competitive development in retailing that assumes that retail institutions pass through an identifiable cycle that includes four distinct stages: (1) introduction, (2) growth, (3) maturity, and (4) decline.

Retail mix is a retailer's combination of merchandise, prices, advertising, location, customer services, selling, and store layout and design that is used to attract customers.

A **reverse auction** involves one buyer who invites bids from several prequalified suppliers.

ROI stands for "return on investment."

Role ambiguity is anxiety caused by inadequate information about job responsibilities and performance-related goals.

Role conflict is the anxiety caused by conflicting job demands.

Routing is the process of directing incoming calls to customer service representatives in which more profitable customers are more likely to receive faster and better customer service.

Royalty is the compensation paid by one firm to another under licensing and franchising agreements.

S

Sales call anxiety is a fear of negative evaluation and rejection by customers.

Sales potential is the share of the market potential that a particular marketer may hope to gain over the long term.

Sales promotion consists of all marketing activities that attempt to stimulate quick buyer action, or, in other words, attempt to promote immediate sales of a product (thereby yielding the name *sales promotion*).

Scale of market entities displays a range of products along a continuum based on their tangibility.

Scrambled merchandising is the handling of merchandise lines based solely on the profitability criterion and without regard to the consistency of the product or merchandise mix.

Search attributes are physical properties that customers can evaluate prior to their purchase decision.

Search engines are mechanisms through which Internet users can automatically search Web sites to find desired information.

Selection criteria are the factors that a firm uses to choose which intermediaries will become members of its marketing channel.

Selective distribution means that a carefully chosen group of intermediaries is used at a particular level in the marketing channel.

Self-concept refers to a person's self-image.

Selling sites are Web sites that provide products for purchase over the Internet.

The **service gap** is the gap between customers' expectations of service and their perception of the service actually delivered, which is a function of the knowledge gap, the standards gap, the delivery gap, and the communications gap.

Service quality is an attitude formed by a long-term, overall evaluation of performance.

Service recovery is a firm's reaction to a complaint that results in customer satisfaction and goodwill.

Service sites are Web sites that provide a customer service interface for a company.

Services are deeds, efforts, or performances.

Servicescapes refers to the use of physical evidence to design service environments.

Sharing involves making key customer information accessible to all parts of the organization and in some cases selling that information to other firms.

Sherman Antitrust Act prohibits any contract, combination, or conspiracy that restrains trade. It was passed by Congress in 1890 in an effort to prevent companies from controlling (monopolizing) an industry.

Shrinkage refers to reduction of merchandise through theft, loss, and damage.

Single-source systems are a measurement of the effectiveness of advertising (whether it leads to increased sales activity). They are unique in that all the relevant data is collected by a single source, processed, and then made available in a readily usable format to retailers and manufacturers.

Situational ethics is that societal condition where "right" and "wrong" are determined by the specific situation, rather than by universal moral principles.

SKU is a stock keeping unit and refers to a distinct merchandise item in the retailer's merchandise assortment.

Social responsiblity is the collection of marketing philosophies, policies, procedures, and actions intended primarily to enhance society's welfare.

Sogoshosha are the trading companies of Japan, including firms such as Sumitomo, Mitsubishi, and Mitsui.

Specialization or division of labor occurs when each participant in the marketing channel focuses on performing those activities at which it is most efficient.

Sponsorship marketing is the practice of promoting the interests of a company and its brands by associating the company with a specific event (e.g., a golf tournament) or a charitable cause (e.g., the Leukemia Society).

Stage-Gate process is a common new product development process that divides the repeatable portion of product development into a time-sequenced series of stages, each of which is separated by a management decision gate. In each stage, a team completes a set of tasks that span the functions involved in product development. At the end of each stage, management reviews the results obtained and, based on the team's ability to meet the objectives in that stage, provides the resources to continue to the next stage ("go"), requests additional work ("recycle"), or stops the project ("kill").

Standardized approach is the approach to international marketing in which products are marketed with little or no modification.

Storage costs are those costs to a firm associated with the act of storing inventory.

Straight rebuy is routine reordering from the same supplier of a product that has been purchased in the past.

Strategic alliances are informal or formal arrangements between two or more companies with a common business objective.

Strategic marketing concept is a company's mission to identify, generate, and sustain competitive advantage through superior positioning and vision.

Subscription is a fee paid by users to be granted access to certain online information or services.

Suggestion selling occurs when the salesperson points out available complementary items in line with the selected item(s), in order to encourage an additional purchase.

Sugging refers to an illegal survey conducted under the guise of research but with the intent of selling.

Supply-chain management is a technique for linking a manufacturer's operations with those of all of its strategic suppliers and its key intermediaries and customers to enhance efficiency and effectiveness (Ch. 6); managing logistical systems to achieve close cooperation and comprehensive interorganizational management so as to integrate the logistical operations of different firms in the marketing channel (Ch. 10).

Supply-side market failure results when the individual activities of a supplier inadvertently lead to destructive effects on the overall supply.

Sustainable competitive advantage is a competitive edge that cannot be easily or quickly copied by competitors in the short run.

Systems concept of logistics entails viewing all components of a logistical system together and understanding the relationships among them.

T

Tacit knowledge is knowledge that is implied by or inferred from actions or statements.

Target markets are those market segments whose needs and demands a company seeks to serve and satisfy.

Targeting involves offering the firm's most profitable customers special deals and incentives.

Theory of dual entitlement holds that consumers believe there are terms in a transaction to which both consumers and sellers are "entitled" over time. Cost-driven price increases are believed to be fair because they allow sellers to maintain their profit entitlement. Demand-driven price increases are not believed to be fair, however, since they allow sellers to increase per-unit profit, while buyers receive nothing in return.

Time, place, and possession utilities are conditions that enable consumers and business users to have products available for use when and where they want them and to actually take possession of them.

Total cost approach is calculating the cost of a logistical system by addressing all of the costs of logistics together rather than individual costs taken separately, so as to minimize the total cost of logistics.

Total cost of ownership considers not only the purchase price but also an array of other factors such as complete life cycle.

Trade allowances, or trade deals, come in a variety of forms and are offered to retailers simply for purchasing the manufacturer's brand or for performing activities in support of the manufacturer's brand.

Trading company is a marketing intermediary that undertakes exporting, importing, countertrading, investing, and manufacturing.

Tragedy of the commons is the name given to the process in which individuals, pursuing their own self-interest, overuse a common good to such an extent that the common good is destroyed.

Transaction-Based Information System (TBIS) captures and analyzes all of the transactions between a company and its customers.

Transaction efficiency refers to designing marketing channels to minimize the number of contacts between producers and consumers.

Trial impact refers to inducing nonusers to try a brand for the first time, or encouraging retrial by consumers who have not purchased the brand for an extended period.

U

Uncertainty avoidance is the extent to which people feel threatened by ambiguous situations and have created beliefs and institutions to try to avoid these feelings.

Uniform delivered pricing means that the seller charges all customers the same transportation cost regardless of their location.

Universal Product Code (UPC) is a bar code on a product's package that provides information read by optical scanners.

Users are the consumers who actually use the product.

V

Validity in customer survey results refers to their accuracy in measuring what they are intended to measure.

VALS™ is a psychographic profiling scheme developed by SRI Consulting Business Intelligence.

Value analysis is a method of weighing the comparative value of materials, components, and manufacturing processes from the standpoint of their purpose, relative merit, and cost in order to uncover ways of improving products, lowering costs, or both.

Value proposition is a program of goods, services, ideas, and solutions that a business marketer offers to advance the performance goals of the customer organization.

Values are end-states or goals one lives for.

Voice of the customer (VOC) is the expression of the preferences, opinions, and motivations of the customer that need to be listened to by managers (Ch. 4); a one-on-one interviewing process to elicit an in-depth set of customer needs (Ch. 8).

W

Wants are desires to obtain more satisfaction than is absolutely necessary to improve an unsatisfactory condition.

Wheel of retailing theory is a pattern of competitive development in retailing which states that new types of retailers enter the market as low-status, low-margin, low-price operators. However, as they meet with success, these new retailers gradually acquire more sophisticated and elaborate facilities, thereby becoming less efficient and vulnerable to new types of low-margin retail competitors who progress through the same pattern.

Wholesalers are persons or establishments that sell to retailers and/or other organizational buyers for industrial, institutional, and commercial use, but do not sell in significant amounts to ultimate consumers.

Wholesaling involves the activities of persons or establishments that sell to retailers and/or other organizational buyers for industrial, institutional, and commercial use, but do not sell in significant amounts to final consumers.

World Trade Organization (WTO) is the institution that administers international trade and investment accords. It supplanted the General Agreement on Tariffs and Trade (GATT) in 1995.

World Wide Web (Web) is a data network system that allows users to interact with documents stored on computers across the Internet.

Literary Credits

P. 14, Figure 1.3   From John H. Lindgren, Jr. and Terence A. Shimp, *Marketing,* 1st ed. ©1996. Reprinted with permission of South-Western College Publishing, a division of Thomson Learning. Fax 800-730-2215.

P. 18, Figure 1.4   From John H. Lindgren, Jr. and Terence A. Shimp, *Marketing,* 1st ed. ©1996. Reprinted with permission of South-Western College Publishing, a division of Thomson Learning. Fax 800-730-2215.

P. 38, Table 2.1   From Worldwatch Institute, *How Much is Enough*, 1993, www.worldwatch.org.

P. 41, Table 2.2   Reprinted by permission of Pearson Education, Inc.

P. 42, Figure 2.2   Reproduced with permission of Ronald E. Berenheim.

P. 44, Figure 2.3   Reprinted by permission of the American Marketing Association.

P. 67, Figure 3.2   ©1994 *World Trade Magazine,* www.worldtrademag.com.

P. 71, Figure 3.3   From Franklin R. Root*, Entry Strategies for International Markets* ©1994 D.C. Heath & Co. This material is used by permission of Jossey-Bass, Inc., a subsidiary of John Wiley & Sons, Inc.

P. 74, Table 3.2   Reprinted with permission of South-Western College Publishing, a division of Thomson Learning. Fax 800-730-2215.

P. 82, Figure 3.5   Reprinted with permission of South-Western College Publishing a division of Thomson Learning. Fax 800-730-2215.

P. 108, Table 4.1   From William Dillon, et al., *Marketing Research in a Marketing Environment*, p. 201 ©1990 Irwin. Reprinted with permission of The McGraw-Hill Companies.

P. 123, Table 4.7   Reprinted with permission of The Conference Board.

P. 147, Figure 5.2   Reprinted with permission of SRI Consulting Business Intelligence. All rights reserved.

P. 177, Box   Courtesy Covisint, LLC.

P. 186, Table 6.4   Reprinted from *Industrial Marketing Management* 8, Gene R. Laczniak, "An Empirical Study of Hospital Buying," p. 61 ©1979, with permission from Elsevier Science.

P. 200, Box   Copyright 1997 *Austin American Statesman.* Reprinted with permission.

P. 209, Figure 7.4   ©University of Chicago Press.

P. 210, Figure 7.5   Copyright ©2002 Esribis. All rights reserved. ESRI Business Information Solutions.

P. 215, Figure 7.9   From Susie Stephenson, "Tackling Teens," *Restaurants & Institutions,* 15 February 1997, 57–60; and "More Than Lunch Money," *Marketing News,* 11 May 1998.

P. 225   Figure reprinted with permission of Geoscape International, Inc.

P. 227, Figure 7.16   From "Today's Global Market: Who is the elusive Global Consumer?" *Chain Store Age*, November 1993, 28–30. Reprinted by permission from *Chain Store Age* (November

1993) Copyright Lebhar-Friedman, Inc., 425 Park Avenue, New York, NY 10022.

P. 241, Figure 8.1   From *Journal of Product Innovation Management*, Vol. 14, Abbie Griffin, "PDMA Research on New Product Development Practices: Updating Trends and Benchmarking Best Practices," pp. 429-258 ©1997. Reprinted with permission from Elsevier Science.

P. 247, Box   Courtesy of the American Marketing Association.

P. 255, Table 8.2   From public presentations and brochures.

P. 262, Figure 8.7   From Peter R. Dickson, *Marketing Management,* 2nd ed. ©1997. Reprinted with permission of South-Western College Publishing, a division of Thomson Learning. Fax 800-730-2215.

P. 266, Figure 8.9   From *Winning at New Products* by Robert G. Cooper, p. 140. Copyright ©1993 by Perseus Books, L.L.C. Reprinted by permission of Perseus Books Publishers, a member of Perseus Books, L.L.C.

P. 269, Figure 8.11   From John H. Lindgren, Jr. and Terence A. Shimp, *Marketing,* 1st ed. ©1996. Reprinted with permission of South-Western College Publishing, a division of Thomson Learning. Fax 800-730-2215.

P. 283, Figure 9.3   Courtesy of the American Marketing Association.

P. 286, Box   Reproduced from *Revolution* magazine with the permission of the copyright owner, Haymarket Business Publications.

P. 290, Table 9.2   Adapted from Mary Jo Bitner, "Servicescapes: The Impact of Physical Surroundings on Customers and Employees," *Journal of Marketing* 56, no. 2 (April 1992): 60. Reprinted by permission of the American Marketing Association.

P. 296, Table 9.3   Reprinted with permission of the American Society for Quality.

P. 302, Figure 9.11   From Dianne Brady, "Why Service Stinks," *Business Week,* 23 October 2000, pp. 120-121.

P. 304, Figure 9.12   Reprinted by permission of the American Marketing Association.

P. 307, Figure 9.14   Reprinted with permission of South-Western College Publishing, a division of Thomson Learning. Fax 800-730-2215.

P. 333, Figure 10.3   Reprinted with permission of South-Western College Publishing, a division of Thomson Learning. Fax 800-730-2215.

P. 352, Table 10.1   From Martha C. Cooper and Lisa M. Ellram, "Characteristics of Supply Chain Management and Implications for Purchasing and Logistics Strategy," *The International Journal of Logistics Management* 4, no. 2 (1993): 16.

P. 354, Table 10.2   From U.S. Census Bureau, *Statistical Abstract of the United States: 2000*, 120th ed. (Washington, D.C.: U.S. Government Printing Office, 2000).

P. 358, Table 10.3   From John T. Mentzer, Roger Gomes, and Robert E. Knapfel, Jr. "Physical Distribution Service: A Fundamental Marketing Concept?" *Journal of the Academy of Marketing Science* (Winter 1988): 55. ©1988 Sage Publications. Reprinted by permission of Sage Publications.

P. 374, Figure 11.1   From U.S. Bureau of the Census, *Statistical Abstract of the United States: 1996,* 116th ed., Washington, D.C., 1996. Table No. 1259. *Retail Trade Sales of Multiunit Organizations, by Kind of Business: 1980–1995,* 766.

P. 387, Figure 11.9   From George Chister, "Solution Selling: The Key to Supermarket Survival," *International Trends in Retailing* (June 1998): 36.

P. 420, Figure 12.1   From Kevin Lane Keller, "Conceptualizing, Measuring, and Managing Customer-Based Brand Equity," *Journal of Marketing* 57 (January 1993): 7. Reprinted with permission of the American Marketing Association.

P. 421, Box   Reprinted with permission from the 4 September 2000 issue of *Advertising Age.* Copyright, Crain Communications Inc. 2000.

P. 435, Figure 12.6   Adapted from *Marketer's Guide to Media,* Fall/Winter 1994–1995, 17, 2 (New York, ADWEEK, 1994). Copyright ©1994 VNU Business Media Inc.

P. 477, Box   Courtesy of the American Marketing Association.

P. 503, Table 14.2   From Samuelson and Nordhaus, *Economics: An Introductory Analysis,* 4th ed. (New York: McGraw-Hill, 1958), 370–374. Reproduced with permission of The McGraw-Hill Companies.

P. 504, Table 14.3   From Samuelson and Nordhaus, *Economics: An Introductory Analysis,* 4th ed. (New York: McGraw-Hill, 1958), 370–374. Reproduced with permission of The McGraw-Hill Companies.

P. 505, Table 14.4   From Samuelson and Nordhaus, *Economics: An Introductory Analysis,* 4th ed. (New York: McGraw-Hill, 1958), 370–374. Reproduced with permission of The McGraw-Hill Companies.

P. 513, Figure 14.7   From Peter R. Dickson, *Marketing Management,* 2nd ed. ©1997. Reprinted with permission of South-Western College Publishing, a division of Thomson Learning. Fax 800-730-2215.

P. 544, Box   ©Copyright Reuters 2001. All rights reserved.

P. 546, Figure 15.6   From http://cyberatlas.internet.com/markets/b2b/article/0,,10091_719571,00.html. Reprinted with permission of Gartner, Inc.

P. 546, Figure 15.7   Data from Jupiter Research.

P. 547, Figure 15.8   Data from TRI's Online Census, TRI

P. 549, Figure 15.9   From http://www.iconocast.com/pdf/ataglance1-01.pdf. Data from Media Metrics, December 2000.

P. 559, Table 15.6   Reprinted with permission of Insight Express.

P. 569, Figure A.1   From John H. Lindgren, Jr. and Terence A. Shimp, *Marketing,* 1st ed. ©1996. Reprinted with permission of South-Western College Publishing, a division of Thomson Learning. Fax 800-730-2215.

P. 570, Figure A.2   Reprinted with permission of Intellvisions Software Ltd., www.intellvisions.com

P. 572, Figure A.4   From John H. Lindgren, Jr. and Terence A. Shimp, *Marketing,* 1st ed. ©1996. Reprinted with permission of South-Western College

Publishing, a division of Thomson Learning. Fax 800-730-2215.

P. 573, Figure A.5   From *Strategic Market Planning: Problems and Analytical Approaches,* by Derek F. Abell and John S. Hammond, p. 213 ©1979 Prentice Hall.

P. 575, Figure A.6   From John H. Lindgren, Jr. and Terence A. Shimp, *Marketing,* 1st ed. ©1996. Reprinted with permission of South-Western College Publishing, a division of Thomson Learning. Fax 800-730-2215.

P. 583   Video Cases from Louis E. Boone and David L. Kurtz, *Contemporary Marketing,* 10th ed. ©2001. Reprinted with permission of South-Western College Publishing, a division of Thomson Learning. Fax 800-730-2215.

Photo and Web Page Credits

P. 3   Nokia and the Xpress-on™ covers shown are registered trademarks of Nokia Corporation.

P. 5   Corbis

P. 6   Richard T. Nowitz/Corbis

P. 8   Hulton Archive/Getty Images

P. 13, Figure 1.2   Top: Digital Imaging Group; middle: Dr. Pepper/Seven Up, Inc.; bottom left: Pepsi, Pepsi-Cola and the Pepsi Globe Design are registered trademarks of Pepsico, Inc. Used by permission; bottom right: Mountain Dew and Dew are registered trademarks of Pepsico, Inc., Mountain Dew Code Red is a trademark of Pepsico, Inc. Used by permission.

P. 16   Digital Imaging Group

P. 20   ©Getty Images/PhotoDisc

P. 21   ©Getty Images/PhotoDisc

P. 23   Courtesy of International Business Machines Corporation

P. 31   Courtesy of www.adbusters.org

P. 32   Photo courtesy of the American Red Cross

P. 34   Location courtesy of bigg's Skytop Pavilion, Cincinnati, OH/Sam A. Marshall Photography

P. 39, Figure 2.1   Courtesy of Ford Motor Company

P. 40   Digital Imaging Group

P. 43   Hulton Archive/Getty Images

P. 47   Bettmann/Corbis

P. 49   Alison Wright/Corbis

P. 52, Figure 2.4   Courtesy of Anheuser-Busch Companies, Inc.

P. 61   ©2002 Index Stock Imagery, Inc./Roberto Santos

P. 64, Figure 3.1   McDonald's Corporation

P. 68   ©Jeff Greenberg/PhotoEdit

P. 72   Reproduced with permission of Yahoo! Inc. © 2000 by Yahoo! Inc. YAHOO! and the YAHOO! logo are trademarks of Yahoo! Inc.

P. 75   ©Getty Images/PhotoDisc

P. 77   Catherine Karnow/Corbis

P. 81   Anna Clopet/Corbis

P. 83, Figure 3.7   Marriott International

P. 87   ©2002 Index Stock Imagery, Inc./Matthew Borkoski

P. 99   Digital Imaging Group

Page numbers followed by f indicate figures; t, tables.

A

Alexander, Jason, 575, 576
Ames, Pat, 583
Ander, Will, 154
Anschuetz, Ned, 203
Artzt, Edwin L., 518, 519
Azar, Jack, 35

B

Bentham, Jeremy, 45
Blinder, Alan, 516
Brinckley, David, 596
Brooks, Andrew L., 589, 590
Brooks, Diana, 522
Browning, Jim, 598
Bryant, Kobe, 413, 431
Buckley, Ed, 595
Burkhardt, Will, 586
Bush, George W., 149

C

Carlin, George, 293
Carteras, Gabrielle, 286
Chambers, John, 164
Chaplin, Charlie, 62
Chesler, Randall M., 161
Clark, G. Edmond, 589
Conran, Terence, 84
Courville, Mary, 601, 602
Crosby, Bing, 393
Cuban, Mark, 460
Czinkota, Michael R., 60

D

Dayton, Matthew, 137
Dell, Michael, 342, 343, 366, 367, 368, 494
Demos, Steve, 412
Dickson, Peter R., 2, 30, 98
Doerr, John, 194
Dole, Bob, 596
Donio, Jim, 587
Doyle, Kathleen, 457, 458
Dreissigacker, Dick, 604
Dreissigacker, Pete, 604
Dunne, Patrick, 370
Dusenberry, Tom, 597
Dyson, Brian, 510

F

Ford, Henry, 7, 502

G

Galvin, Christopher, 2
Gantner, Erica, 466

Garrity, Mary Carol, 508
Gates, Bill, 51
Gault, Stanley, 88
Gibara, Samir, 88
Gier, Randy, 603
Giuliani, Rudolph, 603
Gleason, Sean, 603
Gluckman, Larry, 604
Goings, E. V., 88
Goodwin, George, 521, 522
Granoff, Peter, 600
Greer, Judy, 604
Griffin, Abbie, 236
Gryfe, Shelley Glick, 591
Gurley, William J., 496

H

Haines, Peter, 605
Hamilton, Charlie, 394
Hamlin, John, 369
Helm, Garith, 325
Hitchcock, Alfred, 62
Hitler, Adolf, 43
Hobbes, Thomas, 43
Hoffman, Douglas K., 278
Hogan, Mark, 222
Hopkins, Tom, 470
Horibe, Emiko, 84
Horibe, Koin, 84
Hume, David, 45
Hutt, Michael D., 162

I

Iverson, Allan, 413

J

Jung, Andrea, 88

K

Kahle, Lynn, 145
Kamen, Dean, 194
Kant, Immanuel, 45
Katz, Misha, 589
Kelley, Jim, 22
Kelly, James, 595
Krishnan, Balaji C., 136

L

Larose, Shawn, 604
Lawson, John, 606
Lazarus, Charles, 84
Lee, Spike, 603
Levin, Douglas, 592, 593
Lindgren, John H., Jr., 536
Lusch, Robert F., 370

M

Maslow, Abraham, 141
McGuire, Hailey, 137

Mead, Dana, 88
Menezes, Victor J., 88
Mill, John Stuart, 45
Miller, Bob, 521
Morgan, David D, 200
Morgan, Tracy, 605
Mt. Joy, Scott, 526
Mundt, Henry, 101
Myers, Glenn, 585

N

Newlands, Bill, 600
Nugent, Jennifer, 154

O

Ogle, Bill, 603
O'Neal, Shaquille, 413

P

Packard, Vance, 30
Partridge, Jessica, 137
Patterson, John, 167
Payton, Billy, 583, 584
Perpich, Rudy, 95
Porter, Michael, 120, 122

R

Rasmussen, Bill, 585
Rhoney, Mark, 595
Roberts, Leonard, 598, 599
Rokeach, Milton, 145
Ronkainen, Ilkka A., 60
Roope, John R. III, 174
Rosenbloom, Bert, 324
Rosso, Jean-Pierre, 88
Rothschild, Steven, 589
Rousseau, Jean-Jacques, 43
Ruth, Babe, 33

S

Scherkenback, Michael, 283
Sekler, Lior, 491, 492
Shah, Rajan, 416
Sheth, Jagdish N., 136
Shimp, Terence A., 410
Sholes, Christopher, 117
Siguaw, Judy A., 456
Simpson, Penny M., 196
Smith, Adam, 5, 33, 38
Smith, Fred, 304
Solomon, Michael, 587, 588
Solomon, Russ, 587
Spears, Britney, 602
Speh, Thomas W., 162
Stasell, Mark, 250
Stephan, Bonnie, 138
Stothart, Betta, 592
Swartz, Jeffrey, 585

T

Tansky, Burton, 583
Taylor, John, 521, 522
Telzrow, Dennis, 599
Thompson, Catherine, 457, 458
Topfer, Mort, 366
Trump, Donald, 603

U

Unanue, Andy, 594
Unanue, Joseph A., 593

Unanue, Prudencio, 593
Urbany, Joel E., 494

W

Walton, Sam, 391, 393
Ward, Ian J., 94
Washington, George, 130

Weiner, Allen, 552
West, William, 137
Williamson, Stephen, 593
Wyne, Jeff, 588, 589

Y

Young, Alan, 607

Page numbers followed by f indicate figures; t, tables.

A

A. C. Nielsen, 103, 114, 116, 124
Accenture, 24, 416
Advanced Micro Devices, 511
AFLAC (American Family Life Insurance Company), 424, 425, 426
A.G.B. McNair, 103
Airbus, 22, 23
Albertson's, 386
Allegheny Pepsi, 521
Amazon.com, 29, 194, 195, 267, 341, 375, 376, 540t, 541, 542, 543f, 551, 552, 556, 600
Ambac International, 494
American Airlines, 117, 292, 296t
American Express, 84, 161, 212, 213
America Online (AOL), 27, 72, 134, 600
Amtrak, 429
Amway, 389
Anderson Consulting, 24, 416
Anheuser-Busch Comapny, 325
Ann Taylor, 377
AOL- Time Warner, 125, 586
Apple, 118, 236, 344, 350, 369
Arbitrage Networks, 516
Arbitron, Inc., 547
Archer Daniels Midland, 522
Arnold Worldwide, 412, 415
Arterial Vascular Engineering, 514
Arthur Andersen, 40, 607
AT&T, 136, 185, 213, 254, 429, 598
Audi of America, 443
Aurora Electronics, 35
Auto Glass Plus, 478
AutoZone, 388
Avero, Inc., 491
Avon Products Inc., 88, 135, 373, 389

B

Bank One, 111, 112t
Barlow Limited, 65t
Barnes & Noble, 29, 341, 375, 388, 511
Bayer, 494, 596
Bearings Inc., 398
Bedas Canadian Ltd., 94
Bed Bath & Beyond, 388
BellSouth, 136
Ben & Jerry's, 5
Berman Technologies, 536
Bertelsmann, 29
Best Buy, 378, 388, 598
Black & Decker, 167, 396, 466
Blockbuster Video, 388
Bloomberg Business Report, 600
Bloomingdale's, 392
Blue Cross and Blue Shield, 282

Body Shop, The, 377
Boeing, 22, 23, 168, 170, 172t, 173, 185, 188, 258
Bombardier Aerospace, 606–7
Bonnie's Hallmark, 138
Booklet Binding, Inc., 515
Boomer Book Company, 394
Booz Allen Hamilton, 558
Borders Books, 341, 511
Boston Consulting Group, 74, 167, 570, 571
Boy Scouts of America, 46
Breakers, The, 476
Bridge, 62
Bridgestone/Firestone, 443, 449
British Airways, 292
Broadcast.com, 460
Budweiser, 51
Burger King, 201, 221, 239, 347
Business Information Solutions, 210

C

C. Itoh, 76
CACI Marketing Systems, 210, 213
Cadbury Schweppes, 83, 296t
CalComp, 254, 255t
Campbell's Soup, 594
Canon, 84
Capitol Records, 331
Case Corp., 88
Caterpillar, 341
CBS, 591
Cemex, S.A., 24, 65t
Centura Bank, Inc., 301
Charles Schwab, 24, 300, 388
ChevronTexaco, 388
Chico's, 386
China National Chemicals Import & Export Corporation, 65t
China State Construction Engineering Corporation, 65t
Christie's, 522
Chrysler, 83, 167, 248, 252, 270, 340, 350, 540t
Circuit City, 388, 598
Cisco Systems Inc., 22, 163, 164, 173, 368, 549, 551
Citic Pacific, Limited, 65t
Citigroup, 88, 172t
Clark Equipment Company, 186
Clear Channel Communications, Inc., 331
Coach, 376
Cobalt Card, 161
Coca-Cola Co., 19, 20, 68, 84, 91, 129, 135, 164, 215, 341, 416, 540, 540t, 568, 569, 574
Coca-Cola Enterprises, 510
Coleman Insights, 547
Colgate-Palmolive, 87, 218, 296t
Columbia Tristar, 62
Companhia Vale do Rio Doce, 65t

Compaq Computer Corporation, 24, 166, 239, 338, 368, 416, 477, 495, 516
Compuserve, 460
Concept2, 604–5
Conoco, 388
Continental Airlines, 296t, 301
Cooper Industries, 167
Coors Brewing Company, 208
Corning Consumer Products Company, 355
Corning Inc., 80, 355
Costco, 330, 371, 372, 376, 378, 403
Covisint, 177
Cox Communications, 136
Crate & Barrel, 377
Crestar Bank, 536
Crosspoint Venture Partners, 161
Cybex International, 605–6

D

Daewoo Corporation, 65t, 81
DaimlerChrysler Corporation, 177, 182, 294, 295, 296t, 542
Danone Group, 510
DEKA Research and Development, 194
dELiA, 386, 388
Dell Computer Corporation, 166, 172t, 175, 190, 327, 338, 342, 343, 366–69, 373, 494, 495, 496, 512, 554, 555f, 588
Deloitte Consulting, 496
Delta, 136
Denny's, 414
Deutsche Telekom, 72
Digital Marketing Services (DMS), 134, 135
Dillard's, 385, 388, 392, 403
Discount City Fireworks, 394
Discovery Channel, 135
Dollar General, 387
Donnelly Corp., 494
Dow Chemical, 170
Dunkin' Donuts, 379
DuPont, 22, 105, 173, 175f, 189, 340, 513, 514
Duracell, 119
Dutch Boy paint, 444

E

E. & J. Gallo Winery, 466
Earthlink, Inc., 416
eBay, 153, 516, 539, 554, 555f
Electrolux, 389
Electronic Data Systems, 24
EMI, 331
Enermetrix, 516
Enersis, S.A., 65t
Enron, 40
Envirocycle, 35
Ericsson, 80, 170
Ernst & Young, 136

ESPN, 421, 585–87
Ethan Allen Interiors Inc., 347, 348, 349
Ethnic Technologies, 225
Excite, 72
Exxon Chemical, 255t

F

F. Hoffmann La Roche, 558
Family Dollar, 380
Federal Express (FedEx), 15, 213, 294, 304, 305f, 327, 540t, 541, 549, 551, 556, 588–89
Federated Stores, 385
FedEx Trade Networks, Inc., 589
Ferro Corporation, 181
Fidelity Investments, 299
Firestone, 32
First Bank of Baltimore, 301
First Pacific Company Limited, 65t
First Pennsylvania Bank, 536
First Union, 301
Fisher-Price, 104, 591–92
Flagstar, Inc., 494
Fleet Financial Group, 212
Food Lion, 443
Footaction USA, 223
Foot Joy, 199, 201
Foot Locker, 223, 385
Ford Motor Company, 80, 83, 88, 91, 136, 167, 173, 174, 175f, 177, 241, 242, 252, 296t, 340, 443, 449
Fox, 62
France Telecom, 72
FreeMarkets Inc., 167
Fresh Samantha, 592–93
Frito-Lay, 20
Fujitsu, 81
Furniture.com, 589–90

G

Gadzooks, 199
Galeries Lafayette, 85
Gap, The, 385
Gartner, Inc., 545, 597
Gateway Computer, 34, 368, 369, 495, 496, 595
GE Capital, 301
General Electric (GE), 136, 170, 189, 195, 263, 340, 549, 570, 573
General Electric Medical Systems, 170f, 170
General Foods Corporation, 261, 403, 456
General Mills, 81, 262, 466, 476
General Motors (GM), 81, 164, 175f, 177, 282, 296t, 339, 340, 429
Geoscape International, 225
Gerland's Food Fair Inc., 212
Gillette, 85, 294

Girl Scouts of America, 46
Godiva, 430
Goodyear Tire and Rubber, 88, 345, 349
Goya Foods, Inc., 593–94
GTE, 306
Guangdong Investment Limited, 65t
Gucci, 335
Guess? Inc., 163, 164
Guidant, 514
Guy Laroche, 84

H

Haggar Clothing Company, 204, 205
Hallmark, 138
Hamilton Bank, 536
Hard Candy Cosmetics, 595
Harley-Davidson, 171, 173, 190, 418, 509, 595
Hasbro, Inc., 597–98
Henkel, 88
Hershey Foods Corporation, 296t, 444
Hertz, 291
Heublein, Inc., 526
Hewlett-Packard, 24, 80, 135, 173, 184, 185, 273, 278, 279, 280, 313, 368, 369, 495, 496, 526, 595
Hickory Farms, 135, 385
H.J. Heinz Company, 263, 296t, 444
Holiday Hospitality Corporation, 381
Home Depot, 36, 348, 388, 396
Honda, 173, 174, 175, 177, 181, 509
Honeywell Inc., 88
Hutchinson Whampoa, Limited, 65t
Hyundai Engineering & Construction Co., 65t
Hyvee, 343

I

IBM, 23, 24, 41, 60, 86, 117, 118, 167, 172t, 173, 174, 184, 188, 268, 293, 368, 416, 514, 516, 519, 551
IBM Global Services, 24, 174
ICOS/Eli Lilly, 596
IGA, 373
Ikea, 299
Information Resource Inc. (IRI), 114, 116, 436
Intel, 166, 167, 170, 188, 242, 306, 443, 495, 511
IntelliQuest, 135
Intellvisions Software Limited (ISL), 569, 570f
International Auto, 536

International Circuit Technology, 181
International Harvester, 250
International Red Cross, 32
International Truck and Engine Corproation, 236, 250
Isotoner, 98

J

J. M. Smucker Company, 175
Jafra Cosmetics, 389
Jardine Matheson Holdings, Limited, 65t
JCPenny, 134, 385, 388
Jefferson National Bank, 536
Johnson Controls, 174, 175f
Johnson & Johnson, 194, 514

K

Keithley Instrument, 255t
Kellogg's, 263
Kenmore, 296t
Kentucky Fried Chicken (KFC), 20, 80, 295, 296t, 595, 603
Keppel Corporation Limited, 65t
Kimberly-Clark, 51
Kleiner Perkins Caufield & Byers, 194
Kmart, 36, 112t, 378, 385, 386, 527
Kodak, 135, 262
Kohlberg Kravis Roberts, 261
Kohl's, 385, 403
Kraft Foods, 261, 456, 467
Kroger, 112t, 154, 386

L

Lakewood Forest Products, 94
Lands' End, 379, 384
Lane Bryant, 379
LEGO systems, 478
Lever Brothers, 395
Levi Strauss, 80, 87, 201, 222
LG Electronics, Incorporated, 65t
Limited, The, 349
Lipton, 80
Liz Claiborne, 47
L.L. Bean, 294, 379, 389, 540t, 543, 588
Lockheed Martin Corporation, 168, 169f
Lowe's, 348, 388, 396
Lucent Technologies, Inc., 22, 136, 516
Lycos, 72

M

M/A/R/C Group, 134
Marks & Spencer, 85, 306, 374–75
Marriott, 84, 105, 165, 472
Marshall Field, 385

Mars Inc., 418
Mary Kay Cosmetics, 389
MasterCard, 101
Mattel, 597
May Company, 385
Maytag, 172, 181, 182, 222, 296t
MBNA, 282
McDonald's, 51, 201, 214, 221,
    222, 224, 239, 246, 261, 291,
    295, 296t, 337, 338, 346, 347,
    348, 431
MCI, 599
MCI WorldCom, 212
McKesson, 117, 397
McKinsey & Company, 476
McLane Company, 397
McMillan Doolittle, 154
Mead Corporation, 185
Mediamark Research, Inc., 435
Media Tech Ventures, 161
Meijer, 36, 154
Microsoft, 27, 51, 125, 129, 131t,
    172t, 298, 338, 517, 600
MicroSolutions, 460
Miller Brewing Company, 222
Mirae, 72
Miramax, 62
Mitsubishi, 76, 80
Mitsui, 76
Motel 6, 296
Motorola, 2, 3, 8, 20, 26, 70, 136,
    170, 185, 218f, 286, 366
MTV, 124
Murray Ohio Manufacturing, 83

N

Napster, 331, 553
National Broadcasting Company,
    161
Navistar, 236, 250
NCR Corporation, 154
Neil Hill, 508, 509
Neiman Marcus, 217, 222, 583–84
Nestlé, 78, 81, 83
Netscape, 194, 338
News Corporation, 62
New World Development Co.,
    Limited, 65t
Nieto Computer Services, 526
Nike, 81, 222, 223, 229, 294, 430
Nissan, 177
Nokia, 2, 3, 170
Nortel, 136
Northwest Airlines, 296t, 523
Nucor Corporation, 514

O

Odwalla Inc., 593
Office Depot, 388
Office Max, 388
Old Navy, 199, 595
Optum, Inc., 606, 607
Oracle, 22, 298f
Owens-Illinois, 175

P

Palm, 236, 237, 244
Panasonic, 104
Parker Hannifin Corp., 278
PeopleSoft, 190
PepsiCo, 80, 129, 215, 341
Peregrine Inc., 516
Perrier, 414
Petroleo Brasileiro S.A.-Petro-
    bras, 65t
Petróleos de Venezuela S.A., 65t
PETRONAS-Petroliam Nasional
    Berhad, 65t
PetsMart, 388
Pfizer, Inc., 429, 596–97
Philip Morris, 32, 261, 429, 444,
    456
Philips, 80, 86
Pillsbury, 136, 177t, 178, 222
Pixar, 15
Pizza Hut, 602–3
Poindexter Systems, 537
Polaroid, 601–2
Pottery Barn, 377
PricewaterhouseCoopers, 476
Procter & Gamble (P&G), 14, 41,
    85, 88, 164, 165, 244, 245,
    262, 270, 273, 310, 347, 395,
    428, 429, 466, 467, 476, 518,
    519, 540, 574
Prudential, 261
Publishers Clearing House, 202
Purex Corporation, 268, 269f

Q

Quaker Oats Company, 114, 343,
    527
Qualcomm, 80

R

R. G. Barry, 98, 100
RadioShack, 598–99
Ralph Lauren, 51, 328
Ramada Franchise Systems, 476
Reebok, 421
Regal Ware, 389
Remington, 117
RestaurantTrade, 491
Right Start, 389
Ritz Carlton, 293
RJR Nabisco, 261
Rocky Top Books, 394
Rolex, 509
Rolling Strong Gym, The, 199
ru4, 537
Rubbermaid, 514
Ryan's Family Steakhouse,
    223–24

S

Saab, 436
Safeway, 291, 349, 386

Saks Incorporated, 373, 383
Sam Miguel Corporation, 65t
Sam's Club, 371, 376, 403
Samsung Electronics Co.,
    Limited, 3, 65t
SAP, 24
Sappi Limited, 65t
Save the Childen Fund (SCF), 56,
    444
Schering-Plough, 596
Schnucks Markets Inc., 343
Sears Roebuck and Company, 36,
    263, 299, 345, 349, 374, 385
Segway Comapny, 194
Sharper Image, 376
Shaw's, 154
Shell Oil, 51, 100
Sherlock Systems, 516
Sherwin-Williams Company, 349
Shomotion, 283
Shougang Group, 65t
Siemens, 3, 80, 81, 86
Simmons Market Research
    Bureau, Inc., 213, 435
Singapore Airlines, 293
Six Continents, 299, 381
Smart & Final, Inc., 398
Snap-on Inc., 398
Snapple Beverage Corporation,
    343
Sony, 62, 104, 331
Sotheby's, 522
Southland Corporation, 350, 351
Southwest Airlines, 478, 512
Spirit Airlines, 523
Sports Authority, 388
Sprint Corporation, 135, 136, 301,
    598, 599
Square D, 136
SRI Consulting Business Intelli-
    gence, 147, 149, 159, 210
SRI International, 147
Staples, 377
Starbucks, 135, 377, 423, 454
Star (Texaco) Enterprise, 536
State Farm Insurance, 309f
Stride Rite, 444
Sumitomo Corporation, 72, 91
Sunkyong Group, 65t
Sun Microsystems, 24, 516

T

Taco Bell, 140, 289, 295, 296t, 379,
    603
Takashimaya, 85
Tandy, 598
TAP Pharmaceuticals, 596
Target, 36, 376, 377, 378, 379, 385,
    386, 392, 403
Tenneco, Inc., 88
Tesco PLC, 24
TGIFriday's, 78
Thames Water, 306
Thompson Doyle Hennessey &
    Everest (TDH&E), 457, 458

3M, 66, 67f, 88, 105, 136, 170, 185, 340, 510
Timberland Company, 584–85
Timex, 509
Tomra Systems, 454
Top of the Ninth, 137
Touche Ross and Company, 536
Tower records, 587–88
Toyota Motor Corporation, 83, 270
Toys "R" Us, 51, 84, 85, 376, 387
TRW, 174, 175f
Tupperware, 88, 373, 389

U

Underwood, 117
Unicom, 295, 296t
United Airlines, 105, 292, 296t, 301, 600
United Parcel Service (UPS), 15, 22, 111, 294, 327, 551, 556, 594–96
United Technologies, 190
Universal, 331
Universo Online, 72
U.S. Postal Service, 195, 233, 234, 429
US Airways, 291, 308

USAirways Groups, Inc., 296t
US Steel, 239
US West Inc., 296t
USX, 175f, 239

V

Veryfine, 592
Victoria's Secret, 544
Volkswagen, 327
Volkswagen of America, 278
Volvo, 141, 430

W

Walgreens, 385
Wal-Mart, 36, 112t, 217, 222, 346, 347, 371, 372, 374, 378, 379, 380, 385, 386, 391, 392, 393, 394, 403, 445, 467, 518, 522, 523, 527
Walt Disney, 15, 20, 241, 293, 294
Wang Laboratory, 118, 500
Warner Brothers, 62, 135, 331
Warner-Lambert, 444
Waterpik, 219f
Webvan, 24
Wells Fargo & Company, 295, 296t, 540, 540t, 542f, 551

Wendys, 347
West Bend, 389
Weyerhaeuser, 222
Whirlpool, 66, 84, 136, 296t
White Wave, 411, 412, 413, 415, 421, 426
Williams Sonoma, 377, 389
Wine.com, 558, 559f, 600–601
Winn-Dixie, 112t
WorldCom, Inc., 301
W.W. Grainger, 398
Wyndham International, 91

X

Xerox, 35, 173, 179f, 185, 190, 223, 255t

Y

Yahoo!, 72, 460, 540t
YMCA, 46
YPF Sociedad Anonima, 65t

Z

Zonagen, 596

Page numbers followed by f indicate figures; t, tables.

A

Accessible markets, 207
Accessories in new product development and product decisions, 239
Accountability of database marketing, 437
Achievers, 148
Actionable markets, 207
Action programs in marketing planning, 575f, 576–77, 580–81
Activities of marketing exchange, 9–10
Actualizers, 148–49
Actual self, 146
Actual services in customer satisfaction, 296
ADA. *See* Americans with Disabilities Act (ADA)
Addressability of database marketing, 437
Advertising, 413, 419, 428–29
　accountability of database marketing, 437
　addressability of database marketing, 437
　brand positioning, 430
　budget, 429
　cost per thousand, 434
　database marketing, 436
　direct advertising, 436–37
　effectiveness assessments, 434–36
　e-marketing, 551–52
　exaggerated comparative price advertising, 523
　flexibility of database marketing, 437
　formal advertising, 168
　gross rating points, 433
　heuristics, 429
　interactive mediums, 434
　international marketing, 84
　mass-media advertising, 419
　measurability of database marketing, 437
　media selection, 432–34, 435f
　message creation, 430–32
　niche marketing, 436
　objective-and-task method, 429
　objectives, 429
　percentage-of-sales method, 429
　sales promotion, 437–39
　single-source systems, 435
　social responsibility, 36–37
　vehicles within mediums, 432
Affiliate programs in e-marketing, 552
After-purchase satisfaction, 379

Agents
　international market entry strategies, 76
　manufacturer's agents, 399
　wholesalers and wholesaling, 396f, 397f, 399
American Automobile Labeling Act, 50t
American Demographics magazine, 101–2
American Marketing Association code of ethics, 43, 44f
Americans with Disabilities Act (ADA), 50t
Amiable social style, 471
Analytical social style, 470–71
Analytic modeling, 506
Anchor stores, 377
Antidumping laws, 69
Anti-trust laws, 49–51
"Approaching the client" in the sales process, 470–71
A priori segmentation, 204
Arousal component of motivation, 140
Atmospherics, 392–94
Attitudes, 149
Attracting customers, 392–93
Attractiveness/strength model in strategic planning, 573–74
Auditing current competitors, 120–24
Audits, change, 125t
Audits, distributor, 125–27
Automatic merchandising machine operators, 390
Average total cost, 498–99
Awareness set of brands, 151
Awareness stage of adoption process, 265

B

Balanced tenancy, 377
Banner ads, 551
Bargaining power of distributors, 120
Bargaining power of suppliers, 120
Bargaining strategy in household decision making, 157
Base prices, 497–98
B2B markets. *See* Business-to-business (B2B) markets and marketing
BCG's product-portfolio analysis, 571–73
B2C markets. *See* Business-to-consumer (B2C) markets
BEA. *See* Break-even analysis (BEA)
"Becoming the customer," 246–47
Behavioral variables in channel structure, 344
Behavior of consumers. *See* Consumer behavior

Behavior of target audience in integrated marketing communications, 419
Behavior segmentation, 212
Believers, 148
Benchmarking, 123
Benefit concept in services marketing, 289
Benefits of product in the sales process, 472
Benefits-sought segmentation, 210–11
"Better marketing," 33
B2G markets. *See* Business-to-government (B2G) markets
Bottom-up budgeting (BU), 427
Brady Law, 50t
Brand association, 422
Brand awareness, 151, 420–21
Brand equity
　e-marketing, 560
　integrated marketing communications, 419–23
　new product development and product decisions, 261–62
Brand extensions, 261–62
Brand image, 420, 422–23
Branding, private labels, 374
Branding decisions, 238, 261–63
Branding in international marketing, 83–84
Branding strategies, 262–63
Brand positioning, 430
Brand recall, 421
Brand recognition, 421
Brand Web sites, 539–40
Break-even analysis (BEA), 501–2
Break-even point, 501
Bridge buying, 441
Brokers
　international market entry strategies, 76
　wholesalers and wholesaling, 396f, 397f, 399
BU. *See* Bottom-up budgeting (BU)
Budgets and budgeting
　advertising, 429
　bottom-up budgeting, 427
　integrated marketing communications, 425–26, 427
　marketing planning, 575f, 576–77, 580–81
　mental budgeting in consumer decision making, 149
Business cases, 256–58
Business customers and price flexing, 514–17
Business districts, 377
Business market segmentation, 222, 227t
　buyer's personal characteristics, 224
　demographics, 223
　operating characteristics, 223
　product use or usage situation, 223–24

Business market segmentation
(*cont.*)
purchasing approaches, 223
situational factors, 224
Business position of products,
573
Business practice improvements
using the Internet, 549–51
Business-to-business (B2B) markets and marketing, 163–64,
188, 538, 545–46
buyer-seller relationships,
173–74
buying power of customers,
166–67
characteristics of business
markets, 171–75
classifying business cus-
tomers, 170
commercial customers, 165
commercial enterprises as customers, 166–67
concentration of customers,
166
definition of business market,
164
demand issues, 171
derived demand, 171
fluctuating demand, 172–73
formal advertising, 168
governmental units as customers, 165, 167–70
institutional buying, 168–70
institutional customers, 165,
168–70
international customers, 165,
169–170
just-in-time, 175
manufacturers, 166
negotiated contracts, 168
organizational buyer requirements, 165–66
organizational buying influences. *See* Organizational
buying influences
organizational buying process.
See Organizational buying
process
purchasing functions, 167
relationship marketing,
173–74
resellers, 166
retailers, 166
reverse auctions, 167
Segway Human Transporter
case study, 194–95
stimulating demand, 173
supply-chain management,
174–75
types of customers, 164–66
wholesalers, 166
Business-to-business products,
238–40
Business-to-consumer (B2C) markets, 539, 547–49, 554t
Business-to-government (B2G)
markets, 539

Buyers
consumer behavior, 138
organizational buyer requirements, 165–66
organizational buying influences. *See* Organizational
buying influences
organizational buying process.
See Organizational buying
process
personal characteristics in
business market segmenta-
tion, 224
seller relationships in business-to-business marketing,
173–74
Buying activities as marketing
exchange, 9
Buying centers, 185–87
Buying power of customers in
business-to-business mar-
keting, 166–67
Buying situation isolation, 185–86
Buying situations analyzed,
178–81

C

Careers
brand management, 416
consumer behavior, 141
delivering service solutions to
IBM customers, 174
development organizations, 53
e-marketing, 558
entertainment transportation,
283
global experience, 88
marketing mix, 341
new product development, 250
niche marketing, 200
pricing, 518
research, 103
retailing, 394
sales, 460, 466
services marketing, 283
Cartels, 522
Cash and carry wholesalers, 398
Cash cows, 572
Cash or payment discounts, 515
Categorical imperative and ethical behavior, 45–46
Category killers, 385f, 387–88
Category management, 394–95
Cause-related marketing
social responsibility, 51–52
sponsorship marketing, 444
CBD. *See* Central business districts (CBD)
CBP. *See* Core benefit proposition
(CBP)
C2C markets. *See* Consumer-to-
consumer (C2C) markets
Celler-Kefauver Antimerger Act,
50t
Census blocks, 115

Central business districts (CBD),
377
Certification of sales forces, 467
Chain store growth, 373–75
Champions in new product development and product deci-
sions, 260
Change agents in international
marketing, 66
Change audits, 125t
Channel captains, 374
Channel research, 124–27
change audits, 125t
distributor audits, 125–27
trade customers, 125–27
Channels and distribution, 14,
326, 358–59
acceptance enhancement
through packaging, 263–64
channel partnerships, 347
conflict in marketing channels,
337–38
contractual VMSs, 348
decision areas for channel
management, 339–51
definition of marketing channel, 326–27
Dell's channel strategy case
study, 366–69
facilitating channel, 326
flows in marketing channels,
335–37
form utility, 326
informal support for channel
members, 347
information flows, 335, 336
international marketing, 84–86
interorganizational context,
338
leadership, 349
learning about member needs
and problems, 346–47
logistics. *See* Logistics
management of marketing
channel, 338–51
marketing mix coordination,
339, 349–50
member motivation, 339,
346–49
member performance evaluations, 339, 350–51
member selection, 339,
344–46
member selection criteria, 345
microbrews, 325
motivating members, 339,
346–49
negotiation flows, 335, 336
ownership flows, 335, 336
perspectives for channel management, 338
power, marketing channel, 337
pricing strategy and, 350
product flows, 335
product positioning strategy
and, 349
promotion flows, 335, 336–37

promotion strategy and, 350
prospective channel members, 345–46
retailers and retailing, 15
social responsibility, 34–36
social systems and, 337–38
strategic alliances, 347
strategy, 14–15, 339–41, 349–50
structure. *See* Channel structure
support for channel members, 347–49
sustainable competitive advantage, 340
system inefficiency, 34–36
time, place and possession utilities, 326
vertical marketing systems, 347–49
wholesalers and wholesaling, 15
Channel structure, 327
alternative structures, 343
behavioral variables, 344
channel intensity, 328–29, 343
channel length, 328, 343
company variables, 344
designing, 339, 342–44
discrepancies between production and consumption, 330–32
discrepancies in assortment, 331
discrepancies in place, 332
discrepancies in quantity, 330–31
discrepancies in time, 331
distribution objectives, 342–43
distribution tasks, 330–34, 343
economics of performing distribution tasks, 332–34
economies of scale and economies of scope, 333
exclusive distribution, 329
external environment variables, 344
facilitating agencies, 327
intensive distribution, 328–29
intermediary types, 330, 343
intermediary variables, 344
management control of distribution, 334–35
market variables, 344
music distribution, 331
optimal structures, 344
product variables, 344
scrambled merchandising, 330
selective distribution, 328–29
specialization or division of labor, 332–33
transaction efficiency, 334
Child Protection Act, 50t
Children
and credit cards case study, 161
household decision making, 156

Choice models in consumer decision making, 152
Clayton Act, 50t
Click throughs, 552
Close-ended questions in the sales process, 472
Cluster analysis, 115
Coaching a sales force, 479
Code law, 69
Codes of conduct for sales forces, 482
Codes of ethics for companies, 41–43
Coding in customer relationship management, 299
Cognitive dissonance in consumer decision making, 154
Cognitive responses in consumer behavior, 143
Cold calling, 469–70
Cold mailing, 108t
Commercial customers, 165, 166–67
Commissions for sales forces, 479–80
Commitment in the sales process, 475
Commoditization, 496
Common law, 69
Communication outcomes in integrated marketing communications, 428
Communications gap in service quality, 303, 304f, 306
Company codes of ethics, 41–43
Company ethic statements, 41, 42f
Company variables in channel structure, 344
Company Web sites, 539–40
Comparative advantage, 9
Compelling experiences for customers, 294
Compensating a sales force, 475f, 479–80
Compensatory choice model in consumer decision making, 152
Competition
integrated marketing communications, 425
marketing environment, 16, 18f, 21
new product development and product decisions, 244, 257
pricing, 495, 500, 508–9, 510–11, 510t
pricing adjustments, 514
research. *See* Competitor research
retailers and retailing, 380–83
segmentation and target markets, 221
Competitive Strategy, 120
Competitor research, 117–19
auditing current competitors, 120–24

bargaining power of distributors, 120
bargaining power of suppliers, 120
benchmarking, 123
current competitors, 120–24
definition of market, 117
dynamic thought, 117
history of the market, 119–20
levels of competition, 117, 118f
market share, 117
mind share, 119
Porter's 5 competitive advantages, 122
Porter's 5 forces of competition, 120
research and development share, 119
static thought, 117
threat of new entrants, 120
threat of new substitutes, 120
voice share, 119
Complementary marketing, 81
Component parts and materials, 239
Concentrated strategy in segmentation and target markets, 208
Concentration of customers, 166
Concentration strategy in international marketing, 73
Concepts in new product development and product decisions, 246
Concept tests in new product development and product decisions, 257
Conflict in family decisions, 156–57
Conflict in marketing channels, 337–38
Conjunctive choice model in consumer decision making, 152
Conquest marketing, 307
Consideration set of brands in consumer decision making, 151
Consultative selling, 459
Consumer behavior, 138, 157–58
arousal component of motivation, 140
buyers, 138
children and credit cards case study, 161
cognitive responses, 143
collecting, 137–38
definition of consumer, 138
describing consumer behavior. *See* Psychographics
drive component of motivation, 140
emotions, 142–43
enduring involvement, 144
goal-object component of motivation, 140

Consumer behavior (*cont.*)
　household decision making. *See* Household decision making
　individual consumer decision making. *See* Consumer decision making
　involvement, 144
　learning, 140
　Maslow's hierarchy of needs, 141–42
　moods, 143–44
　motivation, 140
　needs of consumers, 139, 140–42
　payers, 138
　perception, 140
　physiological responses, 143
　psychographics. *See* Psychographics
　roles of consumers, 138
　situational involvement, 144
　users, 138
　wants of consumers, 139
Consumer Credit Protection Act, 50t
Consumer decision making, 149–50
　alternative evaluation, 151f, 152–53
　awareness set of brands, 151
　choice models, 152
　cognitive dissonance, 154
　compensatory choice model, 152
　conjunctive choice model, 152
　consideration set of brands, 151
　disjunctive choice model, 152
　elimination by aspects choice model, 153
　evoked set of brands, 151
　exit responses, 154
　external stimuli, 150
　heuristics, 151–52
　information search, 151–52
　internal stimuli, 150
　lexicographic choice model, 152
　loyalty responses, 154, 155
　marketer source of information, 151
　mental budgeting, 149
　noncompensatory choice model, 152
　nonmarketer source of information, 151
　postpurchase behavior, 151f, 154–55
　problem recognition, 150–51
　purchase, 151f, 153
　self-service at point of sale, 154
　voice responses, 154–55
Consumer-oriented sales promotions, 414, 441

Consumer product development and decisions, 238
Consumer Product Safety Act, 50t
Consumer protection laws, 49–51
Consumer research, 100–101
　census blocks, 115
　cluster analysis, 115
　cold mailing, 108t
　control sample, 114
　convenience quota sample, 110
　convenience samples, 110–11
　customer satisfaction, 108–9
　customer visits in business-to-business marketing, 105–6
　database mining, 116
　decision support systems, 116–17
　demographics, 107
　direct mailing, 108t
　electronic data interchange, 117
　electronic observational research, 114–16
　European Article Numbering, 114
　focus group research, 106–7
　geodemographic information, 115
　hands-on consumer research, 104
　interval scale, 111
　mail panels, 108t
　mall intercept surveys, 108t
　moderators for focus groups, 106
　motivational research, 105
　nonresponse or participation bias, 110
　omnibus surveys, 110
　open-ended questions, 111
　panels of households, 110
　personal in-home surveys, 108t
　plastic money, 101
　pretests, 113
　process, 101, 102f
　qualitative consumer research, 104–5
　question design, 111–14
　random sample, 109–10
　ratio scale, 111
　reliability, 111
　sampling, 109–11
　secondary data analysis, 101–4
　sugging, 111
　survey research, 107–9
　telephone surveys, 108t
　Transaction-Based Information Systems, 117
　Universal Product Code, 114
　validity of result, 111
　voice of the customer, 104
Consumers. *See also* Customers behavior. *See* Consumer behavior

decision making. *See* Consumer decision making
　external consumers, 146
　final consumers, 15
　internal consumers, 146
　price flexing, 517–21
　research. *See* Consumer research
　sales promotion, 441
Consumer-to-consumer (C2C) markets, 539
Consumption satiation, 4, 5–6
Contacts in integrated marketing communications, 417
Contact with customers between sales, 308
Contract manufacturing, 81
Contractual arrangements in foreign direct investing, 80–81
Contractual VMSs, 348
Contribution margin, 501
Control sample in consumer research, 114
Convenience products, 238, 239t
Convenience quota sample in consumer research, 110
Convenience samples in consumer research, 110–11
Convenience stores, 385f, 388
Core benefit proposition (CBP), 236, 241–42
Corporate culture and sales forces, 476
Corporate sponsorships, 443
Cost per thousand (CPM) in advertising, 434
Cost-plus pricing, 497–500
Costs
　average total cost, 498–99
　e-marketing, 549–50, 558–60
　estimating costs, 215
　handling costs, 550
　marginal costs, 505
　obsolescence costs, 550
　pricing, 494–95
　procurement costs, 550
　storage costs and e-marketing, 550
Couponing, 519
CPM. *See* Cost per thousand (CPM) in advertising
Credence attributes in services marketing, 284
Credit card customer direct mailing case study, 233–34
Credit cards and children case study, 161
CRM. *See* Customer relationship management (CRM)
Cross-docking, 355
Culture
　global market segmentation, 226–27
　international marketing, 66, 67f
Current competitor research, 120–24

Customer-oriented sales force, 464
Customer prototypes, 252–53
Customer relationship management (CRM), 299
  coding, 299
  limitations of, 301–2
  outcomes, 299–301
  red-lining, 302
  routing, 299, 300
  sales, 461
  sharing, 299, 301
  targeting, 299, 301
Customer retention, 306–7
  conquest marketing, 307
  contact between sales, 308
  delivery process monitoring, 308
  discretionary effort, 310
  distributive justice, 310, 311
  installation of products, 308–9
  interactional justice, 310
  leaky bucket theory, 307
  perspective, 308
  polygamous loyalty, 307
  procedural justice, 310–11
  service guarantees, 310
  service recovery, 310–11
  standing behind the product, 309–10
  tactics, 307–8
  training of customers, 308–9
  trust building, 308
Customers. *See also* Consumers
  attracting customers, 392–93
  "becoming the customer," 246–47
  buying power of customers in business-to-business mar-keting, 166–67
  compelling experiences for customers, 294
  concentration of, 166
  defined, 14
  goal advancement in organiza-tional buying influences, 184
  institutional customers, 165, 168–70
  international customers, 165, 169–170
  late majority customers, 264, 267f
  "living with customers" in new product development and product decisions, 247–49
  loyalty in retailing mix, 393
  needs defined in new product development and product decisions, 245–46
  need understanding in new product development and product decisions, 246
  new product development and product decision success, 242

visits in business-to-business marketing, 105–6
Customer satisfaction, 295
  actual services, 296
  benefits of, 297–98
  consumer research, 108–9
  customer relationship man-agement. *See* Customer relationship management (CRM)
  definition of, 296
  importance of, 297
  new product development and product decisions, 242
  perceived services, 296
  service quality distinguished, 302–3
  TARP figures, 297
Customer service
  e-marketing, 551, 560
  logistics, 357–58
Customer surveys, 506
Customization in price flexing, 516–17, 520–21

D

Database marketing, 436, 437
Database mining, 116
Database sources of segmenta-tion data, 212–13
Data mining, 212
Deciders, 186, 187
Decision making by consumers. *See* Consumer decision making
Decision support systems (DSS), 116–17
Decline stage of product life cycle, 265t, 268
Decline stage of retail life cycle, 382f, 383
Definition of marketing, 9
Degree of individualism in inter-national marketing, 66
Delayed rewards, 441
Delivery gap, 303, 304f, 305–6
Delivery process monitoring, 308
Demand, 501
  analytic modeling, 506
  break-even analysis, 501–2
  break-even point, 501
  business-to-business market-ing, 171
  contribution margin, 501
  customer surveys, 506
  demand schedules, 502, 503f, 503t, 504t
  elastic demand, 503, 504t
  elasticity coefficient, 502
  elasticity of demand, 501, 502–4
  experiments, 506
  fluctuating demand, 172–73
  forecasting, 214
  heterogeneous demand, 198

  inelastic demand, 502–3
  managerial judgments, 506
  marginal costs, 505
  marginal revenues, 505
  profit maximization, 504–7
  social responsibility, 39
  target return pricing, 500
  total contributions, 504
  unitary elasticity, 504
Demographics
  business market segmenta-tion, 223
  consumer research, 107
  price flexing, 519
  segmentation and target mar-kets, 208–9
Department stores, 385
Derived demand, 171
Design considerations in interna-tional marketing, 83
Desk jobbers, 398
DEWKS, 19t
Differentiation
  retailers and retailing, 379–80
  segmentation and target mar-kets, 207–8, 215
  selling process differentiation, 379
  servicescape, 292–93
Diffusion process in product life cycle, 266–67
DINKS, 19t
Direct advertising, 436–37
Direct exporting and importing, 76
Direct mail, 108t
Direct mail case study, 233–34
Direct sellers, 389
Discount department stores, 385
Discounters, 385
Discounts, 515, 516
Discrepancies between produc-tion and consumption and channel structure, 330–32
Discrepancies in assortment and channel structure, 331
Discrepancies in place and chan-nel structure, 332
Discrepancies in quantity and channel structure, 330–31
Discrepancies in time and chan-nel structure, 331
Discretionary effort in customer retention, 310
Disjunctive choice model in con-sumer decision making, 152
Displacement in international market entry strategies, 78
Disposal enhancement through packaging, 263
Distribution. *See* Channels and distribution
Distributive justice in customer retention, 310, 311
Distributor audits, 125–27
Distributor bargaining power, 120

Distributors, industrial, 398
Distributors and international
    market entry strategies, 76
Diversification strategy in interna-
    tional marketing, 73
Diverting in sales promotions,
    441
"Dogs," 572–73
"Doing the most good for the
    most people," 45
Drive component of motivation,
    140
Driver social style, 470, 471f
Drop-shippers, 398
DSS. *See* Decision support sys-
    tems (DSS)
Dual entitlement theory, 510
Dynamic thought in competitor
    research, 117

E

"Eaches," 357
EAN. *See* European Article Num-
    bering (EAN)
Early adopters, 264, 267f
Early majority customers, 264,
    267f
Economic environment, 16, 18f,
    20
    global market segmentation,
        226
    organizational buying influ-
        ences, 183–84
Economic order quantity (EOQ),
    355, 356f
Economics of performing distri-
    bution tasks, 332–34
Economies of scale and
    economies of scope, 333
EDI. *See* Electronic data inter-
    change (EDI)
EDLP. *See* Every day low pricing
    (EDLP)
Effectiveness
    advertising, 434–36
    integrated marketing commu-
        nications, 428
    marketing environment, 21
    social responsibility, 33–40
Efficiency
    marketing environment, 21
    retailing mix, 393–94
    social responsibility, 33–40
    transaction efficiency, 334
EFT. *See* Electronic funds transfer
    (EFT)
80/20 principle, 212
Elastic demand, 503, 504t
Elasticity coefficient, 502
Elasticity of demand, 501,
    502–4
Electronic brochures, 558
Electronic commerce, 545–49
Electronic data interchange (EDI)
    consumer research, 117
    e-marketing, 545

Electronic funds transfer (EFT),
    545
Electronic intermediaries, 554
Electronic observational research,
    114–16
Electronic shopping, 17, 390–91
Elimination by aspects choice
    model, 153
E-marketing, 537, 561
    advertising, 551–52
    affiliate programs, 552
    banner ads, 551
    benefits of, 560
    brand equity, 560
    business practice improve-
        ments using the Internet,
        549–51
    business-to-business markets
        and marketing. *See* Busi-
        ness-to-business (B2B) mar-
        kets and marketing
    business-to-consumer mar-
        kets, 539, 547–49, 554t
    business-to-government mar-
        kets, 539
    click throughs, 552
    company/brand sites, 5
        39–40
    consumer-to-consumer mar-
        kets, 539
    cost reductions, 549–50
    costs of, 558–60
    customer service, 551, 560
    defined, 538
    definition of Internet, 538
    definition of World Wide Web
        (Web), 538
    development opportunities,
        551
    drawbacks of, 558–60
    electronic brochures, 558
    electronic commerce, 545–49
    electronic data interchange,
        545
    electronic funds transfer, 545
    electronic intermediaries, 554
    extranets, 538, 545
    fashion shows, 544
    government-to-consumer mar-
        kets, 539
    handling costs, 550
    history of Internet, 538
    information sites, 539, 540t,
        543–45
    information transfer benefits
        of, 560
    Internet hosts, 547
    Internet's history, 538
    intranets, 538, 545
    inventory reduction, 550–51
    limited audience, 559
    market development opportu-
        nities, 551
    marketing mix, 556–58
    music, 553
    obsolescence costs, 550
    online product vending, 554

    personal selling, 557
    place, 556
    portals, 538
    price, 556
    procurement costs, 550
    product development opportu-
        nities, 551
    products, 556
    profit models, 551–55
    promotion, 556–58
    prospective customers, 560
    resistance to change, 560
    résumé case study, 566
    search engines, 545
    selling sites, 539, 540t, 541–43
    service sites, 539, 540–41
    storage costs, 550
    subscriptions, 552–53
    terms, 538
    types of Internet sites,
        539–45
EMCs. *See* Export management
    companies (EMCs)
Emotional motives in organiza-
    tional buying influences,
    187
Emotions in consumer behavior,
    142–43
Enduring involvement in con-
    sumer behavior, 144
Environment. *See* Marketing
    environment
EOQ. *See* Economic order quan-
    tity (EOQ)
ERM. *See* Event-related market-
    ing (ERM)
E-services, 278–79
Estimating costs, 215
E-tailing, 390–91
Ethical behavior, 40–41
    American Marketing Associa-
        tion code of ethics, 43, 44f
    categorical imperative, 45–46
    company codes of ethics,
        41–43
    company ethic statements, 41,
        42f
    "doing the most good for the
        most people," 45
    ethical vigilance, 48
    issue spotting, 47–48
    normal good, 45
    Nuremberg trials, 42–43
    personal ethics checklist,
        47–48
    pricing, 521–22, 523–24
    principle of utility, 45
    sales force, 482
    situational ethics, 46
    social contracts, 45
    theories of marketing ethics,
        43–46
    values, sources of, 46–47
EU. *See* European Union (EU)
European Article Numbering
    (EAN), 114
European Union (EU), 68

Event-related marketing (ERM), 444
Every day low pricing (EDLP), 519
Evoked set of brands in consumer decision making, 151
Evolution of marketing, 25
    activities of marketing exchange, 9–10
    alternative to traditional view of, 8–9
    buying activities, 9
    comparative advantage, 9
    exchange principle, 9
    exchange process view of marketing, 9–10
    financing activities, 10
    fostering trust with trading partners, 10
    grading activities, 10
    marketing era, 7–8
    obtaining market information activities, 10
    production era, 6–7
    relationship marketing era, 7f, 8
    risk taking activities, 10
    sales era, 7
    selling activities, 9
    standardization activities, 10
    storing activities, 10
    traditional view of, 6–8
    transporting activities, 9
Evolution of markets via spontaneous economic combustion, 4–6
Exaggerated comparative price advertising, 523
Exchange activities, 9–10
Exchange principle, 9
Exchange process view of marketing, 9–10
Exclusive distribution, 329
Executive summaries in marketing planning, 575, 578
Existing customers
    new product development and product decisions, 244
    profiling, 213
Exit responses in consumer decision making, 154
Experience attributes in services marketing, 284
Experiencers, 148
Experiential programs in integrated marketing communications, 418
Experiments, demand, 506
Exporting, 75–76
Export management companies (EMCs), 76
Expressive social style, 471
Expropriation, 77
External consumers, 146
External factors in segmentation, 208
External marketing environment, 16, 18–22, 82–83, 344

External stimuli in consumer decision making, 150
Extranets, 538, 545

F

Facilitating agencies, 327
Facilitating channel, 326
Facilitating the service process, 291
Failure of products, 243–44
Fair Packaging and Labeling Act, 50t
Families and household decision making, 155–57
Family brand name strategy, 262–63
Family life cycle (FLC), 209
Features of products
    new product development and product decisions, 238
    sales process, 472
Federal Trade Commission Act, 50t
Field selling, 465–67
Final consumers, 15
Financial success in new product development and product decisions, 242
Financing activities as marketing exchange, 10
FLC. *See* Family life cycle (FLC)
Flexibility
    database marketing, 437
    pricing, 495
Flexible presentations of products, 472–73
Flows in marketing channels, 335–37
Flow-through distribution, 355
Fluctuating demand, 172–73
FOB pricing, 515
Focus group research, 106–7
Following up in the sales process, 475
Forecasting
    new product development and product decisions, 247
    segmentation and target markets, 214
Foreign direct investment, 78–81
Foreign direct investors, 78–79
Formal advertising, 168
Form utility
    channels and distribution, 326
    strategy, 12
For-profit services marketing, 282t
Forward buying, 441
Franchises
    international market entry strategies, 77–78
    sales promotion, 441, 442f
Free choice, 33
Freedom and social responsibility, 33

Free on board (FOB) pricing, 515
Free-standing inserts (FSIs), 519
Freestanding retailers, 377f, 378–79
FSIs. *See* Free-standing inserts (FSIs)
Fulfilleds, 148
Full ownership of a company, 79
Full-service merchant wholesalers, 397–98

G

Gatekeepers, 186
Generalized averages in segmentation and target markets, 213
General merchandise wholesalers, 397
Geodemographics
    consumer research, 115
    segmentation and target markets, 210
Geographical organization of sales forces, 481
Geographic pricing, 515
Geographic segmentation, 209–10, 519
GE's attractiveness/strength model, 573–74
Globalization
    international marketing. *See* International marketing
    market segmentation. *See* Global market segmentation
Global market segmentation, 224–25, 227t
    cultural factors, 226–27
    economic factors, 226
    intermarket segmentation, 227
    language considerations, 225
    legal/political factors, 226
Goal-object component of motivation, 140
Goal-setting in pricing, 509–11
Good cause marketing, 51–54
Goods
    product defined, 12
    services marketing, 282, 284–88
Gouging laws, 524
Governmental units as customers, 165, 167–70
Government services marketing, 282t
Government-to-consumer (G2C) markets, 539
Grading activities as marketing exchange, 10
Gray marketing, 84
Gross margin, 376
Gross margin percentage, 375–76
Gross rating points (GRPs), 433
Group forces in organizational buying, 183, 185–87

Growth stage of product life cycle, 265t, 267
Growth stage of retail life cycle, 382–83
Growth vector model, 570–71
GRPs. *See* Gross rating points (GRPs)
GUPPIES, 19t

H

Handling costs, 550
Hands-on consumer research, 104
Hard sell, 461
Heterogeneity in services marketing, 288
Heterogeneous demand, 198
Heterogeneous markets, 206
Heuristics
  advertising, 429
  consumer decision making, 151–52
Hidden Persuaders, The, 30
Hierarchy of effects, 423–24
History of marketing. *See* Evolution of marketing
History of the Internet, 538
History of the market research, 119–20
Household decision making, 155
  bargaining strategy, 157
  children's influence, 156
  conflict in family decisions, 156–57
  families and, 155–57
  persuasion strategy, 157
  politicking strategy, 157
  problem solving strategy, 156
  steps in family buying decisions, 156

I

Idea generation and screening stage of new product development, 254–56, 255t
Ideal self, 146
Ideas, 12
Identification function of packaging, 263
Identification of target international markets, 70–73
Identifying client needs, 471–72
Image reinforcement, 441, 442f
IMC. *See* Integrated marketing communications (IMC)
Immediate rewards, 441
Implementing marketing programs worldwide, 86–88
Importing, 75–76
Inbound telemarketers, 464
Incentives in sales promotions, 437
Indirect exporting and importing, 75–76

Individual adoption process in the product life cycle, 264–66
Individual brand name strategy, 262
Individual forces in organizational buying, 183, 187
Individual markets, 199–201
Industrial distributors, 398
Industry attractiveness in strategic planning, 573–74
Inefficient targeting, 37
Inelastic demand, 502–3
Influencers in organizational buying, 186
Informal support for channel members, 347
Information flows, 335, 336
Information function of packaging, 263
Information search in consumer decision making, 151–52
Information transfer benefits of e-marketing, 560
Information Web sites, 539, 540t, 543–45
Innovators, 264, 267f
Inseparability in services marketing, 285–87
Installation of products and customer retention, 308–9
Installations in new product development and product decisions, 239–40
Institutional buying, 168–70
Institutional customers, 165, 168–70
Instrumental values, 145
Intangibility in services marketing, 282, 285
Intangible dominant in services marketing, 282
Integrated marketing communications (IMC), 412, 415–17, 445–47
  advertising. *See* Advertising
  behavior of target audience, 419
  bottom-up budgeting, 427
  brand association, 422
  brand awareness, 420–21
  brand equity, 419–23
  brand image, 420, 422–23
  brand recall, 421
  brand recognition, 421
  budget, 425–26, 427
  communication outcomes, 428
  competition, 425
  consumer-oriented sales promotions, 414, 441
  contacts, 417
  effectiveness evaluations, 428
  elements of, 417–19
  experiential programs, 418
  features of, 417–19
  hierarchy of effects, 423–24
  intended market, 423

  managing the process, 426–28
  mass-media advertising, 419
  media strategies, 427
  message formulation and implementation, 427–28
  milk sales, 411–12
  mix of tools, 423–26
  objectives, 423–25, 426
  participants in, 415
  personal selling, 413
  point-of-purchase communications, 414, 444–45
  positioning statement, 427
  positioning strategy, 427
  product life cycle, 425
  product's nature, 425
  publicity, 413–14
  public relations. *See* Public relations
  pull strategy, 426
  push strategy, 426
  recycling kiosks case study, 454–55
  relationship building, 418
  return on investment, 419
  sales promotion. *See* Sales promotion
  speaking with a single voice, 418
  sponsorship marketing. *See* Sponsorship marketing
  synergy, 418
  target market selection, 426
  tools, 413–14, 423–26
  top-down budgeting, 427
  trade-oriented sales promotions, 414, 440–41
Intellectual property rights, 69
Intended market in integrated marketing communications, 423
Intensive distribution, 328–29
Interactional justice in customer retention, 310
Interactive mediums, 434
Intermarket segmentation, 227
Intermediaries
  electronic intermediaries, 554
  international market entry strategies, 75, 76
  types in channel structure, 330, 343
  variables in channel structure, 344
Internal consumers, 146
Internal marketing environment, 16, 17–18
Internal stimuli in consumer decision making, 150
International customers, 165, 169–170
International market entry strategies, 75
  agents, 76
  complementary marketing, 81
  contract manufacturing, 81

contractual arrangements in foreign direct investing, 80–81
direct exporting and importing, 76
displacement, 78
distributors, 76
exporting, 75–76
export management companies, 76
expropriation, 77
foreign direct investment, 78–81
foreign direct investors, 78–79
franchising, 77–78
full ownership of a company, 79
importing, 75–76
indirect exporting and importing, 75–76
international intermediaries, 75, 76
joint ventures, 79–80
licensing, 76–78
licensing agreements, 76
multinational corporations, 78
outsourcing, 81
ownership types in foreign direct investing, 79–81
profit repatriation limitations, 79
royalties, 76
sogoshosha, 76
strategic alliances, 80
trading companies, 76
International marketing, 62–63, 89
advertising copy considerations, 84
antidumping laws, 69
branding considerations, 83–84
change agent, 66
chopsticks case study, 94–96
code law, 69
common law, 69
company abilities, 82
concentration strategy, 73
cultural environment, 66, 67f
degree of individualism, 66
design considerations, 83
distribution decisions, 84–86
diversification strategy, 73
entry strategies. See International market entry strategies
environment of, 66–70, 82–83
EU, 68
globalization approach, 82
gray marketing, 84
identification of target international markets, 70–73
implementing marketing programs worldwide, 86–88
intellectual property rights, 69
International Organization for Standardization, 83

Internet portals, 72
labeling considerations, 84
legal and political environment, 69–70
level of equality, 66
macroenvironmental influences, 82–83
management process, 86–87
managerial commitment, 73, 81
marketing mix adjustments, 82–86
market potential, 70
material achievement, 66
MERCOSUR, 68
motivations to go abroad, 73–75
multidomestic approach, 82
multinational firms from developing countries, 64, 65t
NAFTA, 68
opportunities and challenges in, 63–66
organizational structures, 87–88
packaging considerations, 84
positioning considerations, 84
pricing decisions, 86
proactive motivations for, 74
process of internationalization, 73–75
product decisions, 83–84
promotion decisions, 84
reactive motivations for, 74–75
sales potential, 71
screening of target international markets, 70–73
socioeconomic environment, 67–69
standardized approach, 82
target market selection, 70–73
uncertainty avoidance, 66
U.S. movies, 61–62
World Trade Organization, 69
International Organization for Standardization (ISO), 83
Internet
banner ads, 551
e-marketing. See E-marketing
gambling case study, 59
marketing research case study, 134–35
portals, 72
sales force, 477
supply chain management, 177
virtual ISP, 286
Interpersonal values, 146
Interval scale in consumer research, 111
Intranets, 538, 545
Introduction stage of product life cycle, 264–67
Introduction stage of retail life cycle, 382
Inventory control, 355

Inventory reduction, 550–51
Inventory turnover, 375–76
Involvement in consumer behavior, 144
ISO. See International Organization for Standardization (ISO)

J

JIT. See Just-in-time (JIT)
Job anxiety, 464
Joint ventures, 79–80
Just-in-time (JIT), 175

K

"Keeping promises" in the sales process, 475
Key buying influentials in organizational buying, 187
Knowledge gap, 303, 304f
Knowledge stage of adoption process, 265

L

Labeling
Fair Packaging and Labeling Act, 50t
international marketing, 84
new product development and product decisions, 264
Labor specialization, 4–5
Laggards in the product life cycle, 264, 267f
Language considerations, 225
Late majority customers, 264, 267f
Laws and political environment, 50t
antidumping laws, 69
anti-trust laws, 49–51
code law, 69
common law, 69
consumer protection laws, 49–51
global market segmentation, 226
gouging laws, 524
international marketing, 69–70
marketing environment, 16, 18f, 20–21
markup laws, 523
pricing, 521–23
red-lining, 302
retailers and retailing, 384
sales force, 482
Leadership in channels and distribution, 349
Leading NPD projects, 259–60
Leaky bucket theory, 307
Learning about member needs and problems, 346–47
Learning in consumer behavior, 140

"Less marketing," 33
Level of equality in international marketing, 66
Levels of competition research, 117, 118f
Lexicographic choice model in consumer decision making, 152
Licensing, 76–78
Licensing agreements, 76
Life cycle of products. *See* Product life cycle
Life cycle of retailing, 382–83
Lifestyle, 147–49
Liking stage of adoption process, 265
Limited problem solving in organizational buying process, 181
Limited-service merchant wholesalers, 398
Line extensions, 240–41
"Living with customers" in new product development and product decisions, 247–49
Location in retailing, 376–79, 380
Logistics, 351
    cross-docking, 355
    customer service, 357–58
    "eaches," 357
    economic order quantity, 355, 356f
    flow-through distribution, 355
    inventory control, 355
    logistical services standards, 357–58
    materials handling, 354–55
    "onesie" transactions, 357
    order cycle time, 355
    order processing, 355
    packaging, 357
    services standards, 357–58
    supply chain management, 351
    systems concept of logistics, 352–57
    total cost approach, 352–53
    transportation, 353–54
    warehousing, 356–57
Loyalty responses in consumer decision making, 154, 155

M

Macroenvironment, 16, 18–22, 82–83, 344
Mail order, 389–90
Mail panels, 108t
Makers, 148
Mall intercept surveys, 108t
Management control of distribution, 334–35
Management of marketing channel, 338–51
Management process in international marketing, 86–87

Management support for NPD, 260
Managerial commitment in international marketing, 73, 81
Managerial judgments about demand, 506
Managing wholesalers, 400
Manufacturers
    business-to-business marketing, 166
    marketing channel members, 14
Manufacturer's agents, 399
Manufacturer's sales branches, 396, 397f
Manufacturing, contract, 81
Marginal costs, 505
Marginal revenues, 505
"Marginals" class and social responsibility, 38
Margins in retailing, 375–76
Market, target. *See* Segmentation and target markets
Market analysis in new product development and product decisions, 257
Market attractiveness in strategic planning, 573–74
Market development
    e-marketing, 551
    new product development and product decisions, 269
    strategic planning, 570–71, 571f
Marketer source of information in consumer decision making, 151
Marketing channels. *See* Channels and distribution
Marketing concept, 10–11
Marketing environment, 16, 18f
    competitive environment, 16, 18f, 21
    DEWKS, 19t
    DINKS, 19t
    economic environment, 16, 18f, 20
    effectiveness, 21
    efficiency, 21
    environmental scanning, 16
    external marketing environment, 16, 18–22, 82–83, 344
    GUPPIES, 19t
    internal marketing environment, 16, 17–18
    international marketing, 66–70, 82–83
    legal/political environment, 16, 18f, 20–21
    macroenvironment, 16, 18–22, 82–83, 344
    microenvironment, 16, 17–18
    MOBYS, 19t
    objectives and resources, 16, 17–18
    PUPPIES, 19t
    SKIPPIES, 19t

    socio-cultural environment, 16, 18–20
    technological environment, 16, 18f, 21–22
    WOOFS, 19t
    yuppies, 19t
Marketing era of history, 7–8
Marketing exchange activities, 9–10
Marketing mix
    adjustments in international marketing, 82–86
    coordination in channels and distribution, 339, 349–50
    e-marketing, 556–58
    place. *See* Place
    price. *See* Pricing
    products. *See* Products
    promotion. *See* Promotion
    segmentation and target markets, 222
    strategy, 11, 12, 14f
Marketing myopia, 284
Marketing planning, 568, 574, 575f
    action program and budget preparation, 575f, 576–77, 580–81
    analysis of the marketing situation, 575, 579
    control procedures, 575f, 577
    executive summary, 575, 578
    objectives, 575f, 576
    opportunity and threat assessments, 575–76
    strategic planning, 574
    strategy formulation, 575f, 576, 580
    trends, 577–78
Marketing strategy. *See* Strategy
Market penetration
    new product development and product decisions, 269
    strategic planning, 570, 571f
Market potential, 70
Market segmentation. *See* Segmentation and target markets
Market share
    competitor research, 117
    success in new product development and product decisions, 242
    targets and pricing, 510
Market skimming, 511
Markup laws, 523
Markup on cost, 499
Markup on retail price, 499
Maslow's hierarchy of needs, 141–42
Mass markets, 199–201
Mass-media advertising, 419
Material achievement in international marketing, 66
Materials handling, 354–55
Maturity stage of product life cycle, 265t, 267

Maturity stage of retail life cycle, 382f, 383

Measurability of database marketing, 437

Measurable markets, 206

Media selection in advertising, 432–34, 435f

Media strategies in integrated marketing communications, 427

Mental budgeting in consumer decision making, 149

Merchant wholesalers, 396–98

MERCOSUR, 68

Message creation in advertising, 430–32

Message formulation and implementation in integrated marketing communications, 427–28

Microenvironment, 16, 17–18

Micromarkets, 200

Miller-Tydings Resale Price Maintenance Act, 50t

Mind share research, 119

Missionary salespeople, 465f, 467

MOBYS, 19t

Modified rebuys in organizational buying, 181

Moods and consumer behavior, 143–44

Motivation
    channels members, 339, 346–49
    consumer behavior, 140
    consumer research, 105
    international marketing, 73–75
    sales forces, 475f, 478–79

Multidomestic approach to international marketing, 82

Multinational corporations, 64, 65t, 78

Music
    distribution and channel structure, 331
    e-marketing, 553

N

NAFTA. *See* North American Free Trade Agreement (NAFTA)

NAICS. *See* North American Industrial Classification System (NAICS)

National account managers, 465–67

National Environmental Policy Act, 50t

National High Blood Pressure Education Program (NHBPEP), 53–54

NBD. *See* Neighborhood business districts (NBD)

Needs of consumers, 139, 140–42

Negotiated contracts, 168

Negotiation flows, 335, 336

Neighborhood business districts (NBD), 377

Never out-of-stock differentiation, 380

New product development and product decisions, 238, 271–72
    accessories, 239
    anthropological excursions, 247–49
    "becoming the customer," 246–47
    brands and branding, 238, 261–63
    business case, 256–58
    business-to-business products, 238–40
    champions, 260
    channel acceptance enhancement through packaging, 263–64
    competitive analysis, 257
    competitively advantaged product, 244
    component parts and materials, 239
    concepts, 246
    concept test, 257
    consumer products, 238
    convenience products, 238, 239t
    core benefit proposition, 236, 241–42
    customer needs, understanding, 246
    customer needs defined, 245–46
    customer prototypes, 252–53
    customer satisfaction success, 242
    customer's perspective on success, 242
    defining new products, 240–44
    definition of new, 240–42
    definition of product, 238
    degree offering case study, 276–77
    detailed financial analysis, 257
    detailed investigation stage, 254f, 255t, 256–58
    developing a competitively advantaged product, 252–59
    development stage, 254f, 258–59
    disposal enhancement through packaging, 263
    e-marketing, 551
    existing customers, 244
    failure of products, 243–44
    family brand name strategy, 262–63
    features of products, 238
    financial success, 242
    forecasting, 247
    growth opportunities, 269–70
    idea generation and screening stage, 254–56, 255t
    identification function of packaging, 263
    individual brand name strategy, 262
    information function of packaging, 263
    installations, 239–40
    international marketing, 83–84
    labeling decisions, 264
    leading NPD projects, 259–60
    line extensions, 240–41
    living with customers, 247–49
    management support for NPD, 260
    market analysis, 257
    market development, 269
    market penetration, 269
    market share success, 242
    observing customers, 247–49
    packaging decisions, 263–64
    personal digital assistants, 236–38
    potential customers, 244
    preliminary investigation stage, 254f, 255t, 256
    pricing, 511–12
    problem discovery, 246–47
    process owners, 260
    product development process, 253
    product development strategy, 252, 270
    product diversification, 270
    product launch stage, 254f, 255t, 259
    product life cycle. *See* Product life cycle
    product line, 268
    product mix, 243, 268–69
    project leaders, 259–60
    project strategy, 243–44, 252–53
    project success, 242–43
    protection function of packaging, 263
    prototypes, 246
    raw materials, 238
    requirements for developing successful new products, 244–52
    shopping products, 238, 239t
    silver bullet success, 243
    specialty products, 238, 239t
    stage-gate processes, 253–59
    strategy, 12–14, 571
    success of new products, 242–43, 244–52
    supplies, 238–39
    tacit knowledge, 247
    talking to customers, 249–52
    technical assessment, 257
    technical performance success, 242
    testing and validation stage, 254f, 255t, 259
    types of products, 238–40

New product development and
    product decisions (*cont.*)
    uncovering unmet needs and
        problems, 245–52
    unrealized customers, 244
    unsought products, 238, 239t
    usage enhancement through
        packaging, 263
    voice of the customer, 249–52
New-task buying situations in
    organizational buying, 180
NHBPEP. *See* National High Blood
    Pressure Education Pro-
    gram (NHBPEP)
Niche marketing
    advertising, 436
    segmentation and target mar-
        kets, 199–200
Noncompensatory choice model
    in consumer decision mak-
    ing, 152
Nonmarketer source of informa-
    tion in consumer decision
    making, 151
Nonprofit services, 282t
Nonresponse bias in consumer
    research, 110
Nonstore-based retailers, 383,
    388–91
Nontraditional locations for retail-
    ers and retailing, 377f
"Normal good," 45
North American Free Trade
    Agreement (NAFTA), 50t, 68
North American Industrial Classi-
    fication System (NAICS),
    170–71
Nuremberg trials, 42–43
Nutritional Labeling and Educa-
    tion Act, 50t

O

Obeying the law and social
    responsibility, 49–51
Objection handling in the sales
    process, 473–74
Objective-and-task method adver-
    tising, 429
Objectives
    advertising, 429
    integrated marketing commu-
        nications, 423–25, 426
    marketing environment, 16,
        17–18
    marketing planning, 575f, 576
    pricing, 509–11
    sales promotion, 439–40
    variance over product life cycle
        and pricing adjustments,
        513–14
Observing customers in new
    product development and
    product decisions, 247–49
Obsolescence costs, 550

Obsolete technology and social
    responsibility, 35
Off-invoice allowance, 440
Omnibus surveys in consumer
    research, 110
"Onesie" transactions, 357
Online product vending, 554
Open-ended questions
    consumer research, 111
    sales process, 472
Operating characteristics in busi-
    ness market segmentation,
    223
Operating expenses of retailers
    and retailing, 376
Order cycle time, 355
Order getters, 465
Order processing, 355
Order takers, 465
Organizational buyer require-
    ments, 165–66
Organizational buying influences,
    183
    buyers, 186, 187
    buying centers, 185–87
    buying situation isolation,
        185–86
    customer goal advancement,
        184
    deciders, 186, 187
    economic influences, 183–84
    emotional motives, 187
    environmental forces, 183–84
    evaluative criteria, 185, 187
    gatekeepers, 186
    group forces, 183, 185–87
    individual forces, 183, 187
    influencers, 186
    key buying influentials, 187
    organizational forces, 183,
        184–85
    organizational positioning of
        purchasing, 185
    purchasing strategy, 185
    rational motives, 187
    relative influence of partici-
        pants, 185
    technological forces, 184
    users, 186
    value proposition, 185
Organizational buying process,
    176–78
    buying situations analyzed,
        178–81
    limited problem solving, 181
    modified rebuys, 181
    new-task buying situations,
        180
    routine problem solving, 180
    search process, 178
    straight rebuys, 180
    supplier selection and perfor-
        mance review, 178, 181–82
    total cost of ownership, 181
    value analysis, 181–82
    weighted point plans, 182

Organizational socialization, 291
Organizational structures in inter-
    national marketing, 87–88
Organization and systems in ser-
    vices marketing, 294
Organization mission, 568–69
Organization of a sales force,
    475f, 481
"Other customers" in services
    marketing, 293–94
Outbound telemarketers, 464
Outcomes in customer relation-
    ship management, 299–301
Outlet numbers, 373–75
Outsourcing, 81
"Overconsumers" class and
    social responsibility, 38
Over-the-counter selling, 465
Ownership flows, 335, 336
Ownership types in foreign direct
    investing, 79–81

P

Packaging
    Fair Packaging and Labeling
        Act, 50t
    identification function of pack-
        aging, 263
    information function of pack-
        aging, 263
    international marketing, 84
    logistics, 357
    new product development and
        product decisions, 263–64
    protection function of packag-
        ing, 263
    servicescape, 291
    usage enhancement through
        packaging, 263
Panels of households in con-
    sumer research, 110
Participation bias in consumer
    research, 110
Payers and consumer behavior,
    138
Payment discounts, 515
PD. *See* Logistics
Penetration strategy, 511–12
Perceived services in customer
    satisfaction, 296
Percentage-of-sales method in
    advertising, 429
Perception and consumer behav-
    ior, 140
Perceptual mapping, 216
Perishability and services market-
    ing, 288
Personal ethics checklist, 47–48
Personal in-home surveys, 108t
Personal selling
    e-marketing, 557
    integrated marketing commu-
        nications, 413
    sales, 459–61

Perspective and customer retention, 308
Persuasion strategy in household decision making, 157
Physical differentiation of the product, 379
Physical distribution (PD). *See* Logistics
Physiological responses and consumer behavior, 143
Place
  decisions and strategy, 14–15
  e-marketing, 556
  product defined, 12
Place utilities, 14, 326
Planned obsolescence and social responsibility, 34
Planning, 567–68, 581
  marketing planning. *See* Marketing planning
  sales process, 470
  strategic planning. *See* Strategic planning
  tactical planning, 568
Plastic money, 101
Point-of-purchase communications
  integrated marketing communications, 414, 444–45
  retailers and retailing, 445
Political environment. *See* Laws and political environment
Politicking strategy in household decision making, 157
Polygamous loyalty and customer retention, 307
Portals, 538
Porter's 5 competitive advantages, 122
Porter's 5 forces of competition, 120
Positioning considerations in international marketing, 84
Positioning statement in integrated marketing communications, 427
Positioning strategy
  integrated marketing communications, 427
  pricing, 508–9, 510t
  segmentation and target markets, 215–22
Possession utilities, 14, 326
Post hoc segmentation, 204
Postpurchase behavior in consumer decision making, 151f, 154–55
Potential buyers and customers
  new product development and product decisions, 244
  social responsibility, 37
Preapproach and planning in the sales process, 470
Predatory pricing, 523
Preference stage of adoption process, 265

Preliminary investigation stage in new product development, 254f, 255t, 256
Presentation of products in the sales process, 472–73
Pretests in consumer research, 113
Price flexing, 514
  alternatives to discounts, 516
  business customers, 514–17
  cash or payment discounts, 515
  consumers, 517–21
  couponing, 519
  customization, 516–17, 520–21
  demographic segments, 519
  discounts, 515, 516
  every day low pricing, 519
  free on board pricing, 515
  free-standing inserts, 519
  geographic pricing, 515
  geographic segments, 519
  price promotions, 517–19
  price shading, 514–15
  prisoner's dilemma, 519
  sales promotion allowances, 515
  segments, 519
  single-pricing, 517
  time segments, 519–20
  uniform delivered pricing, 515
  usage segments, 519
  value pricing, 519
  volume discounting, 515
Pricing, 497, 508f, 522, 525
  adjustments. *See* Pricing adjustments
  average total cost, 498–99
  base prices, 497–98
  cartels, 522
  channels and distribution, 350
  commoditization, 496
  competitive position, 495, 500, 508–9, 510–11, 510t
  competitive strategy positioning continuum, 508
  cost, 494–95
  cost-plus pricing, 497–500
  definition of price, 497
  Dell Computer, 494–97
  demand considerations. *See* Demand
  e-marketing, 556
  ethics, 521–22, 523–24
  exaggerated comparative price advertising, 523
  flexibility, 495
  goal-setting, 509–11
  gouging laws, 524
  grocery pricing case study, 532–33
  international marketing, 86
  legal issues, 521–23
  market share targets, 510
  market skimming, 511
  markup laws, 523

markup on cost, 499
markup on retail price, 499
new product pricing, 511–12
objectives, 509–11
penetration strategy, 511–12
positioning strategy, 508–9, 510t
predatory pricing, 523
price discrimination, 522
price-fixing, 522
price-quality judgments, 512
price skimming, 511
profit maximization, 511
resale price maintenance, 522–23
ROI, 509–10
segmentation and target markets, 217
Sherman Antitrust Act, 522
stabilization of price and margin objective, 510
standard markup approach, 499–500
strategy, 14
survival pricing, 511
target return pricing, 500
theory of dual entitlement, 510
Pricing adjustments, 512, 513f
  competitive price moves, 514
  objectives vary over product life cycle, 513–14
  price flexing. *See* Price flexing
Principle of utility, 45
Prisoner's dilemma, 519
Private label branding, 374
Proactive marketing public relations, 442–43
Proactive motivations for international marketing, 74
Probing questions in the sales process, 471–72
"Problem children" in strategic planning, 572
Problem discovery in new product development, 246–47
Problem recognition in consumer decision making, 150–51
Problem solving strategy in household decision making, 156
Procedural justice and customer retention, 310–11
Process owners and new product development and product decisions, 260
Procurement costs, 550
Product flows, 335
Production era of history, 6–7
Product life cycle, 264, 265f
  awareness stage, 265
  decline strategies, 265t, 268
  diffusion process, 266–67
  early adopters, 264, 267f
  early majority customers, 264, 267f
  growth strategies, 265t, 267

Product life cycle (*cont.*)
  individual adoption process, 264–66
  innovators, 264, 267f
  integrated marketing communications, 425
  introduction strategies, 264–67
  knowledge stage, 265
  laggards, 264, 267f
  late majority customers, 264, 267f
  liking stage, 265
  maturity strategies, 265t, 267
  preference stage, 265
  product diffusion, 266
  purchase stage, 265
Product line organization of sales forces, 481
Product-portfolio analysis, 571–73
Products
  defined, 12, 238
  development and decisions. *See* New product development and product decisions
  diversification, 270, 571
  e-marketing, 556
  life cycle. *See* Product life cycle
  nature of and integrated marketing communications, 425
  positioning, 11, 218, 219, 220, 349
  presentations in the sales process, 472–73
  sales force knowledge, 476
  use or usage situations, 223–24
  variables and channel structure, 344
Professional salespeople, 465
Professional selling method, 469
Professional services marketing, 282t
Profiling selected segments, 213–14
Profitability potential assessments in segmentation and target markets, 214–15
Profit center approach to compensation of sales forces, 480
Profit maximization
  demand, 504–7
  pricing, 511
Profit models and e-marketing, 551–55
Profit repatriation limitations in international markets, 79
Project leaders in new product development and product decisions, 259–60
Project strategy in new product development and product decisions, 243–44, 252–53
Project success in new product development and product decisions, 242–43

Promotion
  e-marketing, 556–58
  flows, 335, 336–37
  international marketing, 84
  strategy, 15–16, 350
Prospecting in the sales process, 469–70
Prospective channel members, 345–46
Prospective customers and e-marketing, 560
Protection function of packaging, 263
Prototypes in new product development and product decisions, 246
Providers of services, 293
Prudence in claim making to customers by sales forces, 482
Psychographics, 145
  achievers, 148
  actualizers, 148–49
  actual self, 146
  attitudes, 149
  believers, 148
  experiencers, 148
  external consumers, 146
  fulfilleds, 148
  ideal self, 146
  instrumental values, 145
  internal consumers, 146
  interpersonal values, 146
  lifestyle, 147–49
  makers, 148
  segmentation and target markets, 210
  self-concept, 146–47
  strivers, 148
  strugglers, 148
  terminal values, 145–46
  VALS, 147–49
  values, 145–46, 147–49
Publicity, 413–14
Public relations, 413–14, 442
  proactive marketing public relations, 442–43
  reactive MPR, 443
Pull strategy in integrated marketing communications, 426
PUPPIES, 19t
"Purchase" in consumer decision making, 151f, 153
Purchase stage of adoption process, 265
Purchasing approaches to business market segmentation, 223
Purchasing functions in business-to-business marketing, 167
Purchasing strategy in organizational buying influences, 185
Push strategy in integrated marketing communications, 426

Q
Qualified sales leads, 469
Qualitative consumer research, 104–5
Quality
  positioning, 217
  services. *See* Service quality
Question design in consumer research, 111–14
Quotas for sales forces, 479

R
Rack jobbers, 398
Random sample in consumer research, 109–10
Rational motives in organizational buying influences, 187
Ratio scale in consumer research, 111
Raw materials
  new product development and product decisions, 238
  scarcity, 4
"Reaching the customer" in retailing, 373
Reactive motivations for international marketing, 74–75
Reactive MPR, 443
Recruiting a sales force, 475–76
Red-lining, 302
Referrals in the sales process, 469
Relationship building and integrated marketing communications, 418
Relationship marketing, 173–74
Relationship marketing era, 7f, 8
Relationship selling, 461
Reliability in consumer research, 111
Repositioning, 222
Resale price maintenance, 522–23
Research, 127–28
  channel research. *See* Channel research
  competitor research. *See* Competitor research
  consumer research. *See* Consumer research
  importance of, 100
  online marketing research, 134–35
  online marketing research case study, 134–35
  slipper market, 98–99
Resellers, 166
Resistance to change and e-marketing, 560
Retailers and retailing, 371–72, 401
  after-purchase satisfaction, 379
  anchor stores, 377
  automatic merchandising machine operators, 390

balanced tenancy, 377
business districts, 377
business-to-business marketing, 166
category killers, 385f, 387–88
central business districts, 377
chain store growth, 373–75
channel captains, 374
competition, 380–83
convenience stores, 385f, 388
Cycle South case study,
406–7
decline stage of life cycle, 382f,
383
department stores, 385
differentiation, 379–80
direct sellers, 389
discount department stores,
385
discounters, 385
electronic shopping, 390–91
e-tailing, 390–91
freestanding retailers, 377f,
378–79
gross margin, 376
gross margin percentage,
375–76
growth stage of life cycle,
382–83
introduction stage of life cycle,
382
inventory turnover, 375–76
laws regulating, 384
life cycle, 382–83
location, 376–79, 380
mail order, 389–90
margins, 375–76
marketing channel members,
15
maturity stage of life cycle,
382f, 383
mix, retail. *See* Retailing mix
neighborhood business districts, 377
never out-of-stock differentiation, 380
nonstore-based retailers, 383,
388–91
nontraditional locations, 377f,
379
operating expenses, 376
outlet numbers, 373–75
physical differentiation of the
product, 379
point-of-purchase communications, 445
private label branding, 374
reaching the customer, 373
retail life cycle, 382–83
scrambled merchandising,
386, 387f
secondary business districts,
377
selling process differentiation,
379
shopping centers/malls,
377–78

specialty stores, 385–86
stock differentiation, 380
store-based retailers, 383–88
street peddling, 388–89
supercenters, 385f, 386–87
supermarkets, 385f, 386
trends, 373–79
types of retail formats, 383–91
vending machines, 390
wheel of retailing, 380–82
Retailing mix, 391
atmospherics, 392–94
attracting customers, 392–93
category management, 394–95
customer loyalty, 393
efficiency, 393–94
shrinkage, 393
SKU, 394–95
Reverse auctions in business-to-
business marketing, 167
Rewards for sales forces, 462–64
Risk taking activities as marketing
exchange, 10
Robinson-Patman Act, 50t
ROI
integrated marketing communications, 419
pricing, 509–10
Role ambiguity and sales forces,
464
Role conflict and sales forces,
463–64
Roles of consumers, 138
Routine problem solving in the
organizational buying
process, 180
Routing and customer relationship management, 299, 300
Royalties, 76

S

Sales, 458, 483–84
commercial real estate, 457–58
consultative selling, 459
customer relationship management, 461
field selling, 465–67
food service industry software
case study, 491–92
force. *See* Sales force
hard sell, 461
over-the-counter selling, 465
personal selling, 459–61
process. *See* Sales process
relationship selling, 461
telemarketing, 464–65
Sales era of history, 7
Sales force, 461
certification, 467
coaching, 479
codes of conduct, 482
commissions, 479–80
compensating, 475f, 479–80
corporate culture, 476
customer-oriented, 464

drawbacks, 462–64
ethics, 482
evaluating, 475f, 480–81
field selling, 465–67
geographical organization,
481
inbound telemarketers, 464
Internet, 477
job anxiety, 464
legal issues, 482
missionary salespeople, 465f,
467
motivating, 475f, 478–79
national account managers,
465–67
order getters, 465
order takers, 465
organization, 475f, 481
outbound telemarketers, 464
over-the-counter selling, 465
product knowledge, 476
product line organization, 481
professional salespeople, 465
profit center approach to compensation, 480
prudence in claim making to
customers, 482
quotas, 479
recruiting, 475–76
rewards, 462–64
role ambiguity, 464
role conflict, 463–64
salaries, 479–80
salary plus commission, 479,
480f
sales call anxiety, 479
sales skills, 476
sexual harassment, 483
straight commission, 479, 480f
straight salary, 479, 480f
suggestion selling, 465
support salespeople, 465f, 467
team selling, 468
technology, 476–78
telemarketing, 464–65
territory allocation, 481
territory potential, 481
training, 475f, 476–78
traits, 464
Sales potential in international
marketing, 71
Sales process, 467–69
amiable social style, 471
analytical social style, 470–71
approaching the client, 470–71
benefits of products, 472
close-ended questions, 472
cold calling, 469–70
commitment, 475
driver social style, 470, 471f
expressive social style, 471
features of products, 472
flexible presentations of products, 472–73
following up, 475
identifying client needs,
471–72

Sales process (*cont.*)
keeping promises, 475
memorized presentations of
products, 472f, 473
objection handling, 473–74
open-ended questions, 472
preapproach and planning, 470
presentation of products,
472–73
probing questions, 471–72
product presentation, 472–73
professional selling method,
469
prospecting, 469–70
qualified sales leads, 469
referrals, 469
social styles, 470–71
supporting evidence, 474
traditional selling method, 467
Sales promotion, 414, 437
advertising, shift from, 437–39
allowances and price flexing,
515
bridge buying, 441
consumer sales promotion,
441
delayed rewards, 441
diverting, 441
forward buying, 441
franchise holding/loading, 441,
442f
growth of, 437–39
image reinforcement, 441,
442f
immediate rewards, 441
incentives, 437
objectives, 439–40
off-invoice allowance, 440
roles of, 439–40
tasks, 439–40
trade allowances or trade
deals, 438
trade promotions, 440–41
trial impact, 441, 442f
Sampling in consumer research,
109–11
SBD. *See* Secondary business
districts (SBD)
SBUs. *See* Strategic business
units (SBUs)
Scrambled merchandising
channel structure, 330
retailers and retailing, 386,
387f
Screening of target international
markets, 70–73
Search attributes in services marketing, 282
Search engines, 545
Search process in organizational
buying, 178
Secondary business districts
(SBD), 377
Secondary data analysis in consumer research, 101–4
Segmentation and target mar-
kets, 198, 204, 205f, 228

accessible markets, 207
actionable markets, 207
advantages of, 201–2, 203t
bases for segmentation,
208–12, 227t
behavior or usage segmentation, 212
benefits-sought segmentation,
210–11
business markets. *See* Business market segmentation
collecting segmentation data,
212–13
competition positioning, 221
concentrated strategy, 208
criteria for successful segmentation, 206–8
data mining, 212
definition of market, 198
definition of market segments
and segmentation, 198
definition of target market and
marketing, 198
demographic segmentation,
208–9
differentiated strategy, 208
differentiation, 207–8, 215
direct mail targeting of credit
card customers, 233–34
disadvantages of, 202–3
80/20 principle, 212
energy drinks, 197–98
estimating costs, 215
existing customer profiling,
213
external database sources of
segmentation data, 213
external factors in segmentation, 208
family life cycle, 209
forecasting demand, 214
generalized averages, 213
geodemographics, 210
geographic segmentation,
209–10
global markets. *See* Global
market segmentation
heterogeneous demand, 198
heterogeneous markets, 206
individual markets, 199–201
integrated marketing communications, 426
internal database sources of
segmentation data, 212–13
international marketing,
70–73
marketing mix, 222
mass markets, 199–201
measurable markets, 206
micromarkets and marketing,
200
need for segmentation deter-
minations, 205–6
niche marketing, 199–200
perceptual mapping, 216
positioning strategy, 215–22
post hoc segmentation, 204

price flexing, 519
price/quality positioning, 217
a priori segmentation, 204
product attribute positioning,
218
product class positioning, 220
product usage positioning,
219
product user positioning, 218
profiling selected segments,
213–14
profitability potential assessments, 214–15
psychographic segmentation,
210
repositioning, 222
screening of target international markets, 70–73
situational segmentation, 211
spidering, 213
strategy and strategic factors,
11, 207–8
substantial markets, 206–7
successful segmentation criteria, 206–8
symbol positioning, 222
total market identification,
204–5
undifferentiated targeting
strategy, 207, 208f
variables in segmentation,
208–12
Segway Human Transporter case
study, 194–95
Selective distribution, 328–29
Self-concept, 146–47
Self-interest of marketers and
unintended consequences
on demand, 39–40
Self-interest of marketers and
unintended consequences
on supply, 37–39
Self-service at point of sale, 154
Selling activities as marketing
exchange, 9
Selling process differentiation,
379
Selling sites and e-marketing,
539, 540t, 541–43
Service guarantees and customer
retention, 310
Service quality, 302–3
communications gap, 303,
304f, 306
customer satisfaction distinguished, 302–3
delivery gap, 303, 304f, 305–6
knowledge gap, 303, 304f
service gap, 303–6
standards gap, 303, 304–5
Servicescape, 289–93
differentiation, 292–93
facilitating the service process,
291
organizational socialization,
291
packaging the service, 291

socializing employees and customers, 291
Service sites and e-marketing, 539, 540–41
Services marketing, 280–81, 311–12
  benefit concept, 289
  compelling experiences for customers, 294
  credence attributes, 284
  customer retention. *See* Customer retention
  customer satisfaction. *See* Customer satisfaction
  definition of services, 12, 281–82
  entertainment transportation, 283
  e-services, 278–79
  experience attributes, 284
  for-profit services, 282t
  goods, 282, 284–88
  government services, 282t
  health care case study, 317–22
  heterogeneity, 288
  inseparability, 285–87
  intangibility, 282, 285
  intangible dominant, 282
  marketing myopia, 284
  nonprofit services, 282t
  organization and systems, 294
  other customers, 293–94
  perishability, 288
  professional services, 282t
  providers of services, 293
  quality. *See* Service quality
  scale of market entities, 282–84
  search attributes, 282
  service providers, 293
  servicescape. *See* Servicescape
  tangible dominant, 282
  virtual ISP, 286
Sexual harassment, 483
Sharing and customer relationship management, 299, 301
Sherman Antitrust Act, 50t, 522
Shopping centers/malls, 377–78
Shopping products and new product development and product decisions, 238, 239t
Shrinkage, 393
Silver bullet success in new product development and product decisions, 243
Single-line wholesalers, 397
Single-pricing, 517
Single-source systems and advertising, 435
Situational ethics, 46
Situational factors in business market segmentation, 224
Situational involvement and consumer behavior, 144
Situational segmentation, 211
SKIPPIES, 19t

SKU, 394–95
Social contracts and ethical behavior, 45
Socializing employees and customers, 291
Social responsibility, 32, 54–55
  advertising wasted, 36–37
  anti-trust laws, 49–51
  "better marketing," 33
  cause-related marketing, 51–52
  consumer protection laws, 49–51
  demand-side market failure, 39
  distribution system inefficiency, 34–36
  efficiency and effectiveness, 33–40
  ethical behavior. *See* Ethical behavior
  free choice, 33
  freedom, 33
  good cause marketing, 51–54
  inefficient targeting, 37
  Internet gambling case study, 59
  "less marketing," 33
  "marginals" class, 38
  National High Blood Pressure Education Program, 53–54
  obeying the law, 49–51
  obsolete technology, 35
  "overconsumers" class, 38
  planned obsolescence, 34
  potential buyers, 37
  self-interest of marketers and unintended consequences on demand, 39–40
  self-interest of marketers and unintended consequences on supply, 37–39
  smoking, 30–31
  socioecological classes, 38
  supply-side market failure, 38
  "sustainers" class, 38
  tragedy of the commons, 37–38
  unneeded products, 33–34
Social styles and the sales process, 470–71
Social systems and channels and distribution, 337–38
Socio-cultural environment, 16, 18–20
Socioecological classes and social responsibility, 38
Socioeconomic environment and international marketing, 67–69
Sogoshosha, 76
"Speaking with a single voice" in integrated marketing communications, 418
Specialization or division of labor, 332–33
Specialty products, 238, 239t
Specialty stores, 385–86

Specialty wholesalers, 397
Spidering, 213
Sponsorship marketing, 414, 443–44
  cause-related marketing, 444
  corporate sponsorships, 443
  event-related marketing, 444
Spontaneous economic combustion, 4
  consumption satiation, 4, 5–6
  labor specialization, 4–5
  raw material scarcity, 4
Stabilization of price and margin objective, 510
Stage-gate processes in new product development, 253–59
Standardization activities as marketing exchange, 10
Standardized approach in international marketing, 82
Standard markup approach, 499–500
Standards gap, 303, 304–5
Standing behind the product and customer retention, 309–10
"Stars" in strategic planning, 572
Static thought and competitor research, 117
Statistical Abstract of the United States, 102
Stimulating demand in business-to-business marketing, 173
Stock differentiation, 380
Storage costs and e-marketing, 550
Store-based retailers, 383–88
Storing activities as marketing exchange, 10
Straight commission for sales forces, 479, 480f
Straight rebuys in the organizational buying process, 180
Straight salary for sales forces, 479, 480f
Strategic alliances
  channels and distribution, 347
  international market entry strategies, 80
Strategic business units (SBUs), 569
Strategic planning, 568, 569f
  attractiveness/strength model, 573–74
  BCG's product-portfolio analysis, 571–73
  business position of products, 573
  cash cows, 572
  "dogs," 572–73
  GE's attractiveness/strength model, 573–74
  growth vector model, 570–71
  industry attractiveness, 573–74
  market attractiveness, 573–74
  market development, 570–71, 571f

Strategic planning (*cont.*)
   marketing plans, 574
   market penetration, 570, 571f
   organization mission, 568–69
   "problem children," 572
   product development, 571
   product diversification, 571
   product-portfolio analysis,
     571–73
   "stars," 572
   strategic business units, 569
   tools, 569–74
Strategy, 11–12, 13f
   Airbus, 22–23
   bargaining strategy in house-
     hold decision making, 157
   best/worst practices, 22–24
   Boeing, 22–23
   branding strategies, 262–63
   Cemex, 24
   channels and distribution,
     14–15, 339–41, 349–50
   concentrated strategy in seg-
     mentation and target mar-
     kets, 208
   concentration strategy in inter-
     national marketing, 73
   deploying assets and capabili-
     ties, 11t
   distribution decisions, 14–15
   diversification strategy in inter-
     national marketing, 73
   family brand name strategy,
     262–63
   form utility, 12
   IBM, 23–24
   international market entry
     strategies. *See* International
     market entry strategies
   marketing mix, 11, 12, 14f
   marketing planning, 575f, 576,
     580
   market segments, 11
   media strategies in integrated
     marketing communications,
     427
   place decisions, 14–15
   planning. *See* Strategic plan-
     ning
   pricing decisions, 14
   product decisions and activi-
     ties, 12–14
   product positioning, 11
   promotion decisions, 15–16
   segmentation and target mar-
     kets, 207–8
   strategic marketing concept,
     22
   target markets, 11
   vision, 12t
   Webvan, 24
Street peddling, 388–89
Strivers, 148
Structure of channels. *See* Channel structure
Strugglers, 148

Subscriptions and e-marketing,
   552–53
Substantial markets, 206–7
Successful segmentation criteria,
   206–8
Success of new products, 242–43,
   244–52
Suggestion selling, 465
Sugging, 111
Supercenters, 385f, 386–87
Supermarkets, 385f, 386
Supplier bargaining power, 120
Supplier selection and perfor-
   mance review, 178, 181–82
Supplies in new product develop-
   ment and product deci-
   sions, 238–39
Supply-chain management
   business-to-business market-
     ing, 174–75
   logistics, 351
Supply-side market failure, 38
Support salespeople, 465f, 467
Survey research, 107–9
Survival pricing, 511
Sustainable competitive advan-
   tage, 340
"Sustainers" class and social
   responsibility, 38
Symbol positioning, 222
Synergy in integrated marketing
   communications, 418
Systems concept of logistics,
   352–57

T

Tacit knowledge in new product
   development and product
   decisions, 247
Tactical planning, 568
Talking to customers in new prod-
   uct development and prod-
   uct decisions, 249–52
Tangible dominant in services
   marketing, 282
Targeting in customer relation-
   ship management, 299, 301
Target markets. *See* Segmenta-
   tion and target markets
Target return pricing
   demand, 500
   pricing, 500
TARP figures, 297
TBIS. *See* Transaction-Based
   Information Systems
   (TBISs)
TD. *See* Top-down budgeting (TD)
Team selling, 468
Technical assessment in new
   product development and
   product decisions, 257
Technical performance success in
   new product development
   and product decisions, 242

Technology
   environment, 16, 18f, 21–22
   fashion shows, 544
   forces in organizational buy-
     ing, 184
   forecasting, 247
   language considerations in
     global market segmenta-
     tion, 225
   music distribution, 331, 553
   obsolete technology and social
     responsibility, 35
   pricing, 521
   sales force, 476–78, 477
   self-service at point of sale,
     154
   virtual ISP, 286
Telemarketing, 464–65
Telephone surveys, 108t
Terminal values, 145–46
Territory allocation of sales
   forces, 481
Territory potential of sales forces,
   481
Testing and validation stage of
   new product development
   and product decisions, 254f,
   255t, 259
Theory of dual entitlement, 510
Threat of new entrants in com-
   petitor research, 120
Threat of new substitutes in com-
   petitor research, 120
Time segments, 519–20
Time utilities, 14, 326
Top-down budgeting (TD), 427
Total contributions and demand,
   504
Total cost approach in logistics,
   352–53
Total cost of ownership in the
   organizational buying
   process, 181
Total market identification, 204–5
Trade allowances or trade deals,
   438
Trade customers, 125–27
Trade-oriented sales promotions,
   414, 440–41
Trading companies and interna-
   tional market entry strate-
   gies, 76
Traditional selling method, 467
Traditional view of the evolution
   of marketing, 6–8
Tragedy of the commons, 37–38
Training of customers, 308–9
Training sales forces, 475f,
   476–78
Traits of sales forces, 464
Transaction-Based Information
   Systems (TBISs), 117
Transaction efficiency, 334
Transportation, 353–54
Transporting activities as market-
   ing exchange, 9

Trial impact in sales promotion, 441, 442f
Truck jobbers, 398
Trust building
    customer retention, 308
    evolution of marketing, 10

U

Uncertainty avoidance in international marketing, 66
Uncovering unmet needs and problems in new product development and product decisions, 245–52
Undifferentiated targeting strategy, 207, 208f
Uniform delivered pricing, 515
Unitary elasticity, 504
Universal Product Code (UPC), 114
Unneeded products and social responsibility, 33–34
Unrealized customers in new product development and product decisions, 244
Unsought products in new product development and product decisions, 238, 239t
UPC. *See* Universal Product Code (UPC)
U.S. Industrial Outlook, 102
Usage enhancement through packaging, 263
Usage segmentation, 212, 519

V

Validity of result in consumer research, 111
VALS, 147–49
Value analysis in organizational buying, 181–82
Value pricing, 519
Value proposition in organizational buying, 185

Values
    instrumental values, 145
    interpersonal values, 146
    psychographics, 145–46, 147–49
    sources of, 46–47
Vending machines, 390
Vertical marketing systems (VMSs), 347–49
Video cases
    Concept2, 604–5
    Cybex International, 605–6
    ESPN, 585–87
    FedEx, 588–89
    Fisher-Price, 591–92
    Fresh Samantha, 592–93
    Furniture.com, 589–90
    Goya Foods, 593–94
    Hasbro, 597–98
    Learjet, 606–7
    Neiman Marcus, 583–84
    Pfizer, 596–97
    Pizza Hut, 602–3
    Polaroid, 601–2
    RadioShack, 598–99
    Timberland, 584–85
    Tower Records, 587–88
    UPS, 594–96
    Wine.com, 600–601
Virtual ISP, 286
Vision and strategy, 12t
VMS. *See* Vertical marketing systems (VMSs)
Voice of the customer (VOC)
    consumer decision making, 154–55
    consumer research, 104
    new product development and product decisions, 249–52
Voice share in competitor research, 119
Volume discounting, 515

W

Wagon jobbers, 398
Wants of consumers, 139

Warehousing, 356–57
Wealth of Nations, The, 5
Web sites. *See also* Internet companies and brands, 539–40
    information Web sites, 539, 540t, 543–45
Weighted point plans in organizational buying, 182
Wheeler-Lea Act, 50t
Wheel of retailing, 380–82
Wholesalers and wholesaling, 371–72, 395, 401
    agents/brokers, 396f, 397f, 399
    business-to-business marketing, 166
    cash and carry wholesalers, 398
    Cycle South case study, 406–7
    desk jobbers, 398
    drop-shippers, 398
    full-service merchant wholesalers, 397–98
    general merchandise wholesalers, 397
    industrial distributors, 398
    limited-service merchant wholesalers, 398
    managing wholesalers, 400
    manufacturer's agents, 399
    manufacturer's sales branches, 396, 397f
    marketing channel members, 15
    merchant wholesalers, 396–98
    rack jobbers, 398
    selecting wholesalers, 399–400
    single-line wholesalers, 397
    specialty wholesalers, 397
    truck jobbers, 398
    types of wholesalers, 396–99
    wagon jobbers, 398
WOOFS, 19t
World Trade Organization (WTO), 69

Y

Yuppies, 19t